THE AMERICAN
PRESIDENCY

Clio Bibliography Series No. 15

Gail Schlachter, Editor
Pamela R. Byrne, Executive Editor

Users of the Clio Bibliography Series may refer to current issues of
America: History and Life *and* Historical Abstracts
for continuous bibliographic coverage of the subject areas
treated by each individual volume in the series.

THE AMERICAN PRESIDENCY

★ ★ ★ ★ a historical bibliography ★ ★ ★ ★

ABC-Clio Information Services

Santa Barbara, California
Oxford, England

Library of Congress Cataloging in Publication Data
Main entry under title:

The American presidency.

  (Clio bibliography series; no. 15)
  Includes index.
  1. Presidents—United States—Bibliography.
  2. United States—Politics and government—
Bibliography. I. ABC-Clio Information Services.
  II. Series. Z1249.P7A47 1984 [E176.1]
  016.973'09'92 83-12245 ISBN 0-87436-370-5

ABC-Clio Information Services, Inc.
2040 Alameda Padre Serra
Santa Barbara, California

Clio Press Ltd.
55 St. Thomas St.
Oxford OX1 1JG, England

Printed and bound in the United States of America.

TABLE OF CONTENTS

PREFACE

The seven brief paragraphs of the United States Constitution defining the power of the President were framed with the intention of creating a political authority capable of providing executive leadership but not powerful enough to dominate the other branches of the Federal Government. Yet, in less than 200 years the Presidency has become the paramount federal institution, and Chief Executives have often been the dominant personalities of their eras, causing historians to periodize American history by presidential name—the Jacksonian Era, the Age of Roosevelt.

Like the powers of the office, the periodical literature on the Presidency has proliferated. *The American Presidency: A Historical Bibliography* (number 15 of the Clio Bibliography Series) is designed to provide bibliographical control for the bulk of this literature that has appeared during the Post-Watergate Era (1973-1982). Its entries are drawn from the ABC-Clio database of citations to articles from some 2,000 periodical titles concerned with history and the related social sciences and humanities.

The editor has reviewed the database with the goal of selecting all entries for inclusion that relate in any way to Presidential Studies. Consequently the user of the volume will find abstracts of articles on the lives of the presidents, which include such topics as family life, religious values, and private as well as public careers; presidential political campaigns and elections; the policies and activities of presidential administrations; and the development of the Executive Branch, including the Office of the President and the Departments. The resulting bibliography consists of 3,489 abstracts of scholarly studies, topical articles, bibliographies, and review essays published in the journal literature.

In one sense this volume provides access to articles on political history. Perusal of its pages, however, also reveals larger contours of American history. A quantitative approach to the contents, for example, shows that about twenty per cent of the entries concerning presidential administrations and the Presidency through the tenure of William McKinley deal with foreign policy. For the period since 1945 the figure is close to fifty per cent. The quantity of the research reflects the changing content of the American past as a young developing nation matured into a position of world leadership. In qualitative terms the abstracts in this bibliography referring to the character of the men chosen for office, the agendas of presidential administrations, and the institutions devised to implement political mandates indicate something of the aspirations of the American people and the efforts deemed appropriate to achieve them.

The entries are organized by chronological period, with each period subdivided by broad subject categories. These subdivisions are largely self-explanatory, but a few words of explication may help to clarify the volume's organization. Abstracts specifically about presidents that focus on their activities as presidents are organized under the "Presidential Administrations" sections; articles on other aspects of the lives of presidents are located under sections labeled "Presidents." Articles on the growth of presidential power, the development of Executive Departments, and related topics are particularly difficult to classify. Entries that seem to treat these topics as facets of the history of presidential administrations have been placed in the "Presidential Administrations" sections while those that seem to emphasize the larger constitutional and historical trends have been assigned to sections labeled "Presidency." Although editorial judgment in many of these cases has been necessarily arbitrary, the organizational integrity of this volume has been insured by a high degree of consistency in assigning entries to the various chapter subsections. Scholars may debate the placement of particular entries, but they can be assured that no matter where the entry is located, it can be readily found by using the subject index.

This volume utilizes ABC-SPIndex—one of the most advanced and comprehensive indexing systems yet developed. ABC-SPIndex allows fast, analytical, and pinpoint access by linking the key subject terms and historical period of each abstract to form a composite index entry that provides a complete subject profile of the periodical article. Each set of index terms is then rotated so that the complete profile appears in the index under each of the subject terms. Thus the number of access points is increased severalfold over conventional hierarchical indexes, and irrelevant material can be eliminated early in the search process. The explanatory note at the beginning of the subject index provides more information about ABC-SPIndex.

Care has been taken to eliminate inconsistencies that might have appeared in the subject index as a result of combining a decade of database material. The subject profile index thus reflects a highly labor-intensive effort—the product of many hours of editing and reediting, and allows easy access to the materials included in this volume. Additional cross-references have been added to ensure fast and accurate searching.

This volume represents the collaboration of a highly skilled and diverse group. Pamela R. Byrne, Executive Editor of the Clio Bibliography Series, directed the project from the initial planning stage through the complex editorial processes of the computer-assisted indexing system and machine-readable database, to the final design and production of the book.

Historian-editor Robert deV. Brunkow selected, organized, and indexed the entries that comprise this volume and at critical points in the editorial process was expertly assisted by other ABC-Clio Information Services editors, Suzanne Robitaille Ontiveros, Lance Klass, and Susan Kinnell.

The Data Processing Services Department, under the supervision of Ken Baser, Director, and Deborah Looker, Production Supervisor, ably manipulated the database to fit the editorial specifications of this bibliography. Most especially, appreciation is extended to the worldwide community of scholars without whose contributions this book would not have been possible.

1. PRESIDENTS, ADMINISTRATIONS, AND THE PRESIDENCY: MULTIPERIOD

1. Adkison, Danny. PRESIDENTIAL VACANCIES AND SECTION TWO OF THE TWENTY-FIFTH AMENDMENT. *Social Sci. J. 1979 16(3): 41-57.* Describes presidential succession and evaluates the effectiveness of Section Two of the 25th Amendment, adopted 1967, which provides for presidential nomination and congressional confirmation of vice-presidents; covers 1789-1970's.

2. Artaud, Denise. DE WILSON À CARTER: MYTHES ET RÉALITÉS DE LA POLITIQUE AMÉRICAINE EN EUROPE [From Wilson to Carter: myths and realities of US policy towards Europe]. *Défense Natl. [France] 1979 35(Jan): 49-62.* Despite European opinion to the contrary, a review of US policy towards Europe, 1913-78, shows that there has been some continuity in US foreign policy.

3. Baker, Gladys L. WOMEN IN THE U.S. DEPARTMENT OF AGRICULTURE. *Agric. Hist. 1976 50(1): 190-201.* In its first decades the US Department of Agriculture hired only a few women, mainly as clerks, librarians, and assistant microscopists. Gradually in the early 20th century a few women made their mark as scientists and in the Office of Home Economics. Since then several women have advanced to important positions, although their percentage in the Department workforce remains small. 48 notes.   D. E. Bowers

4. Balutis, Alan P. THE PRESIDENCY AND THE PRESS: THE EXPANDING PRESIDENTIAL IMAGE. *Presidential Studies Q. 1977 7(4): 244-251.* Using the front pages of the *New York Times* and the *Buffalo Evening News,* continues and confirms Elmer Cornwell's (b. 1924) study of the mass media during 1885-1957 indicating that the president's image in the struggle for political hegemony is expanding. The pattern for Congress, on the other hand, is one of short-term fluctuations but a steady downward trend in frequency of appearance in these papers. Some balancing by the media is necessary or the presidency will retain its advantage in the struggle for hegemony. 4 tables, 21 notes.
                                                                J. Tull

5. Banner, James M., Jr. HISTORIANS AND THE IMPEACHMENT INQUIRY: A BRIEF HISTORY AND PROSPECTUS. *Rev. in Am. Hist. 1976 4(2): 139-149.* Review article prompted by C. Vann Woodward, ed., *Responses of the Presidents to Charges of Misconduct* (New York: Dell, 1974); discusses the role of historians in 1974 in compiling evidence for the Impeachment Inquiry of the House Judiciary Committee.

6. Barenboim, P. D. VETO PREZIDENTA SSHA [The American president's veto]. *Sovetskoe Gosudarstvo i Pravo [USSR] 1977 (12): 96-99.* A critical look at the powers of veto enjoyed by the presidents of the United States since George Washington.

7. Bates, J. Leonard. WATERGATE AND TEAPOT DOME. *South Atlantic Q. 1974 73(2): 145-159.* In both the Teapot Dome Scandal and the Watergate Scandal the executive branch attempted to withhold evidence which Congress tried to discover. Compares the roles of Senators Thomas J. Walsh and Samuel J. Ervin. In the earlier period the scandals occurred because Secretary of the Interior Albert B. Fall and others took payoffs; the men around Nixon were not interested in personal gain. "The methods by which Fall exploited both the Navy Department and the marines are reminiscent of the later manipulations of the Federal Bureau of Investigation, the Central Intelligence Agency, the Internal Revenue Service, and other agencies." 4 notes.
                                                                E. P. Stickney

8. Berens, John F. THE FBI AND CIVIL LIBERTIES FROM FRANKLIN ROOSEVELT TO JIMMY CARTER: AN HISTORICAL OVERVIEW. *Michigan Academician 1980 13(2): 131-144.* The history of the Federal Bureau of Investigation since the presidency of Franklin D. Roosevelt, whose mandates in 1936 and 1939 "opened the door to massive FBI surveillance of Americans who deviated from the established and normal politics of the day," has adequately shown the dangers to individual civil liberties of the FBI's programs.

9. Berger, Harriet F. APPOINTMENT AND CONFIRMATION TO THE NATIONAL LABOR RELATIONS BOARD: DEMOCRATIC CONSTRAINTS ON PRESIDENTIAL POWER? *Presidential Studies Q. 1978 8(4): 403-417.* Using the National Labor Relations Board (NLRB) as a case study, examines the presidential power of appointment to independent regulatory commissions and the effectiveness of the Senate's power of confirmation as a restraint on the President. Since the establishment of the NLRB in 1935, members have enjoyed long tenure and frequent reappointment with only perfunctory review by the Senate. While the Boards tend to reflect the orientation of the President, the absence of deep ideological differences and the influence of the regulated parties ensures stability and limited Senate review. Chart, 59 notes.
                                                                S. C. Strom

10. Berger, Raoul. EXECUTIVE PRIVILEGE IN LIGHT OF *UNITED STATES V. NIXON.* *Maryland Historian 1975 6(2): 67-78.* Traces the history of executive privilege which was recognized in *United States* v. *Nixon* (US, 1974). Contends that no basis for executive privilege exists in the constitution nor is intent to establish executive privilege evidenced in the commentary of the framers of the constitution. Based on primary and secondary constitutional law sources; 70 notes.
                                                                G. O. Gagnon

11. Boller, Paul F., Jr. RELIGION AND THE U.S. PRESIDENCY. *J. of Church and State 1979 21(1): 5-21.* Examines the religions of American presidents. Five presidents from James A. Garfield through Jimmy Carter have been born-again Christians. Most have been church members, the largest number (six) being Episcopalians. Calvin Coolidge and Dwight D. Eisenhower became church members after election to the presidency. Some 11 presidents were not affiliated with any religion. Religion was a major issue in only three or four elections. Secondary sources; 50 notes.   S

12. Brigman, William E. THE EXECUTIVE BRANCH AND THE INDEPENDENT REGULATORY AGENCIES. *Presidential Studies Q. 1981 11(2): 244-261.* Analyzes presidential influence over the independent regulatory commissions. In theory, the commissions can act as constraints on the president, but in practice there is a considerable amount of leverage the president can use on the commissions. Appointment power, budget review, and control over the commissions' access to the courts, are some of the more potent leverages. This analysis serves as a corrective to the myth that commissions enjoy greater freedom from presidential control than the departments. Covers the 20th century. Based on a paper presented to the 1979 Summer Seminar for College Teachers. Primary sources; table, 45 notes.   A. Drysdale

13. Brodie, Fawn M. THE PRESIDENTIAL HERO: REALITY OR ILLUSION. *Halcyon 1981: 1-16.* Draws from the careers and personalities of selected US presidents, beginning with George Washington, to put into better perspective the image of the president as hero, an especially illusory image since the administration of Richard M. Nixon.

14. Bryson, Thomas A. A BICENTENNIAL REASSESSMENT OF AMERICAN-MIDDLE EASTERN RELATIONS. *Australian J. of Pol. and Hist. [Australia] 1978 24(2): 174-183.* A consideration of the ethnic factor in American relations with the Middle East, concentrating on the efforts of Greeks, Armenians, and Zionists. Appeals by the small US Greek community in the 1820's were met by official neutrality but private goodwill. The 52,000-strong Armenian community got some influential support for the abortive plan for a US Mandate in Armenia 1919. Zionists proved the most successful lobbyists: President Harry S. Truman endorsed partition and de facto recognition of Israel in 1948, against State Department advice, to secure electoral advantage. Criticizes the recent "special relationship" with Israel in the context of wider Middle East interests. Documented from monographs and articles; 65 notes.
                                                                W. D. McIntyre

15. Burk, Robert F. NEW PERSPECTIVES FOR PRESIDENTIAL LIBRARIES. *Presidential Studies Q. 1981 11(3): 399-410.* Starting with Franklin D. Roosevelt, the cult of the presidency has been reflected and supported by the different presidential libraries. The impact of Roosevelt upon the presidency caused many to feel that a separate library and museum should be built housing his papers. Although it faced congressional opposition, the establishment of the Roosevelt library in 1940 had a tremendous impact on the development of the presidential cult. Gerald R. Ford's new library offers hope for a postimperial approach to presidential libraries, but at their bases, these libraries are still political. 46 notes.
D. H. Cline

16. Burnham, James. AND THE SWORD. *Marine Corps Gazette 1960 44(10): 10-14.* Examines how the war powers of Congress and the President have changed since the promulgation of the Constitution of the United States, with particular reference to the ability of contemporary presidents to wage war without Congress's expressed consent by dubbing war a "police action."

17. Burstein, Paul. POLITICAL ELITES AND LABOR MARKETS: SELECTION OF AMERICAN CABINET MEMBERS, 1932-72. *Social Forces 1977 56(1): 189-201.* An empirical regularity has not been satisfactorily explained: since the administration of John Adams, those appointed to top political positions in the United States have had similar, high-status backgrounds. The article attempts to explain this finding by applying to presidential appointments insights gained from the study of labor markets, treating the president as an employer trying to fill positions with minimum expenditure of resources. Presidents appear to appoint similar sorts of people because they share both ends and means in making appointments. Presidents select appointees primarily on the basis of competence and in order to make political payoffs of specified types. In addition, they use screening devices commonly used by employers to choose among job candidates: they appoint people they know personally, people who are highly visible, and people who fit specified ascriptive criteria.
J

18. Burton, Agnes Rose. POLITICAL PARTIES: EFFECT ON THE PRESIDENCY. *Presidential Studies Q. 1981 11(2): 289-298.* Suggests that political parties are necessary for a republican form of government and that they act as a constraint on the president. Discusses the purpose of parties and their roles in the election process and in Congress to support this thesis. Considers possble infringements on party functions of the media and interest groups. Studies the relationship of the Jefferson and Eisenhower presidencies with political parties. Primary sources; 46 notes.
A. Drysdale

19. Burton, William L. DOES CORRUPTION PAY? *Midwest Q. 1976 18(1): 53-63.* Discusses the effect of corruption on political parties. Watergate provides a model indicating that when corruption in a national party is exposed that party suffers in the next election. Earlier examples do not bear out this theory. Corruption was a public issue during the administrations of Presidents Ulysses S. Grant and Warren Harding, yet the party in power during the scandals maintained its political position in the following election. Corruption is rarely the only election issue. Voters often are more concerned with other issues. Historically, the exposure of corruption has not been a serious handicap to a national party. Biblio.
S. J. Quinlan

20. Campbell, A. E. THE FOREIGN POLICY OF A DEMOCRACY. *Hist. J. [Great Britain] 1974 17(2): 443-447.* Review article on: Milton Plesur's *America's Outward Thrust: Approaches to Foreign Affairs, 1865-1890* (DeKalb, Illinois: North Illinois U. Press, 1971); Otis L. Graham's *The Great Campaigns: Reform and War in America, 1900-1928* (Englewood Cliffs, New Jersey: Prentice-Hall, 1971); Sidney Bell's *Righteous Conquest: Woodrow Wilson and the Evolution of the New Diplomacy* (Port Washington, New York: Kennikat Press, 1972); Charles Chatfield's *For Peace and Justice: Pacifism in America, 1914-1941* (Knoxville, Tennessee: U. of Tennessee Press, 1971); Michael G. Fry's *Illusions of Security: North Atlantic Diplomacy, 1918-1922* (U. of Toronto Press, 1972); Joseph S. Tulchin's *The Aftermath of War: World War I and U.S. Policy Toward Latin America* (New York University Press, 1971); Gloria J. Barron's *Leadership in Crisis: FDR and the Path to Intervention* (Port Washington, New York: Kennikat Press, 1973); and Robert J. Maddox's *The New Left and the Origins of the Cold War* (New

Jersey: Princeton U. Press, 1973). All are adequate within their limits, but all fail to examine American foreign policy within the context of the overriding circumstantial constraints which dictate policy.
G. L. Owen

21. Cantor, Milton. WAR IS THE HEALTH OF THE PRESIDENCY. *R. in Am. Hist. 1974 2(3): 322-330.* Examines the warmaking powers of the presidency from the origins of the warmaking clause in the Constitution through "episodes that helped shape the warmaking power" in the 18th-20th centuries to the abuses of power by Lyndon B. Johnson and Richard M. Nixon, in a review of Jacob Javits' and Don Kellermann's *Who Makes War: The President Versus Congress* (New York: William Morrow & Co., 1973) and Arthur M. Schlesinger, Jr.'s *The Imperial Presidency* (Boston: Houghton Mifflin, 1973).

22. Carpenter, Ronald H. and Jordan, William J. STYLE IN DISCOURSE AS A PREDICTOR OF POLITICAL PERSONALITY FOR MR. CARTER AND OTHER TWENTIETH CENTURY PRESIDENTS: TESTING THE BARBER PARADIGM. *Presidential Studies Q. 1978 8(1): 67-78.* Reexamines James D. Barber's theory as expressed in *The Presidential Character: Predicting Performance in the White House* (Englewood Cliffs, N.J.: Prentice-Hall, 1972), that personality shapes performance. Attempts to develop specific tools for predicting presidential behavior through analysis of rheoitrcal type. Word frequency as measured by the Type-Token-Ratio is a more accurate indicator of presidential personality than the representational meaning which is subject to changing situational exigencies. Analysis of word repetition in first Inaugural Addresses since 1900 confirms the relationship between low levels of motivation and high lexical diversity. This technique is used to analyze President Jimmy Carter and indicates that he has a more passive personality than originally assumed, but confirmed by early performance in office. 41 notes.
S. C. Strom

23. Ceaser, James W. POLITICAL PARTIES AND PRESIDENTIAL AMBITION. *J. of Pol. 1978 40(3): 708-739.* The recent decline in the role of parties during presidential elections is a direct result of decisions by party commissions and state legislatures to open the nomination process. Both the authors of *The Federalist Papers* and the originators of permanent party competition (notably Martin Van Buren) sought electoral processes which regulated candidate behavior. On the contrary, Populist and Progressive movements (and Woodrow Wilson) sought a system which would elevate a dynamic leader above his party. A balance between these positions maintained the mixed system of candidate-oriented primaries and organization-dominated selection procedures until the post-1968 Democratic Party reforms. Primary and secondary sources; 59 notes.
A. W. Novitsky

24. Ceaser, James W.; Thurow, Glen E.; Tulis, Jeffrey; and Bessette, Joseph M. THE RISE OF THE RHETORICAL PRESIDENCY. *Presidential Studies Q. 1981 11(2): 158-171.* This century has seen the rise of the rhetorical presidency primarily as a result of three factors: a modern doctrine of presidential leadership, the modern mass media, and the modern presidential campaign. A look at recent events shows failures of the current doctrine, and it is perhaps time for a discussion of alternatives. For a change to occur, there must first be a change in the selection process, the presidents should reduce the number of their speeches, and the character of their speeches must change. The problem with the rhetorical presidency extends to the basic questions of how our nation is governed. 42 notes.
A. Drysdale

25. Chastenet, Jacques. LA PRESIDENCE DES ÉTATS-UNIS [The Presidency of the United States]. *Nouvelle Rev. des Deux Mondes [France] 1976 (12): 527-533.* Traces the evolution of the office and powers of the Presidency from the ratification of the Constitution to the term of Jimmy Carter.

26. Chester, Edward W. BEYOND THE RHETORIC: A NEW LOOK AT PRESIDENTIAL INAUGURAL ADDRESSES. *Presidential Studies Q. 1980 10(4): 571-582.* A widespread belief is that presidential inaugural addresses are mediocre at best. However, an examination of the content of 19th-century addresses reveals a strong emphasis on the Constitution, isolationism, and the condition of the Indian. But recent addresses have tended to be long on rhetoric and short on content, thus defying classification. Based on the inaugural addresses; 46 notes.
D. H. Cline

27. Christensen, Bonniejean. STYLE IS THE MAN: A SAMPLING OF PROSE FROM PRESIDENTIAL INAUGURAL ADDRESSES. *North Dakota Q. 1980 48(1): 5-27.* Analyzes presidential inaugural addresses to compare and contrast the style, sentence structure, and characteristics, from George Washington to Jimmy Carter.

28. Christenson, Reo M. PRESIDENTIAL LEADERSHIP OF CONGRESS: TEN COMMANDMENTS POINT THE WAY. *Presidential Studies Q. 1978 8(3): 257-268.* The success of a President depends on his ability to lead Congress and the application of certain principles can enhance his effectiveness with that body. Examples during 1932-77 illustrate these "Ten Commandments." A president must know the personalities and power centers in Congress, develop a sense of timing, establish legislative priorities, consult with Congressional party leaders before launching policy initiatives, nurture his legislative programs, have a good legislative liaison staff, respect Congress as an equal institution, seek bipartisan support for his programs, compromise, and propose sound legislative packages. 37 notes.   S. C. Strom

29. Cloud, Preston. THE IMPROBABLE BUREAUCRACY: THE UNITED STATES GEOLOGICAL SURVEY, 1879-1979. *Pro. of the Am. Phil. Soc. 1980 124(3): 155-167.* The US Geological Survey, although a bureau of the Department of Interior, is the nation's most eminent federal scientific agency. It was founded in 1879 with a staff of 47 employees, including 18 eminent geologists. The author describes the development of the survey, its directors, and other important personalities related to it. 12 illus., biblio.   H. M. Parker, Jr.

30. Cochrane, James L. THE U.S. PRESIDENTIAL LIBRARIES AND THE HISTORY OF POLITICAL ECONOMY. *Hist. of Pol. Econ. 1976 8(3): 412-427.* Describes these libraries and their importance for historians of political economy. Established in 1938 by Franklin D. Roosevelt, there are now six, containing papers and microfilms from White House Central Files and other departments and agencies. Additionally, there is an oral history program, recording members of former Administrations. Access to sources is sometimes difficult or impossible. 20 notes, ref.   J. Tull

31. Cohen, Jeffrey. PRESIDENTIAL PERSONALITY AND POLITICAL BEHAVIOR: THEORETICAL ISSUES AND AN EMPIRICAL TEST. *Presidential Studies Q. 1980 10(4): 588-599.* Analyzes presidents of the past century in terms of four personality traits: power motivation, achievement motivation, and James Barber's active-passive and positive-negative characteristics. In testing Barber's theory, mixed results appear, particularly with the active-passive dimension. It is important to examine a number of personality traits as well as the contemporary political environment to achieve a fuller understanding of presidential personality. 5 tables, fig., 42 notes.   D. H. Cline

32. Collat, Donald S.; Kelley, Stanley, Jr.; and Rogowski, Ronald. THE END GAME IN PRESIDENTIAL NOMINATIONS. *Am. Pol. Sci. Rev. 1981 75(2): 426-435.* A simple, empirically derived rule accounts well for the outcome of multiballot, majority-rule conventions in the period 1848-1948, and the same rule would have enabled one to predict correctly the outcome of all contested presidential nominations since 1952 before any candidate had achieved majority support in the Associated Press's polls of delegates. The rule's success suggests two conclusions about the behavior of delegates: 1) that their guesses about outcomes are based on objective cues, similarly interpreted, and 2) that the trend in voting for candidates, in addition to the level of support they attract, is an important element of such cues. Delegates in recent years do not contrast sharply with their predecessors in their predilection for bandwagon voting.   J

33. Coughlan, Margaret N. LIVES OF GREAT MEN ALL REMIND US . . . . *Q. J. of the Lib. of Congress 1981 38(4): 265-275.* Antebellum books for American children were based on the lives of such heroes as George Washington, Benjamin Franklin, and Andrew Jackson. The authors invented incidents in the lives of these great men to inspire virtues such as industry, piety, and honesty in young Americans. Secondary sources; 19 notes.   J. Powell

34. Craig, Gordon A. THE UNITED STATES AND THE EUROPEAN BALANCE. *Foreign Affairs 1976 55(1): 187-198.* From the beginning of the republic Americans have thought that there should be as little involvement as possible with Europe. But, from George Washington's ending of the French alliance to Henry Kissinger's statements on Communist components serving in NATO molders of US foreign policy have enmeshed policies with Europe. America has not shrunk from involvement whenever its interests were at stake.   R. Riles

35. Crews, Clyde F. THE POLITICAL GATEWAY TO THE SOUTH: PRESIDENTS IN LOUISVILLE. *Filson Club Hist. Q. 1982 56(2): 181-200.* Provides brief descriptions of the visits of 27 presidents, from James Monroe to Jimmy Carter, to Louisville, Kentucky. None of the visits resulted in any major historical events. Based on contemporary newspapers; 68 notes.   G. B. McKinney

36. Curtis, Kenneth M. THE PRESIDENCY: AN IMPERFECT MIRROR. *Presidential Studies Q. 1981 11(1): 28-31.* The presidency has always been the vivid reflection of both our fears and our most cherished hopes. Based on the author's experience as US ambassador to Canada.   D. H. Cline

37. Damon, Allan L. A LOOK AT THE RECORD: THE CABINET. *Am. Heritage 1976 27(3): 50-53, 90-91.* A brief history of the role of the cabinet in the executive branch of the government. Members of the cabinet are subordinate, and consequently rarely achieve great notoriety. The lack of constitutional directives has resulted in the determination of the cabinet's role largely by the will of the presidents. Includes a resumé of the types of persons (527 to date) who have served in the cabinet, and a brief history of each of the current executive departments.
                                              J. F. Paul

38. Damon, Allan L. PRESIDENTIAL ACCESSIBILITY. *Am. Heritage 1974 25(3): 60-63, 97.* Examines accessibility of various presidents to the press and public.   S

39. Damon, Allan L. PRESIDENTIAL EXPENSES. *Am. Heritage 1974 25(4): 64-67, 94-95.* A short history of the growth in Presidential expenses since 1789, including the President's salary, housing and servants, White House staff, transportation, protection, retirement, and other costs.   S

40. Damon, Allan L. VETO. *Am. Heritage 1974 25(2): 12-15, 81.* Chronological overview of presidents' use of the veto.   S

41. Daniels, O. C. Bobby. THE BICENTENNIAL: CONTRADICTIONS IN AMERICAN DEMOCRACY. *Black Scholar 1976 7(10): 2-6.* Sees contradictions inherent in the Declaration of Independence, the Constitution, and the Presidency. A passage of the initial draft of the Declaration of Independence condemning slavery was deleted from the final draft by slaveholders. This indicates that the black American was never supposed to share the unalienable rights given to white Americans. The Constitution has as its moral guardians blacks and women, although both were excluded from its writing. The blacks' constant struggle for civil rights has strengthened the nation and the Constitution. Presidents from Washington to Ford have reflected racism; even men such as Jefferson and Lincoln are frequently pictured as friends of the Negro only because of the historical myths that surround them. Based on primary and secondary sources; illus., 6 notes.   B. D. Ledbetter

42. Davison, Kenneth E. THE AMERICAN PRESIDENCY: A BIBLIOGRAPHICAL ESSAY. *Am. Studies (Lawrence, KS) 1973 12(1): 16-23, (2): 28-44.* Part I. Reviews the holdings of presidential papers in the Library of Congress, publication projects, and the development of presidential libraries. Part II. An annotated bibliography organized in seven categories: contemporary sources, general bibliographies, diaries and autobiographies, recordings and pictorial works, general histories, monographs, and biographies. The quantity and quality of studies are increasing rapidly.   L. L. Athey

43. Devol, Edward. FROM THOMAS JEFFERSON TO CYRUS VANCE. *Foreign Service J. 1977 54(11): 6-10.* Discusses the position of Secretary of State, 1793-1977.

44. Donner, Frank. HOW J. EDGAR HOOVER CREATED HIS INTELLIGENCE POWERS. *Civil Liberties Rev. 1977 3(6): 34-51.*

Discusses the evolution of the intelligence operations and powers of the Federal Bureau of Investigation between 1934 (when the Bureau investigated Nazism in the United States) and 1976.

45. Dumbrell, John W. and Lees, John D. PRESIDENTIAL POCKET-VETO POWER: A CONSTITUTIONAL ANACHRONISM? *Pol. Studies [Great Britain] 1980 28(1): 109-116.* Analyzes the little-noticed but significant conflict between the US executive and Congress over President Richard M. Nixon's use of the pocket (indirect) veto, 1970-74. Intended as a modified form of the absolute veto, this provision was little used until 1929; precedents were established in 1929 and 1938. An appellate court decision of 1974 went against the executive, which finally conceded defeat in 1975. The episode illustrates the potential for anachronisms to exist in the US constitution and the increasing role played by the courts in adjudicating executive-legislative disputes. Based on congressional, presidential, Supreme Court, and appellate court papers; 27 notes.   D. J. Nicholls

46. Durbin, Louise. INAUGURATION WAS NO BIG DEAL AT FIRST. *Smithsonian 1977 7(10): 101-111.* Discusses milestones in the presidential inauguration proceedings. Mentions categories of location, inauguration balls, addresses, parades, receptions, administration of oath, and media handling. Secondary sources; 10 illus.   K. A. Harvey

47. Edwards, George C., III. THE PRESIDENT, THE MEDIA AND THE FIRST AMENDMENT. *Presidential Studies Q. 1982 12(1): 42-47.* To understand the formation of the American Constitution, it is necessary to understand the tyranny experienced by the colonists. This led to the adoption of the Bill of Rights, particularly the 1st Amendment. Based on the author's experience as chief judge of the US Court of Appeals.   D. H. Cline

48. Edwards, George C., III. THE QUANTITATIVE STUDY OF THE PRESIDENCY. *Presidential Studies Q. 1981 11(2): 146-150.* Although the American presidency is a prime research topic for political scientists, progress in understanding it has been slow. A greater use of quantitative analysis could improve the standards of research and thus generate more respect for work done in this area. Many questions concerning the presidency are conducive to quantitative analysis. There is sufficient data for research, and access to this data is improving. Covers 1789-1980. 2 notes.   A. Drysdale

49. Engeman, Thomas S. PRESIDENTIAL STATESMANSHIP AND THE CONSTITUTION: THE LIMITS OF PRESIDENTIAL STUDIES. *Rev. of Pol. 1982 44(2): 266-281.* Studies such as Richard Neustadt's *Presidential Power* (1960) and Richard Pious's *The American Presidency* (1979) provide useful analyses of various elements of the presidency; however, they do not fully explain the nature of the executive. The nature of presidential government can be better understood by studying the opinions of "Publius" in the *Federalist* and the statesmanship of Lincoln as they relate to constitutional separation of powers, executive prerogative, and impeachment. While prerogative operates as the true source of executive power, providing the president with the necessary power to govern in the face of political inertia, impeachment acts as the ultimate legislative power and insures democracy. The successful president combines knowledge of democratic principles with the prudent use of his prerogative powers under the Constitution. 44 notes.
                                                      G. A. Glovins

50. Fairbanks, James David. THE PRIESTLY FUNCTIONS OF THE PRESIDENCY: A DISCUSSION OF THE LITERATURE ON CIVIL RELIGION AND ITS IMPLICATIONS FOR THE STUDY OF PRESIDENTIAL LEADERSHIP. *Presidential Studies Q. 1981 11(2): 214-232.* Despite the intentions of the Founding Fathers to separate church and state, there exists a civil religion centering on the president. As this religion consists of the ultimate values of American society, the presidency's moral dimension lies in responding to the citizens' needs, including spiritual needs. Relevant extracts from inaugural addresses are cited. To guide future empirical research, a series of propositions concerning civil religion, political leadership, and the moral role of the president are presented. Covers 1789-1980. Based on a paper presented to the 1979 Summer Seminar for College Teachers. Primary sources; 80 notes.
                                                       A. Drysdale

51. Falk, Gerhard. OLD CALVIN NEVER DIED: PURITANICAL RHETORIC BY FOUR AMERICAN PRESIDENTS CONCERNING PUBLIC WELFARE. Plesur, Milton, ed. *An American Historian: Essays to Honor Selig Adler* (Buffalo: State U. of N.Y., 1980): 183-190. Discusses the themes of Calvinism and the work ethic from Max Weber's *The Protestant Ethic and the Spirit of Capitalism* (1905) as expressed in the rhetoric of Franklin D. Roosevelt, Herbert C. Hoover, Lyndon B. Johnson, and Richard M. Nixon; 1905-79.

52. Finkelstein, Leo, Jr. THE CALENDRICAL RITE OF THE ASCENSION TO POWER. *Western J. of Speech Communication 1981 45(1): 51-59.* President Franklin D. Roosevelt's first inaugural address in 1933 marked a change in both the style and substance of inaugural addresses: because agreement occurs more easily at higher levels of abstraction, addresses have become more abstract so as to appeal to an increasingly pluralistic society; and to cope with crises such as the Great Depression of 1929 and with threats of armed conflict and Cold War, speeches have placed less emphasis on America's greatness than on the faith necessary to preserve that greatness.

53. Fischer, Roger A. PINBACK PUT-DOWNS: THE CAMPAIGN BUTTON AS POLITICAL SATIRE. *J. of Popular Culture 1980 13(4): 645-653.* Reviews presidential campaign buttons from the McKinley-Bryan contest of 1896 to the 1976 Carter-Ford election. The quantity of such buttons apparently diminished in times of widespread national unrest (e.g., in 1916 and 1920), but in each of the 21 presidential election battles fought during this period, campaign buttons continued, in their own way, the long tradition of American political satire. 2 photos, 16 notes.   D. G. Nielson

54. Fisher, Louis. FLOUTING THE CONSTITUTION. *Center Mag. 1977 10(6): 13-19.* Discusses executive power, its connection with veto power in terms of the US Constitution, 1800-1976.

55. Fredman, L. E. WHY GREAT MEN ARE, OR ARE NOT, ELECTED PRESIDENT: SOME BRITISH VIEWS OF THE PRESIDENCY. *Presidential Studies Q. 1980 10(3): 296-305.* Using James Bryce's *The American Commonwealth* (1888) as a starting point, examines the British view of the presidency and those who have held the office. Bryce and succeeding scholars such as Harold Laski, Dennis Brogan, and Marcus Cunliffe all compared Great Britain's and America's institutions to issue warnings or statements about the nature of the two systems. Many of these scholars have attempted to devise a system to rank presidents, but such systems usually have been overrated and biased. There is no ideal test of greatness; ideals and standards vary greatly. 24 notes.
                                                      D. H. Cline

56. Freitag, Peter J. THE CABINET AND BIG BUSINESS: A STUDY OF INTERLOCKS. *Social Problems 1975 23(2): 137-152.* A study of US Cabinet Secretaries during 1897-1973 supports C. Wright Mills's contention that there is a high degree of interchange of personnel between the elites of corporate and political institutions. In the executive branch elite businessmen are the rule rather than the exception. The exchange of positions of leadership provides a mechanism of communication between government and business, and able administrators in government will have to be businessmen. 6 tables, ref.   A. M. Osur

57. Fullington, Michael Gregory. PRESIDENTIAL MANAGEMENT AND EXECUTIVE SCANDAL. *Presidential Studies Q. 1979 9(2): 192-202.* Provides evidence to support the position that presidential scandal is experienced due to ineffective management by the president of staff and advisors, and traces the history of management sciences since 1927.

58. Fullington, Michael Gregory. PRESIDENTIAL STAFF RELATIONS: A THEORY FOR ANALYSIS. *Presidential Studies Q. 1977 7(2-3): 108-114.* Managerial skill is perhaps the most important factor which determines presidential effectiveness. The President must receive the information necessary for informed decisionmaking, and he must have a competent staff to implement his decisions. The author investigates the use of managerial science theories for improving presidential performance, and suggests the use of André L. Delbecq's decisionmaking theories—routine, creative, and negotiated decisionmaking. Presidents from Franklin D. Roosevelt to Richard M. Nixon are viewed in the context of Delbecq's typologies. Secondary sources; 2 tables, 50 notes.
                                                        R. D. Hurt

59. Funston, Richard. GREAT PRESIDENTS, GREAT JUSTICES? *Presidential Studies Q. 1977 7(4): 191-199.* Explores whether there is a correlation between great presidents and great Supreme Court justices appointed by them. The study uses evaluations on greatness drawn up a decade ago in a survey of historians. Establishing from these a mean prestige rating for appointees, a justice-president ratio and an index of judicial recruitment, concludes that there is no correlation between President and Justice appointees with respect to greatness. 5 tables, 13 notes.   J. Tull

60. Gawthrop, Louis C. ADMINISTRATIVE RESPONSIBILITY: PUBLIC POLICY AND THE WILSONIAN LEGACY. *Policy Studies J. 1976 5(1): 108-113.* Discusses administrative responsibility and ethics in public administration during the 20th century.

61. Genovese, Michael A. DEMOCRATIC THEORY AND THE EMERGENCY POWERS OF THE PRESIDENT. *Presidential Studies Q. 1979 9(3): 283-289.* Discusses the problem of reconciling presidents' emergency powers during crises with the principles of democracy, from when John Locke defined presidential power as executive "prerogative" until Jimmy Carter's presidency through 1979.

62. George, Alexander L. ASSESSING PRESIDENTIAL CHARACTER. *World Pol. 1974 26(2): 234-282.* James David Barber's trenchant analysis of the styles of eleven Presidents (in his *The Presidential Character: Predicting Performance in the White House, 1972*) contributes much to an understanding of their performance in that office and illuminates the ways in which personality expresses itself in political behavior. Less successful is Barber's effort to develop a theory for predicting performance in the Presidency well enough to contribute to the assessment of candidates for that office. The personality theory he employs for this purpose is insufficiently developed and insufficiently validated to carry the burden of prediction.   J

63. Gilbert, Robert E. DEATH AND THE AMERICAN PRESIDENT. *Politico [Italy] 1977 42(4): 719-741.* Comparing statistics for differential mortality and average life expectancy, the author argues that US presidents, vice-presidents, and defeated presidential candidates are notably short-lived in comparison with the general white male population, and even more disadvantaged in terms of longevity when compared to white male members of Congress and the Supreme Court, who are drawn from the same socioeconomic strata. The explanation for this phenomenon seems to be both the inner tensions of men who are driven to take upon themselves the ordeal of running for president and the incredible stress and "mental anguish" of the office itself. As Dr. Hans Kraus concludes, "tension is the killer" of presidents, usually by leading to cardiovascular disease. 76 notes.   J. C. Billigmeier

64. Gustafson, Merlin. THE PRESIDENTIAL LIBRARIES: SOME IMPRESSIONS. *Manuscripta 1974 18(3): 155-165.* Discusses the historical development of five libraries which have been constructed as repositories for presidential papers; the Herbert Hoover Presidential Library in West Branch, Iowa, the Franklin D. Roosevelt Library in Hyde Park, New York, the Harry S. Truman Library in Independence, Missouri, the Dwight D. Eisenhower Library in Abilene, Kansas, and the Lyndon Baines Johnson Library in Austin, Texas. Examines the general facilities available in each, their importance as sources of religious and political history, and their value to the writers of Catholic history. 21 notes.   I. Fenlon

65. Gustafson, Merlin. THE PRESIDENT'S MAIL: IS IT WORTHWHILE TO WRITE TO THE PRESIDENT? *Presidential Studies Q. 1978 8(1): 36-44.* Examines the methods used to screen and process citizen mail received by presidents from Herbert Hoover to Dwight Eisenhower. Presidential mail is divided into three levels, only the first of which reaches the president. Numerically small, this segment came overwhelmingly from influential persons. Letters in the second level, which are handled by top presidential advisors, were also from elites but the president lacked the time or desire to respond personally. The bulk of presidential mail is from ordinary citizens and receives noncommital acknowledgement from staff. Specific problems and mail handling techniques of various administrations are discussed. Predicts letters will continue to be screened and channelled upward according to their relative importance. 26 notes.   S. C. Strom

66. Hagan, Charles B. THE STORY OF AN UNBALANCED GOVERNMENT. *World Affairs 1977 140(1): 67-77.* The shift in power and influence from the legislative to the executive branch during the 20th century climaxed with the Watergate scandal.

67. Haley, P. Edward. COMPARATIVE INTERVENTION: MEXICO IN 1914 AND THE DOMINICAN REPUBLIC IN 1965. *Australian J. of Pol. and Hist. 1974 20(1): 32-44.* Compares President Wilson's intervention in Mexico in 1914 and President Johnson's in the Dominican Republic in 1965 against a background of US military intervention in the 20th century. Suggests that the characteristic American reaction to foreign revolution is neither defense of self-determination nor exploitation. Rather the US has sought to devise and put into operation a liberal democratic alternative to radical social revolution. This predates the Cold War and great power status and is determined by the beliefs of American leaders, domestic political needs, the policymakers' comprehension of the situation, capability, and a favorable international situation. Documented from monographs and memoirs.

W. D. McIntyre

68. Halliday, E. M. CARVING THE AMERICAN COLOSSUS. *Am. Heritage 1977 28(4): 18-27.* The carving of the profiles of Lincoln, Washington, Jefferson, and Theodore Roosevelt on Mount Rushmore was a lengthy project conceived and directed by Gutzon Borglum (1923-39) and later his son. 8 illus.   B. J. Paul

69. Handberg, Roger. PRESIDENTIAL PREDICTIONS OF SUPREME COURT JUSTICES' BEHAVIOR. *J. of Pol. Sci. 1980 7(2): 146-149.* Presidential predictions of Supreme Court appointees' future behavior is accurate over the short run. Liberal presidents have had the greatest difficulty in predicting judicial performance in terms of the appointees' liberalism/conservatism. When the president is not diverted by other variables, such as friendship ties or political expediency, predictions entering the selection process are very successful. Covers 1795-1980. Primary sources; 2 tables, 10 notes.   T. P. Richardson

70. Hanson, Robert. HAIL TO THE CHIEFS: OUR PRESIDENTIAL LIBRARIES. *Wilson Lib. Bull. 1981 55(8): 576-583.* Compares the six libraries dedicated to recent presidents and their times: the Franklin D. Roosevelt Library, Hyde Park, New York (1940), the Harry S. Truman Library and Museum, Independence, Missouri (1957), the Dwight D. Eisenhower Library, Abilene, Kansas (1962), the Herbert Hoover Presidential Library and Museum, West Branch, Iowa (1962), the Lyndon Baines Johnson Library, Austin, Texas (1971), and the John Fitzgerald Kennedy Library, Boston, Massachusetts (1979).

71. Harris, Irving D. THE PSYCHOLOGIES OF PRESIDENTS. *Hist. of Childhood Q. 1976 3(3): 337-350.* Eminent men such as Presidents act in accordance with personal psychologies largely shaped by position in the family as children. First sons, such as Lyndon B. Johnson, have a high sense of self-worth, while later sons, such as Richard M. Nixon, have a lower self-regard bordering on inferiority. The self-image often is reflected in the ways the President pictures the nation in his public statements. Other leaders included in this analysis are Kennedy, Madison, Hamilton, Jay, Polk, Lincoln, Wilson, Franklin D. Roosevelt, Truman, and McKinley, as well as some foreign leaders. First sons are more likely to lead nations to war. Secondary sources; 10 notes.

R. E. Butchart

72. Holzer, Harold. LINCOLN AND WASHINGTON: THE PRINTMAKERS BLESSED THEIR UNION. *Register of the Kentucky Hist. Soc. 1977 75(3): 204-213.* In trying to save his country, Abraham Lincoln often invoked the name of George Washington. As a result, portraitists often featured them together. Secondary sources; 5 illus., 18 notes.   J. F. Paul

73. Hughes, Arthur J. "AMAZIN' JIMMY AND A MIGHTY FORTRESS WAS OUR TEDDY": THEODORE ROOSEVELT AND JIMMY CARTER, THE RELIGIOUS LINK. *Presidential Studies Q. 1979 9(1): 80-83.* Both Theodore Roosevelt and Jimmy Carter claimed a strong belief in God, referred repeatedly to their faith, professed a sense of mission in their political functions, and had heroes (Oliver Cromwell and Hyman Rickover, respectively) with similar senses of mission.

74. Hugins, Walter E. MORALISM IN AMERICAN FOREIGN POLICY: FROM JEFFERSON TO JIMMY CARTER. *Issues and Studies [Taiwan] 1978 14(9): 57-69.* Jimmy Carter's foreign policy is attempting to merge the pragmatism which governed policy until the late 19th century with the moralism that basically governed it in the 20th century.

75. Huitt, Ralph K. CONGRESS: RETROSPECT AND PROSPECT. *J. of Pol. 1976 38(3): 209-227.* Studies Congress since its founding. The evolution of the modern Congress rests on two fundamental concepts: federalism and the separation of powers. These principles have been influenced by party leadership, by how the President has related to Congress, and by the balance of power between the Presidency and Congress. Assesses the limits and potential of Congressional accomplishment under the American system. 16 notes.   R. V. Ritter

76. Isetti, Ronald E. THE CHARTER MYTH OF AMERICA: A STUDY OF POLITICAL SYMBOLISM IN THE INAUGURAL ADDRESSES OF THE PRESIDENTS. *Cithara 1976 16(1): 3-17.* The Presidents have looked upon America not merely as a young nation in a new land, but as Israel in the New World, a biblical vision that was born of the experience of the Protestant settlers of the 17th century, who left England (as it were, Egypt) to found their righteous New Jerusalems, under charter from God, in the American wilderness.

77. Ivie, Robert L. PRESIDENTIAL MOTIVES FOR WAR. *Q. J. of Speech 1974 60(3): 337-345.* "The vocabulary of American Presidents is analyzed to locate the images, or vocabularies of motives, that they project in justification of war. Kenneth Burke's dramatism provides the methodological resources to chart and synthesize the language of Madison, Polk, McKinley, Wilson, Roosevelt, Truman, and Johnson in selected war messages and to discover that their vocabulary establishes a rigid and truncated pattern of justification for war."   J

78. Johnson, M. Glen. HUMAN RIGHTS AND UNITED STATES FOREIGN POLICY. *India Q. [India] 1978 34(4): 471-490.* George Washington "clearly eschewed the use of human rights as a guide to the making of foreign policy . . . [which] was to be the dominant principle of US policy throughout the 19th century, and exerted a profound influence over it well into the 20th century." Woodrow Wilson elevated human rights to a higher level of priority than ever before; since then, all American political leaders have been Wilsonians. Human rights was one of many factors which led to the Cold War and contributed more than other factors to its intensity and duration. Henry A. Kissinger and other US diplomats were active behind the scenes in promoting better observance of human rights in other countries. The door was kept open for political refugees seeking a land in which human rights were fully observed. Gives various definitions of human rights and discusses problems and risks. 8 notes.   E. P. Stickney

79. Kaiser, Frederick M. PRESIDENTIAL ASSASSINATIONS AND ASSAULTS: CHARACTERISTICS AND IMPACT ON PROTECTIVE PROCEDURES. *Presidential Studies Q. 1981 11(4): 545-558.* Since 1804, attacks on presidents have been occurring with more frequency, forcing the Secret Service to almost continually reexamine its procedures. The service has responded by increasing its cooperation with the Federal Bureau of Investigation and the National Security Agency, and by greatly increasing its protective activities of different individuals. From its origins as an anticounterfeiting organization in the 1890's, the Secret Service has expanded and continually modified its methods. But, it is still an agency with limited law enforcement authority, and thus it remains restricted. Table, 62 notes.   D. H. Cline

80. Kamath, M. V. THE FUNCTIONING OF THE AMERICAN POLITICAL SYSTEM. *India Q.: J. of Int. Affairs [India] 1976 32(3): 303-314.* Analyzes the structure and operations of the political system from the period of the framing of the US Constitution to the Watergate scandal. Believes that the rise of executive power has come largely due to the exigencies. The founding fathers sought to build into the Constitution a system of checks and balances which would avoid either the tyranny of the legislature or the executive.   S. H. Frank

81. Kampelman, Max M. CONGRESS, THE MEDIA, AND THE PRESIDENT. *Pro. of the Acad. of Pol. Sci. 1975 32(1): 85-97.* This overview of difficulties in mass media conveyance of presidential and Congressional activities emphasizes the important role of the press in presenting informative analysis and in influencing public opinion, 19th-20th centuries.

82. Kaspi, André. ÉLECTIONS AMÉRICAINES: LE TRIOMPHE DES "MÉDIOCRES"? [The US elections: triumph of mediocrity?]. *Histoire [France] 1980 (26): 91-93.* The President of the United States is elected every four years, and every four years the old theme appears: good candidates are rare.

83. Kehl, James A. WHITE HOUSE OR ANIMAL HOUSE? *South Atlantic Q. 1980 79(4): 343-354.* A tongue-in-cheek comment on the influence of pets and other animals in and around the White House. The most significant was FDR's Fala. Nixon's Checkers played a prominent part, for he was the only gift the family had received, and Nixon was going to keep him. His famous "Checkers Speech" was his first attempt at stonewalling. Nixon is also remembered for receiving two Chinese pandas, to the dismay of environmentalists. And it was Theodore Roosevelt who popularized the Teddy Bear—almost to the point of making the doll obsolete. Eisenhower had his problems with dogs, but his greatest difficulty came with the White House lawn squirrels who constantly threatened his putting green. His efforts to evict them were not only futile, but ired many groups.   H. M. Parker, Jr.

84. Kislov, A. K. BELYI DOM I SIONISTSKOE LOBBI [The White House and the Zionist lobby]. *Voprosy Istorii [USSR] 1973 (1): 48-61.* The author discloses the interrelations between the White House and the Zionist lobby over the past fifty years, tracing the influence exerted by the Zionists on the political life of the U.S.A. in general and their ties with the White House, beginning with the Presidency of Woodrow Wilson, in particular. Considerable attention is devoted in the article to the causes of this influence which becomes especially pronounced during election campaigns, as well as to the methods employed by the Zionists in their activity. The author stresses that the Zionists' possibilities to secure at definite stages the introduction of certain correctives beneficial for them in the U.S. foreign policy line are not unlimited. In the final analysis the decision to further one or another concrete course of action remains the prerogative of the U.S. authorities which express the interests of the capitalist class as a whole. That is why the determinative aspect of relations between the Zionist lobby and the White House is the need for international Zionism to adapt itself to the interests of American imperialism.   J

85. Koenig, Louis W. REASSESSING THE "IMPERIAL PRESIDENCY." *Pro. of the Acad. of Pol. Sci. 1981 34(2): 31-44.* Discusses writings about the American "imperial presidency." Presidents since Washington have seen it as anything but imperial. 17 notes.
                    T. P. Richardson

86. Koppes, Clayton R. FROM NEW DEAL TO TERMINATION: LIBERALISM AND INDIAN POLICY, 1933-1953. *Pacific Hist. Rev. 1977 46(4): 543-566.* In Indian policies there was only a selective continuity of liberalism from the New Deal to the Fair Deal. Roosevelt's commissioner of Indian affairs (1933-45), John Collier, considered the loss of community the major problem of modern society. His Indian policy was in the same spirit as other early New Deal policies and programs which sought to foster cooperation and community rather than competition and individualism. By World War II liberal support for such programs had greatly eroded. The Truman administration allowed Indian policy to return to its earlier emphasis on assimilation, in keeping with the Fair Deal's own emphasis on economic prosperity and individual competition and on individual civil rights and freedom from group identity. Based on documents in the National Archives, Yale University Library, Library of Congress, and Truman Library, and on published primary and secondary sources; 39 notes.   W. K. Hobson

87. Koschal, Stephen. PRESIDENTIAL BOOK COLLECTING. *Manuscripts 1976 28(4): 284-291.* Describes the book collecting habits of Presidents through Gerald R. Ford. Comments on the availability and value of books either owned or inscribed by each President. Illus.
                    D. A. Yanchisin

88. Krukones, Michael G. PREDICTING PRESIDENTIAL PERFORMANCE THROUGH POLITICAL CAMPAIGNS. *Presidential Studies Q. 1980 10(4): 527-543.* Using the actions of presidents between 1912 and 1972, studies the degree to which candidates adhered to campaign promises once they had been elected president. During this period, approximately 70%-80% of the promises, as transmitted by the popular media, were kept by the men once they had entered office. This indicates that the public can make an intelligent choice between different candidates based on their policy promises as candidates. 5 tables, 48 notes.
D. H. Cline

89. Kunzle, David. 200 YEARS OF THE GREAT AMERICAN FREEDOM TO COMPLAIN. *Art in Am. 1977 65(2): 99-105.* Discusses the art of political cartooning, especially aimed at the presidency, highlighting an exhibition, "The American Presidency in Political Cartoons, 1776-1976" at the University Art Museum, Berkeley, 1976.

90. LaFontaine, Charles V. GOD AND NATION IN SELECTED U.S. PRESIDENTIAL INAUGURAL ADDRESSES, 1789-1945. *J. of Church and State 1976 18(1): 39-60, (3): 503-521.* Part I. Suggests that the Presidential Inaugural addresses are a religious statement, in that they constitute the nation's statement of faith. Studies the addresses of George Washington, John Adams, Thomas Jefferson, Abraham Lincoln, Woodrow Wilson, and Franklin Roosevelt. Limits of the study are discussed, indicating that a full study would require examination of all writings of presidents and of their times. The addresses all pay attention to the deity in some form. The most popular term is "God," followed by "providence." "Jesus Christ" and "Christian" do not appear often. Stressed is the view that God is considered a part of the ruling group and government. The government reflects the will of God to some extent. There is a summary of the doctrine of deity found in the addresses, with 9 points, and a summary of the views on the nation and the deity with 17 points. The Civil War caused the first major revision of American concepts of the deity. 65 notes. Part II. Presidents to the time of Abraham Lincoln thought of America as a chosen land, divinely favored. With Lincoln and the Civil War, change occurred. God was chastising the people for their faults and Lincoln saw the war as God's way of reestablishing the nation as it had been. James A. Garfield wanted Congress to respect the religious scruples of the citizens, but at the same time, not to allow any church to usurp power. William McKinley saw God's will in America's obtaining an empire from the Spanish War. Woodrow Wilson went back to Lincoln's view of restoration in 1913. Franklin Roosevelt followed a similar theme in 1933. From this we can see a national theology developing. 1) America as a chosen people and 2) America as an example to the world. 129 notes.
E. E. Eminhizer

91. Lea, Jimmy. THE PRESIDENCY: AUXILIARY AND PRIMARY LIMITS. *Southern Q. 1976 14(2): 133-149.* Examines the direct and indirect powers associated with the American presidency, since the writing of the Constitution. Focuses on existing judicial and legislative methods and alternatives for preventing the growth and abuse of executive power. Social, cultural, and technological factors and developments could influence public attitudes toward power and the presidency. 61 notes.
R. W. Dubay

92. LeClaire, Charles A. THE MARINES HAVE LANDED. *Marine Corps Gazette 1959 43(7): 24-30.* Describes the constitutional implications of decisions by the US government to dispatch US Marines on combat missions to foreign lands, and comments on how the matter has been viewed by US presidents since Thomas Jefferson.

93. Lee, Jong R. PRESIDENTIAL VETOES FROM WASHINGTON TO NIXON. *J. of Pol. 1975 37(2): 522-546.* Employs multiple regression to analyze historical patterns of presidential vetoes and congressional overriding. One basic finding is that both the frequency of vetoes and success of congressional efforts to override are largely responsive to congressional experience of a president and objective changes in the political situation. Over 40 percent of variance in the presidential vetoes is accounted for by previous congressional membership of the president, party control of the Congress, and degree of electoral support, whereas variance in overriding actions is significantly accounted for by party control, midterm election, level of military force, and price instability.
J

94. Lee, Jong R. RALLYING AROUND THE FLAG: FOREIGN POLICY EVENTS AND PRESIDENTIAL POPULARITY. *Presidential Studies Q. 1977 7(4): 252-256.* Records public opinion about presidents in 53 short-term policy events, from Franklin D. Roosevelt to Gerald Ford. In the six categories employed, the President's popularity tended to go up immediately but soon slip back. Events having relatively lasting impact on presidential popularity are wars and military crises. It is more difficult to explain variations in duration of popularity changes than the changes themselves. 2 tables, ref.
J. Tull

95. Leiter, William M. THE PRESIDENCY AND NON-FEDERAL GOVERNMENT: THE BENEFACTOR-AVERSION HYPOTHESIS, THE CASE OF PUBLIC ASSISTANCE POLICIES IN THE NEW DEAL AND NIXON ADMINISTRATIONS. *Presidential Studies Q. 1980 10(4): 636-644.* Tests the benefactor-aversion hypothesis, where presidential administrations view state and local governments as responsible for governmental ills, for its validity during the Roosevelt and Nixon administrations. In both of these cases, the hypothesis holds true. Both administrations felt that the inferior governments were not living up to their responsibility and were the cause of the majority of problems. 30 notes.
D. H. Cline

96. Lengle, James I. DIVISIVE PRESIDENTIAL PRIMARIES AND PARTY ELECTORAL PROSPECTS, 1932-1976. *Am. Pol. Q. 1980 8(3): 261-277.* Using two different units of analysis, this article examines the impact of divisive presidential primaries on party electoral prospects. First, an examination of state-level data from 1932 to 1976 shows that divisive presidential primaries hurt both parties' chances of winning those same states in the November general election. This effect is stronger for Democrats and remains even after controlling for incumbency and state party orientation. Second, an examination of survey data collected in 1972 and 1976 shows that supporters of losing contenders are likely to defect in general elections. Here again, the effect is present for both parties, but more pronounced for Democrats.
J

97. Lindop, Edmund. "A NATIONAL NEED": MUSIC AND THE PRESIDENTS. *Am. Hist. Illus. 1975 10(8): 4-9, 46-50.* Describes the musical tastes of US Presidents and asserts that from colonial times to the present day presidents have regarded music a vital national asset.

98. Lindsey, David. THE PRESIDENT: SELECTION AND PERFORMANCE. *Mankind 1981 6(10): 26-30.* Reviews recent books on American presidential politics: James David Barber's *The Pulse of Politics: Electing Presidents in the Media Age* (New York: Norton, 1980), John M. Blum's *The Progressive Presidents: Theodore Roosevelt, Woodrow Wilson, Franklin D. Roosevelt, Lyndon B. Johnson* (New York: Norton, 1980), and Michael R. Beschloss's *Kennedy and Roosevelt: The Uneasy Alliance* (New York: Norton, 1980). Together, these works provide important insights into the presidential election process, presidential power, and how American chief executives have sought to combine the quests for a better society in the United States and for a more tolerable world order. 7 illus.
C. D. Geist

99. Linkugel, Wil A. and Sellen, Robert W. THE PRESIDENTIAL CANDIDATE IN BEHALF OF HIMSELF. *South Atlantic Q. 1976 75(3): 290-311.* The intense focus upon individual presidential candidates is a recent tradition in American politics. Most candidates, from George Washington to Woodrow Wilson in 1912, have maintained a degree of seclusion from the rough spectacle of presidential campaigns. Even after he broke the tradition in 1916, Wilson ceased campaigning after his chief opponent, Theodore Roosevelt, was hospitalized from an assassination attempt. Herbert Hoover made good use of the new media of radio, but Franklin Roosevelt became its master. Subsequently, television theatrics made the presidential race less one of parties and issues and more one of personality and charisma. Primary and secondary sources; 49 notes.
W. L. Olbrich

100. Locander, Robert. THE ADVERSARY RELATIONSHIP: A NEW LOOK AT AN OLD IDEA. *Presidential Studies Q. 1979 9(3): 266-274.* The traditional adversary relationship between presidents and the press is not always applicable; traces the relationships between press and Presidents Franklin D. Roosevelt through Gerald R. Ford.

101. Locander, Robert. THE PRESIDENT, THE PRESS, AND THE PUBLIC: FRIENDS AND ENEMIES OF DEMOCRACY. *Presidential Studies Q. 1978 8(2): 140-150.* Defines the democratic roles of the Presidency, the Press, and the public and contrasts them with realistic and authoritarian behavior alternatives. Historical examples show how each of these participants can act democratically or undemocratically under different circumstances. Watergate proves that a democratic press and public can remove an authoritarian President. The growing power of Congress and special interest groups indicates that future Presidents will follow a realistic pattern of behavior. American voters show greater issue consistency and independence. The press, with its unrestrained and growing public influence, may be the greatest threat to democracy in the future. 2 fig., 30 notes.   S. C. Strom

102. Longley, Lawrence D. THE ELECTORAL COLLEGE. *Current Hist. 1974 67(396): 64-69, 85-86.* Explains how the electoral college works, what criticisms have been directed against it, and what reforms have been suggested. One of eight articles in this issue on political reform.   S

103. Loss, Richard. ALEXANDER HAMILTON AND THE MODERN PRESIDENCY: CONTINUITY OR DISCONTINUITY? *Presidential Studies Q. 1982 12(1): 6-25.* Tests the thesis of Edward Corwin and Clinton Rossiter that a continuity between the teachings of Alexander Hamilton and the modern theory of presidential power exists. Hamilton's thoughts cannot be seen as a primary or secondary source, however, for the theories of presidential power espoused by Theodore Roosevelt, Woodrow Wilson, and Corwin. They reduced Hamilton's complex theory to a simple quest for power, and they abandoned his belief in natural law, Christianity, moderation, and virtue. 106 notes.
          D. H. Cline

104. Loss, Richard. EDWARD S. CORWIN: THE CONSTITUTION OF THE DOMINANT PRESIDENCY. *Presidential Studies Q. 1977 7(1): 53-65.* Edward S. Corwin's writings emphasized a living, flexible, changing Constitution. Corwin criticized the Founding Fathers for not anticipating contemporary problems. The Constitution should meet the needs of the majority. A dominant President, actively engaged in social planning, could fulfill these needs and serve as a power center for a living Constitution. Corwin opposed the rigidity of the courts. He exaggerated the constitutional competence of Congress and the Presidency. Covers the period 1914-60. Based on Corwin's writings; 123 notes.
          R. D. Hurt

105. Lovely, Louise. THE EVOLUTION OF PRESIDENTIAL LIBRARIES. *Government Publ. Rev. 1979 6(1): 27-36.* Surveys the disposition of presidential papers and their retention in presidential libraries, documents use by students and researchers, and summarizes reports for the National Study Commissions on Records and Documents of Federal Officials, 1929-78.

106. Massaro, John. "LAME-DUCK" PRESIDENTS, GREAT JUSTICES? *Presidential Studies Q. 1978 8(3): 296-302.* Examines the lame-duck hypothesis that an unfavorable political situation in the Senate forces a president to nominate Supreme Court candidates of above average quality. Richard Funston's "greatness" ratings (see abstract 59) of Supreme Court justices appointed during the final year of a presidential term are compared with the overall average and found to be significantly higher. The likelihood of rejection forces lame-duck presidents to choose more qualified candidates with fewer ideological or party considerations. 4 tables, 14 notes.   S. C. Strom

107. McCoy, Donald R. TRENDS IN VIEWING HERBERT HOOVER, FRANKLIN D. ROOSEVELT, HARRY S. TRUMAN, AND DWIGHT D. EISENHOWER. *Midwest Q. 1979 20(2): 117-136.* Briefly appraises the historical and biographical literature on the presidents from Herbert Hoover to Dwight D. Eisenhower, 1928-74.

108. McDonough, John; Jacobs, Richard F.; and Hoxie, R. Gordon. WHO OWNS PRESIDENTIAL PAPERS? *Manuscripts 1975 27 (1): 2-11.* In a panel discussion on presidential papers, McDonough spoke about the fate of presidential papers and those in the Library of Congress, Hoxie spoke about the attitude of Presidents toward their papers, and the editor summarized Jacobs' comments about presidential libraries and recent developments in legislation regarding the papers of public officials. 17 notes.   D. A. Yanchisin

109. McGuire, John R. THE FOREST SERVICE: CONSERVER OF AMERICA'S FORESTS. *J. of NAL Assoc. 1978 3(3-4): 72-76.* History of the Forest Service of the US Department of Agriculture since 1876; focusing on the changes instituted by the Forest Reserve Act (US, 1891) and the Organic Administration Act (US, 1897), new responsibilities of the Forest Service under the administration of Theodore Roosevelt, and conservation progress under national legislation until 1976.

110. McKay, Pamela R. PRESIDENTIAL PAPERS: A PROPERTY ISSUE. *Lib. Q. 1982 52(1): 21-40.* The dramatic change which occurred in the ownership of presidential papers due to litigation surrounding former President Nixon's papers is the underlying theme in this discussion of the property aspects of presidential papers from George Washington to the present. The paper begins with the Supreme Court case *Nixon v. Administrator of General Services* (US 1977). Additional topics include a description of presidential papers, a survey of past practice and law regarding the ownership and control of presidential papers, and the pro and con arguments of presidential ownership.   J/S

111. Mead, Walter J. THE NATIONAL ENERGY PROGRAM EVALUATED. *Current Hist. 1978 75(438): 9-12, 31-33.* Lists 11 federal energy policies of administrations since the 1930's whose conflicting emphases indicate the need for a comprehensive energy program, and evaluates the chances for success of President Jimmy Carter's energy program.

112. Merrill, Jeffrey. PLANNING FOR NEW HEALTH HUMAN-POWER. *Social Policy 1975 6(3): 36-43.* Discusses similarities and differences between present health care issues and those of the Roosevelt Administration and the Works Progress Administration in 1935.

113. Musto, David F. CONTINUITY ACROSS GENERATIONS: THE ADAMS FAMILY MYTH. Albin, Mel, ed. *New Directions in Psychohistory: The Adelphi Papers in Honor of Erik H. Erikson* (Lexington, Mass.: Heath, 1980): 117-129. Discusses the extent to which people are influenced by their environments, situating this dilemma in the family's quest for identity and continuity across generations. Examines four generations of the Adams family, beginning with John and Abigail Adams in 1764, attempting to understand the family's intergenerational internal stream of identity, the "family myth," and how it relates to the wider culture. Such a myth can be forged in a stressful historical period, continue for several generations as an inherited set of attitudes, and eventually be reconstructed under the impact of an incongruous environment. Secondary sources; 23 notes.   J. Powell

114. Nelson, Michael. JAMES DAVID BARBER AND THE PSYCHOLOGICAL PRESIDENCY. *Virginia Q. Rev. 1980 56(4): 650-667.* Examines and criticizes James David Barber's psychological theories about the American presidency in his *The Presidential Character* (1972) and *The Pulse of Politics.* In the first, Barber argues that character is the most important thing about presidents and that they can be classified as active or passive and positive or negative. In the second, Barber insists that the public's election moods, conflict, conscience, and conciliation, recur in order over 12-year cycles. Barber's belief is that election reform can best come from media journalism if it can engage readers' interest and give "greater attention to the character of the candidates."
          O. H. Zabel

115. Neumann, Robert G. LEADERSHIP: FRANKLIN ROOSEVELT, TRUMAN, EISENHOWER, AND TODAY. *Presidential Studies Q. 1980 10(1): 10-19.* Looks at the presidency of the United States from the point of view of leadership. The ability to lead intelligently affects not only America but other countries as well. Criteria of presidential leadership within the US political system should be established; the Roosevelt, Truman, Eisenhower, and Carter presidencies are tested against suggested criteria. The Carter presidency, so viewed, has been a troublesome one. Based on official records and research; 13 notes.
          G. E. Pergl

116. Nikolayev, Y. THE URGENT DEMAND OF THE TIME. *Int. Affairs [USSR] 1974 (11): 14-18.* Discusses trends in US foreign

policy with the USSR 1919-70's, including recent diplomacy of the Nixon administration and Secretary of State Henry A. Kissinger.

117. Nikolayev, Y. US DIPLOMATIC SERVICE: PAST AND PRESENT. *Int. Affairs [USSR] 1977 (7): 118-132.* Reviews the history of the US Foreign Service. The Service is a product of American politics: various cliques and factions fought for control at the time of the Revolutionary War, a factor which has become a permanent part of the American system. The key factor influencing American foreign policy has been militaristic imperialism. Because of the central position of this factor, American presidents have relied much more on military advisers than on the professional service. After 1945, the United States actively and openly sought world domination, a policy which crumbled during the Johnson and Nixon administrations. At present, American diplomats are hesitantly learning to live in a world of peaceful detente, but it remains to be seen how successful they will be. 34 notes. V. L. Human

118. Oh, John C. H. THE PRESIDENCY AND PUBLIC WELFARE POLICY. *Presidential Studies Q. 1978 8(4): 377-390.* A President's policy effectiveness depends on 1) widespread perception of a crisis, 2) public perception of the President's philosophy and commitment, 3) the public's understanding of the proposed policy, and 4) an effective relationship with Congress. These elements are reviewed in the context of presidents' welfare policy since 1933, including Roosevelt's Aid to Dependent Children (ADC), Truman's Aid to Families with Dependent Children (AFDC), the Kennedy-Johnson War on Poverty and "self-help" services strategy, and Nixon's Family Assistance Plan (FAP). Concludes that the outlook for Carter's welfare reform package is not good. 2 tables, 44 notes. S. C. Strom

119. Olson, Dolores. PRESIDENTIAL REORGANIZATION. *Presidential Studies Q. 1981 11(4): 526-544.* Since the Franklin D. Roosevelt administration, reorganization has been a major theme, but few significant improvements have been made. The current organization is too burdensome and carries with it too much public scorn. 60 notes, biblio. D. H. Cline

120. O'Neill, James E. WILL SUCCESS SPOIL THE PRESIDENTIAL LIBRARIES? *Am. Archivist 1973 36(3): 339-351.* The Presidential Library system began in 1938 with the plans for the Roosevelt Library in Hyde Park, New York, and now includes libraries for Hoover, Truman, Eisenhower, Kennedy, and Johnson. The libraries have successfully preserved presidential papers (papers of earlier presidents have been lost or destroyed), have given legal title to the papers to the United States, and have made the papers available to researchers on equal terms and with little delay. They also contain museum items. Problems include large volumes of material and access to restricted manuscripts, but the library system will probably continue to function as it is now. Based on secondary sources; 13 notes. D. E. Horn

121. Orman, John. THE MACHO PRESIDENTIAL STYLE. *Indiana Social Studies Q. 1976/77 29(3): 51-60.* Traces the evolution of the office of the president as an embodiment of the aspirations of the American people, concluding that the result has been a necessary revolutionary machismo attached to the office, 1787-1977.

122. Parris, Judith H. CONGRESS IN THE AMERICAN PRESIDENTIAL SYSTEM. *Current Hist. 1974 66(394): 259-263.* Views Congress as the "durable partner" of the presidency. One of six articles in this issue on "The American Presidency." S

123. Peabody, Robert L.; Ornstein, Norman J.; and Rohde, David W. THE UNITED STATES SENATE AS A PRESIDENTIAL INCUBATOR: MANY ARE CALLED BUT FEW ARE CHOSEN. *Pol. Sci. Q. 1976 91(2): 237-258.* Analyze the Senate's role in developing vice-presidential and presidential candidates. The implications of this role for the operation of the Senate and its policy process are discussed. J

124. Pederson, William D. AMNESTY AND PRESIDENTIAL BEHAVIOR: A "BARBERIAN" TEST. *Presidential Studies Q. 1977 7(4): 175-183.* Explores the role of American presidential behavior in granting amnesty, using a modified Barberian typology (activeness and flexibility). It is found that amnesty is a tradition depending on presiden-

tial character, with James David Barber's (b. 1930) "active-positives" issuing more than half of all formal amnesties. Such a study indicates that the informed citizen might also be able to determine candidate behavior without psychological expertise. 2 tables, 22 notes, biblio. J. Tull

125. Petras, James. PRESIDENT CARTER AND THE "NEW MORALITY." *Monthly Rev. 1977 29(2): 42-50.* Analyzes historical antecedents of Jimmy Carter's "new morality" approach to foreign policy, since Woodrow Wilson's administration.

126. Pika, Joseph A. MOVING BEYOND THE OVAL OFFICE: PROBLEMS IN STUDYING THE PRESIDENCY. *Congress & the Presidency 1981-82 9(1): 17-36.* Discusses problems in separating the person from the office, evaluates the literature on the subject, and presents two research strategies for studying the presidency.

127. Pilcher, George William. POWER, THE PRESIDENCY, AND THE FOUNDING FATHERS. *Colorado Q. 1976 25(3): 253-265.* Discusses the power imbued in the office of the President by the Founding Fathers of the United States; assesses the 10 greatest presidents and the characteristics which they had in common, one of the primary ones being accusations (while in power) of corruption of the use of power; covers the revolutionary period through 1976 drawing comparisons between Jefferson and Nixon.

128. Pious, Richard M. THE EVOLUTION OF THE PRESIDENCY: 1789-1932. *Current Hist. 1974 66(394): 241-245, 271-272.* One of six articles in this issue on "The American Presidency." S

129. Polenberg, Richard. HISTORIANS AND THE LIBERAL PRESIDENCY: RECENT APPRAISALS OF ROOSEVELT AND TRUMAN. *South Atlantic Q. 1976 75(1): 20-35.* Franklin D. Roosevelt and Harry S. Truman, usually praised by historians for their liberal achievements, have recently come under strong revisionist attacks. This revisionism is the combined result of access to previously classified manuscript materials, popularization of New Left attitudes, and disillusion with the presidency following Vietnam and Watergate. Revisionists find that neither president went far enough in reform attempts, especially in civil liberties. Methods used by Roosevelt and Truman to achieve policy goals severely compromised their success; for example, Truman is now seen as a defender of McCarthyism. Finally, their liberal goals are seen as sops to the masses while they shored up corporate capitalist elitism. While some concession to popularity is always due, some of these attacks amount to wishful thinking and hindsight. Based on secondary sources; 57 notes. W. L. Olbrich

130. Polsby, Nelson W. AGAINST PRESIDENTIAL GREATNESS. *Commentary 1977 63(1): 61-63.* Once inaugurated, presidents tend to seek a place in the ranks of so-called great presidents. Historians who choose members of the presidential hall of fame seem to prefer and admire activist presidents who seek expansion of presidential power. The last president to argue against an activist view of the office was Dwight D. Eisenhower. The danger of rhetoric and pretension in a president seeking history's heights is that the administration loses touch with reality and wastes true opportunities to govern well. Primary and secondary sources. S. R. Herstein

131. Powers, Richard Gid. ONE G-MAN'S FAMILY: POPULAR ENTERTAINMENT FORMULAS AND J. EDGAR HOOVER'S F. B. I. *Am. Q. 1978 30(4): 471-492.* Discusses the public relations efforts and image creation methods employed by J. Edgar Hoover during 1930's-60's. The emphasis in early years via every medium of the entertainment industry was of the tough cop, sophisticated, and uncorruptible who always got his man, achieving justice as living proof that crime did not pay and that the Federal Bureau of Investigation was effective protection for the American public from its "public enemies." A shift to moralism and an overlay of domesticity as an important part of the public relations pitch made the operatives especially vulnerable whenever one made a misstep. 42 notes. R. V. Ritter

132. Raphalides, Samuel J. THE PRESIDENT'S USE OF TROOPS IN CIVIL DISORDER. *Presidential Studies Q. 1978 8(2): 180-187.* Examines the President's constitutional and statutory authority to use federal troops during civil disorders. Articles I and IV of the Constitution

plus various statutes passed since 1789 and surviving in sections 331-333 of Title 10 of the United States Code provide for federal intervention with or without a state's request. Semantical inconsistencies have given the President broad discretionary powers in determining what constitutes "domestic violence." Historic examples of federal intervention are discussed including the Whisky Rebellion, the Pullman Strike of 1894, and the civil rights disorders of the 1960's. Despite the reluctance of Presidents to exercise these extensive powers, there is concern about possible abuses. The National Emergencies Act (US, 1976) addresses this concern, but more should be done to define the circumstances where intervention may be employed. 43 notes, biblio.   S. C. Strom

133. Reed, Randal Penn. FOREIGN POLICY AND THE INITIATION OF WAR: THE CONGRESS AND THE PRESIDENCY IN THE DISPUTE OVER WAR POWERS. *Potomac Rev. 1973 6(1): 1-29.* Covers 1787-1972.

134. Relyea, Harold C. NATIONAL EMERGENCY POWERS: A BRIEF OVERVIEW OF PRESIDENTIAL SUSPENSIONS OF THE HABEAS CORPUS PRIVILEGE AND INVOCATION OF MARTIAL LAW. *Presidential Studies Q. 1977 7(4): 238-243.* Chronicles outstanding examples of executive power to suspend habeas corpus and invoke martial law. The issue of his right to suspend habeas corpus is based on precedent, not being clearly outlined in the Constitution. Martial law has often merely meant placing soldiers at the disposal of civil authorities. Hawaii was placed under both martial law and suspension of habeas corpus by its governor at the outbreak of hostilities with Japan, a condition lasting until late 1944. An open question is whether a congressional declaration or presidential proclamation would be mandatory for suspension or martial law in case of wars or national emergencies. 19 notes.
                                                        J. Tull

135. Riccards, Michael P. THE PRESIDENCY: IN SICKNESS AND IN HEALTH. *Presidential Studies Q. 1977 7(4): 215-231.* Chronicles diseases of the 35 deceased presidents in terms of political decisions and events. Those serving after 1861 had a decidedly shorter life span than their age cohorts, due perhaps to executive stress and physical ailments they brought to the office. Medical reports on presidents should be more candid. 3 tables, 40 notes.   J. Tull

136. Roberts, John W. RECORDS OF THE OFFICE OF MANAGEMENT AND BUDGET: A NEGLECTED SOURCE FOR DIPLOMATIC HISTORY RESEARCH. *Soc. for Hist. of Am. Foreign Relations. Newsletter 1982 13(2): 2-7.* Briefly traces the history of the Office of Management and Budget from its formation in 1921, and focuses on its value for diplomatic historians as the records from 1910 through 1972 are now in the National Archives.

137. Rogin, Michael Paul. THE KING'S TWO BODIES: ABRAHAM LINCOLN, RICHARD NIXON, AND PRESIDENTIAL SELF-SACRIFICE. *Massachusetts Rev. 1979 20(3): 553-573.* "The King has in him two bodies," wrote Edmund Plowden. President Richard M. Nixon (b. 1913) had, like George III (1738-1820), a monarchial view of his powers. In justification Nixon turned to President Abraham Lincoln (1809-1865), who was reviled as "dictator" and "despot." Nixon's sacrifice was offered to bind Watergate's wounds; Lincoln's made him our political Christ. Nixon, Lincoln, and President Woodrow Wilson (1856-1924), imagined themselves as founders. Nixon lived his presidential life at Wilson's desk, but he prepared his presidential death at Lincoln's. Lincoln's sacrifice gained the country's love; he became its lamb of God. Nixon's drew the country's hate; he was its scapegoat. Based on presidential papers, government documents, and newspapers; 10 notes.
                                                        E. R. Campbell

138. Ross, Russell M. and Schwengel, Fred. AN ITEM VETO FOR THE PRESIDENT? *Presidential Studies Q. 1982 12(1): 66-79.* The idea of an item veto for the president has been supported by past presidents and others throughout the 20th century, and it is an idea whose time has come. This authority, which would allow a president to reject specific items within legislation, would help eliminate budgetary fat, and would restore to the president some of the veto power usurped by Congress. 43 notes.   D. H. Cline

139. Rourke, Francis E. EXECUTIVE FALLIBILITY: PRESIDENTIAL MANAGEMENT STYLES. *Administration and Society 1974 6(2): 171-177.* Compares the management styles of Hoover, Kennedy, Johnson and Nixon, concluding that "the costs of secrecy to the Nixon presidency (1968-74) have been enormous."   S

140. Royster, Vermont. AMERICAN POLITICS: 1932-1972. *Am. Scholar 1973 42(2): 205-214.* Richard M. Nixon's presidential landslide in 1972 amid Democratic congressional gains can only be explained by the steady erosion of Democratic Party power since 1936. Harry S. Truman's minority of the popular vote made 1948 an historic election. Kennedy also was a minority president. The Johnson victory was not seen as a durable resurgence of the Democratic Party. Nixon in 1968 won with only 43.4 percent of the popular vote. "The Republican failure to build a solid national majority has been a major factor in midcentury American politics, right up to the election of 1972 . . . there is no proof that the nation is ready yet to award to either party that sought-for mandate to govern."   E. P. Stickney

141. Schapsmeier, Edward L. and Schapsmeier, Frederick H. FARM POLICY FROM FDR TO EISENHOWER: SOUTHERN DEMOCRATS AND THE POLITICS OF AGRICULTURE. *Agric. Hist. 1979 53(1): 352-371.* Analyzes political alignments and policies in the South since the New Deal. Regardless of historic Jeffersonian principles, Southern agriculture pragmatically supported federal intervention, and resisted major reform of the post-New Deal parity-price-support acreage allotment system, thereby giving tacit approval for enlarging other aspects of the welfare state. They also were able to defy Presidents Roosevelt, Truman, and Eisenhower on the substance of farm programs. Added to this, southern power in Congress was evidenced in the use of seniority, parliamentary skill, and adroitness at forming voting coalitions. By such means they played a vital role in the formulation of major farm programs of the period. 71 notes. Comment by John E. Lee, Jr., pp. 372-376.
                                                        R. V. Ritter

142. Schlesinger, Arthur M., Jr. I POTERI DEL PRESIDENTE NEGLI STATI UNITI: DAI PADRI FONDATORI A PEARL HARBOR [The powers of the president in the United States: from the founding fathers to Pearl Harbor]. *Comunità [Italy] 1979 33(181): 1-94.* Traces the growing influence of presidential power in foreign policy and the accompanying changes in the nature of the presidency, 1776-20th century; excerpted from the first part of the author's *The Imperial Presidency.*

143. Schröder, Hans-Jürgen. AMERIKA ALS MODELL? DAS DILEMMA DER WASHINGTONER AUSSENPOLITIK GEGENÜBER REVOLUTIONÄREN BEWEGUNGEN IM 20. JAHRHUNDERT [America as a model? The dilemma of Washington's foreign policy toward revolutionary movements in the 20th century]. *Hist. Zeitschrift [West Germany] 1979 Beiheft 5: 189-242.* Discusses difficulty of combining a democratic domestic policy with traditionally expansive foreign economic and territorial policies. In the 1960's and 1970's, American historians such as William Appleman Williams, Walter LaFeber, Gordon Levin, and Arno Mayer have examined this theme critically. Of special interest is the fear of revolutionary movements in sensitive territories, especially Latin America. Woodrow Wilson's policy was especially limited in alternatives to opposition to revolution. These trends continued through Roosevelt, Truman, and Kennedy, but with expressions of the notion that the United States should be the cornerstone of democratic social alignments. 135 notes.   G. H. Davis

144. Schulte Nordholt, J. W. DE AMERIKAANSE CONSTITUTIE EN HET PRESIDENTSCHAP [The American constitution and the presidency]. *Kleio [Netherlands] 1975 16(11): 671-675.* Discusses the conflicting tendencies of "idealism" (trust) and "realism" (distrust) in American political history. The constitution, a product of distrustful politicians, provided a system of checks and balance. The executive has become increasingly independent of the legislative branch; mentions advantages and disadvantages of such a development. Cites the press and public opinion, bolstered by idealism, as a counterweight to maintain a democratic society. Compares Wilson's idealism, with its redeeming qualities, to Nixon's extreme manifestation of distrust which led to his downfall.   R. C. Alltmont

145. Scott, Frank D. PRESIDENTIAL YACHTS. *Nautical Res. J. 1974 20(3): 119-128.* A catalogue and description of presidential yachts from 1873 to 1961. S

146. Sheppard, William F. THE FOREIGN SERVICE. *Marine Corps Gazette 1974 58(1): 38.* Tells the history of the Foreign Service from 1775 to 1975. S

147. Shienbaum, Kim Ezra. IDEOLOGY VS. RHETORIC IN AMERICAN POLITICS. *Midwest Q. 1979 21(1): 21-32.* First published in *Midwest Quarterly* in 1975 (see abstract 12A:5509). The homogeneity of American ideology as seen in its political environment has limited the possibility of meaningful political change. Therefore, "this nation is only able to respond to crisis in symbolic terms—with rhetoric, not substantive action." An examination of the Jeffersonian revolution of 1800, the Jacksonian revolution of 1828, the New Nationalism, the New Freedom, the New Deal, Kennedy's New Frontier, Johnson's Great Society and Nixon's New American revolution reveals no radical change commensurate with the rhetoric. The symbolism of rhetoric took the place of action. Selective bibliography. R. V. Ritter

148. Sloss, Frank H. THE VICE PRESIDENTS: FORGOTTEN MEN. *Am. Hist. Illus. 1974 9(8): 12-19.* Surveys American Vice Presidents and notes that they are generally selected for political advantage rather than ability. While contributing little to the hard core of history, these men have added an element of color. Some have been scoundrels, others have been unjustly treated as such, and seven have died in office. 8 photos. V. L. Human

149. Smith, Gary N. ST. LOUIS HOSTS THE POLITICAL CONVENTIONS. *Gateway Heritage 1981 1(4): 10-17.* St. Louis hosted Democratic national nominating conventions in 1876, 1888, 1904, and 1916, as well as the national Republican convention of 1896 and a national Populist convention in the same year. Because of easy railroad access to St. Louis, the city's elegant hotels and expansive meeting facilities, and Democratic political sensitivity to the "Solid South," the Democratic Party frequently selected St. Louis for its conclaves. 13 photos. H. T. Lovin

150. Smith, Kathy B. THE REPRESENTATIVE ROLE OF THE PRESIDENT. *Presidential Studies Q. 1981 11(2): 203-213.* In a democracy, an elected representative can assume a role somewhere between the two extremes of a "delegate" and a "trustee." The president, as a national representative, must assume both the passive role of "chief of state," and the active role of insuring the public welfare. Through writings of previous presidents, their interpretation of their role emerges. There was an emphasis on their active role, and a noticeable absence of any reference to the symbolic function. Covers 1789-1980. Based on a paper presented to the 1979 Summer Seminar for College Teachers; 74 notes. A. Drysdale

151. Smylie, Robert F. THE U.S. AND THE USSR: RELIGIOUS LIBERTY AS A HUMAN RIGHT. *Worldview 1977 20(9): 26, 33-35.* Recounts issues of religious freedom in the USSR that have faced American presidents from Wilson to Carter.

152. Starostin, E. V. and Kabochkina, T. S. PREZIDENTSKIE BIBLIOTEKI V SISTEME ARKHIVNOI SLUZHBY SSHA [The presidential libraries in the US archive system]. *Sovetskie Arkhivy [USSR] 1978 (6): 78-86.* Views the book collections of American presidents since George Washington (1789-97) and asks whether they are personal or national property.

153. Stathis, Stephen W. and Moe, Ronald C. AMERICA'S OTHER INAUGURATION. *Presidential Studies Q. 1980 10(4): 550-570.* Vice Presidential inaugurations have been distinguished by their wide diversity in character and format. History offers few precedents for the place of inauguration, the officer administering the oath, the inaugural speech's content, or the date of the ceremony. The ritual is accepted without question and with little notice, and herein lies the power of this office and its importance in the US governmental system. Table, 76 notes. D. H. Cline

154. Stathis, Stephen W. PRESIDENTIAL DISABILITY AGREEMENTS PRIOR TO THE 25TH AMENDMENT. *Presidential Studies Q. 1982 12(2): 208-215.* Prior to the 25th Amendment, transition of power agreements were inconsistent and often ill-defined. Eisenhower in 1958 firmly decided when a president's disability warranted the assumption of presidential powers and duties by the vice-president. This model was followed by succeeding presidents until the adoption of the 25th Amendment. 36 notes. D. H. Cline

155. Sterling, Carleton W. ELECTORAL COLLEGE MISREPRESENTATION: A GEOMETRIC ANALYSIS. *Polity 1981 13(3): 425-449.* Explores the interaction of voter coalitions and rules for electing the president, to elucidate normative and empirical issues in the proposal to substitute direct election for the electoral college system. Using a geometric scheme, the author analyzes the biases in the present system, challenges its claims, and illustrates his argument with a dissection of the critical 1860 election. J/S

156. Sterling, Carleton W. THE ELECTORAL COLLEGE AND THE IMPACT OF POPULAR VOTE DISTRIBUTION. *Am. Pol. Q. 1974 2(2): 179-204.* Statistical information indicates that the electoral college does not bias presidential elections in favor of liberal candidates. S

157. Stinson, Steven A. THE FEDERAL BUREAU OF INVESTIGATION: ITS HISTORY, ORGANIZATION, FUNCTIONS AND PUBLICATIONS. *Government Publ. Rev. 1979 6(3): 213-240.* Overview of federal investigative activities since 1790, leading up to the present-day Federal Bureau of Investigation; includes FBI functions, activities, major publications, and the continual controversy over FBI activities.

158. Tagg, James D. LESSER PRESIDENTS. *Can. Rev. of Am. Studies [Canada] 1980 11(2): 211-222.* The American Presidency Series of the Regents Press of Kansas so far contains interpretive surveys of eight US presidents. Six of the volumes deal with so-called lesser presidents John Adams, James Buchanan, William H. Taft, Warren G. Harding, and Dwight D. Eisenhower. All were among America's less successful chief executives for essentially the same reasons. 20 notes.

H. T. Lovin

159. Tatalovich, Raymond. ELECTORAL VOTES AND PRESIDENTIAL CAMPAIGN TRAILS, 1932-1976. *Am. Pol. Q. 1979 7(4): 489-497.* Studies the impact of the Electoral College system on presidential campaigning during 1932-76. Three variables are analyzed: size, competition, and region. It is hypothesized that candidates will concentrate on larger, more competitive states. And the data show that both parties allocate proportionately more campaign "stops" to larger states than to medium-size or small states. However, when controls are imposed for both size and competition, it is determined that size is the stronger variable. When the context is less competitive, campaigning is still targeted to larger states, with their wealth of electoral votes. A partisan difference in strategy does exist, moreover. Democrats give proportionately more attention than Republicans to the larger states whereas the GOP concentrates more campaigning on small states. A regional shift in campaigning is noted. J

160. Taylor, John M. PRESIDENTIAL LETTERS. *Manuscripts 1975 27(1): 51-63.* Contains extracts from the writings of eight presidents read by their descendants at the annual meeting of the Manuscripts Society: George Washington by John Augustine Washington; John Adams and John Quincy Adams by Thomas B. Adams; Thomas Jefferson by Thomas Jefferson Eppes; William Henry Harrison by William Henry Harrison, Jr.; Rutherford B. Hayes by Webb Cook Hayes III; Benjamin Harrison by John Scott Harrison; and Franklin D. Roosevelt by Eleanor Roosevelt Seagraves. Illus. D. A. Yanchisin

161. Theoharis, Athan G. THE FBI'S STRETCHING OF PRESIDENTIAL DIRECTIVES, 1936-1953. *Pol. Sci. Q. 1976-77 91(4): 631-647.* Details the history of presidential directives issued between 1936 and 1953 bearing on the FBI's authority to investigate dissident political activities. He concludes that because presidential supervision of the FBI was inadequate, the FBI was able to self-define the scope of its authority. J

162. Thomson, Peggy. THE INAUGURAL TRAPPINGS ON VIEW. *Smithsonian 1973 3(10): 38-43.* Presidential inauguration Bibles and ball gowns dating from 1789 are on display at the Smithsonian Institute.   S

163. Thornburgh, Richard L. THE FEDERAL ROLE IN CRIMINAL LAW ENFORCEMENT. *Current Hist. 1976 70(417): 249-252, 273.* Traces the federal government's crime control efforts, particularly through the Justice Department, since 1789, focusing on the department's dramatic expansion in the 1930's.

164. Tubbesing, Carl D. VICE PRESIDENTIAL CANDIDATES AND THE HOME STATE ADVANTAGE: OR, "TOM WHO?" WAS TOM EAGLETON IN MISSOURI. *Western Pol. Q. 1973 26(4): 702-716.* Examination of presidential election results from 1836 to 1972 indicates that the vice-presidential candidate is of limited help in winning the election in that candidate's home state.

165. Ulmer, S. Sidney. SUPREME COURT APPOINTMENTS AS A POISSON DISTRIBUTION. *Am. J. of Pol. Sci. 1982 26(1): 113-116.* Jimmy Carter is the only president serving at least four years who failed to make a single appointment to the US Supreme Court. Vacancies in the court have followed a Poisson distribution in the inclusive period 1790-1980. Probabilities based on the Poisson function are provided for the Carter experience and other possible contingencies.   J

166. Vlasikhin, V. A. GENERAL'NYI ATTORNEI I GENERAL'-NYI SOLISITOR V GOSUDARSTVENNOM MEKHANIZME S.SH.A. [The Attorney General and the Solicitor General in the US machinery of state]. *Sovetskoe Gosudarstvo i Pravo [USSR] 1979 (5): 111-116.* Discusses the power of the US attorney general, or "Super Sheriff," instituted in 1789, and of the US solicitor general.

167. Wade, Jennifer. AT HOME WITH THE ELEGANCE OF 18TH-CENTURY AMERICA: THE DIPLOMATIC RECEPTION ROOMS OF THE UNITED STATES DEPARTMENT OF STATE. *Art & Antiques 1982 6(4): 88-95.* Describes the interiors of the State Department's diplomatic reception rooms, which exemplify the finest 18th-century styles.

168. Walker, Thomas G. and Hulbary, William E. THE SUPREME COURT SELECTION PROCESS: PRESIDENTIAL MOTIVATIONS AND JUDICIAL PERFORMANCES. *Western Pol. Q. 1980 33(2): 185-196.* Students of the federal judiciary have devoted considerable attention to the process of selecting individuals for the United States Supreme Court. Much of this research has examined the factors motivating a President to elevate a particular person to the Court from among all other individuals available. The present study analyzes the impact of presidential motivations on the quality of judge selected. By searching biographical and historical records, the reasons prompting presidential nominations were compiled for all of the members of the Supreme Court from John Jay through Thurgood Marshall. These motivating factors fell into three categories: Traditional Criteria, Political Criteria, and Professional Qualifications Criteria. These selection variables were then analyzed in relation to the justices' subsequent performances on the Court (based upon the Blaustein/Mersky Supreme Court performance ratings). This analysis allowed us to evaluate the relative impact of various presidential motivations on the quality of judicial performance.   J

169. Walton, Hanes, Jr. and Gray, C. Vernon. BLACK POLITICS AT THE NATIONAL REPUBLICAN AND DEMOCRATIC CONVENTIONS 1868-1972. *Phylon 1975 36(3): 269-278.* Contrary to popular, and some scholarly opinion, black influence at the national conventions has been at times considerable. Reviews past and contemporary attempts by blacks to influence Republican and Democratic Convention proceedings. Finds that from 1868 to 1936, blacks, being mainly

Republican, determined several Republican presidential nominations. After 1936, shifting their allegiance to the Democratic Party, they began to influence that party. In 1964 and 1968 black voters overwhelmingly supported the Democratic Party. 26 notes.   R. V. Ritter

170. Wasserman, Benno. A CRITICAL ANALYSIS OF THE FOREIGN OFFICE. *Contemporary Rev. [Great Britain] 1974 224(1296): 27-34.* Analyzes the British Foreign Office and the American State Department in the 20th century, to establish the extent to which their organization is conducive to war.

171. Wells, Ronald. AMERICAN PRESIDENTS AS POLITICAL AND MORAL LEADERS: A REPORT ON FOUR SURVEYS. *Fides et Hist. 1978 11(1): 39-53.* Reports on a replication of Arthur M. Schlesinger's 1948 and 1962 polls of American historians to determine their rankings of American presidents. In the replication, two groups were polled: British scholars concerned with American Studies; and Christian historians associated with the Conference on Faith and History. The remarkable similarities in the results of the four polls are discussed. Secondary sources and survey results; table, 23 notes.
                                                                R. E. Butchart

172. Westin, Alan F. and Hayden, Trudy. PRESIDENTS AND CIVIL LIBERTIES FROM FDR TO FORD: A RATING BY 64 EXPERTS. *Civil Liberties Rev. 1976 3(5): 9-35.* Offers the opinions of 64 experts concerning the impact of Franklin D. Roosevelt, Harry S. Truman, Dwight D. Eisenhower, John F. Kennedy, Lyndon B. Johnson, Richard M. Nixon, and Gerald R. Ford as presidents on civil liberties.

173. Whitfield, Stephen J. THE PERTINENCE OF GARRY WILLS. *Am. Q. 1981 33(2): 232-242.* Reviews Wills's *The Second Civil War: Arming for Armageddon* (1968), *Nixon Agonistes: The Crisis of the Self-Made Man* (1970), *Bare Ruined Choirs: Doubt, Prophecy, and Radical Religion* (1972), *Inventing America: Jefferson's Declaration of Independence* (1978), and *Confessions of a Conservative* (1979). Wills is pertinent because he reopens questions about the meaning of liberalism. 4 notes.   D. K. Lambert

174. Williams, Irving G. THE AMERICAN VICE PRESIDENCY. *Current Hist. 1974 66(394): 254-258, 273-274.* Reviews the history of the vice presidency since 1787. One of six articles in this issue on "The American Presidency."   S

175. Wilson, James Q. REAGAN AND THE REPUBLICAN REVIVAL. *Commentary 1980 70(4): 25-32.* Compares the rise of Ronald Reagan and the New Republicans to the 1896 election and William Jennings Bryan's similar appeal to the Democratic Party, an election that resulted in a major realignment of the political parties; events of the 1960's and 1970's may signal the Fourth Great Awakening, because the First Great Awakening (1730-60), the Second Great Awakening (1800-30), and the Third Great Awakening (1890-1920) were all preceded by religious and cultural upheavals similar to those of the 1960's and 1970's.

176. —. EXHIBIT: "THE GREAT AUTUMNAL MADNESS": CAMPAIGNING FOR THE PRESIDENCY. *Chicago Hist. 1980 9(3): 166-167.* Illustrates and comments on items from a 1980 Chicago Historical Society exhibit of "banners, buttons, broadsides, clothing, and other objects" from presidential campaigns during 1860-1920.

177. —. THE INTER-AMERICAN IDEA IN THE UNITED STATES: A HISTORICAL APPROACH. *Américas 1976 28(5): s1-s16.* Biographical sketches of Thomas Jefferson, James Monroe, Henry Clay, John Quincy Adams, Woodrow Wilson, James Brown Scott, Cordell Hull, Franklin D. Roosevelt, and John F. Kennedy stress each one's dedication to friendship and cooperation with Latin America, 1823-1961.

2. FROM WASHINGTON THROUGH MCKINLEY

Presidents of the Revolutionary Generation, 1789-1821

178. Andrews, Robert Hardy. HOW THE CIA WAS BORN. *Mankind 1975 5(4): 14-15, 68.* Comments on Thomas Jefferson's attitude toward the intelligence service in the American Revolution, 1775-83.

179. Appleby, Joyce. THE NEW REPUBLICAN SYNTHESIS AND THE CHANGING POLITICAL IDEAS OF JOHN ADAMS. *Am. Q. 1973 25(5): 578-595.* The rightward shift in the political philosophy of John Adams (1735-1826) resulted from his European exposure during 1779-86 to the intellectual ferment surrounding Jean Louis De Lolme's (1740-1807) defense of the English constitution against the radical democratic theories of Baron Anne Robert Turgot (1727-1817). Adams, with a cosmopolitanism understated in current historiography, assumed the universality of political science, believing a conservative reformism based on De Lolme's thought could save Americans from the follies of radical egalitarianism. 38 notes. W. D. Piersen

180. Appleby, Joyce. WHAT IS STILL AMERICAN IN THE POLITICAL PHILOSOPHY OF THOMAS JEFFERSON? *William and Mary Q. 1982 39(2): 287-309.* Thomas Jefferson did not embody the agrarian conservatism of classical republicanism. Rather, Jefferson advocated commercial exploitation of agriculture. His dislike of institutions and privilege and his extolling of the self-actualizing capacities of the individual remove him from the "country party" mold into which recent historians have put him. Jefferson's vision combined materialism and the new morality. Jefferson's ideas are compared to Montesquieu's *Spirit of the Laws.* 71 notes. H. M. Ward

181. Babu, B. Ramesh. THE EPHEMERAL AND THE ETERNAL IN *THE FEDERALIST. Indian J. of Am. Studies [India] 1979 9(1): 3-14.* Explores the enduring political themes found in the 85 essays of Alexander Hamilton, James Madison, and John Jay published as *The Federalist.* Such themes include: union and liberty, the federal system of government, the separation of powers, the system of checks and balances, and elections. In all this, the single overriding concern was the freedom of the individual. The complex system of government was proposed to secure the blessings of liberty. In the mixture of the ephemeral and the eternal found in *The Federalist,* the latter outweighs the former. 17 notes. L. V. Eid

182. Bailyn, Bernard. 1776: A YEAR OF CHALLENGE: A WORLD TRANSFORMED. *J. of Law and Econ. 1976 19(3): 437-466.* Surveys significant publications in 1776, including works by Edward Gibbon, Thomas Paine, Jeremy Bentham, John Adams, and most important, Adam Smith's *Wealth of Nations.* Describes these books within the context of the flood of peasant emigration that alarmed Great Britain, and of worsened Anglo-American relations which made the American Revolution inevitable. 47 notes. C. B. Fitzgerald

183. Banes, Ruth A. THE EXEMPLARY SELF: AUTOBIOGRAPHY IN EIGHTEENTH CENTURY AMERICA. *Biography 1982 5(3): 226-239.* The autobiographies of John Woolman, John Adams, Thomas Jefferson, and Benjamin Franklin employ three literary devices to obscure self importance: a justification for writing, parable form to illustrate important principles, and allusions to the power of Divine Providence. These conventions work together to establish an autobiographical form and present a shared self-conception: the exemplary self. While the 18th-century religious autobiography reaffirmed a universe of verities, the secular autobiographer served his public by clarifying and expounding upon important aspects of American history. In each case early American autobiographers emphasize universal principles, while diminishing individual importance. J/S

184. Banning, Lance. THE MODERATE AS REVOLUTIONARY: AN INTRODUCTION TO MADISON'S LIFE. *Q. J. of the Lib. of Congress 1980 37(2): 162-175.* Traces James Madison's (1751-1836) political career from 1774, when he served as a member of the Orange County, Virginia, committee of safety, through his terms in the Virginia council of state, the Virginia state assembly, the Confederation Congress, the Constitutional Convention, and the House of Representatives, through his terms as secretary of state under Thomas Jefferson from 1801 to 1808, and finally as president from 1809 to 1817. Notes his major contributions, including the Virginia Plan, the Constitution, *The Federalist,* the Bill of Rights, and the Virginia Resolutions. Examines his political ideas, including his early attempts to strengthen the central government and his later attempts to limit the federal government's authority and to define states' rights; his creation, with Thomas Jefferson, of the nation's first political party; his early criticism of and reaction against Hamiltonian policy and his later acceptance of some of its elements; and the problems he encountered with the War of 1812. 14 illus. A. R. Souby

185. Barnes, Howard A. THE IDEA THAT CAUSED A WAR: HORACE BUSHNELL VERSUS THOMAS JEFFERSON. *J. of Church and State 1974 16(1): 73-83.* Discusses differing conceptions of church and state between Congregationalist Horace Bushnell and Thomas Jefferson in the early to mid-19th century, emphasizing issues in racism, individualism and morality.

186. Baron, Sherry. THOMAS JEFFERSON: SCIENTIST AS POLITICIAN. *Synthesis 1975 3(1): 6-21.* Thomas Jefferson's understanding of the Enlightenment helped him develop a group of axiomatic principles, such as his belief in natural rights, a moral instinct, utility, and experimentation. These principles guided his approach to problems both in science and in government. Based on secondary sources; 69 notes. M. M. Vance

187. Barrett, Wayne. GEORGE AND BETSY AND POLLY AND PATSY AND SALLY . . . AND SALLY . . . AND SALLY. *Smithsonian 1973 4(8): 90-99.* Discusses George Washington's romances (1750's-99) and his love for Sally Cary Fairfax, a married woman. S

188. Beloff, Max. THE SALLY HEMINGS AFFAIR: A "FOUNDING FATHER." *Encounter [Great Britain] 1974 43(3): 52-56.* Three recent books on Thomas Jefferson [Leonard W. Levy's *Jefferson and Civil Liberties: The Darker Side* (Harvard U. Pr., 1963), Dumas Malone's *Jefferson the President: Second Term* (Little, Brown, 1974), and Fawn M. Brodie's *Thomas Jefferson, An Intimate History* (Norton)], taken together, give a more personal view of Jefferson as a human being. Discusses the relationship of Jefferson and Hemings.

189. Berens, John F. "LIKE A PROPHETIC SPIRIT": SAMUEL DAVIES, AMERICAN EULOGISTS, AND THE DEIFICATION OF GEORGE WASHINGTON. *Q. J. of Speech 1977 63(3): 290-297.* During the Early National Period (1789-1815), American eulogists drew upon a homegrown "prophecy" by the Reverend Samuel Davies to give George Washington's legend as the providential agent of Heaven validity and vitality, thus satisfying the new nation's "need for national symbols and its psychological and spiritual craving for a common father figure."

190. Bezayiff, David. LEGAL ORATORY OF JOHN ADAMS: AN EARLY INSTRUMENT OF PROTEST. *Western Speech 1976 40(1): 63-71.* "Between 1768 and 1770 Adams used the courtroom to set forth the principles justifying the cause of rebellion," particularly in his defense of the British soldiers involved in the Boston Massacre (1770).

191. Bottorff, William K. MR. JEFFERSON TOURS NEW ENGLAND. *New-England Galaxy 1979 20(3): 3-7.* Thomas Jefferson, then Minister to France, visited Connecticut in the summer of 1784, part of a tour of New England before his departure for Europe to make commercial treaties.

192. Bourke, Paul F. THE PLURALIST READING OF JAMES MADISON'S TENTH FEDERALIST. *Perspectives in Am. Hist. 1975*

9: 271-295. In his 10th *Federalist*, James Madison exhibited a modern understanding of the character of political groupings and their inherent machinations. Many modern pluralists have cited the 10th *Federalist* as evidence of Madison's early perception of political expression, but the author believes this lifts Madison out of historical perspective. Calls for a reexamination of the accuracy of pluralists' views. 28 notes.

W. A. Wiegand

193. Boyd, Julian P. JEFFERSON'S EXPRESSION OF THE AMERICAN MIND. *Virginia Q. R. 1974 50(4): 538-562.* Concludes that Jefferson's "A Summary View of the Rights of British America" (1774) was written for presentation by Patrick Henry, an effective orator. It argued, as did his less well-known Declaration of Rights, that Parliament had no authority over the American colonies. Probably Jefferson's purpose was to achieve his object—forceful oral presentation of his advanced view—"by indirection rather than by confrontation."

O. H. Zabel

194. Branson, Roy. MADISON AND THE SCOTTISH ENLIGHTENMENT. *J. of the Hist. of Ideas 1979 40(2): 235-250.* Parallels James Madison's ideas about society and politics with those of David Hume, Adam Smith, John Millar, and Adam Ferguson. The essay concludes that Madison synthesized the Lockean view that government is controlled by majorities with the Scottish understanding that society is "full of active occupational, political, and commercial groups achieving moderate reforms." Published primary and secondary sources; 77 notes.

D. B. Marti

195. Brodie, Fawn M. THOMAS JEFFERSON'S UNKNOWN GRANDCHILDREN. *Am. Heritage 1976 27(6): 28-33, 94-99.* Thomas Jefferson, married only once, had two families. The second family, by his quadroon slave, Sally Hemings, numbered seven children, from a liaison lasting 38 years. Their disappearance and that of their progeny resulted from several factors, including Jefferson's desire that they eventually "escape" into white society. Much information has recently come to light concerning Jefferson's other family. Family lines are traced from each of the children. Based on primary and secondary sources; 2 illus., 36 notes.

J. F. Paul

196. Cable, Mary and Prager, Annabelle. THE LEVYS OF MONTICELLO. *Am. Heritage 1978 29(2): 30-39.* After Thomas Jefferson's death in 1826, Monticello was sold in 1831 and quickly fell into disrepair. Purchased by Uriah Philips Levy in 1836, little was done to preserve the home. Levy's will left the property to the United States but with too many strings attached. One of Levy's nephews, Jefferson Monroe Levy, bought the property in 1879 and began to restore it. By the turn of the century, the house was sound again, and public clamor to make it a national shrine mounted and in 1923, the Thomas Jefferson Memorial Association bought the property. In 1954, the house underwent a complete renovation. But for J. M. Levy, the house might have been lost to history. 14 illus.

J. F. Paul

197. Calhoon, Robert M. JOHN ADAMS AND THE PSYCHOLOGY OF POWER. *Rev. in Am. Hist. 1976 4(4): 520-525.* Review article prompted by Ralph Adams Brown's *The Presidency of John Adams* (Lawrence: U. of Kansas Pr., 1975) and Peter Shaw's *The Character of John Adams* (Chapel Hill: U. of North Carolina Pr., 1976); discusses Adams as a representative of early American political behavior and conceptions of power in the political arena, 1760's-1801.

198. Campbell, Janet. THE FIRST AMERICANS' TRIBUTE TO THE FIRST PRESIDENT. *Chronicles of Oklahoma 1979 57(2): 190-195.* Attending the 4 July 1848 cornerstone laying for the Washington Monument were delegates from the Cherokee, Chickasaw, Stockbridge, Creek, and Choctaw nations. Several of these groups contributed money for the monument and others promised to contribute part of the stone. When the monument finally was completed in 1884, it bore a memorial stone only from the Cherokee. Secondary sources; 2 photos, 9 notes.

M. L. Tate

199. Cappon, Lester J. JARED SPARKS: THE PREPARATION OF AN EDITOR. *Massachusetts Hist. Soc. Pro. 1978 90: 3-21.* A study of the background of Jared Sparks, historian and editor of documents pertaining to colonial and revolutionary America, particularly the papers

of George Washington. Sparks, an 1815 graduate of Harvard College and a Unitarian minister, received training as editor of the *North American Review* and *The Unitarian Miscellany*. This literary experience helped him formulate his controversial style as an historical editor when he began to collect, copy, and edit the Washington manuscripts, including those at Mount Vernon. Based on the Jared Sparks Papers at the Houghton Library of Harvard University and other primary sources; 81 notes.

G. W. R. Ward

200. Carey, George W. MAJORITY TYRANNY AND THE EXTENDED REPUBLIC THEORY OF JAMES MADISON. *Modern Age 1976 20(1): 40-54.* Once government shifts from a relatively passive instrumentality operative within a narrow sphere to an instrumentality for the advancement of interests and purposes of broad scope, the best one can hope for consistent with Madisonian theory is that the true interests of the country reside somewhere within the depths of the forces which propel the dominant interest coalitions. Based on primary and secondary sources; 7 notes.

M. L. Lifka

201. Carey, George W. SEPARATION OF POWERS AND THE MADISONIAN MODEL: A REPLY TO THE CRITICS. *Am. Pol. Sci. Rev. 1978 72(1): 151-164.* This article critically examines the commonly held proposition that Madison advocated separation of powers as a means of thwarting majority rule, or, conversely, of protecting identifiable minority interests. Rather, Madison's chief purpose in advancing the doctrine of separation of powers—one which was shared by the majority of his contemporaries—was to prevent governmental tyranny whose characteristic feature was seen as arbitrary and capricious rule resulting in government of men, not of laws. Many modern critics' analyses of the Madisonian model (most notably, Burns, Dahl, and advocates of a responsible party system) are seriously deficient because they fail to take into account this dimension of the model. Madison's writings, principally in *The Federalist*, as well as his remarks at the Philadelphia convention, clearly indicate that one of his central concerns was simultaneously to provide for protection against governmental tyranny and to guarantee popular control of government. This article examines in some detail certain critical aspects of this endeavor.

J

202. Carpenter, Joseph. THE BICENTENNIAL AND THE BLACK REVOLUTION: IS IT A MYTH OR A REALITY? *Negro Hist. Bull. 1976 39(1): 496-499.* The American Revolution must be reinterpreted to replace racism and economic exploitation with new values based on the bonds of blackness. George Washington and Thomas Jefferson were racist slaveowners who fathered children by black slave women. Both represented the colonial industrialists and the Virginia power elite. It is an American tragedy that they now symbolize the struggle for human rights while true revolutionaries, such as James Otis, Thomas Paine, Crispus Attucks, and Salem Poor, are ignored. Secondary sources; 5 illus., 16 notes.

W. R. Hively

203. Cauthen, Irby B., Jr. "A COMPLETE AND GENEROUS EDUCATION": MILTON AND JEFFERSON. *Virginia Q. Rev. 1979 55(2): 222-233.* Discusses John Milton's dislike of his education at St. Paul's and Cambridge and his short pamphlet, *Of Education,* in which he outlined a physical and intellectual curriculum which would provide "a complete and generous education." It called for a dramatic renovation and revolution in education. There were great similarities, and some differences, in the educational program Thomas Jefferson sponsored 200 years later. Milton's proposals were the "culmination of the English Renaissance" and Jefferson's "the epitome of the American Enlightenment." They "join in the insistence upon civic leadership and personal integrity."

O. H. Zabel

204. Chaudhuri, Joyotpaul. JEFFERSON'S UNHEAVENLY CITY: A BICENTENNIAL LOOK. *Am. J. of Econ. and Sociol. 1975 34(4): 397-410.* Discusses the modern concepts in Thomas Jefferson's political theory and reveals philosophical differences between Jefferson and John Locke.

205. Chaudhuri, Joyotpaul. JEFFERSON'S UNHEAVENLY CITY: AN INTERPRETATION. Chaudhuri, Joyotpaul, ed. *Non-Lockean Roots of American Democratic Thought* (Tucson: U. of Arizona Pr., 1977): 17-29. Though most often compared with John Locke's ontological dualism, Thomas Jefferson's epistemology and political thought antici-

pated modern concerns regarding rights, property, and consent and are best characterized as Stoic realism bolstered by empirical verification.

206. Cheatham, Edgar and Cheatham, Patricia. REUNION AT MONTICELLO. *Early Am. Life 1977 8(6): 40-43.* Discusses the friendship between the Marquis de Lafayette and Thomas Jefferson, 1777-1824 throughout the American Revolution and Jefferson's tenure in France; ends with a reunion meeting which took place at Jefferson's home, Monticello, Virginia, in 1824.

207. Chianese, Mary Lou. THOMAS JEFFERSON: ENLIGHTENED AMERICAN. *Daughters of the Am. Revolution Mag. 1975 109(5): 417-423.* Reexamines the life and ideas of Thomas Jefferson (1743-1826), author of the Declaration of Independence and the Statute of Virginia for Religious Freedom and founder of the University of Virginia.   S

208. Childs, Catherine Murtaugh. VIRGINIA PATRIARCH: GEORGE WASHINGTON AND HIS AIDES. *Daughters of the Am. Revolution Mag. 1980 114(4): 446-449.* Discusses the duties and careers of General George Washington and his aides-de-camp including Edmund Randolph, George Baylor, Joseph Reed, Robert Hanson Harrison, Samuel Webb, William Grayson, William A. Washington, and Thomas Mifflin during and after the American Revolution, 1775-1794.

209. Clarfield, Gerald H. JOHN ADAMS: THE MARKETPLACE, AND AMERICAN FOREIGN POLICY. *New England Q. 1979 52(3): 345-357.* John Adams (1735-1826) was not an isolationist but accepted mercantilism and "believed that the key to an effective foreign policy lay in the successful manipulation of the American marketplace." During the Revolution, liberal economic doctrine fit American needs and he advocated it, believing the prospect of trade would lead nations to aid America. European policy after the war led him to abandon free trade and to favor an American navigation system like Britain's. Based on Adams's writings and secondary sources; 29 notes.   J. C. Bradford

210. Cole, Adelaide M. ABIGAIL ADAMS: A VIGNETTE. *Daughters of the Am. Revolution Mag. 1979 113(5): 494-499.* Biography of Abigail Adams (1744-1818), wife of John Adams and mother of John Quincy Adams.

211. Cole, Adelaide M. MARTHA WASHINGTON: THE FIRST FIRST LADY. *Daughters of the Am. Revolution Mag. 1979 113(2): 136-140.* Discusses Martha Dandridge Custis Washington (1732-1802), and her childhood, early marriage (1749) to Daniel Parke Custis (d. 1757), and subsequent marriage (1759) to George Washington.

212. Colket, Meredith B., Jr. GEORGE WASHINGTON AND HIS VISION OF THE WEST. *Daughters of the Am. Revolution Mag. 1975 109(5): 406-411, 423.* Discusses George Washington's interest in opening the Ohio Valley to trade and settlement, 1750's-90's.   S

213. Conniff, James. THE ENLIGHTENMENT AND AMERICAN POLITICAL THOUGHT: A STUDY OF THE ORIGINS OF MADISON'S *FEDERALIST NUMBER 10. Pol. Theory 1980 8(3): 381-402.* James Madison's innovations in political theory have not been recognized, as scholars have attempted to tie him to Enlightenment ideology; responding to the needs particular to the American experience, he determined that effective authority rather than virtue was central to republicanism, as recorded in *Federalist No. 10.*

214. Conniff, James. ON THE OBSOLESCENCE OF THE GENERAL WILL: ROUSSEAU, MADISON, AND THE EVOLUTION OF REPUBLICAN POLITICAL THOUGHT. *Western Pol. Q. 1975 28(1): 32-58.* James Madison revolutionized the political theory of the Republican form of government in *Federalist #10.* Republican theory before Madison's formulation was based on classical examples and on the idea that society could achieve an objective good. In addition it was thought that a Republic must have a homogeneous population and possess a small land area. The author shows how Jean Jacques Rousseau fitted into this pattern. The varied population and great expanse of the United States made it difficult for the Federalists to defend the new Constitution. Madison's solution was to reject the idea of the government enacting the general will and to maintain that its job was to balance

competing interests. In that case the stronger the central government was and the greater was the size of the country, the smaller the chance that any social group could gain unacceptable levels of power. Based on published works including the *Federalist Papers*; 116 notes.

G. B. McKinney

215. Cooke, J. W. JEFFERSON ON LIBERTY. *J. of the Hist. of Ideas 1973 34(4): 563-576.* Explains and illustrates Thomas Jefferson's ideas of freedom or liberty. Jefferson's only attempt at a formal definition of freedom, in 1819, was an uncharacteristically colorless and abstract statement. Normally his ideas of liberty were expressed in connection with other ideas which engaged his philosophical attention. His understanding of liberty was many-sided; but finally was "negative" and "conventional . . . original only in detail and emphasis." Based on secondary sources, including Jefferson's letters; 12 notes.   D. B. Marti

216. Cooke, Jacob E. THE COLLABORATION OF TENCH COXE AND THOMAS JEFFERSON. *Pennsylvania Mag. of Hist. and Biog. 1976 100(4): 468-490.* Tench Coxe and Thomas Jefferson had complementary characters and interests. They collaborated on several reports, and Coxe influenced Jefferson's instructions to agents abroad. National self-sufficiency appealed to both. Coxe supported Alexander Hamilton and Jefferson but was ultimately jettisoned by both. Based on Coxe Papers, Historical Society of Pennsylvania; Madison Papers, Library of Congress; other primary and secondary sources; 63 notes.

T. H. Wendel

217. Cooney, Charles F. GEORGE WASHINGTON IS NOT BURIED HERE. *Am. Hist. Illus. 1980 15(7): 48-49.* Story of the empty tomb in the basement of the Capitol building in Washington, D.C., which was intended for the remains of George Washington and Martha Washington, who are both buried in the family burial vault at Mt. Vernon; 1799-1832.

218. Cormier, Raymond J. FOREIGN LANGUAGES AND THE FOUNDING FATHERS OF AMERICA. *Daughters of the Am. Revolution Mag. 1978 112(5): 452-457.* Speculates on the Founding Fathers's speaking abilities in foreign languages, notably, John Adams, George Washington, Thomas Jefferson, Benjamin Franklin, and other less famous figures, 1760's-70's.

219. Cox, James M. JEFFERSON'S AUTOIOGRAPHY: RECOVERING LITERATURE'S LOST GROUND. *Southern Rev. 1978 14(4): 633-652.* Thomas Jefferson's autobiography, first published in 1830 as *Memoir,* is indeed an autobiography by literary standards, and not merely a historical memoir.

220. Cullen, Joseph P. WASHINGTON AT MOUNT VERNON. *Am. Hist. Illus. 1974 9(2): 4-11, 45-48.* Reviews the life of George Washington in his home at Mount Vernon, Virginia. He lived simply, despite the huge plantation he owned. Washington was basically a farmer; no other life appealed to him as much. He introduced new crop and animal strains, endeavored to build up the land, even discontinuing profitable money crops which were hard on the soil. Visitors were numerous after the War of Independence, but entertainment was simple. Despite Washington's care and expertise, the farm eventually failed to show a profit, and after his term in the presidency, Washington was too old to properly care for it. 13 illus., photo.   V. L. Human

221. Cunliffe, Marcus. SYMBOLS WE MADE OF A MAN NAMED GEORGE WASHINGTON. *Smithsonian 1981 12(11): 74-81.* Discusses the folklore and symbolic status of George Washington, which grew after his death, as reflected in American painting and other objects of art.

222. Cunliffe, Marcus. THOMAS JEFFERSON AND THE DANGERS OF THE PAST. *Wilson Q. 1982 6(1): 96-107.* Thomas Jefferson drew selectively from past wisdom to support his idea of the new American Republic, 1771-1825.

223. Dabney, Virginius and Kukla, Jon. THE MONTICELLO SCANDALS: HISTORY AND FICTION. *Virginia Cavalcade 1979 29(2): 52-61.* Examines Thomas Jefferson's reputation and the validity of claims that the slave Sally Hemings bore his children.

224. Daiker, Virginia. THE CAPITOL OF JEFFERSON AND LA-TROBE. *Q. J. of the Lib. of Congress 1975 32(1): 25-32.* Benjamin Henry Latrobe (1764-1820) was the only well-trained professional architect in the country. Thomas Jefferson disagreed with Latrobe over the lighting of the House of Representatives chamber. After the War of 1812, Latrobe was hired to rebuild the Capitol and, "as Jefferson was no longer President, was able to construct his cupolas on both wings." Based upon correspondence of Jefferson and Latrobe. Illus., 19 notes.
E. P. Stickney

225. Davis, Edwin S. THE RELIGION OF GEORGE WASHINGTON: A BICENTENNIAL REPORT. *Air U. R. 1976 27(5): 30-34.* Discusses George Washington's religious beliefs and the role that these beliefs played in the development of the Chaplain's corps of the US Army. Several examples of Washington's faith and interest in religious matters are cited by the author. Based on *The Writings of George Washington* and other published works; 20 notes.
J. W. Thacker, Jr.

226. Dawidoff, Robert. THE FOX IN THE HENHOUSE: JEFFERSON AND SLAVERY. *Rev. in Am. Hist. 1978 6(4): 503-511.* Review article prompted by John Chester Miller's *The Wolf by the Ears: Thomas Jefferson and Slavery* (New York: Free Pr., 1977) which discusses Thomas Jefferson's views on slavery.

227. deChambrun, René. WASHINGTON, SECOND PÈRE DE LAFAYETTE [Washington, a second father to Lafayette]. *Nouvelle Rev. des Deux Mondes [France] 1981 (12): 579-588.* The president of the French Sons of the American Revolution, a descendant of the Marquis de Lafayette (1757-1834) tells of the close relations between his ancestor, who served in the Continental Army, and General George Washington, using documents found at the Château Lagrange, Lafayette's mansion.

228. D'Elia, Donald J. JEFFERSON, RUSH, AND THE LIMITS OF PHILOSOPHICAL FRIENDSHIP. *Pro. of the Am. Phil. Soc. 1973 117(5): 333-343.* Discusses the opposing points of view of Thomas Jefferson and Benjamin Rush on matters such as "the nature of man, the problem of evil, God, science, history, and the ideal commonwealth." Nurtured in the spirit of the Enlightenment when they first met in Philadelphia in 1775, both discovered that they were growing further apart philosophically through the correspondence they maintained until shortly before Rush's death in 1813. Primary sources; 61 notes.
C. W. Olson

229. Deren, Štefica. NASTANAK I RAZVOJ JEFFERSONOVIH REPUBLIKANACA [Origins and development of Jefferson's republicans]. *Politička Misao [Yugoslavia] 1972 9(4): 403-414.* Analyzes Thomas Jefferson's role in the grouping of antifederalists and his contribution in the formation and growth of the Democratic-Republican Party.

230. Devine, Francis E. OSTRACISM IN POPULAR GOVERNMENT: BURKE AND ADAMS. *Southern Q. 1975 14(1): 17-20.* Compares the political philosophies of American John Adams (1735-1826) and Englishman Edmund Burke (1729-97). Focuses on the view of how best to control individual ambition for power within a democratic commonwealth. Adams, the more democratic-minded, held that the talents and energies of ambitious leaders could be most effectively utilized for the public good when such persons were ostracized or isolated in a political body called a senate. When surrounded by others of similar ability, such persons could not dominate and become authoritarian. Government thereby retains the service of its most outstanding citizens and yet remains securely popular. 20 notes.
R. W. Dubay

231. Dewey, Frank L. THOMAS JEFFERSON AND A WILLIAMSBURG SCANDAL: THE CASE OF *BLAIR* V. *BLAIR.* *Virginia Mag. of Hist. and Biog. 1981 89(1): 44-63.* Presents Thomas Jefferson's argument in this 1773 Virginia case where the widow of Dr. James Blair sued her brother-in-law, as executor of Dr. Blair's estate, for her dowry. Precedents were against the estate, but Jefferson and his colleagues argued that because the marriage was not consummated, it was nominal only. They further asserted that Mrs. Blair, who had been legally denied separate maintenance while Dr. Blair was alive, was guilty of deceit in her marriage contract. Jefferson's account is fully printed here for the first time. His appeals to English and international law, literature and the Bible in defense of Blair men were, ultimately, for the losing side. 50 notes.
P. J. Woehrmann

232. Dewey, Frank L. THOMAS JEFFERSON'S NOTES ON DIVORCE. *William and Mary Q. 1982 39(1): 212-223.* Jefferson prepared notes intended to be used on behalf of Dr. James Blair of Williamsburg for a petition to the legislature for divorce. Blair died on 26 December 1772. No legislation for the divorce was introduced during the session of February-April 1772 (the next session was March 1773). Jefferson's notes outline the case that Jefferson would have made to the legislature. The author explains Jefferson's references to treatises on international law and Scripture, and the annotation points specifically to Jefferson's sources. Reproduces the document. Based on books in Jefferson's library; 57 notes.
H. M. Ward

233. Dewey, Frank L. THOMAS JEFFERSON'S LAW PRACTICE. *Virginia Mag. of Hist. and Biog. 1977 85(3): 289-301.* Despite the contention of virtually every biographer that Thomas Jefferson practiced extensively in the county courts as well as the General Courts, there is no evidence that he ever was concerned with the former. To have done so would have violated both the law and Jefferson's own ideas on the subject. The myth that he practiced in most of the colony's county courts stems from a misinterpretation of Jefferson's Casebook, Fee Book, and account books. Based on Jefferson material in the Huntington Library, his published papers, and secondary accounts; 40 notes.
R. F. Oaks

234. Dewey, Frank L. THE WATERSON-MADISON EPISODE: AN INCIDENT IN THOMAS JEFFERSON'S LAW PRACTICE. *Virginia Mag. of Hist. and Biog. 1982 90(2): 165-176.* In 1769, Virginia lawyer Thomas Jefferson acted as counsel to a group of clients who proposed to use existing land statutes to their advantage in a get-rich-quick scheme. Apparently Jefferson did not play any part in the plan's conception; however, he would have collected a large sum of money had it succeeded. As it was, the scheme failed and Jefferson left his law practice a few years later, possibly disillusioned by clients who did not pay their bills. Based on Virginia legal records and statutes, Jefferson's account book, and secondary sources; 53 notes.
D. J. Cimbala

235. Dickson, Charles Ellis. JAMES MONROE'S DEFENSE OF KENTUCKY'S INTERESTS IN THE CONFEDERATION CONGRESS: AN EXAMPLE OF EARLY NORTH/SOUTH PARTY ALIGNMENT. *Register of the Kentucky Hist. Soc. 1976 74(4): 261-280.* Political party divisions may have begun earlier than generally believed. James Monroe defended the interests of the West, particularly Kentuckians, in Congress under the Articles of Confederation. In the debates over negotiations under way with Spain in regard to the use of the Mississippi River, as early as 1785 Monroe and others fought diligently to protect the future economic development of the region. Primary and secondary sources; 60 notes.
J. F. Paul

236. Diggins, John P. SLAVERY, RACE AND EQUALITY: JEFFERSON AND THE PATHOS OF THE ENLIGHTENMENT. *Am. Q. 1976 28(2): 206-228.* Jefferson's inner vacillation on the question of racial equality may have had its psychic roots in his racist phobias or in social pressures, but his ambiguous moral philosophy also reveals two contrary strains in the thought of the Enlightenment. These ideas are that the human mind can draw its principles from the nature of things and that the mind can impose its rational will and moral imagination on the environment. Based primarily on Jefferson's writings and secondary sources.
N. Lederer

237. Donnelly, Marian C. JEFFERSON'S OBSERVATORY DESIGN. *J. of the Soc. of Architectural Hist. 1977 36(1): 33-35.* Discusses Thomas Jefferson's design for the Montalto observatory which was never erected but which combined his interests in landscape design, geometry, and scientific observation. Points out his interest in medieval motifs and his dependence on traditional 18th-century definitions of an observatory. Contrasts the observatory of David Rittenhouse of Philadelphia with Jefferson's design. 21 notes.
M. Zolota

238. Draper, Theodore. HUME & MADISON: THE SECRETS OF FEDERALIST PAPER NO. 10. *Encounter [Great Britain] 1982 58(2): 34-47.* Examines James Madison's debt to David Hume for the concept of the "extended republic" which Madison used as a guiding principle and check against factionalism in Federalist No. 10; and comments on 20th-century studies of this connection by Douglass Adair (in 1957) and Garry Wills in his *Expanding America: The Federalist* (1981).

239. Edward, C. JEFFERSON, SULLIVAN, AND THE MOOSE. *Am. Hist. Illus.* 1974 9(7): 18-19. Relates how Thomas Jefferson, with the assistance and cooperation of his friend John Sullivan, Governor of New Hampshire, succeeded in his attempt to convince Georges, Comte de Buffon, the leading French naturalist of the day, that North American mammals were not "typically small and degenerate compared to their European counterparts," by shipping from Boston to Paris the carcass of a moose that was about seven feet high. This amusing episode in 18th-century international diplomacy was eventually completed at a cost of 46 pounds, 7 shillings, 10 and 1/2 pence sterling. Photo, illus.

D. D. Cameron

240. Einhorn, Lois J. BASIC ASSUMPTIONS IN THE VIRGINIA RATIFICATION DEBATES: PATRICK HENRY VS. JAMES MADISON ON THE NATURE OF MAN AND REASON. *Southern Speech Communication J.* 1981 46(4): 327-340. Discusses Antifederalist Henry Clay's assumptions that man and government were inherently evil, and that to an absolutist, reasoning was unnecessary, and James Madison's assumptions that man was a combination of good and bad, and a balanced government could control people, based on his support of the power of reason and logical thinking; focuses on their speeches at the Virginia Ratification Convention on the Federal Constitution in 1788.

241. Ferguson, Henry N. THE MAN WHO SAVED MONTICELLO. *Am. Hist. Illus.* 1980 14(10): 20-27. Discusses the design and construction of Thomas Jefferson's Virginia home, Monticello, which he designed and built in 1809, and traces the estate's history from Jefferson's death in 1826 and Uriah Phillips Levy's acquisition and renovation of it in 1836, to its present upkeep by the Thomas Jefferson Memorial Foundation.

242. Ferguson, Robert A. "MYSTERIOUS OBLIGATIONS": JEFFERSON'S *NOTES ON THE STATE OF VIRGINIA*. *Am. Literature* 1980 52(3): 381-406. *Notes on the State of Virginia* (London, 1787) represents Thomas Jefferson's attempt to define America as a republic, utilizing themes and techniques common to Enlightenment thinkers of the 18th century. Jefferson demonstrates how the compilation of factual knowledge would lead to a larger coherence. The legal philosophy of the Enlightenment and English common law provided Jefferson with a structure with which he could connect the natural world (America) and the political order (the new Republic). *Notes* deserves critical attention because it possesses both theme and structure that reflect Jefferson's mastery of Enlightenment thought. Table, 58 notes.

T. P. Linkfield

243. Fleming, Thomas. MONTICELLO'S LONG CAREER—FROM RICHES TO RAGS TO RICHES. *Smithsonian* 1973 4(3): 62-69. Theodore Fred Kuper, a Russian immigrant, helped restore Thomas Jefferson's home, Monticello, 1826-1935.

S

244. Flexner, James Thomas. "THE MIRACULOUS CARE OF PROVIDENCE": GEORGE WASHINGTON'S NARROW ESCAPES. *Am. Heritage* 1982 33(2): 82-85. Five times during his military career, George Washington escaped close encounters with death. For this, he thanked Providence and considered himself lucky. The narrow escapes are chronicled in this article. Illus.

J. F. Paul

245. Fohlen, Claude. JEFFERSON ET LA FRANCE [Jefferson and France]. *Rev. des Travaux de l'Acad. des Sci. Morales et Pol. et Comptes Rendus de ses Séances [France]* 1976 129(2): 553-567. Thomas Jefferson was the only one of the founding fathers to remain a consistent admirer of France. That was largely the result of his experiences while US minister to France during 1785-89. He was impressed favorably by his introduction to refined Parisian life, his conversations with the intellectual elite, and his visits to sites of ancient ruins. He reacted less favorably to the class structure and the political, economic, and religious abuses of the Old Regime. Though he sought close diplomatic ties to France based on mutual material interests, he was above all an American patriot.

J. R. Vignery

246. Funston, Janet and Funston, Richard. CESARE BECCARIA E I PADRI FONDATORI AMERICANI [Cesare Beccaria and the American Founding Fathers]. *Storia e Politica [Italy]* 1976 15(4): 688-704. The ideas against capital punishment and torture expressed by Cesare Beccaria (1738-94) in his famous 1764 book *Dei delitti e delle pene* [On crimes and punishments] were widely known in America. John Adams, Thomas Jefferson, and James Madison read and were influenced by it. The Declaration of Independence itself is, to a great extent, a synthesis of Beccaria's ideas on European feudalism. Based on secondary works; 50 notes.

A. Canavero

247. Gaintner, J. Richard. 250TH BIRTHDAY ANNIVERSARY: GEORGE WASHINGTON 1732-1799. *J. of the Lancaster County Hist. Soc.* 1981 85(2): 50-62. Reprints the author's *A Story of George Washington in Postage Stamps, Envelopes, Postcards and Postmarks* (1932), written to commemorate Washington's 200th birthday, and covering notable historical data beginning with Washington's birth in 1732.

248. Gál, István. A HUNGARIAN CONTACT OF BENJAMIN FRANKLIN. *New Hungarian Q. [Hungary]* 1973 15(53): 158-162. János Zinner, a Hungarian scholar who corresponded with Benjamin Franklin during the American Revolution, compiled biographical and historical notes on Franklin as well as the revolutionary war which came to rest in the private library of Ferenc Széchényi; includes a letter to Franklin and excerpts from Zinner's biographical sketches of Franklin and George Washington, 1755-78.

249. Garrett, Wendell D. BICENTENNIAL OUTLOOK: THE MONUMENTAL FRIENDSHIP OF JEFFERSON AND ADAMS. *Historic Preservation* 1976 28(2): 28-35. Describes the "bramble-strewn and thicket-tested friendship" of Thomas Jefferson and John Adams which, lasting from 1775 until their deaths on 4 July 1826, "is unparalleled in American history." 2 illus., 4 photos. R. M. Frame III

250. Gittleman, Edwin. JEFFERSON'S "SLAVE NARRATIVE": THE DECLARATION OF INDEPENDENCE AS A LITERARY TEXT. *Early Am. Literature* 1974 8(3): 239-256. The controlling unity of the Declaration of Independence is provided by the theme of slavery, and Thomas Jefferson intended that the final "grievance" on slavery (subsequently deleted by the Congress) be the most shocking and accusatory possible. Suppressed throughout the declaration, the theme of slavery nevertheless controls the rhetoric, structure, and meaning. Based on primary and secondary sources; 23 notes.

D. P. Wharton

251. Gleason, Gene. ROYALL TYLER'S BLIGHTED ROMANCE. *New-England Galaxy* 1976 18(2): 43-49. Describes the friendship of Royall Tyler with Mrs. Abigail Adams and her daughter Abigail Amelia which in time blossomed into a romance between Tyler and the daughter. This romance lasted between 23 December 1782 and 11 August 1785.

P. C. Marshall

252. Gleason, Gene. YOUNG JOHN ADAMS COMES TO WORCESTER. *New-England Galaxy* 1974 16(2): 3-10. Portrays John Adams' (1735-1826) brief career as a schoolmaster in Worcester, Massachusetts 1755-58. Adams, recently graduated from Harvard, experimented with teaching methods, studied law under James Putnam for two years, and in 1758 returned to his hometown, Braintree (now Quincy), as its first trained lawyer. 2 illus.

P. C. Marshall

253. Glenn, Patricia. WAKEFIELD. *Early Am. Life* 1979 10(2): 30-33. Describes the interior design and architecture of Wakefield, an 1825 replica of the birthplace of George Washington located in Florence, Alabama.

254. Golladay, V. Dennis. JEFFERSON'S "MALIGNANT NEIGHBOR," JOHN NICHOLAS, JR. *Virginia Mag. of Hist. and Biog.* 1978 86(3): 306-319. John Nicholas, Jr. (ca. 1758-1836), usually refrained from politics, but his few partisan activities alienated his neighbor Thomas Jefferson. Nicholas, one of the few Federalists in Republican Albemarle County, through his involvement in the Langhorne affair in 1797-98 contributed to the final break between Jefferson and former President Washington. Based on Nicholas's correspondence and on secondary works; 42 notes.

R. F. Oaks

255. Goode, Cecil E. GILBERT SIMPSON: WASHINGTON'S PARTNER IN SETTLING HIS WESTERN PENNSYLVANIA LANDS. *Western Pennsylvania Hist. Mag.* 1979 62(2): 149-166. Traces the friendship of George Washington and Gilbert Simpson from their

childhood in 1740, and discusses their partnership in settling Washington's land in southwest Pennsylvania, which Simpson proposed in 1772. The partnership was dissolved in 1784; Simpson bought the land and owned it until he died in 1794.

256. Govan, Thomas P. ALEXANDER HAMILTON AND JULIUS CAESAR: A NOTE ON THE USE OF HISTORICAL EVIDENCE. *William and Mary Q. 1975 32(3): 475-480.* Takes to task prominent historians (Dumas Malone, Julian P. Boyd, and Douglass Adair) who have stressed Alexander Hamilton's admiration of Julius Caesar, finding that the evidence does not support this contention. Except in one instance Hamilton's references to Caesar "uniformly carry an opprobrious connotation." To Hamilton, Thomas Jefferson was a Caesar in disguise. Based on the Hamilton papers; 19 notes.   H. M. Ward

257. Grampp, William D. ADAM SMITH AND THE AMERICAN REVOLUTIONISTS. *Hist. of Pol. Econ. 1979 11(2): 179-191.* Adam Smith and American revolutionaries such as Thomas Jefferson similarly stressed the importance of nationalism and utilitarianism, 1770's-90's.

258. Gribbin, William. A REPLY OF JOHN ADAMS ON EPISCOPACY AND THE AMERICAN REVOLUTION. *Hist. Mag. of the Protestant Episcopal Church 1975 44(3): 277-283.* In 1824 Jedidiah Morse published his *Annals of the American Revolution; or, A record of the causes and events which produced, and terminated in the establishment and independence of the American republic*. Included in this work was a letter written by John Adams, "Episcopacy, a Cause of the Revolution." The Episcopalians immediately replied to Adams' charge. One such respondent was "W," who was Rev. George Weller, rector of St. Stephen's chapel, North Sassafras, Maryland. Reproduces the letter, with minor editorial annotations. It refutes Adams' claim, concluding that at his advanced age, Adams might better utilize his time in preparing for the world to come rather than in reliving events of his younger days. 8 notes.   H. M. Parker, Jr.

259. Guinness, Desmond. THOMAS JEFFERSON: VISIONARY ARCHITECT. *Horizon 1979 22(4): 51-55.* Receiving inspiration from Classic architecture as well as the French Visionary architects, Thomas Jefferson set out to design a model university, which became the University of Virginia.

260. Hallam, John S. HOUDON'S *WASHINGTON* IN RICHMOND: SOME NEW OBSERVATIONS. *Am. Art J. 1978 10(2): 72-80.* By examination of some correspondence and other data never before used in connection with studies of Jean Antoine Houdon's statue of *Washington* in Richmond, Virginia, seeks a more integrated coverage of several facets of the commission and its execution, and placement, ca. 1784-96. It relates to problems of Neoclassicism, state portraiture, Republican iconography, and its place in the artistic history of France and the new American nation. The statue (ca. 1788-91) embodies an amalgamation of ideas from American sources—Peale, West, Jefferson, and Washington himself, infused by Houdon's own genius. 9 illus., 31 notes.   R. V. Ritter

261. Hamowy, Ronald. JEFFERSON AND THE SCOTTISH ENLIGHTENMENT: A CRITIQUE OF GARRY WILLS'S *INVENTING AMERICA: JEFFERSON'S DECLARATION OF INDEPENDENCE*. *William and Mary Q. 1979 36(4): 503-523.* Takes issue with Garry Wills's thesis (New York: 1978) that Thomas Jefferson's philosophical views in the Declaration of Independence are derived from the Scots Enlightenment—the works of Thomas Reid, David Hume, Adam Smith, Lord Kames, Adam Ferguson, and Francis Hutcheson—rather than from the influence of John Locke. Sees similarities in language of the Declaration with the Scots philosophers, but says that they reflect statements in Locke's writings. The author criticizes Wills's use of booklists. There is no evidence that Jefferson was even remotely familiar with the Scots philosophers at the time of writing the Declaration. The author clarifies the meaning of certain phrases in the Declaration, such as the "pursuit of happiness." Collates the Declaration of Independence and Jefferson's writings with the works of Locke and the Scots philosophers. 69 notes.   H. M. Ward

262. Hanchett, William. BOOTH'S DIARY. *J. of the Illinois State Hist. Soc. 1979 72(1): 39-56.* Reviews the evidence presented in a book

and film, *The Lincoln Conspiracy* (1977), to the effect that a gigantic conspiracy was responsible for the assassination of President Abraham Lincoln, and that John Wilkes Booth was set up for the blame. The case rests on missing pages in Booth's diary, which the men behind the movie claim have been recovered, although they have failed to produce them. Covers evidence that contradicts such a view, and closes with the argument that Secretary of War Edwin M. Stanton suppressed the diary for the purpose of preventing ex-rebels and sympathizers from making a martyr of Booth. 10 illus., 40 notes.   V. L. Human

263. Handler, Edward. "NATURE ITSELF IS ALL ARCANUM": THE SCIENTIFIC OUTLOOK OF JOHN ADAMS. *Pro. of the Am. Phil. Soc. 1976 120(3): 216-229.* Although he founded the American Academy of Science and the Massachusetts Agricultural Society, and generally aided all organized pursuit of science in America, John Adams denied the importance of pure science. Instead, he concentrated on practical applications in agriculture, manufactures, and commerce because he possessed a chastened sense of the limits of science and an awareness of its ambiguous results. His fundamental outlook, Christian and classical in its roots, was that science and technology, despite their promises of ameliorations, could not redeem human life. Despite his dedication to the advancement of science in America, Adams's attitudes contributed to the continued backwardness of 19th century American scientific research. Based on primary and secondary sources; 29 notes.   W. L. Olbrich

264. Hill, C. William. CONTRASTING THEMES IN THE POLITICAL THEORIES OF JEFFERSON, CALHOUN, AND JOHN TAYLOR OF CAROLINE. *Publius 1976 6(3): 73-92.* Examines the views of federalism and political theory of John Taylor, Thomas Jefferson, and John Calhoun; Taylor's belief in philosophic rationalism (natural rights perceived and applied through reason) was and is a basic distinguishing factor between him and the other two.

265. Hoeveler, J. David, Jr. THOMAS JEFFERSON AND THE AMERICAN "PROVINCIAL" MIND. *Modern Age 1981 25(3): 271-280.* Traditional interpretation views Thomas Jefferson as having read and wholly imbibed John Locke's *Second Treatise* on government, helping stamp its individualistic ideals on the American political mind. Garry Wills, however, in *Inventing America*, regards Jefferson as influenced by Scottish Enlightenment democratic and social philosophy. Jefferson, then, established the priority of community over the claims of individual sovereignty. Yet another possibility for understanding Jefferson is that he perceived in the philosophy of the Scots a usable defense of provincial culture and provincial values. Jefferson's thought must be understood within the context of 18th-century American provincial culture. His concepts endure because the clash between provincial and cosmopolitan culture continues. Based on the writings of Thomas Jefferson and Garry Wills and secondary sources; 30 notes.   R. D. Rahmes

266. Hoffmann, John. QUERIES REGARDING THE WESTERN RIVERS: AN UNPUBLISHED LETTER FROM THOMAS JEFFERSON TO THE GEOGRAPHER OF THE UNITED STATES. *J. of the Illinois State Hist. Soc. 1982 75(1): 15-28.* In a previously unpublished letter to Thomas Hutchins written in 1784, Thomas Jefferson requested information concerning flooding on the Missouri, Mississippi, Illinois, Ohio, and Wabash rivers. He also noted a major error in Hutchins's estimate of the size of the Ohio watershed. Hutchins, a native of New Jersey, had been appointed geographer to the United States in 1781 after surveying and charting the Ohio, Mississippi, and Gulf Coast frontiers during the American Revolution. Jefferson used a map by Hutchins in his *Notes on Virginia* and shared Hutchins's enthusiasm for the trans-Allegheny land and rivers, arguing the advantages of the Potomac over the Hudson River in linking the Ohio territory to the Atlantic Ocean. 3 illus., 2 maps, 22 notes.   A. W. Novitsky

267. Homans, George C. JOHN ADAMS AND THE CONSTITUTION OF MASSACHUSETTS. *Pro. of the Am. Phil. Soc. 1981 125(4): 286-291.* In a three-month period in 1779, John Adams wrote out the constitution for Massachusetts, working on the kitchen table of his farmhouse. The brevity of time expended indicates that he had already done his homework. His draft was modified but slightly by the subsequent convention. Discusses Adams's political thinking: his distrust of political thinkers, utopians, and pure democracy; his belief in the system of checks

and balances; his admiration of the British Constitution; and his adherence to bicameral legislature, which would represent both the gentlemen and the simplemen. Above all he insisted on a government by laws, not men. Since 1780 the Constitution has been much amended, but it is still recognizably what Adams had in mind. Based largely on Adams's *Works;* 22 notes.   H. M. Parker, Jr.

268. Hortin, Mellie Scott. BICENTENNIAL LADY: FIRST IN THE HEARTS OF HER COUNTRYMEN. *Daughters of the Am. Revolution Mag. 1975 109(2): 100-102.* Brief sketch of Martha Washington and her role in the American Revolution.   S

269. Hoskins, Janina. "A LESSON WHICH ALL OUR COUNTRYMEN SHOULD STUDY": JEFFERSON VIEWS POLAND. *Q. J. of the Lib. of Congress 1976 33(1): 29-46.* Thomas Jefferson maintained a remarkably intense contact with Poland and personally knew many Poles. "Poland, in her effort to avoid dissolution at the hands of her aggressive neighbors, drew some inspiration from the American point of view that Jefferson embodies, while in America the Polish example served to remind the founders of the new nation of the dangers of a failure of national unity." Illus., 71 notes.   E. P. Stickney

270. Huntley, William B. JEFFERSON'S PUBLIC AND PRIVATE RELIGION. *South Atlantic Q. 1980 79(3): 286-301.* In a study of Thomas Jefferson's religion, one must distinguish between the public and the private. In his public life, his faith can be found in such writings as the Declaration of Independence, the Virginia Bill Establishing Religious Freedom, and the *Notes on the State of Virginia.* His private religion is found in his letters, where he worked out a religion, including an ethic and a theology which he submitted for discussion to friends, particularly John Adams, Joseph Priestley, and Benjamin Rush. Discusses Jefferson's religion in four themes: personal experience with the holy, creation of community through myth and ritual, daily living that expresses cosmic law, and spiritual freedom through discipline. Based on *The Adams-Jefferson Letters,* ed. Cappon; *Writings of Jefferson,* ed. Bergh; *Letters of Benjamin Rush,* ed. Butterfield, secondary sources; 45 notes.
                                H. M. Parker, Jr.

271. Huston, James H. ROBERT YATES' NOTES ON THE CONSTITUTIONAL CONVENTION OF 1787: *CITIZEN GENET'S EDITION. Q. J. of the Lib. of Congress 1978 35(3): 173-182.* Two pages of the notes taken during the Constitutional Convention of 1787 by Robert Yates and copied by John Lansing, Jr., were found in the papers of Edmond C. Genet in the Manuscript Division of the Library of Congress. Comparison with the 1821 publication edited by Genet, *Secret Proceedings and Debates of the Convention Assembled at Philadelphia in the Year 1787, . . . from Notes taken by the late Robert Yates, . . . and copied by John Lansing, . . . ,* reveals that Genet took many liberties with the original Yates-Lansing notes, rendering the published version inaccurate, incomplete, and polemical, portraying James Madison in an unfavorable light. Madison recognized some of the inaccuracies, but changed his own notes to agree with the published version in many places. Madison's notes published in 1840 and the Yates-Lansing published notes are the primary sources of information about the Constitutional Convention of 1787; both must now be examined more carefully, as parts may be unreliable. Based on documents in the Rare Book and Special Collections Division of the Library of Congress and secondary sources; 7 illus., 16 notes.   A. R. Souby

272. Israel, John and Hochman, Steven H. DISCOVERING JEFFERSON IN THE PEOPLE'S REPUBLIC OF CHINA. *Virginia Q. Rev. 1981 57(3): 401-419.* This article is subdivided into three short essays. Israel (pp. 401-406) describes his contacts with Chinese visitors to the University of Virginia since 1976 and his 1980 discovery of, and correspondence with, the Chinese historian Liu Zuochang (Liu Tso-ch'ang), apparently "China's sole Jefferson expert." Hochman (pp. 406-414) reviews Liu's "Thomas Jefferson's Ideas of Democracy" and finds it a surprisingly favorable assessment of Jefferson despite some biases and omissions. Israel (pp. 414-419) completes the trilogy with reflections on Marx and Jefferson in the People's Republic.   O. H. Zabel

273. Jackson, Donald. GEORGE WASHINGTON'S BEAUTIFUL NELLY. *Am. Heritage 1977 28(2): 80-85.* Eleanor Parke Custis was George Washington's step-granddaughter, but he regarded her as a

daughter for she grew up in his household. Although Nelly was adored and pampered as a child, her adulthood was sad and difficult, in part because she never developed self-reliance. 5 illus.   B. J. Paul

274. Jillson, Calvin C. THE REPRESENTATION QUESTION IN THE FEDERAL CONVENTION OF 1787: MADISON'S VIRGINIA PLAN AND ITS OPPONENTS. *Congressional Studies 1981 8(1): 21-41.* Discusses the elements of James Madison's Virginia Plan, which would strengthen nation authority over states' rights, presented at the Constitutional Convention of 1787, focusing on the controversy over the issue of representation in Congress.

275. Johnson, Richard R., ed. PATIENCE AND PLANNING: A LETTER FROM GEORGE WASHINGTON. *Pacific Northwest Q. 1979 70(1): 20-23.* Presents the text of a letter from George Washington to Third New Jersey Regiment Colonel Elias Dayton on 21 July 1780 during a critical period in the American Revolution. 4 photos, 11 notes.
                                M. L. Tate

276. Kaplan, Lawrence S. REFLECTIONS ON JEFFERSON AS A FRANCOPHILE. *South Atlantic Q. 1980 79(1): 38-50.* In spite of the effort of some scholars (Gilbert Chinard, Dumas Malone, Merrill Peterson) to separate myth from reality, there will always be a residual suspicion of weakness in Thomas Jefferson's feelings for France. Yet his love for France was far less evident than a visceral dislike of the common enemy—the Federalists at home and Great Britain abroad. While his widely advertised love of the French only slightly compromised his position as a public man, in his writings Jefferson provided sufficient material to keep alive the topic for future historians and politicians to debate. Based on the published and edited writings of Jefferson and secondary studies; 36 notes.   H. M. Parker, Jr.

277. Katcher, Philip. "THEY BEHAVED LIKE SOLDIERS": THE THIRD VIRGINIA REGIMENT AT HARLEM HEIGHTS. *Virginia Cavalcade 1976 26(2): 64-69.* Discusses the Virginia Regiment (3rd) at the battle of Harlem Heights in 1776, which, because of the tired and defeated nature of the troops, General George Washington never intended to engage in, much less to win.

278. Katz, Stanley N. THOMAS JEFFERSON AND THE RIGHT TO PROPERTY IN REVOLUTIONARY AMERICA. *J. of Law and Econ. 1976 19(3): 467-488.* Jefferson believed widespread landowning and a farming economy essential to a republic. His Viginia legislation (prohibiting entail, primogeniture, etc.) exemplified his brief-lived dream of pure republicanism in government. His vision, enacted as the Articles of Confederation, survived only during 1776-87. Based on primary and secondary sources; 52 notes.   C. B. Fitzgerald

279. Knudson, Jerry. JEFFERSON THE FATHER OF SLAVE CHILDREN? ONE VIEW OF THE BOOK REVIEWERS. *Journalism Hist. 1976 3(2): 56-58.* Examines Fawn M. Brodie's thesis in *Thomas Jefferson, An Intimate History* (New York, 1974) that Jefferson fathered five children by his slave Sally Hemings, and its reception by the critics.

280. Koch, Adrienne. JAMES MADISON AND THE LIBRARY OF CONGRESS. *Q. J. of the Lib. of Congress 1980 37(2): 159-161.* James Madison (1751-1836), regarded as the "father of the Constitution," was also the first to propose a Library of Congress. He drew up the first book list of the legislators' library, worked to get Thomas Jefferson's private library for the nation, and worked closely with the Librarian of Congress. A philosopher-statesman, Madison advocated the American experiment and combined theory and practice into a new political institution based on his knowledge of human nature and the normal course of social change. His native intelligence, reasoning power, command of learning, and devotion to liberty combined to allow him to make his unique contributions.   A. R. Souby

281. Kukla, Jon. FLIRTATION AND *FEUX D'ARTIFICES:* MR. JEFFERSON, MRS. COSWAY, AND FIREWORKS. *Virginia Cavalcade 1976 26(2): 52-63.* Examines a minor flirtation between Thomas Jefferson (when he was American Ambassador to France) and Maria Cosway (the wife of an eccentric Englishman, 1786-89; discusses fireworks, a popular form of entertainment in France, and one which Jefferson and Cosway witnessed.

282. Ladenson, Alex. "I CANNOT LIVE WITHOUT BOOKS": THOMAS JEFFERSON, BIBLIOPHILE. *Wilson Lib. Bull. 1978 52(8): 624-631.* Discusses the importance of books to the education of Thomas Jefferson, the building of his personal library starting in the 1770's, its classification system, its sale in 1814, and attempts at rebuilding in the 1820's.

283. Laska, Vera. THE MANY-SPLENDORED CORRESPONDENCE OF ABIGAIL AND JOHN ADAMS. *New England Social Studies Bull. 1976/77 34(1): 11-13.* Short discussion of the letters between John and Abigail Adams, 1762-84.

284. Leveque, Lawrence L. GENERAL GEORGE WASHINGTON AND THE REVOLUTION: A SELECT BIBLIOGRAPHY. *Indiana Social Studies Q. 1975 28(1): 5-13.*

285. Levitsky, Ihor. THE TOLSTOY GOSPEL IN THE LIGHT OF THE JEFFERSON BIBLE. *Can. Slavonic Papers [Canada] 1979 21(3): 347-355.* Comparison of both the rationale and the content of Leo Tolstoy's *Christ's Christianity* (London, 1855) and Thomas Jefferson's *The Life and Morals of Jesus of Nazareth* (Washington, 1904) reveals a remarkable similarity. Both considered that the essential moral teachings of Jesus had been overlaid by a tradition begun by Paul the Apostle that concealed the essence of Christianity and turned it in a detrimental direction. This unorthodox approach was no problem to Jefferson in view of his ability to adjust to public expediencies. For Tolstoy, with his sense of responsibility to conviction, these views created many tensions. Primary sources; 27 notes. R. V. Ritter

286. Lewis, Clayton W. STYLE IN JEFFERSON'S *NOTES ON THE STATE OF VIRGINIA*. *Southern Rev. 1978 14(4): 668-676.* Thomas Jefferson's style in his *Notes On the State of Virginia* (which was written in 1781-82 but not published until 1789) achieves literary as well as historical status.

287. Lint, Gregg L. JOHN ADAMS ON THE DRAFTING OF THE TREATY PLAN OF 1776. *Diplomatic Hist. 1978 2(3): 313-320.* Discusses the sources used by John Adams in preparing the Plan of Treaties of 1776, a document intended most immediatley as a model for America's hoped-for treaty with France—a treaty which Adams insisted should be strictly commercial in nature. After preparing Articles 1-13 with the help of two old volumes of limited relevance—Adams was greatly assisted by the loan from Benjamin Franklin of a very helpful book from which he was able to lift almost verbatim the remainder of the treaty, judiciously selected. This second section consisted wholly of material from treaties already in force between France and Britain. Based on primary sources, including the very volume lent by Franklin to Adams, with Franklin's marginal X's beside treaty articles to which he wished to direct Adams's attention; 19 notes. L. W. Van Wyk

288. Luker, Ralph E. GARRY WILLS AND THE NEW DEBATE OVER THE DECLARATION OF INDEPENDENCE. *Virginia Q. Rev. 1980 56(2): 244-266.* Conservative Garry Wills's *Inventing America,* initially praised for its new interpretation of the Declaration of Independence, has recently been seriously criticized. Wills, a distributist (favoring more equal distribution of property to prevent state centralization), portrays Jefferson as less liberal and individualist than has been thought. Recent critics include various conservative scholars: neoconservative Kenneth Lynn, traditionalist Harry Jaffa, and libertarian Ronald Hamoway. Each vigorously attacks Wills's view, seeking in Thomas Jefferson "their own highest values." O. H. Zabel

289. Luttrell, Clifton B. THOMAS JEFFERSON ON MONEY AND BANKING: DISCIPLE OF DAVID HUME AND FORERUNNER OF SOME MODERN MONETARY VIEWS. *Hist. of Pol. Econ. 1975 7(2): 156-173.* Discusses the banking and economic theory of Thomas Jefferson 1775-1816, emphasizing the similarity to the thought of philosopher David Hume.

290. Lynn, Kenneth S. FALSIFYING JEFFERSON. *Commentary 1978 66(4): 66-71.* Criticizes Garry Wills's *Inventing America* for being more inventive than scholarly in its assertion that Thomas Jefferson, in writing the Declaration of Independence, was influenced by communitarian philosophers of the Scottish Enlightenment, rather than Lockean individualism, which is the thesis of Carl Becker's classic, *The Declaration of Independence.*

291. Mabee, Charles. THOMAS JEFFERSON'S ANTI-CLERICAL BIBLE. *Hist. Mag. of the Protestant Episcopal Church 1979 48(4): 473-481.* Thomas Jefferson's unpublished "scissors-and-paste" treatment of the gospels during 1813-20 reveals him as an American, not a Marcionite, and as a declericalizer rather than a demythologizer. In endeavoring to rid the scriptures of what he deemed to be priest-ridden interpretations, Jefferson inadvertently grasped one of the basic themes of the gospels: truth is not as it appears in this world. Demonstrates this by drawing attention to the positioning of the gospel passages in Jefferson's work. Thomas Jefferson thus emerges in the "prophetic and apologetic spirit of a true devotee of Jesus." Based on Jefferson's letters and secondary sources; 21 notes. H. M. Parker, Jr.

292. MacConkey, Dorothy Ingling. BICENTENNIAL PRESIDENTS AND THEIR ROLE MODELS: A SOCIOLOGICAL VIEW. *Daughters of the Am. Revolution Mag. 1976 110(5): 508-512, 642.* Presents key biographical factors in the personal lives of early US Presidents, including George Washington, Thomas Jefferson, John Adams, James Madison, and James Monroe.

293. Malone, Dumas. MR. JEFFERSON'S PRIVATE LIFE. *Pro. of the Am. Antiquarian Soc. 1974 84(1): 65-72.* Reprints a letter written by Ellen Randolph Coolidge in 1858 to her husband concerning the personal life of her grandfather, Thomas Jefferson, and countering certain allegations made against his character, particularly the story initially circulated by journalist James Thomson Callender, that Jefferson had fathered children by one of his slaves, Sally Hemings. 14 notes. B. L. Fenske

294. Marienstras, Elise. THOMAS JEFFERSON ET LA NAISSANCE DES ÉTATS-UNIS [Thomas Jefferson and the birth of the United States]. *Histoire [France] 1980 (19): 30-39.* Jefferson, a philosopher of the Enlightenment, refused to grant human rights to Indians and Negroes; favored states' rights, but was an authoritarian president; and, although proagrarian, promoted US industrialization. J

295. McCoy, Drew R. JEFFERSON AND MADISON ON MALTHUS: POPULATION GROWTH IN JEFFERSONIAN POLITICAL ECONOMY. *Virginia Mag. of Hist. and Biog. 1980 88(3): 259-276.* Tries to account for Thomas Jefferson and James Madison's partial favoring of the views of Thomas Robert Malthus, in spite of their basic Republic optimism for the future of the United States. Madison, who discussed Malthus with Robert Owen, saw the supplying of foreign markets as a means of employing surplus domestic labor, thus mitigating the effect of America's population on its material resources. 55 notes. P. J. Woehrmann

296. McCoy, Drew R. MADISON'S AMERICA: POLITY, ECONOMY, AND SOCIETY. *Q. J. of the Lib. of Congress 1980 37(2): 259-264.* Examines James Madison's (1751-1836) concerns about the republican government, which he felt depended on a populace socially and economically independent, equal and virtuous, and thus able to work for the common or public good and not susceptible to "bribery, corruption, and factious dissension." Madison realized that even with America's great expanses of arable land, the rapid growth of population would lead to the necessity for manufacturers, thus creating a class of dependent laborers and landless persons unable to secure material and economic independence. Madison feared that this inequality and dependence of part of the populace would be a threat to the republic. Concludes that the spirit and substance of Madison's republic has indeed been lost, judging by today's problems of unemployment, lack of social and economic independence, and widespread voter apathy. 18 notes. A. R. Souby

297. McCoy, Drew R. REPUBLICANISM AND AMERICAN FOREIGN POLICY: JAMES MADISON AND THE POLITICAL ECONOMY OF COMMERCIAL DISCRIMINATION, 1789 TO 1794. *William and Mary Q. 1974 31(4): 633-646.* The development of American commercial policy was connected with the rise of political parties. Madison's views on manufactures and his reasons for discrimination, reflected his Republican ideology. Actually Madison wanted an unrestricted international order which would expand the human mind and humanity.

American economic independence would not exclude Americans from foreign markets. Also describes Hamilton's conception of a sectionally interdependent economy as a means for the United States to contend for reciprocity, rather than Madison's coercive proposals. Based on primary and secondary sources; 42 notes.   H. M. Ward

298. McCoy, Drew R.   THE VIRGINIA PORT BILL OF 1784. *Virginia Mag. of Hist. and Biog. 1975 83(3): 288-303.* In an attempt to bring economic independence to Virginia after the Revolution, James Madison led a drive to restrict the state's trade to a few enumerated ports. Madison hoped to create port cities, ending Virginia's dependence on Philadelphia and Baltimore and reducing the influence of British merchants on the state's trade. Though his port bill passed the legislature, opposition from nonfavored areas of the state delayed its implementation and amended it to emphasize potential revenue. Madison, meanwhile, shifted his attention from the state to the national level in his attempt to achieve economic self-sufficiency. Based on published editions of the Madison and Jefferson papers, county petitions in the Virginia State Library, and secondary sources; 62 notes.   R. F. Oaks

299. Medlin, Dorothy.   THOMAS JEFFERSON, ANDRÉ MOREL-LET, AND THE FRENCH VERSION OF *NOTES ON THE STATE OF VIRGINIA. William and Mary Q. 1978 35(1): 85-99.* Jefferson was furious with André Morellet's translation of his *Notes on the State of Virginia* (published in France, 1788). Morellet rearranged and edited the work. Jefferson objected to printing errors, stylistic changes, and substantial changes. Compares the two versions, with examples of changes. Morellet's edition actually added clarity and many of Jefferson's objections were uncalled for. Jefferson's criticisms reveal more about him than the translator, namely that he had more pride in authorship than he admitted. Quotes passages from both editions. Based on Jefferson's correspondence; 43 notes.   H. M. Ward

300. Meschutt, David.   THE ADAMS-JEFFERSON PORTRAIT EXCHANGE. *Am. Art J. 1982 14(2): 47-54.* During 1785-86, while John Adams was minister to England and Thomas Jefferson was minister to France, the two men became friends. Each hired American painter Mather Brown, a student of Benjamin West, to paint a portrait to keep for themselves, and one to exchange with the other. The history of these four paintings is complex; Jefferson got a replica, not the original, for himself. Today both portraits the men had of themselves are lost. Based on the Jefferson Papers in the Library of Congress; 4 plates, 53 notes.
J. J. Buschen

301. Meschutt, David.   GILBERT STUART'S PORTRAITS OF THOMAS JEFFERSON. *Am. Art J. 1981 13(1): 2-16.* Gilbert Stuart (1755-1828) painted Thomas Jefferson from life on three occasions, once at Philadelphia in 1800 and twice at Washington in 1805. Confusion has clouded the history of these portraits because of Stuart's devious and sometimes fraudulent business practices. The first picture has disappeared. The "Edgehill Jefferson," reputed to be the second, was actually a copy of 1821. The "Bowdoin Jefferson" (1805) was the second portrait, and the "Madison Jefferson" (1805) the third. All other portraits of Jefferson are copies of the two 1805 paintings. Based on the Jefferson Papers in the Library of Congress and other primary sources; 11 plates, 55 notes.   J. J. Buschen

302. Meyers, Marvin.   REVOLUTION AND FOUNDING: ON PUBLIUS-MADISON AND THE AMERICAN GENESIS. *Q. J. of the Lib. of Congress 1980 37(2): 192-200.* James Madison (1751-1836), writing as "Publius" in *The Federalist*, defended the work of the Philadelphia convention of 1787 against charges of a counterrevolutionary coup by saying that they were working under the supreme authority of the people and their rights to point out a system capable of securing the country's happiness, a system which the people would approve or disapprove. His view of history as a graveyard of lost republican hopes led him to understand that "a measure of popular and local liberty . . . must be reconciled with that full measure of authority necessary to secure the rights, the safety, and the happiness of society." The problem of the republic was that the right of the people to institute new government was accompanied by their right to alter and aoblish old government. Madison warned that the instability of government must be protected against or the republic could not last. 3 illus., 19 notes.   A. R. Souby

303. Midgley, Louis.   THE BRODIE CONNECTION: THOMAS JEFFERSON AND JOSEPH SMITH. *Brigham Young U. Studies 1979 20(1): 59-67.* A look at the treatment accorded two books by Fawn M. Brodie. The first, a 1946 account of Mormon Joseph Smith, has been held by scholars at large to be a true and accurate account of the founder's life. Only Mormons objected, and they were accused of self-interest and brushed aside. Brodie's most recent book deals with the life of President Thomas Jefferson, and critics have wasted no time in pointing out its many shortcomings. Interestingly, their criticisms fairly parallel those of Mormons against the Joseph Smith production, suggesting that perhaps non-Mormon scholars should take another look at it.
V. L. Human

304. Miller, Randall M.   THE FOUNDING OF A FATHER: JOHN ADAMS AND THE APPOINTMENT OF GEORGE WASHINGTON AS COMMANDER-IN-CHIEF OF THE CONTINENTAL ARMY. *Maryland Historian 1973 4(1): 13-23.* Reexamines John Adams' description of the selection of George Washington as commander-in-chief. Contemporary accounts and events support Adams' contention that Washington was chosen for political reasons. He was radical enough for the North, and a Virginian, which satisfied southern delegates' concerns. Based on primary sources; 38 notes.   G. O. Gagnon

305. Miller, Sue Freeman.   MR. JEFFERSON'S PASSION: HIS GROVE AT MONTICELLO. *Hist. Preservation 1980 32(2): 32-35.* The Thomas Jefferson Memorial Foundation decided in 1977 to fund the Monticello curator's project for the recreation of Jefferson's grove on the Virginian mountainside. Because Jefferson rarely specified the particular placement of plants, the new grove cannot reproduce the original. Plants and trees mentioned in Jefferson's plans are once more growing in the grove, however, and Rudy J. Favretti, the landscape architect who redesigned it, suggests that Jefferson's own botanical experiments may continue as new shoots vie for survival in untried soil. Already visitors can appreciate the serenity of the grounds, in spirit, at least, as Jefferson felt it. 8 photos.   S

306. Mintz, Max M.   HORATIO GATES, GEORGE WASHINGTON'S RIVAL. *Hist. Today [Great Britain] 1976 26(7): 419-428.* Discusses the military strategy of Continental Army General Horatio Gates in the battle of Saratoga, and George Washington's and Congress' opposition to his plans for the invasion of Canada, 1777-80.

307. Moore, John Hammond.   THAT "COMMODIOUS" ANNEX TO JEFFERSON'S ROTUNDA: WAS IT REALLY A NATIONAL MAUSOLEUM? *Virginia Cavalcade 1980 29(3): 114-123.* The Annex added to Thomas Jefferson's Rotunda at the University of Virginia between 1851 and 1853 was destroyed by fire along with the Rotunda in 1895 and never restored; describes its designer, architect Robert Mills (1781-1855), and some of his other buildings. The Rotunda was restored in the 1970's to Jefferson's original floor plan.

308. Moore, Virginia.   DOLLEY MADISON: QUEEN OF SOCIETY, DEBT-RIDDEN WIDOW. *Smithsonian 1979 10(8): 173-185.* Describes the social life of Dolly Payne Madison after the death of James in 1836 until her own demise in 1849.

309. Morgan, Edmund S.   GEORGE WASHINGTON: THE ALOOF AMERICAN. *Virginia Q. Rev. 1976 52(3): 410-436.* Aloofness, self-interest, honor, and daring were characteristics of Washington. All contributed to his ability to lead effectively in the Revolution and to set domestic and foreign policies of the new constitutional government. Then and now "Americans honor the father of their country from a respectful distance."   O. H. Zabel

310. Morgan, Robert J.   MADISON'S ANALYSIS OF THE SOURCES OF POLITICAL AUTHORITY. *Am. Pol. Sci. Rev. 1981 75(3): 613-625.* James Madison believed that political institutions are not the effects of conflicts among private groups in society. He traced political authority to human nature. It is the ultimate source of both public opinion and the motives which impel some individuals to hold government offices. Prudently contrived governmental institutions can moderate the countervailing tendencies arising from these two sources of authority, although they are necessarily in a state of continuing tension. Strict accountability of representatives to the whole range of diverse opinion in society is in conflict with the tendency of government to become autonomous.
J/S

311. Morgan, Robert J. MADISON'S THEORY OF REPRESENTATION IN THE TENTH FEDERALIST. *J. of Pol.* 1974 36(4): 852-885. Madison's tenth *Federalist* has been interpreted by the progressives and their heirs as proof that the Constitution is a barrier to majority rule, especially by political parties responsive to a landless urban electorate. Pluralists have construed it so as to demonstrate that majority rule is rendered benign when an increase in the size of a democratic system spontaneously multiplies and diversifies political groups. In [this essay the author] argues that the essay contains a probabilistic causal theory of representation intended to prove that some fundamental cleavages can be stabilized in a federal republic by electing legislators in large, heterogeneous districts. Madison revised republican theory to prove that constitutional government is just and stable because it incorporates all interests into the legislative process on a continuing basis, contrary to the theories of Harrington, Hume, and Montesquieu.   J

312. Morison, Samuel Eliot. THREE GREAT LADIES HELPED ESTABLISH THE UNITED STATES. *Smithsonian* 1975 6(7): 96-103. Presents biographies of Abigail Adams, Mercy Otis Warren, and Martha Washington, focusing on their letters, feminism, and contributions to the American Revolution.

313. Ney, Virgil. WASHINGTON'S CONTINENTAL ARMY. *Daughters of the Am. Revolution Mag.* 1976 110(6): 827-837. Discusses the organizational structure of the Continental Army under George Washington during the American Revolution, showing Washington's improvements.

314. Nordham, George Washington. GEORGE WASHINGTON: A REMEMBRANCE ON THE 250TH ANNIVERSARY OF HIS BIRTH. *Daughters of the Am. Revolution Mag.* 1982 116(2): 84-88. A biography of George Washington noting what made him a great man.

315. Nyquist, Ewald B. THE SWEDISH CONNECTION: SAMUEL VON PUFENDORF AND THE AMERICAN REVOLUTION. *Swedish Pioneer Hist. Q.* 1977 28(4): 252-258. Samuel von Pufendorf influenced the American Founding Fathers with his book, *On the Law of Nature and Nations,* published in 1672 in Lund, Sweden. Pufendorf, although a German, spent 18 years in Sweden as a teacher, author, royal historiographer, and secretary of state under King Charles XI. His book was very controversial, possibly because it contained so many ideas in its 1,300 pages that different readers could find different quotes to sustain conflicting beliefs. The obligation of the citizen to the state was emphasized, but he also warned rulers about taxing people too heavily. Pufendorf returned to Germany in 1688 and died in Berlin in 1694. By the middle of the 18th century, Pufendorf was considered an important enough writer to be taught in several of the colonial American colleges. Many of the founders of our nation read him, including John Jay, Alexander Hamilton, and James Madison. Thomas Jefferson quoted him at length by 1770. It is believed that George Washington owned a copy of the book and it was one of the earliest acquisitions of the Library Company of Philadelphia, of which Benjamin Franklin was the chief founder. Based on the writings of Pufendorf and his biography written in 1965 by Leonard Krieger.   C. W. Ohrvall

316. O'Brien, Matthew C. JOHN ESTEN COOKE, GEORGE WASHINGTON, AND THE VIRGINIA CAVALIERS. *Virginia Mag. of Hist. and Biog.* 1976 84(3): 259-265. Though novelist John Esten Cooke is usually associated with the Civil War, he also wrote several novels set in pre-Revolutionary Virginia. His themes included both a longing for the Cavalier past, embodied in men such as George Washington, and a democratic disdain for the evils of the aristocratic class system. 4 notes.   R. F. Oaks

317. Ogburn, Floyd, Jr. STRUCTURE AND MEANING IN THOMAS JEFFERSON'S *NOTES ON VIRGINIA. Early Am. Literature* 1980 15(2): 141-150. Suggests a novel approach to understanding Jefferson's *Notes on the State of Virginia* (1784-85) by emphasizing key passages on nature and the arrangement of nouns and verbs in those passages. Nature is central for Jefferson's meaning and structure, and he uses nouns and verbs to suggest the idea of a quest for nature. Man's objective and subjective quest for nature is Jefferson's thesis in *Notes.* 15 notes.   T. P. Linkfield

318. Palmer, Lilla Rachel. GEORGE AND MARTHA: HOST AND HOSTESS. *Daughters of the Am. Revolution Mag.* 1979 113(5): 528-531, 640. Discusses the hospitality of George and Martha Washington before and during his presidency, and their lives before they married in 1759.

319. Peden, William. THE JEFFERSON MONUMENT AT THE UNIVERSITY OF MISSOURI. *Missouri Hist. Rev.* 1977 72(1): 67-77. Thomas Jefferson designed his own tombstone. Vandals gradually reduced the Monticello gravesite until 1883, when the government replaced the original stone with a more imposing monument. The University of Missouri was one of many supplicants seeking the old obelisk and base. The monument, which has been standing at several campus sites since 1885, was given to the university to commemorate Jefferson's long interest in state-supported education and because the school was the first state university in the Louisiana Purchase Territory. Primary and secondary sources; illus., 16 notes.   W. F. Zornow

320. Peterson, Merrill D. DUMAS MALONE: THE COMPLETION OF A MONUMENT. *Virginia Q. Rev.* 1982 58(1): 26-31. Malone, editor of *The Dictionary of American Biography,* in 1943 began his six-volume biography, *Jefferson and His Time,* which was completed in 1981. As a critical biography it presents Jefferson's faults and errors without trivializing him and without imposing the author's prejudices upon the reader. Based upon diligent research, this monumental work both relates Jefferson to his time and covers his many-sidedness. "The dominant image that emerges . . . is not new. It is the old image of the Apostle of Liberty."   O. H. Zabel

321. Peterson, Merrill D. MR. JEFFERSON'S "SOVEREIGNTY OF THE LIVING GENERATION." *Virginia Q. Rev.* 1976 52(3): 437-447. Viewing the French Revolution, Thomas Jefferson developed his theory of the "sovereignty of the living generation" which denied that the dead can bind the living. His theory is pertinent in the Bicentennial Era as Americans consider the balance of change and conservation in the American Experiment.   O. H. Zabel

322. Pickens, Buford. MR. JEFFERSON AS REVOLUTIONARY ARCHITECT. *J. of the Soc. of Architectural Historians* 1975 34(4): 257-279. Discusses Thomas Jefferson's architectural designs for buildings in Virginia between 1769 and 1809.

323. Pilling, Ron. " . . . PERMIT ME AGAIN TO SUGGEST THAT YOU RECEIVE THE OLIVE BRANCH . . . " *Am. Hist. Illus.* 1980 15(8): 30-35. In December 1811, Benjamin Rush finally ended the long feud between ex-presidents John Adams and Thomas Jefferson; covers 1796-1811.

324. Powell, J. H. GENERAL WASHINGTON AND THE JACK ASS. *South Atlantic Q.* 1977 76(4): 409-423. Long convinced that mules were the best draft animals, George Washington spent many years trying to develop a superior strain. Had he not been the famous general and President, he never would have succeeded. Spanish mules—the world's best at that time—were a royal monopoly and it took the machinations of the Marquis de Lafayette to get the embargo lifted. Although the two jacks Washington received never lived up to his desires in showing profits, they did sire the American mule still in use today.   W. L. Olbrich

325. Rabinowitz, Howard. "THE WASHINGTON LEGEND 1865-1900: THE HEROIC IMAGE IN FLUX." *Am. Studies (Lawrence, KS)* 1976 17(1): 5-24. The Civil War provided Americans with a reason to reconsider the founders, and the late nineteenth century was a critical era in the evolution of the Washington legend. Those persons who feared a decline in morals and in religious conviction emphasized a need to resort to the wisdom of Washington. At the same time a new generation of writers, disciples of the German "scientific" school, tried to depict Washington as he really was. Yet an entirely new image of George Washington never really emerged. Based on primary and secondary sources; 66 notes.   J. Andrew

326. Ravier, Xavier. THOMAS JEFFERSON ET LA LANGUE D'OC [Thomas Jefferson and the Occitan language]. *Ann. du Midi [France]* 1978 90(136): 41-52. The letter sent by Thomas Jefferson from

Aix-en-Provence, March 28, 1787, to his secretary and confidant W. Short, contains a passage of considerable importance for those who study the Midi. It is nothing less than, from the pen of the man who will become the third president of the United States, an enthusiastic praise of the Occitan language. The text, remarkable in more than one way, contains, in particular concerning the history of linguistic thought, a number of propositions which the comparative schools of the early 19th century will take up and develop.   J

327. Reardon, Paul C. THE MASSACHUSETTS CONSTITUTION MARKS A MILESTONE. *Publius 1982 12(1): 45-55.* The constitution of the state of Massachusetts, ratified in 1780, is an important historical document, as it had a profound effect on the ratification of the Federal Constitution. John Adams was the draftsman of the Massachusetts constitution after becoming an expert by studying constitutions, both ancient and modern. In drafting the Massachusetts constitution, he borrowed from the Pennsylvania Declaration and the 1776 Virginia Bill of Rights. Primary sources; 27 notes.   J. Powell

328. Reid, John Phillip. A LAWYER ACQUITTED: JOHN ADAMS AND THE BOSTON MASSACRE. *Am. J. of Legal Hist. 1974 18(3): 189-207.* Discusses John Adams in the context of the American common-law tradition, with particular attention to his words and actions during the Boston Massacre of 1770.   S

329. Richardson, E. P. A LIFE DRAWING OF JEFFERSON BY JOHN TRUMBULL. *Maryland Hist. Mag. 1975 70(4): 363-371.* Argues that a pencil sketch of Thomas Jefferson found 40 years ago among Benjamin Henry Latrobe's papers and commonly attributed until now to Latrobe, was actually the work of John Trumbull, probably in August or early September 1786. At that time Trumbull stayed with Jefferson in Paris and the two consulted on details for Trumbull's famous painting of *The Declaration of Independence*. This life study is especially unique because it shows Jefferson when he was happy, "sparkling with life, intelligence, and pleasure." After the 1790's he and the artist were estranged over political views, and Trumbull and Latrobe, it is shown, had much contact through the next few years so the sketch could easily have changed hands. Includes Jefferson's own sketch of the floor plan of the Philadelphia State House, and modifications made by Trumbull in the finished painting, and in the positioning of the figures. Reprinted from *The American Art Journal* 1975 7(2). Primary and secondary sources; 5 illus, 11 notes.   G. J. Bobango

330. Richardson, E. P. A LIFE DRAWING OF JEFFERSON BY JOHN TRUMBULL. *Am. Art J. 1975 7(2): 4-9.* Discusses a pencil drawing of Thomas Jefferson originally attributed to Benjamin Henry Latrobe, but now identified as the work of John Trumbull. 8 illus.

331. Rinaldi, Nicholas. GEORGE WASHINGTON AT HOME IN VIRGINIA. *Early Am. Life 1977 8(1): 11-17.* Excerpts from the personal diaries and letters of George Washington which remark on the weather, activities at Mount Vernon, acquaintances, and his marriage to Martha Dandridge Custis during 1760-86.

332. Rinaldi, Nicholas. GEORGE WASHINGTON AT HOME IN VIRGINIA. *Early Am. Life 1977 8(2): 69-71.* Conglomeration from 1797-99 of Washington's notes to himself and to friends, short journal excerpts, and last will and testament.

333. Risjord, Norman K. THE COMPROMISE OF 1790: NEW EVIDENCE ON THE DINNER TABLE BARGAIN. *William and Mary Q. 1976 33(2): 309-314.* Reprints a note sent through James Madison by Thomas Jefferson, inviting Tench Coxe to dinner on 6 June 1790. The dinner was a political one at which a compromise was reached on the location of the nation's capital and federal assumption of state war debts. These decisions led to a Pennsylvania-Virginia alliance. Describes the events following the compromise. Based on letters located in the Tench Coxe Papers at the Historical Society of Pennsylvania. 16 notes.
                                                                H. M. Ward

334. Ritcheson, Charles R. THE FRAGILE MEMORY: THOMAS JEFFERSON AT THE COURT OF GEORGE III. *Eighteenth-Century Life 1981 6(2-3): 1-16.* Contemporary accounts of Thomas Jefferson's visit to the English court of George III in 1786 show that Jefferson

misrecollected and made errors in his *Autobiography,* written at age 78.

335. Ritcheson, Charles R. THE FRAGILE MEMORY: WHAT REALLY HAPPENED WHEN THOMAS JEFFERSON MET GEORGE III. *Am. Heritage 1981 33(1): 72-77.* On 17 March 1786, Thomas Jefferson met George III at the king's levee. Jefferson's account, recorded years later in his *Autobiography,* indicates a failure of memory, but his reports of being snubbed have been embellished in later writings on the subject. Yet, it appears there was no snub, nothing out of the ordinary. Jefferson's account was based at least in part on his undying hatred for the king. 4 illus.   J. F. Paul

336. Royster, Charles. A BATTLE OF MEMOIRS: LIGHT-HORSE HARRY LEE AND THOMAS JEFFERSON. *Virginia Cavalcade 1981 31(2): 112-127.* Discusses the attacks by Henry "Light-Horse Harry" Lee, on Thomas Jefferson in Lee's *Memoirs of the War* (1812), which deprecated Jefferson's war leadership while governor of Virginia during the British invasion; a staunch Federalist, Lee blamed all of his and the Federalists' personal and political losses on Jeffersonian Republicanism.

337. Rutland, Robert A. MADISON'S BOOKISH HABITS. *Q. J. of the Lib. of Congress 1980 37(2): 176-191.* Examines James Madison's (1751-1836) book-buying habits and discusses the books Madison owned or probably owned, based on the list he made in 1783 of "books proper for the use of Congress," works he quoted in his writings, the catalogue of books that Thomas Jefferson bought for him during his stay in Paris from 1785 to 1789, and Madison's pamphlet collection at the University of Virginia. Thomas Jefferson's influence on Madison's reading interests is noted, as well as Madison's concern for books of knowledge, to be used for a purpose, rather than books of a frivolous nature. Based on the Madison Papers in the Manuscript Division of the Library of Congress; 12 illus., 7 notes.   A. R. Souby

338. Saunders, Frances W. EQUESTRIAN WASHINGTON FROM ROME TO RICHMOND. *Virginia Cavalcade 1975 25(1): 4-13.* Discusses the planning, erection, and unveiling of statues and monuments of George Washington in Richmond 1784-1868, emphasizing the sculpture of Thomas Crawford.

339. Schnitter, Helmut. PLANTAGENBESITZER, GENERAL, PRÄSIDENT: ZUM 250. GEBURTSTAG VON GEORGE WASHINGTON [Plantation owner, general, president: on the 250th birthday of George Washington]. *Militärgeschichte [East Germany] 1982 21(1): 86-88.* Sketches the life and career of George Washington, emphasizing his role as general and his support of the rising American bourgeoisie, which developed into a powerful, rich, and brutal ruling class. Washington was part of the antifeudal, antiabsolutist struggle for liberation of the middle classes, the true inheritance of which is fulfilled today in the struggle of the revolutionary workers' movement in the United States against exploitation, suppression, war, and race discrimination. Illus., 8 notes.   H. D. Andrews German.

340. Schultz, Harold S. JAMES MADISON: FATHER OF THE CONSTITUTION? *Q. J. of the Lib. of Congress 1980 37(2): 215-222.* Praises James Madison (1751-1836) for his character and mind, his influences at the Constitutional Convention of 1787, and his concern for nationalism, republicanism, stability, and the protection of the private property rights of individuals, but feels that he cannot truly be considered the Father of the Constitution because he was not able to achieve what he thought was most important in the new plan of government and did not contribute either to the "Great Compromise" or to the provision for the judicial veto of state and federal laws. Madison's major influence was in his insistence on a strong national government elected by popular vote. 2 illus.   A. R. Souby

341. Selby, John E. RICHARD HENRY LEE, JOHN ADAMS, AND THE VIRGINIA CONSTITUTION OF 1776. *Virginia Mag. of Hist. and Biog. 1976 84(4): 387-400.* Richard Henry Lee's discussions of independence with John Adams in the fall of 1775 convinced Lee of the value of Adams' approach to constitution making for newly independent states. Lee then began a campaign in Virginia to convince doubters in that colony that a republican government would not cause internal dislocation. The most important result of Lee's effort was the Virginia Constitu-

tion of 1776. Based on a recently discovered handbill in the Williams C. Library, the Adams Papers, and the published papers of several contemporary Virginians; illus., 48 notes.   R. F. Oaks

342. Shalhope, Robert E.   THOMAS JEFFERSON'S REPUBLICANISM AND ANTEBELLUM SOUTHERN THOUGHT.   J. of Southern Hist. 1976 42(4): 529-555. The traditional view that reactionary forces appeared in the South around the 1820's, prompting the South to repudiate Jeffersonian liberalism in favor of militant conservativism, does not give adequate attention to Thomas Jefferson's own ideas. A deeper understanding of republican ideology and Jefferson's agrarian republicanism allows comprehension of the clash between the changing dynamic nature of the nation and the more static southern pastoral republicanism. Meanwhile, throughout the first half of the 19th century, the North moved toward a republicanism consistent with its economic growth and maturation. Hence, better insight into antebellum America is gained by recognizing that no sharp break occurred in southern thought, but rather a transformation of northern ideas.   T. Schoonover

343. Shaw, Peter.   JOHN ADAMS' CRISIS OF CONSCIENCE. J. of the Rutgers U. Lib. 1980 42(1): 1-25. Uncertainty and wavering marked John Adams's (1735-1826) mind during 1761-76. The mystery of his state of mind was not cleared up in his voluminous reminiscences but does throw light on the vicissitudes of patriotism in the years before Independence. In an effort to penetrate the mystery the author examines Adams's relationships with leading patriot James Otis, Jr. (1725-83), and Thomas Hutchinson (1711-80), who served as representative of the British ministry in Massachusetts throughout the prerevolutionary disturbances. 48 notes.   R. Van Benthuysen

344. Sheehan, Bernard W.   JEFFERSON AND THE WEST. Virginia Q. Rev. 1982 58(2): 345-352. Reviews Donald Jackson's Thomas Jefferson and the Stony Mountains (1981). Summarizes Jefferson's consuming interest in the American West. Although never west of Virginia, Jefferson played a central role in opening the West from the revolutionary era through the early 19th century. Important facets of his interest included exploration (the Lewis and Clark Expedition) and his preoccupation with the Indians.   O. H. Zabel

345. Shiriaev, B. A.   TOMAS DZHEFFERSON I AMERIKANSKAIA KONSTITUTSIIA [Thomas Jefferson and the American constitution]. Vestnik Leningradskogo U.: Seriia Istorii, Iazyka i Literatury [USSR] 1977 (8): 49-55. The atmosphere and the style of work of the constitutional convention strongly emphasized its antidemocratic tendencies. Thomas Jefferson understood some of the reasons for this, while admitting that the constitution had its good and its bad articles. The absence of a bill of rights, however, troubled him. He was compelled to compromise and accept many of the articles that he disagreed with, but on the condition that a bill of rights be added to the document. 21 notes.   G. F. Jewsbury

346. Shively, Frances Clark.   GEORGE WASHINGTON AND HENRY LEE. Daughters of the Am. Revolution Mag. 1977 111(5): 467-471, 574. Discusses the close personal and political friendship between Henry Lee and George Washington throughout the colonial period, through the American Revolution, and during the period of Washington's presidency, 1753-1812.

347. Sifton, Paul G.   THE PROVENANCE OF THE THOMAS JEFFERSON PAPERS. Am. Archivist 1977 40(1): 17-30. When Thomas Jefferson died in 1826, his papers passed to his grandson. Subsequently, his public papers have been acquired by the government. Papers deemed "private" remained with the family and were lost or scattered among family members, private collectors, and historical societies. Since 1829 several collections of Jefferson papers have been published. The edition started in 1950 under the editorship of Julian Parks Boyd will be the most complete to date.   G.-A. Patzwald

348. Sifton, Paul G.   RECENT ADDITIONS TO THE JAMES MADISON PAPERS AT THE LIBRARY OF CONGRESS. Q. J. of the Lib. of Congress 1980 37(2): 265-273. "Since the completion of the microfilm edition of the Library's James Madison (1751-1836) Papers in 1964, the Manuscript Division has acquired more than a dozen additional Madison items. The more significant additions acquired over these past

15 years date from 1781 to 1834 and include letters to and from Madison and papers ranging in topic from President Washington's method of communicating to the Senate to the Virginia Convention of 1829. The papers document Madison's interest in a wide array of topics, including Russo-American relations, the arts, agricultural societies, the problem of preserving presidential letters, the University of Virginia, the genius of Philip Freneau, and the Bonus Bill question." Based on the James Madison Papers in the Library of Congress; 5 illus, 4 notes.
A. R. Souby

349. Simpson, Lewis P.   THE ART OF THOUGHT IN VIRGINIA. Early Am. Literature 1979-80 14(3): 253-268. By the late 18th century, Virginia's intellectual consciousness had developed a diverse model based on rationality and secular morality. the process began with Captain John Smith and culminated with Thomas Jefferson, who harmonized with the tone and temper of his age. Depends heavily upon two seocndary works by Richard Beale Davis: Intellectual Life in Jefferson's Virginia, 1780-1830 (1964); and Intellectual life in the Colonial South, 1585-1763 (1978). Based on an essay presented to the Modern Language Association, 30 December 1978; 18 notes.   T. P. Linkfield

350. Skaggs, David Curtis.   THE GENERALSHIP OF GEORGE WASHINGTON.   Military R. 1974 54(7): 3-10. Discusses the military capability of George Washington during the American Revolution.

351. Smylie, James H.   THE PRESIDENT AS REPUBLICAN PROPHET AND KING: CLERICAL REFLECTIONS ON THE DEATH OF WASHINGTON.   J. of Church and State 1976 18(2): 233-252. From a study of 50 sermons and 440 eulogies at the death of Washington in 1799, sees the following conclusions: 1) Divine providence was good to America by giving it a Republican leader and making him great, 2) the clergy legitimized the presidential office from the Bible. God had spoken through the Scriptures. They compared Washington with Moses, David, and others, and 3) Washington was a pious man, thankfully. The mystique they wrapped Washington and his office in has made it difficult to criticize either Washington or his successors. 45 notes.
E. E. Eminhizer

352. Sognnaes, Reodar F.   AMERICA'S MOST FAMOUS TEETH. Smithsonian 1973 3(11): 47-51. Discusses the construction of George Washington's false teeth.   S

353. Sogrin, V. V.   BIOGRAFII OTTSOV-OSNOVATELEI SSHA V AMERIKANSKOI ISTORIOGRAFII 1970-KH GODOV [Biographies of the Founding Fathers of the United States in American historiography during the 1970's]. Novaia i Noveishaia Istoriia [USSR] 1980 (1): 154-163. Reviews recent biographies of Thomas Paine, Thomas Jefferson, Alexander Hamilton, George Washington, Samuel Adams, and Benjamin Franklin. The author characterizes each biography briefly, mentioning over 25 works. All of them are imbued with the current official American line: consensus is stressed while social conflict is neglected. 39 notes.
D. N. Collins

354. Sogrin, V. V.   DZHEIMS MEDISON: KLASSOVAIA SUSHCHNOST' POLITIKI KOMPROMISSA [James Madison: class as the essence of the policy of compromise]. Novaia i Noveishaia Istoriia [USSR] 1978 (3): 124-144. Describes the political life and philosophy of President James Madison (1751-1836) and takes issue with American studies including Irving Brant's James Madison (6 vols., Indianapolis, Bobbs-Merrill, 1941-61). None have exhaustively and correctly explained his complex, zigzagging political course. The true explanation of his seemingly paradoxical and unprincipled behavior is the fact that Madison's evolution reflected the contradictions in the historical development of the young American republic, primarily the conflict between two ruling social classes: the trade and business-oriented bourgeoisie and slave-holding plantation owners. Primary and secondary Amerian sources; 60 notes.
N. Frenkley

355. Stagg, J. C. A.   JAMES MADISON AND THE COERCION OF GREAT BRITAIN: CANADA, THE WEST INDIES, AND THE WAR OF 1812.   William and Mary Q. 1981 38(1): 3-34. The motive for the War of 1812 was not so much expansionism as to limit Great Britain's naval and commercial powers that could be used against the United States. James Madison's position was in response to the 1st Earl of Shef-

field's pamphlet, *Observations on the Commerce of the American States* (1784), which became the basis of British policy in restricting American commerce. Canada was to be developed like the former American colonies. American retaliatory commercial actions leading to the War of 1812 are examined. Notes British efforts to promote the growth of Canada. Based on Madison's papers, contemporary writings, and diplomatic archival material; 118 notes.

H. M. Ward

356. Steele, Thomas J. THE FIGURE OF COLUMBIA: PHILLIS WHEATLEY PLUS GEORGE WASHINGTON. *New England Q. 1981 54(2): 264-266.* Traces the heritage behind Phillis Wheatley's creation of the figure Columbia in her poem "To his Excellency George Washington." Columbia's character was clearly drawn from Phoebus Apollo and Athene, for all traits Wheatley assigned to Columbia appear in William King's *An Historical Account of the Heathen Gods and Heroes Necessary for the Understanding of the Ancient Poets*, a popular 18th-century English work. Columbia represented Phoebus Apollo, the goddess of strategy and generals and thus a representation of Washington, and Athene, the goddess of poetry and poets and thus a representation of the poetess herself. 2 notes.

R. S. Sliwoski

357. Stegeman, John and Stegeman, Janet. PRESIDENT WASHINGTON AT MULBERRY GROVE. *Georgia Hist. Q. 1977 61(4): 342-346.* Describes the friendship between George Washington and Caty Greene, wife of General Nathanael Greene, during the American Revolution, which led to Washington's visit to her plantation, Mulberry Grove, in 1791. Describes Mulberry Grove in 1972. Based on primary and secondary sources; 8 notes.

G. R. Schroeder

358. Stevens, Michael E. THOMAS JEFFERSON, INDIANS, AND MISSING PRIVY COUNCIL JOURNALS. *South Carolina Hist. Mag. 1981 82(2): 177-185.* Two extracts from the South Carolina Privy Council Journals (published earlier without these two extracts) explained the council's reaction to Indian raids and the work of Thomas Jefferson as South Carolina's financial agent. On 27 September 1787, at the request of Governor Thomas Pinckney, the council called for General Andrew Pickens to obtain satisfaction from the Indians for the murder and property damage committed. The second extract revealed the council's sanction of Jefferson as South Carolina's agent in Europe; furthermore the council ordered him to execute an ordinance to fund and discharge South Carolina's foreign debt. Based on South Carolina Privy Council journals and the governor's messages in the Department of Archives and History of South Carolina; 13 notes.

R. H. Tomlinson

359. Stolba, K. Marie. MUSIC IN THE LIFE OF THOMAS JEFFERSON. *Daughters of the Am. Revolution Mag. 1974 108(3): 196-202.*

360. Storch, Neil T. ADAMS, FRANKLIN AND THE ORIGIN OF CONSULAR REPRESENTATION. *Foreign Service J. 1975 52(10): 11-13.* Foreign relations with France and the recommendations of John Adams and Benjamin Franklin prompted Congress to establish the office of US Consul in 1780.

S

361. Stuart, Reginald C. THOMAS JEFFERSON AND THE FUNCTION OF WAR: POLICY OR PRINCIPLE? *Can. J. of Hist. [Canada] 1976 11(2): 155-171.* Thomas Jefferson and other Founding Fathers were heirs to the idea that it was just to defend the state. Evidence shows that Jefferson "sailed much closer to the wind of power politics than scholars generally appreciate.... Negotiation with, and not annihilation of, the enemy was the objective." Jefferson regarded the War of 1812 as an instrument of last resort after the failure of the embargo, but still one of policy because it related to the survival of the state. He saw the War of 1812 as a just war. 54 notes.

E. P. Stickney

362. Stuart, Reginald C. THOMAS JEFFERSON AND THE ORIGINS OF WAR. *Peace and Change 1976 4(2): 22-27.* Thomas Jefferson, though optimistic during the American Revolution, began a slow evolution toward pessimism 1783-1812, concerning the origin of war; eventually he believed in pacifism yet felt that war stemmed from economic, political, and basic human conditions.

363. Tauber, Gisela. RECONSTRUCTION IN PSYCHOANALYTIC BIOGRAPHY: UNDERSTANDING THOMAS JEFFERSON. *J. of Psychohistory 1979 7(2): 189-207.* A psy-

choanalytic interpretation of the life of Thomas Jefferson in which his needs to express himself and his wish not to do so were reflected in his penchant for paraphrasing renowned writers. Creative expression, however, conflicted with his active participation in politics. His unique contributions in political writing are explained on this basis. Presented at the convention of the International Psycho-analytical Association, New York City, 7-9 June 1979.

M. R. Strausbaugh

364. Taylor, Robert J. JOHN ADAMS: LEGALIST AS REVOLUTIONIST. *Massachusetts Hist. Soc. Pro. 1977 89: 55-71.* Through a detailed study of many legal sources, John Adams slowly derived a revolutionary view of the English government before 1776. Central to his view were the definition of Parliament and the relationship of the liberty of the colonists to the power of the King. He concluded that the colonies were outside Parliament's jurisdiction and that allegiance to the King was not due him in a political capacity. Based on the Adams Papers at the Massachusetts Historical Society and on other primary sources; 41 notes.

G. W. R. Ward

365. Treadway, Sandra Gioia. POPES CREEK PLANTATION: BIRTHPLACE OF GEORGE WASHINGTON. *Virginia Cavalcade 1982 31(4): 192-205.* History of Popes Creek plantation, 60 miles downriver from Mount Vernon, from 1656-57, when Washington's great-grandfather John Washington settled nearby, until the present, including the reconstruction of the home.

366. Troianovskaia, M. O. TOMAS DZHEFFERSON I POLITICHESKAIA BOR'BA NA PERVOM KONTINENTAL'NOM KONGRESSE (K ISTORII FORMIROVANIIA POLITECHESKIKH FRAKTSII) [Thomas Jefferson and the political struggle at the First Continental Congress (to the history of the formation of political factions)]. *Vestnik Moskovskogo U., Seriia 8: Istoriia [USSR] 1980 (4): 54-66.* Jefferson's "General View" was widely acclaimed but did not win the support of the Continental Congress at first. His condemnation of the slave trade, his insistence on natural rights, and his unique theory of emigration were not acceptable when the Congress was under the influence of Joseph Galloway. But by October 1775, the Declaration of Rights and Complaints was stated and the decision to establish an Association was accepted. This Declaration, based on Jefferson's "General View," is one of the most important documents in US history. 47 notes.

D. Balmuth

367. Watson, Francis J. B. AMERICA'S FIRST UNIVERSAL MAN HAD A VERY ACUTE EYE. *Smithsonian 1976 7(3): 88-95.* Examines Thomas Jefferson's love of classic art, architecture, and functional items, sparked by his tours through parts of Europe, 1784-1807; pictures some of Jefferson's collected pieces.

368. Watson, Ross. THOMAS JEFFERSON'S VISIT TO ENGLAND, 1786. *Hist. Today [Great Britain] 1977 27(1): 3-13.* Discusses Thomas Jefferson's travel and visit to Great Britain while serving as US ambassador to France in 1786; includes his financial problems and his visits to gardens in London, Twickenham, Cobham, Weybridge, and Caversham.

369. Weber, Paul J. JAMES MADISON AND RELIGIOUS EQUALITY: THE PERFECT SEPARATION. *Rev. of Pol. 1982 44(2): 163-186.* Traces the writings of James Madison through his career, during 1780-1830, as political theorist, constitutional architect, president, and retired statesman. Madison consistently stressed the principle of equal separation in matters of public policy regarding church and state. Religious liberty did not demand structural separation; however, it was important that it remain free of government coercion and totally disestablished so that each citizen could enjoy equality. Finally, it was Madison's contention that religious liberty should enjoy equal protection and promotion, much as those other natural rights of life and property. 70 notes.

G. A. Glovins

370. Welles, Edward O., Jr. GEORGE WASHINGTON SLEPT HERE . . . AND HERE'S HOW IT REALLY LOOKED. *Hist. Preservation 1982 34(3): 22-27.* Describes how scientific analysis was used to determine colors originally used to paint the interior of George Washington's Mount Vernon in order to restore the interiors; surprisingly, the colors were quite bright.

371. Wensyel, James W.   THE BADGE OF MILITARY MERIT. *Am. Hist. Illus. 1982 17(3): 26-31, 46.* Account of what little is known about General George Washington's design of the Revolutionary War Badge of Military Merit, or the Purple Heart Medal, presented to three documented recipients Washington considered to be his best soldiers, Sergeant Elijah Churchill, Sergeant William Brown, and Sergeant Daniel Bissell, and possibly one undocumented and unknown recipient.

372. Wensyel, James W.   THE NEWBURGH CONSPIRACY. *Am. Heritage 1981 32(3): 40-47.* Traces what is known about the rumored attempt on the part of army officers to force Congress to meet their needs for pay and provisions and the role of the "nationalists" in government in their effort to strengthen the central government. George Washington, Alexander Hamilton, Henry Knox, Gouverneur Morris, and others were involved. Ultimately, it was Washington who dissuaded his officers from taking the law into their own hands, establishing the primacy of civilian control over the military. 6 illus.   J. F. Paul

373. Wettstein, A. Arnold.   RELIGIONLESS RELIGION IN THE LETTERS AND PAPERS FROM MONTICELLO. *Religion in Life 1976 45(2): 152-160.* Discusses anti-sectarianism and the conception of religion and Christianity in the letters of Thomas Jefferson, 1784-1800.

374. Whitridge, Arnold.   THE MIRACLE OF INDEPENDENCE. *Hist. Today [Great Britain] 1974 24(6): 380-387.* Describes the difficulties faced by George Washington in creating an army and leading it to victory.

375. Wiggins, James Russell.   JULIAN PARKS BOYD. *Massachusetts Hist. Soc. Pro. 1980 92: 160-163.* Julian Boyd, who had a distinguished career as a scholar, librarian, and historian at Princeton University, died on 28 May 1980. In 1944, Boyd began the massive task of editing the Jefferson papers. With accuracy the paramount object, Boyd meticulously mined the papers and managed to complete 20 volumes before his death. It was his firm determination to produce the definitive edition so that scholars of the future would never need to duplicate the effort. More importantly, it was Boyd's desire to have Thomas Jefferson understood as clearly as possible.
G. A. Glovins

376. Williams, T. Harry.   ON THE COUCH AT MONTICELLO. *Rev. in Am. Hist. 1974 2(4): 523-529.* Review article prompted by Fawn Brodie's *Thomas Jefferson: An Intimate History* (New York: W. W. Norton and Co., 1974) which focuses on the book's unconventional nature as a biography. Outlines Brodie's use of psychological and psychoanalytical techniques, points out interpretive problems involved when using such techniques, and asserts that Brodie has misused them. Especially discusses Brodie's explication of Jefferson's sexual life, particularly her interpretation of the relation between his liaison with Sally Hemings and his attitudes and actions concerning slavery. Based on secondary sources; 4 notes.   A. E. Wiederrecht

377. Wills, Garry.   GEORGE WASHINGTON AND "THE GUILTY, DANGEROUS AND VULGAR HONOR." *Am. Heritage 1980 31(2): 4-11.* After the American Revolution, Henry Knox formed an influential society of retired military officers called the Society of the Cincinnati which so closely allied itself to George Washington that he almost failed to attend the 1787 Constitutional Convention simply because the society would also be present in Philadelphia.

378. Wills, Garry.   MASON WEEMS, BIBLIOPOLIST. *Am. Heritage 1981 32(2): 66-69.* An excerpt from *Cincinnatus: George Washington and the Enlightenment,* to be published in 1982, analyzes the writings and motives of Mason Locke Weems (1759-1825). 4 illus.
J. F. Paul

379. Wilson, Douglas L.   THE AMERICAN *AGRICOLA:* JEFFERSON'S AGRARIANISM AND THE CLASSICAL TRADITION. *South Atlantic Q. 1981 80(3): 339-354.* Calls attention to an aspect of Thomas Jefferson's agrarian ideal that has been consistently glossed over by historians: the influence of classical writers and the classical tradition on his ideas about agrarian life. The life which appealed to Jefferson was in the georgic mode, where happiness is closely related to hard work and where the farmer actively participates in the cycle of nature. Such was not

a fantasy for Jefferson, for he had seen it acted out in the colonial countryside. For Jefferson, the promise of American life was not the prospect of idleness, political disengagement, or economic indifference; it was rather the image of the noble husbandman in Virgil's *Georgics*—who was industrious, virtuous, and self-reliant. Based on the writings of Jefferson and citations from classical writers; 35 notes.   H. M. Parker, Jr.

380. Wolfe, Maxine G.   WHERE MONROE PRACTICED LAW. *Am. Bar Assoc. J. 1973 59(11): 1282-1284.* The house where James Monroe practiced law in Fredericksburg, Virginia, is now the James Monroe Museum and Memorial Library, perpetuating the memory of the statesman and philosopher.

381. Wolff, Philippe.   JEFFERSON ON PROVENCE AND LANGUEDOC. *Pro. of the Ann. Meeting of the Western Soc. for French Hist. 1975 3: 191-205.* Documents the travels of Thomas Jefferson in southern France in 1787, largely through his correspondence with William Short and his daily journal. Demonstrates Jefferson's concern with social and economic conditions in the pre-Revolutionary period as well as his practical observations on such technical subjects as agricultural methods and linguistic patterns. Shows his historical appreciation of architecture, painting, and sculpture. 56 notes.   J. Brown

382. Wolff, Philippe.   LE VOYAGE DE THOMAS JEFFERSON EN PROVENCE ET LANGUEDOC EN 1787 [Thomas Jefferson's travels in Provence and Languedoc in 1787]. *Ann. Hist. de la Révolution Française [France] 1976 48(4): 595-613.* In the spring of 1787, Thomas Jefferson, American ambassador to France since 1784, spent four months touring southern France. His diary and correspondence reveal that his interests during these months ranged from agriculture and trade to classical architecture and the "provençal" language. He also showed himself a keen and sympathetic observer of social conditions in prerevolutionary France. The author concludes, however, that Jefferson's basic affinity with the liberal aristocracy and his eventual disaffection with the course of the French Revolution can be read between the lines in these writings. Primary and secondary sources; 59 notes.   P. T. Newton

383. Wood, Gordon S.   HISTORIANS AND DOCUMENTARY EDITING. *J. of Am. Hist. 1981 67(4): 871-877.* Reviews two editions of John Adams's papers: Robert J. Taylor, Mary-Jo Kline, and Gregg L. Lint's *Papers of John Adams,* (Cambridge: Harvard University Press, 1977), and Robert J. Taylor, Gregg L. Lint, and Celeste Walker's *Papers of John Adams,* (Cambridge: Harvard University Press, 1979). The first collection covers September 1755 to April 1775, while the second covers May 1775 through August 1776. The volumes contain illustrations, maps, notes, and indexes. Note.   T. P. Linkfield

384. Woodward, Isaiah A., ed.   EVENTS PRIOR TO AND DURING THE DAY GENERAL GEORGE WASHINGTON RESIGNED AS COMMANDER IN CHIEF OF THE CONTINENTAL ARMY— 1783. *West Virginia Hist. 1977 38(2): 157-161.* Ceremonies in several different towns honored George Washington in December 1783 just before he resigned as commander in chief of the Continental Army. Primary sources; 2 illus., 14 notes.   J. H. Broussard

385. Wright, Esmond.   THE POLITICAL EDUCATION OF JAMES MADISON. *Hist. Today [Great Britain] 1981 31(Dec): 17-23.* Examines the background and attitudes of James Madison, including his consistent dislike of Indians and religious radicalism, and contrasts him with such contemporaries as Jefferson and Hamilton.

386. Wunderink, A.   UIT DE DIPLOMATIEKE CORRESPONDENTIE VAN JOHN ADAMS [From the diplomatic correspondence of John Adams]. *Spiegel Hist. [Netherlands] 1981 16(11): 583-588.* In 1780 John Adams came to The Hague as the first diplomatic representative from the United States to the Dutch Republic. His correspondence from the first two years of his residence illustrates not only the international situation of the late 18th century but also attitudes, problems, and personalities of the Dutch Republic in its closing days. Primary sources; 4 illus.   C. W. Wood, Jr.

387. Yarbrough, Jean.   FEDERALISM IN THE FOUNDATION AND PRESERVATION OF THE AMERICAN REPUBLIC. *Publius 1976 6(3): 43-61.* That James Madison and Alexander Hamilton

distrusted federalism may explain some of the difficulties of present-day politicians dealing with federalism.

388. Yarbrough, Jean. REPRESENTATION AND REPUBLICANISM: TWO VIEWS. *Publius 1979 9(2): 77-98.* Examines the political theories of Antifederalists Melancton Smith and Richard Henry Lee, and Federalists James Madison and Alexander Hamilton during the 1780's, focusing on the latter pair. The Antifederalists believed that the public good was served when representatives reflected and had to reconcile private interests, while the Federalists believed that representatives could rise to serve the public good regardless of their private interests. Hamilton and Madison adopted the British interest in virtual representation to meet the requirements of republicanism. The British conceived that an official was representative if he shared the interests of his constituents and that consequently the disfranchisement of large sections of the population did not matter, while the Federalists refined representation by extending the electoral districts: by increasing the ratio of constituents to representatives they insured that the best men would be elected and still allowed widespread suffrage. Unlike the British they contended that representation was based on election and not on mutuality of interest. 46 notes.   S

389. Yoder, Edwin M. THE SAGE AT SUNSET. *Virginia Q. Rev. 1982 58(1): 32-37.* Briefly examines Jefferson's life after leaving the presidency as presented in Dumas Malone's *The Sage of Monticello.* He remained strongly in favor of both republicanism and the imperial extension of the nation. Plagued by private debt (he sold his private library to the nation for $25,000 and it became the nucleus of the Library of Congress), "he hated public debt" as well. He was also concerned by the implications of the Missouri Compromise and favored emancipation. His fondest concern was the new University of Virginia. In this volume one has the "chronicle of one distinguished octogenarian by another . . . ."
                                            O. H. Zabel

390. —. GEORGE WASHINGTON IN 19TH-CENTURY POPULAR ART. *Am. Hist. Illus. 1980 15(5): 35-39.* Brief introduction discussing George Washington's likeness as a theme for 19th-century popular art in America, followed by exemplary reproductions of watercolors, medals, ceramics, oils, etc.

391. —. [POLITICAL THOUGHT OF THOMAS JEFFERSON]. *Chinese Studies in Hist. 1981 14(3): 3-37.*
Israel, John. AN INTRODUCTION TO LIU THO-CH'ANG'S "THE DEMOCRATIC THOUGHT OF THOMAS JEFFERSON," *pp. 3-6.* A short sketch of the life and writings of Liu Zuochang (Liu Tho-ch'ang) (1921) and his position as the foremost Jefferson scholar in China.
Liu Zuochang. THE DEMOCRATIC THOUGHT OF THOMAS JEFFERSON, *pp. 7-37.* Explains the positive and negative aspects of such Jeffersonian ideals as the separation of powers, the right of revolution, checks and balances, an agrarian-based society, and the importance of human freedom. Based on Jefferson's writings and the analysis of his biographers; 15 notes.
                                            A. C. Migliazzo

Presidents of the Manifest Republic, 1821-1901

392. Adler, Selig. THE OPERATION ON PRESIDENT MCKINLEY. Plesur, Milton, ed. *An American Historian: Essays to Honor Selig Adler* (Buffalo: State U. of N.Y., 1980): 37-49. Details the surgery performed on President William McKinley in 1901 after he was shot by Leon F. Czolgosz, from the notes saved by Dr. Charles G. Stockton, one of several physicians who assisted during the operation.

393. Aragonnès, Claude. LINCOLN ASSASSINÉ: UN DRAME SHAKESPEARIEN [Lincoln assassinated: a Shakespearian drama]. *Miroir de l'Hist. [France] 1959 (120): 1574-1584.* Describes the last days of President Abraham Lincoln, 8-14 April 1865, and his assassination in a theater, by an actor, John Wilkes Booth.

394. Armour, Rollin S. SIDELIGHTS ON FLORIDA BAPTIST HISTORY: THE WINTER ASSEMBLY AT UMATILLA AND A CONNECTION WITH THE ASSASSINATION OF PRESIDENT LINCOLN. *Baptist Hist. and Heritage 1973 8(4): 225-231.* Two notes; one about the establishment of Southern Baptist winter assembly grounds; the other about the son of a Baptist pastor, convicted for his part in the assassination of Lincoln.   S

395. Baer, Emily Angel. WORDS AND DEEDS: LINCOLN AS LITERARY ARTIST, A HISTORIOGRAPHICAL SURVEY. *Lincoln Herald 1981 83(3): 695-704.* Presents a survey of the literature on Lincoln as a writer of 19th-century American literature in three phases: 1900-20's, 1930-60, and 1960-1970's; includes Daniel K. Dodge's *Abraham Lincoln: Master of Words,* Luther E. Robinson's *Abraham Lincoln as a Man of Letters,* Roy P. Basler's *A Touchstone for Greatness,* Herbert J. Edwards and John E. Hankins's *Lincoln the Writer: The Development of his Literary Style,* David Anderson's *Abraham Lincoln,* and numerous others.

396. Barnard, Harry. BIOGRAPHICAL MEMORIES, *INRE* RBH. *Hayes Hist. J. 1978 2(2): 89-96.* Harry Barnard, author of *Rutherford B. Hayes and His America,* writes of his experiences while living at Fremont, Ohio, for five years researching his biography; library facilities; availability and variety of primary source material; assistance from Webb Cook Hayes (1890-1957); and, interesting facets of Hayes's life and family which prior to this publication were unknown. Barnard discusses this biography as a model of psychohistory. Taken from a speech by Barnard at the Hayes Historical Society, Spiegel Grove, on June 1, 1978. 7 illus., 10 notes.   J. N. Friedel

397. Basler, Roy P. THE EVOLUTION OF ABRAHAM LINCOLN'S HANDWRITING. *Manuscripts 1973 25(1): 2-11.* Despite all the modifications and variations in personal handwriting, it remains a remarkably acute form of individual identification—"no less than finger prints." Remarks on this quality as it applies to the uncovering of forgeries, with particular emphasis on the Tobin and Huber facsimiles of the Bixby letter—a purported Lincoln letter to Mrs. Bixby, the original of which has never appeared. Presents facsimiles of Lincoln manuscripts at (approximate) five-year intervals 1826-65. Illus.
                                            D. A. Yanchisin

398. Basler, Roy P. LINCOLN, BLACKS, AND WOMEN. Davis, Cullom; Strozier, Charles B.; Veach, Rebecca Monroe; and Ward, Geoffrey C., ed. *The Public and the Private Lincoln: Contemporary Perspectives* (Carbondale: So. Illinois U. Pr., 1979): 38-53. Relates Abraham Lincoln's personal contacts with blacks including Frederick Douglass and William H. Johnson, and women, including Anna Ella Carroll and Anna E. Dickenson, especially during his presidential years. His relations with blacks were "almost models of democratic correctness and friendly courtesy." Raised in a masculine world, however, he could not treat intelligent women as his equals. 33 notes.   S

399. Bauer, Charles J. LINCOLN AND SAM MUSICK'S BRIDGE. *Lincoln Herald 1974 76(2): 94-96.* Abraham Lincoln's first bill enacted into law in 1828 benefitted an early Lincoln supporter, Sam Musick. Musick operated a ferry over Salt Creek and wanted to build a toll bridge instead for the New Salem-Jacksonville road in Sangamon County, Illinois. Another early Lincoln supporter, Coleman Smoot, suggested rural bills for which Lincoln could campaign and later make into legislative bills.   A. C. Aimone

400. Bernard, Kenneth A. HERMAN MELVILLE, THE CIVIL WAR AND THE ASSASSINATION. *Lincoln Herald 1979 81(4): 268-269.* Reprints Herman Melville's "The Martyr," a short poem included in his volume of war poetry, *Battle-Pieces and Aspects of the War* (1866), and comments on an essay on Reconstruction that appeared in the same volume.

401. Beveridge, John W. LINCOLN'S VIEWS ON SLAVERY AND BLACKS AS EXPRESSED IN THE DEBATES WITH STEPHEN A. DOUGLAS. *Lincoln Herald 1981 84[i.e., 83](3[i.e., 4]): 791-800.* Briefly traces American history from 1774 in order to provide a background for the 1858 debates between Abraham Lincoln, Illinois Republican candidate for the US Senate, and Democratic candidate Stephen A.

Douglas, focusing on Lincoln's arguments against slavery, which demonstrated his brilliant logic.

402.   Blake, May Belle.   MARTIN VAN BUREN: FIRST AMERICAN PRESIDENT TO BE CHOSEN FROM NEW YORK STATE. *Daughters of the Am. Revolution Mag. 1975 109(5): 450-452.* Describes personal events in the life of Martin Van Buren (1782-1862) in New York.
S

403.   Blue, Merle D.   SLEUTHING LINCOLN MYTHS. *Indiana Social Studies Q. 1976 29(1): 43-51.* Discusses falsehoods and folk myths in 19th- and 20th-century historical writings and biographies of Abraham Lincoln.

404.   Boller, Paul F., Jr.   THE LAUGHING AND THE LITERARY LINCOLN.   *Social Sci. 1980 55(2): 71-76.* Abraham Lincoln was the only president who was both humorist and literary artist. Lincoln's funny stories not only entertained people; they also helped him make important points. Lincoln was utterly without malice, but he was the most vilified of all our presidents. His sense of humor, however, as well as his deep devotion to democratic ideals, led him to respond to personal attacks with tolerance and magnanimity. And he enshrined his democratic faith in some of the most beautiful English prose ever written. 36 notes.   J

405.   Bolt, Robert.   VICE PRESIDENT RICHARD M. JOHNSON OF KENTUCKY: HERO OF THE THAMES—OR THE GREAT AMALGAMATOR?   *Register of the Kentucky Hist. Soc. 1977 75(3): 191-203.* Richard M. Johnson, a hero of the War of 1812, gained prominence for reportedly killing the Indian leader Tecumseh in 1813. This reputation gained him the Democratic vice-presidential nomination in 1836. His fathering of two children by his black mistress almost prevented him from winning the election. Johnson had been a member of the Kentucky legislature, the House of Representatives, and the Senate. His election to the vice-presidency was decided by the Senate. Primary and secondary sources; 35 notes.   J. F. Paul

406.   Boritt, G. S.   ANOTHER NEW LINCOLN TEXT? SOME THOUGHTS CONCERNING AN OUTRAGEOUS SUGGESTION ABOUT ABRAHAM LINCOLN "CORPORATION LAWYER." *Lincoln Herald 1975 77(1): 27-32.* Abraham Lincoln may have written the portion of Illinois state auditor Jesse K. Dubois's 1858 report which summarized the state's position in a suit against the Illinois Central Railroad while he represented that railroad. The evidence is circumstantial, but Lincoln acted in accordance with accepted legal practice. Based on primary and secondary works; 4 photos, 8 notes, appendix.
B. J. LaBue

407.   Boritt, G. S.   LINCOLN'S OPPOSITION TO THE MEXICAN WAR.   *J. of the Illinois State Hist. Soc. 1974 67(1): 79-100.* Abraham Lincoln's law partner and biographer, William H. Herndon, maintained that Lincoln committed "political suicide" because of his Mexican War stand. Later historians adopted Herndon's theory uncritically. However, Lincoln's opposition to the Mexican War had as firm an ethical foundation as did his antislavery beliefs. Based on Lincoln's collected works, biographies, and Illinois period newspapers; chart, 4 photos, 49 notes.
A. C. Aimone

408.   Boritt, G. S.   THE RIGHT TO RISE.   Davis, Cullom; Strozier, Charles B.; Veach, Rebecca Monroe; and Ward, Geoffrey C., ed. *The Public and the Private Lincoln: Contemporary Perspectives* (Carbondale: So. Illinois U. Pr., 1979): 57-70. An underlying theme in Abraham Lincoln's thought was his conviction that men should rise according to their ability. His economic policy calling for internal improvements and state banks was designed to promote commerce and industry. These avenues of enterprise, rather than agriculture, led to economic opportunity. After the Kansas-Nebraska Act of 1854, Lincoln turned his attention from economics to slavery, but his concern was still over the right to rise. His military policy during the Civil War was conducted by the same principle, leading to rapid promotions and demotions of military officers. To a large degree, Lincoln viewed the war as a judgment against a nation which did not reward laborers according to their merits. 39 notes.   S

409.   Borst, William A.   LINCOLN'S HISTORICAL PERSPECTIVE.   *Lincoln Herald 1974 76(4): 195-203.* Examines the views which

Abraham Lincoln held of the importance of history to the American people and the national character, 1858-65.

410.   Bradford, M. E.   DIVIDING THE HOUSE: THE GNOSTICISM OF LINCOLN'S POLITICAL RHETORIC.   *Modern Age 1979 23(1): 10-25.* Abraham Lincoln's development as a rhetorician suggests that his public career can be divided in two. Lincoln of the Whig years was heir of the Enlightenment with his faith in necessity and his suspicion that he knows its disposition for the future. He showed a streak of rhetorical dishonesty in his use of an *ad hominem* mask. The second Lincoln, artificial Puritan 1854-61, was gnostic in his purchase on American politics. Regrettably, whenever our leaders succumb to the temptation to take the easy way to power, they partake as heirs in the Lincoln legacy and join with him in once again dividing the house. Primary and secondary sources; 85 notes.   M. L. Lifka

411.   Bradford, M. E.   THE HERESY OF EQUALITY: BRADFORD REPLIES TO JAFFA.   *Modern Age 1976 20(1): 62-78.* Challenging Harry Jaffa's interpretation of Lincoln's reading of the Declaration of Independence, Bradford argues that equality is the antonym of every legitimate conservative principle. Based on primary and secondary sources; 49 notes.   M. L. Lifka

412.   Branton, Harriet K.   ANOTHER ALBUM LEAF BY JOHN QUINCY ADAMS.   *Western Pennsylvania Hist. Mag. 1977 60(4): 415-418.* Reprints a poem written by John Quincy Adams to Mary E. Rhey, a young woman he met while traveling to Cincinnati, Ohio, 1843.

413.   Breiseth, Christopher N.   LINCOLN, DOUGLAS, AND SPRINGFIELD IN THE 1858 CAMPAIGN.   Davis, Cullom; Strozier, Charles B.; Veach, Rebecca Monroe; and Ward, Geoffrey C., ed. *The Public and the Private Lincoln: Contemporary Perspectives* (Carbondale: So. Illinois U. Pr., 1979): 101-120. Abraham Lincoln and Stephen A. Douglas did not debate in Springfield, but the town and central Illinois were crucial for the election of the state legislature and selection of US senators. Of the local newspapers, the *Illinois State Journal* supported Lincoln while the *Illinois State Register* supported Douglas. The *Journal* had trouble explaining Lincoln's position on Negro equality while the *Register* harped on Negrophobia and the fear that Lincoln's hostility to slavery meant abolitionism and ultimately civil war. The *Register* was instrumental in swinging central Illinois behind the Democrats. 61 notes.
S

414.   Bridges, Roger D., ed.   LINCOLNIANA: THREE LETTERS FROM A LINCOLN LAW STUDENT.   *J. of the Illinois State Hist. Soc. 1973 66(1): 79-87.* Gibson W. Harris was Abraham Lincoln's and William H. Herndon's first clerk and law student. Three of Harris' abridged letters describe politics in 1846 as observed by a pro-Whig member. Harris became a businessman rather than a lawyer. The Illinois Mormon troubles and the 1846 local, state, and national election campaigns are described. Harris gives one of the earliest accounts of Lincoln's storytelling. 3 illus., 23 notes.   A. C. Aimone

415.   Butterfield, L. H.   TENDING A DRAGON-KILLER: NOTES FOR THE BIOGRAPHER OF MRS. JOHN QUINCY ADAMS. *Pro. of the Am. Phil. Soc. 1974 118(2): 165-178.* A sketch intended for the eventual biographer of Louisa Catherine Johnson Adams (1775-1852), married for "more than five decades to one of the most trying of men," John Quincy Adams, and the grandmother of Henry Adams. Born in London to a family of Maryland background, she lived an extraordinarily varied life. No biography of her has been written because her papers have been closed to the public. 7 figs., 50 notes.
C. W. Olson

416.   Cain, Marvin R.   LINCOLN AS SOLDIER OF THE UNION: A REAPPRAISAL.   *Lincoln Herald 1981 83(4, i.e., 1): 592-603.* Discusses the military experience of President Abraham Lincoln from his enlistment in the Illinois militia in April 1832 until July 1832, focusing on his feelings about the horror of war coupled with his understanding of military matters and his "enthusiasm for the movement of armies and the planning of battles" during the Civil War.

417.   Carlson, Richard G., ed.   GEORGE P. PETERS' VERSION OF THE BATTLE OF TIPPECANOE (NOVEMBER 7, 1811).   *Vermont*

Hist. 1977 45(1): 38-43. The image of William Henry Harrison as the decisive victor over Tecumseh at Tippecanoe (in Indiana) was initiated by Harrison and exaggerates the facts. The battle, instigated by Harrison, did not end Indian raids and was closer than the commander reported. The account of Lieutenant George P. Peters adds details not found elsewhere. 14 notes.   T. D. S. Bassett

418. Carson, S. L.   THE OTHER TRAGIC LINCOLN: ROBERT TODD.   *Manuscripts 1978 30(4): 242-259.* Death and tragedy followed Robert Todd Lincoln throughout his life. Despite his feelings of inadequacy and intense privacy, he was a successful man in his own right. Perhaps if his life had been less tragic, he might have been less of a private man and freer with his father's papers. Certainly in spite of the myths about the Lincoln assassination, the papers guarded so zealously by his son contained no hint of a conspiracy. 18 notes, illus.
                                                                      D. A. Yanchisin

419. Cash, Kenneth P.   A REAL LOOK AT THE REAL LINCOLN. *Lincoln Herald 1981 84[i.e., 83](3[i.e., 4]): 801-803.* Criticism of Gore Vidal's "A Look At The Real Lincoln," published in the 8 February 1981 issue of the *Cleveland Plain Dealer,* which dispels Vidal's contentions that Lincoln rejected Christianity, was illegitimate, and gave his wife, Mary Ann Todd Lincoln, syphilis.

420. Chambrun, René de.   "UN FRANÇAIS CHEZ LES LINCOLN" [A Frenchman with Lincoln]. *Nouvelle Rev. des Deux Mondes [France] 1976 (10): 68-82.* Introduces two letters written in April 1865 by Adolphe de Chambrun to his wife in France immediately before and after the assassination of President Abraham Lincoln.

421. Clar, Bayard S.   A SERMON BY PHILLIPS BROOKS ON THE DEATH OF ABRAHAM LINCOLN.   *Hist. Mag. of the Protestant Episcopal Church 1980 49(1): 37-50.* Contains the 1893 text of the sermon which Phillips Brooks, 30-year-old rector of Boston's Holy Trinity Church, preached to his Philadelphia congregation on 23 April 1865, following Lincoln's assassination nine days earlier. The sermon vaulted Brooks into national prominence as a preacher. He was a strong antislavery advocate, as the sermon reveals. In it Brooks pointed out that slavery was the curse of the nation. 2 notes.
                                                                      H. M. Parker, Jr.

422. Cochrane, Elizabeth.   NELLIE BLY VISITS SPIEGEL GROVE: MRS. RUTHERFORD B. HAYES' QUIET HOME AT FREMONT, OHIO.   *Hayes Hist. J. 1976 1(2): 133-144.* Elizabeth Cochrane (later, Seaman), the famous journalist better known as "Nellie Bly," was commissioned by the *New York World* to visit the homes of all former First Ladies for an article. Lucy Webb Hayes was not present during Cochrane's visit to Spiegel Grove. Lucy Elliott Keeler, the President's cousin, served as hostess and guide. Cochrane's account, as well as biographical data on the author, are included. Primary sources; 28 photos, 6 notes.   J. N. Friedel

423. Colling, B. F.   CAMPAIGN FOR FORTS HENRY & DONELSON.   *Conflict 1974 (7): 28-39.* Discusses Ulysses S. Grant's strategy and the Union victories at these Tennessee forts in 1862.   S

424. Cooney, Charles F., ed.   AT THE TRIAL OF THE LINCOLN CONSPIRATORS: THE REMINISCENCES OF GENERAL AUGUST V. KAUTZ.   *Civil War Times Illus. 1973 12(5): 22-31.*

425. Crady, Wilson.   INCIDENT OF DESTINY.   *Lincoln Herald 1981 83(3): 730-733.* Brief biographies of the author's father, John W. Crady, and Austin Gollaher (d. 1898), both of Knob Creek in Larue County, Kentucky; focuses on the story of Gollaher's rescue of young Abraham Lincoln from drowning in the creek.

426. Crane, James L.   GRANT FROM GALENA.   *Civil War Times Illus. 1979 18(4): 26-29.* The Reverend James L. Crane, chaplain of the 21st Illinois Volunteers in 1861, later wrote a detailed and flattering description of the unit's "bold and daring" commander, a colonel from Galena, Illinois, by the name of Ulysses S. Grant (1822-85).

427. Croce, Lewis H.   WAS LINCOLN PREPARED FOR THE PRESIDENCY?   *Lincoln Herald 1976 78(4): 160-163.* Discusses

Abraham Lincoln's scant political experience prior to attaining the presidency, but emphasizes his native intelligence, shrewdness, ability to make quick judgments, and great physical strength as characteristics which enabled him to assume the office with few problems, 1861.

428. Current, Richard N.   GRANT WITHOUT GREATNESS. *Rev. in Am. Hist. 1981 9(4): 507-509.* Reviews William S. McFeely's *Grant: A Biography* (1981).

429. Current, Richard N.   THE LINCOLN PRESIDENTS. *Presidential Studies Q. 1979 9(1): 25-35.* Abraham Lincoln, a favorite past president for a number of subsequent officeholders to quote when justifying or suggesting a political maneuver, also had his favorite statesmen, among them Thomas Jefferson, Zachary Taylor, and Henry Clay.

430. Curtis, David.   EARLY FAILURE OF A CONQUERING HERO.   *Pacific Hist. 1975 19(4): 356-362.* Attributes the resignation of Ulysses S. Grant from the Army in 1854 to his commanding officer, separation from family, location, low pay, and drinking problem. Secondary sources; illus., 6 notes.   G. L. Olson

431. David, Beverly R.   SELLING THE SUBSCRIPTION BOOK. *Hayes Hist. J. 1977 1(3): 192-200.* During the 1870's, the sale of subscription books, those for which a definite market was created before or after publication by soliciting individual orders, reached its zenith as a commercial enterprise. Subscription salesmen included such noted individuals as Rutherford B. Hayes, Jay Gould, and P. T. Barnum. The authors and publishers generally benefited financially from this industry, but not the sales agents. Details the role and financial problems of the sales agents. Primary and secondary sources; 6 illus., 26 notes.
                                                                      J. N. Friedel

432. Davis, William C.   BEHIND THE LINES.   *Civil War Times Illus. 1977 16(5): 33-37.* Discusses the authenticity of an upcoming motion picture, "The Lincoln Conspiracy." Makers of the movie used unreliable data, sometimes outright forgeries, and pieced it together to suggest a tremendous conspiracy which is entirely unproven. The fault lies not with the movie moguls, who are trying to make money, but with a gullible public obsessed with conspiracies and unwilling to search out reliable source material for verification. 3 photos.   V. L. Human

433. DeBirny, Cecile Ream.   VINNIE REAM.   *Daughters of the Am. Revolution Mag. 1973 107(2): 88-103.* Sculptress Vinnie Ream Hoxie (1847-1914) modelled Lincoln and Farragut.   S

434. Dowding, Nancy E.   SANDBURG THE BIOGRAPHER. *Lincoln Herald 1979 81(3): 159-162.* Discusses the American poet Carl Sandburg's successful biography of Abraham Lincoln, which accurately captures Lincoln's personality and the times in which he lived. The biography is in two volumes entitled *Abraham Lincoln, "The Prairie Years"* (New York: Harcourt, Brace and Co., 1926), and *Abraham Lincoln, "The War Years"* (New York: Harcourt, Brace and Co., 1939).

435. Durham, Harriet F.   LINCOLN'S SONS AND THE MARFAN SYNDROME.   *Lincoln Herald 1977 79(2): 67-71.* Abraham Lincoln was an unsuspecting victim of the hereditary disorder known as Marfan Syndrome, and was a doomed man even without John Wilkes Booth. Because of the hereditary factor involved, several of Lincoln's ancestors and descendants must have carried the disorder to some degree. Recent research by Harold Schwartz, M.D., has shown that Marfan traits were evident in all of Lincoln's sons and in the only grandchild. Though no concrete conclusion can be made, Marfan Syndrome was probably a factor in the early death of three of Lincoln's four sons—William, Thomas, and Edward. 4 photos, diagram, biblio.
                                                                      T. P. Linkfield

436. Eckert, Edward K.   THE MC CLELLANS AND THE GRANTS: GENERALSHIP AND STRATEGY IN THE CIVIL WAR.   *Military Rev. 1975 55(6): 58-67.* Analyzes the types of general officers in the Union Army during the Civil War. The "McClellans" were unwilling to fight unless all odds appeared to be in their favor. By failing to understand the political nature of the war, they were a threat to the Union. The "Grants," meanwhile, were daring. Because of their ability to understand the political nature of the war, they were the keys to the Union victory. Primary and secondary sources; 2 illus., 5 notes.
                                                                      J. K. Ohl

437. Eisendrath, Joseph L. LINCOLN'S FIRST APPEARANCE ON THE NATIONAL SCENE, JULY, 1847. *Lincoln Herald 1974 76(2): 59-62.* Most historians overlook Abraham Lincoln's July 1847 appearance at the Rivers and Harbors Convention in Chicago, Illinois. Because of a dearth of materials, Lincoln's first appearance at a national convention attempting to resolve a national issue has been either dropped or lightly sketched. Based on a sketch published in 1882 by Robert Fergus of Chicago and contemporary newspaper accounts; illus.
                                                                A. C. Aimone

438. Elazar, Daniel J. THE CONSTITUTION, THE UNION, AND THE LIBERTIES OF THE PEOPLE: ABRAHAM LINCOLN'S TEACHING ABOUT THE AMERICAN POLITICAL SYSTEM AS ARTICULATED BY HIM ON HIS TOUR FROM SPRINGFIELD TO WASHINGTON IN FEBRUARY, 1861. *Publius 1978 8(3): 141-175.* President-elect Abraham Lincoln's month-long journey from his home in Springfield, Illinois, to Washington, D.C., climaxed in Philadelphia where he spoke on Washington's birthday, 1861, at Independence Hall and culminated in his inaugural addresss; in the latter, a careful and conservative speech as compared to his spontaneous, emotional one in Philadelphia, Lincoln reiterated the theme of his journey—that the union must be preserved, and, by drawing support from both nationalist and federalist perspectives, prepared the nation for an assertion of authority on the part of the federal government and for the restoration of its services to the seceding states.

439. Ellsworth, Edward W. LINCOLN AND THE EDUCATION CONVENTION: EDUCATION IN ILLINOIS—A JEFFERSONIAN HERITAGE. *Lincoln Herald 1978 80(2): 69-78.* Thomas Jefferson's support for universal education in a democracy provided the inspiration for Illinoisans who worked to implement that principle during 1820-55. Simultaneously, Abraham Lincoln sought a career for himself and broadened his educational horizons. In 1834 Lincoln represented Sangamon County at the Illinois General Education Convention. He developed a philosophy of education that suited not only his personal career requirements, but also those of a rapidly developing Illinois. He combined the Jeffersonian spirit of education for civic responsibility and progressive citizenship with the utilitarian needs of the frontier. 2 photos, 31 notes.
                                                                T. P. Linkfield

440. Ely, James W., Jr. ANDREW JACKSON AS TENNESSEE STATE COURT JUDGE, 1798-1804. *Tennessee Hist. Q. 1981 40(2): 144-157.* The future general and president served almost six years on the highest court in Tennessee, the Superior Court of Law and Equity. Although he had little legal training, Jackson apparently was an effective jurist who used much common sense and frontier psychology. Most cases before the court were civil and were seldom of widespread concern. Jackson's resignation is usually considered to have been due to poor health and low pay. However, he was never happy in the law and thereafter sought advancement in the fields of planting, business, the military, and politics. Mostly court records and correspondence; 67 notes.
                                                                C. L. Grant

441. Ely, James W., Jr. THE LEGAL PRACTICE OF ANDREW JACKSON. *Tennessee Hist. Q. 1979 38(4): 421-435.* Andrew Jackson began reading law in 1784 in Salisbury, North Carolina. In 1788 he took a post as prosecutor in Nashville, Tennessee, where as elected Attorney General of the Metro District from 1788-96 he had a 62% conviction rate. A prodigious litigant on his own, Jackson also won two-thirds of his suits in private practice. If he never democratized the law, he won considerable success and reputation as a lawyer. Based on Metro District Superior Court, Minute Book, and other sources; 3 tables, 78 notes.
                                                                W. D. Piersen

442. Endy, Melvin B. ABRAHAM LINCOLN AND AMERICAN CIVIL RELIGION: A REINTERPRETATION. *Church Hist. 1975 44(2): 229-241.* Abraham Lincoln was in many important respects a preeminent prophet of American civil religion. His conception of revelation and providence and his attitudes toward Negroes and Southern slavery caused him to compromise significantly on his stance concerning the distance between church and state. Thus he was a less impressive spokesman for what he called the central idea of the American experiment, democracy. His flaw may be an inevitable product of a civil religion whose vocational consciousness is informed primarily by the biblical myth of the chosen nation. 66 notes.   M. D. Dibert

443. Engel, Bernard F. LINCOLN'S DEATH AS SEEN IN VERSE. *Lincoln Herald 1981 84[i.e., 83](3[i.e., 4]): 804-807.* Discusses the numerous memorial verses written to commemorate Abraham Lincoln's death in April 1865, including James Russell Lowell's "Ode," Walt Whitman's "When Lilacs Last in the Dooryard Bloom'd," S. Weir Mitchell's "Lincoln," Phoebe Cary's "Peace," and Julia Ward Howe's "Parricide."

444. Ensor, Allison R. LINCOLN, MARK TWAIN, AND LINCOLN MEMORIAL UNIVERSITY. *Lincoln Herald 1976 78(2): 43-51.* Abraham Lincoln and Mark Twain never met nor is it likely that Lincoln ever read any of Twain's writings. Twain used Lincoln to personify the ideals of the past that he felt the country was turning away from. This apothesosis of Lincoln earned Twain an invitation to preside at a Lincoln Birthday Celebration to raise funds for Lincoln Memorial University. The Reverand A. A. Myers changed his Harrow School to the Lincoln Memorial University in 1897 when General Oliver Otis Howard promised he would help the institution. The 1901 fund raiser was successful and Howard asked Twain to preside over another one celebrating the hundredth anniversary of Lincoln's birthday, to be held 11 February 1909. Twain declined but wrote a letter endorsing the project. Primary and secondary sources; 2 illus., 3 facsimiles, 25 notes.
                                                                B. J. LaBue

445. Erickson, Gary Lee. THE LAST YEARS OF WILLIAM HENRY HERNDON. *J. of the Illinois State Hist. Soc. 1974 67(1): 101-119.* William H. Herndon's years after Abraham Lincoln's death in 1865 were filled with economic struggles and unjust rumors about his personal life. The well-read Herndon was elected as a local school board president and campaigned for agricultural reforms. Because Herndon wrote about the most controversial aspects of Lincoln's life, the former law partner was discredited despite his thorough search of Lincoln's life. Based on the Trainor family Herndon papers, contemporary newspapers, and monographs; 2 photos, 66 notes.   A. C. Aimone

446. Erler, Edward J. THE AMERICAN TRADITION. *Polity 1975 7(3): 378-385.* A. J. Beitzinger's *A History of Political Thought* (New York: Dodd, Mead & Co., 1972), Reo M. Christenson's *Heresies Right and Left: Some Political Assumptions Reexamined* (New York: Harper & Row, 1973), Thomas O'Brien Hanley's *The American Revolution and Religion: Maryland 1770-1800* (Washington, D. C.: Catholic U. Pr., 1971), and Harry V. Jaffa's *Crisis of the House Divided: An Interpretation of the Lincoln-Douglas Debates* (Seattle: U. of Washington Pr., 1973) consider a unique American tradition based on the abstract principle of equality.   W. R. Hively

447. Eulenberg, Ed. THE CHICAGO HISTORICAL SOCIETY'S LINCOLN DIORAMA. *Chicago Hist. 1974 3(2): 88-91.*

448. Faust, Richard H. ANOTHER LOOK AT GENERAL JACKSON AND THE INDIANS OF THE MISSISSIPPI TERRITORY. *Alabama R. 1975 28(3): 202-217.* Disputes the oft-repeated contention that Andrew Jackson was an Indian-hater as being "overly simplistic" and failing to allow for "other of his attitudes and motivations." Jackson adopted an Indian boy, drew sharp distinction between friendly and hostile Indians, befriended individuals and tribes on several occasions, and generally deplored brutality and barbarity. Frontier conditions dictated Jackson's policies, which can be summed up as security for the United States and protection for the Indians. Primary and secondary sources; 47 notes.   J. F. Vivian

449. Fehrenbacher, Don E. LINCOLN AND THE WEIGHT OF RESPONSIBILITY. *J. of the Illinois State Hist. Soc. 1975 68(1): 45-56.* Abraham Lincoln's deep love for Shakespearean tragedy, especially *Richard III*, *King Lear*, and *Macbeth* was not surprising given his involvement in issues of power and politics similar to those analyzed by the playwright. *Macbeth*, with its overtones of guilt and personal responsibility for tragic events, made the greatest impression on Lincoln. Considers Lincoln's career to have embodied a Shakespearean irony in that his rise from obscurity to the highest office in the land was a partial cause for the tragedy of the Civil War.   N. Lederer

450. Fehrenbacher, Don E. LINCOLN'S LOST LOVE LETTERS. *Am. Heritage 1981 32(2): 70-80.* In 1928, Wilma Frances Minor offered to share with the *Atlantic Monthly* her information on the "true love

story" of Abraham Lincoln and Ann Rutledge, based on letters in her family's possession. Although some were suspicious from the start, the *Atlantic* eventually published three articles by Minor. Owner and editor Ellery Sedgwick, though later knowing the letters were forgeries, refused to acknowledge publicly even Minor's confession. 8 illus.

J. F. Paul

451. Fleischman, Richard K. THE DEVIL'S ADVOCATE: A DEFENSE OF LINCOLN'S ATTITUDE TOWARD THE NEGRO, 1837-1863. *Lincoln Herald 1979 81(3): 172-186.* Discusses Abraham Lincoln's attitudes toward slavery in the United States from 1837 to 1863 in light of the attitudes toward blacks at the time; while not a proabolitionist in his early political career, Lincoln was committed to the nonextension of slavery.

452. Foner, Eric. A NEW ABRAHAM LINCOLN? *Rev. in Am. Hist. 1979 7(3): 375-379.* Review of G. S. Boritt's *Lincoln and the Economics of the American Dream* (Memphis: Memphis State U. Pr., 1978) considers the impact of Abraham Lincoln's attitudes toward economics and social mobility on his actions as a politician and president, 1840's-64.

453. Fox-Genovese, Elizabeth. PSYCHOHISTORY VERSUS PSYCHODETERMINISM: THE CASE OF ROGIN'S JACKSON. *R. in Am. Hist. 1975 3(4): 407-418.* Michael Paul Rogin's *Fathers and Children: Andrew Jackson and the Subjugation of the American Indian* (New York: Alfred A. Knopf, 1975) "offers Jackson as a key to understanding the transition from customary to market society in the United States; he offers Indian removal as the American experience of 'primitive accumulation'; and he offers Jacksonian democracy as a unique formulation of nineteenth-century liberalism."

454. Fredrickson, George M. A MAN BUT NOT A BROTHER: ABRAHAM LINCOLN AND RACIAL EQUALITY. *J. of Southern Hist. 1975 41(1): 39-58.* Abraham Lincoln has been viewed as both a Negrophobe and a champion of racial equality. An examination of his racial attitudes within the intellectual context of his times and the political pressures they exerted reveals that he consistently held a racial philosophy between the two extremes throughout his public life. Beginning with his affiliation with Henry Clay's moderate position on slavery, Lincoln's speeches show a moral opposition to slavery and an acceptance of the basic humanity of blacks coupled with an underlying emotional commitment to whiteness and white supremacy. He recognized that his denial of black citizenship, though inconsistent with his basic political doctrine of natural rights, was a political necessity. Because he felt that white prejudice made social and political equality and racial harmony impossible, he advocated colonization as the only alternative. Based on speeches, letters, and secondary sources; 57 notes.   S

455. Fredrickson, George M. THE SEARCH FOR ORDER AND COMMUNITY. Davis, Cullom; Strozier, Charles B.; Veach, Rebecca Monroe; and Ward, Geoffrey C., ed. *The Public and the Private Lincoln: Contemporary Perspectives* (Carbondale: So. Illinois U. Pr., 1979): 86-98. Abraham Lincoln basically was guided by a legalist-rationalist conservatism that sought to inculcate respect for law by demonstrating the rational principles underlying the legal and constitutional order. He held to the concept of a procedural community in which decisions were rendered by the well-trained based on tested procedures. He distrusted the excesses of Jacksonian democracy, for mere majoritarianism might go beyond the reach of legal authority. He also rejected the emotionalism of evangelicals who conceived of the existence of a moral community. After the Kansas-Nebraska Act (US, 1854), however, his level of moral passion was aroused. During the Civil War he merged the concepts of legal order, majoritarian democracy, and a religious sense of American destiny. He viewed the North as a popular democracy whose people could be trusted because they were committed to law and stability. The war war in accordance with divine purpose so it could legitimately arouse religious emotions. 33 notes.   S

456. Fries, Sylvia D. ABRAHAM LINCOLN AND THE LANGUAGE OF SECTIONAL CRISIS. *Lincoln Herald 1977 79(2): 61-66, (3): 104-109.* Part I. Lincoln's intellectual concepts and speeches reflected contemporary ideas and issues that his constituents could relate to. This was especially true of slavery and the sectional crisis of the 1850's. His abstract approach to slavery as an evil coincided with that of a generation

of northern reformers. Abraham Lincoln also defined the American Dream, the pursuit of freedom or equal opportunity, in practical Hegelian terms his constituents could understand. Slavery constituted an artificial barrier to what America could become because it not only exploited black labor, but it also degraded free white labor. Slavery, therefore, must not expand westward into the territories. 25 notes. Part II. Since Lincoln viewed the preservation of the Union and free soil as inseparable issues, he was convinced that a crisis was a necessary solution regarding slavery. He evolved an association of his own role in such a solution with that of the "public mind." When the Civil War finally came, Lincoln could justify it not only as God's will, with Lincoln as one of God's instruments, but also as a necessary step toward the realization of American democracy. Lincoln utilized both rational and romantic thought to defend his concept of the Union and eventually to justify its preservation. 20 notes.

T. P. Linkfield

457. Gallardo, Florence. 'TIL DEATH DO US PART: THE MARRIAGE OF ABRAHAM LINCOLN AND MARY TODD. *Lincoln Herald 1982 84(1):3-10.* Criticizes the 1885 book, *Life of Lincoln,* by William H. Herndon in collaboration with Jesse W. Weik, that includes a negative account of the marriage between Abraham Lincoln and Mary Todd Lincoln; it was regarded as absolutely true until 1947, when the Lincoln papers were made available and documented another version of their admittedly difficult marriage from 4 November 1842 until his assassination in 1865.

458. Geary, James W. ANOTHER LOST LINCOLN LETTER: THE PRESIDENT AS PRAGMATIST OR HUMANITARIAN? *Lincoln Herald 1974 76(3): 149-151.* Discusses a routine letter requesting Major General John E. Wool to look into a report that 400 sick soldiers in Baltimore were allegedly without shelter. The letter was written on 13 July 1862 just four days before Lincoln approved the Militia Act and shortly after the North's disastrous Peninsula Campaign. Based on the Lincoln letter in the Wool Papers of the New York State Library; illus.

A. C. Aimone

459. Geer, Emily Apt. LUCY W. HAYES AND THE NEW WOMEN OF THE 1880'S. *Hayes Hist. J. 1980 3(1-2): 18-26.* Lucy Webb Hayes, wife of Rutherford B. Hayes and first lady from 1877-81, had contact with many "new women" of the 1880's, including the journalists Mary Clemmer Ames, Emily Edson Briggs ("Olivia"), Austine Snead, Elizabeth Cochrane ("Nellie Bly"), and Laura Holloway, the suffragists Elizabeth Cady Stanton, Susan B. Anthony, Phoebe Couzins, and Belva Ann Lockwood, the temperance leader Frances Willard, the botantist Rachel L. Bodley, and the Paiute Indian leader Sarah Winnemucca. Although Lucy Hayes's perception of her role as a promoter of social harmony prevented her from meeting the demands and expectations of the most militant of these, most respected her as a gracious and skillful hostess, one who refused to serve wine in the White House, and as an able leader of the Women's Home Missionary Society of the Methodist Church. Based on primary sources; 2 illus., 4 photos, 45 notes.

E. L. Keyser

460. Geer, Emily Apt. LUCY WEBB HAYES AND HER INFLUENCE UPON HER ERA. *Hayes Hist. J. 1976 1(1): 22-35.* Reexamination of primary sources dispels the false images surrounding Lucy Webb Hayes (1831-89). Though nicknamed "Lemonade Lucy," and the first First Lady to be a college graduate, she did not support publicly the temperance movement, woman suffrage, or higher education for women. Her ideas and actions were consistent with established social codes; however, her husband's position extended her influence beyond her family and friends. Lucy Hayes was a transitional figure, rather than a representative of the new "Woman Era." Based on primary snd secondary sources; 9 illus., 73 notes.

J. N. Friedel

461. Geer, Emily Apt. THE RUTHERFORD B. HAYES FAMILY. *Hayes Hist. J. 1978 2(1): 46-51.* Compares the 19th-century family with the present era, by examining the family of Rutherford B. Hayes and Lucy Hayes; until Hayes' election to the Presidency (1877), their family life was typical of politically active, upper middle-class families of their age. Comparing the Hayes family with our own, using the factors of health, familial affection, living conditions, educational and recreational opportunities, religious training, and individual development, rejects the notion of the 19th century as the "golden age" of the American family. Primary and secondary sources; 3 photos, 23 notes.

J. N. Friedel

462. George, Joseph, Jr. THE LINCOLN WRITINGS OF CHARLES P. T. CHINIQUY. *J. of the Illinois State Hist. Soc. 1976 69(1): 17-25.* Examines the claims of the anti-Catholic Charles P. T. Chiniquy (1809-99), a client of Abraham Lincoln in 1856 who later claimed to be a friend of Lincoln and an authority on his religious beliefs, particularly his alleged anti-Catholicism. Chiniquy's claims of a Catholic plot to assassinate Lincoln are false, but several historians have accepted his less sensational but equally unfounded writings about Lincoln's religion. Chiniquy autobiography, Lincoln's *Collected Works,* court records; 2 illus., 45 notes.   J/S

463. Gholson, Sam C. THE ARTIST AS BIOGRAPHER. *Hayes Hist. J. 1978 2(2): 119-131.* Studies three artists as biographers. The 19th-century William Garl Browne and William M. Chase each painted full-length portraits of President Hayes during his lifetime, and exemplified divergent aesthetic trends of Victorian years. Critiques each painting, elaborating on the artist as the physiological psychologist; i.e., believing that the inner personality of the individual can be communicated by the painting. Chase's psychological portrait had some shortcomings. Gholson relates his own research, motives, and techniques in painting a posthumous portrait of Hayes (1976). Primary sources; 12 illus., 24 notes.   J. N. Friedel

464. Gienapp, William E. LINCOLNIANA: THE 1856 ELECTION: AN UNPUBLISHED LINCOLN LETTER. *J. of the Illinois State Hist. Soc. 1977 70(1): 18-21.* In an 1856 letter to US Senator Lyman Trumbull, Lincoln gives his reactions to the nominations of John Charles Frémont for President and William H. Bissell for Illinois governor. 3 illus., 6 notes.   J/S

465. Graebner, Norman A. THE APOSTLE OF PROGRESS. Davis, Cullom; Strozier, Charles B.; Veach, Rebecca Monroe; and Ward, Geoffrey C., ed. *The Public and the Private Lincoln: Contemporary Perspectives* (Carbondale: So. Illinois U. Pr., 1979): 71-85. Throughout his political career, Abraham Lincoln advocated national development through internal improvements. As a state legislator in Illinois, he proposed road construction and navigation aids. As an attorney, he took on railroad clients including the Illinois Central Railroad, and promoted railroad development within the state. 39 notes.

466. Gutman, Richard J. S. [LINCOLN IN FILMS].
A ROSTER OF EARLY LINCOLN IMPERSONATORS: LINCOLN'S IMAGE IN THE CINEMA, 1900-1930. *Lincoln Herald 1976 78(4): 139-146.* Discusses actors, especially George A. Billings, Walter Huston, and Benjamin Chapin, who played the role of Abraham Lincoln.
THREE OUTSTANDING "ABES": LINCOLN'S IMAGE IN THE CINEMA, 1931-77. *Lincoln Herald 1978 80(3): 122-132.* Discusses portrayals of Lincoln by Henry Fonda (1939), Raymond Massey (1940), and Hal Holbrook (1974-75).   G. A. Hewlett/T. P. Linkfield

467. Hanchett, William. THE EISENSCHIML THESIS. *Civil War Hist. 1979 25(3): 197-217.* Chemist-turned-historian Otto Eisenschiml (1880-1963) professed scientific objectivity for his *Why Was Lincoln Murdered?* (Boston, Mass.: Little, Brown, 1937), but even though he did raise many important questions that historians had ignored, he nevertheless distorted the evidence in his book, in which he theorized about the culpability of Secretary of War Edwin M. Stanton based on the little-researched Lincoln assassination Investigation and Trial Papers in the Judge Advocate-General's Office in the War Department. Scrutinizes Eisenschiml's thesis point-by-point and finds it wanting. Eisenschiml himself brought up evidence against some of his own points. Based on official and secondary sources; 65 notes.   S

468. Harrison, Lowell H. AN AUSTRALIAN REACTION TO LINCOLN'S DEATH. *Lincoln Herald 1976 78(1): 12-17.* During the Civil War Melbourne had been pro-Confederate. Two of the three daily newspapers had been also pro-Confederate. After learning of Abraham Lincoln's death on 23 June 1865, *The Age, The Argus,* and *The Herald* ran editorials that recognized Lincoln's place in history and noted the problems that lay before the reunited country. The editorials are included in the article; 2 illus., 2 notes.   B. J. LaBue

469. Harrison, Lowell H. "OLD MAN ELOQUENT" TAKES THE FLOOR. *Am. Hist. Illus. 1978 13(10): 22-31.* Following his defeat by Jackson in the presidential election of 1828, John Quincy Adams was elected to the House of Representatives where he served 1831-48 working diligently and gaining the nickname "Old Man Eloquent."

470. Havlik, Robert J. ABRAHAM LINCOLN AND THE TECHNOLOGY OF "YOUNG AMERICA." *Lincoln Herald 1977 79(1): 3-11.* Abraham Lincoln's interest in mechanical devices reflected the technological changes in America before the Civil War. He was especially interested in technological improvements for agriculture and transportation. Lincoln even patented a device for lifting grounded boats over river shoals. Because of his interest in science and technology and also his pragmatic attitude toward change, Lincoln adjusted easily to the changing American environment. 4 illus., 41 notes.   T. P. Linkfield

471. Hay, Robert P. "AND TEN DOLLARS EXTRA, FOR EVERY HUNDRED LASHES ANY PERSON WILL GIVE HIM, TO THE AMOUNT OF THREE HUNDRED": A NOTE ON ANDREW JACKSON'S RUNAWAY SLAVE AD OF 1804 AND ON THE HISTORIAN'S USE OF EVIDENCE. *Tennessee Hist. Q. 1977 36(4): 468-478.* In 1804 Andrew Jackson ran an ad for a runaway slave in the Nashville *Tennessee Gazette.* In the 173 years since, biographers of Jackson and students of southern slavery have often failed to find this unusual ad or have misued it when they did. The fact that the ad is being placed in the definitive edition of the Andrew Jackson papers for all researchers to see will help historians make a more balanced assessment of Jackson's attitude toward slaves. Primary and secondary sources; 26 notes.   M. B. Lucas

472. Hickey, Donald R. ANDREW JACKSON AND THE ARMY HAIRCUT: INDIVIDUAL RIGHTS VS. MILITARY DISCIPLINE. *Tennessee Hist. Q. 1976 35(4): 365-375.* In 1801 Thomas Butler, a Federalist who wore his hair in a queue, was courtmartialed for refusing to cut his hair. Andrew Jackson and other friends from middle Tennessee came to his defense. A petition signed by seventy-five of the leading citizens of Nashville was sent to President Thomas Jefferson objecting to the persecution of Colonel Butler. Although the President promised the charge would be downplayed, Butler was convicted. Primary and secondary sources; 39 notes.   M. B. Lucas

473. Hickey, James T. LINCOLNIANA: A SMALL RECEIPT REVEALS A LARGE STORY. *J. of the Illinois State Hist. Soc. 1982 75(1): 73-80.* Reproduces the receipt written by Abraham Lincoln involving a foreclosure against William Walters, a leading Springfield Democrat, editor and publisher of the *Illinois State Register,* and neighbor of Lincoln. In 1839 Walters purchased property at 8th and Market streets from Peter Van Bergen, but fell behind in payments by 1842. Van Bergen, in turn, was in debt to Joshua F. Speed, Lincoln's client. Lincoln brought suit for Van Bergen against Walters, but arranged to purchase the property for Speed, who agreed to hold it until Walters could repurchase it. In 1843, Charles H. Lamphier, Walters's brother-in-law, assumed the purchase, and he received the deed to the property in 1845. 6 illus., 15 notes.   A. W. Novitsky

474. Hickey, James T. LINCOLNIANA: SOME ROBERT LINCOLN LETTERS ON THE "DREADFUL STATUE" BY GEORGE GREY BARNARD. *J. of the Illinois State Hist. Soc. 1980 73(2): 132-139.* Discusses the controversy surrounding the sculpture of Abraham Lincoln by George Grey Barnard, commissioned in 1910 as a gift for the city of Cincinnati, and reprints letters from Robert Todd Lincoln regarding the proposal made by a group, led by the family of former President William Howard Taft in 1917, to erect replicas of the statue in London and other European capitals. Robert Lincoln's efforts to prevent this had limited success: a replica was finally erected in Manchester, England, in 1922. 3 photos, reproduction, 11 notes.   G. V. Wasson

475. Hickey, James T. "OWN THE HOUSE TILL IT RUINS ME": ROBERT TODD LINCOLN AND HIS PARENTS' HOME IN SPRINGFIELD. *J. of the Illinois State Hist. Soc. 1981 74(4): 279-296.* Between 1865 and 1887, Robert Todd Lincoln exhibited extraordinary interest, concern, and irritation over the tenants of the family home in Springfield. Correspondence centers on repairs, taxes, and rent in arrears. For two years, the property may have been a boardinghouse. In 1883,

Osborn Hamiline Oldroyd occupied the house as a "Memorial Hall" to house his collection of Lincolniana. The state of Illinois purchased the house in 1887, and, Democratic Governor John Peter Altgeld appointed Herman Hofferkamp as custodian in 1892. Robert Lincoln's final visit occurred at the centennial commemoration of his father's birth on 12 February 1909. 8 illus., 25 notes.   A. W. Novitsky

476. Hickey, James T. ROBERT S. TODD SEEKS A JOB FOR HIS SON-IN-LAW, ABRAHAM LINCOLN. *J. of the Illinois State Hist. Soc. 1979 72(4): 273-276.* In 1843 Abraham Lincoln represented his father-in-law, Robert Smith Todd, in a case against Nathaniel A. Ware, a speculator from whom Todd had contracted to purchase land in 1841. In an 1844 letter to another son-in-law, Ninian W. Edwards, Todd revealed his knowledge and approval of Lincoln's political ambitions as well as his willingness to help him. Based on the manuscript collection of Robert Todd Lincoln in the Illinois State Historical Library and the Lincoln Law Case files of the Herndon-Weik Collection, Library of Congress; 2 illus., 4 notes.   E. L. Keyser

477. Hickey, James T. ROBERT TODD LINCOLN AND THE "PURELY PRIVATE" LETTERS OF THE LINCOLN FAMILY. *J. of the Illinois State Hist. Soc. 1981 74(1): 59-79.* The papers of Abraham Lincoln were held by Elizabeth Todd Grimsley, Clark Moulton Smith, and William H. Herndon. After his assassination, his White House papers were brought to Bloomington by David Davis at the request of Robert T. Lincoln. Robert, determining that family papers should not be available for public inspection, safeguarded them. Many family papers, stored in his law office, were destroyed in the Chicago fire of 1871. Examination of the surviving papers was conducted by Charles Sweet until Robert Lincoln transferred them from Chicago to Hildene, his Vermont estate, between 1911 and 1918. In 1919, he presented eight trunks, forming the base of the *Collected Works of Abraham Lincoln,* to the Library of Congress. Robert Todd Lincoln Beckwith recently distributed the last of the Hildene material to close friends and various historical agencies. 16 illus., 41 notes.   A. W. Novitsky

478. Holzer, Harold. HOW THE PRINTMAKERS SAW LINCOLN: NOT-SO-HONEST PORTRAITS OF "HONEST ABE." *Winterthur Portfolio 1979 14(2): 143-170.* American engravers during 1858-66 helped to popularize the image of Abraham Lincoln making him a well-known political candidate, the Great Emancipator, and the martyred President. Many of the prints are fakes or pirated copies of original works. The "portraits" associated the man with union and democracy. Based on the Lincoln papers, contemporary periodicals and other primary sources; 36 illus., 43 notes.   N. A. Kuntz

479. Holzer, Harold. SOME VIEWS OF THE LINCOLN HOME: OLD AND "NEW." *Lincoln Herald 1980 82(3): 483-486.* Reproduces prints and a photograph of Abraham Lincoln's two-story home in Springfield, Illinois, ca. 1860-66.

480. Hurt, James. ALL THE LIVING AND THE DEAD: LINCOLN'S IMAGERY. *Am. Literature 1980 52(3): 351-380.* Analyzes Abraham Lincoln's speeches by relating the actual words to Lincoln's personality and to images such as filial rivalry, time, and the earth. During his years in New Salem, Illinois (1831-37), Lincoln forged a new identity for himself by rejecting his father's values. The images in Lincoln's speeches reflect not only his own emotional experiences, but also those of a post-heroic America. Based on *Herndon's Life of Lincoln* (1949) and works by Erik H. Erikson and George B. Forgie; 36 notes.   T. P. Linkfield

481. Hurwitz, Michael R. THE LINCOLN CONSPIRACY REEXAMINED. *Manuscripts 1978 30(2): 108-111.* Refutes the conclusions of the Sunn Classics Pictures book by David Balsinger and Charles Sellier, Jr., and film production of *The Lincoln Conspiracy*.   D. A. Yanchisin

482. Hyman, Harold M. NEITHER IMAGE BREAKER NOR BROKER BE. *Rev. in Am. Hist. 1978 6(1): 72-79.* Review article prompted by Stephen B. Oates's *With Malice Toward None: The Life of Abraham Lincoln* (New York: Harper & Row, 1977).

483. Illick, Joseph E. JOHN QUINCY ADAMS: THE MATERNAL INFLUENCE. *J. of Psychohist. 1976 4(2): 185-195.* The role of Abigail Adams in forming the character of her son, John Quincy Adams, has been neglected, while the parallels between his career and philosophy and that of his father, John Adams, are noted. An examination of John Quincy Adams' childhood and adolescence shows that his mother, rather than his father, set his emotional tone. Primary sources; 23 notes.   R. E. Butchart

484. Isacsson, Alfred. A STUDY OF LOUIS J. WEICHMANN. *Lincoln Herald 1978 80(1): 25-38.* Louis J. Weichmann, a principal witness in the conspiracy trial of 1865, suffered from a mental disorder in an advanced stage when he wrote his *A True History of the Assassination of Abraham Lincoln and of the Conspiracy of 1865* 30 years after Abraham Lincoln's death. Weichmann's advanced paranoia prevented him from placing the events of 1865 in their proper perspective; consequently he created his own reality in his book. Obsessed with the delusion that he possessed truth and virtue, Weichmann distorted the facts, events, and people surrounding the assassination to fit his predetermined thesis. Photo, 80 notes.   T. P. Linkfield

485. Johannsen, Robert W. THE LINCOLN-DOUGLAS CAMPAIGN OF 1858: BACKGROUND AND PERSPECTIVE. *J. of the Illinois State Hist. Soc. 1980 73(4): 242-262.* Discusses the events leading up to the election of Stephen A. Douglas as US senator from Illinois in 1858. At this time factions in the United States were deeply divided over the slavery question, and the campaign between Abraham Lincoln and Douglas assumed an important role as they were symbolic of the anti- and proslavery positons. Douglas won the election, but the victory for the Democrats only heightened the division over the slavery question. Primary sources; 58 notes.   J. Powell

486. Jones, Maldwyn A. JOHN QUINCY ADAMS. *Hist. Today [Great Britain] 1980 30(Nov): 5-8.* Traces John Quincy Adams's political career, stressing his failure as a president and his more successful service in the House of Representatives; 1783-1848.

487. Jones, Terry L. GRANT'S CANALS IN NORTHEAST LOUISIANA. *North Louisiana Hist. Assoc. J. 1979 10(2): 7-17.* A summary of Ulysses S. Grant's unsuccessful, but not unrealistic, attempts to enhance Union chances for victory in the Vicksburg campaign by building canals in northeastern Louisiana. The unpredictability of the Mississippi River was the main reason for the failure of the project. 53 notes.   J. F. Paul

488. Kauffman, Mike. FORT LESLEY MC NAIR AND THE LINCOLN CONSPIRATORS. *Lincoln Herald 1978 80(4): 176-188.* The Washington Arsenal (now known as Fort Lesley J. McNair) played a key role in the Lincoln murder story. Sixteen people eventually were imprisoned in the Arsenal (also called the Old Penitentiary); four of those eight who were tried were hanged. The four who hanged, plus John Wilkes Booth, were buried temporarily on Arsenal grounds. The only surviving part of the Arsenal is Building 20 at Fort McNair, the building where the Lincoln conspiracy trial was held. 2 diagrams, 9 photos, 66 notes.   T. P. Linkfield

489. Kaye, Jacqueline. JOHN QUINCY ADAMS AND *THE CONQUEST OF IRELAND*. *Éire-Ireland 1981 16(1): 34-54.* After losing to Andrew Jackson in the presidential election of 1828, John Quincy Adams broke off all personal dealings with him even though they had been friends of long standing. The reason for this severance is revealed in Adams's *The Conquest of Ireland,* a poem written in 1831 in four Byronic cantos that condemned Dermot MacMurrogh, the 12th-century king of Leinster who bargained away Ireland to the English and helped them conquer it after he had been expelled from Ireland by another king angered by his adultery. Adams was genuinely sympathetic to Irish independence, but he also wished to compare MacMurrogh and Jackson, whose marriage to Mrs. Rachel Robards before she had been legally divorced was a prominent issue in the campaign of 1828. Adams believed that respect for the family unit affected respect for public morality. 48 notes.   D. J. Engler

490. Keiser, David S. LINCOLN'S ANCESTORS CAME FROM IRELAND! *Lincoln Herald 1977 79(4): 146-150.* Establishes the genea-

logical connection between Martha Lyford and Samuel Lincoln, who was the Emancipator's first ancestor named *Lincoln* to reach America. Martha Lyford, daughter of the Reverend John Lyford, arrived at Plymouth Colony in 1624 from Armagh, Ireland. She may possibly have been born in Ireland. Samuel Lincoln arrived at Boston in 1637 from England. In 1649 Samuel Lincoln married Martha Lyford, and from this marriage Abraham Lincoln descended. 2 charts, 24 notes.

                                         T. P. Linkfield

491. Kerp, Thomas Bland. WERE THE LINCOLN CONSPIRATORS DEALT JUSTICE? *Lincoln Herald 1978 80(1): 38-46.* The eight Abraham Lincoln assassination alleged conspirators, especially Edwin Spangler, Dr. Samuel Mudd, and Samuel Arnold, were deprived of due process of law. In 1866 Federal judge Willard Hull decided in *United States v. Commandant of Fort Delaware* that because the Civil War had ended, civilians could not be tried before a military commission, and he ordered the civilians in question released. This established a precedent that should have applied in the cases of Arnold, Mudd, and Spangler, who were imprisoned on the Dry Tortugas, Florida. Instead, another judicial decision, *Ex parte Mudd et al.* (1868), deprived the three civilians of their constitutional right of due process. 9 photos, 35 notes.

                                         T. P. Linkfield

492. Keys, Thomas Bland. LINCOLN'S VOICE FROM THE GRAVE: A SPIRITUALISTIC CONVERSATION WITH CARL SCHURZ. *Lincoln Herald 1975 77(2): 121-123.* Carl Schurz, summoned to Washington, D.C. by President Andrew Johnson in 1865, assumed it was to discuss the President's plan for reconstructing North Carolina. The night before the meeting, during a seance, Abraham Lincoln supposedly told him the true nature of the meeting and made several prognostications that eventually came true. Based on primary and secondary sources; illus., 17 notes.   B. J. LaBue

493. King, Willard L. THE CASE THAT MADE LINCOLN. *Lincoln Herald 1981 84[i.e., 83](3[i.e., 4]): 786-790.* Discusses Abraham Lincoln's defense of Henry B. Truett, who was tried in 1838 for the murder of Dr. J. M. Early; Lincoln successfully defended Truett, even though Lincoln had been admitted to the bar only the year before.

494. Kubicek, Earl C. THE LINCOLN CORPUS CAPER. *Lincoln Herald 1980 82(3): 474-480.* Biography of Terrance Mullen (b. 1849), one of the men charged and found guilty of an attempt to steal the body of Abraham Lincoln in Springfield, Illinois, in exchange for the release from prison of counterfeiter Ben Boyd on the night of the presidential election in 1876.

495. Kurth, Madelyn. MARY LINCOLN. *Daughters of the Am. Revolution Mag. 1978 112(2): 90-91, 126.* Discusses Mary Todd Lincoln's relationship with Abraham Lincoln, 1846-65.

496. Larson, Robert and Larson, Sylvia. NEW ENGLAND REMEMBERS MR. LINCOLN. *Lincoln Herald 1980 82(3): 422-437.* Presents a guide to memorials, artifacts, and memorabilia of and to Abraham Lincoln in Connecticut, Rhode Island, Massachusetts, New Hampshire, Maine, and Vermont.

497. Lewis, Theodore B., ed. ENOCH LEWIS'S ACCOUNT OF LINCOLN'S SECRET JOURNEY FROM HARRISBURG TO PHILADELPHIA, FEBRUARY 22, 1861. *Lincoln Herald 1974 76(3): 148-149.* Two letters between Enoch Lewis, General Superintendent of the Pennsylvania Railroad and Allen Pinkerton, detective, debate whether Allen or John A. Kennedy, Superintendent of the New York Metropolitan Police, should be credited with saving Abraham Lincoln's life in 1861. Lewis disclaimed popular illustrations and newspaper reports of the day depicting President-elect Lincoln in various disguises. Based on original letters of the editor; 8 notes.   A. C. Aimone

498. Lindsey, Richard A. LINCOLN AND SHIELDS. *Lincoln Herald 1978 80(2): 65-69.* In September 1842 Abraham Lincoln was involved in a curious and farcical affair with James Shields, state auditor of Illinois. The affair involved the publication of three letters (one authored by Lincoln) attacking Shields's public and private reputation. The affair led to a challenge, but both sides achieved a compromise to avoid a duel. Shields and Lincoln later became friends, and after Lincoln

became President, he named Shields a brigadier general in the Union Army. Photo, 7 notes.   T. P. Linkfield

499. Loux, Arthur F. THE MYSTERY OF THE TELEGRAPH INTERRUPTION. *Lincoln Herald 1979 81(4): 234-237.* William H. Heiss, Sr., Superintendent of the commercial telegraph in Washington, D.C., was at Ford's Theater on the night of Abraham Lincoln's assassination and shut down commercial telegraph operations within 10 minutes of the shooting to allow the government, via the military telegraph, maximum latitude.

500. Marchman, Watt P. COLLEGE COSTS: WHAT RUTHERFORD B. HAYES SPENT AS A STUDENT AT KENYON, 1838-1841. *Hayes Hist. J. 1978 2(1): 14-19.* A financial record of three of the four years Rutherford B. Hayes was a student at Kenyon College, in Gambier, Ohio (1838-41). Includes a record of money received from his mother and his uncle, Sardis Birchard; a capitulation of expenditures for his freshman and sophomore years, October 1838 to 5 August 1840; itemized accounts of daily expenses for the sophomore year, and the junior year from 5 October 1840, through August 1841; and a capitulation of the junior year. An itemized account of the senior year exists for only September and early October 1841. Primary sources; 3 photos.   J. N. Friedel

501. Marchman, Watt P. RUTHERFORD B. HAYES IN LOWER SANDUSKY, 1845-1849. *Hayes Hist. J. 1976 1(2): 122-132.* Examines Rutherford B. Hayes' life and early legal career in Lower Sandusky, Ohio. Cites reasons for this geographical selection, his later motives for moving to Cincinnati to expand his legal practice, and the change of the town's name to Fremont. Primary sources; 4 illus., 25 notes.

                                         J. N. Friedel

502. Marchman, Watt P. RUTHERFORD B. HAYES AS PAINTED BY WILLIAM MERRITT CHASE: THE DOCUMENTARY STORY. *Hayes Hist. J. 1976 1(1): 36-44.* One of the two full-length portraits of Rutherford B. Hayes which were painted from life was completed by William Merritt Chase (1849-1916) of Indiana in 1882. The planning for the portrait, its description, the painter's manners, and his New York City studio, are documented by correspondence to and from Hayes. The Chase portrait is located at Harvard's Langdell Hall. Based on primary sources; 5 illus., 14 notes.   J. N. Friedel

503. Marcus, Robert D. JAMES A. GARFIELD: LIFTING THE MASK. *Ohio Hist. 1979 88(1): 78-83.* Examines the character of James A. Garfield, 20th President, as analyzed in Margaret Leech and Harry J. Brown's *The Garfield Orbit* and Allan Peskin's *Garfield.* Though the books differ in their approach to the subject, both show the man to be a product of his time—the Gilded Age—neither worse nor better than his fellow leaders who built their careers by intense study of complicated issues, not merely by partisanship. Leech and Brown provide insight into Garfield's youth which is lacking in the Peskin work. His career comes through as a case study of the way war (in this case the Civil War) may produce moral exhaustion. Illus., 2 notes.   H. F. Thomson

504. Markowitz, Arthur M., ed. TRAGEDY OF AN AGE: AN EYEWITNESS ACCOUNT OF LINCOLN'S ASSASSINATION. *J. of the Illinois State Hist. Soc. 1973 66(2): 205-211.* Reprints an overlooked account of Abraham Lincoln's assassination, that of Roeliff Brinkerhoff (1828-1911), a general in the Quartermaster Corps. Brinkerhoff's seat gave him a view of the president's theater box and thus of the assassination. The account also describes the capture of John Wilkes Booth at Richard H. Garrett's farm and Sergeant Boston Corbett's shooting of Booth. Based on Brinkerhoff's autobiography; illus., 11 notes.

                                         A. C. Aimone

505. Massey, Mary Elizabeth. MARY TODD LINCOLN. *Am. Hist. Illus. 1975 10(2): 4-9, 44-48.* Discusses Mary Todd Lincoln's life of neurotic behavior (1819-82) and evaluates contemporary media criticism of her.

506. McGhee, James E. THE NEOPHYTE GENERAL: U.S. GRANT AND THE BELMONT CAMPAIGN. *Missouri Hist. R. 1973 67(4): 465-483.* Discusses the controversial first campaign of General Ulysses S. Grant (1822-85) at Belmont, Missouri, 7 November 1861. In charge of most of southeast Missouri and southern Illinois, Grant

prepared to face a strong threat from the forces of Major General Leonidas Polk and Brigadier M. Jeff Thompson. With raw forces, Grant moved against the rebels at Belmont in order to protect Colonel Richard Oglesby, basing his orders on erroneous reports about Confederate movements. Casualties were high, and while damage was done to the Confederate army, Grant's troops barely escaped destruction. Grant's inexperience was obvious, but he learned from his mistakes and Belmont demonstrated his "aggressiveness, initiative and determination." Based on Grant's memoirs, US goverment documents, contemporary newspaper reports, and secondary sources; 9 illus., map, 60 notes. N. J. Street

507. McMurtry, R. Gerald. IN THE LINCOLN MEMORIAL UNIVERSITY COLLECTION ... PRESENTATION COPY OF JAMES RUSSELL LOWELL'S "COMMEMORATION ODE." *Lincoln Herald 1974 76(1): 36-39.* An interesting rare book in the Lincoln Memorial University collection is James Russell Lowell's "Ode Recited at the Commemoration of The Living and Dead Soldiers of Harvard University July 21, 1865." It is one of 50 privately printed copies inscribed by Lowell with his poem, "Abraham Lincoln, July, 1865." It is considered one of the rarest Lincoln publications. Explains why and how Lowell wrote this poem. 2 illus. A. C. Aimone

508. Morris, Walter J. JOHN QUINCY ADAMS'S GERMAN LIBRARY, WITH A CATALOG OF HIS GERMAN BOOKS. *Pro. of the Am. Phil. Soc. 1974 118(4): 321-333.* Comments on John Quincy Adams the bibliophile. Adams collected books from age 11 and augmented his collection through his travels, diplomatic assignments in Europe, and close attention to catalogues and book sales. His collection forms the bulk of the Adams library at the Adams National Historic Site. Particular emphasis is given to the collection of German books which he began collecting in 1781. 20 notes, biblio. C. W. Olson

509. Morrison, Katherine L. A REEXAMINATION OF BROOKS AND HENRY ON JOHN QUINCY ADAMS. *New England Q. 1981 54(2): 163-179.* The career of John Quincy Adams provided a lens through which Henry and Brooks Adams could look back upon their family and nation. Exchanges in their letters over Brooks's manuscript, "Life of John Quincy Adams," indicate moral and intellectual positions between the brothers that are more divergent than previously believed. Flattering comments included in the letters cannot be taken seriously. The evidence is even stronger that Henry never supplied much intellectual material for Brooks. Primary sources; 36 notes. R. S. Sliwoski

510. Morrissey, Charles T. THE PERILS OF INSTANT HISTORY: JOSIAH G. HOLLAND'S BIOGRAPHY OF ABRAHAM LINCOLN. *J. of Popular Culture 1973 7(2): 347-350.* Holland's biography of Lincoln was affected by his high esteem for Lincoln and resulted in a dubious portrayal of the assassinated leader. S

511. Myers, Elisabeth P. WRITING A JUVENILE BIOGRAPHY OF PRESIDENT HAYES. *Hayes Hist. J. 1978 2(2): 97-101.* Myers, author of many American biographies for children, relates details of her meeting with Henry Regnery, publisher and editor of the Henry Regnery Company, and how she wrote a juvenile biography of Rutherford B. Hayes (1969). Discusses Myers's selection of Hayes as the subject of her biography, and the extent of her preliminary readings and research. 7 illus. J. N. Friedel

512. Neely, Mark E., Jr. ABRAHAM LINCOLN'S NATIONALISM RECONSIDERED. *Lincoln Herald 1974 76(1): 12-28.* Studies historians' judgments since 1870 about Abraham Lincoln's nationalism. Daniel Webster and Lincoln had similar ideas about the origins of the American nation. Lincoln looked to Henry Clay to develop ideas about the founding fathers. Based on Lincoln and Clay writings and on monographs; notes. A. C. Aimone

513. Neely, Mark E., Jr. AMERICAN NATIONALISM IN THE IMAGE OF HENRY CLAY: ABRAHAM LINCOLN'S EULOGY ON HENRY CLAY IN CONTEXT. *Register of the Kentucky Hist. Soc. 1975 73(1): 31-61.* As with most political eulogies, Lincoln's eulogy on Henry Clay, delivered on 6 July 1852, has been treated with disdain by historians. Numerous eulogies on Clay are discussed with emphasis on those by Lincoln and William H. Seward. Lincoln's eulogy, serving also as a Fourth of July address, linked Clay's life to a consistent history of

opposition to slavery. Criticizing both extremes, Lincoln's eulogy was thus more harsh and strident than others. It was, in effect, another indication of Lincoln's strong nationalistic impulse. Based on primary and secondary sources; illus., 42 notes. J. F. Paul

514. Neely, Mark E., Jr. LINCOLN AND THE MEXICAN WAR: AN ARGUMENT BY ANALOGY. *Civil War Hist. 1978 24(1): 5-24.* Gives an historiographical analysis of Abraham Lincoln's opposition to the Mexican War. Compares Albert Beveridge's ideas in *Abraham Lincoln, 1809-1858* (1928): that Lincoln, an inexperienced politician, was overwhelmed by experienced eastern Whigs, forgot the expansionist sentiments of his Illinois constituents, and opposed the war, with G. S. Boritt's contention that Lincoln's antiwar sentiments stemmed from moral grounds, and were not disputed by his constituents. Analyzes the inconsistencies in the records of Lincoln's stand on the war, and concludes that Lincoln's position on the war reflected that of the Whig Party, and "he picked his way through the political solutions to the Mexican War with a politician's care." S

515. Neely, Mark E., Jr. WAR AND PARTISANSHIP: WHAT LINCOLN LEARNED FROM JAMES K. POLK. *J. of the Illinois State Hist. Soc. 1981 74(3): 199-216.* Abraham Lincoln, the lone Whig congressman from Illinois, bitterly opposed the policies of the James K. Polk administration, especially the prosecution of the Mexican War. Economic principles and the increase of presidential power, rather than territorial expansion or slavery, decisively separated the two. The Polk administration polarized and crystallized Lincoln's political thought, intensifying his partisanship. His opposition to the war was based, not on international rights, but on the threat to the US Constitution. Both presidents led the country to military victory, were personally involved in determining strategy, and repudiated dissent. 8 illus., 52 notes.
A. W. Novitsky

516. Nugent, Walter. OUR MARTYRED PRESIDENT. *Rev. in Am. Hist. 1979 7(1): 79-84.* Review article prompted by Allan Peskin's *Garfield: A Biography* (Kent, Ohio: Kent State U. Pr., 1978).

517. Oates, Stephen B. WHY SHOULD THE SPIRIT OF MORTAL BE PROUD? *Am. Hist. Illus. 1976 11(1): 32-41.* "Why should the spirit of mortal be proud" is the first line of Lincoln's favorite poem, *Mortality,* which stressed the transitory nature of human life. Abraham Lincoln's advice to potential lawyers was: "Resolve to be honest at all events and if in your judgement you cannot be an honest lawyer, resolve to be honest without being a lawyer." He enjoyed practicing law during 1837-60 and hoped to do so again after his presidency. Although he was scrupulously fair in establishing his fee, the large volume of Lincoln's business made his law practice financially successful. Most of his practice was in the 14 counties of middle Illinois' 8th circuit. Lincoln was lucid, logical, appealed to the jury's sense of fair play, and reduced complex issues to the simplest propositions. 10 illus., map. D. Dodd

518. Oates, Stephen B. WILDERNESS FUGUE: LINCOLN'S JOURNEY TO MANHOOD ON THE KENTUCKY AND INDIANA FRONTIER. *Am. West 1976 13(2): 4-13.* Presents a narrative account of Abraham Lincoln's boyhood from his earliest memories in Kentucky, the Indiana sojourn, and the early Illinois years, 1814-31. Adapted from a forthcoming biography. 5 illus., biblio. D. L. Smith

519. Ostendorf, Lloyd. FACES LINCOLN KNEW—PHOTOGRAPHS FROM THE PAST. *Lincoln Herald 1977 79(1): 29-32.* William Florville, who opened the first barbershop in Springfield in 1832, developed a unique and long relationship with Abraham Lincoln. Florville, a light-skinned black from Haiti, was a hard-working barber and a good businessman in real estate. Lincoln was a steady customer for Florville, and the barber's legal advisor and attorney. Both men had humble beginnings, but they succeeded in their respective vocations in Springfield, Illinois. Photo. T. P. Linkfield

520. Ostendorf, Lloyd. HISTORY OF A LINCOLN BED. *Lincoln Herald 1981 83(3): 733-736.* Traces the history and ownership of a walnut spool bed from the Lincoln home of the 1850's given to a family servant, Mariah Vance, who worked for the Lincolns from 1850 to 1860.

521. Ostendorf, Lloyd and Holzer, Harold. THE JOHN HENRY BROWN MINIATURE OF LINCOLN: A CRITICAL RE-ASSESSMENT (AND A CONTROVERSY OVER PRIMACY EXPLAINED). *Lincoln Herald 1976 78(2): 78-81.* Discusses the discovery in 1976 of the (supposedly) first portrait of Abraham Lincoln by John Henry Brown, completed in 1860, which the authors claim was the 5th or 6th portrait of Lincoln.

522. Ostendorf, Lloyd. LINCOLN AND THE HOBLITS. *Lincoln Herald 1975 77(1): 49-52.* Two generations of the Hoblit family of Logan County, Illinois, were friends of Abraham Lincoln. Lincoln frequently visited the Hoblits. Based on documentation provided by the Hoblit family; illus., 2 photos, 5 notes.
                                                              B. J. LaBue

523. Ostendorf, Lloyd. A RELIC FROM HIS LAST BIRTHDAY: THE MILLS LIFE-MASK OF LINCOLN. *Lincoln Herald 1973 75(3): 79-85.* One of the latest items of Lincolniana is a rediscovered 1865 plaster cast of Abraham Lincoln's face. The mask was made by sculptor Clark Mills on Lincoln's birthday, two months before Lincoln's death. The author acquired it after going through several auction houses and background authenticity research. Describes the history of death masks. Based on correspondence with Lincoln specialists; 2 photos, 14 notes.
                                                              A. C. Aimone

524. Owsley, Harriet Chappell. DISCOVERIES MADE IN EDITING THE PAPERS OF ANDREW JACKSON. *Manuscripts 1975 27(4): 274-279.* Discusses the correspondence of Andrew Jackson with extracts relating to the earliest business account found in his papers, dated 1 March 1790, made with Melling Woolley of the Spanish town of Natchez. The unpaid account led the editors to several important discoveries in the correspondence of Jackson with Thomas Irwin, Ebenezer Rees, and George and Robert Cochran. A great deal more work is required in the Spanish archives and "more information about Jackson's business dealings in Natchez is needed." Illus., 2 notes.   D. A. Yanchisin

525. Paludan, Phillip S. LINCOLN, THE RULE OF LAW, AND THE AMERICAN REVOLUTION. *J. of the Illinois State Hist. Soc. 1977 70(1): 10-17.* Analyzes Abraham Lincoln's "political religion" as revealed through his *Collected Works.* That religion was based on his self-proclaimed reverence for law and the constitutional system. He saw the crucial test of democracy as a balance between liberty and order. 2 illus., 18 notes.   J

526. Parsons, Lynn Hudson. "A PERPETUAL HARROW UPON MY FEELINGS": JOHN QUINCY ADAMS AND THE AMERICAN INDIAN. *New England Q. 1973 46(3): 339-379.* Explores John Quincy Adams' changing attitudes toward Indian affairs. In his Plymouth oration of 1802 he said that the Indians, as hunting rather than agrarian communities, had no right to stand in the way of the white man. But in the 1820's he considered both removal and assimilation inadmissible solutions. In the 1830's his attitude changed further. His opposition to Indian removal drew great support. In 1841 he rejected appointment as Chairman of the House Committee on Indian Affairs, declaring US Indian policy to be "among the most heinous sins of this nation," and a "harrow upon my feelings." 120 notes.   E. P. Stickney

527. Parsons, Lynn Hudson. CENSURING OLD MAN ELOQUENT: FOREIGN POLICY AND DISUNION, 1842. *Capitol Studies 1975 3(1): 89-106.* Discusses the 1842 attempted censure of John Quincy Adams in the House of Representatives for advocating dissolving the Union.

528. Parsons, Lynn Hudson. THE "SPLENDID PAGEANT": OBSERVATIONS ON THE DEATH OF JOHN QUINCY ADAMS. *New England Q. 1980 53(4): 464-465.* John Quincy Adams died on 23 February 1848. His death coincided with the implementation of national telegraph services, the beginning of the Revolution of 1848 in France, and the receipt by President Polk of the Treaty of Guadelupe, which ended the Mexican War. Thus Adams's death was celebrated nationwide in a national ritual that simultaneously celebrated American unity and values. Adams was praised as a son of the American Revolution, a model Yankee, Puritan, and Christian statesman. Primary sources, 69 notes.
                                                              J. Powell

529. Payne, Alma J. WILLIAM DEAN HOWELLS AND OTHER EARLY BIOGRAPHERS OF RUTHERFORD B. HAYES. *Hayes Hist. J. 1978 2(2): 78-88.* Surveys the first half century of writing about Hayes: three hastily written campaign biographies issued in 1876, by Russell H. Conwell, James Q. Howard, and William Dean Howells; Charles Richard Williams's 1914 scholarly and standard life; and Hamilton J. Eckenrode's 1930 poorly researched and disappointing political biography. Howells's book is examined in greater detail. Analyzes the philosophy and significance of these early works interpreting Rutherford B. Hayes. Primary and secondary sources; 9 illus., 32 notes.
                                                              J. N. Friedel

530. Peckham, Charles A. THE OHIO NATIONAL GUARD AND ITS POLICE DUTIES, 1894. *Ohio Hist. 1974 83(1): 51-67.* Though it was poorly armed, the guard maintained an excellent record during the turbulent year of 1894. Governor William McKinley provided leadership, and the troops moved quickly to keep peace in the face of major fires, lynch mobs, and labor unrest. Primary and secondary sources; 9 illus., 52 notes.
                                                              S. S. Sprague

531. Peskin, Allan. FROM LOG CABIN TO OBLIVION. *Am. Hist. Illus. 1976 11(2): 25-34.* Born in a log cabin in 1831 and educated at Western Reserve Eclectic Institute in Hiram, Ohio, and at Williams College in Massachusetts, James A. Garfield became a successful orator, an ordained minister, a college president, a state senator in the Ohio legislature, a major general in the Union Army, a Republican congressman, and a US Senator, before being elected President over the Democrat, Winfield Scott Hancock, in 1880. Garfield was shot by Charles J. Guiteau who believed God chose him to do the act in order "to unite the Republican party, forestall another civil war, and incidentally, publicize Guiteau's latest book." Garfield suffered for 80 days before succumbing. He aroused the nation's sympathy and became "what he had never been in health: a genuine folk hero." A grief-stricken nation contributed over a quarter of a million dollars to erect a monumental crenelated turret to house his remains; but he was soon forgotten, and his entire generation was pushed into "undeserved oblivion." 12 illus.   D. Dodd

532. Peskin, Allan. JAMES A. GARFIELD, HISTORIAN. *Historian 1981 43(4): 483-492.* President James A. Garfield had broad historical interests and anticipated many of the directions later taken by professional historians. Examines Garfield's early interest in history, his readings and writings on the subject, and his efforts promoting the subject. Garfield was ill at ease with the grand literary histories of the 19th century, and he looked instead for large patterns of historical development, in particular he anticipated both quantification and social history. Primary sources; 43 notes.   R. S. Sliwoski

533. Peskin, Allan. THE "LITTLE MAN ON HORSEBACK" AND THE "LITERARY FELLOW": GARFIELD'S OPINIONS OF GRANT. *Mid-America 1973 55(4): 271-282.* Traces the rivalry between James A. Garfield and Ulysses S. Grant. Garfield disliked Grant's ignoring him in the matter of a postmastership, opposed Grant's Santo Domingo scheme, and disapproved of the corruption of Grant's administration. Tempted to bolt the Republican Party in 1872, Garfield nevertheless preferred Grant to Horace Greeley, but led the anti-Grant forces in 1880. As president, Garfield purged many of Grant's friends. Based on the Garfield Papers in the Library of Congress, published sources, and secondary works; 62 notes.   T. H. Wendel

534. Planck, Gary R. "DEEP POOL OF BLACK SILENCE": ABRAHAM LINCOLN, TRAGIC HERO. *Lincoln Herald 1976 78(2): 62-65.* Abraham Lincoln's life and character match Alonzo Myers' definitions for great tragedy and great tragic heroes as set forth in his book *Tragedy: A View of Life* (1956). Secondary sources; illus., 16 notes.
                                                              B. J. LaBue

535. Planck, Gary R. LINCOLN AND BAILEY: A FORGOTTEN FRIENDSHIP. *Lincoln Herald 1974 76(3): 143-147.* The Reverend Gilbert S. Bailey was a neighbor of Abraham Lincoln in Springfield, Illinois. Bailey was prominent in organizing Baptist churches in Illinois, to one of which Lincoln contributed. Bailey was also active in missionary work and church organization and education. He helped to lay the foundations for the University of Chicago. Based on newspaper sources; illus., 32 notes.   A. C. Aimone

536. Planck, Gary R. LINCOLN ASSASSINATION: THE "FOR-GOTTEN" INVESTIGATION: A. C. RICHARDS, SUPERINTEN-DENT OF THE METROPOLITAN POLICE. *Lincoln Herald 1980 82(4): 521-539.* Utilizes overlooked sources to examine the role of A. C. Richards, superintendent of Washington, D.C.'s metropolitan police force, in the investigation and trial of the conspirators involved in the murder of President Lincoln.

537. Planck, Gary R. LINCOLN'S ASSASSINATION: MORE "FORGOTTEN" LITIGATION—EX PARTE MUDD (1868). *Lincoln Herald 1974 76(2): 86-90.* Dr. Samuel A. Mudd, sentenced to hard labor for life at Fort Jefferson, Dry Tortugas Island, for his involvement in Abraham Lincoln's assassination, fought a legal battle for his release. Mudd had hoped to gain his freedom either by the Supreme Court case of *Ex parte Miligan* or by presidential proclamations of amnesty. Neither appeal worked, although Dr. Mudd's medical service rendered during a yellow fever epidemic gained his release through President Andrew Johnson. Based on secondary works; illus., 21 notes.
A. C. Aimone

538. Plummer, Mark A. THE HERNDON-OGLESBY EX-CHANGE ON THE CHARACTER OF LINCOLN. *Lincoln Herald 1977 79(4): 169-173.* In January and February of 1866, William Herndon and Richard J. Oglesby exchanged four letters on the personality and character of Abraham Lincoln. Herndon, Lincoln's last law partner, was gathering material for a book, which was not published until 1889. Oglesby was the Governor of Illinois and had been an early Lincoln booster. The four letters are part of the Oglesby Collection at the Illinois State Historical Society and are reprinted in full. Both men agreed that Lincoln was a good but not a perfect man. 2 photos, 25 notes.
T. P. Linkfield

539. Pressly, Thomas J. WRITINGS ABOUT ABRAHAM LIN-COLN IN THE 1970S: A REVIEW ARTICLE. *Pacific Northwest Q. 1981 72(2): 72-75.* Seven books published during the 1970's indicate that the "Lincoln theme" has not been exhausted by historians. Especially noteworthy is Stephen Oates's *With Malice Toward None* which offers a well-organized, well-written and balanced treatment of Lincoln, and is particularly enlightening on his family relationships. Equally valuable is David Potter's *The Impending Crisis, 1848-1861,* which traces the development of Lincoln's racial attitudes, and David Nichols's *Lincoln and the Indians* which examines one aspect of those attitudes. Women and ethnic historians may soon offer additional perspectives on the Lincoln theme. 5 notes.
M. L. Tate

540. Prucha, Francis Paul. GENERAL JACKSON, EXPANSION-IST. *Rev. in Am. Hist. 1978 6(3): 331-336.* Review article prompted by Robert V. Remini's *Andrew Jackson and the Course of American Empire, 1767-1821* (New York: Harper & Row, 1977).

541. Pukl, Joseph M., Jr. JAMES K. POLK'S CONGRESSIONAL CAMPAIGNS, 1829-1833. *Tennessee Hist. Q. 1981 40(4): 348-365.* James K. Polk developed his political savvy in Tennessee congressional politics during his 1829, 1831, and 1833 campaigns. As a Jackson loyalist, Polk opposed the national bank. To maintain middle Tennessee support he won a mail route change and explained his votes against the pension bills as protests against their too restrictive nature. His popularity meant he often ran unopposed. Based on the *Correspondence of James K. Polk* and other primary sources; 46 notes.
W. D. Piersen

542. Pukl, Joseph M., Jr. JAMES K. POLK'S EARLY CONGRES-SIONAL CAMPAIGNS OF 1825 AND 1827. *Tennessee Hist. Q. 1980 39(4): 440-458.* In 1824 James K. Polk declared himself a candidate for the 19th Congress, which was to convene in December 1825. His campaign in Tennessee's Sixth district endorsed internal improvements, with the qualification that a state must grant permission for federal improvements within its borders. On 4 and 5 August 1825, he was elected. Congressman Polk kept in touch with his constituents, using every advantage of incumbency to keep his name before the public. In the 1827 elections Polk invited the public to examine his record. He was reelected. Primary sources; 41 notes.
J. Powell

543. Quimby, Rollin W. LLOYD LEWIS MISREADS THE PREACHERS. *Lincoln Herald 1973 75(1): 3-10.* Historian Lloyd

Lewis argued in his *Myths After Lincoln* that Union clergymen were Lincoln's chief mythmakers. However, Lewis rearranged quoted sermons on Lincoln's death to fit his thesis. Lincoln's lowly birth, clear thinking, kindness and honesty plus the idea that the Lord took Lincoln away at the right time were basic mythmaking ideas that Lewis' use of rhetorical materials distorted. A chronological examination of the surviving Civil War sermons, church resolutions, and newspaper and magazine articles shows that nothing new was said by either clergy or editors after Lincoln's death. Based on contemporary church papers, reports and sermons, and secondary sources; 31 notes.
A. C. Aimone

544. Quinn, Yancey M., Jr. JACKSON'S MILITARY ROAD. *J. of Mississippi Hist. 1979 41(4): 335-350.* Details the interest of Andrew Jackson in a road between New Orleans and his Nashville headquarters after the War of 1812. The conflict had shown the pressing need for a shorter route and better transportation between the two cities. These factors, coupled with the interruption of communications on the Natchez Trace and the role played by Mississippi, Tennessee, and Kentucky militia, led him to recommend construction. Discusses congressional approval and appropriations as well as the important individuals in surveying and constructing the road. Included are primary descriptions of the region and the route by the surveyors and the completion of the project on 17 May 1820.
M. S. Legan

545. Quitt, Martin H. JACKSON, INDIANS, AND PSYCHOHIS-TORY. *Hist. of Childhood Q. 1976 3(4): 543-551.* Review article prompted by Michael Paul Rogin's *Fathers and Children: Andrew Jackson and the Subjugation of the American Indian* (New York: 1975). Rogin's volume is disappointing and fails to support his assertion that Indian dispossession was the central feature of the Jacksonian period, and to adequately delineate the psychological forces in Andrew Jackson's personality that explain his Indian policy or the national cult built around him. 8 notes.
R. E. Butchart

546. Randall, Robert L. HEALTHY IDEALIZATION OF ABRAHAM LINCOLN. *Lincoln Herald 1978 80(4): 188-191.* Defines four characteristics of "healthy idealization" scholars can use for guidance. Healthy idealization of Abraham Lincoln would recognize both his "transcedent specialness" and his humanness. Scholars who indulge in healthy idealization of Lincoln wish to become part of his specialness without surrendering their self-esteem or individuality. 17 notes.
T. P. Linkfield

547. Randall, Robert L. LINCOLN'S CRISES: A PSYCHO-HIS-TORICAL INTERPRETATION. *Lincoln Herald 1977 79(3): 116-121.* Abraham Lincoln's struggle to maintain his own psychological equilibrium became wedded with his desire to preserve the nation's union. A series of traumatic blows, such as his mother's death, made Lincoln not only emotionally vulnerable but also psychologically fragmented for the rest of his life. In an attempt to maintain psychological equilibrium and protect his vulnerable, nuclear self, Lincoln sought identification with a public cause. He was able to join his struggle of preserving personal self-union with the broader public struggle of preserving the nation's civil union. Abraham Lincoln needed this identification for his own emotional and psychological survival. 22 notes.
T. P. Linkfield

548. Read, Harry. "A HAND TO HOLD WHILE DYING": DR. CHARLES A. LEALE AT LINCOLN'S SIDE. *Lincoln Herald 1977 79(1): 21-26.* US Army Assistant Surgeon Charles Augustus Leale, who regarded Abraham Lincoln as the "Savior of his Country," was the first doctor to enter the presidential box at Ford's Theater on 14 April 1865. His subsequent diagnosis and treatment of the President remained the model, even though other doctors were also in attendance. After leaving the army in 1866, Dr. Leale pursued a distinguished career in civilian medicine. He died in 1932 at the age of 90. 2 photos.
T. P. Linkfield

549. Reeves, Thomas C. THE SEARCH FOR THE CHESTER ALAN ARTHUR PAPERS. *Manuscripts 1973 25(3): 171-185.* Arthur "was extremely sensitive to personal criticism, and carried his penchant for seclusion to an extreme." So successfully did he, his associates, and his family hide his papers from contemporary journalists and future historians that, "For six decades a search was carried out for the Arthur papers, and only in late 1970 was it possible to believe with much certainty

that it had concluded successfully." Reviews the story of the dispersion and recovery of the Arthur papers with regard to the issue of presidential papers and their public nature. Based in part on interviews; illus., 26 notes.   D. A. Yanchisin

550. Remini, Robert V.   THE FINAL DAYS AND HOURS IN THE LIFE OF GENERAL ANDREW JACKSON.   *Tennessee Hist. Q. 1980 39(2): 167-177.* A few days after the death of his foster father Andrew Jackson in 1845, Andrew Jackson, Jr., the adopted son, wrote a detailed account of that death. It provides an extraordinary record of the dying hero's last days, describing both tremendous physical suffering and deep commitment to Christianity. These two aspects are frequently overlooked or ignored by biographers. Based on the letter of Andrew Jackson, Jr., to A. O. P. Nicholson in the Miscellaneous Jackson Papers, New York Historical Society; Jackson Papers in the Huntington Library; Jackson Papers in the Pierpont Morgan Library; and secondary studies; illus., 24 notes.   H. M. Parker, Jr.

551. Richman, Michael.   THE LONG LABOR OF MAKING NATION'S FAVORITE STATUE.   *Smithsonian 1977 7(11): 54-61.* Sketches the life of sculptor Daniel Chester French (1850-1931) and summarizes the history of the statue of Abraham Lincoln in the Lincoln Memorial. The Lincoln Memorial Commission was established in 1911 and Henry Bacon was chosen as architect. In 1914, the Commission appointed French as sculptor for the Lincoln statue. Traces the development of the statue from its model form through its casting and carving and the congressional appropriations for a lighting system in September 1926. Secondary sources; 8 illus.   K. A. Harvey

552. Rietveld, Ronald D., ed.   AN EYEWITNESS ACCOUNT OF ABRAHAM LINCOLN'S ASSASSINATION.   *Civil War Hist. 1976 22(1): 60-69.* Provides a previously unpublished memoir of an eyewitness, Frederick A. Sawyer, to President Abraham Lincoln's assassination, on 14 April 1865, in Ford's Theater. The brief note was written a few hours after the attack was made. Sawyer was sitting in the orchestra seats just beneath the presidential box, heard the fatal shot, and saw John Wilkes Booth leap to the stage although at the time he did not know it was Booth. He describes the panic in the theater and the mood of gloom which quickly seized the District of Columbia. Sawyer did not hear Booth shout "Sic Semper Tyrannis," although he records that someone else heard such a cry.   E. C. Murdock

553. Rietveld, Ronald D.   LINCOLN AND THE POLITICS OF MORALITY.   *J. of the Illinois State Hist. Soc. 1975 68(1): 27-43.* Abraham Lincoln became convinced that the fight against slavery was a moral struggle by 1854. He emphasized the incompatibility of the institution existing in a free country throughout his political involvement in the 1850's, especially in his struggle for political office with the pragmatic Democrat Stephen A. Douglas. Lincoln's stand on the immorality of slavery was attuned to the intellectual climate of the time and was a great aid in making him a viable presidential candidate in 1860.
N. Lederer

554. Riley, Stephen T.   MANUSCRIPTS IN THE MASSACHUSETTS HISTORICAL SOCIETY.   *Massachusetts Hist. Soc. Pro. 1980 92: 100-116.* The Reverend Jeremy Belknap (1744-1798), an indefatigable manuscript collector and one of the society's principle founders, believed that historical documents needed a decent repository to insure their existence and safety. Among the major acquisitions discussed are the Adams Family Papers, the Winthrop Family Papers, George Washington's Newburgh Address of March 1783, and a considerable collection of Thomas Jefferson's manuscripts (over 70 volumes), including the original manuscript of *Notes on the State of Virginia*.   G. A. Glovins

555. Robbins, Peggy.   ANDREW AND RACHEL JACKSON.   *Am. Hist. Illus. 1977 12(5): 22-28.* Discusses the love relationship between Andrew Jackson and Rachel Robards (later to become Jackson's wife), the scandal it produced, and the use of the relationship as anti-Jackson political fodder, 1788-1828.

556. Robbins, Peggy.   THE LINCOLNS AND SPRITUALISM.   *Civil War Times Illus. 1976 15(5): 4-10, 46-47.* Discusses the involvement of Mary Todd Lincoln in spiritualism and the effect which this had on Abraham Lincoln, 1848-64.

557. Robertson, Deane and Robertson, Peggy.   THE PLOT TO STEAL LINCOLN'S BODY.   *Am. Heritage 1982 33(3): 76-83.* In an effort to win the release from prison of his best counterfeit-bill engraver, James Kinealy plotted in 1876 to steal the body of Abraham Lincoln and exchange it for the freedom of Ben Boyd and some cash. A Secret Service agent foiled the plot. Two of the would-be thieves were arrested and imprisoned by Illinois officials. 6 illus.   J. F. Paul

558. Robertson, James O.   HORATIO ALGER, ANDREW CARNEGIE, ABRAHAM LINCOLN, AND THE COWBOY.   *Midwest Q. 1979 20(3): 241-257.* Discusses the transformation of America's male heroes from independent frontiersmen and pioneers who fought Indians and settled rural America, to the urban rags-to-riches giants of industrial America, and the acceptance of the new heroes by Americans.

559. Roper, Donald M.   MARTIN VAN BUREN AS TOCQUEVILLE'S LAWYER: THE JURISPRUDENCE OF POLITICS.   *J. of the Early Republic 1982 2(2): 169-189.* Discusses the law career of Martin Van Buren as a member of the New York State Bar, a state senator, a judge on the Court of Errors, and as a state attorney general. Van Buren was a lawyer-politician, attuned to public opinion and able to use his legal ability to further his political ambition in an era when the bar was a means of advancement. He defended the emerging doctrine of legal positivism and he was an advocate of the 19th-century trend that placed an emphasis on policy, instrumentalism, and legislative law. Primary and secondary sources; 69 notes.   G. A. Glovins

560. Satz, Ronald N.   REMINI'S ANDREW JACKSON (1767-1821): JACKSON AND THE INDIANS.   *Tennessee Hist. Q. 1979 38(2): 158-166.* Reviews Robert V. Remini's *Andrew Jackson and the Course of American Empire, 1767-1821* (New York: Harper & Row, 1977) by examining Remini's handling of Andrew Jackson's (1767-1845) early experiences with Tennessee Indians, Jackson's treatment of the Indians as a military commander, his conduct as a treaty negotiator, and his relations with the Seminoles while he was territorial governor of Florida. Motivated by security considerations and interests in land speculation, Jackson worked for removal but remained paternalistic in his personal dealings with the Indians. 20 notes.   W. D. Piersen

561. Schelin, Robert C.   A WHIG'S FINAL QUEST: FILLMORE AND THE KNOW-NOTHINGS.   *Niagara Frontier 1979 26(1): 1-11.* History of the American, or Know-Nothing, Party in the United States, which originated in European anti-Catholicism and American nativism, becoming a political force in the 1850's; focuses on the Party's nomination of ex-President Millard Fillmore as presidential candidate at the 1856 nominating convention, and his vain attempts, as a pro-Union candidate, to resurrect the Whig Party.

562. Schlup, Leonard.   DEMOCRATIC TALLEYRAND: ADLAI STEVENSON AND POLITICS IN THE GILDED AGE AND PROGRESSIVE ERA.   *South Atlantic Q. 1979 78(3): 182-194.* Adlai Stevenson (1835-1914), 23d Vice President, has been largely neglected by historians; yet in his day he was considered a very shrewd politician. He has remained an enigma largely because his political letters have not been found. Cites 16 of his letters, which bring to light certain of his characteristics. They were written during 1876-1908 and disclose his reactions to various events, the support he sought or gave, his concern over political developments, and his determination to serve the Democratic Party. A faithful party member, he was no maverick. He served as a transitional figure between the conservative tradition of Democracy under Cleveland to the progressive brand under Bryan and Wilson. But his most lasting contribution was the founding of an American political dynasty. Based on Stevenson's correspondence located in scattered collections; 30 notes.
H. M. Parker, Jr.

563. Schweikart, Larry.   THE MORMON CONNECTION: LINCOLN, THE SAINTS, AND THE CRISIS OF EQUALITY.   *Western Humanities Rev. 1980 34(1): 1-22.* Briefly traces concepts of equality during the Enlightenment, then discusses these ideas in 19th-century America, particularly among the Mormons, led by Joseph Smith, who relocated numerous times to pursue without harrassment their own ideas of equality; focuses on the Mormons' influence on Abraham Lincoln's political career, and his ideas on equality, slavery, and polygamy, from 1840 to the early 1860's.

564. Sewell, Richard H. LINCOLN AND THE "POSTHEROIC" GENERATION. *Rev. in Am. Hist. 1980 8(1): 52-56.* Review essay of George Forgie's *Patricide in the House Divided: A Psychological Interpretation of Lincoln and His Age* (New York: W. W. Norton and Co., 1979); mid-1820's-61.

565. Sherwood, John. ALFRED WHITAL STERN: IN PURSUIT OF THE LINCOLN LEGEND. *Q. J. of the Lib. of Congress 1981 38(2): 108-116.* Profiles Lincolniana collector and millionaire Alfred Whital Stern (1882-1961). Not a Lincoln scholar, Stern became interested in Abraham Lincoln in 1923 when he chanced to read *The Uncollected Letters of Abraham Lincoln* (1917), edited by Gilbert A. Tracy. This book began a collection so compelling that Stern left his job as vice-president of B. Kuppenheimer, a men's clothing manufacturer, became an independent investor, and devoted himself to collecting Lincolniana. His most prized item was Lincoln's 1863 letter to Major General Joe Hooker, naming him head of the Army of the Potomac. This letter, along with 5,200 other items in Stern's collection, was presented to the Library of Congress in 1953. Based on interviews with Alfred Whital Stern's heirs and personal acquaintances; 6 illus.
A. R. Souby

566. Shulsinger, Stephanie. THE MAGNIFICENT MADMAN. *New-England Galaxy 1978 19(4): 30-37.* John Quincy Adams, member of the US House of Representatives during 1831-48, challenged the institution of slavery. Notes Adams's efforts to present abolitionist petitions, the Southern imposition of the "gag rule" to table all petitions, and the end of the "gag rule" in 1842. 2 illus.
P. C. Marshall

567. Silverman, Jason H. "IN ISLES BEYOND THE MAIN": ABRAHAM LINCOLN'S PHILOSOPHY ON BLACK COLONIZATION. *Lincoln Herald 1978 80(3): 115-122.* From the early 1850's until his death in 1865, Abraham Lincoln advocated colonization in conjunction with emancipation as the best solution to the nation's racial problem. Both Thomas Jefferson and Henry Clay, who had enthusiastically supported colonization, provided Lincoln with inspiration. All of Lincoln's efforts to implement black colonization had failed by 1864, but he never abandoned this program as the best solution. He justified his position on political, economic, and moral grounds, claiming that both races would benefit from separation. Lincoln merely assumed that blacks would rather leave America than remain as second-class citizens. 4 photos, 28 notes.
T. P. Linkfield

568. Simon, John Y. and James, Felix. ANDREW JOHNSON AND THE FREEDMEN. *Lincoln Herald 1977 79(2): 71-75.* In 1863 Secretary of War Stanton created the American Freedmen's Inquiry Commission to study the complex problem of the increasing number of free blacks, made wards of the government because of the war. One of the persons the commission interviewed was Andrew Johnson, military governor of Tennessee. As a staunch Unionist, Johnson favored emancipation as a wartime necessity, but he scorned any measure which would give free blacks special protection or assistance from the national government. Includes Johnson's personal testimony before the commission. Photo, 13 notes.
T. P. Linkfield

569. Simon, John Y. GRANT AT BELMONT. *Military Affairs 1981 45(4): 161-166.* The battle at Belmont, Missouri, on 7 November 1861, is important because the Union force was commanded by Ulysses S. Grant. Both sides claimed victory; neither deserved to. Grant had taken advantage of the confusion surrounding the change of command in the Western Department to look for a fight. The results of the inconclusive battle at least established Grant as a fighting general entitled to continue command and taught him a few lessons. Also, Belmont illustrated a few of the qualities which carried him to greater successes. Based on Civil War records and other primary sources; note.
A. M. Osur

570. Sklar, Kathryn Kish. VICTORIAN WOMEN AND DOMESTIC LIFE: MARY TODD LINCOLN, ELIZABETH CADY STANTON, AND HARRIET BEECHER STOWE. Davis, Cullom; Strozier, Charles B.; Veach, Rebecca Monroe; and Ward, Geoffrey C., ed. *The Public and the Private Lincoln: Contemporary Perspectives* (Carbondale: So. Illinois U. Pr., 1979): 20-37. Examines efforts by prominent Victorian women to limit the size of their families and their public and private activities to arrive at a qualitative rather than quantitative definition of motherhood, during 1830-80. Harriet Beecher Stowe's strategy was to

abstain from sex, in part to punish her philandering husband, undertake a literary career, and foster women's education. Elizabeth Cady Stanton, like Stowe, practiced family planning and worked for feminist domestic reform, seeking the legal equality of women. Mary Todd Lincoln's approach was total commitment to her husband and children. In part she practiced family planning to aid her husband's political career, and she was indulgent of her children. She did not separate domestic from public life, participating in the political sector on Abraham's behalf, but she was unable to build an autonomous career. 40 notes.
S

571. Smith, John David. CONTRIBUTIONS OF LOUIS A. WARREN TO LINCOLN SCHOLARSHIP. *Lincoln Herald 1978 80(2): 95-101.* Louis A. Warren is the most prolific of Lincoln scholars. He was Director of the Lincoln Library and Museum in Fort Wayne, Indiana, from 1928 until his retirement in 1956. This is the first complete compilation of his publications on Abraham Lincoln. The bibliography is divided into five sections: books, edited publications, pamphlets, articles, and book reviews. Each section is arranged chronologically.
T. P. Linkfield

572. Sprague, Ver Lynn. MARY LINCOLN: ACCESSORY TO MURDER. *Lincoln Herald 1979 81(4): 238-242.* Mary Todd Lincoln was largely responsible for General Ulysses S. Grant's absence from Ford's Theater the night her husband was shot, and was also responsible for the appointment of White House bodyguard John Parker, who deserted his post that night.

573. Stathis, Stephen W. and Roderick, Lee. MALLET, CHISEL, AND CURLS. *Am. Heritage 1976 27(2): 44-47, 94-96.* Vinnie Ream Hoxie (1847-1914), who had been sculpting a bust of President Abraham Lincoln before his death, received a commission from Congress in 1866 to do a full-length statue of him. Although caught up in the impeachment of President Johnson, she finished the statue in 1871. 6 illus.
B. J. Paul

574. Steers, Edward, Jr. *INTER ARMA SILENT LEGES:* THE MILITARY TRIAL OF THE LINCOLN CONSPIRATORS. *Lincoln Herald 1981 83(3): 719-730.* Discusses the use of military commissions instead of civil courts during Abraham Lincoln's presidency, from 25 April 1861, when Lincoln authorized General Winfield Scott to suspend the privilege of the writ of habeas corpus under certain circumstances and culminating in the execution of the four conspirators in Lincoln's assassination on 7 July 1865 by order of a military commission, a decision deemed illegal based on the 1866 Supreme Court's *ex parte Milligan* decision.

575. Stern, Madeleine B. A BOOK FROM GARFIELD'S LIBRARY: THE PREFACE TO A PREFACE. *Q. J. of the Lib. of Congress 1973 30(3): 205-209.* Reprints President James Abram Garfield's preface of 1874 to *The Executive Power,* a translation of a book by Charles Adolphe de Pineton, Marquis de Chambrun. The original French edition, a gift of the author to President Garfield, is now in the Rare Book Division of the Library of Congress. Illus., 13 notes.
E. P. Stickney

576. Strozier, Charles B. THE SEARCH FOR IDENTITY AND LOVE IN YOUNG LINCOLN. Davis, Cullom; Strozier, Charles B.; Veach, Rebecca Monroe; and Ward, Geoffrey C., ed. *The Public and the Private Lincoln: Contemporary Perspectives* (Carbondale: So. Illinois U. Pr., 1979): 3-19. Though acquiring a reputation as an Illinois legislator, Abraham Lincoln was inept in business, changing jobs frequently during the 1830's. His indecision in defining his professional life occurred at the very time he feared intimacy, as exemplified by his relations with Mary Owen and Mary Todd, the latter with whom he broke his engagement before finally marrying in 1842. 85 notes.
S

577. Suppiger, Joseph E. THE INTIMATE LINCOLN, PART I: THE BOY. *Lincoln Herald 1981 83(4, i.e., 1): 604-614.* Reports on the personal life and values of Abraham Lincoln, tracing his geneaology to 1619, and focusing on his childhood in Kentucky, 1809-19.

578. Suppiger, Joseph E. THE INTIMATE LINCOLN. *Lincoln Herald 1981 84[i.e., 83](2): 668-676, (3): 737-746, (3[i.e., 4]): 774-785; 1982 84(1): 26-37.* Part II: GROWING UP IN INDIANA. Focuses on

Abraham Lincoln's boyhood in Indiana during 1817-28. Part III. ON THE ILLINOIS FRONTIER. Describes the Lincoln family's arrival in New Salem, Illinois in 1830 and their life there until 1832. Part IV. FROM NEW SALEM TO VANDALIA. Traces Lincoln's life from 1832, when he ran for the Illinois legislature, to 1837. Part V. LIFE IN SPRINGFIELD, 1837-1840. Lincoln entered into law practice with J. T. Stuart, and furthered his political career as a Whig legislator.

579. Suppiger, Joseph E. LINCOLN LEGENDS. *Lincoln Herald 1979 81(1): 33-38.* Provides several examples of popular biographies of Abraham Lincoln published from 1863 to the early 1900's.

580. Suppiger, Joseph E. THE OFFICIAL OPENING OF THE ABRAHAM LINCOLN LIBRARY AND MUSEUM. *Lincoln Herald 1977 79(2): 47-52.* On 4 June 1977 the Abraham Lincoln Library and Museum was officially opened on the campus of Lincoln Memorial University in Harrogate, Tennessee. The building contains one of the world's most spectacular collections of Lincolniana, including rare books, furniture, and works of art. The opening of this library and museum was an opportunity for the university to rededicate the spirit and purpose of its founders. 7 photos.　　　　　　　　　　T. P. Linkfield

581. Suppiger, Joseph E. PRIVATE LINCOLN AND THE SPY BATTALION. *Lincoln Herald 1978 80(1): 46-49.* After serving for a month as a captain in the Illinois militia during the Black Hawk War of 1832, Abraham Lincoln volunteered for three successive tours of duty in an outfit known as the "Spy Battalion." This elitist and very irregular group of "Independent Rangers" was supposed to gather information for the regular army concerning the Indians' movements in Illinois and Wisconsin. Lincoln was unemployed at the time and enjoyed serving as a "spy," although apparently he never fired his musket at an Indian. He served from 29 May to 10 July 1832.　　　　　　T. P. Linkfield

582. Taylor, John M. ASSASSIN ON TRIAL. *Am. Heritage 1981 32(4): 30-39.* Discusses the trial of Charles Guiteau, the assassin of President James A. Garfield, a trial in which the defense claimed insanity. The national atmosphere and the case presented by the prosecution combined to produce a guilty verdict. At his execution, Guiteau convinced some of the legitimacy of his insanity plea. 10 illus.　　　　J. F. Paul

583. Taylor, John M. "WITH MORE SORROW THAN I CAN TELL": A FUTURE PRESIDENT TURNED ON HIS COMMANDER. *Civil War Times Illus. 1981 20(1): 20-29.* Explores the deteriorating relationship between James A. Garfield and his commander Major General William S. Rosecrans over the latter's delay in engaging southern troops, a delay which led to crushing defeat for the Union at Chickamauga Creek, Tennessee, in 1863, and to Rosecrans' ouster from his post, and set the stage for hostile relations between Rosecrans and Garfield from then on.

584. Temple, Wayne C. LINCOLN'S JOINT RESOLUTIONS. *Lincoln Herald 1981 84[i.e., 83](2): 641-645.* Discusses President-elect Abraham Lincoln's "Joint Resolution on Federal Relations," drafted in Springfield before Lincoln went to Washington, D.C. and passed by the Illinois General Assembly in February 1861.

585. Temple, Wayne C. TINSMITH TO THE LATE MR. LINCOLN: SAMUEL S. ELDER. *J. of the Illinois State Hist. Soc. 1978 71(3): 176-184.* Authenticates several tools as the ones used by craftsman Samuel S. Elder on 4 May 1865 to seal Abraham Lincoln's coffin for burial in Springfield, Illinois. Until now, the tools—knife, solder, and soldering irons—had been held by National Park Service officials at the museum at Ford's Theatre, Washington, D.C. The author's research was begun at their suggestion. The author bases his claims on reminiscences of the Lincoln funeral services, public records, and Springfield sources on the Elder family. Traces the tools from Elder's hands to Washington. 4 illus., map, 44 notes.　　　　　　　　　　　　　　J/S

586. Temple, Wayne C. TWO MORE DAYS IN THE LIFE OF A. LINCOLN. *Lincoln Herald 1978 80(4): 159-161.* Although scholars know Abraham Lincoln's exact whereabouts for most of his life, brief periods of time are still missing, such as late 1835 and early 1836. Archer G. Herndon's merchandising record for his store in Springfield, Illinois, fills the gap for two days during these periods. On Monday, 7 December

1835, while traveling to the State Legislature at Vandalia, Lincoln purchased an item on account at Herndon's store. On 21 January 1836, on the return trip from Vandalia, Lincoln paid for the item. Herndon's account book is kept at the Illinois State Archives. Photo, 13 notes.
　　　　　　　　　　　　　　T. P. Linkfield

587. Temple, Wayne C. U.S. GRANT IN MILITARY SERVICE FOR THE STATE OF ILLINOIS. *Lincoln Herald 1981 83(3): 705-708.* Discusses Ulysses S. Grant's military service for the state of Illinois in the capacity of acting military aide to the governor, and later as colonel of the 21st Infantry Regiment, Illinois State Militia during April-July 1861.

588. Theodore, Terry C. THE CIVIL WAR ON THE NEW YORK STAGE FROM 1861-1900. *Lincoln Herald 1972 74(1): 34-40.* Discusses dramatic treatment as it reflected public opinion toward contemporary leaders such as Major Robert Anderson, U. S. Grant, and Stonewall Jackson, and (occasionally) Abraham Lincoln, Robert E. Lee, and Jefferson Davis. 16 notes.　　　　　　A. C. Aimone

589. Thweatt, John H. THE JAMES K. POLK PAPERS. *Tennessee Hist. Q. 1974 33(1): 93-98.* A collection of papers from the James K. Polk home in Columbia, Tennessee, has been recently deposited in the Tennessee State Library and Archives. It consists of about 800 items covering 1825-49, and provides information on presidential appointments, Polk's cotton plantations in Mississippi, slavery, White House dinners, and other matters involving the President.　　M. B. Lucas

590. Tilly, Bette B. THE JACKSON-DINSMOOR FEUD: A PARADOX IN A MINOR KEY. *J. of Mississippi Hist. 1977 39(2): 117-131.* Describes an 1811-12 quarrel between Andrew Jackson and Silas Dinsmoor, the Choctaw Indian agent who, in the Mississippi Territory along the Natchez Trace, had begun strictly enforcing an 1802 federal law which required passports of US citizens traveling through Indian territory. Jackson's protests may have been partly responsible for the replacement of Dinsmoor in 1814. The quarrel was publicized by anti-Jackson forces in the presidential campaign of 1828 but was not effective propaganda. 18 notes.　　　　　　　　J. W. Hillje

591. Treadway, William E. THE ESTATE OF ABRAHAM LINCOLN. *Lincoln Herald 1974 76(1): 7-11.* Lincoln's estate was executed by his friend David Davis. Although Lincoln died without a will, Justice Davis ably invested the inheritance for Mary Todd Lincoln and her sons Robert Todd and Thomas. Robert Lincoln inherited collectively $138,675 from his father, mother, and brother. Based on probate files in the Illinois State Historical Library; photo, notes.　　　　　　A. C. Aimone

592. Tucker, Glenn. LINCOLN'S JESSE W. WEIK. *Lincoln Herald 1975 77(1): 3-15, (2): 72-86.* Part I. Jesse W. Weik wrote and did considerable research for William H. Herndon's *The History and Personal Recollections of Abraham Lincoln as Originally Written by William H. Herndon and Jesse W. Weik* (1889). Primary and secondary works; photo, 23 notes. Part II. Weik, the writer in the William Herndon-Jesse Weik collaboration, also collected and preserved many stories and recollections of Lincoln. Many of the stories, herein recounted, appeared in other publications by Weik. 2 illus., 22 notes.　　B. J. LaBue

593. Tucker, Glenn. WAS LINCOLN A CONVERTED CHRISTIAN? *Lincoln Herald 1976 78(3): 102-108.* Speculates on the veracity of a claim made by Methodist Church minister James F. Jacquess that in 1847 he was responsible for the conversion to Christianity of Abraham Lincoln in Springfield, Illinois.

594. Turner, Thomas R. DID WEICHMANN TURN STATE'S EVIDENCE TO SAVE HIMSELF?: A CRITIQUE OF A TRUE HISTORY OF THE ASSASSINATION OF ABRAHAM LINCOLN. *Lincoln Herald 1979 81(4): 265-267.* Review of Floyd Risvold, ed., *A True History of the Assassination of Abraham Lincoln and the Conspiracy of 1865* by Louis J. Weichmann (New York: Knopf, 1975), a manuscript by one of the witnesses at the Lincoln assassins' trial.

595. Turner, Thomas R. PUBLIC OPINION AND THE ASSASSINATION OF ABRAHAM LINCOLN. *Lincoln Herald 1976 78(1): 17-24, (2): 66-76.* Part I. Many modern writers discussing the Lincoln

assassination have tried to develop a theory of a conspiracy among Northern leaders and have ignored the reactions of contemporaries who felt Secretary of War Edwin M. Stanton handled the post-assassination crises adequately. The "sensational dime press" and the clergy both contributed to stirring up public opinion against the South. Many of the supposedly suppressed facets of the assassination and subsequent investigations appeared in the press. Primary and secondary sources; 32 notes. Part II. The historians' sympathy for those conspiring to assassinate Abraham Lincoln was not shared by contemporaries. Five members of the military commission signed a clemency plea in the case of Mrs. Mary E. Surratt but Judge Holt withheld this information from President Andrew Johnson when he signed the sentence. It is doubtful that Johnson would have acted differently had he known about the plea. Public opinion favored the sentence. During the civil trial of John Surratt public opinion shifted from belief in his guilt to confusion and doubt after the defense made its case. Primary and secondary sources; 83 notes.   B. J. LaBue

596. Turner, William E.   HAYES ALBUM: FOURTEEN PANELS DEPICTING SCENES FROM THE LIFE OF PRESIDENT HAYES. *Hayes Hist. J. 1976 1(1): 45-59.* Explains the personal life and presidency of Rutherford B. Hayes (1822-93) through reproductions of William E. Turner's 14 mural-size illustrations of selected incidents in Hayes' life. Commissioned in January 1971 by the Rutherford B. Hayes Library, these illustrations include Hayes' law studies and wedding; the defense of Rosetta Amstead, a slave; military service during the Civil War; the Spiegel Grove residence; the 1877 presidential inauguration; his silver wedding anniversary; the invention of the telephone and the phonograph; presidential receptions for American Indians, and the ambassador from China; and the great western tour (1880).   J. N. Friedel

597. Unsigned.   WILLIAM HENRY HARRISON: FIRST GOVERNOR OF INDIANA TERRITORY. *Indiana Hist. Bull. 1973 50(2): 15-19.* William Henry Harrison (1773-1841) studied medicine but later turned to the Army, where his tutor was Anthony Wayne. Harrison became secretary of the Northwest Territory in 1798 and governor of the new Indiana Territory in 1800. When he was Indian Commissioner, his land policy gained him the opposition of Tecumseh, whom he defeated in battle in 1811. During the War of 1812, Harrison commanded the Northwestern Army. He served in both houses of Congress and became president in 1841, but died after one month in office. 4 illus.
J. F. Paul

598. Waksmundski, John.   GOVERNOR MC KINLEY AND THE WORKING MAN. *Historian 1976 38(4): 629-647.* Unlike earlier Republican Party leaders, Ohio governor William McKinley (1843-1901) sought to align himself and his party with the working class. Elected in 1891, McKinley asked the legislature to enact laws on railroad worker safety, right of employees to join labor organizations, and arbitration. McKinley was reelected in 1893 with improved Republican vote totals in counties with a substantial worker voting bloc. McKinley's careful actions dealing with striking coal miners during the 1893 depression enabled him to keep labor support. Notes.   M. J. Wentworth

599. Wert, Jeffry D.   OLD HICKORY AND THE SEMINOLES. *Am. Hist. Illus. 1980 15(6): 28-35.* Without official US approval, Andrew Jackson invaded and captured Spanish Florida in 1818, defeating the Seminole Indians and angering Great Britain and Spain.

600. West, Richard Samuel.   THE KENYON EXPERIENCE OF R. B. HAYES. *Hayes Hist. J. 1978 2(1): 6-13.* Summarizes Rutherford B. Hayes's student experiences at Kenyon College (1838-42), in Gambier, Ohio. Hayes's college years transformed a boy, apathetic to higher education, into a mature young man, strongly committed to obtaining the benefits of a sound college program. Examines the Kenyon curriculum and the qualifications of its staff, Hayes' participation in extracurricular as well as academic events and groups, and his relationship with classmates and faculty. Primary sources; 7 illus., 13 notes.
J. N. Friedel

601. Westwood, Howard C.   THE SINGING WIRE CONSPIRACY: MANIPULATION OF MEN AND MESSAGES FOR PEACE. *Civil War Times Illus. 1980 19(8): 30-35.* By controlling the telegraph system at his headquarters, General Ulysses S. Grant (1822-85) influenced, for his own purposes, the Hampton Roads Peace Conference in Virginia in February 1865.   D. P. Jordan

602. Wilson, Robert E.   OLD TIPPECANOE IN BOGOTÁ. *Foreign Service J. 1978 55(1): 12-13, 30.* William Henry Harrison, minister plenipotentiary and envoy extraordinary to Gran Colombia, 1829-30, was asked to leave the country by the Colombian government because of his fraternization with rebels, foreknowledge of an attempted insurrection, generally insurrectionary sentiments, and an insulting letter written to General Santander.

603. Wolf, George D.   LINCOLN, THE MASTER POLITICIAN. *Lincoln Herald 1979 81(3): 163-168.* Describes Abraham Lincoln's political career from his defeat as a candidate for the Illinois state legislature in 1832, until his death in 1865 while President.

604. Zinsmeister, Robert, Jr.   THE PIGEON CREEK BAPTIST CHURCH. *Lincoln Herald 1978 80(4): 161-163.* The Pigeon Creek (Indiana) Baptist Church helped shape Abraham Lincoln's character during his formative years. Thomas Lincoln and his son Abraham helped build the church in 1822. Abraham Lincoln never joined the Pigeon Creek Baptist Church, but there is evidence that he was its janitor. The church, a simple log structure, was razed about 1880. Photo.

T. P. Linkfield

605. —.   "THE COMING RUDE STORMS" OF LINCOLN WRITINGS: WILLIAM H. HERNDON AND THE LINCOLN LEGEND. *J. of the Illinois State Hist. Soc. 1978 71(1): 66-70.* A letter by former Illinois Governor Richard J. Oglesby to Herndon compliments him on his December 1865 "Analysis of the Character of Abraham Lincoln." In 1873 Herndon attacked the popular 1870's belief that Lincoln was a Christian. 2 illus., 13 notes.   J

606. —.   "EVERYBODY LIKES TO SHAKE HANDS WITH HIM": LETTERS OF ELBRIDGE ATWOOD. *J. of the Illinois State Hist. Soc. 1979 72(2): 139-142.* Three letters of Elbridge Atwood, a Springfield resident, describe the generally favorable attitude toward Abraham Lincoln in 1860 and at the time of Lincoln's funeral. Illus., 5 notes.   E. P. Stickney

607. —.   A LINCOLN PRESIDENTIAL LIBRARY ISSUE: COLONEL HARLAND SANDERS CENTER FOR LINCOLN STUDIES. *Lincoln Herald 1973 75(2): 43, 44-48, 50-67, 75-76.*
Sanders, Harland and Sanders, Claudia.   WHY WE BELIEVE IN THE NEED FOR A CENTER OF LINCOLN STUDIES AT THE LINCOLN MEMORIAL UNIVERSITY, pp. 43-44.
McMurtry, R. Gerald.   A BRIEF HISTORY OF A GREAT LINCOLN COLLECTION, pp. 45-46.   Discusses the Lincoln Memorial University library's contributors and provides anecdotes about collecting.
Newman, Ralph G.   THE IMPORTANCE TO ALL AMERICANS OF A CENTER FOR LINCOLN STUDIES, pp. 47-48.   Emphasizes Lincoln scholars of the past.
Petz, Weldon.   SOME VIEWS ON THE LINCOLN AND CIVIL WAR COLLECTION OF THE LINCOLN MEMORIAL UNIVERSITY, pp. 50-52.
Hamilton, Holman.   LINCOLN MEMORIAL UNIVERSITY AND THE LINCOLN COLLECTION, pp. 53-54.
Temple, Wayne C.   THE IMPORTANCE OF THE LINCOLN COLLECTION AT LINCOLN MEMORIAL UNIVERSITY, pp. 55, 76.   Appeals for an Abraham Lincoln presidential library and describes the university's holdings.
Watson, Stuart L.   LINCOLN LIVES IN APPALACHIA, pp. 56-57, 76.   Describes Lincoln Memorial University in Harrogate, Tennessee. Illus.
McClelland, Stewart W.   THE URGENCY OF PRESERVING AND USING THE VAST LINCOLN ERA COLLECTION AT THE LINCOLN MEMORIAL UNIVERSITY, p. 58.
Rankin, Frank C.   THE LINCOLN COLLECTION: A HALLOWED WELLSPRING OF HISTORY, p. 59.
Suppiger, Joseph E.   SOME NEW AND EXCITING USES FOR THE LINCOLN COLLECTION OF THE LINCOLN MEMORIAL UNIVERSITY, pp. 60-61.
Wolfe, Richard J.   A VISIT WITH THE LINCOLN COLLECTION OF THE LINCOLN MEMORIAL UNIVERSITY, JUNE 1973, p. 62.

Watson, Stuart L.   ENLARGED OPPORTUNITIES FOR LINCOLN STUDIES, p. 63.

Williams, Frank J.   THE LINCOLN ERA COLLECTION OF THE LINCOLN MEMORIAL UNIVERSITY: AN OASIS FOR RESEARCHERS AND WRITERS, pp. 64, 75.

Welch, Frank W.   LINCOLN AND CURRENT AMERICAN HIGHER EDUCATION, pp. 65, 75.

Murray, Crosby.   MY VIEWS OF THE LINCOLN COLLECTION OF THE LINCOLN MEMORIAL UNIVERSITY, pp. 66-67.

A. C. Aimone and S

608.   —.   LINCOLNIANA.   *J. of the Illinois State Hist. Soc. 1975 68(4): 368-369.* Reproduction of a plat and ledger including documentation of land lot purchase and sale in Springfield, Illinois, by Abraham Lincoln 1837-53. Plat and ledger reproduced from originals in Elijah Iles Papers in Illinois State Historical Library.   N. Lederer

609.   —.   LINCOLNIANA.   *J. of the Illinois State Hist. Soc. 1979 72(1): 70-71.* Announcement of a gift of Lincoln family memorabilia by Robert Todd Lincoln Beckwith to the Illinois State Historical Library. Beckwith, the only surviving direct descendant of President Abraham Lincoln, has included in the donation subject files compiled by Robert Todd Lincoln, and books, artworks, and personal effects. This series of materials is the largest single private collection known. 5 photos.   V. L. Human

610.   —.   [ULYSSES S. GRANT VISITS JAPAN, 1879].   *Am. Hist. Illus. 1981 16(3): 36-45.*
Finn, Dallas.   GRANT IN JAPAN,   *pp. 36-37, 40-45.*
Grant, Julia Dent.   MRS. GRANT REMEMBERS JAPAN, *pp. 38-39.*
Accounts of General Ulysses S. Grant and Mrs. Grant's 1879 trip to Japan for both private and official reasons after Grant had served two terms as president.

Presidential Campaigns

611.   Ambacher, Bruce.   GEORGE M. DALLAS, CUBA, AND THE ELECTION OF 1856.   *Pennsylvania Mag. of Hist. and Biog. 1973 97(3): 318-332.* By appointing George M. Dallas the American Minister to Great Britain, President Franklin Pierce silenced an influential critic of the administration's Cuban policy. Pierce's action also had the effect of removing Dallas, a potential presidential contender, from competing against him in his unsuccessful quest for the Democratic nomination in 1856. Primary and secondary sources; 47 notes.   E. W. Carp

612.   Baetzhold, Howard G.   MARK TWAIN STUMPS FOR HAYES.   *Hayes Hist. J. 1976 1(2): 111-114.* Impressed by Rutherford B. Hayes's campaign promise to reform the civil service system, and to serve only one term as President, Mark Twain was persuaded by William Dean Howells, the editor of the *Atlantic Monthly,* to give a speech in support of the Republican Party's presidential candidate of 1876. This speech, as it appeared in the *New York Times,* 2 October 1876, is reprinted in its entirety. Although Twain's enthusiasm for Hayes cooled with the passage of time, in 1876 he was one of his staunchest supporters. Primary and secondary sources; photo, 7 notes.   J. N. Friedel

613.   Baum, Dale.   "NOISY BUT NOT NUMEROUS": THE REVOLT OF THE MASSACHUSETTS MUGWUMPS.   *Historian 1979 41(2): 241-256.* In a pioneering electoral study, Lee Benson challenged the accepted notion that the Mugwumps influenced enough Republican votes toward Cleveland to defeat Blaine; instead he suggested that the decline of Republican votes in Massachusetts from 1880-84 was best explained by support for Benjamin F. Butler. Reexamines this hypothesis through a more detailed analysis of Massachusetts voting returns by ecological regression. Argues that Butler failed to attract Republican votes, and that apathy was more important in the decline of Republican fortunes. Exaggerated importance given to restore political factions plus unsophisticated procedures for estimating voting patterns from aggregate statistics have combined "to give the celebrated bolt of the Mugwumps an importance out of proportion to their raw numerical strength, not only in the 1880's but also later in accounts of the period by many historians." Primary and secondary sources; 9 tables, 29 notes.   R. S. Sliwoski

614.   Belohlavek, John M.   THE DEMOCRACY IN A DILEMMA: GEORGE M. DALLAS, PENNSYLVANIA, AND THE ELECTION OF 1844.   *Pennsylvania Hist. 1974 41(4): 391-411.* Discusses the events leading to the Democratic nomination of former Senator George M. Dallas for the vice-presidency in 1844 and the role Dallas played in formulating party strategy during the campaign. Based on the Polk and Dallas papers; illus., 26 notes.   D. C. Swift

615.   Benedict, Michael Les.   SOUTHERN DEMOCRATS IN THE CRISIS OF 1876-1877: A RECONSIDERATION OF REUNION AND REACTION.   *J. of Southern Hist. 1980 46(4): 489-524.* C. Vann Woodward's thesis that Reconstruction represented an effort by northern capitalists to secure their interests against a revived agrarianism has remained strongly embedded in the textbooks and synthesis works despite general agreement that racial rather than economic issues determined the course of Reconstruction. An analysis of the House votes on the proposed filibuster of late February 1877 reveals that both northern and southern Democrats defected from the Democratic ranks. Thus, fear of violence rather than any economic bargaining played the major role in the events of 1877. Based on personal manuscripts of congressmen and newspapers; 2 tables, 93 notes, 2 appendixes.   T. D. Schoonover

616.   Bennett, W. Lance and Haltom, William.   ISSUES, VOTER CHOICE, AND CRITICAL ELECTIONS.   *Social Sci. Hist. 1980 4(4): 379-418.* Analyzes the McKinley-Bryan presidential election of 1896 to test a number of current theories of voting behavior. Emphasizes the format and rhetoric of campaigns rather than issues or sociocultural appeal. William McKinley was more successful than William Jennings Bryan in his appeal to individual interests, in the openness and breadth of his rhetoric, and in appearing less partisan and divisive. This suggests some modification of "critical election" theory, especially for ethnocultural and issue-centered advocates. Based on newspapers and secondary sources; notes, biblio.   L. K. Blaser

617.   Blue, Frederick J.   CHASE AND THE GOVERNORSHIP: A STEPPING STONE TO THE PRESIDENCY.   *Ohio Hist. 1981 90(3): 197-220.* Discusses the career of Salmon P. Chase during 1850-73, particularly his election as governor of Ohio in 1855 and his unrelenting bid to capture the Republican nomination for the presidency. As Ohio's governor, Chase managed to maintain a national prominence by subordinating state issues to national ones. Although he was a leader in the formation of the antislavery party, he ultimately failed to secure the presidential nomination because his stands on sectional issues, his obvious personal ambition, his past partisan record, and his inability to establish a smoothly functioning political machine alienated the moderates and conservatives within the Republican Party. Based on the Salmon P. Chase Papers at the Library of Congress, the Ohio Historical Society and the Historical Society of Pennsylvania, various archival collections of Harvard University and the Massachusetts Historical Society; photo, 74 notes.   L. A. Russell

618.   Bohmer, David A.   STABILITY AND CHANGE IN EARLY NATIONAL POLITICS: THE MARYLAND VOTER AND THE ELECTION OF 1800.   *William and Mary Q. 1979 36(1): 27-50.* Contends, from examination of electoral and population data from all of Maryland's counties for the presidential election of 1800, that there was no substantial realignment. Nor was there any significant increase in voter participation. Voting patterns were similar in elections during 1796-1816. Most persons, however, who switched their voting preference in 1800 from that of the off-year election in 1798 voted for Jefferson. Evaluates ethnic voting patterns. Federalist strength still remained in Maryland after the election of 1800. Consults poll lists and federal and local records; 39 notes.   H. M. Ward

619.   Boritt, G. S.   WAS LINCOLN A VULNERABLE CANDIDATE IN 1860?   *Civil War Hist. 1981 27(1): 32-48.* Suggests that if Abraham Lincoln's "Honest Abe" image had been tarnished by the revelation of his activities as a corporation lawyer for the Illinois Central Railroad, a bank and a bond scheme, it might have swayed enough voters for him to lose the presidential election in 1860. Based on correspondence, newspapers, and secondary sources; table, 44 notes.   G. R. Schroeder

620. Brescia, Anthony M. THE ELECTION OF 1828: A VIEW FROM LOUISVILLE. *Register of the Kentucky Hist. Soc. 1976 74(1): 51-57.* Warden Pope (1772-1838) of Louisville, a lawyer, a friend of Jackson, and a foe of Clay, wrote a lengthy letter to a Congressman (later governor) Charles A. Wickliffe (1788-1868). In the letter Pope expressed his concern over the upcoming presidential election. Based on primary and secondary sources; 15 notes.   J. F. Paul

621. Briceland, Alan V. THE PHILADELPHIA AURORA, THE NEW ENGLAND ILLUMINATI, AND THE ELECTION OF 1800. *Pennsylvania Mag. of Hist. and Biog. 1976 100(1): 3-36.* During the election of 1800, Thomas Jefferson and the Republicans were accused by the high Federalist clergy of being agents of the Order of Illuminati, a European anti-Christian sect which through control of the societies of Freemasonry was blamed for overthrowing Church and state in revolutionary France. Writing in the *Aurora*, 1798-1800, Episcopal clergyman John C. Ogden (d. 1800) helped counteract this Federalist propaganda by portraying New England, the birthplace and main support of Jefferson's opponent, John Adams, as dominated by an intolerant clerical-political aristocracy. Turning the tables on the Federalist clergy, Ogden began in 1799 to freely refer to to the Federalist clergy as the New England Illuminati, imputing to their antimasonry a desire to destroy religious liberty in America. Thus, in the minds of the *Aurora* readers Jefferson was associated with freedom of religion while Adams was tarred with the brush of religious bigotry. Based on primary and secondary sources; 117 notes.   E. W. Carp

622. Brumgardt, John R. "OVERWHELMINGLY FOR 'OLD ABE' ": SHERMAN'S SOLDIERS AND THE ELECTION OF 1864. *Lincoln Herald 1976 78(4): 153-159.* War weariness seemed to spell the end of Republican hegemony in the presidential election of 1864, but propaganda alleging that peace would bring disunion, and heavy support from troops under General William Tecumseh Sherman, helped Abraham Lincoln win.

623. Cochran, William C. "DEAR MOTHER: ..." AN EYEWITNESS REPORT ON THE REPUBLICAN NATIONAL CONVENTION OF 1876. *Hayes Hist. J. 1976 1(2): 88-97.* Presents an eyewitness account of the Republican Party Convention of 1876, in Cincinnati, and traces how James G. Blaine, initially the most widely supported candidate, lost the nomination to Rutherford B. Hayes of Ohio. The role of the press, rumors about the candidates, and the attempt of Blaine supporters to force a vote for President and Vice-President, are highlighted as deciding factors in the nomination of Hayes. Primary source; 4 illus.
                    J. N. Friedel

624. Collins, Bruce W. THE DEMOCRATS' ELECTORAL FORTUNES DURING THE LECOMPTON CRISIS. *Civil War Hist. 1978 24(4): 314-331.* President James Buchanan exasperated and soured northern Democrats by his pro-slavery actions, but he did not destroy party popular support. Stephen A. Douglas fought for the 1860 presidential nomination because he believed that a less extreme prosouthern policy could keep a political coalition and assure his electoral victory. All that he had to do was to isolate the southern extremists. Modern historians have misread congressional party strength and politics. Published primary and secondary sources; 55 notes.   R. E. Stack

625. Crouch, Barry A. AMOS A. LAWRENCE AND THE FORMATION OF THE CONSTITUTIONAL UNION PARTY: THE CONSERVATIVE FAILURE IN 1860. *Hist. J. of Massachusetts 1980 8(2): 46-58.* Examines the role of Amos A. Lawrence, a cotton manufacturer, in organizing the Constitutional Union Party in 1860, an attempt to save the union by offering a moderate presidential candidate. Despite Lawrence's efforts, John Crittenden did not become a national candidate for that office and the movement failed. Based on the papers, letters, and diaries of Amos A. Lawrence, and secondary sources; illus., 34 notes.
                    W. H. Mulligan, Jr.

626. Curry, Earl R. PENNSYLVANIA AND THE REPUBLICAN CONVENTION OF 1860: A CRITIQUE OF MC CLURE'S THESIS. *Pennsylvania Mag. of Hist. and Biog. 1973 97(2): 183-198.* In 1892 Whig politician and journalist Alexander K. McClure recorded that William H. Seward was prevented from securing the presidential nomination at the Republican National Convention of 1860 by the Pennsylvania delega-

tion's refusal to support him. Pennsylvania was recognized, and rightly so, as the Keystone State—an essential state to carry in any national election. According to McClure, Pennsylvania's leaders realized that if Seward was nominated, strong opposition from Pennsylvania's Know-Nothings spelled ultimate defeat for the national ticket. Contrary to McClure's thesis, however, the Know-Nothings were so weak in Pennsylvania by 1860 that Republican leaders did not even feel it necessary to consider their views. Republican leaders did not support Seward because they feared that his outspoken attacks on slavery would become the chief focus of the campaign, thereby obscuring the tariff issue—which topic the Republican leaders wanted to make the dominant campaign issue. Based on primary and secondary sources; 46 notes.   E. W. Carp

627. Daly, James J. WILLIAM JENNINGS BRYAN AND THE RED RIVER VALLEY PRESS, 1890-1896. *North Dakota Hist. 1975 42(1): 27-37.* The Republican newspapers saw Bryan as an anti-Christ, a fool, a danger to American freedoms, an anarchist, and a disloyal American. Before his nomination as Democratic Presidential candidate, Bryan was either ignored, treated neutrally, or slightly disparaged in the Red River Valley press; yet following his nomination, the free-wheeling and outspoken Republican editors vilified him. The few Democratic newspapers came to his defense but they were a fairly insignificant minority in a heavily Republican area. Based on primary newspaper research and secondary sources.   N. Lederer

628. Daniels, James D. AMOS KENDALL: KENTUCKY JOURNALIST, 1815-1829. *Filson Club Hist. Q. 1978 52(1): 46-65.* Narrates the early life and career of Jacksonian newspaper editor and politician Amos Kendall. After graduating from Dartmouth, Kendall moved to Kentucky and became a political ally of Henry Clay and editor of the Frankfort *Argus of Western America.* Despite his association with Clay, Kendall attacked the United States Bank as early as 1818 and supported debt relief in Kentucky after 1819. Kendall opposed the election of John Quincy Adams in 1824, and, after a break with Clay, initiated the "corrupt bargain" controversy that weakened Adams in the election of 1828. Kendall supported Andrew Jackson in 1828 and helped to carry Kentucky for him. Documented from Kendall's *Autobiography,* the Jackson Papers at the library of Congress, and the *Argus.* 45 notes.
                    G. B. McKinney

629. Edwards, Tom. THE PRESIDENTIAL CANDIDATE WHO DIDN'T GO WEST. *New-England Galaxy 1975 16(4): 37-42.* Chronicles Horace Greeley's participation in politics since 1860, focusing on his work in presidential elections and his eventual candidacy in 1872.

630. Ewing, Gretchen Garst. DUFF GREEN, INDEPENDENT EDITOR OF A PARTY PRESS. *Journalism Q. 1977 54(4): 733-739.* In 1826 Duff Green became an editor of the *United States Telegraph* of Washington, D.C., a widely read newspaper that strongly promoted Andrew Jackson and John C. Calhoun during the 1828 presidential campaign. Throughout the campaign Green maintained financial and editorial control over the *Telegraph* and took personal risks to expand the paper's circulation and, despite the opposition of other Jackson supporters, to endorse Calhoun. Green's editorials projected an attractive image of Jackson, but they also exemplify, in their criticism of Green's opponents, the personal and vitriolic style in partisan journalism of the time. Based on the Green editorials and on secondary sources; 30 notes.
                    R. P. Sindermann, Jr.

631. Ewing, Gretchen Garst. DUFF GREEN, JOHN C. CALHOUN, AND THE ELECTION OF 1828. *South Carolina Hist. Mag. 1978 79(2): 126-137.* Prior to the election of 1828, Duff Green, editor of the Washington *United States Telegraph,* a newspaper created primarily to encourage Andrew Jackson's bid for the Presidency, printed several editorials and favorable reports about the vice-presidential candidate, John C. Calhoun and, as many claimed, seemed more interested in the promotion of Calhoun's political career than Jackson's.

632. Fischer, Roger A. THE REPUBLICAN PRESIDENTIAL CAMPAIGNS OF 1856 AND 1860: ANALYSIS THROUGH ARTIFACTS. *Civil War Hist. 1981 27(2): 123-137.* Historians, arguing from various printed documents, have claimed that the 1856 Republican Party campaign (John C. Frémont, presidential candidate) was a single-issue, ideological campaign while Abraham Lincoln's in 1860 was a multi-

issue one and more personality-oriented. These descriptions are corroborated by the analysis of banners, buttons, and other artifacts from the two campaigns. Based on campaign artifacts and secondary sources; 37 notes.
G. R. Schroeder

633. Ford, Trowbridge H. THE POLITICAL CRUSADE AGAINST BLAINE IN 1884. *Mid-America 1975 57(1): 38-55.* James G. Blaine's defeat was a matter of neither ideology nor sociology, but of his unknowingly becoming a pawn in a plot by Edwin L. Godkin and A. V. Dicey to bring American pressure to bear on Great Britain to grant Ireland home rule. Included were important Englishmen and Irish Americans. But the Irish were divided, and Blaine failed to respond, and ultimately Godkin utilized the British and Irish press to achieve Grover Cleveland's narrow victory. Based on the Godkin Papers, Houghton Library, and secondary sources; 72 notes.
T. H. Wendel

634. Geary, James W. CLEMENT L. VALLANDIGHAM VIEWS THE CHARLESTON CONVENTION. *Ohio Hist. 1977 86(2): 127-134.* Reproduces a previously unpublished letter from Clement L. Vallandigham to Alexander H. Stephens discussing the Democratic National Convention of April 1860. Held in Charleston, South Carolina, this convention was organized to select a Presidential candidate and platform. However, the delegates were hopelessly split over the choice of Stephen A. Douglas and his popular sovereignty program throughout the convention, and many delegates, both northern and southern, left before the convention formally adjourned ten days after it began. Vallandigham, secretary to the Charleston Convention, wrote this letter after the convention had ended and it reveals an eye-witness view of the occasion. The letter is housed at Emory University. 2 illus., 25 notes.
J

635. Gienapp, William E. THE CRIME AGAINST SUMNER: THE CANING OF CHARLES SUMNER AND THE RISE OF THE RE-PUBLICAN PARTY. *Civil War Hist. 1979 25(3): 218-245.* South Carolina Democratic Congressman Preston S. Brooks's caning of Massachusetts Republican Senator Charles Sumner on the Senate floor on 22 May 1856, after Sumner had made scathing personal attacks on Brooks's relative, South Carolina Democratic Senator Andrew P. Butler, created even more support for the fledgling Republican Party than did the repeal of the Missouri Compromise and the troubles in the Kansas Territory. Describes the instant, rampant, and deep-seated indignation in the North, protest meetings, Republican themes, the destruction of Millard Fillmore's chances in the 1856 election, and John Frémont's good showing in that election. The caning caused such political and sectional animosity that it "was a major landmark on the road to civil war." 97 notes.
S

636. Gould, Lewis L. CHARLES WARREN FAIRBANKS AND THE REPUBLICAN NATIONAL CONVENTION OF 1900: A MEMOIR. *Indiana Mag. of Hist. 1981 77(4): 358-371.* Describes the unsuccessful political maneuvering involved in the attempt by Charles W. Fairbanks and Marcus Hanna to prevent the Republican vice presidential nomination from going to Theodore Roosevelt in 1900. Although many Republican leaders wanted Fairbanks, the pressure of New York Republican leaders to get Theodore Roosevelt out of New York and the unwillingness of President William MacKinley to openly express his preference for Fairbanks prevented the latter from receiving the nomination. 26 notes; 2 pictures, 2 cartoons.
A. Erlebacher

637. Hackett, Derek L. A. THE DAYS OF THIS REPUBLIC WILL BE NUMBERED: ABOLITION, SLAVERY, AND THE PRESIDENTIAL ELECTION OF 1836. *Louisiana Studies 1976 15(2): 131-160.* The presidential campaign of 1836 between Democratic candidate Martin Van Buren (1782-1862) and Whig candidate Hugh Lawson White (1773-1840) is significant because it marks the breakup of the dominant Democratic Party and inaugurates a national two-party system. In Louisiana, as an example, this situation came about for ideological reasons, especially the fear that a northerner such as Van Buren would be unable or unwilling to defend slavery. Newspapers in Louisiana during the campaign are filled with articles about fears of slave uprisings such as the "Murrell Conspiracy" of 1835 and attempts at abolition. Articles, letters to the editor, and editorials on these themes dominate in discussions of the election. Based on letters and papers in Louisiana State U. Library, Louisiana legislative records, Louisiana newspaper accounts, and secondary sources; table, 90 notes.
J. Buschen

638. Hackett, Derek L. A. "VOTE EARLY! BEWARE OF FRAUD!" A NOTE ON VOTER TURNOUT IN PRESIDENTIAL AND GUBERNATORIAL ELECTIONS IN LOUISIANA, 1828-1844. *Louisiana Studies 1975 14(2): 179-188.* Examines the estimates of voter eligibility and turnout in Louisiana during the Age of Jackson by Richard McCormick, Joseph Tregle, Perry Howard, and Emmett Asseff. Discovers wide differences in the estimates of these writers. Points out the errors in the studies, gives new estimates, and depicts avenues for future research. Primary sources and secondary sources; table, 28 notes.
B. A. Glasrud

639. Hanna, William F., III. ABRAHAM LINCOLN'S 1860 VISIT TO RHODE ISLAND. *Lincoln Herald 1979 81(3): 197-201.* Describes Abraham Lincoln's two visits to Rhode Island in 1860 in the months before the 1860 presidential election, and discusses the political climate in Rhode Island during 1860 when the state's Republicans were split between the conservatives and the moderates.

640. Hanna, William F., III. THIS SIDE OF THE MOUNTAINS: ABRAHAM LINCOLN'S 1848 VISIT TO MASSACHUSETTS. *Lincoln Herald 1978 80(2): 56-65.* In September 1848 Abraham Lincoln made a purely political trip to Massachusetts before heading home to Illinois. Promoting the presidential candidacy of Zachary Taylor, Lincoln made 12 speeches in 11 days. The tour was an attempt to unite a state Whig Party badly splintered by a "free soil" element. Lincoln became cognizant of how deeply troubled the North was over the slavery issue. Citizens of Massachusetts benefited from hearing a first-class, Western stump speaker at his best. Photo, 51 notes.
T. P. Linkfield

641. Hay, Robert P. THE AMERICAN REVOLUTION TWICE RECALLED: LAFAYETTE'S VISIT AND THE ELECTION OF 1824. *Indiana Mag. of Hist. 1973 69(1): 43-62.* Lafayette's visit to the United States, which started in 1824, became closely linked to the presidential election of that year. Americans desperately desired to return to Revolutionary days, and Lafayette represented a spiritual return to those days. Nostalgia dominated the campaign; homage to Lafayette was, in a sense, homage to the Revolutionary patriots. The rhetoric of presidential campaigners and of Lafayette was retrospective. Lafayette's visit and the election of 1824, won by John Quincy Adams (1767-1848), were interrelated chapters in the United States' quest for national self-awareness. 45 notes.
N. E. Tutorow

642. Hay, Robert P. THE PILLORYING OF ALBERT GALLATIN: THE PUBLIC RESPONSE TO HIS 1824 VICE-PRESIDENTIAL NOMINATION. *Western Pennsylvania Hist. Mag. 1982 65(3): 181-202.* Presents a brief background to the exemplary political career of the Jeffersonian Republican Albert Gallatin, tails his humiliating experience as the vice-presidential nominee in 1824 on the ticket with William H. Crawford; Gallatin faced public protest and ridicule after tirelessly serving his adopted country for nearly 40 years, resulting in his withdrawal from the race.

643. Hinckley, Ted C. THE POLITICS OF SINOPHOBIA: GARFIELD, THE MOREY LETTER, AND THE PRESIDENTIAL ELECTION OF 1880. *Ohio Hist. 1980 89(4): 381-399.* Presidential elections of the late 19th century often provided a necessary outlet to public tensions and articulated public issues that would influence subsequent legislation; the presidential struggle of 1880 provides an example that magnified Americans' anti-Chinese labor feelings with the controversy over the "Morey Letter." James A. Garfield's purported letter to H. L. Morey, first published in New York City's *Truth* and endorsed as genuine by Democratic leaders Abram S. Hewitt and William H. Barnum, threatened to anathematize the Republican candidate to western voters already panicked by the negotiation of the Burlingame Treaty, increased Chinese immigration, and the 1870's business depression. Although proven to be a forgery, the letter revealed the Chinese labor question to be a volatile issue in the voters' minds and accelerated the passage of the 1882 Chinese Exclusion Act. Based on the papers of James A. Garfield, Ohio Historical Society Archives, the collections of the Rutherford B. Hayes Memorial Library, and other primary sources. 2 illus., 50 notes.
L. A. Russell

644. Holzer, Harold. AN ALL-PURPOSE CAMPAIGN POSTER. *Lincoln Herald 1982 84(1): 42-45.* Discusses the three political posters

rendered by the lithography firm of H. H. Lloyd & Company of lower Manhattan, New York City, for the 1860 campaign: the pro-Lincoln "National Republican Chart," the "Political Chart" that portrayed a number of political candidates of different political persuasions, and the "National Political Chart" issued after Lincoln's victory.

645. Holzer, Harold. HOW AMERICA MET MR. LINCOLN: ENGRAVINGS AND LITHOGRAPHS FROM THE FIRST LINCOLN CAMPAIGN. *Nineteenth Cent. 1980 6(1): 52-57.* Describes the cheap portraits of Abraham Lincoln produced after he won the Republican presidential nomination in 1860.

646. Holzer, Harold. THE IMAGEMAKERS: PORTRAITS OF LINCOLN IN THE 1860 CAMPAIGN. *Chicago Hist. 1978-79 7(4): 198-207.* In need of an image improvement because of his 'homely' countenance, Abraham Lincoln posed for a portrait by Chicago photographer Samuel M. Fassett which was in turn made into a popularly distributed lithograph by Chicago artist Edward Mendel and used during the 1860 presidential campaign.

647. Horowitz, Murray M. BENJAMIN F. BUTLER: SEVENTEENTH PRESIDENT? *Lincoln Herald 1975 77(4): 191-203.* In 1885 Benjamin F. Butler wrote an article for the October issue of *North American Review* claiming he had refused an offer to run as President Lincoln's second-term Vice-President. Louis Taylor Merill in the March 1947 issue of *Mississippi Valley Historical Review* assessed the evidence and concluded that the story was essentially true. This author does not accept the Merill thesis. In early 1864 Lincoln's reelection was not guaranteed. Butler was a viable dark horse candidate for the presidential nomination. The offer was made by Simon Cameron during a meeting at Fort Monroe in March 1864. There is evidence that the meeting was requested by Butler. Cameron's letter to Lincoln after the meeting only mentions the conversation in the concluding sentence, not the expected action of an emissary on such an important mission. The lack of contemporary evidence to the contrary forces the conclusion that Butler made up the story. Based on primary and secondary sources; illus., 41 notes.

B. J. LaBue

648. Horowitz, Murray M. "THE MOST QUIET ELECTION": BEN BUTLER COMES TO NEW YORK. *Lincoln Herald 1973 75(4): 148-151.* November 8, 1864 was a crucial election day. Major General Benjamin Franklin Butler was dispatched to New York City to curb fraud at the polls in the Democrat stronghold. Butler insured order in the city with his troops so the election would be neither disrupted nor stolen. He accomplished his mission and the Empire State was safeguarded for President Abraham Lincoln. Based on Butler's *Private and Official Correspondence* and the Stanton papers in the Library of Congress; 6 notes.

A. C. Aimone

649. Horowitz, Robert F. JAMES M. ASHLEY AND THE PRESIDENTIAL ELECTION OF 1856. *Ohio Hist. 1974 83(1): 4-16.* James M. Ashley aimed to create a national machine favoring Salmon P. Chase's candidacy. Though Chase established a power base by becoming governor, his Free Soil/Know-Nothing ties made him unelectable. Ashley played a major role in bringing about a national convention with a party platform in line with Chase's views. Primary and secondary sources; 2 illus., 74 notes.

S. S. Sprague

650. Howe, John. POLITICS IN THE EARLY REPUBLIC AND THE ELECTION OF 1800. *Rev. in Am. Hist. 1975 3(3): 316-321.* Provides a review essay of Daniel Sisson's *The American Revolution of 1800* (New York: Knopf, 1974), which evaluates the book's contributions to understanding the development of early American politics, and which analyzes the book's merit as an examination of political ideology.

651. Howland, Glenn C. ORGANIZE! ORGANIZE! THE LINCOLN WIDE-AWAKES IN VERMONT. *Vermont Hist. 1980 48(1): 28-32.* Republicans supported Abraham Lincoln and Hannibal Hamlin in 1860 with local paramilitary Wide-Awake clubs, organized by young men, with bands, uniforms, parades, flag raisings, torches, lanterns and banners, in massive numbers, and financially supported by businessmen. The Chittenden County Wide-Awakes marched in Burlington early in September, climaxed by a steamboat excursion to a Plattsburgh rally. At their Chester rally in June, a Seward delegate to the Chicago Convention

explained the early Vermont switch to Lincoln. The clubs helped build the enthusiastic solidarity of the large Vermont Republican majority that year. 15 notes referring to family letters and a newspaper.

T. D. S. Bassett

652. James, Edward T. BEN BUTLER RUNS FOR PRESIDENT: LABOR, GREENBACKERS, AND ANTI-MONOPOLISTS IN THE ELECTION OF 1884. *Essex Inst. Hist. Collections 1977 113(2): 65-88.* Before the 1954 accession by the Library of Congress of Benjamin F. Butler's (1818-1893) papers, scholars inadequately understood his campaign as a third-party presidential candidate in 1884. Even with support from the Anti-Monopoly Convention, Greenbackers, and labor, Butler's People's Party failed to stop Grover Cleveland's nomination at the Democratic convention and subsequent election. Discusses causes for failure, chiefly the Republican subsidy. Based on the Butler Papers, primary and secondary sources; 3 illus., photo, 78 notes.

R. S. Sliwoski

653. Kremm, Thomas W. CLEVELAND AND THE FIRST LINCOLN ELECTION: THE ETHNIC RESPONSE TO NATIVISM. *J. of Interdisciplinary Hist. 1977 8(1): 69-86.* Politics in Cleveland, Ohio, on the eve of the Civil War did not revolve exclusively around the question of slavery extension. Accepted theories on the election do not adequately explain ethnic voting patterns in the city. The major division within the electorate was one of Catholics versus non-Catholics. The Republican Party was as much an anti-Catholic coalition as it was an anti-slavery extension organization and non-Catholic voters, ethnic and native-American, voted accordingly. Newspapers and printed sources; 8 tables, 19 notes.

R. Howell

654. Lander, Byron G. MISSOURI AND THE PRESIDENTIAL ELECTION OF 1828. *Missouri Hist. Rev. 1977 71(4): 419-435.* The presidential election in Missouri has been viewed as a contest between the supporters of democracy and aristocracy. An examination of party organization, supporters, issues and personal attacks shows that such a clear distinction did not exist. Andrew Jackson and John Quincy Adams did not differ on basic policies, and so their supporters concentrated on making personal attacks on the opponent candidate. The voters must have known no great issues were at stake, because more than 40 percent of them did not bother to vote. Primary and secondary sources; illus., 71 notes.

W. F. Zornow

655. Leff, Michael C. and Mohrmann, G. P. LINCOLN AT COOPER UNION: A RHETORICAL ANALYSIS OF THE TEXT. *Q. J. of Speech 1974 60(3): 346-358.* "Seeking the presidential nomination, Lincoln attempts to ingratiate himself with a Republican audience, and after an extensive attack upon Douglas, he creates a mock debate with the South and appeals for Republican unity. Each section features controlled argument, builds in intensity, and rests upon an association between Republican and the founding fathers, Lincoln using arrangement, argument, and style to associate self and party with the fathers and to dissociate self and party from his chief rivals."

J

656. Leitman, Spencer L. THE REVIVAL OF AN IMAGE: GRANT AND THE 1880 REPUBLICAN NOMINATING CAMPAIGN. *Missouri Hist. Soc. Bull. 1974 30(3): 196-204.* Analyzes maneuvers by admirers and Stalwart factionalists to obtain the Republican Party's presidential nomination in 1880 for Ulysses S. Grant (1822-85). The boom for Grant foundered on the shoals of intraparty factionalism and widespread antipathy toward a third presidential term for Grant. Based on newspapers and secondary sources; 41 notes.

H. T. Lovin

657. Lowden, Lucy. NEW HAMPSHIRE AT CHICAGO—1860: "THE ONLY FIT AND PROPER NOMINATION...." *Hist. New Hampshire 1974 29(1): 20-41.* Examines the New Hampshire delegation's decision at the Republican National Convention to vote for the presidential nomination of Abraham Lincoln instead of William H. Seward.

S

658. Lunde, Erik S. THE AMBIGUITY OF THE NATIONAL IDEA: THE PRESIDENTIAL CAMPAIGN OF 1872. *Can. Rev. of Studies in Nationalism [Canada] 1978 5(1): 1-23.* The 1872 presidential campaign in the United States, pitting the incumbent Ulysses S. Grant against newspaper editor Horace Greeley, also represented a clash be-

tween two views of the American nation and of nationalism. The Republicans supporting Grant saw the Civil War as a great triumph which had bound the United States into a united nation, linked not only by sentiment but by rapidly increasing stretches of roads, railways, telegraph lines, and other modes of communication. The Democrats, among whom were many former Confederates, and their Liberal Republican allies, among whom were Carl Schurz and Greeley himself, looked upon the war as a tragedy and upon Republican centralism with distaste. America needed to recapture the unity and the purity of prewar days through reconciliation and respect for the autonomy of the states. The elections of 1872 saw Greeley's benevolent image of nationalism defeated by the centralizing, "blood and iron" concept of Grant and his Republicans, but the latter's triumph would be short-lived; the Liberal vision would win in the end. 46 notes.   J. C. Billigmeier

659. Lunde, Erik S.   THE CONTINUED SEARCH FOR NATIONAL UNITY: THE UNITED STATES PRESIDENTIAL CAMPAIGN OF 1876.   *Can. Rev. of Studies in Nationalism [Canada] 1981 8(1): 131-149.* The contest between Samuel J. Tilden and Rutherford B. Hayes in the year of the American centennial was the occasion for a renewed surge of nationalist spirit. Still suffering from the legacy of the Civil War, the political parties disagreed on the exact nature of nationalism, the role of government, and regionalism; only increased disunity resulted from the polemics. 43 notes.   R. Aldrich

660.   McCrary, Peyton; Miller, Clark; and Baum, Dale.   CLASS AND PARTY IN THE SECESSION CRISIS: VOTING BEHAVIOR IN THE DEEP SOUTH, 1856-1861.   *J. of Interdisciplinary Hist. 1978 8(3): 429-457.* Analyzes voting behavior and the realignment process in southern states, 1856-61, through the use of multiple ecological regression, to estimate individual voting behavior from the aggregate data. The first stage of the realignment process occurred in the 1860 presidential election, and the second stage was marked by the collapse of the Constitutional Coalition Union under the impact of the secession crisis. There is little clear-cut evidence of class alignments in voting behavior on the eve of the Civil War. The realignment was selective and the drop in voter turnout affected certain constituencies more than others, but it is clear that the bulk of the secessionist vote came directly from supporters of John C. Breckinridge. 9 tables, 40 notes.   R. Howell

661.   Mering, John V.   THE CONSTITUTIONAL UNION CAMPAIGN OF 1860; AN EXAMPLE OF THE PARANOID STYLE.   *Mid-America 1978 60(2): 95-106.* Studies the Constitutional Union Party campaign in 1860, using as a basis the "paranoid" style of politics as articulated by the late Richard Hofstadter. The Constitutional Unionists were paranoid in that they did not see much difference between the Republicans and the abolitionists. Although they opposed secession, they saw the Republicans as an organized conspiracy to abolish slavery and acted accordingly during the campaign. Based on campaign speeches and diaries; 45 notes.   J. M. Lee

662.   Meyer, Lysle E.   PIONEER REPUBLICANS JOIN THE FRAY: ASPECTS OF THEIR FIRST PRESIDENTIAL NOMINATING CONVENTION OF 1856.   *Lincoln Herald 1975 77(1): 15-26.* Amidst the social turmoil and the dissolution of the Whig Party in the early 1850's emerged the Republican Party. The party began at the local level in 1854, and by the fall of that year had organizations in the Mississippi Valley and some eastern states. A national convention to nominate candidates for President and Vice-President was held in Philadelphia in 1856. The party nominated John C. Frémont for President and William L. Dayton for Vice-President. Based on primary and secondary sources; 7 illus., 68 notes.   B. J. LaBue

663.   Miglian, Robert Murken.   CALIFORNIA'S REACTION TO THE DISPUTED PRESIDENTIAL ELECTION OF 1876.   *J. of the West 1976 15(1): 9-28.* Unlike in the East, in California there was little reaction to the Hayes-Tilden election. Provides résumés of the party platforms for 1876, and the election returns.   R. Alvis

664.   Mohrmann, G. P. and Leff, Michael C.   LINCOLN AT COOPER UNION: A RATIONALE FOR NEO-CLASSICAL CRITICISM.   *Q. J. of Speech 1974 60(4): 459-467.* "Genre theory can serve as a corrective to certain defects in 'neo-Aristotelian' rhetorical criticism. Analysis of the theory and practice of neo-Aristotelian critics reveals the

lack of adequate standards for rhetorical evaluation. This deficiency is directly correlated with their neglect of the classical conception of oratorical genres. Using our critique of Lincoln's Cooper Union Address as an example, we argue that reference to oratorical genres can provide a more precise focus for criticism."   J

665.   Nadler, Solomon.   THE GREEN BAG: JAMES MONROE AND THE FALL OF DEWITT CLINTON.   *New York Hist. Soc. Q. 1975 59(3): 202-225.* Evidence that President James Monroe exerted presidential power to influence his reelection campaign in 1820 may be seen in the decline of DeWitt Clinton's influence in New York and national politics. Clinton had been elected governor in 1817 and hoped to use that office as a base for a presidential campaign. However, Monroe used his appointive power and other political devices for weakening Clinton and was so successful that the Governor did not seek reelection in 1822. Despite Clinton's censure of the administration for interference in state politics, a censure which was included in his "Green Bag Message," he was eliminated as a presidential possibility and Monroe's reelection was assured. Primary sources; 3 illus., 43 notes.   C. L. Grant

666.   Nelson, Larry E.   BLACK LEADERS AND THE PRESIDENTIAL ELECTION OF 1864.   *J. of Negro Hist. 1978 63(1): 42-58.* The presidential campaign and election of 1864 was marked by political campaigning by Afro-American leaders. Although generally denied the vote, they spoke publicly to the central issue of the campaign: the fate of black people after the Civil War. Although the Republican Party received support as the lesser of two racist evils, the political culture of Afro-Americans had its beginnings in the election of 1864. Based on periodical literature of 1864 and secondary material; 88 notes.

N. G. Sapper

667.   Olmsted, Roger.   THE CIGAR-BOX PAPERS: A LOCAL VIEW OF THE CENTENNIAL ELECTORAL SCANDALS.   *California Hist. Q. 1976 55(3): 256-269.* Describes the presidential campaign of 1876 as seen from the editorials and cartoons of *Harper's Weekly* and San Francisco's new magazine, *The Wasp.* Thomas Nast's cartoons in *Harper's Weekly* were generally pro-Republican, while *Wasp* cartoonist G. Frederick Keller favored the Democrats. Keller's primary occupation was designing cigar-box labels, as the publishers of *The Wasp* also manufactured cigar-boxes. Of the two styles, Nast's was the more pungent, but Keller's improved over the course of the campaign and election which saw frauds committed on a massive scale. Through manipulation of the electoral commission created to determine which contested votes to accept, supporters of Rutherford B. Hayes saw their candidate enter the White House rather than Democrat Samuel J. Tilden. Throughout the controversy *The Wasp* exercised a moderate view favorable to reform. Based on cartoons from *Harper's Weekly* and *The Wasp,* and editorials from those magazines and from other periodicals; illus.

A. Hoffman

668.   Osborne, Thomas J.   WHAT WAS THE MAIN REASON FOR CLEVELAND'S ELECTION VICTORY IN 1884?   *Northwest Ohio Q. 1973 45(2): 67-71.* The election of 1884 was decided in New York State. Suggests where James Gillespie Blaine (1830-93) might have obtained the 575 votes he needed to carry New York and to defeat Grover Cleveland (1837-1908) for the presidency. The most logical place seemed to be in the upstate counties which were heavily populated with Republicans, but heavy rainstorms in several of those counties kept voters from the polls. Oneida County was the most likely source of the needed votes. It had a large Republican voting strength, and it experienced no severe rainstorms to keep voters at home, but Blaine failed to gain the necessary votes there because New York boss Roscoe Conkling (1829-88) campaigned against him. 24 notes.   W. F. Zornow

669.   Payne, Alma J.   THE *ASHTABULA SENTINEL* AND THE ELECTION OF 1876.   *Hayes Hist. J. 1976 1(2): 98-110.* Outlines the role of the *Ashtabula Sentinel* throughout the election campaign of 1876. It was the first newspaper to propose Rutherford B. Hayes as the Republican Party's presidential candidate. Details the relationship of the early career and the political ideals of its editor, William Cooper Howells, and the *Sentinel*'s support for Hayes. Once Hayes was nominated, the articles aimed at weakening the foundation of the Democratic platform, as opposed to defending Hayes. Primary sources; illus., 4 photos, 75 notes.

J. N. Friedel

670. Phillips, Kim T. THE PENNSYLVANIA ORIGINS OF THE JACKSON MOVEMENT. *Pol. Sci. Q. 1976 91(3): 489-508.* Discusses the earliest sources of support for Andrew Jackson as a presidential nominee in 1824. Finds that economic discontent in the aftermath of the panic of 1819 was central to the campaign to nominate Jackson, who was seen as a potential reformer of the system of banking and business privilege. J

671. Pocock, Emil. WET OR DRY? THE PRESIDENTIAL ELECTION OF 1884 IN UPSTATE NEW YORK. *New York Hist. 1973 54(2): 174-190.* Grover Cleveland (1837-1908) won the presidential election of 1884 because he carried New York State but his plurality there was only 1,143 votes out of more than 1.1 million votes over James Gillespie Blaine (1830-93). Minimizes the usual explanations of Blaine's defeat in New York State: the Mugwump bolt, the rains that held down the turnout, and Reverend Samuel D. Burchard's "rum, Romanism and rebellion" remark that alienated the Irish in New York City. The election returns show that John P. St. John, the Prohibition Party candidate, drew 25,006 votes of which 18,665 were in normally Republican upstate New York and were enough to defeat Blaine. Primary and secondary sources; 4 illus., 7 tables, 19 notes. G. Kurland

672. Rable, George C. SOUTHERN INTERESTS AND THE ELECTION OF 1876: A REAPPRAISAL. *Civil War Hist. 1980 26(4): 347-361.* Southerners, especially in Louisiana and South Carolina, were far more interested in the election of Democratic governors in 1876 (Francis J. Nicholls and Wade Hampton respectively) than in who became president. They saw Samuel J. Tilden as a weak character and refused to fight to have him elected. They were willing to accept Rutherford B. Hayes as president, if they could oust the Republican governors from their states. Based on correspondence and other sources; 31 notes. G. R. Schroeder

673. Ratcliffe, Donald J. THE ROLE OF VOTERS AND ISSUES IN PARTY FORMATION: OHIO 1824. *J. of Am. Hist. 1973 59(4): 847-870.* The presidential election of 1824 in Ohio was a race among three candidates: Henry Clay, Andrew Jackson, and John Quincy Adams. Historians have traditionally viewed that election, narrowly won by Clay, as one in which ambitious politicians created catch-all party organizations designed to attract voters who were insensitive to political issues or ideology. In fact, issues were of predominant importance, and political organizations were built around constituency interests. Clay attracted votes from counties hoping to benefit from his "American system" of federally-supported internal improvements, Adams got support from New Englanders repelled by Clay's involvement in slavery, and Jackson gathered support from depression-ridden Cincinnati, Scotch-Irish and German voters, and a general antipolitical animus. These alignments continued into the Whig Democrat era. 4 tables, 69 notes. K. B. West

674. Raybeck, Joseph G. A MYTH RE-EXAMINED: MARTIN VAN BUREN'S ROLE IN THE PRESIDENTIAL ELECTION OF 1816. *Pro. of the Am. Phil. Soc. 1980 124(2): 106-118.* In 1842 Jabez D. Hammond created a myth when he wrote that Martin Van Buren's open support of Daniel D. Tompkins for president had been false; that he had secretly supported James Monroe. Retracing the maze of political developments in the first half of 1816 in both Albany and Washington, the author reveals that Van Buren did indeed support Tompkins as long as Tompkins felt he had a chance for the nomination. Based on the Martin Van Buren Papers (Library of Congress), contemporary New York State and Washington newspapers, and other primary and secondary sources; 78 notes. H. M. Parker, Jr.

675. Rickert, William E. HORACE GREELEY ON THE STUMP: PRESIDENTIAL CAMPAIGN OF 1872. *Western Speech 1975 39(3): 175-183.* Discusses reactions to Horace Greeley's participation in his own campaign for the presidency, a habit which prior to Greeley's efforts had been considered out of the question. S

676. Scherr, Arthur. THE "REPUBLICAN EXPERIMENT" AND THE ELECTION OF 1796 IN VIRGINIA. *West Virginia Hist. 1976 37(2): 89-108.* Both parties in 1796 believed a victory by the other would endanger the nation's survival. Federalists emphasized northern objections to another Virginia President, and their electoral candidates took an

antiparty attitude by saying they would use their own best judgement in choosing a President. Republicans claimed that the South needed a friendly President, and they helped undermine the old politics of personal deference by pledging themselves openly to Thomas Jefferson so the voters could make a direct choice of candidates. Based on newspapers and secondary sources; 51 notes. J. H. Broussard

677. Scherr, Arthur. THE SIGNIFICANCE OF THOMAS PINCKNEY'S CANDIDACY IN THE ELECTION OF 1796. *South Carolina Hist. Mag. 1975 76(2): 51-59.* During the campaign of 1796 federalists and Republicans seriously considered Thomas Pinckney of South Carolina for president. His election might have enabled Jeffersonians and Hamiltonians to settle their differences rather than polarizing the nation into two political parties as did the election of John Adams. Primary sources; 38 notes. R. H. Tomlinson

678. Schlup, Leonard. ADLAI E. STEVENSON AND THE PRESIDENTIAL ELECTION OF 1896. *Social Sci. J. 1977 14(2): 117-128.* Examines the unifying role which Adlai E. Stevenson had on the Democratic Party in the presidential election of 1896, including the stand which he took on the otherwise confusing currency issue.

679. Schlup, Leonard. ADLAI E. STEVENSON'S CAMPAIGN VISITS TO KENTUCKY IN 1892. *Register of the Kentucky Hist. Soc. 1977 75(2): 112-120.* Adlai Ewing Stevenson (1835-1914), the Democratic vice-presidential nominee in 1892, was born and raised near Herndon, Kentucky. During the summer of 1892, candidate Stevenson campaigned widely for the ticket, including at least two visits to the state of his birth. He was well-received and Kentucky voted for the Cleveland-Stevenson ticket in its victorious election. Primary and secondary sources; 22 notes. J. F. Paul

680. Schlup, Leonard. ADLAI E. STEVENSON'S CAMPAIGN VISITS TO WEST VIRGINIA. *West Virginia Hist. 1977 38(2): 126-135.* Adlai E. Stevenson (1835-1914) campaigned twice in West Virginia as a Vice Presidential candidate. In 1892 he denounced the McKinley Tariff and the Force Bill, waging an unusually energetic campaign. He also issued his acceptance letter for the nomination and tried to ease conservative fears of his Greenbacker past by endorsing sound money. Running again in 1900, he emphasized attacks on trusts and imperialism. Primary and secondary sources; 26 notes. J. H. Broussard

681. Schlup, Leonard. ADLAI E. STEVENSON AND THE SOUTHERN CAMPAIGN OF 1892. *Q. Rev. of Hist. Studies [India] 1977-78 17(1): 7-14.* Reviews vice-presidential candidate Adlai E. Stevenson's efforts to hold the solid south for the Democratic Party during the presidential election of 1892. Farm economics were unfavorable; southern states threatened to go for the Populist candidate. Stevenson campaigned in North Carolina and Virginia, and when he was finished, victory was assured. He was successful because: 1) his family was from the south, 2) Republicans and Populists refused to merge, 3) the Populists nominated a northerner repugnant to the south, and 4) he played heavily on the racial issue to overcome economic fears. Ref. V. L. Human

682. Schlup, Leonard. ADLAI E. STEVENSON AND THE 1900 CAMPAIGN IN DELAWARE. *Delaware Hist. 1977 17(3): 191-198.* As the vice-presidential candidate on the William Jennings Bryan ticket in 1900, Adlai Stevenson of Illinois played the role of party accommodator, trying to win over conservative Democrats to Bryan. In mid-October, 1900, he made several significant speeches in Delaware, focusing on foreign policy, and ignoring local issues such as the John Addicks controversy in Delaware. Argues that Stevenson was anti-expansionist and, in many ways, backward in his conception of American foreign policy. Although his speeches were well attended, the Democrats did not carry the state. 17 notes. R. M. Miller

683. Schlup, Leonard. ADLAI E. STEVENSON AND THE 1892 CAMPAIGN IN VIRGINIA. *Virginia Mag. of Hist. and Biog. 1978 86(3): 345-354.* Democratic Vice-Presidential nominee Adlai E. Stevenson campaigned vigorously in Virginia during the 1892 campaign. His efforts headed off a serious threat by the Populist Party and helped carry the state for the Democratic Party. Based on manuscript material, newspapers, and secondary accounts; 26 notes. R. F. Oaks

684. Schlup, Leonard. ADLAI E. STEVENSON AND THE PRESIDENTIAL CAMPAIGN OF 1900. *Filson Club Hist. Q. 1979 53(2): 196-208.* Adlai E. Stevenson won the Democratic vice-presidential nomination in 1900 despite little organized efforts on his behalf. As Grover Cleveland's Vice-President from 1893 to 1897, Stevenson had become identified with the conservative wing of the party. At the same time, he was a moderate supporter of increased silver money. Thus, he was acceptable to the reform Democrats and presidential candidate William Jennings Bryan. Based on the Stevenson, Bryan, and Carter Harrison Papers; 34 notes.   G. B. McKinney

685. Schlup, Leonard. ADLAI E. STEVENSON AND THE 1892 CAMPAIGN IN ALABAMA. *Alabama R. 1976 29(1): 3-15.* Vice-presidential nominee Adlai E. Stevenson was instrumental in preserving the Democratic majority in the South in 1892. He spent two months campaigning in five southern states, including Alabama. His speeches consistently portrayed the Federal Elections Bill (1890), although twice defeated, as indicative of the direct threat that awaited regional interests should the Republicans recapture the White House. Stevenson's efforts successfully neutralized the Populist challenge. Primary and secondary sources; 22 notes.   J. F. Vivian

686. Schlup, Leonard. BRYAN'S PARTNER: ARTHUR SEWALL AND THE CAMPAIGN OF 1896. *Maine Hist. Soc. Q. 1977 16(4): 189-211.* Describes the role played by Arthur Sewall, wealthy shipbuilder from Bath, Maine, as the vice-presidential nominee on the Democratic ticket in 1896. Sewall's selection by the Democratic Party was doubly unwise since Sewall was unknown nationally, and Maine, with few electors, constituted no power base. 60 notes.   P. C. Marshall

687. Schlup, Leonard. CHARLES A. TOWNE AND THE VICE-PRESIDENTIAL QUESTION OF 1900. *North Dakota Hist. 1977 44(1): 14-20.* Charles A. Towne of Minnesota was an ardent silverite and William Jennings Bryan's own choice for running mate on the Democratic ticket in 1900. Following the Populists' nomination of Bryan for President and Towne for Vice President, the Democrats were pressured by their Free Silver wing to adopt the same ticket. Counterpressures from the Eastern wing of the Party and more conservative factions prevailed. Towne's supporters lost to those of Adlai E. Stevenson at the Democratic National Convention. Towne nevertheless campaigned hard for the ticket and probably would have been offered a cabinet position had Bryan won the election.   N. Lederer

688. Schlup, Leonard. GROVER CLEVELAND AND HIS 1892 RUNNING MATE. *Studies in Hist. and Society 1977 2(1-2): 60-74.* Discusses the political activity of Adlai Ewing Stevenson during 1888-92, particularly his role in Grover Cleveland's 1892 presidential campaign. Stevenson was selected as Cleveland's running mate, and was a moderate force who represented Democratic Party liberals. Coming from Illinois, Stevenson attracted votes from the Midwest; Cleveland was from the East. Stevenson was on very cordial terms with Cleveland, who had nominated him for a judgeship in 1889 before leaving office during his first presidential term. Stevenson's campaigning in the South was extremely important in 1892 because Populist forces were eroding the strength of the Democrats. Discusses antecedents of the Democratic Convention, where Stevenson played an important role in nominating Cleveland, and his activity leading up top the victory of their ticket. Stevenson's earlier support of a "soft" money policy was his only vulnerable position; he publicly modified his views to conform with the Party platform. 59 notes.

689. Schlup, Leonard. POLK AND CLAY: THE POLITICS OF TEXAS IN 1844. *Q. Rev. of Hist. Studies [India] 1979 18(4): 211-217.* The only 19th-century presidential campaign that was dominated by a foreign affairs issue was the 1844 contest between James K. Polk of Tennessee and Henry Clay of Kentucky. The controversy was based on the general theme of manifest destiny and specifically, the annexation of Texas and war with Mexico. Clay wavered in his position, but Polk endorsed the annexation; Polk defeated Clay with a 38,000-vote margin. Primary sources; 36 notes.   W. T. Walker

690. Schlup, Leonard. RELUCTANT EXPANSIONIST: ADLAI E. STEVENSON AND THE CAMPAIGN AGAINST IMPERIALISM IN 1900. *Indiana Social Studies Q. 1976 29(1): 32-42.* Discusses foreign policy attitudes of Democratic Party Presidential and Vice-Presidential candidates William Jennings Bryan and Adlai E. Stevenson in the 1900 election, emphasizing the Philippines.

691. Schofield, Harold A. THE *NEW NATION* AND ITS EDITOR: A NEW PERSPECTIVE ON FREMONT'S WITHDRAWAL FROM THE PRESIDENTIAL CAMPAIGN OF 1864. *Lincoln Herald 1974 76(4): 203-207.* Gustave Paul Cluseret, editor of the *New Nation,* and an editorial published in 1864 discouraging John C. Frémont from challenging Abraham Lincoln's presidency in the 1864 presidential election, caused Frémont to withdraw.

692. Shook, Cynthia. RICHARD PARKS BLAND: ALMOST A CANDIDATE. *Missouri Hist. R. 1974 68(4): 417-436.* Discusses the involvement of Missouri congressman Richard Parks Bland (1835-99) in the Free Silver movement and the Democratic nomination in 1896. Bland led the silverites in Congress for 20 years, and all his major efforts were for this cause, including the Bland-Allison Act (1878) and opposition to the Sherman Silver Purchase Act (1890). In 1895 the silverites actively sought control of the Democratic Party and many pro-silver men endorsed Bland as their presidential candidate. A seating and platform battle between gold and silver Democrats took place at the national convention, but the silver men took control. Bland was nominated, but eventually defeated by William Jennings Bryan for numerous reasons, particularly because he did not actively take part in the campaign in his behalf. Based on contemporary newspaper reports, documents of the Democratic Party, primary and secondary sources; 5 illus., 5 photos, 42 notes.   N. J. Street

693. Smith, Thomas A. GOVERNOR HAYES VISITS THE CENTENNIAL. *Hayes Hist. J. 1977 1(3): 159-163.* Republican presidential nominee Governor Rutherford B. Hayes visited the Centennial Exposition in Philadelphia on Ohio Day, 26 October 1876. Includes the public speeches by Hayes at this celebration. Primary sources; 5 illus., 8 notes.   J. N. Friedel

694. Stanley, Gerald. RACISM AND THE EARLY REPUBLICAN PARTY: THE 1856 PRESIDENTIAL ELECTION IN CALIFORNIA. *Pacific Hist. R. 1974 43(2): 171-187.* Develops the thesis that California Republicans in the presidential election of 1856 were concerned over the geographical expansion of the black race rather than matters relating to freedom and racial equality. Republicans repeatedly declared that they opposed the extension of slavery because it would encroach upon the rights of the white race. "They never disapproved of slavery because of its injustice to the slave. . . . It was the geographical location, not the status of black Americans that vexed California's Republicans in 1856." 67 notes.   R. V. Ritter

695. Stanley, Gerald. THE SLAVERY ISSUE AND ELECTION IN CALIFORNIA, 1860. *Mid-America 1980 62(1): 35-45.* In the 1860 four-party presidential election, Republicans won 32% of the total vote. The Republican Party campaigned against the extension of slavery because it encroached upon the rights of nonslave-owning whites in the West. Furthermore, they linked slavery and race to other issues such as homesteads, railroads, and daily overland mail in a deliberate appeal to race prejudice. The Democratic Party was divided, but exploitation of the slavery and race issues was the decisive factor in the Republican victory. Notes.   M. J. Wentworth

696. Stern, Norton B. LOS ANGELES JEWISH VOTERS DURING GRANT'S FIRST PRESIDENTIAL RACE. *Western States Jewish Hist. Q. 1981 13(2): 179-185.* During the 1868 presidential race between Republican Ulysses S. Grant and Democrat Horatio Seymour, both sides in Los Angeles tried to attract Jewish voters. Democrats reminded Jews of Grant's infamous General Order No. 11, expelling Jews, as a class, from the Department of Tennessee in 1862—supposedly for illegal cotton speculation. Republicans charged the County Board of Supervisors, mostly Democrats, of assigning higher tax assessment to the property of Jews. The election verified the Democratic affiliation of Los Angeles' Jews, who voted overwhelmingly for Seymour. Based on newspaper accounts; 34 notes.   B. S. Porter

697. Sullivan, John. INDECOROUS ARGUMENT: THE USE OF MADISON AND MONROE IN THE ELECTION OF 1828. *South-*

ern Speech Communication J. 1980 45(4): 378-393. When political opponents of Andrew Jackson put forth the names of James Madison and James Monroe (against both of their wills), the mode in which the two responded reaffirmed the limits of decorous argument and helped to establish the role played by former presidents in presidential elections and campaigns; 1828.

698. Theisen, Lee Scott. A "FAIR COUNT" IN FLORIDA: GENERAL LEW WALLACE AND THE CONTESTED PRESIDENTIAL ELECTION OF 1876. *Hayes Hist. J. 1978 2(1): 20-30.* General Lew Wallace, author of *Ben Hur,* and a member of the Republican committee to recount the Florida votes in the 1876 presidential election, played a significant role in the electoral outcome of this state, and in the victory of Rutherford B. Hayes. In exchange for his efforts, Wallace's appointment as governor of the New Mexico Territory took almost two years; in the meantime, he became embroiled in Indiana state politics. Offers insight into the contested 1876 presidential election, state politics of the era, and the complicated late 19th-century spoils system. Primary sources; 7 illus., 31 notes.   J. N. Friedel

699. Turner, John J. and D'Innocenzo, Michael. THE PRESIDENT AND THE PRESS: LINCOLN, JAMES GORDON BENNETT AND THE ELECTION OF 1864. *Lincoln Herald 1974 76(2): 63-69.* The *New York Herald* editor, James Gordon Bennett, was critical of President Abraham Lincoln's policies regarding blacks. Many Lincoln historians propose that Lincoln got Bennett to soften the *Herald's* editorials with the offer of the French ambassadorship in 1864. If such pre-election maneuvering was attempted, Bennett failed to help gain New York City votes for Lincoln. Based on *New York Herald* papers and secondary works; 33 notes.   A. C. Aimone

700. Vazzano, Frank P. THE LOUISIANA QUESTION RESURRECTED: THE POTTER COMMISSION AND THE ELECTION OF 1876. *Louisiana Hist. 1975 16(1): 39-57.* Upon the initiative of Rep. Clarkson N. Potter (D-NY), a Congressional commission was formed in 1878 to investigate charges of fraud in the presidential election of 1876. The investigation revolved largely around the incriminating testimony of James E. Anderson, who revealed a sordid tale of Republican fraud and voter intimidation in Louisiana. The tables were turned on Potter, however, with the disclosure of substantial Democratic fraud in Florida and South Carolina. The majority of the Commission declared that Republican fraud had cheated Tilden out of the presidency in 1876, but no action was ever taken by Congress. "If anything, the Potter investigation only reenforced what Republicans and Democrats already believed—that their party won the presidency in 1876." Based principally on primary sources; 87 notes.   R. L. Woodward, Jr.

701. Warner, Lee H. NATHANIEL HAWTHORNE AND THE MAKING OF THE PRESIDENT—1852. *Hist. New Hampshire 1973 28(1): 20-36.* Dark horse Franklin Pierce (1804-69), needing a campaign biography, accepted the offer of Nathaniel Hawthorne (1804-64), a former fellow student at Bowdoin, whom he had helped to custom house appointments. The image Hawthorne presented was of a stalwart Mexican War officer, "an upright family man . . . a competent legislator and an able lawyer," with moderate views on current issues. It was "a hard book to write," said Hawthorne, because of Pierce's mediocrity. He drew on his fictional characters for this subject's "sunny" childhood, and dubious battle record, and on the popular revolutionary record of his father, Benjamin Pierce. Hawthorne lauded Pierce's resistance to abolition and other reforms which were thought good in themselves, but destructive of social equilibrium. Using an unfamiliar form, with few sources, Hawthorne hacked out an inferior product in 10 weeks and in 1853 was rewarded with the consulship at Liverpool. 4 illus., 41 notes.
                                                        T. D. S. Bassett

702. Warner, Lee H. WITH PIERCE AND HAWTHORNE, IN MEXICO. *Essex Inst. Hist. Collections 1975 111(3): 213-220.* In authoring an 1852 campaign biography of Franklin Pierce, Nathaniel Hawthorne had special difficulty in writing about Pierce's less-than-illustrious military career during the Mexican War, 1847.

703. Webb, Ross A. THE BRISTOW PRESIDENTIAL BOOM OF 1876. *Hayes Hist. J. 1976 1(2): 78-87.* Traces the unsuccessful efforts of Benjamin Helm Bristow, an ardent reformer from Kentucky and Secre-

tary of the Treasury during the Grant administration, to gain the Republican Party's presidential nomination in June 1876. Bristow continued to support his party by campaigning extensively for the election of Rutherford B. Hayes. Gives insight into the political maneuvering and compromises between the Democrats and Republicans, and within the Electoral Commission, in selecting Hayes as President. Primary sources; 6 illus., 38 notes.
                                                        J. N. Friedel

704. Williams, David A. CALIFORNIA DEMOCRATS OF 1860: DIVISION, DISRUPTION, DEFEAT. *Southern California Q. 1973 55(3): 239-252.* Recounts California's participation in the 1860 Democratic National Convention. Heavily pro-slavery and anti-Stephen A. Douglas, California and Oregon supported the Southern states at the Charleston meeting. Although Douglas supporters were in the majority at the convention, they lacked the two-thirds vote necessary to put their candidate and platform across. On a number of key issues California voted on the side of the South, and after 57 ballots the deadlocked convention adjourned. When it met again in Baltimore 45 days later, California and the southern states walked out. The Baltimore convention went on to nominate Douglas, while California and the southern states nominated John C. Breckinridge at a rump convention in Richmond. In November California narrowly went for Lincoln and the Republicans. Primary and secondary sources; 40 notes.   A. Hoffman

705. Wolff, Gerald W. THE OHIO FARMER-LABOR VOTE IN THE ELECTION OF 1896: A CASE STUDY. *Northwest Ohio Q. 1975 47(3): 100-119.* Republicans and Democrats wooed farmers and labor for the presidential election of 1896.

706. Yzenbaard, John H. H. P. SCHOLTE AND THE 1856 PRESIDENTIAL CAMPAIGN IN MICHIGAN. *Annals of Iowa 1973 42(1): 28-40.* Discusses Henry (Hendrick) P. Scholte's promotion of James Buchanan and John Cabell Breckinridge, Democratic candidates for president and vice-president from Michigan in the campaign of 1856, and traces Scholte's abilities as a leader to 1846 when he led a group of Dutch coreligionists to Iowa to settle his community of Pella, where he led his followers in spiritual and secular matters.

707. —. AN APOLOGY TO EDWARD MENDEL: THE ORIGINAL OF LINCOLN'S LETTER FOUND IN CHICAGO. *Chicago Hist. 1979 8(2): 78-79.* Provides a brief biography of Prussian-born lithographer Edward Mendel (1827-84), who established himself in business in Chicago as a lithographer, mapmaker, and engraver, and discusses in particular the letter from Abraham Lincoln thanking Mendel for the 1860 lithograph portrait of Lincoln.

708. —. [THE COMPROMISE OF 1877]. *J. of Am. Hist. 1973 60(1).*
Peskin, Allan. WAS THERE A COMPROMISE OF 1877?, pp. 63-75.
    C. Vann Woodward's *Reunion and Reaction: The Compromise of 1877 and the End of Reconstruction* (Boston: Little, Brown & Co., 1951), contains the classic and almost universally accepted interpretation of the far-reaching compromise wherein southern Democrats accepted Hayes as president in return for withdrawal of federal troops, support for internal improvements in the South, assurance of federal subsidies, appointment of a southerner as postmaster general, and the admission that the South alone could resolve its racial problems. Argues that these terms of the "compromise" were not complied with, that no compromise in fact existed, and that the southern Democrats were outwitted by Republicans.
Woodward, C. Vann. YES, THERE WAS A COMPROMISE OF 1877, pp. 215-223. The Compromise of 1877 was as real as that of 1850, the major terms were complied with, particularly home rule for the South, and if anyone was outwitted it was the Republicans. 49 notes.   K. B. West

709. —. THE HARRISON BANDWAGON. *Am. Heritage 1975 26(6): 18-27.* A selection of song sheets from the 1840 presidential campaign of William Henry Harrison. From the book *Music for Patriots, Politicians, and Presidents* by Vera Brodsky Lawrence (New York: Macmillan, 1975). 10 illus.   B. J. Paul

710. —. PRAISE FOR THE "MOST AVAILABLE CANDIDATE." *J. of the Illinois State Hist. Soc. 1978 71(1): 71-72.* A letter

from Scott County Chairman Nathan Knapp to Illinois Secretary of State Ozias M. Hatch praises Abraham Lincoln as "the biggest man in the lot" of Republicans in 1859. Illus., 7 notes.   J

Presidential Administrations: New Nation to New Empire

General

711. Borden, Morton. A NEO-FEDERALIST VIEW OF THE JEFFERSONIANS. *Rev. in Am. Hist. 1977 5(2): 196-202.* Review article prompted by Forrest McDonald's *The Presidency of Thomas Jefferson* (Lawrence: U. Pr. of Kansas, 1976).

712. Boston, Ray. THE IMPACT OF "FOREIGN LIARS" ON THE AMERICAN PRESS (1790-1800). *Journalism Q. 1973 50(4): 722-730.* Examines the influence of British exile journalists, who vilified John Adams and the Federalists, on the Democratic-Republican press, run by William Duane (1790-1800).   S

713. Brauer, Kinley J. SEWARD'S "FOREIGN WAR PANACEA": AN INTERPRETATION. *New York Hist. 1974 55(2): 133-57.* On 1 April 1861 Secretary of State William Henry Seward sent President Lincoln a note urging the United States to precipitate a war with a major European power in order to create a wave of popular patriotism that would bring the seceded states of the South back into the federal Union. Most historians have viewed Seward's proposal as a lapse of sanity, but Brauer makes an attempt to rehabilitate Seward's foreign war panacea. He sees it as a consistent policy designed to prevent European trade with the seceded states, drive Spain from Santo Domingo, prevent European interference in Latin American affairs, and use the threat of foreign war to strengthen the hand of southern Unionists. Seward did not want war, but sought to use the threat of war to solve the nation's domestic crisis. Based on William Henry Seward Papers, primary, and secondary works; 7 illus., 47 notes.   G. Kurland

714. Bruns, Roger. ASSASSINATION ATTEMPT OF PRESIDENT ANDREW JACKSON. *West Tennessee Hist. Soc. Papers 1977 31: 33-43.* On 30 January 1835, on the steps of the US Capitol, Richard Lawrence attempted to kill President Andrew Jackson. This was the first attempt on the life of a President. The attacker was wrestled to the ground by the crowd and Jackson. Jackson's friends endeavored to find conspiracy as a motive, but the later investigation ruled this out. Lawrence suffered from the delusion that he was King of England and was found not guilty by reason of insanity. Based on proceedings of the trial in congressional documents and newspaper accounts; 3 pictures, 30 notes.   H. M. Parker, Jr.

715. Clarfield, Gerard. PROTECTING THE FRONTIERS: DEFENSE POLICY AND THE TARIFF QUESTION IN THE FIRST WASHINGTON ADMINISTRATION. *William and Mary Q. 1975 32(3): 443-464.* The introduction of the Tariff of 1792, implementing ideas from Hamilton's "Report on Manufactures," resulted in opposition led by James Madison. Alexander Hamilton viewed Madison and his Virginia followers as trying to limit the powers of the Treasury Department. Hamilton linked the need for military appropriation for the Indian campaigns to the necessity of a high tariff. Examines the Indian war and public attitudes toward it, discussing the lengthy debate in Congress over the bill "for the protection of the frontiers," and a new tariff law. Based chiefly on the *Annals of Congress* and the Washington, Jefferson, and Hamilton papers; 73 notes.   H. M. Ward

716. Crackel, Theodore J. JEFFERSON, POLITICS, AND THE ARMY: AN EXAMINATION OF THE MILITARY PEACE ESTABLISHMENT ACT OF 1802. *J. of the Early Republic 1982 2(1): 21-38.* Investigates Thomas Jefferson's military policies in light of the Military Peace Establishment Act (US, 1802). Closer scrutiny reveals that the act proposed economies in army size with actually negligible financial expenditures. The true thrust of the act was to purge the army officer corps of its most vocal Federalist support and replace it with men of Republican

sympathies. The act reinstated the rank of colonel in order to dilute the strength of the senior officers; it jettisoned key Federalist officers in the internal administration and control network, and transferred responsibilities to newly created civilian positions filled with Republicans. The act restructured the artillery corps and infantry companies to accommodate the appointment of junior grade Republican officers. Finally, it authorized the creation of West Point for the purpose of educating and training a Republican officer corps. Primary and secondary sources; 2 plates, table, 37 notes.   G. A. Glovins

717. Current, Richard N. LINCOLN, THE CIVIL WAR, AND THE AMERICAN MISSION. Davis, Cullom; Strozier, Charles B.; Veach, Rebecca Monroe; and Ward, Geoffrey C., ed. *The Public and the Private Lincoln: Contemporary Perspectives* (Carbondale: So. Illinois U. Pr., 1979): 137-146. Abraham Lincoln was the heir of the Puritans and later thinkers who believed that the United States was a model for the rest of the world. He consequently accepted the possibility of civil war to prove that the American experiment with self-government had not failed. 20 notes.   S

718. Davison, Kenneth E. THE SEARCH FOR THE HAYES ADMINISTRATION. *Hayes Hist. J. 1978 2(2): 107-118.* Examines four reasons why the American public's knowledge about Hayes is so sparse. Davison recounts biographical adventures encountered during a 10-year search of documents and artifacts associated with the Hayes administration; his efforts resulted in *The Presidency of Rutherford B. Hayes* (1972). Painstaking genealogical searches uncovered facts about Hayes's cabinet officers, the Supreme Court, and his personal friends; use of material culture supplemented written records. Research conclusions concerning the disputed 1876 election and the special features of the biography are listed. Describes the character and integrity of a traditionally misunderstood president. Primary sources; 11 illus., 20 notes.   J. N. Friedel

719. Dearmont, Nelson S. FEDERALIST ATTITUDES TOWARD GOVERNMENTAL SECRECY IN THE AGE OF JEFFERSON. *Historian 1975 37(2): 222-240.* Shows that the issue of secrecy in government is a bedrock question dating not merely from the Nixon and other recent administrations, but back to the early years of the Constitution when controversies over foreign policy (Jefferson's embargo, acquisition of West Florida, war with Britain in 1812), parliamentary practice (voting the previous question), and the increasing use of closed congressional sessions led to popular suspicion of governmental power, and debate of the doctrine that publicity is essential to republicanism. Although traditionally associated with advocacy of aristocratic principles, the Federalists took the affirmative in this debate in part, perhaps, because they learned the importance of publicity to an out-of-office party during Jefferson's administration. Annals of Congress, 1789-1824; 57 notes.   N. W. Moen

720. Deren, Štefica. PODRIJETLO AMERIČKOG STRANAČKOG SUSTAVA (S POSEBNIM OSVRTOM NA RAZVOJ FEDERALISTA) [The origins of the American party system (with special regard to the development of the federalists)]. *Politička Misao [Yugoslavia] 1972 9(2-3): 216-228.* Examines the antagonisms between George Washington and Alexander Hamilton on one side, and Thomas Jefferson on the other, which split the nation between federalists and antifederalists (later republicans), and argues that the major reason for the short existence of federalists was the conflict between Hamilton and John Adams, and not any external factors.

721. DeSantis, Vincent P. GROVER CLEVELAND: ANOTHER LOOK. *Hayes Hist. J. 1980 3(1-2): 41-50.* Historians continue to rate Grover Cleveland as a "near great" president, the ablest and most respectable between Abraham Lincoln and Theodore Roosevelt. During his two terms in office, 1885-89 and 1893-97, however, Cleveland's character—his energy, honesty, and devotion to duty—more than his accomplishments established his claim to greatness. Although a Democrat, he accepted the Whig-Republican hands-off attitude toward legislation and thus failed to give leadership to Congress. Based on primary sources; 2 illus., photo, 30 notes.   E. L. Keyser

722. Eckert, Edward K. EARLY REFORM IN THE NAVY DEPARTMENT. *Am. Neptune 1973 33(4): 231-245.* A study of Navy

Department reforms under William Jones, fourth Secretary of the Navy (1813-14). Most significant was his recommendation to Congress for the creation of a board of naval commissioners, patterned after the British Navy Office, and accepted by Congress in 1815. In two years Jones had "reformed his department as far as he could under the existing laws by weeding out the personnel whose presence harmed the establishment and by continually checking on those who remained." At the end of his term he proposed a coordinated system of reform which opened the way to the efficient functioning he envisioned. 40 notes.

R. V. Ritter

723. Eggert, Gerald G. "I HAVE TRIED SO HARD TO DO RIGHT." *Am. Hist. Illus. 1978 12(9): 10-23.* Stephen Grover Cleveland (1837-1908) of New York defeated Blaine for the Presidency in 1884. A Democratic reformer known for thoroughness and integrity, Cleveland used the veto "to do right." Vetoing pension bills cost him the support of the GAR and possibly the 1888 election, but he defeated Harrison in an 1892 rematch. The Panic of 1893, Coxey's Army's march, the Pullman Strike, and Hawaiian and Cuban expansion moves occupied his second term. Cleveland retired to "Oakview" in Princeton, New Jersey. His dying words furnished the title and theme of the article. Cleveland was philosophically conservative, politically lucky, and mentally unimaginative, but morally honest. Secondary sources; 14 illus.

D. Dodd

724. Fehrenbacher, Don E. LINCOLN AND THE CONSTITUTION. Davis, Cullom; Strozier, Charles B.; Veach, Rebecca Monroe; and Ward, Geoffrey C., ed. *The Public and the Private Lincoln: Contemporary Perspectives* (Carbondale: So. Illinois U. Pr., 1979): 121-136. Reviews Abraham Lincoln's views on government and constitutional principles. Though the Civil War consolidated federal power to an unprecedented degree, Lincoln did not enter the war with the intention of remodeling the relationship of federal and state governments; his reconstruction program was designed to restore the prewar system even if it meant that the freedmen would be at the mercy of their old masters. He upheld the right of judicial review but did not support judicial supremacy. Though he extended emergency powers of the presidency, he displayed little legislative leadership as he followed the Whig principle that government initiative lay with the legislature. His belief in government by the people was stronger than his belief in the union, for he agreed in advance to abide by the election of 1864. 22 notes.

S

725. Fisher, Everett. THE GARFIELD CENTENNIAL. *Manuscripts 1981 33(2): 138-143.* Obtaining documents relating to the ill-fated presidency of James A. Garfield has presented some unusual problems. Illus.

D. A. Yanchisin

726. Fisher, Louis. GROVER CLEVELAND AGAINST THE SENATE. *Congressional Studies 1979 7(1): 11-25.* Examines the Senate's exercise of its investigative power, President Grover Cleveland's interpretation of his power to withhold certain documents and to suspend and remove civil officers, the partisan collision between a Democratic president and a Republican Senate, the Constitutional procedure for impeachment, and the politics of patronage and civil service reform, 1884-86.

727. Goodman, Paul. PERSPECTIVES ON THE PRESIDENCY AND THE PARTIES IN THE 1790'S. *Rev. in Am. Hist. 1975 3(1): 71-76.* Review article prompted by Rudolph M. Bell's *Party and Faction in American Politics: The House of Representatives, 1789-1801* (Westport, Conn.: Greenwood Pr., 1973) and Forrest McDonald's *The Presidency of George Washington* (Lawrence: U. Pr. of Kansas, 1974).

728. Gould, Lewis L. WILLIAM MC KINLEY AND THE EXPANSION OF PRESIDENTIAL POWER. *Ohio Hist. 1978 87(1): 5-20.* Analyzes the presidency of William McKinley. Argues that McKinley was shrewd, intelligent, and hard-working, and that he significantly contributed to the expansion of presidential power during his administration. He handled the demands that international changes and domestic pressures were placing on the American government and led the way for a strong executive leadership carried on by Theodore Roosevelt. Primary and secondary sources; 43 notes.

N. Summers

729. Harrison, Lowell H. THE PRESIDENT WITHOUT A PARTY. *Am. Hist. Illus. 1981 16(1): 12-21.* Originally a Democrat, John Tyler joined the amorphous Whig Party that formed in the 1830's, was elected vice president on the Whig ticket in 1840, and became the first vice president to succeed to the presidency (when William Henry Harrison died); when policy differences with other Whigs expelled him from the party, Tyler was forced to govern without party support.

730. Hyman, Harold M. MARS AND THE CONSTITUTION. *Civil War Times Illus. 1973 12(3): 36-42.* The debate over Lincoln's constitutional power to wage the Civil War.

S

731. Jackson, Donald. JEFFERSON, MERRIWETHER LEWIS, AND THE REDUCTION OF THE UNITED STATES ARMY. *Pro. of the Am. Phil. Soc. 1980 124(2): 91-96.* By the time of Thomas Jefferson's inauguration, the US Army had been reduced from 5,400 to 2,700 men. Most of the officer corps was Federalist. Anxious to put Republicans in top civilian posts and to retain in the military those officers who were sympathetic with the Republican Party, Jefferson selected Captain Meriwether Lewis to expel incompetents and to identify officers as Federalist or Republican. A sheet with symbols used to screen officers was recently identified as written in Lewis's hand. It is thus obvious that Jefferson originally hired Lewis for a purpose beyond training for the transcontinental expedition. So when Lewis did set out on his famous expedition with Clark in 1803, he had the satisfaction of knowing that he had served his president and his party in a rather unusual way. Based on the Jefferson Papers (Library of Congress) and other primary and secondary materials; 2 tables, 2 fig., 16 notes.

H. M. Parker, Jr.

732. Jeffreys-Jones, Rhodri. THE MONTREAL SPY RING OF 1898 AND THE ORIGINS OF "DOMESTIC" SURVEILLANCE IN THE UNITED STATES. *Can. R. of Am. Studies [Canada] 1974 5(2): 119-134.* Chronicles responses by the William McKinley administration to potentially serious espionage by a Spanish "spy ring" at Montreal during the Spanish-American War. Lyman Gage (1836-1927) directed the wartime American counterintelligence work. In these operations, John Wilkie (1860-1934) was "America's master spy." Wilkie's agents, using questionable methods, dealt with the menace posed by the Spanish "spy ring." Based on Canadian and American archival sources; 54 notes.

H. T. Lovin

733. Jones, Robert F. GEORGE WASHINGTON AND THE POLITICS OF THE PRESIDENCY. *Presidential Studies Q. 1980 10(1): 28-35.* One of the oldest extra-official roles of the president is that of leader of his political party. The only president who could not be labeled a party leader was the first: George Washington. Nevertheless, he did not remain entirely above politics; in 1794 he joined the Federalists. At the end of his administration he embraced politics propagated by extreme, or Hamiltonian, Federalists. His acceptance of their politics started the politicizing of the presidency. 29 notes.

G. E. Pergl

734. Ketcham, Ralph. JAMES MADISON: THE UNIMPERIAL PRESIDENT. *Virginia Q. Rev. 1978 54(1): 116-136.* Describes Madison's concern with balancing the limitation of the power of government, especially the executive powers in wartime, with "the good use . . . that could be made of power in a republican government." Madison's critical insight evolved as he helped fashion the executive power in the Constitution, served in his public career, and carried out the executive's duties "in time of war, international turmoil, and disharmony."

O. H. Zabel

735. Kleber, Louis C. JOHN TYLER: TENTH PRESIDENT. *Hist. Today [Great Britain] 1975 25(10): 697-703.* Discusses John Tyler, 10th President of the United States, 1841-45, whose term witnessed a charge of impeachment and the acquisition of Texas.

736. Lindsey, David. REHABILITATING THE PRESIDENTS: GARFIELD, ARTHUR, MCKINLEY. *Rev. in Am. Hist. 1982 10(1): 72-77.* Reviews Justus D. Doenecke's *The Presidencies of James A. Garfield & Chester A. Arthur* (1981), and Lewis L. Gould's *The Presidency of William McKinley* (1980).

737. Marchman, Watt P., ed. THE "MEMOIRS" OF THOMAS DONALDSON. *Hayes Hist. J. 1979 2(3-4): 157-265.* Reprints the journal-like notes kept by Thomas Corwin Donaldson for 1872-93, which provide a lively, behind-the-scenes record of political and social life in Washington. The bulk of the entries focus on the period 1877-79 and

Donaldson's relationship with President Rutherford B. Hayes and James G. Blaine. Based on an original manuscript owned by the Indiana Historical Society; 26 photos.   J. Cushnie

738. Maxwell, Jerry H. THE BIZARRE CASE OF LEWIS PAINE. *Lincoln Herald 1979 81(4): 223-233.* Discusses Lewis T. Powell, known as Lewis Paine, or Payner, who attempted to assassinate Secretary of State William H. Seward and was hanged with the conspirators in the assassination of Lincoln.

739. McDonald, Forrest. A MIRROR FOR PRESIDENTS. *Commentary 1976 62(6): 34-41.* The presidency combines dual functions. The administrative and executive functions are involved in formulating and implementing policy. The other function is ceremonial. Often the ritualistic aspect is considered less important in evaluating performance. However, the ceremonial aspects of the job perhaps are more important than the governing aspects. George Washington's greatest contribution to the presidency was his position as a bridge between monarchy and republicanism. Thomas Jefferson republicanized the monarchical aspects of the job. Washington and Jefferson illustrate that the burden of the presidency elongates and changes during a second term and is thus too great a psychological burden. Primary and secondary sources.
                                                             S. R. Herstein

740. McFeely, William S. THE JACKSONIAN NAVAL PERSON IN LINCOLN'S CABINET. *R. in Am. Hist. 1974 2(3): 394-401.* The influence of Jacksonian Democrats in the political history of the 1820's-1870's is illustrated in John Niven's biography of Gideon Welles, Secretary of the Navy during the Civil War, *Gideon Welles: Lincoln's Secretary of the Navy* (New York: Oxford U. Pr., 1973).

741. McGinty, Brian. "CASTINE" AND MR. LINCOLN. *Civil War Times Illus. 1977 16(7): 26-35.* Discusses the relationship between President Abraham Lincoln and writer Noah Brooks. Something of a wanderer and business failure, Brooks was writing for a Sacramento, California, newspaper when the Civil War began. He went to Washington as a reporter and for three years wrote of events in Washington for California readers. He became perhaps the closest friend Lincoln had. More than three decades after the President's death, Brooks wrote a series of lengthy articles about him, later condensed into a book, which provides much of what is known about the human side of Lincoln. 9 photos.
                                                             V. L. Human

742. Miller, Richard G. THE TARIFF OF 1832: THE ISSUE THAT FAILED. *Filson Club Hist. Q. 1975 49(3): 221-230.* The tariff issue posed many dangers for the Democratic Party in the election of 1832, but adroit political action by Andrew Jackson eliminated the potential dangers. Jackson was under pressure from southern Democrats to reduce or end the tariff rates passed in 1828. Henry Clay championed manufacturing interests and Western farmers, claiming that the Democrats reflected only southern farmers. On the other side, John C. Calhoun threatened to lead a Southern nullification movement if the tax was not defeated. Jackson defused the issue by backing a moderate reduction of the tariff that proved to be so popular that Clay supported it and Calhoun was unable to rally the South to his position. Documentation comes from manuscripts at the Library of Congress including the Clay and Jackson Papers; 41 notes.   G. B. McKinney

743. Murphy, William J., Jr. JOHN ADAMS: THE POLITICS OF THE ADDITIONAL ARMY, 1798-1800. *New England Q. 1979 52(2): 234-249.* Clarifies provisions of army legislation during the Quasi War, takes issue with the traditional view that John Adams (1735-1826) opposed raising an army during the war, and confirms the belief that Adams used army appointments as a political tool in the election of 1800. Adams did not oppose enlarging the regular army or raising a provisional one during the spring and summer of 1798, but he did lose interest in the new forces after George Washington (1732-1799) forced him to name Alexander Hamilton (1757-1804) second in command and refused to allow the appointment of Republican officers. In February 1799 Adams began to reaffirm his influence over appointments and from then on consistently attempted to use military appointments to make political gains. Primary and secondary sources; 32 notes.   J. C. Bradford

744. Niven, John. GIDEON WELLES AND NAVAL ADMINISTRATION DURING THE CIVIL WAR. *Am. Neptune 1975 35(1): 53-66.* Some contemporaries and historians have considered Gideon Welles "a token Secretary of the Navy" and thought his dynamic assistant, Gustavus Vasa Fox, was "the real power in the Navy Department." However, Navy Department files and Welles' diary and correspondence reveal that Welles was the Navy Department's chief policymaker and administrator. Based on manuscripts and secondary sources; 27 notes.
                                                             G. H. Curtis

745. Peskin, Allan. PRESIDENT GARFIELD AND THE RATING GAME: AN EVALUATION OF A BRIEF ADMINISTRATION. *South Atlantic Q. 1977 76(1): 93-102.* James A. Garfield's 120 active days in office do not allow for sufficient analysis of his presidential ability. However, from his previous actions and writings, his possibilities can be measured. Garfield's qualifications were excellent; his four years as chairman of the House Appropriations Committee capped his highly active and popular political career. He probably would not have promoted any strong legislative program; he felt that was the province of Congress. In his political appointments, Garfield faced a nightmare of demands from both parties and from the Senate. He was apparently equal to this struggle and would have strengthened the Presidency against both the parties and the Congress. By the modest goals he set himself, Garfield would have been a fairly good President. 22 notes.
                                                             W. L. Olbrich

746. Peterson, Merrill D. PROCESS AND PERSONALITY IN JEFFERSON'S ADMINISTRATION. *Rev. in Am. Hist. 1979 7(2): 189-198.* Review article prompted by Noble E. Cunningham, Jr.'s *The Process of Government under Jefferson* (Princeton, N.J.: Princeton U. Pr., 1978) and Robert M. Johnstone, Jr.'s *Jefferson and the Presidency: Leadership in the Young Republic* (Ithaca, N.Y.: Cornell U. Pr., 1978).

747. Reese, Lee Fleming. ANDREW JOHNSON: 17TH PRESIDENT OF THE UNITED STATES. *Daughters of the Am. Revolution Mag. 1974 108(1): 18-20.*

748. Schlup, Leonard. PRESIDENTIAL DISABILITY: THE CASE OF CLEVELAND AND STEVENSON. *Presidential Studies Q. 1979 9(3): 303-310.* Discusses the lack of a systematic means for the transfer of power from president to vice-president in emergencies until the 25th Amendment was passed in 1967, using President Grover Cleveland and his Vice-President Adlai E. Stevenson in 1893 as an example.

749. Skeen, C. Edward. MR. MADISON'S SECRETARY OF WAR. *Pennsylvania Mag. of Hist. and Biog. 1976 100(3): 336-355.* Analyzes the performance of the Secretary of War, John Armstrong, Jr. (1758-1843), during the War of 1812. Although Armstrong excessively interfered with his commanders and "lacked to a degree the scope and drive of a good administrator," the War Department was made more efficient under his charge and the beginnings of a staff system first appeared." Primary and secondary sources; 39 notes.   E. W. Carp

750. Smith, Carlton B. CONGRESSIONAL ATTITUDES TOWARD MILITARY PREPAREDNESS DURING THE MONROE ADMINISTRATION. *Military Affairs 1976 40(1): 22-25.* Examines the military policy of the Monroe administration and congressional attitudes toward military preparedness. Three factors affecting the discussion were: the economic situation, the traditional hostility toward standing armies in peacetime, and the possibility of future wars. Overall, Monroe's administration made positive accomplishments in providing a system of defense, successfully convincing the majority of the threat of future war. Based on primary and secondary sources; 30 notes.   A. M. Osur

751. Smith, Dwight L., ed. ROBERT LIVINGSTON STANTON'S LINCOLN. *Lincoln Herald 1974 76(4): 172-180.* Reprints personal remembrances which Robert Livingston Stanton had of Abraham Lincoln, 1861-64.

752. Spiller, Roger J. CALHOUN'S EXPANSIBLE ARMY: THE HISTORY OF A MILITARY IDEA. *South Atlantic Q. 1980 79(2): 189-203.* John C. Calhoun served as Secretary of War in James Monroe's cabinet, 1817-25. He inherited the problem of an American suspicion toward a large standing army, something with which George Washington

himself had grappled. Washington had proposed a skeleton army, a stage higher than militia. Winfield Scott had envisioned a reduced army into which recruits could be assimilated in the event of war. Calhoun proposed an expansible army based on that of the French under Napoleon, whereby a basic cadre of 6,000 officers and men could be expanded into 11,000 without adding additional officers or companies. His task was to convince Congress that political and military expediency were not always mutually exclusive in a democratic republic. Congress pretty well scuttled Calhoun's proposal, but he is best known because of this idea. Stillborn though it was, the concept of the expansible army survived the Civil War. Based on published *Papers of John C. Calhoun;* Letters Received by the Secretary of War relating to Military Affairs, National Archives Record Group 107, microcopy 221; Vandeventer Papers, William L. Clements Library, University of Michigan; Swift Papers, Library of U.S. Military Academy; 37 notes.   H. M. Parker, Jr.

753. Stark, Cruce. THE HISTORICAL IRRELEVANCE OF HEROES: HENRY ADAMS' ANDREW JACKSON. *Am. Literature 1974 46(2): 170-181.*

754. Stathis, Stephen W. JOHN TYLER'S PRESIDENTIAL SUCCESSION: A REAPPRAISAL. *Prologue 1976 8(4): 223-236.* John Tyler was the first Vice President to succeed to the Presidency because of the incumbent's death in office. The Constitution contained no firm guidelines concerning either the manner in which such a succession should take place or the actual legal position of the new office-holder. Many observers felt that if a President died in office, the Vice President should act as an interim Chief Executive until an election for the office could be held. However, upon Harrison's death, Tyler moved quickly to assume the full mantle of the Presidency, and quieted possible opposition by adroitly handling and misleading the Whig leadership. Given his swift and capable maneuverings, it would have been difficult for the Whigs to remove him. Primary and secondary sources.   N. Lederer

755. Strozier, Charles B. LINCOLN'S LIFE PRESERVER. *Am. Heritage 1982 33(2): 106-108.* Humor was both a part of Abraham Lincoln's personality and a purposeful part of his political style. His anecdotal humor has been described as his "life preserver." Covers 1860-65. Illus.   J. F. Paul

756. Sweeney, Martin A. THE PERSONALITY OF LINCOLN THE WAR PRESIDENT. *Social Studies 1974 65(4): 164-167.* Recounts memorable events of Lincoln's presidency and attributes his success in office to strong qualities of personality rather than to political expertise and statesmanship. Great qualities of character were evidenced by his important decisions. Good, compassionate, honest, hard-working, rational, master grammarian, taskmaster: all are appropriate descriptions of this great personality. 20 notes.   L. R. Raife

757. Taylor, John M. COMPASSION IS ALWAYS DUE TO AN ENRAGED IMBECILE. *Am. Hist. Illus. 1976 10(10): 14-20.* General Winfield Scott unsuccessfully opposed arming Jefferson Davis' regiment with Whitney rifles in the Mexican War. As a senator Davis later unsuccessfully opposed the promotion of Scott to Lieutenant-General in the lame duck days of the Millard Fillmore administration. The past disagreements were basic to the feud which became overt and vile during the Franklin Pierce administration when Davis was Secretary of War and Scott was Commanding General of the Army. Primary and secondary sources; 8 illus.   D. B. Dodd

758. Theodore, Terry C. PRESIDENT LINCOLN ON THE CONFEDERATE STAGE. *Lincoln Herald 1976 78(4): 147-152.* Abraham Lincoln was portrayed as a villain, an illiterate, morally corrupt, and a destroyer of liberty.

759. Thompson, Harry C. THE SECOND PLACE IN ROME: JOHN ADAMS AS VICE PRESIDENT. *Presidential Studies Q. 1980 10(2): 171-178.* Examines the experience of John Adams as this country's first vice-president. The vice-presidency had few designated powers, and in many ways was relegated to an inferior position. Adams grew frustrated with the position, but recognized its importance when, as vice-president, he stated: "In esse [in actuality] I am nothing—but in posse [in potentiality] I am everything." 28 notes.   D. H. Cline

760. Thomson, Harry C. THE FIRST PRESIDENTIAL VETOES. *Presidential Studies Q. 1978 8(1): 27-32.* Discusses the early history of the veto during the presidency of George Washington. After considering action against several bills including the establishment of the national bank, Washington invoked the first presidential veto on 5 April 1792 against a bill reapportioning the House of Representatives. The grounds were constitutional and compromise legislation was quickly adopted. In February 1797, a second veto was applied to a bill for the reduction of the Army. Washington based his action on military considerations and again his veto was upheld proving the viability of the constitutional division of authority. 5 notes.   S. C. Strom

761. Trickey, Katharine Shelburne. YOUNG HICKORY AND SARAH. *Daughters of the Am. Revolution Mag. 1974 108(5): 430-434.* Describes the presidential term of James K. Polk.   S

762. Wheare, K. C. WALTER BAGEHOT. *Pro. of the British Acad. [Great Britain] 1974 60: 173-198.* Walter Bagehot (1826-77) criticized the American constitution and the policies of Lincoln, developed a theory of national character, and "invented" the English constitution. 87 notes.   E. L. Furdell

763. Williamson, James R. ALEXANDER JAMES DALLAS: FORGOTTEN SECRETARY OF WAR, MARCH-AUGUST 1815. *Daughters of the Am. Revolution Mag. 1980 114(3): 296-299.*

764. Wills, Garry. WASHINGTON'S FAREWELL ADDRESS: AN EIGHTEENTH-CENTURY "FIRESIDE CHAT." *Chicago Hist. 1981 10(3): 176-179.* Puts into political context the rhetoric of national unity used by George Washington in his "Farewell Address" of 1796.

765. —. CONTEMPORARY ESTIMATES OF PRESIDENT HAYES. *Hayes Hist. J. 1978 2(2): 132-138.* A documentary section sampling judgments on Hayes and his administration at his death in 1893. As a whole, the spirit of the press was friendly in its estimates of the character of Hayes and the merits of his administration. Includes 22 excerpts from 1893 newspapers.   J. N. Friedel

766. —. THOMAS CORWIN DONALDSON. *Hayes Hist. J. 1979 2(3-4): 150-156.* Highlights the career of Thomas Corwin Donaldson, special attention being given to his relationship with President Rutherford B. Hayes. Specific mention is made of political appointments, interest in minerals, Americana, and collecting art. A list of the works in his collection is included. Photo.   J. Cushnie

Domestic Affairs

767. Abrams, Rochonne. MERIWETHER LEWIS: TWO YEARS WITH JEFFERSON, THE MENTOR. *Missouri Hist. Soc. Bull. 1979 36(1): 3-18.* President Thomas Jefferson detached Meriwether Lewis (1774-1809) from active US Army service to become Jefferson's private secretary, a post that Lewis held 1801-03. A useful servant whom Jefferson kept at his elbow, Lewis learned from Jefferson many arts, from social elegance to polished language to political sagacity. Most of all, the impressionable Lewis came to share Jefferson's dreams of westward American expansion. Based on archival materials and secondary sources; 3 photos, 34 notes.   H. T. Lovin

768. Albright, Claude. DIXON, DOOLITTLE, AND NORTON: THE FORGOTTEN REPUBLICAN VOTES. *Wisconsin Mag. of Hist. 1975-76 59(2): 90-100.* Discusses US Senators James Dixon of Connecticut, James R. Doolittle of Wisconsin, and Daniel S. Norton of Minnesota, three Republicans who voted for the acquittal of President Andrew Johnson during his impeachment trial in 1868. Although most historians mention seven Republicans who abandoned their party to support acquittal along with a Democratic minority, the author argues that Dixon, Doolittle, and Norton should be added to the list. He believes that these moderate Republicans over the length of their careers represented their party more closely than their radical colleagues in Congress. 8 illus., 4 tables, 34 notes.   N. C. Burckel

769. Anderson, Ken. THE ROLE OF ABRAHAM LINCOLN AND MEMBERS OF HIS FAMILY IN THE CHARLESTON RIOTS DURING THE CIVIL WAR. *Lincoln Herald 1977 79(2): 53-60.* On 28 March 1864 a serious riot occurred in Charleston, Illinois between Unionist Republicans and local Copperheads. Even though several Union soldiers were either killed or wounded, this was not a draft riot. Lincoln had practiced law in the area and had several relatives living there, two of whom were arrested for participating in the riot. Fifteen Copperhead civilians were shipped to Delaware for military trial, but Lincoln transferred them back to the civil authorities in Illinois. Dennis Hanks, Lincoln's second cousin, claimed credit for obtaining their release. 4 photos, biblio. T. P. Linkfield

770. Arconti, Steven J. TO SECURE THE PARTY: HENRY L. DAWES AND THE POLITICS OF RECONSTRUCTION. *Hist. J. of Western Massachusetts 1977 5(2): 33-45.* Henry L. Dawes was a moderate Republican congressman, until 1875, when he was elected to the Senate. He initially supported President Andrew Johnson; but after the president's veto of the Civil Rights Act of 1866 he became convinced that Johnson had to be removed in order to save the Republican Party from factionalism, and the country from disunion. Illus., 56 notes. W. H. Mulligan, Jr.

771. Ashton, J. Hubley. LINCOLNIANA: A GLIMPSE OF LINCOLN IN 1864. *J. of the Illinois State Hist. Soc. 1976 69(1): 67-69.* Describes Abraham Lincoln's attempts to reconcile his duties as commander-in-chief with mercy in a case involving relief of a farmer who could not meet the terms of an Army contract. Based on Ashton's reminiscences; illus., 3 notes. J

772. Bakeless, John. LINCOLN'S PRIVATE EYE. *Civil War Times Illus. 1975 14(6) 22-30.* Discusses the career of William Alvin Lloyd, personal agent for President Lincoln in Richmond during the Civil War. S

773. Barney, William L. JOHNSON AND RECONSTRUCTION: SWINGING AROUND THE CIRCLE AGAIN. *Rev. in Am. Hist. 1980 8(3): 366-371.* Review essay of Albert Castel's *The Presidency of Andrew Johnson* (Lawrence: Regents Pr. of Kansas, 1979), Patrick W. Riddleberger's *1866: The Critical Year Revisited* (Carbondale: Southern Illinois U. Pr., 1979) and James E. Sefton's *Andrew Johnson and the Uses of Constitutional Power,* edited by Oscar Handlin (Boston: Little, Brown, 1980).

774. Beeton, Beverly. THE HAYES ADMINISTRATION AND THE WOMAN QUESTION. *Hayes Hist. J. 1978 2(1): 52-56.* Rutherford B. Hayes was not an advocate of women's rights; opposing the enfranchisement of women, he viewed women as an elevating influence on men. Despite the efforts of the National Woman Suffrage Association and the American Woman Suffrage Association, Hayes maintained a traditional view of women which was incompatible with political participation. The movement to outlaw the Mormon practice of polygamy, and Congress' move to take away the vote from women in Utah, resulted in Mormon women visiting President and Mrs. Hayes, and sending numerous petitions to Congress. Hayes supported Congress on the Mormon question. Secondary sources; 4 illus., 7 notes. J. N. Friedel

775. Benedict, Michael Les. A NEW LOOK AT THE IMPEACHMENT OF ANDREW JOHNSON. *Pol. Sci. Q. 1973 88(3): 349-367.* "Benedict's interpretation of the impeachment of President Andrew Johnson destroys the conventional textbook wisdom which portrays Johnson as a martyred president unjustifiably pilloried by a vindictive Congress. Benedict shows that the decision to impeach was made reluctantly after a series of presidential actions over the years convinced even the most conservative members of Congress that impeachment was the only means left for defending their constitutional prerogatives." J

776. Bennett, James D. JOSEPH HOLT: RETRENCHMENT AND REFORM IN THE POST OFFICE DEPARTMENT, 1859-1860. *Filson Club Hist. Q. 1975 49(4): 309-322.* Kentuckian Joseph Holt was James Buchanan's Postmaster General during 1859-60. He had come to the attention of the President as an efficient Commissioner of Patents. The spoils system, turnover of top personnel, and rapid expansion of postal service made administration of the Post Office extremely difficult. In an attempt to contain costs Holt renegotiated inflated transportation contracts, fired post masters, and cut back service to many rural villages. Despite his efforts to reform the postal situation, Holt was not successful and he was forced to report the Department's largest deficit in 1860. Based on newspapers and Holt's annual Post Office reports; 71 notes. G. B. McKinney

777. Bernard, Kenneth H. LINCOLN AND THE CIVIL WAR AS VIEWED BY A DISSENTING YANKEE OF CONNECTICUT. *Lincoln Herald 1974 76(4): 208-214.* Expresses the dissenting opinion of Richard Harvey Phelps of Connecticut, an ardent member of the Democratic Party who opposed the Civil War and Abraham Lincoln's running of it on nearly all fronts.

778. Berwanger, Eugene H. ROSS AND THE IMPEACHMENT: A NEW LOOK AT A CRITICAL VOTE. *Kansas Hist. 1978 1(4): 235-242.* Edmund Ross (1826-1907) was one of seven Republicans who voted to acquit President Andrew Johnson (1808-75). His vote had less to do with idealism than it did with a belief that an attempt was being made to destroy his political career. He intimated that the trial had degenerated into a scheme by certain Republicans to retain control of the government through patronage. Letters to President Johnson reveal the degree to which Ross believed this to be true. A letter from Henry C. Whitney (1831-1905) to the editor of the Burlington *Kansas Patriot* on 13 June 1868 reveals the degree to which Ross feared Kansas Senator Samuel C. Pomeroy (1816-91) and Representative Sidney Clarke (1831-1909) were conspiring to turn out all of Ross's friends after the conviction of Johnson. Illus., 35 notes. W. F. Zornow

779. Berwanger, Eugene. THREE AGAINST JOHNSON: COLORADO REPUBLICAN EDITORS REACT TO RECONSTRUCTION. *Social Sci. J. 1976 12(3): 149-158.* The three leading Republican newspapers of Colorado, finding President Andrew Johnson's Reconstruction overtures to Democrats political treason, attacked him as an odious character in 1865-67.

780. Bloom, Robert L. THE GETTYSBURG ADDRESS. *Lincoln Herald 1981 84[i.e., 83](3[i.e., 4]): 765-774.* Examines the extraordinary wording of the Gettysburg Address phrase by phrase, presented by President Abraham Lincoln at the dedication of the Gettysburg cemetery on 19 November 1863.

781. Bone, Beverly. EDWIN STANTON IN THE WAKE OF THE LINCOLN ASSASSINATION. *Lincoln Herald 1980 82(4): 508-521.* Reassesses some accepted historical views on the actions and involvement of Secretary of War Edwin M. Stanton during the capturing, imprisonment, and trials of the people involved in the assassination of President Abraham Lincoln.

782. Bormann, Ernest G. FETCHING GOOD OUT OF EVIL: A RHETORICAL USE OF CALAMITY. *Q. J. of Speech 1977 63(2): 130-139.* The Puritan preachers developed a recurring rhetorical form in which calamity was seen as God's punishment for sins, a retribution which carried with it the implicit promise of a better future once the sin had been propitiated. This pattern appeared during subsequent times of national trial, particularly wars, and was extensively used by Abraham Lincoln in his efforts to hold the Union together during the Civil War. Based on primary and secondary sources; 22 notes. E. C. Bailey

783. Bradford, M. E. THE LINCOLN LEGACY: A LONG VIEW. *Modern Age 1980 24(4): 355-363.* President Abraham Lincoln was less than the noble leader that his platform rhetoric and history make him out to be. He led the North into war so that he could implement his domestic political priorities at the expense of his soldiers in the field. Furthermore his "freeing" of the slaves won for him and Northerners in general the role of pious emancipators. However, only minimal alterations in the conditions of the Negroes came about. He passed legislation to restrict the flow of Negroes to the North, and exploited black labor through his representatives in the South. 24 notes. J. Powell

784. Breiseth, Christopher N. LINCOLN AND FREDERICK DOUGLASS: ANOTHER DEBATE. *J. of the Illinois State Hist. Soc. 1975 68(1): 9-26.* Despite Abraham Lincoln's view of the issue of Civil

War from the stance of a unionist and Frederick Douglass' from that of a spokesman for black rights, the two men reached a common understanding of slavery as being destructive of the founding principles of the nation as well as of the humanity of blacks. Douglass' initial hesitation over accepting Lincoln's humanity was overcome through his firsthand appraisal of the president, while Lincoln gradually came to a realization of the need to abolish slavery to win the war and to establish the fundamental rights of blacks to achieve a meaningful peace.

N. Lederer

785. Bridges, Robert D. JOHN SHERMAN AND THE IMPEACHMENT OF ANDREW JOHNSON. *Ohio Hist. 1973 82(3/4): 176-191.* Sherman was horrified by the idea of a strong president. He was a practical politician who believed Johnson a threat to radical reconstruction and to the idea of balance of power. Based on primary and secondary sources; 3 illus., 38 notes.   S. S. Sprague

786. Bridges, Roger D. LINCOLN REACTS TO THE CIVIL WAR. *Lincoln Herald 1979 81(2): 63-77.* Abraham Lincoln's reactions to the course of the Civil War included infringement on individual rights, destruction and confiscation of private property, continued bloodshed, and virtual avoidance of the slavery issue, but they were aimed at preserving the Union and assuring the future of democracy.

787. Brown, Russel K. AUGUSTA ARSENAL IN THE NULLIFICATION CRISIS OF 1832. *Richmond County Hist. 1982 14(2): 18-26.* Discusses General Winfield Scott's fear of an attack on the Augusta Arsenal by the South Carolina militia during the Nullification Crisis; and focuses on the measures taken by President Andrew Jackson to enforce the law.

788. Brownlow, Paul C. THE NORTHERN PROTESTANT PULPIT AND ANDREW JOHNSON. *Southern Speech Communication J. 1974 39(3): 248-259.* The tactics used by Protestant clergy exaggerated Andrew Johnson's characteristics and gave a distorted image of him.

S

789. Brumgardt, John R. PRESIDENTIAL DUEL AT MIDSUMMER: THE "PEACE" MISSIONS TO CANADA AND RICHMOND, 1864. *Lincoln Herald 1975 77(2): 96-102.* To silence critics and to capitalize on supposed discontent in the North, Jefferson Davis in 1864 sent Jacob Thompson and Clement C. Clay as emissaries to Canada. They were to give the appearance of a South willing to negotiate for peace. Abraham Lincoln, at the insistence of Horace Greely, offered to meet with any emissary authorized to discuss reunion and emancipation. The emissaries were unable to meet Lincoln's conditions, but some Northern leaders believed Lincoln had deliberately stifled the Southern initiative. Southern leaders had hoped for just such results thinking they would weaken Lincoln's chances for reelection in 1864. Lincoln countered the southern initiative by sending James F. Jacquess and James R. Gilmore on an unofficial mission to Richmond to propose reunion, emancipation, amnesty, and compensation to slaveholders owning less than 50 slaves. Davis said the South would accept only independence. Gilmore and Jacquess returned north and published an account of their discussions with Davis. With the South's true intentions made clear Lincoln had little trouble winning reelection. Based on primary sources; illus., 33 notes.   B. J. LaBue

790. Buice, David. LINCOLN'S UNISSUED PROCLAMATION. *Prologue 1978 10(3): 153-169.* Abraham Lincoln's failure to make a public commitment on behalf of the Five Civilized Tribes resident in the Indian Territory during the Civil War caused them great hardships. Many of these Indians supported the Confederacy owing to geographical proximity and to the lack of tangible aid and counsel from the Union. William P. Dole, commissioner of Indian affairs for the Union, failed to obtain Union troops to hold the Indians in line, while pro-Union Indian refugees in Kansas were compelled to exist without Union aid or support. After meeting with Cherokee Indian leader John Ross in 1862, Lincoln drafted a letter to Ross and a proclamation to the Five Civilized Tribes which would have established a promising new approach to relations between the government and the Indians. The documents were never issued. Based on archival research.   N. Lederer

791. Cain, Marvin R. RETURN TO REPUBLICANISM: A REAPPRAISAL OF HUGH SWINTON LEGARÉ AND THE TYLER PRESIDENCY. *South Carolina Hist. Mag. 1978 79(4): 264-280.* Despite the difficulty of forming a political coalition after the death of William H. Harrison, the Tyler administration, depending on the expertise of Attorney General Hugh Swinton Legaré, was able to revitalize republicanism and begin a movement to break the polarization between the Congress and the presidency, 1841-43.

792. Chandler, Robert J. THE RELEASE OF THE *CHAPMAN* PIRATES: A CALIFORNIA SIDELIGHT ON LINCOLN'S AMNESTY POLICY. *Civil War Hist. 1977 23(2): 129-143.* In October 1863, three southern sympathizers were convicted in San Francisco of attempting to sail the schooner *J. M. Chapman* as a commerce raider. Their release provided a knotty problem for President Abraham Lincoln's amnesty policy. The case appears to have "broadened his amnesty to include those on trial and those already convicted." Lincoln took this chance to further his program. The President finally retreated from his liberality in 1864, but the case contributed to the California Unionists' distaste for civil law and reliance on arbitrary military arrests. Based on newspapers, US government documents and archival and secondary sources.   R. E. Stack

793. Chuinard, E. G. THOMAS JEFFERSON AND THE CORPS OF DISCOVERY: COULD HE HAVE DONE MORE? *Am. West 1975 12(6): 4-13.* Discusses points of criticism of Thomas Jefferson and his handling of certain elements of the Lewis and Clark expedition: lack of concern about some medical aspects of the expedition, not sending a trained naturalist with the expedition, not ensuring a captain's commission he had promised to William Clark, not sending a ship to the mouth of the Columbia River to bring the expedition home, not preserving the appurtenances of the expedition, and permitting Lewis and Clark to keep their journals (official Army records) which might have been lost and never published. The only substantive and reasonable criticisms of Jefferson, however, are his failure to press for immediate publication of the journals, and his lack of interest in directing that all appurtenances of the expedition be saved. 11 illus., note.   D. L. Smith

794. Clark, Thomas D. THE JACKSON PURCHASE: A DRAMATIC CHAPTER IN SOUTHERN INDIAN POLICY AND RELATIONS. *Filson Club Hist. Q. 1976 50(3): 302-320.* Explains the diplomatic efforts of Andrew Jackson and Isaac Shelby to purchase the Chickasaw reservation located between the Tennessee and Mississippi Rivers in western Tennessee and Kentucky in 1818. The Chickasaws proved extremely reluctant to give up their treaty rights, and only by using bribery and verbal threats were Jackson and Shelby able to carry out their mission. Based on published government documents and the published correspondence of Jackson and John C. Calhoun; 84 notes.

G. B. McKinney

795. Colgate, Gilbert, Jr. THE DAY THE WAR ENDED. *Civil War Times Illus. 1980 19(2): 42-44.* By 18 March 1865, the Reverend Thomas Cox Teasdale (1808?-91) had secured the signatures of Presidents Jefferson Davis (1808-89) and Abraham Lincoln (1809-65) on a document that would have allowed southern cotton to be sold in the North to aid an orphanage in Mississippi; Teasdale dallied, however, and the war ended before he could capitalize on his unique opportunity.

D. P. Jordan

796. Collier, Bonnie B. A NEW LINCOLN LETTER. *Yale U. Lib. Gazette 1974 48(3): 192-194.* Comments on Abraham Lincoln's letter of 29 April 1864, addressed to Colonel Francis B. Loomis, a New London manufacturer, in response to Loomis' offer to finance the garrisoning of Fort Trumbull, one of New London's two Revolutionary forts. Lincoln refused the offer but praised Loomis for his patriotism. Illus., 7 notes.

D. A. Yanchisin

797. Cooke, Jacob E. TENCH COXE, ALEXANDER HAMILTON, AND THE ENCOURAGEMENT OF AMERICAN MANUFACTURES. *William and Mary Q. 1975 32(3): 369-382.* Examines the contributions of Tench Coxe, Assistant Secretary of the Treasury, to Alexander Hamilton's "Report on Manufactures" of December 1791. Compares Coxe's hastily prepared single draft with Hamilton's several drafts. Most of Coxe's proposals were adopted. Coxe showed more inter-

est in cooperation between industry and agriculture, whereas Hamilton was more inclined to favor the dominance of industry. Notes Coxe's role in the formation of the Society for Establishing Useful Manufactures, its problems in operation, and reasons for failure. Based on the Coxe manuscript collection and Hamilton papers; 81 notes.   H. M. Ward

798.   Cooney, Charles F.   SEWARD'S SAVIOR: GEORGE F. ROBINSON.   *Lincoln Herald 1973 75(3): 93-96.* Private George Foster Robinson, a night nurse to the convalescing Secretary of State William Henry Seward, helped ward off Lewis Payne, a would-be assassin. For saving him and for being a key witness in the trial of the conspirators, Seward gave Robinson a clerkship in the Treasury Department. Robinson gained further rewards through political connections with the Seward family, Senator Hannibal Hamlin, and others, and eventually became a paymaster lieutenant colonel. Based on Robinson's Military Service Record file in the National Archives and on the *Congressional Globe;* 20 notes.
                    A. C. Aimone

799.   Court, Susan J.   SALMON P. CHASE AND ABRAHAM LINCOLN.   *Cincinnati Hist. Soc. Bull. 1981 39(4): 251-260.* Discusses President Abraham Lincoln's nominations of Ohioan Salmon P. Chase as Secretary of the Treasury in 1861 and as Chief Justice of the United States Supreme Court in 1864 despite their frequent disagreements on policy, the Civil War, and Lincoln's federal administration; 1848-64.

800.   Crofts, Daniel W.   A RELUCTANT UNIONIST: JOHN A. GILMER AND LINCOLN'S CABINET.   *Civil War Hist. 1978 24(3): 225-249.* After Abraham Lincoln's election, William H. Seward consulted northern and southern moderates and decided to center his strategy to divide the South on a Upper-South Unionist in the Cabinet. At Seward's urging, Lincoln preferred North Carolina Congressman John Adams Gilmer. Gilmer insisted to Lincoln that he precede the cabinet gesture by shelving the territorial issue. Gilmer became enmeshed in Seward's power struggle with Salmon P. Chase. Lincoln's inaugural draft and Chase's victory forced Gilmer's refusal to serve. He pursued peaceful compromise, advocating "no coercion" of the South, no "collision of arms." Lincoln's relief of Sumter ended his hopes. Primary and secondary sources; 48 notes.   R. E. Stack

801.   Crofts, Daniel W.   THE UNION PARTY OF 1861 AND THE SECESSION CRISIS.   *Perspectives in Am. Hist. 1977-78 11: 325-376.* The Union Party, which took political shape in the upper South between Abraham Lincoln's election and his decision to move on Fort Sumter, had political potential. Party members did not want to secede, and most residents of the upper south shared their views. If Lincoln had not forced their hand by his decision on Sumter, the Civil War might have been averted.   W. A. Wiegand

802.   Cullen, Joseph P.   THE PEOPLE'S DAY.   *Am. Hist. Illus. 1979 14(2): 30-33.* Describes the gala inauguration of Andrew Jackson in 1829, which was the beginning of the end of Eastern control of politics and signalled the rise of the West's political influence.

803.   Curtis, James C.   ANDREW JACKSON: SYMBOL FOR WHAT AGE?   *Rev. in Am. Hist. 1980 8(2): 194-199.* Review essay of Richard B. Latner's *The Presidency of Andrew Jackson: White House Politics, 1829-1837* (Athens: U. of Georgia Pr., 1979).

804.   Curtis, James C.   IN THE SHADOW OF OLD HICKORY: THE POLITICAL TRAVAIL OF MARTIN VAN BUREN.   *J. of the Early Republic 1981 1(3): 249-267.* Ironically, the administration of Martin Van Buren, Andrew Jackson's second vice-president, is usually dismissed as a continuation of Jacksonian policies. A new breed of party politician, Van Buren valued party over personal loyalty, and preferred to seek party goals through cooperation rather than confrontation with Congress. Ill at ease with Jackson's presidential style, Van Buren acted during his own administration to build party unity and rededicate the Democratic Party to states' rights. The Panic of 1837, however, led him to reject ineffectively controlled state banks for the federally managed subtreasury system. Accused of executive excess, portrayed as a lover of power, Van Buren misjudged the popular appeal of the Whig Party Log Cabin Campaign of 1840, losing to the other hero of the War of 1812, William Henry Harrison. Based on Van Buren and Jackson papers and secondary literature; 40 notes.   C. B. Schulz

805.   Dahl, Curtis.   THE CLERGYMAN, THE HUSSY, AND OLD HICKORY: EZRA STILES ELY AND THE PEGGY EATON AFFAIR.   *J. of Presbyterian Hist. 1974 52(2): 137-155.* The Peggy Eaton affair had considerable effect on the Democratic Party, the presidency of Andrew Jackson, and the ambitions of prominent politicians. Explains the role of the Presbyterian clergyman the Reverend Dr. Ezra Stiles Ely in the scandal. 64 notes.   D. L. Smith

806.   Davison, Kenneth E.   ALBUM: THE WHITE HOUSE DURING THE HAYES ERA.   *Hayes Hist. J. 1977 1(4): 263-269.* The Hayes administration (1877-81) restored a natural, simple dignity and sincerity not only to White House social functions, but to its interior decorations and furnishings as well. Contains a sampling of rare and unusual photographs of White House rooms and views during the Hayes's occupancy, and of the Grand Dukes of Russia's visitation to the United States (April, 1877). 16 illus.   J. N. Friedel

807.   Davison, Kenneth E.   THE HAYES GREAT WESTERN TOUR OF 1880.   *Hayes Hist. J. 1980 3(1-2): 95-104.* The unprecedented Great Western Tour of 1880 took President Rutherford B. Hayes and his family by rail from their home in Ohio through most of the western states. Illus., 19 photos, map.   E. L. Keyser

808.   Davison, Kenneth E.   PRESIDENT HAYES AND THE REFORM OF AMERICAN INDIAN POLICY.   *Ohio Hist. 1973 82(3/4): 205-214.* The conclusion of the last major Indian war, the defeat of the movement to return the Indian Bureau to the Department of War, and the appointment of reform-minded Carl Schurz as Secretary of the Interior all led to a new turn in Indian policy. An investigation led to firings and reform. All Indian traders had to be bonded and licensed, and Indian education improved. Despite bad publicity from mismanagement of the removal of the Poncas and the issuance of Helen Hunt Jackson's *A Century of Dishonor,* conditions for the Indians improved under the administration of President Hayes. Based on primary and secondary sources; 3 illus., 25 notes.   S. S. Sprague

809.   Dearing, Mary R.   THE ROLE OF THE G.A.R. IN THE CONSTITUTIONAL CRISIS OF 1867-1868.   Karsten, Peter, ed. *The Military in America: From the Colonial Era to the Present* (New York: Free Pr., 1980): 173-183. Discusses the role of the Grand Army of the Republic, an organization of Union veterans, as standby protection for President Andrew Johnson, who was threatened with impeachment and a coup by Radical Republicans during 1867-68.

810.   Delaplaine, Edward S.   LINCOLN AFTER TANEY'S DEATH.   *Lincoln Herald 1977 79(4): 151-157.* Chief Justice Roger B. Taney, one of the most disliked men of his time, died at age 87 in 1864. President Abraham Lincoln attended the short funeral service at Taney's Washington home, but absented himself from the High Mass and burial service at Frederick, Maryland. Most cabinet officials refused to attend any of the services in Taney's honor. The hatred against Taney took many years to subside. By contrast, Lincoln's memory assumed the proportions of a legend almost immediately after his assassination. 3 photos.
                    T. P. Linkfield

811.   Dillon, Rodney E., Jr.   DON CARLOS BUELL AND THE UNION LEADERSHIP.   *Lincoln Herald 1980 82(2): 363-373.* Story of the charges of disloyalty and military incompetence against Major General Don Carlos Buell during the Civil War in 1862; his attempts to clear his name and attack his critics, including Union generals Ulysses S. Grant and William T. Sherman, Republican leaders in Congress, President Lincoln's administration, and the governors of Indiana, Illinois, Ohio, and Tennessee, continued to attract attention until his death in 1898.

812.   Domer, Thomas.   THE ROLE OF GEORGE S. BOUTWELL IN THE IMPEACHMENT AND TRIAL OF ANDREW JOHNSON.   *New England Q. 1976 49(4): 596-617.* A combination of party animosity, concern for Negro suffrage in the South, and a genuine fear that Andrew Johnson was conspiring to seat, by force if necessary, a Congress controlled by Democrats and representatives from the southern states as well as to seize control of the government, prompted Congressman George S. Boutwell of Massachusetts to lead the drive to impeach the president. Based on congressional records and newspapers; 51 notes.
                    J. C. Bradford

813. Dubovitski, G. A. THE DEMOCRATIC PARTY AND THE POLITICAL STRUGGLE IN THE UNITED STATES DURING THE PRESIDENCY OF M. VAN BUREN (1836-1840). *Soviet Studies in Hist. 1980 19(1): 61-86.* Translation of an article that first appeared in *Vestnik Moskovskogo Universiteta, Seriia 8. Istoriia 1979.* 62 notes.
S

814. Dubovitski, G. A. DEMOKRATICHESKAIA PARTIIA I POLITICHESKAIA BOR'BA V S.SH.A. V PERIOD PREZIDENTSTVA M. VAN-BIURENA (1836-1840) [SIC] [The Democratic Party and political struggle in the U.S.A. in the presidency of M. Van Buren]. *Vestnik Moskovskogo U., Seriia 8: Istoriia [USSR] 1979 (3): 43-57.* The depression of 1837-43 occurred during Martin Van Buren's presidency. The Democrats took over some of the ideas of the "locofocos" and proposed a variety of policies. Democrats favored an independent federal treasury, hard money, a reduced role for the government in the economy, and a liberal policy for the sale of public lands to encourage settlement; they opposed tariffs. The Southern plantation owners liked the Democratic emphasis on a weak central government. John C. Calhoun tried to get the party to take a pro-slavery position but this struggle over slavery took place after Van Buren. During his presidency, the Southerners were happy with the Democratic emphasis on economic policy and a weak central government. 62 notes.
D. Balmuth

815. Englund, Donald R. INDIANS, INTRUDERS, AND THE FEDERAL GOVERNMENT. *J. of the West 1974 13(2): 97-105.* The federal government had pledged to protect the Cherokee Indians from intruders in the Treaties of 1835 and 1866 but "there were numerous and prominent signs that the government actually wanted to expedite white intrusion into the Cherokee Nation. Several provisions of the Treaty of 1866 . . . made the area attractive to whites." More detrimental were a series of administrative actions instituted by the Department of the Interior dealing with the right of the Cherokee government to determine the identity and legal status of intruders. This indicated "that the government was not sincere in its avowed policy of actively removing intruders." 26 notes.
D. D. Cameron

816. Erickson, Gary Lee. LINCOLN'S CIVIL RELIGION AND THE LUTHERAN HERITAGE. *Lincoln Herald 1973 75(4): 158-171.* In 1862 various social resolutions concerning the nation were adopted by the General Synod Convention of the Evangelical Lutheran Church, held in Lancaster, Pennsylvania. They were presented to President Lincoln on 13 May 1862. Discusses the background of the social resolutions, the resolutions themselves, and Lincoln's response. Lincoln believed it mandatory to have dialogue with theologians; he cordially received church representatives. Based on the Minutes of the General Synod Convention, 6 May 1864, Baser's *Collected Works of Abraham Lincoln,* and secondary sources; 72 notes.
A. C. Aimone

817. Ewers, John C. PIPES FOR THE PRESIDENTS. *Am. Indian Art Mag. 1981 6(3): 62-70.* Recounts some famous incidents involving Indians, white men, and the Indian pipe of peace, given to Father Pierre Marquette and most Presidents and government officials up through the 19th century.

818. Farrell, Richard. PROMOTING AGRICULTURE AMONG THE INDIAN TRIBES OF THE OLD NORTHWEST, 1789-1820. *J. of NAL Assoc. 1978 3(1-2): 13-18.* The federal program outlined by Secretary of War Henry Knox in 1789, to civilize American Indians, is considered a failure; it included promoting agriculture to traditional hunters-gatherers and was carried out by Catholic, Quaker, and Moravian groups in the Old Northwest.

819. Fehrenbacher, Don E. ONLY HIS STEPCHILDREN: LINCOLN AND THE NEGRO. *Civil War Hist. 1974 20(4): 293-310.* An analysis of Abraham Lincoln's racial attitudes toward Negroes. Asserts that Lincoln's most oft-quoted remarks suggesting racial prejudice have been torn from context, distorting his true thinking. These remarks were made in the 1858 debates with Senator Stephen A. Douglas and were prompted by the political circumstances of that campaign. Lincoln never again spoke so strongly on the subject. Moreover, his support of colonization was most pronounced in 1862 on the eve of the Emancipation Proclamation, and "may have been part of the process of conditioning the public mind for the day of jubilee."
E. C. Murdock

820. Ferguson, Clyde R. CONFRONTATION AT COLERAINE: CREEKS, GEORGIANS, AND FEDERALIST INDIAN POLICY. *South Atlantic Q. 1979 78(2): 224-243.* Details a meeting at Coleraine on St. Mary's River, which was an American outpost just across from Spanish Florida and on the Creek Indians' side of the temporary boundary in the State of Georgia. Numerous factors contributed to making the meeting difficult—state's rights, the Federalist centralizing of Indian policy, the role of the federal government in affairs that appeared to abridge the claims of a state. In the end, the Treaty of Coleraine, signed 29 June 1796, reflected the success of the federal commissioners in attaining the goals of the Washington administration, a setback to Georgia's claims. Much of the work was later undone by the Jeffersonians who emphasized the role of the State at the expense of Indians. Based largely on American State Papers, Indian Affairs, other primary sources, and secondary monographs; 48 notes.
H. M. Parker, Jr.

821. Foner, Eric. ANDREW JOHNSON AND RECONSTRUCTION: A BRITISH VIEW. *J. of Southern Hist. 1975 41(3): 381-390.* Publication of two letters by British Minister Frederick Bruce to British Foreign Secretary George Villiers, Earl of Clarendon, with an introductory and analytical preface. Bruce was reporting an interview with President Andrew Johnson, relating his understanding of the President's policies and ideas. Reconstruction policies were foremost; Johnson opposed Negro suffrage and participation in government. He even wanted white suffrage limited. Britain wanted to improve relations with the United States and feared the Fenian movement. 14 notes.
V. L. Human

822. Friedman, Jean E. and Shade, William G. JAMES M. PORTER: A CONSERVATIVE DEMOCRAT IN THE JACKSONIAN ERA. *Pennsylvania Hist. 1975 42(3): 189-204.* James M. Porter, brother of Pennsylvania Governor David Porter, served briefly in 1843 as President John Tyler's Secretary of War until the Senate refused to confirm his appointment. Though not an important political figure, this Pennsylvania Democrat provides a case study of a politician, wed to traditional political values, who rejected the new political culture which was characterized by highly disciplined parties. James Porter supported the economic nationalism of Henry Clay and voted for him in the 1824 presidential election. In 1828 Porter supported John Quincy Adams for president. Porter joined the Democratic Party in large measure because he objected to the anti-Masonic and moralistic tone of the Pennsylvania Whigs. His brief tenure as a cabinet officer grew out of Tyler's efforts to forge a link with the David Porter faction of Pennsylvania Democrats. Illus., 50 notes.
D. C. Swift

823. Frisch, Morton J. HAMILTON'S REPORT ON MANUFACTURES AND POLITICAL PHILOSOPHY. *Publius 1978 8(3): 129-139.* The tension in American political tradition between liberty and equality can be found in the opposition between Alexander Hamilton's case for manufacturing, as expressed in his Report on Manufactures (1791), and Thomas Jefferson's case for agriculture: Hamilton, in the tradition of John Locke and David Hume, felt men should be free to develop individual talents and accumulate property through commerce and industry, even if it led to inequality, whereas Jefferson, in the tradition of Jean Jacques Rousseau, felt a society of self-sufficient small farmers would best promote virtue, equality, and governmental stability.

824. George, Joseph, Jr. "A CATHOLIC FAMILY NEWSPAPER" VIEWS THE LINCOLN ADMINISTRATION: JOHN MULLALY'S COPPERHEAD WEEKLY. *Civil War Hist. 1978 24(2): 112-132.* In 1859 New York Archbishop John J. Hughes made John Mullaly's new *Metropolitan Record* his "official" organ, if there were no identification with party. Mullaly distrusted abolitionists but supported Lincoln and the Union until the January 1863 Emancipation Proclamation. Archbishop Hughes severed connections with the *Record* in March 1863. Mullaly joined the Copperhead press; he was bitterly anti-Lincoln and a "peace at any price" Democrat. He was arrested for resisting the 1864 draft. Supporting McClellan, he feared the worst. Racism seems to have been Mullaly's main motivation; added were religious fears of Know-Nothingism and Irish economic self-interest. Newqspaper and secondary sources; 57 notes.
R. E. Stack

825. George, Joseph, Jr. CHARLES J. STILLÉ: "ANGEL OF CONSOLATION." *Pennsylvania Mag. of Hist. and Biog. 1961 85(3): 303-*

315. Describes public disillusionment with Abraham Lincoln's handling of the Civil War after 1862, and explores the impact that the pamphlet "How a Free People Conduct a Long War," written by Charles Janeway Stillé in 1862, had in bolstering northern hopes.

826. George, Joseph, Jr. PHILADELPHIA'S *CATHOLIC HER-ALD* EVALUATES PRESIDENT LINCOLN. *Lincoln Herald 1980 82(3): 447-453.* Discusses the largely Democratic and anti-Lincoln *Catholic Herald,* a weekly published for the Irish Catholics of Philadelphia beginning in January 1833; it became the *Catholic Herald and Visitor* in 1856-63, and was finally renamed *The Universe: Catholic Herald and Visitor;* it ceased publication in the late 1860's.

827. Govan, Thomas P. FUNDAMENTAL ISSUES OF THE BANK WAR. *Pennsylvania Mag. of Hist. and Biog. 1958 82(3): 305-315.* Summarizes the issues leading to the destruction of the 2d Bank of the United States during President Andrew Jackson's term, and the battle between Jackson and the bank's president, Nicholas Biddle, about whether the United States should have a controlled financial and credit system.

828. Gragg, Larry. THE REIGN OF KING MOB, 1829. *Hist. Today [Great Britain] 1978 28(4): 236-241.* Describes the preparation and events of the inauguration of Andrew Jackson, 1829.

829. Greene, Larry A. THE EMANCIPATION PROCLAMATION IN NEW JERSEY AND THE PARANOID STYLE. *New Jersey Hist. 1973 91(2): 108-124.* New Jersey's description as the northernmost of southern states is reinforced by its reaction to the Emancipation Proclamation. The state legislature passed "Peace Resolutions" which denied Lincoln's power to free slaves and advocated a peace settlement with the Confederacy. New Jerseyites' reverence for private property, white workers' job security, opposition to amalgamation, and a desire for limited black population were all challenged by the Emancipation Proclamation. Based on primary and secondary sources; 7 illus., 27 notes.
E. R. McKinstry

830. Guthrie, Blaine A., Jr. A VISIT BY THAT CONFIDENTIAL CHARACTER—PRESIDENT MONROE. *Filson Club Hist. Q. 1977 51(1): 44-48.* Consists of excerpts from the journal of Guerdon Gates. On 4 September 1817, Gates recorded the visit of President James Monroe to Washington, Pennsylvania. The journal is found in the Sullivan-Gates Family Papers at the Filson Club, Louisville, Kentucky. Editorial notes come from published sources; 11 notes.
G. B. McKinney

831. Hagan, William T. CIVIL SERVICE COMMISSIONER THEODORE ROOSEVELT AND THE INDIAN RIGHTS ASSOCI-ATION. *Pacific Hist. R. 1975 44(2): 187-200.* Theodore Roosevelt, US Civil Service Commissioner during 1889-95, contributed to the improvement of the Indian Service and acted as an ally to the Indian Rights Association (I.R.A.). A major contributing factor was the similarity in background between Roosevelt and I.R.A. leader Herbert Welsh. Welsh requested and received Roosevelt's help in placing Indian Office personnel under Civil Service and in lobbying with Congress, the Commissioner of Indian Affairs, and the Secretary of the Interior on Indian Office personnel matters and on stopping white incursions on Indian land. Based on I.R.A. Papers, Historical Society of Pennsylvania; 61 notes.
W. K. Hobson

832. Hahn, Dan F. and Morlando, Anne. A BURKEAN ANALYSIS OF LINCOLN'S SECOND INAUGURAL ADDRESS. *Presidentiual Studies Q. 1979 9(4): 376-379.* Rhetorical analysis of Abraham Lincoln's Second Inaugural Address suggests why the speech had little resonance in 1865, notwithstanding its subsequent renown. Time-bound, bitter after the Civil War, Lincoln's audience could not transcend contemporary circumstances which included, as always, assumptions about the attribution of blame. Lincoln's speech attempted to replace political passions with divine compassion. Noble rhetoric could not, however, negate the real, if uncharitable, reactions to war. 4 notes.
P. M. Cohen

833. Hall, Claude H. ABEL PARKER UPSHUR: AN EASTERN SHOREMAN REFORMS THE UNITED STATES NAVY. *Virginia Cavalcade 1974 23(4): 29-37.* Discusses Secretary of the Navy and Secretary of State Abel Parker Upshur's role in the modernization and expansion of the Navy during the Tyler administration, 1841-44.

834. Hall, Kermit L. ANDREW JACKSON AND THE JUDI-CIARY: THE MICHIGAN TERRITORIAL JUDICIARY AS A TEST CASE, 1828-1832. *Michigan Hist. 1975 59(3): 131-151.* Local partisan demands, community pressure, and concern for judicial integrity guided Andrew Jackson's appointments to the Michigan bench, but national political priorities played a more important role. The President's willingness to subordinate local interests to national party development when making territorial court appointments indicates that substantial factional cohesion had developed by the early 1830's. But Jackson acted not merely out of political expediency, for he refused to remove opposition jurists summarily, preferring instead to make appointments only as terms expired. Based on primary and secondary sources; 3 illus., 70 notes.
D. W. Johnson

835. Hanchett, William. THE WAR DEPARTMENT AND BOOTH'S ABDUCTION PLOT. *Lincoln Herald 1980 82(4): 499-508.* Reevaluates sources that led Otto Eisenschiml and researchers influenced by him to the conclusion that the War Department knew about a conspiracy, conceived by John Wilkes Booth, to kidnap President Abraham Lincoln in the spring of 1865.

836. Harrison, Lowell H., ed. JOHN C. UNDERWOOD, REMINIS-CENCES OF INTERVIEWS WITH SENATOR CHARLES SUM-NER, PRESIDENT ABRAHAM LINCOLN, AND JUDGE THOMAS CORWIN. *Lincoln Herald 1974 76(1): 29-34.* An anecdotal account of Underwood's (1840-1913) three meetings with Lincoln and meetings with Sumner and Corwin, mostly concerning Civil War prisoner-of-war exchanges. Describes Underwood's Confederate service and his postwar careers as a civil engineer and as a politician (lieutenant governor of Kentucky, 1875-79). Based on biographical sources and Underwood's papers; photo, notes.
A. C. Aimone

837. Harrison, Lowell H. LINCOLN AND COMPENSATED EMANCIPATION IN KENTUCKY. *Lincoln Herald 1982 84(1): 11-17.* Discusses President Abraham Lincoln's attempt to persuade the four loyal slave states to accept some form of compensated emancipation to bind them closer to the Union, focusing on Lincoln's interest in Kentucky, which, of the four, had the most slaves; Kentucky rejected this plan and subsequent proposals which continued to infuriate Kentuckians; 1861-65.

838. Hattaway, Herman and Jones, Archer. LINCOLN AS MILI-TARY STRATEGIST. *Civil War Hist. 1980 26(4): 293-303.* Abraham Lincoln used an orthodox military strategy, relying on the advice of Henry W. Halleck and other conventional soldiers. Because Lincoln realized the importance of defense and the futility of attacking a firmly entrenched army, he concentrated on activities in the West and waited for Lee to make a move, hoping to be able to break Lee's communications and damage his army. Covers 1862-63. Based on Lincoln correspondence and *Official Records of the Union and Confederate Armies;* 22 notes.
G. R. Schroeder

839. Hattaway, Herman and Jones, Archer. THE WAR BOARD, THE BASIS OF THE UNITED STATES FIRST GENERAL STAFF. *Military Affairs 1982 46(1): 1-5.* During the Civil War, Secretary of War Edwin M. Stanton created the War Board, an embryonic American version of a general staff consisting of the heads of the various army bureaus. Under General Henry W. Halleck, the War Board functioned effectively in facilitating logistical support, and this gave the North an important edge in the war. The structure was similar to von Moltke's contemporary Prussian staff, but, because it was entirely informal, the model disappeared at the end of the war. Primary sources; 14 notes.
A. M. Osur

840. Hayes, Webb C. and Marchman, Watt P. THE FIRST DAYS OF THE HAYES ADMINISTRATION: INAUGURATION TO EASTER SUNDAY, 1877. *Hayes Hist. J. 1977 1(4): 230-262.* A brief account of the presidential election of 1877 preceeds a detailed, composite record of the daily events in Rutherford B. Hayes' life, during the month of his inauguration, March, 1877. The account reveals the strenuous schedule of the First Family, the congressional and cabinet leadership, Hayes' pursuit by office-seekers, and the intricacies of concluding Reconstruction. Key episodes and numerous prominent political figures are graphically portrayed both in the documentary text and the accompa-

nying drawings and photographs. Based on contemporary newspaper accounts and correspondence, the diaries of Rutherford B. Hayes and his son, Webb C. Hayes. 26 illus.

J. N. Friedel

841. Henry, Milton Lyman, Jr. PRE-CIVIL WAR COMPROMISE EFFORTS: A RE-EVALUATION. *Louisiana Studies 1973 12(1): 376-382.* Reappraises the peace efforts on the eve of the Civil War. Details one effort touched on only lightly by most historians: the House Committee of Thirty-three. The report of this committee was the most statesmanlike of all, though it failed to gain the approval of President Lincoln. 13 notes.

G. W. McGinty

842. Hickey, James Thomas. LINCOLNIANA: A FAMILY DIVIDED. *J. of the Illinois State Hist. Soc. 1977 70(1): 22-26.* Reproduces and explains a letter written in July, 1865, by Lizzie Green Maynard, daughter of *United States Telegraph* (D.C.) publisher Duff Green, to a Springfield, Illinois, cousin, Helen Dodge Edwards. The letter illustrates the desperate hostility of Maynard, a Georgian, for Abraham Lincoln and the entire North. The letter describes the burning of Richmond and mentions the execution of Confederate John Yates Beall. 2 illus., 20 notes.

J/S

843. Hinton, Wayne K. MILLARD FILLMORE, UTAH'S FRIEND IN THE WHITE HOUSE. *Utah Hist. Q. 1980 48(2): 112-128.* Millard Fillmore's moderate attitude when he became president after Zachary Taylor's death in July 1850 temporarily settled the slavery question in the territories. Favoring local rule, Fillmore appointed Mormons to four of seven of Utah's teritorial offices, and made Brigham Young governor. Considering controversy over Young's authoritarian rule and over John M. Bernhisel's election as territorial delegate to be attempts to discredit his administration, Fillmore continued his support of the Mormons. In 1874, Utahans renamed the new territorial seat Fillmore in his honor. Based on Journal History, LDS Archives; 8 illus., 53 notes.

J. L. Hazelton

844. Holman, Tom. WILLIAM G. COFFIN, LINCOLN'S SUPERINTENDENT OF INDIAN AFFAIRS FOR THE SOUTHERN SUPERINTENDENCY. *Kansas Hist. Q. 1973 39(4): 491-514.* Coffin was caught in the struggle between the North and South for control of Indian Territory. He insisted that every effort should be made to provide for the protection and well-being of the Indians in the territory during the times the Confederates drove them into Kansas and while they were returned to the territory under military protection. Coffin's dealings with the Indians, certain military commanders, his subordinates, the War Department, the Interior Department, and the Bureau of Indian Affairs reveals a story of wartime uncertainty. Agrees that the Indians suffered greatly and were used in ways that made their anguish greater, but concludes that their plight would have been infinitely worse had it not been for Coffin's constructive work. Based on books, articles and manuscripts in the Indiana Historical Society and National Archives; 55 notes.

W. F. Zornow

845. Holzer, Harold. THE BEARDING OF THE PRESIDENT, 1860: THE PORTRAITISTS PUT ON HAIRS. *Lincoln Herald 1976 78(3): 95-101.* Having decided, at the suggestion of Grace Bedell, to grow a beard following his election in 1860, Abraham Lincoln appeared in the nation's capitol, presenting a problem for portrait painters who had to follow the variant lengths and in some cases add beards to beardless portraits, 1860-61.

846. Holzer, Harold. HOHENSTEIN: LINCOLN'S "PRINT DOCTOR." *Lincoln Herald 1974 76(4): 181-186.* Discusses Anton Hohenstein, a lithographer in Philadelphia who gained notoriety for having pirated and "doctored" more prints of Abraham Lincoln for the Philadelphia press than any other lithographer of his time, 1860's.

847. Holzer, Harold. LINCOLN AND HIS PRINTS: "A VERY INDIFFERENT JUDGE." *Lincoln Herald 1975 77(4): 203-211.* Lincoln was a very reticent critic of the likenesses made of him while he was President. However, he recognized the political value of the likenesses and never refused an artist or photographer a sitting. Discusses many of the prints and photographs, and traces their lineage. Based on primary and secondary sources; 8 illus., 42 notes.

B. J. LaBue

848. Holzer, Harold. LINCOLN AND THE OHIO PRINTMAKERS. *Ohio Hist. 1980 89(4): 400-419.* Discusses regional influences in the printmakers' and publishers' portrayals of Abraham Lincoln at four major junctions in his career: his nomination to the presidency in 1860, his arrival in Washington as the new president and sporting a new beard, his 1862 announcement of the Emancipation Proclamation, and his state funeral in 1865. The Lincoln prints issued by Ohio printmakers mirror all of the strengths and weaknesses of the infant industry and are unique in that, although they reflected the ebb and flow of public demand for portraits of the president, some of the Ohio prints were highly original, occasionally experimental, and in one case directly influenced by Lincoln himself. The printmakers of Ohio, and the nation, gave the mythification of President Lincoln tangible form and widespread visibility and defined a martyr's place in American archive and folklore. Based on the collections of the Louis A. Warren Lincoln Library and Museum, the Library of Congress, the New York Public Library, and other primary sources; 20 illus., 34 notes.

L. A. Russell

849. Holzer, Harold. LINCOLNIANA: LINCOLN AND THE PRINTMAKERS. *J. of the Illinois State Hist. Soc. 1975 68(1): 74-84.* American printmakers were compelled to change their portraitures of Abraham Lincoln because of his changing physical appearance during his presidency and his varying image as held by the American people. The results were sometimes ludicrous as print publishers rushed to capitalize on his nomination, election, important events during his presidency, and assassination. On occasion printmakers superimposed Lincoln's head on the portraits of other worthies in the interest of speed. The varied manner in which Lincoln was depicted reflected the changing image of the president in the eyes of the American public.

N. Lederer

850. Holzer, Harold and Ostendorf, Lloyd. THE LONG LOST LINCOLNS. *Civil War Times Illus. 1979 18(2): 32-41.* Presents, with commentary, a series of "hitherto-unknown, unpublished or long misidentified pictures of the Great Emancipator." 8 illus.

D. P. Jordan

851. Holzer, Harold. PRESIDENTIAL PROXIMITY: 'MUSICAL CHAIRS' IN LINCOLN EMANCIPATION PRINTS. *Lincoln Herald 1978 80(3): 148-153.* The public demand for paintings and prints of key historic events in President Lincoln's administrations inspired both official works and pirated versions. In 1864 Francis Bicknell Carpenter (1830-1900) depicted in his *First Reading of the Emancipation Proclamation of President Lincon* the official version of the seating arrangement during that historic moment. By showing the proximity of the cabinet members to Lincoln, Carpenter suggested a number of political currents and also each official's abolitionist leanings. Alexander Hay Ritchie (1822-95) produced an exact duplicate of Carpenter's painting in an official folio print. In 1866 Edward Herline produced a pirated version of Ritchie's print to capitalize upon the growing demand for prints depicting Lincoln's reading his Emancipation Proclamation to his cabinet. 4 photos, 19 notes.

T. P. Linkfield

852. Holzer, Harold. PRINTMAKERS PROCLAIM FREEDOM: THE EMANCIPATION IN ENGRAVINGS AND LITHOGRAPHS. *Lincoln Herald 1977 79(1): 11-21.* Printers and lithographers faced a number of frustrations in trying to meet the public demand for pictures of Abraham Lincoln. They were particularly hard-pressed after Lincoln issued the Emancipation Proclamation in 1862 because this document assured him a unique place in history, and they wanted to capitalize on the situation. Emancipation prints based on photographs and paintings not only filled a great public demand, but they also had an impact no other medium could equal. Evidence suggests that engravings based on photographs were the most popular. 10 illus., 50 notes.

T. P. Linkfield

853. Holzer, Harold. WHEN LINCOLN PURCHASED AN EMANCIPATION ENGRAVING. *Lincoln Herald 1981 83(4 [i.e., 1]): 617-620.* Presents evidence indicating that President Abraham Lincoln was the first to collect the engraving, *First Reading of the Emancipation Proclamation before the Cabinet,* by Alexander Hay Ritchie (1822-95), ca. 1864, based on the painting commemorating the Emancipation Proclamation by Francis Bicknell Carpenter.

854. Holzer, Harold. WHITE HOUSE LINCOLNIANA: THE FIRST FAMILY'S PRINT OF THE LINCOLNS. *Lincoln Herald 1974 76(3): 132-138.* A comparative study of the author's and the White House's little-known lithographs of Abraham Lincoln's family. The publishing house of Joseph Hoover of Philadelphia hired French lithographer, George Spokny, to make contrived portraits of the Lincoln family. Although not accurate, the prints are a unique example of the versatility and ingenuity of America's printmakers. Based on the two lithographs and correspondence; illus., 15 notes.   A. C. Aimone

855. Hoogenboom, Ari and Hoogenboom, Olive. FRANCIS PRESTON BLAIR AND THE IMAGE OF ANDREW JACKSON. *Rev. in Am. Hist. 1981 9(1): 76-81.* Review essay of Elbert B. Smith's *Francis Preston Blair* (1980); 1830-79.

856. Horowitz, Murray M. "THAT PRESIDENTIAL GRUB": LINCOLN VERSUS HIS GENERALS. *Lincoln Herald 1977 79(4): 157-168.* President Abraham Lincoln was acutely aware of the political threat posed by various Union generals during the Civil War. The tangled intrigues and machinations of men like McClellan, Butler, and Frémont were crucial not only for his own survival as president but for the maintenance of civilian control as well. This was true in late 1862 and early 1863 when rumors circulated concerning the dictatorial designs of Generals McClellan and Hooker. The political situation reached its nadir in 1864 when Lincoln admitted that the greatest threat to his reelection would come from a general. The Democrats nominated McClellan, but Lincoln, aided by important Union victories, easily defeated him. In his political struggles against his generals, Lincoln displayed superior ability as a strategist. Photo, 42 notes.   T. P. Linkfield

857. Howard, Thomas W. PETER G. VAN WINKLE'S VOTE IN THE IMPEACHMENT OF PRESIDENT ANDREW JOHNSON: A WEST VIRGINIAN AS A PROFILE IN COURAGE. *West Virginia Hist. 1974 35(4): 290-295.* Despite resolutions from the West Virginia legislature favoring the impeachment of Andrew Johnson, Senator Peter G. Van Winkle voted against conviction. His legal opinion that Johnson had done nothing justifying removal from office ignored the political side of the issue. Based on primary sources; 16 notes.   J. H. Broussard

858. Hoxie, Frederick E. REDEFINING INDIAN EDUCATION: THOMAS J. MORGAN'S PROGRAM IN DISARRAY. *Arizona and the West 1982 24(1): 5-18.* Thomas Jefferson Morgan served as commissioner of Indian affairs during 1889-93. He brought reform through a national Indian school system of day, primary, grammar, and high schools to give the young people gateways "from the desolation of the reservation into assimilation with our national life." While assimilation continued to be the goal after Morgan, the content of Indian schooling made a dramatic change from holistic to vocational training. The new reformers called for simple training and manual labor so that the Indians could become self-supporting. They were no longer expected to achieve a "fraternal" relationship with white society. The scientific racism applied to other minorities was imposed on Indians as well. This was a step in the direction of the present cultural pluralism. 7 illus., 29 notes.   D. L. Smith

859. Hubbell, John T. JEREMIAH SULLIVAN BLACK AND THE GREAT SECESSION WINTER. *Western Pennsylvania Hist. Mag. 1974 57(3): 255-274.* Attorney General Jeremiah Sullivan Black urged President James Buchanan to arm the federal forts in South Carolina during the secession crisis that led to the Civil War.   S

860. Hummel, Jeffrey Rogers. THE JACKSONIANS, BANKING, AND ECONOMIC THEORY: A REINTERPRETATION. *J. of Libertarian Studies 1978 2(2): 151-165.* Reinterprets Andrew Jackson's war against the Second Bank of the United States.

861. Hyman, Harold M. LINCOLN AND CONGRESS: WHY NOT CONGRESS AND LINCOLN? *J. of the Illinois State Hist. Soc. 1975 68(1): 57-73.* Recent research on the role of Congress during the Civil War has provided valuable evidence regarding basic institutional arrangements, procedures, and power structures. In order to further historical analysis in this area during Abraham Lincoln's presidency, quantitative techniques for the retrieval of information must be employed. Unemployed historians could provide the working staff for developing standard index categories and the construction of a nationwide computerized finding aid.   N. Lederer

862. Jensen, Richard E., ed. COMMISSIONER THEODORE ROOSEVELT VISITS INDIAN RESERVATIONS, 1892. *Nebraska Hist. 1981 62(1): 85-106.* Reprints a report prepared by Civil Service Commissioner Theodore Roosevelt on his trip in the fall of 1892 to the Omaha, Winnebago, and Santee reservations in Nebraska; Pine Ridge, Cheyenne River and Yankton in South Dakota; and the Haskell Institute in Kansas. Roosevelt concluded that the Indian Commissioner needed greater power and responsibility and that the Secretary of the Interior and others should have no authority to appoint agents.   R. Lowitt

863. Johnson, Ludwell H. JEFFERSON DAVIS AND ABRAHAM LINCOLN AS WAR PRESIDENTS: NOTHING SUCCEEDS LIKE SUCCESS. *Civil War Hist. 1981 27(1): 49-63.* Because the North won the Civil War, Abraham Lincoln always is regarded as a greater war president than Jefferson Davis. But a comparison of the two men's records in areas such as military strategy and knowledge and cabinet choices, where Davis is usually criticized, demonstrates that Davis was at least as good a president, if not a better one than Lincoln. Secondary sources; 35 notes.   G. R. Schroeder

864. Jones, Howard. THE ATTEMPT TO IMPEACH DANIEL WEBSTER. *Capitol Studies 1975 3(1): 31-44.* Discusses the House of Representatives' 1846 attempt to retroactively impeach Daniel Webster for misconduct as Secretary of State.

865. Joshi, Manoj K. LINCOLN, LABOUR AND THE CIVIL WAR. *Indian J. of Am. Studies [India] 1979 9(1): 44-53.* Distinguishes between Abraham Lincoln's often-quoted statements of concern for the industrial worker and his rejection in practice of these same workers in time of industrial strife. Laboring classes around the world judged Lincoln favorably; even Karl Marx lauded Lincoln's reelection in 1864. However, Lincoln's conservative view of society would not allow him to sympathize with the inflation-fueled sufferings of the working class during the Civil War. 21 notes.   L. V. Eid

866. Joynt, Robert H. ABRAHAM LINCOLN AND THE CAPTURE OF NORFOLK. *Lincoln Herald 1974 76(2): 69-79.* President Abraham Lincoln first exposed himself to enemy fire while directing the overall Union army and naval forces attacking Norfolk, Virginia in 1862. It was an example of Lincoln's strategic abilities and use of his powers as commander-in-chief. The capture of the Confederacy's major naval yard also resulted in the destruction of the dangerous ironclad *Merrimack.* Based on the *Official Records,* Army and Navy, and secondary works; illus., 58 notes.   A. C. Aimone

867. Keeler, Lucy Elliot. EXCURSION TO BALTIMORE, MD., AND WASHINGTON, D.C., JANUARY 18-FEBRUARY 15, 1881. *Hayes Hist. J. 1976 1(1): 5-21.* Lucy Keeler, 16, describes her Baltimore and Ohio Railroad excursion from Fremont (Ohio) to Baltimore (Maryland) and Washington, D.C. (18 January-15 February 1881). Cousin to President Rutherford B. Hayes, she gives insight into the lifestyle of the First Family, and 19th-century society. She describes the furnishings, decorations, and rooms of the first and second floors of the White House, and other federal buildings. Based on excerpts from Lucy Keeler's diary; 10 illus., 2 diagrams, 37 notes.   J. N. Friedel

868. Kelsey, Harry. ABRAHAM LINCOLN AND AMERICAN INDIAN POLICY. *Lincoln Herald 1975 77(3): 139-148.* Indian policy under Abraham Lincoln during the Civil War was not a major concern of the government; in fact there was no clearly defined federal policy. Lincoln and his Commissioner of Indian Affairs, William P. Dole, believed in both assimilation of the Indian into white society and the need for continuing the treaty process to protect the rights of the Indians. However, they believed this process should be carried out on large reservations far removed from white settlements. In pursuit of this goal several treaties were negotiated with the Indian tribes of the plains, but none were ratified by Congress. Shortly after Lincoln's assassination Congress began abolishing the treaty process. Based on primary and secondary sources; 5 illus., 19 notes.   B. J. LaBue

869. Kilar, Jeremy W. ANDREW JOHNSON "SWINGS" THROUGH MICHIGAN: COMMUNITY RESPONSE TO A PRESIDENTIAL CRUSADE. *Old Northwest 1977 3(3): 251-273.* President Andrew Johnson (1808-1875) included southern Michigan in his "swing around the circle" of 1866 attempting to advance his moderate reconstruction policy. Speaking in Detroit and eight other towns he was defended by the Democratic press, attacked by the Republican. His press relations were bad, and he was upstaged by the military heroes who accompanied him. In spite of this Johnson won some favorable results in areas visited. The Democrats carried Wayne County (Detroit) and barely lost other counties along Johnson's route. Based on newspaper reports and secondary works; map, 67 notes.   J

870. Kilar, Jeremy W. "THE BLOOD-RUGGED ISSUE IS IMPEACHMENT OR ANARCHY": MICHIGAN AND THE IMPEACHMENT AND TRIAL OF ANDREW JOHNSON. *Old Northwest 1980 6(3): 245-269.* Examines the process in Michigan between 1865 and 1868, which created the eventual consensus for the impeachment of President Andrew Johnson. Johnson's intransigence against congressional Reconstruction policies was used by politicians and the press to persuade the people to support impeachment. The study of the impeachment campaign in Michigan demonstrates the depth and diversity of the antipathy displayed against Johnson by the populace. It also provides an insight into the process by which consensus may be developed within the body politic. Based on the Blair Papers in the Burton Historical Collection at the Detroit Public Library and other primary sources; 67 notes.   P. L. McLaughlin

871. King, Jeffery S. A MEMORABLE SPECTACLE; LINCOLN'S MEETING WITH PLAINS INDIANS ON MARCH 27, 1863. *Lincoln Herald 1979 81(1): 20-27.* Describes the events which culminated in a meeting between President Abraham Lincoln and several tribes of Plains Indians on 27 March 1863 in an attempt to secure peace with the Indians of the southwestern United States.

872. King, Willard L. LINCOLN AND THE ILLINOIS COPPERHEADS. *Lincoln Herald 1978 80(3): 132-137.* Early in the Civil War, Illinois was the most ardent prowar Union state. Even local Democrats, to avoid disloyalty, refused to campaign against Abraham Lincoln in 1862. After Lincoln's Emancipation Proclamation in 1863, Illinois Democrats began to repudiate and condemn him. A majority of them became Copperheads and caused considerable trouble south of Springfield. Because Lincoln hated slavery, he refused to abandon his policy, even though friends told him it would cost him reelection in 1864. After the war a few Illinois Democrats were still considered Copperheads, a word implying disloyalty. 2 photos.   T. P. Linkfield

873. Klein, Philip S. PATRIOTIC MYTHS AND POLITICAL REALITIES: BUCHANAN AND THE ORIGINS OF THE CIVIL WAR. *Lock Haven R. 1974 (15): 65-78.* The uproar over the Lecompton Constitution (Kansas, 1857-58), and the policy of President James Buchanan in the last months of his term. A re-examination of historical data.   S

874. Krug, Mark M. LINCOLN, THE REPUBLICAN PARTY AND THE EMANCIPATION PROCLAMATION. *Hist. Teacher 1973 7(1): 48-61.* The Emancipation Proclamation was a turning point in the Civil War because it made slavery a central issue. Lincoln had a long record of criticizing slavery, and he wished to see it abolished. He was not forced to issue the proclamation by the Radicals; rather, he issued it to help the military situation and to right a moral wrong. The proclamation was endorsed by all factions of the Republican Party. Based on primary and secondary sources; 49 notes.   P. W. Kennedy

875. Kurtz, Henry I. THE IMPEACHMENT OF ANDREW JOHNSON. *Hist. Today [Great Britain] 1974 24(5): 299-306, (6): 396-405.*

876. Latner, Richard B. THE EATON AFFAIR RECONSIDERED. *Tennessee Hist. Q. 1977 36(3): 330-351.* When Jackson went to Washington he found a political struggle going on between Martin Van Buren and John C. Calhoun, and each faction had to be represented in the Cabinet. As his administration progressed, the Eaton Affair emerged, and the two factions divided over the issue. The unimportant Eaton Affair soon came to symbolize positions based on more significant issues, such as the tariff question. Primary and secondary sources; 61 notes.
                                                       M. B. Lucas

877. Latner, Richard B. THE KITCHEN CABINET AND ANDREW JACKSON'S ADVISORY SYSTEM. *J. of Am. Hist. 1978 65(2): 367-388.* Uses traditional historical methods and selected social sciences methods to explain the nature of Andrew Jackson's advisory system. The so-called kitchen cabinet, as depicted by Jackson's opposition and by many historians, did not exist. Instead, the kitchen cabinet was similar to an early prototype of a Presidential White House staff, though the comparison is imperfect. The kitchen cabinet was "part of the enlargement of presidential power that occurred under Jackson." As president, Jackson devised an advisory system that was both close-knit and flexible, like a system of interlocking circles, and that reflected his military experience. The kitchen cabinet was a central part of this flexible system with Jackson at the center. 70 notes.   T. P. Linkfield

878. Latner, Richard B. THE NULLIFICATION CRISIS AND REPUBLICAN SUBVERSION. *J. of Southern Hist. 1977 43(1): 19-38.* Andrew Jackson distorted the nature of the nullification crisis by viewing the conflict as one derived from ambition and personalities. Jackson also erroneously considered the nullification leaders in conspiracy to thwart or destroy republicanism. Thus Jackson never recognized the real self-defense motivation of Southerners like Calhoun in defending the institution of slavery during the nullification crisis. Based on archival and primary and secondary sources; 68 notes.   T. D. Schoonover

879. Lieberman, Carl. GEORGE WASHINGTON AND THE DEVELOPMENT OF AMERICAN FEDERALISM. *Social Sci. 1976 51(1): 3-10.* The origins and development of American federalism can be explained by reference to such factors as the existence of a common culture, favorable geographical conditions, and the shared experience of a war for independence. However, the actions of national leaders, including the president of the United States, have also affected the development of the federal system. This article describes some of the ways in which George Washington influenced the federal order while serving as the country's first chief executive.   J

880. Lloyd, William B. ALBERT GALLATIN: AMERICA'S GENEVA CONNECTION. *Swiss Am. Hist. Soc. Newsletter 1982 18(1): 12-29.* Albert Gallatin (1761-1849) was a native of Geneva, Switzerland who came to America in 1780. He became an expert in Indian ethnography, and his influence led to the founding of the American Ethnological Society of New York in 1842. He developed an interest in politics and became Thomas Jefferson's presidential campaign manager. He was secretary of the treasury for 12 years under Jefferson and James Madison, and he headed the American delegation to end the War of 1812.
                                                              S

881. Mackinnon, William P. THE GAP IN THE BUCHANAN REVIVAL: THE UTAH EXPEDITION OF 1857-58. *Utah Hist. Q. 1977 45(1): 36-46.* The writings comprising the current revival of interest in James Buchanan rely excessively on Philip S. Klein's eastern-oriented biography, *President James Buchanan.* This leaves a gap in understanding the Utah Expedition (1857-58) and Buchanan's Mormon policy. Norman F. Furniss' study of Buchanan's western policies can be used as a foundation for a much needed, thorough analysis of the decision to intervene in Utah, related cabinet deliberations, and the impact of both on Buchanan's handling of the southern secession crisis. Primary and secondary sources; 2 illus., 34 notes.   J. L. Hazelton

882. MacLaury, Judson. THE SELECTION OF THE FIRST US COMMISSIONER OF LABOR. *Monthly Labor R. 1975 98(4): 16-19.* Examines President Chester A. Arthur's problems in choosing the first US Commissioner of Labor, and how his eventual choice, Carroll Wright, performed successfully for 20 years.   S

883. Maness, Lonnie E. and Chesteen, Richard D. THE FIRST ATTEMPT AT PRESIDENTIAL IMPEACHMENT: PARTISAN POLITICS AND INTRA-PARTY CONFLICT AT LOOSE. *Presidential Studies Q. 1980 10(1): 51-62.* Studies the role of impeachment in the American constitutional system. Sixty-six impeachment attempts reached the investigative stage; many others never advanced beyond their introduction. Some involved presidents; the first (1843) was against President John Tyler, the second and third were against President Herbert C. Hoover in 1932 and 1933. Already in 1787, voices were warning that impeachment power could be abused for partisan reason. 65 notes.
                                                            G. E. Pergl

884. Marr, William L.   ON THE ECONOMICS OF LINCOLN'S PROPOSAL FOR COMPENSATED EMANCIPATION. *Am. J. of Econ. and Sociol. 1976 35(1): 105-107.* Andrew Weintraub argued (see abstract 12A:2807) that the cost to the North of compensating the Southern planter for freeing his slaves would have been greater than the costs of the Civil War to the North. Such a view, according to Marr, is overstated. The value of the marginal product and land values are just as likely to rise with the emancipation of southern slaves instead of reducing land values as Weintraub suggested. The case is not as one-sided as Weintraub indicated.   P. Travis

885. Martin, David A.   METALLISM, SMALL NOTES, AND JACKSON'S WAR WITH THE B.U.S. *Explorations in Econ. Hist. 1974 11(3): 227-247.* Analysis of the ideology and legislative program of the Metallists (1820-37) proves that the Bank War was a complex controversy involving not only the structure of banking and the control of the quantity of money, but also the nature of monetary systems and the proper composition of the circulating media of exchange. Based on published documents, magazines, memoirs, and secondary accounts.
                                                              P. J. Coleman

886. Martin, David L.   WHEN LINCOLN SUSPENDED HABEAS CORPUS. *Am. Bar Assoc. J. 1974 60(1): 99-102.* "In 1861 Lincoln and Taney clashed over the president's suspension of habeas corpus."   J

887. Mayo, Edward L.   REPUBLICANISM, ANTIPARTYISM, AND JACKSONIAN PARTY POLITICS: A VIEW FROM THE NATION'S CAPITAL. *Am. Q. 1979 31(1): 3-20.* Describes the antiparty campaigns of Joseph Gales, Jr., and William Winston Seaton during Andrew Jackson's presidency. These long-time editors of the Washington, D.C., *National Intelligencer* had been steeped in the republican antipartyism of the Virginia presidents. Therefore, their long, sharp editorial criticisms depicted Jacksonian partisan politics in terms of factions, as divisive, and pictured such extraconstitutional organizations as Jackson's Kitchen Cabinet in conspiratorial terms. Their viewpoint may be regarded as reflective of a large number of Americans at the time, given their long experience, even though their audience was primarily of the elite. Based on *National Intelligencer* backfiles; 57 notes.
                                                              D. G. Nielson

888. McCarthy, G. Michael.   THE FOREST RESERVE CONTROVERSY: COLORADO UNDER CLEVELAND AND MCKINLEY. *J. of Forest Hist. 1976 20(2): 80-90.* The McRae Bill of 1893, in answer to President Grover Cleveland's call for protection of America's forests, precipitated the first serious conservation confrontation between the federal government and the West. Westerners in Congress rallied around Henry M. Teller of Colorado to defeat the bill in 1896. Cleveland retaliated by creating 13 new forest reserves in 1897, 10 days before leaving office. The Pettigrew Amendment, championed by Teller and other Westerners as a compromise advantageous to lumbering and grazing interests, passed in June 1897 to become the Forest Management Act. Enforcement of the regulations for forest management proved impossible. Corrupt practices among federal and state enforcement agencies and general disregard of the law by settlers and industry led to a state of complete deterioration on all Colorado reserves by 1899. 10 illus., map, 50 notes.
                                                              L. F. Johnson

889. McCrary, Royce C., Jr.   "THE LONG AGONY IS NEARLY OVER": SAMUEL D. INGHAM REPORTS ON THE DISSOLUTION OF ANDREW JACKSON'S FIRST CABINET. *Pennsylvania Mag. of Hist. and Biog. 1976 100(2): 231-242.* Contains six letters from Secretary of the Treasury Samuel Delucenna Ingham to Attorney General John Macpherson Berrien, discussing the Eaton Affair and the dissolution of Jackson's first cabinet. Transcribed from the John Macpherson Berrien Papers, Southern Historical Collection, University of North Carolina Library; 36 notes. With a short introduction; 2 notes.
                                                              E. W. Carp

890. McLoughlin, William G.   THOMAS JEFFERSON AND THE BEGINNING OF CHEROKEE NATIONALISM, 1806 TO 1809. *William and Mary Q. 1975 32(4): 547-580.* Traces origins and growth of Cherokee nationalism. The treaties of Willstown in 1806 ceded vast Cherokee territory in Tennessee, which led to a crisis among the Cherokees over the validity of the treaties. Discusses the role of Thomas Jefferson,

Col. Return J. Meigs, and others in attempting to force Indian removal. In 1809 the Cherokees were reunited and took a stand against boundary arrangements and Jefferson's proposals for the Indians to be removed and become free simple farmers. Based on War Department and Indian Agency archives and secondary sources; 87 notes.   H. M. Ward

891. McMurry, Richard.   THE PRESIDENTS' TENTH AND THE BATTLE OF OLUSTEE. *Civil War Times Illus. 1978 16(9): 12-24.* Creating a loyal state government in Florida was part of the presidential politics of 1864. Supporters of Salmon P. Chase were trying to win backing in Florida. Lincoln was also aware of the need for political support in Florida. Thus a military campaign was waged to gain control of Florida. Discusses the invasion of the Union army under Brigadier General Thurman Seymour, with emphasis on the battle of Olustee, from which Confederate Brigadier General Joseph Finegan emerged the victor. Comments on the treatment of captured Union black troops. The federal defeat prevented the immediate organization of Florida as a free state and adversely affected Chase's chances for the presidential nomination.
                                                              H. M. Ward

892. Meerse, David E.   BUCHANAN'S PATRONAGE POLICY: AN ATTEMPT TO ACHIEVE POLITICAL STRENGTH. *Pennsylvania Hist. 1973 40(1): 37-57.* President James Buchanan's (1791-1868) policy of selective rotation or the "rule of rotation" was partly a response to the fact that the previous national administration had also been Democratic. Rotation was not applied extensively in the South. In the North, selective rotation was applied to unify the party. The administration was even willing to subordinate past political friendship to demonstrated political strength. Provides case studies. Based on the Buchanan papers and other manuscript collections; illus., 33 notes.   D. C. Swift

893. Meerse, David E.   ORIGINS OF THE BUCHANAN-DOUGLAS FEUD RECONSIDERED. *J. of the Illinois State Hist. Soc. 1974 67(2): 154-174.* A survey-analysis of the 1857 Senator Stephen A. Douglas and President James Buchanan patronage formula which meant nominations would not be reappointed. Douglas' patronage candidates are reviewed and recent historical interpretation of both Douglas and Buchanan is discussed. Based on Douglas and Buchanan published papers and contemporary newspapers plus scattered papers of less known political figures; 33 notes.   A. C. Aimone

894. Meerse, David E.   PRESIDENTIAL LEADERSHIP, SUFFRAGE QUALIFICATIONS, AND KANSAS: 1857. *Civil War Hist. 1978 24(4): 293-313.* Two versions of James Buchanan's Kansas policy have emerged among historians. Allan Nevins's "melodramatic" version has Buchanan submitting a constitution for ratification by bona fide residents. Initially firm, he retreats before a prosouthern Cabinet Directory and southern denunciations. Roy F. Nichols's "legalist" version has Buchanan submitting only "slavery" to voters, becoming distracted by the financial panic of 1857, and accepting the Lecompton Constitution. Both agree on presidential lack of leadership. However, on examination, Buchanan, striving to hold the middleground by accepting de facto slavery settlement, submitted the constitution with the idea of popular amendment. He showed consistency and decisiveness throughout. Published primary and secondary sources; 45 notes.   R. E. Stack

895. Michel, Dorothy.   "THAT THIS NATION SHALL NOT PERISH FROM THIS EARTH." *Lincoln Herald 1978 80(3): 141-143.* President Abraham Lincoln did not deliver his famous address at the First National Soldiers' Cemetery near Gettysburg, Pennsylvania, for political reasons. He wanted to inspire the living, reaffirm his faith in the North's cause, and give some meaning to the costly battle itself. Lincoln's Gettysburg Address has been accepted as one of the supreme masterpieces of English eloquence, the only speech to have its own memorial. Photo.   T. P. Linkfield

896. Miles, Edwin A.   THE FIRST PEOPLES' INAUGURAL: 1829. *Tennessee Hist. Q. 1978 37(3): 293-307.* Compares several of the incidents in the inaugurations of Presidents Andrew Jackson and Jimmy Carter. Relates the background of Jackson's campaign, his journey to Washington, and many incidents surrounding the inauguration; the selection of a cabinet, the invasion by hordes of westerners, the parade, the receptions, the inauguration itself, and the balls. Most of the material treating the inaugural events is taken from Washington, New York, and Philadelphia newspapers; 62 notes.   H. M. Parker, Jr.

897. Miller, Bud. THE INCIDENT. *Lincoln Herald 1980 82(1): 342-343.* Illustrates the story of a dying soldier who was visited by Abraham Lincoln in a military hospital after the battle of Chancellorsville during the Civil War in May 1863; Lincoln wrote a letter to the soldier's parents before the soldier died.

898. Miller, William Lee. LINCOLN'S SECOND INAUGURAL: THE ZENITH OF STATECRAFT. *Center Mag. 1980 13(4): 53-64.* This brief Inaugural Address displayed Abraham Lincoln's skills as a writer, compassionate leader, and mediator, and demonstrated his faith in God and country. Primary sources.
J. R. Grant

899. Miscamble, William G. ANDREW JOHNSON AND THE ELECTION OF WILLIAM G. ("PARSON") BROWNLOW AS GOVERNOR OF TENNESSEE. *Tennessee Hist. Q. 1978 37(3): 308-320.* Thomas B. Alexander's *Thomas A. R. Nelson of East Tennessee* (p. 123) implied that the wartime cordial relationship between Andrew Johnson and William G. Brownlow was a little more than a temporary marriage of convenience. Challenges this view by examining the circumstances by which Brownlow was elected governor of Tennessee in 1865. Johnson's role was crucial in ensuring that his former political enemy would become Tennessee's first postwar civil governor. Examines in depth Johnson's role in effecting Brownlow's election. Suggests that the later differences between the two men may have resulted from Johnson's removal from the Tennessee scene. Based on the Andrew Johnson Papers, Library of Congress, newspapers, and secondary sources; 62 notes.
H. M. Parker, Jr.

900. Moulton, Gary E. JOHN ROSS AND W. P. DOLE: A CASE STUDY OF LINCOLN'S INDIAN POLICY. *J. of the West 1973 12(3): 414-423.* Reviews the relationship of Cherokee Chief John Ross and Commissioner of Indian Affairs William P. Dole during the Lincoln administration. The Cherokee Indians had fought with the Confederacy and Ross was distrustful of government efforts to ameliorate his tribes poor living conditions. Measures were underway when Lincoln was assassinated, and Dole consequently lost his job. 33 notes.
V. L. Human

901. Mugleston, William F. ANDREW JACKSON AND THE SPOILS SYSTEM: AN HISTORIOGRAPHICAL SURVEY. *Mid-America 1977 59(2): 117-125.* Reviews the literature on Andrew Jackson and the spoils system from James Parton to the present. Though the spoils system was established earlier, many writers attributed it to Jackson because of their hostility toward him. Beginning with Erik M. Eriksson in the 1920's this view changed and historians reassessed Jackson's policies of office-holding with a more balanced view. Though the debate continues, the distortions of the past have moderated. Based on secondary sources; 28 notes.
J. M. Lee

902. Myers, James E. LINCOLN AND THE JEWS. *Midstream 1981 27(2): 26-29.* Discusses Abraham Lincoln's just treatment of the Jews, especially in the chaplaincy controversy of 1861-62, and the anti-Semitic activities of General Ulysses S. Grant.

903. Neeley, Mary Ann. MONTGOMERY, 1885-1887: THE YEARS OF JUBILEE. *Alabama Rev. 1979 32(2): 108-118.* Civic improvements—street lights, paved streets and sidewalks, trolley line, piped water, telephone service—came to Montgomery with a rush in the mid-1800's. President Grover Cleveland's stopover there on 20 October 1887 coincided with a sense of fulfillment and post-Civil War satisfaction. Primary and secondary sources; 27 notes.
J. F. Vivian

904. Neely, Mark E., Jr. ABRAHAM LINCOLN AND BLACK COLONIZATION: BENJAMIN BUTLER'S SPURIOUS TESTIMONY. *Civil War Hist. 1979 25(1): 77-83.* In a reminiscence in *Butler's Book* (1892), Benjamin F. Butler quoted Abraham Lincoln as still insisting after February 1865 that black colonization was the only peaceful solution to American racial strife. Examination of the incident reveals impossibilities and questionable aspects: Butler did not see Lincoln at this time; Butler was not in Lincoln's good graces and was in no way an adviser; Butler contradicts Lincoln's known appreciation of black support and desire to reward it with the suffrage and his distrust of disbanded Southern whites. The whole business is "entirely a phantasy." Secondary sources; 27 notes.
R. E. Stack

905. Nelson, Paul David. FROM INTOLERANCE TO MODERATION: THE EVOLUTION OF ABRAHAM LINCOLN'S RACIAL VIEWS. *Register of the Kentucky Hist. Soc. 1974 72(1): 1-9.* Restates the debate over Lincoln's attitude towards blacks and concludes that Lincoln showed greater flexibility after 1863 after abandoning his belief in colonization. Lincoln appeared to have moved considerably to the left, although the evidence is still not conclusive. He would have moved even further had northern and southern whites let him. Based on primary and secondary sources; 31 notes.
J. F. Paul

906. Nichols, David A. THE OTHER CIVIL WAR: LINCOLN AND THE INDIANS. *Minnesota Hist. 1974 44(1): 2-15.* The timing of Indian crises sometimes had an impact on decisions and events far beyond their immediate context during the presidency of Abraham Lincoln. Aside from his immediate response to these occasions, Lincoln in his Indian policy was involved in a contradiction. This was expressed succinctly in his 1864 annual message to Congress: his desire to make the West "secure for the advancing settler, and to provide for the welfare of the Indian." Assimilation was the only hope for the Indian. 9 illus., 62 notes.
D. L. Smith

907. Nieman, Donald G. ANDREW JOHNSON, THE FREEDMEN'S BUREAU AND THE PROBLEM OF EQUAL RIGHTS 1865-1866. *J. of Southern Hist. 1978 44(3): 399-420.* During late 1865 one of the newly created Freedmen's Bureau's chief concerns was providing legal protection for freedmen. Given the racism of the restored southern law enforcement and judicial officials, blacks could expect summary justice. Bureau head General Oliver O. Howard was sensitive to the threat to black legal rights in the South, but he was unwilling and unable to oppose President Andrew Johnson's plan to restore southern governments to authority as soon as possible. Johnson basically opposed and resisted the efforts of the Bureau's field agents to expand the Bureau's jurisdiction over court cases involving blacks; he thus hampered efforts to provide legal protection to the ex-slaves. Manuscript and printed primary and secondary sources; 60 notes.
T. D. Schoonover

908. Oates, Stephen B. "THE MAN OF OUR REDEMPTION": ABRAHAM LINCOLN AND THE EMANCIPATION OF THE SLAVES. *Presidential Studies Q. 1979 9(1): 15-25.* Abraham Lincoln's political evolution from opposition to political rights for blacks (in the fear that his own political career might be affected) to steadfast belief in emancipation and equal rights led to his Emancipation Proclamation in 1863.

909. Oates, Stephen B. THE SLAVES FREED. *Am. Heritage 1980 32(1): 74-83.* A step-by-step account of President Abraham Lincoln's move toward emancipation. Responding to pressures from radical Republicans, Lincoln agreed to demands that the Civil War result in the eradication of the South's peculiar institution. His role in that effort, from the war's beginning to the passage of the 13th Amendment by Congress in 1865, is covered. 11 illus.
J. F. Paul

910. Oates, Stephen B. TOWARD A NEW BIRTH OF FREEDOM: ABRAHAM LINCOLN AND RECONSTRUCTION, 1854-1865. *Lincoln Herald 1980 82(1): 287-296.* Examines the phases of Abraham Lincoln's reconstruction program beginning in 1854 when the Kansas-Nebraska Act nullified the Missouri Compromise line, in terms of Lincoln's view of the Founding Fathers, and the ideals of the American Republic.

911. Oder, Broeck N. ANDREW JOHNSON AND THE 1866 ILLINOIS ELECTION. *J. of the Illinois State Hist. Soc. 1980 73(3): 189-200.* President Andrew Johnson and the 36th Congress disagreed over Reconstruction. Johnson supported rapid readmission of the ex-Confederate states. The Republican Congress favored a more gradual policy. With the congressional elections of 1866 only a few months away, Johnson made a speaking tour of the United States in order to create a Democratic Congress that would favor his policy. This article discusses his tour of Illinois and the probable effects of his tour in voting in that state. Though he may have inspired increased voting by his tour, he did not influence the voter's minds as he had hoped. Based on archival material and other primary sources; 3 tables, 27 notes.
J. Powell

912. Olsen, Otto H. ABRAHAM LINCOLN AS REVOLUTIONARY. *Civil War Hist. 1978 24(3): 213-224.* Evaluates Abraham Lincoln as achieving revolutionary results, not as any radical or extremist personality. His was a strong human welfare commitment with relentless pursuit of basic social transformatin within American society. Slavery expansionism threatened the national structure and ideals. Lincoln insisted he was returning to the past, but he knew better that he was engineering a basic social change. Southerners realized the revolutionary threat. Lincoln was no extremist nor did he anticipate war; his very moderate success threatened slavery dangerously. His firmness finally opposed even the national majority on peace. The war's impact was revolutionary, and Lincoln guided it. Based on secondary sources; 34 notes. R. E. Stack

913. Ostendorf, Lloyd. LINCOLN IN STEREO. *Civil War Times Illus. 1976 14(10): 4-9.* Discusses the discovery of the second half of a stereoscopic photographic slide of Abraham Lincoln taken in 1863.

914. Parish, P. J. LINCOLN AND FORT SUMTER. *Hist. Today [Great Britain] 1961 11(4): 262-270.* Discusses the crisis at Fort Sumter in 1861 in the context of Abraham Lincoln's early days as US president, stressing the opposition of William H. Seward (1801-72), his Secretary of State.

915. Parker, Iola B. WHISKEY CREEK KEEPS RUNNING, BUT ONLY WITH WATER. *Smithsonian 1974 5(3): 82-89.* Soon after George Washington became President, Secretary of the Treasury Alexander Hamilton decided to raise money by taxing whiskey distilling, which "stirred up a hornets' nest in the Pennsylvania hills, where farmers reacted to it so violently that their protest became known as the Whiskey Rebellion. . . . When Thomas Jefferson became President, however, one of his first acts was to repeal the excise tax. . . . Over the years the excise, under various names, has crept back and increased. The tax on whiskey is now more than a hundred times what it was when the 'whiskey boys' balked at paying it." 5 illus. D. D. Cameron

916. Peltier, Michel. UN TÉMOIN FRANÇAIS CHEZ LINCOLN: ADOLPHE DE CHAMBRUN [A French witness close to Lincoln: Adolphe de Chambrun]. *Écrits de Paris [France] 1977 365: 27-29.* The letters (1865-68) of Adolphe de Chambrun, a liberal Frenchman and northern sympathizer, reveal a profound respect for Abraham Lincoln and a detailed knowledge of Civil War events.

917. Perman, Michael. A PRESIDENT AND HIS IMPEACHMENT. *R. in Am. Hist. 1975 3(4): 462-466.* Hans L. Trefousse in *Impeachment of a President: Andrew Johnson, the Blacks, and Reconstruction* (Knoxville: U. of Tennessee Pr., 1975) feels that Andrew Johnson was "not simply a forceful and aggressive politician but a skillful one too" in pursuing his conservative brand of Reconstruction, 1865-68.

918. Peskin, Allan. PRESIDENT GARFIELD AND THE SOUTHERN QUESTION: THE MAKING OF A POLICY THAT NEVER WAS. *Southern Q. 1978 16(4): 375-386.* Republican Presidents after the Civil War were in the unenviable position of wanting, but having no means, to ensure that Negro rights won in the war would not be lost. Force was rejected, but no other policy could be found. President James A. Garfield had witnessed the failures of Presidents Grant and Hayes in this respect. A former Radical, but more importantly a preacher and teacher, Garfield, by means of a massive aid-to-education program, resolved to counter southern claims that Negroes were too ignorant to vote. Other matters were more pressing, and no sooner had he gotten them under control than he was assassinated. Garfield's program died stillborn. 38 notes. V. L. Human

919. Peskin, Allan. PRESIDENT GARFIELD RECONSIDERED. *Hayes Hist. J. 1980 3(1-2): 35-40.* Before his assassination by Charles Guiteau, newly-elected president James A. Garfield, by siding with James G. Blaine against Roscoe Conkling and the Stalwart faction, moved the Republican Party toward the industrialized future and world leadership, including greater involvement in the Developing Nations. Garfield also intended to reform the civil service and deal with southern and racial problems, but he was mourned less for what he had done and intended to do than for embodying old-fashioned national characteristics. Based on primary sources; 4 illus., photo, 7 notes. E. L. Keyser

920. Poland, Charles P., Jr. ABRAHAM LINCOLN AND CIVIL LIBERTIES: A REAPPRAISAL. *Lincoln Herald 1974 76(3): 119-132.* Explores President Abraham Lincoln's attitude on the Constitution and his attempt to square unconstitutional acts with the Constitution. Lincoln contended that the application of the Constitution was not the same in times of "rebellion or invasion" as in peacetime. Civil liberty policies during the administration were left for his cabinet secretaries and the military to handle. Lincoln violated the Constitution in order to preserve the Union. Based on Lincoln's collective works and J. G. Randall's works; illus., 93 notes. A. C. Aimone

921. Purcell, L. Edward. THE FALL OF AN IOWA HERO. *Palimpsest 1976 57(5): 130-145.* Describes circumstances surrounding the impeachment trial of William W. Belknap, Secretary of War from 1869 until his resignation in 1876. Charges of corruption and bribery stemming from a patronage appointment at Fort Sill, Indian Territory, led to Belknap's downfall. The historical evidence neither wholly implicates nor clears Belknap, who steadfastly refused until his death in 1890 to comment publicly or privately on his possible guilt. 7 illus., 3 photos, note on sources. D. W. Johnson

922. Rable, George C. FORCES OF DARKNESS, FORCES OF LIGHT: THE IMPEACHMENT OF ANDREW JOHNSON AND THE PARANOID STYLE. *Southern Studies 1978 17(2): 151-173.* The impeachment of President Andrew Johnson (1808-75) began over implementation of Congress' Reconstruction orders. Partisan passion overshadowed constitutional issues, and the two sides in the controversy came to see one another as morally evil and engaged in dark conspiracies to subvert liberty. Charges were made that Johnson was involved in Lincoln's assassination and was attempting to rule dictatorially. Johnson saw himself as a martyr for freedom, fighting against unconstitutional Congressional activities. The removal of Secretary of War Edwin M. Stanton (1814-69) was based on highly ambiguous wording. Legally Johnson was right. Primary and secondary sources; table, 61 notes. J. Buschen

923. Richards, Leonard L. THE JACKSONIANS AND SLAVERY. Perry, Lewis and Fellman, Michael, ed. *Antislavery Reconsidered: New Perspectives on the Abolitionists* (Baton Rouge: Louisiana State U. Pr., 1979): 99-118. Examines the charge by John Quincy Adams that his defeat by Andrew Jackson in the presidential election of 1828 was a defeat rather than a victory for democracy and concludes that Adams's claim is not without merit. While northern and southern Democrats presented a generally solid front of anti-Negro and proslavery sentiment, northern Whigs were divided on these issues. Jackson's Indian policy and political maneuvers, even in engineering the election of the northerner Martin Van Buren as president, were consistently more advantageous to the South than to the North. 27 notes. S

924. Robert, Joseph C. THE HON. WILLIAM WIRT: THE MANY-SIDED ATTORNEY GENERAL. *Supreme Court Hist. Soc. Y. 1976: 51-60.* Brief biography of Attorney General William Wirt (1772-1834), who, in the administration of James Monroe, was the first attorney general to serve as a cabinet officer; notes his career in law.

925. Robinson, A. H. ON THE FIELD OF GETTYSBURG. *Contemporary Rev. [Great Britain] 1972 221(1281): 204-206.* Discusses the immediate background of Abraham Lincoln's Gettysburg Address of 1863.

926. Roelofs, H. Mark. THE GETTYSBURG ADDRESS: AN EXERCISE IN PRESIDENTIAL LEGITIMATION. *Presidential Studies Q. 1978 8(3): 226-236.* Analyzes the legitimation function of the American presidency whereby the governed are persuaded willingly to place trust and power in their leader. As an example of legitimation, Abraham Lincoln's Gettysburg Address is shown to replicate the Biblical covenant renewal ceremony aimed at restoring a community's sense of divine unity in a time of crisis. In the Hebraic tradition, Lincoln was interpreting the historic meaning of Gettysburg. Charismatically and through artful use of words, a president binds and compels his followers. Questions how and under what circumstances other presidents have undertaken legitimation functions and with what success. 12 notes. S. C. Strom

927. Rohrs, Richard C. PARTISAN POLITICS AND THE AT-
TEMPTED ASSASSINATION OF ANDREW JACKSON. *J. of the
Early Republic 1981 1(2): 149-163.* In January 1835, an unemployed
housepainter, Richard Lawrence, attempted to kill President Andrew
Jackson, but both of his pistols misfired. Despite early evidence that
Lawrence was insane, partisan attempts to link this attack to Jackson's
political foes led to a Senate committee investigation into Jackson's accusations, later dismissed, against Mississippi Senator George Poindexter.
The opposition press used the incident to call attention to incompetence
and corruption in Jackson's administration, even suggesting Jacksonian
Democrats had staged the attack. The clamor died down in the aftermath
of Lawrence's April 1835 acquittal by reason of insanity. Based on
contemporary newspaper accounts, correspondence, and Senate records;
45 notes.   C. B. Schulz

928. Scheina, Robert L. BENJAMIN STODDERT, POLITICS,
AND THE NAVY. *Am. Neptune 1976 36(1): 54-68.* Stoddert was
extremely partisan in his "high Federalist" politics, but when he served
as Secretary of the Navy (1798-1801) he supported President John Adams
rather than the Hamiltonian Federalists. Furthermore, "Stoddert was a
Federalist second and Secretary of the Navy first. When the two conflicted, the Navy won out." Based on manuscript and published sources;
57 notes.   G. H. Curtis

929. Schelbert, Leo. ALBERT GALLATIN, 1761-1849, A GENE-
VAN IN THE AMERICAN ENLIGHTENMENT: AN ESSAY IN
INTERPRETATION. *Swiss Am. Hist. Soc. Newsletter 1982 18(1):
33-45.* "America's Forgotten Statesman," Albert Gallatin (1761-1849),
was not just an American Jeffersonian; he remained a Genevan who felt
"at home in the general climate of the American Enlightenment, but
[pursued] an independent course that had been charted for him by his
Genevan education"; discusses the American Enlightenment and Gallatin's world view, political philosophy, and practice of politics.

930. Schlup, Leonard. AUGUSTUS HILL GARLAND: GILDED
AGE DEMOCRAT. *Arkansas Hist. Q. 1981 40(4): 338-346.* Prints
seven letters (1885-88) to President Grover Cleveland from his attorney
general Augustus Hill Garland, Arkansas lawyer and politician. The
topics include politics as well as personal matters. Includes a brief survey
of Garland's career. Based on the letters and secondary sources; photo,
21 notes.   G. R. Schroeder

931. Schlup, Leonard. VICE-PRESIDENT STEVENSON AND
THE POLITICS OF ACCOMMODATION. *J. of Pol. Sci. 1979 7(1):
30-39.* Adlai Ewing Stevenson (1835-1914), Vice-President of the United
States from 1893 to 1897, based his political philosophy upon accommodation; as reformer and conformer he conciliated differences within the
Democratic Party. Stevenson's most lasting contribution to American
politics was in founding a political dynasty; he thrust his family onto the
political stage and developed a tradition of service to the nation that has
continued to the present. Based on published sources and interviews; 31
notes.   T. P. Richardson

932. Schlup, Leonard S. VILAS, STEVENSON AND DEMO-
CRATIC POLITICS 1884-1892. *North Dakota Q. 1976 44(1): 44-52.*
The closely connected political careers of two midwestern Democrats—
William Freeman Vilas of Wisconsin (1840-1908) and Adlai E. Stevenson
of Illinois (1835-1914)—revolved around the political campaigns (1884
and 1892) and administrations of President Grover Cleveland.

933. Sharp, James Roger. ANDREW JACKSON AND THE LIM-
ITS OF PRESIDENTIAL POWER. *Congressional Studies 1980 7(2):
63-80.* Discusses the conflict between Congress and Andrew Jackson in
1833 over his attempts to increase executive power which resulted in his
censure by the Senate; covers 1789-1834.

934. Shofner, Jerrell H. ANDREW JOHNSON AND THE FER-
NANDINA UNIONISTS. *Prologue 1978 10(4): 211-223.* The Civil
War measure levying taxes on real property in Confederate areas taken
over by Union forces resulted in large-scale forced sales of land in the
Fernandina area, on Amelia island, in northeastern Florida. Many freedmen and southern Unionists gained property at the expense of absentee
landowners and the Florida Railroad Company. The resultant political
and legal controversy over these land sales and efforts of former landown-

ers to regain their property retarded economic growth in the area until
the 1890's. The pro-Conservative Democrat actions of President Andrew
Johnson affected southern Unionists who subsequently returned to the
political camp of their erstwhile enemies who had supported secession.
Based mainly on primary sources in the National Archives.

                                                        N. Lederer

935. Singletary, Michael W. THE NEW EDITORIAL VOICE FOR
ANDREW JACKSON: HAPPENSTANCE OR PLAN? *Journalism
Q. 1976 53(4): 672-678.* Investigates the background of the appointment
of Francis Preston Blair, Sr., as editor of the administration newspaper,
the *Globe,* in 1830, and concludes that the Thomas Hart Benton version
of the appointment as a rather off-hand and impulsive decision by President Jackson to invite Blair from Kentucky is not entirely accurate.

936. Skeen, C. Edward. MONROE AND ARMSTRONG: A
STUDY IN POLITICAL RIVALRY. *New-York Hist. Soc. Q. 1973
57(2): 121-147.* As James Monroe's latest biographer makes clear, Monroe's consuming interest was politics and his desire for the presidency was
overwhelming. Often unnoticed, however, has been his willingness to
"play politics" by sometimes rather dubious means. An illustration is the
relationship between Monroe and John Armstrong, Jr., a potential rival
as Madison's successor. As members of Madison's cabinet, the two constantly worked to lessen each other's influence and hamper each other's
discharge of official duties. Considering his abilities and personality,
Armstrong probably would have had little success as secretary of war; yet
there seems to be ample evidence that, deliberately or not, Monroe undermined his efforts during the War of 1812. The struggle, obviously, was
decided in Monroe's favor. Based on primary sources, including Monroe
Papers; 4 illus., 49 notes.   C. L. Grant

937. Smith, Merritt Roe. GEORGE WASHINGTON AND THE
ESTABLISHMENT OF THE HARPERS FERRY ARMORY.
Virginia Mag. of Hist. and Biog. 1973 81(4): 415-436. The selection of
Harpers Ferry as the site for a federal armory resulted from President
George Washington's desire to promote the economy of the Potomac
River Valley. Advised by close friends who would benefit economically
from the selection, Washington overrode adverse opinions and continued
to press for Harpers Ferry, even in retirement. In the antebellum period
the armory did promote the region's economy, but was not an efficient
government installation. Based primarily on the published and unpublished Washington papers; 99 notes.   R. F. Oaks

938. Stathis, Stephen W. DR. BARTON'S CASE AND THE
MONROE PRECEDENT OF 1818. *William and Mary Q. 1975 32(3):
465-474.* President James Monroe was subpoenaed by George M. Dallas,
judge advocate of a naval court martial in Philadelphia, to testify concerning his conversations with Dr. William P. C. Barton, charged with making unauthorized criticisms of military hospital conditions. Basing his
opinion on the precedent of the trial of Aaron Burr, the Attorney General
ruled that a President did not have to appear in person. The court held
for the defendant, but Monroe's written response came only after the
court had reached its verdict of a "mild reproof" to Barton. Indicates that
the case was a precedent for the Watergate investigations of 1973-74.
Based on national archives of the Monroe and various court records; 44
notes.   H. M. Ward

939. Stein, Nathaniel E. GEORGE WASHINGTON, P. R. MAN.
Manuscripts 1976 28(3): 225-228. George Washington was an admirer
and correspondent of British agriculturalist Sir John Sinclair. On 11
December 1796, Washington wrote Sinclair in response to the Englishman's inquiry about the availability of landed estates in America; Washington's letter is an accurate guide to the people, resources, and land
in America.   D. A. Yanchisin

940. Stepanova, O. L. IMPICHMENT [Impeachment]. *Voprosy Istorii [USSR] 1974 (11): 217-220.* Impeachment, in Great Britain and the
United States, means the misuse of power by a serving member of the
lower ranks of Parliament or Congress and the judgment given by members of the higher ranks. Examines the case of President Andrew Johnson's impeachment in the United States after the simultaneous end of the
Civil War and the death of President Lincoln in 1865. Describes the case
and considers its significance at the time and its relevance to present-day
politics, with reference to work on the subject by John F. Kennedy. Based
on US secondary works on subject; 16 notes.   L. Smith

941. Sullivan, John. THE CASE OF "A LATE STUDENT": PICTORIAL SATIRE IN JACKSONIAN AMERICA. *Pro. of the Am. Antiquarian Soc. 1973 83(2): 277-286.* Reviews the uses of political satire in cartoons during Andrew Jackson's administrations. Curiously, nearly all of the cartoons came from Jackson's opponents, who claimed that Jacksonians did not have enough sense to understand them and therefore did not respond. Jackson's supporters were able to create a superhuman image by embellishing actual facts. They had neither patience with, nor use for, sophisticated and mythical arguments. 2 photos, 29 notes.
V. L. Human

942. Suppiger, Joseph E. LINCOLN AND POPE. *Lincoln Herald 1975 77(4): 218-222.* John Pope, son of Judge Nathaniel Pope, a good friend of President Lincoln, replaced General McClellan as commander of the Army of Virginna 26 June 1862, in Missouri and Mississippi. Losing the Second Battle of Bull Run, Pope was relieved of command and sent to a post in Minnesota. An Indian uprising led by Little Crow in autumn 1862 was suppressed by Pope. A military court sentenced 303 Indians to be hanged, but Lincoln intervened; 38 were hanged, however. Pope's last assignment under Lincoln was as Military Commander of Missouri. Based on primary and secondary sources; illus., 30 notes.
B. J. LaBue

943. Sweig, Donald. A CAPITAL ON THE POTOMAC: A 1789 BROADSIDE AND ALEXANDRIA'S ATTEMPTS TO CAPTURE THE CHERISHED PRIZE. *Virginia Mag. of Hist. and Biog. 1979 87(1): 74-104.* Discusses the widely circulated and reprinted broadside's influence on the location of the national capital, and prints in an appendix the text, along with a draft by David Stuart, determined to be the author through handwriting and textual analysis. Gives factual and inferred connections between the broadside, and the Potowmack Company and George Washington. Washington, who was interested in Potomac navigation and Alexandria's development, chose the exact site of the Federal district, and included Alexandria. Map, 45 notes, appendix.
P. J. Woehrmann

944. Swindler, William F. JOHN TYLER'S NOMINATIONS: "ROBIN HOOD," CONGRESS AND THE COURT. *Supreme Court Hist. Soc. Y. 1977: 39-43.* Discusses President John Tyler's six nominations to the Supreme Court; only Chief Justice Samuel Nelson of New York was confirmed, because Tyler, a Democrat, was opposed by the Whig-controlled Senate during 1844-45.

945. Symonds, Craig L. LINCOLN AND THE STRATEGY OF UNION. *Naval War Coll. R. 1975 27(5): 63-70.* The American Civil War represented both a radical departure from conventional warfare of the past and a dramatic portent of warfare in the future. By recognizing this fact, Abraham Lincoln became its master, able to use its variety of economic, social, military, and political elements to ensure his objective of national reunion.
J

946. Tajima, Keiji. HAMIRUTON KEIZAI SEISAKU NO SHITEKI BUNSEKI: KŌGYŌ SEISAKU O CHŪSHIN TO SHITE [A historical analysis of Alexander Hamilton's economic policy: with special reference to Hamilton's industrial policy]. *Shakaikeizaishigaku (Socio-Economic Hist.) [Japan] 1978 44(1): 25-49.* Emphasizes Secretary of the Treasury Alexander Hamilton's industrial policy rather than his financial policy; 1789-95.

947. Taylor, John M. REPRESENTATIVE RECRUIT FOR ABRAHAM LINCOLN. *Civil War Times Illus. 1978 17(3): 34-35.* President Abraham Lincoln financed a recruit for the Union Army in 1864, hoping to encourage others to do the same. John Summerfield Staples (1844-88) was enlisted as a "representative recruit" upon payment of $500 by the President. Primary sources; illus. N. A. Kuntz

948. Tenney, Craig D. TO SUPPRESS OR NOT TO SUPPRESS: ABRAHAM LINCOLN AND THE CHICAGO *TIMES. Civil War Hist. 1981 27(3): 248-259.* Discusses the circumstances surrounding the arrest of Clement L. Vallandigham in May 1863 and the suppression of the Chicago *Times* in June 1863, both for repeated expressions of disloyal opinion, by order of General Ambrose E. Burnside. Lincoln's decision to revoke the *Times* order was apparently motivated by political considerations. Based on newspaper, other primary, and secondary sources; 63 notes.
G. R. Schroeder

949. Tilberg, Frederick. THE LOCATION OF THE PLATFORM FROM WHICH LINCOLN DELIVERED THE GETTYSBURG ADDRESS. *Pennsylvania Hist. 1973 40(2): 179-191.* Reviews evidence suggesting that the platform from which Lincoln delivered the Gettysburg Address was at the highest point in the cemetery, where the national monument now stands. Based on newspapers and government documents; 2 illus., map, 47 notes.
D. C. Swift

950. True, Marshall. A RELUCTANT WARRIOR ADVISES THE PRESIDENT: ETHAN ALLEN HITCHCOCK, ABRAHAM LINCOLN AND THE UNION ARMY, SPRING 1862. *Vermont Hist. 1982 50(3): 143-150.* Ethan Allen Hitchcock not only had 40 years of army service but also was a respected military scholar and tactician when he was recalled to Washington as an adviser to Abraham Lincoln. His advice regarding the strengthening of George B. McClellan's troops in the Peninsular Campaign against Richmond was not taken, and the Shenandoah Valley was left vulnerable to Stonewall Jackson's attack. Hitchcock resigned in disgust. Based on the Hitchcock and Crofut Papers in the Library of Congress and secondary works; 27 notes.

951. Tucker, Edward L., ed. THE ATTEMPTED ASSASSINATION OF PRESIDENT JACKSON: A LETTER BY RICHARD HENRY WILDE. *Georgia Hist. Q. 1974 58(Supplement): 193-199.* Reprints a letter from Richard Henry Wilde, a member of the House of Representatives, to his brother, John Walker Wilde, describing the attempted assassination of Andrew Jackson. The letter reflects the conflicting opinions current at the time concerning the details of the assassination attempt. Richard Lawrence, the would-be assassin, was mentally deranged. His attempt on Jackson's life was foiled by two guns which misfired. Lawrence was then rescued from Jackson and the crowd who attempted to kill him, was placed on trial, and spent the remainder of his life in various mental hospitals. Based on primary sources; 7 notes.
M. R. Gillam

952. Turner, Arlin. ELIZABETH PEABODY VISITS LINCOLN, FEBRUARY, 1865. *New England Q. 1975 48(1): 116-124.* This copy of a letter by Elizabeth Peabody to her nephew, Horace Mann, Jr., tells of two calls on Abraham Lincoln in February, 1865, at the White House, with extensive historical and critical notes appended. She was impressed with his kind and generous spirit, his simple and open manner with people showing genuine interest and concern. The notes show that details regarding possible impending peace negotiations and prisoner exchanges are remarkably accurate. 13 notes.
R. V. Ritter

953. Turner, L. C. F. THE GRAND STRATEGY OF THE CIVIL WAR. *Australian J. of Pol. and Hist. [Australia] 1980 26(1): 57-70.* A survey of the historiography of the Civil War, followed by judgements on the strategic decisions of Jefferson Davis and Abraham Lincoln. British writers led the way until after World War II. They brought out the importance of the western theater and the role of movement, and the suggestion that Sherman's Georgia campaign foreshadowed the German blitzkrieg of World War II. Among American historians since 1945, Douglas Southall Freeman praised Lee, T. Harry Williams exalted Lincoln and Grant, David Donald drew attention to the impact of Jomini, and Grady McWhiney criticized Lee's obsession with offensive tactics. On the decisions of the rival presidents, Davis (an ex-officer) is praised for his decisions early in the war and is shown to be aware of the importance of the west, but to be slow to make decisions which might have saved the South after Gettysburg and Vicksburg. Lincoln is pictured as a poor strategist, who redeemed himself in 1864 by leaving military decisions to Grant, "the principal architect of the northern victory." 61 notes.
W. D. McIntyre

954. Waksmundski, John. WILLIAM MC KINLEY AND THE RAILROAD WORKERS: INSIGHT INTO POLITICAL STRATEGY. *West Virginia Hist. 1974 36(1): 37-39.* A letter to William McKinley from West Virginia labor leader S. W. Murphy asking McKinley's help in an 1893 labor dispute shows that at least one labor group viewed him as its friend. Primary sources; 3 notes.
J. H. Broussard

955. Walsh, Francis R. THE BOSTON *PILOT* REPORTS THE CIVIL WAR. *Hist. J. of Massachusetts 1981 9(2): 5-16.* Analyzes the reporting of the Civil War and of President Lincoln's policies in the

Boston *Pilot*, the leading Irish Catholic newspaper of the period. The paper tried to balance support of the Union with its opposition to emancipation, while maintaining Irish American patriotism. Based on issues of the *Pilot* and secondary sources; 39 notes.

W. H. Mulligan, Jr.

956. Warren, Donald R. THE U.S. DEPARTMENT OF EDUCATION: A RECONSTRUCTION PROMISE TO BLACK AMERICANS. *J. of Negro Educ. 1974 43(4): 437-451.* In 1867, the federal task of social policymaking in guaranteeing schooling to Negroes narrowed to the ineffective Department of Education.

957. Warren, Louis and Tilberg, Frederick. HAVE WE DONE LINCOLN JUSTICE AT GETTYSBURG? *Civil War Times Illus. 1976 15(4): 10-17.* The authors debate where at the Gettysburg Battleground Abraham Lincoln delivered his address in 1863.

958. Weaver, Bill. THAT BRIEF BUT PLEASANT KENTUCKY INTERLUDE: ANDREW JOHNSON'S "SWING AROUND THE CIRCLE," 1866. *Filson Club Hist. Q. 1979 53(3): 239-249.* Details President Andrew Johnson's visit to Louisville, Kentucky, on 11 September 1866. After a turbulent tour of the mid-western states, Johnson was greeted by an enthusiastic crowd of 50,000 in Louisville. In his few hours in the city he made a short public address and attended a political dinner. Based on Louisville newspapers; 37 notes.   G. M. McKinney

959. Wessling, Wolfgang. GRUNDZÜGE DER POLITISCHEN GEDANKENWELT ABRAHAM LINCOLNS [Characteristic features in Abraham Lincoln's political outlook]. *Geschichte in Wissenschaft und Unterricht [West Germany] 1969 20(5): 257-267.* Presents Lincoln's political thoughts as determined by the contradiction between maintaining the Union of the States and the liberation of the slaves. He was a careful tactician who declared the abolition of slavery only when it was necessary to exhaust all potentialities in order to inflict hardship upon the Confederacy, and to strengthen and justify his own concerns. 34 notes.   St. Boehnke

960. Westwood, Howard C. THE JOINT COMMITTEE ON THE CONDUCT OF THE WAR: A LOOK AT THE RECORD. *Lincoln Herald 1978 80(1): 3-15.* The Joint Congressional Committee on the Conduct of the Civil War, which functioned from December 1861 to May 1865, was a balanced, broadly representative group and does not deserve the condemnation it has received from historians and presidents such as Woodrow Wilson. Instead of attacking Abraham Lincoln personally or undermining the executive branch, the committee supported him, especially during 1863. The committee operated in a bipartisan fashion, and its investigative activities were perfectly legitimate during the Civil War. Photo, 69 notes.   T. P. Linkfield

961. Westwood, Howard C. LINCOLN AND THE HAMPTON ROADS PEACE CONFERENCE. *Lincoln Herald 1979 81(4): 243-256.* President Abraham Lincoln's personal presence at the Hampton Roads Conference in February 1865 probably was prompted by considerations of the future politics of reconstruction.

962. Wiener, Jonathan M. RECONSTRUCTION POLITICS AND SOUTHERN CLASS STRUCTURE. *Rev. in Am. Hist. 1980 8(2): 240-245.* Review essay of Herman Belz's *Emancipation and Equal Rights: Politics and Constitutionalism in the Civil War Era* (New York: W. W. Norton, 1978) and Peyton McCrary's *Abraham Lincoln and Reconstruction: The Louisiana Experiment* (Princeton, N.J.: Princeton U. Pr., 1978); 1850's-80's.

963. Wood, Harry. HOW BOTH ABRAHAM LINCOLNS HELPED FOUND ARIZONA. *Lincoln Herald 1976 78(3): 109-118.* Association through various family connections (one of which was acquainted with Abraham Lincoln's grandfather whose name he bore) led Charles Debrille Posten, an advocate for Arizona territorial status, to the president and eventually to the successful granting of territorial status in 1863. Discusses other connections between Lincoln and Arizona.

964. Zaitseva, N. D. DEMOKRATICHESKIE REFORMY PREZIDENTA T. DZHEFFERSONA (1800-1804 GG.) [The democratic reforms of President T. Jefferson (1800-04)]. *Vestnik Leningradskogo U.:*

Seria Istorii, Iazyka, i Literatury [USSR] 1978 8(2): 64-69. A survey of Thomas Jefferson's reforms during 1801-04 which concludes that the reforms were dictated by the existing conditions of the development of capitalism and the emerging bourgeois liberalism. The state structure by the end of his presidency was undoubtedly unique in comparison with the monarchist form of government to be found in the powerful governments of that time. 12 notes.   G. F. Jewsbury

965. —. ANDREW JACKSON'S ADVICE TO THE CHEROKEES. *J. of Cherokee Studies 1979 4(2): 96-97.* Cherokee removal was consistently pursued as a major policy by Andrew Jackson throughout his career. In 1835, in advice to the Cherokee Indians, he forcibly reiterated this policy. He was convinced that the Cherokees had no choice but to remove west of the Mississippi or face extinction. Reproduced from *The Alleghany Democrat* (Alleghany, New York), 7 April 1835.

J. M. Lee

966. —. THOMAS JEFFERSON'S ADVICE TO THE CHEROKEES. *J. of Cherokee Studies 1979 4(2): 64-66.* Shortly before his retirement in 1809, Thomas Jefferson delivered two speeches to a Cherokee delegation. In the first, he advised the adoption of laws and industrious pursuits; in the second, he indicated a preference for Cherokee removal to the west of the Mississippi. Reproduced from *The National Intelligencer and Washington Advertiser,* 10 March 1809.

J. M. Lee

Foreign Affairs

967. Alvarez Pedroso, Antonio. LA DOCTRINA DE MONROE Y CUBA [The Monroe Doctrine and Cuba]. *R. Interamericana R. [Puerto Rico] 1974 4(1): 46-56.* John Quincy Adams convinced President Monroe not to cooperate with the British against the projects of the Holy Alliance in the New World from fear than an alliance with Great Britain might prevent the United States from annexing Cuba should the opportunity arise. Based on primary and secondary sources; 21 notes.

J. Lewis

968. Anderson, David L. THE DIPLOMACY OF DISCRIMINATION: CHINESE EXCLUSION, 1876-1882. *California Hist. 1978 57(1): 32-45.* Traces the steps leading to the Chinese Exclusion Act (1882). The 1868 Burlingame Treaty had established the right of free immigration of Chinese to America. Pressures on Congress to prohibit Chinese immigration resulted in passage of a law limiting to 15 the number of Chinese on incoming ships; President Hayes vetoed the law. The US minister to China, George Seward, was removed because of his opposition to Chinese exclusion. In his place a diplomatic mission led by James B. Argell went to China in 1880 to revise the Burlingame Treaty. After some hard bargaining the Argell Treaty was agreed on, replacing free immigration with the right of Congress to "regulate, limit, or suspend" the immigration of Chinese laborers, while exempting students, merchants, and tourists. The treaty was approved, and was immediately followed by seven bills to exclude Chinese. President Chester A. Arthur vetoed a bill suspending immigration for 20 years but approved a substitute bill excluding Chinese for 10 years. The Chinese government, plagued by pressures from other countries and internal problems, could not retaliate. The episode reveals the use of treaties and international law to provide legitimacy for arbitrary actions against a weak country. Primary and secondary sources; illus., photos, 46 notes.   A. Hoffman

969. Anderson, Stuart. RACIAL ANGLO-SAXONISM AND THE AMERICAN RESPONSE TO THE BOER WAR. *Diplomatic Hist. 1978 2(3): 219-236.* Racial Anglo-Saxonism was a prominent rhetorical feature of the powerful minority in the United States which supported the British cause in South Africa. Secretary of State John Hay, an admirer of Cecil Rhodes, and Theodore Roosevelt, who was of Dutch descent and thus preferred to speak of the English-speaking rather than of the Anglo-Saxon race, were among this minority. When the fortunes of war turned against the Boers in early 1900, the Darwinian theme of survival of the fittest was increasingly invoked. The issue was virtually dead by the time of the 1900 election. Primary sources; 50 notes.   L. W. Van Wyk

970. Bell, Rudolph M. MR. MADISON'S WAR AND LONG-TERM CONGRESSIONAL VOTING BEHAVIOR. *William and Mary Q. 1979 36(3): 373-395.* By analyzing roll-call voting on foreign policy of Congress, 1789-1812, it is shown that the 12th Congress that voted for war in 1812 was following consistent, traditional voting patterns, and therefore the partisan vote for war does not especially reflect weak leadership of President James Madison. Six hundred roll calls were investigated. No district changed voting alignments regularly. The opposition group in Congress was national, though with a majority of its members from New England. Also tested are fluctuations in wholesale prices of certain commodities in various locations, so as to determine the extent of economic motives in voting. Based on Congressional records; 9 tables, 18 notes, appendix-District (by state) Success Scores, 1789-1812.
H. M. Ward

971. Belohlavek, John M. ANDREW JACKSON AND THE MALAYSIAN PIRATES: A QUESTION OF DIPLOMACY AND POLITICS. *Tennessee Hist. Q. 1977 36(1): 19-29.* When an American trading ship was captured by hostile natives in Sumatra in 1831, President Andrew Jackson sent a naval vessel to investigate. Captain John Downes decided to attack the pirates which led to more than 100 native casualties, including women and children. Anti-Jackson journalists denounced the use of force without attempting to negotiate and a press battle ensued. Once Jackson released the documents of the case to a congressional committee, the issue faded. Americans' interest in the Sumatra massacre was purely domestic politics. Primary and secondary sources; 15 notes.
M. B. Lucas

972. Belohlavek, John M. "LET THE EAGLE SOAR!": DEMOCRATIC CONSTRAINTS ON THE FOREIGN POLICY OF ANDREW JACKSON. *Presidential Studies Q. 1980 10(1): 36-50.* Eight years of Andrew Jackson's presidency witnessed the revival of this office that had stagnated since Jefferson's departure in 1809. Jackson's diplomacy could be called energetic, sometimes imaginative, and often successful. During his two terms the United States involved itself in no foreign wars. Jacksonian diplomacy was characterized by the president himself, not by his cabinet. Based on official documents; 41 notes, 2 appendixes.
G. E. Pergl

973. Benjamin, Thomas. RECENT HISTORIOGRAPHY OF THE ORIGINS OF THE MEXICAN WAR. *New Mexico Hist. Rev. 1979 54(3): 169-181.* Surveys the continuing trends and new interpretations since the mid-1960's. Three basic interpretations are discussed, including the Whig thesis, which held that President James K. Polk (1795-1849) was responsible for the war, and the Democratic thesis, which maintained that Mexico was to blame. A third group of studies, which transcends the Whig-Democratic argument, is more evenhanded and significantly improves the quality of Mexican War historiography. A closer look at the origins of the Mexican War is essential to the study of American expansionism and of Mexican and Hispanic-American politics and national character. 48 notes.
P. L. McLaughlin

974. Bergquist, Harold E., Jr. JOHN QUINCY ADAMS AND THE PROMULGATION OF THE MONROE DOCTRINE, OCTOBER-DECEMBER, 1823. *Essex Inst. Hist. Collections 1975 3(1): 37-52.* George Canning, the British foreign secretary, suggested "a joint Anglo-American statement to warn the Holy Allies not to try to subvert the independence of the new Latin American nations." Adams opposed the idea and conceived the noncolonization principle. These principles of American non-interference in strictly European affairs (such as Greece) and of European non-interference in the affairs of the independent American states constitute the Monroe Doctrine of 1823 included in the presidential address. By taking this action independently of England Monroe wrote that it was done in a manner more conciliatory to Russia and the other countries. 41 notes.
E. P. Stickney

975. Bickerton, Ian J. JOHN HAY'S OPEN DOOR POLICY: A RE-EXAMINATION. *Australian J. of Pol. and Hist. [Australia] 1977 23(1): 54-66.* Details the background to Secretary of State John Hay's China policy of 1899-1901 and suggests that recent revisionist interpretations are incorrect. Marilyn Young (1969) and Raymond Esthus (1959) deemed that the Open Door policy concerned commerce, finance, and politics, and suggested that, while the rhetoric stressed Open Door, in reality US policy soon became a pragmatic one of securing only equal access for US trade. An examination of the Philander C. Knox, Francis M. Huntington Wilson, Willard Straight, William Rockhill, and Hay Papers indicates that the Open Door and opposition to foreign spheres were consistently pursued.
W. D. McIntyre

976. Calkin, Homer L. A 1900 LOOK AT FOREIGN RELATIONS OF THE UNITED STATES. *Soc. for Hist. of Am. Foreign Relations. Newsletter 1979 10(3): 9-12.* Presents a memorandum written in 1900 by chief clerk William H. Michael, following his meeting with Secretary of State John Milton Hay, concerning the two-year delay in the selection and publication of US foreign relations documents for 1898, and the results of his recommendations.

977. Cole, Terrence. THE STRANGE SAGA OF THE PRESIDENT'S DESK. *Am. Heritage 1981 32(6): 62-64.* The presidential desk in the Oval Office was given to President Rutherford B. Hayes by Queen Victoria in 1880. Made from the remains of a British ship, *Resolute,* the desk was given to the United States because of an earlier American action returning the lost ship to England. 5 illus.
J. F. Paul.

978. Cortada, James W. SPANISH VIEWS ON ABRAHAM LINCOLN, 1861-1865. *Lincoln Herald 1974 76(2): 80-85.* Spain watched Abraham Lincoln closely because of United States interest in annexing Spanish Cuba and Lincoln's views on slavery. Gabriel Garcia Tassara, Spanish minister to the United States, wrote regularly to Madrid informing Spanish officials and newspaper editors of Lincoln's views and the American Civil War. Reaction in Spain to Lincoln's assassination was great, due to his popularity there. Based on Spanish Foreign Office Archives, National Archives, Records of the Department of State and contemporary Spanish newspapers; 25 notes.
A. C. Aimone

979. Crapol, Edward P. JOHN QUINCY ADAMS AND THE MONROE DOCTRINE: SOME NEW EVIDENCE. *Pacific Hist. Rev. 1979 48(3): 413-418.* A recently discovered letter from John Quincy Adams to Richard Rush discloses that Adams wrote President Monroe's declaration in the message of December 1823 (Monroe Doctrine), including the noncolonization paragraph, to check both Russian and British designs in North and South America. 15 notes.
R. N. Lokken

980. Cress, Larry D. THE JONATHAN ROBBINS INCIDENT: EXTRADITION AND THE SEPARATION OF POWERS IN THE ADAMS ADMINISTRATION. *Essex Inst. Hist. Collections 1975 111(2): 99-121.* Great Britain charged that Jonathan Robbins was involved in a mutiny in 1797 and asked for his extradition under the Jay Treaty. Robbins claimed he was an American citizen. In a full examination of the incident and the controversy surrounding it, the author finds that Robbins was probably correct. The significance of the case is in the extradition debate, which clarified and institutionalized the issue constitutionally. It also forced a critical examination of the constitutional relationship between the executive and judiciary branches which had long-range repercussions. Based on trial records, letters, newspapers, congressional records, and secondary sources; 72 notes.
R. M. Rollins

981. Davis, Robert R., Jr. PELL-MELL: JEFFERSONIAN ETIQUETTE AND PROTOCOL. *Historian 1981 43(4): 509-529.* When elected president in 1800, Thomas Jefferson "pushed the doctrine of republican simplicity to its logical extreme in a system of etiquette and protocol," which he dubbed "pell-mell." His "Canons of Etiquette" formulated in November 1803 attempted to strip diplomatic etiquette and protocol of its legendary formality and punctiliousness. Jefferson's republican virtues created a social war with the British foreign minister Anthony Merry, which had profound repercussions. When Jefferson realized that his extremism in matters of diplomatic etiquette may have pushed Merry and the Spanish ambassador Yrujo to the brink of conspiracy with Aaron Burr, he modified his strict adherence to republican simplicity after the election of 1804. Primary sources; 87 notes.
R. S. Sliwoski

982. Dell, Christopher. RECONSTRUCTION, HAD LINCOLN LIVED. *Lincoln Herald 1979 81(4): 257-265.* President Abraham Lincoln's reconstruction policies would have been more like those of the Radicals than traditional historiography has allowed.

983. Dillon, Merton L. POLK, EXPANSIONISM, AND MORAL-ITY. *R. in Am. Hist. 1974 2(3): 389-394.* David M. Pletcher's *The Diplomacy of Annexation: Texas, Oregon, and the Mexican War* (Columbia: U. of Missouri Pr., 1973) examines the diplomacy of imperialism and James K. Polk in the 1830's and 1840's, and John H. Schroeder's *Mr. Polk's War: American Opposition and Dissent, 1846-1848* (Madison: U. of Wisconsin Pr., 1973) focuses on the inefficacy of congressional and public antiwar sentiment.

984. Dumbauld, Edward. INDEPENDENCE UNDER INTERNA-TIONAL LAW. *Am. J. of Int. Law 1976 70(3): 425-431.* During the incumbency of George Washington as President and of Thomas Jefferson as Secretary of State, the foundations were laid for according to neutral nations those rights sanctioned by international law.

R. J. Jirran

985. Fohlen, Claude. JEFFERSON ET L'ACHAT DE LA LOUI-SIANE [Jefferson and the Louisiana Purchase]. *Histoire [France] 1978 (5): 75-77.* Review article of Alexander De Conde's *This Affair of Louisi-ana* (New York: Scribner's, 1976).

986. Fry, Joseph A. SILVER AND SENTIMENT: THE NEVADA PRESS AND THE COMING OF THE SPANISH-AMERICAN WAR. *Nevada Hist. Soc. Q. 1977 20(4): 222-239.* Analyzes editorials about Cuban affairs in 25 Nevada newspapers before the Spanish-American War. All papers criticized Spanish rule in Cuba and most disagreed with Cuban policies of President William McKinley (1843-1901). Papers sup-porting free silver resorted to yellow journalism and advocated war with Spain to improve Nevada's economy. Republican papers called for war with Spain but cited principally self-defense and humanitarian reasons. Based on newspaper and secondary sources; 2 photos, 108 notes.

H. T. Lovin

987. Fry, Joseph A. WASHINGTON'S FAREWELL ADDRESS AND AMERICAN COMMERCE. *West Virginia Hist. 1976 37(4): 281-291.* The endorsement of free trade in George Washington's 1796 Farewell Address was Alexander Hamilton's work. Hamilton thought British trade and capital were vital to America's growth and he had opposed for years all Republican attempts to discriminate against Great Britain and divert commerce to France. He used the Farewell Address to marshall Washington's prestige behind the policy of continued depen-dence on British trade. Based on primary and secondary sources; 34 notes.

J. H. Broussard

988. Fry, Joseph A. WILLIAM MCKINLEY AND THE COMING OF THE SPANISH-AMERICAN WAR: A STUDY OF THE BE-SMIRCHING AND REDEMPTION OF AN HISTORICAL IMAGE. *Diplomatic Hist. 1979 3(1): 77-97.* Traces the historiography on Presi-dent William McKinley (1897-1901) and his role in the coming of the Spanish-American War (1898). McKinley was neither "so weak, pliable, and expedient as his critics suggest" nor "so purposeful or so masterfully in control as portrayed by his supporters." Secondary sources; 64 notes.

T. L. Powers

989. Gelfand, Lawrence E. REVIVALS OF A DIPLOMAT AND A WAR: JOHN W. FOSTER AND THE SPANISH-AMERICAN CON-FLICT. *Rev. in Am. Hist. 1982 10(1): 99-104.* Reviews Michael J. Devine's *John W. Foster: Politics and Diplomacy in the Imperial Era, 1873-1917* (1981), on the career of the secretary of state under Benjamin Harrison, and diplomat David F. Trask's *The War with Spain in 1898* (1981), on America's emergence as a world power.

990. Gilley, B. H. "POLK'S WAR" AND THE LOUISIANA PRESS. *Louisiana Hist. 1979 20(1): 5-24.* As reflected in the editorials in their state newspapers, Louisianians welcomed the outbreak of the Mexican War in 1846. They hailed the war as part of America's Manifest Destiny to spread republican institutions (though not necessarily slavery), and they expected their own Zachary Taylor to end the hostilities quickly. They became disillusioned with the war, however, when President James K. Polk failed to prosecute it vigorously and played politics with military appointments, and when the war changed from defending American fron-tiers and punishing aggressors to annexing new territory. Louisianians favored the cession of New Mexico and California but not acquiring all of Mexico. Primary and secondary sources; 49 notes.

L. N. Powell

991. Golladay, V. Dennis. THE UNITED STATES AND BRITISH NORTH AMERICAN FISHERIES, 1815-1818. *Am. Neptune 1973 33(4): 246-257.* A study of the diplomatic struggle between the United States and Great Britain over American rights to fish off the coast of British America and the Newfoundland banks. The American case was handled largely by James Monroe, Secretary of State (and President, 1817-25), and John Quincy Adams, one of the Ghent commissioners (1814) and shortly to be minister to Britain. Both nations compromised their positions, with the United States the largest beneficiary. Knowing that Britain was anxious for settlement, the United States had a main tactic of delay. 49 notes.

R. V. Ritter

992. Gould, Lewis L. THE REICK TELEGRAM AND THE SPAN-ISH-AMERICAN WAR: A REAPPRAISAL. *Diplomatic Hist. 1979 3(2): 193-199.* A telegram of 25 March 1898 from William C. Reick, editor of the New York *Herald,* to John Russell Young, Librarian of Congress, noting that businessmen now supported war with Spain over Cuba, has been prominently used by revisionist historians to explain why President William McKinley decided to go to war. The telegram, how-ever, has been overvalued; it did not reach the White House in time to affect the decision, and it was only one of many documents received by the president.

S

993. Graebner, Norman A. LESSONS OF THE MEXICAN WAR. *Pacific Hist. Rev. 1978 47(3): 325-342.* Until the Treaty of Guadalupe Hidalgo arrived, President James K. Polk faced a dilemma which histori-ans have not recognized. He was unable to obtain a territorial settlement with Mexico despite the apparent military victory. He faced mounting expansionist pressure from fellow Democrats and mounting antiexpan-sionist and antiwar criticism from Whigs. Polk's insistence on maintain-ing a reasonable middle ground helped make the treaty possible. The lessons: "military invasions of backward countries . . . can be more easily productive of military than diplomatic success" and "the transition from war to peace can be rendered smooth and relatively permanent only by terms of peace that are limited, tangible, and precise." Based on manu-script sources, *Congressional Globe,* and newspapers; 39 notes.

W. K. Hobson

994. Graebner, Norman A. THE MEXICAN WAR: A STUDY IN CAUSATION. *Pacific Hist. Rev. 1980 49(3): 405-426.* US claims against Mexico and the Texas boundary dispute did not justify war in 1846. President James K. Polk's exertion of military and diplomatic pressure on Mexico was intended to further negotiations, but the John Slidell mission produced a crisis. Fearing American encroachments at the Rio Grande and in Upper California, Mexico sought British protection. Great Britain advised Mexican restraint in relations with the United States. Dreading war, Mexico outwardly displayed belligerence, but did not endanger US security. The presence of General Zachary Taylor's forces on the Rio Grande opposite the Mexican village of Matamoros triggered the war. Polk's desire to acquire California necessitated the employment of power. Based on the Polk Papers, US and British diplo-matic correspondence, and other primary sources; 46 notes.

R. N. Lokken

995. Gustafson, Milton O. THE MONROE DOCTRINE. *Manu-scripts 1975 27(1): 12-17.* Discusses the origin of the Monroe Doctrine in the 34 handwritten pages of Monroe's annual state of the union mes-sage presented to Congress 2 December 1823. 3 notes.

D. A. Yanchisin

996. Halle, Louis J. PEOPLE VS. GOVERNMENT: THE DUAL-ITY OF AMERICAN FOREIGN POLICY. *Foreign Service J. 1976 53(1): 2-6, 21-23.* Discusses the neutral policy toward France of President George Washington and his Cabinet in 1792-93, which was in clear opposition to the popular wave of French sympathy in the United States.

997. Hammett, Hugh B. THE CLEVELAND ADMINISTRATION AND ANGLO-AMERICAN NAVAL FRICTION IN HAWAII, 1893-1894. *Military Affairs 1976 40(1): 27-32.* Discusses the attempts of the Cleveland administration to maintain a tight rein on the US fleet in the Pacific. Over-zealous naval officers, in pursuing diplomatic affairs, took action in opposition to the British that had serious domestic and interna-tional consequences. Moreover, an annexation decision, the rightful pre-rogative of the President and his Cabinet, was, in essence, taken by naval

officers in Honolulu. This event emphasized that political and military functions should be kept separate, with the military as an instrument rather than an originator of diplomacy. Primary and secondary sources; 51 notes.   A. M. Osur

998. Hune, Shirley. POLITICS OF CHINESE EXCLUSION: LEG-ISLATIVE EXECUTIVE CONFLICT, 1876-1882. *Amerasia J. 1982 9(1): 5-28.* Examines the political battles leading to the passage of the Chinese Exclusion Act (US, 1882), which restricted the immigration of Chinese into the United States. While there was domestic support for such legislation by 1876, it could only be approved after the Executive Branch had secured a suitable international climate. Secondary sources; 43 notes.
                                                              E. S. Johnson

999. Jones, Howard. ANGLOPHOBIA AND THE AROOSTOOK WAR. *New England Q. 1975 48(4): 519-539.* The Maine-Canada boundary dispute of 1837-39 arose from vague passages in the existing treaty. Each side claimed the disputed territory, tempers flared, and troops were sent, but no shooting occurred. President Martin Van Buren sent Winfield Scott to work out a compromise. A neutral area was created and the controversy gradually died down. Great Britain and the United States should have used this time to work out a permanent settlement, but nothing was done. War was avoided simply because neither side wanted it. 30 notes.   V. L. Human

1000. Kushner, Howard I. THE RUSSIAN-AMERICAN DIPLO-MATIC CONTEST FOR THE PACIFIC BASIN AND THE MONROE DOCTRINE. *J. of the West 1976 15(2): 65-80.* Discusses the events leading up to President James Monroe's message to Congress in December, 1823, which became the Monroe Doctrine. Proposes that the policies laid out in the Monroe Doctrine were aimed at Russia rather than at Great Britain, but even more directly at domestic foes. The 1821 ukase, issued by Tsar Alexander I, closed the entire Northwest Coast of America. This challenge was answered directly and in no uncertain terms by diplomatic messages. A contingent in Congress called for direct action. The Monroe Doctrine was the answer to this demand. Also involved were the Presidential aspirations of Henry Clay and John Quincy Adams.
                                                              R. Alvis

1001. Kushner, Howard I. "THE STRONG GOD CIRCUMSTAN-CE": THE POLITICAL CAREER OF JOHN HAY. *J. of the Illinois State Hist. Soc. 1974 67(4): 362-384.* John Milton Hay (1838-1905) was assistant secretary to Abraham Lincoln (1861-65), secretary of the American legation in Paris (1865-67), *chargé d'affaires* in Vienna (1867-68), secretary to the American legation in Madrid (1869-70), assistant secretary of state (1879-81), ambassador to Great Britain (1897-98), and secretary of state (1898-1905). Concludes, contrary to Hay's own claims, that Hay was an active seeker of political office. Based on the John Hay Papers (Brown University), the William H. Seward Papers (University of Rochester), the Henry Adams Papers (Boston), documents from the Library of Congress, and secondary sources; 9 photos, 76 notes.
                                                              N. J. Street

1002. Mannix, Richard. GALLATIN, JEFFERSON, AND THE EMBARGO OF 1808. *Diplomatic Hist. 1979 3(2): 151-172.* Though Thomas Jefferson was closely identified with the Embargo of 1808, he was unaware of its provisions and did not oversee the bill through Congress. Indeed, he expected to go to war. James Madison suggested the embargo, and Albert Gallatin, though he personally opposed it, managed the bill through Congress. Its unpopularity diminished his influence and he left the capital in 1813. Based on documents in the Library of Congress and published primary and secondary sources; 48 notes.   S

1003. Matthewson, Timothy M. GEORGE WASHINGTON'S POL-ICY TOWARD THE HAITIAN REVOLUTION. *Diplomatic Hist. 1979 3(3): 321-336.* The Haitian slave revolt in 1791 endangered America's substantial commerce with that island, strained Franco- and Anglo-American relations, and threatened the racial stability of the South. Because of these multiple threats to American interests, and because of a general antipathy to slave revolts, the administration of President George Washington sought to suppress the uprising by supplying arms, ammunition, provisions, and money to Haiti's white planters. This unsuccessful effort was America's only attempt to quash a foreign slave revolt. 36 notes.   T. L. Powers

1004. McAfee, Ward. A RECONSIDERATION OF THE ORIGINS OF THE MEXICAN-AMERICAN WAR. *Southern California Q. 1980 62(1): 49-65.* Examines some of the diplomatic issues that helped bring on the Mexican War, suggesting that James K. Polk did not deliberately provoke war with Mexico. The failure of John Slidell's mission was due in part to the ineptitude of American Consul John Black and Mexican Foreign Minister Manuel de la Peña to define precisely what their governments sought from negotiations. This confusion caused the United States to believe that Mexico was rudely rejecting the resumption of full diplomatic relations when Mexico had specifically requested negotiations on the Texas issue only. Another source of confusion has been the orders sent to Zachary Taylor ordering him to the Rio Grande; historians have misread the sequence of letters concerning those orders. Polk had had high hopes for the success of the Slidell mission and was angry and frustrated by its failure. 43 notes.   A. Hoffman

1005. McWilliams, Tennant S. PETITION FOR EXPANSION: MO-BILE BUSINESSMEN AND THE CUBAN CRISIS, 1898. *Alabama R. 1975 28(1): 58-63.* More than 50 Mobile businessmen and companies petitioned President William McKinley in May 1897, to work for the restoration of peace in Cuba and thereby to safeguard "a most valuable" but disrupted commercial market. Reproduces the petition, for the first time. Primary and secondary sources; 6 notes.   J. F. Vivian

1006. Nelson, Anna Kasten. SECRET AGENTS AND SECURITY LEAKS: PRESIDENT POLK AND THE MEXICAN WAR. *Journalism Q. 1975 52(1): 9-14.* Discusses President James K. Polk's diplomatic attempts (1846-47) to end the war with Mexico. Newspapers were expanding in circulation; war correspondents and the telegraph made secret diplomacy difficult. Attempted secret missions using General Santa Anna, Alexander J. Atocha, and Nicholas P. Trist were quickly reported by the press, however, Polk managed to send Moses Y. Beach, owner and publisher of the New York *Sun*, to Mexico in secrecy. Primary and secondary sources; 29 notes.   K. J. Puffer

1007. Peltier, Michel. JAMES MONROE, L'HOMME D'UNE DOCTRINE [James Monroe, man of a doctrine]. *Ècrits de Paris [France] 1979 (387): 76-82.* A brief biography and review of James Monroe's political career, focusing on the Monroe Doctrine and its ramifications.

1008. Peskin, Allan. BLAINE, GARFIELD AND LATIN AMER-ICA. *Americas (Acad. of Am. Franciscan Hist.) 1979 36(1): 79-89.* As Secretary of State under James A. Garfield, James G. Blaine launched a policy of active Pan-Americanism. He was probably influenced more than generally realized by Garfield, who as a congressman had previously expressed very similar positions. Based on the Garfield Papers in Library of Congress, and on other primary sources; 46 notes.
                                                              D. Bushnell

1009. Pletcher, David M. RECIPROCITY AND LATIN AMER-ICA IN THE EARLY 1890'S: A FORETASTE OF DOLLAR DIPLO-MACY. *Pacific Hist. Rev. 1978 47(1): 53-89.* Studies the negotiations for reciprocal trade agreements with Latin America by Benjamin Harrison's Secretary of State, James G. Blaine, in 1891 and 1892. Eight agreements were signed affecting Latin America, although attempts were made to sign with all countries and dependencies. The two most important were signed with Brazil and with Spain for Cuba and Puerto Rico. Both Blaine's motives and the obstacles he faced resembled those of later US diplomatic efforts in Latin America. This supports those historians who argue for a broad continuity of US Latin American policy before and after 1898. Based on documents in the National Archives, the Library of Congress, and the British Foreign Office, and published primary and secondary sources; 74 notes.   W. K. Hobson

1010. Polk, John Fleming. VERA CRUZ, 1847: A LESSON IN COMMAND. *Marine Corps Gazette 1979 63(9): 61-66.* The successful US siege of Vera Cruz, Mexico, which involved amphibious warfare and other land and sea operations, with very few US casualties, was the result of an excellent chain of command and cooperation among President James K. Polk, Secretary of War William L. Marcy, Major General Winfield Scott, and Commodore David Connor.

1011. Rosen, Stephen Peter. ALEXANDER HAMILTON AND THE DOMESTIC USES OF INTERNATIONAL LAW. *Diplomatic Hist. 1981 5(3): 183-202.* Hamilton was a man patently more concerned with international power than with international forms. The question why his pamphlets and discussions are dominated by references to treaties and the law of nations finds an answer in the fact that international law is only a reflection of international reality. Legalism in foreign policy is a way of getting citizens to accept unpalatable foreign policy decisions and reducing the divergence between the tendencies of republican government and the necessities of international relations. 42 notes.

J. V. Coutinho

1012. Sanders, Neill F. "UNFIT FOR CONSUL"?: THE ENGLISH CONSULATES AND LINCOLN'S PATRONAGE POLICY. *Lincoln Herald 1980 82(3): 464-474.* Discusses the work of each of the seven men appointed to consular posts in England to gather intelligence about English contraband shipping to the Confederacy during the Civil War; the men were not particularly capable of serving as agents, but aided the Union cause anyway; 1861-63.

1013. Sanders, Neill F. "WHEN A HOUSE IS ON FIRE": THE ENGLISH CONSULATES AND LINCOLN'S PATRONAGE POLICY. *Lincoln Herald 1981 83(4, i.e., 1): 579-591.* President Abraham Lincoln's appointments to consulates at Glasgow, Newcastle, Dublin, Belfast, and Cork were based on political influence and loyalty to the party even though Seretary of State William Seward wanted appointees to serve as agents in an intelligence gathering network in Great Britain to provide information about military shipments to the Confederacy; the consuls did provide information that eventually contributed to the Union victory; 1861-63.

1014. Sarbaugh, Timothy Jerome. A MORAL SPECTACLE: AMERICAN RELIEF AND THE FAMINE, 1845-1849. *Éire-Ireland 1980 15(4): 6-14.* Convinced that British misrule, landlordism, and Church of Ireland compulsory tithing were the causes of misery in Ireland, the American private sector contributed about $1 million (much of it through the Society of Friends in Dublin), including at least 118 shiploads of supplies, for famine relief in Ireland. The US government, however, contributed no funds, but only the use of two rundown public vessels to ship private relief funds to Ireland. One House bill calling for the appropriation of $500,000 in relief died in committee. A similar bill passed the Senate but lost in the House because of the knowledge that President James K. Polk would veto it. Polk held that the US Constitution did not provide for such use of public money. Secondary sources, the *Congressional Globe,* and Polk's diary; 31 notes.

D. J. Engler

1015. Schoonover, Thomas. THE MEXICAN MINISTER DESCRIBES ANDREW JOHNSON'S "SWING AROUND THE CIRCLE." *Civil War Hist. 1973 19(2): 149-161.* The text of two dispatches sent to his home government by Matías Romero, Mexican minister to the United States, on 2 and 7 September 1866. Romero accompanied President Andrew Johnson on his "swing around the circle," and these notes focus attention on the overlooked though important matter of United States-Mexico relations during the 1866 election campaign.

E. C. Murdock

1016. Schroeder, John H. CONGRESS AND OPPOSITION TO THE MEXICAN WAR. *Capitol Studies 1975 3(1): 15-30.* Discusses congressional opposition to President James Polk and the Mexican War, 1846-48, emphasizing the activities of Whigs and Democrats led by John C. Calhoun.

1017. Shewmaker, Kenneth E. DANIEL WEBSTER AND THE POLITICS OF FOREIGN POLICY, 1850-1852. *J. of Am. Hist. 1976 63(2): 303-315.* Daniel Webster deliberately used foreign policy to promote national unity under the Compromise of 1850. His most significant manipulation came with the inherited "Hülsemann Letter" that protested American "intervention" in the Hungarian rebellion. Webster's decision to foment a quarrel with Austria in order to tout the superiority of the American political system has been severely criticized, but he risked little to ease domestic tensions. American lives and commerce were involved in Spain's capture of filibusters in Cuba, and Webster acted more prudently, even though a confrontation could have gained more domestic mileage than the Austrian affair. Primary and secondary sources; 65 notes.

W. R. Hively

1018. Shewmaker, Kenneth E. "UNTAUGHT DIPLOMACY": DANIEL WEBSTER AND THE LOBOS ISLANDS CONTROVERSY. *Diplomatic Hist. 1977 1(4): 321-340.* In the mid-19th century, Peruvian guano became a popular fertilizer in the United States despite high prices set by the Peruvian government, which held a monopoly on guano exports from islands off its coast. It held some of these, the Lobos Islands, in reserve. In June 1852, James Jewett, an American entrepreneur, wrote to Secretary of State Daniel Webster to determine if these islands were open to exploitation by American citizens. Webster replied that they were, and offered Jewett a naval escort. Soon a kind of guano rush was under way, with 40 ships en route for the Lobos. Meanwhile, the Peruvian government and its American sympathizers built a convincing case for exclusive Peruvian sovereignty over the islands, Webster withdrew the offer of a naval escort, and the affair was settled amicably. Archival materials and secondary sources; 82 notes.

L. W. Van Wyk

1019. Shewmaker, Kenneth E. THE "WAR OF WORDS": THE CASS-WEBSTER DEBATE OF 1842-43. *Diplomatic Hist. 1981 5(2): 151-164.* Provides a concise account of the controversy between Secretary of State Daniel Webster and Lewis Cass, US minister to France, occasioned by a critical remark by Webster concerning Cass. The debate is important to the history of American foreign policy. It touched on basic questions concerning international law and America's traditional isolationist policy. Based on primary material in the National Archives, Washington, DC, and the Daniel Webster collection at Dartmouth College, Hanover, New Hampshire; 54 notes.

J. V. Coutinho

1020. Shi, David E. SEWARD'S ATTEMPT TO ANNEX BRITISH COLUMBIA, 1865-1869. *Pacific Hist. Rev. 1978 47(2): 217-238.* When Secretary of State William H. Seward negotiated the purchase of Alaska in 1867, he intended it as the first step in a comprehensive plan to gain control of the entire northwest Pacific coast. Seward was a firm believer in Manifest Destiny, primarily for its commercial advantages to the United States. Seward expected British Columbia to ask for annexation and Britain to accept this in exchange for the *Alabama* claims. Growing Canadian nationalist sentiment in British Columbia, American preoccupation with Reconstruction, and American lack of interest in territorial expansion or in funding a transcontinental railroad link to British Columbia, combined to doom the plan in 1868. Based on American, Canadian, and British unpublished private and diplomatic papers and on newspapers; 90 notes.

W. K. Hobson

1021. Soler, Ricaurte. DE NUESTRA AMERICA DE BLAINE A NUESTRA AMERICA DE MARTI [From our America of Blaine to our America of Martí]. *Casa de las Américas [Cuba] 1980 20(119): 9-61.* Investigates the historical and social bases of the anti-imperialist attitudes of Luperón, Hostos, Betances and Martí, which evolved when the autonomy of the Dominican Republic, Puerto Rico and Cuba was threatened by North American colonial and imperialistic expansion in the late 19th and early 20th centuries. Attention is focused on the concept of Latin American nationhood formulated by José Martí (1853-95), the Cuban patriot. This is contrasted with the idea of Pan-Americanism promoted by James Blaine (1830-93), who took the first initiative to organize an inter-American congress under US auspices in 1881. 159 notes.

P. J. Durell

1022. Spetter, Allan B. HARRISON AND BLAINE: NO RECIPROCITY FOR CANADA. *Can. Rev. of Am. Studies [Canada] 1981 12(2): 143-156.* Although the Benjamin Harrison administration concluded tariff reciprocity agreements with eight nations, reciprocity negotiations with Canada stalled in 1891-92. President Harrison and Secretary of State James G. Blaine hesitated, fearing political repercussions from American agrarians if concessions were made to Canada. Probably Harrison and Blaine's Anglophobia also influenced the outcome of the negotiations, and Canada's negotiators to the end resisted the inclusion of reciprocity on manufactured articles in any treaty. Based on printed and archival primary materials and scondary sources; 38 notes.

H. T. Lovin

1023. Spivak, Burton. REPUBLICAN DREAMS AND NATIONAL INTEREST: THE JEFFERSONIANS AND AMERICAN FOREIGN POLICY. *Soc. for Hist. of Am. Foreign Relations. Newsletter 1981 12(2): 1-21.* Discusses Thomas Jefferson's anglophobia, his rejection of a politics based on commercial enterprise, and the essential failure of the Jeffersonians' foreign policy, which refused to recognize the legitimacy of English demands and maintained that American self-interest was incompatible with republican community.

1024. Stagg, J. C. A. THE COMING OF THE WAR OF 1812: THE VIEW FROM THE PRESIDENCY. *Q. J. of the Lib. of Congress 1980 37(2): 223-241.* Examines James Madison's (1751-1836) policies toward Great Britain in his attempt to make Great Britain respect America and its stance in world trade and politics. Madison hoped that policies of peaceable coercion, including the Virginia Port Bill of 1784, tariff and tonnage duties, the nonimportation laws of 1806-11, and the embargo of 1807-09, would lead to a settlement of the problems between Great Britain and America. The author examines why these policies failed to achieve the desired result, citing both international reactions and developments and those on the domestic front, especially the malcontent within the Republican party during Madison's term as president. When Madison became convinced in April-July 1811 that these policies would not work, he decided that the only recourse was to prepare for war with Great Britain. Based on Madison Papers Microfilm and Jefferson Papers Microfilm, Manuscript Division, Library of Congress, *Annals of Congress,* and other sources; 14 illus., 52 notes.　　　　A. R. Souby

1025. Stagg, J. C. A. JAMES MADISON AND THE "MALCONTENTS": THE POLITICAL ORIGINS OF THE WAR OF 1812. *William and Mary Q. 1976 33(4): 557-585.* Discounts previous interpretations of the causes of the War of 1812. Also considers the roles of Congress and the War Hawks as less decisive than other historians have believed. Granting the importance of the crisis in Anglo-American relations, Stagg emphasizes the disunity and dissension within the Republican Party against Madison and his foreign and domestic policies. Middle state politicians resented the domination of Virginians in national politics. The "malcontents" thought Madison soft on Great Britain. Out of expediency Madison moved to the position of his critics. The war helped to restore unity in the Republican Party. Based on personal correspondence, newspapers, and foreign affairs documents; 102 notes.　　　H. M. Ward

1026. Stern, Norton B. and Kramer, William M. A PRE-ISRAELI DIPLOMAT ON AN AMERICAN MISSION, 1869-1870. *Western States Jewish Hist. Q. 1976 8(3): 232-242.* Rabbi Hayyim Zevi Sneersohn (1834-82) spent several years traveling the world lecturing about the Holy Lands with the goal of gaining support for the establishment of a Jewish homeland in Palestine. In 1869 he succeeded in having President Grant send a Jew to work in the American consulate in Jerusalem. In 1870 President Grant sent another Jew as US consul in Rumania. Rabbi Sneersohn wanted Jews in these posts because he believed they would be able to help their fellow Jews in areas of oppression. His lectures were well attended. 29 notes.　　　　　R. A. Garfinkle

1027. Stuart, Reginald C. JAMES MADISON AND THE MILITANTS: REPUBLICAN DISUNITY AND REPLACING THE EMBARGO. *Diplomatic Hist. 1982 6(2): 145-167.* The failure of the embargo against Great Britain caused a crisis within the divided Democratic Republican Party in 1809. James Madison, a passive leader, wanted Congress to formulate a more vigorous policy. The militant Madison supporters, joined by the "invisibles," urged limited reprisals. Federalists, Quids, and conservative Republicans prevented extreme measures. Voting patterns and the militants' diversity indicate that party affiliation was more significant than region. The majority wanted the embargo repealed and Republican unity maintained, but shrank from war and accepted the Non-Intercourse Act (US, 1809). The militants, by suggesting an active policy in 1809, took the first step toward establishing a consensus for war. Based on the papers of James Madison, *Annals of Congress,* and other primary sources; table, 43 notes.　　　　T. J. Heston

1028. Tagg, James D. BENJAMIN FRANKLIN BACHE'S ATTACK ON GEORGE WASHINGTON. *Pennsylvania Mag. of Hist. and Biog. 1976 100(2): 191-230.* Beginning in 1792, Benjamin Franklin Bache (1769-98), grandson of the American *philosophe* and editor of Philadelphia's *General Advertiser and Aurora,* attacked George Washington's conduct of public affairs. Bache's vituperation reached its height in August 1795 after Washington signed the Jay Treaty. To Bache, the signing represented the ultimate betrayal of republican principles; it ignored the will of the people and it broke relations with France, the most

progressive nation in the world. Although patronage considerations and economic self-interest contributed to Bache's dislike of Washington, the prime factor was Bache's adherence to "radical republican and democratic principles and his belief that Washington had undermined these principles." Based on primary and secondary sources; 123 notes.
　　　　　　　　　　　　　　　　　　　　　　　　E. W. Carp

1029. Thomas, Robert Charles. ANDREW JACKSON VERSUS FRANCE: AMERICAN POLICY TOWARD FRANCE, 1834-1836. *Tennessee Hist. Q. 1976 35(1): 51-64.* Andrew Jackson (1767-1845) nearly provoked a war with France over the Spoliation Claims against deprivations to American shipping during the Napoleonic Wars. Jackson was not, as is often presumed, a "mere tool in the hands of his party or advisors." Rather, his policy clearly reflected his personality, his limited diplomatic experience, his prejudice against foreigners, and an exalted sense of American power and morality characteristic of the time. Opposition to war by commercial interests was ineffective; Congress offered only partisan recriminations. Fortunately, some of Jackson's close advisers—most notably Vice President Martin Van Buren (1782-1862)—restrained him. Based on primary and secondary sources; 69 notes.
　　　　　　　　　　　　　　　　　　　　　　　　W. R. Hively

1030. Turner, Justin G. LINCOLN AND THE CANNIBALS. *Lincoln Herald 1975 77(4): 212-218.* On the afternoon of 13 January 1864 Jonathan Whalon, first officer of the whaling ship *Congress,* was captured by the residents of Hiva Oa, an island of the archipelago Marquesas. The capture and plan to eat Whalon was to avenge a raid by a Peruvian slave ship. Whalon's rescue was effected by Reverend James Hunnewell Kekela, a Hawaiian missionary stationed on the island. Secretary of State Seward or President Lincoln approved the expenditure of $500 for gifts to all involved in the rescue. Based on primary and secondary sources; illus., 17 notes.　　　　　　　　　　　B. J. LaBue

1031. Wilbur, W. Allan. ALEXANDER HAMILTON: THOUGHT AND ACTION IN THE EARLY REPUBLIC. *Maryland Historian 1973 4(1): 59-64.* Reviews Gilbert L. Lycan's *Alexander Hamilton and American Foreign Policy: A Design for Greatness* (Norman: U. of Oklahoma Press, 1970) and Gerald Stourzh's *Alexander Hamilton and The Idea of Republican Government* (Stanford, California: Stanford U. Press, 1970). Each study contributes to a clear understanding of the duality of Alexander Hamilton. Based on secondary sources; 3 notes.
　　　　　　　　　　　　　　　　　　　　　　　　G. O. Gagnon

1032. —. [THE MAKING OF THE MONROE DOCTRINE]. *Diplomatic Hist. 1981 5(1): 53-73.*
Ammon, Harry. THE MONROE DOCTRINE: DOMESTIC POLITICS OR NATIONAL DECISION?, *pp. 53-70.* Dissents from Ernest B. May's thesis, expressed in *The Making of the Monroe Doctrine* (1975), that the Monroe Doctrine was an expression of domestic political imperatives (particularly, the presidential ambitions of three members of President James Monroe's cabinet) rather than of American national interests. There is inadequate evidence to support May's conclusion, and his contention is inconsistent with "what we know about the character, opinions, and personal relationships of the president and his cabinet." 65 notes.
May, Ernest R. RESPONSE TO HARRY AMMON, *pp. 71-73.* Reiterates and defends his thesis.　　　　　　　T. L. Powers

The Presidency: Definition

1033. Berger, Raoul. JEFFERSON V. MARSHALL IN THE BURR CASE. *Am. Bar Assoc. J. 1974 60(6): 702-706.* "A hard look at the Burr case shows Chief Justice Marshall's willingness to exercise judicial review of claims of executive privilege."　　　　　　　　　　　　J

1034. Boyett, Gene W. DEVELOPING THE CONCEPT OF THE REPUBLICAN PRESIDENCY, 1787-1788. *Presidential Studies Q. 1977 7(4): 199-208.* Concerns the conflicting views of the presidency during 1787-88. Antifederalists, particularly, feared the office as potentially monarchical, while Federalists pointed out obvious differences between their concept of a president and the British crown. Other fears concerned the mingling of branches of government, as in treaty making, and the presidential power of veto. Providing for presidential impeachment undercut proponents of a multiple rather than a unitary executive branch. There was, however, almost unanimous agreement on the president's indirect election. The result was a strong, though limited, executive, independent of Congress, but not controlled by the people. 85 notes.

J. Tull

1035. Brogan, Hugh. TOCQUEVILLE AND THE AMERICAN PRESIDENCY. *J. of Am. Studies [Great Britain] 1981 15(3): 357-375.* French politician and writer, Alexis de Tocqueville visited the United States during the 1830's. He called on President Andrew Jackson on 19 January 1832. Subsequently, Tocqueville wrote *Democracy in America* which was published in English in 1835-40. In this work and others, he underrated the significance of the US presidency. He also denied the legitimacy of political parties, seeing only their vulgarities and potential for suppressing liberty. 42 notes.   H. T. Lovin

1036. Cohen, Michael. RELIGIOUS REVIVALISM AND THE ADMINISTRATIVE CENTRALIZATION MOVEMENT. *Administration and Soc. 1977 9(2): 219-232.* The late 19th-century administrative centralization movement, which emphasized the centralizing of unified departments in the executive branch of government, began in an era of intense religious revivals and was promoted by such leading figures as Woodrow Wilson, Luther Gulick, and John Fairlie, who were greatly influenced by the social and political reform tradition of Calvinism.

1037. Grossman, Joel B. THE POLITICS OF FEDERAL JUDICIAL SELECTION: HISTORICAL PERSPECTIVES ON NEW DEVELOPMENTS. *Rev. in Am. Hist. 1981 9(3): 370-376.* Review essay of Kermit L. Hall's *The Politics of Justice: Lower Federal Judicial Selection and the Second Party System, 1829-61* (1979).

1038. Grossman, Jonathan and MacLaury, Judson. THE CREATION OF THE BUREAU OF LABOR STATISTICS. *Monthly Labor R. 1975 98(2): 25-31.* Details the 20 years of legislative crusading by American labor organizations which preceded the establishment of the first national labor statistics agency in 1885.   S

1039. Holtz, Milton E. AGRICULTURAL ADMINISTRATION UNDER THE PATENT OFFICE 1836-1862. *South Dakota Hist. 1975 5(2): 123-149.* Predecessors to the Department of Agriculture grew out of the US Patent Office. During 1836-49 that office was within the Department of State. Its commissioners suggested support for the agricultural branch of American industry. In time appropriations, small at first, were granted for various purposes useful in disseminating information and material, especially to farmers. In 1849 the Patent Office was transferred to the Department of the Interior with a subsequent increase in the Agriculture Division. Much work was done in researching new techniques as well as plants and animals useful for agriculture. Though some of the introductions proved unusable, agriculture in the country was improved immeasurably by the guidance and promotion of this agency. In 1862, full departmental status was accorded agriculture, although executive cabinet-level representation was not forthcoming until 1889. Based on secondary sources; 6 photos, table, 71 notes.

A. J. Larson

1040. Jillson, Calvin C. PRESIDENTIAL POWER: THE EXECUTIVE IN REPUBLICAN GOVERNMENT: THE CASE OF THE AMERICAN FOUNDING. *Presidential Studies Q. 1979 9(4): 386-402.* The question of the proper relationship between the executive and legislative branches of a republican government dominated much of the Constitutional Convention of 1787. Factor analysis of roll-call voting during the debates over the structure of the executive branch, both before and after the compromise of 4 September, shows that political coalitions essentially and firmly determined the nature and length of the argument, as well as its ultimate resolution. The Electoral College has functioned in ways unimagined by Founding Fathers ignorant of how politics could and would change over time, but the relative success of the system accounts for its survival despite perennial criticism. 4 tables, diagram, 20 notes.

P. M. Cohen

1041. Ketcham, Ralph. PARTY AND LEADERSHIP IN MADISON'S CONCEPTION OF THE PRESIDENCY. *Q. J. of the Lib. of Congress 1980 37(2): 242-258.* James Madison (1751-1836) was concerned that faction and political parties posed the greatest threat to free republican government. In the Constitution, he strove not only to provide for an executive who would be able to recognize and possess the virtue to uphold the common good, but also to provide the means for keeping such an executive virtuous, that is, impartial, non-partisan, and able to pursue the public interest over private concerns. Madison was willing to put some restraints on direct, free government in order to provide for such leadership that he considered vital to the public good. Early (pre-1829) presidents tried to be antiparty, patriotic, with a positive conception of national leadership to provide for good republican government. Madison was guided by such a conception of the presidency as he first devised and then filled the office. 15 illus., 16 notes.   A. R. Souby

1042. Ketcham, Ralph. THE TRANSATLANTIC BACKGROUND OF THOMAS JEFFERSON'S IDEAS OF EXECUTIVE POWER. *Studies in Eighteenth-Century Culture 1982 11: 163-180.* During 1789-1829 the first six presidents of the United States, especially Thomas Jefferson, were torn in their interpretations of executive authority between the Augustan model of patriot leadership supplied by Alexander Pope, Jonathan Swift, and Lord Bolingbroke and the new republican politics of Daniel Defoe, Robert Walpole, and Adam Smith. Aware of the dangers of both tyranny and anarchy, Jefferson tried to achieve both a mild government mindful of the needs of the people and a positive government capable of directing them so as to produce a good society. For this reason he emphasized improving the quality of the people's understanding so that they, and not their leaders alone, could work for the public interest. Primary sources; 16 notes.   E. L. Keyser

1043. Koritansky, John C. ALEXANDER HAMILTON'S PHILOSOPHY OF GOVERNMENT AND ADMINISTRATION. *Publius 1979 9(2): 99-122.* Alexander Hamilton's political theory, 1787-90's, was aptly categorized by his opponents as monocratic, for he stressed the power of the executive and bureaucracy. Covers Hamilton's views on representation, political aristocracy, and the role of the national government. 34 notes.   S

1044. Langran, Robert W. SEPARATE AND OPPOSED. *Supreme Court Hist. Soc. Y. 1977: 70-78; 1978: 91-96, 120.* Part 1. PRESIDENTS VERSUS THE COURTS. Details a number of 19th-century cases between the president and the Supreme Court over the power of the Judiciary and the Executive Branch, including *Marbury v. Madison*, 1803 (John Marshall and Thomas Jefferson), *United States v. Burr*, 1807 (Marshall and Jefferson), *Kendall v. United States,* 1838 (the court and Andrew Jackson), the Civil War Prize Cases, 1863 (Roger Brooke Taney and Abraham Lincoln), the Reconstruction cases, 1866-67 (Justice Chase and Andrew Johnson), and *Field v. Clark,* 1892 (John Harlan and the Presidency). Part 2. CONGRESS VS. THE COURT. Discusses conflicts between the legislative and judicial branches of government as exhibited in such cases as *Marbury v. Madison* (1803) and *Stuart v. Laird* (1803).

1045. Patterson, Kirby W. THE MAKING OF A PRESIDENT: THE THINKING IN 1787. *Am. Bar Assoc. J. 1974 60(11): 1357-1362.* "The nation is now in the unique position of having a president chosen with the approval of Congress and will soon have a vice president who must receive similar approval. But this situation is not an aberration. Many members of the Constitutional Convention of 1787 favored just such a plan, and its advantages are worth considering today."   J

1046. Rhodes, Irwin S. WHAT REALLY HAPPENED TO THE JEFFERSON SUBPOENAS. *Am. Bar Assoc. J. 1974 60(1): 52-54.* "While counsel and courts in the Watergate Tapes Case relied for their opposing positions on the rulings of Chief Justice Marshall in the Burr case, they didn't go beyond the reports of that case in Federal Cases. By failing to do adequate research, they missed the contemporaneous shorthand reporting of the case. This account demonstrates that Marshall ruled that the courts may not review a president's assertion of executive privilege."   J

1047. Riccards, Michael P. THE PRESIDENCY AND THE RATIFICATION CONTROVERSY. *Presidential Studies Q. 1977 7(1): 37-46.* During the debate over ratifying the Constitution of 1787, Federalists and Antifederalists argued over the role of the Presidency, discussing the President's relationship with the Senate, term of office, and treaty, pardoning, veto, and military powers. Federalists and Antifederalists chose George Washington for President and drafted the Bill of Rights to protect against abuses of executive power. Based on Federalist and Antifederalist pamphlets, letters, addresses, and legislative debates; 39 notes.   R. D. Hurt

1048. Roy, William G.   THE PROCESS OF BUREAUCRATIZATION IN THE U.S. STATE DEPARTMENT AND THE VESTING OF ECONOMIC INTERESTS, 1886-1905.   *Administrative Sci. Q. 1981 26(3): 419-433.* As bureaucratization occurred in the State Department, the interests of the financial-industrial care industries became more vested while those of other industries remained stable or decreased.

1049. Stevens, Robert D.   DOCUMENTS IN THE GILDED AGE: RICHARDSON'S *MESSAGES AND PAPERS OF THE PRESIDENTS.*   *Government Publ. Rev. 1974 1(3): 233-240.* Relates a fascinating, but somewhat sordid story of the circumstances surrounding the publication of *Messages and Papers of the Presidents* in 1900. The role of James Daniel Richardson of Tennessee as chairman of the House Committee on Printing and as a compiler of the set of 10 volumes is described in absorbing detail. His attempts to privately copyright a commercial edition and to make money from what was originally an official compilation were devious at best and are described in a series of incidents which placed Congress in a false position. Ainsworth R. Spofford, as retired Librarian of Congress and as editor of the index to the set, was an unwitting accessory to the strange events leading to the commercial exploitation of these government documents by Richardson and his publisher. The authors point out that librarians continue to lend their names to publishing projects of dubious merit and contribute to their exaggerated claims.   J

1050. Stuart, Reginald C.   WAR POWERS OF THE CONSTITUTION IN HISTORICAL PERSPECTIVE.   *Parameters 1980 10(4): 65-71.* The war clauses of the American Constitution, which divide the powers to declare and wage war between Congress and the president, were an outgrowth of the idealism and pragmatism of the 18th century. The separation of powers was based on perception that most wars occurred due to disputes between monarchs rather than because of national interests. Yet, the framers and ratifiers of the Constitution also recognized that an armed defense was a necessity. "There was a rough consensus that the country was weak and vulnerable, that republicanism was worth defending, that specific interests should be pursued, and that future wars were likely." Based on letters and other writings of the framers and ratifiers of the Constitution, and on secondary sources; 27 notes.
                                                                   L. R. Maxted

1051. Turner, John J., Jr.   THE REVOLUTION, THE FOUNDING FATHERS, AND THE ELECTORAL COLLEGE.   *West Georgia Coll. Studies in the Social Sci. 1976 15: 31-42.* Discusses the Constitutional Convention in 1787, particularly the Founding Fathers' decision to choose a president through the electoral college.

1052. Turner, John J., Jr.   THE TWELFTH AMENDMENT AND THE FIRST AMERICAN PARTY SYSTEM.   *Historian 1973 35 (2): 221-237.* The 12th Amendment partly was intended to extend and strengthen the safeguards against factionalism which were institutionalized in the Electoral College. In fact, the amendment facilitated the emergence of the modern party system by legalizing party control of both officers in the executive branch. Shows the state of opinion about political parties at this stage in American history. Based on records of the Constitutional Convention, the Federalist papers, and secondary sources; 61 notes.   N. W. Moen

1053. Vivian, James F.   THE COMMERCIAL BUREAU OF AMERICAN REPUBLICS, 1894-1902: THE ADVERTISING POLICY, THE STATE DEPARTMENT, AND THE GOVERNANCE OF THE INTERNATIONAL UNION.   *Pro. of the Am. Phil. Soc. 1974 118(6): 555-566.* Although 18 governments were represented in the International Union and the Commercial Bureau of the American Republics, the United States was in charge of the Bureau's organization and administration. Examines the controversial advertising program for the Bureau's *Monthly Bulletin*, initiated by director Clinton Furbish, and his successor, Joseph P. Smith's *Commercial Directory of American Republics*, both as budgetary means in the face of a reluctant Congress and as "an intergovernmental experiment in hemispheric affairs." The chief threat to the Bureau came from business interests, but this was ultimately met. Reorganization of the Bureau with State Department assistance set the stage for the permanent Pan American Union in 1910. 57 notes.
                                                                   C. W. Olson

3. FROM ROOSEVELT THROUGH ROOSEVELT

Presidents of the Mid-Passage

1054. Alsop, Joseph. ROOSEVELT REMEMBERED. *Smithsonian 1982 12(10): 38-49.* A memoir on the life and presidency of Franklin D. Roosevelt to commemorate his birth in 1882.

1055. Altherr, Thomas L. THE AMERICAN HUNTER-NATU-RALIST AND THE DEVELOPMENT OF THE CODE OF SPORTS-MANSHIP. *J. of Sport Hist. 1978 5(1): 7-22.* By 1900, an idealistic type of hunter developed, the hunter-naturalist. He championed the code of ethics known as sportsmanship. Upper class sportsmen sought to dignify hunting for sport, and to check the savage hunting impulse. Patrician sportsmen embarked on their own search for order by regulating themselves and the commercial hunters. There had always been a close influence of nature upon hunting, and the earliest US naturalists, John James Audubon and Alexander Wilson, were hunters. Before the Civil War, the abundance of game made restraints unnecessary, but after the Civil War, and especially during the 1880's and 1890's, there was a formal emergence of the code of sportsmanship. Theodore Roosevelt was the leading hunter-naturalist of his day. Antihunting critics into the mid-20th century scoffed at the hunters' commitment to nature, and challenged the validity of the hunter-naturalist ideal. 63 notes. M. Kaufman

1056. Beasley, Maurine. LORENA A. HICKOK: JOURNALISTIC INFLUENCE ON ELEANOR ROOSEVELT. *Journalism Q. 1980 57(2): 281-286.* Lorena A. Hickok (1893-1968) was instrumental in developing Eleanor Roosevelt's relationship with female reporters which led to her being the first president's wife to receive regular, extensive news coverage, as well as being the first to regularly grant interviews. Hickok's friendship with Mrs. Roosevelt compromised her position as an Associated Press reporter and eventually led to her departure from journalism. The two women remained fast friends throughout their lives. Hickok was aided by Mrs. Roosevelt in finding jobs, both in and out of government, after ending her career as a reporter. Based on correspondence and Hickok's biography of Mrs. Roosevelt; 57 notes. J. S. Coleman

1057. Beliavskaia, I. A. TEODOR RUZVEL'T: EKSPANSIIA I REFORMA [Theodore Roosevelt: expansion and reform]. *Novaia i Noveishaia Istoriia [USSR] 1973 (5): 112-126; 1974 (1): 123-137.* Part I. Studies the political career of Theodore Roosevelt. His youth, legal training, and early political activity in the 1880's are discussed, together with his private life, to illustrate his lack of business success and his successive political ventures. His support for economic expansion dated from the time of his first post in Washington (1897) and continued through his governorship of New York until his election to the Presidency in 1901. Study of his Presidency then demonstrates Roosevelt's approach to the problems of trust regulation, the color bar, and foreign policy, in which he supported the expansion of American influence to the Far East and Latin America. Primary and secondary sources; 63 notes. Part II. Examines the career of Theodore Roosevelt from 1904 till his death in 1919. He furthered the aggressive desires of powerful American imperialism, and formed a government of "old predatory powers" in the international political arena. Despite personal charm, magnetism, and courage, he was politically neither honest nor principled, but a typical clear-sighted, intelligent, versatile, bourgeois activist. He paved the way for the United States' diplomatic role in world politics in the 20th century. Secondary sources; 44 notes. C. R. Pike/L. Smith

1058. Best, Gary Dean. AN EVANGELIST AMONG SKEPTICS: HOOVER'S BID FOR THE LEADERSHIP OF THE GOP, 1937-1938. *Pro. of the Am. Phil. Soc. 1979 123(1): 1-14.* Immediately after the smashing defeat which the Republican Party suffered in 1936, Herbert C. Hoover laid plans for a conference of Republican leaders for early 1938 to revitalize the party and to establish a basic philosophy true to the party's historical position which would be an affirmative alternate to the coercion of the New Deal. Alfred M. Landon opposed this effort, viewing it as a ploy of Hoover to gain the nomination in 1940. Delineates the moves and countermoves of these two party leaders. Ultimately Hoover

was forced to compromise, both from the timing of the conference as well as in establishing a basic Republican philosophy. The Republicans were highly successful in the 1938 elections, and both men took the credit. Based on the correspondence found in the Hoover Papers (Hoover Presidential Library) and the Landon Papers (Kansas State Historical Society) and contemporary newspaper accounts; 112 notes. H. M. Parker, Jr.

1059. Best, Gary Dean. HERBERT HOOVER AS TITULAR LEADER OF THE GOP, 1933-35. *Mid-America 1979 61(2): 81-97.* After the 1932 election Herbert C. Hoover was the discredited leader of the Republican Party. Between March 1933 and March 1935 he kept a self-imposed public silence on political affairs. In March 1935 he issued an off-the-cuff statement to a Tucson newspaper on the Roosevelt administration's abandonment of the gold standard. Later the same month he issued a letter to the California Republican Assembly attacking the New Deal. This ended his two-year silence, yet Hoover remained discredited. 86 notes. J. M. Lee

1060. Best, Gary Dean. HERBERT HOOVER'S TECHNICAL MISSION TO YUGOSLAVIA, 1919-20. *Ann. of Iowa 1974 42(6): 443-459.* With the expiration of the American Relief Administration in 1919, Herbert Hoover proposed that the transportation section be continued in Austria, Poland, Czechoslovakia, and Yugoslavia with US technical experts serving in an advisory capacity. The Yugoslavian operation was the least successful of the four. The chief American technical advisor, Colonel William G. Atwood, was instructed to obtain railroad materials and financing in the United States, to cooperate with technical advisors elsewhere in reestablishing international transportation relations, and to advise on the reopening of old mines destroyed in World War I, and the opening of new ones. Yugoslavian cabinet crises complicated Atwood's efforts and the mission was shut down in September 1920. Primary and secondary sources; 60 notes. C. W. Olson

1061. Best, Gary Dean. TOTALITARIANSIM OR PEACE: HERBERT HOOVER AND THE ROAD TO WAR, 1939-1941. *Ann. of Iowa 1979 44(7): 516-529.* Before the Japanese attack on Pearl Harbor, Herbert C. Hoover opposed US involvement in World War II. Hoover's opposition stemmed from diverse causes: his Quaker background, his experiences in World War I, his perception of the Communist USSR as a totalitarian government as more objectionable than Nazi Germany and Fascist Italy, and his fear that US involvement in the war would bring about domestic regimentation even greater than the New Deal. The United States could best serve the cause of freedom, said Hoover repeatedly, by remaining aloof from a war between totalitarian nations. Primary and secondary sources; 2 photos, 30 notes. P. L. Petersen

1062. Blakey, George T. CALLING A BOSS A BOSS: DID ROOSEVELT LIBEL BARNES IN 1915? *New York Hist. 1979 60(2): 195-216.* Theodore Roosevelt, defendant in a $50,000 libel suit brought against him by William Barnes, Jr., used the courtroom as a forum for his attack on political bossism and corruption, defense of democratic principles against political machine rule, and an attempt to restore his political prestige. Barnes, long influential in New York Republican politics, sued Roosevelt for having publicly called him a corrupt political boss. The trial revealed the contrasting political styles and philosophies of the principals. Based on the New York State Supreme Court trial records. 10 illus., 45 notes. R. N. Lokken

1063. Cane, Guy. SEA POWER—TEDDY'S "BIG STICK." *US Naval Inst. Pro. 1976 102(8): 40-48.* Following their first meeting in 1888, Alfred Thayer Mahan and Theodore Roosevelt developed a special relationship marked by close friendship and mutual respect. In this relationship Mahan exerted a powerful influence on Roosevelt by serving as a sounding board, a one-man think tank, a gifted proponent of navalism, and a mirror image of his own views on the application of sea power in world politics. Based on primary and secondary sources; 5 illus. J. K. Ohl

1064. Cooper, John Milton, Jr. WOODROW WILSON: THE ACADEMIC MAN. *Virginia Q. Rev. 1982 58(1): 38-53.* His reputation as an academic political scientist who became president has "distorted views of Wilson's academic years." As a university president he is often pictured incorrectly as a leader of an educational counterreformation. Actually, he revamped Princeton's undergraduate curriculum, began the "preceptorial system," and proposed a novel undergraduate living plan. The major thrust of his college presidency was putting Princeton at the forefront of American universities. Fewer parallels and patterns, psychological and otherwise, exist between his Princeton presidency and his later career than have been asserted.   O. H. Zabel

1065. Corgan, Michael T. MAHAN AND THEODORE ROOSEVELT: THE ASSESSMENT OF INFLUENCE. *Naval War Coll. Rev. 1980 33(6): 89-97.* Discusses an article by Peter Karsten (see abstract 14A:860); disputes Karsten's conclusion that Theodore Roosevelt used Alfred Thayer Mahan, arguing that Mahan greatly influenced Roosevelt's political and naval strategy during the first two decades of the 20th century.

1066. Dailey, Wallace Finley. THE THEODORE ROOSEVELT COLLECTION AT HARVARD. *Manuscripts 1977 29(3): 146-154.* "Theodore Roosevelt is the most prolific author among the American Presidents, not simply in his Presidential capacity, but in his own right as historian, naturalist, and social philosopher." In contrast to the Roosevelt Collection at the Library of Congress, which is mainly composed of letterpress copy books and carbon copies, the Collection at Harvard is the original library and archives of Roosevelt. The Harvard Collection began in 1919-20 as the Roosevelt Memorial Library at the Roosevelt Homeplace, but in 1943 it came to Harvard. In 1976 an exhibition was put together for the dedication of the Theodore Roosevelt Gallery in the Pusey Library, which reflected the many facets of Roosevelt: 1) the Harvard Man; 2) the Ranchman; 3) the Rough Rider; 4) the Family Man; 5) the Public Servant; 6) the Strenuous Man; 7) the Naturalist; and 8) the Man of Letters. Illus.   D. A. Yanchisin

1067. Davis, Glenn. [THE CHARACTER OF THEODORE ROOSEVELT].
THE EARLY YEARS OF THEODORE ROOSEVELT: A STUDY IN CHARACTER FORMATION. *Hist. of Childhood Q. 1975 2(4): 461-492.* A Freudian interpretation of the personality formation of Theodore Roosevelt. Starting with a study of Roosevelt's father and mother prior to their courtship, traces influences on the young Roosevelt. Concludes that he developed an oral rage as a result of maternal deprivation, and psychosomatic asthma. By maturity he had successfully integrated psychic defenses against this rage into his character, while his brother, Elliott Roosevelt, never came to terms with his own psychological make-up. Based on primary and secondary sources; 116 notes.
THE MATURATION OF THEODORE ROOSEVELT: THE RISE OF AN "AFFECTIVE LEADER." *Hist. of Childhood Q. 1975 3(1): 43-74.* Seeks to link the character formed in childhood with the public man. Roosevelt's aggressiveness in public life and ruthlessness whether hunting or warring were linked to repressed rage toward his parents. Roosevelt stood as an archetypal personality of the Progressive age. Based on primary and secondary sources; 139 notes.   R. E. Butchart

1068. Davis, Kenneth S. SYMBOLIC JOURNEY. *Antioch Rev. 1979 37(3): 259-276.* Describes Eleanor Roosevelt's tour of Great Britain, Belgium, and France with her two sons, Franklin, Jr. (Brother) and John, and two close friends, Nancy Cook and Marion Dickerman, 1929.

1069. Deane, Hugh. HERBERT HOOVER AND THE KAILAN MINES SWINDLE. *Eastern Horizon [Hong Kong] 1981 20(5): 34-38.* Traces Herbert C. Hoover's role in the British takeover of the Chinese Engineering and Mining Company, from the Boxer Rebellion of 1900 to the legal proceedings during his campaign in 1928, which called into question Hoover's involvement in the affair.

1070. Doenecke, Justus D. THE ANTI-INTERVENTIONIST TRADITION: LEADERSHIP AND PERCEPTIONS. *Literature of Liberty 1981 4(2): 7-67.* Presents a bibliographical essay on such leading anti-interventionists as Senator Robert A. Taft, Herbert C. Hoover, Charles A. Lindbergh, Jr., Anne Morrow Lindbergh, Senator William E. Borah, Senator Hiram Johnson, and Senator Gerald P. Nye, and presents a bibliography of anti-interventionist thought and activities; 1929-41.

1071. Dyer, Thomas G. AARON'S ROD: THEODORE ROOSEVELT, TOM WATSON, AND ANTI-CATHOLICISM. *Res. Studies 1976 44(1): 60-68.* Discusses Theodore Roosevelt's rebuke of Georgia politician Thomas E. Watson's anti-Catholicism in letters in 1915.

1072. Fischer, Robert and Gay, James T. A POST-MORTEM OF THEODORE ROOSEVELT IN HISTORICAL WRITINGS, 1919-1929. *Mid-America 1974 56(3): 139-159.* A review of the literature published on Theodore Roosevelt in the decade after his death exposes the majority of this early writing as nonhistorical or noncritical, and reveals that Roosevelt and his record were clouded in adulation. Among the kinds of materials examined are biographies of Roosevelt as well as contemporary personalities, memories, and special studies of aspects of the man or specific problems of his day. The aspect evaluated most extensively and accurately was Roosevelt's foreign policy. Based on secondary literature; 72 notes.   T. D. Schoonover

1073. Franks, Kenny A., ed. ROOSEVELT: RANCHING ADVENTURES IN THE DAKOTAS. *Great Plains J. 1974 14(1): 87-103.* A brief editor's introduction is followed by selections from Theodore Roosevelt's observations on cattle raising on the Great Plains in the 1880's especially at Medora, North Dakota, and with drawings by Frederic Remington. The observations include descriptions of the semiarid West, the life-style of cowboys and ranchers, the cattle drives, roundups, and the three essentials for a range: grass, water, and shelter. Roosevelt foresaw the devastation which would follow a severe winter on an overcrowded pasture such as occurred in 1886-87. 6 illus., 30 notes.
                                   O. H. Zabel

1074. Friedel, Frank. FRANKLIN D. ROOSEVELT AT HARVARD. *New England Social Studies Bull. 1977-78 35(2): 35-48.* Anecdotes of Franklin D. Roosevelt's student years at Harvard University, 1901-04.

1075. Garcia, George F. HERBERT HOOVER AND THE ISSUE OF RACE. *Ann. of Iowa 1979 44(7): 507-515.* Many blacks considered President Herbert C. Hoover a racist. Hoover did accept "the pseudo science of the social Darwinists" that placed the black race on a lower rung of the evolutionary ladder. His overseas experiences as a mining engineer, moreover, tended to strengthen his belief in the superiority of the white race. Tempering Hoover's racism, however, was his view that part of Negroes' "backwardness" was environmental. Hoover believed that social progress for black Americans could, within limits, be managed and speeded up through conscious and scientifically based social change. But in the area of race, as in many other areas, Hoover sought to use the government not as an instrument of reform but as an agency for promoting private action. Thus, as President, Hoover did not challenge racial segregation. Primary and secondary sources; 29 notes.
                                   P. L. Petersen

1076. George, Juliette L. and George, Alexander L. *WOODROW WILSON AND COLONEL HOUSE:* A REPLY TO WEINSTEIN, ANDERSON, AND LINK. *Pol. Sci. Q. 1981-82 96(4): 641-665.* Defends George and George's *Woodrow Wilson and Colonel House: A Personality Study* (1956), which Arthur S. Link, Edwin A. Weinstein, and James William Anderson characterized as "an essentially incorrect interpretation of the personality of Woodrow Wilson and its effect on his career." The authors defend their characterization on the basis of new evidence, and call into question Weinstein, Anderson, and Link's hypothesis that beginning in 1896 Wilson suffered from a series of strokes. The new data supporting George and George's defense is appended. 58 notes, appendix.   J. Powell

1077. Gillespie, Veronica M. T. R. ON FILM. *Q. J. of the Lib. of Congress 1977 34(1): 39-57.* The large collection of Theodore Roosevelt films in the Library of Congress is now being cataloged and is "a bonanza of primary source material for those scholars investigating the historic, political, and social roles of women during the first decades of the 20th century." Gives a classified list of selected titles. Illus., 15 notes.
                                   E. P. Stickney

1078. Gurewitsch, Edna P. REMEMBERING MRS. ROOSEVELT: AN INTIMATE MEMOIR. *Am. Heritage 1981 33(1): 10-19.* An interview with Edna P. Gurewitsch whose husband, David, was Eleanor Roosevelt's personal physician from White House days until her death in 1962. The author, who with her husband was close to Mrs. Roosevelt in her last years, spoke of Eleanor's attitudes toward Franklin, politics, and Dr. Gurewitsch. 8 illus.   J. F. Paul

1079. Hauptman, Laurence M. GOVERNOR THEODORE ROOSEVELT AND THE INDIANS OF NEW YORK STATE. *Pro. of the Am. Phil. Soc. 1975 119(1): 1-7.* Theodore Roosevelt's Indian-hating attitude was really an expression of sentiments held by most eastern reformers of his day. They believed that the Indian could be saved only by destroying most of his ethnic heritage. Examination of Roosevelt's attitudes towards the New York state Indians while working with the Indian Rights Association, and his instigation of the Commission of 1900, show that Roosevelt did not want to eradicate the Indian, but to assimilate him into the mainstream of white culture. Based on primary and secondary sources; 32 notes.   W. L. Olbrich

1080. Havig, Alan. PRESIDENTIAL IMAGES, HISTORY, AND HOMAGE: MEMORIALIZING THEODORE ROOSEVELT, 1919-1967. *Am. Q. 1978 30(4): 514-532.* The Roosevelt Memorial Association was organized in 1919, the same year as Theodore Roosevelt's death. Discusses its efforts to establish a memorial in Washington, D.C., at the south end of one of the two intersecting axes which include the White House, the Washington Monument, the Lincoln Memorial, and the Capitol. Hermann Hagedorn, Director of the R.M.A., was a strong promoter of the idea, engaging in extensive fund raising and an unhistorical inflation of the Roosevelt image. The proposal was defeated by the assigning of the site to a Jefferson Memorial. However Roosevelt was remembered by naming Analostan Island, "Theodore Roosevelt Island" and establishing a memorial to him there in its very appropriate wilderness setting. It was left to private endeavor in the form of the monumental sculptures on Mount Rushmore to memorialize Roosevelt on a par with Washington, Jefferson, and Lincoln. 32 notes.   R. V. Ritter

1081. Herring, Pendleton. WOODROW WILSON: A PRESIDENT'S READING. *Historic Preservation 1975 27(3): 38-42.* Surveys Wilson's lifetime reading interests in connection with a project at the Woodrow Wilson House (1915) in Washington, D. C., to "gather selectively the titles that meant most" to Wilson. Notes many authors and titles. 4 photos.   R. M. Frame III

1082. Hoxie, R. Gordon. HERBERT HOOVER: MULTINATIONAL MAN. *Presidential Studies Q. 1977 7(1): 49-52.* Surveys Herbert C. Hoover's public life during 1917-46. During World War I he was the US Food Administrator. He again coordinated food supplies for 38 war-torn nations following World War II. Although President Hoover favored arbitration and conciliation in foreign affairs, he never hesitated to use force when American security was threatened. Franklin D. Roosevelt pursued aspects of Hoover's foreign policy, such as maintenance of a Pacific battleship fleet and nonvoting membership in the League of Nations' Advisory Committee on the Far East. Based on Hoover's memoirs and on secondary sources; 18 notes.   R. D. Hurt

1083. James, Edith. EDITH BOLLING WILSON: A DOCUMENTARY VIEW. Deutrich, Mabel E. and Purdy, Virginia C., ed. *Clio Was a Woman: Studies in the History of American Women* (Washington, D.C.: Howard U. Pr., 1980): 234-240. A selection of the letters of Edith Bolling Wilson, wife of Woodrow Wilson, indicates one resource available for the study of a first lady. Edith Wilson struggled to maintain a balance between public obligations and private need, as her letters reveal. A discussion summary follows. 19 notes.   J. Powell

1084. James, J. C. THE FRANKLIN D. ROOSEVELT LIBRARY. *Manuscripts 1973 25(1): 38-40.* Members of the Manuscripts Society during their 25th annual meeting, 6 October 1973, visited the first and oldest of the presidential libraries. Summarizes the library's development and organization, its substantial holdings, and its research use. Illus.
D. A. Yanchisin

1085. Johnson, James P. HERBERT HOOVER AND DAVID COPPERFIELD: A TALE OF TWO CHILDHOODS. *J. of Psychohistory 1980 7(4): 467-475.* Herbert C. Hoover's favorite book was Charles Dickens's *David Copperfield.* The parallel lives of Dickens and Hoover included early loss, poverty, and authoritarian severity. Dickens dealt with this experience through his writings, and Hoover dealt with it through the work ethic.   F. F. Harling

1086. Kilmartin, Thomas W. THE LAST SHALL BE FIRST: THE AMHERST COLLEGE DAYS OF CALVIN COOLIDGE. *Hist. J. of Western Massachusetts 1977 5(2): 1-12.* Discusses President Calvin Coolidge's years at Amherst College based on his own writings and those of his classmates. Illus., 79 notes.   W. H. Mulligan, Jr.

1087. Kirwan, Kent Aiken. THE CRISIS OF IDENTITY IN THE STUDY OF PUBLIC ADMINISTRATION: WOODROW WILSON. *Polity 1977 9(3): 321-343.* The "identity crisis" of the field of public administration leads Kent Kirwan to go back to the beginnings and re-examine Woodrow Wilson's "The Study of Administration." His endeavor to explain the rejection of Wilson's theory by recent students and their lack of success in developing a more usable science leads him to a new appreciation of Wilsonian thought and the conclusion that a return to Wilson's priorities is called for.   J

1088. Knee, Stuart E. ROOSEVELT AND TURNER: AWAKENING IN THE WEST. *J. of the West 1978 17(2): 105-112.* Theodore Roosevelt's *Winning of the West* and Frederick Jackson Turner's "The Significance of the Frontier in American History" both reached essentially the same conclusions. The frontier experience was an evolutionary advance in a form of government developed by men whose characters and social patterns were shaped in the forests. Both men were hostile to industrialism, but while Turner took the Populist view that looked back to a golden age of agrarianism, Roosevelt, the progressive, looked forward to a stage beyond agrarianism where the nation would be equal with the world's great powers. Primary and secondary sources; photo, 53 notes, biblio.   B. S. Porter

1089. Knock, Thomas J. "HISTORY WITH LIGHTNING": THE FORGOTTEN FILM *WILSON. Am. Q. 1976 28(5): 523-543.* The decision of Darryl F. Zanuck to produce *Wilson* for Twentieth Century Fox in 1944 was based on his belief that the United States' failure to join the League of Nations following World War I had brought about the subsequent global conflict and that a postwar international organization could produce a lasting peace. The film was then the most expensive in history, and it lost a considerable amount of money. Liberals and Democrats favorably viewed the film, and it enjoyed a considerable popularity among East Coast audiences. Republicans attacked the movie as pro-Roosevelt and as propaganda for his fourth term. There was poor audience attendance in the American interior. The film did add to the contemporary historiographical interest in Wilson.   N. Lederer

1090. Kollock, Will. THE STORY OF A FRIENDSHIP: MARK SULLIVAN AND HERBERT HOOVER. *Pacific Hist. 1974 18(1): 31-48.* Describes the friendship between Mark Sullivan and Herbert Hoover during Hoover's years in the White House and after. Sullivan, a journalist, advised President Hoover during his troubles with the press corps and continued as both friend and confidant after Hoover was defeated by Franklin Roosevelt in 1932. Both men spoke out against the New Deal and remained close friends until Sullivan's death in 1952. 81 notes.   S

1091. Kraft, Barbara S. and Smythe, Donald. HOW T. R. TRIED IN VAIN TO FIGHT IN WORLD WAR I. *Smithsonian 1973 4(7): 54-61.* Theodore Roosevelt wanted to lead a company of troops during World War I.   S

1092. Lash, Joseph P. ELEANOR ROOSEVELT'S ROLE IN WOMEN'S HISTORY. Deutrich, Mabel E. and Purdy, Virginia C., ed. *Clio Was a Woman: Studies in the History of American Women* (Washington, D.C.: Howard U. Pr., 1980): 243-253. Recounts Eleanor Roosevelt's career. Raised by a grandmother who was the epitome of Victorian female dependence and helplessness, Mrs. Roosevelt did not have a childhood upbringing which nurtured traits of independence and militancy. She was influenced in her conception of how women should participate in political life by her aunt, Mrs. Cowles, emerging as a champion of women's rights. She was also influenced to become more of a public person by the US entry into World War I and by the discovery of her husband's romance with Lucy Mercer. During the 1920's she became a leader in her own right with active participation in many organizations. The New Deal years represented a high point in women's participation in politics and government, largely because of Mrs. Roosevelt. A discussion summary follows. Based on a personal acquaintance with Mrs. Roosevelt; 26 notes.

J. Powell

1093. Maddox, Robert J. TEDDY ROOSEVELT AND THE ROUGH RIDERS. *Am. Hist. Illus. 1977 12(7): 8-19.* Discusses Theodore Roosevelt's Rough Riders, the first Volunteer Cavalry in San Antonio, Tampa, and Cuba. Describes the charge up Kettle Hill during the Spanish-American War. Primary and secondary sources; 12 illus.

D. Dodd

1094. Marion, David E. ALEXANDER HAMILTON AND WOODROW WILSON ON THE SPIRIT AND FORM OF A RESPONSIBLE REPUBLICAN GOVERNMENT. *Rev. of Pol. 1980 42(3): 309-328.* Many current scholars, fearful of the reascendancy of an imperial presidency, have often cited Woodrow Wilson and Alexander Hamilton as American political writers who supported centralized government. Close reading, however, reveals startling differences between the two. "By returning to the political thought of Hamilton and Wilson we can deepen our understanding of the competing arguments on behalf of rule based on popular opinion in a system fashioned to promote the efficient implementation of the majority will and rule based on the deliberate will of the community in a system intended to moderate and even check illiberal, unreasonable, or uninformed popular inclinations." 40 notes.

L. E. Ziewacz

1095. Mattson, Robert Lee. POLITICS IS UP! GRIGSBY'S COWBOYS AND ROOSEVELT'S ROUGH RIDERS, 1898. *South Dakota Hist. 1979 9(4): 303-315.* Political influence played a vital role in the organization, recruiting, equipping, and internal promotions of the three cowboy regiments authorized by Congress during the Spanish-American War in 1898. While Melvin Grigsby, Jay L. Torrey, and Leonard Wood (1860-1927) were authorized to recruit and command regiments, the effects of political pressure caused the Rough Riders regiment led by Wood and Theodore Roosevelt (1858-1919) to gain immortality while the others became lost in obscurity. Although Theodore Roosevelt's courage and ability cannot be denied, his political influence may have been more important in his becoming a war hero than any of his other qualities. Based on the Grigsby Papers at the Center for Western Studies, Augustana College, Sioux Falls, South Dakota, and other primary sources; 4 photos, 44 notes.

P. L. McLaughlin

1096. McCoy, Donald R. THE BEGINNINGS OF THE FRANKLIN D. ROOSEVELT LIBRARY. *Prologue 1975 7(3): 137-150.* Franklin Delano Roosevelt (1882-1945) had no doubt that his presidential papers were private property. After consulting with his adviser Frank C. Walker and national archivist Robert Connor, Roosevelt decided to construct a private depository at Hyde Park financed by public subscription, and to donate the building, some land, and his papers to the federal government. Samuel Eliot Morison (1887-1976) was an important academic consultant. Roosevelt's precedent was followed by his successors. The resulting concentration of materials in scattered institutions is a mixed legacy for historians. Those who are interested in studying more than one presidential administration must travel long distances. Primary and secondary sources; 5 illus., 3 photos, 37 notes. W. R. Hively

1097. Mendel, Roberta. WOODROW WILSON: LIVING MARTYR. *Daughters of the Am. Revolution Mag. 1976 110(3): 332-335, 352.* Summarizes the life of Thomas Woodrow Wilson (1856-1924), 28th President of the United States.

1098. Morris, Edmund. THE CYCLONE ASSEMBLYMAN. *Am. Heritage 1979 30(2): 34-43.* Excerpts from author's biography of Theodore Roosevelt chronicling Roosevelt's early days in the New York Assembly in 1882. The youngest member of the legislature soon glimpsed the combination between politics and business, and led several reform efforts. 9 photos.

J. F. Paul

1099. Mrozek, Donald J. PROGRESSIVE DISSENTER: HERBERT HOOVER'S OPPOSITION TO TRUMAN'S OVERSEAS MIL-

ITARY POLICY. *Ann. of Iowa 1976 43(4): 275-291.* In late 1950, Herbert C. Hoover broke sharply with the overseas military policies of the Truman Administration. For Hoover, the "creation of a large, permanent military force overseas represented an internationalization of the dole that he had criticized during the tenure of Franklin D. Roosevelt." Disturbed by the lukewarm support of European allies for the American involvement in Korea and by the prospect of an Eisenhower presidential candidacy, Hoover called for limits to American commitments overseas. He also called for an end to bipartisan foreign policy. Describes the former president as one of the last progressives, a true follower of Woodrow Wilson, although Truman's defenders and others dismissed Hoover as a relic from the pre-World War II period of isolation. "Because Hoover's protest failed, there was no workable alternative to the administration's policy, which allowed for increasingly elaborate military involvement around the world." Based on correspondence and speech drafts in the Hoover Papers and secondary sources; 40 notes.

P. L. Petersen

1100. Mulder, John M. WILSON THE PREACHER: THE 1905 BACCALAUREATE SERMON. *J. of Presbyterian Hist. 1973 51(3): 267-284.* Woodrow Wilson's baccalaureate sermon at Princeton University emphasized his religious faith and its application. S

1101. Murakata, Akiko. THEODORE ROOSEVELT AND WILLIAM STURGIS BIGELOW: THE STORY OF A FRIENDSHIP. *Harvard Library Bull. 1975 23(1): 90-108.* Reviews the three decades of correspondence (1887-1919) between Theodore Roosevelt and William Sturgis Bigelow. Suggests their friendship in which their mutual friend, Senator Henry Cabot Lodge, figured prominently, had great impact on the nation's cultural and political history. Based on the Theodore Roosevelt papers at the Manuscript Division of the Library of Congress; 2 illus., 62 notes. L. Smith

1102. Nash, George H. THE SOCIAL PHILOSOPHY OF HERBERT HOOVER. *Ann. of Iowa 1980 45(6): 478-496.* Not only did Herbert Hoover lead a life rich in accomplishment but he also reflected upon the circumstances which made his many careers possible. His world travels as a mining engineer gave Hoover ample opportunity to ponder the contrast he perceived between the Old World and the New. Eventually Hoover's writings and speeches came to embody a social philosophy, or ideology, that explained the greatness of the United States and stressed individualism and the need for equal opportunity. Based on Hoover's published writings and speeches and the Commission for the Relief on Belgium Papers, Hoover Institution, Stanford University, Palo Alto, California; 4 photos, 31 notes.

P. L. Petersen

1103. Ness, Gary C. PROVING GROUND FOR A PRESIDENT: WILLIAM HOWARD TAFT AND THE PHILIPPINES 1900-1905. *Cincinnati Hist. Soc. Bull. 1976 34(3): 205-223.* Discusses the public life of William Howard Taft in the decade before his presidential inauguration in 1909, when his service in the Philippines led him to become the "embodiment of the ongoing national effort to reconcile overseas expansion with the strong and generally contradictory, domestic impulses of political liberalism and social reform," and whose subsequent stance in international relations affected American foreign policy for the following 75 years.

1104. Ness, Gary C. WILLIAM HOWARD TAFT AND THE GREAT WAR. *Cincinnati Hist. Soc. Bull. 1976 34(1): 6-23.* Reprints seven letters recently acquired by the Cincinnati Historical Society between William Howard Taft and his mother-in-law, Katherine Rocker Wulsin, concerning World War I, 1917-18.

1105. Neu, Charles E. THE SEARCH FOR WOODROW WILSON. *Rev. in Am. Hist. 1982 10(2): 223-228.* Review essay of Edwin A. Weinstein's *Woodrow Wilson: A Medical and Psychological Biography* (1981); covers 1856-1924.

1106. Olson, James S. THE PHILOSOPHY OF HERBERT HOOVER: A CONTEMPORARY PERSPECTIVE. *Ann. of Iowa 1976 43(3): 181-191.* Herbert C. Hoover believed that the United States constituted "the most magnificent society in the history of the World, for it had achieved a unique synthesis of enlightened individualism and equality of opportunity." Yet Hoover realized that during the Industrial Revolution tremendous economic power had come to rest with the supercorporations; thus he was willing to accept the progressive concept of a regulatory state. The result was a dualism in his philosophy. He desired to lead the country down the middle road between laissez faire on one hand and an activist, coercive, corporate state on the other. Hoover's fears of massive governmental intervention prevented him from effectively meeting the political issues of the depression, but the problem of the modern corporate state in America today affirms that Hoover was "guilty of nothing more than farsightedness." Based on Hoover's published writings and secondary sources; 14 notes. P. L. Petersen

1107. Pechatnov, Vladimir O. ZA KULISAMI VYRABOTKI "NOVOGO KURSA" (F. FRANKFURTER-U. LIPPMAN) [Behind the scenes of the New Deal (F. Frankfurter-W. Lippmann)]. *Voprosy Istorii [USSR] 1979 (7): 112-123.* Analyzes the debates and discussions among Franklin D. Roosevelt, Felix Frankfurter (1882-1965), Walter Lippmann (1889-1974), and others on the eve of the New Deal (1932). THe writings of Frankfurter released in 1945 show clearly that the New Deal temporarily quieted the economic crisis of the 1930's; the United States would remain a capitalist society. At the same time one cannot hide the fact that the outcome of the experiment continued to remain uncertain. Finally the economic success of the New Deal could not be proved because World War II completely changed the nature of the economic crisis of the 1930's. Based on correspondence between FDR and Frankfurter, the Walter Lippmann letters, and the Perkins Collection; 62 notes. J. L. Evans

1108. Perry, Phillip M. WITH CALVIN COOLIDGE IN NORTHAMPTON. *New-England Galaxy 1977 18(3): 37-43.* Discusses Calvin Coolidge's life in Northampton, Massachusetts from March 1929 after he left the presidency until his death on 5 January 1933. His reactions to visitors were described by his secretary, Herman Beaty, and by his chauffeur, John Bukoski. Illus. P. C. Marshall

1109. Pollin, Burton R. THEODORE ROOSEVELT TO THE RESCUE OF THE POE COTTAGE. *Mississippi Q. 1980-81 34(1): 51-60.* Traces disinterest in preserving the little cottage in Fordham in New York City that Edgar Allan Poe had rented for many years to the calumniation he suffered at the hands of journalists such as Horace Greeley and credits the interest Theodore Roosevelt took in the Poe cottage with its eventual preservation and designation as an important historical site.

1110. Potts, Louis W. WHO WAS WARREN G. HARDING? *Historian 1974 36(4): 621-645.* A study of the numerous and diverse evaluations of Warren G. Harding (1865-1923) that have come into print since the beginning of his presidency. Balances the generally accepted low estimates of Harding as a man, leader, and politician with the extensive revisionism which has been attempted repeatedly, taking note of all major studies which have been published in the interval. Recognition of constructive achievements along with the severe weaknesses go back to 1923. 82 notes. R. V. Ritter

1111. Rae, John B. THE HERBERT HOOVER COLLECTION OF MINING AND METALLURGY. *Technology and Culture 1980 21(4): 614-616.* Describes the 1,010 rare books (most of them from 1470 to 1900) in this collection at the Sprague Memorial Library at Harvey Mudd College in Claremont, California. C. O. Smith, Jr.

1112. Rhoads, William B. FRANKLIN D. ROOSEVELT AND DUTCH COLONIAL ARCHITECTURE. *New York Hist. 1978 59(4): 430-464.* President Franklin D. Roosevelt paralleled Thomas Jefferson in his interest in architecture. After his polio attack in 1921 FDR became active in preserving the historical and pictorial records of colonial Dutch houses, and he undertook the revival of Dutch fieldstone architecture in Dutchess County. As president he directed the architects of the Treasury Department to design new post offices in Dutchess and Ulster counties in conformity with local Dutch architectural traditions. Shows how involved FDR was in planning the architectural details of Hudson Valley buildings constructed during his presidency, including the Franklin D. Roosevelt Library at Hyde Park. 8 illus., 78 notes. R. N. Lokken

1113. Ricard, Serge. MEMOIRS OF SELF-RIGHTEOUSNESS: THE AUTOBIOGRAPHY OF THEODORE ROOSEVELT. *Rev.*

Française d'Etudes Américaines [France] 1982 7(14): 277-289. Discusses President Theodore Roosevelt's life and career from 1881-1915, and details aspects of the contemporary corporate and political scene.

1114. Ricard, Serge. THEODORE ROOSEVELT AVANT LA PRÉSIDENCE: ANALYSE D'UNE PENSÉE POLITIQUE [Theodore Roosevelt before the presidency: analysis of one political thought]. *Can. Rev. of Am. Studies [Canada] 1981 12(2): 157-172.* From 1882 to 1901, Theodore Roosevelt wrote extensively, his writings ranging from historical treatises to philosophical works. There he vented his expansive interests, displayed the breadth of vision that became one of his presidential hallmarks, and recorded his political thinking as it evolved over two decades. Roosevelt's political musings pegged him as a product of American political traditions, his conclusions firmly confined to the mainstream. Roosevelt's moralistic concerns formed one common denominator of his thought, and this quality reflected his adherence to the conventional and denoted his acceptance of the New England Puritan heritage. Based on Roosevelt's writings; 11 notes. H. T. Lovin

1115. Richardson, Elmo R. CONSERVATION AS A POLITICAL ISSUE: THE WESTERN PROGRESSIVES' DILEMMA, 1909-1912. *Pacific Northwest Q. 1958 49(2): 49-54.* Examines the complex manner in which the issue of conservation of natural resources affected politics in the Far Western States during 1909-12, with particular reference to the attitude of Theodore Roosevelt and the Progressives.

1116. Robinson, Forrest G. THE ROOSEVELT-WISTER CONNECTION: SOME NOTES ON THE WEST AND THE USES OF HISTORY. *Western Am. Literature 1979 14(2): 95-114.* Theodore Roosevelt and Owen Wister, who were long-time friends, had a mutual interest in Western history. Their writings strongly portrayed this interest since both wanted national unity to win over the threat of sectionalism. Also, they tried to describe national aspirations and to produce a popular conception of the American hero. At a luncheon in the early 1890's Wister assured Roosevelt that he would do his best to interpret the West through works of imagination. In doing this, he frequently consulted Roosevelt's writings in order to show the flexibility of Roosevelt's public image. M. Genung

1117. Rochefort, David A. THE WESTERN MORATORIUM OF THEODORE ROOSEVELT. *North Dakota Q. 1981 49(3): 42-56.* Describes Theodore Roosevelt's years during 1884-86 in North Dakota where he lived the life of a cowboy in order "to seek a respite from adult roles and obligations associated with the East and to experiment with an identity marked by divergent intellectual and physical preoccupations."

1118. Ross, Irwin. FIFTEEN SECONDS OF TERROR. *Am. Hist. Illus. 1975 10(4): 10-13.* Discusses Giuseppe Zangara's attempted assassination of President-elect Franklin D. Roosevelt in Miami, Florida, in 1933.

1119. Russell, Francis. THE SHADOW OF WARREN HARDING. *Antioch Rev. 1978 36(1): 57-76.* Describes the discovery (at Marion, Ohio, in 1963) of President Warren G. Harding's letters to Carrie Phillips during their love affair from 1905 to 1920, and the problems the letters presented to biographers and protectors of Harding's reputation.

1120. Saunders, Frances W. LOVE AND GUILT: WOODROW WILSON AND MARY HULBERT. *Am. Heritage 1979 30(3): 69-77.* Woodrow Wilson's relationship with Mary Hulbert, from their first encounter in Bermuda in 1907 to Wilson's marriage to Edith Galt in 1915, is traced. Hulbert's understanding at the time of the death of Wilson's first wife in 1914, and her loyalty when Wilson married Galt, are stressed. The correspondence was purchased from Hulbert by Ray Stannard Baker and Bernard Baruch and was ultimately given to the Library of Congress. 10 illus. J. F. Paul

1121. Schacht, John N. FOUR MEN FROM IOWA. *Palimpsest 1982 63(1): 30-31.* Summarizes the lives and careers of President Herbert C. Hoover, United Mine Workers President John L. Lewis, Secretary of Agriculture Henry A. Wallace, and New Deal administrator and presidential advisor Harry Hopkins.

1122. Schacht, John N. THE IOWA ENVIRONMENT. *Palimpsest 1982 63(1): 4-5.* Analyzes the environment of Iowa from the mid-1870's to the mid-1890's to discover why "a disproportionate share of the influential people in the 1930's [Herbert C. Hoover, John L. Lewis, Henry A. Wallace, and Harry Hopkins] came from Iowa."

1123. Schacht, John N. A TIME OF PREPARATION. *Palimpsest 1982 63(1): 6-11.* Focuses on the education and careers of four Iowans: President Herbert C. Hoover, United Mine Workers President John L. Lewis, Secretary of Agriculture Henry A. Wallace, and New Deal administrator and presidential advisor Harry Hopkins.

1124. Schlup, Leonard, comp. and ed. SELECTED LETTERS OF SENATOR MCCUMBER TO FORMER PRESIDENT TAFT CONCERNING THE LEAGUE OF NATIONS. *North Dakota Hist. 1979 46(3): 15-23.* Ten letters to William Howard Taft reveal that North Dakota Senator Porter J. McCumber and President Taft were leaders of the Republican senators who supported the League of Nations. Together they advocated certain reservations to be incorporated in articles 10 and 15 of the treaty, which it was hoped would mollify the opponents of the League. Other items of concern in the correspondence were: 1) the guarantee of US policy and rights under the Monroe Doctrine, 2) the number of votes in the Council allotted to Great Britain, and 3) the unanimous vote in the Council to refer a problem to the Assembly. Other senators with whom McCumber was working were McNary, Cummins, Kellogg, Hale, and Lenroot. 7 illus., 3 photos, 2 charts, 47 notes, ref.
                                                                    H. F. Thomson

1125. Schullery, Paul. A PARTNERSHIP IN CONSERVATION: THEODORE ROOSEVELT AND YELLOWSTONE. *Montana 1978 28(3): 2-15.* Theodore Roosevelt became a staunch supporter and defender of wildlife conservation and Yellowstone National Park in the 1880's. With George Bird Grinnell and others, Roosevelt founded the Boone and Crockett Club and worked to preserve Yellowstone National Park as the "park for the people." He opposed railroad construction through the Park and worked to secure passage of the National Park Protective Act, 1894. As President, he visited Yellowstone from 8-24 April 1903, to relax, study wildlife, and view preservation efforts. Naturalist John Burroughs accompanied Roosevelt. As informally as possible, Roosevelt toured the Park, devoting particular attention to its wildlife. He also dedicated the stone arch entrance at Gardiner, Montana. Historians have mistakenly credited Roosevelt's 1903 visit with making the President a conservationist. In truth, he already held those beliefs. The visit merely provided lessons and inspiration. Thereafter he worked to expand all National Parks and to establish the National Park Service. Based on published letters and writings of Roosevelt and Burroughs, secondary works, and unpublished materials in the Yellowstone Park Reference Library; 13 illus., 40 notes, biblio.   R. C. Myers

1126. Shannon, David A. THE MAKING OF A PRINCETON PRESIDENT, 1896-1902: AN ESSAY REVIEW. *Pacific Northwest Q. 1974 65(4): 184-186.* Reviews Arthur S. Link's *The Papers of Woodrow Wilson*, Volume 10, 1896-98 (Princeton: Princeton U. Press, 1971, Volume 11, 1971, Volume 12, 1972). Concentrates on Woodrow Wilson's professorial career at Princeton University, the University of Virginia's interest in him as chairman of the faculty, Wilson's negotiations with the board of Princeton, their maneuvers to eliminate President Francis Landey Patton, and the election of Wilson to the Princeton presidency as Patton's successor.   R. V. Ritter

1127. Silver, Thomas B. COOLIDGE AND THE HISTORIANS. *Am. Scholar 1981 50(4): 501-517.* Calvin Coolidge was an educated, dignified, decent, moral, patriotic, and deeply democratic human being. He was enormously popular, elected by large majorities every time he ran except once. This is in sharp contrast to the popular images drawn by Samuel E. Morrison, Arthur Schleisinger, Jr., and others.
                                                                    F. F. Harling

1128. Silverman, Eliane Leslau. REFORM AS A MEANS OF SOCIAL CONTROL: THEODORE ROOSEVELT AND WOMEN'S SUFFRAGE. *Atlantis [Canada] 1976 2(1): 22-36.* Discusses the idea that woman suffrage as a means of radical reform actually became a tool for middle class males to gain social and political control, citing Theodore Roosevelt's attitudes towards women's suffrage as an example of men's scorn for women's political involvement, 1899-1919.

1129. Smith, Ronald A. SPORT, POLITICS, AND HARVARD: A LITTLE LESSON IN HONOR FOR TEDDY ROOSEVELT. *New England Q. 1981 54(3): 412-416.* Theodore Roosevelt, Harvard class of 1880, was particularly sensitive to losses sustained by Harvard to Yale in sporting events. When two members of the Harvard crew were dismissed in June 1908 for stealing a book from the library, Roosevelt pleaded with Harvard's president, Charles William Eliot, to temper their punishment. Their exchanges became public when the *New York Times* published the telegrams. While Roosevelt was furious over the leak, Eliot would not stand for interference from anyone, and by taking Roosevelt to task upheld the moral integrity of Harvard. Primary sources; 13 notes.
                                                                    R. S. Sliwoski

1130. Stewart, William J. OPENING CLOSED MATERIAL IN THE ROOSEVELT LIBRARY. *Prologue 1975 7(4): 239-241.* In recent years restricted documents have been a major source of conflict between researcher and archivist. The Franklin D. Roosevelt Library's declassification project began in January 1970. Archivists used their own discretion to open donor-restricted files, and gradually received guidelines for declassifying agency-restricted and security classified material. More than 99% of the library's holdings, excluding Secret Service files, are now open. Scholarly interest in the Roosevelt era is still growing; research visits to the library have increased 30% over the previous five-year period.
                                                                    W. R. Hively

1131. Taft, Charles P. WILLIAM HOWARD TAFT: MY FATHER THE CHIEF JUSTICE. *Supreme Court Hist. Soc. Y. 1977: 5-10.* Reminiscences about Supreme Court Chief Justice William H. Taft, tracing his career from the late 19th century to 1930.

1132. Taggart, Robert J. WOODROW WILSON AND CURRICULUM REFORM. *New Jersey Hist. 1975 93(3-4): 99-114.* Woodrow Wilson, President of Princeton University, admired the tutor-student educational system of Oxford and Cambridge and believed that general education was best for Princetonians. He advocated quadrangles as the basis for student life, and criticized eating clubs as hindrances to sober reflection. Wilson felt Princeton should deemphasize its graduate program. Faculty, alumni, and trustees argued effectively against Wilson's ideas so they were never implemented. Wilson failed at educational reform because his plans did not coincide with Princeton's goals. Based on primary and secondary sources; 5 illus., 2 maps, 30 notes.
                                                                    E. R. McKinstry

1133. Weinstein, Edwin A.; Anderson, James William; and Link, Arthur S. WOODROW WILSON'S POLITICAL PERSONALITY: A REAPPRAISAL. *Pol. Sci. Q. 1978-79 93(4): 585-598.* Reviews the literature on Woodrow Wilson's personality, concentrating on the book *Woodrow Wilson and Colonel House* by Alexander and Juliette George. The authors contend that the Georges' book is based on incorrect assumptions about the relationship between Wilson and his father and offer an alternative view of the dynamics of Wilson's political personality.   J

1134. Wert, Jeffry D. THEODORE ROOSEVELT: PATRON SAINT OF DRY SUNDAYS. *Am. Hist. Illus. 1982 17(2): 30-35.* Describes the reforms initiated by president of the New York City Police Board, Theodore Roosevelt, especially his order to officers to enforce the 38-year-old Sunday Excise Law prohibiting the sale of alcohol between midnight Saturday and midnight Sunday; this effort, designed to break the control of Tammany Hall boss Patrick "King" Callahan and his cronies, failed, and Roosevelt left the board in 1897 with the Tammany politicians still in control.

1135. Whitaker, W. Richard. THE NIGHT HARDING DIED. *Journalism Hist. 1974 1(1): 16-19.* Examines how the press reported the death of President Warren G. Harding on the night of 2 August 1923.

1136. Willoughby, William R. THE ROOSEVELT CAMPOBELLO INTERNATIONAL PARK COMMISSION. *Dalhousie R. [Canada] 1974 54(2): 289-297.* Roosevelt Campobello International Park in New Brunswick is a significant milestone in the evolution of Canadian-American friendship in that it is truly an international park. Earlier parks at Waterton-Glacier (Alberta-Montana) and International Peace Garden (Manitoba-North Dakota) are operated by the two countries as separate entities. The land for the park was given by Dr. Armand Hammer who had bought it from the Roosevelt family. Both countries had thought of the site as a park at one time or another, but both had rejected it. The problem was one of Canadian land with US historical interest. A joint commission plus Hammer's offer as a gift was the ideal solution, with the costs of development equally shared. 18 notes.   C. Held

1137. Wolfe, Christopher. WOODROW WILSON: INTERPRETING THE CONSTITUTION. *Rev. of Pol. 1979 41(1): 121-142.* A comparative analysis of early and recent Supreme Court decisions indicates a difference in the "manner in which the Constitution is interpreted." An examination of Woodrow Wilson's interpretation of the Constitution indicates that the modern Supreme Court has assumed judicial legislative power in most cases which is a great departure from its original mission which was to reflect "the popular will embodied in the Constitution." 14 notes.   L. Ziewacz

1138. Živojinović, Dragoljub R. TEODOR RUZVELT I POLITIKA SJEDINJENIH AMERIČKIH DRŽAVA PREMA JUGOISTOČNOJ EVROPI, 1917-18 GODINE [Theodore Roosevelt and the US policy toward Southeastern Europe, 1917-18]. *Vojnoistorijski Glasnik [Yugoslavia] 1973 24(1): 79-101.* Describes Roosevelt's special interest in events in Southeast Europe and his demand for a greater American commitment there during World War I with a declaration of war against Austro-Hungary, Turkey, and Bulgaria.   J. Bamber

1139. —. A FRANKLIN D. ROOSEVELT SYMPOSIUM: THREE PAPERS OBSERVING THE 100TH ANNIVERSARY OF HIS BIRTH. *Presidential Studies Q. 1982 12(1): 48-65.*
Roosevelt, James. STAFFING MY FATHER'S PRESIDENCY: A PERSONAL REMINISCENCE, *pp. 48-49.*
Helicher, Karl. THE EDUCATION OF FRANKLIN D. ROOSEVELT, *pp. 50-53.* Describes the formal education of Roosevelt, who viewed school as a means to an end and never an intense experience in itself. 17 notes.
Sheffer, Martin S. THE ATTORNEY GENERAL AND PRESIDENTIAL POWER: ROBERT H. JACKSON, FRANKLIN ROOSEVELT, AND THE PREROGATIVE PRESIDENCY, *pp. 54-65.* Franklin Roosevelt used Attorney General Robert H. Jackson to constitutionalize his presidential power. In three areas—the removal of members of the Tennessee Valley Authority, the acquisition of naval and air bases, and in the stressing of executive privilege—Jackson acted as a partisan advocate for the president. 83 notes.
                    D. H. Cline

1140. —. "MAINTENANCE OF PEACE IN ARMENIA": A SENATORIAL SUBCOMMITTEE DEBATES SJR 106, "THE WILLIAMS RESOLUTION," 1919. *Armenian Rev. 1981 34(2): 199-217, 4(4): 412-427.* Continued from a previous article (see entry 19A:7763). Part 3. A meeting of the US Senate Subcommittee on Foreign Relations took place on 10 October 1919 to discuss American options and responsibilities in dealing with the problems in Armenia; includes a statement by Prime Minister Ohannes Kachasnouni of the Armenian Republic. Part 4. Presents a series of documents dealing with the Senate's consideration of humanitarian and military aid for the Armenian Republic in 1919, emphasizing the views and efforts of Senators John Sharp Williams and Warren G. Harding.

Presidential Campaigns

1141. Anderson, Fenwick. HAIL TO THE EDITOR-IN-CHIEF: COX VS. HARDING, 1920. *Journalism Hist. 1974 1(2): 46-49.* The presidential election campaign of 1920 between two journalists, Republican Warren G. Harding and Democrat James M. Cox, demonstrated the lack of objectivity in newspapers run by the two candidates.

1142. Bailey, John W., Jr. THE PRESIDENTIAL ELECTION OF 1900 IN NEBRASKA: MC KINLEY OVER BRYAN. *Nebraska Hist. 1973 54(4): 561-584.* Bryan won his home state over McKinley in 1896 by more than 13,000 votes, but lost it in 1900 by more than 7,000 votes. Prosperity, the decline of Populism, the intensive Republican campaign in the state, and Bryan's partial neglect of his home state all explain the results in 1900.   R. Lowitt

1143. Bauman, Mark K. PROHIBITION AND POLITICS: WARREN CANDLER AND AL SMITH'S 1928 CAMPAIGN. *Mississippi Q. 1977-78 31(1): 109-118.* Distaste for mixing religion and politics and a desire not to draw attention to anti-Prohibition elements led Methodist Episcopal Church, South, senior bishop Warren Candler to instruct the clergy in his church not to become involved in the presidential election of 1928 between Catholic, anti-Prohibition candidate Alfred E. Smith and Herbert H. Hoover.

1144. Blair, John L. CALVIN COOLIDGE AND THE ADVENT OF RADIO POLITICS. *Vermont Hist. 1976 44(1): 28-37.* Radio came into political use with Calvin Coolidge, "and it was largely the President who made it" prominent. By November 1924, more than 500 stations beamed to 3,000,000 receiving sets. Coolidge could conduct his campaign from the White House. His party spent over $100,000 for broadcasts when prime time cost $5,000 an hour. His inauguration was the first ever broadcast; some 20,000,000 heard his 1927 Washington's Birthday address. Charles Michelson of the Democratic New York *World* concluded that Coolidge had "the perfect radio voice." Coolidge seized the chance to focus public attention on the Presidency. Based on Coolidge Papers, magazines, and monographs; 32 notes.   T. D. S. Bassett

1145. Blayney, Michael Stewart. HONOR AMONG GENTLEMEN: HERBERT PELL, FRANKLIN ROOSEVELT, AND THE CAMPAIGN OF 1936. *Rhode Island Hist. 1980 39(3): 95-102.* Herbert Pell, a Knickerbocker patrician, was linked to Franklin D. Roosevelt by ties of class, liberalism, antibusiness sentiment, a Hudson River estate near Roosevelt's, and an association dating back to their student days at Harvard. In the 1936 presidential campaign Pell served as a defender of Roosevelt against the charges that he was an enemy to his class. Based on papers in public repositories and private hands, interviews, and published documents; 4 illus., 40 notes.   P. J. Coleman

1146. Bradford, Richard H. RELIGION AND POLITICS: ALFRED E. SMITH AND THE ELECTION OF 1928 IN WEST VIRGINIA. *West Virginia Hist. 1975 36(3): 213-221.* In the 1928 Democratic presidential primary, New York Governor Alfred E. Smith faced Missouri Senator James A. Reed in West Virginia. Although Smith never set foot in the state while Reed campaigned vigorously, and although Smith was a Catholic running in a 95% Protestant state, he won the primary, 82,000 to 76,000. In November, Hoover won; but West Virginia had been a Republican state for some time, and Smith did better than previous Democratic candidates. Based on newspapers and secondary sources; 50 notes.   J. H. Broussard.

1147. Carter, Paul A. DEJA VU; OR, BACK TO THE DRAWING BOARD WITH ALFRED E. SMITH. *Rev. in Am. Hist. 1980 8(2): 272-276.* Review essay of Allan J. Lichtman's *Prejudice and the Old Politics: The Presidential Election of 1928* (Chapel Hill: U. of North Carolina Pr., 1979).

1148. Coletta, Paolo E. BRYAN AT BALTIMORE, 1912: WILSON'S WARWICK. *Nebraska Hist. 1976 57(2): 200-225.* Detailed examination of William Jennings Bryan's crucial role in the 1912 Democratic Party convention. As a result of his stance in opposing any candidate who had the support of "the financiers of Wall Street," Woodrow Wilson was able on the 46th ballot to secure the nomination.
                    R. Lowitt

1149. Feinman, Ronald L. THE PROGRESSIVE REPUBLICAN SENATE BLOC AND THE PRESIDENTIAL ELECTION OF 1932. *Mid-America 1977 59(2): 73-91.* During the early 1930's the progressive Republican Senate bloc consisted of 12 senators from Midwestern and Western states. Most of them opposed Herbert Hoover's policies and sought options which would further progressivism. A third party alternative was rejected. Several considered opposing Hoover in the 1932 primaries, but this failed to materialize. Only two of the 12, Charles McNary of Oregon and Arthur Capper of Kansas, actively supported Hoover during the Presidential campaign. The others remained neutral or supported Roosevelt as the most progressive candidate. Based on archival material; 43 notes.   J. M. Lee

1150. Gould, Lewis L. THEODORE ROOSEVELT, WILLIAM HOWARD TAFT, AND THE DISPUTED DELEGATES IN 1912:

TEXAS AS A TEST CASE. *Southwestern Hist. Q. 1976 80(1): 33-56.* Reexamines Texas' 40 disputed delegates to the 1912 Republican national convention. Texas party leaders split between President William Howard Taft and ex-President Theodore Roosevelt, but the Taft group claimed nearly all the delegates. The Republican national convention rejected a Roosevelt challenge and gave Taft 31 of the 40 votes. Impartial analysis of each district indicates that a fair division would have been 21 for Roosevelt, 19 for Taft, but both factions were interested in political advantage rather than fairness. Based on primary sources; table, 49 notes.
J. H. Broussard

1151. Grant, Philip A., Jr. ESTABLISHING A TWO-PARTY SYSTEM: THE 1932 PRESIDENTIAL ELECTION IN SOUTH DAKOTA. *Presidential Studies Q. 1980 10(1): 73-79.* Among the foremost farm states involved in the presidential election of 1932 was South Dakota. With four electoral votes, it became somewhat of a barometer of midwestern, even national, political sentiment. Franklin D. Roosevelt's candidacy in the 1932 election unquestionably benefited from the discontent prevailing in South Dakota over the state's economic conditions. South Dakotans cast their votes against Herbert C. Hoover, favoring a change in national leadership. This is how the genuine two-party system began in the state. 47 notes.
G. E. Pergl

1152. Grant, Philip A., Jr. THE PRESIDENTIAL ELECTION OF 1932 IN MISSOURI. *Missouri Hist. Soc. Bull. 1979 35(3): 164-170.* During 1918-30, the Missouri electorate consistently chose Republican candidates for most national and state offices. But, in the 1932 elections, Democratic nominees prevailed because Missouri voters were angry with the Herbert C. Hoover administration failures to cope with the Great Depression. Showing their displeasure, electors voted more against Hoover than for Franklin D. Roosevelt. Based on governmental publications and newspaper sources; table, 43 notes.
H. T. Lovin

1153. Grant, Philip A., Jr. THE PRESIDENTIAL ELECTION OF 1932 IN WESTERN MASSACHUSETTS. *Hist. J. of Western Massachusetts 1980 8(1): 3-13.* Franklin D. Roosevelt's success in western Massachusetts in the 1932 presidential election was related to widespread discontent with the regional economy, gains by the Democratic Party in the 1928 Al Smith campaign, and the unity and strength of that party in the region. Based on newspapers, convention proceedings, and secondary sources; 37 notes.
W. H. Mulligan, Jr.

1154. Grant, Philip A., Jr. THE PRESIDENTIAL ELECTION OF 1932 IN IOWA. *Ann. of Iowa 1979 44(7): 541-550.* Franklin D. Roosevelt's resounding defeat of Herbert C. Hoover in the 1932 presidential election in traditionally Republican Iowa was the result of profound discontent over the precarious state of Iowa's economy. Roosevelt's victory was extremely helpful to many Democratic Party candidates for state, congressional, and legislative offices. The presidential election of 1932 marks the beginning of a genuine two-party system in Iowa. Primary and secondary sources; photo, 39 notes.
P. L. Petersen

1155. Hammersmith, Jack L. FRANKLIN ROOSEVELT, THE POLISH QUESTION, AND THE ELECTION OF 1944. *Mid-Am. 1977 59(1): 5-17.* Examines Democratic Party strategies to retain Polish American voters in 1944. The Republicans made major gains in the 1942 congressional elections and concentrated on winning ethnic minorities, especially Polish Americans, in 1944. Roosevelt and the Democrats took special care to retain and woo the Polish Americans by keeping the Polish-Russian question at arm's length and appealing to the special interests of Poles. Although Roosevelt won by the narrowest margin ever, it was perhaps the Polish-American vote which contributed the most to his victory. Primary and secondary sources; 66 notes.
J. M. Lee

1156. Hammond, John L. NEW APPROACHES TO AGGREGATE ELECTORAL DATA. *J. of Interdisciplinary Hist. 1979 9(3): 473-492.* Comparative analysis between elections can compensate for certain kinds of measurement error and is the only way in which long-term and short-term components of the vote can be separated in aggregate data. It is necessary in understanding voting behavior that the two be separated. This is illustrated with respect to the 1928 Herbert C. Hoover-Al Smith presidential campaign in Minnesota. The religious issue (Smith was a Catholic), not the liquor question, determined voters' response to the 1928 campaign, and this can only be determined by comparative analysis. Explanatory and from printed sources; 3 tables, 27 notes.
R. Howell

1157. Haney, James E. BLACKS AND THE REPUBLICAN NOMINATION OF 1908. *Ohio Hist. 1975 84(4): 207-221.* Joseph B. Foraker was a strong candidate for the Republican presidential nomination in 1908 among blacks, who regarded him as their agent in repudiating the dishonorable discharge of 167 black soldiers for alleged involvement in a disturbance at Brownsville, Texas in 1906. When Taft was nominated, many blacks in the North opposed him because of his views on Negro suffrage, the reduction of Southern representation in the House, and the Brownsville Affair; but a campaign of black journalists on behalf of Taft was highly successful. With the race arrayed in his favor, blacks could expect political rewards. Illus., 56 notes.
E. P. Stickney

1158. Heinemann, Ronald L. "HARRY BYRD FOR PRESIDENT": THE 1932 CAMPAIGN. *Virginia Cavalcade 1975 25(1): 28-37.* Discusses the political campaign of Virginia governor Harry Flood Byrd for the presidential nomination of the Democratic Party convention in Chicago in 1932, emphasizing his competition with Franklin D. Roosevelt.

1159. Huston, James A. POLITICS IN MID-TWENTIETH CENTURY AMERICA. *Current Hist. 1974 67(395): 20-23, 40-42.* Analyzes influences on presidential nominations and elections 1920-48, including issues, personalities, and historical forces. One of seven articles in this issue on the two-party system.
S

1160. Hynes, Terry. MEDIA MANIPULATION AND POLITICAL CAMPAIGNS: BRUCE BARTON AND THE PRESIDENTIAL ELECTIONS OF THE JAZZ AGE. *Journalism Hist. 1977 4(3): 93-98.* Studies the marketing and promotion of Republican presidential candidates Calvin Coolidge and Herbert C. Hoover, in 1924 and 1928, through the work and writings of advertising executive Bruce Barton.

1161. Jakoubek, Robert E. A JEFFERSONIAN'S DISSENT: JOHN W. DAVIS AND THE CAMPAIGN OF 1936. *West Virginia Hist. 1974 35(2): 145-153.* John W. Davis, the 1924 Democratic presidential nominee, believed in a limited federal government. He supported Franklin D. Roosevelt in 1932 but feared the liberalism of the first Hundred Days. He helped form the anti-New Deal American Liberty League and as a constitutional lawyer argued many cases against New Deal measures. Although Davis distrusted the Republican Party, he decided finally to openly oppose Roosevelt's re-election in 1936. Afterward, he stood apart from both parties. Based on Davis' private papers; 45 notes.
J. H. Broussard

1162. Jensen, Richard. THE CITIES REELECT ROOSEVELT: ETHNICITY, RELIGION, AND CLASS IN 1940. *Ethnicity 1981 8(2): 189-195.* Analyzing poll results, the author argues that Franklin D. Roosevelt's urban coalition was based largely on ethnic groups. While class and union support played a role, ethnicity was the key factor. 7 tables, 7 notes.
T. W. Smith

1163. Kleppner, Paul and Baker, Stephen C. THE IMPACT OF VOTER REGISTRATION REQUIREMENTS ON ELECTORAL TURNOUT, 1900-16. *J. of Pol. and Military Sociol. 1980 8(2): 205-226.* This article tests the hypothesis that the imposition of personal registration requirements largely accounted for the post-1896 decline in voter turnout. The laws were found to depress turnout, but neither they nor other legal factors proved as important as electoral competitiveness. That was especially evident in the nation's urban-industrial area. There the social character of the active electorate changed markedly after 1896. Regression models of the 1900-16 turnout decline show the effects of an age-cohort replacement process, and one that was especially marked among younger voters of immigrant parents. That age-structured electoral demobilization was primarily a behavioral response to the "System of 1896."
J

1164. Koeniger, A. Cash. THE POLITICS OF INDEPENDENCE: CARTER GLASS AND THE ELECTION OF 1936. *South Atlantic Q. 1981 80(1): 95-106.* In the 1936 presidential election, Carter Glass of Virginia ran considerably behind Franklin D. Roosevelt in vote-gathering. He essentially sat out the campaign because he could not support the New Deal. His role in the election marked the beginning of a hallmark in Virginia politics for the next three decades. Unable to reconcile his conservative convictions with the presidential candidate and national platform of his party, yet wedded to Democratic traditions, Glass took the only course that would enable him to maintain his integrity and remain a Democrat. His conduct met the approval of the Virginia electorate. It would be emulated and refined in the famed "golden silence" of Harry F. Byrd. Based on the Carter Glass Papers and the Harry F. Byrd Papers (both in the University of Virginia), the R. Walton Moore Papers (Franklin D. Roosevelt Library), and contemporary newspaper accounts; 27 notes.

H. M. Parker, Jr.

1165. Krasnov, I. M. PREZIDENTSKIE VYBORY V SSHA 1924G: IZ ISTORII AMERIKANSKOGO BURZHUAZNOGO PAR-LAMENTARIZMA [The US presidential election of 1924: from the history of the American bourgeois parliamentary system]. *Novaia i Noveishaia Istoriia [USSR] 1979 (6): 60-69.* Analyzes the American presidential election campaign of 1924 which was won by Calvin Coolidge (1872-1933), arguing that the real selection process took place behind the scenes and was determined by the forces of monopoly capital; candidates approved by the ruling business class were presented to the public as the most worthy citizens, thus confirming the sham nature of American two-party democracy. Based on the personal papers of past presidents, especially those of Coolidge held by the American Library of Congress, also other primary sources; 28 notes.

R. J. Ware

1166. Kyvig, David E. RASKOB, ROOSEVELT, AND REPEAL. *Historian 1975 37(3): 469-487.* A prohibition repeal advocate, John J. Raskob exploited his chairmanship (1928-32) of the Democratic National Committee to secure repeal of the 18th Amendment. In so doing he collided with the presidential course of Franklin D. Roosevelt who mistakenly questioned the political wisdom of making any party commitment to repeal. However, Raskob was successful, first at the Democratic National Convention of 1932 with passage of a strong anti-prohibition plank to which Roosevelt gave opportunistic endorsement, and finally with the actual repeal on 5 December 1933. 83 notes.

1167. Levi, Steven C. THE MOST EXPENSIVE MEAL IN AMERICAN HISTORY. *J. of the West 1979 18(2): 62-73.* In the summer of 1916 Charles Evans Hughes, Republican candidate for president, attempted to bring disaffected Progressives back into the Republican Party. His campaign in California coincided with a period of labor unrest in San Francisco. Hughes unwisely followed the advice of conservative Republicans and attended a banquet in an antiunion restaurant on 19 August 1916. This act marked Hughes as an enemy of labor and was a major cause of his failure to carry California in the presidential election. Based on newspapers and other published sources; 4 photos, 59 notes.

B. S. Porter

1168. Lichtman, Allan J. CRITICAL ELECTION THEORY AND THE REALITY OF AMERICAN PRESIDENTIAL POLITICS, 1916-40. *Am. Hist. R. 1976 81(2): 317-351.* Using both quantitative and traditional historical methods, this study applies critical election theory to presidential elections, 1916-40. Focusing on the Smith-Hoover encounter of 1928, it reinterprets electoral politics during these years, challenging the notion that 1928 was either a critical election or an important component of a critical era of electoral change. It also questions the logical and empirical validity of critical election theory and argues for a broader vision of electoral change and stability in the United States. The study relies upon a quantitative data base of all 2058 counties outside the confederate South. Variables measured for the counties include presidential election returns and a variety of social and economic indicators. For selected counties the data also include primary election returns and statistics of party registration.

A

1169. Lisenby, William Foy. BROUGH, BAPTIST, AND BOMBAST: THE ELECTION OF 1928. *Arkansas Hist. Q. 1973 32(2): 120-131.* Charles Hillman Brough, a prominent Arkansas educator and political figure, clashed with anti-Smith Baptists on prohibition and the teaching of evolution.

S

1170. Margulies, Herbert F. LA FOLLETTE, ROOSEVELT AND THE REPUBLICAN PRESIDENTIAL NOMINATION OF 1912. *Mid-Am. 1976 58(1): 54-76.* Despite Robert Marion La Follette's claims to the contrary, it was he and not Theodore Roosevelt who played a double game during the nomination campaign. Following the successful 1910 fall elections, La Follette created the National Progressive Republi-

can League to work toward replacement of Taft. La Follette's strategy of a united front against Taft collapsed as Roosevelt's candidacy slowly emerged. The ill La Follette, advised by his wife, accused the Roosevel-tians of treachery and continued the race. Ultimately, La Follette preferred Wilson's victory to that of his rivals; he was again the leading progressive Republican. Based on the La Follette Family Collection, Library of Congress and other MS. sources, and on published sources and secondary works; 78 notes.

T. H. Wendel

1171. Margulies, Herbert F. IRVINE L. LENROOT AND THE RE-PUBLICAN VICE-PRESIDENTIAL NOMINATION OF 1920. *Wisconsin Mag. of Hist. 1977 61(1): 21-31.* Irvine L. Lenroot was a moderately progressive Republican senator from Wisconsin who was twice approached about accepting the vice presidential nomination on a Harding ticket. The first time he declined, and the second time he did not have a chance to respond because the convention moved to nominate Calvin Coolidge. Margulies argues that had Harding's preference for Lenroot been made clear to the delegates prior to the nomination of vice presidential candidates, "neither Wisconsin's unpopularity, nor the conservatism of the delegates and popularity of Coolidge, nor the smoldering resentment against the Senators" would have prevented a Lenroot nomination. 5 photos, 29 notes.

N. C. Burckel

1172. Martinson, David L. COVERAGE OF LA FOLLETTE OFFERS INSIGHTS FOR 1972 CAMPAIGN. *Journalism Q. 1975 52(3): 539-542.* The news coverage of Senator Robert Marion LaFollette's presidential campaign 1924 sheds light on that of George S. McGovern. The moderate *New York Times* disagreed with LaFollette on issues. The *Chicago Tribune* believed he would destroy America. The St. Louis *Post Dispatch* could not support a Democrat and an isolationist. News columns contained much negative coverage. The press may categorize candidates so that the electorate fails to receive the image the candidate is trying to project. Primary sources; 22 notes.

K. J. Puffer

1173. McCarthy, G. Michael. THE BROWN DERBY CAMPAIGN IN WEST TENNESSEE: SMITH, HOOVER, AND THE POLITICS OF RACE. *West Tennessee Hist. Soc. Papers 1973 (27): 81-98.* The hard-fought political campaign between Alfred E. Smith and Herbert C. Hoover in Tennessee dredged up racial, religious, ethical, and political mud and ultimately resulted in Hoover's breaking the solid South for the first time since Reconstruction.

1174. McCarthy, G. Michael. SMITH VS. HOOVER: THE POLITICS OF RACE IN WEST TENNESSEE. *Phylon 1978 39(2): 154-168.* When the Democrats in 1928 nominated for President of the United States Al Smith of New York, a big-city, Catholic, anti-prohibition, pro-immigration, professional politician, there were wide defections in parts of the South, which was overwhelmingly rural and small-town, Protestant, prohibitionist, and anti-immigration. Herbert Hoover won over many southern Democrats because he was from a rural background, was a Protestant, a prohibitionist, and an old stock American. West Tennessee resisted this anti-Smith trend for racial reasons. Blacks were one-third the population in West Tennessee, and the whites feared that they might become politically powerful. The Republican Party had always been the party of the blacks, and in 1928 it reinforced this image by including in its platform a strong anti-lynching plank. The result was white, Democratic solidarity behind Al Smith. Of the 19 counties west of the Tennessee River, only 4 went for Hoover. 71 notes.

J. C. Billigmeier

1175. McGuire, Jack B. ANDREW HIGGINS PLAYS PRESIDENTIAL POLITICS. *Louisiana Hist. 1974 15(3): 273-284.* Discusses the political work of Andrew J. Higgins, a Louisiana-born campaign worker for the Democratic Party, and his work in helping to elect Franklin D. Roosevelt and Harry S. Truman, 1944.

1176. Melcher, Daniel P. THE CHALLENGE TO NORMALCY: THE 1924 ELECTION IN CALIFORNIA. *Southern California Q. 1978 60(2): 155-182.* Analyzes the influence of the La Follette Progressive Party ticket on California in the 1924 presidential election. The third party movement was supported by Republicans who failed to share in Coolidge prosperity, including workers in the depressed gold, timber, and agricultural industries, plus urban working class voters. Their vote was a protest against the upper and middle class orientation of the Republican party; disaffected Democrats also turned to the Progressives in the belief that the Democratic party failed to represent their needs. The La Follette ticket provided the means for a major realignment in the electorate as Republicans went through the Progressive Party in 1924 and into the Democratic party in 1928. "More than any other factor, the election of 1924 turned on the economic well-being of the electorate." Thus the Progressives were not a reminder of prewar reform as much as the beginnings of what by 1932 became a Democratic coalition. Census and voting records, contemporary and secondary published works; 6 tables, 59 notes.

A. Hoffman

1177. Melosi, Martin V. POLITICAL TREMORS FROM A MILITARY DISASTER: 'PEARL HARBOR' AND THE ELECTION OF 1944. *Diplomatic Hist. 1977 1(1): 79-95.* Discusses the debate between Republicans and the Roosevelt administration over personal responsibility for the Pearl Harbor disaster. Republicans failed, however, to make this a vital issue in the 1944 presidential campaign. Criticism of Franklin D. Roosevelt's policies was difficult to achieve while the nation was still at war. Republican presidential nominee Thomas E. Dewey was "reluctant to make a stand on an issue that smacked of disloyalty," and he could not "exploit one spectacular issue—the breaking of the Japanese code— which might give the Republican criticisms legitimacy." Furthermore, the Roosevelt administration effectively denied the release of information which might aid the Republicans. Primary and secondary sources; 49 notes.

G. H. Curtis

1178. Misse, Fred B. FRANKLIN ROOSEVELT AND THE POLISH VOTE IN 1944. *Midwest Q. 1980 21(3): 317-332.* During 1944, as Soviet replaced German domination in eastern Europe, Polish Americans were increasingly distrustful of the policy of President Franklin D. Roosevelt toward Poland and the USSR. Because he did not wish to alienate Josef Stalin and endanger his own hopes for postwar Soviet-American cooperation, Roosevelt sought to keep the Polish question out of the election of 1944. Roosevelt skillfully neutralized the potential Polish American political defection by meeting with key Polish American spokesman Charles Rozmarek, who in turn publicly endorsed Roosevelt. Based on the Roosevelt papers and other primary sources; 23 notes, biblio., appendix.

M. E. Quinlivan

1179. Mugleston, William F. THE 1912 PROGRESSIVE CAMPAIGN IN GEORGIA. *Georgia Hist. Q. 1977 61(3): 233-245.* The situation of the Progressive Party in Georgia was representative of the problems Theodore Roosevelt had throughout the South during the campaign of 1912. White southerners were particularly suspicious of Progressive attitudes toward Negroes, which caused party splits in Georgia and three other states. This third party and its supporters were very weak in campaign ability and received little support in the South. Their position was even more difficult since they were opposing Woodrow Wilson who was a southern Democrat. Primary and secondary sources; 27 notes.

G. R. Schroeder

1180. Murray, Robert K. THE DEMOCRATS VS. FRUSTRATION CITY: IT WAS NO MIX. *Smithsonian 1976 7(1): 48-55.* Reviews a chapter in Robert K. Murray's *The 103rd Ballot: The Democrats and the Disaster in Madison Square Garden* (Harper-Row, 1976), concerning the Democratic convention in New York City in 1924, a convention which reflected American social cleavage, e.g. urban vs. agricultural, wet vs. dry, and featured the candidacy of William Gibbs McAdoo (1863-1941) and Alfred E. Smith (1873-1944). Many favorite sons were antagonistic about the convention location, and this, plus misunderstanding, influenced the candidates and the convention results. By 10 July (the convention began 24 June) the delegates, after voting for 59 different persons on 103 Presidential ballots (both records), reached a compromise. 6 illus., 20 photos.

K. A. Harvey

1181. Partin, John W. ROOSEVELT, BYRNES, AND THE 1944 VICE-PRESIDENTIAL NOMINATION. *Historian 1979 42(1): 85-100.* Reviews the internecine strife that enveloped the 1944 vice-presidential nomination between James F. Byrnes and Henry A. Wallace. Franklin D. Roosevelt very consciously played them off against each other so that Harry S. Truman could be nominated. Roosevelt was able to enter the campaign with the support of his entire party, but he had done nothing to repair the schisms in the Democratic Party that would remain to plague his successors. Primary sources; 34 notes.

R. S. Sliwoski

1182. Patenaude, Lionel V. THE GARNER VOTE SWITCH TO ROOSEVELT: 1932 DEMOCRATIC CONVENTION. *Southwestern Hist. Q. 1975 79(2): 189-204.* Describes the complex political negotiations which led to the release of the delegates pledged to John Nance Garner and the nomination of Franklin D. Roosevelt on the fourth ballot at the Democratic Convention in Chicago, 1 July 1932. Sam Rayburn was the key man, aided by William Gibbs McAdoo head of the California delegation, and James A. Farley, Roosevelt's campaign manager. It was Roosevelt who made the decision to run with Garner; Garner accepted the vice-presidency "reluctantly and only as a party-saving gesture." 10 illus., 22 notes.

C. W. Olson

1183. Petersen, Peter L. THE RELUCTANT CANDIDATE: EDWIN T. MEREDITH AND THE 1924 DEMOCRATIC NATIONAL CONVENTION. *Palimpsest 1976 57(5): 146-156.* Des Moines publisher Edwin T. Meredith, widely regarded as a satisfactory compromise candidate at the deadlocked 1924 Democratic Party Convention, was rejected by Al Smith because Meredith unyieldingly supported William G. McAdoo. Subsequently, Meredith declined the vice-presidential nomination, although his strong business, labor, and agricultural ties probably would have produced more votes than did nominee Charles Bryan. Meredith, who might have had a later chance at the presidential nomination, died prematurely in 1928. Illus., 7 photos, note on sources.

D. W. Johnson

1184. Petersen, Peter L. STOPPING AL SMITH: THE 1928 DEMOCRATIC PRIMARY IN SOUTH DAKOTA. *South Dakota Hist. 1974 4(4): 439-454.* Rural "dry" Democrats failed to defeat Al Smith's nomination in 1928 in the first primary of the year. Although Smith won by less than 2,000 votes, opposition among Democrats nationwide melted away after the attempt in South Dakota. The attempt failed owing to the well-established Smith campaign, the reluctance of Thomas Walsh of Montana to announce his candidacy, and the ascendency of the urban East. Internally, South Dakota Democrats patched up differences to reelect the state's first Democratic governor. 3 photos.

A. J. Larson

1185. Prindle, David F. VOTER TURNOUT, CRITICAL ELECTIONS, AND THE NEW DEAL REALIGNMENT. *Social Sci. Hist. 1979 3(2): 144-170.* Empirically tests "critical election" theory, using quantitative analysis of material from Wisconsin, Pennsylvania, and the city of Pittsburgh, during the New Deal era. Democratic Party mobilization or increasing voter turnout was more important than party switching or voter realignment. No single election or sharply defined time period stands out as critical. Covers 1912-40. Based on local election returns, census data, voter registration lists, and other primary materials; 11 tables, 9 graphs.

L. K. Blaser

1186. Qualls, J. Winfield. THE 1928 PRESIDENTIAL ELECTION IN WEST TENNESSEE: WAS RACE A CHIEF FACTOR? *West Tennessee Hist. Soc. Papers 1973 (27): 99-107.* Statistical analysis of the impact of black voting in Tennessee indicates that lack of organization and split political party affiliation demoted the black vote to a relatively innocuous position in the list of factors affecting the presidential election outcome in 1928.

1187. Rorvig, Paul. CLASH OF THE GIANTS: THE 1912 PRESIDENTIAL ELECTION. *Am. Hist. Illus. 1979 14(7): 12-15, 42-46.* Describes the events surrounding the 1912 presidential election in the United States, beginning in 1910, and discusses those competing for the office; Theodore Roosevelt, William Howard Taft, and Woodrow Wilson.

1188. Ross, Hugh. JOHN L. LEWIS AND THE ELECTION OF 1940. *Labor Hist. 1976 17(2): 160-189.* The breach between John L. Lewis and Franklin D. Roosevelt in 1940 originated from domestic and foreign policy concerns. The struggle to organize the steel industry, and after 1938, business attempts to erode Walsh-Healy and the Fair Labor Standards Act provided the backdrop for the feud. But activities of Nazi agents, working through William Rhodes Davis, increased Lewis' suspicions of Roosevelt's foreign policy and were important in the decision to support Wendell Willkie. Based on correspondence, German foreign policy documents, and published sources; 63 notes.

L. L. Athey

1189.   Ryan, Thomas G.   ETHNICITY IN THE 1940 PRESIDENTIAL ELECTION IN IOWA: A QUANTITATIVE APPROACH. *Ann. of Iowa 1977 43(8): 615-635.* After a statistical analysis of voting patterns in selected Iowa counties in 1936 and 1940, supports the traditional assumption of a large-scale defection of German American voters from Franklin D. Roosevelt. The data do not support, however, interpretations such as those of Robert E. Burke or Malcolm Moos which attribute Democratic losses between 1936 and 1940 to farm dissatisfaction, or the interpretations of Harold F. Gosnell or Warren Moscow which emphasize the general defection of Catholics from the Roosevelt coalition. Primary and secondary sources; 10 tables, 27 notes.

P. L. Petersen

1190.   Sarasohn, David.   THE ELECTION OF 1916: REALIGNING THE ROCKIES. *Western Hist. Q. 1980 11(3): 285-305.* Woodrow Wilson's electoral victory in the election of 1916 is traditionally explained as a consequence of the split in the Republican Party and of the unique wartime circumstances. Outside the Old South, Wilson and the Democratic Party gained their most sweeping victories in the eight Rocky Mountain states. The conventional explanations are not satisfactory for the mountain states. Here the voters saw fundamental long-range issues at stake and responded emphatically; they remained in the Democratic ranks throughout the 1920's. 6 tables, 34 notes.

D. L. Smith

1191.   Schlup, Leonard.   ALTON B. PARKER AND THE PRESIDENTIAL CAMPAIGN OF 1904. *North Dakota Q. 1981 49(1): 48-60.* Brief biography of Democratic Party presidential nominee in 1904, Alton Brooks Parker (1852-1926), focusing on his political career, particularly the circumstances surrounding his defeat by Teddy Roosevelt.

1192.   Schlup, Leonard.   COE I. CRAWFORD AND THE PROGRESSIVE CAMPAIGN OF 1912. *South Dakota Hist. 1979 9(2): 116-130.* Coe Isaac Crawford (1858-1944), elected successively as a Republican Governor and Senator between 1907 and 1915, was the founder of the progressive movement in South Dakota. During the Republican Party split in 1912 Crawford supported Theodore Roosevelt while officially remaining within the Republican Party and used his influence to aid the cause of reform. When Roosevelt carried South Dakota by 10,000 votes, Crawford saw the results as a progressive victory. Although defeated by the Republican stalwarts in the 1914 senatorial primary, Crawford left behind a legacy of progressive reform in South Dakota. Primary sources; 3 illus., 5 photos, 29 notes.

P. L. McLaughlin

1193.   Schnell, J. Christopher.   MISSOURI PROGRESSIVES AND THE NOMINATION OF F.D.R. *Missouri Hist. R. 1974 68(3): 269-279.* Reexamines the basis of support by Missouri Democratic delegates of Franklin D. Roosevelt for the presidential nomination in 1932. Many historians claim that the influence of Kansas City boss Thomas J. Pendergast swung Missouri support to Roosevelt. The support, however, was the result of efforts by a group of Wilsonian progressives, including many anti-Pendergast forces, led by Ewing Y. Mitchell, William Hirth, Judge Eldridge Dearing, and Louis Gualdoni. Pendergast had publicly supported the favorite son candidate, James A. Reed. The pro-Roosevelt group was well organized and had strong rural and "outstate" support. At the national convention the Missouri delegation increased its support of Roosevelt with each ballot, and all of the initial Missouri support came from these non-Pendergast forces. Based on contemporary newspaper reports, primary and secondary sources; 5 photos, 28 notes.

N. J. Street

1194.   Schuyler, Michael W.   DROUGHT AND POLITICS 1936: KANSAS AS A TEST CASE. *Great Plains J. 1975 15(1): 2-27.* Analyzes the various drought relief and long-range agricultural programs of the New Deal in 1936 in Kansas. It is difficult to assess the influence of the drought on the presidential race between Franklin D. Roosevelt and Alfred M. Landon. However, the Roosevelt administration appears to have benefited in several ways. Primary and secondary sources; 9 illus., 62 notes.

O. H. Zabel

1195.   Snyder, Robert E.   HUEY LONG AND THE PRESIDENTIAL ELECTION OF 1936. *Louisiana Hist. 1975 16(2): 117-143.* The rise in popularity of Huey Long's Share Our Wealth movement caused Franklin D. Roosevelt and his supporters well-founded concern as the election of 1936 approached, not because Long (1893-1935) had any chance of winning the presidency, but because his candidacy could have given a strong Republican a better chance. Moreover, Long's movement would have kept other pro-Roosevelt politicians from winning office. Based on primary and secondary sources; 73 notes.

R. L. Woodward

1196.   Spencer, Thomas T.   AUXILIARY AND NON-PARTY POLITICS: THE 1936 DEMOCRATIC PRESIDENTIAL CAMPAIGN IN OHIO. *Ohio Hist. 1981 90(2): 114-128.* Discusses the 1936 presidential campaign in Ohio, and the successful Democratic Party strategy of going outside the party to attract voters by organizing auxiliary and nonparty committees. Especially important in appealing to labor, blacks, farmers, and women, Democratic auxiliary committees such as the Non-Partisan Labor League, the Good Neighbor League, and Roosevelt's All-Party Agricultural Committee helped to counter criticism of the New Deal by attracting those voters with a vital stake in its success. Although Democratic fears of losing the Midwestern states were exaggerated, the campaign appeal of such organizations led to their becoming a "vital part of the Democratic coalition in future elections." Based on the collections of the Franklin D. Roosevelt Library, Hyde Park, New York, the National Archives and Records Service, the University of Iowa, and other primary sources; illus., 42 notes.

L. A. Russell

1197.   Spencer, Thomas T.   BENNETT CHAMP CLARK AND THE 1936 PRESIDENTIAL CAMPAIGN. *Missouri Hist. Rev. 1981 75(2): 197-213.* Clark won the Missouri senatorial election in 1932 without any help from the Democratic machine in Kansas City. His votes against New Deal bills often made him a thorn in President Franklin D. Roosevelt's side, but the president and party leaders recognized his ability and selected him for an important role in 1936. As chairman of the rules committee for the Democratic National Convention, Clark found his assignment to lead the fight against the two-thirds rule an easy one, since no strong support for the rule developed. His most challenging assignments were to deliver campaign speeches and to chair the Committee of One, an auxiliary organized to solicit support from individuals outside the regular party structure. Based on secondary sources, newspapers, James A. Farley Papers, Library of Congress, Frank Walker Papers, University of Notre Dame, Emil Hurja Papers and the Democratic National Committee Records, Franklin D. Roosevelt Library; illus., 37 notes.

W. F. Zornow

1198.   Spencer, Thomas T.   THE GOOD NEIGHBOR LEAGUE COLORED COMMITTEE AND THE 1936 DEMOCRATIC PRESIDENTIAL CAMPAIGN. *J. of Negro Hist. 1978 63(4): 307-316.* The Good Neighbor League Colored Committee, along with the Colored Voters Division of the Democratic Party, was a vital force in making Afro-Americans part of the Franklin D. Roosevelt coalition in 1936. Since 1936, blacks have continued to play an important part in Democratic campaigns. Based upon records in the Franklin D. Roosevelt Presidential Library; 32 notes.

N. G. Sapper

1199.   Spencer, Thomas T.   "LABOR IS WITH ROOSEVELT": THE PENNSYLVANIA LABOR NON-PARTISAN LEAGUE AND THE ELECTION OF 1936. *Pennsylvania Hist. 1979 46(1): 3-16.* In Pennsylvania, the Labor Non-Partisan League contributed much to Franklin D. Roosevelt's 1936 victory through its contributions, voter canvassing drives, and propaganda. Organized at the national level by John L. Lewis and Sidney Hillman, the league was comprised largely of C.I.O. unions and was intended to assure the president's reelection and function as a spokesman for liberalism. In 1943, it became the C.I.O.'s Political Action Committee. Based on the Pennsylvania Non-Partisan League Papers and other materials; 3 photos, 32 notes.

D. C. Swift

1200.   Spencer, Thomas T.   THE NEW DEAL COMES TO THE "GRANITE STATE": THE 1936 DEMOCRATIC PRESIDENTIAL CAMPAIGN IN NEW HAMPSHIRE. *Hist. New Hampshire 1980 35(2): 186-201.* Franklin D. Roosevelt surprised many political observers in defeating Alfred Landon in the 1936 presidential election in New Hampshire. Roosevelt's personal popularity and the success of New Deal relief and recovery programs probably account for the victory. The president carried only three of New Hampshire's 10 counties, but he carried populous Hillsborough County by more than 11,000 votes. Relief and recovery programs employed more than 9,000 workers in New Hampshire in the fall of 1936, mainly in urban areas. 34 notes.

D. F. Chard

1201. Spencer, Thomas T. THE ROOSEVELT ALL-PARTY AGRICULTURAL COMMITTEE AND THE 1936 ELECTION. *Ann. of Iowa 1979 45(1): 44-57.* Strategists for the Democratic Party in 1936 believed that the midwestern farm belt was crucial to Franklin D. Roosevelt's reelection bid. In August 1936, the Franklin D. Roosevelt All-Party Agricultural Committee was formed. William Settle of Indiana was chairman. Other important members included Representative Marvin Jones of Texas, William Bradley of Iowa, and Paul Porter, chief of the Agricultural Adjustment Administration's press section. A study of the All-Party Agricultural Committee's activities in 1936 justifies several conclusions. First, Democratic leaders saw the farm vote as important and sought to bring farmers into the Roosevelt coalition. Second, the Committee was able to counter criticisms of New Deal agricultural policy. Finally, farmers were politically active in 1936 and many saw Roosevelt as their best hope for the future. 28 notes.   P. L. Petersen

1202. Stagner, Stephen. THE RECALL OF JUDICIAL DECISIONS AND THE DUE PROCESS DEBATE. *Am. J. of Legal Hist. 1980 24(3): 257-272.* Theodore Roosevelt, at the advent of his presidential campaign of 1912, called for the revision or recall of state supreme court decisions when they went against majority opinion. The author presents a description and assessment of the debate over the recall of judicial decisions within the law profession from the legal periodicals of the period. Lawyers as a group did not castigate Roosevelt's position. While the spokesmen of the American Bar Association ridiculed it, law professors and judges supported his plan as an antidote to the perversion of the 14th Amendment that had made due process "a wall against state action." Based on published speeches and legal periodicals; 44 notes.
                     L. A. Knafla

1203. Stickle, Warren E. THE REPUBLICAN CAMPAIGN OF 1940. *New Jersey Hist. 1975 93(1-2): 43-57.* In 1940 Jerseymen voted nationally for a president and elected their governor. Discusses the discord and disunity of Wendell Willkie's primary and general election campaigns symbolized by the many statewide Willkie Clubs, reviews the heated G.O.P. gubernatorial primary battle between former governor Harold G. Hoffman and state senator Robert Hendrickson, the eventual winner; and summarizes the contest between Henrickson and Charles Edison, the Democratic standard bearer. Republican Party losses in both elections are blamed on extensive party factionalism. Based on primary and secondary sources; 6 illus., 27 notes.   E. R. McKinstry

1204. Swanson, Jeffrey L. THAT SMOKE-FILLED ROOM: A UTAHN'S ROLE IN THE 1920 GOP CONVENTION. *Utah Hist. Q. 1977 45(4): 369-379.* Reed Smoot, (1862-1941), Utah senator during 1903-33, played a pivotal role in writing the platform and in the presidential nomination at the 1920 Republican Party Convention. As a member of the platform subcommittee, he submitted Elihu Root's compromise plank which avoided a direct stand on the League of Nations, thus averting a party split. He pushed the nomination of Harding at the meeting of seven senators in George Harvey's smoke-filled hotel room. He placated other candidates to keep party unity. Primary and secondary sources; 2 illus., 40 notes.   J. L. Hazelton

1205. Tarter, Brent. A FLIER ON THE NATIONAL SCENE, HARRY F. BYRD'S FAVORITE-SON PRESIDENTIAL CANDIDACY OF 1932. *Virginia Mag. of Hist. and Biog. 1974 82(3): 282-305.* Former Virginia Governor Harry F. Byrd ran as a favorite-son candidate for President in 1932, primarily to consolidate his control over the Democratic political machinery in his state and to prevent national issues, such as prohibition, from splitting his supporters. Byrd's candidacy also reflected his suspicion of front runner Franklin D. Roosevelt, and his participation in an anti-Roosevelt movement nearly succeeded. Based on primary and secondary sources; cartoon, 44 notes.   R. F. Oaks

1206. Tingley, Ralph R. BRASS BANDS AND HUZZAHS: POLITICS AT THE CORN PALACE, 1908. *South Dakota Hist. 1982 12(1): 32-47.* Recounts the activities on three successive days in September 1908, when three presidential candidates visited the Corn Palace in Mitchell, South Dakota. The Corn Palace and business district of Mitchell were especially decorated for the campaigning of Democrat William Jennings Bryan, Republican William Howard Taft, and Prohibitionist Eugene W. Chafin during the annual Corn Palace celebration. Primary sources; 7 photos, 44 notes.   P. L. McLaughlin

1207. Tingley, Ralph R. CHARLIE, THE "OTHER BRYAN," IN SOUTH DAKOTA, 1924. *Nebraska Hist. 1979 60(4): 556-566.* Discusses Democratic Vice-Presidential nominees in South Dakota, particularly Charles Wayland Bryan, younger brother of William Jennings Bryan. The Democratic Party in South Dakota carried only 13 percent of the vote.   R. Lowitt

1208. Tingley, Ralph R. PODIUM POLITICS IN SIOUX FALLS, 1924: DAWES VERSUS LAFOLLETTE. *South Dakota Hist. 1980 10(2): 119-132.* Recounts the presidential campaign of 1924 and its impact on South Dakota as seen from Sioux Falls. Charles Gates Dawes (1865-1951), the Republican Vice Presidential candidate, and Wisconsin Senator Robert Marion LaFollette (1855-1925), running as an independent presidential candidate, staged rallies in Sioux Flls within a few weeks of each other. Since South Dakota was considered LaFollette territory, Dawes attemped to paint LaFollette as a radical while praising South Dakota. In the final analysis, even though the LaFollette rally was more enthusiastic and better attended, Republican organization outweighed the emotion of the LaFollette forces and the Republican Party carried South Dakota. Based on newspapers and other primary sources; 2 illus., 3 photos, 24 notes.   P. L. McLaughlin

1209. Tyson, Carl N. "I'M OFF TO COOLIDGE'S FOLLIES": WILL ROGERS AND THE PRESIDENTIAL NOMINATIONS, 1924-1932. *Chronicles of Oklahoma 1976 54(2): 192-198.* Discusses press coverage and political commentary by Will Rogers about the national political conventions of 1924, 1928, and 1932.

1210. Williams, Brian. PETTICOATS IN POLITICS: CINCINNATI WOMEN AND THE 1920 ELECTION. *Cincinnati Hist. Soc. Bull. 1977 35(1): 43-70.* Though highly organized for precinct and educatory purposes, women voters in Cincinnati, Ohio, during the 1920 presidential election did not subscribe to a specific ideology and hence made no great impact on voting patterns in the state.

1211. Wingo, Barbara C. THE 1928 PRESIDENTIAL ELECTION IN LOUISIANA. *Louisiana Hist. 1977 18(4): 405-415.* Although Alfred E. Smith's majority in Louisiana in 1928 (76.3%) was very similar to Democratic majorities in that state in the 1920 and 1924 elections, the composition of his support was markedly different. Reviews and analyzes the election, showing that his strength was in the "wet," Catholic, southern part of the state rather than in the "dry," Protestant north. Black participation remained a factor in the state's Republican Party. Notes some similarities in the support for Smith and Huey P. Long. Primary sources; 3 tables, 66 notes.   R. L. Woodward, Jr.

1212. Zink, Steven D. CULTURAL CONFLICT AND THE 1928 PRESIDENTIAL CAMPAIGN IN LOUISIANA. *Southern Studies 1978 17(2): 175-197.* Religious differences had played an accepted but subordinate role in Louisiana politics until 1928. Al Smith (1873-1944), the Democratic nominee for president, represented for many an East Coast, Catholic, evilly urban supporter of alcoholic beverages. The typical Southern solidarity in voting based on race was broken as patterns show a clear difference between Catholic and Protestant parishes in Louisiana. Strong anti-Catholic bias is reflected in the newspapers. The division was not based on religion itself, but on issues such as prohibition that reflected religious attitudes. Primary and secondary sources; 2 tables, 84 notes.
                     J. Buschen

Presidential Administrations: Age of Reform

General

1213. Allison, Hildreth M. DUBLIN GREETS A PRESIDENT. *Hist. New Hampshire 1980 35(2): 202-206.* On Saturday, 27 August 1910, President William H. Taft visited his friend, Secretary of the Treasury Franklin MacVeagh, at MacVeagh's home in Dublin, New Hampshire. Other guests on the occasion included Governor Henry B. Quimby of New Hampshire and British Ambassador James Bryce. Taft planted a maple tree to commemorate the visit, and presided over a grand soiree at the MacVeagh mansion that evening. On Sunday the Tafts attended worship at the First Congregational (Unitarian) Church. After lunch, Taft motored back to Beverly without incident. Illus., 6 notes.

D. F. Chard

1214. Anderson, Donald F. THE LEGACY OF WILLIAM HOWARD TAFT. *Presidential Studies Q. 1982 12(1): 26-33.* William H. Taft is unique not only because he served as both president and chief justice of the Supreme Court but also because his career path to these positions consisted almost entirely of appointed political posts. Taft's actions stemmed from belief in constitutional democracy and the separation of powers, conviction that political parties were essential elements of a democratic society, and perception of the danger of radical majoritarianism. Taft was a literalist who believed in a strong presidency, but he was unable to transform that belief into effective electoral political policy. 12 notes.

D. H. Cline

1215. Arnold, Peri E. THE "GREAT ENGINEER" AS ADMINISTRATOR: HERBERT HOOVER AND MODERN BUREAUCRACY. *Rev. of Pol. 1980 42(3): 329-348.* Contrary to most scholars' interpretations, Herbert C. Hoover was a modern rather than a traditional administrator. "Hoover offers the lesson that government might be better attacked for what it does rather than for the means through which it operates." 51 notes.

L. E. Ziewacz

1216. Balch, Stephen H. DO STRONG PRESIDENTS REALLY WANT STRONG LEGISLATIVE PARTIES? *Presidential Studies Q. 1977 7(4): 231-238.* Describes Woodrow Wilson's (1856-1924) strategies in fragmenting the strong legislative party he inherited. He believed in strong executive leadership rather than strong party leadership and systematically undermined the strength of prominent floor leaders, making a number of alternative figures accountable to him. The result was a decentralization in the House of Representatives that lasted for some time. 35 notes.

J. Tull

1217. Bellush, Jewel. OLD AND NEW LEFT REAPPRAISALS OF THE NEW DEAL AND ROOSEVELT'S PRESIDENCY. *Presidential Studies Q. 1979 9(3): 243-266.* Briefly discusses the differences between the Old and the New Left, and focuses on both groups' opinion of Franklin D. Roosevelt's presidency and his New Deal.

1218. Blair, John L. COOLIDGE THE IMAGE-MAKER: THE PRESIDENT AND THE PRESS, 1923-1929. *New England Q. 1973 46(4): 499-522.* Analyzes the reasons for President Calvin Coolidge's remarkable rapport with the press. Prosperity and the absence of grating political issues played a role, but the President's personality was more important. He liked reporters, was attentive to their wants and needs, never avoided questions, and enjoyed being photographed. Coolidge established the modern press conference. He acted alone, without the corps of public relations experts which developed later. 69 notes.

V. L. Human

1219. Braeman, John. THE HISTORIAN AS ACTIVIST: CHARLES A. BEARD AND THE NEW DEAL. *South Atlantic Q. 1980 79(4): 364-374.* American historian Charles A. Beard supported the first two administrations of Franklin D. Roosevelt, despite occasional trepidation. But when Roosevelt geared up for the 1940 campaign, Beard scathingly denounced the New Deal's failures. Long before Pearl Harbor he predicted that Roosevelt was determined to bring the United States into war with Hitler, either directly or by provoking a war with Japan. Beard's growing disillusionment with the New Deal roughly paralleled that of many liberal intellectuals. Even his commitment to isolationism was typical. What distinguished Beard was the depth and intensity of his bitterness. Based on the Beard File (microfilm), DePauw University Archives; the Roosevelt Papers, Franklin D. Roosevelt Library; Beard's letters and writings, and secondary materials; 26 notes.

H. M. Parker, Jr.

1220. Butow, R. J. C. THE FDR TAPES. *Am. Heritage 1982 33(2): 8-24.* For 11 weeks during the fall of 1940, Franklin D. Roosevelt used a tape recorder to protect against misquotation by the press, even though he disliked the idea of taping conversations. The article discusses how the taping system came about and its use, and concludes with examples of the information recorded. Roosevelt's thoughts on foreign policy, the election of 1940, political appointments, and civil rights are among the items recorded. 14 illus.

J. F. Paul

1221. Dalton, Kathleen. WHY AMERICA LOVED THEODORE ROOSEVELT: OR CHARISMA IS IN THE EYES OF THE BEHOLDERS. *Psychohistory Rev. 1979 8(3): 16-26.* Theodore Roosevelt, despite upper class origins, appealed to many so-called common people because he was able to appeal to their hearts. He was a charismatic leader. Examining Roosevelt's support by reality-oriented followers, the author sees him as appealing to those who sought symbolic mastery of a complex industrial society. Embodying masculine assertiveness, Roosevelt symbolized the triumph of the will. He offered many Americans the sense of mastery they needed to cope with change and uncertainty. Roosevelt as hero may have prevented the growth of radicalism, because he offered symbolic if not real solutions to personal and social problems. 93 notes.

J. M. Herrick

1222. Dayer, Roberta Allbert. STRANGE BEDFELLOWS: J. P. MORGAN & CO., WHITEHALL AND THE WILSON ADMINISTRATION DURING WORLD WAR I. *Business Hist. [Great Britain] 1976 18(2): 127-151.* At the beginning of World War I, US Treasury Secretary William McAdoo and others in the Wilson administration were very suspicious of J. P. Morgan & Co.'s role as British agent for purchasing and banking. When the United States entered the war this gave way to close collaboration, in the course of which Morgan received financial concessions. Uses unpublished papers of Willard Straight (1880-1918), Thomas Lamont (1870-1948), British Treasury Records, and Arthur James Balfour (1848-1930), British Museum; 140 notes.

B. L. Crapster

1223. Errico, Charles J. THE NEW DEAL, INTERNATIONALISM AND THE NEW AMERICAN CONSENSUS, 1938-1940. *Maryland Hist. 1978 9(1): 17-31.* Contrasts Republican victories in the 1938 elections with the Democratic victories of 1940. Franklin D. Roosevelt, prompted by James Farley and Henry Wallace, emphasized the need for national unity in a time of international crisis even while continuing the unpopular domestic policies which had caused defeat in 1938. Based on correspondence and secondary sources; illus., 43 notes.

G. O. Gagnon

1224. Glad, Paul W. HAIL TO THE CHIEF! *R. in Am. Hist. 1975 3(4): 477-482.* Discusses the historiography on Herbert Hoover in this review of Martin L. Fausold and George T. Mazuzan, eds. *The Hoover Presidency: A Reappraisal* (Albany: State U. of New York Pr., 1974), a collection of papers from a symposium at the State University of New York at Geneseo; and Joan Hoff Wilson's *Herbert Hoover: Forgotten Progressive* (Boston: Little, Brown, 1975), a biography.

1225. Henderson, F. P. FDR AT WARM SPRINGS. *Marine Corps Gazette 1982 66(7): 54-58.* Based on the author's experiences, describes President Franklin D. Roosevelt's frequent trips to the National Polio Foundation Center at Warm Springs, Georgia, where he went for therapy accompanied by a detachment of Marines from the base at Quantico, Virginia; focuses on an occasion when the president invited a number of Marines to join him for cocktails.

1226. Holley, I. B., Jr. THE MANAGEMENT OF TECHNOLOGICAL CHANGE: AIRCRAFT PRODUCTION IN THE UNITED STATES DURING WORLD WAR II. *Aerospace Hist. 1975 22(3): 161-165.* From an article previously published in *Revue d'Historie de la deuxieme guerre mondiale.* The fall of France in 1940 triggered an expansion in the war production effort in the United States. Lack of coordination in specifications between purchasers caused the creation of the Joint Aircraft Committee in the fall of 1940 to coordinate United States services and British purchases. In addition, President Roosevelt created the National Defense Advisory Commission. Because it was only "advisory" in nature it was not too effective. In December, 1940 he created the Office of Production Management. Describes the work of the aircraft industry under the OPM and concludes that the study of the operation of these controlling bodies can help in preparing future agencies to do their jobs better. Based on Senate Committee Hearings and secondary sources; photo., 8 notes.

C. W. Ohrvall

1227. Hone, Thomas and Friedman, Norman. INNOVATION AND ADMINISTRATION IN THE NAVY DEPARTMENT: THE CASE OF THE *NEVADA* DESIGN. *Military Affairs 1981 45(2): 57-62.* In 1911, Congress authorized the construction of two battleships, the *Nevada* and the *Oklahoma.* Their design became the standard for every battleship developed and built afterward by the US Navy. The design actually developed was one which a distant but informed observer would not have anticipated, given the history of the navy's battleship design process to that date. Instead, the design process encouraged innovation and coordination and reflected the importance and the administrative authority of the General Board. US Naval Records and other primary sources; 15 notes.   A. M. Osur

1228. Johnson, James P. HERBERT HOOVER: THE ORPHAN AS CHILDREN'S FRIEND. *Prologue 1980 12(4): 193-206.* That Herbert C. Hoover was orphaned before he was 10 was a key factor in his life. As an apparent result of his unhappy childhood, Hoover developed a passion for working with and for children. This passion was evidenced throughout his life, resulting in such efforts as organizing large-scale assistance to civilian war victims as director of the Committee for Relief in Belgium, setting up a European Children's Fund to feed starving children as director of the American Relief Agency, providing food to millions of Russians during 1921-23 under the Food and Remittance Plan, combining private volunteer groups into the American Child Health Association, and convening 2,500 delegates to a National Conference on Child Health as President. Based on Hoover public statements, Presidential personal papers, President Hoover files, newspapers, and interviews; illus., 10 photos, 84 notes.   M. A. Kascus

1229. Kaufman, Burton I. WILSON'S "WAR BUREAUCRACY" AND FOREIGN TRADE EXPANSION. *Prologue 1974 6(1): 19-31.* Details the numerous boards and committees established 1917-21 to promote foreign trade expansion. Most important was "the formation of the Central Foreign Trade and Economic Liaison Committees . . . because of what it suggests about the European influence on administration policy. In brief, the administration's perception of economic developments in Europe accentuated the movement in the United States toward greater government coordination and centralization of economic activity. This, in turn, had serious consequences for Wilson's postwar economic plans." 50 notes.   D. D. Cameron

1230. Láng, Imre. A ROOSEVELT-KORMÁNYZAT ELSŐ ÉVÉNEK GAZDASÁGPOLITIKAI DILEMMÁJA [The economic policy dilemma of the first year of the Roosevelt administration]. *Századok [Hungary] 1974 108(1): 136-185.* The Roosevelt administration considered the solution of the world economic crisis to lie in the regulation of the US economic policy, as an internal affair. He introduced the New Deal with the Agricultural Adjustment Act (US, 1933) and the National Industrial Recovery Act (US, 1933). In 1933, the gold standard was abandoned. All this led to economic isolationism. Yet this was an inevitable step to take. At the London Conference of 1933, the antagonism between the United States and the Gold Standard countries led by France was sharpened. This year was, however, an episode that pushed the Open Door policy temporarily into the background, but the latter was revived after 1934 as proposed by Foreign Secretary Cordell Hull. Primary sources; 135 notes.   R. Hetzron

1231. LePore, Herbert P. PRELUDE TO PREJUDICE: HIRAM JOHNSON, WOODROW WILSON, AND THE CALIFORNIA ALIEN LAND LAW CONTROVERSY OF 1913. *Southern California Q. 1979 61(1): 99-110.* Describes how the California legislature passed the Webb-Heney Act (1913), the first alien land law in the United States. President Taft, in securing the Treaty of Commerce and Navigation with Japan in 1911, dissuaded Governor Hiram W. Johnson from actively sponsoring anti-alien land ownership legislation which would embarrass the federal government. Taft's successor, Woodrow Wilson, for such possible reasons as his Southern background or desire to capture California in 1916, made little tangible effort to stop Johnson or the legislature from enacting an alien land law. Once the law was passed, Wilson took no action to have its constitutionality challenged by the federal courts or to sponsor federal legislation overruling the state. Despite rationalizations of economic rivalry and alleged Japanese dominance in California agriculture, the actual reason for support of the law by white Californians was racial prejudice, an attitude both Johnson and Wilson found useful for their own political gain. Primary and secondary sources; 45 notes.
                                                    A. Hoffman

1232. Margulies, Herbert F. THE COLLABORATION OF HERBERT HOOVER AND IRVINE LENROOT, 1921-1928. *North Dakota Q. 1977 45(3): 30-46.* Discusses the personal and political friendship between Irvine L. Lenroot and Herbert Hoover while the former was a Senator from Wisconsin and the latter held various cabinet posts until his election to the presidency; includes discussion of their collaboration on foreign affairs, agricultural issues, and the economy.

1233. Mervin, David. WOODROW WILSON AND PRESIDENTIAL MYTHS. *Presidential Studies Q. 1981 11(4): 559-564.* Contrary to popular belief, not all presidents have been workaholics. Examination of the early six months of the Wilson administration shows that although Wilson was busy with work, he was able to continually relax. Everything did not depend on the man in the White House, and he was not unremittingly bound to his desk working on every policy detail. Based mainly on private papers and diaries; 35 notes.   D. H. Cline

1234. Moore, James R. SOURCES OF NEW DEAL ECONOMIC POLICY: THE INTERNATIONAL DIMENSION. *J. of Am. Hist. 1974 61(3): 728-744.* In the earliest months of the New Deal, Franklin D. Roosevelt developed his pragmatic economic policies within an international dimension. He and his economic advisors advocated schemes for global public works programs backed by continued American loans, stabilization of currency exchange rates at devalued levels, a tariff "truce," and settlement of the thorny war debts issue. Pressed by a Congress that advocated inflationary action and faced with an attitude of non-cooperation from France and Britain, Roosevelt turned to a frankly nationalistic economic policy. 50 notes.   K. B. West

1235. Morris, Edmund. THEODORE ROOSEVELT, PRESIDENT. *Am. Heritage 1981 32(4): 4-15.* Four character traits—aggressiveness, righteousness, pride, and militarism—strongly affected Theodore Roosevelt's posture and actions as president. The author applauds Roosevelt for his refusal to run again in 1908, and notes with approval that Roosevelt "loved being President and was so good at his job that the people loved him. . . ." 9 illus.   J. F. Paul

1236. O'Brien, Patrick G. and Rosen, Philip T. HOOVER AND THE HISTORIANS: THE RESURRECTION OF A PRESIDENT. *Ann. of Iowa 1981 46(2): 83-99.* Revisionist historians in the decade of the 1970's have confirmed and expanded upon the consensus era literature, which depicted Herbert C. Hoover as a reform and activist political leader. Increasingly, historians recognize both Hoover's failures and his accomplishments, and the result has been a more balanced picture. 23 notes, biblio.   P. L. Petersen

1237. O'Brien, Patrick G. and Rosen, Philip T. HOOVER AND THE HISTORIANS: THE RESURRECTION OF A PRESIDENT. PART I. *Ann. of Iowa 1981 46(1): 25-42.* Once vilified as a callous and inept reactionary, a newer and kinder image of Herbert C. Hoover has begun to emerge. Since the middle 1960's, revisionist historians have attempted to resurrect Hoover's reputation. This revisionism is attributable, in part, to the opening of the Herbert Hoover Presidential Library in West Branch, Iowa, to researchers in 1966, and to a waning of enthusiasm for the New Deal among historians. Secondary sources; 28 notes. Article to be continued.   P. L. Petersen

1238. Peltier, Michel. AVRIL 1945: ROOSEVELT EST MORT [April 1945: Roosevelt is dead]. *Écrits de Paris [France] 1975 (346): 21-26.* Recounts the rise to power of Franklin D. Roosevelt, on the 30th anniversary of his death, noting in particular the blunders he committed in negotiations with the USSR.

1239. Peterson, Barbara Bennett. FDR'S "QUARTERBACKING" OF U.S. NAVAL POLICY IN THE PACIFIC 1933-39. *Pacific Historian 1973 17(1): 61-72, (2): 60-73.* Discusses Franklin D. Roosevelt's naval strategy in the Pacific area.   S

1240. Rader, Frank J. THE WORKS PROGRESS ADMINISTRATION AND HAWAIIAN PREPAREDNESS, 1935-1940. *Military Affairs 1979 43(1): 12-17.* Early preparedness activities of the Works Progress Administration (WPA) in Hawaii and other territories proved to be an indication of a changing US foreign policy. President Franklin D. Roosevelt took several surreptitious steps to strengthen the nation's outer defense network; one such move was the transfer of the Hawaiian WPA to War Department control in 1938. Thus, military projects would receive top priority in the allocation of relief funds and labor. Based on WPA records and secondary sources; 35 notes.   A. M. Osur

1241. Sargent, James E. F. D. R., FOREIGN POLICY, AND THE DOMESTIC-FIRST PERSPECTIVE, 1933-1936: AN APPRAISAL. *Peace and Change 1975 3(1): 24-29.* Evaluates the policies of Franklin Delano Roosevelt's first term as president.   S

1242. Saunders, Frances W. "NO PALE, COLD SCHOLAR": JOHN SINGER SARGENT'S PORTRAIT OF WOODROW WILSON. *Virginia Cavalcade 1980 30(2): 52-59.* In May 1917, after US entry into World War I, the National Gallery of Ireland, in Dublin, commissioned US President Woodrow Wilson as the subject of a portrait by John Singer Sargent.

1243. Shulimson, Jack and Cosmas, Graham A. TEDDY ROOSEVELT AND THE CORPS' SEA-GOING MISSION. *Marine Corps Gazette 1981 65(11): 54-61.* Discusses efforts led by navy Commander William F. Fullam and aided by Commander William S. Sims, to reform the navy and remove the Marine Corps, then operating under the Navy Department, from service as guards on navy ships and form the corps into permanent battalions with its own transports, focusing on President Theodore Roosevelt's agreement with the reformers and legislation "requiring return of the Marine guards to the ships of the fleet."

1244. Sirevåg, Torbjørn. THE NEW DEAL OF WAR. *Am. Studies in Scandinavia [Norway] 1975 7(2): 81-99.* The political opponents of Franklin D. Roosevelt perceived that American involvement in World War II would allow him to create a "Super-New Deal" domestically. Conceivably, wartime controls would (and did) become permanent features of New Deal programs. The Japanese attack rallied Roosevelt's political opponents by strengthening their suspicions of his motivations. A portion of the text is to become part of a monograph on the eclipse of the New Deal, 1940-45.   P. D. Travis

1245. Skau, George H. FRANKLIN D. ROOSEVELT AND THE EXPANSION OF PRESIDENTIAL POWER. *Current Hist. 1974 66(394): 246-248, 274-275.* One of six articles in this issue on "The American Presidency."   S

1246. Spackman, S. G. F. ROOSEVELT. *Hist. Today [Great Britain] 1980 30 (June): 38-43.* Analyzes Franklin D. Roosevelt's policies from the 1920's to his death in 1945 and concludes that he did much to create the modern presidency and to make the diplomatic transition from the balance of power system to that of the superpowers.

1247. Steele, Richard W. THE PULSE OF THE PEOPLE: FRANKLIN D. ROOSEVELT AND THE GAUGING OF AMERICAN PUBLIC OPINION. *J. of Contemporary Hist. [Great Britain] 1974 9(4): 195-216.* Franklin D. Roosevelt deliberately constructed and carefully maintained his channels to "those groups outside government whose attitudes at a given time might have a significant impact on his political plans." He monitored the press, used informants, encouraged the American people to write to him, and gathered intelligence from the Democratic National Committee and the State Directors of the Office of Government reports. He watched the opinion polls and studied analyses of them. He even established an Office of Facts and Figures for the sake of propaganda. All were utilized to great advantage during World War II. Primary sources; 37 notes.   M. P. Trauth

1248. Vinogradov, K. B. and Sergeev, V. V. VUDRO VIL'SON V DNI VOINY I MIRA   [Woodrow Wilson in war and peace]. *Novaia i Noveishaia Istoriia [USSR] 1975 (5): 122-134.* A political portrait of the US President who played an important part in securing the US entry into World War I shows the reasons behind the unexpected political fiasco of this leader. [Article to be continued].   J

1249. Walter, John C. CONGRESSMAN CARL VINSON AND FRANKLIN D. ROOSEVELT: NAVAL PREPAREDNESS AND THE COMING OF WORLD WAR II, 1932-40. *Georgia Hist. Q. 1980 64(3): 294-305.* Franklin D. Roosevelt, although former assistant secretary of the Navy, favored a decrease rather than a buildup in naval power

after he became president. This brought him into conflict with Georgia Congressman Carl Vinson, chairman of the House Naval Affairs Committee, who favored a strong navy and expansion. Vinson's persistence, despite Roosevelt's opposition, resulted in the United States being somewhat better prepared for World War II. Based on correspondence, newspapers, and secondary sources; 40 notes.   G. R. Schroeder

1250. Wilson, John R. M. THE QUAKER AND THE SWORD: HERBERT HOOVER'S RELATIONS WITH THE MILITARY. *Military Affairs 1974 38(2): 41-47.* Although personally close to his military leaders, Herbert Hoover was a foe of militarism. He believed in preparedness but viewed national defense as the capability to *prevent* an enemy landing in the United States or the Western Hemisphere. Because he opposed large military expenditures during the Depression the Navy suffered greatly, especially in its building programs, while the Army was less affected. Hoover's selection of General Douglas MacArthur as Chief of Staff proved to be outstanding. Based on Hoover's and others' personal papers and official documents; 20 notes.   K. J. Bauer

Domestic Affairs

1251. Allen, William R. IRVING FISHER, F.D.R., AND THE GREAT DEPRESSION. *Hist. of Pol. Econ. 1977 9(4): 560-587.* Presents Professor Fisher's (1867-1947) analysis and prescriptions for the Great Depression. Perhaps "the country's greatest scientific economist," he favored monetary remedies for the depression: reflation and stabilization of the dollar. He proposed 100% reserves against demand deposits in commercial banks, thus enabling monetary authorities to control the volume of money. His efforts were seconded by other leading economists, but the imminence of World War II blocked possible completion. 114 notes.   J. Tull

1252. Anderson, Adrian. PRESIDENT WILSON'S POLITICIAN: ALBERT SIDNEY BURLESON OF TEXAS. *Southwestern Hist. Q. 1974 77(3): 339-354.* Studies the tenure, 1913-21, of Texan Albert Sidney Burleson as postmaster general for President Woodrow Wilson. Burleson (1863?-1937) was selected more for his political skill than for his administrative ability. He often supported Wilson's policies out of loyalty, not from conviction. Although he contributed to the reform of progressivism, his primary guide was the demands of power politics, not reform. 55 notes.   D. L. Smith

1253. Annunziata, Frank. THE PROGRESSIVE AS CONSERVATIVE: GEORGE CREEL'S QUARREL WITH NEW DEAL LIBERALISM. *Wisconsin Mag. of Hist. 1974 57(3): 220-233.* George Creel (1876-1953) was a progressive Democrat long before his appointment as chairman of the Committee on Public Information during World War I, and he remained an important progressive well into the New Deal. Although an early advocate of Roosevlet and the New Deal, (in his post as chairman of the National Advisory Board, Works Progress Administration), Creel turned passionately against both during the war years 1940-45. The causes of that change in attitude included his resentment of certain advisors close to Roosevelt, his failure to win an important administrative post during the war, and the death of his first wife. Ideologically, he felt that the New Deal, by moving to create a welfare state that accommodated demands of organized interest groups, had abandoned the major tenets "of the neutral regulatory progressive state." He then called unsuccessfully for a conservative coalition of southern Democrats and Republicans to reverse the trend, and he was disappointed with the policies of both Presidents Truman and Eisenhower. 3 photos, 61 notes.   N. C. Burckel

1254. Antognini, Richard. THE ROLE OF A. P. GIANNINI IN THE 1934 CALIFORNIA GUBERNATORIAL ELECTION. *Southern California Q. 1975 57(1): 53-86.* Analyzes how A. P. Giannini, founder and head of the Bank of America, switched from traditional support of the Republican Party to endorsement of the Roosevelt candidacy in 1932, and eventual backing of the Republican gubernatorial candidate in 1934. Giannini came into conflict with the Federal Reserve Board, the head of San Francisco's Federal Reserve Bank, and the Reconstruction Finance Corporation. Unhappy with the Hoover Administration, Giannini endorsed Franklin D. Roosevelt in 1932; and in return

Roosevelt promised to support policies friendly to Giannini's needs. After Upton Sinclair captured the 1934 Democratic gubernatorial nomination, the Giannini forces and Republican candidate Frank Merriam reached an agreement which permitted support of Merriam without damaging relations with the Roosevelt Administration. Primary and secondary sources, including the Bank of America Archives; 86 notes.   A. Hoffman

1255. Armbrester, Margaret E. JOHN TEMPLE GRAVES II: A SOUTHERN LIBERAL VIEWS THE NEW DEAL. *Alabama Rev. 1979 32(3): 203-213.* John Temple Graves II (1892-1961), syndicated columnist with the Palm Beach *Times,* warmly supported the New Deal until President Franklin D. Roosevelt proposed Supreme Court reorganization and Congress passed the Fair Labor Standards Act. Graves's support cooled thereafter, chiefly on grounds of Wilsonian idealism, southern self-interest, and states' rights. Primary and secondary sources; 39 notes.   J. F. Vivian

1256. Babu, B. Ramesh. UNEMPLOYMENT INSURANCE IN THE UNITED STATES: AN ANALYSIS OF THE BEGINNING. *J. of the U. of Bombay [India] 1975-76 44-45(80-81): 139-172.* The Social Security Act (US, 1935), which provided for unemployment insurance, was part of Franklin D. Roosevelt second New Deal. Although intended to counter criticism from the left, the Act was in fact a middle-of-the-road policy. It was preceded in 1934 by two attempts at unemployment insurance which failed to secure Congressional approval: the Wagner-Lewis Bill, intended to encourage the states to provide benefits, and the Lundeen Bill, which proposed coverage for persons who had been unable to secure employment for a minimum period. The Committee on Economic Security, appointed in 1934 to advise Roosevelt on social security, placed more emphasis on job creation than on unemployment insurance. They recommended a federal-state system based on tax credits. The Social Security Act, based on their recommendations but modified somewhat by the House of Representatives and the Senate, became law on 14 August 1935. Although the unemployment insurance provisions, criticized by the left and the right, were less impressive than some of its others, the Act as a whole was a major development in the evolution of the United States as a welfare state. Published government documents, contemporary newspapers and journals and secondary works; 87 notes.
                                                        J. F. Hilliker

1257. Berkowitz, Edward D. and McQuaid, Kim. BUREAUCRATS AS "SOCIAL ENGINEERS": FEDERAL WELFARE PROGRAMS IN HERBERT HOOVERS'S AMERICA. *Am. J. of Economics and Sociol. 1980 39(4): 321-335.* Historians interested in 20th century American reform often seek to analyze the ideologies of political leaders separately from the institutions that these same leaders created. Such emphases on ideas, as opposed to actions, has, for example, led "revisionist" American historians to argue that the presidencies of Herbert Hoover and Franklin D. Roosevelt were "conceptually continuous." Our examination of the major social welfare programs undertaken by the federal government in the 1920's disputes this claim. Examination of the operations of the federal bureaucracy instead of the rhetoric of politicians demonstrates the existence of decided policy difference between the Hoover and Roosevelt eras. "Efficiency" analogues dominant during the Hoover era were replaced with "direct service-provider" approaches which created a clear distinction between private and public welfare programs. Elements of "continuity" between the two eras have been overdrawn. Background is provided for increased understanding of some of the policy implications of America's contemporary welfare debate—particularly about "rehabilitation" strategies and/or rationales for action in the social welfare field.   J

1258. Bhana, Surendra. AN ATTEMPT BY THE ROOSEVELT ADMINISTRATION TO "REINFORCE" SELF-GOVERNMENT IN PUERTO RICO: THE ELECTIVE GOVERNOR BILL OF 1943. *Rev. Interamericana [Puerto Rico] 1973 2(4): 559-573.* World War II and internal politics in Puerto Rico influenced the Roosevelt administration to allow Puerto Ricans to elect their own governor. Congress opposed self-government in Puerto Rico and blocked enabling legislation during 1943-44. Primary and secondary works; 74 notes.   J. Lewis

1259. Billington, Monroe. THE ALABAMA CLERGY AND THE NEW DEAL. *Alabama Rev. 1979 32(3): 214-225.* Quantitative analysis of 327 Alabama clergy who responded to President Franklin D. Roose-

velt's special query of September 1935. More than three-fourths supported the New Deal, notably for pragmatic rather than ideological reasons. Contradictions also were evident, chiefly between desired social services and disliked higher taxes. Primary and secondary sources; tables, 10 notes.   J. F. Vivian

1260. Billington, Monroe and Clark, Cal. THE MASSACHUSETTS CLERGY AND THE NEW DEAL. *Hist. J. of Massachusetts 1980 8(2): 12-29.* Analyzes the response of 363 Massachusetts clergymen to a letter from President Franklin D. Roosevelt in 1935 asking their advice on social problems. The clergymen were generally favorable to the New Deal, especially its relief programs. Manuscript letters in Franklin D. Roosevelt Library and secondary sources; 6 tables, 14 notes.
                                                    W. H. Mulligan, Jr.

1261. Bishirjian, Richard J. CROLY, WILSON, AND THE AMERICAN CIVIL RELIGION. *Modern Age 1979 23(1): 33-38.* If salvation is thought to be intramundane, political life takes on new historical importance as it becomes enveloped in the history of salvation, and politics becomes the field of prophecy. Two who represent extreme eschatological aspirations in the American millenarianism were Herbert Croly and Woodrow Wilson. Based on author's *A Public Philosophy Reader* (1979).   M. L. Lifka

1262. Blanchard, Margaret A. THE FIFTH-AMENDMENT PRIVILEGE OF NEWSMAN GEORGE BURDICK. *Journalism Q. 1978 55(1): 39-46, 67.* Invoking the Fifth, rather than the First, Amendment, George Burdick of the New York *Tribune* refused in 1914 to answer a federal grand jury's questions about the sources of his paper's stories on the dealings of a customs appointee of President Woodrow Wilson. Burdick refused the presidential pardon issued to encourage him to cooperate with Assistant US Attorney Frank Carstarphen. Federal district judge Learned Hand held that the pardon could not be refused. The Supreme Court in *Burdick* v. *United States* (US, 1915) ruled, however, that because a pardon imputes guilt, no one can be forced to accept one. Primary and secondary sources; 41 notes.   R. P. Sindermann, Jr.

1263. Braeman, John. THE MAKING OF THE ROOSEVELT COALITION: SOME RECONSIDERATIONS. *Can. Rev. of Am. Studies [Canada] 1980 11(2): 233-253.* Six recent publications attempt anew to assess Franklin D. Roosevelt's New Deal of the 1930's: Kristi Andersen's *The Creation of a Democratic Majority, 1928-1936* (Chicago, 1979), Barbara Blumberg's *The New Deal and the Unemployed: The View from New York City* (Lewisburg, Pa., 1979), Sidney Fine's *Frank Murphy: The Detroit Years* (Ann Arbor, 1975) and *Frank Murphy: The New Deal Years* (Chicago, 1979), John W. Jeffries's *Testing the Roosevelt Coalition: Connecticut Society and Politics in the Era of World War II* (Knoxville, Tenn., 1979), and Martha H. Swain's *Pat Harrison: The New Deal Years* (Jackson, Miss., 1978). 37 notes.   H. T. Lovin

1264. Bremer, William W. ALONG THE "AMERICAN WAY": THE NEW DEAL'S WORK RELIEF PROGRAMS FOR THE UNEMPLOYED. *J. of Am. Hist. 1975 62(3): 636-652.* Describes the ideal of a constructive and psychologically supportive work relief program formulated by New Deal administrators and social workers, including Harry Hopkins, William Matthews, and Homer Folks, and its partial and temporary implementation in the Civil Works Administration of 1933-34. Political and budgetary pressures soon ended the CWA experiment. Instead, more traditional relief practices were adopted which kept work relief less attractive than private employment and retained the animus of charity. New Dealers did not view work relief as a permanent policy which guaranteed a "right to work." Based on collected papers, journals, and secondary works; 70 notes.   J. B. Street

1265. Brinkley, Alan. THE NEW DEAL: PRELUDE. *Wilson Q. 1982 6(2): 50-61.* Discusses reform traditions during 1900-33, which influenced Franklin D. Roosevelt's New Deal policies.

1266. Brown, Lorraine. FEDERAL THEATRE: MELODRAMA, SOCIAL PROTEST, AND GENIUS. *Q. J. of the Lib. of Congress 1979 36(1): 18-37.* Recounts the history of the Federal Theatre Project of the Works Progress Administration from its establishment in 1935 until its demise in 1939. Implemented by Harry L. Hopkins, director of the WPA, and directed by Hallie Flanagan, the Federal Theatre Project was begun

to relieve unemployed theater people during the depression. Theatre centers nationwide produced a wide variety of plays independently and simultaneously, including works by Sinclair Lewis, George Bernard Shaw, and Eugene O'Neill. The Federal Theatre Project produced both regional and national projects and struggled against censorship and cuts in funds for four years before it was ended for political reasons. Based on the Federal Theatre Project Collection at the Library of Congress; 15 photos, 39 notes.
                                                                A. R. Souby

1267. Brown, Richard C. MARK SULLIVAN VIEWS THE NEW DEAL FROM AVONDALE. *Pennsylvania Mag. of Hist. and Biog. 1975 99(3): 351-361.* Mark Sullivan, a widely read syndicated political columnist, felt that New Deal principles were a threat to the peaceful way of life epitomized by his farm at Avondale, Pennsylvania. An early supporter of Franklin D. Roosevelt, Sullivan became a cautious critic of the presidents. By the end of Roosevelt's first term he felt there were "serious flaws in Roosevelt's character and performance." 39 notes.
                                                                C. W. Olson

1268. Candeloro, Dominic. LOUIS F. POST AND THE RED SCARE OF 1920. *Prologue 1979 11(1): 41-55.* In 1920 as Assistant Secretary of Labor, 71-year-old Louis F. Post successfully thwarted the arbitrary and capricious enforcement of the Alien Anarchist Act (US, 1918), by which scores of foreign-born radicals were deported under the aegis of Attorney General Mitchell Palmer and his assistant J. Edgar Hoover. Post, a long-time sympathizer with left-wing causes and a public admirer of the Russian Revolution, came under intensive Congressional scrutiny for his stand and an effort was made to remove him from office through impeachment proceedings. The effort failed, owing in large part to Post's own inspired defense of his position before Congressional committees. Post's insistence that due process and a rigid adherence to law mark governmental operations against foreign-born radicals did a great deal to stem the tide of wanton and arbitrary deportation of dissenters resident in the United States. Based mainly on research in the National Archives.
                                                                N. Lederer

1269. Christie, Jean. NEW DEAL RESOURCES PLANNING: THE PROPOSALS OF MORRIS L. COOKE. *Agric. Hist. 1979 53(3): 597-606.* Morris L. Cooke, independently wealthy former advisor to Pennsylvania Governor Gifford Pinchot, served as head of a number of New Deal agencies dealing with land and water conservation. Cooke's approach to conservation was a regional one. He believed in the watershed and river valley as the smallest division of a conservation unit. Cooke served with the Rural Electrification Administration and other government agencies until the era of conservation reform ended under President Harry S. Truman, who was preoccupied with the Korean War. Primary and secondary sources; 23 notes.
                                                                R. T. Fulton

1270. Cobb, James C. THE BIG BOY HAS SCARED THE LARD OUT OF THEM. *Res. Studies 1975 43(2): 123-125.* Examines Franklin D. Roosevelt's unsuccessful attempt in 1938 to purge the Democratic Party of conservative congressmen, particularly Walter F. George of Georgia.
                                                                S

1271. Cobb, James C. NOT GONE, BUT FORGOTTEN: EUGENE TALMADGE AND THE 1938 PURGE CAMPAIGN. *Georgia Hist. Q. 1975 59(2): 197-209.* Discusses the political career of Georgia Democratic governor Eugene Talmadge, 1926-38, emphasizing President Franklin D. Roosevelt's 1938 intervention to remove him from power due to attacks on the New Deal.

1272. Collins, Robert M. POSITIVE BUSINESS RESPONSES TO THE NEW DEAL: THE ROOTS OF THE COMMITTEE FOR ECONOMIC DEVELOPMENT, 1933-1942. *Business Hist. Rev. 1978 52(3): 369-391.* Argues that previous scholars have not sufficiently noted the efforts of business elements that attempted to arrange a detente with the Roosevelt administration during the 1930's. One expression of this effort was the government's Business Advisory Council, a second was those businessmen who came to embrace the Keynesian solution of deficit spending, and a third spawned from academic-business dialogues initiated at the University of Chicago in 1936. All three of these sources played a role in the eventual formation of the Committee for Economic Development in 1942. The establishment of the CED was essentially the product of long-developing trend toward business-government collaboration

begun years before. Based on private papers and published business periodicals; 90 notes.
                                                                C. J. Pusateri

1273. Conkin, Paul K. HONEYMOON FOR A SOPHOMORE. *R. in Am. Hist. 1974 2(3): 429-436.* The fourth volume of Frank Freidel's biography *Franklin D. Roosevelt: Launching the New Deal* (Boston: Little, Brown and Co., 1973) focuses on Roosevelt's political leadership and economic policy during the New Deal.

1274. Conrad, David E. CREATING THE NATION'S LARGEST FOREST RESERVE: ROOSEVELT, EMMONS, AND THE TONGASS NATIONAL FOREST. *Pacific Hist. Rev. 1977 46(1): 65-83.* President Theodore Roosevelt and George T. Emmons, a retired career naval officer interested in Alaskan native art and forest conservation, collaborated to bring the Tongass National Forest in Alaska into existence in 1902. It was the largest forest reserve in the United States. The collaboration was based on a long-standing friendship between the two men. Normal bureaucratic and legal procedures were circumvented. Based on documents in National Archives, Library of Congress, and Field Museum of Natural History, on published documents and on secondary sources; map, 62 notes.
                                                                W. K. Hobson

1275. Crosby, Earl W. PROGRESSIVE SEGREGATION IN THE WILSON ADMINISTRATION. *Potomac Rev. 1973 6(2): 41-57.* Racial segregation was supported by the southern Progressive Movement as well as the federal government during Woodrow Wilson's administration (1913-21).

1276. Crosson, David. JAMES S. CLARKSON AND THEODORE ROOSEVELT, 1901-1904: A STUDY IN CONTRASTING POLITICAL TRADITIONS. *Ann. of Iowa 1974 42(5): 344-360.* Theodore Roosevelt's appointment of James S. Clarkson as surveyor of the Port of New York renewed Clarkson's political career. A Radical Republican, as opposed to the Progressivism of the President, Clarkson nevertheless used his post to gather information about New York City's business and financial elites and to organize labor and minority support for the President. Clarkson's success certainly contributed to Roosevelt's election in 1904.
                                                                C. W. Olson

1277. Cuff, Robert D. THE DILEMMAS OF VOLUNTARISM: HOOVER AND THE PORK-PACKING AGREEMENT OF 1917-1919. *Agric. Hist. 1979 53(4): 727-747.* Herbert C. Hoover's appointment as Food Administrator during World War I tested his belief in voluntary restraint of business. Recalcitrant pork packers who wanted to extract the maximum profit from wartime business made it difficult to control prices. But in order to justify his philosophy, Hoover was forced to defend the packers against the Federal Trade Commission and others in the administration who wanted sweeping reform of the industry and greater government control. The short wartime crisis and its accompanying prosperity made his voluntary approach look more successful than it would be during the Great Depression. 53 notes.
                                                                D. E. Bowers

1278. Cuff, Robert D. THE POLITICS OF LABOR ADMINISTRATION DURING WORLD WAR I. *Labor Hist. 1980 21(4): 546-569.* The US Department of Labor was more effective in resisting bureaucratic invasions from the emergency war agencies during World War I than many other executive departments. The department won a major political victory when President Woodrow Wilson named the Secretary of Labor head of the government's wartime administration for labor policies in January 1918; yet, the Labor Department never really succeeded in acquiring actual administrative control of the government's labor policies. Based on the William B. Wilson Papers and other primary sources; 48 notes.
                                                                L. F. Velicer

1279. Cuff, Robert D. WE BAND OF BROTHERS—WOODROW WILSON'S WAR MANAGERS. *Can. R. of Am. Studies 1974 5(2): 135-148.* Analyzes policy-making and management practices by the War Council in 1918. Created by Woodrow Wilson in March 1918, the Council attempted to mobilize efficiently America's resources for war purposes. Unlike its successors since 1918, the Council tempered its use of power with "moral concern" that its powers were not abused. Based on primary and secondary sources; 39 notes.
                                                                H. T. Lovin

1280. Culbert, David H. "CROAK" CARTER: RADIO'S VOICE OF DOOM. *Pennsylvania Mag. of Hist. and Biog. 1973 97(3): 287-317.* During the period 1935-38 Boake Carter, radio news commentator, achieved enormous popularity and influence through his caustic and slightly irresponsible criticism of Franklin D. Roosevelt and the New Deal. One of the first news analyzers on commercial radio, Carter saw his popularity and power go into a sudden and mysterious eclipse after 1938. In the process of successfully attacking Roosevelt's administration, Carter revealed for the first time the immense power of radio as a medium for political criticism. Primary and secondary sources; 91 notes.
E. W. Carp

1281. Danbom, David B. THE AGRICULTURAL EXTENSION SYSTEM AND THE FIRST WORLD WAR. *Historian 1979 41(2): 315-331.* When the United States entered World War I there was a great need to mobilize the American economy, especially in agriculture. The traditional individualism of farmers, however, and the disorganized and isolated nature of the countryside presented serious problems for mobilization. The task of mobilization fell to the Department of Agriculture and the assignment by design and default to the county agents who had been working in rural areas since 1902 trying to improve the farm and home practices of rural people through adult education. Soon these agents became engaged in duties not related to their traditional roles—conducting propaganda campaigns, organizing and running Liberty Loan campaigns, and organizing Red Cross and YMCA fund drives. When the war ended the extension system was much stronger, but questionable whether they, or higher prices, were more responsible for increased production. Primary and secondary sources; 57 notes.
R. S. Sliwoski

1282. Daniel, Cletus E. AGRICULTURAL UNIONISM AND THE EARLY NEW DEAL: THE CALIFORNIA EXPERIENCE. *Southern California Q. 1977 59(2): 185-215.* Argues that the Franklin D. Roosevelt administraton, in the first phase of its New Deal policies, undercut the development of agricultural unionism in California. New Deal economic planners at first envisioned a harmonious relationship between employers and workers brought about through active federal mediation under the National Industrial Recovery Act (NIRA). Although New Deal labor policy dramatically changed after the end of the NIRA and the passage of the Wagner Act, California's agricultural labor movement suffered irreparably from the involvement of George Creel, self-styled NIRA mediator, in the San Joaquin cotton strike of October 1933. Creel effected a compromise which the Communist-led union accepted, and the chance to create an effective agricultural workers' union was lost. The Department of Labor sent Pelham Glassford to mediate labor disputes in the Imperial Valley. In 1934 he undercut the union by endorsing a company union, only to find that employers rejected both federal involvement and the company union. Thus the New Deal, remembered for its liberalism and reform, promoted the destruction of a vigorous effort to organize California agriculture. Primary and secondary sources; 68 notes.
A. Hoffman

1283. Davis, Kenneth S. THE BIRTH OF SOCIAL SECURITY. *Am. Heritage 1979 30(3): 38-51.* A history of the adoption of the Social Security Act (US, 1935). Essentially a conservative approach, the plan was limited in its scope by President Franklin D. Roosevelt and some of his closest advisors. Based on plans developed in Wisconsin and Ohio, and stimulated by the efforts of demagogues like Huey P. Long and Francis Townsend, the Roosevelt administration gradually realized the strong national support for such a proposal, but then made certain that it was limited in both cost and coverage. 19 illus.
J. F. Paul

1284. Davis, Kenneth S. INCIDENT IN MIAMI. *Am. Heritage 1980 32(1): 86-95.* An account of the attempted assassination of Franklin D. Roosevelt by Giuseppe Zangara in Miami, Florida, on 15 February 1933. Zangara wounded several persons, including Chicago's Mayor Anton Cermak who died on 6 March. Zangara was tried and executed. Roosevelt refused to let the incident unnerve him. 12 illus.
J. F. Paul

1285. Davis, Polly Ann. ALBEN W. BARKLEY'S PUBLIC CAREER IN 1944. *Filson Club Hist. Q. 1977 51(2): 143-157.* Examines the conflict between President Franklin D. Roosevelt and Senate Democratic Majority Leader Alben W. Barkley over a tax bill in February 1944. Roosevelt vetoed H.R. 3687 on 21 February because it did not raise

enough revenue. Barkley, who regarded the bill as the best measure obtainable, made a major Senate speech on 23 February, called on Congress to override the veto, and then resigned as Majority Leader. The immediate result was the overwhelming passage of the legislation and the unanimous reelection of Barkley as Majority Leader. The speech helped Barkley to be reelected to the Senate in 1944, but it prevented him from receiving the Vice Presidential nomination that same year. Based on newspapers and the Barkley papers; 66 notes.
G. B. McKinney

1286. Davis, Polly Ann. COURT REFORM AND ALBEN W. BARKLEY'S ELECTION AS MAJORITY LEADER. *Southern Q. 1976 15(1): 15-31.* Examines 1937 judiciary reform and the contest for majority leadership in the US Senate which involved Byron P. Harrison and Alben W. Barkley. President Franklin D. Roosevelt's court pack fight receives primary consideration. The results of both struggles are evaluated. Concludes that the situations helped factionalize the Democratic Party. 53 notes.
R. W. Dubay

1287. Dawson, Nelson L. LOUIS D. BRANDEIS, FELIX FRANKFURTER, AND FRANKLIN D. ROOSEVELT: THE ORIGINS OF A NEW DEAL RELATIONSHIP. *Am. Jewish Hist. 1978 68(1): 32-42.* The Brandeis-Frankfurter partnership influencing national political events began in 1917 (re the appointment of an economic "czar"). By the 1920's the extensive correspondence between them included politics, law, and Zionism. By 1933, Frankfurter acted as the intermediary between Brandeis and Roosevelt. The intellectual relation of these three men demonstrates the importance of personal contact as a source of political influence and the truth of their philosophy's central thesis: that the richest sources of a democracy are the individuals in public service.
F. Rosenthal

1288. Day, David S. HERBERT HOOVER AND RACIAL POLITICS: THE DEPRIEST INCIDENT. *J. of Negro Hist. 1980 65(1): 6-17.* Oscar DePriest, the first black congressman since 1901, was the focal point of considerable controversy when his wife was invited to the Congressional Wives tea party in the White House by Mrs. Herbert Hoover. On the heels of this event, DePriest organized a "musicale and reception" to raise $200,000 for the NAACP and invited Congressional Republicans and heightened the racial controversy of 1929. The Hoover administration was concerned with preserving its electoral gains in the South and DePriest's aim was to enhance the political strength of blacks, especially that of Oscar DePriest. Based on primary sources in the Herbert Hoover Presidential Library; 46 notes.
N. G. Sapper

1289. Dorsett, Lyle W. FRANK HAGUE, FRANKLIN ROOSEVELT AND THE POLITICS OF THE NEW DEAL. *New Jersey Hist. 1976 94(1): 23-35.* Frank Hague was not pro-Roosevelt at the 1932 convention, but he enthusiastically supported him in the general election and helped deliver New Jersey's electoral votes to the Democratic ticket. Hague's political power was again demonstrated in his control of the New Deal's WPA and FERA programs in New Jersey. Abuses of the programs soon became common and the President's personal distaste for the Jersey City mayor grew. Roosevelt supported Charles Edison for governor in 1940, hoping to circumvent Hague with a friend in Trenton. As time passed it became evident that Hague could be embarrassed but not destroyed. Based on primary and secondary sources; 4 illus., 27 notes.
E. R. McKinstry

1290. Drake, Douglas C. HERBERT HOOVER, ECOLOGIST: THE POLITICS OF OIL POLLUTION CONTROL, 1921-1926. *Mid-Am. 1973 55(3): 207-228.* Commerce Secretary Herbert Hoover, representing conflicting shipping and fishing interests, initiated an antipollution bill 7 June 1924. Although it died on the books, it nevertheless represented the birth of the modern ecology movement. An earlier conference covened by Hoover led to complex congressional hearings and politicking in which the American Petroleum Institute played a significant role. Major legislative issues included inclusion of shore plants, separators, and enforcement. Delay and compromises were the politics of oil pollution control. Based on the Herbert Hoover Papers, Herbert Hoover Presidential Library, and printed sources. 44 notes.
T. H. Wendel

1291. Eagles, Charles W. TWO "DOUBLE V'S": JONATHAN DANIELS, FDR, AND RACE RELATIONS DURING WORLD

WAR II. *North Carolina Hist. Rev. 1982 59(3): 252-270.* American blacks' wartime hopes and expectations were articulated in a 1942 *Pittsburgh Courier* article on the "Double V": victory over the Axis powers and victory over domestic racial discrimination, particularly in civilian employment and in the military. President Franklin D. Roosevelt's less explicit "Double V" was military victory abroad and political victory at home. White Southern liberal newspaperman Jonathan W. Daniels of Raleigh, as presidential administrative assistant during 1943-45, helped Roosevelt execute this vague policy and, simultaneously, aided blacks in making limited strides toward decreasing racial discrimination. Based primarily on the Roosevelt and Daniels papers, Daniels's published writings, and interviews; 10 photos, 41 notes. T. L. Savitt

1292. Ebner, Michael H. "WINNING... IT'S THE ONLY THING": FDR VERSUS BOSTON. *Rev. in Am. Hist. 1978 6(1): 120-125.* Review article prompted by Charles H. Trout's *Boston, the Great Depression, and the New Deal* (New York: Oxford U. Pr., 1977).

1293. Edwards, John Carver. HERBERT HOOVER'S PUBLIC LANDS POLICY: A STRUGGLE FOR CONTROL. *Pacific Historian 1976 20(1): 34-45.* During the 1920's, Republicans developed few positive programs for dealing with Western lands. Herbert C. Hoover's Secretary of Interior, Ray Lyman Wilbur, supported efforts to turn lands over to states for administration, as recommended by a special committee headed by James R. Garfield. Opponents, such as Gifford Pinchot, raised the specter of Teapot Dome, and the plan was defeated. Primary and secondary sources; 3 illus., 16 notes. G. L. Olson

1294. Ellis, Richard N. "INDIANS AT IBAPAH IN REVOLT": GOSHIUTES, THE DRAFT AND THE INDIAN BUREAU, 1917-1919. *Nevada Hist. Soc. Q. 1976 19(3): 163-170.* Traces the development of unrest and opposition of Goshiute Indians against Bureau of Indian Affairs administrators who directly supervised the Goshiute Indian Reservation. Bureau investigators charged erroneously that Goshiute resistance to military service was the fundamental cause of the friction. Based on United States archival sources; 23 notes. H. T. Lovin

1295. Fausold, Martin L. PRESIDENT HOOVER'S FARM POLICIES 1929-1933. *Agric. Hist. 1977 51(2): 362-377.* The relationship between Herbert C. Hoover's concept of corporatism and its political implementation explains to a large degree the failures in farm policymaking during his presidency. Compares Hoover's farm program attempts with the speeches and actions of his Democratic political rival Franklin D. Roosevelt. Primary and secondary sources; 65 notes. R. T. Fulton

1296. Feder, Donald. BENITO AND FRANKLIN. *Reason 1982 14(4): 29-32.* Claims that Franklin D. Roosevelt's New Deal economic policies paralleled Benito Mussolini's fascistic policies for Italy in that the political framework of welfare liberalism was constructed in the early 1930's by men who espoused a collectivist ideology similar to that of Fascism.

1297. Ficken, Robert E. GIFFORD PINCHOT MEN: PACIFIC NORTHWEST LUMBERMEN AND THE CONSERVATION MOVEMENT, 1902-1910. *Western Hist. Q. 1982 13(2): 165-178.* The 1902 disastrous forest fires in Washington and Oregon and the accompanying human casualties precipitated intense public interest in the prevention of future disasters. Large timber owners headed a conservation movement to secure government protection of their threatened holdings from disaster, mismanagement, and the more radical forms of environmental preservation. The lumbermen found themselves allies of the nation's chief forester, Gifford Pinchot. This era came to a close in 1910, when Pinchot was dismissed by the William Howard Taft administration and when the anti-Taft dominated national conservation congress of that year called for increased federal regulation. These initiated a period of intense enmity between lumbermen and regulation-oriented conservationists. 64 notes. D. L. Smith

1298. Ficken, Robert E. POLITICAL LEADERSHIP IN WARTIME: FRANKLIN D. ROOSEVELT AND THE ELECTIONS OF 1942. *Mid-America 1975 57(1): 20-37.* Franklin D. Roosevelt mainly remained aloof during the 1942 campaign, fearing to alienate the Kelly machine in the Illinois race and staying clear of Democratic Party disputes in Texas and Pennsylvania. The Democratic setback in 1942 showed how decayed the party was becoming. Primary and secondary sources; 85 notes. T. H. Wendel

1299. Ficken, Robert E. PRESIDENT HARDING VISITS SEATTLE. *Pacific Northwest Q. 1975 66(3): 105-114.* President Warren G. Harding's appearance in the Pacific Northwest during July 1923 followed a successful but harried tour of Alaska. Addressing crowds in Seattle, Harding praised the future statehood prospects for Alaska, while simultaneously warning that he would not tolerate ruinous exploitation of its natural resources. Soon after leaving the city, the president became ill and died several days later in San Francisco. The resultant outpouring of grief was especially evident in Seattle, where even his critics joined in the eulogies. The praise, however, evaporated in the light of administrative scandals and his trip was quickly forgotten. Yet Harding's tour had created a legacy of promoting Alaska, advocating the Roosevelt-Pinchot brand of conservation, and modifying state politics in Washington. Primary sources; 46 notes. M. L. Tate

1300. Fisch, Dov. THE LIBEL TRIAL OF ROBERT EDWARD EDMONDSON: 1936-1938. *Am. Jewish Hist. 1981 71(1): 79-102.* Covers events leading to, and Jewish reaction to, the 1936-38 libel trial of anti-Jew publisher Robert Edward Edmondson. Attacking high-ranking Jews in Franklin D. Roosevelt's administration as leading the nation to Communism, Edmondson even claimed that secretary of Labor Frances Perkins was a Russian Jew. Both conservative and liberal Jews hailed New York Mayor Fiorello La Guardia for instituting libel charges in 1936. But two years of delay altered Jewish opinion, and in 1938 three major Jewish organizations, seeking to prevent making a "martyr" of Edmondson, joined the American Civil Liberties Union in defending him. Edmondson claimed victory and resumed publishing, only to be indicted during World War II for sedition and conspiracy. Based on New York City Municipal Archives and other primary sources; 104 notes. R. A. Keller

1301. Fischhoff, Baruch. INTUITIVE USE OF FORMAL MODELS: A COMMENT ON MORRISON'S "QUANTITATIVE MODELS IN HISTORY." *Hist. and Theory 1978 17(2): 207-210.* Responds to an article by Rodney J. Morrison, correcting the error that assumes in statistical reasoning that probability has a memory. 7 notes. D. A. Yanchisin

1302. Funigiello, Philip J. THE BONNEVILLE POWER ADMINISTRATION AND THE NEW DEAL. *Prologue 1973 5(2): 89-97.* Discusses the administration of the BPA from its establishment in 1937 to the interconnection of all electric utilities in the Pacific Northwest in 1942. Problems treated include the outworking of a federal power policy, the conflict between private and public power interests, and bureaucratic clashes with government officials and agencies. Based on primary sources; 31 notes. D. G. Davis, Jr.

1303. Garcia, George F. BLACK DISAFFECTION FROM THE REPUBLICAN PARTY DURING THE PRESIDENCY OF HERBERT HOOVER, 1928-1932. *Ann. of Iowa 1980 45(6): 462-497.* During the presidency of Herbert Hoover, several factors contributed to growing black defections from the ranks of the Republican Party: Hoover's efforts to strengthen the southern wing of his party by purging black Republicans from leadership positions; his nomination of John J. Parker, a North Carolina judge with a racist past, to the Supreme Court; the president's failure to condemn the segregation of Gold Star mothers during a War Department sponsored trip to American cemeteries in France; and the reduction of black military units. By 1932 much of the black press was portraying Hoover as a racist and a shift of black allegiance from the Republicans to the Democrats was underway even before Franklin D. Roosevelt took office. Based on the Colored Question file, Presidential Papers, Herbert Hoover Presidential Library, West Branch, Iowa, and other primary sources; 40 notes. P. L. Petersen

1304. Garraty, John A. THE NEW DEAL, NATIONAL SOCIALISM, AND THE GREAT DEPRESSION. *Am. Hist. R. 1973 78(4): 907-944.* Compares government methods for coping with the Great Depression in Hitler's Germany and Roosevelt's United States. Nazi and New Deal antidepression policies displayed striking similarities and were distinct from those of other industrial nations. Focuses on the years 1933 to 1936. Of the two, the Nazis were the more successful; by 1936 the depression was substantially over in Germany, but far from finished in the United States. "However, neither regime solved the problem of maintaining prosperity without war." 6 figs., 71 notes.   R. V. Ritter

1305. Garvey, Daniel E. SECRETARY HOOVER AND THE QUEST FOR BROADCAST REGULATION. *Journalism Hist. 1976 3(3): 66-70, 85.* Examines the role of Secretary of Commerce Herbert C. Hoover in the formulation of regulations to control American broadcasting, particularly the Radio Act (US, 1927).

1306. Gatewood, Willard B., Jr. THEODORE ROOSEVELT AND ARKANSAS, 1901-1912. *Arkansas Hist. Q. 1973 32(1): 3-24.* Covers race relations and the Republican Party.

1307. Gengarelly, W. Anthony. SECRETARY OF LABOR WILLIAM B. WILSON AND THE RED SCARE, 1919-1920. *Pennsylvania Hist. 1980 47(4): 311-330.* During the red scare of 1919-20, Secretary of Labor William B. Wilson permitted subordinates and Attorney General A. Mitchell Palmer to violate the rights of immigrants in deportation procedures. Legislation placed deportation matters under Secretary Wilson, who previously had established just guidelines for them. While Wilson was on a brief leave of absence in 1920, Assistant Secretary Louis F. Post cancelled 1,140 deportation warrants and moved to rectify earlier abuses of power. Upon his return, Wilson backed Post in these efforts. Based on Wilson papers, Labor Department archives, other government documents, and secondary sources; 2 photos, 51 notes.   D. C. Swift

1308. Giddens, Paul H. THE NAVAL OIL RESERVE, TEAPOT DOME AND THE CONTINENTAL TRADING COMPANY. *Ann. of Wyoming 1981 53(1): 14-27.* Traces the Teapot Dome Scandal beginning in 1921 when Secretary of the Interior Albert Fall received control over the naval oil leases from the secretary of the navy. Despite immediate complaints from Senator Robert LaFollette, Congress was slow to investigate the questionable transfer, and President Calvin Coolidge offered little help when the question was again raised in 1923. Senator Thomas Walsh kept the issue before a congressional committee and in 1924 uncovered the financial connection between Fall and oil magnates Edward Doheny and Harry Sinclair. Amid the unraveling of the scandal, three cabinet officers resigned and Fall went to prison. Based on congressional studies of naval oil leases; 4 photos, 84 notes.   M. L. Tate

1309. Giglio, James N. ATTORNEY GENERAL HARRY M. DAUGHERTY AND THE UNITED GAS IMPROVEMENT COMPANY CASE, 1914-1924. *Pennsylvania Hist. 1979 46(4): 346-367.* In 1922 and 1923, Attorney General Harry M. Daugherty terminated antitrust actions against the Philadelphia-based United Gas Improvement Company, a street lighting trust. Although indictments had been obtained, there were weaknesses in the government's case. Yet, Daugherty's decision was based largely upon political considerations and his friendship for the trust's attorneys. Based on the Wheeler Committee Investigation of Daugherty; photo, 58 notes.   D. C. Swift

1310. Ginzl, David J. LILY-WHITES VERSUS BLACK-AND-TANS: MISSISSIPPI REPUBLICANS DURING THE HOOVER ADMINISTRATION. *J. of Mississippi Hist. 1980 42(3): 194-211.* Discusses the origin of intraparty factionalism among Mississippi Republicans during Herbert C. Hoover's race for the presidency in 1928. This struggle between the lily-whites and black-and-tans was dominated by considerations of race and party patronage. Persisting throughout the Hoover administration, the strife continued to dominate Republican Party politics in Mississippi over the next three decades. Perry W. Howard, one of the highest ranking blacks in the federal government, a national committeeman, and leader of the black-and-tans, remained a focal point in the struggle over the state's patronage and control of the Republican Party machinery. Based on Hoover Presidential Papers and several other collections housed in the Herbert Hoover Presidential Library; 35 notes.   M. S. Legan

1311. Ginzl, David J. PATRONAGE, RACE AND POLITICS: GEORGIA REPUBLICANS DURING THE HOOVER ADMINIS-

TRATION. *Georgia Hist. Q. 1980 64(3): 280-293.* Accusations of irregularities in the dispensing of Republican Party patronage and the collection of "contributions" in Georgia resulted in the rise of political factions that struggled for control of the state party throughout Hoover's presidency. Factions were also based on race. Based on correspondence, newspapers and secondary sources; 30 notes.   G. R. Schroeder

1312. Ginzl, David J. THE POLITICS OF PATRONAGE: FLORIDA REPUBLICANS DURING THE HOOVER ADMINISTRATION. *Florida Hist. Q. 1982 61(1): 1-19.* Herbert Hoover's presidential sweep in 1928 raised hopes of returning Republicans to state offices. The Depression retarded reorganization efforts. The Hoover administration failed to heal rifts within the state and demonstrated political ineptness in dispensing patronage. Florida state Republican leaders resented outside interference. The result was confusion and division with the loss of all hope for reestablishing the party within the state. Based on the Hoover Presidential Papers (Hoover Presidential Library, West Branch, Iowa), state newspapers, and other sources; 4 fig., 45 notes.   N. A. Kuntz

1313. Glazier, Kenneth M. W. E. B. DU BOIS' IMPRESSIONS OF WOODROW WILSON. *J. of Negro Hist. 1973 58(4): 452-459.* This previously unpublished essay by W. E. B. Du Bois, written in response to a query from a researcher seeking information about Woodrow Wilson, provides insights into Du Bois' struggles for black equality. The essay is in the Hoover Institution on War, Revolution, and Peace.   N. G. Sapper

1314. Goldberg, Joseph P. FRANCES PERKINS, ISADOR LUBIN, AND THE BUREAU OF LABOR STATISTICS. *Monthly Labor Rev. 1980 103(4): 22-30.* Secretary of Labor Frances Perkins's influence on the Bureau of Labor Statistics was evidenced by her initiating a review of the Bureau's statistics and choosing Isador Lubin as Commissioner of Labor Statistics under Franklin Roosevelt's New Deal, both which improved and modernized the Bureau; covers 1920's-40's.

1315. Gould, Allan B. "TROUBLE PORTFOLIO" TO CONSTRUCTIVE CONSERVATION: SECRETARY OF THE INTERIOR WALTER L. FISHER, 1911-1913. *Forest Hist. 1973 16(4): 4-12.* In the aftermath of the Ballinger-Pinchot controversy, President William Howard Taft wisely chose Walter Lowrie Fisher (1862-1935), a progressive Republican and urban reformer, to succeed Secretary of the Interior Richard Achilles Ballinger. Fisher had opposed the administration's policies, but Taft knew he would not yield "to Pinchot and his fanatics." Fisher's conservation philosophy was one of "constructive conservation," a policy of pragmatism and enlightened compromise. By the end of Taft's administration Fisher had restored public confidence in the Interior Department and had influenced future federal resource policies. Based on personal papers, correspondence, newspapers, and secondary sources; 2 illus., 2 photos, 32 notes.   D. R. Verardo

1316. Gould, Lewis L. WESTERN RANGE SENATORS AND THE PAYNE-ALDRICH TARIFF. *Pacific Northwest Q. 1973 64(2): 49-56.* A study of the western range senators' insistence on a tariff on hides and their influence in shaping the final form of the Payne-Aldrich Tariff (1909). The struggle exposed the east-west sectionalism in the Republican Party, and a review of the contest reveals: 1) a monolithic conservative senatorial bloc obscuring economic and personal forces, 2) the centrality of the tariff as an issue for Progressive politics, and 3) the fact that William H. Taft deserves more credit for effective presidential leadership than he has usually received. 43 notes.   R. V. Ritter

1317. Gower, Calvin W. THE STRUGGLE OF BLACKS FOR LEADERSHIP POSITIONS IN THE CIVILIAN CONSERVATION CORPS: 1933-1942. *J. of Negro Hist. 1976 61(2): 123-135.* The efforts of Negroes to gain equal opportunities through leadership positions in the Civilian Conservation Corps were not successful. This experience reflects the general failure of Afro-Americans to obtain significant improvement for themselves during the New Deal. Based on the records of the Civilian Conservation Corps; 24 notes.   N. G. Sapper

1318. Grossman, Jonathan. BLACK STUDIES IN THE DEPARTMENT OF LABOR, 1897-1907. *Monthly Labor Rev. 1974 97(6): 17-27.* Between 1897 and 1903 the Labor Department, in collaboration with

Atlanta University, produced a series of investigations about the condition of blacks in America; but with changed leadership and in a climate of racial strife, the effort had been abandoned by 1907.

1319. Gustafson, Merlin. PRESIDENT HOOVER AND THE NATIONAL RELIGION. *J. of Church and State 1974 16(1): 85-100.* Discusses the extent to which Christianity, specifically Protestantism, was considered the "national religion" in the religious attitudes of President Herbert C. Hoover, 1928-32, emphasizing church and state issues.

1320. Guth, James L. HERBERT HOOVER, THE U.S. FOOD ADMINISTRATION, AND THE DAIRY INDUSTRY, 1917-1918. *Business Hist. Rev. 1981 55(2): 170-187.* The "milk question" during World War I offers a good case study in business and government relations. Herbert C. Hoover as administrator of the Food Administration mediated a three-cornered struggle between producers, distributors, and consumers. At first reluctant to intervene and treating the matter as a problem for local government, Hoover finally settled on limited intervention in selected urban markets in 1918 initially through public fact-finding commissions and then by quiet negotiations between producers and dealers. While Hoover's policy was marked by its ambiguous and inchoate qualities, it did serve the symbolic purpose of both convincing consumers something was being done about high milk prices and fostering more stable producer-distributor relations in the postwar years. Based mainly on federal records and other archival materials; 44 notes.
C. J. Pusateri

1321. Guzda, Henry P. FRANCES PERKINS' INTEREST IN A NEW DEAL FOR BLACKS. *Monthly Labor Rev. 1980 103(4): 31-35.* Discusses Secretary of Labor Frances Perkins's commitment to making blacks' welfare a top priority of the Labor Department, 1933-45.

1322. Guzda, Henry P. LABOR DEPARTMENT'S FIRST PROGRAM TO ASSIST BLACK WORKERS. *Monthly Labor Rev. 1982 105(6): 39-44.* The Division of Negro Economics was formed in 1917 as part of the Department of Labor to recruit black workers for the war effort at the state and local levels, particularly in the Northern industrial cities where the division met with the greatest success; the program ended in 1921 when a new administration and a new head of the Labor Department without interest in promoting equal opportunity employment took over.

1323. Habibuddin, S. M. THEODORE ROOSEVELT'S ATTITUDE TOWARD THE JUDICIARY. *Indian J. of Pol. [India] 1975 9(1): 20-32.* Examines relations between Theodore Roosevelt (in and out of office) and the Supreme Court, 1901-12, and assesses the anti-Courtism of liberal and progressive political groups who favored certain social and economic legislation.

1324. Hall, Alvin L. POLITICS AND PATRONAGE: VIRGINIA'S SENATORS AND THE ROOSEVELT PURGES OF 1938. *Virginia Mag. of Hist. and Biog. 1974 82(3): 331-350.* Examines President Franklin D. Roosevelt's attempt in 1938 to strip Virginia Senators Harry F. Byrd and Carter Glass of federal patronage and give it to anti-Byrd Democrats in Virginia. Byrd and Flood countered with the issue of "Senatorial Courtesy," and the overwhelming support they received in the senate dealt a serious blow to the already diminished prestige of the president. Based on primary and secondary sources; cartoon, 71 notes.
R. F. Oaks

1325. Hall, Tom G. WILSON AND THE FOOD CRISIS: AGRICULTURAL PRICE CONTROL DURING WORLD WAR I. *Agric. Hist. 1973 47(1): 25-46.* Political pressures led the Wilson administration to impose controls on wheat prices in 1917. This policy held prices low enough to keep workers from striking and high enough to provide incentives to farmers. It also showed farmers that government intervention could work in their favor without altering the structure of American agriculture. Based on archival material, Congressional records, and newspapers and magazines; 53 notes.
D. E. Brewster

1326. Harrington, Jerry. SENATOR GUY GILLETTE FOILS THE EXECUTION COMMITTEE. *Palimpsest 1981 62(6): 170-180.* Brief biograhy of Iowa Congressman Guy M. Gillette, focusing on his election in 1932 on the Democratic ticket, his two terms in office from 1933 to 1936, and his election to the Senate in 1936; during the election, Franklin D. Roosevelt campaigned against Gillette and other dissident Democrats who did not wholeheartedly accept the New Deal.

1327. Harris, J. Will. MR. HOOVER AND MR. COOLIDGE—COLLEGE FUND-RAISING IN THE 1920'S. *R. Interamericana R. [Puerto Rico] 1973 3(2): 166-172.* A portion of the memoirs of Dr. J. Will Harris (1876-1956), published under the title *Riding and Roping: The Memoirs of J. Will Harris* (Inter-American U. Press, 1974). Dr. Harris, founder of Inter-American University of Puerto Rico in 1912, spent much of his earlier years soliciting money for his college. He met many of the most important and wealthiest individuals of his day and related their ability to thwart fund raisers such as himself. 9 notes.
J. A. Lewis

1328. Hass, Edward F. DEPRESSION AND NEW DEAL IN URBAN AMERICA. *J. of Urban Hist. 1981 7(4): 507-514.* This review essay covers Sidney Fine's *Frank Murphy: The Detroit Years;* Lyle W. Dorsett's *Franklin D. Roosevelt and the City Bosses;* and Charles H. Trout's *Boston, the Great Depression, and the New Deal.* Political scientists have for some time described the elections of 1928-36 as realigning elections which changed the country from being Republican to Democratic. This basic and sustaining political shift was made possible by the forging of the New Deal coalition of Southern Dixiecrats, unionists and other workers, liberal intellectuals, and Democratic politicians. These works describe the forging of the urban link of the coalition. 6 notes.
T. W. Smith

1329. Hauptman, Laurence M. BIG DEAL? *J. of Ethnic Studies 1981 9(2): 119-123.* Reviews Donald L. Parman's *The Navajos and the New Deal* (1976), Kenneth R. Philp's *John Collier's Crusade for Indian Reform, 1920-1954* (1977), and Graham D. Taylor's *The New Deal and American Indian Tribalism: The Administration of the Indian Reorganization Act, 1934-1945* (1980). Taken together, the works show that "historians have finally begun to take the sizeable Indian criticism of New Deal policies more seriously than in the past," and tend more to agree with those Native Americans who "have looked askance at the . . . legacy of the Collier years."
G. J. Bobango

1330. Hauser, Robert E. "THE GEORGIA EXPERIMENT": PRESIDENT WARREN G. HARDING'S ATTEMPT TO REORGANIZE THE REPUBLICAN PARTY IN GEORGIA. *Georgia Hist. Q. 1978 62(4): 288-303.* When Warren G. Harding won the presidential election of 1920, he began planning to extend the Republican Party in the South, beginning in Georgia. Many members of the two factions in the existing Georgia party refused to unite behind John Louis Philips, Harding's man. This opposition, plus scandal, led to Republican defeat in the congressional election of 1922. Eventually the experiment failed and the old leadership, particularly Henry Lincoln Johnson, returned to power. Primary sources; 56 notes.
G. R. Schroeder

1331. Hawley, Ellis W. HERBERT HOOVER, THE COMMERCE SECRETARIAT, AND THE VISION OF AN "ASSOCIATIVE STATE," 1921-1928. *J. of Am. Hist. 1974 61(1): 116-140.* In the 1920's Hoover sought to expand the Commerce Department as the directing agency of economic development. He believed that efficient government agencies staffed by experts and connected with a multitude of trade associations and volunteer agencies could provide for a flexible response to social problems such as housing and child care and stimulate economic productivity without the coercion of a swollen bureaucracy. The department dealt with informational and promotional activities, sought to stabilize industry, encouraged cooperation with labor in areas such as unemployment and hours, and urged industrial "self-government" to stave off government intervention. The vision was dimmed by the depression but has relevance for those exploring solutions to current problems. 88 notes.
K. B. West

1332. Helmer, William J. THE DEPRESSION DESPERADOS: A STUDY IN MODERN MYTH-MAKING. *Mankind 1975 5(2): 40-46.* Criminals such as John Dillinger spurred the Justice Department and the Federal Bureau of Investigation to modernize and coordinate the efforts of law enforcement agencies in 1933-34.

1333. Hendrickson, Kenneth E. THE NATIONAL YOUTH AD-MINISTRATION IN SOUTH DAKOTA: YOUTH AND THE NEW DEAL, 1935-1943. *South Dakota Hist. 1979 9(2): 130-151.* The National Youth Administration (NYA), between its creation in 1935 and its demise in 1943, provided part-time employment for needy high school and college students and relief work for youth not in school. Although often caught up in political and bureaucratic difficulties, the NYA in South Dakota experienced its greatest success and popularity between 1937 and 1940 under Anna C. Struble as State Youth Director. The NYA program in South Dakota gave assistance and relief to thousands of youngsters and their families and demonstrated that the federal system can work effectively for the welfare of all the people. Primary sources; 6 photos, 35 notes.   P. L. McLaughlin

1334. Hochheiser, Sheldon. THE EVOLUTION OF U.S. FOOD COLOR STANDARDS, 1913-1919. *Agric. Hist. 1981 55(4): 385-391.* Federal regulation of synthetic food colors began after passage of the Food and Drug Act (US, 1906) when the Agriculture Department drew up a short list of dyes known to be safe. This list omitted oil soluble dyes, making it difficult for butter and margarine manufacturers to color their products. After years of tests by the Agriculture Department, four dyes were approved in 1918; but two of them were soon found unsafe and subsequently were withdrawn. Based on government records; 28 notes.
D. E. Bowers

1335. Howard, Vincent W. WOODROW WILSON, THE PRESS, AND PRESIDENTIAL LEADERSHIP: ANOTHER LOOK AT THE PASSAGE OF THE UNDERWOOD TARIFF, 1913. *Centennial Rev. 1980 24(2): 167-184.* Examines Woodrow Wilson's use of publicity and media in demonstrating his strength and leadership in the first major piece of legislation passed in his administration. As a reform measure, the Underwood Tariff seemed assured of passage, given Wilson's access to executive patronage and a Democratic majority in Congress, along with the Progressive Republican support for a reduced tariff. But Wilson took the opportunity to gain national newspaper coverage through his denunciation of lobbyists, delivering his message personally to Congress—a return to a practice last used by John Adams—and making an elaborate ceremony of his signing the bill into law. Thus Wilson, in an episode that lacked real substance, made the most of his opportunity to show a dramatic beginning to his administration and strong presidential leadership. Based largely on coverage of 10 daily newspapers and secondary studies; 28 notes.   A. Hoffman

1336. Ingram, Earl, ed. THE FEDERAL RELIEF ADMINISTRA-TION IN LOUISIANA. *Louisiana Hist. 1973 14(2): 194-201.* Describes and evaluates the more than 500 files of the Louisiana Emergency Relief Administration, 1933-35, located in the Louisiana State Archives. The files are valuable sources of data on relief administration in the state and are categorized under 10 major headings: Administrative (44 files); Individual correspondence (61 files); Correspondence between the central office in New Orleans and city, parish, and district offices (80 files); "Wages and wages committee" of the various parishes (70 files); Local, parish, state, and federal aid (17 files); Agriculture and various farm relief programs (43 files); Transient bureau and transients (29 files); Community cooperatives and self-help agencies (11 files); College student aid (5 files); and Miscellaneous reports.   R. L. Woodward, Jr.

1337. Inouye, Arlene and Susskind, Charles. "TECHNOLOGICAL TRENDS AND NATIONAL POLICY," 1937: THE FIRST MODERN TECHNOLOGY ASSESSMENT. *Technology and Culture 1977 18(4): 593-621.* The 1937 report, begun in 1934 during Franklin D. Roosevelt's administration, was a continuation of efforts of the Herbert C. Hoover administration. "Its goal was to highlight new inventions that might affect living and working conditions in the United States during the following ten to 25 years." 98 notes.   C. O. Smith

1338. Jensen, Billie Barnes. WOODROW WILSON'S INTERVEN-TION IN THE COAL STRIKE OF 1914. *Labor Hist. 1974 15(1): 63-77.* Assesses the factors which caused Woodrow Wilson to intervene with federal troops in the Colorado coal fields strikes of 1914. All parts of the country pressured President Wilson to intervene. His mediation attempts failed, partly as a result of mineowners obstinacy. Union and congressional outcries also increased pressure, while newspapers were generally in favor of sending federal troops. After the "Ludlow Massacre"

pressure became so intense that Governor Elias Ammons finally requested federal intervention, and Wilson ordered troops in. Wilson and Ammons are characterized as men "pushed by the events." Based on the Woodrow Wilson papers in the Library of Congress. 59 notes.
L. L. Athey

1339. Johnson, James P. THE WILSONIANS AS WAR MANAG-ERS: COAL AND THE 1917-18 WINTER CRISIS. *Prologue 1977 9(4): 193-208.* Arguments that Wilsonians were excellent administrators during World War I are not bolstered by a study of government actions regarding the coal supply. Government bureaucrats, led by Fuel Administrator Harry A. Garfield, seriously jeopardized the availability of coal to industrial, business, and consumer interests through actions based on their antagonism toward coal producers, whom they regarded as seeking to unduly profit from the war emergency. A series of administrative blunders based on this attitude toward coal owners led to the Garfield order of 17 January 1918, which for 15 days, caused a cessation of manufacturing east of the Mississippi in order to unsnarl the railroad loading imbroglio and to conserve fuel. The temporary stoppage of manufacturing adversely affected industrial war production, while it did not materially improve the situation concerning the desired goals. In this matter, the Wilsonian administrators revealed a lack of understanding of economic realities and the problems inherent in the incorporation of ideology into government operations. Based on research in National Archives.   N. Lederer

1340. Johnson, Roger T. PART-TIME LEADER: SENATOR CHARLES L. MCNARY AND THE MCNARY-HAUGEN BILL. *Agric. Hist. 1980 54(4): 527-541.* Republican Senator Charles L. McNary of Oregon sponsored the McNary-Haugen bill during the Calvin Coolidge administration, to deal with the problem of farm surpluses by setting up a government board to dispose of surpluses and establish a two-tiered domestic-world price system. McNary, however, showed only moderate interest in the bill and was more willing to compromise its controversial features to meet Coolidge's objections than most of its supporters. After Coolidge twice vetoed the bill, McNary was able to get a weaker version, the Agricultural Marketing Act (US, 1929), signed by President Herbert C. Hoover. The 1929 Act established a Federal Farm Board to assist agricultural cooperatives in stabilizing prices by buying surpluses. Based on McNary's letters and on periodical sources; 35 notes.
D. E. Bowers

1341. Jones, Gene Delon. THE ORIGIN OF THE ALLIANCE BE-TWEEN THE NEW DEAL AND THE CHICAGO MACHINE. *J. of the Illinois State Hist. Soc. 1974 67(3): 253-274.* In 1932, the Chicago political machine had tried to shout down Franklin D. Roosevelt's nomination, but by 1940, Mayor Edward J. Kelly could refer to him as "our beloved President." The "politics of relief" had allied Roosevelt with the bosses, to the dismay of reformers. Kelly's overwhelming mayoral victory in 1935 put him in excellent position to demand a large share of New Deal relief funds for Chicago. It also convinced Roosevelt that machine support was necessary to carry Illinois in 1936. Primary and secondary sources; 2 illus., 3 photos, 76 notes.   L. Woolfe

1342. Kalin, Berkley. YOUNG ABE FORTAS. *West Tennessee Hist. Soc. Papers 1980 (34): 96-100+.* Abe Fortas (b. 1910) had a meteoric rise in the federal government. Ten letters to Hardwig Peres (Memphis attorney, author, and merchant) illustrate Fortas's intelligence, wit, gift of phrase, and varied interests. Peres had helped Fortas get into the Yale Law School in the early 1930's. One of Franklin D. Roosevelt's "bright young men," Fortas was appointed Undersecretary of the Interior in 1942, at age 32. This caused a small storm, and he resigned to enter the military, much against Roosevelt's desires, only to be discharged a month later for medical causes. Letters are from the Mississippi Valley Collection, Memphis State University, Tennessee.
H. M. Parker, Jr.

1343. Kalmar, Karen L. SOUTHERN BLACK ELITES AND THE NEW DEAL: A CASE STUDY OF SAVANNAH, GEORGIA. *Georgia Hist. Q. 1981 65(4): 341-355.* Discrimination plagued lower-class blacks in Savannah during the New Deal programs of the 1930's. Any complaints made to the national Works Progress Administration (W.P.A.) were referred back to the state W.P.A. and were explained away rather than solved. Members of the black elite never supported other blacks in their attempts to gain justice. Based on Works Progress Administration papers; 38 notes.   G. R. Schroeder

1344. Kane, Richard D. THE FEDERAL SEGREGATION OF THE BLACKS DURING THE PRESIDENTIAL ADMINISTRATIONS OF WARREN G. HARDING AND CALVIN COOLIDGE. *Pan-African J. [Kenya] 1974 7(2): 153-171.* Condemns the federal government for its discrimination against black Americans during 1897-1927, particularly those blacks employed by the federal government. Cases of abuse are cited in all administrations during that era. 102 notes.   H. G. Soff

1345. Kelly, Lawrence C. ANTHROPOLOGY AND ANTHROPOLOGISTS IN THE INDIAN NEW DEAL. *J. of the Hist. of the Behavioral Sci. 1980 16(1): 6-24.* The use of anthropological techniques to analyze problems in American society was a product of the late 1920's and the New Deal era. A major stimulus to the development of this "applied anthropology" was a series of projects initiated by John Collier in the Bureau of Indian Affairs beginning in 1935. Four of these experiments, the Applied Anthropology Unit, the Soil Conservation Service experiment on the Navajo reservation, the Technical Cooperation-Bureau of Indian Affairs soil conservation work on other Indian reservations, and the Indian Education, Personality, and Administration Research Project, are the subject of this article.   J

1346. Kelly, Lawrence C. CHOOSING THE NEW DEAL INDIAN COMMISSIONER: ICKES VS. COLLIER. *New Mexico Hist. R. 1974 49(4): 269-284.* Many persons were surprised and some expressed dismay when President-elect Franklin D. Roosevelt in the spring of 1933 appointed two relative unknowns to high positions in the Interior Department. Harold Ickes, a Bull Moose Republican, was named Secretary and John Collier, who had consistently criticized federal Indian policy, was appointed Commissioner of Indian Affairs. The two men were not friends and were critical of each other. Notes.   J. H. Krenkel

1347. Kertman, G. L. BOR'BA V RESPUBLIKANSKOI PARTII SSHA PO VOPROSAM NALOGOVOI POLITIKI (1925-1928) [The struggle in the US Republican Party on tax policy (1925-28)]. *Vestnik Moskovskogo U., Seriia 8: Istoriia [USSR] 1980 (5): 42-55.* Among the Republicans there was a division on the income tax system. Andrew W. Mellon, the Secretary of the Treasury under Calvin Coolidge, wanted to lower taxes to encourage production. The issue of the inheritance tax also became important but a compromise, which retained it, was passed in 1926. By 1927, the growth in the size of the government and governmental expenses, as well as the proposal of agrarian Republicans to establish an agricultural stabilization fund, forced the "Old Guard" and Coolidge to keep the inheritance tax. 76 notes.   D. Balmuth

1348. Kleiler, Frank M. THE WORLD WAR II BATTLES OF MONTGOMERY WARD. *Chicago Hist. 1976 5(1): 19-27.* Discusses Montgomery Ward's Chairman of the Board, Sewell Avery, and his steadfast refusal to comply with arbitration set down by the War Labor Board in an attempt to settle a strike of Ward workers, which led to Franklin Roosevelt's order for US Army troops to seize the Ward plant, 1941.

1349. Koeniger, A. Cash. CARTER GLASS AND THE NATIONAL RECOVERY ADMINISTRATION. *South Atlantic Q. 1975 74(3): 349-364.* The usual view of New Deal liberals calmly carrying out the programs of earlier Progressives is not borne out in the example of Senator Carter Glass' struggle with the National Industrial Recovery Act and its administrative organization, the National Recovery Administration. Glass despised the program and fought it until the Supreme Court ruled it unconstitutional. Glass, like many Progressives, viewed the New Deal not as a reform program building evolutionarily on the past, but rather as a complete break with the past and the beginning of Fascist collectivism. This argument was at the heart of his objections. 38 notes.   V. L. Human

1350. Koeniger, A. Cash. THE NEW DEAL AND THE STATES: ROOSEVELT VERSUS THE BYRD ORGANIZATION IN VIRGINIA. *J. of Am. Hist. 1982 68(4): 876-896.* Modifies two interpretations of President Roosevelt's patronage feud with the Byrd machine in Virginia during the middle and late 1930's: James T. Patterson's *The New*

Deal and the States: Federalism in Transition (1969) and James MacGregor Burns's *Roosevelt: The Lion and the Fox* (1956). Senator Byrd's "organizaton" was even less secure than Patterson claimed it was, but the US Senate viewed Roosevelt's attempt to undermine Byrd's supremacy in Virginia's Democratic Party as an attack on its procedures. Had Roosevelt pressed his attack, as Burns claimed he should have, he might have damaged seriously his leadership ability in Congress. Based on the Harry F. Byrd Papers, the Carter Glass Papers, and the Franklin D. Roosevelt Papers; 74 notes.   T. P. Linkfield

1351. Koerselman, Gary H. SECRETARY HOOVER AND NATIONAL FARM POLICY: PROBLEMS OF LEADERSHIP. *Agric. Hist. 1977 51(2): 378-395.* Herbert C. Hoover, as secretary of commerce, demonstrated more genuine concern for the primary food producers than did the leaders of the dominant farm organizations. Hoover believed that an agricultural policy must be a part of a broader national economic policy that was operational without the McNary-Haugen Act. Primary and secondary sources; 72 notes.   R. T. Fulton

1352. Koistinen, Paul A. C. MOBILIZING THE WORLD WAR II ECONOMY: LABOR AND THE INDUSTRIAL-MILITARY ALLIANCE. *Pacific Hist. R. 1973 42(4): 443-478.* Examines the junior partnership role of organized labor during World War II through agencies such as the War Production Board and the War Manpower Commission. Challenges the theory that big labor became the equal of the business community or the military establishment. War production set records, but industrial unrest increased as the industrial and military complex successfully maintained the status quo. The Roosevelt administration avoided supporting changes not only because they might interfere with the overseas war effort, but also because the administration was committed to preserving the corporate capitalist system. Labor was no match for its opponents. 66 notes.   C. W. Olson

1353. Kozenko, B. D. VUDRO VIL'SON: BURZHUAZNYI REFORMATOR [Woodrow Wilson: bourgeois reformer]. *Voprosy Istorii [USSR] 1979 (4): 133-147.* During his first two years in office, President Woodrow Wilson introduced a number of reforms: the Federal Reserve System and the income tax. Despite his positivist philosophy and respect for American democracy, the progressive content of his political policies was extremely limited. He was a vain and egocentric man, and, as V. I. Lenin noted, his reformism was essentially petit bourgeois and he completely failed to understand class struggle. Covers 1913-21. Secondary sources; 99 notes.   B. Holland

1354. Krueger, Thomas A. NEW DEAL HISTORIOGRAPHY AT FORTY. *R. in Am. Hist. 1975 3(4): 483-488. The New Deal* (Columbus: Ohio State U. Pr., 1975), edited by John Braeman, Robert H. Bremner, and David Brody, is a collection of essays on New Deal topics, volume 1 dealing with New Deal ideology, business, and a wide variety of labor policy, etc., on the national level; volume 2 covering the economic and political reform of the New Deal in state governments in the 1930's and 1940's.

1355. Kruman, Marie W. QUOTAS FOR BLACKS: THE PUBLIC WORKS ADMINISTRATION AND THE BLACK CONSTRUCTION WORKER. *Labor Hist. 1975 16(1): 37-51.* Harold Ickes instituted quotas for hiring skilled and unskilled blacks in construction financed through the Public Works Adminstration (PWA). Resistance from employers and unions was partially overcome by negotiations and implied sanctions. Although results were ambiguous, the plan helped provide blacks with employment, especially among unskilled workers. Based on files of the PWA in the National Archives; tables of compliance, 30 notes.   L. L. Athey

1356. Lambert, C. Roger. HOOVER, THE RED CROSS AND FOOD FOR THE HUNGRY. *Ann. of Iowa 1979 44(7): 530-540.* By 1932 the question of food for hungry Americans had become one of the most controversial issues of the presidency of Herbert C. Hoover. Hoover believed that food relief was the responsibility of local charity organizations aided and supported by local government. This put great pressure upon the American Red Cross. Initially, national leaders of the Red Cross were reluctant to accept responsibility for Depression victims, but public opinion and congressional action eventually forced the organization to assume the broader relief role exemplified by its distribution of surplus wheat in 1932. Hoover's half-hearted acceptance of the surplus wheat distribution damaged his reputation as a humanitarian and helped to "destroy" the Hoover presidency. Primary and secondary sources; 2 photos, 28 notes.   P. L. Petersen

1357. Lambert, C. Roger. THE ILLUSION OF PARTICIPATORY DEMOCRACY: THE AAA ORGANIZES THE CORN-HOG PRODUCERS. *Ann. of Iowa 1974 42(6): 468-477.* Discusses the New Deal efforts under Secretary of Agriculture Henry A. Wallace to create farmer support and involvement in a program to control commodity production. The economic situation was particularly acute in the interrelated hog and corn-growing sector. Iowa farmers created a pressure group under the leadership of Roswell Garst and Donald Murphy, the editor of *Wallaces' Farmer.* They supported production control in return for federal cash assistance, as in the Agricultural Adjustment Act (1933). 31 notes.   C. W. Olson

1358. Lear, Linda J. HAROLD L. ICKES AND THE OIL CRISES OF THE FIRST HUNDRED DAYS. *Mid-America 1981 63(1): 3-17.* Harold L. Ickes, Secretary of the Interior, strove valiantly, but unsuccessfully, March through May 1933 to persuade President Roosevelt and Congress to approve far reaching regulatory legislation to deal with the chaos within the oil industry. Ickes lobbied for the Marland-Caper Bill, which called for strict federal control, yet Roosevelt supported the most general controls. These appeared as an amendment to an industrial recovery bill.   M. J. Wentworth

1359. Lee, Bradford A. THE NEW DEAL RECONSIDERED. *Wilson Q. 1982 6(2): 62-76.* Assesses the economic efficacy of Franklin D. Roosevelt's New Deal; during 1933-38 it had little effect, and in the end alienated business and the Farm Bureau.

1360. Leiter, William M. THE PRESIDENCY AND NON-FEDERAL GOVERNMENT: FDR AND THE PROMOTION OF STATE LEGISLATIVE ACTION. *Presidential Studies Q. 1979 9(2): 101-121.* Discusses the promotion of state legislative action on federal programs from 1933 to 1941 during the presidency of Franklin D. Roosevelt, and compares this to federal promotion of legislative action in a nonfederal sphere in the 1960's and 1970's.

1361. Lepawsky, Albert. THE PLANNING APPARATUS: A VIGNETTE OF THE NEW DEAL. *J. of the Am. Inst. of Planners 1976 42(1): 16-32.* Despite a lack of sophistication in the field of economic planning, the New Deal remains the high watermark of American planning thought and planning practice. This was most apparent in the realm of social and socioeconomic planning, including social security; in the planned use and development of natural resources and the related field of ecologic-environmental planning; in the correlation of national plans with local, state, regional, and international, including strategic, planning; and in the realm of political planning, that is, in the realization of progressive societal values through innovative public policy and adaptive planning technique. In search of a causative explanation for this unique American experience in the use of political intelligence and administrative expertise, the author offers this vignette of the New Deal and its planning apparatus.   J

1362. Lowitt, Richard. HENRY A. WALLACE AND THE 1935 PURGE IN THE DEPARTMENT OF AGRICULTURE. *Agric. Hist. 1979 53(3): 607-621.* Newly published excerpts from Secretary of Agriculture Henry A. Wallace's diary for January and February 1935 which show his position during the purge of the Agricultural Adjustment Administration when Chester Dale fired Jerome Frank and other liberal lawyers in the Office of the General Counsel. The liberals wanted to force cotton planters to keep the same tenants on the land. Also includes three related memoranda. 21 notes.   D. E. Bowers

1363. Lowitt, Richard. THE NEW DEAL. *Pacific Northwest Q. 1977 68(1): 25-30.* Reviews the two-volume work *The New Deal,* edited by John Braeman, et al. (Ohio State U. Pr., 1975). Volume I contains 11 essays covering the effects of New Deal policies on the national level, including impact studies on agriculture, labor, corporate capitalism, fiction, blacks, and the legal profession. Volume II offers 13 articles on New Deal programs at the state and local levels. These assume a political orientation and clearly indicate that the success and failure of Franklin

D. Roosevelt's policies rested on the political forces far below the national level. 4 photos.   M. L. Tate

1364. Lowitt, Richard. "ONLY GOD CAN CHANGE THE SUPREME COURT." *Capitol Studies 1977 5(1): 9-24.* Examines Franklin D. Roosevelt's attempts at reorganization of the judiciary in 1937 and the support, albeit lukewarm, lent by George W. Norris, to get the 75th Congress to yield to Roosevelt's wishes.

1365. Lowitt, Richard. "PRESENT AT THE CREATION": GEORGE W. NORRIS, FRANKLIN D. ROOSEVELT AND THE TVA ENABLING ACT. *East Tennessee Hist. Soc. Publ. 1976 48: 116-126.* Describes the birth of the Tennessee Valley Authority from the resolution introduced by George W. Norris, 9 March 1933, calling for the development of the Tennessee Valley to the naming of the Norris Dam, 1 August 1933. Based on printed sources and the Papers of Franklin D. Roosevelt and George W. Norris; 25 notes.   D. A. Yanchisin

1366. Lucas, Stephen E. THEODORE ROOSEVELT'S "THE MAN WITH THE MUCK-RAKE": A REINTERPRETATION. *Q. J. of Speech 1973 59(4): 452-462.* "An acknowledged landmark of American public address, Theodore Roosevelt's 'The Man with the Muck-Rake' has long resisted adequate interpretation, largely because historians and rhetoricians have not resolved the apparent anomaly between Roosevelt's conservative remarks on journalism and his 'progressive' proposals for economic reform. Examining Roosevelt's rhetorical intentions resolves the anomaly, reveals the thematic unity of the address and explains its meaning as rhetorical action."   J

1367. Lunardini, Christine A. STANDING FIRM: WILLIAM MONROE TROTTER'S MEETINGS WITH WOODROW WILSON, 1913-1914. *J. of Negro Hist. 1979 64(3): 244-264.* William Monroe Trotter met twice with Woodrow Wilson—in November 1913 and in November 1914. Intensification of segregation in the federal bureaucracy, despite Wilson's campaign promises to the contrary, prompted Trotter's concern. Based on the Wilson Collection at Princeton University and the Wilson Papers in the Library of Congress; 13 notes.   N. G. Sapper.

1368. Lunardini, Christine A. and Knock, Thomas J. WOODROW WILSON AND WOMAN SUFFRAGE: A NEW LOOK. *Pol. Sci. Q. 1980-81 95(4): 655-671.* Reinterprets the role of Woodrow Wilson in the passage of the 19th Amendment guaranteeing women the right to vote. Wilson, originally opposed to the amendment, was converted through the efforts of women suffragists and became an advocate of critical importance.   J

1369. Mal'kov, Viktor Leonidovich. GARRI GOPKINS: STRANITSY POLITICHESKOI BIOGRAFII [Harry Hopkins: the pages of political biography]. *Novaia i Noevishaia Istoriia [USSR] 1979 (2): 124-144.* Discusses the life, activity, and ideas of Harry Hopkins, one of the closest advisors to President Franklin D. Roosevelt and the main proponent of the New Deal policies in the United States in the 1930's. Prior to his political career, Hopkins worked for charity organizations in New York and this enabled him to understand the limitations of the system of private monopoly capitalism. After Roosevelt's 1932 victory, he supervised the new administration's policies for alleviation of poverty and unemployment. Hopkins's influence grew but he realized that a mere tinkering with the system produced insignificant results incommensurable with the disastrous products of the great depression. Article to be continued. 82 notes.   V. Sobeslavsky

1370. Marcello, Ronald E. THE SELECTION OF NORTH CAROLINA'S WPA CHIEF, 1935: A DISPUTE OVER POLITICAL PATRONAGE. *North Carolina Hist. R. 1975 52(1): 59-76.* State political issues were involved in Harry Hopkins's selection of a North Carolina Works Progress Administration chief. The Roosevelt administration owed favors to North Carolina's senators, Robert L. Doughton and Josiah Bailey. Doughton and Bailey favored conservative candidates, not wholly committed to the New Deal, and opposed certain liberal political rivals. At the last minute a compromise candidate, George W. Coan, Jr., appeared and was accepted by all factions. Based on interviews, personal papers, newspaper accounts, published government documents, and secondary sources; 6 illus., 61 notes.   T. L. Savitt

1371. Maze, John and White, Graham. HAROLD L. ICKES: A PSY-CHOHISTORICAL PERSPECTIVE. *J. of Psychohistory 1981 8(4): 421-444.* Analyzes the political career of Harold L. Ickes (1874-1952) by studying parental influences mentioned in his diary and autobiography. Ickes was secretary of the Interior Department during 1933-46. He unhappily identified with his mother and somewhat unsuccessfully sought the affection of his father. Politics and religion interested Ickes's mother, whereas his father had suffered an early defeat at an elective office when his son campaigned for him. Ickes later backed many losing politicians, perhaps trying not to "triumph over" his father. Ickes may have unconsciously patterned himself after his mother in his fanatic pride in office, his meticulous honesty, and his childlike devotion to Franklin D. Roosevelt. Based on the diary and autobiography of Harold L. Ickes and the Harold L. Ickes Papers (Library of Congress); 51 notes.

L. F. Velicer

1372. McAndrew, William J. "WEIGHING A WILD-CAT ON THE KITCHEN SCALES": CANADIANS EVALUATE THE NEW DEAL. *Am. Rev. of Can. Studies 1974 4(2): 23-45.* Anti-Americanism, a strong theme in Canadian attitudes toward the United States, shows through in their interpretation of the New Deal, which takes one of two attitudes; disillusionment over Roosevelt's initial rejection of the internationalist option in lieu of stimulating domestic economy, and argument over whether the New Deal actually represented continuity or discontinuity in the overall sweep of American policy, 1930's.

1373. McCoy, Donald R. THE CRUCIAL CHOICE: THE APPOINTMENT OF R. D. W. CONNOR AS ARCHIVIST OF THE UNITED STATES. *Am. Archivist 1974 37(3): 399-413.* The American Historical Association played a major role in President Franklin D. Roosevelt's choice of R. D. W. Connor as first Archivist. Wishing to forestall a political appointment, J. Franklin Jameson of the Library of Congress and AHA President William E. Dodd chose Robert Digges Wimberly Connor of the University of North Carolina as a suitable candidate. Connor received the appointment because of the AHA's support and because his supporters "were better organized to court Roosevelt" than those of the other candidate, Dunbar Rowland of Mississippi. Primary and secondary sources; 32 notes.

J. A. Benson

1374. McDonnell, Janet. COMPETENCY COMMISSIONS AND INDIAN LAND POLICY, 1913-1920. *South Dakota Hist. 1980 11(1): 21-34.* The Department of the Interior, between 1913 and 1920, established several Indian competency commissions to determine which Indians were able to manage their own affairs so that they could be released from government control. The policy, although intended to promote Indian self-support and independence, actually led to their pauperization and the disintegration of the Indian estate. Approximately 20,000 Indians were persuaded or forced to accept deeds of ownership for their land allotments. The government had not relieved itself of its responsibility nor improved the condition of the Indians because most of them sold the land and became destitute. Based on the Major James McLaughlin Papers located at the Assumption Abbey Archives in Richardton, North Dakota, and other primary sources; 3 photos, 38 notes.

P. L. McLaughlin

1375. McFarland, Charles K. and Neal, Nevin E. THE RELUCTANT REFORMER: WOODROW WILSON AND WOMAN SUFFRAGE, 1913-1920. *Rocky Mountain Social Sci. J. 1974 11(2): 33-43.*

1376. McGuire, Phillip. JUDGE HASTIE, WORLD WAR II, AND ARMY RACISM. *J. of Negro Hist. 1977 62(4): 351-362.* William Hastie, the first Afro-American appointed to the federal bench as US District Court Judge for the Virgin Islands (1937-39), left the deanship of the Howard University Law School to serve as a civilian aide to the Secretary of War (1940-43). Although Secretary Henry L. Stimson asked Hastie to be responsible for all black military personnel, most of Hastie's activities related to the US Army. The aide resigned in 1943 in protest against the racism of the military establishment. The integration of the armed forces by executive order in 1948 was the legacy of Hastie's efforts. Based on primary materials in the Library of Congress, National Archives, the Yale University Library, and secondary sources; 34 notes.

N. G. Sapper

1377. McGuire, Phillip. JUDGE HASTIE, WORLD WAR II, AND THE ARMY AIR CORPS. *Phylon 1981 42(2): 157-167.* In October 1940, Secretary of War Henry L. Stimson appointed Judge William Henry Hastie civilian aide to the secretary. He was to locate problems in race relations in the armed services and recommend remedial action. He learned early that this did not include eliminating segregation and discrimination. He refused to remain silent even though his ineffectiveness was a source of constant frustration. In January 1943 he resigned because of the racism and traditionalism which prevented progressive change.

A. G. Belles

1378. McGuire, Phillip. JUDGE WILLIAM H. HASTIE CIVILIAN AIDE TO THE SECRETARY OF WAR, 1940-1943. *Negro Hist. Bull. 1977 40(3): 712-713.* Evaluates William H. Hastie's fight against racism in the armed forces during World War II. Although unable to convince the War Department to integrate the Army, he helped bring about military reform: the admission of Blacks to officer candidate schools, acceptance of Blacks as blood donors, integration of some recreational facilities, the commissioning of black doctors in the Army Medical Reserve, the training of black pilots as heavy bombardment fliers, the participation of black schools in the Air Force enlistment program, and the beginning of experiments with integrated units. Based on the author's unpublished dissertation; photo, note, biblio.

R. E. Noble

1379. Melosi, Martin V. NATIONAL SECURITY MISUSED: THE AFTERMATH OF PEARL HARBOR. *Prologue 1977 9(2): 75-89.* Throughout World War II, the Roosevelt Administration sought to retain absolute secrecy over the circumstances resulting in the Japanese bombing of Pearl Harbor, in order to preserve vital aspects of national security, especially in regard to intelligence operations. The administration attempted to end growing public interest in the matter by casting all blame upon the military commanders on the scene, Admiral Husband E. Kimmel and Major General Walter C. Short, blaming them for failing to take proper precautions to meet the surprise attack. Roosevelt's obfuscation of this issue had the result of generating more public suspicions of the manner in which the war was being conducted and of providing the Republican opposition with a readymade political issue which they were not slow to exploit. Largely based on Congressional hearings and materials in the National Archives.

N. Lederer

1380. Metcalf, Evan B. SECRETARY HOOVER AND THE EMERGENCE OF MACROECONOMIC MANAGEMENT. *Business Hist. R. 1975 49(1): 60-80.* The origins of federal government management of the economy lies in policies developed by Herbert Hoover while he was Secretary of Commerce in the 1920's. His program included the establishment of public employment offices, public works planning, unemployment insurance, and the encouragement of voluntary action on the part of business to stabilize employment and capital investment. Based on Hoover papers, government documents, and secondary sources; 39 notes.

C. J. Pusateri

1381. Michelman, Irving S. A BANKER IN THE NEW DEAL: JAMES P. WARBURG. *Rev. Int. d'Hist. de la Banque [Italy] 1974 8: 35-59.* James P. Warburg, scion of one of the great German Jewish banking houses in the United States, was one of the few Wall Streeters to become part of the FDR administration. Drawn into the frantic preparations to reopen the banks in March 1933, Warburg became a delegate to the World Economic Conference in London, only to resign shortly after his appointment. Roosevelt made it clear that domestic monetary policy could not be compromised by international agreements. Roosevelt's decision to take the United States off the gold standard and to accept legislation which gave him far-reaching power to increase the money supply led Warburg to break with the administration. A successful polemicist and writer, Warburg became associated with the anti-New Deal faction and the Liberty League. Secondary sources; 24 notes.

D. McGinnis

1382. Miller, James Edward. A QUESTION OF LOYALTY: AMERICAN LIBERALS, PROPAGANDA, AND THE ITALIAN-AMERICAN COMMUNITY, 1939-1940. *Maryland Hist. 1978 9(1): 49-71.* Examines the extensive effort of the Roosevelt administration to counter Fascist support among the Italian Americans. Despite massive efforts by the Office of War Information, conservative Italians remained in control of media and Italian fraternal organizations. The fear of fifth column activity was baseless. The entire campaign was led by liberals and illustrates the increasing tendency of liberals to turn to the government to achieve their ends. Based on US archives and secondary sources; 3 illus., 59 notes.   G. O. Gagnon

1383. Miller, John E. PROGRESSIVISM AND THE NEW DEAL: THE WISCONSIN WORKS BILL OF 1935. *Wisconsin Mag. of Hist. 1978 62(1): 25-40.* Uses the controversy surrounding the unsuccessful Wisconsin Works Bill as a means of studying the leadership of Governor Philip F. LaFollette; "the anomalous relationship between the Wisconsin progressives and the New Deal; the effectiveness of President Franklin Delano Roosevelt's strategy in co-opting potential left-wing opposition; and the declining influence of the states within the federal system." 10 illus., 43 notes.   N. C. Burckel

1384. Miller, M. Sammy. WOODROW WILSON AND THE BLACK JUDGE. *Crisis 1977 84(2): 81-86.* Discusses the reappointment of Robert H. Terrell to the municipal bench of the District of Columbia. Although the District Bar Association rated him the best Municipal Court judge, Woodrow Wilson's racist policies and his concern for southern congressmen made his reappointment doubtful. Eventually he was nominated and confirmed in April 1914.

1385. Miscamble, Wilson D. THURMAN ARNOLD GOES TO WASHINGTON: A LOOK AT ANTITRUST POLICY IN THE LATER NEW DEAL. *Business Hist. Rev. 1982 56(1): 1-15.* Thurman W. Arnold headed the Antitrust Division of the Justice Department during 1938-43. He was appointed by Franklin D. Roosevelt, who was not enthusiastic about a vigorous antitrust campaign and who did not expect Arnold to launch one. Roosevelt's attitude toward Arnold's campaign was ambivalent, merely permitting and not supporting it. When the demands of World War II production came into conflict with Arnold's activities, FDR offered, and Arnold accepted, a seat on the US Court of Appeals. FDR's failure to strongly support Arnold was a result of the New Deal's lack of a considered economic program and philosophy in its later years. Based on periodical material and published memoirs; illus., 60 notes.   C. J. Pusateri

1386. Mitchell, Virgil L. THE LOUISIANA UNEMPLOYED AND THE CIVIL WORKS ADMINISTRATION. *Red River Valley Hist. Rev. 1980 5(3): 54-67.* Because federal relief programs instituted in 1932 in Louisiana to offset the effects of the Depression had failed to produce the desired results, President Roosevelt created the Civil Works Administration to aid the destitute through the winter of 1933-34 or until they could be absorbed by the Public Works Administration then being formed.

1387. Morison, Elting E. THEODORE ROOSEVELT APPOINTS A JUDGE. *Massachusetts Hist. Soc. Pro. 1957-60 72: 309-322.* Describes the events leading up to Theodore Roosevelt's appointment of Charles Hough to be a federal judge in the southern district of New York in 1906.

1388. Morrison, Rodney J. FRANKLIN D. ROOSEVELT AND THE SUPREME COURT: AN EXAMPLE OF THE USE OF PROBABILITY THEORY IN POLITICAL HISTORY. *Hist. and Theory 1977 16(2): 137-146.* Uses the historical problem of Roosevelt's attempt to pack the Supreme Court to support Fogel's arguments in favor of quantitative methods for more than economic history. Probability theory shows that Schlesinger's claim for the inevitability of Roosevelt's action was biased, subjective, and erroneous. 6 tables, 26 notes.   D. A. Yanchisin

1389. Mullins, William H. SELF-HELP IN SEATTLE, 1931-1932: HERBERT HOOVER'S CONCEPT OF COOPERATIVE INDIVIDUALISM AND THE UNEMPLOYED CITIZENS' LEAGUE. *Pacific Northwest Q. 1981 72(1): 11-19.* The Unemployed Citizens' League (UCL) of Seattle, Washington, created in 1931, closely paralleled President Herbert C. Hoover's call for voluntary, self-help programs to solve the problems of the Depression. Mayor Robert Harlin agreed with the program and appointed I. F. Dix to coordinate public and private relief efforts. Initial UCL success in creating jobs was shortlived, however, as internal strife, local politics, loss of funding sources, and the leftward turn of UCL leaders undermined its efforts. By the end of 1932 the organization had lost its popular following and its power. Primary sources; 3 photos, 39 notes.   M. L. Tate

1390. Murray, Lawrence L. BUREAUCRACY AND BI-PARTISANSHIP IN TAXATION: THE MELLON PLAN REVISITED. *Business Hist. Rev. 1978 52(2): 200-225.* Disagrees with the traditional portrait of Andrew W. Mellon as an archconservative Secretary of the Treasury who successfully advocated a tax reduction program that primarily benefited his own higher income constituency. The Mellon tax approach would have been the basis of Treasury Department policy even if the Democrats had won the 1920 election, because it was the product of earlier departmental bureaucratic planning and not Mellon's own initiative. Based principally on government documents and private papers; 98 notes.   C. J. Pusateri

1391. Murray, Richard K. THE PRESIDENT UNDER FIRE. *Am. Hist. Illus. 1974 9(5): 32-40.* The Teapot Dome Scandal in the administration of President Warren G. Harding, 1923-24, shook up the Justice Department.

1392. Myhra, David. REXFORD GUY TUGWELL: INITIATOR OF AMERICA'S GREENBELT NEW TOWNS, 1935 TO 1936. *J. of the Am. Inst. of Planners 1974 40(3): 176-188.* "Between 1935 and 1936, the United States Department of Agriculture (USDA) initiated a public housing program that resulted in the construction of planned new communities called Greenbelt Towns. The prime mover behind this effort was Rexford Tugwell. The significance of this idea was his advanced concept of resettling the rural poor in planned towns at the edge of urban areas. Tugwell recognized, earlier perhaps than many of his colleagues, the 'push-pull' tendencies emerging in American society in the 1930s. Arguing that urban growth was inevitable, Tugwell's Greenbelt concept was to demonstrate how housing could be surrounded with a more pleasing environment in order to accommodate the expanding rural to urban migration. In less than two years Tugwell's Resettlement Administration planned and constructed three new communities and litigated a fourth. By all standards, these accomplishments demonstrate an unprecedented speed record for action by a bureaucracy."   J

1393. Nelsen, Clair E. HERBERT HOOVER, REPUBLICAN. *Centennial R. 1973 17(1): 41-63.* Herbert Clark Hoover's political collapse was due largely to his relationship with the Republican party. His failure to affiliate with the Republicans until 1920 and his liberal and internationalist stance affronted the "Old Guard," who opposed his selection as secretary of commerce in 1921. Although Hoover was head of the Republican party after winning the 1928 presidential nomination, he did not become part of it. As president, he often diverged from Republican policy and lost congressional support. Hoover's efforts at governmental intervention during the Depression made him a "transitional figure in American politics between the old and the new ideas of government." He had been elected to maintain the status quo and his failure was "the party's excuse for repudiating him in 1932." 40 notes.   A. R. Stoesen

1394. Nuechterlein, James A. THE POLITICS OF CIVIL RIGHTS: THE FEPC, 1941-46. *Prologue 1978 10(3): 171-191.* Despite his lack of a strong political commitment to civil rights, Roosevelt bent to black pressures in 1941 to establish the Fair Employment Practices Committee through Executive Order 8802. The FEPC had no direct enforcement powers to curb job discrimination in war industries and was therefore forced to rely on other governmental agencies to cancel the war contracts of offenders. The principal weapon of the committee was publicity generated through media exposure of their hearings. Placing the FEPC under the supervision and control of hostile Paul V. McNutt, director of the War Production Board, in 1942 brought tensions between the committee and other government agencies to a head. An explosion resulted from McNutt's cancellation of committee hearings into railroad employment discrimination. Roosevelt was forced to step in, reconstituting the FEPC with a larger budget but still without enforcement powers. Between 1943 and the committee's demise in 1946, the body was under continual Congressional attack from conservative Southern Democrats who ended the FEPC in 1946. Based on research in the National Archives.   N. Lederer

1395. Ohl, John Kennedy. GENERAL HUGH S. JOHNSON AND THE WAR INDUSTRIES BOARD. *Military Rev. 1975 55(5): 35-48.* Describes the efforts of General Hugh S. Johnson to integrate the military and industrial sectors during World War I. As a member of the War

Department General Staff and the War Industries Board, Johnson helped reorganize the Army supply system and educated fellow officers in the need to accept businessmen as partners in mobilization. Primary and secondary sources; 7 illus., 50 notes.   J. K. Ohl

1396. Olson, James S. REHEARSAL FOR DISASTER: HOOVER, THE R.F.C., AND THE BANKING CRISIS IN NEVADA, 1932-1933. *Western Hist. Q. 1975 6(2): 149-161.* Despite the pump priming of millions of dollars by the Reconstruction Finance Corporation into the ailing Nevada banking institutions in the 1932-33 crisis, the bottom fell out of the state's banking structure and its liquid assets were quickly depleted. A state banking holiday failed to relieve the situation and Nevada was in serious difficulty. Nevada's experience was a rehearsal for the national banking crisis at the time of transition from the Herbert C. Hoover to the Franklin D. Roosevelt presidency. It generated some policy change by the Hoover administration, and reinforced the idea that the federal government would have to pour fresh capital into troubled banks. 27 notes.   D. L. Smith

1397. Patenaude, Lionel. VICE PRESIDENT JOHN NANCE GARNER: A STUDY IN THE USE OF INFLUENCE DURING THE NEW DEAL. *Texana 1973 11(2): 124-144.* Explores the impact which John Nance Garner, as vice president, had on New Deal policies; details relations between Garner and Franklin D. Roosevelt, 1933-38. 87 notes.

1398. Pellanda, Anna. GLI ASPETTI MONETARI E CREDITIZI DEL NEW DEAL: RIFLESSI SULLA CONTEMPORANEA REALTÀ ITALIANA [Monetary and financial aspects of the New Deal: their relation to contemporary Italian reality]. *Econ. e Storia [Italy] 1977 24(4): 506-513.* Compares Franklin D. Roosevelt's monetary and financial policy with that of Benito Mussolini, 1922-36. The common aim was for monetary stability. The economist Irving Fisher visited Mussolini in 1927 and Roosevelt in 1933. The economic policies of these political leaders were antiquantitativist, or neo-Keynesian, because their intervention was not merely monetary. From 1925 to 1936 Mussolini made war on private banks. The contemporary American press praised the foundation of the Istituto Mobiliare Italiano (IMI) in 1931 and the Istituto per la Ricostruzione Industriale (IRI) in 1932, which were two instruments of control similar to Roosevelt's Reconstruction Finance Corporation. Secondary sources; 34 notes.   F. Busachi

1399. Phillips, Edward Hake. TEDDY ROOSEVELT IN TEXAS, 1905. *West Texas Hist. Assoc. Year Book 1980 56: 58-67.* Describes President Theodore Roosevelt's celebrated visit to Texas in 1905 for a reunion of his Rough Riders in San Antonio.

1400. Philp, Kenneth R. THE NEW DEAL AND ALASKAN NATIVES, 1936-1945. *Pacific Hist. Rev. 1981 50(3): 309-327.* The Indian Reorganization Act of 1934 delayed social justice for Alaskan Indians, Aleuts, and Eskimos. New Deal policy was to create new reservations, but most Alaskan aborigines were small family groups resident on town lots in villages, lacked tribal cohesiveness, and were Americanized and of mixed blood. The attempt to create reservations failed because of native opposition. Natives received benefits from the Alaska Reorganization Act (US, 1936), but Interior Department inefficiency created problems. The Interior Department's intention to protect the natives' fishing and hunting rights probably erred in failing to obtain the full cooperation of the Congress and the Justice Department. Based on records of the Solicitor's Office, Alaska Native rights, other sources in the National Archives, and other primary sources; 87 notes.   R. N. Lokken

1401. Platschek, Hans. ROOSEVELTS MALER [Roosevelt's painters]. *Frankfurter Hefte [West Germany] 1975 30(7): 49-64.* During the New Deal, thousands of artists were given jobs painting public buildings; the style, which can still be seen on the walls of post offices and courthouses throughout the land, is a heroic, historical one, reminiscent of contemporary Russia's Socialist Realism.

1402. Plesur, Milton. THE REPUBLICAN CONGRESSIONAL COMEBACK OF 1938. Plesur, Milton, ed. *An American Historian: Essays to Honor Selig Adler* (Buffalo: State U. of New York, 1980): 167-182. Causes of the Republican Party's comeback in the congressional elections of 1938 included that party's attempts to unify itself and to shed its reactionary image, dangerous setbacks to the economy starting in

1937, a purge in the Democratic Party, President Franklin D. Roosevelt's ill-fated attempt to remodel the Supreme Court, labor unrest, popular dissatisfaction with contradictions and complexities in the New Deal, and Roosevelt's foundering anti-isolationist foreign policy. The election of 1938 represented not a rejection of the New Deal, however, but a call to moderation in which the Democrats and Roosevelt suffered reverses even as the Republicans began to join them in a trend toward progressivism that would see the election of a Republican president 14 years later. 49 notes. Abridged from *Review of Politics* 1962 24(3): 525-562.   S

1403. Polenberg, Richard. ROOSEVELT, CARTER, AND EXECUTIVE REORGANIZATION: LESSONS OF THE 1930'S. *Presidential Studies Q. 1979 9(1): 35-46.* Lessons pertaining to scientific management, the nature of bureaucracy and the bureaucratic ethos, planning, congressional review, presidential power, and public opinion in executive reorganization learned by the Franklin D. Roosevelt administration during 1937-38 are of value to the Jimmy Carter administration, which seeks similar reforms.

1404. Porter, David. THE BATTLE OF THE TEXAS GIANTS: HATTON SUMNERS, SAM RAYBURN, AND THE LOGAN-WALTER BILL OF 1939. *Texana 1974 12(4): 349-361.* The Logan-Walter Bill would have restricted the power of the executive agencies, thus limiting the power of President Roosevelt's New Deal. Two of the most influential members of the House of Representatives—both from Texas —took different sides in the heated debate on the bill; Hatton Sumners supported the bill and Sam Rayburn opposed the bill. Although the bill passed Congress, Roosevelt vetoed it, and his veto could not be overridden. Based on primary and secondary sources; 22 notes.

B. D. Ledbetter

1405. Powers, Richard Gid. THE ATTORNEY GENERAL AND THE G-MAN: HOLLYWOOD'S ROLE IN HOOVER'S RISE TO POWER. *Southwest Rev. 1977 62(4): 329-346.* Examines the effects of Hollywood films, especially *G-Men* (1935), on J. Edgar Hoover's rise to prominence, and Attorney General Homer Cummings's eclipse; Cummings, not Hoover, had been primarily responsible for the government's success against crime.

1406. Pursell, Carroll W., Jr. GOVERNMENT AND TECHNOLOGY IN THE GREAT DEPRESSION. *Technology and Culture 1979 20(1): 162-174.* The New Deal, in the new agencies it set up and the reports they issued, began with doubts about the good effects of rapid technological change. But by 1940, as exemplified in the Tennessee Valley Authority and the Rural Electrification Administration, it encouraged most citizens to conform to the new technologies, offered some form of special welfare to those who were not benefitted, and "eschewed any serious attempt at national planning." 31 notes.   C. O. Smith

1407. Rader, Frank J. HARRY L. HOPKINS, THE AMBITIOUS CRUSADER: AN HISTORICAL ANALYSIS OF THE MAJOR INFLUENCES ON HIS CAREER, 1912-1940. *Ann. of Iowa 1977 44(2): 83-102.* Examines "leading conditioners" of New Dealer Harry Hopkins's (1890-1946) development from "an ambitious relief administrator into the selfless assistant president of the war years." Discusses Hopkins's family and his formal education at Grinnell College, his progressive views and social work career, the impact of his chronic poor health, his political ambitions, and "the emergency-charged ambiance of the New Deal years." Based on secondary and primary sources, including the Hopkins Papers at the Franklin D. Roosevelt Library; 3 photos, 59 notes.

P. L. Petersen

1408. Raper, Arthur F. THE SOUTHERN NEGRO AND THE NRA. *Georgia Hist. Q. 1980 64(2): 128-145.* Discusses the effect of the National Recovery Administration's wage regulations on Negro labor in the South in 1933-34, including wage differentials between North and South, benefits and disadvantages to Negroes, Negroes' fears, employers' evasion of the rules, and why employees went along with lower wages. This article was written in 1934. Based on fieldwork.

G. R. Schroeder

1409. Reading, Don C. NEW DEAL ACTIVITY AND THE STATES, 1933 TO 1939. *J. of Econ. Hist. 1973 33(4): 792-810.* New Deal per capita federal expenditures varied widely by state and region;

western mountain states received the highest allocations. Percentage of decline in real income, rather than the absolute income of a region, corresponds with New Deal allocations. Regression analysis suggests that New Deal agencies distributed funds in a pattern contributing to relief, recovery, and improved use of natural resources, but not to effect reform by equalizing income. The South, which Roosevelt proclaimed the "Nation's Number One Economic Problem," received the lowest per capita allocations in nearly all programs. Raises questions about political motivations behind the varying allocations and their economic impact. Based on primary and secondary sources; 4 tables, 11 notes, biblio., appendix.
W. R. Hively

1410. Reeves, William D. PWA AND COMPETITIVE ADMINISTRATION IN THE NEW DEAL. *J. of Am. Hist. 1973 60(2): 357-372.* The competitive theory of administration developed by Franklin Delano Roosevelt has often been admired as producing efficiency. In the case of the Public Works Administration (PWA), however, the competition over the size of expenditure, the selection of the administrator, and the appointment of staff at the state level, led to delays and to the ultimate failure of PWA as a recovery instrument. As director of the budget, Lewis Douglas overrode the views of leading senators in reducing appropriations to $3,500,000,000 and in transferring much of that money to other agencies in lieu of their own specific appropriations. The cautious and penurious Harold Ickes won out over the more imaginative Hugh S. Johnson as chief of public works administration. Political competition between rival Democratic state organizations and between Democrats and Progressive Republicans led to delays in implementing PWA efforts on the local level. 60 notes.
K. B. West

1411. Rinn, Fauneil J. PRESIDENT HOOVER'S BAD PRESS. *San Jose Studies 1975 1(1): 32-44.* Lists the factors that contributed to the alienation between Herbert Hoover and the press during his administration.
S

1412. Rison, David. FEDERAL AID TO ARKANSAS EDUCATION: 1933-1936. *Arkansas Hist. Q. 1977 36(2): 192-200.* The depression profoundly affected the Arkansas public schools. As the tax base withered, schools closed and teachers failed to receive salaries. The Federal Emergency Relief Administration (FERA) intervened with financial support to keep schools open. The Arkansas legislature did little to raise money within the state to support education, despite warnings from FERA administrator Harry Hopkins. Hopkins finally suspended relief funds until a state tax law was passed to raise school funds. Based on newspaper accounts and manuscript letters in the National Archives; 25 notes.
T. L. Savitt

1413. Robbins, William G. HERBERT HOOVER'S INDIAN REFORMERS UNDER ATTACK: THE FAILURES OF ADMINISTRATIVE REFORM. *Mid-America 1981 63(3): 157-170.* President Herbert C. Hoover was less interested in Indian affairs than in administrative reform. It was left to Interior Secretary Ray Wilbur and Indian Commissioners Charles J. Rhoads and J. Henry Scattergood to grapple with the failures of allotment alleged in the Meriam Report of 1928. Generally the trio reflected the wishes of the assimilationist Indian Rights Association and Board of Indian Commissioners, and clashed with both John Collier and the American Indian Defense Association, who felt the Indian bureaucracy was weak in defending the Indian from commercial exploitation, and in providing for his material care. The Indian himself was in a measure lost in administrative reorganization and in increasing preoccupation with the Depression. The Hoover and Wilbur Papers; 59 notes.
P. J. Woehrmann

1414. Roberts, George C. WOODROW WILSON, JOHN W. KERN AND THE 1916 INDIANA ELECTION: DEFEAT OF A SENATE MAJORITY LEADER. *Presidential Studies Q. 1980 10(1): 63-73.* Overall Democratic Party relations between Woodrow Wilson and his first Senate leader warrant more extensive examination; John W. Kern, the personification of social justice, backed up Wilson's legislative program. The 1916 Indiana election, with Wilson and Kern electoral partners, clearly illuminates their relationship. It also indicates why Kern lost his bid for reelection. 77 notes.
G. E. Pergl

1415. Rodabaugh, Karl. CONGRESSMAN HENRY D. CLAYTON AND THE DOTHAN POST OFFICE FIGHT: PATRONAGE AND

POLITICS IN THE PROGRESSIVE ERA. *Alabama Rev. 1980 33(2): 125-149.* Examines the spoils system at the local political level through the reform of civil service, and the administrations of William Howard Taft and Woodrow Wilson in order to shed light on the removal of Byron Trammell Dothan, Alabama's postmaster. Trammell had supported Theodore Roosevelt at the 1912 Republican National Convention. Despite the influence of Alabama Congressman Henry D. Clayton, Taft removed Trammell from office, and the spoils systems claimed another victim. Primary sources; 41 notes.
J. Powell

1416. Rosen, Philip T. BROADCASTING: THE POLITICS OF INNOVATION. *Continuity 1981 (3): 51-61.* Examines the government's struggle to regulate a budding radio industry and discusses the actions taken by the Navy Department, the Post Office Department, and the Commerce Department to impose controls on radio broadcasting. Ultimately Secretary of Commerce Herbert C. Hoover was successful in wresting control of radio broadcasting from the navy and post office by exercising licensing power.
W. A. Wiegand

1417. Ross, B. Joyce. MARY MC LEOD BETHUNE AND THE NATIONAL YOUTH ADMINISTRATION: A CASE STUDY OF POWER RELATIONSHIPS IN THE BLACK CABINET OF FRANKLIN D. ROOSEVELT. *J. of Negro Hist. 1975 60(1): 1-28.* Argues that the 1930's rather than the 1960's should be termed the beginning of the "Second Reconstruction" because of the revival of federal support for racial equality. The existence of a so-called New Deal "Black Cabinet" was illustrated by the career of Mary McLeod Bethune with the National Youth Administration (NYA). As Director of the NYA's Division of Negro Affairs, Bethune was a symbol of black aspiration in the earliest years of the "Second Reconstruction." Based on primary sources in the records of the NYA in the National Archives; 39 notes.
N. G. Sapper

1418. Ryan, Halford Ross. ROOSEVELT'S FIRST INAUGURAL: A STUDY OF TECHNIQUE. *Q. J. of Speech 1979 65(2): 137-149.* In his first inaugural speech, Franklin D. Roosevelt (1882-1945) three times reworked a text by Raymond Moley. His changes tended to strengthen three major rhetorical devices: scapegoating, military metaphor, and a carrot-and-stick approach to Congress. His techniques parallel those of Hitler, but Roosevelt never sought the dictatorial power achieved by the German leader. Primary and secondary sources; 91 notes.
E. Bailey

1419. Ryan, Halford Ross. ROOSEVELT'S FOURTH INAUGURAL ADDRESS: A STUDY OF ITS COMPOSITION. *Q. J. of Speech 1981 67(2): 157-166.* The author clarifies the confusion about the authorship of Franklin D. Roosevelt's fourth inaugural, and studies the speech drafts to determine which thoughts were his and which were contributed by speechwriters.
J

1420. Sadler, Charles. "POLITICAL DYNAMITE": THE CHICAGO POLONIA AND PRESIDENT ROOSEVELT IN 1944. *J. of the Illinois State Hist. Soc. 1978 71(2): 119-132.* Considers the creation and operation of the Polish-American Congress, founded by moderate groups in Buffalo, New York, to rally support for an independent Poland. National in membership and headquartered in Chicago, the Congress was treated deferentially by Franklin D. Roosevelt and some ethnic-minded officials in industrial states, but failed in the end to influence foreign policy. Based on Congress documents, State Department files, and Polish-American newspapers; 3 illus., map, 63 notes.
J

1421. Salmond, John A. POSTSCRIPT TO THE NEW DEAL: THE DEFEAT OF THE NOMINATION OF AUBREY W. WILLIAMS AS RURAL ELECTRIFICATION ADMINISTRATOR IN 1945. *J. of Am. Hist. 1974 61(2): 417-436.* In January 1945, Franklin D. Roosevelt nominated Alabama-born Aubrey W. Williams to be director of the Rural Electrification Administration. Williams had had experience as a social worker and relief administrator for several New Deal agencies, and was recognized as a capable administrator. However, his identification with the poor and the black incurred the opposition of right wing Republicans and Democrats such as Senator Kenneth McKellar, who accused him of Communist sympathies. Williams' forthright defense of racial equality in employment merited the animosity of bigots like Senator Theodore G. Bilbo, while liberal Republicans, under pressure for supporting Henry Wallace's nomination as Secretary of Commerce, sought to prove party loyalty by opposing Williams. The alignment of forces foreshadowed difficulties for the liberal programs of President Truman and point up the importance of domestic politics during World War II. 83 notes.   K. B. West

1422. Saloutos, Theodore. NEW DEAL AGRICULTURAL POLICY: AN EVALUATION. *J. of Am. Hist. 1974 61(2): 394-416.* An analysis of the manifold aspects of New Deal farm policy demonstrates that efforts of the first Agricultural Adjustment Administration to raise prices to parity were not very successful, that acreage reduction was countered by expansion of yield per acre, that relatively few acres of crop land subject to erosion were in fact covered by plans of the Soil Conservation Service, and that the concept of the second AAA's "ever normal granary" did develop reserves and seemed to operate successfully. In spite of the "agricultural establishment," more was done for tenant farmers, sharecroppers, and farm laborers than is commonly supposed. On the whole, the New Deal constituted "the greatest innovative epoch in the history of American agriculture." 72 notes.   K. B. West

1423. Sargent, James E. FDR AND LEWIS W. DOUGLAS: BUDGET BALANCING AND THE EARLY NEW DEAL. *Prologue 1974 6(1): 33-43.* Analyzes why the personal, political, and policymaking relationships of President Franklin D. Roosevelt and Lewis W. Douglas, director of the budget, changed and deteriorated during 1933-34. "In terms of their policy relationship, Douglas believed that the government must consistently adhere to orderly spending and economizing on the grounds that maintaining United States credit superseded and buttressed the entire recovery program. . . ." The president's "halfway commitments prevented him from determining whether he or Douglas was right about the federal government's capacity to spend America into prosperity during peacetime." Douglas' resignation was accepted on 30 August 1934.
                                                    D. D. Cameron

1424. Sargent, James E. ROOSEVELT'S ECONOMY ACT: FISCAL CONSERVATISM AND THE EARLY NEW DEAL. *Congressional Studies 1980 7(2): 33-51.* Analyzes the origins and decline of Franklin D. Roosevelt's fiscal conservatism as embodied in the Economy Act (US, 1933).

1425. Schacht, John N. THE DEPRESSION AND AFTER. *Palimpsest 1982 63(1): 12-29.* Examines the expertise and opinions of President Herbert C. Hoover, United Mine Workers President John L. Lewis, Secretary of Agriculture Henry A. Wallace, and New Deal administrator and presidential advisor Harry Hopkins.

1426. Schnell, J. Christopher. NEW DEAL SCANDALS: E. Y. MITCHELL AND F. D. R.'S COMMERCE DEPARTMENT. *Missouri Hist. R. 1975 69(4): 357-375.* Assistant Secretary of Commerce Ewing Young Mitchell worked to eliminate corruption and to streamline the four agencies under his direction to reduce waste and the number of political appointees. He ran afoul of the president when his investigations brought in some damning evidence against Boss Thomas J. Pendergast of Kansas City. Franklin D. Roosevelt was not a true Progressive. Although he had crusaded against big city machines, FDR refused to support Mitchell's fight against one of his most productive allies. The same story was repeated in other cities where FDR sacrificed Progressive principles in favor of seeking aid from political machines. Based on primary and secondary sources; illus., 42 notes.   W. F. Zornow

1427. Schön, Donald A. PUBLIC SERVICE ORGANIZATIONS AND THE CAPACITY FOR PUBLIC LEARNING. *Int. Social Sci. J. [France] 1979 31(4): 682-695.* Focusing on the Works Progress Administration (WPA), examines how public service organizations implement and sometimes change the public policy they are designed to follow.

1428. Schwartz, Bonnie Fox. NEW DEAL WORK RELIEF AND ORGANIZED LABOR: THE CWA AND THE AFL BUILDING TRADES. *Labor Hist. 1976 17(1): 38-57.* The Civil Works Administration, a first attempt at work relief, faced immediate problems of hiring and wage practices in their relationship to the American Federation of Labor's building trades. Under the leadership of John Carmody federal regulations attempted to protect labor's right to organize and uphold the prevailing wage rates, while mollifying the opposition of local employers.

The CWA provided a "first forum" to alleviate organized labor's suspicions of work relief. Based on the CWA papers and the oral memoir of John Carmody; 41 notes.   L. L. Athey

1429. Sears, James M. BLACK AMERICANS AND THE NEW DEAL. *Hist. Teacher 1976 10(1): 89-105.* A discussion of black support for Franklin D. Roosevelt and the New Deal. Blacks, disenchanted with the Hoover administration, anticipated inclusion in New Deal efforts to create jobs for the unemployed. Blacks benefitted from the New Deal in perhaps greater measure than they had anticipated. Without specifically committing himself, Roosevelt gave black Americans a stake in the governmental process. Black political and religious leaders, the black press and organizations, and Roosevelt's charisma helped place Negroes firmly in the Democratic party. Based on primary and secondary sources; 63 notes, biblio.   P. W. Kennedy

1430. Seltzer, Alan L. WOODROW WILSON AS "CORPORATE LIBERAL": TOWARD A RECONSIDERATION OF LEFT REVISIONIST HISTORIOGRAPHY. *Western Pol. Q. 1977 30(2): 183-212.* Examination of Woodrow Wilson's opposition to artificial combination, the Justice Department's antitrust prosecutions, Wilson's foreign trade policies, and his speeches on foreign trade reveals that Wilson supported vigorous antitrust policy, contrary to left revisionist interpretations.

1431. Severn, John K. and Rogers, William Warren. THEODORE ROOSEVELT ENTERTAINS BOOKER T. WASHINGTON: FLORIDA'S REACTION TO THE WHITE HOUSE DINNER. *Florida Hist. Q. 1976 54(3): 306-318.* Most white southerners, including Floridians, condemned Theodore Roosevelt for inviting Booker T. Washington to a White House dinner. They felt that blacks should not be denied legal rights, but were not entitled to social equality. Roosevelt never made a public apology and, indeed, continued to rely on Washington's advice. Washington did not discuss the event publicly, but the incident tended to strengthen his position among blacks. Based mainly on newspaper accounts; 46 notes.   P. A. Beaber

1432. Sherfy, Marcella M. THE NATIONAL PARK SERVICE AND THE FIRST WORLD WAR. *J. of Forest Hist. 1978 22(4): 203-205.* The National Park Service, established in 1916, faced a severe threat during World War I. The nation wanted access to the natural resources of individual parks, and Congress was reluctant to appropriate money needed for the protection and administration of parks. But Director Stephen T. Mather and especially Assistant Director Horace M. Albright charmed Congress and waged a vigorous campaign to attract tourists to parks ("See America First"), thus overcoming the crisis and laying the groundwork for an expanded and more secure park system and agency in subsequent years. Part of a theme issue on forestry and the World War I era. 2 illus.   R. J. Fahl

1433. Sivachev, N. V. NA 96-M S'EZDE AMERIKANSKOI ISTORICHESKOI ASSOTSIATSII [96th meeting of the American Historical Association]. *Voprosy Istorii [USSR] 1982 (5): 151-158.* Reviews proceedings of this annual meeting, held in Los Angeles 28-30 December 1981, and describes American reactions to Soviet papers by I. P. Dement'ev et al. on the US two-party system and by N. V. Sivachev on inter- and intra-party changes under President Franklin D. Roosevelt. While conceding the highly professional character of the Soviet studies, American historians disagreed with some theoretical and methodological postulates and noted basic differences between the Soviet (materialistic) and American (cultural) approaches to history. 8 notes.   N. Frenkley

1434. Sivachev, N. V. "NOVYI KURS" F. RUZVEL'TA [The Roosevelt New Deal]. *Voprosy Istorii [USSR] 1981 (9): 45-63.* A survey of the main trends of American historiography on the New Deal that analyzes the economic, social, and political aspects of the New Deal policy as a process of the development of US monopoly capitalism into state-monopoly capitalism. The reforms in industry, agriculture, finance, labor relations, unemployment relief, and the introduction of the social security system are discussed. Reveals the role of the working class and democratic forces in winning social legislation, analyzes political struggle and the substantial changes in the two party system in the second half of the 1930's.   J

1435. Sivachev, N. V. RABOCHAIA POLITIKA PRAVI-TEL'STVA SSHA V NACHALE VTOROI MIROVOI VOINY (SEN-TIABR' 1939 G.-DEKABR' 1941 G.) [The labor policy of the US government at the beginning of World War II, September 1939-December 1941]. *Vestnik Moskovskogo U., Seriia 9: Istoriia [USSR] 1971 26(6): 18-37.* During this 27-month period the liberal-progressive labor policy of the 1930's (Wagner Act, etc.) began a reactionary shift led by Congressman Smith of Virginia. The large corporations sought strict limitations on the rights of labor unions, all in the interest of national defense. The National Labor Relations Board was instituted to handle disputes. When strikes continued to occur, President Franklin D. Roosevelt called out military forces on two occasions to work in defense-related industries in the absence of striking workers. In 1940 the National Defense Advisory Commission (NDAC) and in 1941 the Office of Production Management (a branch of the NDAC) were created. By 7 December 1941, the reactionary forces had won. 106 notes.   G. E. Munro

1436. Skocpol, Theda and Finegold, Kenneth. STATE CAPACITY AND ECONOMIC INTERVENTION IN THE EARLY NEW DEAL. *Pol. Sci. Q. 1982 97(2): 255-278.* Discusses the failure of the National Recovery Administration and the relative success of the Agricultural Adjustment Administration (AAA) in the 1930's, to underline the greater capacity of the US government to intervene in the agricultural, rather than in the industrial, economy. Both administrations promised much during the early New Deal, but only the goals of the AAA were attainable. 75 notes.   J. Powell

1437. Smith, Brian Lee. THEODORE ROOSEVELT VISITS OKLAHOMA. *Chronicles of Oklahoma 1973 51(3): 263-279.* Recounts Theodore Roosevelt's visits to Oklahoma during 1900-12, describing his relationship to the issue of Oklahoma statehood and the local Progressive Party.   S

1438. Smith, Elaine M. MARY MCLEOD BETHUNE AND THE NATIONAL YOUTH ADMINISTRATION. Deutrich, Mabel E. and Purdy, Virginia C., ed. *Clio Was a Woman: Studies in the History of American Women* (Washington, D.C.: Howard U. Pr., 1980): 149-177. The National Youth Administration existed during 1935-44 primarily to assist youth aged 16 to 24 in getting work. Mary McLeod Bethune persuaded the agency to recognize Negro leadership both by expanding the Office of Negro Affairs and by employing black administrative assistants in more than 25 states. Under her aegis, too, it addressed blacks' needs notably through the Special Graduate and Negro College Fund. She also promoted a policy which assured blacks the same defense training and placement opportunities as whites. A discussion summary follows. 107 notes.   J. Powell

1439. Snyder, J. Richard. HOOVER AND THE HAWLEY-SMOOT TARIFF: A VIEW OF EXECUTIVE LEADERSHIP. *Ann. of Iowa 1973 41(7): 1173-1189.* Evaluates Herbert Hoover's executive leadership during consideration of the Hawley-Smoot Tariff of 1930.   S

1440. Spencer, Thomas T. THE AIR MAIL CONTROVERSY OF 1934. *Mid-America 1980 62(3): 161-172.* The 1934 air and ocean mail contracts controversy involved the Hoover administration's award of contracts to private air carriers without competitive bids. A congressional resolution, passed before Franklin D. Roosevelt took office in March 1933, set up a special Senate investigation committee led by Hugo Black. The Black committee began public hearings in January 1934; and the Post Office Department began its own investigation leading to Postmaster General James A. Farley's decision to cancel the existing contracts in February 1934. The US Army Air Corps handled the mail amid much criticism. By the end of March 1934 the administration had decided to return airmail to private contractors until Congress could write new legislation. Roosevelt failed to follow the cancellation order with reform proposals, yet his actions did point out the shift toward greater government regulation in the 1930's. Based on previously unused manuscript records such as the United States Senate, 74th Congress, Special Committee to Investigate Air Mail and Ocean Mail Contracts.   M. J. Wentworth

1441. Stratton, David H. TWO WESTERN SENATORS AND TEA-POT DOME: THOMAS J. WALSH AND ALBERT B. FALL. *Pacific Northwest Q. 1974 65(2): 57-65.* Both Albert B. Fall, an intensely partisan Republican, and Thomas J. Walsh, an equally partisan Democrat, were molded and shaped in frontier environments, with western ideas about conservation and public lands. However, Fall "always remained an unredeemed 19th-century exploiter," but "Walsh was a man who combined party loyalty with a strict personal morality." Moreover, Fall "viewed government as a sort of concurrent majority of special interests with himself as their minister plenipotentiary." Walsh, as chairman of the senatorial committee investigating Teapot Dome oil leases, thoroughly and relentlessly followed every shred of evidence "which finally opened up the case revealing Edward L. Doheny and Harry F. Sinclair as the source of Fall's new-found affluence." Fall became the first US cabinet member to close his career in prison, while Walsh became nationally famous. 40 notes.   R. V. Ritter

1442. Strong, Elizabeth. SCIENCE AND THE EARLY NEW DEAL: 1933-1935. *Synthesis 1982 5(2): 44-63.* In the summer of 1933 President Roosevelt created a Science Advisory Board, made up of university and industrial scientists, with Karl Compton as chairman, to study technical problems of governmental agencies. The board responded to requests from several agencies. It also developed a proposal for a Recovery Program for Science, requesting funds to support research as a background for public works and to relieve unemployment among scientists. This proposal aroused sharp opposition, and the board was terminated in 1935. Its assigned duties were turned over to the National Academy of Science. Mainly secondary sources; 67 notes.   M. M. Vance

1443. Swain, Martha H. THE LION AND THE FOX: THE RELATIONSHIP OF PRESIDENT FRANKLIN D. ROOSEVELT AND SENATOR PAT HARRISON. *J. of Mississippi Hist. 1976 38(4): 333-359.* Describes the development (1928-37), cooling (1937-39), and renewal (1938-41) of the political friendship of Franklin D. Roosevelt and Mississippi Democratic Senator Pat Harrison, chairman of the powerful Committee on Finance. Harrison's problems with Roosevelt stemmed partly from policy disagreements, especially on taxation, and partly from the President's personality and methods. "In dealing with another master strategist . . . FDR often met his match." Based on primary sources, especially newspapers and the papers of Harrison and Roosevelt; 67 notes.   J. W. Hillje

1444. Syrett, John. ROOSEVELT VS. FARLEY: THE NEW YORK GUBERNATORIAL ELECTION OF 1942. *New York Hist. 1975 56(1): 51-81.* Examines the 1942 gubernatorial election that marked the end of Democratic Party solidarity in New York state politics. Anti-Roosevelt forces, led by James A. Farley, split the state party and guaranteed the election of Republican Thomas E. Dewey. President Franklin D. Roosevelt, although concerned about the New York election, failed to provide adequate leadership for pro-Roosevelt forces desiring a stronger Democratic candidate for governor than Farley-backed John J. Bennett, Jr. 5 illus., 59 notes.   R. N. Lokken

1445. Szasz, Ferenc M. WHEELER AND HOLY CROSS: COLORADO'S "LOST" NATIONAL MONUMENTS. *J. of Forest Hist. 1977 21(3): 133-144.* The Antiquities Act (1906) "was one of the most significant conservation measures of the entire Progressive era." Theodore Roosevelt used it to establish 17 national monuments, including Wheeler National Monument in 1908. It had been recommended for monument status by forest supervisor Frank C. Spencer. In 1919 Father Joseph Carrigan helped organize the Holy Cross Association, and Herbert Hoover designated Holy Cross Mountain a national monument in 1929. Both were declassified in 1950, Wheeler because of its inaccessibility and Holy Cross because it had never attracted the anticipated interest of Christians. Based on documents in the US Forest Service Archives, Denver, and on primary and secondary sources; 4 illus., 57 notes.   F. N. Egerton

1446. Tarter, Brent. "ALL MEN ARE EQUAL BEFORE FISHES": HERBERT HOOVER'S CAMP ON THE RAPIDAN. *Virginia Cavalcade 1981 30(4): 156-165.* Details Herbert C. Hoover's motives for establishing a presidential retreat on the headwaters of the Rapidan River in Virginia in 1929, traces Camp Rapidan's history and offers a parallel by discussing briefly a similar country refuge from the pressures of Washington, D.C., life founded by President Franklin D. Roosevelt at Camp David.

1447. Taylor, Graham D. ANTHROPOLOGISTS, REFORMERS, AND THE INDIAN NEW DEAL. *Prologue 1975 7(3): 151-162.* Bureau of Indian Affairs Commissioner John Collier has been considered as one of the New Deal administrators who applied social sciences principles to the federal government for the first time. However, his analysis of Indian culture was prescriptive rather than descriptive. Collier was not completely successful in his reversal of previous policies aimed at assimilating Indians into white society. Anthropologists who shared his reformist commitment to preserve traditional cultures functioned effectively in the bureaucracy; those committed to professional academic standards and current methodology encountered hostility. The hypothesis of conflict between old-line administrators and young reformers is simplistic and inaccurate. Based on primary and secondary sources; 2 photos, 51 notes.
                                                                    W. R. Hively

1448. Taylor, Graham D. THE TRIBAL ALTERNATIVE TO BUREAUCRACY: THE INDIAN'S NEW DEAL, 1933-1945. *J. of the West 1974 13(1): 128-156.* A critical analysis of the steps taken under the new Commissioner of Indian Affairs, John Collier, to change what had become "a frightening example of an arrogant, corrupt, and undirected bureaucracy" that left the Indians "mired in poverty and despair." Proponents of the New Deal saw the Indian tribes as a convenient "laboratory" for experimenting with planned political and economic development. Although Collier attempted "a genuine and farsighted effort to bridge a cultural chasm and allow the Indians to build a new society on the foundations of traditional institutions," the reorganization foundered on the lack of understanding of Indian tribal and political patterns and the great variety represented. The result was "a revival of bureaucratic control and Congressional exploitation." 54 notes.
                                                                    R. V. Ritter

1449. Turnbaugh, Roy. THE FBI AND HARRY ELMER BARNES: 1936-1944. *Historian 1980 42(3): 385-398.* The Federal Bureau of Investigation's investigation of historian, reformer, and political commentator Harry Elmer Barnes from 1936 to 1944 reveals much about the motives and priorities of that organization. Initially, Barnes was branded by the FBI as an enemy for his criticism of that agency's failure to pursue organized crime. His opposition to America's entry into World War II before Pearl Harbor and his growing alienation from the Roosevelt administration kept alive the agency's interest in his activities. An ill-considered speech in October 1942 before the Rotary Club in Utica, New York, allowed the FBI to take its revenge by trying to brand him as a seditionist; yet he was not prosecuted in the Sedition Trial of 1944. The entire Barnes affair was more than simply FBI chief J. Edgar Hoover's animosity toward Barnes. In essence, Hoover's attitudes toward hostile criticism had so pervaded the Bureau by 1936 that relatively obscure speeches drew tremendous attention. Primary sources; 44 notes.
                                                                    R. S. Sliwoski

1450. Valerina, A. F. POLITICHESKAIA BOR'BA V SSHA V 1937G. VOKRUG PROEKTA REOFRMY VERKHOVNOGO SUDA [The political struggle in the United States in 1937 over the plan to reform the Supreme Court]. *Vestnik Moskovskogo U., Seriia 8: Istoriia [USSR] 1978 (4): 36-54.* President Franklin D. Roosevelt's plan to reform the Supreme Court caused severe struggles in every stratum of American society and cast its shadow on the latter years of the New Deal. The conservative majority in the Supreme Court, and the conservatives in both parties in Congress, wished to prevent the federal government from interfering in state politics. Strengthened by an election victory in 1936, Roosevelt set about limiting the Court's powers. His proposals were not unconstitutional, nor were they without precedent. Attacks on the reform were based on conservative fears that it might just be the prelude to more radical developments. Defeated, the President felt that he had won the war; however, a neoconservatism was developing which was to have a great effect on American politics after World War II. Based on the Congressional Record and on published documents and secondary sources; 144 notes.
                                                                    D. N. Collins

1451. Vaughn, Stephen. FIRST AMENDMENT LIBERTIES AND THE COMMITTEE ON PUBLIC INFORMATION. *Am. J. of Legal Hist. 1979 23(2): 95-119.* The Committee on Public Information, created on 13 April 1917 to create propaganda for the federal government during World War I, became involved with censorship. Topics include the work of publicist Arthur Bullard, who was responsible for its creation, cabinet discussions and congressional debates, the role of its executive head,

George Creel, and his relationship with the Wilson administration and the press, the problem of liberalism, and conflicting historiographical interpretations. 84 notes.
                                                                    L. A. Knafla

1452. Ward, Robert D. and Brogdan, Frederick W. THE REVOLT AGAINST WILSON: SOUTHERN LEADERSHIP AND THE DEMOCRATIC CAUCUS OF 1920. *Alabama Hist. Q. 1976 38(2): 144-157.* Discusses President Woodrow Wilson's struggle for military training before the war and particularly his struggle in 1920 to maintain universal military training and a 500,000-man army. Views his defeat on this issue as more important than the loss of the League of Nations. 37 notes.
                                                                    E. E. Eminhizer

1453. Warren-Findley, Jannelle. MUSICIANS AND MOUNTAINEERS: THE RESETTLEMENT ADMINISTRATION'S MUSIC PROGRAM IN APPALACHIA, 1935-37. *Appalachian J. 1979-80 7(1-2): 105-123.* Led by left-winger Charles Seeger of the Composers' Collective in New York City, the New Deal Resettlement Administration's music program in Appalachia intended "to integrate music, participation in the arts, and political education into a coherent whole which would enable resettled farmers, unemployed miners, impoverished lumbermen, and their families to take control of their own lives and situations."

1454. Weiss, Stuart. LEO T. CROWLEY: PRAGMATIC NEW DEALER. *Mid-America 1982 64(1): 33-52.* Recounts the public career of Leo T. Crowley, especially in Franklin D. Roosevelt's administration, 1934-45. Crowley came from a business, banking, and political advisory background in Wisconsin, loyally served Roosevelt as head of the Federal Deposit Insurance Corporation, as Alien Property Custodian, and as an expert on upper Midwest politics among other jobs. Roosevelt resisted, or ignored, persistent criticism of Crowley, centering on his private banking operations. When Roosevelt died, Crowley lost his political support, and President Truman allowed Crowley's positions either to expire or did not reappoint him. More sources are needed to write a definitive analysis of this New Dealer who sought historical obscurity. Based partly on the Crowley Papers and the Roosevelt Papers; 102 notes.
                                                                    P. J. Woehrmann

1455. Whitaker, W. Richard. HARDING: FIRST RADIO PRESIDENT. *Northwest Ohio Q. 1973 45(3): 75-86.* Warren G. Harding (1865-1923) best summarized his attitude toward radio when he said that it was an excellent way to bring the government closer to the people and the people closer to the government and to those temporarily charged with official responsibility. KDKA in Pittsburgh broadcast election returns in 1920, Harding's inaugural was broadcast in 1921, a radio greeting was beamed to 28 countries on 5 November 1921, and Harding's address on 11 November 1921 at the entombment of the Unknown Soldier was broadcast in New York and San Francisco. In 1923 a number of his speeches during the fatal trip to Alaska and the Far West were broadcast. A complex system of telephones and telegraphs kept him in touch with the public while he was in the continental United States; wireless radio kept him in touch in Alaska. Based on articles, books, and the Harding Papers in the Ohio Historical Society; 33 notes.
                                                                    W. F. Zornow

1456. Wilcox, Marguerite Bone. [1923 PRESIDENTIAL VISIT TO ALASKA]. *Alaska J. 1973 3(4): 194-203.*
A PRESIDENT VISITS ALASKA, *pp. 194-198.*
PRESIDENTIAL VISIT, 1923, *pp. 199-203.*
Discusses President Warren G. Harding's visit to Alaska in 1923.

1457. Williams, David. "THEY NEVER STOPPED WATCHING US": FBI POLITICAL SURVEILLANCE, 1924-1936. *UCLA Hist. J. 1981 2: 5-28.* Demonstrates that during 1924-36 Federal Bureau of Investigation Director J. Edgar Hoover violated a restriction on surveillance activities imposed by Attorney General Harlan Fiske Stone. Although Hoover officially declared that the FBI was not interested in political opinions protected by law, he continued to direct political surveillance activities until 1936, when President Franklin Roosevelt approved an expansion of the FBI's function. Hoover justified surveillance in the name of national security. The American Civil Liberties Union, Trade Union Education League, and mass political demonstrations attracted Hoover's attention. Only a vigilant Congress can prevent such constitutional abuses, by adopting an FBI charter prohibiting such surveillance and holding the agency accountable for its actions. Primary and secondary sources; 53 notes.
                                                                    A. Hoffman

1458. Wilson, Joan Hoff. HOOVER'S AGRICULTURAL POLICIES, 1921-1928. *Agric. Hist. 1977 51(2): 335-361.* Herbert C. Hoover was one of the few public figures of the 1920's who anticipated the conflict of a domestic farm policy with the promotion of unlimited economic expansion. He tried to bring farm production in line with what he overestimated to be an ever-increasing domestic demand. As such he has been much misunderstood by historians. Primary and secondary sources; 56 notes.   R. T. Fulton

1459. Winfield, Betty Houchin. F. D. R.'S PICTORIAL IMAGE, RULES AND BOUNDARIES. *Journalism Hist. 1978-79 5(4): 110-114.* Studys Franklin D. Roosevelt's photographic image during the 1930's, as it was controlled by certain rules and guidelines designed not to show his physical handicap.

1460. Winfield, B. H. FRANKLIN D. ROOSEVELT'S EFFORTS TO INFLUENCE THE NEWS DURING HIS FIRST TERM PRESS CONFERENCES. *Presidential Studies Q. 1981 11(2): 189-199.* Examination of the record number of press conferences held during Franklin D. Roosevelt's first term as president, 1933-37, reveals specific tactics used to control information about himself and his administration. He used the press as a conduit for accurate information to the public and for making his assignment an important one. Roosevelt managed the flow of information by planting questions and also by his own personality. Even when the press became his adversary, he used it more than it abused him. This control shows one aspect of his great political skill. Primary sources; 115 notes.   A. Drysdale

1461. Winfield, Betty Houchin. MRS. ROOSEVELT'S PRESS CONFERENCE ASSOCIATION: THE FIRST LADY SHINES A LIGHT. *Journalism Hist. 1981 8(2): 54-55, 63-70.* Discusses Eleanor Roosevelt's formation of the Press Conference Association and encouragement of women's press conferences, originally Associated Press reporter Lorena Hickok's idea, to help women reporters keep their jobs by writing about something besides society news during the Depression.

1462. Wolf, T. Phillip. BRONSON CUTTING AND FRANKLIN ROOSEVELT: FACTORS IN PRESIDENTIAL ENDORSEMENT. *New Mexico Hist. Rev. 1977 52(4): 317-334.* Roosevelt did not endorse the reelection of New Mexico's Bronson M. Cutting to the US Senate in 1934. Such liberal senators as Hiram W. Johnson (California), George W. Norris (Nebraska), and Robert Marion La Follette, Jr. (Wisconsin), were endorsed by the President. Roosevelt did not endorse Cutting because Cutting did not endorse F. D. R. until two weeks before the election. Roosevelt and Cutting did not agree on veterans' benefits. The chief reason for Roosevelt's unwillingness to endorse Cutting was the weakness of the Democratic Party in New Mexico. 51 notes.
                                              J. H. Krenkel

1463. Woodward, Earl F. HON. ALBERT B. FALL OF NEW MEXICO. *Montana 1973 23(1): 14-23.* Traces the rise of Albert Bacon Fall (1861-1944) from minor political offices to the positions of senator from New Mexico and secretary of the interior under President Warren Gamaliel Harding. Fall's stormy career culminated in conviction for accepting bribes in the Teapot Dome oil scandal. Contemporary press and the writings of the principals; illus., 16 notes.   S. R. Davison

1464. Wright, Esmond. HOW RELEVANT IS THE NEW DEAL? *Encounter [Great Britain] 1982 58-59(6-1): 92-99.* Examines the development of the New Deal, focusing on the activities of presidents Herbert C. Hoover and Franklin D. Roosevelt, of John Maynard Keynes, and of others involved in this economic program; criticizes recent British suggestions that elements of the New Deal be applied to Britain's economic problems.

1465. Yodfat, Aryeh. HAMAAVAK NEGED HOZEH-HASAHAR HARUSI-AMERIKAI MISHNAT 1911 BIGLAL AFLAYAT YEHUDIM AMERIKAIYIM BERUSIAH [The 1911 struggle against the Russo-American trade agreement because of discrimination against American Jews in Russia]. *Shvut [Israel] 1978 6: 24-33.* An 1832 trade agreement between the United States and Russia was abrogated in December 1911 by the US government in reaction to Russian refusal to issue entry visas to American Jews wanting to visit Russia. The public debate in the United States over this so-called Passport Question brought in its wake a more general concern with the conditions of Russian Jews. The Russians themselves were surprised at America's seeming capitulation to its Jewish population, but in fact neither the Taft nor the Wilson administrations allowed the abrogation to adversely affect trade relations with Russia. Primary sources; 54 notes.   T. Sassoon

1466. Zieger, Robert H. THE CAREER OF JAMES J. DAVIS. *Pennsylvania Mag. of Hist. and Biog. 1974 98(1): 67-89.* James John Davis' (1873-1947) career as US Secretary of Labor and senator from Pennsylvania (1930-45) has been largely neglected by historians. As Secretary of Labor under Presidents Harding, Coolidge, and Hoover, Davis earned a reputation for moderation, although he was rarely consulted as an advisor and thus had little impact on economic policy. As a moderately liberal Republican Senator for 15 years, Davis was noted by his colleagues for "his uncanny ability to maintain himself in public office rather than for intellectual distinction, legislative prowess, or political courage." Based on primary and secondary sources; 42 notes.   E. W. Carp

1467. Zieger, Robert H. HERBERT HOOVER, THE WAGE-EARNER, AND THE "NEW ECONOMIC SYSTEM," 1919-1929. *Business Hist. Rev. 1977 51(2): 161-189.* Herbert Hoover regarded the labor issue as the greatest challenge facing American capitalism, feared union militancy as "wasteful and authoritarian," and favored employee representation systems in industry. During the 1920's, however, he was "curiously silent" on the subject, apparently unwilling to seriously examine the real nature of representation plans. Attributes this inaction in large part to Hoover's natural affinity for the new corporate managers who were the sponsors of welfare capitalism and company-sponsored unions. Based on Hoover papers and writings as well as other contemporary sources; 62 notes.   C. J. Pusateri

1468. —. THE BATTLE FOR THE FUTURE. *Am. Hist. Illus. 1979 14(4): 38-39, 42-44.* The State Department and the War Department, wanting to insure that business, industry, jobs, farms, and cities grew and prospered, during World War II campaigned to convince Americans and the world that big is better.

1469. —. THE CONTRIBUTIONS TO ECONOMICS AND ECONOMIC POLICY OF LAUCHLIN CURRIE IN THE 1930'S. *Hist. of Pol. Econ. 1978 10(4): 507-548.*
Jones, Byrd L. LAUCHLIN CURRIE, PUMP PRIMING, AND NEW DEAL FISCAL POLICY, 1934-1936, *pp. 509-524.* Traces the career of Lauchlin Currie, who joined the New Deal government. He understood Keynesianism and sought to convince the government that economic theory could be applied to improve society, 1920's-36.
Currie, Lauchlin. COMMENTS ON PUMP PRIMING, *pp. 525-533.* Memorandum, ca. February-March 1935, on the benefits of government spending to rebuild the economy by stimulating production.
Currie, Lauchlin and Krost, Martin. FEDERAL INCOME-INCREASING EXPENDITURES, 1932-1935, *pp. 543-540.* Memorandum, ca. November 1935, on determining the appropriate time during the business cycle to introduce deficit spending to increase personal income.
Currie, Lauchlin. COMMENTS AND OBSERVATIONS, *pp. 541-548.* The author describes how he became a Keynesian and his role in convincing New Dealers of the salutary effects of deficit spending, 1930's.

Foreign Affairs

1470. Accinelli, Robert D. THE HOOVER ADMINISTRATION AND THE WORLD COURT. *Peace and Change 1977 4(3): 28-36.* Discusses Herbert Hoover's strategy (1929-33) to secure senatorial support for US membership in the Permanent Court of International Justice.

1471. Accinelli, Robert D. LINK'S CASE FOR WILSON THE DIPLOMATIST. *Rev. in Am. Hist. 1981 9(3): 285-294.* Reviews Arthur S. Link's *Woodrow Wilson: Revolution, War, and Peace* (1979), focusing on Woodrow Wilson's role as diplomat.

1472. Accinelli, Robert D. THE ROOSEVELT ADMINISTRA-TION AND THE WORLD COURT DEFEAT, 1935. *Historian 1978 40(3): 463-478.* On 29 January 1935, the US Senate refused to sanction American membership in the World Court, thus climaxing one phase of a fierce struggle over American involvement in European affairs. Discusses many of the reasons traditionally given for the defeat, but focuses on the failure of the Roosevelt administration to be more forceful in defense of the World Court. Believes that the President, preoccupied with domestic considerations, provided only timid leadership in the Court fight which could have been carried with more resourceful management. Concludes that this failure set the stage for the high tide of isolationism in the mid-thirties.
M. S. Legan

1473. Accinelli, Robert D. WAS THERE A "NEW" HARDING? WARREN G. HARDING AND THE WORLD COURT ISSUE. *Ohio Hist. 1975 84(4): 168-181.* Many writers claim that Warren G. Harding, as a result of his presidential responsibilities, came to display greater initiative and determination. But, judged on the basis of his handling of the World Court issue, he had not changed much, though he took personal charge of the proposal for membership in the World Court, no longer leaving the initiative in the hands of Secretary of State Charles Evans Hughes. He was evidently prepared "to make major concessions to the anti-Court faction in order to keep the party together and to facilitate Senate approval of membership. . . . On the Court issue it was the "old" Harding that gained the upper hand in the end." Illus., 53 notes.
E. P. Stickney

1474. Adams, D. K. MESSERSMITH'S APPOINTMENT TO VIENNA IN 1934: PRESIDENTIAL PATRONAGE OR CAREER PROMOTION? *Delaware Hist. 1978 18(1): 17-27.* George Strausser Messersmith (1883-1960) was a career diplomat who was appointed to the important post in Vienna in 1934. His understanding of German, his experience as consul general in Berlin, his understanding of the complex issues surrounding the rise and strength of Nazi power and of America's international role made him a good candidate for the ambassador's post in Vienna. However, it was also political influence, Franklin D. Roosevelt's interest in promoting the professionalism of the foreign service, and his own lobbying which led to his appointment. Messersmith Papers and documents in the National Archives. 51 notes.
R. M. Miller

1475. Aga Rossi, Elena. GLI STATI UNITI E LA DIVISIONE DELL'EUROPA [The United States and the division of Europe]. *Storia Contemporanea [Italy] 1979 10(6): 1165-1177.* Examines the basis of the postwar order in Europe through an analysis of the political objectives pursued by the Allies, with reference to the diplomacy between Roosevelt, Churchill, and Stalin. Historians have underestimated the differences and divisions between the United States and Great Britain and have overemphasized unity and commonality of interests. Essential for an understanding of the present structure of Europe is an awareness of the different attitudes of the two western allies toward the future of the continent and the predominant influence of the United States in laying the foundations of the postwar reorganization. Based on the National Archives, Washington, and Public Record Office, London, and other sources; 35 notes.
P. J. Durell

1476. Alvarez, David J. THE DEPARTMENT OF STATE AND THE ABORTIVE PAPAL MISSION TO CHINA, AUGUST 1918. *Catholic Hist. Rev. 1976 62(3): 455-463.* The State Department's response to the establishment of diplomatic relations between China and the Vatican illuminates America's Far Eastern policy during World War I. Alarmed over the penetration of German influence into Siberia, the State Department intervened with the Chinese to block the reception of Monsignor Petrelli, a Germanophile, as papal nuncio. Concerned also with possible Japanese expansion into China, the Department cooperated with France to prevent the acceptance of any papal representative. France claimed a protectorate over Catholics in the Far East, and the Department supported this claim in order to buttress European influence in China and counter Japanese influence.

1477. Ambrosius, Lloyd E. THE ORTHODOXY OF REVISIONISM: WOODROW WILSON AND THE NEW LEFT. *Diplomatic Hist. 1977 1(3): 199-214.* Calls orthodox the New Left interpretation of the Cold War. Woodrow Wilson's (1856-1924) internationalism and view of American leadership in world affairs provided the intellectual framework of the Cold War. In essence, New Left historians did not go beyond Wilson's concepts in their revisionist critiques. In effect, the pluralist critique was more radical, going beyond Wilson's vision of a Pax Americana. 51 notes.
J. Tull

1478. Ambrosius, Lloyd E. WILSON, CLEMENCEAU AND THE GERMAN PROBLEM AT THE PARIS PEACE CONFERENCE OF 1919. *Rocky Mountain Social Science J. 1975 12(2): 69-80.*

1479. Anderson, Irvine H., Jr. THE 1941 *DE FACTO* EMBARGO ON OIL TO JAPAN: A BUREAUCRATIC REFLEX. *Pacific Hist. R. 1975 44(2): 201-231.* Heretofore unused documents reveal that President Franklin D. Roosevelt did not intend to terminate Japan's oil supply when he froze funds in July 1941. He correctly anticipated that Japan would attack the Netherlands East Indies if oil was cut off, but Roosevelt allowed the order to be written as all-inclusive so that policy could be changed day-to-day without issuing further orders. Neither the public nor the British, Dutch, or Japanese were given a clear idea of the American policy. This ambiguity allowed a bureaucracy biased against Japan, specifically the Foreign Funds Control Interdepartmental Committee, to establish a de facto oil embargo which Roosevelt and Cordell Hull supported by mid-September out of fear that a relaxation would be interpreted as a sign of weakness. Based on government documents at the Federal Records Center, Suitland, Maryland and the National Archives, private papers at Hoover Institution and Yale University, and other primary and secondary sources; 107 notes.
W. K. Hobson

1480. Artaud, Denise. SUR L'ENTRE-DEUX-GUERRES: WILSON A LA CONFERENCE DE LA PAIX (1919) [On the interwar period: Wilson at the peace conference, 1919]. *Rev. d'Hist. de la Deuxième Guerre Mondiale [France] 1981 31(124): 97-107.* American feelings of rivalry with British financial interests and Woodrow Wilson's lack of realism in dealing with British war debts were the chief causes of the failure of European financial reconstruction at the Paris peace conference in 1919. Based on writings of John Maynard Keynes and other economic history sources; 34 notes.
G. H. Davis

1481. Avery, Laurence G. MAXWELL ANDERSON'S REPORT ON FRANK COBB'S INTERVIEW WITH WOODROW WILSON: DOCUMENTARY SOURCE. *North Dakota Q. 1977 45(3): 5-14.* Reprints the manuscript version of an interview said to have occurred between Woodrow Wilson and Frank I. Cobb on the day Wilson delivered his war message to the Congress in 1917; Wilson discusses the heads of the Allied powers and his opinion on the chances which the Allies have in defeating Germany.

1482. Bailey, Thomas A. THE WOODROW WILSON WORSHIPERS. *Soc. for Hist. of Am. Foreign Relations. Newsletter 1981 12(4): 13-15.* Discusses the historical controversies surrounding Woodrow Wilson and his negotiations in the Paris Peace Settlements.

1483. Balfour, Michael. THE ORIGIN OF THE FORMULA: "UNCONDITIONAL SURRENDER" IN WORLD WAR II. *Armed Forces and Soc. 1979 5(2): 281-301.* There is some uncertainty whether the formula "unconditional surrender" had been given serious study before being enunciated by President Franklin D. Roosevelt at his Casablanca press conference. A careful consideration of all pro and con factors affecting its advisability as a basis for achieving early surrender and the best possible foundation for postwar settlements would suggest, given the personalities and circumstances involved, that an adequate change in the character of the peace to be achieved was not an available option. Primary sources; 37 notes.
R. V. Ritter

1484. Baram, Phillip. THE DEPARTMENT OF STATE'S OUTLOOK AND EXPECTATIONS IN THE MIDDLE EAST, 1919-1945. *Jerusalem J. of Int. Relations [Israel] 1977 2(3): 1-22.* US foreign policy toward the Middle East, 1919-45, wooed the Arab-Moslem majority (at the cost of alienating minorities in the area and other powers) in order to elevate national prestige, private enterprise abroad, and State Department status in domestic political life.

1485. Baram, Phillip. UNDERMINING THE BRITISH: DEPARTMENT OF STATE POLICIES IN EGYPT AND THE SUEZ CANAL BEFORE AND DURING WORLD WAR II. *Historian 1978 40(4):*

631-649. In Egypt, friendly competition existed between Britain and the United States in the political, military, economic, and public relations areas as British strength gained or diminished. Overall, however, US wartime relations with Egypt as conducted by the State Department's Division of Near Eastern Affairs and by the Foreign Service were limited and secondary. Even the State Department's postwar planning for Egypt was deliberately passive. No question of competition existed over the Suez Canal, however. The State Department's view was that the Canal was totally a British military responsibility, essentially separate from Anglo-American relations in the rest of Egypt.   M. S. Legan

1486. Bartlett, Merrill and Love, Robert William, Jr. ANGLO-AMERICAN NAVAL DIPLOMACY AND THE BRITISH PACIFIC FLEET, 1942-1945. *Am. Neptune 1982 42(3): 203-216.* In the spring of 1942, Great Britain pressed the United States to take offensive actions in the Pacific to force Japanese withdrawal from the Indian Ocean. American launched raids helped accomplish this and led Japan to plan an attack on Midway Island. When the United States asked Britain to make diversionary attacks to weaken the Japanese attacks on Midway and the Solomon Islands the British refused. In 1944, after the tide had turned, Britain demanded a role in a major naval operations in the Central Pacific. American naval leaders rightly saw that Britain was motivated by a wish to increase its postwar influence and objected, insisting Britain be limited to the Malaya area, but Franklin D. Roosevelt backed Britain, and it was given a role. Based on records in the Naval Historical Division and National Archives in Washington, in the FDR Library at Hyde Park, and elsewhere; 60 notes.   J. C. Bradford

1487. Benjamin, Jules R. THE NEW DEAL, CUBA, AND THE RISE OF A GLOBAL FOREIGN ECONOMIC POLICY. *Business Hist. Rev. 1977 51(1): 57-78.* Revises the conventional thesis that isolationism characterized early New Deal foreign policy. US involvement in Cuba increased during this period, and this helped to establish precedents for the global outlook of American policy in the 1940's and beyond. The new policy was especially visible in the use of the Reconstruction Finance Corporation and the Export-Import Bank to promote American interests. Based on State Department and other US governmental records; 39 notes.   C. J. Pusateri

1488. Ben-Zvi, Abraham. AMERICAN PRECONCEPTIONS AND POLICIES TOWARD JAPAN, 1940-1941: A CASE STUDY IN MISPERCEPTION. *Internat. Studies Q. 1975 19(2): 228-248.* An attempt to develop a new typology of American policymakers involved in US-Japanese relations during 1940 and 1941. The typology consists of three major categories: 1) the globalist-realists, Henry Stimson, Henry Morgenthau, and Stanley Hornbeck, 2) the globalist-idealists like Cordell Hull, and 3) the nationalist-pragmatists, Franklin D. Roosevelt and Joseph Grew. 5 notes.   G. J. Boughton

1489. Bernstein, Barton J. THE QUEST FOR SECURITY: AMERICAN FOREIGN POLICY AND INTERNATIONAL CONTROL OF ATOMIC ENERGY, 1942-1946. *J. of Am. Hist. 1974 60(4): 1003-1044.* Overriding the objections of some scientists, the administration of Franklin D. Roosevelt made the decision *not* to share atomic secrets with the USSR. Henry Stimson considered promising such secrets in return for an opening of Soviet society, and had F.D.R. lived he might quite possibly have used "atomic diplomacy" to ease America's postwar role. President Truman later saw the United States as a trustee for the awesome weapon. Although at times he seemed disposed to listen to Stimson and Acheson who suggested a more open and direct approach to the Soviet Union, he was averse to sharing secrets that might end America's nuclear monopoly. The Acheson-Lilienthal report was so amended by Bernard Baruch (with provisions for inspections and giving up veto power in the UN) as to make it obviously unacceptable to the Soviet military chief. The climate of political opinion in 1946 made it difficult for the United States to offer any proposal which might have been acceptable to the Soviet Union. The controversy over atomic energy was both cause and consequence of the Cold War. 81 notes.   K. B. West

1490. Bernstein, Barton J. ROOSEVELT, TRUMAN, AND THE ATOMIC BOMB: A REINTERPRETATION. *Pol. Sci. Q. 1975 90(1): 23-69.* Reinterprets the Roosevelt and Truman policies on the construction and use of atomic weapons. Concludes that FDR's decisions to treat the bomb as a legitimate weapon and to exclude the Soviets from a nuclear

partnership prepared the way for the Truman administration's atomic bombing of Japan, the toughening of policy at Potsdam, and the postwar practice of atomic diplomacy.   J

1491. Bernstein, Barton J. THE UNEASY ALLIANCE: ROOSEVELT, CHURCHILL, AND THE ATOMIC BOMB, 1940-1945. *Western Pol. Q. 1976 29(2): 202-230.* Reinterprets the wartime Anglo-American relationship on atomic energy, defined primarily by Roosevelt and Churchill. Atomic energy represented, potentially, the cornerstone of a postwar Anglo-American entente in which only these "two policemen" (the United States and Great Britain) would have the atomic bomb. Roosevelt was a shrewd administrator in this important area, as revealed by his wartime foreign policy: his understanding of power, his attitudes toward the Soviet Union, his view of the United Nations, and his expectations about the postwar world. He was not naïve or innocent, but astute, about power in international affairs. He was not a Wilsonian internationalist but a firm believer in big-power politics. Based on the recently declassified American and British archives.   J/S

1492. Best, Gary Dean. THE JEWISH "CENTER OF GRAVITY", AND SECRETARY HAY'S ROMANIAN NOTES. *Am. Jewish Arch. 1980 32(1): 23-34.* Personal liberty for Jews in Romania was steadily reduced through government edict between 1880 and 1900, even though Romania had been a party to the 1878 Treaty of Berlin. By 1901, many immigrants from Romania were entering the United States. The oppression and subsequent immigration drew the attention of wealthy and influential American Jews, notably Jacob H. Schiff and Oscar Straus, who tried to persuade the Theodore Roosevelt administration to express displeasure at the events in Romania. American efforts were futile because of lack of support from European allies, but the mere act of American opposition (through the strongly worded but misdirected communication by Secretary of State John Milton Hay) placed the United States in a leading role in mediating the world's differences. Primary sources; 2 illus., 41 notes.   T. Koppel

1493. Biber, Dušan. BRITANSKA IN AMERIŠKA POLITIKA O ITALIJANSKO-JUGOSLOVANSKI MEJI V DRUGI SVETOVNI VOJNI [British and American policy concerning the Italian-Yugoslav frontier during World War II]. *Zgodovinski Časopis [Yugoslavia] 1980 34(4): 431-441.* Analyzes the origin and repercussions of the British verbal guarantees to the royal Yugoslav government in 1941 that the British government would support Yugoslav demand for revision of the Yugoslav-Italian frontier. President Roosevelt was skeptical about the expediency of such a guarantee, the restoration of Yugoslavia on the whole, Stalin's suggestions in 1941, and the restraint of the British policy toward the demands for revision of the frontier. The author describes the resistance of Marshal Tito, who didn't want Yugoslavia to be involved in the policy of the spheres of interest. Presented at the Round Table of the American and Yugoslav Historians in Plitvice, Yugoslavia, 4-6 August 1980.   J/S

1494. Biskupski, M. B. POLAND IN AMERICAN FOREIGN POLICY, 1918-1945: "SENTIMENTAL" OR "STRATEGIC" FRIENDSHIP? A REVIEW ARTICLE. *Polish Am. Studies 1981 38(2): 5-15.* Attempts to prove that Poland has had few true friends among US leaders. These leaders may have been sympathetic but seldom offered support for strategic reasons of benefit to Poland. They helped Poland because they happened to be helping other countries as well, and only during periods of congruent interest. Such long-established friends of Poland as Woodrow Wilson, Herbert Hoover, and Franklin D. Roosevelt lose lustre in this context, but US Ambassador to Poland, A. J. Drexel Biddle holds his own. Primary and secondary sources in Polish and English; 25 notes.   S. R. Pliska

1495. Black, Gregory D. *KEYS OF THE KINGDOM:* ENTERTAINMENT AND PROPAGANDA. *South Atlantic Q. 1976 75(4): 434-446.* Uses the history of *The Keys of the Kingdom,* a 1944 20th Century-Fox movie about early 20th-century missionary life in China, to show the Office of War Information's (OWI) involvement in American wartime film industry. Only with the greatest persuasion could the filmmakers conceive of Chinese society in terms other than the mysterious East, but the stereotyping forced on them by the government agency was equally unrealistic. The OWI was promoting Franklin D. Roosevelt's concept of China as a fourth world power and obviously used this movie to improve relations between Washington and Chungking. Primary and secondary sources; 19 notes.   W. L. Olbrich

1496. Blayney, Michael Stewart. HERBERT PELL, WAR CRIMES, AND THE JEWS. *Am. Jewish Hist. Q. 1976 65(4): 335-352.* Herbert Claiborne Pell, a Harvard classmate of Franklin D. Roosevelt, was one of Roosevelt's political appointees in various foreign service posts. Pell was an early and vigorous denouncer of Nazi policies; his letters to the President stand in marked contrast to the restrained style and attitude of the State Department. His 1943 appointment to the UN War Crimes Commission led almost from the beginning to increased conflict with the State Department, which did not agree with his definition of war crimes and atrocities. The question whether crimes against Jews, regardless of location and nationality, came within the jurisdiction of the commission was another issue that divided Pell and the Department. All of this led to his abrupt dismissal in 1945. 45 notes.   F. Rosenthal

1497. Block, Robert Hoyt. SOUTHERN CONGRESSMEN AND WILSON'S CALL FOR REPEAL OF THE PANAMA CANAL TOLL EXEMPTION. *Southern Studies 1978 17(1): 91-100.* In 1913, President Woodrow Wilson (1856-1924) asked Congress to remove American exemption from tolls for use of the Panama Canal. Although the Hay-Pauncefote Treaty of 1901 had called for usage by all nations "on terms of entire equality," Congress established rates, in 1912, exempting American ships. The British protested, and Wilson decided to seek repeal. This was in opposition to the Democratic Party platform and Wilson's own views of a year earlier. To secure passage, Wilson enlisted the aid of southern congressmen and government officials, who supported him primarily out of party loyalty. In both houses, southern Democrats voted for repeal to a larger degree than northern Democrats. Primary and secondary sources; 46 notes.   J. Buschen

1498. Braeman, John. POWER AND DIPLOMACY: THE 1920'S REAPPRAISED. *Rev. of Pol. 1982 44(3): 342-369.* Post-World War II historiography of diplomacy in the 1920's produced a legalist-moralist indictment that consistently attacked Republican administrations for their failure to support Wilsonian peace and security arrangements, such as the League of Nations. It also has generated a realist indictment blaming the Republicans for their faithful adherence to a diplomacy that favored business interests and persuasion rather than the reality of force and military preparedness, particularly in view of the Japanese military threat. The difficulty with the realist indictments rests with its ignorance of America's overwhelming economic dominance in the 1920's and the unusual security it enjoyed. The 1920's should not be confused with the 1930's, a time when technology and weaponry shifted the balance of power. The diplomacy of the 1920's was realistic and adequate given the circumstances. Secondary sources; 61 notes.   G. A. Glovins

1499. Brune, Lester H. CONSIDERATIONS OF FORCE IN CORDELL HULL'S DIPLOMACY, JULY 26 TO NOVEMBER 26, 1941. *Diplomatic Hist. 1978 2(4): 389-405.* The Japanese occupation of much of Indochina in mid-1941 resulted in Secretary of State Cordell Hull's disillusionment with the prospects for successful negotiations, but resulted also in a decision—to defend the Philippines when hostilities commenced—which laid upon him the task of continuing negotiations solely for the military purpose of buying time. Hull, who never seemed to appreciate the practical connections between diplomatic and military considerations, was not the man for this job, and he bungled it rather badly. On 26 November Hull and Roosevelt, reversing a war council decision of the previous day, scrapped plans to offer the Japanese a few token concessions, and thus abandoned the effort to extend negotiations until American preparations were complete in February or March 1942. Published primary and secondary sources; 48 notes.
                                    L. W. Van Wyk

1500. Bryson, Thomas A. ROOSEVELT'S QUARANTINE SPEECH, THE GEORGIA PRESS AND THE BORG THESIS: A NOTE. *Australian J. of Pol. and Hist. 1975 21(2): 95-98.* Franklin D. Roosevelt delivered the quarantine speech in Chicago on 5 October 1937 as a response to Japanese military operations in China, and German and Italian involvement in Spain and Ethiopia respectively. Dorothy Borg maintained that the speech, contrary to popular interpretation, did not represent a sharp change in policy, or anticipate the use of economic sanctions, but was an attempt to avoid war. Roosevelt was not attempting

to establish a form of Wilsonian collective security but probably envisaged collective neutrality. He dropped plans to "quarantine" aggressors because of the intense opposition of leading isolationists. This thesis is tested by sampling 65 Georgian newspapers. The editors misrepresented the speech and read more into it than was intended, but the evidence suggests that it was primarily public opinion, rather than a few isolationists, which caused Roosevelt to forego plans to curb belligerent acts by the Axis powers. Primary and secondary sources; 22 notes.
                                    R. G. Neville

1501. Burton, D. H. THEODORE ROOSEVELT AND THE "SPECIAL RELATIONSHIP" WITH BRITAIN. *Hist. Today [Great Britain] 1973 23(8): 527-535.* Discusses Anglo-American diplomacy during the presidency of Theodore Roosevelt.

1502. Cary, Otis. THE SPARING OF KYOTO: MR. STIMSON'S "PET CITY." *Japan Q. [Japan] 1975 22(4): 337-347.* There have been a number of stories told about why the city of Kyoto was not heavily bombed by the US air forces during World War II or why the city was spared from nuclear attack even though its name had appeared high on the list of target cities prepared by various US air commanders. One story credits Florence Denton, a long-time teacher at Dōshisha Women's College, as the person responsible for having Kyoto removed from the target lists. Another credits Langdon Warner, from Harvard's Fogg Museum. A third gives credit to Professor Edwin O. Reischauer, also of Harvard University. It was really Henry L. Stimson, US Secretary of War in 1945, who caused Kyoto to be removed from the US target lists, and he did so with President Truman's knowledge and approval. 20 notes.
                                    A. N. Garland

1503. Chan, Kit-cheng. THE UNITED STATES AND THE QUESTION OF HONG KONG, 1941-45. *J. of the Hong Kong Branch of the Royal Asiatic Soc. [Hong Kong] 1979 19: 1-20.* Discusses the US attitude concerning the conflict between Great Britain and China over Hong Kong during World War II. The United States did not view British claims to Hong Kong with sympathy because Franklin D. Roosevelt fervently desired an end to colonialism and imperialism and because the US government feared that if the United States was perceived as favoring the British, China and Chiang Kai-shek would cease fighting the Japanese and thereby weaken Allied efforts in the Asian theater. Relies on the letters and papers of several figures involved in the negotiations, including Stanley K. Hornbeck, Joseph W. Ballantine, and Henry Morgenthau; 72 notes.   G. V. Wasson

1504. Chan, Loren B. FIGHTING FOR THE LEAGUE: PRESIDENT WILSON IN NEVADA, 1919. *Nevada Hist. Soc. Q. 1979 22(2): 115-127.* Thwarted by resistance from the US Senate to the post-World War I Versailles Treaty, President Woodrow Wilson (1856-1924) appealed to the American people to side with him. In September 1919, he renewed that appeal at Reno, Nevada, where Democratic politicians and most of the populace cheered him. But that warm public reception masked widespread opposition in Nevada to the treaty, and many Nevadans as well as the state's two US Senators deserted Wilson when the showdown came between the President and the Senate. Based on government documents, newspapers, and secondary sources; 57 notes.
                                    H. T. Lovin

1505. Chi, Madeleine. CHINA AND UNEQUAL TREATIES AT THE PARIS PEACE CONFERENCE OF 1919. *Asian Profile [Hong Kong] 1973 1(1): 49-61.* Analyzes China's failures to achieve its goals in the Paris Peace Conference in 1919. The allied powers encouraged China to seek territorial control over the Shantung Peninsula and the annulment of the unequal treaties. Japan had seized German holdings in China during World War I and in the unequal treaties, imposed extraterritoriality, spheres of influence, and foreign control over customs, postal, and trading authorities. Japan prevailed in its claims for the former German special concessions in China and in the Pacific islands north of the equator. To secure the establishment of the League of Nations Woodrow Wilson yielded in his initial support for Chinese diplomatic positions. British and French diplomats were unwilling to yield any imperial prerogatives. Refusing to sign the humiliating Versailles Peace Treaty, the Chinese delegates resigned. Based on official diplomatic documents and secondary sources; 71 notes.   S. H. Frank

1506. Cigliana, Carlo. PAGINE DISCUSSE DELL'ULTIMO CON-FLITTO MONDIALE: I PRECEDENTI DI PEARL HARBOR [Pages of the last world conflict examined: the precedents of Pearl Harbor]. *Riv. Militare [Italy] 1969 25(6): 701-715.* The attack on Pearl Harbor was neither unexpected nor unprovoked; in April 1941, Franklin D. Roosevelt believed it was in America's best interests to hinder Japanese efforts in Southeast Asia while waiting for America to become strong enough to launch an offensive against Japan.

1507. Clements, Kendrick A. EMISSARY FROM A REVOLU-TION: LUIS CABRERA AND WOODROW WILSON. *Americas (Acad. of Am. Franciscan Hist.) 1979 35(3): 353-371.* Though Woodrow Wilson preferred Venustiano Carranza and the Constitutionalists in their struggle against the regime of Victoriano Huerta in Mexico, Carranza rejected Wilson's demand for guarantees of good behavior as a form of intervention. By sending the able Luis Cabrera to Washington as special agent, Carranza helped induce Wilson to relax the arms embargo on Mexico and otherwise favor the Constitutionalists without explicit concessions in return. On two subsequent occasions Cabrera served Mexico well as a representative in the United States. Covers 1914-17. Based on US and British diplomatic records and on Mexican published sources; 51 notes.   D. Bushnell

1508. Clements, Kendrick A. "A KINDNESS TO CARRANZA": WILLIAM JENNINGS BRYAN, INTERNATIONAL HAR-VESTER, AND INTERVENTION IN YUCATÁN. *Nebraska Hist. 1976 57(4): 479-490.* Examines William Jennings Bryan's role as Secretary of State in endorsing a plan for military intervention in Yucatán which would benefit the International Harvester Corporation. Bryan's assistance to the "harvester trust," a corporation he formerly denounced, was indicative of a developing pattern in Wilsonian diplomacy, as well as an example in which Bryan's "moral diplomacy" shifted to "moral imperialism." Covers the period 1913-15.   R. Lowitt

1509. Clements, Kendrick A. WOODROW WILSON'S MEXICAN POLICY, 1913-15. *Diplomatic Hist. 1980 4(2): 113-136.* Woodrow Wilson's Mexican policy was not the attempt to force the Mexican Revolution into a "liberal-capitalist" mold which most historians have discerned. Wilson (1856-1924) sought to use American power to prevent domination of Mexico by any foreign power, including the United States. Although he would have preferred an American-style system there, he did not attempt to force his choice upon the Mexican people, whom he perceived as struggling valiantly against "the interests." "Despite mistakes and misunderstandings, ... the result was a policy vastly more practical and successful than most historians have realized." 81 notes.
                                                  T. L. Powers

1510. Coletta, Paolo E. THE DIPLOMACY OF THEODORE ROOSEVELT AND WILLIAM HOWARD TAFT. Haines, Gerald K. and Walker, J. Samuel, ed. *American Foreign Relations: A Historiographical Review* (Westport, Conn.: Greenwood Pr., 1981): 91-113. Surveys the literature on the administrations of Theodore Roosevelt and William H. Taft, noting the continuing controversy over Roosevelt's diplomatic policies among consensus, realist, and radical historians, and the agreement over Taft's foreign policies. Secondary sources; 65 notes.
                                                  J. Powell

1511. Coletta, Paolo E. A QUESTION OF ALTERNATIVES: WILSON, BRYAN, LANSING, AND AMERICA'S INTERVENTION IN WORLD WAR I. *Nebraska Hist. 1982 63(1): 33-57.* A careful examination of American diplomacy leading to intervention in 1917 from the perspective of William Jennings Bryan, Secretary of State during 1913-15. Primarily manuscript sources.   R. Lowitt

1512. Conway, John S. A GERMAN NATIONAL REICH CHURCH AND AMERICAN WAR PROPAGANDA. *Catholic Hist. Rev. 1976 62(3): 464-472.* In 1941 American sources obtained a secretly circulated pamphlet from Germany outlining a plan to abolish Christianity and substitute a National Reich Church complete with Nazi symbols, liturgies and ideology. Franklin D. Roosevelt used this for his propaganda campaign, designed to attack Nazi Germany and to denounce the persecution of the Churches. He assumed that this plan was an official Nazi proposal and used it to win over opponents, particularly American Roman Catholics. In fact, Gestapo reports showed that the

proposal stemmed from a pro-Nazi fanatic. But, the anticlerical and anti-Christian aspects of the program closely resembled the Gestapo's own plans.

1513. Cook, Charles O., Jr. THE PACIFIC COMMAND DIVIDED: THE "MOST UNEXPLAINABLE" DECISION. *US Naval Inst. Pro. 1978 104(9): 55-61.* There has never been a satisfactory explanation as to why the command in the Pacific during World War II was not united under one commander. Two military theaters of operation were established —the Southwest Pacific headed by General Douglas MacArthur and the Pacific Ocean Areas commanded by Admiral Chester W. Nimitz. From the available evidence, it seems clear that President Franklin D. Roosevelt had lost faith in General MacArthur as a result of the latter's actions during the battle for the Philippines, 1941-42, and did not think that MacArthur could be trusted with the increased authority of an undivided Pacific command. The decision to divide the Pacific appears to have been the President's, and the Joint Chiefs of Staff because they knew how he felt, gave him the plan that was put into effect in March 1942. Primary and secondary sources; 5 photos, 14 notes.
                                                  A. N. Garland

1514. Cooper, John Milton, Jr. "AN IRONY OF FATE": WOODROW WILSON'S PRE-WORLD WAR I DIPLOMACY. *Diplomatic Hist. 1979 3(4): 425-437.* Review article of Arthur S. Link, ed., *The Papers of Woodrow Wilson,* vols. 27-30 (Princeton, N.J., 1978-79), which covers 1913-14.

1515. Cooper, John Milton, Jr. "THE WARRIOR AND THE PRIEST": TOWARD A COMPARATIVE PERSPECTIVE ON THEODORE ROOSEVELT AND WOODROW WILSON. *South Atlantic Q. 1981 80(4): 419-428.* In his *Ideals and Self-Interest in America's Foreign Relations* (1953), Robert E. Osgood utilized Nietzsche's distinction between warrior and priest as a model, which offers three important insights in viewing Theodore Roosevelt and Woodrow Wilson personally and in their approaches to politics. Osgood noted that both were intellectuals, both sought political careers because of personal characteristics that stemmed from childhood, and in both instances foreign policy played a major role in shaping their administration policies. It would appear that Wilson emerges as the priest, Roosevelt as the warrior. Contradictions exist in each of Osgood's analyses, however, and use of Nietzschean symbols demonstrates that Wilson is indeed the warrior, and Roosevelt is the priest. Secondary sources, 14 notes.   H. M. Parker, Jr.

1516. Cooper, John Milton, Jr. WOODROW WILSON THROUGH ALIEN EYES. *Reviews in Am. Hist. 1975 3(3): 359-364.* Review article prompted by Patrick Devlin's *Too Proud to Fight: Woodrow Wilson's Neutrality* (New York: Oxford U. Pr., 1974); places the book within historiographical context, outlines the book's content, and evaluates the book's character sketch of Wilson and its treatment of the neutrality issue.

1517. Cuff, Robert D. HERBERT HOOVER, THE IDEOLOGY OF VOLUNTARISM AND WAR ORGANIZATION DURING THE GREAT WAR. *J. of Am. Hist. 1977 64(2): 358-372.* Volunteers were widely used to staff government agencies in the United States during World War I. Voluntarism was successful because of the hasty and incomplete mobilization of American resources, because of the lofty ideals and dedication of professional businessmen serving the government, and because voluntarism was uniquely suited to the country's need for central authority and cooperation without aggrandizing the federal government. Herbert C. Hoover's tenure as administrator of the Food Administration shows the force that voluntarism could have in securing goods for war. Primary and secondary sources; 35 notes.   J. W. Leedom

1518. DeWitt, Howard A. HIRAM JOHNSON AND EARLY NEW DEAL DIPLOMACY, 1933-1934. *California Hist. Q. 1974 53(4): 377-386.* Assesses Hiram Johnson's influence in directing American foreign policy toward isolationism in the 1930's. Although dismissed as self-seeking by some historians, Johnson sincerely worked to avoid war through a highly restrictive foreign policy. He sponsored legislation banning loans to nations that defaulted on their war debts and pressed for an arms embargo resolution that would apply impartially to all belligerents. President Roosevelt, concerned with the passage of domestic reforms in the early stages of the New Deal, acceded to Johnson's views in these areas. The Nye Committee thus had a major precedent in Johnson as a successful promoter of isolationist policies. Based on primary and secondary sources; illus., photos, 35 notes.   A. Hoffman

1519.   DeWitt, Howard A.   THE "NEW" HARDING AND AMERICAN FOREIGN POLICY: WARREN G. HARDING, HIRAM W. JOHNSON, AND PRAGMATIC DIPLOMACY.   *Ohio Hist. 1977 86(2): 96-114.* An analysis of Warren G. Harding's relationship with Senator Hiram W. Johnson of California reveals that Harding remained a conciliatory, compromising politician who did not significantly expand the role of the President in foreign affairs. The author concludes, however, that Harding's dealings with the isolationist-minded Johnson illustrated the President's skill as a practical politician who aided the smooth course of Republican foreign policy in the 1920's by pursuing middle-of-the-road policies. Based on manuscript, newspaper, and secondary sources; 3 illus., 70 notes.   J

1520.   Dodd, Thomas J.   LOS ESTADOS UNIDOS EN LA POLITICA NICARAGUENSE: ELECCIONES SUPERVISADAS 1928-1932   [The United States in Nicaraguan politics: supervised elections, 1928-32].   *Rev. del Pensamiento Centroamericano [Nicaragua] 1975 30(148): 5-102.* Details US involvement in Nicaragua, 1927-32, focusing on supervision of elections during the period, including presidential elections of 1928 and 1932, legislative elections of 1930, and municipal elections of 1931. While US financial intervention (1912-27) had been highly successful, political stability had not been achieved, owing to the clear US preference for Conservatives before 1927. Henry Stimson attempted to solve this problem by providing free elections with participation of the Liberals, who assumed power following the election of 1928. But the United States also worked subtly to prevent Liberal José M. Moncada from continuing in power beyond 1932. The election of Juan B. Sacasa was seen favorably in Washington for it achieved that goal, enabling the United States to withdraw gracefully and to reach an agreement with Augusto Sandino to end his guerrilla warfare. The primary US motive was to maintain stability in Nicaragua, but the supervision of elections caused a change in the US *modus operandi* to support "popular will" and the Liberals. Stimson's efforts to make Nicaragua a "North America in miniature" were not successful, but they served US interests. Based on author's dissertation, primary and secondary sources; 465 notes, biblio.   R. L. Woodward

1521.   Doenecke, Justus D.   BEYOND POLEMICS: AN HISTORIOGRAPHICAL RE-APPRAISAL OF AMERICAN ENTRY INTO WORLD WAR II.   *Hist. Teacher 1979 12(2): 217-251.* Revisionism is a continual process, particularly in this controversial subject area. The earliest works were by historians and writers such as Beard, Barnes, and Tansil who opposed Roosevelt's interventionism. Internationalist historians who followed defended the basic Roosevelt diplomacy. The key work in this school was by Langer and Gleason. Recently economic factors, particularly in regard to Japan, have received much attention, but the study of religious, ethnic, psychological and emotional factors have continued to be neglected. 156 notes.   L. C. Smith

1522.   Doerries, Reinhard R.   AMERIKANISCHE AUSSENPOLITIK IM KARIBISCHEN RAUM VOR DEM ERSTEN WELTKRIEG   [American foreign policy in the Caribbean prior to World War I].   *Jahrbuch für Amerikastudien [West Germany] 1973 18: 62-77.* American intervention and expansionism in the pre-World War I Caribbean did not mark an abrupt turning point in American foreign policy but can be comprehended within the context of the Monroe Doctrine. In the era of New Imperialism the interests and security of the United States as the leading power in the Western Hemisphere were threatened, particularly by Germany, which did not recognize the Monroe Doctrine and chose Mexico as the focal point of its meddling policies in Latin America. The contrast between Woodrow Wilson's salvation of the Mexican Revolution and other American interventions in the Caribbean at the time shows the complex reality determining American policies in this area. Based on secondary sources; 88 notes.   G. Bassler

1523.   Doerries, Reinhard R.   [GERMANY AND THE UNITED STATES AFTER WORLD WAR I].   *Central European Hist. 1975 8(4): 370-374.* Reviews *Deutsche Revolution und Wilson-Frieden: Die Amerikanische und Deutsche Friedensstrategie Zwischen Ideologie und Machtpolitik 1918/19* (Düsseldorf: Drotse, 1971) by Klaus Schwabe and *Deutschland und die Reparationen 1918/19: Die Genesis des Reparation-*

sproblems in Deutschland Zwischen Waffenstillstand und Versailer Friedensschluss* (Stuttgart: Deutsche Verlags-Anstalt, 1973) by Peter Krüger. Schwabe's study helps correct a long-distorted image of Woodrow Wilson and sheds new light on many of the negotiations which went on in 1918 between Berlin and Washington. Krüger's work is thorough in looking at reparations from Germany's point of view, but it unfortunately ignores the international forces at work.   C. R. Lovin

1524.   Donnelly, J. B.   PRENTISS GILBERT'S MISSION TO THE LEAGUE OF NATIONS COUNCIL, OCTOBER, 1931.   *Diplomatic Hist. 1978 2(4): 373-387.* The appearance on 16 October 1931 of Prentiss B. Gilbert, US Consul at Geneva, at an emergency session of the Council of the League of Nations, created high hopes that war between Japan and China, which had broken out on the night of 18-19 September, could be checked. Gilbert was under orders from Secretary of State Henry L. Stimson to join in calling for peace under the aegis of the Kellog-Briand Pact to which the United States was a signatory (it had not signed the League Covenant). The pact was indeed invoked, but when the session ended on 24 October, little concrete progress toward peace had been made. A series of bad transatlantic telephone connections between Stimson and Gilbert, and the former's sensitivity to isolationist criticism at home hampered the American effort. Based on archival and other primary sources; 71 notes.   L. W. Van Wyk

1525.   Dorwart, Jeffery M.   THE ROOSEVELT-ASTOR ESPIONAGE RING.   *New York Hist. 1981 62(3): 307-322.* President Franklin D. Roosevelt obtained intelligence of military importance as early as 1933 from Vincent Astor and other members of the ROOM, an informal secret society of men high in the social register. After 1939, the ROOM, code-named the CLUB, supplied Roosevelt with intelligence information and in many quiet ways aided Great Britain's war effort. In March 1941, Roosevelt appointed Astor area controller of intelligence work in New York. After Pearl Harbor the Roosevelt-Astor espionage ring ended. Former members of the ROOM were engaged in the army's Military Intelligence Division, Office of Strategic Services, or antisubmarine and convoy routing duty. Based on manuscripts in the Franklin D. Roosevelt Library and other primary sources; 3 illus., 22 notes.
                                                        R. N. Lokken

1526.   Eismeier, Dana L.   U.S. OIL POLICY, JAPAN, AND THE COMING OF WAR IN THE PACIFIC, 1940-1941.   *Michigan Acad. 1982 14(4): 359-367.* The policy adopted by Great Britain and by President Franklin D. Roosevelt of continued oil shipments to Japan, combined with limited restrictions and threats, delayed possible war in 1940 until late 1941 when the United States was better prepared both materially and psychologically; oil diplomacy allowed Roosevelt to control US entry into the war until the United States could make a more viable military commitment to the Allied cause.

1527.   Etzold, Thomas H.   FISCAL DIPLOMACY: THE HOUSE OF MORGAN, THE STATE DEPARTMENT, AND THE REPARATION LOANS.   *Peace and Change 1975 3(2/3): 109-112.* Describes the positions of the State Department and the Morgan Guaranty Trust Co. with regard to World War I reparations in the 1930's.

1528.   Etzold, Thomas H.   PROTECTION OR POLITICS? "PERDICARIS ALIVE OR RAISULI DEAD."   *Hist. 1975 37(2): 297-304.* When the Moroccan bandit Raisuli kidnapped a presumed American citizen, Ion Perdicaris, in May 1904, Secretary of State John Hay and President Theodore Roosevelt responded in such flamboyant terms that historians have regarded the incident more as a means to attract favorable attention on the eve of a national Republican nominating convention than as an example of a government protecting an individual citizen. Relying principally upon State Department records in the National Archives, this study shows that Roosevelt and Hay had cause to be impatient due to Moroccan delays, and that the incident has more consequence than has been attributed to it because it was one of the events that ultimately led the French to exert more control over the government in Tangier. 18 notes.   N. W. Moen

1529.   Fay, Bernard.   "UN GRAND AMI DE LA FRANCE: FRANKLIN DELANO ROOSEVELT"   ["A great friend of France: Franklin Delano Roosevelt"].   *Écrits de Paris [France] 1974 (339): 46-50.* President Roosevelt championed the cause of France, even before America entered World War II and as early as 1938.

1530. Feingold, Henry L. WHO SHALL BEAR GUILT FOR THE HOLOCAUST: THE HUMAN DILEMMA. *Am. Jewish Hist. 1979 68(3): 261-282.* Analyzes the inability to save Jewish lives during the Holocaust and indicts the Roosevelt administration, the Vatican, the British government, other governments, and American Jewry's leadership. Political and military priorities were compounded by the sheer impossibility for most Americans, including Jews, to absorb what was happening, even as late as December 1944. F. Rosenthal

1531. Fischer, Robert. HENRY CABOT LODGE AND THE TAFT ARBITRATION TREATIES. *South Atlantic Q. 1979 78(2): 244-258.* In August 1911 President William H. Taft had his Secretary of State, Philander C. Knox, conclude two arbitration treaties with Great Britain and France. They acknowledged the Senate's voice in the special agreement to submit each dispute to settlement, but they also provided that all differences were to be submitted to the Hague Court or other tribunal. Further, whenever there was a disagreement between the two parties as to what was subject to arbitration, the question would be submitted to a Joint High Commission. Republican Senator Henry Cabot Lodge viewed Taft's policy as challenging the Senate's prerogatives in the conduct of foreign affairs as well as the taproots of traditional American foreign policy. Delineates the debates as well as the correspondence between Lodge and Theodore Roosevelt, who opposed the treaties. Finally, the matter of a tribunal ascertaining whether something was subject to arbitration was removed, and the Senate approved the amended treaties. Based on the Roosevelt Papers (Library of Congress), Lodge Papers (Massachusetts Historical Society), *Congressional Record* and secondary studies; 36 notes. H. M. Parker, Jr.

1532. Floto, Inga. COLONEL HOUSE IN PARIS: THE FATE OF A PRESIDENTIAL ADVISER. *Am. Studies in Scandinavia [Norway] 1973/74 6(1/2): 21-45.* This historiographical article discusses the break between President Woodrow Wilson and Colonel Edward M. House in 1919 as well as House's competency as an international negotiator. Evaluation is made of numerous historical and psychological works, including Charles Seymour, *The Intimate Papers of Colonel House* (1928); Ray Stannard Baker, *Woodrow Wilson and World Settlement* (1923); Alexander and Juliette L. George, *Woodrow Wilson and Colonel House. A Personality Study* (1956); and the author's own work, *Colonel House in Paris: A Study of American Policy at the Paris Peace Conference 1919* (1973). Based on various private manuscript collections and secondary sources; 64 notes. J. E. Findling

1533. Fohlen, Claude. THE FOREIGN POLICY OF F. D. ROOSEVELT: SOME REFLECTIONS. *Amerikastudien/American Studies [West Germany] 1976 21(1): 109-118.* Franklin D. Roosevelt had a very personal way of conducting foreign policy, relying less and less on the State Department and more and more on his own instinct and information which reached him through various channels. He was always looking for the support of public opinion. Behind all his decisions was a desire to build a strong international organization which he wanted to be dominated by the big powers. 20 notes. G. Bassler

1534. Fowler, John G., Jr. COMMAND DECISION. *Military Rev. 1979 59(6): 2-6.* General George C. Marshall balanced personal career goals against professional responsibilities. Though he desired the field command of the Allied invasion of Europe in World War II, Marshall refused to allow personal preferences to influence President Franklin D. Roosevelt's decision. Roosevelt decided that Marshall's global strategic vision and diplomatic ability made him indispensible as US Army chief of staff. The field command was given to Dwight D. Eisenhower. 17 notes. J. Moore

1535. Francis, Michael J. THE UNITED STATES AT RIO, 1942: THE STRAINS OF PAN-AMERICANISM. *J. of Latin Am. Studies [Great Britain] 1974 6(1): 77-95.* Explains why at the Rio Conference (1942) a rupture of diplomatic relations with the Axis powers rather than a joint declaration of war or a unanimous termination of relations with the Axis was recommended. In explaining this outcome, the author focuses on the domestic and foreign policy considerations of representatives from Chile, Argentina, and Brazil. Different analyses of Latin American realities, plus sharp personal rivalry between Under Secretary Sumner Welles and Secretary Cordell Hull, added to the difficulties of the United States in obtaining the unanimous break which Hull thought more desir-

able. Based on the US National Archives, Department of State, and *Foreign Relations of the United States* and some secondary works; 95 notes. K. M. Bailor

1536. Freedman, Lawrence. THE STRATEGY OF HIROSHIMA. *J. of Strategic Studies [Great Britain] 1978 1(1): 76-97.* Follows the Roosevelt Administration's decisionmaking on the operational use of the first atomic bombs. Cities were attacked because of the lack of significant military targets and to increase the bomb's shock value over conventional strategic bombing, and not for experimental value or to intimidate the Soviet Union. The bombing of Nagasaki was the logical extension of the decision to use the bomb in the first place. Primary sources; 45 notes. A. M. Osur

1537. Gaines, Anne-Rosewell J. POLITICAL REWARD AND RECOGNITION: WOODROW WILSON APPOINTS THOMAS NELSON PAGE AMBASSADOR TO ITALY. *Virginia Mag. of Hist. and Biog. 1981 89(3): 328-340.* Records the circumstances surrounding the 1913 appointment of wealthy Washington, D.C., and Virginia literary figure, Thomas Nelson Page. Wilson and Page had ties at the University of Virginia, and Page had chaired Wilson's inauguration committee. Page, a friend of Theodore Roosevelt and William Howard Taft, became increasingly sympathetic to Progressivism. His friends solicited the London post for him, but Page professed disinterest. By April, Page desired a diplomatic position, which he received in June. Page served Wilson loyally for six years. Based on the Wilson and Page papers; 61 notes. P. J. Woehrmann

1538. Gandi, Vera. I LIMITI DELL'INTERNAZIONALISMO WILSONIANO [The limits of Wilsonian internationalism]. *Comunità [Italy] 1981 35(183): 96-152.* Reviews Woodrow Wilson's ideas on the international order, his doctrinaire idealism, and his evolution from a British-type liberalism to the "New Freedom." Italian.

1539. Genizi, Haim. JAMES MCDONALD AND THE ROOSEVELT ADMINISTRATION. Artzi, Pinhas, ed. *Bar-Ilan Studies in History* (Ramat-Gan, Israel: Bar-Ilan U. Pr., 1978): 285-306. Assesses the career of James McDonald (1886-1964) and his assistance to Jewish refugees in the 1930's. In 1933, the League of Nations set up a High Commission for Refugees; America put McDonald forward as a candidate, although it wanted to remain isolationist. As High Commissioner, McDonald found little support in America; he resigned after the Nuremberg decrees in 1935. Franklin D. Roosevelt became more helpful to the Jews after the German annexation of Austria in 1938. He set up the President's Advisory Committee, with McDonald as chairman and as liaison between the State Department and the social services. Various countries were suggested for the Jewish national home, but many European consuls and the State Department objected. For his strenuous efforts on the Jews' behalf, he was awarded the Gottheil Medal for Services to American Jewry. Based on archive sources and secondary works; 114 notes. A. Alcock

1540. George, Brian T. THE STATE DEPARTMENT AND SUN YAT-SEN: AMERICAN POLICY AND THE REVOLUTIONARY DISINTEGRATION OF CHINA, 1920-1924. *Pacific Hist. Rev. 1977-46(3): 387-408.* Historians have failed to analyze the reasons for State Department distaste for Sun Yat-sen in the latter part of his career. The main reasons were the view that Sun's activities had an unstabilizing effect which raised problems for the successful implementation of the United States' Open Door policy. Sun was not seen as a revolutionary and a nationalist, but as a megalomaniacal troublemaker who was primarily responsible for China's failure to unify peacefully and reform politically under warlord control. Based on documents in MSS. collections and the National Archives and on published primary sources; 67 notes. W. K. Hobson

1541. Gerome, Frank. SECRETARY OF STATE PHILANDER C. KNOX AND HIS GOOD WILL TOUR OF CENTRAL AMERICA, 1912. *Secolas Ann. 1977 8: 72-83.* Secretary of State Knox visited Central America, Venezuela, and several Caribbean islands in 1912. The purpose of the trip was to lessen tension in the Caribbean and to duplicate the success of Elihu Root's tour of South America in 1906. Although the trip was interesting, it accomplished very little in aiding US policy and understanding of the Caribbean. 41 notes. J. Lewis

1542. Giffin, Frederick C. THE RUDOWITZ EXTRADITION CASE. *J. of the Illinois State Hist. Soc. 1982 75(1): 61-72.* In October 1908, Ernest von Schilling, the Russian consul in Chicago, demanded the extradition of Christian Ansoff Rudowitz, a refugee who had participated in the Revolution of 1905. Upon the arrest of Rudowitz, massive public agitation for his release centered in Chicago among radicals, but quickly spread throughout the nation as attention focused on American relations with the government of Tsar Nicholas II and the establishment of a precedent abolishing political asylum in the United States. On 7 December, Commissioner Mark A. Foote ordered the extradition but he was overruled on 26 January 1909 by Secretary of State Elihu Root, who noted the political nature of Rudowitz's offenses. 6 illus., 35 notes.
A. W. Novitsky

1543. Gilderhus, Mark T. PAN-AMERICAN INITIATIVES: THE WILSON PRESIDENCY AND REGIONAL INTEGRATION, 1914-1917. *Diplomatic Hist. 1980 4(4): 409-423.* During his first term of office, 1913-17, President Woodrow Wilson sought to institute a policy of Pan-American regional integration. He and his aides envisioned for the Americas a functioning network of trade and investment coordinated with a united resistance to potential European intervention. A related Pan-American treaty would provide for a multilateral police force to maintain order in the hemisphere. Although American trade within the hemisphere did grow, amateurish American diplomacy and Latin American fears of US domination doomed the vision. 43 notes.
T. L. Powers

1544. Girard, Jolyon P. CONGRESS AND PRESIDENTIAL MILITARY POLICY: THE OCCUPATION OF GERMANY, 1919-1923. *Mid-America 1974 56(4): 211-220.* Although Congress was unwilling to take the drastic step of cutting off funds for the United States Army of Occupation in Germany after World War I, it continually exerted pressure on Presidents Woodrow Wilson and Warren G. Harding to withdraw the troops. During the winter of 1922-23 when it appeared that France and Germany might become involved in conflict, dragging the United States in because of the presence of its troops, the Senate voted 57 to six (with 33 not voting), in favor of a resolution declaring that the sense of the Senate was for immediate withdrawal. The increasingly more vehement congressional opposition prompted Harding to act. Based on primary and secondary sources; 33 notes.
T. D. Schoonover

1545. Gorokhov, A. FRANKLIN ROOSEVELT ON US-SOVIET RELATIONS. *Int. Affairs [USSR] 1972 (6): 67-69.* Cites Franklin D. Roosevelt as the first American president to realize the importance of maintaining open and friendly relations between the United States and the USSR, 1933-45.

1546. Gould, Lewis L. A FAN LETTER TO THEODORE ROOSEVELT. *Rev. in Am. Hist. 1980 8(3): 377-381.* Review essay of Frederick W. Marks III's *Velvet on Iron: The Diplomacy of Theodore Roosevelt* (Lincoln: U. of Nebraska Pr., 1979); 1902-15.

1547. Gow, Douglas R. HOW DID THE ROOSEVELT COROLLARY BECOME LINKED TO DOMINICAN REPUBLIC? *Mid-America 1976 58(3): 159-165.* Examines the link between the Roosevelt Corollary of 1904 and American intervention in the Dominican Republic in 1905. Concludes that the link was an accident of timing which led the public and subsequent historians to think they were related. Suggests that the Corollary was devised with Venezuela, Panama, and Cuba in mind. Roosevelt did not mention the Dominican Republic in the 1904 campaign or in his State of the Union message of 6 December 1904. Speeches by Elihu Root in announcing the Corollary led the public to think that it resulted in the subsequent intervention in the Dominican Republic. Primary and secondary sources; 21 notes.
J. M. Lee

1548. Habibuddin, S. M. FRANKLIN D. ROOSEVELT'S ANTI-COLONIAL POLICY TOWARDS ASIA: ITS IMPLICATIONS FOR INDIA, INDO-CHINA AND INDONESIA (1941-45). *J. of Indian Hist. [India] 1975 53(3): 497-522.* Examines the anticolonial policies of President Franklin D. Roosevelt with special emphasis on India, Indo-china, and Indonesia. Roosevelt's support of Asian aspirations for national independence reflected a commitment to humanitarian ideals. The strategic importance of India after the Japanese capture of the British, French, and Dutch colonies in Asia prompted American officials to urge

concessions from the British. Roosevelt wanted the imperialistic powers of Europe to follow the American example in the Philippines and grant independence to subject nationalities. By the end of World War II, however, American anticolonialist policy became passive, particularly after the publication of the William Phillips letter on India in the summer of 1944. War Department and Navy interests were opposed to any trusteeship system which would weaken American control of strategic islands in the Pacific Ocean. Although the Netherlands gave a wartime pledge of greater autonomy to its Asian colonies, neither France nor England indicated any willingness to liquidate overseas empires. Asian nationalists were inspired by the American president's continuing efforts in their behalf. Secondary sources; 105 notes.
S. H. Frank

1549. Haight, John McVickar, Jr. FDR'S "BIG STICK." *US Naval Inst. Pro. 1980 106(7): 68-73.* From late 1937 to early 1938, President Franklin D. Roosevelt tried to find some way to blunt Japan's aggression in China. As he intimated privately to close associates and publicly in the famous Quarantine Speech in Chicago in early October 1937, he wanted a naval blockade of Japan. He realized, though, that he needed American public opinion behind him before proceeding and that unless he could get Great Britain to commit the British fleet, a blockade of Japan would be unsuccessful and damage US interests in the Far East. Despite the Japanese attack on the USS *Panay* in China in December 1937, Roosevelt failed to rally the American people. When Prime Minister Neville Chamberlain rebuffed Roosevelt's suggestion about using the British fleet, the blockade idea died. A preliminary version of this article appeared in the *Pacific Historical Review*, May 1971 (see abstract 10:489). 5 photos, 14 notes.
A. N. Garland

1550. Haines, Gerald K. THE ROOSEVELT ADMINISTRATION INTERPRETS THE MONROE DOCTRINE. *Australian J. of Pol. and Hist. [Australia] 1978 24(3): 332-345.* Franklin D. Roosevelt and his advisers selectively used the Monroe Doctrine to legitimize and support their objectives. In the 1930's, they converted it into a common hemispheric defense policy, but avoided the term "Monroe Doctrine" in favor of "continental solidarity" or "Pan American unity." By 1938, assurances had been given to Canada. In 1940, British and French colonies west of the International Dateline had been included, and Greenland and West Africa were also considered. By the late 1930's, military officials planned to deny to enemies bases from which they could threaten the United States or the Panama Canal, and business executives supported the administration's desire to counter German or Japanese economic or cultural penetration in Latin America. Based on Department of State archives and on the Roosevelt and Hull Papers; 69 notes.
W. D. McIntyre

1551. Haines, Gerald K. UNDER THE EAGLE'S WING: THE FRANKLIN ROOSEVELT ADMINISTRATION FORGES AN AMERICAN HEMISPHERE. *Diplomatic Hist. 1977 1(4): 373-388.* The Franklin D. Roosevelt administration evolved a comprehensive program for minimizing the influence of the Axis Powers in Latin America. Secret police of friendly nations were trained by FBI agents, and Axis aid to local military forces was displaced by American aid. Newspapers, firms, and radio stations thought to be pro-Axis were blacklisted; e.g., American firms were told to restrict their tax deductible Latin American advertising to friendly newspapers and stations. Government censorship was encouraged, while the region was blanketed with pro-American propaganda. Beginning in 1940, the US effort was coordinated by the Office of the Coordinator of Inter-American Affairs headed by Nelson A. Rockefeller. Based on archival and secondary sources; 60 notes.
L. W. Van Wyk

1552. Harbutt, Fraser. THE AMERICAN FOREIGN SERVICE AND THE APPROACH TO COLD WAR. *Rev. in Am. Hist. 1981 9(4): 431-536.* Review essay of Hugh De Santis's *The Diplomacy of Silence: The American Foreign Service, the Soviet Union, and the Cold War, 1933-1947* (1980).

1553. Harper, James W. HUGH LENOX SCOTT Y LA DI-PLOMACIA DE LOS ESTADOS UNIDOS HACIA LA REVOLU-CIÓN MEXICANA [Hugh Lenox Scott and the diplomacy of the United States toward the Mexican revolution]. *Hist. Mexicana [Mexico] 1978 27(3): 427-445.* The response of Woodrow Wilson to the Mexican Revolution was the first chapter in the response of North American diplomacy to the nationalist revolutions of the 20th century. Through

Hugh Lenox Scott, Wilson rejected full-scale and direct intervention and sought to establish a reasonably efficient and friendly government in Mexico through support of Pancho Villa and his partisans. This objective was frustrated by Carrranza's victory over Villa in central Mexico in 1915. Recognizing the failure of indirect intervention, Scott still maintained a moderate position and opposed military intervention. Scott's rejection of military intervention in Mexican affairs belies usual claims that Wilson engaged in "idealistic imperialism."

F. J. Shaw, Jr.

1554. Harris, Ruth R. THE "MAGIC" LEAK OF 1941 AND JAPANESE-AMERICAN RELATIONS. *Pacific Hist. Rev. 1981 50(1): 77-96.* As the result of a British communications lapse in April 1941, the German embassy in Washington knew that American cryptoanalysts had broken the Japanese diplomatic code. In May, American naval intelligence learned of the leak from a decoded Japanese message from Berlin to Tokyo. Until 1 November, delivery of intercepted Japanese messages to the White House was curtailed, and, inadequately informed, President Franklin D. Roosevelt made diplomatic mistakes that worsened relations with Japan. In August, American naval intelligence did not inform the president that the Japanese had decided not to transmit highly secret policy decisions because of danger of interception. Decoded Japanese messages in the fall of 1941 contained information that misled American officials. Based on Japanese diplomatic messages in national Archives and other primary sources; 44 notes.   R. N. Lokken

1555. Harrison, Benjamin T. CHANDLER ANDERSON AND BUSINESS INTERESTS IN MEXICO: 1913-1920: WHEN ECONOMIC INTERESTS FAILED TO ALTER U.S. FOREIGN POLICY. *Inter-American Econ. Affairs 1979 33(3): 3-23.* Chandler Anderson was an international attorney who represented business interests in Mexico during Woodrow Wilson's presidency; Chandler failed to win Wilson's support in protecting American commercial interests, 1913-20.

1556. Harrison, Richard A. A PRESIDENTIAL *DEMARCHE*: FRANKLIN D. ROOSEVELT'S PERSONAL DIPLOMACY AND GREAT BRITAIN, 1936-37. *Diplomatic Hist. 1981 5(3): 245-272.* During the mid-30's, Roosevelt made an unsuccessful attempt to prevent World War II and to establish a cooperative partnership with Great Britain. Though unsuccessful, it was the precursor of the Anglo-American relationship that emerged during the war. It also demonstrated both the creative advantages and dangers of personal presidential diplomacy. Based on primary material in the Public Record Office, London, and other British archives; 88 notes.   J. V. Coutinho

1557. Hartig, Thomas H. ROBERT LANSING AND EAST ASIAN-AMERICAN RELATIONS: A STUDY IN MOTIVATION. *Michigan Academician 1974 7(2): 191-199.* Examines Secretary of State Robert Lansing's foreign policy, particularly toward Japan, prior to World War I.   S

1558. Hera, Florin and Bullitt, William C. PENTRU PREȘEDINTE: PERSONAL ȘI CONFIDENȚIAL [For the President: personal and confidential]. *Magazin Istoric [Romania] 1978 12(9): 37-42.* Extracts from William C. Bullitt's *For the President: Personal and Secret Correspondence Between Franklin D. Roosevelt and William C. Bullitt* (1973) translated into Romanian with an introduction and commentary, noting the isolationism of this US ambassador to the USSR and then France; 1933-41.

1559. Hindman, E. James. THE GENERAL ARBITRATION TREATIES OF WILLIAM HOWARD TAFT. *Historian 1973 36(1): 52-65.* A study of William Howard Taft's efforts involving arbitration treaties signed by the United States, Great Britain, and France on 4 August 1911. Opposition was led by Theodore Roosevelt and implemented in the Senate through amendments that destroyed the effectiveness of the treaties. "Taft's arbitration efforts were rejected amid an atmosphere of suspicion and partisan policies." 71 notes.

R. V. Ritter

1560. Hitchins, Keith. WOODROW WILSON AND THE UNION OF TRANSYLVANIA WITH RUMANIA, 1917-1918. *Rev. Roumaine d'Hist. [Romania] 1979 18(4): 803-810.* The evolution of Woodrow Wilson's attitude toward the aspirations of the subject nationalities of Austria-Hungary, and especially those of the Romanians of Transylvania, moved from a belief that Austria would respond more to peace overtures if assured that the empire would be left intact, to the conviction by 1918 that self-determination was more important than any economic or strategic considerations. Examines the work of the American Preparatory Commission, or "the Inquiry," and its influence on American policy, as well as the effect of the mission of Vasile Stoica and Romanian American propaganda on Washington's war aims. Ultimately Wilson would be guided primarily by the expressed will of the subject peoples. National Archives, secondary material; 26 notes.   G. J. Bobango

1561. Hodge, Larry G. AMERICAN DIPLOMACY TOWARDS TRANSCAUCASIA DURING THE RUSSIAN REVOLUTION, MARCH 1917-MARCH 1918. *New Rev.: A J. of East-European Hist. [Canada] 1975 15(1-2): 20-38.* The United States became involved in Transcaucasia only through wartime necessity. The American consul at Tiflis, Felix Willoughby Smith, impressed the plight of the Caucasian front, the threat of Moslem Turkey, and the disruption caused by the German supported Bolsheviks upon the State Department. American foreign policy towards the area gradually shifted from a preoccupation with World War I to a desire to establish a stable local government. Transportation problems and the Western Front preoccupation kept the Americans powerless to prevent the Central Powers from dominating the Caucasus. Primary and secondary sources; 76 notes.

W. L. Olbrich

1562. Hoernel, David. LAS GRANDES CORPORACIONES Y LA POLÍTICA DEL GRAN GARROTE EN CUBA Y A MÉXICO [Large corporations and the Big Stick policy in Cuba and Mexico]. *Hist. Mexicana [Mexico] 1980 30(2): 209-246.* During the late 19th century, the interests and overseas activities of many financial and industrial corporations frequently clashed with those of their governments. The rhythm of these clashes affected US policy in Cuba and Mexico. Theodore Roosevelt's Big Stick policy was the fruit of his alliance with financial and industrial groups opposed to the largest trusts. Taft's "Dollar Diplomacy" reflected his effort to restore domestic financial stability by cultivating the largest trusts. Wilson's reaction to the Madero assassination reflected not only moral outrage but the widening rift between the US government and US financial interests allied to German financial interests. Based on documents in the National Archives and secondary works.

F. J. Shaw, Jr.

1563. Hogan, Michael J. INFORMAL ENTENTE: PUBLIC POLICY AND PRIVATE MANAGEMENT IN ANGLO-AMERICAN PETROLEUM AFFAIRS, 1918-1924. *Business Hist. R. 1974 48(2): 187-205.* Studies the development of a *modus operandi* for handling oil rich areas in the post-World War I period. The US State Department abandoned unilateralism in favor of a policy that encouraged multinational, especially Anglo-American, management of petroleum resources by private business leaders. This policy was followed in Persia, Mesopotamia, and Latin America. Nationalism, neutrality, and the "open door," were redefined to accommodate the new vision of expert management and cooperative capitalism. "In practice, the dream of an 'all-British' system and the American vision of an open door world had come out as an informal Anglo-American entente, institutionalized at the private level, surrounded with the mystique of enlightened capitalism and masked behind tortured concessions to competitive symbols." 64 notes.

R. V. Ritter

1564. Holbo, Paul S. PRESIDENTS, PROFESSORS, AND ASIAN POLICY, 1899-1945. *Rev. in Am. Hist. 1980 8(2): 277-283.* Review essay of Noel H. Pugach's *Paul S. Reinsch: Open Door Diplomat in Action* (Millwood, N.Y.: KTO Pr., 1979), Michael Schaller's *The U.S. Crusade in China, 1938-1945* (New York: Columbia U. Pr., 1979), and Richard E. Welch, Jr.'s *Response to Imperialism: The United States and the Philippine-American War, 1899-1902* (Chapel Hill: U. of North Carolina Pr., 1979).

1565. Hosoya, Chihiro. JAPANESE-AMERICAN RELATIONS. *Pacific Hist. 1979 23(4): 9-27.* Japanese Prime Minister Konoe Fumimaro's idea of a summit conference with Franklin D. Roosevelt in October 1941 was intended to work out a settlement in the Pacific area. Some historians have placed the blame for Pearl Harbor on the State Department's cool reception to Konoe's proposal, but through his 1934 trip to the United States Konoe had so alienated important American business-men and statesmen that his actions as prime minister were suspect, and this was what prevented Roosevelt from proceeding with the conference with Konoe.   H. M. Parker, Jr.

1566. Hourihan, William J.   THE BIG STICK IN TURKEY: AMERICAN DIPLOMACY AND NAVAL OPERATIONS AGAINST THE OTTOMAN EMPIRE, 1903-1904. *Naval War Coll. Rev. 1981 34(5): 78-88.* Missionary societies formed a single issue group in American politics. Their influence, the reported assassination of an American diplomat in Beirut, an impending presidential election, and a Turkish pasha unwilling to receive the American minister because of "important visits to the harem" gave Theodore Roosevelt an opportunity to demonstrate American seapower. If its lessons were lost on the Otto-man Empire, they were not in the capitals of Europe.   J/S

1567. Iakovlev, N. N.   F. ROOSEVELT: PROPONENT OF COL-LABORATION WITH THE SOVIET UNION. *Soviet Studies in Hist. 1974 12(4): 3-29.* President Roosevelt's recognition of the USSR in 1933 and his policy of cooperation with the Soviet Union against fascism were dictated by his astute understanding of *Realpolitik* and his ability to see the true interests of the United States beyond the reactionary prejudices of many segments of American and Western European society during 1933-45.

1568. Ibarra, Jorge.   AGOSTO DE 1906: UNA INTERVENCIÓN AMAÑADA [August 1906: clever intervention]. *Rev. de la Biblioteca Nac. José Martí [Cuba] 1973 15(1): 161-186.* Studies the growth of US imperialism and colonial politics in Cuba, 1901-06, and factors contribut-ing to the fall of the government of President Thomás Estrada Palma in 1906, stressing Theodore Roosevelt's reluctance to intervene.

1569. Iriye, Akira.   THE MAKING OF A *REALPOLITIKER.* *Rev. in Am. Hist. 1980 8(1): 109-114.* Review essay of Robert Dallek's *Franklin D. Roosevelt and American Foreign Policy, 1932-1945* (New York: Oxford U. Pr., 1979).

1570. Jablon, Howard.   CORDELL HULL, HIS "ASSOCIATES," AND RELATIONS WITH JAPAN, 1933-1936. *Mid-America 1974 56(3): 160-174.* Cordell Hull did not exercise the control over US foreign policy in the mid-1930's which he has claimed, but was a force in some areas, such as commercial matters. In Far Eastern policy he continued the programs of his predecessor, Henry L. Stimson, without substantial modification. Franklin D. Roosevelt's concern with domestic matters permitted Hull a freer rein in foreign policy. However, when Hull gained this freedom, it was often paradoxically surrendered to his Division heads. Since the Division heads were staunch Stimson men, Hull was advised to continue the policy toward Japan adopted by his predecessor. As a result, foreign policy of the mid-1930's remained inflexible and unimaginative. Based on manuscript and printed primary and secondary sources; 63 notes.   T. D. Schoonover

1571. James, Edith.   WILSONIAN WARTIME DIPLOMACY: THE SENSE OF THE SEVENTIES. Haines, Gerald K. and Walker, J. Samuel, ed. *American Foreign Relations: A Historiographical Review* (Westport, Conn.: Greenwood Pr., 1981): 115-131. Reviews World War I historiography of the 1970's, especially Woodrow Wilson's wartime diplomacy, tracing many current concerns—intervention, self-determina-tion, economic expansion, economic regulation, government candor, in-ternational cooperation—to their origins in this era. The 1970's scholarship of the period calls for multiarchival research, multinational perspectives, multicausal analysis, and multidimensional explanations. American involvement in World War I can no longer be seen as stemming strictly from political interests or from purely economic motives, but rather from a complex combination of factors involving national security, moral and legal issues, and diplomatic and economic influences. Second-ary sources; 45 notes.   J. Powell

1572. Jones, Kenneth Paul.   DISCORD AND COLLABORATION: CHOOSING AN AGENT GENERAL FOR REPARATIONS. *Diplomatic Hist. 1977 1(2): 118-139.* Discusses the Calvin Coolidge ad-ministration's attempts to appoint an Agent General for German Repara-tions and the resulting controversy and repercussions. Emphasizes both discord and collaboration between public officials and private financiers

such as J. P. Morgan, in the promotion of American economic diplomacy. Covers 1923-24. 93 notes.   G. H. Curtis

1573. Kahn, Gilbert N.   PRESIDENTIAL PASSIVITY ON A NON-SALIENT ISSUE: PRESIDENT FRANKLIN D. ROOSEVELT AND THE 1935 WORLD COURT FIGHT. *Diplomatic Hist. 1980 4(2): 137-159.* In 1935, the US Senate seemed ready to approve American membership in the Permanent Court of International Justice (World Court). The issue was not a vital one, and President Franklin D. Roose-velt (1882-1945) had little to lose and much to gain by actively supporting the treaty of adherence. His failure to exercise decisive leadership in this, his first major foreign policy fight, allowed anti-World Court forces to prevail in the Senate. It further permitted the growth in the Senate of an isolationist sentiment which would cause him great problems on later foreign policy issues which were vital, and encouraged legislative indepen-dence of executive authority. 93 notes.   T. L. Powers

1574. Kane, N. Stephen.   BANKERS AND DIPLOMATS: THE DI-PLOMACY OF THE DOLLAR IN MEXICO, 1921-1924. *Business Hist. R. 1973 47(3): 335-352.* Examines the cooperative relations between American investment bankers, the US State Department, and Mexico, illustrating the interdependency of the dollar and diplomacy in the 1920's. Secretary of State Charles Evans Hughes used conditional recognition and financial pressure in the form of loan bans and closed markets to force Mexico to come to terms with the US both politically and economically. The International Committee of Bankers on Mexico, representing holders of defaulted securities and working closely with the diplomats, achieved their goals of a settlement with Mexico wherein the debt would be paid. Diplomatic recognition came later. Mexican political instability hindered financial relations and eventually the Lamont-de la Huerta Agreement (1922) was suspended by Mexico. Dollar diplomacy achieved immediate American ends but later proved self-defeating. Based on US Government documents, ICBM papers, contemporary newspaper reports, and other primary and secondary sources; 55 notes.   N. J. Street

1575. Kane, N. Stephen.   CORPORATE POWER AND FOREIGN POLICY: EFFORTS OF AMERICAN OIL COMPANIES TO IN-FLUENCE UNITED STATES RELATIONS WITH MEXICO, 1921-1928. *Diplomatic Hist. 1977 1(2): 170-198.* Two case studies of the interaction between American oil companies and the US Department of State indicate that the companies "failed to exert effective influence on the foreign policy process" in their efforts to protect their foreign invest-ments in Mexico. The State Department's position concerning Mexico's petroleum legislation was actually based on "the Department's long-standing commitment to the concept of fair treatment of United States citizens and their capital abroad in the fields of trade and investment within the framework of generally accepted principles of international law." Based on primary and secondary sources; 89 notes.

G. H. Curtis

1576. Keating, John S.   MISSION TO MECCA: A POSTSCRIPT. *US Naval Inst. Pro. 1978 104(4): 74-77.* On 14 February 1945, President Franklin D. Roosevelt met with King Ibn Saud of Saudi Arabia on the Great Bitter Lake at the Suez Canal. As a result of the three-hour meet-ing, the two men signed a memorandum in which they expressed their mutual desires to agree. The memorandum was not given to the press and only a few copies were prepared. Little was said of its contents until 1954. In that year, Colonel William A. Eddy, a retired Marine Corps officer, published a book in which he gave the details of the meeting. Eddy had been US minister plenipotentiary to Saudi Arabia in 1945 and had been with King Ibn Saud at the meeting. In fact, he had acted as the kings's interpreter. The author quotes extensively from Colonel Eddy's book. He also points out the difficult position the United States was in as the question of an independent state of Israel was being discussed in the years immediately following the war. 4 photos.   A. N. Garland

1577. Kernek, Sterling J.   WOODROW WILSON AND NA-TIONAL SELF-DETERMINATION ALONG ITALY'S FRONTIER: A STUDY OF THE MANIPULATION OF PRINCIPLES IN THE PURSUIT OF POLITICAL INTERESTS. *Pro. of the Am. Phil. Soc. 1982 126(4): 243-300.* Examines President Wilson's handling of Italian boundary questions at the Paris Peace Conference in a manner that illustrates his flexibility as well as his ability to manipulate principles in the pursuit of self-interests. Challenges certain widespread interpretations of his statesmanship in general and his conduct of relations with Italy at the conference in particular. His idealism in international relations has emerged more memorable than his pursuit of political advantages. In all the postwar diplomacy, Wilson's one primary goal was the League of Nations, and all else was subordinated to it. Based on unpublished (Woodrow Wilson Papers, Library of Congress) as well as published primary sources (basically memoirs of persons at the Paris Conference), and secondary sources; biblio., map, 221 notes.

H. M. Parker, Jr.

1578. Kim, Won Mo. THEODORE ROOSEVELT'S KOREAN POLICY IN THE FAR EAST, 1901-1905. *J. of Social Sci. and Humanities [South Korea] 1976 (43): 99-116.* Describes Theodore Roosevelt's view of Asian power politics and his policy toward the independence of Korea in the aftermath of the Russo-Japanese War. Roosevelt regarded Russia as America's foremost rival in Asia, but he could not directly confront Russian attempts at Asian hegemony. He thus backed Japanese efforts to control the strategic Korean peninsula; the Taft-Katsura agreement of 1905 reflected the policy. With the withdrawal of the American legation from Seoul and the refusal of the Secretary of State to receive a Korean protest mission, Korea's fate was sealed. English-language sources; 144 notes.

D. M. Bishop

1579. Kimball, Warren F. CHURCHILL AND ROOSEVELT: THE PERSONAL EQUATION. *Prologue 1974 6(3): 169-182.* Reviews the personal correspondence between President Franklin D. Roosevelt and Prime Minister Winston Churchill. Nearly all of the voluminous correspondence has been preserved and presents a remarkable portrait of relations between the two world leaders. These relations were generally amicable, but the few disagreements were of a fundamental nature. Churchill resented playing a secondary role and was very distrustful of Soviet motives. It is doubtful if their friendship could have withstood the rigors of postwar problems. 3 photos, 45 notes.

V. L. Human

1580. Kimball, Warren F. THE MYTHICAL YALTA MYTH. *Soc. for Hist. of Am. Foreign Relations. Newsletter 1982 13(2): 21-23.* Examines the issue of the relationship between Poland and the USSR as discussed at the 1945 Yalta Conference attended by Winston Churchill, Franklin D. Roosevelt, and Joseph Stalin.

1581. Kimball, Warren F. and Bartlett, Bruce. ROOSEVELT AND PREWAR COMMITMENTS TO CHURCHILL: THE TYLER KENT AFFAIR. *Diplomatic Hist. 1981 5(4): 291-311.* The secrecy surrounding the 1940 espionage case involving the arrest and imprisonment of Tyler Kent, an anti-Semitic and anti-Roosevelt code clerk at the American embassy at London who passed confidential documents to Axis agents, fueled revisionist speculation that the affair concealed evidence of a Winston Churchill-Franklin D. Roosevelt conspiracy to involve the United States in the war. The evidence, released in 1972, does not support a conspiracy thesis. While the papers conveyed by Kent indicate Anglo-American naval cooperation, they also show Roosevelt's reticence to become more involved without congressional and public approval. Their release in 1940 would have merely embarrassed the prime minister and president. Based on US State Department records and other primary sources; 46 notes.

T. J. Heston

1582. Kimball, Warren F. THE ROOSEVELT RIDDLE: STILL ANOTHER VIEW. *Rev. in Am. Hist. 1976 4(3): 458-463.* Review article prompted by *The Diaries of Edward R. Stettinius, Jr., 1943-1946* (Thomas M. Campbell and George C. Herring, eds.; New York: New Viewpoints, 1975); discusses American foreign policy under Roosevelt, 1943-45.

1583. Kottman, Richard N. HERBERT HOOVER AND THE ST. LAWRENCE SEAWAY TREATY OF 1932. *New York Hist. 1975 56(3): 314-346.* Describes President Herbert Hoover's negotiations with Canada of the St. Lawrence Seaway Treaty of 1932. Negotiations were politically complicated by New York state's and Chicago's interests in several aspects of the proposed seaway. Based on recently opened manuscripts in the United States, Canada, and Great Britain; 5 illus., 61 notes.

R. N. Lokken

1584. Kottman, Richard N. HERBERT HOOVER AND THE SMOOT-HAWLEY TARIFF: CANADA, A CASE STUDY. *J. of*

Am. Hist. 1975 62(3): 609-635. Analyzes the role of President Herbert C. Hoover and the Smoot-Hawley Tariff of 1930 in the deterioration of Canadian-American relations. Hoover's insensitivity to nationalist feeling and agricultural interests in Canada, reflected in his signing of the Smoot-Hawley Tariff, led to tariff retaliation, prolonged neglect of the St. Lawrence seaway project, and the Liberal electoral defeat in Canada in 1930. Recent scholarship which attempts to rehabilitate Hoover's image faces a contradiction in Hoover's handling of Canadian-American relations, 1929-33. Based on Hoover's writings, documents in the public archives of Canada, records of the Department of State, newspapers, journals, and secondary works; 117 notes.

J. B. Street

1585. Kottman, Richard N. THE HOOVER-BENNETT MEETING OF 1931: MISMANAGED SUMMITRY. *Ann. of Iowa 1974 42(3): 205-221.* Examines the 1931 Washington summit conference between Herbert Hoover and Canadian Prime Minister R. B. Bennett against a background of several areas of dispute, including tariff protection, prohibition, restriction of laborers from Canada into the United States, and joint development of the St. Lawrence River. The January 1931 visit of Bennett did nothing to settle national differences, and activities of the press raised false hopes. 41 notes.

C. W. Olson

1586. Kramer, Paul. NELSON ROCKEFELLER AND BRITISH SECURITY COORDINATION. *J. of Contemporary Hist. [Great Britain] 1981 16(1): 73-88.* An executive order of President Franklin D. Roosevelt, 16 August 1940, created the Office of Coordinator of Commercial and Cultural Relations between the American Republics, and appointed Nelson A. Rockefeller as head. The covert purpose of the new office was cooperation with British Security Coordination to eliminate Nazi agents and businesses from the Americas. The British also hoped to induce the United States to join the Allied side in the war. A precedent of covert activity was thus established to be applied later to the Office of Strategic Services and the Central Intelligence Agency. Based on a personal interview and published primary sources; 19 notes.

M. P. Trauth

1587. Lael, Richard L. STRUGGLE FOR RATIFICATION: WILSON, LODGE, AND THE THOMSON-URRUTIA TREATY. *Diplomatic Hist. 1978 2(1): 81-102.* Within a year of taking office, Woodrow Wilson succeeded where his predecessors had failed, negotiating a treaty stabilizing US-Colombian relations strained by American activities in Panama since 1903. In concluding the agreement, Wilson made every effort to placate the Columbians, who had rejected earlier treaties, but neglected his own Senate. Henry Cabot Lodge (1850-1924) and other senators, perceiving in the pact a condemnation of Theodore Roosevelt's Panama policies, delayed ratification for seven years. Only a native threat to American oil interests in Colombia moved the Senate finally to approve the treaty. Primary sources; 94 notes.

T. L. Powers

1588. LaFeber, Walter. ROOSEVELT, CHURCHILL, AND INDO-CHINA, 1942-1945. *Am. Hist. R. 1975 80(5): 1277-1295.* During 1942-44 Franklin D. Roosevelt hoped to place the French colonies in Southeast Asia under an international trusteeship after the war. He further hoped that China would become the "policeman" in the area, and that the United States could work through China to stabilize and develop Southeast Asia. The president believed that once this precedent was established and China became a great power, the British colonies would also be given their independence and opened to world trade. Roosevelt thought little of the French and strongly disliked the new French leader, General Charles de Gaulle. Fully realizing Roosevelt's plans, Winston Churchill and the British Foreign Office concluded by 1943 that they needed de Gaulle's cooperation if British interests in Asia and Europe were to be protected after the war. As they worked to undercut Roosevelt's policy, they were helped by European specialists in the US Department of State, who also wanted to restore French power, and, most important, by the near-collapse of the Chinese government in 1944. After the summer of 1944 Roosevelt gave up in large measure on Chiang Kai-shek, and as he did so (and as Southeast Asia became less important to American military strategy), he slowly allowed the French to return to Southeast Asia. Above all, Roosevelt wanted an orderly, non-revolutionary Southeast Asia open to Western interests. It was therefore not illogical that when his trusteeship plan failed, he allowed the colonial powers to reenter the area.

A

1589. Leutze, James. THE SECRET OF THE CHURCHILL-ROOSEVELT CORRESPONDENCE SEPTEMBER 1939-MAY 1940. *J. of Contemporary Hist. [Great Britain] 1975 10(3): 465-491.* A careful examination of the Roosevelt-Churchill file does not disclose a plot on the American side to get the USA in the war to help Britain. The revelations of the letters do include the spy case of Tyler Gatewood Kent, a code clerk in the American embassy, who had hundreds of classified documents in his possession when he was arrested and convicted in London in 1940. Kent had felt that Franklin D. Roosevelt was trying to involve the USA in the war while openly saying the opposite to the American people. More importantly, it is now clear that the United States broke neutrality, among other ways, by informing the British of German ship movements in the neutrality zone, of movements of Japanese ships, and of miscellaneous intelligence picked up in Berlin and Tokyo. An appendix lists FDR messages to Winston Churchill and Churchill messages to Roosevelt, 11 September 1939 to 20 May 1940. 89 notes.   M. P. Trauth

1590. Lewis, Tom T. FRANCO-AMERICAN RELATIONS DURING THE FIRST MOROCCAN CRISIS. *Mid-America 1973 55(1): 21-36.* France wished to use the Entente Cordiale to further French "peaceful penetration" of Morocco, without alarming Germany or appearing to violate the 1880 Madrid Convention. Theodore Roosevelt, though slightly gravitating toward France, feared that French colonialism would lead to a Franco-German war. William II appealed for American support of the Moroccan open door and an international conference, to which Roosevelt ultimately influenced France to agree. In a unilateral action, Roosevelt offered an American plan for the contested supervision of the Moroccan police and trade, an initiative that helped alter Germany's designs and led to the Algeciras Treaty. Roosevelt's basic policy orientation remained consistent: prevention of a European war. Based on archival, published official documents, letters, and secondary works; 67 notes.   T. H. Wendel

1591. Liang, Chin-tung. PATRICK HURLEY: THE CHINA MEDIATOR. *Bull. of the Inst. of Modern Hist. Acad. Sinica [Taiwan] 1977 6: 329-353.* Describes the attempts by General Patrick J. Hurley to mediate between Jiang Jieshi (Chiang Kai-shek) and Mao Zedong while serving as US ambassador to China from 1944 to 1945. His pro-Chiang stance was consistently opposed by officers in the State Department, notably John Carter Vincent. US indirection in China policy strengthened Mao's demand for a coalition government, which Chiang resisted. Hurley resigned in 1945 and was replaced by General George C. Marshall. Based on documents in Tachi Archives, vol. 6, Foreign Relations of the United States, vol. 6-7, 1944-45; 83 notes.   C. C. Brown

1592. Link, A. S. INGA FLOTO, *COLONEL HOUSE IN PARIS: A STUDY IN AMERICAN FOREIGN POLICY AT THE PARIS PEACE CONFERENCE 1919.* [Inga Floto's *Colonel House in Paris: A study in American foreign policy at the Paris Peace Conference 1919. Hist. Tidsskrift [Denmark] 1978 78(1): 335-337.* Reviews, in English, Floto's book (Århus: Universitetsforlaget, 1973), which shows that Colonel Edward Mandell House was a poor diplomat who failed to keep Woodrow Wilson properly informed. The cause of the break between Wilson and House was House's disloyalty to Wilson when, without the President's knowledge, he agreed to shelve the League of Nations, joining Georges Clemenceau in moving to an agreement on a preliminary treaty on French terms.   M. A. Bett/S

1593. Little, Douglas J. TWENTY YEARS OF TURMOIL: ITT, THE STATE DEPARTMENT, AND SPAIN, 1924-1944. *Business Hist. Rev. 1979 53(4): 449-472.* Previous writers on American multinational corporations have underestimated the important role of the US government in protecting overseas business operations. The history of the International Telephone and Telegraph Corporation (ITT) in Spain illustrates this governmental role, because ITT's ability to survive the successive Spanish governmental upheavals in the 1930's depended in large part on the mediating efforts of the US State Department. Specifically, only threats of rejecting Spain's application for Export-Import Bank credit by the State Department forced Franco to renew ITT's franchise in 1939 rather than turning it over to Nazi interests. Based largely on State Department records in the National Archives; 65 notes.
                                                C. J. Pusateri

1594. Lowenstein, Sharon. A NEW DEAL FOR REFUGEES: THE PROMISE AND REALITY OF OSWEGO. *Am. Jewish Hist. 1982 71(3): 325-341.* Recounts the establishment in June 1944 of the Oswego Emergency Refugee Shelter in New York to receive 1000 Hitler victims, primarily from Hungary. Urged on by Henry Morgenthau, Jr., and Peter Bergson, Franklin Roosevelt set up the War Refugee Board in January, 1944, under the Treasury rather than the less cooperative State Department, and it quickly advocated temporary havens in the United States, Palestine, and elsewhere, to receive all evacuable refugees. But the Roosevelt administration, facing stiff political opposition, scaled down the venture, pressured England to open Palestine also, and delayed long enough to garner sufficient public support before acting. By then Hungarian Jewish deportations to Auschwitz were already underway. Based on Papers of the War Refugee Board, Henry Morgenthau, Jr., Diaries, Franklin D. Roosevelt Library, and other primary sources; 52 notes.
                                                R. A. Keller

1595. Lowenthal, Mark M. ROOSEVELT AND THE COMING OF THE WAR: THE SEARCH FOR UNITED STATES POLICY 1937-42. *J. of Contemporary Hist. [Great Britain] 1981 16(3): 413-440.* Between the extreme views of Franklin Delano Roosevelt as either plotter or statesman falls the interpretation of Roosevelt as improvisor, whose policy decisions fit into three consecutive periods. During the search for influence, October 1937 to May 1940, he hoped to use US power either to prevent or limit war. May 1940 to December 1941 was marked by a search for ways of saving Great Britain. Curiously, throughout this period, he expected Japan to remain neutral. The search for strategy from December 1941 to January 1943 was bedeviled by Roosevelt's failure to lay down broad policy decisions as perimeters of action either for the diplomats or for the military. Based on archival sources; 73 notes.
                                                M. P. Trauth

1596. Maddux, Thomas R. UNITED STATES-SOVIET NAVAL RELATIONS IN THE 1930'S: THE SOVIET UNION'S EFFORTS TO PURCHASE NAVAL VESSELS. *Naval War Coll. Rev. 1976 29(2): 28-37.* Once a president establishes an official policy, its implementation requires the cooperation and support of subordinate officers in the bureaucracy. Starting in 1936, the USSR made repeated efforts to purchase naval vessels from the United States. Although President Franklin D. Roosevelt officially approved the Russian proposal to purchase a battleship and two destroyers, to be built in US shipyards, in order to improve relations with Moscow, the Navy opposed it for several reasons. Navy opposition successfully delayed construction until 1939 when America's own shipbuilding program preempted available construction facilities.
                                                J

1597. Maddux, Thomas R. WATCHING STALIN MANEUVER BETWEEN HITLER AND THE WEST: AMERICAN DIPLOMATS AND SOVIET DIPLOMACY, 1934-1939. *Diplomatic Hist. 1977 1(2): 140-154.* Most American diplomats residing in the USSR during the late 1930's agreed that Soviet Russia was an unacceptable ally, despite a general difference in assessment of Soviet policy between Soviet specialists, such as George F. Kennan, and other American officers, such as William C. Bullitt. Consequently, they opposed President Franklin D. Roosevelt's efforts to promote Soviet-American cooperation. Furthermore, their evaluations of the 1930's tended to mold their interpretation of Soviet actions after 1945. Unfortunately, these diplomats underestimated the importance of Stalin's overtures to the West and thus failed to fully exploit the possibility of undermining Soviet cooperation with Nazi Germany. Based on primary and secondary sources; 43 notes.
                                                G. H. Curtis

1598. Mal'kov, Viktor Leonidovich. GARRI GOPKINS: STRANITSY POLITICHESKOI BIOGRAFII [Harry Hopkins: pages from a political biography]. *Novaia i Noveishaia Istoriia [USSR] 1979 (3): 108-126, (4): 129-144.* Part II. In 1938 Franklin D. Roosevelt's foreign policy was fluctuating, and he shifted priorities away from social welfare toward a buildup of armaments and maintenance of America's international standing. Hopkins believed that admonitions to Hitler were useless and dangerous. He was an influence behind Roosevelt's decision to run for the presidency a third time. In March 1941 he became an official advisor to Roosevelt and attended cabinet meetings. Hopkins was relieved when war on the Eastern Front broke out, as this took pressure off England. Nevertheless, he always had words of praise for the Soviet

Union's courage. 78 notes. Part III. A treaty of mutual agreement was signed on 11 June 1942 between the USSR and the United States but the second front did not appear immediately. In the autumn and winter of 1942 Hopkins was already beginning to dwell on postwar Soviet-American relations and sought to make the world more stable for American ambitions. This tendency was apparent in the Teheran declaration of 1943 when the United States, Britain, and the Soviet Union agreed to continue to work together in a peaceful world. Hopkins's influence on American political strategy declined sharply from the end of 1944. During his career he was attacked by conservatives, but he always defended a conservative position. He died on 29 January 1946. 69 notes.   L. J. Seymour

1599. Mal'kov, Viktor Leonidovich. SPETSSLUZHBY SSHA I "UMIRNAIA INITSIATIVA" FON PAPENA V 1943 G. [The Office of Strategic Services and von Papen's peace initiative in 1943]. *Novaia i Noveishaia Istoriia [USSR] 1980 (3): 122-140.* Toward the end of World War II, anti-Soviet movements in Great Britain and the United States became increasingly influential. In 1943 US agents met emissaries of the Third Reich in Turkey. Franz von Papen, German ambassador to Turkey, saw his mission as the division of the anti-Nazi coalition, and the formation of alliances between Great Britain, the United States, and Germany against the USSR. Such an alliance was advocated in the United States by George Earle. The author's claim rests on an intelligence report from Istanbul (declassified in the United States in 1976), which records the US-Nazi meeting, and which is here reproduced in Russian translation. Uses archival sources in the Franklin D. Roosevelt Library; 76 notes.   J. S. S. Charles

1600. Margulies, Herbert F. THE SENATE AND THE WORLD COURT. *Capitol Studies 1976 4(2): 37-52.* Examines political dealings between Calvin Coolidge and the Senate in Coolidge's attempt to foster support for the World Court, 1923-24.

1601. Marks, Frederick W., III. MORALITY AS A DRIVE WHEEL IN THE DIPLOMACY OF THEODORE ROOSEVELT. *Diplomatic Hist. 1978 2(1): 43-62.* The quest for virtue was a major motivating force in Theodore Roosevelt's (1858-1919) life. His idea of virtue was a very personal one, conditioned by "the spirit of the age," but his convictions were strong and genuine. Nearly all the major diplomatic conflicts in which he was involved derived from what he perceived as a betrayal of his trust by other parties. In this light, such "big stick" incidents as the Panama Canal Zone acquisition, the Alaska boundary dispute, and the dispatch of the Great White Fleet take on a different hue. 52 notes.   T. L. Powers

1602. Martin, Bernd. AMERIKAS DURCHBRUCH ZUR POLITISCHEN WELTMACHT: DIE INTERVENTIONISTISCHE GLOBALSTRATEGIE DER REGIERUNG ROOSEVELT, 1933-1941 [America's breakthrough to world power: the interventionist global strategy of the Roosevelt administration, 1933-41]. *Militärgeschichtliche Mitteilungen [West Germany] 1981 (2): 57-98.* Traces the evolution of American foreign, military, and economic policy in opposition to the Axis powers. Escalation of this opposition came not only with the appearance of a threat to the Western Hemisphere, but in the Roosevelt adminstration's anticipation of Hitler's concept of global envelopment. Fears of German success in the USSR then produced the final unraveling of neutrality prior to US entry into World War II. Secondary sources; 231 notes.   K. W. Estes

1603. Mashberg, Michael. DOCUMENTS CONCERNING THE AMERICAN STATE DEPARTMENT AND THE STATELESS EUROPEAN JEWS, 1942-1944. *Jewish Social Studies 1977 39(1-2): 163-182.* A collection of documents from the papers of Franklin D. Roosevelt's wartime Secretary of the Treasury, Henry M. Morgenthau, Jr., indicates the efforts of the Treasury Department to investigate and bring to the attention of the President the role of State Department officials in preventing any tangible efforts to rescue European Jewry from extermination at the hands of the Nazis. Treasury Department investigators, especially general counsel Randolph E. Paul, believed that the State Department prevented Jewish rescue through procrastination and failure to act, that it refused to work with private rescue agencies, that it prevented public disclosure of news about the exterminations, and that it covered up its role in regard to the Jewish situation. The actions of Morgenthau and his staff finally resulted in the creation of the War

Refugee Board and efforts to retrieve refugees from the hands of the Nazis. Based on documents in the Franklin D. Roosevelt Library.
          N. Lederer

1604. Mason, Julian. OWEN WISTER AND WORLD WAR I: APPEAL FOR PENTECOST. *Pennsylvania Mag. of Hist. and Biog. 1977 101(1): 89-102.* Reviews Owen Wister's attitude toward President Woodrow Wilson and World War I. Wister, a Republican, had been fond of Wilson in the early years but rebelled against the latter's reluctance to get involved in World War I and his neutrality in word but not in deed. Wister composed a scorching sonnet, blasting the President, which evoked strong, though mixed, reviews. Himself a German, Wister published a booklet which compared peaceful prewar Germany with the monster nation that had evolved. Wister simply could not understand why America did not rise in defense of the small states of Europe. 44 notes.   V. L. Human

1605. Matray, James I. AN END TO INDIFFERENCE: AMERICA'S KOREAN POLICY DURING WORLD WAR II. *Diplomatic Hist. 1978 2(2): 181-196.* After Pearl Harbor, it became evident to US policymakers that future peace in Asia would depend upon postwar stability in Korea. Thanks to 40 years of Japanese domination of the country, an independent government of inexperienced and unprepared Koreans would probably have been unable to maintain that stability in the face of British imperialism, Chinese expansionism, and Soviet Communism. President Franklin D. Roosevelt advocated an international trusteeship for postwar Korea, believing that such an arrangement would bring stability without encouraging imperialism, while preparing Koreans for eventual independence. 67 notes.   T. L. Powers

1606. Matsuda, Takeshi. WILSON SEIKEN TO WALL STREET: TAIKA ROKKAKOKU SHAKKANDAN DATTAI MONDAI O CHŪSHIN TO SHITE [The Wilson administration and Wall Street]. *Seiyō Shigaku [Japan] 1979 (112): 1-17, (113): 33-43.* Examines the historical significance of President Woodrow Wilson's statement of 18 March 1913 withdrawing from the Sextuple Consortium to China. Considers the American Bankers group's attitudes toward Chinese loans during the Taft administration, and reviews Wilson's opposition to participation in the consortium. Emphasizes Wilson's view that it was necessary to curtail the influences of international financial capitalists in Wall Street in order to open the Chinese door. Primary sources, including papers by Willard Straight and Thomas W. Lamont; 122 notes.   Y. Aoki

1607. Matz, Eliahu. POLITICAL ACTIONS VS. PERSONAL RELATIONS. *Midstream 1981 27(4): 41-48.* Attempts to analyze the various interpretations of the creation of the War Refugee Board on 22 January 1944 by Franklin D. Roosevelt, and contributes a fresh view based on facts overlooked by most historians.

1608. Matzozky, Eliyho. AN EPISODE: ROOSEVELT AND THE MASS KILLING. *Midstream 1980 26(7): 17-19.* Examines the attitudes of Franklin D. Roosevelt's administration toward the known destruction of European Jews and Jewish pressure for an active rescue policy.

1609. Mazur, Zbigniew. ZACHODNIA GRANICA POLSKI W KONCEP-CJACH DEPARTAMENTU STANU PODCZAS II WOJNY ŚWIATOWEJ [Poland's western borders as conceptualized by the State Department during World War II]. *Przegląd Zachodni [Poland] 1980 35(5-6): 104-128.* The US policy on border changes attempted to delay decisions till the peace conference. Meanwhile, State Department committees prepared position papers inimical to Polish interests. Poland was to be rewarded with few German possessions, yet was to reciprocate by ceding Polish land. Americans feared that concessions to Poland would induce French and Dutch demands in the West. Such border changes would fuel German hatred, and increase German financial dependence on the Allies. Chaos might ensue. When Roosevelt agreed to Soviet demands on Polish eastern territories some recompense in the West was necessary. After Roosevelt's death, Truman agreed to borders on the Oder and on the Neisse, but he resisted the western (Lusatian) Neisse, insisting on the eastern (Klodzka) Neisse, but matters were no longer determinable by America alone. Based on primary publications and State Department papers.   M. Krzyzaniak

1610. Metallo, Michael V. AMERICAN MISSIONARIES, SUN YAT-SEN, AND THE CHINESE REVOLUTION. *Pacific Hist. Rev. 1978 47(2): 261-282.* American missionaries greeted the 1911 Chinese Revolution optimistically, expecting it would improve prospects for the expansion of Christianity. Missionaries also expected the new China to model its political, social, and economic institutions after those of the United States. Sun Yat-sen was especially esteemed. The American business and diplomatic communities in China viewed the revolution far less positively, influencing the William Howard Taft administration's nonrecognition policy. Woodrow Wilson was more sympathetic to the missionary viewpoint, extending diplomatic recognition to China in May 1913. From 1913 on, American missionaries withdrew support from Sun Yat-sen and extended support to elements in China which stood for stability and order rather than for extending the revolution. Based on private papers of missionary societies, documents in the National Archives and Library of Congress, and missionary newspapers; 81 notes.
W. K. Hobson

1611. Miller, James Edward. THE POLITICS OF RELIEF: THE ROOSEVELT ADMINISTRATION AND THE RECONSTRUCTION OF ITALY, 1943-44. *Prologue 1981 13(3): 193-208.* Discusses the difficulties encountered by President Franklin D. Roosevelt in his reelection bid of 1944, their effects on policy initiatives, and the repercussions both on the American position in Italy and in Italian-American internal politics. The New Deal gave Italy only limited aid, but politically it was significant in that it committed the United States to a major role in Italian affairs. Within one year of the Roosevelt-Churchill statement at the end of the Quebec Conference (September 1944), which fell far short of US objectives, the United States had assumed a position of primacy in Italian affairs. Based on Roosevelt's personal letters, 1928-45, Roosevelt Papers, records of the Office of Strategic Services, and newspapers; 13 photos, 61 notes.
M. A. Kascus

1612. Mitchell, David. WOODROW WILSON AS "WORLD SAVIOUR." *Hist. Today [Great Britain] 1976 26(1): 3-14.* Discusses President Woodrow Wilson's role in establishing the League of Nations at the 1918-19 Paris Peace Conference, emphasizing possible negative aspects of his moral idealism.

1613. Mitchell, Kell. THE UNITED STATES' GREEK POLICY AT THE PARIS PEACE CONFERENCE, JUNE-DECEMBER, 1919. *North Dakota Q. 1979 47(3): 30-44.* The US policy involved the questions of territory in Epirus, Thrace, western Asia Minor, and the Aegean islands; the US delegation at the conference, after the treaty of Versailles was signed and President Wilson returned to the United States, was headed by Secretary of State Robert Lansing, then by Commissioner Henry White, and finally by Frank L. Polk.

1614. Mooney, Christopher F. MORAL CONSENSUS AND LAW. *Thought 1976 51(202): 231-254.* In order to gain popular support for the position taken on the German sinking of the *Lusitania* in 1915, Woodrow Wilson sought to generate a moral consensus against unannounced submarine attacks on belligerent cruisers (no such precedent existed in international law because of the newness of submarine warfare) which required that he insist upon the freedom of US citizens to travel freely aboard foreign vessels and conceal the fact that the *Lusitania* was carrying ammunition to the British.

1615. Moore, James R. WOODROW WILSON AND POST-ARMISTICE DIPLOMACY: SOME FRENCH VIEWS. *Reviews in Am. Hist. 1974 2(2): 207-213.* French scholars have suggested three new perspectives on Wilsonian postarmistice diplomacy: the Anglo-American quest for hegemony, the effect of diplomatic quandary and military collapse on shaping the armistice, and the isolation of a too-personalized American executive. 10 notes.
W. D. Piersen

1616. Moore, Jamie W. NEW DEAL DIPLOMACY: PARADIGMS AND MODELS. *Peace and Change 1975 3(1): 30-42.*

1617. Moynihan, Daniel P. MORALITY AND AMERICAN FOREIGN POLICY: WAS WOODROW WILSON RIGHT? *Foreign Service J. 1974 51(9): 8-12, 24-25.* Defends Woodrow Wilson's acceptance of the "American definition of citizenship as a matter not of blood or soil or religious faith, but of adherence to political norms."
S

1618. Murray, G. E. Patrick. "UNDER URGENT CONSIDERATION": AMERICAN PLANES FOR GREECE, 1940-1941. *Aerospace Hist. 1977 24(2): 61-69.* German advances in Europe, and especially the fall of France in June 1940, threatened Greece. Athens assumed an Italian attack and needed enough air power to counter 500 Italian planes. In June 1940, the Greek government turned to the United States as a source of planes, but delivery did not begin until April 1941, too late to help the Greeks. The failure to assist Greece illuminates the problems of the Roosevelt administration in establishing an "arsenal for democracy." Says "that if delivery had not taken so long, the planes might have become something more than a symbolic gesture." Based on State Department Records; 35 notes.
A. M. Osur

1619. Myers, Duane. THE UNITED STATES AND AUSTRIA, 1918-1919: THE PROBLEM OF NATIONAL SELF-DETERMINATION. *Pro. of the South Carolina Hist. Assoc. 1975: 5-15.* Discusses the problem of national self-determination as it applied to Austria at the Paris Peace Conference of 1919 and the role of Woodrow Wilson in the final outcome. The Austrian Germans thought that they would be treated as the other nationalities of the old Hapsburg Empire and were bitterly disappointed. Wilson made little effort to secure national self-determination for the Austrians, favoring instead the claims of the allies and the former subject nationalities of the Empire. Based on published sources; 20 notes.
J. Thacker, Jr.

1620. Neumann, William L. ROOSEVELT'S FOREIGN POLICY DECISIONS, 1940-1945. *Modern Age 1975 19(3): 272-284.* On difficult questions which required a strong and courageous stand, Franklin D. Roosevelt evaded action and stalled by lying to all parties in order to preserve surface tranquility. Based on primary documents and secondary sources; 40 notes.
M. L. Lifka

1621. Nikol, John and Holbrook, Francis X. NAVAL OPERATIONS IN THE PANAMA REVOLUTION 1903. *Am. Neptune 1977 37(4): 253-261.* Questions whether the US role in the Panama Revolution was haphazardly arranged by President Theodore Roosevelt. US Navy records, plus other evidence, suggest that Roosevelt indeed had arranged for the "taking" of Panama. Such evidence indicates, for example, that there was "a planned deployment of United States naval units immediately prior" to the revolution. Based primarily on the Area Files of the Naval Record Collection (Record Group 45); 18 notes.
G. H. Curtis

1622. Ninkovich, Frank. CULTURAL RELATIONS AND AMERICAN CHINA POLICY, 1942-1945. *Pacific Hist. Rev. 1980 49(3): 471-498.* United States-China cultural relations were hampered by Guomindang (Kuomintang) politics and US failure to understand Chinese culture. The State Department originally emphasized extending practical assistance to China in technical fields, but the Guomindang politicized the technical training of Chinese students. American intellectuals opposed the technically oriented cultural program and the Guomindang's effort to modernize China without accepting Western liberal ideas. The State Department's later humanities-oriented cultural program was also obstructed by Guomindang politics. The US assumption that the diffusion of Western liberal ideas among Chinese intellectuals would result in a strong, democratic China resulted in intractable differences between the United States and China. Based on US State Department Papers, Papers of the American Library Association, and other primary sources; 46 notes.
R. N. Lokken

1623. Ninkovich, Frank. IDEOLOGY, THE OPEN DOOR, AND FOREIGN POLICY. *Diplomatic Hist. 1982 6(2): 185-208.* Uses various social science methodologies in exploring Open Door ideology. The Open Door concept reflected all facets of 19th century liberalism. A pacific ideology, it emphasized nonpolitical commercial and cultural expansion. Paradoxically, many proponents of the Open Door Policy advocated an "open world" with its interventionist tendencies. The ideological orientations of Jane Addams and Woodrow Wilson illustrate this inconsistency. Addams consistently held to the fundamental ideology that the world was naturally internationalist, even if politicians failed to recognize it as such. Wilson's operative ideology, Wilsonianism, led him to attempt to construct an internationalist world, by force where necessary. Based on the papers of Woodrow Wilson and other primary sources; 50 notes.
T. J. Heston

1624. Noelte, Earl. L'ÉBLOUISSEMENT PROVOQUÉ L'IMAGE DE LA RUSSIE: OU LE REFLET DE L'OPINION PUBLIQUE DANS LA POLITIQUE ÉTRANGÈRE DE FRANKLIN D. ROOSE-VELT À L'ÉGARD DE L'UNION SOVIÉTIQUE DE 1941 À 1945 [The fascination with the image of Russia: the influence of public opinion on Franklin D. Roosevelt's policy toward the Soviet Union, 1941-45]. *Relations Int. [France] 1975 (4): 137-154.* After Hitler's armies attacked the USSR on 22 June 1941, the US government and media saw in the USSR a potential ally in the struggle against the Axis, and went to work rehabilitating the image of the USSR and its dictator, Joseph Stalin. President Roosevelt repeatedly stressed his view that Communist Russia was less of a threat to democracy, religion, and Western civilization than was Nazi Germany. As Soviet armies came closer to Central Europe, and the USSR's hegemonic intentions towards Eastern Europe became clearer, Roosevelt did little. Still bedazzled by his image of a basically friendly, beneficent Russia, he failed to alert the American people to the true nature of Soviet imperialism and its plans. 63 notes.

J. C. Billigmeier

1625. Norton, Douglas M. THE OPEN SECRET: THE U.S. NAVY IN THE BATTLE OF THE ATLANTIC, APRIL-DECEMBER 1941. *Naval War Coll. Rev. 1974 26(4): 63-83.* The issues of Executive secrecy and the role of the Commander in Chief versus the congressional right to declare war are not unique to the years of the Indochina war. The preservation of England in 1941 demanded U.S. involvement in the naval battle for the Atlantic long before the declaration of war with Germany. Due almost entirely to Presidential action, often undertaken in secret without approval of either the Congress or the public, the operations were a possible infringement on the warmaking powers of Congress. At the same time they were important to saving England.

J

1626. Offner, Arnold A. APPEASEMENT REVISITED: THE UNITED STATES, GREAT BRITAIN, AND GERMANY, 1933-1940. *J. of Am. Hist. 1977 64(2): 373-393.* American historians have followed Cordell Hull's belief that the economic similarities between the United States and Great Britain made them natural allies, and natural antagonists with Germany. Yet during 1936-40, German and American trade increased, as did American investments in Germany. Hull's statement also belies consistent attempts by the United States to appease Germany's economic and political ambitions. Franklin Roosevelt and his foreign policy advisor, Sumner Welles, were willing to grant Germany a sphere of influence in Central and Eastern Europe in return for disarmament talks and nonaggression pacts. American attempts at appeasing Axis appetites continued until March 1940. Primary and secondary sources; 79 notes.

J. W. Leedom

1627. Okuneva, M. A. "DOKTRINA T. RUZVEL'TA" I ANTIIM-PERIALISTICHESKOE DVIZHENIE V LATINSKOI AMERIKE V NACHALE XX VEKA [The "doctrine of T. Roosevelt" and the anti-imperialist movement in Latin America in the beginning of the 20th century]. *Voprosy Istorii [USSR] 1975 (6): 76-92.* Drawing on a number of new archive materials, the author shows the U.S. imperialist expansion in Latin America at the beginning of the 20th century. The article reveals the true nature and significance of Theodore Roosevelt's doctrine directed against the national independence of the Latin American peoples and basically aimed at protecting the interests of the monopolies, intensifying the exploitation of the working class and all the other sections of the toiling population in Latin American countries. The new documents cited by the author convincingly refute the spurious assertions of American historiography that there is no criticism or any opposition in Latin America to Roosevelt's interpretation of the Monroe Doctrine and effectively bear out Lenin's conclusion about the widespread discontent caused by this doctrine among broad segments of the population in Latin America. The article also highlights the steady growth of the anti-imperialist movement in Latin America at the beginning of this century and the prominent part played in it by the working class.

J

1628. Ostrower, Gary B. THE AMERICAN DECISION TO JOIN THE INTERNATIONAL LABOR ORGANIZATION. *Labor Hist. 1975 16(4): 495-504.* Support for American membership in the International Labor Organization arose from the Department of Labor under Frances Perkins. With the support of the Department of State and Franklin D. Roosevelt, opposition from isolationist sentiment and financial conservatives was overcome by 1934. Suggests that the New Deal may have been less isolationist than generally characterized. Based on archives of Departments of Labor and State; 23 notes.

L. L. Athey

1629. Ostrower, Gary B. SECRETARY OF STATE STIMSON AND THE LEAGUE. *Historian 1979 41(3): 467-482.* Kent G. Redmond's article, "Henry Lewis Stimson and the Question of League Membership," *The Historian* 1963 25: 211-212, which finds Henry L. Stimson favorable to US membership in the League of Nations, is erroneous. Actually, Stimson's attitude toward collective security and toward American membership in the League appeared both erratic and confused during his State Department service of 1929-33. Uses the Manchurian Crisis to demonstrate Stimson's wavering between cooperating with the League and ignoring it, thus mirroring his countrymen's old isolationism and new desire for collective security. Any consistency in Stimson's support for the League stems from his statements after leaving the State Department. 43 notes.

R. S. Sliwoski

1630. Padvaiskas, Edmund R. WORLD WAR II RUSSIAN-AMERICAN RELATIONS AND THE BALTIC STATES: A TEST CASE. *Lituanus 1982 28(2): 5-27.* During the early years of World War II, the US government refused to recognize the forcible incorporation of the Baltic States of Estonia, Latvia, and Lithuania into the Soviet Union in 1940. President Franklin D. Roosevelt maintained especially stiff resistance to the diplomatic pressure for recognition exerted by both the USSR and Great Britain throughout the first half of 1942, as the latter two countries prepared to sign a treaty of alliance. But at the Teheran Conference with Stalin late in 1943, Roosevelt, increasingly concerned about the future of Soviet-American relations, finally ceased making an issue of the Baltic States. Based on US State Department records and diplomatic memoirs; 47 notes.

J. H. Krukones

1631. Parzen, Herbert. THE ROOSEVELT PALESTINE POLICY, 1943-1945. *Am. Jewish Arch. 1974 26(1): 31-65.* "It is astonishing to what degree the President's private views . . . reflected the opinions of the State Department officials in charge of Middle Eastern affairs and even of the political leaders of the Arab states as pictured in the current consular dispatches to Washington."

J

1632. Patterson, David S. THE UNITED STATES AND THE ORIGINS OF THE WORLD COURT. *Pol. Sci. Q. 1976 91(2): 259-277.* Describes and interprets the attempts of American lawyers and government officials to establish a world court in the two decades before 1920. Ironically, President Woodrow Wilson nearly subverted this long-term American effort at the Paris Peace Conference and only reluctantly acquiesced in the provision for the Permanent Court of International Justice in the Covenant of the League of Nations.

J

1633. Penkower, Monty Noam. JEWISH ORGANIZATIONS AND THE CREATION OF THE U.S. WAR REFUGEE BOARD. *Ann. of the Am. Acad. of Pol. and Social Sci. 1980 (450): 122-139.* Confronted by the Holocaust, the Anglo-American Alliance moved slowly to meet this unique tragedy during World War II. Refusing the initial appeal of Jewish organizations in the free world that food and medical packages be dispatched to the ghettos of Europe, London and Washington argued that supplies would be diverted for the Germans' personal use or would be granted the Jews just to free the Third Reich from its "responsibility" to feed them. A license granted in December 1942 for such shipments had minimal effect. The World Jewish Congress' subsequent plan to rescue Jews through the use of blocked accounts in Switzerland received the US Treasury Department's approval in mid-1943, but the State Department and the British Foreign Office procrastinated further. Jewish groups failed at times to measure up to the catastrophe but the fundamental obligation lay with the Allied councils of war, which discriminated in their unwillingness to save a powerless European Jewry. The persistence of Treasury Secretary Henry Morgenthau, Jr., and his staff in bypassing State and ultimately confronting Franklin D. Roosevelt in January 1944, along with increasing calls from Congress and the public for a presidential rescue commission, resulted in the executive creation of the US War Refugee Board. The lateness of the hour and Hitler's ruthless determination to complete the murder of all the Jews of Europe made the odds for the new board's success more than questionable.

J

1634. Pogue, Forrest C. LA CONDUITE DE LA GUERRE AUX ETATS UNIS (1942-1945): SES PROBLEMES ET SA PRATIQUE [The conduct of the war in the United States (1942-45): Problems and practices]. *Rev. d'Hist. de la Deuxième Guerre Mondiale [France] 1975 (100): 67-94.* During World War II the United States had to improvise a world strategy and the structures to pursue it. Under pressure from General George C. Marshall the War Department was reorganized as was the Marine Corps. The Joint Chiefs of Staff was formed and Franklin D. Roosevelt worked out his own mode of supervision. Although he avoided detailed operational direction, he was explicit in opposing support for Charles de Gaulle's claims to leadership. Roosevelt's principal adviser, Harry Hopkins, was a crucial link between the president and the military. Surveys other aspects of US government conduct including the lack of planning for maintenance of troops abroad after the war. 11 notes.
G. H. Davis

1635. Pollock, Fred E. ROOSEVELT, THE OGDENSBURG AGREEMENT, AND THE BRITISH FLEET: ALL DONE WITH MIRRORS. *Diplomatic Hist. 1981 5(3): 203-220.* The Ogdensburg Agreement, signed by Roosevelt and Canadian Prime Minister William Lyon Mackenzie King on 17 August 1940, announced the formation of the Permanent Joint Board on Defense (PJBD). The agreement was hailed as an attempt to strengthen North American defenses rather than as a move toward intervention in the European war, which it actually was. Roosevelt wanted to gain control over the British fleet in the event of a German invasion of Great Britain. Once the German invasion was canceled and the British fleet was safe, he quickly lost interest in the PJBD. Based on primary material in the Public Archives of Canada, the FDR Library, and the London Public Record Office; 60 notes.
J. V. Coutinho

1636. Pomerance, Michla. THE UNITED STATES AND SELF-DETERMINATION: PERSPECTIVES ON THE WILSONIAN CONCEPTION. *Am. J. of Internat. Law 1976 70(1): 1-27.* Idealists blame Woodrow Wilson for the failure of the principle of self-determination; realists consider it an impractical moralistic slogan; radicals believe it is a disguise for economic imperialism. Actually, the principle is ambiguous and provides no assistance in defining the scope of "self," or what, when, or how "self" will determine. Wilson believed the League of Nations would settle these questions. Based on published documents and secondary sources; 132 notes.
M. I. Elzy

1637. Raat, William Dirk. THE DIPLOMACY OF SUPPRESSION: *LOS REVOLTOSOS,* MEXICO, AND THE UNITED STATES, 1906-1911. *Hispanic Am. Hist. Rev. 1976 56(4): 529-550.* During the Roosevelt and Taft administrations and the latter years of Díaz' presidency in Mexico, both governments cooperated in the suppression of socialism and revolution in Mexico as a means of protecting capital investments, especially in the northern Mexican states. Both were guilty of covert activities which violated the civil liberties of revolutionary leaders. Discusses the steps taken in suppressing such activities, all of which contributed to Madero's overthrow of the Mexican government in 1911. Madero successfully undermined the efficiency of the international police and espionage structure by gaining the open sympathy of many US citizens and Mexicans living along the border. 66 notes.
R. V. Ritter

1638. Rabe, Stephen G. ANGLO-AMERICAN RIVALRY FOR VENEZUELAN OIL, 1919-1929. *Mid-America 1976 58(2): 97-110.* General Juan Gómez encouraged foreign development of Venezuelan oil. Great Britain responded first, followed by the United States. Gómez sued the Shell Company for contractual noncompliance. Subsequently, American Minister McGoodwin misconstrued his instruction concerning the Venezuelan concession. Gómez annulled the court's anti-Shell decision, but after 1921 America and England cooperated in the Middle East and Venezuela. With new American fields, the US government relaxed, though Herbert Hoover demanded continued vigilance. The US State Department did act in accord with the Open Door Policy in the German-based Stinnes and other monopoly threats, though it excepted the American monopolies which came to dominate in Venezuela by 1929. Based on State Department records (Group 59), National Archives, Foreign Office Correspondence, and Public Record Office papers (London), and on secondary sources; 42 notes.
T. H. Wendel

1639. Raffo, Peter. THE ANGLO-AMERICAN PRELIMINARY NEGOTIATIONS FOR A LEAGUE OF NATIONS. *J. of Contemporary Hist. [Great Britain] 1974 9(4): 153-176.* President Woodrow Wilson and British Conservative politician, Lord Robert Cecil, dominated the League of Nations Commission at the Paris Peace Conference (1919). In September 1916 Cecil drew up the *Memorandum* of first principles to govern postwar peace-keeping machinery. Included was a "Conference of Powers." The idea germinated, to emerge in Lloyd George's declaration of 5 January 1918 and Woodrow Wilson's Fourteen Points of 8 January 1918. But during most of 1918 there was little Anglo-American cooperation on the drafting of a practical proposal for a League of Nations. Each side worked on its own. The evidence points to the fact that Wilson was more interested in the shape of the Covenant than its actual provisions, which turned out to be largely the British contribution. Wilson's role in the final Covenant of the League was less than usually has been assumed. Archival and published primary sources; 67 notes.
M. P. Trauth

1640. Ray, Deborah Wing. THE TAKORADI ROUTE: ROOSEVELT'S PREWAR VENTURE BEYOND THE WESTERN HEMISPHERE. *J. of Am. Hist. 1975 62(2): 340-358.* Describes the tactics used by Franklin D. Roosevelt, Hopkins, advisors, and Pan American Airways to circumvent Lend-Lease and neutrality restrictions to set in operation the Takoradi air route across the South Atlantic Ocean to West Africa and on to Cairo in 1941. The Takoradi route was crucial to the British war effort in the Middle East, and, after Pearl Harbor, to the allied war effort world-wide. The episode was a clear example of Roosevelt's tactics before American entry into the war. Based on memoirs, documents in the National Archives and the Roosevelt library, records of the State Department, strategic studies, and secondary works; 82 notes.
J. B. Street

1641. Reynolds, David. COMPETITIVE CO-OPERATION: ANGLO-AMERICAN RELATIONS IN WORLD WAR TWO. *Hist. J. [Great Britain] 1980 23(1): 233-245.* Studies six books dealing with the special relationship between the United States and Great Britain, 1939-45, initiated by Sir Winston Churchill and Franklin D. Roosevelt, which consisted of cooperation between the countries as they bargained for supremacy.

1642. Reynolds, David. FDR ON THE BRITISH: A POSTSCRIPT. *Massachusetts Hist. Soc. Pro. 1978 90: 106-110.* In 1938-39, a letter by President Franklin D. Roosevelt containing seemingly negative opinions of Lord Lothian's attitude toward Adolf Hitler came to the attention of the British government. This letter caused some reconsideration of Lothian's incipient appointment as ambassador to the United States, and nearly cost him his position. However, Roosevelt had nothing against Lothian (who was subsequently appointed and served with distinction)— he was merely trying to stiffen Britain's attitude toward Hitler, and encourage them to fight on. Based on correspondence in numerous archives and repositories, and on published diaries; 22 notes.
G. W. R. Ward

1643. Rhodes, Benjamin D. HERBERT HOOVER AND THE WAR DEBTS, 1919-33. *Prologue 1974 6(2): 130-144.* Settlement of World War I war debts devolved early about the person of Herbert Hoover who originally favored a conciliatory approach, but was forced by political considerations to reverse his course. Election to the presidency and the coming of the Great Depression again caused Hoover's reversion to the soft-line position, with opposition in Congress remaining adamant. Hoover further failed to win over president-elect Roosevelt to his viewpoint, which represented the end of the line for his program. 46 notes.
V. L. Human

1644. Riste, Olav. AN IDEA AND A MYTH: ROOSEVELT'S FREE PORTS SCHEME FOR NORTH NORWAY. *Americana Norvegica IV: Norwegian Contributions to Am. Studies (Oslo: Universitets forlaget, 1973), pp. 379-397.* Denies that at a White House meeting between President Franklin Delano Roosevelt and Norwegian Foreign Minister Trygve Lie on 12 March 1943, Roosevelt acted as an intermediary for Soviet demands for ports in North Norway. "Our contention that Lie must have misunderstood the President, and that in fact the Soviet Union had not expressed any 'desires or demands' involving Norwegian territory, is further confirmed by a study of the debate on Soviet war aims that took place among the Allies from the autumn of 1941 onwards. The available evidence suggests that North Norway became the first target for Roosevelt's speculations on the topic of free ports. One piece of evidence also indicates that he may have conceived the idea early in 1942—precisely at the time when the President was casting about for ways to satisfy Soviet desires for expansion short of annexation." 34 notes.

D. D. Cameron

1645. Roberts, Stephen S. THE DECLINE OF THE OVERSEAS STATION FLEETS: THE UNITED STATES ASIATIC FLEET AND THE SHANGHAI CRISIS, 1932. *Am. Neptune 1977 37(3): 185-202.* The Japanese assault on Shanghai, January 1932, marked the decline in influence of the European and US navies stationed in China. The Western nations' confrontation with Japan "brought into the naval balance the entire Japanese navy"—thus rendering ineffective their small station fleets. Focuses on the roles of US Asiatic Fleet commander Admiral Montgomery Meigs Taylor and Secretary of State Henry L. Stimson, indicating "a fundamental disagreement between the two in their interpretation of the Far Eastern crisis." Based primarily on Admiral Taylor's papers and government records; 44 notes.   G. H. Curtis

1646. Rockaway, Robert A. THE ROOSEVELT ADMINISTRATION, THE HOLOCAUST, AND THE JEWISH REFUGEES. *Rev. in Am. Hist. 1975 3(1): 113-118.* Review article prompted by Saul S. Friedman's *No Haven for the Oppressed: United States Policy toward Jewish Refugees, 1938-1945* (Detroit, Mich.: Wayne State U. Pr., 1973).

1647. Rubin, Barry. ANGLO-AMERICAN RELATIONS IN SAUDI ARABIA, 1941-45. *J. of Contemporary Hist. [Great Britain] 1979 14(2): 253-267.* From 1941 to 1945, Saudi Arabia repeatedly played off the Americans against the British in order to get financial aid from both Great Britain and the United States. Great Britain was accused of trying to undermine American interests. The US State Department's Near East Affairs Division, animated by national self-righteousness and anti-imperialism, while being prodded by the US oil companies, misread British intentions and involved the United States in a five-year plan "on the assumption that America would have to undertake entire responsibility for aid." Based on British Foreign Office and US State Department Archives; 44 notes.   M. P. Trauth

1648. Sabki, Hisham. WOODROW WILSON AND SELF-DETERMINATION IN THE ARAB MIDDLE-EAST. *J. of Social and Pol. Studies 1979 4(4): 381-399.* Discusses the impact of Woodrow Wilson's championing of the concept of national self-determination among the Arabs of the Ottoman Empire, 1915-20.

1649. Sadler, Charles. THE AMERICANS, EAST PRUSSIA, AND THE ODER-NEISSE LINE. *Mid-America 1979 61(3): 159-177.* Describes the activities of the State Department's Advisory Committee on Post-War Foreign Policy, and its influence on US negotiators at Potsdam. The Subcommittee on Territorial Problems, chaired by Dr. Isaiah Bowman, identified Polish boundaries as the most important problem. Largely prewar boundaries were at first recommended, but Under-Secretary Sumner Welles forced further studies. US willingness, as early as 1942, to see East Prussia transferred to Poland from Germany prepared the way for acquiescence in the more radical Oder-Niesse boundary change at war's end. During 1944-45, the Committee lost influence due to Welles's resignation. The present boundaries were established due to the realities of Soviet occupation. Based on State Department records and secondary sources; 60 notes.   J. M. Lee

1650. Safford, Jeffrey J. EDWARD HURLEY AND AMERICAN SHIPPING POLICY: AN ELABORATION ON WILSONIAN DIPLOMACY, 1918-1919. *Historian 1973 35(4): 568-586.* Woodrow Wilson's foreign policy after World War I aimed at building a moral and constitutional world peace modeled along the lines of market-oriented capitalism, and achieved by means of an expanding American political economy. This study of Edward Nash Hurley's objectives as chairman of the US Shipping Board and member of Wilson's War Council supports this interpretation. Based largely upon Hurley's addresses, publications, and his papers at the University of Notre Dame Library. 62 notes.

N. W. Moen

1651. Sandos, James A. PANCHO VILLA AND AMERICAN SECURITY: WOODROW WILSON'S MEXICAN DIPLOMACY RE-

CONSIDERED. *J. of Latin Am. Studies [Great Britain] 1981 13(2): 293-311.* Against a background of border disturbances for which the US government considered Venustiano Carranza ultimately responsible, Pancho Villa raided New Mexico in early 1916. Woodrow Wilson sent John J. Pershing with troops to break up and disperse Villa's bands (accomplished by June 1916) and, indirectly, to force Carranza to secure the border. Carranza, under serious internal pressure from dissidents taxing his resources, managed to cope with Villa and secure the border by early 1917. As a result, Wilson ordered Pershing to withdraw. By allowing Carranza to arouse nationalism against the invasion the punitive expedition had politically helped him, ultimately influencing 20th century Mexican government. US and Mexican archives; 89 notes.

M. A. Burkholder

1652. Schäfer, Peter. KOLLEKTIVE SICHERHEIT ODER APPEASEMENTPOLITIK. ZUR AUSSENPOLITIK DER ROOSEVELT-REGIERUNG BIS ZUR MITTE DER DREISSIGER JAHRE [Collective security or appeasement policy: on the foreign policy of the Roosevelt administration until the mid-thirties]. *Wissenschaftliche Zeitschrift der Humboldt-Universität zu Berlin. Gesellschafts- und Sprachwissenschaftliche Reihe [East Germany] 1973 22(1-2): 81-94.* In 1933 the Roosevelt administration adopted a policy of appeasement toward Nazi Germany. This line did not change until 1936, when the US government realized the aggressive strategy of Nazism. Published documents and secondary literature; 70 notes.   R. Wagnleitner

1653. Schwabe, Klaus. WOODROW WILSON AND GERMANY'S MEMBERSHIP IN THE LEAGUE OF NATIONS, 1918-19. *Central European Hist. 1975 8(1): 3-22.* Describes Woodrow Wilson's changes in attitude concerning Germany's membership in the League of Nations, 1918-19. Wilson first believed that Germany should be a member, 2) then that she should not, 3) then that Germany should only be admitted to the League when she disarmed. Wilson "reacted to changing circumstances" in changing his views. Published and unpublished sources; 65 notes.

C. R. Lovin

1654. Sealander, Judith. IN THE SHADOW OF GOOD NEIGHBOR DIPLOMACY: THE WOMEN'S BUREAU AND LATIN AMERICA. *Prologue 1979 11(4): 236-250.* Sketches the relationship between the Good Neighbor Policy and the Women's Bureau of the Labor Department, which was established in 1920, in respect to United States-Latin American relations. The bureau, a "ghetto of talented women" who were both bureaucrats and feminists, sought Latin American connections specifically under the direction of Mary Cannon. The Good Neighbor Policy wanted to improve understanding between nations, and ulteriorly, keep Latin America pro-US. Cannon tried to both be a good-will ambassador and develop a network of Latin American labor officials who would support her. Her tours of foreign countries helped accomplish these aims. Publicly she praised the status quo in these countries; privately she advocated better rights and working conditions for women. Primary sources; 6 photos, 60 notes.   S

1655. Sellen, Robert W. WHY PRESIDENTS FAIL IN FOREIGN POLICY: THE CASE OF WOODROW WILSON. *Social Studies 1973 64(2): 64-77.* Recounts memorable and significant events in the life of Wilson and discusses his failure in foreign policy, which perhaps was due to his lack of understanding of foreign affairs. 31 notes.

L. R. Raife

1656. Sessions, Gene A. THE CLARK MEMORANDUM MYTH. *Americas (Acad. of Am. Franciscan Hist.) 1977 34(1): 40-58.* The memorandum on the Monroe Doctrine drawn up by J. Reuben Clark for Secretary of State Frank Kellogg in 1928 depicted the doctrine as an expression of US self-defense and did not explicitly renounce rights of intervention in Latin America (as often stated). It had some impact on Senate debates concerning the Kellogg Pact, but little if any on the evolution of US Latin American policy. 65 notes.   D. Bushnell

1657. Sessions, Gene A. NONINTERVENTION AND THE FALL OF CIUDAD JUÁREZ, 1911. *Rev. Interamericana [Puerto Rico] 1975 5(2): 236-249.* President Taft's administration has often been described as one willing to use force to impose its will on Latin America. Yet Taft's decision not to intervene in Mexico after the seizure of Ciudad Juárez in 1911 by rebel forces, even when American life and property suffered,

sheds doubt on this old interpretation. Primary and secondary sources; 36 notes.
                                                                    J. A. Lewis

1658. Shepardson, Donald E.   THEODORE ROOSEVELT AND WILLIAM II: THE NEW STRUGGLE FOR ATLANTIC SUPREMACY.   Parker, Harold T., ed. *Problems in European History* (Durham, North Carolina, Moore Publ., 1979): 165-176. Reviews German-American relations from the accession of William II (1888) to the funeral of Edward VII (1910), attended by William and former president Theodore Roosevelt, with special emphasis on the relationship of these two leading figures. Roosevelt could combine bombast with consummate perceptiveness and practical wisdom, while William could not. The first fruit of his constitutional lack of discretion was the Franco-Russian alliance of 1894. The American president at first may have admired William, but the latter's behavior during the Moroccan crisis (1904-07) and the Second Hague Conference (1907), and in two interviews in 1908 with a *New York Times* reporter, suppressed by Roosevelt, raised a storm of protest inside Germany, convincing Roosevelt that the German Kaiser was lacking in elementary prudence. Ref.
                                                                    L. W. Van Wyk

1659. Sherwin, Martin Jay.   THE ATOMIC BOMB AND THE ORIGINS OF THE COLD WAR: U.S. ATOMIC ENERGY POLICY AND DIPLOMACY, 1941-'45.   *Am. Hist. R. 1973 78(4): 945-968.* An examination of recently opened atomic energy files indicates that President Franklin Delano Roosevelt left no definitive statement on the postwar role of the atomic bomb. Nevertheless, the policies he chose from among the alternatives of international control, advocated by his science advisors, and an Anglo-American postwar monopoly, urged by Churchill, indicates that the potential postwar diplomatic value of the bomb began to shape his atomic energy policies as early as 1943. The assumption that the bomb could be used to secure postwar diplomatic aims was carried over to the Truman administration. Suggests that historians have exaggerated Roosevelt's confidence in (and perhaps his commitment to) amicable postwar relations with the Soviet Union. In light of this study, the widely held assumption that Truman's attitude toward the atomic bomb was substantially different from Roosevelt's must also be revised.
                                                                    A

1660. Smallwood, James.   BANQUO'S GHOST AT THE PARIS PEACE CONFERENCE: THE UNITED STATES AND THE HUNGARIAN QUESTION.   *East European Q. 1978 12(3): 289-307.* Historians Arno J. Mayer and N. Gordon Levin agree that the American delegation to the Paris Peace Conference in 1919 was genuinely concerned about Bolshevism in Europe. Describes the reactions of American advisors to the Communist takeover in Hungary by Bela Kun. Concludes that Woodrow Wilson understood the causes of Bolshevism better than any of his advisers, but was limited in what he could do by a number of factors. He would have been willing for Kun's government to coexist with others in that area, but actions taken by allies and associated powers as well as attitudes of his own staff prevented carrying out this policy. Based on published documents and secondary sources; 91 notes.
                                                                    C. R. Lovin

1661. Smith, M. J. J.   F. D. R. AND THE BRUSSELS CONFERENCE, 1937.   *Michigan Acad. 1981 14(2): 109-122.* Discusses the role of Franklin D. Roosevelt in undermining the Brussels Conference of the Nine Power Treaty signatories in 1937 in the context of the undeclared Sino-Japanese War and the imminent outbreak of World War II.

1662. Spector, Ronald.   ALLIED INTELLIGENCE AND INDOCHINA, 1943-1945.   *Pacific Hist. Rev. 1982 51(1): 23-50.* The need for continuous intelligence from Indochina by American and British commanders in the Far East prompted US intelligence agents to cooperate with whatever forces could provide the best information. Such activities conflicted with official policies in Washington. These agents cooperated with the French at a time when President Franklin D. Roosevelt's policy was to avoid involvement with French colonialism in Indochina. When the Japanese coup of March 1945 made it obvious that the French could no longer operate in Vietnam, the intelligence community became involved with the Viet Minh, although Washington policy favored French resumption of sovereignty in Indochina. Based on Wedemeyer files, National Archives, and other primary sources; 95 notes.
                                                                    R. N. Lokken

1663. Stathis, Stephen W.   MALTA: PRELUDE TO YALTA.   *Presidential Studies Q. 1979 9(4): 469-482.* Despite President Franklin D. Roosevelt's fear that an Anglo-American meeting before the Yalta Conference might antagonize the USSR, such a meeting eventually took place. Yielding to British Prime Minister Winston Churchill's wishes, Roosevelt agreed to a meeting of the Joint Chiefs of Staff on Malta at the end of January 1945. Military matters such as Eisenhower's plan for the crossing of the Rhine, the occupation of Germany, and the Polish question received attention. Probably by Roosevelt's design, substantive political issues were not addressed. 69 notes.
                                                                    S

1664. Tate, Michael L.   PERSHING'S PUNITIVE EXPEDITION: PURSUER OF BANDITS OR PRESIDENTIAL PANACEA?   *Americas (Acad. of Am. Franciscan Hist.) 1975 32(1): 46-71.* Discusses Woodrow Wilson's decision for intervention in Mexico, 1916, as a reflection of his general foreign relations attitude toward all of Latin America, and evaluates the resultant animosity between Mexico and the United States which hastened nationalization of foreign petroleum interests in Mexico.

1665. Tobia, Bruno.   IL PARTITO SOCIALISTA ITALIANO E LA POLITICA DI W. WILSON (1916-1919)   [The Italian Socialist Party and the policy of Woodrow Wilson, 1916-19].   *Storia Contemporanea [Italy] 1974 5(2): 275-303.* The Italian Socialist Party opposed Italy's entrance into World War I and continued this opposition throughout the conflict. When Woodrow Wilson first proposed his peace proposals, later crystalized in the Fourteen Points, the reaction of Italian Socialists was favorable. Wilson's ideas seemed very close to those of the Socialists. The results of the Paris Peace Settlements disappointed them, however. Versailles was a victory for the international bourgeoisie rather than for Wilson's idealism. 82 notes.
                                                                    J. C. Billigmeier

1666. Toškova, Vitka.   THE POLICY OF THE UNITED STATES TOWARDS THE AXIS SATELLITES (1943-1944).   *Bulgarian Hist. Rev. [Bulgaria] 1979 7(2): 3-26.* Dealing with peace overtures from Romania, Hungary, and Bulgaria exercised the State Department from early 1943. That the satellites were differently committed to the Axis influenced their approaches to the Allies, who were not in agreement among themselves, Roosevelt's call for unconditional surrender being the chief stumbling block. In the end, events overtook discussions. The Western powers could not spare resources for a Balkan campaign, and it was left to the advancing Russian forces to apply in practice their democratic views on the attitude to be adopted. Based on published and unpublished documents from US National Archives; 145 notes.
                                                                    J. P. H. Myers

1667. Trask, David F.   REMARKS FOR THE BICENTENNIAL LECTURE SERIES, U.S. DEPARTMENT OF STATE MAY 1, 1981: WOODROW WILSON AND THE COORDINATION OF FORCE AND DIPLOMACY.   *Soc. for Hist. of Am. Foreign Relations. Newsletter 1981 12(3): 12-19.* Discusses the importance of coordinating force and diplomacy by statesmen, and the seriousness of World War I for world alliances and divisions; focuses on President Woodrow Wilson's successful decision to use military force and failures in postwar diplomacy.

1668. Trask, David F.   WOODROW WILSON AND THE RECONCILIATION OF FORCE AND DIPLOMACY: 1917-1918.   *Naval War Coll. R. 1975 27(4): 23-31.* "In their studies of Woodrow Wilson and the First World War, most historians have assumed that the near-pacifist Wilson had little appreciation for the concept of force as an extension of diplomacy. On more careful investigation, however, it becomes apparent that Wilson not only developed realistic and clearly articulated war goals but that he was able to coordinate his larger diplomatic purpose with the use of force perhaps better than any war President before or since."
                                                                    J

1669. Travis, Paul D.   GORE, BRISTOW AND TAFT: REFLECTIONS ON CANADIAN RECIPROCITY, 1911.   *Chronicles of Oklahoma 1975 53(2): 212-224.* Attempts by Canada and the United States to negotiate reciprocal trade agreements in 1911 produced considerable reaction from the agricultural Midwest. Favoring the measure was Democratic Senator Thomas Gore of Oklahoma who faced stiff opposition from Republican Senator Joseph Bristow of Kansas. Debate went beyond the tariff issue into the structure of party politics as Bristow led Insurgent

Republicans in opposition to President Taft who promoted the compromise agreement. In the election of 1912 Kansas and other Republican strongholds dumped Taft and supported the successful Democratic candidate Woodrow Wilson. Based on primary and secondary sources; 68 notes.   M. L. Tate

1670. Trow, Clifford W. "SOMETHING DESPERATE IN HIS FACE":WOODROW WILSON IN PORTLAND AT THE"VERY CRISIS OF HIS CAREER." *Oregon Hist. Q. 1981 82(1): 40-64.* Describes the events of President Woodrow Wilson's visit to Portland, Oregon, on 15 September 1919 during his swing around the country to raise support for the League of Nations. Also included is a discussion of the opposition to the League covenant as it stood voiced by various senators, and the positions of Oregon senators Charles L. McNary and George E. Chamberlain. Based on newspapers and secondary sources; 6 photos, 77 notes.
G. R. Schroeder

1671. Trow, Clifford W. "TIRED OF WAITING": SENATOR ALBERT B. FALL'S ALTERNATIVE TO WOODROW WILSON'S MEXICAN POLICIES, 1920-1921. *New Mexico Hist. Rev. 1982 57(2): 159-182.* Examines the attempts by many interests, political and private, to influence to recognition of Mexico by the United States during the administration of President Woodrow Wilson. Albert B. Fall of New Mexico, chairman of the Senate subcommittee to investigate Mexican affairs, led the opposition to the "watchful waiting" attitude of the president. Based on the Albert B. Fall Papers in the Henry E. Huntington Library, San Marino, California, and other primary sources; photo, 74 notes.   A. C. Dempsey

1672. Tulchin, Joseph S. WHEN DIPLOMATS BECOME HISTORIANS. *R. in Am. Hist. 1975 3(2): 241-248.* Dana G. Munro's *The United States and the Caribbean Republics 1921-1930* (Princeton, N.J.: Princeton U. Pr., 1974) defends the foreign policy of the State Department in which he served in the Caribbean in the 1920's.

1673. Utley, Jonathan G. UPSTAIRS, DOWNSTAIRS AT FOGGY BOTTOM: OIL EXPORTS AND JAPAN, 1940-41. *Prologue 1976 8(1): 17-28.* Historians have generally failed to investigate the manner in which the cautious foreign policy toward Japan formulated by President Roosevelt and Secretary of State Cordell Hull was implemented at lower levels of the foreign service bureaucracy. Lower echelon administrators such as Assistant Secretary of State Dean Acheson favored a stronger and more aggressive attitude toward Japan than did their superiors and they changed the whole character of their instructions to reflect their personal views. Acheson and independent agencies like the Foreign Funds Control Committee prevented Japan from obtaining the oil supplies to which it was entitled under the conditions laid down by the president and the secretary of state. Based on secondary and government archival records.
N. Lederer

1674. Van Meter, Robert H., Jr. THE WASHINGTON CONFERENCE OF 1921-1922: A NEW LOOK. *Pacific Hist. Rev. 1977 46(4): 603-624.* Historians have ignored the influence of the depression of 1920-21 on American policy at the Washington Conference on the Limitation of Armaments, 1921-22. The depression did influence American policy. Secretary of Commerce Herbert C. Hoover and other top Harding administration officials were convinced that international disarmament would promote economic stabilization and recovery in Europe, which, in turn, would help restore prosperity to the United States by increasing the overseas market for American goods, especially agricultural goods. Based on numerous manuscript and published primary sources; 51 notes.
W. K. Hobson

1675. Villa, Brian Loring. THE ATOMIC BOMB AND THE NORMANDY INVASION. *Perspectives in Am. Hist. 1977-78 11: 463-502.* Franklin D. Roosevelt skillfully refrained from bringing Great Britain into confidence on the atomic bomb project until Winston Churchill openly committed himself to a cross-channel invasion. Although FDR had acted the country squire, his business methods were ingenious and effective. This conclusion contradicts the school of thought which argues that Roosevelt was inept at diplomacy and weak on goals and objectives. Other Roosevelt diplomatic decisions should be reexamined in light of these findings.   W. A. Wiegand

1676. Villa, Brian Loring. THE U.S. ARMY, UNCONDITIONAL SURRENDER, AND THE POTSDAM PROCLAMATION. *J. of Am. Hist. 1976 63(1): 66-92.* Examines the critical factors affecting the timing of the Japanese surrender. Clarifies the politico-military position assumed by Roosevelt, the Congress, and the US Army. Conflicts arising from differing goals (Roosevelt desired "the rooting out of evil philosophies"; the Army wanted military supremacy) and semantic interpretations ("surrender" was unknown to the Japanese) delayed peace. 69 notes.
V. P. Rilee

1677. Vivian, James F. THE "TAKING" OF THE PANAMA CANAL ZONE: MYTH AND REALITY. *Diplomatic Hist. 1980 4(1): 95-100.* One of President Theodore Roosevelt's most reputed actions was his reputed boast that he "took Panama," (or the isthmus, or the canal zone), starting construction of the canal while Congress debated the question. There is doubt that he ever made that claim. Newspaper accounts of the relevant speech vary greatly, and the President's own text, still in his private papers, reads, "I took *a trip to* the isthmus . . . " Emphasis added. Historians should hesitate before using this episode to exemplify Roosevelt's thinking. 18 notes.   T. L. Powers

1678. Vivian, James F. WILSON, BRYAN, AND THE AMERICAN DELEGATION TO THE ABORTIVE FIFTH PAN AMERICAN CONFERENCE 1914. *Nebraska Hist. 1978 59(1): 56-69.* The Fifth Pan American Conference scheduled to convene in Santiago, Chile, on 29 November 1914, was cancelled because of reverberations emanating from World War I in Europe. Woodrow Wilson, sympathetic to the calling of the conference, carefully selected (with suggestions by Bryan) the American delegation. Examines the delegation in detail and speculates on the position that members would have taken had the conference met as scheduled.   R. Lowitt

1679. Watt, Donald. ROOSEVELT AND NEVILLE CHAMBERLAIN: TWO APPEASERS. *Internat. J. [Canada] 1973 28(2): 185-204.* Although Franklin Delano Roosevelt's sources of information and perspective on Europe were different from Neville Chamberlain's, their assessments of the international order and what to do about it were remarkably similar. 62 notes.   R. V. Kubicek

1680. Wiegand, Wayne A. AMBASSADOR IN ABSENTIA: GEORGE MEYER, WILLIAM II AND THEODORE ROOSEVELT. *Mid-America 1974 56(1): 3-15.* George von Lengerke Meyer (1858-1918), US Ambassador to Italy and Russia before World War I, established a close personal relationship with the Emperor William II, not unlike the relationship which developed between German Ambassador Speck von Sternberg and Theodore Roosevelt. The relationship between Meyer and William II served to improve general relations between Germany and the United States and was a factor in prompting William to exert influence on the tsar to submit to US mediation of the Russo-Japanese War in 1905. Based on manuscript, and primary and secondary sources; 28 notes.   T. D. Schoonover

1681. Williams, J. E. THE JOINT DECLARATION ON THE COLONIES: AN ISSUE IN ANGLO-AMERICAN RELATIONS, 1942-1944. *British J. of Int. Studies [Great Britain] 1976 2(3): 267-292.* Compares British and American attitudes toward colonialism and imperialism in regard to British colonies in Southeast Asia 1942-44; examines the Roosevelt administration's unsuccessful attempt to form a Joint Declaration between the two nations toward the colonies.

1682. Williams, Joyce G. THE RESIGNATION OF SECRETARY OF STATE ROBERT LANSING. *Diplomatic Hist. 1979 3(3): 337-343.* Presents the entire text of a memorandum by Edith Bentham, secretary to Edith Bolling Galt Wilson, the wife of President Woodrow Wilson, concerning the 11 February 1920 resignation of Wilson's Secretary of State, Robert Lansing. The memo seems to suggest that Mrs. Wilson and Joseph Tumulty (Wilson's secretary), both of whom disliked Lansing, took advantage of the president's illness and isolation following his massive stroke on 2 October 1919 to engender bad feeling between the two men. The memo is from a recently opened collection of papers in the Library of Congress.   T. L. Powers

1683. Williams, William Appleman. DEMYSTIFYING COLD WAR ORTHODOXY. *Sci. and Soc. 1975 39(3): 346-351.* Based on a review of works by George C. Herring, Jr., and Thomas G. Paterson, it is concluded that the confrontation between the United States and the USSR would have been different under Roosevelt from that which occurred under Truman but that the commitment to the global Open Door was as much a part of Roosevelt's refusals to make firm agreements with Stalin in 1941-42 and 1944, as it was of Truman's call in 1945 for the internationalization of the Danube and the Open Door in Manchuria.

N. Lederer

1684. Wolk, Herman S. THE OVERLORD DISPUTE: PRELUDE TO D-DAY: THE BOMBER OFFENSIVE. *Air Force Mag. 1974 57(6): 60-65.* Reconstructs the controversy between the Allied military commanders and Winston Churchill and Franklin D. Roosevelt over the use of airpower in the Normandy invasion, Operation Overlord, 1944, and the compromise which was worked out.

1685. Woods, Randall B. HULL AND ARGENTINA: WILSONIAN DIPLOMACY IN THE AGE OF ROOSEVELT. *J. of Inter-Am. Studies and World Affairs 1974 16(3): 350-371.* In 1943 the United States was anxious to force Argentina to break diplomatic relations with the Axis powers. Washington prodded Argentine President Pedro Ramírez into a diplomatic split with Germany, but then the State Department refused to furnish Ramírez with the proof that some of his military officers were linked to the Nazis. Without this proof the Ramírez government fell to pro-Axis forces. Secretary of State Cordell Hull refused to assist Ramírez because Hull, a product of Wilsonian diplomacy, believed in a clear delineation between right and wrong, saw the Ramírez government as wrong, and thought it deserved to fall. Based on State Department documents, memoirs, newspapers and secondary sources; 11 notes, biblio.

J. Thomas

1686. Woods, Randall B. TERRORISM IN THE AGE OF ROOSEVELT: THE MISS STONE AFFAIR, 1901-1902. *Am. Q. 1979 31(4): 478-495.* In September 1901, Ellen M. Stone (1846-1927), an American Congregationalist missionary, was kidnapped and held for ransom by a group of Macedonian nationalists called the Internal Macedonian Revolutionary Organization. During her captivity, the Roosevelt administration, the American public, and Stone's organization, the American Board Commissioners for Foreign Missions, struggled with the issues of international political terrorism. A $66,000 ransom raised by public donations was ultimately accepted by the nationalists, who then freed Stone in February 1902. The ransom helped finance a Macedonian rebellion in August 1903 that was quickly suppressed by the Turks. Based on Department of State papers, the Papers of the American Board Commissioners for Foreign Missions, and other primary sources; 69 notes.

D. K. Lambert

1687. Woytak, Richard A. ROOSEVELT'S EARLY FOREIGN POLICY REFLECTED IN POLISH DISPATCHES FROM WASHINGTON (1932-1933). *Polish Rev. 1976 21(3): 217-224.* Roosevelt's foreign policy eventually served to strengthen ties between the United States and Europe, including Poland.

1688. Wright, Esmond. THE FOREIGN POLICY OF WOODROW WILSON: A RE-ASSESSMENT. *Hist. Today [Great Britan] 1960 10(3): 149-157, (4): 223-231.* Part I. WOODROW WILSON AND THE FIRST WORLD WAR. Analyzes the stages by which Woodrow Wilson passed from neutrality to crusading political intervention on behalf of democracy. Part II. WILSON AND THE DREAM OF REASON. Considers Wilson's European policy in 1919 stressing his idealism and the shortcomings of his diplomatic methods which led to the failure of his policies abroad and at home.

1689. Young, Lowell T. FRANKLIN D. ROOSEVELT AND AMERICA'S ISLETS: ACQUISITION OF TERRITORY IN THE CARIBBEAN AND IN THE PACIFIC. *Historian 1973 35(2): 205-220.* The anticolonialist Roosevelt, who favored U.S. withdrawal from the Philippines, who was in a special way an imperialist who favored U.S. acquisition of tiny, remote, mostly uninhabited islands outside the Western Hemisphere which were suitable for use as naval bases and refueling stations. He met the problem of international rivalry by proposing Pan-American trusteeships for strategically situated islands in Latin American waters. Outside this hemisphere, the president favored direct U.S. control, a policy which brought him into conflict with Britain and Japan. Based on letters and papers in the Roosevelt library; 49 notes.

N. W. Moen

1690. Young, Lowell T. FRANKLIN D. ROOSEVELT AND THE EXPANSION OF THE MONROE DOCTRINE. *North Dakota Q. 1974 42(1): 23-32.*

1691. Yü, Yüh-chao. SHIH-T'ING-SHENG PU CH'ENG-JÊN CHU-I CHIH YAN-CHIU [A study of Henry Stimson's doctrine of "Non-Recognition"]. *Shih-ta Hsüeh-pao (Bull. of National Taiwan Normal U.) [Taiwan] 1981 26: 353-380.* Henry L. Stimson's doctrine of nonrecognition for the Japanese puppet-state of Manchukuo developed from an initially conciliatory approach to Japanese aggression in Manchuria in September 1931 to a sternly worded nonrecognition principle in January 1932. Unfortunately, this doctrine had little effect on Japanese aggression in China, largely because it did not receive the support of the European powers and because President Herbert Hoover refused to back the doctrine with military force. Nevertheless, Stimson's doctrine did help to bar the Japanese puppet-state of Manchukuo from receiving international recognition, thus giving China indirectly legal as well as moral support in her efforts to recover Manchuria. Based on Stimson's *Diary* and *The Far Eastern Crisis,* the Lytton Report, and secondary sources; 64 notes, biblio.

R. C. Houston

1692. Zelaya, José Santos and Centeno, José, ed. REFUTACIÓN DE LAS AFIRMACIONES DEL PRESIDENTE TAFT [Refutation of the assertions of President Taft]. *Casa de las Américas [Cuba] 1975 15(88): 102-115.* José Santos Zelaya, president of Nicaragua (1893-1909), defends his administration against President Taft's assertion that Zelaya was an "international criminal" who had to be removed. Zelaya claims that the US desired territorial expansion and economic exploitation and utilized the Monroe Doctrine as a pretext. According to the ex-president, the United States favored internal rebellions to set up governments favorable to its interests—conduct that violated the Treaty of Washington (1907). Argues that US intervention in Nicaragua was the first step in seeking the colonization of Latin America. Zelaya defended his country's interests, but considered the struggle hopeless and therefore resigned to prevent useless bloodshed. After his departure US political and economic influence became most evident. The final vindication came when the new government, which was no friend of Zelaya, refused to brand him an international criminal. 22 notes.

H. J. Miller

1693. Živojinović, Dragan R. POPE BENEDICT XV'S PEACE EFFORTS (1914-1917). Bosworth, Richard and Cresciani, Gianfranco, ed. *Altro Polo: A Volume of Italian Studies* (Sydney: U. of Sydney, 1979): 71-104. The peace efforts of Pope Benedict XV, who became pope in September 1914, were rejected by both sides, as each suspected the pope of working for the other side. Initially he worked at enlisting the support of US President Woodrow Wilson in ending World War I on the basis of *status quo ante bellum,* but Wilson's efforts at preserving Anglo-French-US friendship, and Germany's efforts to eliminate Wilson as a mediator, worked also at eliminating the pope in the same role. The author discusses the intricacies of diplomacy; Wilson did not want to cooperate with the pope, and Benedict XV and Cardinal Gasparri favored continued US neutrality which was "a kind of support to the Central Powers." The Vatican's continued appeal to and confidence in Germany's support was unshaken, although Germany always took a negative attitude toward Vatican initiatives. 93 notes.

S

1694. Zobrist, Benedict K. RESOURCES OF PRESIDENTIAL LIBRARIES FOR THE HISTORY OF THE SECOND WORLD WAR. *Military Affairs 1975 39(2): 82-85.* Numerous papers and records from varied sources are contained in the Presidential Libraries, offering unique opportunities for researchers interested in World War II. Major sources are available at the Hoover, Roosevelt, Truman, Eisenhower, and Kennedy Libraries. 8 notes.

A. M. Osur

1695. Zolov, A. V. AMERIKANSKII IZOLIATSIONISM I PRINIATIE ZAKONA O NEITRALITETE 1935 GODA [American isolationism and the enactment of the Neutrality Act (1935)]. *Vestnik Moskovskogo U., Seriia 8: Istoriia [USSR] 1979 (1): 32-44.* Isolationists were divided into four groups. The liberal democratic group feared that war would end domestic reform. The left radical groups feared that war would impede socialism in America. The conservatives feared that war would bring social reform and wanted the United States to be an arbiter of a Europe weakened by war. Fascists such as Fr. Coughlin, Long, and Hearst constituted a fourth group. President Franklin D. Roosevelt saw that isolationist sentiment was strong and so acted cautiously in dealing with the Neutrality Act. Roosevelt did win a concession from Congress that the embargo on the shipment of military goods would last only six months. Many groups in America were happy at the passage of the bill. 81 notes.　　　　　　　　　　　　　　　D. Balmuth

1696. —. THE DIPLOMATIC HISTORY OF THE OPENING OF THE SECOND FRONT IN EUROPE (1941-1944). *Int. Affairs [USSR] 1974 (5): 93-102, (7): 121-126, (10): 107-114.* Continued from *Int. Affairs* 1970 (4,7,12). Discusses the USSR's diplomatic attempts to involve Great Britain and the United States in the opening of a second front in Europe during World War II in 1942-43, emphasizing aspects of military strategy and the roles of Winston Churchill and Franklin D. Roosevelt.

1697. —. [FRANKLIN D. ROOSEVELT AND HIS FOREIGN POLICY CRITICS]. *Pol. Sci. Q. 1979 94(1): 15-35.*
Steele, Richard W. FRANKLIN D. ROOSEVELT AND HIS FOREIGN POLICY CRITICS. *pp. 15-32.* Reexamines the actions and attitudes of President Franklin D. Roosevelt toward critics of his foreign policy just before and in the early years of American entry in World War II. According to Steele, Roosevelt viewed what was mere dissent as evidence of subversion and disloyalty.
Schlesinger, Arthur M., Jr. A COMMENT ON "ROOSEVELT AND HIS FOREIGN POLICY CRITICS." *pp. 33-35.* Takes issue with Steel's analysis, contending that presidential critics fared much better under the Roosevelt administratikon than under earlier wartime administrations such as Lincoln's and Woodrow Wilson's.
　　　　　　　　　　　　　　　　　　　　　　　　　J

1698. —. [WORLD WAR II: 30 YEARS AFTER]. *Survey [Great Britain] 1975 21(1/2): 1-42.*
Dallek, Robert. ALLIED LEADERSHIP IN THE SECOND WORLD WAR: ROOSEVELT, *pp. 1-10.* Franklin D. Roosevelt's personal views did not determine US policy. Quite the contrary, Roosevelt himself mirrored American public opinion. He followed the US public from pacifism to neutralism, although he himself was never an isolationist. His call for unconditional surrender grew out of official and unofficial thinking, and while his skepticism about postwar cooperation with the USSR was growing, he never let on to the public. Roosevelt also followed American fantasies about China's role, and when the American public wanted a new Wilsonian League after the war instead of Roosevelt's world policed by the Great Powers, he also went along. Based on secondary sources; 18 notes.
Dallin, Alexander. ALLIED LEADERSHIP IN THE SECOND WORLD WAR: STALIN, *pp. 11-19.* Joseph Stalin did not win the victory nor was the victory won despite him, but as a symbol of wartime leadership he would have had to have been invented had he not existed. There is no record of any great military ability, but he did mobilize the Russian people. As the head of the Party and the government his behavior exhibited his personal needs more than those of the system. He excelled in using people and in making concessions and then taking them back. The same tactics also applied to the Allies, but Stalin never lost sight of the fact that a clash with them was inevitable. Based on secondary sources; 23 notes.
Dilks, David. ALLIED LEADERSHIP IN THE SECOND WORLD WAR: CHURCHILL, *pp. 19-29.* Winston Churchill was a man with a profound sense of history, and "he was incapable of looking at an issue except in its historical setting." The memory of the slaughter of World War I led him to distrust the military, and he would have looked at German terms had they been offered in 1940. Churchill preferred indirection and one of his greatest contributions may have been getting the invasion of France postponed until 1944, and even then it succeeded only by a narrow margin. Although Stalin fooled him over Poland, his view of Russia was not one of implacable hostility. Based on archival material, memoirs and secondary sources; 12 notes.
Kennan, George F. COMMENT, *pp. 29-36.* Roosevelt's policy by 1940 was to force Japan and Germany into moving against the US; thereby making a war inevitable. For all his charm and political skill, his ability to lead during the war, when it came to foreign policy Roosevelt was a superficial, ignorant dilettante, a man with a severely limited intellectual horizon. Churchill probably had the

most straightforward task; he was fighting for Britain's survival. Stalin, until 1943, was also fighting for survival—his, and in his acts he did not so much deceive the Western leaders as they deceived themselves.
Seton-Watson, Hugh. REFLECTIONS, *pp. 37-42.* A comparison of 1815 and 1945, while directly opposite in result is also strikingly similar in many respects. Yet whatever may be fashionable in the West, Cold War, peaceful coexistence, detente, the reality of the Soviet Empire remains the same.　　　　　R. B. Valliant

The Presidency: Bureaucratic Expansion

1699. Arnold, Peri E. EXECUTIVE REORGANIZATION & THE ORIGINS OF THE MANAGERIAL PRESIDENCY. *Polity 1981 13(4): 568-599.* Explores the efforts of various executive reorganization plans in this century, especially those predating the Brownlow Committee of 1936-37, to deal with the issue of augmenting the managerial capacity of the presidency. The primary function of the several executive reorganization schemes is to reduce and mask conflict over the changing relationship of the president to Congress and to administration.　　J/S

1700. DeNovo, John A. THE ENIGMATIC ALVEY A. ADEE AND AMERICAN FOREIGN RELATIONS, 1870-1924. *Prologue 1975 7(2): 69-80.* Alvey Augustus Adee (1842-1924) was the administrative support of the State Department, 1870-1924. He provided six presidents and their secretaries of state with continuity in foreign policy and insights to a rich diplomatic tradition. His functions included counseling on substantive problems of diplomacy and international law, overseeing the mechanics of the State Department, and drafting and censoring diplomatic messages. As second assistant of state, he epitomized the public administrator, executing rather than originating policies and basing his conservative policy recommendations on historical precedent and the political attitudes of those he served. 66 notes.　　T. Simmerman

1701. Grossman, Jonathan. THE ORIGIN OF THE U.S. DEPARTMENT OF LABOR. *Monthly Labor Rev. 1973 96(3): 3-7.* Labor leaders campaigned for the creation of a federal Labor Department in the United States from 1864 until their aim was achieved in 1913.

1702. Hone, Thomas C. and Mandeles, Mark David. MANAGERIAL STYLE IN THE INTERWAR NAVY: A REAPPRAISAL. *Naval War Coll. Rev. 1980 32, i.e. 33(5): 88-101.* Critiques an essay by historian Waldo Heinrichs, "The Role of the United States Navy" in *Pearl Harbor as History,* edited by Dorothy Berg and Shumpei Okamoto (New York: Columbia U. Pr., 1973), disputing Heinrichs's hypothesis "about the way in which peacetime navies, as institutions, will and must plan and prepare for a war" which he supports by discussing Navy Department policy during 1929-41.

1703. Powe, Marc B. THE AMERICAN GENERAL STAFF (1903-1916). *Military Rev. 1975 55(4): 71-89.* The American General Staff was developed in 1903 by Secretary of War Elihu Root and William H. Carter to help the nation prepare for war. It was an imperfect device, but through the years it played a key role in modernizing the Army. When the United States entered World War I, the General Staff was able to respond with facts and plans; its experienced officers served with distinction in both Washington and France. Based on primary and secondary sources; 13 illus., 63 notes.　　　　　　　J. K. Ohl

1704. Powe, Marc B. AMERICAN MILITARY INTELLIGENCE COMES OF AGE. *Military Rev. 1975 55(12): 17-30.* Traces the accomplishments of Ralph H. Van Deman in institutionalizing military intelligence in the United States War Department. Serving in several capacities, Van Deman, in the period between the turn of the century and World War I, created a complete intelligence system, coordinating at national level all available assets. In addition, he developed a doctrine which gave the intelligence system life. Primary and secondary sources; 7 illus., 44 notes.
J. K. Ohl

1705. Schultz, L. Peter. WILLIAM HOWARD TAFT: A CONSTI-TUTIONALIST'S VIEW OF THE PRESIDENCY. *Presidential Studies Q. 1979 9(4): 402-414.* An examination of the theory of presidential power advanced by William Howard Taft casts doubt on the prevalent assumption that strict adherence to the Constitution implies severely limited presidential authority. Citing John Marshall, Taft argued that political law substantively differed from law properly treated in the courts. Execution of treaties, for example, as well as decisions required of the commander in chief, involved the political discretion of the president, whose quasi-legislative and quasi-judicial responsibilities were in such cases beyond dispute. Theodore Roosevelt's stewardship theory is perhaps unduly broad; Taft's arguments suggest that the constitutionalist's view is not so narrow as presumed. 102 notes.   S

1706. Werking, Richard Hume. SELLING THE FOREIGN SER-VICE: BUREAUCRATIC RIVALRY AND FOREIGN-TRADE PROMOTION, 1903-1912. *Pacific Hist. Rev. 1976 45(2): 185-208.* Studies the efforts made by federal agencies to expand foreign trade. Spearheaded by the Department of State, the agencies urged merchants and manufacturers to enter foreign markets and to support appropriations and other legislation for revamping the foreign service. They also regularly supplied information about foreign markets to American businessmen. The Department of Commerce and Labor was created in 1903 to "foster, promote, and develop the foreign and domestic commerce." This introduced an element of competition and rivalry into the expansion effort. 41 notes.   R. V. Ritter

1707. Williams, David. THE BUREAU OF INVESTIGATION AND ITS CRITICS, 1919-1921: THE ORIGINS OF FEDERAL PO-LITICAL SURVEILLANCE. *J. of Am. Hist. 1981 68(3): 560-579.* Federal Bureau of Investigation surveillance of political dissent originated with American involvement in World War I, not with the Cold War. Investigations by J. Edgar Hoover, chief of the General Intelligence Division during the Red Scare, were systematic and pervasive and revealed the extreme antiradicalism in the bureau. Hoover learned that Congress and the president would tolerate the bureau's antiradical activities as long as they remained secret. Based in part on FBI files secured through the Freedom of Information Act; 49 notes.   T. P. Linkfield

4. FROM TRUMAN TO REAGAN'S FIRST YEARS

Presidents of Recent America

1708. Acheson, Dean. "DEAR BOSS": UNPUBLISHED LETTERS FROM DEAN ACHESON TO EX-PRESIDENT HARRY TRUMAN. *Am. Heritage 1980 31(2): 44-48.* The author, who served as Secretary of State under Harry S. Truman from 1949 to 1953, kept up a lively and unusual correspondence with the former president after both men left office; 1953-65.

1709. Allen, Mark. JAMES E. CARTER AND THE TRILATERAL COMMISSION: A SOUTHERN STRATEGY. *Black Scholar 1977 8(7): 2-7.* Jimmy Carter was groomed for the presidency by the Trilateral Commission. Carter joined the commission in 1973 and was then elected to its governing board. The commission is a "private American, European, Japanese Initiative on Matters of Common Concern," and is composed of some of the most powerful and richest financial and corporate interests in the world. Big business will dominate Carter's administration at the expense of the Black American. — B. D. Ledbetter

1710. Ambrose, Stephen E. EISENHOWER AND THE INTELLIGENCE COMMUNITY IN WORLD WAR II. *J. of Contemporary Hist. [Great Britain] 1981 16(1): 153-166.* Dwight D. Eisenhower entered World War II practically innocent of the intricacies of intelligence gathering; he left the war "a highly sophisticated and effective user of all these techniques." In fact, throughout the European campaign he had almost as good a grasp of German order of battle as Hitler, and sometimes better. He learned from Ultra and other deciphering of German messages; he was also informed by residents outside Germany who were antagonistic to Nazi occupation (although he did not get information from persons residing within Germany). Eisenhower became skilled in deceiving the Germans about Allied strength and possible landing sites. He pretended that the Normandy landing was a feint and that Pas de Calais and Norway were the real invasion sites. Finally, Eisenhower used well the covert operations of the French Resistance. Based on a personal interview and printed primary sources; 37 notes. — M. P. Trauth

1711. Ambrose, Stephen E. EISENHOWER, THE INTELLIGENCE COMMUNITY AND THE D-DAY INVASION. *Wisconsin Mag. of Hist. 1981 64(4): 261-277.* Reviews Dwight D. Eisenhower's preparations for the Normandy invasion on 6 June 1944, including his use of British intelligence, his skill in selecting an invasion site, and his patience in dealing with Allied military leaders. Emphasizes the role of intelligence in deceiving the Germans about the Allies' order of battle, combat leadership, and landing site in the successful invasion. 31 notes, 11 illus. — N. C. Burckel

1712. Baranovski, V. STRATEGIIA, VEDUSHCHAIA V TUPIK [Strategy leading to a dead end]. *Mirovaia Ekonomika i Mezhdunarodnye Otnosheniia [USSR] 1981 (2): 131-139.* Criticizes Richard M. Nixon's *The Real War* (1980), which discusses US and Soviet military strategy and foreign policy options since World War II. Russian.

1713. Beisel, David R. TOWARD A PSYCHOHISTORY OF JIMMY CARTER. *J. of Psychohistory 1977 5(2): 202-238.* Although the media has portrayed the Carter family as an ideal family, Jimmy Carter's biography suggests that the family was marked by distant parents, a sense of abandonment, and family disengagement. The Carters' unconscious denial and reaction formation created the idealized family myth that the Carters projected to the media. The public, which felt abandoned after the Nixon resignation, has responded to that image because it meets their group-fantasy needs. The positive image contributed to the narrow electoral victory over Gerald Ford, but does not indicate a leader with true nurturing potential. Primary and secondary sources; 73 notes. — R. E. Butchart

1714. Bethell, Thomas N. EARL WARREN: ON THE MOB'S PAYROLL? *Washington Monthly 1976 8(1): 35-46.* Continued criticism of the Warren Commission Report on the Kennedy killing—in the form of Robert Sam Anson's *They've Killed the President!* (Bantam Books, 1975) and *The Assassinations: Dallas and Beyond* (Random House/Vintage, 1976), edited by Peter Dale Scott, Paul H. Hoch, and Russell Statler—says more about the urge to oppose official writ than about the merits of the case itself.

1715. Billington, Monroe. LYNDON B. JOHNSON AND BLACKS: THE EARLY YEARS. *J. of Negro Hist. 1977 62(1): 26-42.* The Johnson presidency, 1963-68, constituted a significant era in the progress of civil rights for blacks. Focuses on Lyndon B. Johnson's early relationships with and attitudes toward blacks and their rights. Questions his sincerity in pressing for civil rights legislation, issuing executive orders, and speaking out publicly. Notes the length of time he held such expressed views, the degree of consistency throughout his career, and the argument that he may have acted through political expediency in yielding to current pressures. 97 notes. — P. J. Taylorson

1716. Bourne, Tom. IN SEARCH OF NIXON. *Horizon 1981 24(2): 42-45.* Biographer Fawn Brodie (1915-81), who shocked her Mormon family and friends first with a biography of Mormon leader Joseph Smith and later with a biography of Thomas Jefferson, completed a biography of Richard M. Nixon in 1980 which traces various psychological themes, such as Nixon's needless lying and unresolved grief and guilt over his brothers' deaths.

1717. Brodie, Fawn M. "I THINK HISS IS LYING." *Am. Heritage 1981 32(5): 4-21.* Excerpts from Fawn M. Brodie's *Richard Nixon: The Shaping of His Character* (1981) in which Richard M. Nixon's role in the trial and conviction (for perjury) of Alger Hiss is retraced, and similarities between the character of Hiss and Nixon are noted. 9 illus. — J. F. Paul

1718. Bullock, Paul. "*RABBITS AND RADICALS*": RICHARD NIXON'S 1946 CAMPAIGN AGAINST JERRY VOORHIS. *Southern California Q. 1973 55(3): 319-359.* An account of the 1946 Congressional campaign between Richard M. Nixon and Congressman Jerry Voorhis, describing the issues and events which contributed to Voorhis' defeat. Nixon campaigned over legitimate issues such as price controls, housing, and labor-management relations, but gained his greatest publicity from a simplistic presentation of artificial issues such as the Political Action Committee endorsement, Voorhis' legislative record, and the telephone smear. Nixon misrepresented the nature of an endorsement from the Political Action Committee and gave out misleading statistics on Voorhis' votes in Congress. A third issue was the controversial smear campaign over the telephone just before election day in which callers alleged Voorhis was a Communist. Nixon might have won on the issues alone, but Republicans had coveted the district for 10 years and made sure of their victory through use of controversial tactics. Based on the author's campaign recollections as a Voorhis supporter, newspapers, personal interviews, and published studies; 40 notes, 4 appendices. — A. Hoffman

1719. Chambers, John Whiteclay, II. PRESIDENTS EMERITUS. *Am. Heritage 1979 30(4): 16-25.* Traces the evolution of the ex-presidency. Until 1958, former presidents had no governmental aid to maintain themselves. Gradually, a small beginning became large, but with the public disaffection with Presidents Johnson and Nixon, some began to question the propriety and the amounts involved. 12 illus. — J. F. Paul

1720. Combs, James. TELEVISION AESTHETICS AND THE DEPICTION OF HEROISM: THE CASE OF THE TV HISTORICAL BIOGRAPHY. *J. of Popular Film and Television 1980 8(2): 9-18.* Popular movie and television biographies in the 1970's depicted heroism of the past in a personal light; for example, ABC television produced the *Ike* miniseries in 1979 with themes of simple virtue, causality, responsibility, and charisma regarding General Dwight D. Eisenhower in World War II.

1721. Culver, John H. GOVERNORS AND JUDICIAL APPOINT-MENTS IN CALIFORNIA. *State Government 1981 54(4): 130-134.* Examines the relationship between the political attitudes of governors Jerry Brown, Ronald Reagan, and Edmund G. Brown, and the judges they have appointed.

1722. Davis, Polly Ann. ALBEN W. BARKLEY: VICE PRESI-DENT. *Register of the Kentucky Hist. Soc. 1978 76(2): 112-132.* After 36 years as a senator, Alben W. Barkley became vice president in 1949. Barkley was an intelligent statesman, a model patriot, an effective public speaker, one of the greatest senators of the 20th century, and a popular vice president. He returned to the Senate in 1955 and died in 1956. Primary and secondary sources; 86 notes.
J. F. Paul

1723. Diamond, Sigmund. ON THE ROAD TO CAMELOT. *Labor Hist. 1980 21(2): 279-290.* Reprints the questions of Congressman John F. Kennedy to (among others) Robert Buse, President of United Automobile Workers of America, Local 248 (UAW-CIO), from the hear-ings of the House Committee on Education and Labor on 1 March 1947. Suggests that Kennedy tried to link the 1946-47 Allis-Chalmers strike in Milwaukee, Wisconsin, to the Communist Party. 6 notes.
L. L. Athey/S

1724. Dyer, Stanford P. and Knighten, Merrell A. DISCRIMINA-TION AFTER DEATH: LYNDON JOHNSON AND FELIX LON-GORIA. *Southern Studies 1978 17(4): 411-426.* Felix Longoria (1919-45), a Mexican American from Three Rivers, Texas, was killed while serving in the US Army in the Philippines. In 1949, when his body was returned to the United States for burial, the only undertaker in Three Rivers refused to handle the funeral because of Longoria's race. When the matter attracted national attention for its discrimination, Lyndon B. Johnson (1908-73), recently elected to the US Senate with support from Mexican Americans, arranged for burial in Arlington National Cemetery. Johnson's support of civil rights began at least this early. Based on Felix Longoria File in LBJ Library, and on other primary and secondary sources; 59 notes.
J. J. Buschen

1725. Easterbrook, Gregg. THE REPUBLICAN SOUL. *Washing-ton Monthly 1981 13(5-6): 13-24.* Discusses the Republican state of mind in 1981, especially as represented by Ronald Reagan, whose life is charac-terized as a kind of Norman Rockwellian idyll that romanticizes Ameri-can life but ignores social problems and the poor; and traces Reagan's life from the Depression era in Illinois to his election as President.

1726. Elovitz, Paul H. THREE DAYS IN PLAINS. *J. of Psychohis-tory 1977 5(2): 175-199.* Interviews Lillian Carter, Gloria Carter Spann, A. D. Davis, and Annie Mae Jones, in Plains, Georgia. Concludes that President Carter has a narcissistic personality with obsessive-compulsive characteristics. 10 notes, 14 photos.
R. E. Butchart

1727. Elzy, Martin I. RESEARCHING AMERICAN DIPLO-MATIC HISTORY AT JOHNSON LIBRARY. *Soc. for Hist. of Am. Foreign Relations. Newsletter 1977 8(4): 17-21.* Several holdings in the collections of the Lyndon Baines Johnson Library in Austin, Texas, per-tain to foreign affairs during Johnson's entire political career, 1937-69.

1728. Etheredge, Lloyd S. PERSPECTIVE AND EVIDENCE IN UNDERSTANDING JIMMY CARTER. *Psychohistory Rev. 1978 6(4): 53-59.* A review article prompted by recent works dealing with Jimmy Carter's upbringing and psychological make-up, and with the psychohistory of the US Presidency. The book *Jimmy Carter and Ameri-can Fantasy: Psychohistorical Essays,* edited by Lloyd de Mause and Henry Ebel (New York: Two Continents/Psychohistory Pr., 1977), con-sists of essays with rather bizarre interpretations of Jimmy Carter's per-sonal history and of the US Presidency, as well as false predictions such as that of de Mause that Carter's psycholgoical make-up will lead him to start a war by 1979. These essays veer off into an Alice-in-Wonderland world where the authors' fantasies take the place of careful analysis.
J. C. Billigmeier

1729. Fenn, Dan H., Jr. LAUNCHING THE JOHN F. KENNEDY LIBRARY. *Am. Archivist 1979 42(4): 429-442.* After overcoming sev-eral land acquisition problems, the John F. Kennedy Library and Mu-seum were located in Boston, adjacent to the University of Massachusetts campus. In addition to the John F. Kennedy papers, the complex houses papers of Kennedy's associates, oral history materials, an audiovisual collection, a library of more than 20,000 political science books, and more than 15,000 museum items. The library's program emphasizes its function as an educational institution and the availability of its resources to all interested persons. 12 photos.
G.-A. Patzwald

1730. Fink, Gary M. and Hilty, James W. PROLOGUE: THE SEN-ATE VOTING RECORD OF HARRY S. TRUMAN. *J. of Interdisci-plinary Hist. 1973 4(2): 207-235.* Reviews the Senate voting record of Harry S. Truman, using cluster analysis and Guttman scaling. His voting pattern suggests that he assumed an ideological position at the center of the party structure. As his power increased, so did the percentage of roll calls on which he failed to respond. It is significant that the change in his voting behavior started well before his 1940 campaign for reelection. 15 figs., 77 notes.
R. Howell

1731. Frantz, Joe B. OPENING A CURTAIN: THE METAMOR-PHOSIS OF LYNDON B. JOHNSON. *J. of Southern Hist. 1979 45(1): 3-26.* About 1,200 oral interviews have produced 10 million words to help us understand the source of Lyndon B. Johnson's social concern. The interviews reveal that the progressive, even liberal, tendencies expressed in the Great Society were not inconsistent with his early thought and activity. While the times and Johnson changed, and while he did make mistakes, there was in fact no metamorphosis in his political philosophy. Based on interviews and published primary materials; 44 notes.
T. D. Schoonover

1732. Frantz, Joe B. WHY LYNDON? *Western Hist. Q. 1980 11(1): 4-15.* Of the geographically western presidents, Lyndon B. Johnson (1908-73) is usually considered the only westerner. (Barry Goldwater is the only defeated presidential candidate who can be considered a west-erner). Johnson looked, talked, and acted like a westerner. Further, he was one of the few western politicians who attained national rather than regional stature. He surmounted his regional boundaries because he learned early to represent national constituencies and to see beyond the West. Illus.
D. L. Smith

1733. Funk, Arthur L. CHURCHILL, EISENHOWER, AND THE FRENCH RESISTANCE. *Military Affairs 1981 45(1): 29-33.* Details the discussions and actions leading up to the employment of the French Resistance against the Germans during World War II. British Prime Minister Winston Churchill was the first to assess the possibilities of the French Resistance and to take speedy if unilateral action on its behalf. General Dwight D. Eisenhower's response to Churchill's enterprising program was brief and too late to affect the French campaigns signifi-cantly. In the end they both supported aid to the French Resistance, but in different places and for different reasons. Covers 1943-44. Based on US and British military records; 39 notes.
A. M. Osur

1734. Furlong, William Barry. MONDALE'S MINNESOTA. *Horizon 1977 20(2): 66-74.* Discusses Minnesota's natural resources and farm beauty, and gives a biography of Vice-President Walter F. Mondale (b. 1928), focusing on his boyhood and political career, and changes for him and his home state.

1735. Giglio, James N. HARRY S. TRUMAN AND THE MULTI-FARIOUS EX-PRESIDENCY. *Presidential Studies Q. 1982 12(2): 239-255.* Examines the career of Truman following his tenure as presi-dent. His views were shaped by an intense partisanship, and he was the first president to extend executive privilege to his later years. However, his partisanship also limited his effectiveness within a split Democratic Party, and he became too tied to his presidential years to be a force in his later years. 82 notes.
D. H. Cline

1736. Grant, Philip A., Jr. THE ELECTION OF HARRY S TRU-MAN TO THE UNITED STATES SENATE. *Missouri Hist. Soc. Bull. 1980 36(2, pt. 1): 103-109.* Of the three Missouri Democrats seeking their party's US senatorial nomination in 1934, only Harry S. Truman (1884-1972) had no prior congressional service, but all were liberals sympathetic to Franklin D. Roosevelt's New Deal. After prevailing in the primary election, Truman ignored opposition attacks on his ties with the Pender-gast political machine, reasserted his fealty to the New Deal, and thun-dered against the rich whose interests Republicans assertedly served.

Truman captured 59.9% of the votes in the general elections. Based on government documents and newspaper sources; 35 notes.

H. T. Lovin

1737. Griffin, Clifford S. THE MAGIC OF RICHARD NIXON. *Rev. in Am. Hist. 1982 10(2): 269-274.* Review essay of Fawn M. Brodie's *Richard Nixon: The Shaping of His Character* (1981); 1920's-70's.

1738. Griffith, Robert. WHY THEY LIKED IKE. *Rev. in Am. Hist. 1979 7(4): 577-583.* Review essay of Dwight David Eisenhower's *The Papers of Dwight David Eisenhower,* Vol. 6, *Occupation, 1945,* edited by Alfred D. Chandler, Jr., et al., and Vols. 7-9, *The Chief of Staff,* edited by Louis Galambos, et al. (Baltimore, Md.: The Johns Hopkins U. Pr., 1978); 1945-1948.

1739. Grothaus, Larry. KANSAS CITY BLACKS, HARRY TRUMAN AND THE PENDERGAST MACHINE. *Missouri Hist. R. 1974 69(1): 65-82.* Many writers have called Harry S. Truman a centrist, a moderate, and a man who failed to appreciate or take action on racial matters until forced to do so by political pressure. During 1922-34, when Thomas Pendergast's machine controlled Kansas City politics, both Truman and Negroes in the city learned to use the machine to advance their interests. Both Truman and the machine were not always correct in dealing with blacks, but they had better records than the city's reform groups. Truman's record as presiding judge of Jackson County and as state director of reemployment was good enough to win 88% of the black vote when he ran for the Senate in 1934. Based on newspapers, books, articles, and papers in the Harry S. Truman Library, the Western Historical Manuscripts Collection, University of Missouri-Columbia, and the Missouri Historical Society, St. Louis; illus., 5 photos, 87 notes.

W. F. Zornow

1740. Haight, David J. and Curtis, George H. ABILENE, KANSAS AND THE HISTORY OF WORLD WAR II: RESOURCES AND RESEARCH OPPORTUNITIES AT THE DWIGHT D. EISENHOWER LIBRARY. *Military Affairs 1977 41(4): 195-200.* The Dwight D. Eisenhower Library has become a major repository for historical materials relating to World War II and has realized the early aims of the Eisenhower Foundation and the people of Abilene. An important collection, nicknamed the "sixteen-fifty-two file," is Eisenhower's Pre-Presidential Papers, 1916-52. The largest, single body of World War II military records is the collection designated "U.S. Army, Unit Record 1940-1950." 5 notes.

A. M. Osur

1741. Hamilton, James W. SOME REFLECTIONS ON RICHARD NIXON IN THE LIGHT OF HIS RESIGNATION AND FAREWELL SPEECHES. *J. of Psychohist. 1977 4(4): 491-511.* An overview of Richard M. Nixon's childhood leads to the conclusion that he has a "basically compulsive character structure with much underlying oral sadism." Various elements of his character and its experiential base in childhood are reflected in the images and themes Nixon used in his resignation and farewell speeches. 30 notes.

R. E. Butchart

1742. Henderson, Phillip. PSYCHOHISTORICAL PERSPECTIVES ON THE PRESIDENCY. *Michigan J. of Pol. Sci. 1981 1(1): 1-11.* Discusses some of the benefits and pitfalls of psychohistory as an approach for studying the presidency through the examination of three works: Bruce Mazlish's *In Search of Nixon* (1973), Doris Kearns's *Lyndon Johnson and the American Dream* (1976), and *Jimmy Carter and American Fantasy: Psychohistorical Explorations* (1977) edited by Lloyd deMause and Henry Ebel.

1743. Iakovlev, N. N. IZ ISTORII KLANA KENNEDI [From the history of the Kennedy clan]. *Voprosy Istorii [USSR] 1970 (9): 113-128.* Discusses the circumstances surrounding the assassination of President John F. Kennedy. Emphasizes the apparent incompetence displayed by the police holding the alleged assassin Lee Harvey Oswald and by the investigatory committee set up by President Johnson. The report produced by this committee was criticized both from the political right and left but the most cogent criticism came from Mark Lane in his book *Rush to Judgement* (New York: 1966). Describes the agreement made between the Kennedy family and W. Manchester about the latter's exclusive right of access to material concerning Kennedy and criticizes the chase for profits in which many other writers engaged. Mentions Robert Kennedy's

ambitions and gives a brief analysis of his character. Article to be continued. Published sources; 45 notes.

S

1744. Ivanov, R. F. DUAIT EIZENKHAUER V GODY VTOROI MIROVOI VOINY [Dwight Eisenhower in World War II]. *Novaia i Noveishaia Istoriia [USSR] 1980 (6): 107-128.* Analyzes the performance of Dwight D. Eisenhower during 1942-45, when he commanded the allied forces in Europe. This is followed by a brief sequel depicting his presidential years. The account is partly based on an interview with Eisenhower's son, John, and his brother, Milton. Despite his avowed proclivity for peace, based on religious views, Eisenhower advocated the use of nuclear weapons to end the Vietnamese War. During World War II he was a realist, but as a president he diverged from this stance. Based on published works and oral interviews; 126 notes.

D. N. Collins

1745. Joe, Barbara E. REAGAN'S WELFARE FRAUD. *Washington Monthly 1980 12(8): 34-36.* Criticizes Governor Ronald Reagan's statistics concerning his attack on the California public welfare system, starting in 1971.

1746. Johnson, James P. THE ASSASSINATION IN DALLAS: A SEARCH FOR MEANING. *J. of Psychohistory 1979 7(1): 105-121.* Reviews the following books on Lee Harvey Oswald and the assassination of John F. Kennedy: Edward J. Epstein's *Legend: The Secret World of Lee Harvey Oswald* (New York: Reader's Digest Pr. and McGraw-Hill Book Co., 1978) and Priscilla Johnson McMillan's *Marina and Lee* (New York: Harper and Row, 1977). Epstein emphasizes elements of the assassination drama indicating a conspiracy directed by the KGB. McMillan focuses on Lee Harvey Oswald's childhood, and the trauma responsible for his solitary, violent acts. 36 notes.

M. R. Strausbaugh

1747. Johnson, James P. NIXON AND THE PSYCHOHISTORIANS. *Psychohistory Rev. 1979 7(3): 38-42.* Reviews Richard Nixon's autobiography, *RN.* Summarizes psychohistorical analysis of Nixon's behavior during childhood, early adulthood, and as President. Examines Nixon's childhood, his relationships with each of his parents and his penchant for tough political maneuverings. Mentions Nixon's illnesses and frequent mistakes as signs of his unstable personality and his sense of martyrdom. Finds *RN* congruent with earlier psychohistorical analyses of Nixon. Reveals Nixon as a man who needed enemies he could fight or get revenge for something they had done to him. 22 notes.

J. M. Herrick

1748. Kahana, Yoram. CAPTAIN HARRY: THE CUSSING DOUGHBOY OF BATTERY D. *Mankind 1977 5(11): 36-41.* Harry S. Truman looked back on his war experience as a battery commander with a good deal of nostalgia and remained very fond of his military compatriots. He was a skilled, successful military leader of men who proved to be a hard taskmaster but also a kindred soul in sharing the miseries of the battlefield with his troops.

N. Lederer

1749. Karl, Barry D. THE NIXON FAULT. *Rev. in Am. Hist. 1979 7(2): 143-156.* Review article prompted by Richard M. Nixon's *RN: The Memoirs of Richard Nixon* (New York: Grosset & Dunlap, 1978).

1750. Kearns, Doris. LYNDON JOHNSON'S POLITICAL PERSONALITY. *Pol. Sci. Q. 1976 91(3): 385-409.* Analyzes the development of Lyndon Johnson's political personality—his characteristic ways of acquiring and using power—and traces the impact of Johnson's personality style on his leadership first as Senate majority leader and then as president promoting domestic reform and escalating the nation's involvement in Vietnam.

J

1751. Keefe, Robert. ON COWBOYS AND COLLECTIVES: THE KENNEDY-NIXON GENERATION. *Massachusetts Rev. 1980 21(3): 551-560.* Examines President John F. Kennedy's *Profiles in Courage* (1955) and President Richard M. Nixon's *Six Crises* (1962). Both men suffered from the common need to belong and the need to be alone. The two leading figures of the post-Eisenhower years seemed a mismatched pair: Boston Brahmin, Californian; Ivy Leaguer, small collegian; Kennedy a devourer of detective novels, Nixon a fan of John Wayne. Their writings mirror that fantasy world. Regional hatreds in Kennedy's work and Communism in Nixon's are seen as dangerous threats to the group.

E. R. Campbell

1752. Kempton, Greta. PAINTING THE TRUMAN FAMILY. *Missouri Hist. R. 1973 67(3): 335-349.* Recalls experiences painting President Harry S. Truman and members of the Truman family for various portraits. 6 illus. N. J. Street

1753. Kirkendall, Richard S. HARRY S. TRUMAN: A MISSOURI FARMER IN THE GOLDEN AGE. *Agric. Hist. 1974 48(4): 467-483.* Truman's years as a farmer in Missouri (1906-17) served to strengthen him physically and emotionally for the future. He was a fortunate farmer who operated an unusual farm in the "golden age" of American agriculture. With growing urbanization, farm prices were rising and Truman's farm was favorably situated. Intersected by two railroads and a highway, the farm was never isolated from the city. Based on primary and secondary sources; 88 notes. R. T. Fulton

1754. Kish, Francis B. CITIZEN-SOLDIER: HARRY S. TRUMAN, 1884-1972. *Military R. 1973 53(2): 30-44.* As a member of the Missouri National Guard and the Officer Reserve Corps, Harry S. Truman was a citizen-soldier for all but six years during 1905-42. During World War I Truman served as a battery commander, and his wartime associates and experiences were important elements in his rise to the presidency. Primary and secondary sources; 6 illus., 53 notes. J. K. Ohl

1755. Klaw, Barbara. LADY BIRD JOHNSON REMEMBERS. *Am. Heritage 1980 32(1): 4-17.* In this interview, Claudia Taylor (Lady Bird) Johnson (b. 1912), the widow of President Lyndon B. Johnson, discusses her life with him and since his death. Comments on the Vietnam War, the vice-presidency, and Watergate. 17 illus. J. F. Paul

1756. Kraminov, D. THE END OF THE WAR IN THE WEST. *Int. Affairs [USSR] 1978 (11): 113-122.* After the Anglo-American troops crossed the Rhine in March 1945, they encountered remarkably little resistance on their way to Berlin, and British Field Marshal Montgomery decided on taking the prize of the German capital, but American General Dwight D. Eisenhower thwarted this plan and held the British and American troops on the banks of the Elbe until the Soviet forces entered Berlin. Then the British and Americans swept in to prevent Soviet encirclement of the city, but Eisenhower's actions created friction between the British and Americans. Article to be continued.

1757. Kurtz, Michael L. LEE HARVEY OSWALD IN NEW ORLEANS: A REAPPRAISAL. *Louisiana Hist. 1980 21(1): 7-22.* Outlines Lee Harvey Oswald's arcane life (1939-63) and demonstrates that many intriguing questions about his five-month stay in New Orleans (April-September 1963) remain unanswered. Returning to his native city in these months shortly before the 22 November assassination of President John F. Kennedy in Dallas, Oswald quickly developed close ties with pro- and anti-Castro groups. Although the Federal Bureau of Investigation and the Central Intelligence Agency had him under close surveillance at this time, significant information on Oswald's Cuban connections is missing from the FBI's John F. Kennedy Assassination Files which were released in December 1977 and January 1978. Based on FBI and CIA files and several confidential interviews; 38 notes. D. B. Touchstone

1758. Lawton, Henry W. MILHOUS RISING. *J. of Psychohistory 1979 6(4): 519-542.* Review article of Richard M. Nixon's *RN: The Memoirs of Richard Nixon* (New York: Grosset and Dunlap, 1978) and David Abrahamsen's *Nixon vs. Nixon: An Emotional Tragedy* (New York: New American Library, 1978). Nixon's volume is self-serving, with its attempts to minimize his misconduct and arouse the reader's pity; Abrahamsen's book, based on interviews and correspondence with people who had known Nixon, ignored Nixon's own writings. He compromised the usefulness of his work through his unbridled bias, overstatement, tendency to treat supposition as truth, and diagnostic fuzziness. 113 notes. S

1759. Ledeen, Michael. HISS, OSWALD, THE KGB AND US. *Commentary 1978 65(5): 30-36.* Discusses information from Allen Weinstein's *Perjury: The Hiss-Chambers Case* and Edward J. Epstein's *Legend: The Secret World of Lee Harvey Oswald.* In both instances, experts were extremely unwilling to accept evidence of KGB espionage. Indeed, a mood of anti-anti-Communism has developed, which may only now be yielding to a more realistic appraisal of the KGB's intelligence ability and the lack of American expertise in counterintelligence. J. Tull

1760. Lewis, Nancy. THE CARTER RECORD. *Change 1976 8(9): 22-25, 64.* Georgia still hugs the bottom of the educational ladder. So what, if anything, can higher education expect of its former governor? J

1761. Lucet, Charles. JIMMY CARTER: RELIGION ET POLITIQUE AUX USA [Jimmy Carter: Religion and politics in the USA]. *Nouvelle Rev. des Deux Mondes [France] 1977 (1): 110-117.* Describes the rise of Jimmy Carter, an almost unknown governor of Georgia, to the Presidency of the United States, and his attempt to mix his Baptist religion with politics.

1762. Marcell, David W. POOR RICHARD: NIXON AND THE PROBLEM OF INNOCENCE. Hague, John A., ed. *American Character and Culture in a Changing World: Some Twentieth-Century Perspectives* (Westport, Conn.: Greenwood Pr., 1979): 325-337. Reflects on archetypes of American innocence created by Benjamin Franklin, whose autobiographical legend incorporated themes of perfectibility, self-help, and success; Henry Thoreau, whose *Walden* advocated transcendental awareness, intuition, individualism, the immediate and natural rather than history and milieu; and F. Scott Fitzgerald, whose Jay Gatsby defied the past for a romantic, vague, decadent, narcissistic dream, for a future founded on self. Richard M. Nixon, legally culpable in the Watergate scandal, may be culturally innocent. Americans characteristically confound ideal and reality, naively, beautifully, but dangerously denying human limitations, fate, and the burden of the past. 13 notes, biblio. P. M. Cohen

1763. Marina, William. SHOOTING DOWN THE CONSPIRACY THEORY. *Reason 1979 11(1): 18-24.* While admitting that the Warren Commission made errors of judgment in its study of President Kennedy's assassination, concludes that alternative theories—especially those suggesting conspiracy—are implausible, and that the Warren Commission's conclusions are basically correct.

1764. Mazon, Mauricio. YOUNG RICHARD NIXON: A STUDY IN POLITICAL PRECOCITY. *Historian 1978 41(1): 21-40.* A psychoanalytical evaluation of the early life of Richard M. Nixon (b. 1913). Discusses childhood traumas that molded Nixon's character and perceptions of himself. For example, Nixon in both youth and adulthood perceived himself to be lonely and isolated. Particularly traumatic to young Nixon was the birth of his brother, Donald, 16 months later, in 1914; Donald successfully competed for his mother's affections. To compensate for these anxieties, Richard Nixon showed his precocity by mastering new words which became his security blanket for home, neighborhood, and school. These early experiences led Nixon to "convert his childhood into an apprenticeship in mastering the demands made by crises and unpredictable situations" in his later political career. M. S. Legan

1765. Miscamble, Wilson D. THE EVOLUTION OF AN INTERNATIONALIST: HARRY S. TRUMAN AND AMERICAN FOREIGN POLICY. *Australian J. of Pol. and Hist. [Australia] 1977 23(2): 268-283.* Traces President Harry S. Truman's foreign policy ideas back to his experiences in World War I, but especially during his middle political career, 1935-45. He read widely in military history. In 1938 he advocated preparedness. In 1939 he attacked the dictators Hitler, Mussolini, and Stalin. During the war he attacked isolationism and spoke out for collective security and membership in the United Nations. The view he espoused as President had evolved in the previous decade. W. D. McIntyre

1766. Nuechterlein, James A. RICHARD NIXON'S CHARACTER AND FATE. *Queen's Q. [Canada] 1979 86(1): 16-25.* Reviews Richard M. Nixon's *RN: The Memoirs of Richard Nixon* (New York: Grosset and Dunlap, 1978). Though Nixon's relative candor is surprising, his lower middle class morality is evident. Life and politics are combat; and despite his impressive talents, there is no indication he would have objected to the Watergate break-in other than on the grounds of imprudence. C. A. D'Aniello

1767. Nurse, Ronald J. TWO FUTURE AMERICAN LEADERS REACT TO THE MIDDLE EAST CRISES OF 1939 AND 1948: A DOCUMENTARY EXERCISE. *Hist. Teacher 1974 8(1): 44-53.* Compares two letters from Palestine summarizing the Arab-Jewish imbroglio.

The first letter was written by John F. Kennedy in 1939, the second by Robert Kennedy in 1948.   P. W. Kennedy

1768. Reedy, George. THE TRUE DAWN OF CIVIL RIGHTS. *Washington Monthly 1982 14(3): 46-51.* Examines the role of then-Senator Lyndon B. Johnson in 1957 in the formulation and passing of the 1957 Civil Rights Act, and discusses the act as the beginning of the civil rights struggle in the United States and its impact on later civil rights legislation.

1769. Renshon, Stanley Allen. PSYCHOLOGICAL ANALYSIS AND PRESIDENTIAL PERSONALITY: THE CASE OF RICHARD NIXON. *Hist. of Childhood Q. 1975 2(3): 415-450.* Review article on James David Barber, *The Presidential Character* (New Jersey: Prentice Hall, 1972); Eli S. Chesen, *President Nixon's Psychiatric Profile* (New York: Peter Wyden, 1973); Bruce Mazlish, *In Search of Nixon* (New York: Basic Books, Inc., 1972); and Arthur Woodstone, *Nixon's Head* (New York: St. Martin's Press, 1972). Evaluates each volume in terms of its contributions to an understanding of Richard M. Nixon's personality, and to the development of a system of psychological assessment of political leaders prior to election to office. Based on secondary sources; 47 notes.   R. E. Butchart

1770. Rosenberg, Bruce A. KENNEDY IN CAMELOT: THE ARTHURIAN LEGEND IN AMERICA. *Western Folklore 1976 35(1): 52-59.* Discusses several legends concerning the death of John F. Kennedy and compares these to similar motifs concerning Arthur of Camelot and national heroes in other countries. Based on primary and secondary sources; 7 notes.   S. L. Myres

1771. Scobie, Ingrid Winther. HELEN GAHAGAN DOUGLAS AND HER 1950 SENATE RACE WITH RICHARD M. NIXON. *Southern California Q. 1976 58(1): 113-126.* Democratic incumbent Sheridan Downey bowed out of the primary race because of ill health; newspaper publisher Manchester Boddy, with support from Downey, unsuccessfully contested Helen Gahagan Douglas for the Democratic nomination. The hotly contested primary race provided Richard M. Nixon with additional political ammunition for the general election. Badly divided, the Democrats ran a poor contest against the Republicans. Nixon, managed by Murray Chotiner, ran an aggressive campaign which included use of smear tactics. These included linking Douglas' voting record with radical Congressman Vito Marcantonio's, accusing her of being soft on Communism, and misrepresenting her political views and associations. By contrast, Douglas' approach was idealistic and defensive. Douglas lost by a 3-2 margin. Nixon might have won on the issues alone, given the disorganization of the Democrats, but that ambitious congressman took no chances. Based on primary and secondary sources; 40 notes.   A. Hoffman

1772. Seelye, John. THE MEASURE OF HIS COMPANY: RICHARD M. NIXON IN AMBER. *Virginia Q. Rev. 1977 53(4): 585-606.* Observes "that when the great man turns historian it will be to rectify his mistakes by a process of revision, reforming his errors, by justifying them." Richard M. Nixon is in the stream of Benjamin Franklin, Frederick Douglass, Horatio Alger and others, as he works on revisionist autobiography.   O. H. Zabel

1773. Shapiro, Walter. A CENTURY OF PROGRESS: MADELEINE LEE, MEET NANCY REAGAN. *Washington Monthly 1981 13(1): 47-49.* Discusses the similarities between Henry Adams's *Democracy,* (1880) about the romance between 58-year-old Republican Senator Silas P. Ratcliffe of Illinois and New York heiress and powermonger Madeleine Lee during the transition "between one lackluster president and another," and Nancy Reagan and the rest of the Reagan administration, excluding President Reagan.

1774. Toner, James H. EXCEPTIONAL WAR, EXCEPTIONAL PEACE: THE 1953 CEASE-FIRE IN KOREA. *Military Rev. 1976 56(7): 3-13.* Examines President-elect Dwight D. Eisenhower and the UN's role in diplomacy and peace negotiations to end the Korean War in 1952-53.

1775. Vose, Clement R. NIXON'S ARCHIVAL LEGACY. *PS 1977 10(4): 432-439.* An overview of developments in archival acquisition following the presidency of Richard M. Nixon, synopsizes court

actions in obtaining the Nixon papers and the Kissinger transcripts, and summarizes the Public Documents Commission's proposed legislation to govern the records of federal officials, 1970-77.

1776. Watters, Pat. PROBING JIMMY CARTER'S CIVIL LIBERTIES RECORD. *Civil Liberties Rev. 1976 3(3): 7-22.* Examines Carter's record in Georgia state politics since the 1950's and finds that his "record on civil rights is laudable" but that his record on civil liberties is fuzzy, and concludes that, as President, Carter "will need constant prodding from civil liberties activists. . . ."

1777. Westin, Alan F. and Shattuck, John. THE SECOND DEPOSING OF RICHARD NIXON. *Civil Liberties R. 1976 3(2): 8-23, 84-96.* Prints excerpts of the deposition given by Richard M. Nixon on 15 January 1976 in the pretrial proceedings of *Halperin et al.* v. *Kissinger et al.,* with comments by John Shattuck, the ACLU lawyer who took the deposition.

1778. Williams, Herbert Lee. I WAS TRUMAN'S GHOST. *Presidential Studies Q. 1982 12(2): 256-259.* A reminiscence by the journalist who helped Harry S. Truman write his memoirs.   D. H. Cline

1779. Williams, T. Harry. HUEY, LYNDON, AND SOUTHERN RADICALISM. *J. of Am. Hist. 1973 60(2): 267-293.* The most radical mass movement and the two most radical politicians of recent history were products of an allegedly conservative, undissenting South. The black civil rights movement broke the "enveloping silence" surrounding race relations in the South and may see a greater acceptance of black equality in that region than in the North. Both Huey Long and Lyndon Johnson were products of non-affluent families in historically radical sections, both strove for economic equality for whites, and both would extend that equality to blacks. Johnson was more manipulative, working successfully within the system, while Long was authoritarian, feeling that the political system frustrated radical change. 61 notes.   K. B. West

1780. Wolin, Howard E. GRANDIOSITY AND VIOLENCE IN THE KENNEDY FAMILY. *Psychohistory Rev. 1979 8(3): 27-37.* Behavior patterns of the Kennedy family, including Joseph, Sr., Rose, Joseph, Jr., John, Robert, and Edward, show evidence of fantasies of omnipotence, invulnerability, and grandiosity. These fantasies are not well-integrated with the ego or the ego-ideal and are therefore expressed in unrealistic and self-destructive actions. The Kennedy sons acted out their parents' unintegrated grandiose fantasies. Parental expectations led to incautious behavior by the Kennedy sons. Cites examples of risk-taking behavior by the Kennedy sons. Edward Kennedy's accident at Chappaquiddick Island may have been an anniversary reaction of Robert Kennedy's death. Secondary sources; ref.   J. M. Herrick

1781. —. CARTER AT THE CENTER. *Center Mag. 1977 10(1): 49-58.* Jimmy Carter presents his reasons for running for the presidency in a 1975 interview; outlines his attitudes and policies toward military expenditures, corporate power, the energy shortage, the tax structure, welfare reform, employment, compulsory health insurance, and government secrecy.

Presidential Campaigns

1782. Aberbach, Joel D. ALIENATION AND VOTING BEHAVIOR TODAY. *Society 1976 13(5): 18-26.* Discusses the relationship between political alienation and voting behavior in the 1968 and 1972 presidential elections, emphasizing factors in the choice of candidates.

1783. Abrams, Burton A. and Settle, Russell F. THE ECONOMIC THEORY OF REGULATION AND PUBLIC FINANCING OF PRESIDENTIAL ELECTIONS. *J. of Pol. Econ. 1978 86(2, pt. 1): 245-258.* Recent changes in campaign finance legislation (passed by a heavily Democratic Congress) are considered within the context of the two competing theories of regulation, the "public-interest" theory and the economic theory of regulation. Empirical evidence is presented in support of the economic theory's explanation for the major regulatory changes in the political process. The evidence suggests that these changes were highly beneficial to the Democratic party and that they were instrumental in Jimmy Carter's defeat of Gerald Ford in the 1976 presidential election.

J

1784.   Abramson, Paul R.   CLASS VOTING IN THE 1976 PRESIDENTIAL ELECTION.   *J. of Pol. 1978 40(4): 1066-1072.* In 1972 there was virtually no relationship between social class and party choice among white voters. The percentage of working-class white major-party voters who supported the Democratic party minus the percentage of middle class white major-party voters supporting the Democrats was 44 in 1948, fell to 20 in 1952, 8 in 1956, rose to 12 in 1960, 19 in 1964, and fell to 10 in 1968 and 2 in 1976 [sic]. Economic, social, and political forces contributed to an increase in class voting in 1976, with the youngest voters manifesting the highest level. Democrats won three of the four elections in which class voting was above the median and lost three of the four in which it was below. Primary and secondary sources; fig., 8 notes.

A. W. Novitsky

1785.   Adams, John Clarke.   LA PAGELLA DI CARTER   [Carter's report card]. *Ponte [Italy] 1981 37(7-8): 625-630.* Jimmy Carter's electoral failure may have been due to the opinions of the voters themselves or to the manipulations of the press; future historians may reevaluate his performance.

1786.   Agnoletti, Enzo Enriques.   L'AMERICA IN UN MONDO OSTILE?   [America in a hostile world?]. *Ponte [Italy] 1980 36(10): 987-990.* Compares Ronald Reagan's election with Dwight D. Eisenhower's, noting similarities (such as the unexpected change in governing party), but in general perceiving it as a defeat of democratic world opinion, with attendant worries about proliferation of right-wing dictatorships, while admitting that Europe may benefit from this change of course in American policy.

1787.   Alter, Jonathan.   ROOTING FOR REAGAN.   *Washington Monthly 1981 12(11): 12-17.* Discusses news coverage of the presidential political candidates in 1976 and 1980, focusing on 1980, when it more often than not tilted toward Ronald Reagan; although the imbalance may have occurred unconsciously, it is true that "reporters who cover winning presidential candidates often end up with better jobs for themselves after the election."

1788.   Altschuler, Bruce E.   KENNEDY DECIDES TO RUN: 1968. *Presidential Studies Q. 1980 10(3): 348-352.* Robert F. Kennedy's delayed decision to enter the 1968 presidential contest was the result of many complex factors. Kennedy would run only if his opposition to President Lyndon B. Johnson's policies was greater than the chances for overwhelming defeat and the possibility of the personal conflict between himself and Johnson obscuring the political conflict. Polls and the perceptions of advisors and other political leaders helped shape the decision, but his late and cautious entry would have caused problems if he had lived to contest the nomination. 28 notes.

D. H. Cline

1789.   Altschull, J. Herbert.   THE JOURNALIST AND INSTANT HISTORY: AN EXAMPLE OF JACKAL SYNDROME.   *Journalism Q. 1973 50(3): 489-496.* Reexamines Theodore H. White's claim in *The Making of the President 1960* that the televised debates between presidential candidates John F. Kennedy and Richard M. Nixon in 1960 were decisive in the election, to exemplify "the jackal syndrome."

S

1790.   Anderson, David L.   CHINA POLICY AND PRESIDENTIAL POLITICS, 1952.   *Presidential Studies Q. 1980 10(1): 79-90.* The election of 1952 was the first presidential contest following the founding of the Communist People's Republic of China in 1949. The Korean War had drawn the United States and China into military conflict, causing much of the 1952 debate to turn on the "loss of China." A new and uncomfortable notion was born in 1952: the United States was no longer the omnipotent champion of democracy. US-Chinese relations were not restored to a friendly basis until the 1970's, when the United States withdrew from the Asian continent. 52 notes.

G. E. Pergl

1791.   Anderson, Donald F.   PRESIDENTIAL AVAILABILITY: A FRAMEWORK FOR FUTURE RESEARCH.   *Presidential Studies Q. 1978 8(4): 341-347.* Borrowing from studies of American political culture and small group leadership, the author builds a theoretical structure for

defining and predicting those qualities which constitute "availability" in presidential candidates. Political culture provides those assumptions, attitudes, and beliefs underlying our political system which prescribe certain roles for presidential candidates and favor certain leadership styles. Small group leadership research identifies variables applicable to the selection of political leaders as 1) personality of the leader, 2) expectations of the electorate, 3) nature of the party, and 4) situational tasks. By combining these leadership functions and selection variables in a matrix, a framework is created for the systematic analysis of candidate availability. Table, 42 notes.

S. C. Strom

1792.   Anderson, James A. and Avery, Robert K.   AN ANALYSIS OF CHANGES IN VOTER PERCEPTION OF CANDIDATES' POSITIONS.   *Communication Monographs 1978 45(4): 354-361.* A panel study of 58 families in five states during the 1976 presidential campaign supports the hypothesis that the family strongly influenced voting preferences but had little effect on patterns of change in member's perception of their own and candidates' positions.

1793.   Annunziata, Frank.   THE REVOLT AGAINST THE WELFARE STATE: GOLDWATER CONSERVATISM AND THE ELECTION OF 1964.   *Presidential Studies Q. 1980 10(2): 254-265.* Barry M. Goldwater's nomination for president by the Republican Party in 1964 contravened the idea that neither party could nominate an intense ideologue and abandon electoral pragmatism. He represented a repudiation of Dwight D. Eisenhower's liberal Republicanism. Instead of deciding just who would govern, Goldwater focused on just what government should or should not do. Goldwater was a man who would rather be right than win, and one who wanted to offer a clear choice to the voters. 57 notes.

D. H. Cline

1794.   Arterton, F. Christopher.   STRATEGIES AND TACTICS OF CANDIDATE ORGANIZATIONS.   *Pol. Sci. Q. 1977-78 92(4): 663-671.* Discusses the strategies and tactics of the Gerald R. Ford and Ronald Reagan candidate organizations. One of five articles on "Exploring the 1976 Republican Convention."

J

1795.   Atkin, Charles K.   EFFECTS OF CAMPAIGN ADVERTISING AND NEWSCASTS ON CHILDREN.   *Journalism Q. 1977 54(3): 503-509.* In a study conducted in 1976 on the basis of advertisements for Jimmy Carter, Gerald Ford, and Ronald Reagan, analysis shows that a strong cognitive and affective impact was made on juvenile television viewers.

1796.   Bailey, George.   HOW NEWSMAKERS MAKE THE NEWS. *J. of Communication 1978 28(4): 80-83.* Discusses the news coverage of presidential campaigns in the United States, based on 1976.

1797.   Baker, Kendall L. and Walter, Oliver.   VOTER RATIONALITY: A COMPARISON OF PRESIDENTIAL AND CONGRESSIONAL VOTING IN WYOMING.   *Western Pol. Q. 1975 28(2): 316-329.* This study is based on a statewide representative sample of 868 individuals. The rational voter is defined as an individual who calculates on the basis of essentially accurate, politically relevant information and ranks the candidates on the basis of this information. Using a technique developed by Martin Fishbein, indices of presidential and congressional attitudes, which include a large number of issue orientation items, are developed; in addition, scales measuring the accuracy of the respondents' perceptions of the issue positions of the congressional and presidential candidates are constructed. The findings of the study indicate that issues play a major role in the voter's electoral decision and that the voter is quite accurate in his perceptions of the candidates' issue positions. These relationships are found to be stronger for the presidential than for the congressional election. Like other recent studies, the authors conclude that voters may be a good deal more rational than has been heretofore assumed.

J

1798.   Beatty, Kathleen Murphy.   COLORADO: INCREASINGLY UNPREDICTABLE.   *Social Sci. J. 1981 18(3): 31-40.* The 1980 elections showed state politics to be business as usual as voters split tickets, electing candidates who showed a mixture of conservative and liberal views and continuing to fragment the party system, while Ronald Reagan won decisively.

1799. Bechtolt, Warren E., Jr.; Hilyard, Joseph; and Bybee, Carl R. AGENDA CONTROL IN THE 1976 DEBATES: A CONTENT ANALYSIS. *Journalism Q. 1977 54(4): 674-681.* Assesses the three televised debates of the 1976 presidential campaign as a source of information about the candidates. Although the reporters who asked questions at the debates appear to have directed the discussions in the first and third sessions, the candidates chose the specific topics of debate almost half of the time. Jimmy Carter generally exercised more control over the debates than Gerald R. Ford. Both candidates spoke almost 40% of the time about their personal qualities and public images. Based on transcripts of the debates. Secondary sources; 8 notes.
R. P. Sindermann, Jr.

1800. Bell, B. Tartt. THE CAMPAIGN FOR THE WHITE HOUSE: 1972. *Contemporary Rev. [Great Britain] 1972 221(1281): 177-183.* A view of the American presidential campaign of 1972, written during the campaign.

1801. Bell, Charles G. CALIFORNIA: THE START OF A NEW ERA? *Social Sci. J. 1981 18(3): 15-30.* Analyzes the results of the 1980 state and national elections with emphasis on the growing conservative electorate, the increased expenditure of seeking state office in California, and the effects of redistricting on future candidates.

1802. Beniger, James R. WINNING THE PRESIDENTIAL NOMINATION: NATIONAL POLLS AND STATE PRIMARY ELECTIONS, 1936-1972. *Public Opinion Q. 1976 40(1): 22-38.* Using the results of 202 Gallup opinion polls and 248 state primary elections, this article develops a general model of presidential nomination campaigns. National public opinion is found to play a major role, and state primaries a much lesser role, in winning the presidential nomination.   J

1803. Bennett, William E. FROM THURMOND TO WALLACE: CHANGING ELECTORAL PATTERNS IN MISSISSIPPI CONSERVATISM. *Southern Q. 1975 14(1): 61-69.* Analyzes voting patterns in the state of Mississippi from 1948-72. Focuses on presidential elections. Evaluates voting trends according to two themes: race and conservativism. Also makes correlations according to income, age, education, occupation, and place of residence. Concludes that as the forces of urbanization, industrialization, and population diversification accelerate in the state, so will the appeal of the Republican Party. 3 tables, 9 notes.
R. W. Dubay

1804. Berquist, Goodwin F. and Golden, James L. MEDIA RHETORIC, CRITICISM, AND THE PUBLIC PERCEPTION OF THE 1980 PRESIDENTIAL DEBATES. *Q. J. of Speech 1981 67(2): 125-137.* Media specialists promoted the 1980 televised debates and then sought to influence public perception through commentary and criticism. They viewed substance as less important than delivery, appearance, and manner; downplayed the significance of incumbency; and concluded that current program formats favored perceived candidate advantage rather than the public interest.   J

1805. Bibby, John F. and Cotter, Cornelius P. PRESIDENTIAL CAMPAIGNING, FEDERALISM AND THE FEDERAL ELECTION CAMPAIGN ACT. *Publius 1980 10(1): 119-136.* The Federal Election Campaign Act (US, 1971), as amended in 1974, 1976, and 1979, put strict limits on contributions, tied national and state expenditure limits to public funding for nomination and general election campaigns, set forth extensive administrative regulations, and directed campaign subsidies to candidates rather than to parties directly. The act assures national party committees a significant role in the individual candidate and general election campaigns even as it strengthens state party organizations. It forces candidate organizations to centralize even as it diffuses money and power within the party system. The act has resulted in the proliferation of primaries, longer campaigns, increased emphasis on centralized spending for national media campaigns, discouragement of grass roots organization, and preservation of the Democratic and Republican parties as the only viable national parties. Based on the *Congressional Record* and current periodical literature; 30 notes.   C. B. Schulz

1806. Biles, Roger. JACOB M. ARVEY, KINGMAKER: THE NOMINATION OF ADLAI E. STEVENSON IN 1952. *Chicago Hist. 1979 8(3): 130-143.* Democratic National Committeeman and Chicago politico Colonel Jacob M. Arvey, got the Democratic presidential nomination for Illinois Governor Adlai E. Stevenson, in 1952; briefly traces Arvey's political career from 1932.

1807. Black, Earl and Black, Merle. THE DEMOGRAPHIC BASIS OF WALLACE SUPPORT IN ALABAMA. *Am. Pol. Q. 1973 1(3): 279-304.* Examines the evolution of the George Wallace constituency in Alabama, 1958-70, showing its importance for Wallace's entry into national politics.

1808. Black, Edwin. ELECTING TIME. *Q. J. of Speech 1973 59(2): 125-129.* "The 1972 presidential campaign revolved around the theme of *time.* This theme organizes Muskie and Humphrey as anachronisms, Kennedy as promissory, McGovern as attempting to sponsor a historical myth, and Nixon as a figure divorced from a personal history."   J

1809. Bohn, Thomas W. BROADCASTING NATIONAL ELECTION RETURNS, 1952-1976. *J. of Communication 1980 30(4): 140-153.* Advanced technology, including that of television, has hardly improved the ritualistic structure of election night broadcasting; as in the early days of radio, experts project, rather than explain, trends and outcomes.

1810. Bonazzi, Tiziano. DAL "POPULISMO" CARTERIANO ALLA VALANGA REAGAN [From Carter's populism to the Reagan landslide]. *Ponte [Italy] 1981 37(1): 20-24.* Explains Jimmy Carter's presidential defeat in 1980 in terms of his ambiguity and failure to define a program that would crystallize the aspirations of a basically conservative majority.

1811. Bormann, Ernest G. THE EAGLETON AFFAIR: A FANTASY THEME ANALYSIS. *Q. J. of Speech 1973 59(2): 143-159.* "To win in 1972 the Democrats needed a unified rhetoric. Their strategy was to emphasize *persona.* The breaking news of Senator Eagleton's mental health, coming at a strategic time, created a fantasy that chained through the electorate and presented the McGovern *persona* as inconsistent, inept, and untrustworthy."   J

1812. Bormann, Ernest G.; Koester, Jolene; and Bennett, Janet. POLITICAL CARTOONS AND SALIENT RHETORICAL FANTASIES: AN EMPIRICAL ANALYSIS OF THE '76 PRESIDENTIAL CAMPAIGN. *Communication Monographs 1978 45(4): 317-329.* Discusses a study investigating the similarity between shared fantasies in small groups and patterns of shared media fantasies among different kinds of voters, using political cartoons appearing during the 1976 presidential campaign to represent the main media fantasy themes.

1813. Boyd, Richard W. DECLINE OF U.S. VOTER TURNOUT: STRUCTURAL EXPLANATIONS. *Am. Pol. Q. 1981 9(2): 133-159.* Decline in turnout in American presidential elections since 1964 results from America's population growing in just those young and old age groups that vote in low rates and from an expanding election calendar across federal, state, and local governments. Tracing individual voter histories across a series of elections provides evidence of a core electorate, which is large as a proportion of the registered electorate and which votes at a reasonably high and equal level.   J/S

1814. Boyett, Joseph H. BACKGROUND CHARACTERISTICS OF DELEGATES TO THE 1972 CONVENTIONS: A SUMMARY REPORT OF FINDINGS FROM A NATIONAL SAMPLE. *Western Pol. Q. 1974 27(3): 469-478.* "In general, the data for the sample suggest that delegates to the 1972 conventions tended to be married, white males in their 40's, who had been active in politics for approximately 16 years."
S

1815. Bradford, Richard H. JOHN F. KENNEDY AND THE 1960 PRESIDENTIAL PRIMARY IN WEST VIRGINIA. *South Atlantic Q. 1976 75(2): 161-172.* Analyzes the 1960 West Virginia Democratic primary in which John F. Kennedy overwhelmingly defeated Hubert H. Humphrey. Kennedy's victory is traced to support from Franklin D. Roosevelt, Jr., a superior campaign organization, effective use of television, appeals to the poor and unemployed, and reverse psychology concerning the Catholic issue. The election had major significance in Kennedy receiving the national party nomination. 69 notes.
R. W. Dubay

1816. Bremner, John Evan. THE WINNING CANDIDATE. *Washington Monthly 1976 8(3): 58-61.* Discusses issues in the political campaigns of presidential candidates Jimmy Carter and Jerry Brown in the Democratic Party in 1976.

1817. Broh, C. Anthony. HORSE-RACE JOURNALISM: RE-PORTING THE POLLS IN THE 1976 PRESIDENTIAL ELECTION. *Public Opinion Q. 1980 44(4): 514-529.* Reporting of public opinion polls conformed to a horse-race image of campaign reporting during the 1976 presidential election. Journalists avoided prediction, reported segments of the sample, selectively compared results, emphasized spectacles, questioned the validity of polling, made a few mistakes, and ignored certain data in their reporting.   J/S

1818. Brown, Clifford W., Jr.; Hedges, Roman; and Powell, Lynda Watts. BELIEF STRUCTURE IN A POLITICAL ELITE: CON-TRIBUTORS TO THE 1972 PRESIDENTIAL CANDIDATES. *Polity 1980 13(1): 134-146.* The study of a political elite, contributors of more than $100 to the 1972 presidential campaign, indicates that the elite are more likely than most citizens to find the liberal-conservative scale relevant to their beliefs, more likely to be consistent on the issues and to support the candidate who shares their preferences on the issues, more likely to be extreme on the liberal-conservative question, but not more likely to be extreme on substantive issues; perhaps the high educational level of the elite makes them more likely than other citizens to be extreme on abstract issues but not extreme on substantive ones.

1819. Brown, Clifford W., Jr.; Hedges, Roman B.; and Powell, Lynda Watts. MODES OF ELITE POLITICAL PARTICIPATION: CON-TRIBUTORS TO THE 1972 PRESIDENTIAL CANDIDATES. *Am. J. of Pol. Sci. 1980 24(2): 259-290.* Contributors of more than $100 to presidential candidates offer unique opportunities for an investigation of elite behavior because they participate both extensively and intensively in political activities. Their activity can be structured around five modes of participation: Campaigning, Giving, Using Good Offices, Voting, and Mobilizing. There are basic similarities in structure between these elite participants and mass participants (as described by Verba and Nie, 1972), despite a wide difference in participation levels. The elite contributors can be aggregated, on the basis of their behavior patterns, into nine clusters that provide not only an empirical typology of campaign contributors, but also a meaningful basis for discrimination with respect to other, non-behavioral, attributes. A predictive model of elite behavior is presented. 2 tables, biblio., 2 appendixes.   J

1820. Bushnell, Eleanore and Driggs, Don W. NEVADA: BUSI-NESS AS USUAL. *Social Sci. J. 1981 18(3): 65-74.* In Nevada state politics the political tradition of electing conservative Democrats to the state legislature and Republicans to national office continued in the general election with the Ronald Reagan landslide victory of 1980.

1821. Campbell, Bruce A. PATTERNS OF CHANGE IN THE PARTISAN LOYALTIES OF NATIVE SOUTHERNERS: 1952-1972. *J. of Pol. 1977 39(3): 730-761.* Southern loyalty to the Democratic Party declined 10 percent during 1952-72. This trend reversed itself only in 1964. Neither in-migration nor out-migration adequately explains the change. During the 1950's, native southern blacks moved toward the Republican Party to support President Eisenhower's integration policies; during the 1960's, they overwhelmingly supported the civil rights positions of Democratic presidents John F. Kennedy and Lyndon B. Johnson. Southern whites, in contrast, moved toward the Republican Party because that party more accurately reflected their attitudes on integration and the expanding power of the federal government. Based on six national presidential election studies by the staff of the Center for Political Studies and other primary and secondary sources; 3 tables, 10 graphs, 31 notes.
                                                        A. W. Novitsky

1822. Campen, Jim. ECONOMIC CRISIS AND CONSERVATIVE ECONOMIC POLICIES: U.S. CAPITALISM IN THE 1980S. *Radical Am. 1981 15(1-2): 33-54.* The Ronald Reagan attack on the sorry state of the economy proved to be successful in the 1980 election. Populist rhetoric notwithstanding, the corporations did face a grim decade in the 1970's. 26 notes, 6 illus.   C. M. Hough

1823. Carmines, Edward G. and Gopoian, J. David. ISSUE COALI-TIONS, ISSUELESS CAMPAIGNS: THE PARADOX OF RATIO-NALITY IN AMERICAN PRESIDENTIAL ELECTIONS. *J. of Pol. 1981 43(4): 1170-1189.* Between 1956 and 1976, Democratic presidential candidates received strong support from voters who took liberal positions on federal aid to education, government provision of health care, and government guarantees of full employment. Republican candidates received support from conservatives on these issues. Since 1964, attitudes toward fair employment and school integration have served as similar predictors of voting behavior. However, candidates continue to avoid substantive campaigns in favor of consensus-building, recognizing the politically harmful effects of issue-oriented appeals. While the existence of issue-oriented electoral coalitions indicates that party cleavage is a long-term and stable element of American politics, popular response to specific presidential candidates may cut across such partisan coalitions. 4 illus., 6 tables, 18 notes.   A. W. Novitsky

1824. Cassel, Carol A. CHANGE IN ELECTORAL PARTICIPA-TION IN THE SOUTH. *J. of Pol. 1979 41(3): 907-917.* Regional differences in presidential voting narrowed from 1952 to 1976 as both black and white females were mobilized into the southern electorate while nonsouthern voting, especially among the younger and less educated, declined. White southern males paralleled nonsouthern whites of both sexes in declining participation, despite the tumultuous period when differences in parties became clear and issue salience was high. The younger noncollege generation was the major source of the decline. 4 illus., table, 16 notes.   A. W. Novitsky

1825. Cassel, Carol A. and Hill, David B. EXPLANATIONS OF TURNOUT DECLINE: A MULTIVARIATE TEST. *Am. Pol. Q. 1981 9(2): 181-195.* Tests explanations of the post-1964 decline in turnout for presidential elections in nonsouthern states. Twelve socioeconomic and attitudinal variables are used to predict validated voting reports collected in conjunction with 1964 and 1976 national election studies. Both regression and probit analyses indicate that political attitudes, like partisanship and concern over the election outcome, have contributed to the decline in turnout; however, education and interest variables have offset the decline attributed to changes in political attitudes. The analysis leaves the puzzle of declining turnout largely unsolved.   J/S

1826. Center, Judith A. 1972 DEMOCRATIC CONVENTION RE-FORMS AND PARTY DEMOCRACY. *Pol. Sci. Q. 1974 89(2): 325-350.* "Analyzes the origins and content of the Democratic party's delegate selection 'reforms' for the 1972 convention. In a sharp attack on the new procedures, Center argues that a convention constituted under the 1972 rules was incapable of choosing a presidential nominee with maximum chance of winning the November general election."   J

1827. Chaffee, Steven H. PRESIDENTIAL DEBATES—ARE THEY HELPFUL TO VOTERS? *Communication Monographs 1978 45(4): 330-346.* Analyzes impact studies, including those of the televised Jimmy Carter-Gerald Ford debates and the 1960 presidential debates, concluding that voters benefit from them.

1828. Chaffee, Steven H. and Choe, Sun Yuel. TIME OF DECISION AND MEDIA USE DURING THE FORD-CARTER CAMPAIGN. *Public Opinion Q. 1980 44(1): 53-69.* This paper challenges the traditional belief that a full presidential political campaign can have only "limited effects" on voting, by identifying a group of voters who make their decisions during the campaign rather than either prior to or very late in the campaign. In a panel study of Wisconsin voters in the 1976 election, 40% were Campaign Deciders. These voters were low in partisanship, but paid close attention to the campaign and the Ford-Carter debates, and voted in accordance with campaign-specific perceptions. By contrast, both Pre-campaign Deciders and Last-minute Deciders voted mainly on the basis of party identification. 4 tables, 5 notes, biblio.   J

1829. Chambers, Raymond L. GUIDELINES FOR CHOOSING A PRESIDENT. *Presidential Studies Q. 1980 10(2): 156-162.* Most voters in America know little about their government, how it works, how it affects their lives, and most political issues, but do know something about the presidency. Thus, the only tool of democracy directly available to the citizens is the presidency. This leads to two major points. First, voters must look for a candidate with experience and proven ability, best gained in long and recent service in Congress. Second, to keep democracy functioning, a strong presidency is needed to overcome obstacles and restrictions inherent in the decisionmaking process. Table, 34 notes.

D. H. Cline

1830. Childs, Richard S. PRESIDENTIAL PRIMARIES NEED OVERHAUL. *Natl. Civic R. 1975 64(1): 14-20.* Argues that presidential primary elections are too expensive and very often do not result in the election of the party's favorite candidate.   S

1831. Clark, Cal and Clark, Janet M. NEW MEXICO: MOVING IN THE DIRECTION OF A REPUBLICAN REALIGNMENT. *Social Sci. J. 1981 18(3): 75-85.* Analyzes the results of the 1980 general election in New Mexico that led to the election of Ronald Reagan and Republican incumbent victories in general; the most interest was generated by the election of Republican Joe Skeen to the House of Representatives, which marked only the third time that a write-in candidate for Congress won.

1832. Claussen, E. Neal. ALBEN BARKLEY'S RHETORICAL VICTORY IN 1948. *Southern Speech Communication J. 1979 45(1): 79-92.* Describes the political events and the rhetorical milieu which led to the nomination of Senator Alben Barkley for the vice-presidency at the 1948 Democratic National Convention.

1833. Corbetta, Piergiorgio. IDENTIFICAZIONE PARTITICA, PROGRAMMA POLITICO E PERSONALITA DEI CANDIDATI NELLE ELEZIONI PRESIDENZIALI AMERICANE DEL 1980 [Party identification, issues, candidates: the American presidential elections, 1980]. *Riv. Italiana di Sci. Pol. [Italy] 1982 12(1): 73-119.* Discusses whether the presidential election of 1980 was a mandate for a new policy for President Reagan or a negative judgment of the Carter presidency. Party identification does not seem to have been a decisive factor in these elections. Of greater importance was the role of political issues: the vote is better predicted from the vicinity of the voter to the positions of Reagan than from the distance of the voter from Carter. For the personality of the candidates similar considerations apply: the vote was determined not so much by the unpopularity of Carter as by the trust felt toward Reagan. The outcome of the election was not only a rejection of the outgoing president but a sign of support for the conservative program of the Republican candidate.   J/S Italian.

1834. Corlew, Robert E., III. FRANK GOAD CLEMENT AND THE KEYNOTE ADDRESS OF 1956. *Tennessee Hist. Q. 1977 36(1): 95-107.* The rapid rise of Frank Goad Clement in Tennessee politics and his choice as keynote speaker for the 1956 Democratic Party convention indicated that his success would continue at the national level. After a fiery speech that received much praise, however, Clement was bitterly disappointed that he received scant consideration for national office. Primary and secondary sources; 26 notes.   M. B. Lucas

1835. Costain, Anne N. AN ANALYSIS OF VOTING IN AMERICAN NATIONAL NOMINATING CONVENTIONS. *Am. Pol. Q. 1978 6(1): 95-120.* Statistically analyzes the response of US political parties to an electoral imperative in their selection of presidential nominees. Discusses whether their choices are made in relation to a balance of issue orientation and electoral interests within the party. Applies the method to both Democratic and Republican conventions. Concludes: "1) There has been a significant increase in the frequency of ideological voting in the selection of presidential nominees; and 2) the major change has occurred in the Democratic party." 8 notes, ref.

R. V. Ritter

1836. Costain, Anne N. CHANGES IN THE ROLE OF IDEOLOGY IN AMERICAN NATIONAL NOMINATING CONVENTIONS AND AMONG PARTY IDENTIFIERS. *Western Pol. Q. 1980 33(1): 73-86.* Linkages between new patterns of voting in American national nominating conventions and attitudinal changes among party activities and identifiers are examined using a bloc analysis of convention voting and Survey Research Center data on the attitudes of party identifiers. For the period from 1956 to 1972, the growing importance of ideological belief in determining party activism parallels the increased prevalence of issue-based convention voting. Similarly, the growing distance in attitudinal surveys between the ideological position

of party activists and identifiers seems to accompany the virtual disappearance of an identifiable bloc of electorally motivated delegate votes. The traditional belief that party conventions search for a nominee who can win the general election for the party seems to have been displaced by a pattern of convention voting in which the issue position of candidates provides the dominant claim on convention votes. The significance of the virtual disappearance of a strong electorally oriented bloc and the growth of ideological factionalism within both parties' conventions is that there now appears to be more pressure to select nominees sharing the issue preferences of the party elite rather than candidates with political positions favored by the majority of voters. 2 tables, 2 fig., 26 notes.   J

1837. Coveyou, Michael R. and Pfeiffer, David G. EDUCATION AND VOTING TURNOUT OF BLACKS IN THE 1968 PRESIDENTIAL ELECTION. *J. of Pol. 1973 35(4): 995-1001.* "The traditional generalization that voter turnout increases monotonically as education increases does not describe the pattern of black turnout in the 1968 presidential election. The very consistency of another pattern, curvilinearity, lends considerable weight to the confidence which we may place in this finding." 2 tables, 13 notes.   A. R. Stoesen

1838. Cragan, John F. FOREIGN POLICY COMMUNICATION DRAMAS: HOW MEDIATED RHETORIC PLAYED IN PEORIA IN CAMPAIGN '76. *Q. J. of Speech 1977 63(3): 274-289.* Using a sample of Peorians, attempts to provide empirical confirmation that people frame reality and cognitively assimilate events in dramatistic form; study is based on three foreign policy dramas or issues (Cold War, Neo-Isolationism, and Power Politics) that appeared in the media between 1946 and 1972.

1839. Cronin, Thomas E. THE DIRECT VOTE AND THE ELECTORAL COLLEGE: THE CASE FOR MESHING THINGS UP! *Presidential Studies Q. 1979 9(2): 144-163.* Discusses the pros and cons of direct popular election of the president, and presents a plan that would combine the main features of both the direct vote and the electoral college, 1960's-70's.

1840. Crotts, Gail. "A SPECTACULAR COUP": TELEVISION AND THE 1948 CONVENTIONS. *Journalism Hist. 1974 1(3): 90-93.* Studies television's coverage of the national political conventions in 1948, and the effect on subsequent televised conventions.

1841. Cyr, A. Bruce. THE CALCULUS OF VOTING RECONSIDERED. *Public Opinion Q. 1975 39(1): 19-38.* "A rational economic hypothesis of the citizen's decision to vote or not vote in US presidential elections has been cited as an example of the replacement of social-psychologically oriented 'empirical generalizations' by axiomatically based deductive propositions in political science. However, close scrutiny shows that the rational (or political) economic paradigm is no more accurate a theory than previously popular systems analysis or functional paradigms. The claimed verification of the original hypothesis was based on an apparently imprecise, ad hoc, ordinal procedure that could not distinguish between the intimately related rational economic and social-psychological hypotheses. A more powerful technique resolves the issue in favor of the latter model for the data used by the original authors."   J

1842. Davis, Leslie K. CAMERA EYE-CONTACT BY THE CANDIDATES IN THE PRESIDENTIAL DEBATES OF 1976. *Journalism Q. 1978 55(3): 431-437.* During the 1976 presidential debates, Jimmy Carter appeared to appeal directly to the public by looking directly at the camera as he spoke, while President Gerald R. Ford conveyed a sense of expertise by speaking directly to the panel of questioners instead. Opinion polls showed Ford winning the first debate, when both candidates looked mainly away from the cameras, but losing the second debate, when the candidates primarily faced the cameras during their speeches. The third debate had no clear result. Based on the polls and on a timing of the speeches; 2 tables, 3 graphs, 11 notes.   R. P. Sindermann, Jr.

1843. DeBats, Donald A. THE EFFECTS OF REFORM ON PARTY: SOME NOTES FROM THE AMERICAN EXPERIENCE. *Pol. Sci. [New Zealand] 1981 33(1): 91-97.* Reviews the following revisionist volumes on the effects of democratic reform on political parties in the United States: Austin Ranney's *The Federalization of Presidential*

Primaries (1978), Jeane J. Kirkpatrick's *Dismantling the Parties: Reflections on Party Reform and Party Decomposition* (1978), Austin Ranney's *The Past and Future of Presidential Debates* (1979), and Martin Diamond's *The Electoral College and the American Idea of Democracy* (1977).

1844. Declercq, Eugene; Hurley, Thomas L.; and Luttbeg, Norman R. VOTING IN AMERICAN PRESIDENTIAL ELECTIONS, 1956-1972. *Am. Pol. Q. 1975 3(3): 222-246.* Evaluates the respective roles of political issues, candidate image, and party image in voting patterns in presidential elections from 1956-72, including methodological questions in sociological theory.

1845. DelaIsla, José. THE POLITICS OF REELECTION: SE HABLA ESPAÑOL. *Aztlán 1976 7(3): 427-451.* Traces the growing power of Hispanic Americans in elections and the appeal of Richard M. Nixon's administration for their support; the policy of revenue sharing meant that federal funds would no longer flow directly to Hispanic groups, so to reduce opposition the administration channeled grants to key Spanish-speaking groups and Republican sympathizers in time to influence the election of 1972.

1846. DeMaio, Gerald and Muzzio, Douglas. THE 1980 ELECTION AND APPROVAL VOTING. *Presidential Studies Q. 1981 11(3): 364-373.* The current method of voting often performs inadequately. This is especially true in a multicandidate election, where the plurality winner often falls short of a majority vote. The 1980 presidential primary and general elections illustrate this perfectly. Plurality voting became "least of evils" voting. An alternate system, the Condorcet criterion, is too unwieldy to be practical. Instead, America should adopt approval voting, where voters could vote for as many of the candidates as they approved of. If this system had been used in the 1980 election, Reagan would have still emerged as a clear winner, but strong support for John Anderson would also have been apparent. Based on ABC News exit poll; 3 tables, 36 notes. D. H. Cline

1847. Denhardt, Robert B. and Jakes, Jay E. THE IMPACT OF DEMOCRATIC PARTY REFORM ON THE SOUTH. *J. of Pol. Sci. 1976 4(1): 36-51.* Guidelines for delegate selection for the 1972 Democratic Party convention adopted the McGovern-Fraser reforms which were committed to nondiscrimination. Adherence to the guidelines was mandatory for seating at the convention. Louisiana's resistance to guidelines became an issue. Southern states complied; the representation was achieved by normative, utilitarian compliance, and by the dynamics of political bargaining and negotiations. Based on participant-observer method by authors working in the McGovern campaign, and on questionnaires; 5 tables, 24 notes. T. P. Richardson

1848. Diamond, Martin. THE ELECTORAL COLLEGE AND THE IDEA OF FEDERAL DEMOCRACY. *Publius 1978 8(1): 63-77.* Presents the author's testimony (given on the last morning of his life, 22 July 1977) before the Constitutional Subcommittee of the Senate Judiciary Committee, on a proposed constitutional amendment providing for direct election of the President. Diamond presents an opening statement and then is questioned by the amendment's sponsor, Senator Birch Bayh. The rhetoric of many academic opponents of the electoral college, Diamond asserts, reveals an aversion to it based on an absurd extent in its mere antiquity. The other major objection to it, that the possibility of the college electing a candidate who fails to receive a popular plurality represents "a loaded pistol to our heads" (the phrase is Estes Kefauver's), is equally absurd—the pistol having gone off, without discernible damage, in 1888. Diamond warns also that the proposed amendment will encourage splinter parties. L. W. Van Wyk

1849. Dobriansky, Lev E. THE UNFORGETTABLE FORD GAFFE. *Ukrainian Q. 1977 33(4): 366-377.* Examines the effect on President Gerald R. Ford's election campaign of his statement on Soviet domination of Eastern Europe during the second campaign debate. Presents evidence to show that this was the deciding mistake in Ford's loss of the presidential election, particularly when viewed with other statements and actions emanating from the Kissinger policy of detente. The Carter administration also has demonstrated a lack of true understanding for the position of Eastern Europe and the other captive nations. 27 notes. K. N. T. Crowther

1850. Doeker, Günther. WAHLSTRATEGIE UND DIE TRANSFORMATION DER DEMOKRATIE IN DEN VEREINIGTEN STAATEN UNTER NIXON [Election strategy and the transformation of democracy in the United States under Nixon]. *Gegenwartskunde [West Germany] 1973 22(3): 303-314.* The election of Richard M. Nixon over McGovern in 1972 was an important step from a liberal democratic to an authoritarian society. Describes certain aspects of Nixon's election strategy—the "managed" election, his isolation from voters—and concludes that the election was a triumph of bureaucracy over democracy. Analyzes the implications of the Watergate scandal for political morality. 3 notes. J. B. Street

1851. Donahue, Bernard F. THE POLITICAL USE OF RELIGIOUS SYMBOLS: A CASE STUDY OF THE 1972 PRESIDENTIAL CAMPAIGN. *R. of Pol. 1975 37(1): 48-65.* The electorate expects a presidential candidate to provide a moral as well as a political program. The use of religious terminology in political rhetoric, although not decisive, can have an impact upon voters. In 1972, Richard M. Nixon relied upon the "symbols of American civil religion," while George S. McGovern relied "heavily upon the Judaeo-Christian, biblical religion." Nixon's speeches, reflecting a combination of the work and Puritan ethic, more successfully appealed to the new majority. Secondary sources; 43 notes. L. E. Ziewacz

1852. Edwards, George C., III. THE IMPACT OF PRESIDENTIAL COATTAILS ON OUTCOMES OF CONGRESSIONAL ELECTIONS. *Am. Pol. Q. 1979 7(1): 94-108.* Presidential coattails are frequently addressed in American politics, but we know little about their impact on the outcomes in elections for the House. Yet it is here that they are most significant. If presidential coattails do affect congressional elections, they can be the cause of increased support for the president (from new representatives of his party) and increased support for policy change (from representatives of a new generation). This research examines the relationship between how well a president runs in a congressional district and the success of the congressional candidate of his party in winning the district. The analysis is done for each of the six presidential elections from 1952 through 1972, and is done separately for the North and South as well as for the country as a whole. In every instance, constituency party strength is controlled in order to isolate the impact of the presidential candidate on the congressional outcome. The basic conclusions are that presidential coattails have had a declining impact on the outcomes in congressional elections since 1952 and that in recent elections their impact has declined to the vanishing point. That, it is argued, is primarily due to the increasing lack of competitiveness of congressional districts. J

1853. Edwards, George C., III. PRESIDENTIAL ELECTORAL PERFORMANCE AS A SOURCE OF PRESIDENTIAL POWER. *Am. J. of Pol. Sci. 1978 22(1): 152-168.* One of the most fertile areas of research in American politics has been that focusing on the vote in presidential elections. Most studies in this area, however, take the presidential vote as the dependent variable. This research carries the analysis further and examines the influence of the presidential vote in a congressional constituency on the support of that constituency's congressman for the President's policies. Using the techniques of causal modeling and path analysis, this article tests for both the direct influence of the presidential vote on presidential support and for its indirect influence through its effect on the party which wins the seat in a congressional district while controlling for the effects of constituency party strength. The basic finding is that presidential electoral performance does influence presidential support, particularly in Democratic presidential years. J

1854. Einsiedel, Edna F. and Bibbee, M. Jane. THE NEWS MAGAZINES AND MINORITY CANDIDATES: CAMPAIGN '76. *Journalism Q. 1979 56(1): 102-105.* Assesses the coverage by *Time, Newsweek,* and *U.S. News and World Report* of Eugene J. McCarthy's third-party presidential candidacy in 1976. The three news magazines divided their campaign coverage evenly between the Democratic and Republican candidates, but devoted relatively little space to articles about McCarthy and other minor candidates. In this coverage of third-party candidates, the magazines showed little bias. Based on magazine articles from September to November 1976 and on secondary sources; 17 notes. R. P. Sindermann, Jr

1855.　Einsiedel, Edna F.　TELEVISION NETWORK NEWS COVERAGE OF THE EAGLETON AFFAIR: A CASE STUDY. *Journalism Q. 1975 52(1): 56-60.* Media performance during the controversy which resulted in the resignation of Senator Thomas Eagleton as Democratic vice-presidential candidate has been criticized. Television network news, however, was not disproportionately negative toward Eagleton. Commentary by the National Broadcasting Company (NCB) was unfavorable, the American Broadcasting Company (ABC) was favorable, and the Columbia Broadcasting System (CBS) was nearly neutral. The Eagleton story was the most important political news story of the time. Based on transcripts of television newscasts; 2 tables, 9 notes.
　　　　　　　　　　　　　　　　　　　　　　K. J. Puffer

1856.　Eisenstein, Zillah.　ANTIFEMINISM IN THE POLITICS AND ELECTION OF 1980. *Feminist Studies 1981 7(2): 187-205.* A feminist analysis of the political significance of Ronald Reagan's 1980 election victory over President Jimmy Carter. Rather than being a landslide for militaristic and antifeminist policies, Reagan's victory "reflects a small, highly mobilized and organized section of the electorate alongside a much larger, disorganized, disenfranchised public which did not vote." Although the party platforms differed significantly on the women's issue, there was "no appreciable difference in the candidates once Carter's record was compared with Reagan's platform." Based on election polls and other sources; 23 notes.　　　　M. E. Quinlivan

1857.　Elzy, Martin I.　ILLINOIS VIEWED FROM THE JOHNSON WHITE HOUSE. *J. of the Illinois State Hist. Soc. 1981 74(1): 2-16.* Illinois, with a large population, significant industrial and agricultural development, and political power, affected both the political career and the presidency of Lyndon B. Johnson. Johnson was defeated for a position on the national ticket at Democratic National Conventions in Chicago in both 1952 and 1956. In 1960, the state's support for John F. Kennedy both frustrated Johnson's presidential candidacy and assured the victory of the Democratic ticket over Richard M. Nixon and Henry Cabot Lodge. During the Johnson presidency, Chicago issues, including race relations, federal aid to cities, and urban riots, dominated domestic policies. While Chicago's Mayor Richard J. Daley attracted the 1968 Democratic convention to his city, the withdrawal from the campaign and absence from the convention of Johnson, in addition to violent confrontations, cast a pall on the closing days of the Johnson administration. 9 illus, 42 notes.
　　　　　　　　　　　　　　　　　　　　　　A. W. Novitsky

1858.　Epstein, Laurily K. and Strom, Gerald.　ELECTION NIGHT PROJECTIONS AND WEST COAST TURNOUT. *Am. Pol. Q. 1981 9(4): 479-491.* News media early projections for the presidential contest are greeted with cries of outrage from losers of lower offices as well as from academics and other interested observers of the political process. Analysis shows, however, that attributing a decline in West Coast turnout to information conveyed by the media ignores the inescapable fact that the decision to vote—on the West Coast or anywhere else—is the result of a complicated combination of factors, none of which is related to information received on election day. Covers 1960-80.　　　　J/S

1859.　Epstein, Leon D.　POLITICAL SCIENCE AND PRESIDENTIAL NOMINATIONS. *Pol. Sci. Q. 1978 93(2): 177-195.* Appraises political scientists' generalizations about presidential nominations before the 1976 nominations and questions the value of these generalizations for future nominations.

1860.　Epstein, Leon D.　WHO VOTED FOR MC GOVERN: THE WISCONSIN CASE. *Am. Pol. Q. 1973 1(4): 465-478.* Discusses voting patterns and support within the Democratic Party for candidate George McGovern in the 1972 presidential election in Wisconsin.

1861.　Erickson, Keith V.　JIMMY CARTER: THE RHETORIC OF PRIVATE AND CIVIC PIETY. *Western J. of Speech Communication 1980 44(3): 221-235.* Presidential candidate Jimmy Carter's professed spiritual beliefs made him trustworthy, served to identify him with evangelicals, generated media attention, and reaffirmed American civic piety and faith for voters; 1976.

1862.　Erickson, Keith V. and Schmidt, Wallace V.　PRESIDENTIAL POLITICAL SILENCE: RHETORIC AND THE ROSE GARDEN STRATEGY. *Southern Speech Communication J. 1982 47(4): 402-421.*

Examines the rose garden strategy, or the curtailing of political campaigning by presidential incumbents in election years; analyzes benefits, liabilities, ethics, and rhetorical and political demands of this strategy in presidential election campaigns.

1863.　Erikson, Robert S.　THE INFLUENCE OF NEWSPAPER ENDORSEMENTS IN PRESIDENTIAL ELECTIONS: THE CASE OF 1964. *Am. J. of Pol. Sci. 1976 20(2): 207-233.* This paper estimates the influence of newspaper endorsements on voting behavior in presidential elections. The analysis focuses on the impact of newspaper endorsements in the 1964 presidential election—the one recent presidential election in which a considerable number of newspapers endorsed the Democratic candidate. Multiple regression analysis of the 1964 vote in 223 northern counties suggests that a Democratic endorsement from the local newspaper added about five percentage points to the 1960-1964 Democratic gain. The same estimate is obtained from an application of two-stage least squares. From this result, along with evidence from other election years, it is argued that newspaper endorsements exert an important influence on the outcomes of presidential elections.　　J

1864.　Evarts, Dru and Stempel, Guido H., III.　COVERAGE OF THE 1972 CAMPAIGN BY TV, NEWS MAGAZINES AND MAJOR NEWSPAPERS. *Journalism Q. 1974 51(4): 645-648, 676.*

1865.　Fairbanks, James David.　REAGAN, RELIGION, AND THE NEW RIGHT. *Midwest Q. 1982 23(3): 327-345.* Studies the influence of the fundamentalist New Right on President Ronald Reagan and on the 1980 election. It is not evident that Reagan encompassed the New Right in his campaigning. Rather, he used religious symbols that had appeal to a large segment of the American population. Politics and religion are very much intertwined in US history. Mainly secondary sources; 14 notes, biblio.　　　　　　　　　　　　　　A. C. Dempsey

1866.　Fairlie, Henry.　LETTER FROM WASHINGTON. *Encounter [Great Britain] 1973 40(1): 11-18.* Discusses the campaign of George S. McGovern in the presidential election of 1972, demonstrating that McGovern failed to capture the Democratic Party because "he was paying almost no attention to the variety and generosity of its impulses over the years which have caused it to do so many great things." Refers in particular to basic attitudes toward foreign policy since 1948 and their role in this election.　　　　　　　　　D. H. Murdoch

1867.　Fant, Charles H.　TELEVISING PRESIDENTIAL CONVENTIONS, 1952-1980. *J. of Communication 1980 30(4): 130-139.* Together, political parties and television networks have adapted procedures and schedules to the tastes of the excitement-hungry audience since 1952, when party conventions first appeared on television.

1868.　Farrell, Thomas B.　POLITICAL CONVENTIONS AS LEGITIMATION RITUAL. *Communication Monographs 1978 45(4): 293-305.* Discusses special problems of major parties in the 1976 election year, and each party's attempts to legitimize itself and its leader through its national convention ritual.

1869.　Felson, Marcus and Sudman, Seymour.　THE ACCURACY OF PRESIDENTIAL-PREFERENCE PRIMARY POLLS. *Public Opinion Q. 1975 39(2): 232-236.* Discusses the accuracy of presidential preference polls taken during primary elections in 1968 and 1972.　　S

1870.　Feltner, Paula and Goldie, Leneen.　IMPACT OF SOCIALIZATION AND PERSONALITY ON THE FEMALE VOTER: SPECULATIONS TESTED WITH 1964 PRESIDENTIAL DATA. *Western Pol. Q. 1974 27(4): 680-692.* Explains origins of distinctly female political attitudes.　　　　　　　　　　　　　　　　S

1871.　Ferling, John E.　HISTORY AS JOURNALISM: AN ASSESSMENT OF THEODORE WHITE. *Journalism Q. 1977 54(2): 320-326.* Reviews Theodore White's *Making of the President* books from the 1960 campaign on, including *Breach of Faith* (New York, 1975), and concludes that their author is a liberal Cold War centrist, and that the books —although they have endured surprisingly well for instant histories—are inconsistent and chaotic in applying the writer's philosophy to the events in his narratives.

1872. Ferree, Myra Marx. A WOMAN FOR PRESIDENT? CHANGING RESPONSES: 1958-1972. *Public Opinion Q. 1974 38(3): 390-399.* An analysis of five political surveys conducted by the American Institute of Public Opinion (the Gallup Poll) from 1958-69 and by the National Opinion Research Center, in its "General Social Survey" in 1972, on the willingness to vote for "a well-qualified woman of your party" for president of the United States. "The sudden change in attitudes toward women seems first, to have come from both men and women, but from women much more dramatically than men. . . . Second, it comes from younger and better educated women. . . . Third, the change comes from those who are already tolerant of other minorities. . . . In summary, we can say that despite the fact that 'voting' for a woman was harder in 1972 than voting for a black . . . it was surely much easier in absolute terms than it had been earlier, and much more predictable and systematic. In general, this seems to have been due to women themselves." 7 tables, 4 notes. D. D. Cameron

1873. Fiorina, Morris P. ECONOMIC RETROSPECTIVE VOTING IN AMERICAN NATIONAL ELECTIONS: A MICRO-ANALYSIS. *Am. J. of Pol. Sci. 1978 22(2): 426-443.* A number of recent studies examine the traditional hypothesis that the electoral fortunes of the incumbent president's party rise and fall in direct relation to fluctuations in the state of the national economy. Typically these studies employ a longitudinal design in which a party's aggregate congressional vote serves as the dependent variable, and various economic indicators serve as independent variables. On balance, the election returns appear to bear some relation to economic conditions, although various disagreements exist. Using data from the 1956 to 1974 SRC election studies this paper attempts to uncover an individual-level basis for the macro-relationship found by earlier studies. Specifically, do citizens vote for or against the incumbent president's party as a function of their personal economic condition? The survey data permit us to conclude that a citizen's personal economic condition affects his presidential vote. For congressional voting, however, the findings are positive until 1960 and negative thereafter. And contrary to some previous research, we find no systematic relationship between a citizen's personal economic condition and his decision to vote or abstain. J

1874. Freshley, Dwight L. MANIPULATING PUBLIC EXPECTATIONS: PRE- AND POSTPRIMARY STATEMENTS IN THE '76 CAMPAIGN. *Southern Speech Communication J. 1980 45(3): 223-239.* Analyzes candidates' modest preelection vote-getting predictions in the 1976 US presidential primaries and their rhetorical choices after elections, depending on the degree of success.

1875. Friedmann, F. G. RENAISSANCE DES POPULISMUS IN DEN USA: GEISTIG-RELIGIÖSE HINTERGRÜNDE DER PRÄSIDENTSCHAFTSWAHLEN [Renaissance of Populism in the USA: Spiritual-religious background of the presidential election]. *Stimmen der Zeit [West Germany] 1976 194(11): 757-765.* Discusses Jimmy Carter's belief in the spiritual foundations of politics, his interest in the ideas of Reinhold Niebuhr, American religious tradition since the Puritans, and the American Populist tradition. Carter emerges also from the folk culture of the South. His faith is a tribute to the spiritual vitality of the United States. R. Stromberg

1876. Frohlich, Norman; Oppenheimer, Joe A.; Smith, Jeffrey; and Young, Oran R. A TEST OF DOWNSIAN VOTER RATIONALITY: 1964 PRESIDENTIAL VOTING. *Am. Pol. Sci. Rev. 1978 72(1): 178-197.* Systematic testing of Downsian voter rationality is accomplished using a computer simulation technique on the 1964 SRC voting survey. The simulation tests both the hypotheses predicting whether an individual will vote and for whom an individual will vote. To evaluate the results of the tests we develop a statistic analogous to Pearson's r. This statistic measures the percentage improvement over a random guess technique. Utilizing this statistic, Downs explains 68.5 percent of the unexplained variance in the voters' choices of party. Three alternative interpretations of the turnout decision are then considered, each premised on a different notion of how the costs of voting are distributed among the voters. Here we use an Engel Curve technique to develop the turnout decision and explain 92 percent of the variance. The importance of the various elements of the Downsian theory are evaluated and, in contrast to some recent conjectures, the probability of making a difference on the outcome of the election is shown to have an effect on the turnout decision. Finally,

to determine the viability of the results, the SRC "6 factor" model is developed in an analogous fashion and used to predict both turnout and direction of vote. J

1877. Fuchs, Lawrence H. THE SENATOR AND THE LADY. *Am. Heritage 1974 25(6): 57-61, 81-83.* Recalls Eleanor Roosevelt's opposition to the presidential nomination of John F. Kennedy and their eventual reconciliation. S

1878. Gerston, Larry N.; Burstein, Jerome S.; and Cohen, Stephan J. PRESIDENTIAL NOMINATIONS AND COALITION THEORY. *Am. Pol. Q. 1979 7(2): 175-197.* Contemporary literature postulates that the success of candidate nomination efforts is closely tied to the "rules of the game." Contrary to this view, the authors contend that important variables intercede between the rules and candidate nomination. These variables fall under the umbrellas of coalition theory. As applied in the article, coalition theory suggests that a presidential nomination is achieved if several qualifying criteria are addressed and met. The successful candidate must have the support of his home state delegation, a strong regional base, and continuous momemtum. With respect to the 1976 nominating events, the authors conclude that coalition theory helps to explain success or failure in securing the presidential nomination. Moreover, the analysis indicates that both nominees would have triumphed under two alternate sets of nomination rules by following the strategy suggested by coalition theory. These findings have important implications for future contests. J

1879. Ginsberg, Benjamin and Weissberg, Robert. ELECTIONS AND THE MOBILIZATION OF POPULAR SUPPORT. *Am. J. of Pol. Sci. 1978 22(1): 31-55.* While elections are normally seen as means by which citizens influence leaders, elections can also be viewed as mechanisms which serve to increase elite control over citizens. The opportunity for citizens to participate in leadership selection may also be an opportunity for leaders to coopt citizens by implicating them in the government's creation. This possibility is tested with data from the 1968 and 1972 American presidential elections by comparing citizens' pre- and post-election attitudes toward the regime, leaders, and policy. The elections' largest impact appeared to occur in attitudes toward the regime. Changes in citizen response are discussed in terms of three mechanisms of attitude change, each of which has different implications for leaders and the regime. J

1880. Gold, Ellen Reid. POLITICAL APOLOGIA: THE RITUAL OF SELF-DEFENSE. *Communication Monographs 1978 45(4): 306-316.* Discusses the emphasis on character defense in the 1976 presidential campaign; trust was a major issue and the media, reacting to their own laxity during the Nixon era, probed more aggressively.

1881. Goldstein, Joel H. CANDIDATE POPULARITY AND CAMPAIGN CONTRIBUTIONS IN THE PRE-NOMINATION STATE OF THE PRESIDENTIAL SELECTION PROCESS: THE CASE OF THE 1976 ELECTION. *Presidential Studies Q. 1979 9(3): 329-333.* Compares the amount of campaign contributions received by presidential contenders with their success in the early caucuses and primaries, using the 1976 presidential election as an example.

1882. Goldstein, Joel H. THE INFLUENCE OF MONEY ON THE PRE-NOMINATION STAGE OF THE PRESIDENTIAL SELECTION PROCESS: THE CASE OF THE 1976 ELECTION. *Presidential Studies Q. 1978 8(2): 164-179.* Explores the relationship between campaign expenditures and electoral success using the 1976 prenomination campaigns for the Republican and Democratic presidential candidacies. For the first time, federal matching funds from the Presidential Election Campaign Fund were available to qualified candidates in the prenomination period. Compares primary votes won or raw votes received in caucus with reported campaign spending by each candidate in each state. Evaluates significant unreported resources such as volunteer workers, candidate's time, independent group spending, media coverage, staff talent, and campaign timing. Heavy spending does not necessarily lead to electoral success or bring proportionate returns, but it is more effective in early primaries when candidates' images are still fluid. 5 tables, 29 notes. S. C. Strom

1883. Goodin, Robert E. CONVENTION QUOTAS AND COMMUNAL REPRESENTATION. *British J. of Pol. Sci. [Great Britain] 1977 7(2): 225-261.* The 1972 reforms of the Democratic Party Convention did little to change the party opinion voiced by delegates stressing the benefits of more democratic representation.

1884. Gopoian, J. David. ISSUE PREFERENCES AND CANDIDATE CHOICE IN PRESIDENTIAL PRIMARIES. *Am. J. of Pol. Sci. 1982 26(3): 523-546.* Employs CBS News and *New York Times* primary election exit surveys for 20 1976 presidential primaries to assess the impact of issue preferences upon candidate choice in presidential primaries. Findings indicate that issue-voting was slightly stronger in the 1976 Republican primaries than in the 1976 Democratic primaries, but that issues generally do not predict the outcomes of the 1976 primaries very well. Some consequences of issue-voting (or the absence thereof) for governing are suggested. J

1885. Graber, Doris A. EFFECT OF INCUMBENCY ON COVERAGE PATTERNS IN THE 1972 PRESIDENTIAL CAMPAIGN. *Journalism Q. 1976 53(3): 499-508.* Replicates a 1968 study showing the high degree of uniformity in campaign coverage among large-circulation newspapers. The same uniformity was in evidence in 1972 but the emphasis changed because of an incumbent team running. Coverage of professional qualities moved ahead of personalities, and foreign policy issues lost the limelight. Uniformity in coverage patterns can be expected in future presidential campaigns. Content analysis of 20 newspapers; 4 tables, 16 notes. E. Gibson

1886. Graber, Doris A. PRESS AND TV AS OPINION RESOURCES IN PRESIDENTIAL CAMPAIGNS. *Public Opinion Q. 1976 40(3): 285-303.* A comparison of campaign news in two successive presidential elections [1968, 1972] reveals major deficiencies in information supply. Newspaper audiences, even more than television viewers, receive confusing, heavily negative information which makes candidate appraisal difficult. Incumbency of one candidate does not lead to substantially greater emphasis on public policy issues and professional qualifications. A pattern of heavy stress on personal characteristics and daily campaign events prevails in all sources. Data come from content analysis of nearly 10,000 campaign stories from network television news and 20 U.S. daily newspapers. J

1887. Graber, Doris A. PRESS COVERAGE AND VOTER REACTION IN THE 1968 PRESIDENTIAL ELECTION. *Pol. Sci. Q. 1974 89(1): 68-100.* "Examines the information about presidential candidates that was available through the press in the 1968 election. She goes on to appraise how useful this information was to the general public in making a prudent presidential selection." J

1888. Graebner, Norman A. PRESIDENTIAL POLITICS IN A DIVIDED AMERICA: 1972. *Australian J. of Pol. and Hist. 1973 19(1): 28-47.* Analysis of the 1972 presidential election suggests that George S. McGovern lost to Richard M. Nixon because the electorate looked to stability and not radical reform. McGovern was nominated at the Democratic Convention because constitutional changes in the party gave exponents of the "New Politics" a larger voice in the Convention than their grass roots support warranted. America's discontents were those of upper middle class intellectuals who were vocal in the media—at most 10% of the population. Workingmen went over to the Republicans, who "offered a defence against unwanted changes and the assurance of social stability." W. D. McIntyre

1889. Granberg, Donald and Seidel, John. SOCIAL JUDGMENTS OF THE URBAN AND VIETNAM ISSUES IN 1968 AND 1972. *Social Forces 1976 55(1): 1-15.* The authors examine data from 1968 and 1972 for possible systematic displacement effects in judgments made of candidates' positions on the issues of urban unrest and Vietnam. There was a pervasive tendency to overestimate the similarity of one's own views and those of the preferred candidate. This occurred to a greater extent for Nixon voters in 1968 and 1972 and Humphrey voters in 1968 than for McGovern voters in 1972 and Wallace voters in 1968. The tendency to overestimate the difference between one's views and those of nonpreferred candidates was much less reliable. From detailed analyses using own position, vote, race, importance, party, and others as control variables, six propositions emerge. Findings are related to balance theory and the Pollyanna hypothesis, and implications are briefly discussed. J

1890. Grant, Philip A., Jr. EDITORIAL REACTION TO THE 1952 PRESIDENTIAL CANDIDACY OF RICHARD B. RUSSELL. *Georgia Hist. Q. 1973 57(2): 167-178.* Senator Richard B. Russell (d. 1971) announced his candidacy for the Democratic presidential nomination on 28 February 1952. Although President Harry S. Truman had not indicated whether he would seek reelection, Russell's move was a southern conservative protest to many of the president's key domestic legislative proposals. Russell was overwhelmingly praised by the press but virtually none predicted success for him. 58 notes. D. L. Smith

1891. Grant, Philip A., Jr. THE 1948 PRESIDENTIAL ELECTION IN VIRGINIA: AUGURY OF THE TREND TOWARDS REPUBLICANISM. *Presidential Studies Q. 1978 8(3): 319-328.* In 1948, the Democrats in Virginia were divided over the presidential nomination of Harry S. Truman whose unpopular civil rights platform prompted the formation of the States Rights Democrats supporting South Carolina Governor J. Strom Thurmond for President. With the split in the Democratic Party, Republican candidate Thomas E. Dewey threatened to carry Virginia. Provides a county-by-county analysis of the vote and attributes Truman's 28,716 plurality to Thurman's weak 10.4% showing and Dewey's failure to campaign in the state. Truman's unimpressive victory is seen as a precursor of future Republican presidential wins in Virginia. Table, 47 notes. S. C. Strom

1892. Grant, Philip A., Jr. THE 1952 MINNESOTA REPUBLICAN PRIMARY AND THE EISENHOWER CANDIDACY. *Presidential Studies Q. 1979 9(3): 311-315.* In a "political miracle," Dwight D. Eisenhower, a write-in candidate, received enough votes to place second behind Harold E. Stassen.

1893. Grant, Philip A., Jr. THE 1952 REPUBLICAN PRESIDENTIAL PRIMARY. *South Dakota Hist. 1977 8(1): 46-58.* The last Republican Party primary before the national convention was held in South Dakota. The state was generally expected to favor Senator Robert A. Taft, the more conservative and isolationistic candidate. Dwight Eisenhower was still in Europe and had not yet openly campaigned. The results gave Taft 50.3% of the votes, barely a slim margin of victory. Assesses the meaning of the vote, based on a wide range of national newspapers, a majority of which felt that Taft's prospects had been somewhat diminished. A minority of them felt neither candidate had benefited. In any case, no major newspaper predicted a winner for the Republican presidential primary. Based on secondary sources; 5 photos, 35 notes. A. J. Larson

1894. Grasmick, Harold G. RURAL CULTURE AND THE WALLACE MOVEMENT IN THE SOUTH. *Rural Sociol. 1974 39(4): 454-470.* Analysis of the 1968 presidential election results in North Carolina. S

1895. Gronbeck, Bruce E. THE FUNCTIONS OF PRESIDENTIAL CAMPAIGNING. *Communication Monographs 1978 45(4): 268-280.* Discusses the practical and social functions of Presidential elections and campaigning, describing political objects and acts which are important symbolically, 1960's-70's.

1896. Gudelunas, William and Couch, Stephen R. WOULD A PROTESTANT OR POLISH KENNEDY HAVE WON? A LOCAL TEST OF ETHNICITY AND RELIGION IN THE PRESIDENTIAL ELECTION OF 1960. *Ethnic Groups 1980 3(1): 1-21.* In the 1960 presidential election in Schuylkill County, Pennsylvania, usually a Republican stronghold, voting polarized along religious lines. Protestants voted Republican in stronger numbers than usual, while Irish Catholics increased their usually heavy Democratic vote. But the East European Catholics, who generally split their vote between the two parties, voted strongly Democratic, giving Kennedy a slim victory in the county. J/S

1897. Hagner, Paul and Mullen, William F. WASHINGTON: MORE REPUBLICAN, YES; MORE CONSERVATIVE, NO. *Social Sci. J. 1981 18(3): 115-129.* The 1980 general election led to the defeat of Democratic incumbent Senator Warren Magnusen and the election of Republican politicians to many state offices as Ronald Reagan received the state's electoral votes.

1898. Haines, Richard L. MONTANA: A MODEST COUNTER-REVOLUTION. *Social Sci. J. 1981 18(3): 51-63.* The 1980 general election victory of Ronald Reagan led to a Republican sweep in the Montana state legislature.

1899. Hajda, Joseph. CHOOSING THE 1960 DEMOCRATIC PRESIDENTIAL CANDIDATE: THE CASE OF THE UNBOSSED DELEGATION. *Kansas Q. 1976 8(2): 71-87.* A Kansas delegate's perspective on the 1960 Democratic National Convention in Los Angeles, and the contest over delegate selection in the race among John F. Kennedy, Stuart Symington, Lyndon B. Johnson, and Adlai E. Stevenson, with a distribution of Kansas votes.

1900. Hammond, Thomas H. ANOTHER LOOK AT THE ROLE OF "THE RULES" IN THE 1972 DEMOCRATIC PRESIDENTIAL PRIMARIES. *Western Pol. Q. 1980 33(1): 50-72.* Lengle and Shafer argue in "Primary Rules, Political Power and Social Change" [see abstract 15A:5036] that the rules of the 1972 Democratic presidential primaries had a major effect on who the nominee was. Had the rules in force been Winner-Take-All, they suggest, Hubert Humphrey might have been the nominee. They also project their 1972-based conclusions into the future and suggest that different rules apportion power among the states in different ways, and with different consequences for the party. Unfortunately, their arguments are unsupported by their own evidence. Biases in their data lead to misleading conclusions. When the biases are corrected, we find that candidates like Humphrey were aided by Proportional rules. Lengle and Shafer also neglect two other variables crucial to understanding presidential primaries: the sequence of primaries and the extent of "ideological crowding" among the candidates. Correction of these and other errors leads to very different predictions about the effects of the rules on the party's future. 5 tables, 4 fig., 33 notes. J

1901. Haney, Richard C. WALLACE IN WISCONSIN: THE PRESIDENTIAL PRIMARY OF 1964. *Wisconsin Mag. of Hist. 1978 61(4): 258-278.* Discusses Alabama Governor George C. Wallace's Democratic presidential primary battle with Wisconsin Governor John Reynolds. Although he lost, Wallace won 34% of the Democratic vote and 25% of the entire presidential primary vote. Three factors contributed to his unexpectedly strong showing: 1) the civil rights issue, 2) Republican crossover votes, and 3) lack of local level party support for Reynolds. 11 illus., 43 notes. N. C. Burckel

1902. Hartman, John J. CARTER AND THE UTOPIAN GROUP-FANTASY. *J. of Psychohistory 1977 5(2): 239-258.* Group-dynamic research indicates that under certain conditions of perceived threat and disintegration, the group becomes utopian, seeking a "messiah" that will bring revitalization. The group-fantasy includes birth trauma imagery. This explains the unity of the 1976 Democratic Party convention, the nomination of Jimmy Carter for President, and the messianic imagery built around him. Primary and secondary sources; 35 notes, 4 illus. R. E. Butchart

1903. Hauser, Stephen K. FRANK ZEIDLER, MILWAUKEE'S PRESIDENTIAL CANDIDATE. *Milwaukee Hist. 1980 3(2): 47-58.* Frank P. Zeidler (b. 1912) joined the Socialist Party during the 1930's in Wisconsin, was elected mayor of Milwaukee in 1948 for a 12-year term, and was nominated by the Socialist Party for the presidency in 1975.

1904. Havick, John J. AMATEURS AND PROFESSIONALS AT THE 1972 DEMOCRATIC CONVENTION. *Polity 1978 10(3): 448-457.* Focuses on party loyalty of delegates supporting winning and losing candidates at the 1972 Democratic Party convention. There was a significant relationship between delegates and changes in their intention to campaign for the ticket. Those supporting losers reduced their commitment, while those favoring winners kept it constant or increased it. Delegates without positions in the party supporting losers lowered commitment more than those holding party positions. Party regulars supported the party; delegates without party ties reduced their commitment. J. Tull

1905. Havick, John J. APPROVAL OF A POLITICAL INSTITUTION: A COMPARISON OF WINNERS AND LOSERS. *J. of Pol. Sci. 1978 6(1): 16-25.* Investigates how winning and losing influence presidential nominating delegates. Winners tend to develop a more favor-able perception of the convention, while losers tend to develop a less favorable perception of the convention process. Based on questionnaire information from convention delegates; 3 tables, 23 notes. T. P. Richardson

1906. Havic, John J. and Heffron, Florence. THE IOWA CAUCUSES: CARTER'S EARLY CAMPAIGN FOR THE PRESIDENTIAL NOMINATION. *Midwest Q. 1978 20(1): 32-48.* Examines Jimmy Carter's early campaign strategy for the 1976 presidential election, focusing on his efforts to achieve success in the Iowa Democratic Party caucuses; covers 1975-76.

1907. Heleniak, Roman. LYNDON JOHNSON IN NEW ORLEANS. *Louisiana Hist. 1980 21(3): 263-275.* On the evening of 9 October 1964, Lyndon B. Johnson, campaigning against Barry M. Goldwater, arrived in New Orleans. After a standard political speech at the Jung Hotel, Johnson spoke extemporaneously to the 1,500-member audience in defense of his support (and of his signing on July 2) of the 1964 Civil Rights Act. He spoke feelingly on the need to lay aside the racial animosities that politically crippled the South, of his goal of "equal opportunity for all, special privileges for none," and—with admiration—of Louisiana's Huey "Kingfish" Long. L. Van Wyk

1908. Hellweg, Susan A. and Phillips, Steven L. A VERBAL AND VISUAL ANALYSIS OF THE 1980 HOUSTON REPUBLICAN PRESIDENTIAL PRIMARY DEBATE. *Southern Speech Communication J. 1981 47(1): 23-38.* Provides a verbal and visual content analysis of the 1980 Houston primary debate between Ronald Reagan and George Bush; reviews verbal factors such as message ambiguity and message reasoning strategies and various visual characteristics associated with the debate.

1909. Herzon, Frederick D. INTENSITY OF OPINION AND THE ORGANIZATION OF POLITICAL ATTITUDES. *Western Pol. Q. 1975 28(1): 72-84.* Opinion intensity is an important factor in helping people organize their political attitudes. For the highly educated, intensity provided the impetus for a high degree of attitude organization, often acting as a spur to political activity. For the less well educated, high intensity led to increased cynicism about the political structure and in the 1968 presidential election to a tendency to vote for George C. Wallace. These conclusions were reached through factor analysis of data provided by the 1970 Center for Political Studies American National Election Study. 6 tables, 18 notes. G. B. McKinney

1910. Hess, Stephen. DOES FOREIGN POLICY REALLY MATTER? *Wilson Q. 1980 4(1): 96-111.* Surveys the presidential campaigns from Dwight D. Eisenhower and Adlai Stevenson in 1952 through Jimmy Carter and Ronald Reagan in 1980, suggesting that foreign policy has become important on election day, dependent on the electorate's basic desire for peace.

1911. Hibbs, Douglas A., Jr. PRESIDENT REAGAN'S MANDATE FROM THE 1980 ELECTIONS: A SHIFT TO THE RIGHT? *Am. Pol. Q. 1982 10(4): 387-470.* Presents evidence from statistical data, statistical models, and electoral surveys indicating strongly that the substantial victory of Reagan and the Republicans in 1980 was the predictable consequence of poor economic performance under Carter and the Democrats and did not represent an ideological "shift to the right" by the electorate. Also discusses the implications of this for public support for the Reagan administration's social and economic program. J/S

1912. Himmelfarb, Milton. ARE JEWS BECOMING REPUBLICANS? *Commentary 1981 72(2): 27-31.* Statistics for 1972-80 clearly demonstrate that Jewish political attitudes are shifting to the right; in 1980, for the first time in a national election, the Democratic candidate received less than half of the Jewish vote.

1913. Hinckley, Barbara. THE INITIALLY STRONGEST PLAYER: COALITION GAMES AND PRESIDENTIAL NOMINATIONS. *Am. Behavioral Scientist 1975 18(4): 497-512.* Studies post-World War II presidential nominations and the conditions which tend to help or hinder the initially strongest candidate (1945-74). S

1914.   Hitchcock, James.   PROPHECY AND POLITICS: ABORTION IN THE ELECTION OF 1976.   *Worldview 1977 20(3): 25-26, 35-37.* Discusses the intrusion of politics into religion, as in the 1976 Presidential election, where pressure was put on Catholics to disregard abortion as a key moral issue, in the interests of Democratic Party loyalty.

1915.   Hitlin, Robert A. and Jackson, John S., III.   ON AMATEUR AND PROFESSIONAL POLITICIANS.   *J. of Pol. 1977 39(3): 786-793.* Rule changes governing delegate selection have substantially altered the demographic composition of Democratic Party national conventions since 1968. Women exhibit less political amateurism than do blacks and youth. While professional politicians predominate among delegates selected by state conventions and committees, amateurs were almost exclusively selected on the district level. Amateurs tend to be more ideological and less pragmatic than professionals. Based on a mail survey to delegates to the 1974 Democratic Mid Term Convention, personal interviews, and secondary sources; 3 tables, 13 notes.   A. W. Novitsky

1916.   Hitlin, Robert A.   SUPPORT FOR CHANGES IN THE CONVENTION SYSTEM: 1968.   *Western Pol. Q. 1973 26(4): 686-701.* The 1972 national convention reforms had their roots in the attitudes of delegates to the 1968 conventions, especially among the Democratic Party.

1917.   Hodgson, Godfrey.   AMERICAN PRESIDENTIAL AND PARTY POLITICS: CHANGES IN SPIRIT AND MACHINE.   *World Today [Great Britain] 1976 32(9): 317-327.* Analyzes trends in American politics and the attitude of the voting public on the eve of the 1976 elections.

1918.   Hofstetter, C. Richard; Zukin, Cliff; and Buss, Terry F.   POLITICAL IMAGERY AND INFORMATION IN AN AGE OF TELEVISION.   *Journalism Q. 1978 55(3): 562-569.* Discusses the relative effect of television advertisements and news programs on the public image of candidates during the 1972 presidential campaign. Regardless of the kind of television exposure of a candidate, the degree of political participation and the amount of information gathered from radio and newspapers appeared to be the major influences in a television viewer's rating of the candidates. Newspapers and radio provided more political information than did television advertisements and programs. Based on a 1972 survey by National Analysts, Inc.; 3 tables, 28 notes.   R. P. Sindermann, Jr.

1919.   Hofstetter, C. Richard and Zukin, Cliff.   TV NETWORK POLITICAL NEWS AND ADVERTISING IN THE NIXON AND MC GOVERN CAMPAIGNS.   *Journalism Q. 1979 56(1): 106-115.* Compares the portrayal of political issues in television network news programs and political advertisements during the 1972 presidential campaign. News coverage was devoted more to events with dramatic appeal than it was to specific positions adopted by candidates Richard Nixon and George McGovern. In both the news reports and the advertising the campaign appeared to be a highly personalized contest, but campaign advertising exposed voters to a more detailed discussion of controversial issues than news coverage did. Based on television network news programs and advertisements broadcast from 10 July to November 1972; 24 notes.   R. P. Sindermann, Jr.

1920.   Holm, John D. and Robinson, John P.   IDEOLOGICAL IDENTIFICATION AND THE AMERICAN VOTER.   *Public Opinion Q. 1978 42(2): 235-246.* This article explores the utility of respondent self-evaluation of ideological position on a liberal-conservative scale as a predictor of vote relative to two other types of predictors: party identification and issue positions. The general conclusion is that ideological self-evaluation identifies an effect that is independent of the other two predictors in the electorate as a whole but that the extent of this effect can vary substantially, depending on the context of the campaign and the social grouping being considered. As expected, its effect was more pronounced in 1972 than 1968, or 1964.   J

1921.   Hopkins, Jerry B.   VIOLENCE IN CHICAGO: AN APPRAISAL OF SOURCES ON THE VIOLENCE RELATED TO THE 1968 DEMOCRATIC CONVENTION.   *Fides et Hist. 1979 12(1): 7-28.* Examines the diverse opinions about the causes of the violence at the Democratic National Convention in Chicago during August 1968.

Among those expressing views were the representatives of the mass media at the convention, who some felt were at least partly responsible for the trouble. This is a clear example of the enormous power wielded by the mass media in their ability to shape and mold public opinion. Christian historians should note such incidents carefully, because they are bound at all times to seek the truth. In so doing, they must use, but must simultaneously treat with skepticism, sources emanating from the mass media, which report often with manipulative intent. Printed primary sources; 43 notes.   J. A. Kicklighter

1922.   Howe, Russell Warren and Trott, Sarah Hays.   THE TRUTH AT LAST: HOW NIXON BEAT HUMPHREY.   *Washington Monthly 1976 8(10): 50-53.* Discusses the influence wielded by Anna Chan Chennault in the reelection campaign of Richard M. Nixon in 1968; word passed by Chennault to South Vietnam President Thieu not to appear at peace talks scheduled slightly prior to the 1968 election gave Nixon the needed shot in the arm to defeat Hubert Humphrey in that race.

1923.   Hrebenar, Ron.   UTAH: THE MOST REPUBLICAN STATE IN THE UNION.   *Social Sci. J. 1981 18(3): 103-114.* With the exception of the election of Democratic candidate for governor Scott Matheson, the Republican Party swept into office throughout Utah with the 1980 election victory of Ronald Reagan.

1924.   Hume, Brit.   JACK ANDERSON AND THE EAGLETON CASE.   *Washington Monthly 1974 6(5/6): 7-22.*

1925.   Humphrey, Craig R. and Louis, Helen Brock.   ASSIMILATION AND VOTING BEHAVIOR: A STUDY OF GREEK-AMERICANS.   *Int. Migration Rev. 1973 7(1): 34-45.* Discusses the roles of ethnicity and assimilation in the voting behavior and identification with the Republican Party of Greek Americans in the 1968 presidential election.

1926.   Hynes, Thomas J., Jr.   "MC GOVERN, COME DOWN": AN ANALYSIS OF SENATOR GEORGE MC GOVERN'S CONFRONTATION WITH DEMONSTRATORS, DORAL BEACH HOTEL, JULY 12, 1972.   *Southern Speech Communication J. 1974 39(3): 269-277.*

1927.   Ions, Edmund.   THE AMERICAN PRIMARY ELECTIONS AND CONVENTIONS OF 1976.   *Parliamentary Affairs [Great Britain] 1977 30(1): 59-68.* Evaluates the American primary system, and the reasons for the successes of Jimmy Carter and Gerald R. Ford in winning their respective party's nomination. Carter drew strength from powerful sources in the historical experience of the Republic: piety and populism. Ford succeeded because of his skillful use of presidential power and patronage, and Ronald Reagan's tactical error in selecting a liberal-republican vice-president.   J. C. Holsinger

1928.   Jackman, Mary R.   THE RELATION BETWEEN VERBAL ATTITUDE AND OVERT BEHAVIOR: A PUBLIC OPINION APPLICATION.   *Social Forces 1976 54(3): 646-668.* The discrepancy between verbal attitude and overt behavior bears both on public opinion research and public policy, but there has been little attempt to study the problem with a natural population in a public opinion context. This paper reviews conceptual issues from the attitude-behavior literature and applies them to a public opinion, voting setting. I argue (a) that a large proportion of white Americans seldom or never experience a personal encounter with blacks, thus restricting their realistic behavior orientations and overt behavior toward blacks largely to the policy sphere, and (b) that many of the key issues discussed in voting studies can be subsumed under the more general concerns of the attitude-behavior literature. Using data from the SRC 1968 Presidential Election Survey, the paper examines the process by which affect and action orientation toward blacks are translated into affect, action orientation (voting intention), and overt behavior (voting decision) toward George Wallace, an independent presidential candidate with a strong anti-civil rights campaign platform.   J

1929.   Jackson, John E.   ISSUES, PARTY CHOICES, AND PRESIDENTIAL VOTES.   *Am. J. of Pol. Sci. 1975 19(2): 161-185.* Discusses the role of issues, and the electorate's evaluation of the political parties' stance on issues, in the US electoral process. Produces a statistical model drawn from data of the 1964 presidential election study of the Survey Research Center. Concludes that the most important influences on the evaluation of parties are the effects of peoples' stance upon issues. Fig., 3 tables.   S. P. Carr

1930. Jackson, John S., III; Brown, Jesse C.; and Brown, Barbara L. RECRUITMENT, REPRESENTATION, AND POLITICAL VALUES: THE 1976 DEMOCRATIC NATIONAL CONVENTION DELEGATES. *Am. Pol. Q. 1978 6(2): 187-212.* Makes comparisons with other recent conventions, all in the context of recent changes in the delegates selection rules. Discusses how the delegate selection rules and/or the group characteristics of the delegates systematically affect the delegates' candidate preferences. Examines other more "political" variables for their relationship to candidates' fortunes. Analyzes why Jimmy Carter was nominated and elected in 1976. 7 tables, fig., 14 notes.
                                                                     R. V. Ritter

1931. Jackson, John S., III. SOME CORRELATES OF MINORITY REPRESENTATION IN THE NATIONAL CONVENTIONS, 1964-1972. *Am. Pol. Q. 1975 3(2): 171-188.* Discusses the extent of minority representation in state delegations to the national Democratic Party conventions, 1964-72, emphasizing the representation of Negroes, women, and youths.

1932. Jackson-Beeck, Marilyn and Meadow, Robert G. THE TRIPLE AGENDA OF PRESIDENTIAL DEBATES. *Public Opinion Q. 1979 43(2): 173-180.* The authors find little support for the view that televised presidential debates address the public's primary political concerns. Though candidates speak directly to the public, and the public is represented by journalists who question the candidates, the research suggests that never the "three shall meet." Based on (1) content analysis of the first 1960 and 1976 presidential debates and (2) secondary analysis of survey data (Gallup and CPS), candidates, journalists, and public appear to have their own separate issue agendas . . . Survey data in this paper were made available by the Roper Center and Inter-University Consortium for Political and Social Research, via the University of Pennsylvania Social Science Data Center. Data for 1976 were originally collected by the Center for Political Studies of the Institute for Social Research, the University of Michigan, under a grant from the National Science Foundation.
                                                                               J

1933. Jacobson, Gary C. PRESIDENTIAL COATTAILS IN 1972. *Public Opinion Q. 1976 40(2): 194-200.* Because Richard Nixon's overwhelming victory in the 1972 presidential election was not accompanied by any significant increase in Republican representation in Congress, it has been assumed that his coattails were exceedingly short. However, analysis of several kinds of evidence suggests that such an assumption is premature and that Nixon's pulling power has been underestimated. An explanation of the failure of Republican gains to materialize as congressional seats may be found in the competitive disadvantages suffered by Republicans in a period of increasingly safe seats.   J

1934. James, Judson Lehman and James, Dorothy Buckton. LESSONS OF WATERGATE: THE NIXON CAMPAIGNS. *Current Hist. 1974 67(395): 30-33, 38.* Discusses the impact of the Watergate scandal on political parties and analyzes Nixon's campaigns of 1968 and 1972. One of seven articles in this issue on the two-party system.   S

1935. Jewell, Malcolm E. A CAVEAT ON THE EXPANDING USE OF PRESIDENTIAL PRIMARIES. *Policy Studies J. 1974 2(4): 279-284.* Selective candidate participation, the inability to gauge voters' alternative choices, and low and unrepresentative turnouts make state primaries an unreliable means of nomination.   S

1936. Jewell, Malcolm E. PRESIDENTIAL SELECTION. *Society 1980 17(5): 48-55.* Analyzes the methods for nominating presidential candidates, arguing that the problems are fundamental, not solved merely by a change of the nominating machinery, but necessitating a logical, systematic process of screening and training presidential candidates.

1937. Johnson, Stephen D. and Tamney, Joseph B. THE CHRISTIAN RIGHT AND THE 1980 PRESIDENTIAL ELECTION. *J. for the Sci. Study of Religion 1982 21(2): 123-131.* Interviews with residents of Muncie, Indiana conducted one week prior to the 1980 presi-

dential election reveal that disproportionate support for Ronald Reagan did not come from the Christian Right but from traditional Republicans with inflation as their major concern.

1938. Johnstone, Christopher Lyle. ELECTING OURSELVES IN 1976: JIMMY CARTER AND THE AMERICAN FAITH. *Western J. of Speech Communication 1978 42(4): 241-249.* Examines Jimmy Carter's reliance on faith and Americans' faith in responsible leadership during the 1976 presidential elections.

1939. Joslyn, Richard A. THE CONTENT OF POLITICAL SPOT ADS. *Journalism Q. 1980 57(1): 92-98.* The author studied 156 television spot ads for presidential, gubernatorial, senatorial, and congressional campaigns, in regard to partisanship, issue content, personality content, and reference to demographic groups. The results indicate that as sources of information on specific issues and candidates' positions, spot ads compare favorably with national television news and surpass certain print sources in terms of conveying a candidate's characteristics or qualities. However, spot ads do not fare well in comparison to debates as information sources on a candidate's policies. In general, spot advertising may be as effective as television and print journalism in informing the electorate. 18 notes.   J. S. Coleman

1940. Kallina, Edmund F. THE STATE'S ATTORNEY AND THE PRESIDENT: THE INSIDE STORY OF THE 1960 PRESIDENTIAL ELECTION IN ILLINOIS. *J. of Am. Studies [Great Britain] 1978 12(2): 147-160.* Incompetence of election judges, partisan manipulations, and election day fraud cost Richard M. Nixon, the Republican presidential candidate, votes in the 1960 US presidential elections in Cook County, Illinois. Of greater impact, more widespread irregularities at the polls harmed Benjamin Adamowski, nominee for Cook County State's Attorney, and in turn reduced his chances of later challenging Mayor Richard J. Daley in a Chicago mayoral race. Of more than 600 election judges who were indicted in 1961 for misconduct, only three were convicted by the courts in 1962. Based on newspaper and secondary sources; 15 notes.
                                                                     H. T. Lovin

1941. Kayden, Xandra. THE POLITICAL CAMPAIGN AS AN ORGANIZATION. *Public Policy 1973 21(2): 263-290.* George Stanley McGovern's 1972 political campaign (presidential) as an organizational structure.   S

1942. Kellerman, Barbara. CAMPAIGNING SINCE KENNEDY: THE FAMILY AS "SURROGATE." *Presidential Studies Q. 1980 10(2): 244-253.* The nature of presidential campaigning changed in 1960. To a large extent, this was done by turning the candidate's family into a permanent political resource. With factors such as the decline of the party, the increase of primaries, the personalization of the presidency, the influence of the media, and cultural changes toward women and families, the candidate's families became much more active. This phenomenon is to the advantage of everyone, and is here to stay. 37 notes.
                                                                     D. H. Cline

1943. Kenski, Henry C. and Dreyer, Edward C. IN SEARCH OF STATE PRESIDENTIAL BELLWETHERS. *Social Sci. Q. 1977 58(3): 498-505.* Following the criteria formulation for bellwether identification, eight states qualify. A 1976 election application is followed by before-the-fact historical experiments to assess the prospective accuracy of the four most promising bellwethers—Delaware, Maryland, Ohio, and Pennsylvania.   J

1944. Kessel, John H. THE SEASONS OF PRESIDENTIAL POLITICS. *Social Sci. Q. 1977 58(3): 418-435.* Texts assumed to be typical of three of the seasons of presidential politics have been investigated through a combination of content analysis and factor analysis. The 1972 platforms and acceptance speeches are taken to be representative of nomination politics, the 1972 campaign speeches of electoral politics, and the 1973 inaugural and State of the Union messages of executive politics. Observes that the nomination season provides a detailed statement of intent emphasizing executive agencies, the electoral season is marked by nonpolicy themes of group appeal and national unity, and the executive season is marked by a return to the imperatives of governance.   J

1945. Kessler, Martha Stout. THE ROLE OF SURROGATE SPEAKERS IN THE 1980 PRESIDENTIAL CAMPAIGN. *Q. J. of Speech 1981 67(2): 146-156.* Surrogate speakers have played active roles in recent election campaigns. This article describes their employment in the 1980 campaign and examines the advantages and disadvantages of their efforts to the presidential candidates, the voters, and to the surrogates themselves.   J

1946. King, James D. COMPARING LOCAL AND PRESIDENTIAL ELECTIONS. *Am. Pol. Q. 1981 9(3): 277-290.* Utilizing voter turnout data from a single national sample, presidential and local electorates are compared. The results point to the similarities between the two, with geographic region and interest in politics being the foremost distinguishing factors. In addition to these variables, strength of partisanship, length of residence in the community, age, and education best discriminate between voters and nonvoters in both presidential and local elections.   J/S

1947. King, Michael. ASSIMILATION AND CONTRAST OF PRESIDENTIAL CANDIDATES' ISSUE POSITIONS, 1972. *Public Opinion Q. 1977-78 41(4): 515-522.* Voter assimilation, the tendency to exaggerate the similarity between their favored candidate's position on issues and their own position, and contrast, the tendency to exaggerate the distance between their nonpreferred candidate's position on issues and their own position, were examined in the University of Michigan Center for Political Studies 1972 national election study. Significant assimilation effects were found on all nine issues considered, for both McGovern and Nixon voters, replicating and extending findings for the Vietnam issue in 1968 election data. Contrast effects occurred primarily on issues which polarized the electorate and on which the candidates were viewed as distinct. Assimilation was enhanced both by party identification and by attraction to preferred candidate. These moderators did not uniformly enhance contrast.   J

1948. King, Susan B. and Peabody, Robert L. CONTROL OF PRESIDENTIAL CAMPAIGN FINANCING. *Pro. of the Acad. of Pol. Sci. 1975 32(1): 180-195.* Describes and assesses the implications which the Federal Election Campaign Act Amendment of 1974 has on presidential electioneering and the two-party system.

1949. Kirkpatrick, Samuel A.; Lyons, William; and Fitzgerald, Michael R. CANDIDATES, PARTIES, AND ISSUES IN THE AMERICAN ELECTORATE: TWO DECADES OF CHANGE. *Am. Pol. Q. 1975 3(3): 247-283.* Discusses changing public opinion and electoral behavior toward political issues, parties, and candidates in presidential elections 1952-72, mentioning ticket-splitting, partisan defection, and the rise of independents.

1950. Kirkpatrick, Samuel A. INTRODUCTION: CHANGE AND STABILITY IN AMERICAN ELECTORAL BEHAVIOR. *Am. Pol. Q. 1975 3(3): 219-221.* Discusses methodological issues in sociological theory regarding the analysis of electoral behavior in presidential voting, 1975.

1951. Klonoski, James and Aiken, Ann. OREGON: STILL LIBERAL BUT SLIPPING. *Social Sci. J. 1981 18(3): 87-101.* In the 1980 general election, Ronald Reagan carried the Republican Party to victory in key races throughout the state, especially the defeat of long-term Congressman Al Ullman by a conservative Republican.

1952. Knoke, David. A CAUSAL SYNTHESIS OF SOCIOLOGICAL AND PSYCHOLOGICAL MODELS OF AMERICAN VOTING BEHAVIOR. *Social Forces 1974 53(1): 92-101.* A path model of the presidential vote involving social variables, party identification, issue orientations, and candidate evaluations is estimated using samples from the 1964 and 1968 elections. Social effects on voting behavior are channeled almost completely through party identification, which has the largest direct effect on the vote. Indirect effects of party identification through candidate evaluations are considerably larger than through issue orientations. The models for both years reveal similar effects, although issues and candidates were more important determinants of the vote in 1964.   J

1953. Krasner, Michael. REAGAN'S MANIPULATED MANDATE. *Social Policy 1981 11(5): 26-28.* Discusses the impact of the

mass media, the nationalization of politics, and the spread of presidential primaries on the mechanism of nominating presidential candidates in the United States from 1824 to 1980, focusing on the events which led to the election of Ronald Reagan in 1980.

1954. Kritzer, Herbert M. and Eubank, Robert B. PRESIDENTIAL COATTAILS REVISITED: PARTISANSHIP AND INCUMBENCY EFFECTS. *Am. J. of Pol. Sci. 1979 23(3): 615-626.* One question raised by recent presidential elections is the failure of the winner to carry into office any sizable number of congressional candidates. This paper suggests that explanations based upon previous theories are inadequate and describes and tests an alternate explanation using SRC-CPS data for five elections. The results show that the proposed alternative fails to account for the results of the elections examined. This failure seems to result from the inability of the Republican Party to capture or hold a large number of voters at the congressional level. Additional analyses indicate that much, though not all, of this apparent asymmetry is a result of incumbency effects in congressional elections.   J

1955. Küchler, Manfred and Wides, Jeffrey W. PERZEPTION DER WIRTSCHAFTSLAGE UND WAHLENTSCHEIDUNG: EINE ANALYSE DER AMERIKANISCHEN PRÄSIDENTSCHAFTSWAHL VON 1976 [Economics and elections: an analysis of the American presidential election of 1976]. *Politische Vierteljahresschrift [West Germany] 1980 21(1): 4-19.* An individual voter's choice of candidate depends not so much on his own economic circumstances as on his assessment of the candidates' competence in economic matters. This factor is found to be three times as important as party allegiance. Because of the current financial crisis and the widespread publicity it receives, economic issues may now be more influential in elections than ever before. A summary of recent American electoral studies is included, as is a comparison of political parties and party allegiances in American and West German elections. 2 tables, 14 notes, biblio.   S. Bonnycastle

1956. Ladd, Everett Carll. THE BRITTLE MANDATE: ELECTORAL DEALIGNMENT AND THE 1980 PRESIDENTIAL ELECTION. *Pol. Sci. Q. 1981 96(1): 1-25.* Examines the behavior of the US electorate in the 1980 presidential election within the context of the long-standing argument over whether party realignment is occurring. It is not realignment but the continued progress of "dealignment" that gives the 1980 election its distinctive cast.   J

1957. Lader, Lawrence. THE WALLACE CAMPAIGN OF 1948. *Am. Heritage 1976 28(1): 42-51.* Summarizes factors leading to the unsuccessful presidential bid by Henry A. Wallace in 1948 and analyzes the campaign. Wallace's split with President Truman became clear in 1946 when he urged the President to take a softer line toward the Soviet Union. His ouster as Secretary of Commerce and the ever-hardening Truman Cold War posture led Wallace to make his bid for the presidency on the Progressive Party ticket. His ties with Communist supporters, his soft line in time of a Cold War, and the President's urging of Democrats not to "waste" their votes, all hurt his chances. 7 illus.   J. F. Paul

1958. Lamare, James W. INTER- OR INTRAGENERATIONAL CLEAVAGE? THE POLITICAL ORIENTATIONS OF AMERICAN YOUTH IN 1968. *Am. J. of Pol. Sci. 1975 19(1): 81-90.* This paper explores whether the generations were divided in political outlook in the late 1960's or whether the younger generation was uniquely split in their political orientations. Using a sample of the 1968 electorate, responses to items concerned with political events, policies, and actors involved in political controversies peculiar to this period as well as voting behavior in the 1968 presidential election are investigated. The findings point to little variation between the generations and only some indication of an intragenerational cleavage peculiar to the young."   J

1959. Land, Guy Paul. JOHN F. KENNEDY'S SOUTHERN STRATEGY, 1956-1960. *North Carolina Hist. Rev. 1979 56(1): 41-63.* The John F. Kennedy 1960 presidential campaign really received its start at the 1956 Democratic Party convention when southern delegates began to perceive the Massachusetts senator as less liberal and less harmful than rival Vice-Presidential nominee Estes Kefauver. Over the next four years Kennedy and his followers designed and followed a "southern strategy" to gain votes for the presidential convention of 1960. They played on the South's anti-unionism, fear of labor racketeering, and pride in America's greatness, to win friends and delegates. But the civil rights crises of the late 1950's, the rise of Lyndon Johnson, and the cultivation of southern moderates lost Kennedy the South at the convention, though not the nomination. He recovered and won the majority of southern electoral votes in the election. Based on personal and public papers of Kennedy, Johnson, and Theodore Sorenson, interviews and oral history tapes, newspaper articles, and secondary sources; 12 illus., 90 notes.

T. L. Savitt

1960. Land, Guy Paul. MISSISSIPPI REPUBLICANISM AND THE 1960 PRESIDENTIAL ELECTION. *J. of Mississippi Hist. 1978 40(1): 33-48.* Investigates the 1960 presidential campaign between Richard Nixon and John Kennedy in Mississippi. Describes the actions of state party leaders at both conventions and during the race. The split in the Democratic Party between the Loyalists led by Senator James O. Eastland and the forces led by Ross R. Barnett calling for independent electors, inspired Republican Party leaders such as Wirt Yerger, Jr., to launch the first serious Republican campaign in the state since Reconstruction. Mississippians, primarily concerned with the racial issue, gave the unpledged elector slate a plurality, but the Republican party emerged from the campaign with stronger urban support which provided a foundation for later expansion.

M. S. Legan

1961. Lang, Gladys Engel and Lang, Kurt. THE FIRST DEBATE AND THE COVERAGE GAP. *J. of Communication 1978 28(4): 93-98.* Discusses the controversy surrounding the first television debate between Jimmy Carter and Gerald R. Ford in 1976; the 27-minute gap in broadcasting the sound occurred because the PA system was connected to the audio broadcast signal to prevent feedback.

1962. Lang, Gladys Engel and Lang, Kurt. IMMEDIATE AND DELAYED RESPONSES TO A CARTER-FORD DEBATE: ASSESSING PUBLIC OPINION. *Public Opinion Q. 1978 42(3): 322-341.* A study during the televised Jimmy Carter-Gerald R. Ford debates compared immediate reactions in a controlled group with delayed "contaminated" reactions of another unstructured viewing group; communication events must be assessed in terms of the total communication environment.

1963. Lavrova, T. V. SOVETSKO-AMERIKANSKIE OTNOSHENIIA I VYBORY 1976 G. V SSHA [Soviet-American relations and the 1976 elections in the USA]. *Voprosy Istorii [USSR] 1979 (12): 66-79.* Examines the approach of different circles in the United States to the problem of Soviet-American relations, which was manifested with particular clarity during the presidential election campaign of 1976. The article contains a detailed analysis of the struggle between different trends in the Republican and Democratic parties around the problem of relations with the USSR at the various stages of presidential elections, and characterizes these parties' programs on the given issue.

J

1964. LeBlanc, Hugh L. and Merrin, Mary Beth. PARTIES, ISSUES, AND CANDIDATES: ANOTHER LOOK AT RESPONSIBLE PARTIES. *Western Pol. Q. 1978 31(4): 523-534.* Previous research has indicated that our political parties have been unable to organize the electorate on the basis of meaningful issue cleavages in the manner envisaged by the responsible party doctrine . . . It has been suggested that voters are now more issue conscious in their presidential choices . . . Based on an analysis of the American electorate from 1960 through 1972, we are led to conclude that the nation is moving away from rather than closer to a responsible party system.

J

1965. Lee, David D. THE SOUTH AND THE AMERICAN MAINSTREAM: THE ELECTION OF JIMMY CARTER. *Georgia Hist. Q. 1977 61(1): 7-12.* Describes how Jimmy Carter's presidential campaign emphasizing human values and attacking strong central government was a product of his southern background. His election demonstrates the new attitude of respect toward the South felt by America as a whole in 1976. Primary and secondary sources; 7 notes.

G. R. Schroeder

1966. Lehnen, Robert G. and Koch, Gary G. ANALYZING PANEL DATA WITH UNCONTROLLED ATTRITION. *Public Opinion Q. 1974 38(1): 40-56.* "Three-wave panel data collected during the 1968 presidential election campaign in Florida and North Carolina are analyzed on the basis of the partial candidate preference information available for some respondents and the complete information obtained from others. A supplemented marginals model based on the general linear approach to categorical data analysis is extended to the situation involving incomplete time data. The final statistical models show no politically significant effects associated with the campaign (time) on the level of citizens' preferences for Hubert Humphrey, Richard Nixon, or George Wallace for seven race and occupation classifications."

J

1967. Leitel, Erich. MACHTKAMPF IN DER HOCHBURG DES IMPERIALISMUS: PRÄSIDENTENWAHLEN IN DEN USA [Power struggle in the center of imperialism: presidential elections in the United States]. *Wissenschaftliche Zeitschrift der Friedrich-Schiller-U. Jena. Gesellschafts- und Sprachwissenschaftliche Reihe [East Germany] 1969 18(4): 149-158.* Reviews the development of the Republican and Democratic Parties since the elections of 1964, the primaries for the 1968 campaign, the programs of the candidates, and the results of the elections.

1968. Leubsdorf, Carl P. THE REPORTER AND THE PRESIDENTIAL CANDIDATE. *Ann. of the Am. Acad. of Pol. and Social Sci. 1976 427: 1-11.* Presidential politics in the United States has undergone a revolution since 1960. Campaigns are longer and more complex. Television has created an emphasis on personality, rather than on issues, and a volatility that can change situations overnight. This has complicated the job of the press, which must concentrate more on assessing where the political situation stands than on merely reporting what candidates are saying. The relationship between reporters and candidates changes during the various stages of the campaign. It is personal and intimate during the period that precedes the election year, less so as the primaries progress. Later attitudes depend in considerable measure on whether the candidate is perceived as having a real chance of winning his party's nomination, and the presidency. By the time of the general election, intimacy is largely gone, but much depends on whether the candidate permits an "open" atmosphere. The 1976 campaign is likely to match two candidates running open campaigns, in contrast to the 1972 contest between the open campaign of George McGovern and the closed campaign of Richard M. Nixon.

J

1969. Levantroser, William F. FINANCING PRESIDENTIAL CAMPAIGNS: THE IMPACT OF REFORM FINANCE LAWS ON THE DEMOCRATIC PRESIDENTIAL NOMINATION OF 1976. *Presidential Studies Q. 1981 11(2): 280-288.* The Campaign Finance Act (US, 1974) and its 1976 amendments were important factors in the nomination of Jimmy Carter as Democratic Party candidate in the 1976 campaign. As the primaries started, all candidates relied on matching funds. For the two-month period that payments were suspended while Congress revised the law, only Carter's financial picture was maintained, giving him a definite advantage. Primary sources, 4 tables, 11 notes.

A. Drysdale

1970. Lewis, Mort R. LINCOLN, STEVENSON AND YOURS TRULY. *Manuscripts 1975 27(4): 280-284.* Reminisces about correspondence with Adlai E. Stevenson, II, and includes the copy of a letter suggesting that Stevenson, the Lincoln admirer, engage Dwight D. Eisenhower in a series of debates over national issues in the 1952 presidential election.

D. A. Yanchisin

1971. Li, Richard P. Y. A DYNAMIC COMPARATIVE ANALYSIS OF PRESIDENTIAL AND HOUSE ELECTIONS. *Am. J. of Pol. Sci. 1976 20(4): 671-691.* This paper attempts a longitudinal comparison of the presidential and the on-year and off-year House elections. Five propositions regarding structural differentiation are tested by fitting a cyclical autoregressive-moving-average model to each of the electoral time series and then comparing their estimated coefficients. The results reveal several general patterns: (1) The House elections contain a more stable basic trend than the presidential elections (largely due to the predominant impact of party and incumbency on House elections). (2) The presidential elections, in contrast, are more responsive to short-term effects than the House elections. (3) The presidential electoral realignments appear stronger than House realignments. (4) The off-year House elections contain a more stable basic trend than the on-year House elections. (5) The on-year House elections, in contrast, are more responsive to short-term disturbances than off-year elections, mostly as a result of presidential coattail effect.

J

1972. Lichtenstein, Allen. DIFFERENCES IN IMPACT BE-TWEEN LOCAL AND NATIONAL TELEVISED POLITICAL CANDIDATES' DEBATES. *Western J. of Speech Communication 1982 46(3): 291-298.* Findings in Albuquerque, New Mexico, during the 1980 campaigns confirm earlier results.

1973. Linnik, V. A. S'EZD V CHIKAGO [Convention in Chicago]. *Voprosy Istorii [USSR] 1978 (6): 113-123.* Describes the government's social and political oppression of and violence against dissidents and innocent but accidentally involved people in the United States. Considers McCarthy's "witch-hunt," and focuses on the aggressive participation of the police in Chicago in 1968 and the Democratic National Convention and riots which took place there, quoting detailed British and American journalists' accounts of particular acts of violence. Outlines the importance of Chicago in American history and politics, and its place in contemporary American society. Discusses the attitude of American students and their attempts to combat government repression. Based on British and American newspaper articles 1968-69, and secondary works; 27 notes.
L. Smith

1974. Lipset, Seymour Martin and Raab, Earl. THE ELECTION AND THE NATIONAL MOOD. *Commentary 1973 55(1): 43-50.* Explains the defeat of Democratic Senator George S. McGovern in the 1972 presidential elections, and analyzes the American electorate at that time.

1975. Loomis, Burdette. ANALYSIS ON DEADLINE: THE 1980 ELECTION. *Policy Studies Rev. 1982 2(1): 136-139.* Reviews Gerald Pomper's *The Election of 1980* (1981), *The American Elections of 1980* (1981), edited by Austin Ranney, and Paul R. Abramson, John H. Aldrich, and David W. Rohde's *Change and Continuity in the 1980 Elections* (1981); all three offer electoral analyses by teams of political scientists who rely upon simple analytical methods, and the studies are directed to an audience of students and informed laypersons.

1976. Lucy, William H. POLLS, PRIMARIES, AND PRESIDENTIAL NOMINATIONS. *J. of Pol. 1973 35(4): 830-848.* Argues "that the concepts of availability and bargaining have not proved useful in predicting winners in the presidential nominating process. Since 1936 there have been several strong relationships between public opinion polls, primaries and presidential nominations. At the 20 national conventions, 1940-1972 the nominee has been the preconvention poll leader 19 times, or 95 percent. The preprimary poll leader became the nominee 85 percent of the time, and preprimary poll leaders continued as the postprimary poll leader 90 percent of the time. Only once has the preprimary poll leader lost primaries and then permanently lost the poll lead. This occurred among the Democratic presidential contenders in 1972." Suggests areas for additional research in candidate and delegate attitudes toward opinion polls. 3 tables, 25 notes.
A. R. Stoesen

1977. Maddox, William S. CANDIDATE IMAGES AMONG VOTERS AND NONVOTERS IN 1976. *Am. Pol. Q. 1980 8(2): 209-220.* An analysis of 1976 data indicates that nonvoters' images of presidential candidates do not differ drastically from the images expressed by voters. Nonvoters respond to fewer candidates and tend to rate some "outsider" figures more positively and "establishment" figures less positively. With regard to most candidates, however, nonvoters' perceptions resemble those of fellow partisan identifiers more than those of fellow nonvoters. Tests of candidate-related explanations of turnout provide more support for the "indifference" and "other preference" hypotheses than for alienation, but the utility of these explanations varies across partisan groupings.
J

1978. Maddox, William S. CHANGING ELECTORAL COALITIONS FROM 1952 TO 1976. *Social Sci. Q. 1979 60(2): 309-313.* Analyzes coalitional factors which significantly affected presidential elections during 1952-76. Coalitions considered are those based on income, race, religion, union, region, urbanism, and age. All have been factors in one election or more, but few have exercised an important influence in all of the elections. Race, union membership, and religion are clearly the dominant indicators of party membership at present; the remaining factors all are pretty much up for grabs in any given election. Table, 4 notes, ref.
V. L. Human

1979. Maggiotto, Michael A. and Pierson, James E. ISSUE PUBLICS AND VOTER CHOICE. *Am. Pol. Q. 1978 6(4): 407-429.* Data suggest that in the 1972 election "salience fails to sharpen the impact of issues and that electoral choice was, fundamentally, a question of candidate images." Finds no systematic evidence to demonstrate that issue salience strengthens the relationships between voter preference on issues and either their evaluations of candidates or their electoral choices. No matter how the problem was analyzed the results showed that the perceived salience of issues "did not have a strong influence upon the overall relationships between issue preference and behavior." Future studies should give attention to alternative ways of measuring "issues." 8 tables, 8 notes, ref.
E. P. Stickney

1980. Malaney, Gary D. and Buss, Terry F. AP WIRE REPORTS VS. CBS TV NEWS COVERAGE OF A PRESIDENTIAL CAMPAIGN. *Journalism Q. 1979 56(3): 602-610.* Compares the coverage by the Associated Press (AP) of the 1972 US presidential campaign with similar reporting by the Columbia Broadcasting System (CBS). AP concentrated more on the issues of the campaign, while CBS focused on the public images of the candidates. Both favorable and unfavorable aspects of the candidates' campaigns received proportionately more attention from AP; CBS reported mostly on relatively neutral, day-to-day developments in the campaign. Based on a content analysis of AP and CBS reports and on secondary sources; 31 notes.
R. P. Sindermann, Jr.

1981. Markus, Gregory B. POLITICAL ATTITUDES DURING AN ELECTION YEAR: A REPORT ON THE 1980 NES PANEL STUDY. *Am. Pol. Sci. Rev. 1982 76(3): 538-560.* Analyzes data from the 1980 National Election Study surveys on the rates at which voters become familiar with presidential candidates and their policy positions, trends in public opinion during the 1980 presidential campaign, and the dynamics of individual attitudes that underlie those trends. The analysis yields support for the retrospective voting model and provides no evidence for the contention that Reagan's victory was the result of his policy or ideological positions.
J/S

1982. Marshall, Thomas R. CAUCUSES AND PRIMARIES: MEASURING REFORM IN THE PRESIDENTIAL NOMINATION PROCESS. *Am. Pol. Q. 1979 7(2): 155-174.* In 1968 battles over delegate selection rules and procedures for the national party conventions erupted anew. During the following decade, reformers advanced multiple standards for the delegate selection and presidential nomination process. While many of these goals have been incorporated into party rules and into state or federal law, little research yet exists by which to evaluate how fully presidential primaries versus caucus convention systems achieve these various standards. A review of the 1976 presidential delegate selection process suggests that presidential primaries and caucus convention systems meet most reform goals equally well, although some differences are found between these two modes of delegate selection.
J

1983. Marshall, Thomas R. DELEGATE SELECTION IN 1976: EVALUATING CAUCUSES AND PRIMARIES. *Natl. Civic Rev. 1977 66(8): 391-396, 432.* In some areas caucuses met party reformers' goals better than primaries; in others the reverse was true. Trade-offs between the systems must be weighed and critical goals determined.
J

1984. McAnaw, Richard L. MICHIGAN'S PRESIDENTIAL PRIMARY. *Michigan Academician 1979 12(1): 3-14.* Features of Michigan's presidential primary system (1972, 1976), notably the open primary, indirect primary, parties on ballot, candidates, and delegate selection and apportionment features, largely resulted from Democratic Party reform, 1970-72.

1985. McAnaw, Richard L. THOSE WHO NOMINATE: THE MICHIGAN DELEGATION TO THE DEMOCRATIC NATIONAL CONVENTION—1972. *Michigan Academician 1974 7(2): 227-252.*

1986. McCarthy, Colman. SHRIVER: THE LIGHTWEIGHT LABEL. *Washington Monthly 1976 8(4): 4-10.* Notes the liberal, progressive political attitudes of Sargent Shriver and his achievements in public life, criticizing him for running his 1976 presidential political campaign on the legacy of his brother-in-law, John F. Kennedy.

1987. McClure, Robert D. and Patterson, Thomas E. SETTING THE POLITICAL AGENDA: PRINT VS. NETWORK NEWS. *J. of Communication 1976 26(2): 23-28.* Discusses public opinion of the relative benefits of newspapers' and television's coverage in the 1972 presidential election, emphasizing the issues of the Vietnam War and political corruption.

1988. McDonnell, Richard A. THE DIRECTION OF THE WALLACE VOTE IN 1972 AND 1976. *Presidential Studies Q. 1981 11(3): 374-383.* Analyzes how the 1968 Wallace vote moved in the two following general elections. Many early supporters of George C. Wallace shifted to Nixon in the 1972 election, and even Jimmy Carter, a Southerner, could not bring them back to the Democratic Party in 1976. In this respect, the early Wallace vote can be seen as a portent for the later Reagan victory. Based on analysis of voting in individual congressional districts; 2 tables, 30 notes.   D. H. Cline

1989. McFeeley, Neil D. and Blank, Robert H. IDAHO: A CONSERVATIVE REPUBLICAN LANDSLIDE. *Social Sci. J. 1981 18(3): 41-50.* The 1980 presidential election of Ronald Reagan carried over onto Idaho state politics and led to the defeat of incumbent Democratic Senator Frank Church and the election of an entirely Republican congressional delegation thanks largely to the efforts of the National Conservative Political Action Committee and the Sagebrush Rebellion movement.

1990. McGrath, Wilma E. and Soule, John W. ROCKING THE CRADLE OR ROCKING THE BOAT: WOMEN AT THE 1972 DEMOCRATIC NATIONAL CONVENTION. *Social Sci. Q. 1974 55(1): 141-150.* "... Find that women delegates were deeply influenced by the women's liberation movement, were keenly aware of sex discrimination in politics and that they were more liberal on questions of public policy than their male counterparts."   J

1991. McGregor, Eugene B., Jr. UNCERTAINTY AND NATIONAL NOMINATING COALITIONS. *J. of Pol. 1978 40(4): 1011-1042.* Until 1952, presidential nominating coalitions were formed during multiballot conventions. Since then, winning coalitions have been formed prior to the completion of the first ballot. Delegates tested the strength of various coalitions on procedural votes prior to the first ballot. Successful nominees were those who defeated opponents in primaries, campaign issues, procedural balloting, and roll-call votes. While bargained side-payments and policy payoffs have continued to be used, they have not been deciding factors. Primary and secondary sources; 5 tables, fig., 53 notes.   A. W. Novitsky

1992. Meadow, Robert G. and Jackson-Beeck, Marilyn. CANDIDATE POLITICAL PHILOSOPHY: REVELATIONS IN THE 1960 AND 1976 DEBATES. *Presidential Studies Q. 1980 10(2): 234-243.* By topically analyzing the 1960 and 1976 debates, the two Democratic candidates are seen to have had greater concern for the lessons of history, social change, and national diversity than the Republican candidates, who expressed concern for smaller government and power, and the increase in influence of the private sector. Through this analysis, we can not only better understand the views of each candidate, but also the person. 9 tables, fig., 7 ref.   D. H. Cline

1993. Meadow, Robert G. CROSS-MEDIA COMPARISON OF COVERAGE OF THE 1972 PRESIDENTIAL CAMPAIGN. *Journalism Q. 1973 50(3): 482-488.* Shows that newspaper and television coverage were highly similar.   S

1994. Meadow, Robert G. ISSUE EMPHASIS AND PUBLIC OPINION: THE MEDIA DURING THE 1972 PRESIDENTIAL CAMPAIGN. *Am. Pol. Q. 1976 4(2): 177-192.* Illuminates the problems of media issue presentation in light of the 1972 election campaign. Issues salient to the public at the time of the campaign are compared with the issues discussed by candidates as they appeared in several news sources. Comparisons among several news sources are made to determine if a constant message was differentially reported across news sources. The media have unique formulae for emphasizing campaign issues. Some editors choose the issues which make the most exciting copy. The public's minor interests fail to be represented.   P. Travis

1995. Meadow, Robert G. and Jackson-Beeck, Marilyn. ISSUE EVOLUTION: A NEW PERSPECTIVE ON PRESIDENTIAL DEBATES. *J. of Communication 1978 28(4): 84-92.* Compares the nationally televised presidential debates of 1960 and 1976 between John F. Kennedy and Richard M. Nixon, and Jimmy Carter and Gerald R. Ford; discusses the topics, issues, and length of the debates.

1996. Meier, Kenneth John. RATIONALITY AND VOTING: A DOWNSIAN ANALYSIS OF THE 1972 ELECTION. *Western Pol. Q. 1980 33(1): 38-49.* This paper analyzes voter rationality during the 1972 general election campaign. The paper argues that rationality is used in different ways by different students of voting. Most studies of voting behavior use synoptic rationality with its high standards to assess voter rationality. After arguing that synoptic rationality demands too much from the voter, the paper presents and operationalizes Downs's *An Economic Theory of Democracy* as a limited approach to rationality. Past performance evaluations of the candidates predict respondent vote intention fairly well. An examination of the relationship between past performance evaluations and vote intention to determine if the voter is rational or rationalizing reveals that both behaviors occur. All voter behavior in choosing candidates, however, cannot be dismissed as rationalization. 6 tables, 2 fig., 31 notes.   J

1997. Merrill, Bruce D. ARIZONA: GROWTH, POLITICS, AND SELF INTEREST. *Social Sci. J. 1981 18(3): 7-13.* In the 1980 election, Arizona state politics and politicians were deeply influenced by the victory of Ronald Reagan, and, in a period of economic crisis and scarce resources, the electorate seemed to be more informed about the political issues.

1998. Merrin, Mary Beth and LeBlanc, Hugh L. PARTIES AND CANDIDATES IN 1972: OBJECTS OF ISSUE VOTING. *Western Pol. Q. 1979 32(1): 59-69.* The "perverse and unorthodox" argument of V. O. Key that the American voter is no fool is today approaching orthodoxy. An impressive number of articles have provided evidence that, begining with the election of 1964, voters have become more issue conscious in their presidential voting choices, more agreed on where the parties stand on issues, and more consistent in their own issue attitudes. Based on an analysis of the 1972 election, the evidence of issue voting, including the degree of agreement on party policy stands and the consistency of voters' own issues attitudes, has been exaggerated.   J

1999. Meyers, Renee A.; Newhouse, Thomas L.; and Garrett, Dennis E. POLITICAL MOMENTUM: TELEVISION NEWS TREATMENT. *Communication Monographs 1978 45(4): 382-388.* A study during the 1976 presidential campaign demonstrates television news media's active concern with candidate momentum, suggesting possible benefits from further research on the relationship between momentum treatment and voter behavior.

2000. Miller, Arthur H. and MacKuen, Michael. LEARNING ABOUT THE CANDIDATES: THE 1976 PRESIDENTIAL DEBATES. *Public Opinion Q. 1979 43(3): 326-346.* In this study of the 1976 televised Carter-Ford debates, the authors find that the debates produced a heightened political awareness in viewers in the critical days just prior to the election. The information obtained from the debates focused largely on candidate competence, performance and personality attributes rather than on issues, but some increase in information on issues and policies can be linked to the debates. The major impact of the debates may have been to reinforce partisan predispositions.   J

2001. Miller, Arthur H. PARTISANSHIP REINSTATED? A COMPARISON OF THE 1972 AND 1976 US PRESIDENTIAL ELECTIONS. *British J. of Pol. Sci. [Great Britain] 1978 8(2): 129-152.* Reemergence of party identification is the significant difference between the two elections.

2002. Minow, Newton N. and Mitchell, Lee M. INCUMBENT TELEVISION: A CASE OF INDECENT EXPOSURE. *Ann. of the Am. Acad. of Pol. and Social Sci. 1976 425: 74-87.* Throughout his term of office, an incumbent president of the United States has ready access to television time which allows him to reach millions of potential voters regularly, conveying both his views and "image" at little or no cost to himself or his political supporters. In contrast, the opposition party and those potential candidates who would challenge the incumbent's reelection have little similar access. An incumbent member of Congress, although not enjoying television access to the same extent as the president, also has a unique television advantage over potential challengers. While Congress prevents broadcast coverage of many of its activities, individual members are able to produce their own television programming to reach voters. This "incumbent television" can be a significant electoral advantage to the officeholder seeking reelection. Moreover, with incumbents dominating television, contrasting political viewpoints and personalities, instead of being presented in rational debate throughout an office term, appear too often only in political "spots" immediately preceding elections. Innovations such as televised National Debates, limited right of reply for the opposition party, government-sponsored broadcast time for presidential candidates, and television coverage of congressional proceedings, would counter this trend and help to fulfill television's potential as a medium for political debate.   J

2003. Miroff, Bruce. PRESIDENTIAL CAMPAIGNS: CANDI-DATES, MANAGERS & REPORTERS. *Polity 1980 12(4): 667-675.* Review article of Stephen Hess's *The Presidential Campaign,* rev. ed. (Washington: Brookings Inst., 1978); Jonathan Moore and Janet Fraser, ed., *Campaign for President: The Managers Look at '76* (Cambridge, Mass.: Ballinger, 1977); Vic Gould's *PR as in President* (New York: Doubleday, 1977); James David Barber, ed., *Race for the Presidency: The Media and the Nominating Process* (Englewood Cliffs, N.J.: Prentice-Hall, 1978); and Steven J. Brams, *The Presidential Election Game* (New Haven: Yale U. Pr., 1978).   S

2004. Montero Gibert, José Ramón. EL MARCO LEGAL DE LA FINANCIACIÓN PÚBLICA DE LAS ELECCIONES EN LOS ESTADOS UNIDOS [The legal framework for public financing of elections in the United States]. *Rev. Española de la Opinión Pública [Spain] 1977 (48): 173-201.* The two models for government intervention in American electoral campaigns are the "laboratory" (government regulation) and the liberal (private initiative). The 1966 test of public financing of presidential campaigns through income tax contributions was suspended in 1967; in 1971, the 1966 act was modified to include limits on many kinds of expenditures. The 1974 act, a radical departure, delegated funds to primaries and conventions, limited contributions and electoral expenses and set up campaign committees responsible to a Federal Election Commission. The Supreme Court in 1976 found portions unconstitutional, so Congress that year modified the act, and presently favors the two major parties. 77 notes.   J. Tull

2005. Murray, Michael D. WALLACE AND THE MEDIA: THE 1972 FLORIDA PRIMARY. *Southern Speech Communication J. 1975 40(4): 429-440.* Studies the relationship between George C. Wallace's success and his selective use of media in Florida and earlier campaigns.   S

2006. Myers, David S. EDITORIALS AND THE ECONOMY IN THE 1976 PRESIDENTIAL CAMPAIGN. *Journalism Q. 1978 55(4): 755-760.* During the US presidential campaign of 1976, the economy was seen by many observers to be the primary concern. The economy also preoccupied 10 major US newspapers during the campaign: more than one-third of the papers' editorial space was devoted to economic problems and the positions of the two candidates—a higher proportion than for any other topic. 2 tables, 39 notes.   R. P. Sindermann, Jr.

2007. Myers, David S. EDITORIALS AND FOREIGN AFFAIRS IN THE 1972 PRESIDENTIAL CAMPAIGN. *Journalism Q. 1974 51(2): 251-257, 296.* A sampling of newspaper editorials on foreign affairs, predominantly the Vietnam War and foreign policy, shows that Richard Nixon was favored and that foreign affairs issues decided the election.   S

2008. Nakamura, Robert T. BEYOND PURISM AND PROFES-SIONALISM: STYLES OF CONVENTION DELEGATE FOLLOW-ERSHIP. *Am. J. of Pol. Sci. 1980 24(2): 207-232.* Research on presidential nominating conventions has explored the relationship between two competing delegate political styles, purism and professionalism, and their impact on follower and candidate behavior. This article proposes a more elaborate theoretical framework, based on the work of Erving Goffman, that seeks to enrich the study of delegate styles by

distinguishing, as separate determinants of style, the effect of candidates' self-presentations from their followers' acceptances of that presentation. Style is treated as a consequence of individual rational calculations about how supporting a candidate will help the person to achieve his or her goals. Styles are differentiated by the distinctive rationales characteristic of particular delegate goals and decisions. Each style or rationale, in turn, influences the delegate's perception and behavior with respect to other convention decisions: such as attitudes toward the platform and the decision to legitimate (accept) a party nominee who was not the person's first choice. This framework is then applied to interviews conducted at the 1976 Republican and Democratic national conventions. Diagram, biblio.   J

2009. Nakamura, Robert T. IMPRESSIONS OF FORD AND REA-GAN. *Pol. Sci. Q. 1977-78 92(4): 647-654.* Examines the images of Gerald Ford and Ronald Reagan that were held by delegates and how these images contributed to, or inhibited, the losing delegates' adjustment to the convention outcome. One of five articles on "Exploring the 1976 Republican Convention."   J

2010. Natoli, Marie D. VICE PRESIDENTIAL SELECTION: THE POLITICAL CONSIDERATIONS. *Presidential Studies Q. 1980 10(2): 163-170.* Examines the relationship between the choice of a party's vice-presidential candidate and internal party politics. Because of the role of a political party as a unifying group, the vice-presidential candidate must be one to help unify the party. At best, he is to help win the White House, and at worst, he is not to contribute to its loss. The choice of the vice-president is not a free choice by the president. It must be made in recognition of the powers of the different factions within the party, and the different beliefs within the electorate. 35 notes.   D. H. Cline

2011. Nelson, Michael C. PARTISAN BIAS IN THE ELECTORAL COLLEGE. *J. of Pol. 1974 36(4): 1033-1048.* The biases of electoral systems have long been objects of concern to political scientists and political reformers. "Partisan Bias in the Electoral College" develops a method for simulating presidential elections to measure the presence and extent of partisan bias in the electoral college. Such a bias, which Michael C. Nelson found to be based on the different distributions of party support among states, would determine the victor when the major-party presidential candidates divided the national popular vote almost evenly between them, as in 1960. Since 1956 the bias has been consistently pro-Democratic and will probably result in a Democratic victory if the 1976 presidential election is as close as that of 1960.   J

2012. Newman, William J. AMERICAN FOREIGN POLICY AND AMERICAN DEMOCRACY. *Rev. in Am. Hist. 1974 2(4): 581-585.* Discusses politics, democracy, and foreign affairs and outlines the content and notes the analytical limitations of Robert A. Divine's *Foreign Policy and U. S. Presidential Elections* (New York: New Viewpoints, 1974), which examines the relation between foreign policy issues and presidential elections 1940-60.

2013. Nice, David. IDEOLOGICAL STABILITY AND CHANGE AT THE PRESIDENTIAL NOMINATING CONVENTIONS. *J. of Pol. 1980 42(3): 847-853.* The stability of ideological voting patterns at national political conventions may be attributed to public opinion, party activists or organizations, or pressure groups, but not to delegate repetition, as turnover has averaged 64% from 1944 to 1968. Despite the increasing reliance on presidential primaries, various convention reforms, and the presence of ideologically committed amateurs, states consistently liberal or conservative before 1968 have remained so in the decade since. New patterns may be the result of new voters, westward migration, or intraparty struggles. 3 tables, 14 notes.   A. W. Novitsky

2014. Nicholas, H. G. THE 1972 ELECTIONS. *J. of Am. Studies [Great Britain] 1973 7(1): 1-15.* An analysis, heavily emphasizing the presidential election, of the 1972 U.S. elections. In 1972, only 55 percent of the eligible voters cast ballots in the presidential election, indicating a significant distaste for politics among the American electorate. Speculates about probable reasons for the voter apathy. Examines the campaign issues, the tactics employed by the forces of Richard Milhous Nixon and George Stanley McGovern, and the "enigmatic" ethnic vote. Widespread "ticket-splitting" in the 1972 elections sharply differentiates this election from earlier electoral contests.   H. T. Lovin

2015. Nikolayev, Y. ON THE OUTCOME OF THE U.S. PRESIDENTIAL ELECTIONS. *Int. Affairs [USSR] 1977 (1): 92-95.* Analyzes the 1976 presidential elections. When the campaigns started, the institutions of American democracy were in a state of crisis. Voters deeply distrusted Washington and official policy. The chief result was that the candidates of the extreme reactionaries who openly advocated an arms race and opposed better relations with the Soviet Union, such as Jackson, Reagan, and Wallace, suffered a debacle. The election proves that American rulers, having taken a realistic view of the world, seek an accommodation with socialism. Based on American newspaper and magazine articles.
W. R. Hively

2016. Oldendick, Robert and Bennett, Stephen E. THE WALLACE FACTOR: CONSTANCY AND COOPTATION. *Am. Pol. Q. 1978 6(4): 469-484.* "The rise of the [George C.] Wallace movement appears to conform to the tendency . . .for third parties to emerge in the midst of national crises which polarize the electorate on one or more issues, but are espoused by an important figure such as the Alabama governor." Analyzes the characteristics of his adherents from 1968 through 1976, and the sources of stability of support. Many people who were classified as Wallace supporters when Hubert H. Humphrey was the Democratic candidate were not so categorized when Jimmy Carter was used; Carter also tended to draw away more support among southerners and bluecollar workers. The Wallace movement was not typical of third parties, because it was kept alive by the personality of an individual. 3 tables, 4 notes, ref.
E. P. Stickney

2017. Ostlund, Lyman E. INTERPERSONAL COMMUNICATION FOLLOWING MCGOVERN'S EAGLETON DECISION. *Public Opinion Q. 1973/74 37(4): 601-610.* Based on a questionnaire given to pedestrians in midtown Manhattan following Senator McGovern's decision to drop Senator Eagleton from the 1972 Democratic ticket following the disclosure of Eagleton's past mental illness. Shows that interpersonal communication played little role in establishing awareness, but that it did occur extensively in reaction to the event. Nearly half of the voters questioned made some attempt to persuade others on some aspect of the controversy. The most important criteria for judging presidential candidates were found to be issues, images, and party. 6 tables, 17 notes.
E. P. Stickney

2018. Paletz, David L. and Elson, Martha. TELEVISION COVERAGE OF PRESIDENTIAL CONVENTIONS: NOW YOU SEE IT, NOW YOU DON'T. *Pol. Sci. Q. 1976 91(1): 109-131.* Reviews various criticisms of the kind of coverage television gives to presidential nominating conventions. Examining 1972 data, the authors conclude that given the nature of television coverage, the nominees of divisive conventions are disadvantaged later at the polls.
J

2019. Parris, Judith H. REFORM IN PRESIDENTIAL NOMINATING PROCEDURES SINCE 1972. *Policy Studies J. 1974 2(4): 253-257.*

2020. Patterson, Thomas E. THE ROLE OF THE MASS MEDIA IN PRESIDENTIAL CAMPAIGNS: THE LESSONS OF THE 1976 ELECTION. *Social Sci. Res. Council Items 1980 34(2): 25-30.* Referring to a series of seven interviews with a core panel of 1,200 voters, January to November 1976, and a content analysis of three television networks (ABC, CBS, and NBC), four major newspapers (Los Angeles *Times,* Los Angeles *Herald-Examiner,* Erie *News,* and Erie *Times),* and two major newsmagazines *(Time* and *Newsweek),* assesses the nature of messages transmitted through the mass media, and their effect on public opinion during the presidential campaign.

2021. Patterson, Thomas E. and McClure, Robert D. TELEVISION AND THE LESS-INTERESTED VOTER: THE COSTS OF AN INFORMED ELECTORATE. *Ann. of the Am. Acad. of Pol. and Social Sci. 1976 425: 88-97.* In pre-television American politics, electoral research documented that less-interested voters paid little attention to newspaper coverage of presidential campaigns. The result was that many Americans went to the polls possessing little information about the candidates and issues. Relying on evidence from a panel survey conducted during the 1972 presidential election, this article challenges the common belief that the widespread appeal of television news has changed this condition and made the low-interest voter much more informed about

presidential elections. In fact, the evidence clearly shows that televised network evening newscasts contribute almost nothing to the low-interest voter's election information. But the evidence also shows that another channel of television communication does inform the less-interested voter —televised political advertising. Televised advertising not only reaches low-interest voters, but also teaches them useful, accurate, issue information. So for a candidate to get his message across to all the voters, he cannot simply rely on free television news time; he must buy costly television advertising time. The implications for campaign financing are obvious.
J

2022. Patton, John H. A GOVERNMENT AS GOOD AS ITS PEOPLE: JIMMY CARTER AND THE RESTORATION OF TRANSCENDENCE TO POLITICS. *Q. J. of Speech 1977 63(3): 249-257.* Jimmy Carter's language in his quest for the presidency did not function chiefly in "a pragmatic, instrumentally strategic sense," but rather operated symbolically to affirm the possibility of newness transcending present conditions.

2023. Pedersen, Johannes T. POLITICAL INVOLVEMENT AND PARTISAN CHANGE IN PRESIDENTIAL ELECTIONS. *Am. J. of Pol. Sci. 1978 22(1): 18-30.* Using evidence from the S.R.C. surveys about voting behavior in the presidential elections 1952-1972, this article reexamines the question whether there are in fact groups in the electorate, defined in terms of their level of political involvement, which play a particularly important role in facilitating electoral change. The findings presented here indicate that the pattern of opinion shifts among apathetic and concerned voters is not uniform across elections but varies significantly according to the special features of the individual campaign. The tendency for apathetic voters to contribute disproportionately to electoral change must be seen not as a generally valid model but as one of a number of possible patterns, each associated with particular combinations of campaign stimuli. Moreover, contrary to the argument that flexibility in the electoral system depends upon the voters with low levels of political involvement, the evidence analyzed here indicates that when the apathetics do contribute especially to electoral change, they serve in effect as agents of systemic stability.
J

2024. Pei, Mario. THE LANGUAGE OF THE ELECTION AND WATERGATE YEARS. *Modern Age 1973 17(4): 387-398.* Provides a tongue-in-cheek description of the misuse of language and linguistic formations coined by Richard M. Nixon and George S. McGovern in the 1972 presidential election and the Watergate scandal.

2025. Pernacciaro, Samuel J. and VanDerSlik, Jack R. AMBITION THEORY AND PRESIDENTIAL ASPIRATIONS: HOW THE SENATORS VOTE. *J. of Pol. Sci. 1976 4(1): 52-65.* Identifies senators who are presidential aspirants of the 91st Congress (1969-70), and studies their roll-call voting records. Focuses on whether there is more homogeneity in the voting of aspirant senators than in the voting of the nonaspirant. Comparison of the variance of scores of "All Democrats" and nonsouthern Democrats shows that presidential aspirants vote with similarity on policy positions, whereas nonaspirants vote in behalf of parochial interests. Aspirants seek to satisfy or reflect the consensus perceived in the national electorate of their own party. 2 tables, 14 notes, appendix.
T. P. Richardson

2026. Peters, Charles. THE IGNORANT PRESS. *Washington Monthly 1976 8(3): 55-57.* Discusses press coverage of the income tax reform issue in political campaigns in the 1976 presidential election, emphasizing the statements of candidate Jimmy Carter.

2027. Petrocik, John R. LEVELS OF ISSUE VOTING: THE EFFECT OF CANDIDATE-PAIRS IN PRESIDENTIAL ELECTIONS. *Am. Pol. Q. 1979 7(3): 303-327.* In the last five years studies of the American electorate have found some evidence that voters have adopted more of the attributes that mark the informed citizen. Increasing concern with issues and a greater correlation between issues and the vote have cheered observers who were always uneasy with what appeared to be a blind commitment to voting for the party. However, other recent studies have indicated that candidates also play a role in the level of issue voting which characterizes any election. These data support an early argument that candidates are a critical variable for the level of issue voting in any election; and that higher levels of issue voting since 1964 may be a

reflection of different candidates rather than greater ideological concern among voters. This article examines the latter possibility. The article presents a typology of elections based on the nature of the candidate-pair; it documents the similarity of elections with like candidate-pairs but unlike electorates; it attempts a tentative assessment of the impact of candidate pairs on the individual voter level; and it applies the hypothesis about candidate-pairing effects to the 1976 election. 4 fig., 15 notes, biblio.
J

2028. Plekhanov, S. M. DVISHENIE DZHORDZHA UOLLESA [The George Wallace Movement]. *Novaia i Noveishaia Istoriia [USSR] 1974 (1): 164-174.* Examines the development and interaction of American right-wing politics in the 1960's and early 1970's and the role of George C. Wallace in unifying such diverse groups as neo-Nazis and some trade unions into the American Independent Party. Wallace's popularity could not resolve inherent contradictions in his policies and most AIP supporters eventually returned to the Republican camp. Primary and secondary sources; 31 notes.
L. Smith

2029. Podhoretz, Norman. THE NEW AMERICAN MAJORITY. *Commentary 1981 71(1): 19-28.* Analysts could have predicted Ronald Reagan's landslide victory in the 1980 presidential campaign had they been more conscious of the connection with 1972: in 1980, Reagan overcame his ultraconservative image to reconstitute Richard M. Nixon's "new Republican majority"; whereas, like George McGovern in 1972, President Jimmy Carter split the Democrats into new and old liberals, disaffecting the latter, many of whom voted for Reagan, who, ironically, "represented the values of growth and strength which the Democratic party had once believed in."

2030. Pomper, Gerald M. NEW RULES AND NEW GAMES IN PRESIDENTIAL NOMINATIONS. *J. of Pol. 1979 41(3): 784-805.* Rule changes provide an important explanation of the surprising features of the 1976 major party conventions, especially the victory of Jimmy Carter and the strong performance of Ronald Reagan. Primaries or preference polls were involved in the selection of 76.9% of the Democrats and 71.5% of the Republicans. Since 1952, politics has become more open with electronic journalism; federal matching funds financed marginal candidates; and the role of conventions shifted from the site of bargaining among state parties to the formal expression of the preferences of an activist electorate. Delegate apportionment has favored the conservative south and southwest for the Republicans and the industrial northeast for the Democrats. 4 tables, 19 notes.
A. W. Novitsky

2031. Pressman, Jeffrey L. and Sullivan, Denis G. CONVENTIONAL REFORM AND CONVENTIONAL WISDOM: AN EMPIRICAL ASSESSMENT OF DEMOCRATIC PARTY REFORMS. *Pol. Sci. Q. 1974 89(3): 539-562.* "Present empirical data which challenge widely expressed assertions that recent Democratic party convention reforms were crucial in the 1972 nomination of George McGovern, that they radically changed convention behavior, and that they were a major factor in the Democratic defeat of that year."
J

2032. Pressman, Jeffrey L. GROUPS AND GROUP CAUCUSES. *Pol. Sci. Q. 1977-78 92(4): 673-682.* Examines the behavior of delegates as participants in organized social groupings, or what the Democrats have come to call "group caucuses" or "affinity caucuses." One of five articles on "Exploring the 1976 Republican Convention."
J

2033. Prysby, Charles L. ELECTORAL BEHAVIOR IN THE U.S. SOUTH: RECENT AND EMERGING TRENDS. Steed, Robert P.; Moreland, Laurence W.; and Baker, Tod A., ed. *Party Politics in the South* (New York: Praeger, 1980): 101-126. Explores the social and psychological bases of Republican voting behavior. Uses data on presidential and congressional election contests in 1972 and 1976 to ascertain the social sources of Republican voting in terms of race, social class, and geography, and psychological bases. Based on data from the University of Michigan's Survey Research Center/Center for Political Studies; 11 tables, 25 notes.
J. Powell

2034. Purnell, Sandra E. POLITICALLY SPEAKING, DO WOMEN EXIST? *J. of Communication 1978 28(1): 150-155.* Examines motivations for women to feature themselves as central or peripheral to public life, through investigation of the presence of women at important

political speeches, presidential debates, and acceptance speeches of the Democrats and Republicans, 1968-76.

2035. Raeithel, Gert. ZUR FOLKLORE DES GELDES [The folklore of money]. *Frankfurter Hefte [West Germany] 1974 29(1): 6-8.* Discusses the handling and uses of large sums of money in the presidential election campaign of 1972 as they have come to light in the Senate investigations of the Watergate scandal. Based on published Watergate hearings.
J. B. Street

2036. Ragsdale, Lyn. THE FICTION OF CONGRESSIONAL ELECTIONS AS PRESIDENTIAL EVENTS. *Am. Pol. Q. 1980 8(4): 375-398.* Contemporary research suggests that voters often base midterm congressional election choices on their evaluations of the president. In short, midterm congressional elections are seen as referenda on presidential popularity. The referendum notion does not, however, adequately address nonpresidential variables, which may be key determinants of the vote. Employing a longitudinal analysis of House and Senate voting in the 1970, 1974, and 1978 elections, this study considers the relative, simultaneous effects of presidential popularity, congressional incumbency, party identification, and voters' perceptions of the candidates. The results indicate that presidential popularity is a relatively weak predictor of individual congressional voting decisions, when nonpresidential variables are also considered. The impact is slightly greater in 1970 and 1974 than in 1978. There also appears to be a somewhat larger effect for Senate than House voting. Yet in all instances, the nonpresidential variables are the major predictors of the congressional vote.
J

2037. Randolph, Eleanor. THE "WHIP-HIS-ASS" STORY, OR THE GANG THAT COULDN'T LEAK STRAIGHT. *Washington Monthly 1979 11(7): 50-51.* Recounts President Jimmy Carter's awkward attempts to leak to the press his statement that he would beat Senator Edward M. Kennedy in the 1980 Democratic presidential campaign.

2038. Rarick, David L.; Duncan, Mary B.; Lee, David G.; and Porter, Laurinda W. THE CARTER PERSONA: AN EMPIRICAL ANALYSIS OF THE RHETORICAL VISIONS OF CAMPAIGN '76. *Q. J. of Speech 1977 63(3): 258-273.* Rhetorical investigation of how campaign organizations and the media dramatized Jimmy Carter's 1976 political campaign in relation to how voters came to see the political process, the candidate, and the issues.

2039. Real, Michael R. POPULAR CULTURE, MEDIA PROPAGANDA, AND THE 1972 "CREEP" CAMPAIGN. *J. of Popular Culture 1974 8(3): 644-652.* Examines the propaganda campaign waged by the Committee to Re-Elect the President (known to its opponents as "CREEP") to reelect President Nixon in 1972 and how it related to and played upon the popular political mind.

2040. Reiter, Howard L. HOW ACCURATE ARE THOSE PROJECTIONS? *Presidential Studies Q. 1982 12(1): 80-83.* The five major news organizations—the *New York Times, Washington Post, Time, Newsweek,* and *US News and World Report*—have become increasingly effective in predicting the outcome of presidential elections. Five factors seem to cause the errors in an organization's selection: a partisan bias on the part of the journalist, the perception of a bandwagon effect, the exaggeration due to the underdog effect, a last minute surge, and simple random error. Based on election forecasts by major newspapers and magazines; 2 tables.
D. H. Cline

2041. Reiter, Howard L. INTRA-PARTY CLEAVAGES IN THE UNITED STATES TODAY. *Western Pol. Q. 1981 34(2): 287-300.* In the 1960's, as realignment seemed imminent, the dominant ideological group within each major American political party split into two groups, one favoring a realignment around newly salient issues, the other wishing to continue traditional strategies. The coexistence of these groups with the minority ideologues within each party—Democratic conservatives and Republican liberals—presents a tripartite cleavage structure, in which fundamental intraparty conflict is over strategy and agenda much more than over ideological differences, as the McGovern-Jackson and Ford-Reagan nominating battles make clear. This scheme methodologically implies that the most efficient taxonomic scheme must include measures of receptivity to realignment, attitudes toward different agendas, and the role of issues in campaigns.
J/S

2042. Reiter, Howard L. WHY IS TURNOUT DOWN? *Public Opinion Q. 1979 43(3): 297-311.* The monotonic decline in turnout in presidential elections since 1960 is the subject of this analysis of survey data. After some common explanations for this decline were rejected, it was discovered that the decline occurred mainly among low-income and low-education whites. Two explanatory hypotheses were examined, but appropriate data for testing them were unavailable; however, in the 1970's nonvoters were more likely than voters at all income levels to express dissatisfaction with the political system. Nonvoting whites are not always a Democratic group, and their voting behavior is unpredictable over time. Their failure to vote may have an especially significant impact on Democratic party policies, and implies that palliatives like reform of voter registration laws may not have the desired effect. J

2043. Roback, Thomas H. AMATEURS AND PROFESSIONALS: DELEGATES TO THE 1972 REPUBLICAN NATIONAL CONVENTION. *J. of Pol. 1975 37(2): 436-468.* Uses Wilson's seminal conception as a guide to develop meaningful interpretation of activist style among activists in a party of the right. An attitudinal index based on Soule and Clarke's 1968 study of Democratic delegates is used to measure amateurism-professionalism in relation to socio-economic characteristics, political socialization and recruitment experiences, incentives for party activism, liberal-conservative ideology, and attitudes toward the attributes of the 1972 nominee. The dangers of amoral party professionalism are discussed in evaluating the role of Republican activist style at the 1972 Convention. J

2044. Roback, Thomas H. MOTIVATING FOR ACTIVISM AMONG REPUBLICAN NATIONAL CONVENTION DELEGATES: CONTINUITY AND CHANGE 1972-1976. *J. of Pol. 1980 42(1): 181-201.* Delegates to the 1972 and 1976 Republican Party conventions were surveyed to determine the motivation of their political activism. The 1972 convention was a programmed ritual to renominate Richard M. Nixon with as much unanimity and as little conflict as possible, but the 1976 convention saw a party deeply wounded by Watergate and facing a bitter contest for the nomination between Gerald R. Ford and Ronald Reagan. Supporters of Nixon and later Ford were traditional Republicans who considered political careers important; in contrast Reagan supporters were self-recruited ideological converts, often from traditionally Democratic regions, who placed little emphasis on personal political careers. 4 tables, 17 notes. A. W. Novitsky

2045. Roberts, Churchill L. FROM PRIMARY TO THE PRESIDENCY: A PANEL STUDY OF IMAGES AND ISSUES IN THE 1976 ELECTION. *Western J. of Speech Communication 1981 45(1): 60-70.* A study conducted in Escambia County, Florida, during the 1976 presidential primary campaign suggests that liking or disliking a candidate precedes the adoption of the candidate's stand on the issues and that the media, rather than creating attitudes, merely furnishes substance for the feelings of like or dislike.

2046. Roberts, Churchill L. MEDIA USE AND DIFFICULTY OF DECISION IN THE 1976 PRESIDENTIAL CAMPAIGN. *Journalism Q. 1979 56(4): 794-802.* Randomly selected registered voters in Escambia County, Florida, were interviewed at intervals during the 1976 presidential campaign. It was found that those attentive to the mass media's coverage of a campaign are more likely to form distinct attitudes toward the candidates than those initially indifferent, who subsequently have difficulty determining which candidate to support. Voters in the latter category are also more likely to be influenced by brief political communications, such as television ads, than by in-depth coverage and analysis, and are more skeptical of the importance of the election's outcome. 3 tables, 6 graphs, 27 notes. J. S. Coleman

2047. Robinson, John P. THE PRESS AS KING-MAKER: WHAT SURVEYS FROM LAST FIVE CAMPAIGNS SHOW. *Journalism Q. 1974 51(4): 587-594, 606.* Shows that voting behavior in 1956-72 was related to newspaper endorsement of presidential candidates. S

2048. Robinson, Michael J. and Zukin, Cliff. TELEVISION AND THE WALLACE VOTE. *J. of Communication 1976 26(2): 79-83.* Discusses television's ability to influence voting patterns of conservatives in coverage of George C. Wallace in the 1968 presidential election.

2049. Rohlfes, Joachim. DIE AMERIKANISCHEN PRÄSIDENTSCHAFTSWAHLEN 1980: KONSERVATIVER AUFBRUCH ODER ANTI-CARTER-PROTEST? [The American presidential election of 1980: conservative revolution or anti-Carter protest?]. *Geschichte in Wiss. und Unterricht [West Germany] 1981 32(4): 205-222.* Explains the 1980 American presidential election with particular emphasis on the legal framework, the short-term political situation, and the images of the three major candidates. This analysis proceeds from the assumption that "elections are a mirror of the political culture of a country." The conclusions summarize the election results in light of the title question, noting how difficult it is to weigh precisely the anti-Carter votes as compared to the popular support of conservative political and social programs, and suggest the possibility of a new "populism" of the American middle classes. 10 notes. L. D. Wilcox

2050. Rose, Douglas D. CITIZEN USES OF THE FORD-CARTER DEBATES. *J. of Pol. 1979 41(1): 214-221.* The television debates during the 1976 presidential elections were a major effort at political communication. Surveys reveal that much of the learning was neutral or applicable to both candidates, not helpful in choosing between them. Likewise, much learning was unfavorable, at best reinforcing a preference for the other candidate. There was a slight advantage for Jimmy Carter, indicating that Gerald R. Ford's inability to communicate why voters should support him was a factor in his loss. Voting behavior was slightly closer to party identification than were expressed preelection preferences. 5 tables, note. A. W. Novitsky

2051. Rose, Richard. CITIZEN PARTICIPATION IN THE PRESIDENTIAL PROCESS. *Society 1978 16(1): 43-48.* Compares political participation in the United States with that of other Western nations, and analyzes electoral systems; based on data since 1960.

2052. Ross, J. Michael; Vanneman, Reeve D.; and Pettigrew, Thomas F. PATTERNS OF SUPPORT FOR GEORGE WALLACE: IMPLICATIONS FOR RACIAL CHANGE. *J. of Social Issues 1976 32(2): 69-91.* Evidence to support the argument that George Wallace's popularity is a product of rising antiblack sentiment is examined with a focus on the evaluation of Wallace by northern whites across a number of national surveys. Demographic characteristics of supporters are examined and the link between racial attitudes and pro-Wallace tendencies is explored. It is concluded that the role of racial prejudice in Wallace's northern support has been exaggerated, that the Wallace phenomenon is a symptom not a cause of structural changes in the political system, and that the party leaders are overreacting to myths about the extent of Wallace's influence. J

2053. Rothenberg, Irene Fraser. CHICANOS, THE PANAMA CANAL ISSUES AND THE REAGAN CAMPAIGN: REFLECTIONS FROM 1976 AND PROJECTIONS FOR 1980. *J. of Ethnic Studies 1980 7(4): 37-49.* Mexican Americans, like many US ethnic groups before them, are beginning to see themselves as a domestic lobby for policies favoring the homeland, as evidenced by the unanimity and intensity of the Mexican American and Spanish-language press opposition to Ronald Reagan's Panama Canal treaties position in the spring of 1976. Content analysis of all available issues of 12 newspapers published between 1 April and 8 June 1976 showed them to be bitterly against Reagan. Any efforts by the ex-governor to revive the issue against the Carter administration in 1980 is certain to provoke a dramatic Chicano response. This group indeed has a better reason than most minorities to look beyond US boundaries in seeking an ethnic identity, living as it does in "conquered Mexico." Contemporary ethnic press, secondary works; 36 notes. G. J. Bobango

2054. Rubin, Richard L. THE PRESIDENCY IN THE AGE OF TELEVISION. *Pro. of the Acad. of Pol. Sci. 1981 34(2): 138-152.* Focuses on how "campaigning for the presidency in the present media environment affects the functioning of the presidency," determining the impact of major increases in the penetration and velocity of mass communications on electoral institutions and the effect changes in the electoral process have had on executive power. Major developments in mass communications have permanently changed the political environment. Fig., 3 notes. T. P. Richardson

2055. Ryan, Thomas G. FARM PRICES AND THE FARM VOTE IN 1948. *Agric. Hist. 1980 54(3): 387-401.* The election of 1948 is often treated as an aberration from the normal political behavior of farmers, who generally vote against incumbents when farm prices fall. Corn is usually singled out to show that farm prices were falling in 1948. But a broad look at 1948 prices proves that most were rising or stable, putting the farmers' greater than usual support for the Democratic Party (and President Truman) in line with the historical trend. Uses price and election data to focus on the political situation in Iowa. 4 tables, 32 notes.
D. E. Bowers

2056. Sabato, Larry J. THE GOVERNORSHIP AS PATHWAY TO THE PRESIDENCY. *Natl. Civic Rev. 1978 67(11): 512-518.* Governorships are one of the four primary pathways to the Presidency, the others being the Senate, the Cabinet and the Vice-Presidency. The other positions held the edge for many years, but the election of 1976 showed that governors will be amply considered in the near future.   J

2057. St. Angelo, Douglas and Dobson, Douglas. CANDIDATES, ISSUES, AND POLITICAL ESTRANGEMENT: A RESEARCH NOTE ON 1968 POLITICAL ACTIVISTS. *Am. Pol. Q. 1975 3(1): 45-59.* Examines the interchange of political issues and personal candidate choice via an analysis of behaviorally-defined activists in the 1968 presidential political campaigns, focusing on the peculiar nature of George Wallace activists.

2058. Schonberger, Howard B. THE GENERAL AND THE PRESIDENCY: DOUGLAS MAC ARTHUR AND THE ELECTION OF 1948. *Wisconsin Mag. of Hist. 1974 57(3): 201-219.* Relies on recently opened archival sources to argue that General Douglas MacArthur wanted the Republican presidential nomination in 1948, encouraged friends and participated in important strategy decisions concerning that abortive campaign. His chief supporters agreed that for MacArthur to have a chance of being chosen the compromise candidate at a convention deadlocked over Thomas E. Dewey and Robert A. Taft, he would first have to win the primary contest in Wisconsin. In that campaign his fortunes rested with Philip F. La Follette, former three-term governor and colonel on MacArthur's staff during World War II. Twice elected governor on the Progressive ticket, La Follette had alienated many regular Republicans who did not appreciate his belated return to the Republican party a decade later. MacArthur ran second in a three-man race, behind Harold Stassen. From that point on, his chances for the nomination were negligible, although he continued to believe he could win at the national convention. 11 illus., 75 notes.   N. C. Burckel

2059. Schreiber, E. M. EDUCATION AND CHANGE IN AMERICAN OPINIONS ON A WOMAN FOR PRESIDENT. *Public Opinion Q. 1978 42(2): 171-182.* During the early 1970s, the increase in willingness of Americans to vote for a woman for president was directly related to education and contrasts with the inverse relationship between education and increases in willingness to vote for a black for president. The contrast indicates that on some issues, the relationship between education and "enlightened" opinions is variable and characterizes mainly the middle stages of such issues' life histories.   J

2060. Schulman, Mark A. and Pomper, Gerald M. VARIABILITY IN ELECTORAL BEHAVIOR: LONGITUDINAL PERSPECTIVES FROM CAUSAL MODELING. *Am. J. of Pol. Sci. 1975 19(1): 1-18.* "Voting theory has been vulnerable to limitations inherent in synchronic survey data analysis. These limitations include lack of longitudinal perspective, overgeneralization from single, unique elections, and the conjoining of new methodologies with synchronic data. To promote comparative longitudinal research using survey data, causal models of the 1956, 1964, and 1972 presidential elections are developed. Methods used include a seven-variable causal model and cohort analysis. The 1956 model supports hypotheses which emphasize electoral stability. Party identification is the dominant influence on the vote, with issue preferences found to be weakly related to party identification or the vote. The 1964 and 1972 models show considerably greater voter responsiveness to political issues. Actual political and behavioral variability over time, rather than the electorate's 'inherent limitations' or methodological inadequacies, are seen as responsible for previous divergent findings."   J

2061. Shaffer, Stephen D. A MULTIVARIATE EXPLANATION OF DECREASING TURNOUT IN PRESIDENTIAL ELECTIONS, 1960-1976. *Am. J. of Pol. Sci. 1981 25(1): 68-95.* An electorate both younger and older, decreased political efficacy, decreased reliance on newspapers for campaign information, and less intense partisan identifications are the most important causes of decreased turnout outside the South after 1960. Increased political distrust and a hypothesized less politically interested electorate are not important factors. The same factors are present in the South, though other forces have led to increased turnout there.   J/S

2062. Shaffer, Stephen D. VOTING IN FOUR ELECTIVE OFFICES: A COMPARATIVE ANALYSIS. *Am. Pol. Q. 1982 10(1): 5-30.* CPS survey data from 1952-78 are used to compare the effects of three predictors on voting for House, Senate, gubernatorial, and presidential candidates. The findings show that, despite a declining effect party identification is still the most important predictor of voting for all four offices; presidential coattails especially serve as a vote guide for the less informed, and are more important in federal than state elections; incumbency is most important to the moderately aware voter, and only since 1966 has it been most important in House elections.   J

2063. Shapiro, Walter. THE INTRACTABLES. *Washington Monthly 1976 8(3): 12-18.* Discusses labor unions' attitudes toward Democratic Party presidential candidate Jimmy Carter in 1976, emphasizing issues involving the AFL-CIO and public welfare.

2064. Shapiro, Walter. THE MC GOVERN CAMPAIGNERS: THEIR DIRTY LITTLE SECRET. *Washington Monthly 1973 5(8): 49-51.*

2065. Shapiro, Walter. THE TRIUMPH AND THE TRIVIA: INSIDE THE CARTER HEADQUARTERS IN PENNSYLVANIA. *Washington Monthly 1976 8(5-6): 31-39.* Follows the work of Tim Kraft, Jimmy Carter's state coordinator for the Pennsylvania primary, as he organized the 1976 political campaign.

2066. Shaw, Malcolm. REINSTATEMENT: THE AMERICAN PRESIDENTIAL ELECTION OF 1976. *Parliamentary Affairs [Great Britain] 1977 30(3): 241-257.* Examines the November 1976 American elections in the context of the well-known election classification devised by Angus Campbell and associates at the Survey Research Center of the University of Michigan. Campbell's scheme is more reliable when applied to congregational elections, but vulnerable in explaining and predicting presidential ones. Points out factors which may have caused Jimmy Carter and Gerald R. Ford to win their party's primaries, and why Carter won the election. Primary and secondary sources; table, 7 notes.
J. C. Holsinger

2067. Sigal, Leon V. NEWSMEN AND CAMPAIGNERS: ORGANIZATION MEN MAKE THE NEWS. *Pol. Sci. Q. 1978 93(3): 465-470.* Views newsmaking during presidential election campaigns as the product of interaction between two organizations: one composed of newsmen, the other of campaigners. He concludes that the news coverage that results from current organizational routines and journalistic conventions may favor the candidacy of outsiders over that of Washingtonians.
J/S

2068. Sigelman, Lee. PRESIDENTIAL POPULARITY AND PRESIDENTIAL ELECTIONS. *Public Opinion Q. 1979 43(4): 532-534.* Examines presidential popularity by way of the Gallup Poll over seven elections, 1940-76.

2069. Simons, Herbert W., Chesebro, James W., and Orr, C. Jack. A MOVEMENT PERSPECTIVE ON THE 1972 PRESIDENTIAL CAMPAIGN. *Q. J. of Speech 1973 59(2): 168-179.* "Employing the 1972 presidential campaign and 'The Movement' as extended examples, tentative hypotheses are offered identifying the relationships between campaigns and movements. Since McGovern's lopsided defeat also constituted a repudiation by the electorate of 'The Movement' on which his candidacy was built, this analysis examines, retrospectively, the options which were open to 'The Movement' and offers hypotheses about relationships between presidential campaigns and protest movements."   J

2070. Sindler, Allan P. COMPLETING A PRESIDENTIAL TERM WITH A SUCCESSOR OF PRESIDENTIAL CALIBER. *Policy Studies J. 1974 2(4): 284-289.* Considers the qualification required for the vice-presidency.

2071. Sirevåg, Torbjørn. THE DILEMMA OF THE AMERICAN LEFT IN THE COLD WAR YEARS: THE CASE OF HENRY A. WALLACE. *Norwegian Contributions to Am. Studies 1973 4: 399-421.* Henry Agard Wallace (1888-1965) was Vice-President of the United States 1941-45 and Secretary of Commerce 1945-46. His futile efforts to establish an alternative to the administration policies propelled him into a battle that highlights the split in the liberal ranks before the election of 1948. His views and activities after 1948 reflect much of the same disillusionment which led many of his one-time supporters to oppose him during the last presidential campaign of the 1940's. Previous attempts to explain the Wallace phenomenon of 1948 have failed largely because commentators have unduly neglected the events and strategies of preceding years. Wallace "followed the same road as did the main body of American liberalism in the Cold War years, only he did so with much less speed but with greater ultimate force. What slowed down the process in the critical years prior to 1948 was his deep commitment to a liberalism whose revival he believed to be imminent, as well as his personal aspirations." 41 notes.
D. D. Cameron

2072. Sittig, Robert F. PRESIDENTIAL PREFERENCE PRIMARIES: THE EFFECT OF AUTOMATIC ENTRY. *Natl. Civic R. 1975 64(6): 296-298, 306.* The American primary system of nomination for public office seems among the least effective of our electoral institutions. Its chief defect has been termed a shortage of candidates and voters. One way to enhance voter choices and improve the system is automatic entry of candidates in certain presidential primary states.
J

2073. Sittig, Robert F. PRESIDENTIAL PRIMARY REFORM: THE 1948 NEBRASKA "ALL-STAR" PRIMARY. *Nebraska Hist. 1970 69(4): 499-519.* In 1948 steps were taken in the Nebraska primary which led to the establishment of the principle that the public may have a role in the process of listing presidential candidates on the ballot. The results of this first testing proved so valuable that the automatic entry of presidential primary candidates was quickly absorbed into the electoral practices of a considerable number of states and has become a part of the presidential selection system.
R. Lowitt

2074. Smith, Craig R. ADDENDUM TO CONTEMPORARY POLITICAL SPEECH WRITING. *Southern Speech Communication J. 1977 42(2): 191-194.* Examines the structures used by Gerald R. Ford in his political speechwriting organization, 1976.

2075. Smith, Craig R. THE REPUBLICAN KEYNOTE ADDRESS OF 1968: ADAPTIVE RHETORIC FOR THE MULTIPLE AUDIENCE. *Western Speech 1975 39(1): 32-39.* The 1968 Republican Party Convention keynote address by Daniel J. Evans illustrated an over-adaptation of rhetoric that appealed to neither conservative nor liberal public opinion.
S

2076. Solerlund, Walter C. and Wagenberg, Ronald H. A CONTENT ANALYSIS OF EDITORIAL COVERAGE OF THE 1972 ELECTION CAMPAIGNS IN CANADA AND THE UNITED STATES. *Western Pol. Q. 1975 28(1): 85-107.* While the American and Canadian federal systems are similar in some respects, a content analysis of editorials written in selected newspapers in the two countries reveals important differences in attitudes toward them. The bicultural society of Canada was reflected in much greater Canadian concern with the stability of their union. The central position of the American presidency was emphasized by the much larger number of references to Richard Nixon and George McGovern in American papers than mention of Pierre Trudeau and Robert Stanfield in Canadian papers. Unexpectedly, there was little difference between the coverage given the parties in each country despite the Canadian parliamentary system of government. Documentation comes from newspapers; 10 tables, 40 notes.
G. B. McKinney

2077. Solomon, Martha. JIMMY CARTER AND *PLAYBOY*: A SOCIOLINGUISTIC PERSPECTIVE ON STYLE. *Q. J. of Speech 1978 64(2): 173-182.* Jimmy Carter's comments in *Playboy* on lust, adultery, and Lyndon Johnson's deceitfulness offended many people because they reflected a shift from a controlled, consultative rhetorical style to an informal one inappropriate to Carter's public image. Interview and secondary sources; 2 tables, 14 notes.
E. Bailey

2078. Soule, John W. and McGrath, Wilma E. A COMPARATIVE STUDY OF PRESIDENTIAL NOMINATION CONVENTIONS: THE DEMOCRATS 1968 AND 1972. *Am. J. of Pol. Sci. 1975 19(3): 501-517.* This is intended to be a longitudinal study of politics at the 1968 and 1972 National Democratic Conventions. Although the casts of delegates, candidates, and issues were different at the two conventions, more generic political variables were available for observation and analysis at both conventions. Selected for comparison were (1) the socioeconomic representativeness of delegates, (2) the ideological positions of delegates, and (3) the stylistic preferences (amateur-professional) of delegates. Data used are based upon sample surveys at the two conventions. Results indicate noticeable changes in delegate characteristics which were accompanied by predictable shifts in ideological and stylistic commitments of delegates.
J

2079. Spalding, Phinizy. GEORGIA AND THE ELECTION OF JIMMY CARTER. *Georgia Hist. Q. 1977 61(1): 13-22.* Analyzes the November 1976 vote for Jimmy Carter by the counties in Georgia. Includes a table of votes cast for Carter and Ford. Primary sources; table, 8 notes.
G. R. Schroeder

2080. Squires, J. Duane. WE ARE WRITING TO SAY . . .: AN ANALYSIS OF A DELEGATE'S MAIL FROM PRIMARY ELECTION TO CONVENTION TIME. *New England Social Studies Bull. 1957 14(3): 3-7, 25.* The author analyzes his constituency mail from 1952 and 1956 when he was a New Hampshire Delegate-at-Large to the Republican Party convention.

2081. Stacks, John F.; Germond, Jack; and Witcover, Jules. HOW THE DEMOCRATS GAVE US REAGAN: THE TEN KEY MOMENTS OF THE 1980 CAMPAIGN. *Washington Monthly 1982 13(12): 8-20.* Discusses 10 mistakes made by President Jimmy Carter and Senator Edward Kennedy during the 1980 presidential campaign that contributed to President Ronald Reagan's election.

2082. Sterling, Carleton W. THE ELECTORAL COLLEGE BIASES REVEALED: THE CONVENTIONAL WISDOM AND GAME THEORY MODELS NOTWITHSTANDING. *Western Pol. Q. 1978 31(2): 159-177.* The biases affecting voter coalitions under the electoral college system of presidential election are revealed by examining the interaction of the electoral rules and specified voter coalitions. The method of analysis is to project core coalitions to the critical points where they win minimal electoral majorities. Because this method facilitates comprehensive analysis of the biases related to policy-oriented coalitions, it tests claims that the electoral system has important policy consequences. This analysis challenges the "conventional wisdom" that electoral rules have contributed to welfare-oriented and generally liberal presidential policies because of alleged biases toward large competitive states supposedly favorable to metropolitan and ethnic minority voters. The conventional wisdom, supported both by traditional scholars and game theorists, erroneously depends on analyses focusing on limited segments of the complex of biases in the system with disproportional attention to so-called "swing voters" at the expense of underlying policy-oriented coalitions.
J

2083. Stimson, James A. BELIEF SYSTEMS: CONSTRAINT, COMPLEXITY, AND THE 1972 ELECTION. *Am. J. of Pol. Sci. 1975 19(3): 393-417.* There is little agreement about the degree to which the American electorate structures its beliefs about salient aspects of the political scene. Disagreement arises in large part from the use of differing concepts of belief structuring. Some researchers look for evidence of consistency, simplicity, and power in belief and do not find it in large measure. Others look for complexity and multidimensionality and do find it. Both believe they are measuring belief sophistication. Both schools expect to find greatest evidence of sophistication among the educated and well informed and least among the uneducated and uninformed. The 1972 electorate is stratified by education and political information, and operational indicators of both "constraint" and "complexity" notions of belief structure are examined.
J

2084. Stone, Chuck. BLACK POLITICAL POWER IN THE CARTER ERA. *Black Scholar 1977 8(4): 6-15.* Discusses the power which black voters had in the election of Jimmy Carter; hypothesizes about black political power in the future.

2085. Strafford, Peter. AMERICA'S PRESIDENTIAL CONTEST. *World Today [Great Britain] 1976 32(10): 358-365.* Examines the 1976 presidential election touching on Jimmy Carter's rise from relative obscurity and the contest in the Republican Party between Gerald R. Ford and Ronald Reagan.

2086. Sudman, Seymour. THE PRESIDENTS AND THE POLLS. *Public Opinion Q. 1982 46(3): 301-310.* Since Franklin D. Roosevelt, presidents have used public opinion polls to aid them in being elected and as input to policy formulation. Several examples of such effective use are presented. Polls may also be misused by presidents simply to enhance presidential popularity. Such actions are generally ineffective either for increasing presidential popularity or for making wise policy decisions.
J/S

2087. Sullivan, Denis G. PARTY UNITY: APPEARANCE AND REALITY. *Pol. Sci. Q. 1977-78 92(4): 635-645.* Explores the ways in which convention behavior contributed to the legitimation of the convention's nominees. One of five articles on "Exploring the 1976 Republican Convention."
J

2088. Sutton, C. David. APPALACHIA AND THE 1980 ELECTION. *Appalachian J. 1981 8(2): 150-154.* Studies Appalachian voting patterns in the 1980 election and says that Ronald Reagan succeeded because he convinced a majority of voters that the social and economic programs of the New Deal had failed and that conservatism should be given a chance.

2089. Swanson, David L. AND THAT'S THE WAY IT WAS? TELEVISION COVERAGE OF THE 1976 PRESIDENTIAL CAMPAIGN. *Q. J. of Speech 1977 63(3): 239-248.* Focusing on the 1976 presidential campaign between Gerald R. Ford and Jimmy Carter, describes "general features of the frame of reference within which television assigns meaning" to the campaign events it reports.

2090. Swanson, David L. POLITICAL INFORMATION, INFLUENCE, AND JUDGMENT IN THE 1972 PRESIDENTIAL CAMPAIGN. *Q. J. of Speech 1973 59(2): 130-142.* "A pilot study of the effects of communication in the 1972 presidential campaign illustrates the utility of the survey research method as an adjunct to the conventional tools of the critic-analyst of campaign persuasion. Findings describe the bases on which voters evaluated the campaign and responded to sources of political information and influence."
J

2091. Swanson, Linda L. and Swanson, David L. THE AGENDA-SETTING FUNCTION OF THE FIRST FORD-CARTER DEBATE. *Communication Monographs 1978 45(4): 347-353.* A study of 83 undergraduates at the University of Illinois during the 1976 presidential campaign suggested that the televised Jimmy Carter-Gerald R. Ford debates caused a synthesis of the students' personal priorities and the priorities emphasized in the debate.

2092. Swauger, John. REGIONALISM IN THE 1976 PRESIDENTIAL ELECTION. *Geographical Rev. 1980 70(2): 157-166.* Thirteen Voting Regions are delineated from 1976 presidential election returns. Traditional areas of party support remain discernible in eroded form. Political cultures, urban-suburban rifts, and historical political divisions help to explain the regional patterns evident in the election results. Regionalism exerted a marked influence on voting behavior, as statistical measures of interregional heterogeneity and intraregional homogeneity attest.
J

2093. Sweeney, James R. THE GOLDEN SILENCE: THE VIRGINIA DEMOCRATIC PARTY AND THE PRESIDENTIAL ELECTION OF 1948. *Virginia Mag. of Hist. and Biog. 1974 82(3): 351-371.* Disturbed by President Harry S. Truman's stand on civil rights, the Democratic Party leadership in Virginia, headed by Senator Harry Flood Byrd, determined to fight Truman's election in 1948. The Byrd organization's strategy was to keep Truman from winning Virginia's

electoral votes by releasing the state's electors from the obligation to vote for the national party nominee, but Byrd's opposition managed to mount a last minute pro-Truman movement which carried the state for the President. Based on primary and secondary sources; 2 cartoons, 52 notes.
R. F. Oaks

2094. Sweeney, James R. REVOLT IN VIRGINIA: HARRY BYRD AND THE 1952 PRESIDENTIAL ELECTION. *Virginia Mag. of Hist. and Biog. 1978 86(2): 180-195.* When Senator Harry F. Byrd, longtime opponent of the policies of Presidents Roosevelt and Truman, decided to support Republican candidate Dwight D. Eisenhower for the Presidency in 1952, he weakened the Democratic Party in Virginia and set off a political revolt in that state that lasted for a quarter century. Based on newspaper accounts and on primary material in the University of Virginia; 40 notes.
R. F. Oaks

2095. Tan, Alexis S. MASS MEDIA USE, ISSUE KNOWLEDGE AND POLITICAL INVOLVEMENT. *Public Opinion Q. 1980 44(2): 241-248.* Examines the interdependence of "relationships between mass media use and interpersonal discussion, and between issue knowledge and campaign participation during the 1976 presidential election." The new image of the US voter shows that he is interested in and informed about political issues and is active in the political campaign. Based on Heise's analytical model, and on telephone interviews in Lubbock, Texas; 3 fig., 6 notes, ref.
S

2096. Teodori, Massimo. L'ECLISSI DELLA SINISTRA AMERICANA: DISSENSO E OPPOSIZIONE NEGLI ANNI '50 [The eclipse of the American Left: dissent and opposition in the 1950's]. *Belfagor [Italy] 1979 34(6): 677-694.* Explores organized radical movements—parties on the Left, labor organizations, social movements, and electoral campaigns—from 1948, when Henry Wallace's Progressive Party was the last fragment of nationally organized left-wing electoral activity, through the McCarthy era, and concluding with the victory of the liberal John F. Kennedy in 1960.

2097. Themens, Robert K. TELEVISION'S PORTRAYAL OF THE 1976 PRESIDENTIAL DEBATES: AN ANALYSIS OF VISUAL CONTENT. *Communication Monographs 1978 45(4): 362-370.* Discusses the favored pictorial treatment of Jimmy Carter during the 1976 televised presidential debates, and President Gerald R. Ford's behavioral contribution to the existing bias.

2098. Tiernan, Robert O. THE PRESIDENTIAL CAMPAIGN: PUBLIC FINANCING ACCEPTED. *Natl. Civic Rev. 1980 69(3): 133-140.* In December 1979 the Federal Election Commission certified the first candidate eligible to receive federal matching funds for the 1980 presidential primary elections. The event occurred in the normal course of preparations for the election and did not cause a bit of controversy, very different from 1976. In four years a major change has been established in law and practice.
J

2099. Trent, Judith S. PRESIDENTIAL SURFACING: THE RITUALISTIC AND CRUCIAL FIRST ACT. *Communication Monographs 1978 45(4): 281-292.* Explores the tactics of contenders for the 1976 presidential nominations, emphasizing the adaptations required of candidates by the changes in campaign financing law and rules for delegate selection after 1974.

2100. Trilling, Richard J. PARTY IMAGE AND ELECTORAL BEHAVIOR. *Am. Pol. Q. 1975 3(3): 284-314.* Discusses the significance of political party image in electoral behavior in presidential elections 1952-72, including the effect of partisanship and voter identification.

2101. Tufte, Edward R. and Sun, Richard A. ARE THERE BELLWETHER ELECTORAL DISTRICTS? *Public Opinion Q. 1975 39(1): 1-18.* "Using election returns from all US counties for 14 presidential elections, this study investigates the utility of election forecasting based on 'bellwether' or 'barometric' electoral districts."
J

2102. Uhlman, Thomas M. and Kritzer, Herbert M. THE PRESIDENTIAL AMBITION OF DEMOCRATIC SENATORS: ITS TIMING AND IMPACT. *Presidental Studies Q. 1979 9(3): 316-329.* Discusses the presidential ambition of 17 Democratic senators from 1952 to 1976 based primarily on a 1966 analysis of presidential seekers by Joseph Schlesinger.

2103. Vile, M. J. C.   THE DECLINING SIGNIFICANCE OF AMERICAN PRESIDENTIAL ELECTIONS.   *Contemporary Rev. [Great Britain] 1980 236(1373): 281-286.* Traces the weakening of the American presidential election system since 1930 and the distintegration of the political parties, finding that weakness may lead to dangerous attempts to demonstrate strength.

2104. Walker, Jack.   PRESIDENTIAL CAMPAIGNS: REFORMING THE REFORMS.   *Wilson Q. 1981 5(4): 88-101.* Discusses the problems of the US presidential nominating process, focusing on how a rapidly changing society since 1960 and campaign reform laws of the early 1970's have contributed to the problems, and suggests remedies which will not help unless individuals and politicians can compromise and restrain themselves from "single-interest politics" and the "pursuit of group entitlements."

2105. Wallace, H. Lew.   ALBEN BARKLEY AND THE DEMOCRATIC CONVENTION OF 1948.   *Filson Club Hist. Q. 1981 55(3): 231-252.* Narrates the events at the 1948 Democratic convention, briefly discussing Alben Barkley's nomination as vice-president of the United States. Based on contemporary newspapers and published autobiographies; photo, 68 notes.   G. B. McKinney

2106. Wallace, H. Lew.   THE TRUMAN-DEWEY UPSET.   *Am. Hist. Illus. 1976 11(6): 20-30.* Examines the presidential election of 1948 in which Harry S. Truman upset Thomas E. Dewey in an unexpected victory.

2107. Wasserman, Ira M.   A REANALYSIS OF THE WALLACE MOVEMENT.   *J. of Pol. and Military Sociol. 1979 7(2): 243-256.* The standard interpretation of the Wallace movement of the 1960s and the 1970s was that it represented a movement of racists and bigots opposed to blacks and other minority groups. An alternative explanation has been that it was a neo-Populist movement that mobilized the masses against the established order within the federal government and the political parties. This paper challenges both of these positions. Employing Baran and Sweezey's classic Marxian analysis of race relations in Monopoly Capital as a theoretical framework, the paper argues that the movement was a potential counterrevolutionary movement which mobilized mass white support against government civil rights policies which directly threatened their vested interests. Calling forth the 'fury of private interests,' the movement attempted to mobilize these groups against government intervention in social areas. The ultimate failure of the movement was brought about by the end of the racial turmoil in the late 1960s.
                                                                    J

2108. Wayne, Stephen J.; Beil, Cheryl; and Falk, Jay.   PUBLIC PERCEPTIONS ABOUT TED KENNEDY AND THE PRESIDENCY.   *Presidential Studies Q. 1982 12(1): 84-90.* Throughout most of 1979, Edward Kennedy was a two-to-one favorite over Jimmy Carter for the Democratic presidential nomination. By the following March, Carter had come back to build an insurmountable lead. The reason for this can be suggested by the popular imagery surrounding Kennedy. The more people thought about his image, the less they liked him as a possible president. Based on a national sample of voters; 5 tables, 10 notes.
                                                                    D. H. Cline

2109. Weinberg, Martha Wagner.   WRITING THE REPUBLICAN PLATFORM.   *Pol. Sci. Q. 1977-78 92(4): 655-662.* Traces the writing of the Republican platform and explains how that process differed from Democratic party platform writing and reflected the particular ideological and structural composition of the Republican Party. One of five articles on "Exploring the 1976 Republican Convention."   J

2110. Weisberg, Herbert F. and Grofman, Bernard.   CANDIDATE EVALUATIONS AND TURNOUT.   *Am. Pol. Q. 1981 9(2): 197-219.* Using thermometer data and the 1976 voter validation study, we investigate the magnitude of indifference, alienation, and satisfaction effects. Overall, we find candidate-based abstention in 1976 to be minimal, suggesting that nonvoting in American presidential elections must be understood in terms of factors unrelated to parties' choices of nominees.
                                                                    J/S

2111. Welsh, Matthew E.   CIVIL RIGHTS AND THE PRIMARY ELECTION OF 1964 IN INDIANA: THE WALLACE CHALLENGE.   *Indiana Mag. of Hist. 1979 75(1): 1-27.* Matthew E. Welsh, former governor of Indiana, discusses his favorite-son candidacy in the Indiana Democratic primary of 1964. Welsh decided to resist the candidacy of Alabama Governor George C. Wallace, fearing that Wallace's candidacy would resurrect racial hatreds in Indiana and reverse recent improvements in race relations. Welsh's successful campaign staunched sentiment against the Civil Rights Act (US, 1964) and set the stage for Lyndon Johnson's nomination as the Democratic presidential nominee. 28 notes.   J. Moore

2112. Wides, Jeffrey W.   PERCEIVED ECONOMIC COMPETENCY AND THE FORD/CARTER ELECTION.   *Public Opinion Q. 1979 43(4): 535-543.*

2113. Williams, Philip and Wilson, Graham K.   THE 1976 ELECTION AND THE AMERICAN POLITICAL SYSTEM.   *Pol. Studies [Great Britain] 1977 25(2): 182-200.* Analyzes the 1976 elections in the United States with a view to their impact on general theories about American elections. Stresses the Democratic Party's selection of a moderate around whom they could unite, while the Republicans engaged in bitter factional struggle. The popular vote was not as close as in other postwar elections, while regional variations were less pronounced and party more important than had been supposed. The discrepancy between Republican Party performance in presidential elections and at other levels is reviewed, with the conclusion that no theory satisfactorily explains the phenomenon. 13 tables, 22 notes.   R. Howell

2114. Williamson, Richard S.   1980: THE REAGAN CAMPAIGN— HARBINGER OF A REVITALIZED FEDERALISM.   *Publius 1981 11(3-4): 147-151.* Briefly reviews Ronald Reagan's acceptance speech at the Republican National Convention, 17 July 1980, in which he stressed the need to balance the budget and limit the growth of government, to increase national defense, and to provide leadership in the government and in the free world. He also expressed his interest in giving more power to state and local governments. He later presented his proposals to revitalize the federal government. Based on speeches by Ronald Reagan; 11 notes.   G. Smith

2115. Wilson, Graham K. and Williams, Phillip.   MR. NIXON'S TRIUMPH.   *Parliamentary Affairs [Great Britain] 1973 26(2): 186-200.* Analyzes the circumstances which contributed to Richard Milhous Nixon's 1972 presidential election victory. The victory resulted primarily from negative reaction to George McGovern's views rather than from Nixon's popularity. Describes the campaigns of both parties and reflects on America's political future. 5 tables, 5 notes.   J. A. Casada

2116. Wimberley, Ronald C.   CIVIL RELIGION AND THE CHOICE FOR PRESIDENT: NIXON IN '72.   *Social Forces 1980 59(1): 44-61.* This study introduces the concept of civil religion to presidential voting research and tests its explanatory power in comparison to traditionally used variables. Civil religion is a view that the nation is subject to a divine will and that its affairs must be evaluated from that perspective. Social scientists and others have described the presidency as a central role in American civil religion. As anticipated from such literature, civil religious persons in political, religious, and community samples were more likely to favor Nixon. Among correlates with favored candidate, civil religion ranked ahead of most other variables and, in certain samples, ahead of party. Civil religion was typically more predictive than church religious factors, social background characteristics, and most political variables.   J

2117. Wise, Sidney.   CHOOSING THE PRESIDENTIAL CANDIDATES.   *Current Hist. 1974 67(396): 52-57, 88.* The proliferation of party primaries, increased television coverage, and higher campaign costs have altered the presidential nominating process. One of eight articles in this issue on political reform.   S

2118. Witcover, Jules.   IOWA: HOW CARTER WON THE FIRST BATTLE.   *Washington Monthly 1977 9(5/6): 68-75.* Jimmy Carter won one of the early caucus states, Iowa, in 1975.

2119. Wolfe, James S.   EXCLUSION, FUSION, OR DIALOGUE: HOW SHOULD RELIGION AND POLITICS RELATE?   *J. of Church and State 1980 22(1): 89-105.* Discusses religion and its relation to politics by contrasting the place of religion in the John F. Kennedy and Jimmy Carter presidential campaigns (1960 and 1976). Dialogue, Carter's approach is the best relation between religion and politics. 29 notes.
E. E. Eminhizer

2120. Wolfe, James S.   THE RELIGIOUS ISSUE REVISITED: PRESBYTERIAN RESPONSES TO KENNEDY'S PRESIDENTIAL CAMPAIGN.   *J. of Presbyterian Hist. 1979 57(1): 1-18.* Most Protestants, Presbyterians included, were apprehensive over the ambivalence of the Roman Catholic Church's position on church and state at the time of John F. Kennedy's race for the presidency in 1960. Divides Kennedy's campaign into three waves: Spring 1959, Spring 1960, and Fall 1960. In each of these major waves Presbyterian laymen and clergy were active when religious issues surfaced. Many thought that Kennedy's Catholicism might be a symbolic detriment in the presidency, but they tended not to worry about it. Most Presbyterians accorded legitimacy to the religious issue; some even examined the deeper question of how religion and politics ought to interact. The main battle lines were formed over the questions of whether the Roman Catholic Church had the aims and means to subvert America and whether as president Kennedy would be party to that subversion. Led by their general assemblies, Presbyterians tended to rule out mere religious affiliation as a basis for judgment and focused on the bearing of Kennedy's religion on his character, record, and policy positions alone as legitimate. Presbyterian religious weekly accounts; 30 notes.
H. M. Parker, Jr.

2121. Wolfinger, Raymond E.; Rosenstone, Steven J.; and McIntosh, Richard A.   PRESIDENTIAL AND CONGRESSIONAL VOTERS COMPARED.   *Am. Pol. Q. 1981 9(2): 245-256.* To explore why turnout in midterm elections is about 18% lower than turnout in presidential contests, the author uses data from the Current Population Surveys conducted by the Bureau of the Census in November 1972 and November 1974, which contain a large number of respondents. Contrary to the prevailing wisdom, the demographic composition of the midterm electorate (with the exception of age) is virtually the same as the larger presidential year electorate.
J/S

2122. Wright, Gerald C., Jr.   BLACK VOTING TURNOUT AND EDUCATION IN THE 1968 PRESIDENTIAL ELECTION.   *J. of Pol. 1975 37(2): 563-568.* In 1973 Michael Coveyou and David Pfieffer reported that black high school graduates voted less often than blacks with only grammar school educations or a college education (see abstract 11A:2085). The logic of this interpretation is seen here as flawed because no persuasive reasons are given for the absence of the high school group, and because the appearance of a voting pattern during one year does not necessarily overturn the long-held generalization that the more education a person has the greater the likelihood that he will vote. Table, 13 notes.
A. R. Stoesen

2123. Wright, Gerald C., Jr.   CONTEXTUAL MODELS OF ELECTORAL BEHAVIOR: THE SOUTHERN WALLACE VOTE.   *Am. Pol. Sci. Rev. 1977 71(2): 497-508.* Many studies have sought to investigate contextual influences on individual electoral behavior using aggregate data. The shortcomings of this approach are discussed, focusing on the relationship between black concentration and southern white support for George Wallace for president in 1968. Through combining aggregate and individual-level data and comparing a series of models, black concentration is found to increase white support for Wallace. Intraregional differences in the relationship between white support for Wallace and local black concentration are equalized when contextual influences at the state level are brought into the analysis. Black concentration contextual effects are independent of those of urbanization, education, or residence in Wallace's home state of Alabama. Relative primary group support for Wallace and relative issue proximity to Wallace are then shown to be the intervening variables linking contextual characteristics and electoral choice.
J

2124. Wrinkle, Robert D. and Polinard, Jerry L.   POPULISM AND DISSENT: THE WALLACE VOTE IN TEXAS.   *Social Sci. Q. 1973 54(2): 306-320.* "Utilizing aggregate data, [the authors] . . . examine the 1968 electoral support for Wallace in Texas in terms of the concepts of populism and racism . . . . Supports the racial interpretation but suggests that the Wallace support was not of the traditional populist nature."
J

2125. Zoll, Donald Atwell.   THE PROSPECTS FOR A CONSERVATIVE MAJORITY.   *Modern Age 1973 17(4): 368-377.* Discusses the significance of Democrat George S. McGovern's defeat in the 1972 presidential election and questions the argument that Republican Richard M. Nixon's victory signaled a new conservative majority.

2126. Zolotukhin, Iu.   START PREZIDENTSKOI KAMPANII V SSHA [The start of the presidential campaign in the USA].   *Mirovaia Ekonomika i Mezhdunarodnye Otnosheniia [USSR] 1976 (3): 92-98.* Discusses the standing of the Republican and Democratic Parties in the 1976 presidential campaign and the political, social, and economic problems facing the candidates.

2127. —.   THE AMERICAN SCENE: THE NATIONAL ELECTIONS OF 1976 AND THE ARMENIAN AMERICANS.   *Armenian Rev. 1976-77 29(4): 413-419.* Surveys the efforts made by the Armenian National Committee of America, the Armenian press, and other representative bodies, to seek commitments from Congressional and other candidates on questions of vital interest to Armenian Americans, preparatory to endorsements of favorable candidates. These candidates were largely successful at the polls. Quotations from editorials and relevant letters carry on the theme. The same approach to the presidential candidates brought responses before and after election from Jimmy Carter which are printed here.
R. V. Ritter

2128. —.   [CAMPAIGN RESOURCE ALLOCATIONS].
Brams, Steven J. and Davis, Morton D.   THE 3/2'S RULE IN PRESIDENTIAL CAMPAIGNING.   *Am. Pol. Sci. Rev. 1974 68(1): 113-134.* The purpose of this article is to assess the effect of the winner-take-all feature of the Electoral College on the allocation of resources by candidates to the states in a presidential campaign. Conceptualizing the campaign as a two-person zero-sum infinite game, it is found that the main effect of this feature is to induce candidates to allocate campaign resources roughly in proportion to the 3/2's power of the electoral votes of each state, which creates a peculiar bias that makes voters living in the largest states as much as three times as attractive campaign targets as voters living in the smallest states. Empirically, it is shown that the 3/2's rule explains quite well the time allocations of presidential and vice-presidential candidates in the 1960, 1964, 1968, and 1972 campaigns; for presidential campaigns in 1976 and 1980, optimal allocations are indicated for all fifty states and the District of Columbia. A comparison with optimal allocations under a system of direct popular-vote election of the president reveals that such a system would be less susceptible to manipulative strategies than the Electoral College as well as being compatible with the egalitarian principle of "one man, one vote."

Colantoni, Claude S.; Levesque, Terrence J.; and Ordeshook, Peter C.   CAMPAIGN RESOURCE ALLOCATIONS UNDER THE ELECTORAL COLLEGE.   *Am. Pol. Sci. Rev. 1975 69(1): 141-154.* This essay addresses the question: Why does the Electoral College bias campaign resource allocations in favor of large states? Using data on candidate trips as well as estimates of the time candidates spend in states, we conclude, first, that much of the apparent empirical support for Brams and Davis's 3/2's hypothesis is an artifact of the candidates' consideration of each state's relative competitiveness and the statistical relationship between size and competitiveness. There is some evidence, however, for a residual bias. That is, after controlling for each state's competitiveness, campaign allocations still appear to favor larger states—at least for the two competitive elections of 1960 and 1968. We attribute that bias to corner solutions to the candidate's maximization problem and to the effects of sequential campaign planning. Thus, while we do not dispute the existence of bias over the course of the entire campaign, the data are consistent with a modified (albeit complex) proportional rule that each candidate applies sequentially during the campaign. Our conclusion is that the unit rule feature of the Electoral College, rather than weighted voting, is the predominant cause of bias.

Brams, Steven J. and Davis, Morton D. COMMENT ON "CAM-PAIGN RESOURCE ALLOCATIONS UNDER THE ELEC-TORAL COLLEGE." *Am. Pol. Sci. Rev. 1975 69(1): 155-156.*
Colantoni, Claude S.; Levesque, Terrence J.; and Ordeshook, Peter C. REJOINDER TO "COMMENT" BY S. J. BRAMS AND M. D. DAVIS. *Am. Pol. Sci. Rev. 1975 69(1): 157-161.* J

2129. —. [DEMOCRATIC DELEGATE SELECTION REFORM]. *Am. Pol. Sci. Rev. 1974 68(1): 27-44.*
Cavala, William. CHANGING THE RULES CHANGES THE GAME: PARTY REFORM AND THE 1972 CALIFORNIA DELEGATION TO THE DEMOCRATIC NATIONAL CON-VENTION, *pp. 27-42.* During 1968-72 the Democratic Party developed new rules governing the selection of delegates to their National Convention. In California the result was a delegation dominated by women, youth, and minorities, but with few party leaders. This produced a change in the strategic environment and hindered George McGovern's efforts to wage an effective electoral campaign. To avoid another electoral loss in 1976, the rules are being revised "to drop the demographic quotas and include more party notables" in delegate selection. 55 notes.
Ranney, Austin. COMMENT, *pp. 43-44.* T. Simmerman

2130. —. [EFFECTS OF ECONOMIC POLICY ON VOTES]. *J. of Law & Econ. 1975 18(3): 781-805.*
Meltzer, Allan H. and Vellrath, Marc. THE EFFECTS OF ECO-NOMIC POLICIES ON VOTES FOR THE PRESIDENCY: SOME EVIDENCE FROM RECENT ELECTIONS, *pp. 781-798.* Estimates the effects of some measures of aggregate economic conditions, tax, and income transfers on the popular votes for President in the elections of 1960, 1964, 1968, and 1972.
Kramer, Gerald H. COMMENT, *pp. 799-780.*
Stigler, George J. COMMENT, *pp. 801-802.*
Meltzer, Allan H. and Vellrath, Marc. REPLY, *pp. 803-805.*

2131. —. JIMMY CARTER: KENNEDY OR KEFAUVER? *Washington Monthly 1976 7(12): 17-21.* Reports on the 1976 political campaign work of Jimmy Carter for the Democratic Party nomination in New Hampshire, Iowa, Florida, and Oregon.

2132. —. [PARTICIPATION IN PRESIDENTIAL ELECTIONS]. *J. of Law & Econ. 1975 18(3): 695-744.*
Ashenfelter, Orley and Kelley, Stanley, Jr. DETERMINANTS OF PARTICIPATION IN PRESIDENTIAL ELECTIONS, *pp. 695-733.* Extensive analysis of the determinants of the probability that individuals will vote in Presidential elections. 7 tables, 2 appendixes.
Wittman, Donald. COMMENT, *pp. 735-741.* Proposes an economic theory of voting behavior.
Stigler, George J. COMMENT, *pp. 743-744.*

2133. —. [REGISTRATION LAWS AND VOTER TURNOUT]. *Am. Pol. Sci. Rev. 1978 72(4): 1360-1362.*
O'Rourke, Timothy G. TRIVIAL SHIFTS IN PRESIDENTIAL ELECTIONS, *pp. 1360-1361.* The article by Steven J. Rosenstone and Raymond E. Wolfinger, "The Effect of Registration Laws on Voter Turnout" gives a good analysis of the political consequences of uniformly permissive registration procedures but has understated the consequences which national election-day registration might have when a presidential election is close.
Rosenstone, Steven J. and Wolfinger, Raymond E. [REPLY], *pp. 1361-1362.* As an abstract possibility a shift of 3/10% could decide an election. However it is most improbable. "Three-tenths of a percentage point is statistically equivalent to zero." R. V. Ritter

2134. —. [VOTING BEHAVIOR AND THE 1972 ELECTION]. *Am. Pol. Sci. Rev. 1976 70(3): 753-849.*
Miller, Arthur H.; Miller, Warren E.; Raine, Alden S.; and Brown, Thad A. A MAJORITY PARTY IN DISARRAY: POLICY POLAR-IZATION IN THE 1972 ELECTION, *pp. 753-778.* Theories of voting behavior attribute varying importance to candidates, parties, and issues in presidential elections. The voting public was better informed on issues in 1972 than ever before, and the Democratic

Party's loss "was the result of the ideological polarization within the Democratic ranks." Based on a study of the Center for Political Studies; 4 tables, 41 notes.
Popkin, Samuel; Gorman, John W.; Phillips, Charles; and Smith, Jeffrey. COMMENT: WHAT HAVE YOU DONE FOR ME LATELY? TOWARD AN INVESTMENT THEORY OF VOTING, *pp. 779-805.* Offers an economic approach to voting behavior in which a voter uses his vote as an investment and is concerned "with what the candidate can be expected to 'deliver' and, thus, the voter looks for signs of competence." In 1972 voters perceived incompetence in the George McGovern campaign's handling of the Thomas Eagleton affair and its approaches to the Vietnam and welfare problems, and withdrew their support. 9 tables, 69 notes.
Steeper, Frederick T. and Teeter, Robert M. COMMENT ON "A MAJORITY PARTY IN DISARRAY," *pp. 806-813.* To separate issues from candidate preferences is often an oversimplification. Voters generally select a candidate based on the candidate's projected ability to solve a problem. 3 tables, note.
RePass, David E. COMMENT: POLITICAL METHODOLOGIES IN DISARRAY: SOME ALTERNATIVE INTERPRETA-TIONS OF THE 1972 ELECTION, *pp. 814-831.* Candidate identification has been the leading factor in voting behavior in the 1952-72 presidential elections. Problems in the use of new methodology and research methods for measuring candidate proximity and ideology led the Center for Political Studies to identify ideology as the key voting factor in the 1972 election. 3 tables, 43 notes.
Miller, Arthur and Miller, Warren E. IDEOLOGY IN THE 1972 ELECTION: MYTH OR REALITY—A REJOINDER, *pp. 832-849.* Challenges the above comments and reaffirms that "issue awareness and policy preferences interacted with the clearly articulated candidate differences to produce a vote heavily laden with ideology and policy concerns . . . 1972 was an ideological election." 4 tables, 53 notes. T. Simmerman

2135. —. [WILLIAMS' AND WILSON'S ANALYSIS OF THE 1976 U.S. ELECTION]. *Pol. Studies [Great Britain] 1978 26(2): 249-253.*
Goodrich, Peter Spang. A COMMENT ON WILLIAMS' AND WIL-SON'S ANALYSIS OF THE 1976 U.S. ELECTION, *pp. 249-253.* The wide gap between presidential and congressional elections in 1976 commented on by Williams and Wilson in their earlier article (see abstract 16A:4569) possibly may be explained in "a new way of dichotomizing U.S. regional groupings." 3 tables, 13 notes.
Williams, Phillip and Wilson, Graham K. A REPLY TO GOODRICH, *p. 253.* Expresses general agreement with the comment but objects to the attribution of views not held. R. Howell

Presidential Administrations: World Leadership

General

2136. Ashbrook, John M. MORE SERIOUS THAN WATERGATE. *East Europe 1974 23(2): 21-25.* Discusses the 1973 House of Representatives' investigation of Helmut Sonnenfeldt's nomination as counselor of the State Department, and the denial to Congress (by executive privilege) of access to needed information, in an attempt to cover up possible intelligence transmittals by Sonnenfeldt since 1958.

2137. Baker, James T. LYNDON JOHNSON: AMERICA'S OEDIPUS? *Southern Humanities R. 1974 8(2): 127-138.* Discusses Lyndon Baines Johnson's place in history and offers an alternative interpretation to that of Eric Goldman's *The Tragedy of Lyndon Johnson* (New York: Knopf, 1969). S

2138. Balfour, Nancy. PRESIDENT NIXON'S SECOND TERM. *World Today [Great Britain] 1973 29(3): 98-107.* "Vietnam is out of the way at last, but America faces pressing international, trading, and monetary, as well as domestic, problems. While decision-making is increasingly concentrated in the White House, the confrontation with Congress will make 1973 a difficult year for the President." J

2139. Barber, James David. AN AMERICAN REDEMPTION: THE PRESIDENTIAL CHARACTER FROM NIXON TO FORD TO CARTER. *Washington Monthly 1977 9(2): 6-38.* Explores the characters of Richard M. Nixon, Gerald R. Ford, and Jimmy Carter in terms of personality and how each fits into the presidential role; excerpts from an upcoming book, *The Presidential Character.*

2140. Barber, James David. THE NIXON BRUSH WITH TYRANNY. *Pol. Sci. Q. 1977-78 92(4): 581-605.* James David Barber reviews his typologies of presidential character and outlines the predictions he published in early, pre-Watergate, 1972 of Richard Nixon's vulnerability to political rigidification if challenged in certain ways. He then describes how Nixon's response to the challenges of Watergate confirmed the earlier predictions.　　　　J

2141. Baroody, William J., Jr. GERALD FORD AND THE NEW POLITICS. *Presidential Studies Q. 1977 7(2-3): 91-95.* Following the Nixon Presidency, the United States faced a crisis of executive authority, legitimacy, and function. Gerald R. Ford's new politics sought to restore confidence in presidential leadership and in the federal government. Ford sought to restore balance between the government and the people. Future leadership requires that government not try to deal with all problems. Instead, the President must create conditions in which individuals can serve with equal dignity in either public or private sectors.
　　　　R. D. Hurt

2142. Baudhuin, E. Scott. FROM CAMPAIGN TO WATERGATE: NIXON'S COMMUNICATION IMAGE. *Western Speech 1974 38(3): 182-189.*

2143. Beck, Kent M. THE KENNEDY IMAGE: POLITICS, CAMELOT, AND VIETNAM. *Wisconsin Mag. of Hist. 1974 58(1): 45-55.* The "*way* that Americans have honored and remembered the thirty-fifth President can tell us much about John F. Kennedy and convey even more about the American experience before and since his passing." He traces the changing attitude of political analysts, historians, and journalists toward the Kennedy administration over the past ten years. Immediate reaction to the slain President's policies was favorable when court histories and first-hand accounts published by his entourage held center stage. As the Vietnam War escalated, revisionists began to see Kennedy's foreign policy as one of the most strikingly negative aspects of his administration. More recently, however, a counter-reaction has set in, emphasizing a more balanced picture of his administration. 5 illus., 52 notes.
　　　　N. C. Burckel

2144. Benoit, William L. RICHARD M. NIXON'S RHETORICAL STRATEGIES IN HIS PUBLIC STATEMENTS ON WATERGATE. *Southern Speech Communication J. 1982 47(2): 192-211.* Identifies nine rhetorical strategies in Nixon's public statements on Watergate in 1973, and their development over time through four general phases.

2145. Benze, James G., Jr. PRESIDENTIAL MANAGEMENT: THE IMPORTANCE OF PRESIDENTIAL SKILLS. *Presidential Studies Q. 1981 11(4): 470-478.* A heavy emphasis on management techniques tends to diminish presidential power. This power is defined as the ability to pursue and implement one's own policies regardless of the positions taken by other policy elites. The best way to do this is to combine strong leadership skills with management techniques. The Carter administration was never able to demonstrate these leadership skills, and thus was unable to gain legitimacy of its programs. 6 tables; 24 notes.　　　　D. H. Cline

2146. Berman, William C. THE GENERAL AS PRESIDENT. *R. in Am. Hist. 1975 3(4): 503-506.* Charles C. Alexander's *Holding the Line: The Eisenhower Era, 1952-1961* (Bloomington: Indiana U. Pr., 1975) favorably assesses Dwight D. Eisenhower's presidency, particularly in foreign policy, in the setting of the Cold War.

2147. Bormann, Ernest G. A FANTASY THEME ANALYSIS OF THE TELEVISION COVERAGE OF THE HOSTAGE RELEASE AND THE REAGAN INAUGURAL. *Q. J. of Speech 1982 68(2): 133-145.* Explores the usefulness of fantasy theme analysis for the study of live coverage of breaking news events by making a critical analysis of the televised reports of the hostage release and the Reagan inaugural address of 20 January 1981. Reveals similarities between rhetorical fantasies and televised news by comparing the subliminal impact of the enactment of the transfer of power and end of the crisis by the coverage of the inaugural and hostage release to the way Reagan's speechwriters used the fantasy type of restoration to meet the needs of a conservative political movement in the 1980's.　　　　J/S

2148. Bosha, Francis J. WILLIAM FAULKNER AND THE EISENHOWER ADMINISTRATION. *J. of Mississippi Hist. 1980 42(1): 49-54.* After receiving the Nobel Prize in Literature for 1949, William Faulkner was asked by the State Department to travel abroad as a goodwill ambassador on four occasions between 1954 and 1961. His national service included a stateside phase: in June 1956, President Dwight D. Eisenhower requested that Faulkner serve as chairman of the Writers' Group of the People-to-People Program. The State Department also asked Faulkner to address the Seventh National Conference of the US National Commission for UNESCO in Denver, Colorado, on 2 October 1959. Describes the effort of Maxwell M. Rabb, Eisenhower's executive assistant campaign manager and future associate counsel to the president, to bring the southern writer's name to the attention of the Eisenhower administration. Discusses the opposition of minority groups to the appointment of Faulkner to work with a Civil Rights Commission and the People-to-People Program.　　　　M. S. Legan

2149. Bouzas, Roberto and Maira, Luis. ALGUNAS CLAVES ECONÓMICAS Y POLÍTICAS PARA EL EXAMEN DE LA ADMINSTRACIÓN REAGAN [Some economic and political keys for an examination of the Reagan administration]. *Investigación Econ. [Mexico] 1981 40(156): 307-337.* To understand the essentials of the Reagan administration and, therefore, its state of opposition to the interests of the developing nations, three things are necessary: to understand the cause of the conservative turn in US politics; to decipher the ideological rhetoric which enabled the Republican Party to defeat the liberal faction in control since the postwar period; and to examine the rationale behind Reagan's political plans, their limits, and the conflicts they may cause. Presented at the 2d Congress of the Association of Third World Economists, Havana 1981; 2 charts, 32 notes.　　　　J. V. Coutinho

2150. Brown, Steven R. RICHARD NIXON AND THE PUBLIC CONSCIENCE: THE STRUGGLE FOR AUTHENTICITY. *J. of Psychohistory 1978 6(1): 93-111.* The public obsession with Richard M. Nixon, particularly with perceived inauthenticity on his part, suggests psychological projection whereby character flaws that cannot be admitted are found to be particularly execrable in another person, and that person is punished for the flaws. A test conducted with students provided support for the thesis that Nixon was a recipient for a projection of inauthenticity. Primary and secondary sources, including the David Frost-Richard Nixon interviews; 2 fig., 25 notes.　　　　R. E. Butchart

2151. Brummett, Barry. PRESIDENTIAL SUBSTANCE: THE ADDRESS OF AUGUST 15, 1973. *Western Speech 1975 39(4): 249-259.* Applies Kenneth Burke's concepts of identification and substance to the 15 August 1973 address of Richard M. Nixon.

2152. Brummett, Barry. TOWARDS A THEORY OF SILENCE AS A POLITICAL STRATEGY. *Q. J. of Speech 1980 66(3): 289-303.* This essay outlines a theory of strategic, political silence. That sort of silence directs public attribution of predictable meanings towards political leaders who unexpectedly refuse to speak in public. Those meanings are mystery, uncertainty, passivity, and relinquishment. The theory is illustrated in a criticism of President Carter's silence from 5 July to 15 July 1979.　　　　J

2153. Bundy, McGeorge. THE HISTORY-MAKER. *Massachusetts Hist. Soc. Pro. 1978 90: 75-88.* A recollection of President John F. Kennedy and the political life of the early 1960's, and an assessment of the way the events and issues of that period—the Cuban missile crisis, the nuclear test ban treaty, the Berlin situation, the Vietnam problem, and others—were viewed then and later by three groups of people: the personalities involved, journalists, and historians. Based on newspaper accounts in *The New York Times,* secondary sources, and the author's recollections; note.　　　　G. W. R. Ward

2154. Bundy, McGeorge. VIETNAM, WATERGATE AND PRESIDENTIAL POWERS. *Foreign Affairs 1979-80 58(2): 397-407.* Review article of Henry Kissinger's *White House Years,* which incorrectly blamed the Vietnam War debacle on the effects of the Watergate Scandal on executive power. The defeat was due to American war weariness, the administration's misunderstanding of the Constitution, and the weakness of South Vietnamese society.   S

2155. Caraley, Demetrios and Greissman, Edythe, eds. SEPARATION OF POWERS AND EXECUTIVE PRIVILEGE: THE WATERGATE BRIEFS. *Pol. Sci. Q. 1973 88(4): 582-654.* "The editors reprint the original legal briefs filed in the historic lawsuit to obtain for grand jury use the tape recordings of presidential conversations concerning the Watergate break-in. While President Nixon's attorneys argue in their brief that if disclosure of the tapes can be compelled by the courts 'the damage to the institution of the Presidency will be severe and irreparable,' the brief of the Special Watergate Prosecutor contends that 'even the highest executive officials are subject to the rule of law' and 'there is no exception for the President from the guiding principle that the public, in pursuit of justice, has a right to every man's evidence.' "   J

2156. Chapel, Gage William. SPEECHWRITING IN THE NIXON ADMINISTRATION. *J. of Communication 1976 26(2): 65-72.* Presents an interview with Nixon administration speechwriter Aram Bakshian dealing with policy statements and editorial supervision in political speechwriting for the White House 1972-75.

2157. Cherne, Leo and Drummond, Roscoe. THE CHALLENGE OF WATERGATE: TWO OFFICERS OF FREEDOM HOUSE DISCUSS THE REINFORCING OF CONSTITUTIONAL GOVERNMENT. *Freedom At Issue 1973 (20): 2-5.* President Nixon must eliminate the scandal in his administration or suffer paralysis of his foreign policy.   S

2158. Chester, Edward W. SHADOW OR SUBSTANCE? CRITIQUING REAGAN'S INAUGURAL ADDRESS. *Presidential Studies Q. 1981 11(2): 172-176.* A comparison of Ronald Reagan's major speeches since 1967 shows a basic consistency in his stand on certain issues. The style of delivery is important, and Reagan has skill in successfully communicating his programs to the general public and creating a climate of opinion that will force Congress to enact the majority of his proposals into law. Primary sources; 22 notes.   A. Drysdale

2159. Chomsky, Noam. THE CARTER ADMINISTRATION: MYTH AND REALITY. *Australian Q. [Australia] 1978 50(1): 8-36.* Offers an assessment of the Carter Administration in the United States, comparing the current administration to administrations since World War II.

2160. Coaldrake, Peter. RONALD REAGAN AND "CABINET GOVERNMENT": HOW FAR A COLLEGIAL APPROACH? *Politics [Australia] 1981 16(2): 276-283.* Examines the contradictions inherent in the concept of a collegial presidency that have thwarted attempts by recent presidents to pursue a cabinet approach to government, focusing on the Carter and Reagan administrations; discusses the role of the White House staff in policymaking under Ronald Reagan.

2161. Davis, Eric L. LEGISLATIVE LIAISON IN THE CARTER ADMINISTRATION. *Pol. Sci. Q. 1979 94(2): 287-302.* Examines the behavior of the White House and departmental legislative liaison staffs during the first years of the Carter administration and attempts to account for its relative lack of legislative success.   J

2162. Davis, Eric L. LEGISLATIVE REFORM AND THE DECLINE OF PRESIDENTIAL INFLUENCE ON CAPITOL HILL. *British J. of Pol. Sci. [Great Britain] 1979 9(4): 465-479.* Discusses the influence of congressional changes on the US President's inability to implement his legislative proposals in 1977-78; stresses the significance of power alterations in the House, the rebirth of a conservative coalition, and the desire of Congress to institute policy independent of the President.

2163. Degler, Carl N. JOHNSON AND KENNEDY: THE PUBLIC VIEW. *Rev. in Am. Hist. 1977 5(1): 130-136.* Review article prompted by Doris Kearns's *Lyndon Johnson and the American Dream* (New

York: Harper & Row, 1976) and Bruce Miroff's *Pragmatic Illusions: The Presidential Politics of John F. Kennedy* (New York: David McKay, 1976).

2164. DeMause, Lloyd. HISTORICAL GROUP FANTASIES. *J. of Psychohistory 1979 7(1): 1-70.* Illustrates historical group fantasies related to the presidencies of Eisenhower, Kennedy, Nixon, and Carter, analyzing them in terms of theoretical, psychoanalytic constructs. Individual experience, translated into shared emotional experience and behavior, explains the cyclical nature of historical events and violent historical acts. Primary sources; 4 illus., 6 charts, 116 notes.
                                                M. R. Strausbaugh

2165. deMause, Lloyd, ed. JIMMY CARTER AND AMERICAN FANTASY. *J. of Psychohistory 1977 5(2): 151-173.* President Jimmy Carter's personality and "the powerful emotional demands of American fantasy" will very likely lead us into a new war by 1979. The national "group-fantasy" is rooted in a birth trauma and repeats its cycle roughly every four years, culminating in war or a war-like catharsis, depending upon the presidential personality. When applied to contemporary conditions and the Carter presidency, war appears imminent. Based on primary and secondary sources; 30 notes, illus., chart.   R. E. Butchart

2166. DeSantis, Vincent P. EISENHOWER REVISIONISM. *R. of Pol. 1976 38(2): 190-207.* Because Dwight D. Eisenhower adhered to middle of the road policies and because he largely accepted the social welfare policies of the previous democratic administrations, he satisfied neither liberals nor conservatives. Early assessments of his administration were largely negative. Recent revisionist studies, including some by his previous detractors, have been very positive and complimentary. In the future, the Eisenhower years will be regarded favorably, since Eisenhower will always be "associated with prosperity, abundance and peace, no mean accomplishments for a military leader." 44 notes.   L. E. Ziewacz

2167. Destler, I. M. THE NIXON SYSTEM: A FURTHER LOOK. *Foreign Service J. 1974 51(2): 9-14, 28-29.* The penchant for secretiveness (1972-73) in bureaucratic, domestic, and international politics shared by Richard M. Nixon and Henry A. Kissinger has "worked against trust of underlings and the conduct of serious dialogue in the political arena."
                                                                        S

2168. Divine, Robert A. ASSESSING LYNDON JOHNSON. *Wilson Q. 1982 6(3): 142-150.* Reviews studies on Lyndon B. Johnson, consisting of earlier books that are mostly pro-Johnson, and a later group that are more critical.

2169. Divine, Robert A. ONLY YESTERDAY? *R. in Am. Hist. 1975 3(4): 507-510.* Jim F. Heath's *Decade of Disillusionment: The Kennedy-Johnson Years* (Bloomington: Indiana U. Pr., 1975) provides a balanced account of the personalities, foreign policy, and social reform of John F. Kennedy and Lyndon B. Johnson.

2170. Drischler, Alvin Paul. GENERAL-PURPOSE FORCES IN THE NIXON BUDGETS. *Survival [Great Britain] 1973 15(3): 119-123.* Discusses procurement funding provisions for conventional forces in the defense budget of the Nixon administration, 1969-73.

2171. Ebel, Henry. BUT WHAT KIND OF BABY IS JIMMY CARTER? *J. of Psychohistory 1977 5(2): 259-269.* Political leaders serve as psychotherapeutic objects for the nation. They symbolize infancy for the nation, and project denied insights into the collective unconscious. President Jimmy Carter, specifically, reflects the insanity of contemporary society.   R. E. Butchart

2172. Eckstein, George Günther. FAZIT AUS WATERGATE [Results of Watergate]. *Frankfurter Hefte [West Germany] 1975 30(5): 21-29.* The crisis of Watergate, which dominated public affairs in the United States during 1973-74, and which continues to capture attention today, has had good and bad results; a threat to free institutions has been removed and the system shown to work, but American foreign policy has been partially paralyzed.

2173. Eisenhower, Dwight D. MR. EISENHOWER'S REVIEW OF HIS PRESIDENCY. *Current Notes on Int. Affairs [Australia] 1961*

32(1-2): 40-51. Annual address by President Eisenhower on the state of the Union; primarily a review of his eight years as President, given on 12 January 1961.

2174. Ekirch, Arthur A., Jr.   EISENHOWER AND KENNEDY: THE RHETORIC AND THE REALITY.   *Midwest Q. 1976 17(3): 279-290.* John F. Kennedy's tremendous popularity has made it difficult to do a critical assessment of his administration since his assassination. Rhetorically, Kennedy promised much during the 1960 campaign, but when viewed in retrospect he accomplished comparatively little. The domestic social programs he promised remained unpassed until the Johnson administration, and his foreign policy exhibited more reckless courage than objective intelligence. A reassessment of Dwight D. Eisenhower's administration indicates that he gave the country a period of stability with little inflation. He ended the Korean War, did not start any new wars, and kept military spending down. Eisenhower did more than he had promised, while Kennedy, by trying to transcend the political institutions of the country, endangered them. Based on secondary sources.   S. J. Quinlan

2175. Erokhin, A. V.   RUBEZHI KLANA KENNEDI [Confines of the Kennedy clan].   *Novaia i Noveishaia Istoriia [USSR] 1973 (4): 127-145.* Investigates the philosophy of the Kennedy family. Much of the vast quantity of material which has been published is unhesitatingly approving; a small proportion reserves its judgment in academic neutrality, and a smaller portion is clearly hostile. American historiography pays too much attention to individuals and too little to developing historical processes such as the crisis of capitalism. In addition there are contradictions in works on the Kennedys, due to the contradictory nature of their world view. Joseph P. Kennedy (1888-1969) believed that capitalism could be saved by the capitalists themselves cleaning it up. He approved of the New Deal as a means of stopping the law of the jungle. Increased state intervention and increased worker-management cooperation were essential to this process. The sons copied their father's world view, but began to assert their own views. By military strategy John F. Kennedy as President tried to prevent the USSR from overtaking the USA and harming its prestige. Positive anti-Communism meant preparing a healthy economic base at home so the Soviet example no longer would look so attractive to the Third World. President Kennedy's antimonopoly activities were done in the interests of the bourgeoisie. The interests of the military-industrial complex often coincided with those of the President. A sequel to follow. Based on secondary sources, with some documentary additions and newspaper references; 66 notes. A sequel will appear.   D. N. Collins

2176. Erokhin, A. V.   T. SORENSEN O KENNEDI I "KENNEDIZME" [T. Sorensen on Kennedy and "Kennedyism"].   *Voprosy Istorii [USSR] 1971 (8): 180-184.* Discusses the views of Theodore Sorensen, one of the most influential figures in the Kennedy administration and an apologist for the Kennedy system of government. Sorensen believes in this century's widening of presidential power beyond that envisaged by the Founding Fathers. According to Sorensen, Lyndon Johnson and Richard Nixon continue the Kennedy legacy. Sorensen advocates strengthening the president's function as the answer to conflict in American society. 24 notes.

2177. Fairbanks, James David.   RELIGIOUS DIMENSIONS OF PRESIDENTIAL LEADERSHIP: THE CASE OF DWIGHT EISENHOWER.   *Presidential Studies Q. 1982 12(2): 260-267.* Eisenhower fully understood the essentially religious demand of his office and was successful in carrying it out. His prayers, church attendance, and friendships with religious leaders all were efforts to set a good example for the rest of the country. This recognition of the religious demands of his office helped give a sense of dignity to his office and unity to the nation. 46 notes.   D. H. Cline

2178. Fallows, James.   THE PRESIDENT AND THE PRESS.   *Washington Monthly 1979 11(8): 9-17.* Fascination with current politics and ignorance of American government history among contemporary politicians and the press impede government effectiveness and substantive reporting on government action; uses examples from the Nixon and Carter campaigns and administrations and their press coverage.

2179. Fisher, Louis.   REPROGRAMMING OF FUNDS BY THE DEFENSE DEPARTMENT.   *J. of Pol. 1974 36(1): 77-102.* Defense budget estimates are of a "highly tentative nature" and reprogramming is a continuous process, yet the Defense Department warns that any tampering with its priorities will upset delicately balanced planning. Each year billions of dollars are shifted after the defense appropriation bill has been passed, and no questions are asked. Calls for bolder questioning of the Pentagon's defense estimates by Congress and additional studies of the "committee veto" and the processes of legislative liaison. Additional inquiry should also be developed in the area of executive branch control in reprogramming actions. 4 tables, 59 notes.   A. R. Stoesen

2180. Fisher, Walter R.   ROMANTIC DEMOCRACY, RONALD REAGAN, AND PRESIDENTIAL HEROES.   *Western J. of Speech Communication 1982 46(3): 299-310.* Proposes "to build on the notion that there is a romantic strain in American history and politics, to suggest characteristics of presidential heroes, to relate Reagan's rhetoric to the romantic tradition, and to speculate on his chances of becoming a presidential hero," and compares Ronald Reagan with Jimmy Carter and John Kennedy.

2181. Flatto, Elie.   THE IMPEACHMENT OF A PRESIDENT: REFLECTIONS ON WATERGATE.   *Contemporary Rev. [Great Britain] 1973 223(1292): 129-131.* Discusses the Watergate hearings of 1973 as a televised public trial, making the impeachment of President Richard M. Nixon seem academic.

2182. Flatto, Elie.   THE IMPEACHMENT OF RICHARD M. NIXON.   *Contemporary Rev. [Great Britain] 1975 226(1310): 146-148.* Reflections on the "trial by television" of President Nixon in 1973-74 and the possible effects of his resignation.

2183. Fry, William F.   THE POWER OF POLITICAL HUMOR.   *J. of Popular Culture 1976 10(1): 227-231.* The efficacy of humor to dilute or resolve problems arising in everyday human experiences is seen in American politics. Examples from the FDR through the Ford eras present some of the better examples, although the Truman and Eisenhower years displayed a rather anxious and self-conscious demeanor, and in the Johnson and later Nixon years, it turned sour.

                                                          D. G. Nielson

2184. Geelhoed, E. Bruce.   EISENHOWER, WILSON, AND DEFENSE POLICY.   *Indiana Social Studies Q. 1978-79 31(3): 5-19.* Discusses policy decisions by President Dwight D. Eisenhower and his Secretary of Defense, Charles E. Wilson, 1953-57.

2185. Geelhoed, E. Bruce.   EXECUTIVE AT THE PENTAGON: RE-EXAMINING THE ROLE OF CHARLES E. WILSON IN THE EISENHOWER ADMINISTRATION.   *Military Affairs 1980 44(1): 1-7.* "Charles E. Wilson was a competent Secretary of Defense, even though a newcomer to federal politics. Wilson understood the economic and social dangers involved in runaway Pentagon spending and therefore sought to stabilize or reduce the level of defense expenditures. He realized the necessity of maintaining civilian control over the military and often restrained the excesses of several important Pentagon service chieftains. In addition, he assumed an administrative post which had frustrated the abilities of his four predecessors and provided the Defense Department with a period of stability in leadership." Covers 1953-57. Primary sources; 49 notes.   A. M. Osur

2186. Gilberg, Sheldon; Eyal, Chaim; McCombs, Maxwell E.; and Nicholas, David.   THE STATE OF THE UNION ADDRESS AND THE PRESS AGENDA.   *Journalism Q. 1980 57(4): 584-588.* Hypothesizing that the president's State of the Union message sets the agenda for the national news media, this study analyzed President Jimmy Carter's 1978 State of the Union speech in order to identify major themes. The major television networks' evening newscasts, as well as the coverage found in the *New York Times* and the Washington *Post,* were studied before and after the speech. The president's speech reflected the media's pre-speech emphases, suggesting that the media set the president's agenda, rather than vice-versa. Table, 17 notes.   J. S. Coleman

2187. Graham, Donald.   THE VICE PRESIDENCY: FROM CIGAR STORE INDIAN TO CROWN PRINCE.   *Washington Monthly 1974 6(2): 41-44.* The vice presidency has boosted Gerald R. Ford's prospects for the 1976 presidential election.   S

2188. Greenstein, Fred I. EISENHOWER AS AN ACTIVIST PRESIDENT: A LOOK AT NEW EVIDENCE. *Pol. Sci. Q. 1979-80 94(4): 575-599.* In an analysis based on recently opened archives, takes sharp issue with the conventional view of Dwight Eisenhower as a passive, unskilled president. According to Greenstein, Eisenhower was an active president who succeeded, albeit much of the time covertly, in putting his personal stamp on public policy.   J

2189. Griffith, Robert. HARRY S. TRUMAN AND THE BURDEN OF MODERNITY. *Rev. in Am. Hist. 1981 9(3): 295-306.* Reviews *The Autobiography of Harry S. Truman,* Robert H. Ferrell, ed. (1980), *Off the Record: The Private Papers of Harry S. Truman,* Robert H. Ferrell, ed. (1980), Harold F. Gosnell's *Truman's Crises: A Political Biography of Harry S. Truman* (1980), *The Truman White House: The Administration of the Presidency, 1945-1953,* Francis H. Heller, ed. (1980), and *The Truman Presidency: The Origins of the Imperial Presidency and the National Security State,* Athan Theoharis, ed. (1979).

2190. Griffith, Robert. TRUMAN AND THE HISTORIANS: THE RECONSTRUCTION OF POSTWAR AMERICAN HISTORY. *Wisconsin Mag. of Hist. 1975 59(1): 20-50.* Reviews the historical literature on President Harry S. Truman's foreign policy, including changing interpretations and evaluations of the Marshall Plan, Truman Doctrine, Point Four, atomic diplomacy, the Korean War, containment, and the origins of the Cold War. Also deals with Truman's domestic policy, highlighting his handling of inflation, domestic security, McCarthyism, housing, civil rights, anti-trust enforcement, and public power programs. Revisionist historians view Truman's administration as a failure because it represented mid-century liberalism which "served only to rationalize an aggressive and militaristic foreign policy, while betraying the cause of social justice at home." Presented at the annual meeting of the Organization of American Historians in 1972. 9 illus., 84 notes, biblio.
                                                                   N. C. Burckel

2191. Harrington, Michael. MR. CARTER'S ARENA: AMERICA AND THE WORLD. *Social Policy 1977 7(4): 4-7.* Examines the liberal leanings of the appointments in the Carter administration within the realm of foreign policy and the conservative-leaning appointments within the realm of domestic and social policy, 1976.

2192. Hart, John. CONGRESSIONAL REACTIONS TO WHITE HOUSE LOBBYING. *Presidential Studies Q. 1981 11(1): 83-91.* The establishment of the White House Office of Congressional Relations during the Eisenhower years was the most significant innovation in Presidential-Congressional relations during the last two decades. During the Kennedy administration, this agency helped win over Congressmen through the use of lobbying, patronage, and influence-wielding efforts. 46 notes.   D. H. Cline

2193. Hawkins, Robert Parker; Pingree, Suzanne; and Roberts, Donald F. WATERGATE AND POLITICAL SOCIALIZATION: THE INESCAPABLE EVENT. *Am. Pol. Q. 1975 3(4): 406-422.* Discusses the impact of the Watergate scandal on the political socialization and attitudes of children in the San Francisco Bay area 1972-73, emphasizing evaluations of President Richard M. Nixon.

2194. Herz, Martin F. MAXWELL GLUCK AND ALL THAT. *Foreign Service J. 1978 55(5): 19-22, 39-43.* Discusses cases of ambassadorships being "purchased" as a result of large campaign contributions, notably during the Eisenhower administration with Maxwell H. Gluck, a businessman appointed as ambassador to Ceylon, and during the Nixon administration when a post to Trinidad and Tobago was promised to J. Fife Symington.

2195. Hibbs, Douglas A., Jr. THE DYNAMICS OF POLITICAL SUPPORT FOR AMERICAN PRESIDENTS AMONG OCCUPATIONAL AND PARTISAN GROUPS. *Am. J. of Pol. Sci. 1982 26(2): 312-332.* Investigates the response of political support for American presidents among occupational and partisan groups to economic and noneconomic events within the framework of a dynamic model of political choice. Reveals the relative sensitivity of different groups' political support to unemployment, inflation, and the real income growth rate as well as to the Vietnam casualties, the Watergate scandal, and international crisis events. The intergroup differences in political responses to the per-

formance variables are sizeable and reflect diverging objective group interests rather than partisan-based perceptions.   J/S

2196. Hooley, John. THE REAGAN PRESIDENCY: A FIRST TESTING. *Antioch Rev. 1981 39(4): 488-500.* Reviews the political attitudes of Ronald Reagan since the passage of tax reform legislation in 1981.

2197. Hurwitz, Leon; Green, Barbara; and Segal, Hans E. INTERNATIONAL PRESS REACTIONS TO THE RESIGNATION AND PARDON OF RICHARD M. NIXON: A CONTENT ANALYSIS OF FOUR ELITE NEWSPAPERS. *Comparative Pol. 1976 9(1): 107-123.* Content analysis of press reaction in *Pravda, Le Monde,* the London *Times,* and *Die Welt* to the resignation and pardon of Richard M. Nixon, 1974.

2198. Hurwitz, Leon. WATERGATE AND DETENTE: A CONTENT ANALYSIS OF FIVE COMMUNIST NEWSPAPERS. *Studies in Comparative Communism 1976 9(3): 244-256.* *Pravda* and *Izvestiia,* in contrast to other Communist newspapers outside the USSR, were more favorable to Nixon during the Watergate affair. Although all the newspapers recognized the importance of the affair and gave it more space than other news from the United States, the Soviet newspapers were either neutral or lenient in their treatment of the United States. Perhaps the intention was to avoid threats to detente. Perhaps too, to condemn Nixon's actions would have encouraged Soviet citizens to question the behavior of their own government. 10 notes.   D. Balmuth

2199. Ivanian, E. A. POSLEDNII KRIZIS PREZIDENTA NIKSONA [President Nixon's last crisis]. *Voprosy Istorii [USSR] 1978 (12): 123-140.* President Richard M. Nixon set out to unite Americans during his Presidency, and by its end they were united: in condemnation of the violations of the Constitution by his administration. Despite unpopularity for his handling of the economy and policy in Indochina, Nixon's smear campaigns against his opponents and genuine foreign policy successes such as his visit to Moscow, unlike his minimally fruitful visit to Peking, ensured his reelection in 1972, though the Watergate scandal ended Nixon's second term of office. Nixon proved a consistent anti-Communist reactionary throughout his career, though political realism led him to improve relations with the USSR. 45 notes.   A. P. Oxley

2200. Jasinowski, Jerry J. THE FIRST TWO YEARS OF THE CARTER ADMINISTRATION: AN APPRAISAL. *Presidential Studies Q. 1979 9(1): 11-15.* Reviews Jimmy Carter's foreign and domestic policy record 1977-78, in light of Congress's increased authority, growth in the number of special interest groups, and spiraling inflation.

2201. Kelly, Alfred H. HISTORY AS THEATER. *Rev. in Am. Hist. 1976 4(1): 132-137.* Review article prompted by Theodore H. White's *Breach of Faith: The Fall of Richard Nixon* (New York: Atheneum, 1975) which documents the personal character of Nixon and the involvement in political corruption which led to his political demise.

2202. Kelly, Frank K. AN UNCOMMON COMMON MAN. *Center Mag. 1973 6(2): 60-63.* Details the presidency of Harry S. Truman.   S

2203. Kenski, Henry C. THE IMPACT OF ECONOMIC CONDITIONS ON PRESIDENTIAL POPULARITY. *J. of Pol. 1977 39(3): 764-773.* Studies of presidential popularity correlated with unemployment indicate that, as unemployment increased, Republicans Dwight D. Eisenhower and Richard M. Nixon were adversely affected while Democrats John F. Kennedy and Lyndon B. Johnson were more strongly supported. This may reflect respective party images. Increases in food prices, particularly the consumer price index, are more accurate predictors of presidential popularity. Based on primary and secondary sources; table, 22 notes.   A. W. Novitsky

2204. Kenski, Henry C. THE IMPACT OF UNEMPLOYMENT ON PRESIDENTIAL POPULARITY FROM EISENHOWER TO NIXON. *Presidential Studies Q. 1977 7(2-3): 114-126.* Discusses the influence of unemployment on Presidents' political popularity from Dwight D. Eisenhower through Richard M. Nixon (1953-74). Economic slump, not unemployment, has the greatest effect on presidential popularity. The rate of unemployment, though, does have a more negative effect on Republican administration than on Democratic ones, and the change in the unemployment rate affects both Republican and Democratic Presidencies. For unemployment to be politically devastating, it would need to reach double-digit figures in an absence of social welfare programs. Gallup polls, newspapers, and secondary sources; 3 tables, 65 notes.　　　　　　　　　　　　　　　　　　　　R. D. Hurt

2205. Kinnard, Douglas. JAMES R. SCHLESINGER AS SECRETARY OF DEFENSE. *Naval War Coll. Rev. 1979 32(6): 22-34.* James R. Schlesinger was the youngest Secretary of Defense and the first to have no prior military experience but service fears that he shared other "whiz kid" attributes were erased (or at least balanced) by his articulation of coherent rationales for U.S. strategic and conventional forces. This evaluation of Schlesinger's tenure is adapted by the author from a chapter in his forthcoming *Five Secretaries of Defense.* [Covers 1973-75].　　　J

2206. Kinnard, Douglas. MCNAMARA AT THE PENTAGON. *Parameters 1980 10(3): 22-31.* The major contributions of Robert S. McNamara as secretary of defense from 1961 to 1968 were the introduction of new managment techniques, such as systems analysis, and the transfer of power from the military services to the secretary and his civilian staff. McNamara also assumed the role of primary supervisor of the Vietnam War. Although he originally supported the military's calls for increased force, by 1966 he was calling for a leveling off of military activity and for the start of negotiations. Based on Defense Department studies, writings and Congressional testimony of McNamara, interviews, and secondary sources; 25 notes.　　　　　　　　　L. R. Maxted

2207. Kinnard, Douglas. PRESIDENT EISENHOWER AND THE DEFENSE BUDGET. *J. of Pol. 1977 39(3): 596-623.* President Dwight D. Eisenhower accepted Harry S. Truman's position that the United States should lead the non-Communist world. However, Eisenhower urged that American military strategy be based on strategic deterrence, not on balanced forces. His 1952 campaign promises to end the Korean War, balance the federal budget, and reduce taxes led to pressure to reduce defense expenditures throughout his two terms, even in the post-Sputnik era. The National Security Council was a forum for achieving consensus, not a decisionmaking body. Continental air defense and conventional forces yielded to the development of resources capable of massive retaliation on the Soviet Union. Based on primary and secondary sources; 58 notes.　　　　　　　　　　　　　　A. W. Novitsky

2208. Kopkind, Andrew. PROMISES, PROMISES. *Working Papers for a New Soc. 1978 6(2): 6-8.* Examines the track record for Jimmy Carter, 1977, and projects what is expected in foreign policy, welfare legislation, defense and national security, and energy and environmental policy.

2209. Kuter, Laurence S. JFK AND LBJ CONSIDER AEROSPACE DEFENSE. *Aerospace Hist. 1978 25(1): 1-4.* The Commander of the North American Aerospace Defense Command during the Kennedy administration describes a briefing he gave to President John F. Kennedy and Vice President Lyndon B. Johnson in the Oval Office of the White House, 8 February 1962. Having failed to obtain what he considered adequate funds for ballistic missiles in the proposed defense budget, he received permission to present his case to the Chief Executive. In his presentation he spoke of the gaps in our defenses and expressed the need for closing this gap. The President thanked him and said that his recommendations would be considered. He did not receive the funds requested and concluded that he "had done everything compatible with our constitutional government." Were he to have proceeded further he would have had to embark on a personal and probably political crusade. 7 photos.　　　　　　　　　　　　　　　　　　C. W. Ohrvall

2210. Leapman, Michael. THE AMERICAN MOOD: 1979: PRESIDENT CARTER'S FIRST 30 MONTHS PROVE A DISAPPOINTMENT. *Round Table [Great Britain] 1979 (276): 343-346.* Outlines the personal characteristics and policies of President Jimmy Carter, 1977-79, and compares them with those of two of his rivals in his second-term campaign, Senator Edward M. Kennedy and Governor Jerry Brown.

2211. Lemann, Nicholas. WHY CARTER FAILS: TAKING THE POLITICS OUT OF GOVERNMENT. *Washington Monthly 1978*

10(6): 12-23. President Jimmy Carter, though moral and intelligent, tends to judge programs and information rather than argue them out and to govern according to procedure and detail rather than politics.

2212. Levine, Henry D. SOME THINGS TO ALL MEN: THE POLITICS OF CRUISE MISSILE DEVELOPMENT. *Public Policy 1977 25(1): 117-168.* Analyzing Defense Department attitudes toward weapons systems and external political events, the decision to pursue development of the cruise missile is studied. Interservice rivalry, White House pressure, and the cruise missile's role in negotiations with USSR, are explored. Employs a cybernetic model of decisionmaking to explain cruise missile development from the late 1960's to 1976. Implications for defense policymaking are drawn. Based on original research and secondary sources; 100 notes, glossary of terms.　　　　　　J. M. Herrick

2213. Linnik, V. A. NEKOTORYE UROKI AMERIKANSKIKH VYBOROV [Some lessons to be learned from the American elections]. *Mirovaia Ekonomika i Mezhdunarodnye Otnosheniia [USSR] 1981 (1): 123-126.* Analyzes the deficiencies of the policy of President Jimmy Carter. Russian.

2214. Locander, Robert. CARTER AND THE PRESS: THE FIRST TWO YEARS. *Presidential Studies Q. 1980 10(1): 106-120.* Examines Jimmy Carter's press relations in the first 24 months of the 39th presidency. (There was a "honeymoon" period during the first nine months of the Carter administration). During 1977-78, Carter became an ambitious and innovative communicator. He borrowed liberally from the communications experiences of Roosevelt, Kennedy, Nixon, and Ford. In many ways he made the media work for him, using, for example, the televised press conference, the fireside chat, and the local media meeting. 3 tables, 54 notes.　　　　　　　　　　　　　　G. E. Pergl

2215. Lynn, Laurence E., Jr. and Smith, Richard I. CAN THE SECRETARY OF DEFENSE MAKE A DIFFERENCE? *Int. Security 1982 7(1): 45-69.* Examines the terms of Robert S. McNamara and of Melvin Laird, who both served as Secretary of Defense, showing the contrasting management procedures and how they affected the development of the US military stance; analyzes the actual influence of these two officials over US military forces, capabilities, and costs, stressing armaments procurement.

2216. Manley, John F. PRESIDENTIAL POWER AND WHITE HOUSE LOBBYING. *Pol. Sci. Q. 1978 93(2): 255-275.* Discusses the renegotiation for the balance of power between Gerald R. Ford and Congress in the aftermath of Nixon and the Watergate scandal; describes contrasting models of presidential power, the problematic and the supremacy.

2217. McAliffe, Mary S. EISENHOWER, THE PRESIDENT. *J. of Am. Hist. 1981 68(3): 625-632.* Since the late 1960's revisionist historians have rejected the image of Eisenhower as an unintelligent, bland, and passive president. Instead they have depicted Eisenhower as a strong, decisive leader who led the United States through the Cold War. Revisionists disagree on such issues as Eisenhower's conservatism, his domestic policy, and his use of the Central Intelligence Agency for clandestine operations overseas. 27 notes.　　　　　　　T. P. Linkfield

2218. McCoy, Donald R. HARRY S. TRUMAN: PERSONALITY, POLITICS, AND PRESIDENCY. *Presidential Studies Q. 1982 12(2): 216-225.* President Truman was superb at delegating authority and at backing up his subordinates when they acted according to his instructions. He had a strong sense of his identity as a president and his separate identity as a politician, and he could usually use these two different personalities at appropriate and advantageous times. This was one of the strongest reasons for his success. Based on documents in the Truman Library; 63 notes.　　　　　　　　　　　　D. H. Cline

2219. McGee, Gale. A CONSTITUTIONAL CRISIS. *Freedom At Issue 1973 (19): 7-8, 21-23.* The Nixon administration's impoundment of public funds threatens the constitutional balance between the executive and congressional branches.　　　　　　　　　　　　　　　　S

2220. McInerney, Thomas J. EISENHOWER GOVERNANCE AND THE POWER TO COMMAND: A PERSPECTIVE ON PRESI-

DENTIAL LEADERSHIP. *Presidential Studies Q. 1981 11(2): 262-270.* Taking on the presidency at a time of war and leading a party weakened and in need of modernization, Dwight D. Eisenhower appears to have been exceptionally adept at governance. He recognized the public's need for confidence in their political institutions, and thus, despite his dismay with the judiciary branch, he did not speak out publicly. Eisenhower took command and let the nation feel it was moving in the right direction. Based on a paper presented to the 1979 Summer Seminar for College Teachers. Primary sources; 39 notes.   A. Drysdale

2221. Medick, Monika. THE NIXON NEW ECONOMIC POLICY: ECONOMIC AND SECURITY INTERESTS IN U.S.-EUROPEAN RELATIONS. *Amerikastudien/Am. Studies [West Germany] 1978 23(1): 73-89.* Considers the formulation of Richard M. Nixon's New Economic Policy (August-December 1971) from the perspective of internal interaction and factionalism in the Nixon administraton and interaction between factions of the administration with Western European auxiliaries. The concept of burden-sharing was the key element in the policy's continuity. Traces American unilateralism and protectionalism displayed in NEP partly to common experiences of advanced industrial societies since 1965 and partly to new developments in American society and foreign policy.   J/S

2222. Meehan, Mary. NIXON'S FLYING FÜHRERBUNKER. *Washington Monthly 1974 6(2): 22-28.* President Richard M. Nixon's flying command post in the event of nuclear war.   S

2223. Merrill, F. T., Jr. HOW CARTER STOPPED PLAYING POLITICS AND LOST THE CONGRESS. *Washington Monthly 1977 9(5-6): 28-30.* Jimmy Carter is experiencing difficulties in getting legislation through Congress primarily because of bad communication with the House of Representatives.

2224. Miroff, Bruce. AFTER CONSENSUS: THE DILEMMAS OF CONTEMPORARY AMERICAN LEADERSHIP, A 1979 VIEW. *Presidential Studies Q. 1981 11(3): 411-423.* From a 1979 viewpoint, American leadership seemed to be in disarray. The consensus from the early 1960's had been cracked, and the whole idea of heroic leadership has become disillusioning. The political structures and coalitions had broken down, and Jimmy Carter seemed to be no longer in control. 43 notes.   D. H. Cline

2225. Mitchell, Franklin D. AN ACT OF PRESIDENTIAL INDISCRETION: HARRY S. TRUMAN, CONGRESSMAN MCDONOUGH, AND THE MARINE CORPS INCIDENT OF 1950. *Presidential Studies Q. 1981 11(4): 565-575.* Immediately after World War II, one of the problems in the structuring of the military department was determining the role and status of the Marine Corps. President Truman, an advocate of a diminished role for the Marines, made a crucial mistake in sending a bluntly worded letter to conservative Republican Congressman Gordon L. McDonough expressing his views. The publication of this letter in the first days of the Korean War not only gave ammunition to Truman's enemies, but also assured the later position of the corps. 71 notes.   D. H. Cline

2226. Moch, Jules. CONVERSATIONS AVEC EINSTEIN, EISENHOWER, KHROUCHTCHEV ET WINSTON CHURCHILL ... [Conversations with Einstein, Eisenhower, Khrushchev, and Winston Churchill ...]. *Nouvelle Rev. des Deux Mondes [France] 1980 (4): 27-34.* The author, a French statesman, recalls his conversations with Albert Einstein in 1932, Dwight D. Eisenhower in 1955, Nikita Khrushchev in 1955, and Winston Churchill in 1942, concerning disarmament.

2227. Moe, Ronald C. SENATE CONFIRMATION OF EXECUTIVE APPOINTMENTS: THE NIXON ERA. *Pro. of the Acad. of Pol. Sci. 1975 32(1): 141-152.* The many legislative actions extending confirmation of presidential appointments beyond cabinet and court positions passed during the Nixon administration indicated the desire on the part of the Senate to assume a greater role in institutional administration.

2228. Morehead, Joe. INTO THE HOPPER: TENNIS ELBOW OF THE SOUL: THE PUBLIC PAPERS OF RICHARD NIXON, 1973-1974. *Serials Librarian 1977 1(3): 207-214.* Discusses Nixon's presidency, impeachment preliminaries, his loss of political base, and his eventual resignation, in light of his public papers.

2229. Morris, Roger. THOMSON, MOYERS, AND BALL: PROPHETS WITHOUT OFFICE. *Washington Monthly 1977 9(4): 45-51.* In Jimmy Carter's administration critics of the Vietnam War were ignored for important national security positions in favor of noncontroversial figures who often had friends in the right places.

2230. Morrow, Lance. WHO IS JIMMY CARTER? *Horizon 1978 21(2): 60-65.* Review of Jimmy Carter's first year in office (1977) indicates some difficult decisions (B-1 bomber, human rights, Panama Canal treaty), yet still a somewhat enigmatic leader.

2231. Mrozek, Donald J. THE TRUMAN ADMINISTRATION AND THE ENLISTMENT OF THE AVIATION INDUSTRY IN POSTWAR DEFENSE. *Business Hist. R. 1974 48(1): 73-94.* Contrary to the opinion that business or military leaders were primarily responsible for the "military-industrial complex" that developed after World War II, the most significant pressure for integrating the airplane industry into national defense planning came from Harry S. Truman and his close advisers, such as Clark Clifford and George Elsey, who were anxious to link business to the military establishment. Smaller businessmen and local politicians also supported this policy, and big business soon realized its economic advantages. 51 notes.   R. V. Ritter

2232. Murdock, Clark A. MC NAMARA, SYSTEMS ANALYSIS AND THE SYSTEMS ANALYSIS OFFICE. *J. of Pol. and Military Sociol. 1974 2(1): 89-104.* "Attempts to answer the question of what was the impact of Secretary of Defense McNamara's managerial innovations — principally Planning-Programming-Budgeting System (PPBS) and systems analysis—both upon the manner in which defense policy was made in the Department of Defense and the decisional criteria underlying defense policy output ... [describes] the policy-making process as it was intended to operate by those who initiated it and examines some of the implications of these innovations ...."   J

2233. Neumann, Gerd. OST-WEST-HANDEL ODER RÜSTUNGSKONJUNKTUR? FRIEDLICHE KOEXISTENZ ODER ESKALATION? ZUR WIRTSCHAFTLICHEN LAGE DER USA IM JAHRE 1949 [East-West trade or arms race? Peaceful coexistence or escalation? Concerning the economic situation of the USA in the year 1949]. *Jahrbuch für Wirtschaftsgeschichte [East Germany] 1976 (4): 31-50.* Industrial production in the United States reached its height in October 1948 and thereafter declined markedly. The ensuing economic crisis lasted only 11 months, but evoked comparisons with the economic situation just before the Great Depression. The Truman Administration reacted in September and October 1949 by increasing US military expenditures and offering assistance to American allies overseas, thus initiating the Cold War. Although the economic crisis ended immediately, Truman's policies ruined East-West trade relationships and precipitated the arms race. US actions thus caused more problems than they solved. Secondary sources; 6 tables, 4 graphs, 86 notes.   R. J. Bazillion

2234. Nocera, Joseph. SAM BROWN AND THE PEACE CORPS: ALL TALK, NO ACTION. *Washington Monthly 1978 10(6): 28-41.* The Peace Corps and VISTA were combined into ACTION by the Nixon administration. Carter appointee Sam Brown could not renovate and rejuvenate ACTION and Peace Corps programs.

2235. Osborne, Leonard L. RHETORICAL PATTERNS IN PRESIDENT KENNEDY'S MAJOR SPEECHES: A CASE STUDY. *Presidential Studies Q. 1980 10(3): 332-335.* Uses a combination of rhetorical analysis and content analysis to conclude that President John F. Kennedy developed a set pattern of arrangement that he tailored to fit his actions. Table, 10 notes.   D. H. Cline

2236. Ostman, Ronald E.; Babcock, William A.; and Fallert, J. Cecilia. RELATION OF QUESTIONS AND ANSWERS IN KENNEDY'S PRESS CONFERENCES. *Journalism Q. 1981 58(4): 575-581.* A content analysis of President John F. Kennedy's 62 press conferences reveals that questioners who followed certain rules for asking questions (as promulgated in journalism texts and guides) received "better" answers than questioners who did not adhere to these rules. 3 tables, 18 notes.   J. S. Coleman

2237. Outrey, Georges. LA DIRECTIVE PRÉSIDENTIELLE NO. 59 [Presidential executive order no. 59]. *Défense Natl. [France] 1980 36(10): 125-130.* Discusses US presidential directives on defense from 1973 and particularly President Jimmy Carter's Executive Order No. 59. 8 notes.

2238. Paletz, David L. and Vinegar, Richard J. PRESIDENTS ON TELEVISION: THE EFFECTS OF INSTANT ANALYSIS. *Public Opinion Q. 1977-78 41(4): 488-497.* The effects of instant analyses of presidential appearances are probed through an experimental study of the CBS television network's coverage of an appearance by President Nixon. Explanations are offered for the kinds of instant analysis Presidents encounter.   J

2239. Paletz, David L. and Entman, Robert M. PRESIDENTS, POWER, AND THE PRESS. *Presidential Studies Q. 1980 10(3): 416-426.* Using as an example the experience of President Jimmy Carter, traces the processes and factors involved in the power relationship between the president and the press. Presidents, because of their position and power, hold several distinct advantages over the press, but for each action a president takes, there is a possibility of an adverse reaction that could undercut the president's position. Carter promised an open presidency for the press, but was soon caught up in many problems with the press. The media can handle any event in many different ways, and as Carter's presidency wore on, the presentation was increasingly troublesome for him. 31 notes.   D. H. Cline

2240. Peters, Charles. WHY JIMMY CARTER DOESN'T HIRE JIMMY CARTERS. *Washington Monthly 1977 8(12): 12-15.* Examines Jimmy Carter's tendencies to make government appointments from a select group, as with Patricia Roberts Harris as Secretary of Housing and Urban Development, 1976.

2241. Polsby, Nelson W. PRESIDENTIAL CABINET MAKING: LESSONS FOR THE POLITICAL SYSTEM. *Pol. Sci. Q. 1978 93(1): 15-25.* Suggests that the pattern of appointments in the Carter cabinet shows the persistence of a type of presidential leadership that the Nixon presidency did not put out of style. The causes of President Carter's brand of leadership are traced to the Democratic nomination process, however, rather than to attitudes about presidential authority that Carter evidently does not share with former president Nixon.   J

2242. Quester, George H. WAS EISENHOWER A GENIUS? *Int. Security 1979 4(2): 159-179.* Builds on the revisionist view of the 1960's to suggest that Dwight D. Eisenhower was more politically astute than is commonly acknowledged, 1950's.

2243. Quimby, Rollin W. AGNEW, THE PRESS, AND THE RHETORICAL CRITIC. *Western Speech 1975 39(3): 146-154.* Discusses Spiro Agnew's resignation from the vice presidency and the difficulties it entailed for both reporters and rhetorical analysts.   S

2244. Randall, Ronald. PRESIDENTIAL USE OF MANAGEMENT TOOLS FROM PPB TO ZBB. *Presidential Studies Q. 1982 12(2): 186-194.* Presidents Johnson, Nixon, and Carter have utilized alphabetical camouflage in their quest for an image of administrative success. These presidents used different management tools politically while effecting no substantive impact on the government or on expenditures. 38 notes.   D. H. Cline

2245. Reich, Michael. WHY CARTER CAN'T REDUCE MILITARY SPENDING. *Monthly Rev. 1977 29(2): 53-58.* Military spending is easily expandable, has an important relationship with major industrial corporations, and appears to be the best method available to President Jimmy Carter for stimulating aggregate demand and economic development.

2246. Reichard, Gary W. EISENHOWER AS PRESIDENT: THE CHANGING VIEW. *South Atlantic Q. 1978 77(3): 265-281.* A broad survey of the changing interpretations of the Eisenhower administration (1953-61). Revisionists have already begun the task of reassessing his presidency. Predicts that the verdict on Eisenhower will be mixed. He will not emerge from forthcoming scholarly studies with a ranking of greatness, but will certainly rank higher on the presidential ladder than histori-

ans previously assumed, somewhere in the middle. Based on historiography of Eisenhower's administration; 46 notes.
                                                        H. M. Parker, Jr.

2247. Richardson, Elmo R. WORKING ON IKE. *Pacific Northwest Q. 1977 68(3): 141-142.* Offers a comparative review of two recent books on the Eisenhower presidency. Charles Alexander's *Holding the Line* (1975) contends that Eisenhower secured an equilibrium acceptable to Americans, but the equilibrium did not survive his administration. Based on partisan secondary sources, this book falls short of Gary Reichard's *Reaffirmation of Republicanism* which precisely analyzes Eisenhower's decisive leadership during the 83rd Congress.   M. L. Tate

2248. Riley, Albert. DECISION IN THE PINEY WOODS. *Georgia Life 1979 5(4): 18-20.* President Dwight D. Eisenhower shot a round of golf in Thomasville, Georgia, in 1956 and decided that he was strong enough to resume the activities dropped after his heart attack.

2249. Roberts, Dick. WHO RULES NIXON? *Internat. Socialist R. 1973 34(10): 6-13.* The Nixon administration's most influential financial supporters.   S

2250. Rockman, Bert A. CARTER'S TROUBLES. *Society 1980 17(5): 34-40.* Discusses major trends affecting presidential governance, President Jimmy Carter's conception of the presidential role as that of an agenda setter and activist, his approach to problems, and his reputed status as an amateur outsider.

2251. Rodgers, Harrell R., Jr. and Lewis, Edward B. STUDENT ATTITUDES TOWARD MR. NIXON: THE CONSEQUENCES OF NEGATIVE ATTITUDES TOWARD A PRESIDENT FOR POLITICAL SYSTEM SUPPORT. *Am. Pol. Q. 1975 3(4): 423-436.* Discusses the extent of elementary and high school students' negative attitudes toward President Richard M. Nixon in light of the Watergate scandal in 1974, emphasizing expressions of cynicism and political distrust.

2252. Rosenberg, Leonard B. LUCK OR DESIGN: THE FALL OF RICHARD M. NIXON. *Politico [Italy] 1975 40(4): 706-709.* The political system itself caused Richard M. Nixon's fall from power because the certainty of impeachment and probability of conviction forced him to resign. The behavior of the military, the media, and business prove the stability of the American political system. The orderly transition of power from Nixon to Gerald Ford is another example. However, the potential for the abuse of power remains.   M. T. Wilson

2253. Rourke, John T. MARSHALL, EISENHOWER AND THE MILITARY MIND. *Military Rev. 1981 61(2): 26-32.* The popular conception is that the military mind advocates massive military solutions, and that those who serve in the upper levels of the military carry this mindset on with them into civilian and governmental positions. The examples of George C. Marshall and Dwight D. Eisenhower counter this thesis. Both were experienced military men, but in civilian life they were usually more moderate and restrained than others around them. This example suggests that the military mind does not subvert the principle of civilian control. Based on documents and writings of Marshall and Eisenhower; 24 notes.   D. H. Cline

2254. Rulon, Philip R. EDUCATION RESEARCH OPPORTUNITIES AT THE EISENHOWER LIBRARY. *Prologue 1978 10(4): 243-251.* Research materials in the Eisenhower Library at Abilene, Kansas, include sources illuminating formative influences in the President's youth which affected his attitudes toward education while President, as well as such influential factors as his military education, tenure while President of Columbia University, and exposure to foreign educational influences while he was on military business. The educational categories best represented among the materials at the Eisenhower Library include those revolving around issues, institutions, individuals, integration, and internationalism, focused during his two terms as President. Many of the informational materials are derived from the ad hoc committees set up by Eisenhower to deliberate on educational matters. The sources as a whole indicate that the Eisenhower years marked an important transitional period in the history of American education. Based mainly on primary sources in the Eisenhower Library.   N. Lederer

2255. Ryan, Halford Ross. HARRY S. TRUMAN: A MIS-DIRECTED DEFENSE FOR MACARTHUR'S DISMISSAL. *Presidential Studies Q. 1981 11(4): 576-582.* In President Harry S. Truman's speech of 11 April 1951 defending his dismissal of General Douglas MacArthur, Truman spent comparatively little time justifying that decision. This was a serious mistake, and an instance in which Truman's persuasive powers fell far short of that needed for strong presidential power. Based primarily on private papers; 42 notes.   D. H. Cline

2256. Savitch, H. V. WHITE HOUSE WATCHING: POLICY, ORGANIZATION & IDEOLOGY AMONG CONTEMPORARY PRESIDENTS. *Polity 1978 11(1): 114-124.* Review article prompted by *The Promise and the Performance: The Leadership of John F. Kennedy* (1975) by Lewis J. Paper, *Pragmatic Illusions: The Presidential Politics of John F. Kennedy* (1976) by Bruce Miroff, *The Plot That Failed: Nixon and the Administrative Presidency* (1975) by Richard P. Nathan, and *Organizing The Presidency* (1976) by Stephen Hess.

2257. Shaffer, William R. A DISCRIMINANT FUNCTION ANALYSIS OF POSITION-TAKING: CARTER VS. KENNEDY. *Presidential Studies Q. 1980 10(3): 451-468.* Studies the political positions of John F. Kennedy and Jimmy Carter since Carter took office in 1977, to test the recent theory that Carter is more a Republican than a Democrat. Although Kennedy was more liberal than Carter in 1978, Carter was every bit as Democratic as Kennedy when compared to Republican positions. Also, like Kennedy, Carter's positions were similar to those of a northern Democrat, and not a southern Democrat (or quasi-Republican.) Ideologically, then, the two men have not been far apart. The differences between them appear to be more personal and stylistic than political and ideological. Uses the roll-call voting record of the Americans for Democratic Action; 12 tables, 6 graphs, 13 notes, 21 ref., 3 appendixes.
                                                                          D. H. Cline

2258. Shull, Steven A. PRESIDENTIAL-CONGRESSIONAL SUPPORT FOR AGENCIES AND FOR EACH OTHER: A COMPARATIVE LOOK. *J. of Pol. 1978 40(3): 753-760.* Presidential support of foreign and domestic policy agencies during the Kennedy, Johnson, and Nixon administrations was compared to congressional support for these agencies. Presidents were generally more supportive of foreign policy agencies; Congress of domestic. There was greater agreement between President and Congress concerning domestic than foreign agencies, possibly attributable to the Vietnam War and congressional assertiveness in foreign affairs. Congress often supported agencies despite presidential opposition, perhaps being more sensitive to agency personnel and pressure group clientele. Primary and secondary sources; 2 tables, 17 notes.
                                                                          A. W. Novitsky

2259. Sigelman, Lee. THE DYNAMICS OF PRESIDENTIAL SUPPORT: AN OVERVIEW OF RESEARCH FINDINGS. *Presidential Studies Q. 1979 9(2): 206-216.* Lists numerous studies (1943-78) on the popular support of American presidents.

2260. Skidmore, Max J. THE TUMULTUOUS DECADE: THE AMERICAN OF THE 1960S. *Indian J. of Am. Studies [India] 1979 9(2): 38-50.* Describes America from the nomination of John F. Kennedy in 1960 to the inauguration of Richard M. Nixon in 1969. In this period of ferment, old ideas mixed with new ideas derived from them. The New Left itself had many antecedents. Consumerism, the civil rights movement, participatory democracy, the peace movement, and the women's movement all had long histories in the intellectual and cultural life of the nation. Nixon's presidency introduced great changes in tone and feeling as much as substance, but the America of the Eisenhower years was irreversibly gone; technology, popular culture, political administrations, and social movements had brought about social change. 6 notes.
                                                                          L. V. Eid

2261. Smith, Craig R. CONTEMPORARY POLITICAL SPEECH WRITING. *Southern Speech Communication J. 1976 42(1): 52-67.* Discusses the roles of researchers, writers, and media consultants in political speechwriting 1968-70's, including the staff structures and rhetorical styles of Richard Nixon, George McGovern, Spiro Agnew, and Ronald Reagan.

2262. Sorensen, Theodore C. WATERGATE AND AMERICAN FOREIGN POLICY. *World Today [Great Britain] 1974 30(12): 497-503.* " . . . Assesses the impact of the Watergate crisis on US relations with the outside world: though the damage was real, it was circumscribed by the healthy constitutional process that brought the discredited executive down."   J

2263. Sorenson, Dale. THE LANGUAGE OF A COLD WARRIOR: A CONTENT ANALYSIS OF HARRY TRUMAN'S PUBLIC STATEMENTS. *Social Sci. Hist. 1979 3(2): 171-186.* Content analysis reveals little change in the rhetoric of President Harry S. Truman's public statements concerning the USSR and domestic communism during 1945-50. Public opinion changed relatively independently of the president's public statements. This finding rejects the revisionist theory that Truman's rhetoric played a major role in increasing the Red Scare hysteria of the 1950's McCarthy era. Based on the published papers of Harry S. Truman; 6 graphs, 19 notes.   L. K. Blaser

2264. Spencer, Martin E. THE IMPERIAL PRESIDENCY AND THE USES OF SOCIAL SCIENCE. *Midwest Q. 1979 20(3): 281-299.* Examines the power amassed by Richard M. Nixon during his presidency (1969-74) in terms of the progression of American history, as discussed in Arthur M. Schlesinger, Jr., *The Imperial Presidency* (Boston, 1973).

2265. Spragens, William C. THE MYTH OF THE JOHNSON "CREDIBILITY GAP." *Presidential Studies Q. 1980 10(4): 629-635.* Through recollections by journalists active during the Johnson administration, Johnson is seen to have enjoyed a brief honeymoon with the press, but by November 1964, relations with the press had deteriorated. However, this deterioration seems to be common in every modern administration. Based on oral histories in the LBJ library; 10 notes.
                                                                          D. H. Cline

2266. Spragens, William C. POLITICAL IMPACT OF PRESIDENTIAL ASSASSINATIONS AND ATTEMPTED ASSASSINATIONS. *Presidential Studies Q. 1980 10(3): 336-347.* Violence against political elites such as presidents is not new, but massive media attention to it has created more problems. A presidential assassination is not just a cataclysmic event for the American public; it can also cause profound political change. John F. Kennedy's assassination helped Lyndon B. Johnson get social legislation passed more easily, but it may have also greatly changed American strategy toward Vietnam. 20 notes.   D. H. Cline

2267. Tani, Andrea. L'AMMIRAGLIO ZUMWALT ED IL SUO TEMPO [Admiral Zumwalt and his times]. *Riv. Marittima [Italy] 1979 112(6): 15-28, (7): 61-72.* Reviews Admiral Elmo R. Zumwalt's term as US Naval Chief of Staff, 1970-74, analyzes some of the issues dealt with in Zumwalt's memoirs *On Watch,* and reviews his proposals for naval reorganization.

2268. Theoharis, Athan G. MCCARTHYISM: A BROADER PERSPECTIVE. *Maryland Hist. 1981 12(2): 1-7.* A historiographical essay urging scholars to avoid simplistic labeling of Cold War scholars. Material unclassified since 1975 reveals that McCarthyism was rooted in institutions of the Executive Branch. Secondary sources, 15 notes.
                                                                          G. O. Gagnon

2269. Toinet, Marie-France. LES ÉTATS-UNIS APRÈS WATERGATE: LE RÈGNE DE L'AMBIGUÏTÉ [The United States after Watergate: The reign of ambiguity]. *Études [France] 1975 342: 63-82.* Studies the residual problems, contradictions, and the indecisiveness which characterize the long-range psychological effect of Richard M. Nixon's resignation on the American people, 1974-75, and on the congressional elections of 1974.

2270. Vasiutovich, V. MILITARISTSKII UGAR V SSHA [Militarist intoxication in the United States]. *Mirovaia Ekonomika i Mezhdunarodnye Otnosheniia [USSR] 1980 (6): 25-37.* Examines US defense spending, 1977-80, showing how the plans of the Carter administration and the military-industrial complex were aggravating world tension. 3 tables, 11 notes. English summary.

2271. Vernant, Jacques. LE PRESIDENT CARTER: MORALISME ET REALITES [President Carter: moralism and realities]. *Défense*

Natl. [France] 1977 33(3): 101-106. Surveys and characterizes the Carter administration in its earliest phase. Secondary sources; 2 notes.

2272. Wasser, Hartmut. VOM PHÄNOMEN DER MEDIOK-RITÄT IN DER AMERIKANISCHEN POLITIK [The phenomenon of mediocrity in American politics]. *Frankfurter Hefte [West Germany] 1981 36(5): 23-30.* The criticism of mediocrity of US presidential politics of Dwight D. Eisenhower, Gerald R. Ford, Jimmy Carter, and Ronald Reagan has a long tradition since Tocqueville (1835), Henry David Thoreau (1847), and James Bryce (1888).

2273. Wayne, Stephen J. RUNNING THE WHITE HOUSE: THE FORD EXPERIENCE. *Presidential Studies Q. 1977 7(2-3): 95-101.* The Gerald R. Ford White House reflected the strengths and weaknesses of the man. Although President Ford was open and accessible, he was overly tolerant and unable to pick quality senior staff. As a reactive rather than an assertive President, Ford had no specific domestic policy before the 1976 campaign. The campaign forced him to clarify his views for the first time, but he was unable to adjust quickly enough. In 1974, Gerald Ford began to restore public trust in the Presidency; by 1976, however, the American people demanded more of a President than openness and honesty. Based on interviews with the White House staff; table, 7 notes.
                                                                    R. D. Hurt

2274. Weaver, David H.; McCombs, Maxwell E.; and Spellman, Charles. WATERGATE AND THE MEDIA: A CASE STUDY OF AGENDA-SETTING. *Am. Pol. Q. 1975 3(4): 458-472.* Discusses the role of the mass media in formulating political attitudes of registered voters in Charlotte, North Carolina, during the revelation of the Watergate scandal in 1972-73.

2275. White, Larry D. NIXON'S PUSH ON THE MARSHMAL-LOW: REORGANIZATION AND WATERGATE, 1968-1974. *Rendezvous 1973-74 8(2): 21-38.* It should not be assumed that efforts to improve bureaucratic efficiency and responsiveness by the Nixon administration were completely in vain. There is, however, reason to believe that those efforts were not highly effective. The bureaucracy reorganization effort promoted increased centralization of power exercised by an "oligarchy" within the presidential advisory system. It also led to limited accessibility to the President by the press, Congress, the Cabinet, and additional members of the advisory staff. Nixon's reliance on "insiders" may have contributed to his problems embodied in the Watergate scandal, the Ellsberg fiasco, and similar controversial incidents.   P. Travis

2276. Wildavsky, Aaron. WAS NIXON TOUGH? DILEMMAS OF AMERICAN STATECRAFT. *Society 1978 16(1): 25-35.* Discusses Richard M. Nixon's actions while President, as both leader of the United States and as foreign policymaker, characterized here as tough, and compares Nixon's tough attitude to other Presidents since Truman in the late 1940's.

2277. Williams, Robert J. HARRY S TRUMAN AND THE AMERICAN PRESIDENCY. *J. of Am. Studies [Great Britain] 1979 13(3): 393-408.* Analyzing the presidency (1945-53) of Harry S Truman (1884-1972) has been difficult in the absence of critical biographies of him, and Truman's "elusive private and political personality" has rendered such an attempt even more hazardous. And scholars, compounding these difficulties, have disagreed about Truman's political beliefs and ethical values. The author reviews the evidence which accounts for the widely contradictory judgments about Truman. Based on secondary sources; 68 notes.   H. T. Lovin

2278. Wolfenstein, E. Victor. THE TWO WARS OF LYNDON JOHNSON. *Pol. and Soc. 1974 4(3): 357-396.* Asserts that a connection grew between the antiwar and antiracism movements during the Johnson years and brought about a raised political consciousness in each group that resulted in the so-called Johnson "credibility gap." Uses Lyndon B. Johnson's *Vantage Point* (1971) and a brief survey of his early life and political career in an attempt to reconcile Marxist and Freudian theoretical differences regarding interests and motives. Secondary sources; 49 notes.   D. G. Nielson

2279. Wright, Esmond. THE UNITED STATES AFTER WATERGATE. *Contemporary Rev. [Great Britain] 1974 225(1306): 231-237.*

Attempts to draw up a tentative balance sheet of the effect of the Watergate scandal and the resignation of President Richard M. Nixon on American politics and foreign relations.

2280. Wright, Robert. EISENHOWER'S FIFTIES. *Antioch Rev. 1980 38(3): 277-290.* Discusses the clash between science and technology and American traditional values during the 1950's; suggests why President Dwight D. Eisenhower's folksy, fatherly image attracted middle American voters; and compares the mood of the country by the late 1950's to "the contemporary sense of discontent with the status quo."

2281. Wyszomirski, Margaret Jane. AN HEROIC PRESIDENCY: A 1981 VIEW. *Presidential Studies Q. 1981 11(3): 424-431.* After many crises, Americans seem to be searching for a hero who has a clear vision of the future and who will lead them to that vision. President Ronald Reagan has placed heavy emphasis on heroes and heroic values. 13 notes.
                                                                    D. H. Cline

2282. Yanarella, Ernest J. THE "TECHNOLOGICAL IMPERA-TIVE" AND THE STRATEGIC ARMS RACE. *Peace and Change 1975 3(1): 3-16.* Discusses the policies of Secretary of Defense Robert S. McNamara in the 1960's and the uncontrollable nature of military technology.   S

2283. Zimmer, Troy A. THE IMPACT OF WATERGATE ON THE PUBLIC'S TRUST IN PEOPLE AND CONFIDENCE IN THE MASS MEDIA. *Social Sci. Q. 1979 59(4): 743-751.* A model analysis of voter attitude changes toward President Richard M. Nixon and the mass media as a consequence of the Watergate Scandal. Results reveal that those who voted for Nixon lost trust in both the President and the media as a result of Watergate, whereas those who voted for George McGovern enjoyed a heightened respect for politicians and the mass media. College-educated voters were less likely to recover their former attitudes. The implications of this study are significant insofar as the mass media are concerned, for they must face the fact that truthful reporting will cause a backlash among a significant portion of the populace. Table, 2 fig.
                                                                    V. L. Human

2284. —. COLD WAR, INFLATION, AND CONTROLS. *Monthly Rev. 1980 31(10): 1-9.* The Carter administration used the hostage crisis in Iran and the Soviet invasion of Afghanistan to justify its opposition to the USSR and its increased defense spending, both of which inflationary measures will enable Jimmy Carter to "clamp on controls in the sacred name of national security."

2285. —. [STAFFING THE CARTER PRESIDENCY]. *Pol. Sci. Q. 1978 93(1): 1-14.*
Neustadt, Richard E. STAFFING THE PRESIDENCY: PREMA-TURE NOTES ON THE NEW ADMINISTRATION, *pp. 1-9.* Reviews President Carter's reorganization of the Executive Office of the president, announced last July. Staff arrangements in and near the White House show both the stamp of inheritance and the impact of President Carter's own special outlook on staffing and organization.
Wellford, Harrison. STAFFING THE PRESIDENCY: AN IN-SIDER'S COMMENTS, *pp. 10-11.* Comments on Neustadt's observations from an "insider's" point of view.
Neustadt, Richard E. A JANUARY 1978 POSTSCRIPT, *pp. 12-14.* Reflects on developments in the Carter Executive Office since last September.   J

2286. —. [THROUGH RUSSIAN EYES: JOHN F. KENNEDY]. *Pol. Sci. Q. 1975 90(1): 117-131.*
Polsby, Nelson W. JFK THROUGH RUSSIAN EYES, *pp. 117-126.* Reviews Anatoli A. Gromyko's *Through Russian Eyes: President Kennedy's 1036 Days* (International Library, 1973), concluding that political inquiry about the US in the USSR is not very advanced.
Ploughman, Piers (pseud.). THE POTBOILER RECONSIDERED: A COMMENT ON "JFK THROUGH RUSSIAN EYES," *pp. 127-130.* Agrees with Polsby, adding that Soviet writing on American politics cannot conform to American scholarly standards, although the book is a good source of information about American politics for Soviet readers.

Polsby, Nelson W. A REJOINDER TO PIERS, *p. 131.* It is "gratuitously patronizing" simply to assume that scholarly standards are still inappropriate for judging Soviet writing on American politics.

J/S

Domestic Affairs

2287. Aberbach, Joel D. and Rockman, Bert A. CLASHING BELIEFS WITHIN THE EXECUTIVE BRANCH: THE NIXON ADMINISTRATION BUREAUCRACY. *Am. Pol. Sci. Rev. 1976 70(2): 456-468.* This article examines two key political beliefs of high level American federal executives: their views on the role of government in providing social services and their views regarding inequities in political representation. Data were collected in 1970 through open-ended interviews with a sample of 126 political appointees and supergrade career civil servants in the domestic agencies. Both of the beliefs analyzed were pertinent to the efforts of the Nixon administration to reorder national priorities and policies. The evidence in the paper establishes differences in the outlooks of administrators depending on agency, job status, and party affiliation. Agency and party affiliation are particularly important variables, and their joint effects on the beliefs examined are substantial. Democratic administrators in the social service agencies were the most liberal and Republicans in the non-social service agencies the most conservative. Our data document a career bureaucracy with very little Republican representation and a social service bureaucracy dominated by administrators ideologically hostile to many of the directions pursued by the Nixon administration in the realm of social policy. The article closed with a discussion of the implications of our findings for future conflicts between the elected executive and the bureaucracy.

J

2288. A.G. LA NOUVELLE POLITIQUE ÉNERGÉTIQUE DES ÉTATS-UNIS [The new energy policy of the United States]. *Défense Natl. [France] 1978 34(2): 105-116.* Examines President Jimmy Carter's energy policy of conservation and conversion and considers the ramifications of nuclear alternatives for world power supply.

2289. Anderson, James E. COORDINATING THE WAR ON POVERTY. *Policy Studies J. 1974 2(3): 174-179.*

2290. Anikin, A. VTOROI GOD "REIGANOMIKI" [The second year of Reaganomics]. *Mirovaia Ekonomika i Mezhdunarodnye Otnosheniia [USSR] 1982 (6): 23-34.* Ronald Reagan's administration has held fast to an experimental economic course, convinced that tax reduction combined with a slowdown in the growth of federal spending and monetary restraint would send the United States into a frenzy of productive activity, a policy conforming with supply-side economic doctrine's monetarist theories, helping the wealthy at the expense of practically everybody else; though welcomed in Great Britain, Reaganomics causes serious negative consequences for West Europe and Japan, where "exported" high interest rates threaten to hinder any recovery. Russian.

2291. Asher, Robert. WHEN WILL THEY EVER LEARN? *Labor Hist. 1974 15(2): 271-275.* Reviews Joseph A. Page and Mary-Win O'Brien's *Bitter Wages* (New York: Grossman Publishers, 1973). The book documents the destruction of the Occupational Safety and Health Act (1970), through nonenforcement in the Nixon years. The failure represents the inherent weakness of accident and prevention systems which depend on broad administrative discretion for enforcement.

L. L. Athey

2292. Azevedo, Ross E. PHASE III—A STABILIZATION PROGRAM THAT COULD NOT WORK. *Q. R. of Econ. and Business 1976 16(1): 7-22.* In January 1973, then-President Richard Nixon abandoned administered wage and price controls for Phase III, a program based on voluntary cooperation and self-enforcement. Unfortunately, from its very inception, Phase III was doomed to be a failure as a stabilization effort. This article details the administrative difficulties and substantive problems associated with the implementation and operation of Phase III and indicates the manner in which they led to its ultimate demise. The article links these difficulties to the costs and frustrations imposed on the business community by Phase III, providing strategic suggestions for future stabilization programs.

J

2293. Bailey, Gil. CONGRESS OR THE WHITE HOUSE: THE CONTEST FOR LEADERSHIP IN ENERGY POLICY. *Cry California 1975 10(3): 13-17.* Reports on the programs by the Ford Administration and the Democratic-controlled Congress to deal with both the economic crisis and energy crisis. As interrelated problems, the crises demand solutions which will not aggravate each other. Proposed programs deal with present emergencies, but long-term planning is badly needed to balance energy demands with economic growth. A diversified transportation system, intelligent land use, and long-range programs for energy development must be determined as to priorities. While the administration has met the current emergencies, Congress may prove influential in promoting energy-saving rather than energy-devouring programs.

A. Hoffman

2294. Barber, Rims and Huttie, Joseph J., Jr. NIXONIAN ECONOMICS: ANOTHER VIEW. *New South 1973 28(2): 72-78.* The Nixon administration's dismantling of poverty programs is putting strains on Mississippi's poor.

S

2295. Bartlett, Bruce. KILLING THE MESSENGER: THE CARTER ADMINISTRATION AND THE FACTS ABOUT OIL AND GAS. *Washington Monthly 1978 10(2): 57-60.* Discusses the replacement of Vincent McKelvey as director of the US Geological Survey following a speech he made asserting that current energy policy stood dangerously close to exhausting oil and gas natural resources—a stand which stated data contrary to Carter administration policy.

2296. Becker, Lee B.; Cobbey, Robin E.; and Sobowale, Idowu A. PUBLIC SUPPORT FOR THE PRESS. *Journalism Q. 1978 55(3): 421-430.* Assesses the influence of political, sociological, and psychological variables on public criticism of the press in the United States during the Watergate affair. The most influential variables were political: degree of support for President Richard Nixon, party affiliation, and ideology. Among those factors, the first was predominant; supporters of Nixon tended to criticize the reporting of the Watergate scandal more severely than did Republicans or conservatives as a whole. Aside from the political factors, the respondents' social status and level of optimism were not significant. Based on Harris and Gallup polls and on surveys by the Roper Public Opinion Research Center and the National Opinion Research Center; 2 tables, graph, 36 notes.

R. P. Sindermann, Jr.

2297. Beckler, David Z. THE PRECARIOUS LIFE OF SCIENCE IN THE WHITE HOUSE. *Daedalus 1974 103(3): 115-134.* The demise of the White House science and technology advisory system during Richard M. Nixon's administration was due more to lack of support than to overt opposition. Gradual structural rearrangements left the advisors detached from both the executive and legislative offices. Years of strain between the executive branch and the intellectual community, disappointment over recent projects, and a suspicion of disloyalty led to the Nixon reorganization plan which dropped the science advisors. Past and potential accomplishments demonstrate the need for a new relationship. Based on secondary sources and committee reports; 5 notes, appendix.

E. McCarthy

2298. Bensman, Joseph. WATERGATE: IN THE CORPORATE STYLE. *Dissent 1973 20(3): 279-280.*

2299. Benson, Ezra Taft. ORAL HISTORY: EZRA TAFT BENSON. *Idaho Heritage 1977 (10): 12-15.* Part II. The author details his roles as an Idaho state administrator, Mormon, organizer of the Idaho Cooperative Council, and Secretary of Agriculture under Dwight D. Eisenhower during 1953-61.

2300. Berkowitz, Edward D. THE HISTORIAN AS POLICY ANALYST: THE CHALLENGE OF HEW. *Public Hist. 1979 1(3): 17-25.* Discusses the contributions of historians in the formation of public policy decisions, using as an example the team of historians recruited by the Office of the Secretary of the Health, Education, and Welfare Department in 1975 to investigate the lack of coordination among disability programs who had $40 billion per year at their disposal, and to propose solutions to make them more efficient and less costly to the federal government, based on a history of compensation programs since the 1910's.

2301. Berkowitz, Edward D. THE POLITICS OF MENTAL RETARDATION DURING THE KENNEDY ADMINISTRATION. *Social Sci. Q. 1980 61(1): 128-143.* President John F. Kennedy's (1917-63) special attention to mental retardation legislation culminated in the passage of the Mental Retardation Amendments of 1963. Motivated by the Kennedy family's interest in mental retardation, the President altered domestic policymaking routines by using the power of his office to push mental retardation to the forefront of health politics. Based on the Myer Feldman Papers, the John F. Kennedy Library Oral History Collection, and secondary works; 28 notes, biblio. L. F. Velicer

2302. Berkowitz, Edward D. and McQuaid, Kim. WELFARE RE-FORM IN THE 1950'S. *Social Service Rev. 1980 54(1): 45-58.* Discusses the Eisenhower administration's policy to use federal money to reform welfare legislation, particularly programs dealing with disability, and notes that this policy was based on those established during the New Deal.

2303. Berman, Bruce J. RICHARD NIXON AND THE NEW COR-PORATE STATE. *Queen's Q. [Canada] 1973 80(3): 425-433.* The growth of corporate capitalism in the United States has enhanced tendencies toward a corporate state. Richard Milhous Nixon's presidency epitomizes this trend and its inherent evils. Trust in American government is declining as the entire political process becomes depersonalized. Watergate symbolizes encroaching corruption and shows how erosion of trust and accompanying social costs are inevitable results of the tyranny of corporate political interests. 10 notes. J. A. Casada

2304. Bernstein, Barton J. TRUMAN ON THE HOME FRONT. *Civil Liberties Rev. 1978 5(1): 50-57.* Reviews Robert J. Donovan's *Conflict and Crisis: The Presidency of Harry S. Truman* (New York: W. W. Norton and Co., 1977), focusing on civil rights issues.

2305. Bernstein, Barton J. TRUMAN, THE EIGHTIETH CON-GRESS, AND THE TRANSFORMATION OF POLITICAL CUL-TURE. *Capitol Studies 1973 2(1): 65-75.*

2306. Bhana, Surendra. PUERTO RICO AND THE TRUMAN AD-MINISTRATION, 1945-47: SELF-GOVERNMENT "LITTLE BY LITTLE." *Prologue 1973 5(3): 155-165.* Describes the politics and policy of gradualism in securing the appointment of a native Puerto Rican governor and the passage of an act permitting Puerto Ricans to elect their governor during the Truman administration, 1945-47. Primary and secondary sources; photo, 39 notes. R. W. Tissing, Jr.

2307. Bickel, Alexander M. WATERGATE AND THE LEGAL ORDER. *Commentary 1974 57(1): 19-25.* Discusses ideological motivation in relation to the Watergate Scandal. S

2308. Billington, Monroe. CIVIL RIGHTS, PRESIDENT TRU-MAN, AND THE SOUTH. *J. of Negro Hist. 1973 58(2): 127-128.* Detects a hardening of white attitudes toward civil rights in the South 1945-52; based on a survey of the public opinion files in the Truman Papers. Based on primary sources in the Truman Library and on secondary sources; 52 notes. N. G. Sapper

2309. Bohne, Regina. UMRISSE EINES "GEHEIME SICHER-HEITSPLANS" [Outlines of a "secret security plan"]. *Frankfurter Hefte [West Germany] 1973 28(10): 699-712.* The Watergate Scandal was only the last phase of widespread, largely illegal, secret security operation launched by the Nixon administration against all sorts of groups and individuals identified as its enemies.

2310. Bosworth, Barry P. THE CARTER ADMINISTRATION'S ANTI-INFLATION PROGRAM. *Pro. of the Acad. of Pol. Sci. 1979 33(3): 12-19.* Presents the economic program of the Carter administration, specifically its anti-inflation measures from the perspective of the Director of the Council on Wage and Price Stability, Barry Bosworth. K. N. T. Crowther

2311. Boyd, Marjorie. IS THE PRESIDENT A PERJURER? *Washington Monthly 1975 7(8): 32-38.* Explores allegations that Gerald R. Ford perjured himself during his confirmation hearings for the vice presidency when he denied sidetracking House investigations of the Watergate Scandal at the order of President Nixon. S

2312. Brademas, John. REVENUE SHARING: THE NATIONAL POLICY DEBATE. *Publius 1976 6(4): 155-159.* Comments on the Nixon administration's policy on revenue sharing and concludes that the plan was a weapon against congressional power, 1968-72.

2313. Brauer, Carl M. KENNEDY, JOHNSON, AND THE WAR ON POVERTY. *J. of Am. Hist. 1982 69(1): 98-119.* Analyzes the motives leading to President Lyndon B. Johnson's declaration of war on poverty in his State of the Union message on 8 January 1964. At the time of President John F. Kennedy's assassination, antipoverty plans included such items as training programs for youth, human services, and a domestic Peace Corps. Styling himself a "Roosevelt New Dealer," President Johnson adopted the poverty issue as his own: not only would it maintain continuity with the Kennedy administration, but it would allow him to develop his own authority and identity as President. Thus the war on poverty was the result of presidential initiative. Based on several personal interviews, the Walter Heller Papers, and documents at the Kennedy Library; 50 notes. T. P. Linkfield

2314. Brown, Bertram S. THE FEDERAL ROLE IN MENTAL HEALTH. *State Government 1977 50(4): 209-213.* Surveys current action by the federal government in research, services, staffing, training, and finance of mental health projects through the Health, Education and Welfare Department, the President's Commission on Mental Health, and the National Institute of Mental Health, 1976-77.

2315. Brozen, Yale. WHY CARTER'S GAME PLAN WON'T WORK. *Reason 1977 8(10): 14-18.* Economic history since the 1920's suggests that Jimmy Carter, in urging increased federal spending as recovery from recessions, is reliving old mistakes; only reduced spending can stop the drain of capital going into financing deficits.

2316. Bullock, Charles S., III, and Stewart, Joseph, Jr. THE JUS-TICE DEPARTMENT AND SCHOOL DESEGREGATION: THE IMPORTANCE OF DEVELOPING TRUST. *J. of Pol. 1977 39(4): 1036-1043.* School desegregation lawsuits by the federal Justice Department during 1964-68 strongly paralleled the geographic location of suits concerning voting rights in 1957-64 throughout the South. Involvement in voting cases was contingent upon black complaints, and enabled Justice to develop a record of trustworthiness. The pattern of suits enforcing the 1964 school desegregation provisions, gradually widening circles from the counties where voting suits had been filed, indicates that without the sanction of Health, Education and Welfare Department regulations, progress in the Deep South would have been slower and less uniform. Primary and secondary sources; map, table, 10 notes. A. W. Novitsky

2317. Bulman, Raymond F. LOVE, POWER, AND THE JUSTICE OF THE U.S. PRESIDENTIAL PARDONS. *J. of Church and State 1979 21(1): 23-38.* Focuses on the legal and ethical issues surrounding Gerald R. Ford's unconditional pardon of Richard M. Nixon and conditional amnesty for Vietnam War resisters and deserters. The Nixon pardon was possibly illegal because it frustrated the completion of the judicial process by pardoning a man before he was convicted. It was unethical because it applied a double standard of justice. Based on the works of Paul Tillich and secondary sources; 27 notes. S

2318. Butler, Broadus N. FOUNDER'S DREAM AND AMERI-CAN REALITY. *Crisis 1977 84(2): 71-79.* The Watergate Scandal was a crisis of moral integrity and leadership. There is a need for intellectual and spiritual leadership as we enter our third century. A. G. Belles

2319. Candee, Dan. THE MORAL PSYCHOLOGY OF WATER-GATE. *J. of Social Issues 1975 31(2): 183-192.* As evidenced in their Senate testimony and other public statements nearly all members of the Nixon team seem to have reasoned at stages 3 and 4 as measured by Kohlberg's sequence of moral development. Indeed, many of the acts of the Watergate participants were "right" or at least "permissible" when viewed from the perspective of these stages. Survey responses of 370 persons not involved in Watergate demonstrate that those who reasoned at stages 3 and 4 agreed with the decisions of the participants more often than did their stage 5 counterparts. This was true regardless of their having supported either Nixon or McGovern. It is concluded that Watergate resulted, in part, because the situational pressures to "win at all costs" were particularly appealing to the stage 3 and 4 persons who comprised the leadership of the Nixon administration.   J

2320. Chizhov, Iu. KRIZIS GOSUDARSTVENNOGO REGULIROVANIIA EKONOMIKI SSHA [Crisis in the government regulation of the US economy]. *Mirovaia Ekonomika i Mezhdunarodnye Otnosheniia [USSR] 1978 (8): 68-79.* Provides a survey of the forms of government regulation of the economy employed in the United States since the 1950's and argues that the policies pursued by the Nixon, Ford, and Carter administrations have failed to solve the growing economic crisis.

2321. Churchill, Mae. CARTER'S BORN-AGAIN WAR ON CRIME. *Social Policy 1978 9(3): 40-45.* Discusses the Carter Administration's attempt to revive the 10-year war on crime, and concludes that the Law Enforcement Assistance Administration (LEAA) has been a failure and should be discontinued.

2322. Clark, Janet M. MORAL PREREQUISITES OF POLITICAL SUPPORT: BUSINESS REACTIONS TO THE WATERGATE SCANDAL. *J. of Pol. Sci. 1979 7(1): 40-61.* A case study of the impact of Watergate on political support indicates a strong relationship between diffuse and specific support. Without sufficient diffuse support, due to the scandal, President Richard M. Nixon was without a solid political base for taking desired actions for improving the economy; it appears that his economic failures rather than his moral shortcomings were of primary concern. Based on editorials and feature articles in major business publications, and on other published materials; 12 tables, 40 notes, 3 appendixes.   T. P. Richardson

2323. Cochrane, James L. ECONOMISTS AND PRESIDENTIAL DECISION MAKING: THE JOHNSON YEARS. *Presidential Studies Q. 1978 8(1): 32-35.* A review of primary source material in the Lyndon B. Johnson Library suggests several promising fields of research for economic historians. The first is the process of presidential decision-making, or more accurately, presidential approval of decisions by ad hoc committees. The role of economists in this process and their relationship with their colleagues outside the Federal Government requires further study to determine needed analytical tools and to test economic theory. A second field of inquiry is the relationship between government economists and politics. How successful were they in transforming ideas into action and at what sacrifice of scientific objectivity? 12 notes.   S. C. Strom

2324. Cole, Richard L. and Caputo, David A. PRESIDENTIAL CONTROL OF THE SENIOR CIVIL SERVICE: ASSESSING THE STRATEGIES OF THE NIXON YEARS. *Am. Pol. Sci. Rev. 1979 73(2): 399-413.* Modern presidents must be attentive to influences of the federal bureaucracy on their policy initiatives and all attempt some measure of bureaucratic control. This article assesses the extent of President Nixon's success in gaining some degree of management control over the bureaucracy through the manipulation of the civil service personnel system. We find that Republicans were, in fact, more likely to be selected to top career positions during the Nixon years. We find also that career executives calling themselves Independents were more likely during the Nixon years than before to resemble Republican executives in their support of Nixon's policies and goals. This is significant to presidential control because of the large number of bureaucrats calling themselves Independents. We conclude that Independent career executives may provide a president with a considerable reservoir of bureaucratic support.   J

2325. Connell, Christopher. UTAH: PROVIDING THE LEADERS AND THE DECISION-MAKERS. *Change 1982 14(5): 20-25, 55.* Discusses the careers of Chairman Orrin Grant Hatch of the Senate Labor and Human Resources Committee, and Terrel Howard Bell, US Secretary of Education; their ties with Utah, the Mormons, and the Reagan administration during 1980-82.

2326. Crane, Sylvia E. NELL'AMERICA DI REAGAN: IL CAMUFFAMENTO DEI "DIRITTI DEGLI STATI" [In Reagan's America: camouflaging states' rights]. *Ponte [Italy] 1981 37(5): 425-431.* The rhetoric of politicians exploits traditional themes in order to disguise

fundamental issues and turn the attention of the public away from important decisions; Ronald Reagan has been exploiting the myth that the very existence of the United States is due to the original states which formed the union, but his honeymoon with Congress is coming to an end.

2327. Crevelli, John P. THE FINAL ACT OF THE GREATEST CONSERVATION PRESIDENT. *Prologue 1980 12(4): 173-191.* Discusses the considerable accomplishments of President Lyndon B. Johnson in nature conservation. In the last days of Johnson's administration, he was advised by Secretary of the Interior Stewart Udall to use his executive power under the Antiquities Act to preserve and reserve seven million additional acres of land. The author analyzes Johnson's decision to recommend only 300,000 acres for conservation, and mentions the role of W. De Vier Pierson, special counsel to the president. Based on Department of the Interior Files, Johnson Papers, National Archives Records, and interviews; 10 photos, 70 notes.   M. A. Kascus

2328. Cronin, Thomas E. MAKING THE PRESIDENCY SAFE FOR DEMOCRACY. *Center Mag. 1973 6(5): 25-31.* Covers the role of Congress and the Presidency.

2329. Cronin, Thomas E. PUTTING THE PRESIDENT BACK INTO POLITICS. *Washington Monthly 1973 5(7): 7-12.* Considers the Watergate scandal and political reform.

2330. DeLuna, P. R. BUREAUCRATIC OPPOSITION AS A FACTOR IN TRUMAN'S FAILURE TO ACHIEVE A COLUMBIA VALLEY AUTHORITY. *Can. Hist. Assoc. Hist. Papers [Canada] 1975: 231-256.* The liberal supporters of Harry Truman wanted low cost Federal electricity for the public while the private power companies wanted to control its distribution. The Bureau of Reclamation and the Army Corps of Engineers used their connections in Congress to prevent the adoption of a Columbia Valley Authority modelled on the Tennessee Valley Authority. Based on Records of the Interior Department and personal papers in the National Archives, government reports, and secondary sources; 95 notes.   G. E. Panting

2331. Demuth, Christopher C. DEREGULATING THE CITIES. *Public Interest 1976 (44): 115-128.* Reviews two recent books, *The Politics of Neglect: Urban Aid from Model Cities to Revenue Sharing,* by Bernard J. Frieden and Marshall Kaplan, and Charles M. Haar's *Between the Idea and the Reality: A Study in the Origin, Fate and Legacy of the Model Cities Program,* concerning the Model Cities program of the Johnson administration, the most unequivocal failure of the Great Society. Also includes the author's own experiences as a staff assistant in the White House during the early days of the Nixon Administration. The Model Cities program attempted to rationalize and redirect federal urban policy. A principle reason for its failure was that the legislation drafted to implement it was based on little more than hope and ideas on how to improve existing programs were highly speculative. Institutional barriers to program coordination were underestimated, and the required participation of citizen groups delayed or halted the flow of funds to model neighborhoods for years. Haar views the arrival of the Nixon Administration as a calamity for the program, while Frieden and Kaplan rightly view Nixon as giving less support than Johnson but nevertheless keeping the basic commitment.   S. Harrow

2332. Donner, Frank. ELECTRONIC SURVEILLANCE: THE NATIONAL SECURITY GAME. *Civil Liberties R. 1975 2(3): 15-47.* All of the attorneys general from Jackson through Brownell dealt with national security wiretapping in the spirit of Ring Lardner's observation that Prohibition is better than no liquor at all.   J

2333. Douglas, William O. and Meeker, Joseph W., ed. NATURE'S CONSTITUTIONAL RIGHTS. *North Am. R. 1973 258(1): 11-14.* Presents, with minor editing, the dissenting opinion of William O. Douglas in *Sierra Club vs. Rogers C. B. Morton, Secretary of the Interior* (US, 1972). The Sierra Club had sued to stop the development of Mineral King Valley, a wilderness area of California's Sierra Nevada, by Walt Disney Enterprises, after the Forest Service, an agency of the Department of Interior, had approved use of the site and the access. The Supreme Court decided against the Sierra Club.   E. P. Costello

2334. Duram, James C. 'A GOOD GROWL': THE EISENHOWER CABINET'S JANUARY 16, 1959 DISCUSSION OF FEDERAL AID TO EDUCATION. *Presidential Studies Q. 1978 8(4): 434-444.* The transcript of the 16 January 1959 Cabinet meeting highlights the conflict within the Dwight D. Eisenhower administration over federal aid to education for classroom construction. Secretary of Agriculture Ezra Taft Benson opposed aid on philosophical grounds, fearing state financial dependency and federal control. Arthur S. Flemming, Secretary of Health, Education and Welfare, took the pragmatic approach, citing the critical classroom shortage. The discussion illustrates President Eisenhower's dilemma and how domestic problems forced him to advocate programs which contradicted his personal political beliefs. 7 notes.
S. C. Strom

2335. Edelman, Marian Wright. SOUTHERN SCHOOLS DESEGREGATION, 1954-1973: A JUDICIAL-POLITICAL OVERVIEW. *Ann. of the Am. Acad. of Pol. and Social Sci. 1973 (407): 32-42.* "Following the *Brown* decisions of 1954 and 1955, the Supreme Court refrained from ordering immediate dismantlement of the dual school system, leaving formulation of specific orders with regard to school desegregation in the hands of district courts. Obstruction and delay resulted, with massive southern resistance and a weak federal response. It was not until passage of the Civil Rights Act of 1964, when federal desegregation standards were adopted, that substantial desegregation could begin. Soon both the Department of Health, Education, and Welfare and the federal courts took a unified stand behind the law, attacking 'free choice' and southern delay. Progress finally seemed at hand. However, under the Nixon administration, federal enforcement efforts have been undercut. Major responsibility for enforcing school desegregation has been shifted from HEW to the slower judicial efforts of the Justice Department. Negative executive leadership has set a tone of national retreat. The current issue of busing and neighborhood schools threatens to erase desegregation progress already made in the South as well as to defeat efforts at making *Brown* a nationally applied policy. However, strong national and local leadership could maintain desegregation progress."
J

2336. Elfin, Margery. VICE-PRESIDENTIAL HOME ON NAVAL OBSERVATORY HILL. *Smithsonian 1977 8(6): 62-69.* In 1974 Congress designated the home built by Leon E. Dessez in 1893 for the Superintendent of the Naval Observatory as the Vice-Presidential residence. The interior of the late-Victorian home displays a surprising collection of contemporary American art chosen by Joan Mondale. Assuming the task of spotlighting the arts as part of her public role, she plans on featuring art from museums in different parts of the country, and working towards "awakening people to the fact that art exists outside large metropolitan areas." 5 illus.
S. R. Quéripel

2337. Engelbourg, Saul. THE COUNCIL OF ECONOMIC ADVISERS AND THE RECESSION OF 1953-1954. *Business Hist. Rev. 1980 54(2): 192-214.* The 1953-54 recession was the first in which a Council of Economic Advisers (CEA) appointed by a Republican President, Dwight D. Eisenhower, recommended policy actions. Despite traditional Republican Party rhetoric, the CEA supported an activist contracyclical approach that helped to establish Keynesianism as a bipartisan economic policy for the nation. Especially important in formulating the CEA response to the recession—accelerating public works programs, easing credit, and reducing taxes—were Arthur F. Burns and Neil H. Jacoby. Based on periodical literature of the period, government records, and the Jacoby Papers at Boston University; 62 notes.
C. J. Pusateri

2338. Epstein, Edward Jay. DID THE PRESS UNCOVER WATERGATE? *Commentary 1974 58(1): 21-24.* Discounts the thesis of Carl Bernstein and Bob Woodward's *All the President's Men* (New York: Simon & Schuster, 1974).
S

2339. Epstein, Edward Jay. THE KROGH FILE—THE POLITICS OF "LAW AND ORDER." *Public Interest 1975 (39): 99-124.* Discusses the rhetoric Richard M. Nixon used in his 1968 presidential campaign and his subsequent crime control policy such as the methadone programs formulated in part by Egil Krogh, Jr.
S

2340. Eskilsson, Sture. RONALD REAGANS EKONOMISKA POLITIK [Ronald Reagan's economic policy]. *Svensk Tidskrift [Sweden] 1981 68(9): 437-445.* Economic questions have dominated President

Reagan's first year in office, as he has given top priority to tax reduction, the struggle against inflation, and the financial basis for a strong defense. He is implementing his preestablished goals and maintaining the leadership style he developed earlier. His success can also be attributed to his mastery of the art of communication.
L. B. Sather

2341. Etzioni, Amitai. MASS PSYCHOLOGY IN THE WHITE HOUSE. *Society 1980 18(1): 82-85.* The author, a former White House senior adviser, reveals some inside deliberations on the suggested balanced budget for 1980-81, and discusses the possible results of its implementation versus other means to stifle inflation.

2342. Fairlie, Henry. THE LESSONS OF WATERGATE—ON THE POSSIBILITY OF MORALITY IN POLITICS. *Encounter [Great Britain] 1974 43(4): 8-27.* Discusses the ramifications of the break-in escapade, 1972-74, in which President Nixon gradually became enmeshed, and through which the corruption of his entire administration was sanctioned, showing that in general public opinion the Watergate scandal was viewed as normal politics.

2343. Fallows, James. BILL MOYERS: HIS HEART BELONGS TO DADDY. *Washington Monthly 1974 6(5/6): 36-50.* Comments on the career of Bill Moyers and his association with Lyndon B. Johnson.
S

2344. Faramazian, R. and Borisov, V. EKONOMICHESKIE ASPEKTY VOENNOI PROGRAMMY REIGANA [Economic aspects of Reagan's military program]. *Mirovaia Ekonomika i Mezhdunarodnye Otnosheniia [USSR] 1982 (8): 26-39.* Russian.

2345. Farrar, Ronald. HARRY TRUMAN AND THE PRESS: A VIEW FROM INSIDE. *Journalism Hist. 1981 8(2): 56-62, 70.* Discusses the diaries of Eben A. Ayers, who served as deputy press secretary to Harry S. Truman, presenting an inside view of Truman and his relationship with the press during 1945-53.

2346. Fisher, Louis. CONGRESS, THE EXECUTIVE AND THE BUDGET. *Ann. of the Am. Acad. of Pol. and Social Sci. 1974 411:102-113.* "During the autumn months of 1972 President Nixon and Congress engaged in a prolonged and bitter struggle over a spending ceiling. The president wanted a limit of $250 billion for fiscal 1973, with complete discretion to cut wherever needed to preserve the ceiling. Congress refused to grant him such broad discretion. This single incident tells one many valuable things about the relative advantages available to the two branches. While factually wide of the mark, the president's offensive against a big-spending Congress proved to be overpowering in the political arena. Congress lacked the capability—and, probably, also the will—to defend itself. The result was a serious collapse in informed and responsible policy making."
J

2347. Flanagan, Robert J. ACTUAL VERSUS POTENTIAL IMPACT OF GOVERNMENT ANTIDISCRIMINATION PROGRAMS. *Industrial and Labor Relations Rev. 1976 29(4): 486-507.* Examines improvement in economic status among minorities during 1960's-72; discusses the part played by the Labor Department and the Office of Contract Compliance, and offers information on future goals.

2348. Fragomen, Austin T., Jr. PRESIDENT CARTER'S AMNESTY AND SANCTIONS PROPOSAL. *Int. Migration Rev. 1977 11(4): 524-532.* Discusses President Jimmy Carter's proposed legislation for undocumented aliens; amnesty should be granted to aliens without intermediary temporary resident status and regardless of how or when they entered; citizen status for foreign workers should be made available after three years, and economic aid to Mexico should be increased.

2349. Frazer, Catherine S. THE TRAGEDY OF WATERGATE. *Midwest Q. 1973 15(1): 8-15.* Considers political ethics.

2350. Friedland, Roger. CLASS POWER AND SOCIAL CONTROL: THE WAR ON POVERTY. *Pol. and Soc. 1976 6(4): 459-489.* Views the War on Poverty as a co-optive program of social control to defuse the political threat of the urban poor and nonwhites to the accommodations between monopoly capital and organized labor in the 1960's.

Analyzes the conditions under which poor and nonwhite groups could influence political outcomes. Through statistical analysis of funding levels provided under War on Poverty programs, argues that the presence of powerful labor and corporate forces attended large allocations of funds to poverty agencies. These new bureaucracies allowed for some influence by poor and nonwhites on their operation, thereby deflecting any real influence upon the traditional class power structure. Based on secondary sources; tables, diagram, 46 notes.   D. G. Nielson

2351. Fry, Brian R. and Stolarek, John S.   THE IMPEACHMENT PROCESS: PREDISPOSITIONS AND VOTES.   *J. of Pol.* 1980 42(4): 1118-1134. The House Judiciary Committee voted three of five bills of impeachment against President Richard M. Nixon in 1974. Members of the committee confronted a problem of information overload and those predisposed to support Nixon may have experienced cognitive dissonance. The attitude of each member on each bill of impeachment could be predicted by: liberal or conservative ideology, party membership, and district's vote for Nixon during the 1972 presidential election. Of 190 votes, 165 were successfully predicted by these criteria. While politics did not determine Nixon's fate, it did condition the interpretation of the Watergate affair. 2 tables, 38 notes.   A. W. Novitsky

2352. Frye, Jon and Gordon, Robert J.   GOVERNMENT INTERVENTION IN THE INFLATION PROCESS: THE ECONOMETRICS OF "SELF-INFLICTED WOUNDS."   *Am. Econ. Rev.* 1981 71(2): 288-294. The on-again and off-again controls of the Nixon administration contributed to inflation. Prices of food and energy and declining production were significant contributing factors. This governmental policy was a self-inflicted wound that had long range damages despite a politically attractive short-term policy of intervention. Biblio.
                    D. K. Pickens

2353. Gaines, Edith.   AT HOME: BUILDING THE WHITE HOUSE COLLECTION.   *Art & Antiques* 1981 4(4): 76-83. The preservation and improvement of the furnishing and decoration of the White House was haphazard at best until Jacqueline Kennedy began efforts to rejuvenate the Executive Mansion in 1961; now Clement E. Conger, curator since 1970, organizes an ambitious project to acquire superb examples of American fine and decorative art.

2354. Gambino, Richard.   WATERGATE LINGO: A LANGUAGE OF NON-RESPONSIBILITY.   *Freedom At Issue* 1973 (22): 7-9, 15-17.

2355. Gass, Oscar.   THE NIXON ECONOMY.   *Worldview* 1973 16(7): 7-14. Overview of the economic policy of the Nixon Administration focuses on industrial competitive deficiency, apparent growth in multinational corporations, and general obfuscation of economic facts and trends for political ends, 1971-73.

2356. Geelhoed, E. Bruce.   WHAT WAS GOOD FOR OUR COUNTRY WAS GOOD FOR GENERAL MOTORS: CHARLES E. WILSON AND THE U.S. SENATE.   *Michigan Hist.* 1980 64(5): 36-43. An examination of the Senate hearing on President Eisenhower's appointment of Charles E. Wilson as Secretary of Defense reveals that the quote widely attributed to Wilson is incomplete, and that Wilson underwent a stronger scrutiny than had George Humphrey who also had been a wealthy industrialist. 5 pictures, 42 notes.   L. E. Ziewacz

2357. Geevskii, I. A.   POKHOD BEDNIAKOV NA VASHINGTON I POLITIKA BELOGO DOMA   [The march of the poor on Washington and the policy of the White House]. *Novaia i Noveishaia Istoriia [USSR]* 1977 (3): 67-78. A study of the March on Washington for Jobs and Freedom during May-June 1968, precipitated by civil unrest during the spring and the assassination of Martin Luther King, Jr. Draws on the published documents from Lyndon B. Johnson's archive to show the president's administrative deliberations and the ensuing government decision to deal with the marchers. Based on the archival publications of the Lyndon Baines Johnson Library and secondary works; 46 notes.   S

2358. Gibson, James W. and Felkins, Patricia K.   A NIXON LEXICON.   *Western Speech* 1974 38(3): 190-198. Analyzes Richard M. Nixon's "Checkers" speech and two Watergate speeches.   S

2359. Godden, Richard and Maidment, Richard.   ANGER, LANGUAGE AND POLITICS: JOHN F. KENNEDY AND THE STEEL CRISIS.   *Presidential Studies Q.* 1980 10(3): 317-331. By the examination of the political rhetoric of the participants, this examines President John F. Kennedy's behavior during the 1962 steel price hike crisis. Despite interpretations that depict him as being overwrought and rattled by the crisis, Kennedy acted as a practical politician. The steel crisis threatened his public standing, and Kennedy felt that the action of the steel industry threatened his reputation as a mediator. His dramatic actions, potentially dangerous in terms of business support, stemmed from his liberal Democratic political reaction to the actions of the steel companies. 44 notes.   D. H. Cline

2360. Goff, David H. and Goff, Linda Dysart.   REGULATION OF TELEVISION ADVERTISING TO CHILDREN: THE POLICY DISPUTE IN ITS SECOND DECADE.   *Southern Speech Communication J.* 1982 48(1): 38-50. Traces the dispute over television advertising aimed at children during 1970-81 as heard by the Federal Trade Commission (FTC); notes the ineffectiveness of regulating agencies and a rapidly evolving regulatory atmosphere in the Reagan administration.

2361. Goldberg, Paul.   EPA IN DISARRAY: MUZZLING THE WATCHDOG.   *Washington Monthly* 1981 13(10): 30-35. Reports that the Reagan administration and Environmental Protection Agency administrator Anne Gorsuch are eliminating many environmental regulations.

2362. Goldfeld, Stephen M. and Blinder, Alan S.   NEW MEASURES OF FISCAL AND MONETARY POLICY, 1958-73.   *Am. Econ. Rev.* 1976 66(5): 780-796. By measuring fiscal and monetary policies on macroeconomic activity, the authors discovered that the Eisenhower administration pursued a stabilizing fiscal program while in the Kennedy-Johnson administration *destabilizing* actions regarding income took place. They also pointed out the disharmony between the White House and the Federal Reserve System when a Democrat is President. 6 tables, 6 figs.   D. K. Pickens

2363. Goldsmith, William W.   BRINGING THE THIRD WORLD HOME.   *Working Papers Mag.* 1982 9(2): 24-30. Discusses the way industrial production has become internationalized in the 1970's and the particular example of President Ronald Reagan's tax and regulatory concessions to induce business to invest in economically depressed areas, called enterprise zones, in order to keep jobs inside the United States.

2364. Goldstein, Walter.   THE POLITICAL FAILURE OF U.S. ENERGY POLICY.   *Bull. of the Atomic Scientists* 1978 34(9): 17-19. Historical reluctance to enact economic planning in peacetime and massive rivalries in Congress led to the demise of President Jimmy Carter's energy proposals to reduce oil imports, conserve national consumption, increase domestic coal production, and limit per capita demand for petroleum, 1976-78.

2365. Gouran, Dennis S.   THE WATERGATE COVER-UP: ITS DYNAMICS AND ITS IMPLICATIONS.   *Communication Monographs* 1976 43(3): 176-186. Discusses the group dynamics of the Watergate scandal of 1972, examining its background, four aspects of the group dynamic process, and the implications of the "group-think" process for American politics.

2366. Grayson, A. G.   NORTH CAROLINA AND HARRY TRUMAN, 1944-1948.   *J. of Am. Studies [Great Britain]* 1975 9(3): 283-300. Analyzes responses in North Carolina to domestic policies of Harry S. Truman, particularly his positions on civil rights, labor, and other controversial issues. The North Carolina electorate at first supported Truman, but he lost support increasingly and was vigorously criticized by some North Carolina Democratic factions. However, he continued to enjoy more support in North Carolina than his contemporaries believed. Based on manuscripts, newspapers, and secondary sources; 76 notes.
                    H. T. Lovin

2367. Gruber, Carol S.   WHITE HOUSE SCIENTIST: MUST THE INSIDER GET OUT?   *Rev. in Am. Hist.* 1978 6(1): 131-137. Review article prompted by George B. Kistiakowsky's *A Scientist at the White House: The Private Diary of President Eisenhower's Special Assistant for Science and Technology* (Cambridge, Mass.: Harvard U. Pr., 1976).

2368. Hah, Chong-do and Lindquist, Robert M.   THE 1952 STEEL SEIZURE REVISITED: A SYSTEMATIC STUDY IN PRESIDENTIAL DECISION MAKING. *Administrative Sci. Q. 1975 20(4): 587-605.* Formulates a coherent framework for analyzing presidential decisionmaking, specifically studying the 1952 seizure of the steel mills by President Harry S. Truman.

2369. Hahn, Dan F.   FLAILING THE PROFLIGATE: CARTER'S ENERGY SERMON OF 1979. *Presidential Studies Q. 1980 10(4): 583-587.* President Jimmy Carter's energy speech of 16 July 1979 has been described as two separate speeches—a sermon on the American loss of confidence and a presentation of his energy program. Instead of being two speeches, however, it should be seen as one speech structured by Carter based on his evangelical and spiritual bias. Table, 24 notes.
D. H. Cline

2370. Handlin, Oscar.   WATERGATE: REFLECTIONS FROM AFAR. *Freedom At Issue 1973 (21): 11-13.* Considers the limitations of Executive Power and discusses political ethics.

2371. Harper, Alan D.   A TRUMAN FOR SOME SEASONS. *R. in Am. Hist. 1975 3(2): 249-253.* Alonzo L. Hamby's *Beyond the New Deal: Harry S. Truman and American Liberalism* (New York: Columbia U. Pr., 1973) and Allen Yarnell's *Democrats and Progressives: The 1948 Presidential Election as a Test of Postwar Liberalism* (Berkeley: U. of California Pr., 1974) examine domestic policy and the presidential election of 1948 to prove Truman's liberalism.

2372. Harrell, Jackson; Ware, B. L.; and Linkugel, Wil A.   FAILURE OF APOLOGY IN AMERICAN POLITICS: NIXON ON WATERGATE. *Speech Monographs 1975 42(4): 245-261.* Discusses the failure of apologetic rhetoric in the statements of President Richard M. Nixon during the Watergate scandal, 1972-74.

2373. Harrington, Michael.   WATERGATE: ON POLITICS AND MONEY. *Dissent 1973 20(3): 278-279.* Discusses campaign finance and John Connally.

2374. Harrison, Cynthia E.   A "NEW FRONTIER" FOR WOMEN: THE PUBLIC POLICY OF THE KENNEDY ADMINISTRATION. *J. of Am. Hist. 1980 67(3): 630-646.* The President's Commission on the Status of Women, created on 14 December 1961 by President John F. Kennedy, was the brainchild of a labor union woman, Esther Peterson. The commission became the centerpiece of the Kennedy administration's actions on behalf of women's issues. Peterson used the commission to advance two important women's causes: elimination of discriminatory practices in the federal Civil Service and equal pay legislation. Although successes in these two areas constituted minor advances for women, they did represent an early challenge to the entire sex-role structure in American society. 45 notes.
T. P. Linkfield

2375. Hart, John.   EXECUTIVE REORGANIZATION IN THE USA AND THE GROWTH OF PRESIDENTIAL POWER. *Public Administration [Great Britain] 1974 52(2): 179-191.* Discusses the role of executive reorganization in the Nixon administration, especially after 1970, focusing on the decline of the Cabinet and the effect this had on Congress.

2376. Hart, John.   KENNEDY, CONGRESS AND CIVIL RIGHTS. *J. of Am. Studies [Great Britain] 1979 13(2): 165-178.* President John F. Kennedy took into account the roadblocks to implementing the broad civil rights plank in the Democratic Party platform of 1960. He campaigned in 1960 not for sweeping civil rights legislation but expanded employment and educational opportunities for minorities. After the election, Kennedy cajoled and bargained with an unreceptive Congress until his "moderate and pragmatic" civil rights proposals were headed for Congressional approval when Kennedy was assassinated in 1963. Archival materials and secondary sources; 39 notes.
H. T. Lovin

2377. Hay, George A. and Kelley, Daniel.   AN EMPIRICAL SURVEY OF THE PRICE FIXING CONSPIRACIES. *J. of Law and Econ. 1974 17(1): 13-38.* Survey of the Department of Justice Antitrust Division cases of price fixing, 1963-73, finds that competition conspiracies correlate with situations where companies are few, concentration high, and the product homogeneous.

2378. Hellman, Louis M.   A HISTORY AND REMINISCENCE OF THE OFFICE OF THE DEPUTY ASSISTANT SECRETARY OF POPULATION AFFAIRS, DEPT. OF HEALTH, EDUCATION, AND WELFARE, 1969-1977. *Bull. of the Hist. of Medicine 1982 56(1): 77-87.* In 1970, Louis M. Hellman became Deputy Assistant Secretary for Population Affairs at the Health, Education, and Welfare Department, and he implemented the Family Planning Act (US, 1970), which came from the Gruening Hearings, 1965-68. Despite an almost impossible bureaucracy, the program accomplished its goal, giving family planning services to five million women who wanted but could not afford them. 11 notes.
M. Kaufman

2379. Henderson, Lenneal J., Jr.   IMPACT OF MILITARY BASE SHUTDOWNS. *Black Scholar 1974 5(2): 9-15.* Documents the impact on black workers of Defense budget cutbacks as announced by Secretary of Defense Elliot Richardson 17 April 1973, and asserts that the decision has obvious political motives; the hardest-hit cities have Democratic Party mayors, legislators, and voting majorities, and a substantial nonwhite population; voted overwhelmingly for Humphrey; and have many black elected officials.
M. T. Wilson

2380. Henry, Patrick.   "AND I DON'T CARE WHAT IT IS": THE TRADITION-HISTORY OF A CIVIL RELIGION PROOF-TEXT. *J. of the Am. Acad. of Religion 1981 49(1): 35-47.* Investigates an often-quoted statement made by President Dwight D. Eisenhower in 1954. Traces the history of the transmission of the statement (on the need for government to be guided by religious values), revealing such problems as documentation, when and where the statement was made, the text of the statement, and the implications drawn from it. Presents the best text possible, as well as the context of the statement. 2 notes.
E. R. Lester

2381. Hentoff, Nat.   LIBRARIANS AND THE FIRST AMENDMENT AFTER NIXON. *Wilson Lib. Bull. 1974 48(9): 724-741.* Richard M. Nixon's administration was responsible for the censorship of libraries and other abuses of the First Amendment which restricted freedom of speech.
S

2382. Hoffman, Wayne and Marmor, Ted.   THE POLITICS OF PUBLIC ASSISTANCE REFORM: AN ESSAY REVIEW. *Social Service R. 1976 50(1): 11-22.* Discusses recent writings about political factors in the anti-poverty and public welfare reform policies of the Nixon administration, 1969-72.

2383. Houstoun, L. O., Jr.   THE CARTER URBAN POLICY A YEAR LATER. *Antioch Rev. 1979 37(2): 134-147.* Reviews the origins of the federal policy which affected President Carter's Urban and Regional Policy Group of 1978, which consists of three elements: 1) increased financial aid to cities, 2) a set of improvements designed to be more sensitive to city revitalization, 3) a new set of financial incentives.

2384. Howe, Irving.   WATERGATE: THE Z CONNECTION. *Dissent 1973 20(3): 275-277.* Considers the film *Z*.

2385. Huddleston, Mark W.   THE CARTER CIVIL SERVICE REFORMS: SOME IMPLICATIONS FOR POLITICAL THEORY AND PUBLIC ADMINISTRATION. *Pol. Sci. Q. 1981-82 96(4): 607-621.* Assesses Carter's Civil Service Reform Act (US, 1978), which established a system of merit pay for midlevel managers, instituted a senior executive service for top administrators, provided a statutory foundation for labor relations in the federal sector, and placed the authority of personnel management in the hands of presidential representatives. The act is presidentially, rather than publicly inclined, however. Further, it discourages cooperation among public officials. Secondary sources; 37 notes.
J. Powell

2386. Hudson, William E.   THE NEW FEDERALISM PARADOX. *Policy Studies J. 1980 8(6): 900-906.* Analyzes the Nixon administration's New Federalism reforms as they affected El Paso, Texas, considered a test case, and concludes that contrary to the stated goals of decentralization, they fostered dependency on the federal government and reduced local autonomy; based on 1966 census and a 1978-79 study of El Paso.

2387. Huitt, Ralph K. WHITE HOUSE CHANNELS TO THE HILL. *Pro. of the Acad. of Pol. Sci. 1975 32(1): 71-84.* Discusses disagreements between Congress and the executive branch about needed legislation, 1974-75.

2388. Hundley, Tom. ADDITIVES ANONYMOUS. *Washington Monthly 1982 13(12): 42-46.* Discusses the Bureau of Alcohol, Tobacco and Firearms's 1980 regulation that would require the listing of ingredients on alcoholic beverages by 1983, which was rejected by the Reagan administration in 1981 because it would cost the alcoholic beverage industry, and ultimately the consumer, too much money; traces the history of this regulation since consumer groups requested it in 1972.

2389. Hunter, Allen. IN THE WINGS: NEW RIGHT ORGANIZATION AND IDEOLOGY. *Radical Am. 1981 15(1-2): 113-138.* The Reagan Administration is being goaded by the organized New Right to fulfill economic and socially conservative goals. These cluster around capitalist free enterprise, the male-headed family, and a white middle-class feeling that it was left behind by the changes of the 1960's. The key figures (Richard Viguerie, Paul Weyrich, Howard Phillips, and John "Terry" Dolan) of the core and single-issue organizations, the growing cluster of New Right religious groups, and the networking practices are all identified. 46 notes, 7 illus.   C. M. Hough

2390. Huttie, Joseph J., Jr. "NEW FEDERALISM" AND THE DEATH OF A DREAM IN MOUND BAYOU, MISSISSIPPI. *New South 1973 28(4): 20-29.* The Nixon administration's "New Federalism" is destroying the Mound Bayou Community Hospital and Health Center.   S

2391. Ingram, Timothy H. ITT AND WATERGATE: THE COLSON CONNECTION. *Washington Monthly 1973 5(9): 32-37.*

2392. Isbell, Florence. CARTER'S CIVIL SERVICE REFORM: 35 PERCENT IFS, BUTS AND MAYBES. *Civil Liberties Rev. 1978 5(1): 6-15.* Analyzes the major principles of President Jimmy Carter's proposed Civil Service Reform Act, his chief legislative goal for 1978.

2393. Ives, C. P. SCHOOLING FOR WATERGATE. *Modern Age 1977 21(3): 289-294.* Because bright young Nixon lawyers had been schooled by left-leaning Yale (and other) professors, they were prepared to try new methods rather than work through old channels; so—just as leftward expostulations in the 40's and 50's based on the philosophies of New Dealers in the 30's caused McCarthyist radicalism—liberal teachers of the 60's caused the Watergate scandal.

2394. Johnson, Neil M. and Lagerquist, Philip D. RESOURCES AT THE HARRY S. TRUMAN LIBRARY ON WESTERN ISSUES AND PROGRAMS. *Government Publ. Rev. 1980 7A(2): 159-166.* Identifies holdings of the Harry S. Truman Library on federal policy toward Indians, 1945-66, water power and supply, 1945-52, migratory labor, 1950-51, Japanese American relocation, 1940-45, and oral history of the presidential campaign of 1948.

2395. Jordan, Vernon E., Jr. A QUESTION OF COMMITMENT: THE BLACK URBAN CRISIS AND THE CARTER ADMINISTRATION. *Black Scholar 1977 9(2): 2-9.* Text of a speech delivered in the summer of 1977 at the Urban League Annual Convention held in Washington. The black vote elected Jimmy Carter, who is not living up to his political campaign promises.   B. D. Ledbetter

2396. Kalven, Harry, Jr. IF THIS BE ASYMMETRY, MAKE THE MOST OF IT. *Center Mag. 1973 6(3): 36-37.* The Nixon administration's attack on the mass media and its reflection on freedom of speech; one of six articles in this issue on "Broadcasting and the First Amendment."   S

2397. Katz, Milton S. E. FREDERICK MORROW AND CIVIL RIGHTS IN THE EISENHOWER ADMINISTRATION. *Phylon 1981 42(2): 133-144.* The first black person to serve in an executive capacity for a US president was named in July 1955. President Dwight D. Eisenhower appointed E. Frederick Morrow as administrative officer for special projects. It was not a popular move in the White House staff. Morrow was unable to get to the president when necessary or assert any

power. Yet he remained in the White House against hostility and kept civil rights issues alive.   A. G. Belles

2398. Kaus, Robert M. HOW THE SUPREME COURT SABOTAGED CIVIL SERVICE REFORM. *Washington Monthly 1978 10(9): 38-44.* President Jimmy Carter was forced to change a proposal for civil service reform, due to the threat of its unconstitutionality.

2399. Kempf, Hubert. LA "REAGANOMICS" A L'EPREUVE DES FAITS [Reaganomics tested by facts]. *Etudes [France] 1982 356(2): 183-197.* Contrasts the economic stances of Jimmy Carter and Ronald Reagan; critiques the Reagan administration for failing to achieve its stated promises and goals. French.

2400. Kenski, Henry C. INFLATION AND PRESIDENTIAL POPULARITY. *Public Opinion Q. 1977 41(1): 86-90.* Explores the impact of inflation on the presidential popularity between Dwight D. Eisenhower and Richard M. Nixon, 1953-72.

2401. Khan, Mohammad Mohabbat. POLITICS OF ADMINISTRATIVE REORGANIZATION: PRESIDENT NIXON'S DEPARTMENTAL REORGANIZATION PROGRAM. *Pol. Sci. Rev. [India] 1980 19(2): 170-180.* President Nixon was determined to improve the federal executive structure, and proposed in his 1971 State of the Union speech to abolish seven executive departments and create four new ones in their place. The proposals from the beginning faced determined resistance from organized interest groups, and Nixon reversed his decision regarding the abolition of the Agriculture Department. The proposals for reorganization aroused opposition both from affected interest groups and from Congress because they were seen as a means of increasing the power of the presidency. Based on official papers and interviews; 10 notes.   D. H. Watson

2402. Kilson, Martin. WHITHER INTEGRATION? *Am. Scholar 1976 45(3): 360-376.* Analyzes integration since World War II, the forces that have furthered it, and the advances still needed. The most phenomenal changes have occurred during the last decade through the impetus given by the civil rights movement, the cultural shifts of the 1960's, and public policy initiatives of the Kennedy and Johnson administrations.   R. V. Ritter

2403. Klumpp, James F. and Hollihan, Thomas A. DEBUNKING THE RESIGNATION OF EARL BUTZ: SACRIFICING AN OFFICIAL RACIST. *Q. J. of Speech 1979 65(1): 1-11.* The rhetorical response to a much-publicized racist joke told by Agriculture Secretary Earl Butz (1909-) focused on the inappropriateness of racist sentiments in public officials. Thus Butz's subsequent resignation served as a ritual sacrifice, condemning public racism and soothing the conscience of an inherently racist society while contributing nothing to the eradication of private racism. Based on newspaper reports and secondary sources; 37 notes.   E. Bailey

2404. Klumpp, James F. and Lukehart, Jeffrey K. THE PARDONING OF RICHARD NIXON: A FAILURE IN MOTIVATIONAL STRATEGY. *Western J. of Speech Communication 1978 42(2): 116-123.* Gerald R. Ford's 8 September 1974 speech pardoning Richard M. Nixon was eloquent but a failure because of moral and legal rhetorical errors.

2405. Kopkind, Andrew. WHY NOT THE BEST? CARTER TO CITIES: PLAY DEAD. *Working Papers for a New Soc. 1978 6(1): 6-9.* Surveys Jimmy Carter's new urban policy which is characterized by few new social programs, little increase in spending, tax incentives in the private sector, little relief for public enterprise and community corporations, use of present tools to solve urban ills, and avoidance of tax redistribution, 1977-78.

2406. Koppes, Clayton R. OSCAR L. CHAPMAN AND MCCARTHYISM. *Colorado Mag. 1979 56(1-2): 35-44.* Explores an attack in September 1950 by conservative Republican freshman Senator Andrew F. Schoeppel (of Kansas) upon the loyalty of Interior Secretary Oscar L. Chapman, a Coloradoan. Chapman, a long-time Interior Department administrator, had been considered one of the more leftist New Dealers. Chapman successfully defended himself before the Senate Committee on Interior and Insular Affairs; the charges were held baseless. Support for him came from the leadership of both parties. He had no more trouble over his loyalty. Primary sources, especially the Senate Committee on Interior and Insular Affairs, *Investigation;* 3 photos, 17 notes.

O. H. Zabel

2407. Kovaleff, Theodore P. DIVORCE AMERICAN-STYLE: THE DU PONT-GENERAL MOTORS CASE. *Delaware Hist. 1978 18(1): 28-42.* In 1948 the US government brought a civil suit against the Du Pont Company to force the company's complete divestiture of its stock in General Motors Corp. and its control of General Motors. The case dragged on through three presidential administrations, eventually leading to a government victory handed down by the Supreme Court. The prosecution of the case by the Eisenhower administration, after the government lost its original suits, demonstrated the administration's commitment to upholding and using the nation's antitrust laws. Based on Antitrust Papers in the Department of Justice Records, Records of the Du Pont Company, and secondary accounts; 66 notes.

R. M. Miller

2408. Kuter, Laurence S. TRUMAN'S SECRET MANAGEMENT OF THE AIRLINES. *Aerospace Hist. 1977 24(3): 181-183.* Personal account of the author's experiences with President Harry S. Truman and his appointment as Chairman of the Civil Aeronautics Board in early 1948. Congress did not approve the appointment because of criticism of the policy of placing military men in civilian positions. In spite of this, Truman's instructions to Kuter were without political manipulation, but stressed that Kuter should take action based on his judgment of the best interests of American civil aviation. Based on Kuter's diary.

A. M. Osur

2409. Laing, Robert B. and Stevenson, Robert L. PUBLIC OPINION TRENDS IN THE LAST DAYS OF THE NIXON ADMINISTRATION. *Journalism Q. 1976 53(2): 294-302.* Telephone surveys of 350 people were conducted during the week of 5-9 August 1974 in Seattle, Washington. The respondents were encouraged to describe the impeachment proceedings and their reactions in personal terms. The results show considerable ambivalence about the resolution of the issue. Material presented on the televised hearings tended to make the viewers more likely to favor impeachment. 6 tables, 4 notes.

E. Gibson

2410. Lamb, Charles M. EQUAL EMPLOYMENT OPPORTUNITY AND THE CARTER ADMINISTRATION. *Policy Studies J. 1979 8(3): 377-383.* Examines why President Jimmy Carter shifted some Equal Employment Opportunity programs from the Civil Service Commission to the Labor Department.

2411. Lang, Gladys Engel and Lang, Kurt. POLLING ON WATERGATE: THE BATTLE FOR PUBLIC OPINION. *Public Opinion Q. 1980 44(4): 530-547.* Case studies of the development and outcome of political controversies, like Watergate, can go a long way toward clarification of the direct and indirect impacts of the polls.

J/S

2412. Lanzillotti, Robert F. and Roberts, Blaine. THE LEGACY OF PHASE II PRICE CONTROLS. *Am. Econ. R. 1974 64(2): 82-87.* Discusses the implementation and economic impact during 1971-72 of the Nixon administration's Phase II price controls.

2413. Lawson, Steven F. and Gelfand, Mark I. CONSENSUS AND CIVIL RIGHTS: LYNDON B. JOHNSON AND THE BLACK FRANCHISE. *Prologue 1976 8(2): 65-76.* President Lyndon B. Johnson was personally committed to working for civil rights for Negroes, but was determined to work within the existing political structure to achieve reform in a gradual, orderly manner. He used the authority of his office to clear away many of the legal barriers to black voting, but his political instincts and his sense of the federal system prevented him from using the Voting Rights Act of 1965 as a catalyst for southern political change. Based on primary and secondary sources.

N. Lederer

2414. Lee, R. Alton. REBUILDING THE WHITE HOUSE. *Am. Hist. Illus. 1978 12(10): 12-19.* By the Truman administration the White House had so deteriorated that the White House architect said he could prove mathematically that it was impossible for the mansion to remain standing. The second floor was particularly weak. The 81st Congress approved the renovation in 1949, and it was completed in 1952. The

building was then structurally sound and had roughly 1.5 million cubic feet, more than 100 rooms, and 19 bathrooms. Primary sources; 8 illus.

D. Dodd

2415. Lemann, Nicholas. JORDAN, GEORGIA, AND THE ESTABLISHMENT. *Washington Monthly 1978 10(2): 36-47.* Discusses the role played by Hamilton Jordan in Jimmy Carter's presidential campaign and administration, 1974-78.

2416. Leuchtenburg, William E. THE LEGACY OF FDR. *Wilson Q. 1982 6(2): 77-93.* Discusses the residual impact of Franklin D. Roosevelt's New Deal on three Democratic presidents: Harry S. Truman, John F. Kennedy, and Lyndon B. Johnson, with special attention to Johnson's Great Society legislation; 1933-68.

2417. Levine, Arthur. "I GOT MY JOB THROUGH CREEP." *Washington Monthly 1974 6(9): 35-46.* Discusses how Civil Service posts were filled during the Nixon administration, 1969-74.

2418. Levitan, Sar A. and Taggart, Robert. THE GREAT SOCIETY DID SUCCEED. *Pol. Sci. Q. 1976-77 91(4): 601-618.* Report on their extensive reevaluation of the Johnson administration's Great Society programs. Their conclusion is that the Great Society programs did not fail —as has been widely charged in recent years—but that despite some deficiencies, the programs led to substantial improvements in the living conditions of the poor, the sick, the elderly, and the members of minority groups.

J

2419. Lewis, Eleanor G. THE HOUSE COMMITTEE ON RULES AND THE LEGISLATIVE PROGRAM OF THE KENNEDY AND JOHNSON ADMINISTRATIONS. *Capitol Studies 1978 6(2): 27-38.* The House Rules Committee, formerly a "cemetery" for certain kinds of bills, became more responsive to administration legislative requests during 1961-69.

2420. Lewis, John D., Jr. AMERICAN GESTAPO: HOW THE BATF IS RIDING ROUGHSHOD OVER CIVIL LIBERTIES. *Reason 1980 11(12): 24-28, 44.* The federal Bureau of Alcohol, Tobacco, and Firearms (BATF), faced with less to enforce after moonshining declined in the 1970's, has stepped up its violations of the civil liberties and the Second Amendment rights of legal firearms owners and dealers through paramilitary-style raids, unjustified confiscations of legal firearms, entrapment, and use of untrustworthy informants.

2421. Light, Alfred R. THE CARTER ADMINISTRATION'S NATIONAL ENERGY PLAN: PRESSURE GROUPS, AND ORGANIZATIONAL POLITICS IN THE CONGRESS. *Policy Studies J. 1978 7(1): 68-75.* Relates the Carter administration's record on energy policy, emphasizing policy formation and relations with Congress, 1977-78.

2422. Light, Alfred R. THE GOVERNORS' PUSH FOR EMERGENCY ENERGY POWERS. *Publius 1980 10(1): 57-67.* The long lines at gas stations in 1979 did not represent a replay of the fuel-energy crisis of 1973. Nevertheless, the stalemate between Congress and the Department of Energy in the development of national energy policy for emergencies led to a large role for state governors and the National Governors Association in designing the Emergency Energy Conservation Act (US, 1979). The governors resisted President Jimmy Carter's executive orders extending more authority to them in gasoline pricing, but they insisted on state flexibility in determining cash fuel assistance programs for winter heating oil. The governors retained a central role for themselves in implementation of federal policy during energy emergencies. Based on government publications and current periodical literature; 25 notes.

C. B. Schultz

2423. Light, Alfred R. THE 1979 ENERGY CRISIS SYMPOSIUM: INTRODUCTION. *Publius 1980 10(1): 43-45.* Summarizes "centrally-directed" federalism evident in symposium articles on energy regulation in this issue. Evaluates 1979 trends toward a Department of Energy monopoly on such regulation in the case of nuclear waste management, in particular through burial of nuclear wastes at the Waste Isolation Pilot Plant in Carlsbad, New Mexico.

C. B. Schulz

2424. Light, Paul C. THE PRESIDENT'S AGENDA: NOTES ON THE TIMING OF DOMESTIC CHOICE. *Presidential Studies Q. 1981 11(1): 67-82.* A president's daily agenda is constantly fluctuating, and directly affects major policy decisions. Usually, a president's agenda is set by the end of his first year in office, and what is established during the first year of his first term is crucial for effectiveness and success. A prime example of this is Jimmy Carter. His failure in his first year to establish a clear agenda doomed his administration. 2 tables, 18 notes, biblio.   D. H. Cline

2425. Linnik, V. A. VIRAZHI VNUTRENNEI POLITIKI DZH. KARTERA [The turns in the domestic policy of J. Carter]. *Mirovaia Ekonomika i Mezhdunarodnye Otnosheniia [USSR] 1979 (5): 108-114.* Studies the specific character of the domestic policy of the Carter administration. Biblio.

2426. Long, F. A. PRESIDENT NIXON'S 1973 REORGANIZATION PLAN NO. 1: WHERE DO SCIENCE AND TECHNOLOGY GO? *Sci. and Public Affairs 1973 29(5): 5-8, 40-42.* Richard M. Nixon's switch of responsibility for the nation's scientific advisory apparatus to the National Science Foundation rather than the President's Science Advisory Committee will have lasting effects on scientific research, especially that concerning military technology.

2427. Longley, Charles H. MC NAMARA AND MILITARY BEHAVIOR. *Am. J. of Pol. Sci. 1974 18(1): 1-22.* "Many studies of civil-military relations employ a case study approach. The present study, however, attempts to generate some empirically based propositions regarding the nature of civil-military relations in America as a preliminary step toward theory building. Content analysis of three sources over the period 1953-64 provides the data with which to investigate the relationship between levels of civilian control and military behavior. Subsequent controls for budgetary allocations are also found to be particularly important for explaining the character of civil-military relations in contemporary America."   J

2428. Lord, Donald C. JFK AND CIVIL RIGHTS. *Presidential Studies Q. 1978 8(2): 151-163.* Examines the executive tools employed by the John F. Kennedy administration to further minority voting rights, employment, and desegregation of public accommodations. While building goodwill among blacks, the limited success of this method in 1961 and 1962 convinced Kennedy of the need for stronger civil rights legislation. Public climate made it impossible to strengthen federal civil rights laws before the racial confrontations of 1963. However, the legislative strategy which secured passage of the Civil Rights Act of 1964 was devised by Kennedy in early 1963. Using the authority of his office and appealing to public opinion, Kennedy persuaded doubtful Senators to support a cloture motion resulting in a defeat for the southern filibuster in 1964. 76 notes.   S. C. Strom

2429. Mancke, Richard B. THE AMERICAN RESPONSE: "ON THE JOB TRAINING?" *Orbis 1980 23(4): 785-801.* Analyzes the Jimmy Carter administration's response to the oil crisis, evaluates several of the programs tried, and discusses why they failed. The policies of strategic storage, waiving the MMT gasoline additive ban, subsidizing middle distillate imports, and standby rationing were begun without proper study and were mismanaged. Covers 1978-present. The author concludes that the present crisis will continue until the United States is able to develop a viable energy policy. Based on published sources; table, 15 notes.   J. W. Thacker, Jr.

2430. Manheim, Jarol B. and Lammers, William W. THE NEWS CONFERENCE AND PRESIDENTIAL LEADERSHIP OF PUBLIC OPINION: DOES THE TAIL WAG THE DOG? *Presidential Studies Q. 1981 11(2): 177-188.* An examination of the scheduling and conduct of presidential news conferences, 1961-75, is used to determine the degree to which presidents alter their behavior in response to changes in their Gallup Poll ratings. There appears to be limited response more in the area of scheduling than in verbal behavior. Primary sources; 4 tables, 7 notes.   A. Drysdale

2431. Marando, Vincent L. A METROPOLITAN LOWER INCOME HOUSING ALLOCATION POLICY. *Am. Behavioral Scientist 1975 19(1): 75-103.* Discusses the development 1970-75 by urban government councils and the Housing and Urban Development Department of location plans for low-income housing, in a special issue entitled "Policy Content and the Regulatory Process."

2432. Mayer, Joseph. WATERGATE FLIMFLAM. *Social Sci. 1974 49(2): 99-103.* Discusses the Watergate scandal, glancing "at factors not generally emphasized in the continuing nationwide ballyhoo . . . with a minimum of speculation about the gaps."   E. P. Stickney

2433. Mayer, Milton. AN AMERICAN BANALITY. *Center Mag. 1975 8(3): 2-5.* Discusses the tragic aspects of Richard M. Nixon and the Watergate scandal.   S

2434. McFadyen, Richard E. THE FDA'S REGULATION AND CONTROL OF ANTIBIOTICS IN THE 1950S: THE HENRY WELCH SCANDAL, FÉLIX MARTÍ-IBÁÑEZ, AND CHARLES PFIZER & CO. *Bull. of the Hist. of Medicine 1979 53(2): 159-169.* In late 1959, Dr. Henry Welch, a high official of the Food and Drug Administration, was charged with conflict of interest involving the federal regulation of antibiotics. The scandal indicated that it was dangerous for the agency to be closely intertwined with the industry it was supposed to regulate. Welch, who was chief regulator of the antibiotics industry, was chief editor of scientific papers sponsored by drug companies and which appeared in periodicals supported by the drug companies' own advertising and purchases of reprints. This went on from 1953 to 1960. The Kefauver investigation revealed the degree to which Welch was indebted to the drug industry, and Welch resigned and received a federal disability pension. In 1962, amendments to the Food and Drug law revised the status of the agency and revitalized its regulation of drugs. 44 notes.   M. Kaufman

2435. McFadyen, Richard E. THALIDOMIDE IN AMERICA: A BRUSH WITH TRAGEDY. *Clio Medica [Netherlands] 1976 11(2): 79-93.* On 12 September 1960 the William S. Merrell Co. applied to the Federal Drug Administration (FDA) for the right to sell thalidomide, a soporific used particularly by pregnant women, on the American market. The FDA's newest medical officer, Dr. Frances Oldham Kelsey, did not approve of marketing the sedative, feeling that the clinical reports supporting the application were testimonials rather than scientific studies. William S. Merrell did, however, receive the right to distribute thalidomide on a limited experimental basis. In the early 1960's the drug caused an epidemic of infant deformities in Europe; in America there were 10 known deformities. While the Justice Department did not follow the FDA's recommendation to bring a criminal case against Merrell, civil action was taken by private citizens. This led to tighter FDA regulation. In 1962 Dr. Kelsey received the Gold Medal Award for Distinguished Federal Civilian Service. 57 notes.   A. J. Papalas

2436. Meier, Kenneth John. CLIENT REPRESENTATION IN USDA BUREAUS: CAUSES AND CONSEQUENCES. *Policy Studies J. 1978 6(4): 484-487.* Assesses benefits derived from interest groups' support for various bureaus of the Agriculture Department, covering 1974-76. One of 16 articles in this issue on agricultural policy.

2437. Metzger, H. Peter. ENVIRONMENTAL ACTIVISTS CAPTURE WASHINGTON. *Reason 1979 11(1): 25-29, 32.* Since Jimmy Carter's inauguration, environmentalists and other public interest activists have been appointed—with the President's blessing—to powerful positions from which they are attempting to ruin the American economy and speed the nation on the road to Socialism.

2438. Middleton, Lorenzo. THE EXECUTIVE BRANCH STUMBLES. *Southern Exposure 1979 7(2): 32-37.* Political variation within presidential administrations since the 1960's has slowed the fairly steady progress toward equality and integration made by the federal courts, and the Health, Education, and Welfare Department.

2439. Miller, Ben R. THE PRESIDENCY AND SEPARATION OF POWERS. *Am. Bar Assoc. J. 1974 60(2): 195-197.* "President Nixon's assertion of executive privilege in the Watergate Tapes case is constitutionally sound."   J

2440. Miroff, Bruce. PRESIDENTIAL LEVERAGE OVER SOCIAL MOVEMENTS: THE JOHNSON WHITE HOUSE AND CIVIL

RIGHTS. *J. of Pol. 1981 43(1): 2-23.* While no other administration achieved as much in the field of civil rights as did that of Lyndon Baines Johnson, when activists defined black emancipation in terms alien to the administration's, the confident exercise of presidential leadership was frustrated. Fearing mass activism and defining the racial issue in terms of consensus politics, the Johnson White House sought a shift in black activity from civil rights to party politics. A black Democratic network was to serve as a means of both riot prevention and electoral gains. The administration lost control over the issue by mid-1966 as the movement turned militant and both the Vietnam War and resistance to it preoccupied Washington. 35 notes.　　　　　　　　　A. W. Novitsky

2441. Mitchell, Clarence. MR. FORD AND CIVIL RIGHTS: A MIXED RECORD. *Crisis 1974 81(1): 7-11.*

2442. Moe, Terry M. REGULATORY PERFORMANCE AND PRESIDENTIAL ADMINISTRATION. *Am. J. of Pol. Sci. 1982 26(2): 197-224.* Investigates the link between presidential administration and the performance of three independent regulatory commissions: the National Labor Relations Board, the Federal Trade Commission, and the Securities and Exchange Commission. Regulatory behavior does shift across administrations, and it varies systematically with presidential partisanship. Presidents apparently do achieve a measure of direction and control over the independent commissions.　　　　　　　　　J/S

2443. Molnar, Thomas. WATERGATE UND DIE FOLGEN [Watergate and the consequences]. *Schweizer Monatshefte [Switzerland] 1974 53(10): 672-675.* Richard M. Nixon's deeds have led to growing cynicism among the American people and could lead to disaster for the Republican Party; he should resign by next summer.

2444. Monroe, Kristen R. INFLATION AND PRESIDENTIAL POPULARITY. *Presidential Studies Q. 1979 9(3): 334-340.* Describes the findings of Samuel Kernell's 1978 analysis of how inflation affected the popularity of the president from 1950 to 1974, concluding that presidential popularity is affected by a gradual response to inflation.

2445. Morgan, Anne Hodges. IS THERE A DOCTOR IN THE HOUSE? . . . OR FOR THE HOUSE? *Rev. in Am. Hist. 1980 8(1): 129-133.* Review essay of William E. Pemberton's *Bureaucratic Politics: Executive Reorganization During the Truman Administration* (Columbia: U. of Missouri Pr., 1979), and Monte M. Poen's *Harry S. Truman Versus the Medical Lobby: The Genesis of Medicare* (Columbia: U. of Missouri Pr., 1979); 1945-50.

2446. Morris, Roger and Sheets, Hal. WHY LEAVE IT TO EARL? *Washington Monthly 1974 6(9): 12-19.* Secretary of Agriculture Earl Butz's inflationary and wasteful policies may lead to food shortages.

2447. Moye, William T. PRESIDENTIAL LABOR-MANAGE-MENT COMMITTEES: PRODUCTIVE FAILURES. *Industrial and Labor Relations Rev. 1980 34(1): 51-66.* Over the last quarter-century, six presidents have sought to encourage labor-management-government collaboration through the creation of advisory committees. This study describes how these committees have grappled with such crucial topics as wage-price stabilization, fiscal and monetary policy, and the employment problems created by technological change. Each of these committees eventually expired for a number of reasons: some presidents ignored them and others viewed them as an exercise in public relations; business and labor representatives sooner or later disagreed with presidential policies and with each other; and those representatives could not speak for all American employers and workers. Nonetheless, the author concludes, the committees produced some concrete achievements, such as recommending or providing important support for certain programs, and they also provided a needed forum in which labor and business leaders could discuss issues of mutual concern.　　　　　　　　　J

2448. Mullaney, Thomas R. A POPULIST IN THE NIXON CABINET. *New York Affairs 1975 2(4): 50-59.* Peter J. Brennan, the New York building trades union leader whom Nixon appointed secretary of labor in 1973 as part of the "Middle America" strategy, left office unhappily early in 1975. This is a personal account of disappointment in high office. Illus.　　　　　　　　　J

2449. Myers, Beverlee A. HEALTH CARE FOR THE POOR. *Pro. of the Acad. of Pol. Sci. 1977 32(3): 68-78.* A study of the development of programs designed to provide a measure of medical care for the poor. The most significant programs were developed during the 1960's as a part of the "War on Poverty" and the "Great Society" programs. Medicare and Medicaid were most important in the latter. Analysis of Medicaid reveals serious impairments of performance and many problems. Concludes that "Medicaid is a poor program for poor people." Its main flaw is its "basic welfare image." There is needed "some form of national health program that treats everyone equally."
　　　　　　　　　R. V. Ritter

2450. Myers, Will S. A LEGISLATIVE HISTORY OF REVENUE SHARING. *Ann. of the Am. Acad. of Pol. and Social Sci. 1975 419: 1-11.* Although the general revenue sharing idea was advanced as a solution to several of federalism's problems, it succeeded in mustering enough support only when it was perceived as the way of coming to the aid of financially hard-pressed local governments. Early revenue sharing bills helped to develop the essential ingredients of a workable distribution system and to sort out proponents and opponents of the idea. Former President Nixon made the revenue sharing idea a matter of serious public policy discussion by earmarking $5 billion of his 1972 budget for the program. His proposal called for a "no-strings" aid distribution on a per capita basis modified for tax effort. Congressman Wilbur Mills developed a counter proposal consisting of aid for local governments, tied mainly to urbanization and a measure of poverty for the purpose of supporting a limited number of program and project areas, and general purpose aid for states, tied mainly to state use of personal income tax. In the course of the legislative process the two approaches were modified substantially. The result is a program that is neither pure "no-strings" sharing of federal revenues nor clearly federal aid to achieve well-defined, overriding national objectives as defined by Congress.　　　　　　　　　J

2451. Nathan, Richard P. THE "ADMINISTRATIVE PRESIDENCY." *Public Interest 1976 (44): 40-54.* Discusses "administrative presidency," a second term strategy of President Nixon whereby he was to gain control over the domestic bureaucracy. He resigned before his plans were fulfilled. Nixon was to have the federal bureaucracy carry out his policy preferences by chosing domestic program managers to the various executive agencies. This management strategy began in 1973 and was to be implemented by a new set of cabinet and sub-cabinet officials. There was a corresponding deemphasis on new domestic legislative initiatives. This plan, designed principally by John Erhlichman, was based upon personnel shifts, budget impoundments and reductions, greater power to the President's trusted lieutenants, and regulation writing. Watergate may have made the "administrative presidency" impossible for some time because of the greater power it gives the President. For the next President, the key to managerial control over the executive establishment will be appointments.　　　　　　　　　S. Harrow

2452. Nathan, Richard P. THE NEW FEDERALISM VERSUS THE EMERGING NEW STRUCTURALISM. *Publius 1975 5(3): 111-129.* Discusses the New Structuralism theory of domestic policy during the 1970's and how it differs from the New Federalism of the Nixon Administration.

2453. Natoli, Marie D. THE MONDALE VICE PRESIDENCY: IS THE DIE CAST? *Presidential Studies Q. 1977 7(2-3): 101-107.* The Vice President now plays a more important role in American government than ever before. The modern Vice President meets the demands of protocol by fulfilling a host of ceremonial roles and by representing the President abroad, and thereby saves the Chief Executive's valuable time. Vice Presidents, however, must maintain a low profile in order to survive, because their functions still depend upon the will of the President. Vice President Walter F. Mondale seems to understand this axiom. Interviews and primary and secondary sources; 28 notes.　　　　　　　　　R. D. Hurt

2454. Natoli, Marie D. THE VICE PRESIDENCY: WALTER MONDALE IN THE LION'S DEN. *Presidential Studies Q. 1978 8(1): 100-102.* Analyzes the surprising role of Vice President Walter F. Mondale in ending the Senate filibusters against deregulation of natural gas in October, 1977. Liberal senators allied with the Carter administration were prevented from introducing delaying amendments by Mondale's parliamentary ruling. Rather than perpetuate a bitter stalemate and alienate Democratic Majority Leader Robert Byrd, the White House chose to permit an unfavorable vote in the Senate and rely on the House to prevent passage. To preserve Carter's consistent public stand, Mondale assumed responsibility for an apparent administration defeat. 8 notes.

S. C. Strom

2455. Nelson, Robert A. and Sheley, Joseph F. CURRENT BIA IN-FLUENCE ON INDIAN SELF-DETERMINATION: A CRIMINAL JUSTICE PLANNING ILLUSTRATION. *Social Sci. J. 1982 19(3): 73-85.* Traces the federal government's domination of American Indians until 1970; notes efforts during the administration of Richard Nixon, that resulted in the Indian Self-Determination and Educational Assistance Act (US, 1975); and discusses the continued domination by the Bureau of Indian Affairs (BIA), citing the BIA's reservation crime control programs.

2456. Nixon, Richard M. THE PRESIDENT'S MESSAGE TO CONGRESS ON EQUAL EDUCATIONAL OPPORTUNITY. *Current Hist. 1972 62(370): 305, 311.* Presents excerpts from President Richard M. Nixon's 1972 message to Congress regarding federal aid to education, busing legislation, and school integration for public schools.

2457. Nuechterlein, James A. WATERGATE: TOWARD A REVISIONIST VIEW. *Commentary 1979 68(2): 38-45.* Discusses the historical inaccuracies and injustices caused by hysteria during and after the Watergate trials, especially as revealed indirectly in *The Terrors of Justice: The Untold Side of Watergate* by Maurice H. Stans, and *To Set the Record Straight: The Break-in, the Tapes, the Conspirators, the Pardon* by John J. Sirica.

2458. Oleinikova, L. V. POLITICHESKAIA BOR'BA V S.SH.A. PO VOPROSAM REORGANIZATSII SISTEMY OBSHCHESTVEN-NOGO VSPOMOSHCHESTVOVANIIA (1969-1972) [The political struggle in the USA on the question of reorganization of the system of public relief (1969-72)]. *Vestnik Moskovskogo U. Seriia 8 Istoriia [USSR] 1976 (5): 33-45.* Among the many plans for public welfare legislation, Richard M. Nixon's proposals in 1969 for a guaranteed annual income represented the viewpoint of the conservative new federalism. Liberals criticized the plan, as did conservatives, but it was accepted by the House in March 1970. In the Senate, the Financial Committee rejected the plan. All that emerged was the Talmadge Act (1972) which required all those 16 or older to accept work proposed for them or forfeit federal aid. Also a new Supplemental Security Income proposal federalized three aid programs to the blind, old, and disabled and guaranteed a minimum of $130 a month to everyone in the program. 40 notes. D. Balmuth

2459. Overland, Doris. THE GREAT WATERGATE CONSPIRACY: A TV BLITZKRIEG? *Contemporary Rev. [Great Britain] 1978 233(1350): 29-32.* Discusses the effect of television on the shaping of American public opinion during the Watergate scandal, 1974.

2460. Paige, Connie. THE REVOLUTION AT VISTA. *Working Papers for a New Soc. 1978 6(2): 34-40.* Examines the rejuvenation of VISTA—Volunteers in Service to America—since the appointment of Sam Brown to the head of ACTION, VISTA's parent organization, concurrent with the Carter administration's support for the program, 1977-78.

2461. Parkhomenko, V. K. OPERATSIIA "KOINTELPRO" [Operation Cointelpro]. *Voprosy Istorii [USSR] 1979 (10): 67-79.* Tells about the secret war waged by the Federal Bureau of Investigation against the dissidents in the U.S.A. Shows the scope of the campaign of persecution launched against the democratic and Left movements in the U.S.A. in the period from the 1950's to the early 1970's, describes the methods employed by the FBI in combating political opponents (counter-intelligence, frame-ups, forgeries) and cites factual material illustrating the violation of the constitutional rights of American citizens. In a number of instances U.S. government officials acted as direct accomplices in the secret operations planned by the FBI in its unlawful war against the dissidents. J

2462. Peters, Charles. BLIND AMBITION AT THE WHITE HOUSE. *Washington Monthly 1977 9(1): 17-21.* Reviews Taylor Branch's *Blind Ambition* (New York: Simon and Schuster, 1976), John

Dean's account of the events of the Watergate cover-up and the pressures extant within the White House staff during the decline of the Nixon Administration, 1972.

2463. Peters, Charles. CONCERNS ABOUT CARTER: AND HIS CHIEF COURTIER. *Washington Monthly 1976 8(10): 2-8.* Discusses the place of Jimmy Carter's press secretary, Jody Powell, in the Carter administration, 1975-76.

2464. Peters, Charles. HOW TO TAKE OVER THE GOVERNMENT. *Washington Monthly 1974 6(7): 15-23.* Discusses the lessons on managing people, processes, and policies of the federal government which Elliot Richardson and his associates learned during 1969-73, praising the Richardson team's excellent management and highest ethics.

S

2465. Petersen, Eugene T. A PRESIDENT VISITS MACKINAC ISLAND IN 1975. *Chronicle 1981 17(2): 4-8.* Recounts President Gerald R. Ford's 18-hour visit to Mackinac Island in midsummer 1975, and focuses on the security and other arrangements for the visit.

2466. Petropoulos, Nikos. GREEK-AMERICAN ATTITUDES TO-WARD AGNEW. *J. of the Hellenic Diaspora 1975 2(3): 5-26.*

2467. Pious, Richard M. SOURCES OF DOMESTIC POLICY INITIATIVES. *Pro. of the Acad. of Pol. Sci. 1975 32(1): 98-111.* Both first-(innovative) and second-stage (procedural) domestic policy initiatives are originating with greater frequency from Congress than from the executive branch, 1970-75, in the wake of the Watergate scandal and fears of presidential imperialism.

2468. Pomper, Gerald M. NIXON AND THE END OF PRESIDENTIAL POLITICS. *Society 1973 10(3): 14-16.* Discusses, in the context of elections, the increasing isolation of the president from partisan politics.

S

2469. Pratt, Henry J. SYMBOLIC POLITICS AND WHITE HOUSE CONFERENCES ON AGING. *Society 1978 15(5): 67-72.* Surveys activities of White House Conferences on Aging (1950, 1961, and 1971); symbolic reassurance and quiescence, not specific actions, were earmarks of the political atmosphere.

2470. Rabi, W. UNE TRAGEDIE AMERICAINE [An American tragedy]. *Esprit [France] 1973 (9): 304-316.* An overview of the Watergate Scandal, and a tentative analysis. During a tour across the United States the author attempted to gauge the change in public opinion about Watergate, from silence to concern, and to explain the growth and impact of the imperial presidency. Sees Watergate as a normal development of post World War II America and the military industrial complex. "The Watergate Affair is therefore a perfectly normal phenomenon in a society founded exclusively on money as the measure of all things."

G. F. Jewsbury

2471. Raeithel, Gert. ART BUCHWALD UND RICHARD NIXON [Art Buchwald and Richard Nixon]. *Frankfurter Hefte [West Germany] 1975 30(5): 30-34.* Columnist Art Buchwald's good-natured but penetrating satire during the Watergate Scandal played a historic role in humorously expressing the disillusionment of the American people.

2472. Randall, Ronald. PRESIDENTIAL POWER VERSUS BU-REAUCRATIC INTRANSIGENCE: THE INFLUENCE OF THE NIXON ADMINISTRATION ON WELFARE POLICY. *Am. Pol. Sci. Rev. 1979 73(3): 795-810.* Many observers routinely assert the relative weakness of presidents before the bureaucracy. The research of this study, guided by a structuralist theory of organizations, provides evidence of the Nixon administration's power to change policy, even over the opposition of the bureaucracy, concerning the Aid to Families with Dependent Children program. The study demonstrates that the management tools available to the president and top officials, when used adroitly, are more powerful than are generally presumed. That presidents can affix their indelible stamps on policy by short-circuiting the legislative process and dominating the bureaucracy is more than a remote possibility. J

2473. Ratcliff, Carter. THE AMERICAN ARTIST FROM LONER TO LOBBYIST. *Art in Am. 1977 65(2): 10-12.* Discusses the attitude which newly elected President Jimmy Carter has taken toward art, symbolized by a collection of modern art recently exhibited in the (Athens) Georgia Museum of Art, "Open to New Ideas: A Collection of New Art for Jimmy Carter"; touches upon the role of the socially and politically oriented artist in the 1970's.

2474. Reedy, George E. THE PRESIDENT AND THE PRESS: STRUGGLE FOR DOMINANCE. *Ann. of the Am. Acad. of Pol. and Social Sci. 1976 427: 65-72.* The relationship between the president of the United States and the American press is very much a function of his personal style. President Lyndon B. Johnson never understood the functioning of the press or its role. For him it was just a public relations outlet for whatever individual or group that was astute enough to manipulate the system. His penchant for trying to outwit the press or to "buy" it created problems for him and led to the credibility gap that dogged him to the end. Yet he was a consummate politician who won his political victories despite his poor relations with the press.
J

2475. Regens, James L. and Rycroft, Robert W. ADMINISTRATIVE DISCRETION IN ENERGY POLICY-MAKING: THE EXCEPTIONS AND APPEALS PROGRAM OF THE FEDERAL ENERGY ADMINISTRATION. *J. of Pol. 1981 43(3): 875-888.* As the Organization of Petroleum Exporting Countries instituted an oil embargo in 1973, the American response centered on technological fixes; concern about the economic, social, and ecological consequences of the new technologies; and citizen demands for social control mechanisms to manage technical policy decisions. The Federal Energy Administration was created in 1974. Its broad discretionary rule-making authority led to an extensive exceptions and appeals program. Of more than 1,500 petitions for exceptions, 70% were denied. The most successful applicants were refiners, while producers, resellers, and retailers were most likely to receive negative decisions. Allegations of corporate elite control over decisions were unfounded. 5 tables, 16 notes.
A. W. Novitsky

2476. Regens, James L. ENERGY CONSERVATION AND THE STATES: APPROACHES TO IMPLEMENTING NATIONAL POLICY. *Publius 1980 10(1): 47-56.* Uncertainty about the energy supply has focused government policy toward energy conservation. A centrally-directed model has dominated the approach of the federal government in formulating policy. Federal policies are implemented through the states, using federal grants to fund such energy conservation activities as weatherization of homes for low-income families, energy audits of public buildings, and development of energy performance standards for new construction. Critics charge that states should have a larger role in developing conservation strategy. The Department of Energy currently administers categorical grant programs for federally-developed standards created under the Emergency Energy Conservation Act of 1979. Based on current periodical literature and government publications; 31 notes.
C. B. Schulz

2477. Reichley, A. James. THE CONSERVATIVE ROOTS OF THE NIXON, FORD, AND REAGAN ADMINISTRATIONS. *Pol. Sci. Q. 1981-82 96(4): 537-550.* Richard M. Nixon, Gerald R. Ford, and Ronald Reagan aligned themselves with social order, nationalism, local control of social services, and cultural and moral traditionalism, all qualities of modern conservatism. This paper reviews the history of the term "conservatism," and discusses the attitudes and ideas that characterize the Nixon, Ford, and Reagan administrations as "conservative." Secondary sources; 16 notes.
J. Powell

2478. Reid, Frank. CONTROL AND DECONTROL OF WAGES IN THE UNITED STATES: AN EMPIRICAL ANALYSIS. *Am. Econ. Rev. 1981 71(1): 108-120.* Without fiscal and monetary restrictions, controls have limited effectiveness. Also, both wages and prices must be equally affected. The historical experience in this area, however, is not encouraging. The Nixon policy did not work. 3 tables, 28 ref., 8 notes.
D. K. Pickens

2479. Riccards, Michael P. RARE COUNSEL: KENNEDY, JOHNSON AND THE CIVIL RIGHTS BILL OF 1963. *Presidential Studies Q. 1981 11(3): 395-398.* Rarely consulted by President John F. Kennedy, Vice-President Lyndon B. Johnson played an integral part in the formulation of the 1963 Civil Rights Bill. During two conversations on 3 June 1963, one with Theodore Sorenson and the other with Norbert Schlei, Johnson strongly advised that the president make a firm commitment to the cause of civil rights. Kennedy followed Johnson's advice and started the advancement in the area of civil rights that Johnson would continue. 6 notes.
D. H. Cline

2480. Riemer, Neal. WATERGATE AND PROPHETIC POLITICS. *R. of Pol. 1974 36(2): 284-297.*

2481. Ritchie, Donald A. REFORMING THE REGULATORY PROCESS: WHY JAMES LANDIS CHANGED HIS MIND. *Business Hist. Rev. 1980 54(3): 283-302.* When James Landis stepped down from his post as Chairman of the Securities and Exchange Commission in 1937, he was convinced of the potential for effective administration inherent in regulatory agencies. His 1938 book, *The Administrative Process,* was the outstanding theoretical celebration of that viewpoint. But in the two decades that followed, his views changed. In 1946 he was appointed Chairman of the Civil Aeronautics Board. The unhappy experience of his trying months in that office plus his later observations while practicing law in Washington, caused Landis to reevaluate his position. As a result, his 1960 report to President-elect John F. Kennedy on regulatory performance focused on administrative deficiencies and stimulated New Frontier reform proposals. Based on Landis Papers in the Library of Congress and on public documents in the National Archives; 54 notes.
C. J. Pusateri

2482. Robins, Leonard. THE PLOT THAT SUCCEEDED. *Presidential Studies Q. 1980 10(1): 99-106.* Insufficient attention has been given to the social policy initiatives of the Nixon administration, and the influence of New Federalism has been hardly appreciated. New Federalism, introduced in 1969, has had ideological consequences. That the New Federalism evolved into a politically successful ideology of social policy conservation remains of primary importance. 36 notes.
G. E. Pergl

2483. Robitscher, Jonas. STIGMATIZATION AND STONEWALLING: THE ORDEAL OF MARTHA MITCHELL. *J. of Psychohistory 1979 6(3): 393-408.* Chronicles the events surrounding Martha Mitchell (wife of John Mitchell, US Attorney General in the Nixon Administration) during and after the break-in at the Democratic National Headquarters (Watergate), focusing on the efforts of the Nixon administration to stigmatize Martha Mitchell as mentally ill in order to discredit her with the press. Based on newspaper accounts and secondary sources; 37 notes.
R. E. Butchart

2484. Rogulev, Iu. N. POLITIKA ADMINISTRATSII TRUMANA V OBLASTI TRUDOVYKH OTNOSHENII V GODY VOINY V KOREE [The politics of the Truman administration in the sphere of labor relations at the time of the Korean War]. *Vestnik Moskovskogo U., Seriia 9: Istoriia [USSR] 1974 29(6): 15-30.* At the time of the Korean War the Truman administration attempted to control wages through the Wage Stabilization Board. In the interest of national unity the anti-communist leaders of the AFL-CIO joined businessmen and government officials on the board. Rising prices and rising profits caused the labor representatives to resign in February 1951, but conciliationist union leaders prevented a permanent split. In the face of working-class pressure the administration agreed in December 1952 to permit wage increases and the business representatives resigned. The incoming Eisenhower administration quickly ended wage regulation. Primary sources; 91 notes.
C. J. Read

2485. Rosen, Carey M. A TEST OF PRESIDENTIAL LEADERSHIP OF PUBLIC OPINION: THE SPLIT-BALLOT TECHNIQUE. *Polity 1973 6(2): 282-290.* There have been few studies of the extent to which a political leader influences attitude formation. Using the proposed Family Assistance Program to test presidential leadership of public opinion, the author found that many people are unwilling to oppose even an unpopular president on a controversial, well-publicized issue. Speculates that only a minority "have made enough of a commitment to their position to offset their commitment to the president." 2 tables, 12 notes.
E. P. Stickney

2486. Rosenberg, Harold. THUGS ADRIFT. *Partisan R. 1973 40(3): 341-348.* Reviews Watergate-related events and personalities and analyzes Richard Milhous Nixon's policy as the politics of cover-up. After citing several literary associations with the Watergate caper, the author concludes that "the Nixon collaborators were moved by an essence beyond speech . . . . I know of nothing more offensive to the sensibility of a free individual than the Hollywood-style metaphysics by which Nixon has glamorized his corrupt invention of a Presidency that exists independently of the President."
D. K. Pickens

2487. Rossi, Mario. LE PROBLEME NOIR AUX ETATS-UNIS ET SON IMPACT SUR LA POLITIQUE AMERICAINE [The problem of the black in the United States and its impact on American politics]. *Defense Natl. [France] 1978 34(1): 81-88.* An analysis of blacks' position in American history, from slavery to integration, informs the American government's moral stand in politics—Carter's religiosity partly explicable in terms of a historic atonement.

2488. Roucek, Joseph S. LA NUEVA POLÍTICA ECONÓMICA DEL PRESIDENTE NIXON [The new economic policy of President Nixon]. *Rev. de Política Int. [Spain] 1972 (119): 59-89.* Discusses Richard M. Nixon's economic policies after 1971 when he inaugurated an era of strict federal direction of the economy in the fields of wages, prices, and unemployment.

2489. Roucek, Joseph S. LA SITUACION DE LAS PROGRAMAS NORTEAMERICANOS DE BIENESTAR SOCIAL [The situation of North American programs of social welfare]. *R. de Pol. Social [Spain] 1973 (100): 77-101.* Discusses US public welfare programs since 1969, focusing on legislation by the Nixon administration on welfare reform, War on Poverty, profiles of poverty, and the minimum wage, and giving an analysis of present tendencies and future problems.

2490. Royster, Vermont. THE PUBLIC MORALITY: AFTER-THOUGHTS ON WATERGATE. *Am. Scholar 1974 43(2): 249-259.* The Watergate Scandal was "an attempt to use governmental power to subvert the political process in the broadest sense of that term." Relates this to the separate indictment of Vice President Spiro T. Agnew. There was nothing original in either crime: kickbacks, bribes, income tax evasion, and a myriad of political dirty tricks and campaign spying. Watergate was unusual in that no money was stolen despite the millions available. Attempts to explain the reasons for this political behavior and countless other forms of political acts as a "lawlessness in pursuit of virtue." The chief concern is that the morality of high government officials reflects the public morality.
C. W. Olson

2491. Salant, Walter S. SOME INTELLECTUAL CONTRIBUTIONS OF THE TRUMAN COUNCIL OF ECONOMIC ADVISERS TO POLICY-MAKING. *Hist. of Pol. Econ. 1973 5(1): 36-49.* A study of the educational program carried on by Harry Truman's Council of Economic Advisers, chaired by Leon Keyserling, and the Council's influence on leading men of affairs. The most important changes were: 1) replacement of a "cyclical model" of the economy by a "growth model," 2) the setting of quantitative targets for the economy, 3) use of the theories of fiscal drag and full-employment budget, 4) recognition of the need for greater flexibility in taxation, and 5) replacement of the notion of unemployment as a structural problem by a realization of a low aggregate demand. 14 notes.
R. V. Ritter

2492. Sale, Kirkpatrick. THE SUNSHINE SYNDICATE BEHIND WATERGATE. *Southern Exposure 1973 1(2): 2-8.* Discusses the relationship between the Nixon administration, the Watergate Scandal, and politics in the Southern states.
S

2493. Schapsmeier, Edward L. and Schapsmeier, Frederick H. WESTERN LIVESTOCK POLICY DURING THE 1950'S. *J. of the West 1975 14(3): 25-32.* Discusses federal livestock policy, 1953-60, the efforts of Ezra Taft Benson to lessen federal controls on the stock industry, the Eisenhower administration's advocacy of graduation in lessening control, and the effects which these had on western cattle market prices. 32 notes.

2494. Scheele, Paul E. PRESIDENT CARTER AND THE WATER PROJECTS: A CASE STUDY IN PRESIDENTIAL AND CONGRES-

SIONAL DECISION-MAKING. *Presidential Studies Q. 1978 8(4): 348-364.* Examines the components of President Jimmy Carter's decision in 1977 to eliminate funding for 19 water resource construction projects from the fiscal year 1978 budget. Carter's unfavorable gubernatorial experience with the Army Corps of Engineers, his campaign position on the environment and federal spending, the support received from environmental groups, the existence of ready-made allies, and his lack of experience with Congress contributed to his decision. The process of placating a hostile and protective Congress cost Carter his tax rebate program and threatened several other bills before compromise was reached. The experience reveals Carter's moralistic, executive-oriented, rational approach to decisionmaking and his adjustment to congressional methods of compromise, patronage, and log-rolling. Table, 79 notes.
S. C. Strom

2495. Schram, Sanford F. POLITICS, PROFESSIONALISM, AND THE CHANGING FEDERALISM. *Social Service Rev. 1981 55(1): 78-92.* Discusses the Nixon administration's New Federalism, especially the views of liberal critics who feared that such programs would increase the influence of state and local politicians at the cost of sacrificing professionalism in these services, and gives evidence that to a certain extent this is in fact happening.

2496. Schuetz, Janice. COMMUNICATIVE COMPETENCE AND THE BARGAINING OF WATERGATE. *Western J. of Speech Communication 1978 42(2): 105-115.* Assesses the bargaining behavior and ability of Richard M. Nixon, H. R. Haldeman, and John Erlichman on 17 April 1973 after John Dean resigned.

2497. Shani, Moshe. U.S. FEDERAL GOVERNMENT REORGANIZATION: EXECUTIVE BRANCH STRUCTURE AND CENTRAL DOMESTIC POLICY-MAKING STAFF. *Public Administration [Great Britain] 1974 52(2): 193-208.* Discusses executive branch reorganization in the Nixon administration since 1970; far-reaching changes in the administrative structure were planned but not carried out when the Watergate scandal became public knowledge.

2498. Shattuck, John H. F. YOU CAN'T DEPEND ON IT: THE CARTER ADMINISTRATION AND CIVIL LIBERTIES. *Civil Liberties Rev. 1978 4(5): 10-27.* Criticizes President Jimmy Carter's performance and his handling of Congress, on civil rights issues, as compared with his campaign rhetoric.

2499. Shichor, David and Ranish, Donald R. PRESIDENT CARTER'S VIETNAM AMNESTY: AN ANALYSIS OF A PUBLIC POLICY DECISION. *Presidential Studies Q. 1980 10(3): 443-450.* Examines the societal implications of Jimmy Carter's pardon for draft dodgers on 21 January 1977. Draft evasion was increasingly legitimized as the anti-Vietnam War movement grew in the 1960's, thus partly justifying their pardon. Deserters were considered in another light, as their cases were decided individually, and this suggests important sociological and political implications, as it seemed to justify different levels of standing within society. 43 notes.
D. H. Cline

2500. Silver, Michael. REGULATIONS THAT ARE KILLING US. *Reason 1978 10(6): 22-25.* Discusses the regulation of drug usage by the Food and Drug Administration; safety and efficacy testing during 1962-71 resulted in many deaths because the agency would not release drugs which it felt did not have enough testing (but were in use in other countries); pending legislation would release drugs after not efficacy but safety tests.

2501. Silvert, Frieda. THE NEW FEDERALISM AND THE NEW CORPORATISM. *Am. Soc. of Int. Law Pro. 1974 68: 198-202.* The "New Federalism" developed by the Nixon administration in the 1960's-70's actually centralized power in the federal government.

2502. Smith, Bruce L. R. and Carroll, James D. REAGAN AND THE NEW DEAL: REPEAL OR REPLAY? *PS 1981 14(4): 758-766.* President Ronald Reagan's success has been in actually enacting budgetary cuts of the approximate magnitude as those proposed by Nixon, Ford, and Carter, though it leaves intact most of the original New Deal approaches.

2503. Sorter, Bruce W. ECONOMIC SANCTIONS OF A MILITARY OPEN HOUSING POLICY AS A FORCE FOR SOCIAL CHANGE. *Urban and Social Change R. 1976 9(1): 18-22.* Evaluates the success of the Defense Department's program to end housing discrimination in the military in 1967-68, emphasizing sociological factors.

2504. Stanfield, Rochelle L. THE DEVELOPMENT OF PRESIDENT CARTER'S URBAN POLICY: ONE SMALL STEP FOR FEDERALISM. *Publius 1978 8(1): 39-53.* In the course of the Jimmy Carter administration's 1977 efforts to develop a new urban strategy, spearheaded by the Urban and Regional Policy Group with HUD Secretary Patricia Roberts Harris as chairman, an increasing awareness of the importance of state governments has emerged. This is due in part to the ideas of White House staffer Stuart E. Eizenstat, directed by the President in late summer to intervene to speed up the strategy-development process, and also to the single-minded efforts of Lawrence O. Houstoun, Jr., chairman of the task force on states and metropolitan regions. As Secretary Harris stated on 2 December, "If there is one thing that has been learned in putting together recommendations for the President, it is that the role of state government is critical." L. W. Van Wyk

2505. Stanfield, Rochelle L. TOWARD AN URBAN POLICY WITH A SMALL-TOWN ACCENT. *Publius 1979 9(1): 31-44.* Analyzes President Jimmy Carter's "New Partnership to Conserve America's Communities," presented to big city mayors on 27 March 1978. Instead of concentrating on run-down large urban centers, the program included all communities regardless of size, "a diffusion of resources at a time of scarcity when targeting was necessary." Carter was attempting to bring consistency into an urban policy noted for its inconsistencies, but some feel he brought confusion. The new program resulted from an awareness on the part of small cities and towns of the availability of federal aid to implement their public needs (many resulting from federal standards). It raises a multitude of questions concerning the relationships of federal, state, city, and local fiscal roles. R. V. Ritter

2506. Stein, Howard F. THE SILENT COMPLICITY AT WATERGATE. *Am. Scholar 1973/74 43(1): 21-37.* Suggests that Americans are blinded to the wider context of the Watergate Scandal by focusing attention on the individual guilt of those involved. Examines the political campaign of 1972 as background and believes that Richard M. Nixon's power was very broadly based. Voters were repelled by the "apocalyptic arrogance of the new Left" and got "what was sought and what was preserved through this election, . . . a stern veneer and a corrupt core, so that one can get away with as much as possible, while righteously punishing those who get away with too much too openly." One social concern emerging from the election was the desire of many Americans for a Hitler to restore social order. Watergate intensified the "fundamental polarity of values that has been a dialectic of American history . . . lineal authority versus individualism." C. W. Olson

2507. Stelzner, Hermann G. FORD'S WAR ON INFLATION: A METAPHOR THAT DID NOT CROSS. *Communication Monographs 1977 44(4): 284-297.* President Gerald R. Ford's war metaphor for fighting inflation in 1974 was a poor choice politically because it reminded the public of the Vietnam War, and a poor choice rhetorically because it did not characterize the actions of the Ford administration.

2508. Stern, Laurence. TWO HENRYS DESCENDING. *Foreign Policy 1975 (18): 168-181.* Changing political forces are undermining the leading roles of Secretary of State Henry Kissinger and Senator Henry Jackson, both of whom have dominated the news lately. Among the factors which are pushing these political giants into the background are: the traditional view of American power has declined in credibility as the result of foreign policy failures, the Congressional revolution has brought liberal, anti-traditionalists into leadership, toppling conservative, hawkish chairmen who were either pro-Kissinger or pro-Jackson, and a diffusion of power centers vis-á-vis foreign policy decisionmaking has enabled other individuals and groups to participate. R. F. Kugler

2509. Stewart, Joseph, Jr. and Bullock, Charles S., III. IMPLEMENTING EQUAL EDUCATION OPPORTUNITY POLICY: A COMPARISON OF THE OUTCOMES OF HEW AND JUSTICE DEPARTMENT EFFORTS. *Administration & Soc. 1981 12(4): 427-446.* The desegregation efforts of both the Health, Education, and Welfare Department and the Justice Department in Arkansas, Georgia, Louisiana, and Texas between 1968 and 1974 failed to achieve equal opportunity in education; touches on the problem in defining and implementing policy.

2510. Stockman, David A. THE WRONG WAR? THE CASE AGAINST A NATIONAL ENERGY POLICY. *Public Interest 1978 (53): 3-44.* The three axioms that underlie Jimmy's Carter's National Energy Plan lack validity: 1) that the exhaustion of conventional fossil fuels is imminent and that "business as usual" in the marketplace is inadequate to cope with the problem, 2) that the world energy marketplace was irremediably impaired by the events of October 1973, and now is dependent on a politically motivated cartel that represents a major national economic and security peril, and 3) that homegrown energy is better for the domestic economy. The creation of a giant bureaucracy to regulate in an area where the supposed problems cannot be validated is a major mistake. R. V. Ritter

2511. Stovall, James Glen. CONFLICT IN THE COLONIES: THE LONDON *TIMES* COVERAGE OF WATERGATE FROM THE BREAK-IN TO THE PARDON. *Gazette [Netherlands] 1979 25(4): 209-218.* The Watergate scandal received full and continuing treatment in the *Times.* In general, there was editorial support for President Richard M. Nixon as the incident began to unfold, but this support crumbled as the disclosures implicated him. However, the field reporters tended to display anti-Nixon sentiments from the outset. This anti-Nixon bias was readily discernible in their reports and illustrates a basic difference between American and British journalism in regard to objectivity. 31 notes. J. S. Coleman

2512. Sylves, Richard T. CARTER'S NUCLEAR LICENSING REFORM VS. THREE MILE ISLAND. *Publius 1980 10(1): 69-79.* The March 1979 nuclear accident at the Three Mile Island power plant of the Pennsylvania Public Utility Commission prevented passage of the Nuclear Siting and Licensing Act, which would have increased state participation in locating and approving construction of nuclear power plants. The bill was sponsored in part to reduce the lead-time in Nuclear Regulatory Commission (NRC) processes of approval from the current 10-12 years. Environmental, nuclear utility, and state government responses to the accident all tend to prolong such licensing and increase separate federal and state regulatory activities, thus increasing potential costs of nuclear power and reducing its potential as a power alternative. Based on US government documents and press reports; fig., 40 notes. C. B. Schulz

2513. Teeter, Dwight L., Jr. KICKING NIXON AROUND ONCE MORE. *Rev. in Am. Hist. 1976 4(4): 607-613.* Review article prompted by William E. Porter's *Assault on the Media: The Nixon Years* (Ann Arbor: U. of Michigan Pr., 1976); discusses the Nixon administration's attack on the news media, 1969-1974.

2514. Teodori, Massimo. VIOLENZA DIFFUSA E VIOLENZA ISTITUZIONALIZZATA IN AMERICA [Diffused violence and institutionalized violence in America]. *Problemi di Ulisse [Italy] 1978 14(86): 88-95.* Discusses the violence of criminals and revolutionaries since 1960 in the United States and its relationship to the violations of civil rights by the police and the Federal Bureau of Investigation, especially during the Nixon Administration.

2515. Terekhov, V. I. RAZVITIE VZGLIADOV RESPUBLIKANTSEV NA ROL' GOSUDARSTVA V EKONOMICHESKOI I SOTSIALNOI ZHIZNI OBSHCHESTVA V PERIOD PREZIDENTSTVA D. EIZENKHAUERA [The development of Republican views on the role of the state in the economic and social life of society in the period of the Presidency of D. Eisenhower]. *Vestnik Moskovskogo U. Seriia 8 Istoriia [USSR] 1976 (5): 35-54.* "Rugged individualism" was still strong in the Republican Party before 1952. Eisenhower preserved the system of state regulation and accepted the state's role in the economy in case of need. The new conservatism formed a consensus with neoliberalism. Some Democrats argued for a more pro-business attitude in the party. Programs in education and space represented the principle of state intervention as expressed in the work of Larson. The right wing remained important in the party. Still, Eisenhower's administration strengthened the position of the Republican Party in the two-party system. 67 notes. D. Balmuth

2516. Theoharis, Athan G. THE TRUMAN ADMINISTRATION AND THE DECLINE OF CIVIL LIBERTIES: THE FBI'S SUCCESS IN SECURING AUTHORIZATION FOR A PREVENTIVE DETENTION PROGRAM. *J. of Am. Hist. 1978 64(4): 1010-1030.* Uses the history of the Federal Bureau of Investigation's preventive detention program to demonstrate the possible lack of effective executive control over internal security policy during the Cold War. Top level bureaucrats in the FBI and the Justice Department may have made policy decisions regarding the compilation and use of lists of suspected subversives without informing the President. The FBI's desire for written authorization from the Justice Department to ignore the restrictions of the Internal Security Act of 1950 may have been pursued without President Truman's knowledge. Bureaucrats, operating in a vacuum, may have made national security decisions without regard to their constitutionality or to the need for high-level authorization. 31 notes.
T. P. Linkfield

2517. Thomas, Dan B. and Baas, Larry A. PRESIDENTAL IDENTIFICATION AND MASS-PUBLIC COMPLIANCE WITH OFFICIAL POLICY: THE CASE OF THE CARTER ENERGY PROGRAM. *Policy Studies J. 1982 10(3): 448-465.* Assesses the success of the Carter administration's energy initiatives in influencing the American public to reduce its consumption of energy.

2518. Thomison, Dennis. TROUBLE IN CAMELOT: AN EARLY SKIRMISH OF KENNEDY'S NEW FRONTIER. *J. of Lib. Hist. 1978 13(2): 148-156.* Relates the story of an apparent attempt by the newly elected President Kennedy to replace L. Quincy Mumford as Librarian of Congress in 1961. Discusses Mumford's accomplishments as Librarian of Congress and the reactions of librarians, the A.L.A., and Congress to this threat to his position, and to the prospect of the position being made political. Primary and secondary sources; 23 notes.
A. C. Dewees

2519. Todd, William B. THE WHITE HOUSE TRANSCRIPTS. *Papers of the Biblio. Soc. of Am. 1974 68(3): 267-296.* A bibliographical analysis of Richard M. Nixon's White House transcripts, which were entitled *The Submission of Recorded Presidential Conversations to the Committee on the Judiciary of the House of Representatives.* S

2520. Ulmer, Melville J. WHAT ECONOMISTS KNOW. *Commentary 1982 74(1): 53-57.* Discusses neo-Keynesian demand-side and supply-side economics in the United States with special reference to the Ronald Reagan administration.

2521. Ungar, Sanford J. J. EDGAR HOOVER LEAVES THE STATE DEPARTMENT. *Foreign Policy 1977 (28): 110-116.* The non-reappointment of Frances Knight as the head of the State Department's Passport Office officially came about because of "organizational anomalies" inherited by the Carter administration. Knight's autocratic handling of the office, plus her refusal to work more closely within the department, made her many enemies. Hers was an entrenched bureaucracy that was insensitive to popular leadership.
H. R. Mahood

2522. Vale, Vivian. THE COLLABORATIVE CHAOS OF FEDERAL ADMINISTRATION. *Government and Opposition [Great Britain] 1973 8(2): 177-194.* Discusses President Richard M. Nixon's attempts at federal government reorganization in the 1970's, emphasizing the executive branch, the Office of Management and Budget, and departmental administration.

2523. Varkey, Ouseph. CRISIS SITUATIONS AND FEDERAL SYSTEMS: A COMPARATIVE STUDY OF AMERICA AND INDIA. *Indian J. of Am. Studies [India] 1979 9(1): 65-79.* Studies two comparable situations where state governments challenged federal governments. Details of the American 1957 segregation crisis in Little Rock, Arkansas, are contrasted with the 1968 conflict between the central Indian government and the united front anti-Congress coalition in Kerala. The American president, with fewer explicit constitutional powers, intervened successfully; the Indian federal executive, with many more explicit constitutional powers, retreated. Constitutions and laws do not by themselves determine the nature of federal-state relations. 73 notes.
L. V. Eid

2524. Vaughan, Philip H. THE TRUMAN ADMINISTRATION'S FAIR DEAL FOR BLACK AMERICA. *Missouri Hist. Rev. 1976 70(3): 291-305.* When he sponsored a Fair Deal in 1949 President Harry S. Truman insisted that a meaningful civil rights program had to be an integral part of it. Such a program was before Congress during 1949 and the first half of 1950. Except for certain provisions of the Housing Act of 1949, Truman had to be content with civil rights' victories achieved by executive order or through the courts. Nevertheless, by continuing appeals to Congress for civil rights legislation, Truman helped reverse the long acceptance of segregation and discrimination by establishing integration as a moral principle. Primary and secondary sources; illus., 47 notes.
W. F. Zornow

2525. Vietor, Richard H. K. THE SYNTHETIC LIQUID FUELS PROGRAM: ENERGY POLITICS IN THE TRUMAN ERA. *Business Hist. Rev. 1980 54(1): 1-34.* Late in World War II, the federal government launched a significant program to develop synthetic fuels in the United States. The factors of energy self-sufficiency and national security were the prime motivators. Following the war, the Truman administration found the promising program under increasing attack from the petroleum industry, which saw its own vested interests threatened by the governmental activity. With the advent of an Eisenhower administration that was philosophically predisposed against such federal efforts and was looking for Democratic programs to terminate, the synthetic fuels project was discontinued in 1954. As a result, an inevitable reliance upon foreign oil imports became a reality. Based primarily on governmental documents; 4 tables, 68 notes.
C. J. Pusateri

2526. Vishnevski, S. "AMERIKANSKII KRIZIS" I POLITIKA NIKSONA [The "American crisis" and Nixon's policy]. *Mezhdunarodnaia Zhizn' [USSR] 1970 17(6): 58-67.* Examines the "New Federalism" and Richard Nixon's difficulties during his administration in solving both internal and external problems, including poverty, racial strife, the cities, and health, which together formed a social, economic, and moral crisis beyond the capacity of the ruling elite. Russian.

2527. Wachtel, Harry H. CAMELOT RECONSIDERED. *Civil Liberties Rev. 1978 5(1): 57-61.* Reviews Carl M. Brauer's *John F. Kennedy and the Second Reconstruction* (New York: Columbia U. Pr., 1977), dealing with Kennedy's civil rights legislation.

2528. Walzer, Michael. WATERGATE WITHOUT THE PRESIDENT. *Dissent 1974 21(1): 5-7.* The Watergate scandal extends past the President to corporations and the mass media. S

2529. White, Lawrence J. THE AUTO POLLUTION MUDDLE. *Public Interest 1973 (32): 97-112.* Discusses the relationship between automotive pollution control measures and the executive, legislative, and judicial branches of the federal government during the 1970's. S

2530. Wicker, Tom. THE WATERGATE COMMITTEE CHAIRMAN'S NEW CLOTHES. *Southern Voices 1974 1(1): 7-9.* Discusses Senator Sam J. Ervin's pro-war, anti-civil rights feelings prior to the Watergate Committee hearings. S

2531. Williams, Robert J. and Kershaw, David A. KENNEDY AND CONGRESS: THE STRUGGLE FOR THE NEW FRONTIER. *Pol. Studies [Great Britain] 1979 27(3): 390-404.* The article attempts to develop an interpretation of some of the more important domestic aspects of the Kennedy administration. In particular, it focuses on Kennedy's relations with Congress and on the difficulty of reconciling his reputation as a skillful politician with his legislative disappointments. Case studies of three important bills reveal a consistent, if unsuccessful, legislative strategy. The manner in which the Kennedy administration has been evaluated is considered and the article concludes by locating the source of Kennedy's legislative difficulties in the circumstances of his nomination campaign. J

2532. Winthrop, Henry. FOCUS ON THE HUMAN CONDITION: POLITICAL IMMORALITY AS A CRISIS OF VALUE. *J. of Human Relations 1973 21(1): 91-120.* Presents a late 1972 assessment of the Watergate Scandal focusing on the electorate and the elected US national congressional and executive officers.
R. J. Jirran

2533. Wolman, Harold L. and Merget, Astrid E.   THE PRESI-
DENCY AND POLICY FORMULATION: PRESIDENT CARTER
AND THE URBAN POLICY.   *Presidential Studies Q. 1980 10(3):
402-415.* Examines different models of presidential staff organization in
order to determine the effect the structure of Jimmy Carter's urban policy
planning had on the eventual policy. The decisionmaking evolved from
an attempt at cabinet government to staff dominance of policy, and the
change in structure resulted in very different types of policy that were
formulated. Table.   D. H. Cline

2534. Wright, Peter M.   WYOMING AND THE O.P.A.: THE
POSTWAR POLITICS OF DECONTROL.   *Ann. of Wyoming 1980
52(1): 25-33.* Immediately after World War II, President Harry S. Truman initiated action through the Office of Price Administration (OPA)
to offset projected economic problems. He hoped to establish a spirit of
cooperation among labor, management, and consumers so that postwar
efforts to boost wages, prices, and purchasing would not produce uncontrolled inflation. A conservative coalition of Republicans and Southern
Democrats, led by Senators Robert A. Taft and Kenneth Wherry, opposed any government controls and called for a return to free enterprise.
As Truman's spokesman in Wyoming, Senator Joseph C. O'Mahoney
worked hard on the state and national level for passage of enabling
legislation, which became a reality on 25 July 1946. Unfortunately, a
spectacular rise in inflation continued, partly due to exceptions in price
and wage controls allowed by Truman. Archival sources; 3 photos, 45
notes.   M. L. Tate

2535. Wróblewski, Andrzej N.   LYNDON B. JOHNSON I JEGO
POLITYKA SPOŁECZNA [Lyndon B. Johnson and his social policy].
Studia Nauk Politycznych [Poland] 1980 (2): 77-100. Discusses President
Lyndon B. Johnson's Great Society formula (1964), based on official
pronouncements of President Johnson published in *Public Papers of the
Presidents of the United States.* Discusses the main programs of Johnson's War on Poverty and their results. Sees a significant discrepancy
between the range of Great Society programs and their real social effects
as viewed by American critics.   J/S

2536. Wrong, Dennis H.   WATERGATE: SYMPTOM OF WHAT
SICKNESS?   *Dissent 1974 21(4): 501-507.* Discusses political culture in
the United States since World War II and its relationship to the Watergate Scandal.   S

2537. Yarnell, Allen.   EISENHOWER AND MCCARTHY: AN AP-
PRAISAL OF PRESIDENTIAL STRATEGY.   *Presidential Studies Q.
1980 10(1): 90-98.* There have been many attempts to explain Dwight D.
Eisenhower's conduct toward Joseph R. McCarthy. The president always
denied involvement in McCarthy's demise, favoring a low-key approach
to the affair. Considering that McCarthy was a major force in American
politics in January 1953, Eisenhower played his hand skillfully while
working to destroy McCarthyism. Based on official documents and other
sources; 57 notes.   G. E. Pergl

2538. Zarefsky, David.   THE GREAT SOCIETY AS A RHETORI-
CAL PROPOSITION.   *Q. J. of Speech 1979 65(4): 364-378.* The Great
Society programs of President Lyndon Johnson reflected commitment to
the quality of life, the idea of affirmative action, and government's role
as stimulus and guarantor of social change. Obstacles to adopting the
programs were overcome by employing conservative themes, claiming a
moral imperative to act, and distinguishing the Great Society from older
programs.   J

2539. Zarefsky, David.   PRESIDENT JOHNSON'S WAR ON POV-
ERTY: THE RHETORIC OF THREE "ESTABLISHMENT" MOVE-
MENTS.   *Communication Monographs 1977 44(4): 352-373.* Most
rhetorical critics feel that social movements arise from disaffected minority groups, but social reform also can be generated from within the
establishment, as shown by President Lyndon B. Johnson's War on Poverty; the rhetorical and activist measures of the War on Poverty were
identical, which indicates a need to study further the rhetoric and origins
of social movements.

2540. Zeisel, Hans.   THE FBI'S BIASED SAMPLING: A STATIS-
TICAL DETECTIVE STORY.   *Sci. and Public Affairs 1973 29(1):
38-42.* Because of biased statistics-keeping methods, 1967-73, which tend

to blame the courts for high criminal recidivism, the Federal Bureau of
Investigation should relinquish its statistics keeping to an independent
agency in the Justice Department.

2541. —.   "CAN YOU HEAR ME MR. PRESIDENT?"   *Can. Dimension [Canada] 1973 9(6): 27-37.* Examines political espionage in the
Nixon administration's Watergate scandal, 1968-72; emphasizes the recruitment of former Central Intelligence Agency members, the ITT affair,
and slush funds.

2542. —.   [ECONOMIC   PERCEPTION   AND   POLITICS].
J. of Pol. 1980 42(1): 49-81.
Shapiro, Robert Y. and Conforto, Bruce M.   PRESIDENTIAL PER-
    FORMANCE, THE ECONOMY, AND THE PUBLIC'S EVAL-
    UATION OF ECONOMIC CONDITIONS, *pp. 49-67.* The
    Survey of Consumer Finances, conducted during 1947-75, exam-
    ined public perception of family financial status, and provided a link
    between national economic conditions and public appraisal of presi-
    dential performance. With three exceptions, the public evaluations
    have more accurately predicted national electoral results than have
    objective economic measures. The three exceptions were the period
    1950-51, which can be explained by Harry Truman's leading
    American into the Korean War; and 1973-74 and 1974-75, when
    Watergate, the resignation of Richard Nixon and his subsequent
    pardon by Gerald Ford led to increases in public disapproval of the
    performances of the three presidents. 2 tables, 5 graphs, 47 notes.
Kenski, Henry C.   ECONOMIC PERCEPTION AND PRESIDEN-
    TIAL POPULARITY: A COMMENT, *pp. 68-75.* The above
    article focuses exclusively on economic factors and ignores salient
    noneconomic factors in advancing a theory of presidential popu-
    larity. Foreign policy events are especially unjustifiably ignored.
    There are also serious methodological problems, particularly in the
    manipulation of statistics. 10 notes.
Shapiro, Robert Y. and Conforto, Bruce M.   ECONOMIC PERCEP-
    TION AND POLITICAL BEHAVIOR: REPLY TO PROFES-
    SOR KENSKI, *pp. 76-81.* Reaffirms that economic perception
    provides an indirect effect of economic performance on presidential
    disapproval, although events influenced by the White House may
    overshadow the impact of economic conditions. 11 notes.
                                                          A. W. Novitsky

2543. —.   ENERGY: 1945-1980: SETTING THE STAGE.   *Wilson
Q. 1981 5(2): 54-69.* According to this adaptation of Chapters 1-3 of
Energy in Perspective: Today's Problems, Yesterday's Solutions (Washington, D.C.: The Brookings Institution, 1981) by Craufurd D. Goodwin
and William J. Barber, the Truman administration (1945-53), because of
peacetime preoccupation with short-term political costs and benefits and
because of fragmentation in the energy sector, failed to develop a coherent
energy policy, despite the realization that the United States was no longer
energy self-sufficient; successor Dwight D. Eisenhower ignored the warnings in William S. Paley's 1952 report, *Resources for Freedom,* the main
energy initiative to emerge from the Truman era, and pursued a free
market policy until increasing oil imports led to surplus which, in turn,
led to quotas and the formation of OPEC.

2544. —.   ENERGY: 1945-1980: FROM JOHN F. KENNEDY TO
JIMMY CARTER.   *Wilson Q. 1981 5(2): 70-90.* According to this
adaptation of chapters 4-9 of *Energy in Perspective,* written by William
J. Barber, James L. Cochrane, Neil de Marchi, and Joseph A. Yager,
Presidents John Kennedy, Lyndon Johnson, Richard Nixon, Gerald
Ford, and Jimmy Carter all failed to develop or gain support for energy
plans that would view each fuel as but a part of the complete energy
picture: President Kennedy made few changes in the federal energy policy
inherited from Eisenhower; President Johnson, responding to transient
political and economic pressures, ignored the threats of impending scarcity, price rises, and growing OPEC strength; President Nixon's Project
Independence, a response to the 1973 gasoline crisis created by the Arab
embargo and OPEC price hikes, was hampered by the concerns of environmentalists, price controls imposed earlier in an attempt to curb inflation, and, finally, by Watergate; President Ford devised a more coherent
energy plan than any of his predecessors but was opposed by a Democratic Congress; and President Carter's energy package, which emphasized reducing energy demand while increasing energy efficiency and
which ignored increasing supply, passed Congress diluted beyond recognition.

2545. —. AN EXCHANGE ON WATERGATE. *Partisan R. 1974 41(4): 645-648.*
Chomsky, Noam. TEA PARTY, pp. 645-647. Argues that government repression during the 1960's was more extreme than under Richard M. Nixon, but because it was directed against the Socialist Workers Party, Black Panthers, Student Nonviolent Coordinating Committee, and the New Left in general, it was accepted. In the Watergate scandal, "Nixon's crime was not the choice of means but the choice of enemies"— the liberal establishment, the political and ideological center.
Phillips, William. TRAUMA, pp. 648. Dissents from Chomsky's interpretation. D. K. Pickens and S

2546. —. [KENNEDY AND CONGRESS]. *Pol. Studies [Great Britain] 1980 28(4): 567-583.*
Hart, John. ASSESSING PRESIDENTIAL LEADERSHIP: A COMMENT ON WILLIAMS AND KERSHAW, *pp. 567-578.* Comments on R. J. Williams and D. Kershaw's article, which assesses President John F. Kennedy's record of legislative leadership, but adds nothing to the now-familiar revisionist argument, seeing the contrast between promise and performance in terms of undesirable concessions to Southern conservatism. The selection of case studies is unbalanced, and the accounts of minimum wage, aid to education, and civil rights programs are inadequate and distorted. The attempt to establish a causal connection between the circumstances of Kennedy's nomination and his failure is based on very slender evidence. 25 notes.
Williams, Robert J. APOLOGISTS AND REVISIONISTS: A REJOINDER TO HART, *pp. 579-583.* What Hart calls revisionism is an amalgam of views from different ideological perspectives and does not really exist. He has detected some errors in the essay, but his approach is too quantitive and much of his comment is irrelevant and inaccurate. If he labels his opponents revisionists, then he himself is an apologist. 8 notes. D. J. Nicholls

2547. —. LYNDON B. JOHNSONS GREAT SOCIETY. [Lyndon B. Johnson's Great Society]. *Kleio [Netherlands] 1978 19(9): 845-489.* President Johnson's "Great Society," announced in 1964 and advocating social reform, failed because of the Vietnam War and because he wanted to avoid controversies. 6 notes. H. P. Waalwijk

2548. —. [PUBLIC OPINION ON IMPEACHMENT]. *Pol. Sci. Q. 1974 89(2): 289-304.*
McGeever, Patrick J. "GUILTY, YES; IMPEACHMENT, NO": SOME EMPIRICAL FINDINGS, pp. 289-300. "Reports and analyzes another opinion survey that reveals a seeming contradiction in adult public opinion: Although some two-thirds of McGeever's sample believed President Nixon seriously culpable in the Watergate affair, about one-half of those who hold the President guilty nevertheless did not call for his removal from office through impeachment or resignation."
Finch, Gerald B. IMPEACHMENT AND THE DYNAMICS OF PUBLIC OPINION: A COMMENT ON "GUILTY, YES; IMPEACHMENT, NO," pp. 301-304. "In a commentary on the McGeever data, speculates that the size of the inconsistent 'Guilty, Yes; Impeachment, No' spectrum of opinion will shrink over time. Finch also predicts that the public's reaction to Watergate is unlikely to produce any permanent shifts in party loyalties among many Americans." J

2549. —. WATERGATE: ITS IMPLICATIONS FOR RESPONSIBLE GOVERNMENT. *Administration and Society 1974 6(2): 155-170.*

Foreign Affairs

2550. Adelman, Kenneth L. A CLANDESTINE CLAN: A REVIEW ESSAY. *Int. Security 1980 5(1): 152-171.* Reviews Thomas Powers's *The Man Who Kept the Secrets: Richard Helms and the CIA* (New York: Alfred A. Knopf, 1979) and Kermit Roosevelt's *Countercoup: The Struggle for the Control of Iran* (New York: McGraw-Hill, 1979) and discusses the recent history of US intelligence operations and the Central Intelligence Agency (CIA).

2551. Adler, Frank J. REVIEW ESSAY: *HARRY S. TRUMAN.* *Am. Jewish Hist. Q. 1973 62(4): 414-425.* Criticizes Margaret Truman's description of the Palestine issue in her biography of her father. The review focuses on the partition question (1946-47) and on the part played by Truman's Jewish friend Eddie Jacobson. Margaret Truman mentions only one White House interview with Jacobson but the presidential records show 24 appointments during this period. Margaret Truman's picture of her father's dispassionate stance on these issues is inaccurate. 47 notes. F. Rosenthal

2552. Ahmad, Eqbal. LA POLÍTICA EXTERIOR NORTEAMERICANA EN LA DÉCADA DE LOS SETENTAS: PANORAMA GENERAL [US foreign policy in the seventies: a general panorama]. *Rev. Mexicana de Ciencias Pol. y Soc. [Mexico] 1975 21(81): 11-31.* Surveys US foreign policy, notably the global strategy of Richard M. Nixon and Henry A. Kissinger, who set the tone for the entire decade.

2553. Alberts, D. J. COUNTERFORCE IN AN ERA OF ESSENTIAL EQUIVALENCE. *Air U. R. 1975 26(3): 27-37.* Examines and evaluates the concept of counterforce in an era of essential equivalence, reviewing the Eisenhower-Dulles doctrine of massive retaliation and the McNamara strategy of flexible response. Concludes that the concept of counterforce is really not new, but something that has been practiced intermittently for many years and is therefore not nearly the major issue that military superiority is. Secondary sources; 24 notes. J. W. Thacker, Jr.

2554. Allen, H. C. QUIET STRENGTH? AMERICAN FOREIGN POLICY UNDER PRESIDENT CARTER. *Round Table [Great Britain] 1977 (266): 146-152.* The Inaugural Address of President Carter highlighted the need for nuclear disarmament and for morality in American foreign policy. The era of Imperial Republicanism has ended. There is a new tone in foreign and domestic policy. C. Anstey

2555. Allen, T. Harrell. U.S.-CHINESE DIALOGUE, 1969-72. *J. of Communication 1976 26(1): 81-86.* Discusses improved relations between the United States and China under the Nixon administration, 1969-72.

2556. Allison, Graham T. COLD DAWN AND THE MIND OF KISSINGER. *Washington Monthly 1974 6(1): 38-49.* Reviews John Newhouse's *Cold Dawn: The Story of SALT* (New York: Holt, Reinhart & Winston, 1973). S

2557. Allison, Graham T. MILITARY CAPABILITIES AND AMERICAN FOREIGN POLICY. *Ann. of the Am. Acad. of Pol. and Social Sci. 1973 (406): 17-37.* "Can the availability of a rapid response capability lead the United States to intervene militarily in situations where, without those ready forces, the U.S. government would decide that military intervention was not required? Secretary of Defense [Robert S.] McNamara said *no;* Senator Richard Russell said *yes.* After examining the basic approaches to weapons selection that led McNamara and Russell to opposite conclusions, this article reviews recent instances—Dienbienphu, Laos, Korea, the Bay of Pigs, and Vietnam—in which the presence or absence of a ready military option may have affected decisions about the use of force. A conclusion about who had the better part of the argument provides a base for drawing some implications concerning the full costs and benefits of military capabilities and the responsibilities of the secretary of defense." J

2558. Alter, Jonathan. REAGAN'S DR. STRANGELOVE. *Washington Monthly 1981 13(4): 10-17.* The views of Richard Pipes, a senior adviser on Soviet and Eastern European affairs with the National Security Council, are unusually negative toward the USSR.

2559. Altherr, Marco. LES ORIGINES DE LA GUERRE FROIDE: UN ESSAI D'HISTORIOGRAPHIE [The origins of the Cold War: a historiographical essay]. *Relations Int. [France] 1977 (9): 69-81.* Notes the extent and the passion of the debate among historians about the origins of the Cold War. Divides opinions into traditional, realist, revisionist, and postrevisionist schools, the revisionists in turn being classified as "hard" and "soft." Reviews leading points of controversy, including eastern Europe, the role of Harry Truman, the atomic bomb, and economic determinism. A conflict of generations with different historical experiences helps explain the historiographical disagreements.

R. Stromberg

2560. Ambri, Mariano. LE ORIGINI DEL 'SISTEMA KISSINGER' [The origins of the "Kissinger system"]. *Civitas [Italy] 1976 27(9): 3-16.* It is evident that the two parts of the doctrine expounded in London in 1975 by Henry A. Kissinger and Helmut Sonnenfeldt are two aspects of a single global vision which must be ascribed to the American Secretary of State. The author analyzes the conceptual importance of the "Kissinger system" when he refers to the part read by Sonnenfeldt, the expert in the problems of eastern Europe. In isolating the chief aspects of such a system, it is clear that the US cannot avoid the development of the USSR, a power with interests not only in Europe but all over the world. But the US can, and must, try to obtain that the USSR strengthens its power or moderates its activities. For Kissinger, to moderate means to acknowledge the legitimate interests of USSR and to give proofs that they are not threatened: as long as the Soviets feel that their legitimate interests are not threatened the risk of further complications is very small. This is the fundamental premise of the system, and includes the right of Moscow to its security belt, that is the socialist countries of Eastern Europe. It is necessary to make the USSR economically competitive on the American market with a differentiated and widespread commerce. According to Kissinger, this is the way of converting Moscow to the advantages and virtues of stability. 	J/S

2561. Arbatov, A. G. NA PUTI V TUPIK [Heading for a blind alley]. *Voprosy Istorii [USSR] 1980 (9): 103-116.* A look at American involvement in Vietnam in the 1960's, focusing on Presidents John F. Kennedy and Lyndon B. Johnson. Emphasizes that this is an account through the "prism of today's politics." In 1968, although there were still a few years of war, the role of the United States was already determined. Vietnam serves as an example of flaws in US foreign policy. Based on *The Pentagon Papers* (1971) and other primary sources; 67 notes.

S. J. Talalay

2562. Arnold, Hugh M. HENRY KISSINGER AND HUMAN RIGHTS. *Universal Human Rights 1980 2(4): 57-71.* Examines Henry A. Kissinger's record in human rights from 1971 to 1976, and suggests that his interests in this area were originally all subservient to his desire to attain national security and a stable international status quo, and that only in the last year (1976) of his term (1973-76) as secretary of state did he exhibit a pronounced interest in human rights.

2563. Aron, Raymond. IDEOLOGY IN SEARCH OF A POLICY. *Foreign Affairs 1982 60(3): 503-524.* Discusses the Reagan administration's ideas, which, during 1981, were searching for a policy. Because there has been a shift in the balance of nuclear and conventional forces in the USSR's favor, the United States wants to update its military arsenal so as to catch up with the Soviets. The Europeans agree that there is a need for American rearmament, but differ in their views as to the form it should take. 2 notes. 	A. A. Englard

2564. Aronson, Shlomo. CARTER AND THE MIDDLE EAST: AN EARLY REPORT CARD. *Jerusalem Q. [Israel] 1977 (4): 31-43.* Analyzes President Jimmy Carter's foreign policy, in particular his Middle East program, describing the background of his nonlinkage approach to international relations, ca. 1967-77.

2565. Astiz, Carlos A. U.S. POLICY AND LATIN AMERICAN REACTION. *Current Hist. 1978 74(434): 49-52, 89.* Under Jimmy Carter the United States has pursued an attitude of benign neglect in foreign relations with Latin America.

2566. Auw, David C. L. COMMITMENT, POLICY LEGACY, AND POLICY OPTIONS: THE U.S.-R.O.C. RELATIONS UNDER REAGAN. *Issues & Studies [Taiwan] 1982 18(3): 8-26.* President Reagan's quiet approach to restoration of mutual trust between Washington and Taiwan is too limited. US foreign policy toward the Republic of China should not be restricted to the Taiwan Relations Act or interest in playing the "China card," but must recognize wider economic and strategic factors that make Taiwan a valuable ally. 30 notes.

J. A. Krompart

2567. Avineri, Shlomo. BEYOND CAMP DAVID. *Foreign Policy 1982 (46): 19-36.* Notes US policy in the Middle East as evident in the Camp David Agreement. Further resolution of Middle Eastern problems must use the agreement as a starting point. 	M. K. Jones

2568. Avineri, Shlomo. PEACEMAKING: THE ARAB-ISRAELI CONFLICT. *Foreign Affairs 1978 57(1): 51-69.* President Jimmy Carter's quest for a quick, comprehensive peace settlement in the Middle East has upset the delicate step-by-step approach that was the hallmark of the Kissinger years. The realities of contemporary world politics dictate that major international problems cannot be immediately or tidily resolved. "Peace cannot be achieved by fiat; it requires a period of gestation and mutual accommodation in which both sides will learn to live with each other, fear each other a little less, and trust each other a little more."

M. R. Yerburgh

2569. Ball, Nicole and Leitenberg, Milton. THE FOREIGN ARMS SALES POLICY OF THE CARTER ADMINISTRATION. *Alternatives 1979 4(4): 527-556.* This paper makes the point that the Carter Administration is continuing the US policy of spreading militarization round the world, particularly in the Third World. During the Nixon and Ford Administrations, arms sales and transfers came to be used routinely as the quid pro quo in diplomacy. As a Presidential candidate, Carter pledged to reduce US involvement in the conventional arms trade. Nonetheless, within a year of his enunciating his "arms sales restraint" policy in May 1977, the Administration proposed an end to the arms ban on Turkey, approved the sale of AWACs to Iran and 200 warplanes to the Mid-East, as well as a myriad of less controversial weapons deals. The dollar ceiling on arms sales has been frequently circumvented. Despite the legislation requiring the cessation of military sales, loans and grants to countries in which there is a "consistent pattern of gross violations of internationally recognized human rights," the Carter Administration continues to supply arms to many of the worst human rights offenders. And despite the Arms Export Control Act of 1976, the Administration has failed to act. It is extremely unlikely that any significant change will occur in the world arms trade despite President Carter's pronouncements against the spiralling arms traffic. 69 notes. 	J

2570. Ball, Nicole and Leitenberg, Milton. THE FOREIGN ARMS SALES OF THE CARTER ADMINISTRATION. *Bull. of the Atomic Scientists 1979 35(2): 31-36.* Despite campaign promises and policy suggestions from the Carter Administration, old rationales for foreign arms sales are still used, arms sales are on the increase, and reduction in arms sales seems unlikely.

2571. Balthazar, Louis. PRESIDENT CARTER AND HUMAN RIGHTS: THE CONTRADICTION OF AMERICAN POLICY. *Int. Perspectives [Canada] 1979 (May-Aug): 22-24.* President Jimmy Carter's campaign for the defense of human rights throughout the world is an expression of a characteristically American trait: a desire to inject morality into foreign policy. This moralistic tradition has historically existed side-by-side with the equally American pursuit of very real material interests. Despite the inherent contradiction, a meaningful position in favor of human rights is possible provided that the United States shows more tolerance towards left-wing governments and concentrates its efforts within the framework of multilateral institutions. Covers 1977-79.

E. S. Palais

2572. Banfi, Arialdo. KISSINGER: FINE DI UN MITO [Kissinger: The end of a myth]. *Ponte [Italy] 1973 29(1): 18-25.* Attacks Henry A. Kissinger's foreign policy during the Vietnam War; criticizes the bombing of Hanoi in December 1972 (before the Paris Peace Accords of January 1973).

2573. Baral, Jaya Krishna. THE *MAYAGUEZ* INCIDENT: A STUDY OF CRISIS MANAGEMENT. *Int. Studies [India] 1980 19(1): 15-41.* Interprets the *Mayaguez* incident of 12-14 May 1975 as a crisis by demonstrating the connection of its two phases—crisis diplomacy and crisis decisionmaking. By resorting to a diplomacy of violence, the United States used the incident to bolster its sagging prestige and to impress its foreign and domestic critics. In the contest among various bureaucratic interests within the national government to influence American policy, Henry A. Kissinger emerged the winner. 47 notes.

T. P. Linkfield

2574. Baral, Jaya Krishna. PARIS TALKS ON VIETNAM AND AMERICAN DIPLOMACY. *Int. Studies [India] 1975 14(3): 375-395.* Studies the shifting interactions of the participants in the Paris accord of 1973, revealing lessons for other international settlements. Self-confidence made each side insincere in negotiations until 1968. Popular pressure forced Lyndon B. Johnson to initiate contacts with Hanoi. In 1969 Richard M. Nixon and Henry A. Kissinger introduced their balance-of-power strategy, with tactics of secrecy, surprise, and shock. They aimed to separate Hanoi from its friends, while initiating troop withdrawals. In 1971 Nixon showed all of his cards: troop withdrawal, maneuvers with Russia and China, and hit-concession pressure on Hanoi. Yet, despite his claims, Nixon had to accept Hanoi's final terms for a ceasefire. Secondary sources; 74 notes.
R. E. Stack

2575. Barnds, William J. UNITED STATES FOREIGN POLICY: THE LEGACY AND THE CHALLENGE. *Worldview 1977 20(1-2): 11-18.* Reviews foreign policy of the Nixon Administration and defines the challenge to be met by the Carter Administration as attention to domestic affairs, formulation of publicly supported foreign policy, development of a public-minded attitude, and coming to grips with the imposition of morality in foreign affairs.

2576. Barnes, Trevor. THE SECRET COLD WAR: THE C.I.A. AND AMERICAN FOREIGN POLICY IN EUROPE, 1946-1956. PART I. *Hist. J. [Great Britain] 1981 24(2): 399-415.* An overview of how the American Central Intelligence Agency influenced US policy in Europe and European affairs, 1946-56. Examines how the CIA interpreted intelligence and pursued covert action. Clandestine activity was conducted against the Communists in Italy and Greece and played an important but not decisive role in defeating the extreme left-wing movements. Based on sources in the National Archives and on secondary sources; 69 notes. Article to be continued.
G. M. Alexander

2577. Barnet, Richard; Dellinger, David and Falk, Richard A. U.S. FOREIGN POLICY IN THE MIDDLE EAST. *J. of Palestine Studies [Lebanon] 1980 10(1): 3-34.* A transcript of a symposium held by the Institute for Palestine Studies in which three prominent American intellectuals participated with Edward Said, a professor at Columbia University, as moderator. The topic was recent developments in US foreign policy and their repercussions on the Palestine question. Several major issues were discussed, such as the Carter administration's hard line toward the USSR, the limited influence of US groups sympathetic to liberation movements, and the administration's policy toward the Arab-Israeli conflict and the Palestinian resistance movement. Based on the transcript of the symposium.
P. J. Mattar

2578. Beard, Robin. THE CARTER ADMINISTRATION'S SALT-II PROPOSALS. *J. of Social and Pol. Studies 1977 2(3): 143-154.* Maintains that so many concessions have been made to the Soviets from the Carter administration's SALT-II proposals that the treaty thus far negotiated will not constrain Soviet strategic capabilities, nor diminish the Soviet threat to the US silo-based ICBM.

2579. Beglova, N. POLITIKA SSHA V IUZHNOI AZII [US policy in South Asia]. *Aziia i Afrika Segodnia [USSR] 1980 (8): 15-18.* Negative influence on the situation in South Asia exerted by the four-year-long activity of Carter's administration is the subject matter of the article. Offers the conclusion that the policy of Carter's administration objectively leads to destabilization in the area.
J/S

2580. Bell, Coral. THE DIPLOMACY OF DETENTE: THE KISSINGER ERA: THE NATURE AND PROVENANCE OF DETENTE. *A. N. U. Hist. J. [Australia] 1976 12: 52-75.* Discusses the strategy pursued by the United States, represented by Henry A. Kissinger in detente policy between 1969 and the mid-1970's.

2581. Bell, Coral. KISSINGER IN RETROSPECT: THE DIPLOMACY OF POWER-CONCERT? *Int. Affairs [Great Britain] 1977 53(2): 202-216.* Although it is difficult to see Henry A. Kissinger's Secretaryship in a proper perspective, he did develop a distinctive tradition in American foreign policy, as did Dean Acheson during the post-1945 period. Whereas Acheson took the United States into Europe and a balance of power coalition, Kissinger tried to transform that coalition into a more flexible concert of powers upon a worldwide basis. This policy,

based upon the 19th-century concert, was designed to promote peaceful change and detente. In spite of the constructive nature of Kissinger's policy, a number of criticisms were advanced against it. These involved questions such as disengagement in Vietnam or the validity of detente. In contrast to Acheson, Kissinger has been less fortunate in his domestic and international colleagues. 5 notes.
P. J. Beck

2582. Bell, Coral. VIRTUE UNREWARDED: CARTER'S FOREIGN POLICY AT MID-TERM. *Int. Affairs [Great Britain] 1978 54(4): 559-572.* At mid-term, it is possible to begin assessing President Jimmy Carter's style and assumptions as a foreign policy decisionmaker, especially as he has avoided being dominated by a Kissinger-type figure. Initially, there seemed to be a revived messianism in American foreign policy, a duty to redeem the world, as seen in the stress upon human rights and upon links with the Third World, although there has often been ambiguity in his policy due to both interventionist and withdrawal tendencies. This ambivalence has encouraged diverse interpretations of his policy, for while some accuse him of inexperience and naiveté, others claim that he has provided American adversaries with an opportunity for gain. His policy has been characterized more by virtuous sentiments than by successful outcomes, as demonstrated by Soviet-American relations in Africa and by the Middle East problem. 5 notes.
P. J. Beck

2583. Bender, Gerald J. ANGOLA: LEFT, RIGHT & WRONG. *Foreign Policy 1981 (43): 53-69.* Continuing a tradition dating at least to 1960, the vacillating policy of President Ronald Reagan's administration toward Angola has alienated virtually every element involved in the conflict, both in Africa and the United States. All agree that a stable Angolan-American relationship would be to the advantage of the United States, but this cannot come about until America recognizes the Marxist-oriented government in Luanda and encourages South Africa to restrain its activities in the area.
T. L. Powers

2584. Ben-Zvi, Abraham. IN PURSUIT OF PEACE IN THE MIDDLE EAST: A JUXTAPOSITION OF AMERICAN STRATEGIES, 1969-79. *Australian J. of Pol. and Hist. [Australia] 1981 27(2): 172-185.* Surveys American attempts to mitigate the Arab-Israeli conflict during the winter of 1969 to summer of 1979, suggesting that American diplomacy vacillated between two approaches: the "comprehensive" or "root" approach and the "step-by-step" or "branch" approach. The former was tried during 1969-71 and 1977-78. The latter approach was tried systematically by Henry A. Kissinger during 1973-75 and as a fall-back position during 1978-79. The step-by-step tactic was the only approach that allowed for some progress. Based on memoirs and contemporary accounts; 23 notes.
W. D. McIntyre

2585. Bérard, Armand. LA FIN DE ROOSEVELT ET LA DOUBLE CAPITULATION [The death of Roosevelt and the double capitulation]. *Nouvelle Rev. des Deux Mondes [France] 1978 (2): 280-289.* Discusses US-European diplomacy, February-August 1945.

2586. Berger, Henry W. BIPARTISANSHIP, SENATOR TAFT, AND THE TRUMAN ADMINISTRATION. *Pol. Sci. Q. 1975 90(2): 221-237.* Explains the emergence of "bipartisanship" in foreign policy in the years after World War II. He demonstrates how Senator Robert Taft refused to concede that his expression of disagreement with certain Truman administration foreign policies was a violation of the spirit of bipartisanship and therefore somehow unpatriotic.
J

2587. Bergsten, C. Fred. THE COSTS OF REAGANOMICS. *Foreign Policy 1981 (44): 24-36.* Although the economic goals of the Reagan administration appear to provide strong support for a more assertive US foreign policy, the actual impact of the Reagan program is creating major economic problems throughout the world, with profound implications for overall US foreign policy. The United States must focus attention on the impact of its economic policy on other countries so as to avoid devastating both its foreign policy and domestic prosperity. Note.
L. J. Klass

2588. Bergsten, C. Fred. U.S. TRADE POLICY AND THE WORLD ECONOMY. *Atlantic Community Q. 1977-78 15(4): 442-449.* Reprints an address made on 18 October 1977 at the Conference on the "Crisis in World Trade" in Washington, D.C., discussing the Carter administration's attempts to maintain open international trade.
J/S

2589. Berman, Sylvan M. THE U. S. FOREIGN POLICY LEGACY OF THE PRE-CARTER ADMINISTRATIONS TO ISRAEL. *Int. Problems [Israel] 1977 16(3-4): 15-27.* Discusses the nature and consequences of the US Middle Eastern policy of the Nixon and Ford administrations, 1969-77.

2590. Berman, William C. GLOBAL GAMES. *Rev. in Am. Hist. 1980 8(4): 561-566.* Review essay of Henry A. Kissinger's *White House Years* (Boston: Little, Brown, 1979); 1969-77.

2591. Bernstein, Barton J. "COURAGE AND COMMITMENT: THE MISSILES OF OCTOBER." *Foreign Service J. 1975 52(12): 9-11, 24-27.* Discusses the 1962 Cuban missile crisis and the pattern of negotiation conducted by President John F. Kennedy and Soviet Premier Nikita Khrushchev in averting nuclear war.

2592. Bernstein, Barton J. THE CUBAN MISSILE CRISIS: TRADING THE JUPITERS IN TURKEY? *Pol. Sci. Q. 1980 95(1): 97-125.* Reassesses the relationship between the US Jupiter missiles in Turkey and the Cuban missile crisis. Concludes that analysts previously missed critical evidence and thus erroneously reported that President Kennedy ordered the removal of the Jupiters from Turkey before the Cuban crisis erupted and that the Kennedy administration considered trading its Jupiters in Turkey only after the Soviets raised the issue.   J

2593. Bernstein, Barton J. THE PERILS AND POLITICS OF SURRENDER: ENDING THE WAR WITH JAPAN AND AVOIDING THE THIRD ATOMIC BOMB. *Pacific Hist. Rev. 1977 46(1): 1-27.* The ambiguous American response to Japan's 10 August 1945 surrender offer strengthened the militarists in Japan and nearly prolonged the war. President Truman and Secretary of State James F. Byrnes were reluctant to retain the Emperor. Byrnes and Truman were concerned about domestic political effects and feared a popular backlash if the surrender terms were not harsh enough. They were therefore willing to consider using a third atomic bomb or mounting a costly invasion of Japan. Secretary of War Henry L. Stimson and Admiral William Leahy urged acceptance of Japan's surrender terms in order to end the war quickly, keep Russia out of the peace settlement, and avoid world-wide horror at the use of a third atomic bomb. Based on documents in numerous manuscript collections; 92 notes.   W. K. Hobson

2594. Bernstein, Barton J. THE POLICY OF RISK: CROSSING THE 38TH PARALLEL AND MARCHING TO THE YALU. *Foreign Service J. 1977 54(3): 16-22, 29.* Discusses foreign policy and military strategy in the Korean War, 1950-52, concentrating on the actions of Harry S. Truman, Dean Acheson, and Douglas MacArthur.

2595. Bernstein, Barton J. SHATTERER OF WORLDS: HIROSHIMA AND NAGASAKI. *Bull. of the Atomic Scientists 1975 31(10): 12-22.* US policymakers in the Roosevelt and Truman administrations had little doubt about the desirability of using atomic weapons both for ending the war in the Pacific and for intimidating the USSR.

2596. Bernstein, Barton J. THE WEEK WE ALMOST WENT TO WAR. *Bull. of the Atomic Scientists 1976 32(2): 12-21.* Discusses military strategy and the actions of President John F. Kennedy and USSR Premier Nikita Khrushchev during the 1962 Cuban Missile Crisis, questioning whether the threat of nuclear war was as great as it was thought to be.

2597. Bernstein, Barton J. THE WEEK WE WENT TO WAR: AMERICAN INTERVENTION IN THE KOREAN CIVIL WAR. *Foreign Service J. 1977 54(1): 6-9, 33-35, (2): 8-11, 33-34.* Part I. Discusses President Harry S. Truman and Secretary of State Dean Acheson's appraisals of the USSR's military aims in Korea as a major factor in the US decision to intervene in the Korean War in June 1950. Part II. Chronicles events occurring during the week preceding the decision to intercede in the Korean conflict, 1950.

2598. Berryman, Phillip. CENTRAL AMERICA'S NEWS VS. U.S. VIEWS. *Freedomways 1981 21(3): 161-170.* Compares socioeconomic realities in Central America with the two approaches to the region's problems adopted by the United States: President Jimmy Carter's view that unresolved social problems in Central America make political change

inevitable and must be countered by supporting moderates in the areas's nations; and President Ronald Reagan's view that considers the region as an arena of US-Soviet confrontation; both stances fail to consider the needs and hopes of the general population.

2599. Bertram, Christoph. AMERICA'S OSTPOLITIK. *European R. [Great Britain] 1973/74 24(1): 23-27.* "The United States has embarked upon a policy of negotiation and arrangement with the Soviet Union. Christoph Bertram seeks an explanation of Nixon's 'new course' and asks whether there are grounds for European apprehension."   J

2600. Bethell, Thomas N. INCIDENTALLY, THE U.N. VOTE WAS RIGHT. *Washington Monthly 1980 12(3): 32-41.* Discusses President Jimmy Carter's panic over (and eventual disavowal of) the United States' and other nations' vote for UN Security Council Resolution 465 (1 March 1980) criticizing Israel for building settlements in occupied Arab territories; stresses his fear that the US vote would cause an uproar among the Jews of New York and would hurt his chances in New York's 25 March presidential primary; and describes presidential political expediency in decisionmaking about Zionism since 1948.

2601. Bhagat, G. SOME NOTES ON MATERIALS RELATING TO JOHN FOSTER DULLES AND INDIA. *Indian Arch. [India] 1975 24(1): 28-39.* Outlines the major developments in Indo-American relations during the tenure of Secretary of State John Foster Dulles, 1953-59. The Cold War climate of the Korean War, the escalating conflict in Indochina, and India's nonalignment policy and refusal to join the South East Asia Treaty Organization (SEATO) contributed to cool relations between Prime Minister Jawaharlal Nehru and Dulles. Provides a complete list of documents at Princeton University relating to Dulles's Indian policy. 2 notes.   S. C. Strom

2602. Bhagat, Sheela. MATERIALS ON INDIA IN THE DWIGHT D. EISENHOWER LIBRARY. *Indian Arch. [India] 1974 23(1-2): 47-60.* Describes specific documents from the General Files, Official Files, Presidential Personal Files, and Miscellaneous Files of the Eisenhower Presidential Library, which pertain to US-Indian relations during the Cold War, 1953-60. Focuses on the relationship between Dwight D. Eisenhower, John Foster Dulles, and Jawaharlal Nehru. Also of interest are the numerous reports by private citizens after touring India, presidential speeches, material on the Food for Peace Program, and correspondence relating to Eisenhower's presidential visit to India in December 1959. 2 notes.   S. C. Strom

2603. Bickerton, Ian J. PRESIDENT TRUMAN'S RECOGNITION OF ISRAEL: TWO VIEWS. *Am. Jewish Arch. 1981 33(1): 141-152.* Reviews Zvi Ganin's *Truman, American Jewry, and Israel* (1979), which explores the activities of the State Department, American Jewish leadership, and the White House in the years just before US recognition of Israel, and Evan M. Wilson's *Decision on Palestine: How the U.S. Came to Recognize Israel* (1979), which describes Truman's decision on Israel as not in the best interests of the United States.   T. Koppel

2604. Birnbaum, Norman. IS THERE A NEW AMERICAN FOREIGN-POLICY CONSENSUS? *Antioch Rev. 1981 39(2): 171-180.* Examines the currently fragmented state of American foreign policy, with a special critique of President Ronald Reagan's view of world politics.

2605. Bishop, Joseph W., Jr. CARTER'S LAST CAPITULATION. *Commentary 1981 71(3): 32-35.* Jimmy Carter's capitulation to Iran's terms for the release of the American hostages opens the United States to further acts of terrorism; Carter should have honored the basic principle that under no circumstances should a government yield to terrorists.

2606. Bissell, Richard E. UNITED STATES POLICY IN AFRICA. *Current Hist. 1977 73(432): 193-195, 224-225.* Assesses the Carter administration's foreign policy and UN Ambassador Andrew Young's record; the political, economic, and social instability of Africa justifies an unorthodox policy emphasizing moral values, human rights, and open diplomacy.

2607. Blechman, Barry M.; Nolan, Janne E.; and Pratt, Alan. PUSHING ARMS. *Foreign Policy 1982 (46): 138-154.* Arms sales and military aid are means used by the USSR and the United States to gain influence in developing nations. Local crises test these Third World nations' ties to the superpowers and can escalate into superpower confrontation. Under the administration of President Jimmy Carter, efforts at the Conventional Arms Transfers Talks (1977-78) by the United States and USSR failed because of strained relations between them and the lack of domestic support for the talks in the United States. M. K. Jones

2608. Block, Fred. ECONOMIC INSTABILITY AND MILITARY STRENGTH: THE PARADOXES OF THE 1950 REARMAMENT DECISION. *Pol. & Soc. 1980 10(1): 35-58.* Examines, from a World System perspective, the militarization of US foreign policy in the Truman years through an analysis of a key document, National Security Council-68 (NSC-68). This document proposed that the urgent need for the creation of an international capitalist economic order in the post-World War II era could be met through increased defense spending. The success of the plan, largely brought about by the Korean crisis, has influenced US foreign policy decisions ever since, and analogies may be seen in Kennedy-Johnson Vietnam policies, and in the Carter administration response to the Afghanistan invasion in late 1979. 35 notes. D. G. Nielson

2609. Bonior, David E. REAGAN AND CENTRAL AMERICA. *SAIS Rev. 1981 (2): 3-11.* Under Ronald Reagan's leadership, US foreign policy in Central America may become anachronistic as it defines these foreign relations in terms of the East-West struggle; together with the leadership of Mexico and Venezuela, alienation caused by US policy mistakes may eclipse US influence in the region.

2610. Borisov, K. INTERVENTSIYA SSHA V DOMINIKAN-SKOI RESPUBLIKE [American intervention in the Dominican Republic]. *Voenno-Istoricheskii Zhurnal [USSR] 1971 (8): 48-57.* Describes American intervention in the Dominican Republic from April 1965 to September 1966, reflecting President Lyndon B. Johnson's statement of May 1965 that the United States would not allow another Communist government in the Western Hemisphere; details the role of the American embassy in organizing the intervention and the massive use of night operations by American troops. The populace in the Dominican Republic were morally and politically unprepared for armed conflict.

2611. Borowski, Harry R. A NARROW VICTORY: THE BERLIN BLOCKADE AND THE AMERICAN MILITARY RESPONSE. *Air U. Rev. 1981 32(5): 18-30.* Analyzes the US military response to the Soviet blockade of surface routes between Berlin and Germany's western zones, revealing that President Harry S. Truman's decision to airlift food and supplies from England to West Germany, instead of using military force to make the Soviets lift their blockade, was the key to his narrow victory in the 1948 election.

2612. Bosch, Juan. SALVADOR ALLENDE EN LAS MEMORIAS DE KISSINGER [Salvador Allende in Kissinger's memoirs]. *Casa de las Américas [Cuba] 1981 22(128): 100-103.* The chapter in Kissinger's *White House Years* devoted to Chile and the overthrow of the Allende government makes it clear that the assassins of Allende would not have dared to do away with the president without the overwhelming power and support of the United States. J. V. Coutinho

2613. Bourgois, Philippe. WHAT U.S. FOREIGN POLICY FACES IN RURAL EL SALVADOR: AN EYEWITNESS ACCOUNT. *Monthly Rev. 1982 34(1): 14-30.* The Cold War ideological dogmatism that the United States pursues regarding Third World national liberation movements, such as in El Salvador, prevents Reagan's administration from accurately assessing the strength of popular movements.

2614. Bovey, John A., Jr. DOVES IN ARMOR: AMERICANS AND THE NOBEL PRIZES. *Foreign Service J. 1974 51(1): 10-11.* Reviews the background of the Nobel Peace Prize and the controversial selection of Henry A. Kissinger in 1974. S

2615. Bovin, A. KEMP-DEVID: ANALIZ DOKUMENTOV [Camp David: an analysis of documents]. *Mirovaia Ekonomika i Mezhdunarodnye Otnosheniia [USSR] 1978 (11): 78-83.* Presents an account of the meeting between President Jimmy Carter, President Anwar Sadat and Prime Minister Menahem Begin at Camp David in September 1978, and of the agreement that was reached on the Middle East situation.

2616. Brach, Hans Günter. AMERIKANISH-SOWJETISCHE BEZIEHUNGEN: VOM KALTEN KRIEG ZUR ENTSPANNUNG? AMERIKANISCHE ENTSPANNUNGSPOLITIK GEGENÜBER DER SOWJETUNION UND CHINA (I) [US-USSR relations: from cold war to detente? US policies of detente toward the USSR and China: Part I]. *Neue Politische Literatur [West Germany] 1979 24(4): 513-548.* While immediate postwar armaments developments were controlled by the United States and the USSR, the explosion of the Chinese nuclear bombs and the increasing ideological differences between China and the USSR have changed the balance of power. Richard Nixon's foreign policy changed the modalities and style of US foreign policy but not US goals. 127 notes. R. Wagnleitner

2617. Braestrup, Peter. THE AMERICAN MILITARY: THE CHANGING OUTLOOK. *Wilson Q. 1979 3(2): 124-130.* Although Jimmy Carter ran for the presidency in 1976 on a platform calling for cuts in defense spending, by 1978 he and Defense Secretary Harold Brown realized that to counter the USSR's steady arms buildup they had to halt the relative US military decline after the Vietnam War and thus proposed a controversial 3% real increase in defense spending.

2618. Brecher, Michael and Geist, Benjamin. CRISIS BEHAVIOR: ISRAEL, 1973. *Jerusalem J. of Int. Relations [Israel] 1978 3(2-3): 197-228.* Analyzes Israel's political responses to the buildup of Syrian and Egyptian armed forces, the October War and the involvement of Henry A. Kissinger and Soviet Premier Aleksei Kosygin in resolving the crisis.

2619. Brecher, Michael. ISRAEL AND THE ROGERS PEACE INITIATIVE. *Orbis 1974 18(2): 402-426.* Discusses the efforts of William Rogers, US Secretary of State, to solve problems in the Middle East, 1969-70.

2620. Brenner, Michael J. THE PROBLEM OF INNOVATION AND THE NIXON-KISSINGER FOREIGN POLICY. *Internat. Studies Q. 1973 17(3): 255-295.* Describes the Nixon administration's adjustment of US foreign policy following America's failure in Vietnam in 1968. S

2621. Brenner, Michael J. PROLIFERATION WATCH: CARTER'S BUNGLED PROMISE. *Foreign Policy 1979 (36): 89-101.* Jimmy Carter deserves credit for being the first American president to tackle forthrightly the problem of nuclear nonproliferation. His tactics and accomplishments in the matter merit less praise. Much of the difficulty derives from the complexity of the problem, but inadequate presidential leadership, leading to an undisciplined government without a definite objective, must also bear blame. Tight organization and clear purpose might enable the administration to realize its promise of containing the spread of nuclear weapons. T. L. Powers

2622. Brodie, Bernard. THE DOMINO THEORY. *Rev. Militaire Générale [France] 1972 (10): 468-478.* The domino theory, first enunciated by President Dwight D. Eisenhower (1890-1969) and used to justify US intervention in Vietnam, was based on the assumption that the appeasement of Nazi Germany was the cause of World War II. The domino theory, however, relies upon two fallacies, namely, that events are both predictable and irremediable, and that the best time for intervention is the present. The inherent fallacy of the theory is exposed by the necessity of exaggerating when stating it, as was done by President Lyndon B. Johnson (1908-73) and by President Richard M. Nixon (1913-). References to published works. J. S. Gassner

2623. Brown, Seyom. AN END TO GRAND STRATEGY. *Foreign Policy 1978 (32): 22-46.* "The current turbulence in Soviet-American affairs is widely attributed to the Carter administration's fickle conduct in this and other important foreign relationships. Critics are demanding a grand strategy that will unify American foreign policy and steady the course of US-Soviet relations. But a single architechtural design may be neither feasible nor desirable; and those who insist on a master strategy for dealing with the Kremlin often fail to take account of the highly complex and contingent nature of US-Soviet interactions." 6 notes. T. L. Powers

2624. Brož, Ivan. K REAGANOVĚ PROGRAMU VÝSTAVBY STRATEGICKÝCH SIL USA PRO 80. LÉTA [Reagan's program of a buildup of US strategic forces for the 1980's]. *Hist. a Vojenství [Czechoslovakia] 1982 31(2): 135-150.* Soviet leadership refuses to accept the supposed subordination of the United States in the strategic arms development in comparison to the USSR. The Pentagon wants to change the present military balance to create better conditions for the advancement toward world domination. Capitalists will use political adventurism to improve economic conditions. Among newly produced smokescreens, to cover the real targets of American militarists, is the October 1981 official publication supporting Ronald Reagan's military buildup. 32 notes.

G. E. Pergl

2625. Brož, Ivan. K VOJENSKOPOLITICKYM FAKTORUM ZAHRANIČNÍ POLITIKY CARTEROVY ADMINISTRATIVY [On military-political factors of Carter administration's foreign policy]. *Hist. a Vojenství [Czechoslovakia] 1978 27(6): 150-164.* Reexamines foreign policy of the Carter administration and explains how this policy is constantly influenced by military-political factors—especially in close connection with the NATO system. The NATO structure creates a bond between West European partners and the main line of US world policy. Also analyzes the US military budget since 1976 and its upward tendency. Based on printed material; 23 notes.

G. E. Pergl

2626. Brundtland, Arne Olav. BETRAKTNINGER OM REAGAN-ADMINISTRASJONENS SIKKERHETS- OG UTENRIK-SPOLITIKK [Reflections on American security policy and foreign affairs handling under the Reagan Administration]. *Int. Pol. [Norway] 1981 (4B): 671-694.* After a presentation of the conceptual basis of the Reagan Administration's attitudes vis-à-vis the Soviet Union regarding security policy and foreign affairs, the author examines more closely American ways and means in the military and foreign policy fields in the pursuit of established aims.

J

2627. Brune, Lester H. THE EISENHOWER ADMINISTRATION AND DEFENSE POLICY. *Armed Forces and Soc. 1980 6(3): 511-516.* Reviews Richard A. Aliano's *American Defense Policy from Eisenhower to Kennedy: The Politics of Changing Military Requirements, 1957-1961* (Athens: Ohio U. Pr., 1975), James R. Killian, Jr.'s *Sputnik: Scientists and Eisenhower: A Memoir of the First Assistant to the President for Science and Technology* (Cambridge, Mass.: MIT Pr.), Douglas Kinnard's *President Eisenhower and Strategy Management: A Study in Defense Politics* (Lexington: U. of Kentucky Pr., 1977), and George B. Kistiakowsky's *A Scientist at the White House: The Private Diary of President Eisenhower's Special Assistant for Science and Technology* (Cambridge, Mass.: Harvard U. Pr., 1976), which all assess the New Look, Dwight David Eisenhower's strategic policy, enacted soon after his inauguration in 1953, which abandoned the large expensive programs of former years in favor of increased air power deterrence and small conventional forces.

2628. Brzezinski, Zbigniew. THE DECEPTIVE STRUCTURE OF PEACE. *Foreign Policy 1974 (14): 35-55.* Except for improving relations with China, the Nixon administration's foreign policy success has declined since 1971.

S

2629. Brzezinski, Zbigniew. LA POLITIQUE ÉTRANGÈRE DES ÉTATS-UNIS: À LA RECHERCHE D'UN OBJECTIF [US foreign policy: Searching for a goal]. *Pol. Étrangère [France] 1973 38(3): 257-284.* Considers opposing currents of US thought on world problems; urges cooperation among industrially advanced nations and discusses President Richard M. Nixon's foreign policy, 1970-72.

2630. Buchan, Alastair. THE IRONY OF HENRY KISSINGER. *Internat. Affairs [Great Britain] 1974 50(3): 367-379.* Analyzes the personality and ideas of Henry A. Kissinger, and relates this to the course of American foreign policy since 1969. Kissinger has maintained the momentum of the latter in the face of internal problems, and the irony is his reliance upon pragmatism and energy rather than his academic background. Based on the writings of Kissinger; 16 notes.

P. J. Beck

2631. Buhite, Russell D. MISSED OPPORTUNITIES? AMERICAN POLICY AND THE CHINESE COMMUNISTS, 1949. *Mid-America 1979 61(3): 179-188.* It has been argued that the United States missed opportunities to establish friendly relations with Chinese

Communists in 1949. Two such possibilities were an overture by Zhou Enlai (Chou En-lai) and an invitation to John Leighton Stuart to visit Beijing (Peking). State Department officials doubted Chou's sincerity and were also concerned with American domestic reaction. The Chinese were constrained by their Marxist-Leninist ideology and by Soviet pressure, to treat America as an enemy. It is not clear if such opportunities really existed. Based on State Department records, *Foreign Relations of the United States,* other primary, and secondary sources; 30 notes.

J. M. Lee

2632. Bull, Hedley. A VIEW FROM ABROAD: CONSISTENCY UNDER PRESSURE. *Foreign Affairs 1979 57(3): 441-462.* Reviews 1978 in terms of American foreign policy developments. Despite a wide range of policies, pressures, and concerns, the Carter administration remained generally consistent with its stated foreign policy objectives. Soviet meddling in Africa and a new surge of American anti-Sovietism, for example, have not dampened President Carter's determination to finalize a SALT II treaty.

M. R. Yerburgh

2633. Bull, Hedley. THE WEST AND SOUTH AFRICA. *Daedalus 1982 111(2): 255-270.* Discusses the USSR's threat to South Africa and the stance of the Reagan Administration in countering it, as well as the reluctance of Western Europe to perceive the Soviet threat in the same way.

2634. Bundy, William P. DICTATORSHIPS AND AMERICAN FOREIGN POLICY. *Foreign Affairs 1975 54(1): 51-60.* Examines the balance maintained between the three basic US foreign policy objectives of 1) security against attack, 2) the maintenance of an international community, and 3) the encouragement of representative government. World War II made opposition to totalitarian dictatorship a cornerstone of US policy, but Richard M. Nixon's administration changed American policy toward democracies and dictatorships with serious consequences at home. American policy toward dictatorships has been uneven and contradictory as exemplified in Greece, the Philippines, and Chile. From a paper read to the American Philosophical Society in 1975.

C. W. Olson

2635. Byers, R. B. THE PERILS OF SUPERPOWER DIPLOMACY: DÉTENTE, DEFENSE, AND ARMS CONTROL. *Int. J. [Canada] 1980 35(3): 520-547.* In 1972 President Richard M. Nixon of the United States and Premier Leonid Brezhnev of the USSR agreed on the basic principles of détente—political coexistence, increased commercial relations, and puruit of arms limitation—and implicitly accepted their linkage. The United States, however, failed to remind the Russians of linkage, a concept which the Russians preferred to ignore, and neither side could credit the other's striving for military parity rather than superiority. Only after the Soviet invasion of Afghanistan did President Jimmy Carter revive the concept of linkage, and his overreaction to the invasion led to the postponement of SALT II. 12 notes.

E. L. Keyser

2636. Caldwell, Dan. DÉTENTE IN HISTORICAL PERSPECTIVE. *Int. Studies Notes 1976 3(4): 17-20.* Examines the historical development of the concept of detente in Europe from 1648 to the 20th century and its relationship to President Richard M. Nixon's and Henry Kissinger's detente policy toward the USSR, 1969-73; emphasizes the recent conversion from Cold War bipolarism to a more fluid balance of power system.

2637. Caldwell, Lawrence T. THE FATE OF STRATEGIC ARMS LIMITATION AND SOVIET-AMERICAN RELATIONS. *Int. J. [Canada] 1981 36(3): 608-634.* Discusses interactions between the United States and the Soviet Union in 1981, in particular, policies since the election of Ronald Reagan. Difficulties with the Strategic Arms Limitation Talks (SALT II) stem from the attitude of the Reagan administration toward the USSR. However, there is a wide range of global issues, alliance temptations, domestic pressures, and technological dynamics which have intruded on the SALT process. Secondary sources; 45 notes.

J. Powell

2638. Campbell, John. EUROPEAN SECURITY AFTER HELSINKI: SOME AMERICAN VIEWS. *Government and Opposition [Great Britain] 1976 11(3): 322-336.* Examines the policy of the Ford administration toward European security as generated by the Conference on Security and Cooperation in Europe, and American public opinion on the subject, 1975.

2639. Campos, Icardo Salvador. PROGRESS IN BILATERAL RELATIONS. *Pro. of the Acad. of Pol. Sci. 1981 34(1): 28-31.* Discusses four major topics of US-Mexican relations that have emerged in the last 10 years: energy, trade, migration, and problems in the border area. A framework to deal with these topics was created by President Jimmy Carter and President José López Portillo, which resulted in a consultative mechanism. The consultative mechanism itself is not a guarantee that bilateral relations will be free of conflict, but it enhances the possibility of resolving issues between the two countries.

T. P. Richardson

2640. Canon, David. INTELLIGENCE AND ETHICS: THE CIA'S COVERT OPERATIONS. *J. of Libertarian Studies 1980 4(2): 197-214.* During the last 30 years the goals of the National Security Act (US, 1947) —to collect and disseminate information—have become distorted, leading the United States to rely increasingly on Central Intelligence Agency covert operations for its intelligence; the most sensible alternative to the status quo, now under fire from conservatives and liberals alike, is to abolish all covert operations, except those involving counterintelligence, and to attempt to gain necessary information through an improved understanding of the cultures, attitudes, and feelings of other nations.

2641. Carlile, Donald E. THE MAYAGUEZ INCIDENT—CRISIS MANAGEMENT. *Military Rev. 1976 56(10): 5-14.* Assesses the diplomatic and strategic options available to President Gerald R. Ford in the seizure of the *Mayaguez* by Cambodian forces in 1975; concludes that experience in crisis decisionmaking is a necessity in current international relations.

2642. Carreras Matas, Narciso. ASUNTOS DE PLANEAMIENTO DE DEFENSA [The business of defense planning]. *Rev. General de Marina [Spain] 1978 194(1): 7-32.* Describes the organizations and process of short- and long-range defense planning in the US Department of Defense. An elaborate planning system is designed to ensure that an effective deterrence, a readiness to fight anywhere under any conditions, and a capability for rapid mobilization will always be available despite constantly changing circumstances. 10 tables. W. C. Frank

2643. Carter, Barry E. THE STRATEGIC DEBATE IN THE UNITED STATES. *Pro. of the Acad. of Pol. Sci. 1978 33(1): 15-29.* In the United States the public and intense debate on SALT contributes to the education of the public on nuclear issues. Chief participants in public debate are the military, the Secretary of Defense, the Secretary of State, the President and his advisers, and Congress. Each has varying amounts of influence and knowledge on the several issues which can impede as well as further debate. Care must be taken to prevent misinformation and misunderstanding while continuing to extend public participation. 10 notes. K. N. T. Crowther

2644. Catudal, Honoré M., Jr. KENNEDY UND DIE BERLINKRISE [Kennedy and the Berlin Crisis]. *Schweizerische Zeitschrift für Geschichte [Switzerland] 1979 29(2): 418-437.* The Berlin Crisis of 1961 was one of the gravest tests of President John F. Kennedy's term in office. Fully aware of the potential for a crisis over Berlin, Kennedy had become involved in contingency planning long before the crisis erupted. Nevertheless, the East German move on 13 August to close all passages from West to East Berlin and to begin the construction of the infamous wall took the West by surprise. Intelligence was defective, and news came in piecemeal. Shock and disorganization prevented Western decisionmakers from taking decisive action. A weak formal protest was delivered only after East Germany had further tightened its control measures on 15 August. The West clearly had been outmaneuvered, and the Allies had lost face with the West Berliners. Generals Lucius Clay and Maxwell Taylor finally prevailed upon Kennedy to send a contingent of 1,500 American soldiers to Berlin. They arrived safely on 20 August to be greeted by Vice President Lyndon B. Johnson, General Clay, and jubilant West Berliners. Based on personal interviews with political actors of the time, and letters to the author; 76 notes. H. K. Meier

2645. Cavalla, Antonio and Maira, Luis. PROPOSICIONES METODOLÓGICAS PARA EL ESTUDIO DE LA POLÍTICA DE ESTADOS UNIDOS HACIA AMÉRICA LATINA [Methodological propositions for the study of US policy toward Latin America]. *Estudios Sociales Centroamericanos [Costa Rica] 1980 9(27): 169-180.* US social scientists chiefly use the rational actor, the organizational processes, or the bureaucratic-governmental model to analyze US foreign policy. Analysis of the fundamental assumptions of US foreign policy and the decisionmaking process shows that, despite apparent resistance, foreign policy does have an ideological focus. 11 notes.

T. D. Schoonover

2646. Chace, James. BISMARCK & KISSINGER. *Encounter [Great Britain] 1974 42(6): 44-47.* Discusses the foreign policy changes made by Henry A. Kissinger since 1968, showing the 19th-century European roots of Kissinger's diplomacy, especially in figures such as Otto von Bismarck.

2647. Chai, Jai Hyung. PRESIDENTIAL CONTROL OF THE FOREIGN POLICY BUREAUCRACY: THE KENNEDY CASE. *Presidential Studies Q. 1978 8(4): 391-403.* The Cabinet and the White House staff constitute alternative mechanisms for presidential control of the bureaucracy. The foreign policy of the John F. Kennedy administration moved from institutionalized decisionmaking originating in the State Department to personalized-centralized control from the White House. The parochialism, inflexible procedures, jurisdictional preoccupations, and autonomy of large bureaucracies coupled with the passive leadership of Secretary of State Dean Rusk forced Kennedy to take personal control of foreign policy. This trend toward presidential involvement in detailed problems and the subsequent growth in White House staff has continued diverting more presidential energy. Calls for a mixed system with a return of authority to the Secretary of State and a revitalization of the Department. 90 notes. S. C. Strom

2648. Chern, Kenneth S. POLITICS OF AMERICAN CHINA POLICY, 1945: ROOTS OF THE COLD WAR IN ASIA. *Pol. Sci. Q. 1976-77 91(4): 631-647.* Reviews the American foreign policy debate of 1945 over the question of intervention in the civil war between the Nationalist and Communist Chinese. The Truman administration failed in its obligation to educate the American public about the near inevitability of Communist victory. J

2649. Cherwitz, Richard A. LYNDON JOHNSON AND THE "CRISIS" OF TONKIN BAY: A PRESIDENT'S JUSTIFICATION OF WAR. *Western J. of Speech Communication 1978 42(2): 93-104.* The rhetoric employed by Lyndon B. Johnson on 4-5 August 1964 in elaborating on the alleged shelling of US ships in the Gulf of Tonkin created an international crisis and limited US foreign policy alternatives.

2650. Chomsky, Noam. "GLI ANNI DELLA CASA BIANCA": LE VERITÀ DI KISSINGER [*White House Years:* Kissinger's truths]. *Ponte [Italy] 1980 36(7-8): 683-708.* Reviews Henry A. Kissinger's *White House Years,* concluding that these memoirs "give the impression of having been written by a rather mediocre manager" who has learned to cover the lack of content with pretentious language and finding it full of evident misstatements of documented facts considered unforgivable in someone who must have seen that documentation regarding both Vietnam and the Middle East.

2651. Chu, Shao-hsien. U.S. STRATEGY AND PEACE IN NORTHEAST ASIA. *Issues and Studies [Taiwan] 1975 11(9): 21-31.* Discusses US military strategy and foreign policy toward Japan, South Korea, and the Republic of China in the 1960's and 70's, emphasizing President Gerald R. Ford and Secretary of State Henry Kissinger's recent attempts to define the US defense perimeter.

2652. Chubin, Shahram. REPERCUSSIONS OF THE CRISIS IN IRAN. *Survival [Great Britain] 1979 21(3): 98-106.* Criticizes US policy toward Iran between 1972 and 1976 and faults President Jimmy Carter's actions during the Iranian revolution.

2653. Chung, Chong-Wook. AMERICA AND THE WORLD: A CRIPPLED GIANT IN TROUBLED WATERS? *Korea & World Affairs [South Korea] 1980 4(4): 571-581.* Discusses the decline of US political and military influence abroad from 1970 to 1980 and examines the role of Henry A. Kissinger in forming the present American foreign policy stance.

2654. Church, Frank. COVERT ACTION: SWAMPLAND OF AMERICAN FOREIGN POLICY. *Bull. of the Atomic Scientists 1976 32(2): 7-11.* Discusses clandestine activities of the Central Intelligence Agency in US foreign policy from 1947-70's, including its possible involvement in assassination plots in Cuba, Chile, and the Congo.

2655. Church, Frank. THE COVERT OPERATIONS. *Center Mag. 1976 9(2): 21-25.* Cites and criticizes the espionage activities of the Central Intelligence Agency in other nations since its establishment in 1947.

2656. Clark, Dick. US POLICY TOWARD AFRICA. *Foreign Service J. 1976 53(7): 9-12.* The author, an Iowa senator, presents his views on Kissinger's new Africa policies, especially in the key countries of Rhodesia, Namibia, and South Africa, and discusses US commitments to an African-American cooperation toward the continued struggle for freedom from colonial rule, racial domination, and economic dependence.

2657. Clarke, Duncan L. ARMS CONTROL AND FOREIGN POLICY UNDER REAGAN. *Bull. of the Atomic Scientists 1981 37(9): 12-19.* The Arms Control and Disarmament Agency established in 1960, has experienced traumatic shifts in leadership and support; these shifts coincide with the acceleration of the arms race, the failure to negotiate reductions, and the Reagan Administration's oversimplification, perpetually blaming the Russians.

2658. Clifford, Clark M. RECOGNIZING ISRAEL: THE 1948 STORY. *Am. Heritage 1977 28(3): 4-11.* Admitting that political considerations are a part of every major policy decision, the author defends Harry S. Truman against revisionist charges on the Palestine question. Suggests that Truman's position was consistent with his long-standing position of favoring the underdog. Serious internal opposition, spearheaded by the Office of Near Eastern and African Affairs in the State Department, hampered the formulation of US policies. 3 illus.
J. F. Paul

2659. Clifford, J. Garry. PRESIDENT TRUMAN AND PETER THE GREAT'S WILL. *Diplomatic Hist. 1980 4(4): 371-385.* President Truman (1945-53) was known both for his love of history and for his amateurish use of it to derive lessons to guide his own decisions. An example of the latter is the case of the political will of Russian Tsar Peter the Great (1682-1725), a notorious forgery concocted during the Napoleonic era for anti-Russian propaganda, purporting to contain a blueprint for Russian domination of the world. Truman's apparent belief in the validity of the document may have influenced his perceptions of Soviet motives and stimulated his "conspicuously simplistic and hostile" behavior toward the USSR immediately after World War II. 56 notes.
T. L. Powers

2660. Cline, Ray S. POLICY WITHOUT INTELLIGENCE. *Foreign Policy 1974-75 (17): 121-135.* Recommends a new policy for the gathering of intelligence data and foreign policy decision-making. The government should rebuild and use effectively the interagency staff system supporting the National Security Council. The President should give more attention to the NSC and intelligence agencies. He should separate the position of Secretary of State from the position of Assistant to the President for National Security Affairs. This latter officer, the Chief of the NSC staff, should once again become a staff agent of the President. Secretary of State Henry A. Kissinger, who has both jobs now, has openly revealed that he favors secrecy. As a result, many effective State people are not participating in decision-making. Under the Nixon Administration, the mishandling of foreign affairs reached a dangerous level. The author, Director of Intelligence and Research in the Department of State (1969-73), protested to Kissinger in regard to calling a military alert in response to an alleged Soviet military action in the Middle East, October 1973. Kissinger acted without all the available information and convinced President Nixon that the danger was greater than it really was.
R. F. Kugler

2661. Coffey, John W. GEORGE KENNAN AND THE AMBIGUITIES OF REALISM. *South Atlantic Q. 1974 73(2): 184-198.* George F. Kennan believed that the USSR was less interested in the spread of communism than in establishing power and dominion in central and Eastern Europe. Analyzes the basic themes in his famous article

(signed "Mr. X.") in *Foreign Affairs*. He did not believe in the reality of a Soviet military threat to Western Europe. He was highly critical of the militarization of American Cold War policy. The concept of realism is not a fruitful one as a clue to Kennan's own thinking or as a theory of foreign policy. 25 notes.
E. P. Stickney

2662. Cohen, Michael J. THE GENESIS OF THE ANGLO-AMERICAN COMMITTEE ON PALESTINE, NOVEMBER 1945: A CASE-STUDY IN THE ASSERTION OF AMERICAN HEGEMONY. *Hist. J. [Great Britain] 1979 22(1): 185-207.* Examines the origins of the Anglo-American Committee in 1945 as one aspect of postwar Anglo-American relations, concluding that this case study reflects the major readjustment within the Atlantic Alliance after the war, namely, the assumption of hegemony by the United States. While the British Labor government of Ernest Bevin pursued a policy of reconciling conflicting Arab and Jewish interests in the Middle East, the American administration of President Harry S. Truman faced the twin demands of appeasing a powerful Jewish electorate and pursuing a policy that would best serve American economic and strategic interests in the area. Ultimately, Britain's postwar bankruptcy and the growing Soviet threat to Europe and Asia pushed Great Britain toward closer association with the United States. Bevin's inability to achieve consensus with the Americans on Palestine led him to surrender the Palestinian mandate in 1947. Based on archival materials in the Public Record Office, published documents in *Foreign Relations of the United States,* and secondary sources; 87 notes.
L. J. Reith

2663. Cohen, Michael J. TRUMAN AND PALESTINE, 1945-1948: REVISIONISM, POLITICS AND DIPLOMACY. *Modern Judaism 1982 2(1): 1-22.* Examines the evolution of the Truman administration's attitude toward the Palestine question, focusing on some of the standard works dealing with this subject.

2664. Cohen, Michael J. TRUMAN AND THE STATE DEPARTMENT: THE PALESTINE TRUSTEESHIP PROPOSAL, MARCH, 1948. *Jewish Social Studies 1981 43(2): 165-178.* Documents published in *Foreign Relations of the United States, 1948, Vol. 5* shed new light on the 19 March 1948 US proposal for temporary UN trusteeship over Palestine. They indicate that the proposal logically culminated an open debate in which all sections of the administration participated, including such figures as George Kennan, Dean Rusk, Loy Henderson, Samuel Kopper, Clark Clifford and George Marshall. By February 1948, President Truman had been convinced that the establishment of a Jewish state in Palestine would antagonize the Arabs, jeopardize US interests, and open the door to Soviet intervention. He later changed his mind because of domestic political considerations. 59 notes.
J. D. Sarna

2665. Cohen, Stephen B. CONDITIONING U.S. SECURITY ASSISTANCE ON HUMAN RIGHTS PRACTICES. *Am. J. of Int. Law 1982 76(2): 246-279.* Section 502B of the Foreign Assistance Act, enacted in 1974, directed that military aid not be given to any government consistently in gross violation of internationally recognized human rights; executive branch failure to implement this directive has resulted in serious controversy surrounding US military support of certain Central and South American regimes.

2666. Cohen, Warren I. AMBASSADOR PHILIP D. SPROUSE ON THE QUESTION OF RECOGNITION OF THE PEOPLE'S REPUBLIC OF CHINA IN 1949 AND 1950. *Diplomatic Hist. 1978 2(2): 213-217.* In response to a 1973 query from a historian, former Ambassador Philip D. Sprouse wrote that the Truman administration recognized the inevitability of a Communist victory in the Chinese civil war and the futility of continuing to send aid to the Kuomintang, because all materials sent would end up with the Communists eventually. The question of extending diplomatic recognition to the Communists was considered, but adverse public opinion, and especially congressional opposition, made such action hazardous and dictated the continuation of existing policy. China's entry into the Korean War ended any possibility that recognition would be offered.
T. L. Powers

2667. Cohen, Warren I. HARRY TRUMAN, CHINA, AND THE COLD WAR IN ASIA. *Rev. in Am. Hist. 1978 6(2): 146-154.* Review article prompted by Stanley D. Bachrack's *The Committee of One Million: "China Lobby" Politics, 1953-1971* (New York: Columbia U. Pr.,

1976), *The Origins of the Cold War in Asia* (New York: Columbia U. Pr., 1977), edited by Yonosuke Nagai and Akira Iriye, and Lewis McCarroll Purifoy's *Harry Truman's China Policy: McCarthyism and the Diplomacy of Hysteria, 1947-1951* (New York: New Viewpoints, 1976).

2668. Coker, Christopher. RETREAT INTO THE FUTURE: THE UNITED STATES, SOUTH AFRICA, AND HUMAN RIGHTS, 1976-8. *J. of Modern African Studies [Great Britain] 1980 18(3): 509-524.* The Carter administration's program for human rights failed to make headway in South Africa for a variety of reasons. The most important of these was American insistence on the extension of political rights to South African blacks, without an effort to win broader citizenship rights for nonwhites, and the failure to extend any guarantees of survival to the white population in a future nonracial South African state. The Vorster government in Pretoria maintains its policy of developing separate national communities in South Africa. Based on newspapers, speeches, and secondary sources; 48 notes.   L. W. Truschel

2669. Colard, Daniel. ZBIGNIEW BRZEZINSKI, LE CONSIELLER SPECIAL "VENU DU FROID" [Zbigniew Brzezinski, the adviser "who came in from the cold"]. *Défense Natl. [France] 1978 34(3): 77-87.* Biographical sketch of President Jimmy Carter's national security adviser; focuses on the "Brzezinski doctrine," which seeks world peace through the institutionalization of American alliances.

2670. Colby, William et al. SECRECY IN AN OPEN SOCIETY. *Center Mag. 1976 9(2): 26-38.* A former director of the Central Intelligence Agency defends the covert operations of that intelligence service in helping the government formulate foreign policy, while other political leaders question some of its clandestine operations since 1947.

2671. Collins, Larry. PROSPECTS OF FOREIGN POLICY UNDER CARTER'S ADMINISTRATION. *Int. Perspectives [Canada] 1977 May-June: 25-30.* Reviews President Jimmy Carter's foreign affairs appointments and statements during 1977; Carter will project foreign policy from domestic themes; US foreign policy must recognize demands for a more equitable world order.

2672. Conover, Pamela Johnston and Sigelman, Lee. PRESIDENTIAL INFLUENCE AND PUBLIC OPINION: THE CASE OF THE IRANIAN HOSTAGE CRISIS. *Social Sci. Q. 1982 63(2): 249-264.* Discusses presidential influence on public opinion, focusing on the Iranian hostage crisis responsiveness in Lexington, Kentucky, "varied depending on the nature of the policy which was being pursued" by Jimmy Carter.

2673. Conyers, John, Jr. WHY NIXON SHOULD BE IMPEACHED. *Black Scholar 1974 6(2): 2-8.* As a member of the House Judiciary Committee, the author maintains that Nixon should have been impeached because of his extension of the Vietnam War and authorization and concealment of Cambodian bombing.

2674. Coogan, John W. and Hunt, Michael H. KENNAN AND CONTAINMENT: A COMMENT. *Soc. for Hist. of Am. Foreign Relations. Newsletter 1978 9(1): 23-25.* Comments on an article by John Lewis Gaddis (see abstract 15A:7912); contrary to Gaddis, the foreign policymaking abilities of George F. Kennan were restricted, especially those pertaining to containment, 1947-49, which were vague and shortsighted.

2675. Coulam, Robert F. THE IMPORTANCE OF THE BEGINNING: DEFENSE DOCTRINE AND THE DEVELOPMENT OF THE F-111 FIGHTER-BOMBER. *Public Policy 1975 23(1): 1-38.* Analysis of Secretary of Defense Robert S. McNamara's attempts to develop a multiservice aircraft, the F-111 fighter-bomber, for limited use in the Vietnam War during the 1960's. Despite agreement by the Navy and Air Force to follow McNamara's plan, the Air Force remained committed to preparation of massive retaliation systems to wage full-scale nuclear war. McNamara's acceptance of the Air Force's demand meant his attempt at weapons systems innovation would be unsuccessful. Based on primary and secondary sources, and interviews with military, congressional, Department of Defense, and military contractor personnel; 88 notes.   J. M. Herrick

2676. Couloumbis, Theodore A. FIVE "THEORIES" REGARDING KISSINGER'S POLICY TOWARD THE CYPRUS CRISIS. *Int. Studies Notes 1975 2(1): 12-17.* Discusses Secretary of State Henry A. Kissinger's perceptions of the military and political crisis in Cyprus, and their relationship to US foreign policy, 1969-74.

2677. Cowhey, Peter F. and Laitin, David D. BEARING THE BURDEN: A MODEL OF PRESIDENTIAL RESPONSIBILITY. *Int. Studies Q. 1978 22(2): 267-296.* Presidential responsibility for decisions in foreign policy varies according to the political structure of the international system, the degree of consensus among the countries involved, and the degree of consensus with the United States. Suggests that a model that incorporates these factors can provide a set of decisionmaking rules for future presidents. Demonstrates how the model works by applying it retrospectively to decisions involving the Marshall Plan, the Multilateral Nuclear Force, the Cuban Missile Crisis and the Vietnam War. Fig., 31 notes.   E. S. Palais

2678. Craig, Richard B. OPERATION INTERCEPT: THE INTERNATIONAL POLITICS OF PRESSURE. *Rev. of Pol. 1980 42(4): 556-580.* Operation Intercept was an American plan to halt or slow the flow of drugs across the Mexican-US border. Adopted by the Nixon administration in 1969, it was poorly planned and administered, and lacked coordination with the Mexican government. It angered businessmen on both sides of the border, antagonized the Mexican government, and disrupted traffic between the countries. The operation was ended after pressure from border state congressmen. Residual benefits, however, included a greater awareness by the Mexican government of its growing drug problem. Letters, interviews, minutes, reports, hearings, and secondary sources; 52 notes.   D. F. Ring

2679. Cromwell, William C. THE MARSHALL NON-PLAN, CONGRESS AND THE SOVIET UNION. *Western Pol. Q. 1979 32(4): 422-443.* Revisionist accounts of the origins of the Marshall Plan suggest that US policymakers sought to exclude the Soviet Union by posing conditions they believed the Russians would reject. This study concludes that whereas US officials hoped and expected that the Soviet Union would not accept the Marshall aid proposal, the conditions posed were not designed to produce this result. For several weeks preceding and following Secretary Marshall's address at Harvard, State Department planning for European assistance remained highly tentative and inchoate. The administration declined to assert strong leadership before Congress in advocating a new European aid program. Rather, it pursued a devolutionary strategy of insisting upon a European generated plan as a condition for further US action. The requirement for collective European initiative, though not intended to exclude the Soviet Union, nevertheless had this effect through the subsequent interplay of British, French, and Soviet diplomacy. 101 notes.   J

2680. Crowl, Philip A. JOHN FOSTER DULLES: THE POLICY BEHIND THE MYTH. *Naval War Coll. R. 1975 27(5): 8-17.* John Foster Dulles, Secretary of State during the Eisenhower years, remains in the memory of most political scientists as the hard-line cold warrior, the visceral enemy of appeasement and author of massive retaliation. However, as is the case with many a popular stereotype—even one created by the subject himself—the facts tend to contradict the tenets of the myth.   J

2681. Dahiya, M. S. INDIA-PAKISTAN AND THE AMERICAN ATTITUDE. *J. of the United Service Inst. of India [India] 1973 103(431): 113-127.* Assesses American policy toward India since 1947. India received attention as the world's most populous democracy, but American aid to Pakistan because of its strategic position and agreement with the Washington line in contrast to India's neutrality disturbed relations. President Kennedy improved relations but US support of Portuguese claims to Goa again caused a rift. This was closed by American support of India against China in 1962, and neutrality in the 1965 India-Pakistan conflict. But the United States completely alienated India by aiding Pakistan in 1971 on the Bangladesh issue. Both countries now "realize the importance of normalization and cementing their relations." Primary and secondary sources; 74 notes.   L. R. Maxted

2682. Dainelli, Luca. IL BICENTENARIO E IL RUOLO DEGLI STATI UNITI NEL MONDO [The bicentennial and the role of the

United States in the world]. *Riv. di Studi Politici Int. [Italy] 1976 43(2): 183-236.* The only hope for the Western world is the United States, which is committed to defend human rights and liberty from Communist attacks. Traces the history of US foreign relations since the birth of the nation, emphasizing US diplomatic relations with Soviet Russia and the European powers since World War II. Criticizes the policies of some US presidents and especially Henry A. Kissinger's conception of detente. The United States may have lost ground to Russia in world power, due to lack of understanding of the ultimate goals of Communist Russia.

A. Sbacchi

2683. Damiloff, Nicholas. KISSINGER AND THE PRESS: A MUTUAL MALAISE. *Foreign Service J. 1976 53(7): 6-8, 17.* Criticizes Henry A. Kissinger and his State Department administration for naivete and audacity with the press, while outlining the real role of the Secretary of State, and remedies needed such as regular briefings of other foreign service officers, more efficient delegation of responsibility, and a greater level of truth in dealing with the press.

2684. D'Attorre, Pier Paolo. GUERRA FREDDA E TRASFORMAZIONI DELLE SOCIETA OCCIDENTALI NELLA STORIOGRAFICA AMERICANA [The cold war and transformations of western societies in American historiography]. *Italia Contemporanea [Italy] 1980 32(140): 83-103.* Surveys books and articles dealing with the origin of the cold war between the USSR and the United States during the presidency of Harry S. Truman (1945-53). These studies highlight the relationship between the cold war and the American political system, the international economic policy of the United States, and European-American ties. Many of the studies written since 1972 have taken either a new Left or an anti-New Left perspective. Primary sources; 42 notes.

E. E. Ryan

2685. David, Charles. LE CONSEIL NATIONAL DE SECURITE ET LA POLITIQUE SUD-AFRICAINE DES ETATS-UNIS DE 1969 A 1976 [The National Security Council and United States foreign policy toward South Africa, 1969-76]. *Etudes Int. [Canada] 1981 12(4): 657-690.* Examines the performance of the National Security Council (NSC) as a policymaking body vis-à-vis the southern African conflict under the Nixon and Ford administrations. Discusses and verifies the hypothesis that the institutionalized system of the NSC gives the president a way to seriously improve his policies by analyzing the range of options and alternatives free of negative bureaucratic influences. 63 notes.

J. F. Harrington

2686. Davidson, Frederic. STRATEGIC ENGAGEMENT AND SINO-AMERICAN TRADE. *SAIS Rev. 1981 (2): 131-140.* Ever since the Nixon administration, responding to the geopolitics of parallel interests, began to normalize relations with China, successive administrations have controlled exports as a matter of foreign policy; export control policy has been manipulated to satisfy China's appetite for Western technology and to punish the USSR for forays into Afghanistan and Africa.

2687. Davis, Nathaniel. THE ANGOLA DECISION OF 1975: A PERSONAL MEMOIR. *Foreign Affairs 1978 57(1): 109-124.* Reflections by the former Assistant Secretary of State for African Affairs who resigned his post in opposition to covert US involvement in Angola. Though Davis had stated repeatedly" . . . that covert military involvement would probably increase the level of violence . . . ," his warning fell on deaf ears; the CIA "Action Plan" was implemented during the summer of 1975. 9 notes.

M. R. Yerburgh

2688. Davis, Vincent. EARLY REAGAN SECURITY POLICY IN A COMPARATIVE PERSPECTIVE: SOME TENTATIVE OBSERVATIONS. *Int. Studies Notes 1981 8(1): 1-6.* Focuses on Reagan's national security policy, both foreign and defense policy positions with emphasis on the military dimensions, since Reagan has stressed this in his first 100 days in office; compares Reagan's administration to Carter's.

2689. Delmas, Claude. IL Y A VINGT-CINQ ANS: LE CONFLICT TRUMAN-MAC ARTHUR [Twenty-five years ago: the Truman-MacArthur conflict]. *Défense Natl. [France] 1976 32(6): 83-98.* The conflict between President Harry S. Truman and General Douglas MacArthur over US foreign policy toward China during the Korean War demonstrates the need for the soldier's subordination to the politician, and their common adherence to clearly defined objectives.

2690. Derian, Patricia M. HUMAN RIGHTS AND AMERICAN FOREIGN POLICY. *Universal Human Rights 1979 1(1): 3-9.* The author, the leading human rights specialist in the State Department, outlines the Jimmy Carter administration's human rights policy, articulated in 1977, and relates it to international concerns.

2691. De Simone, Silvio. DA NIXON A FORD: L'EVOLUZIONE DELLA POLITICA AMERICANA VERSO LA CINA, DALLA DOTTRINA DI GUAM AL DOPO VIETNAM [From Nixon to Ford: the evolution of American policy toward China from the Guam Doctrine to post-Vietnam]. *Mondo Cinese [Italy] 1976 4(15): 85-123.* Considers the history of the prospective in which the United States has observed China, from the 1950's to the 1970's. Examines the internal reasons and the international objectives for the change in US policy, and outlines the content of the "about-face." Ascribes various motives to explain this normalization and the progressive abandonment of Taiwan on the part of the Americans, including the circumstance of strategic importance, and how, for the United States, China constitutes a cushion between itself and Soviet expansionism.

J/S

2692. Destler, I. M. TREATY TROUBLES: VERSAILLES IN REVERSE. *Foreign Policy 1978-79 (3): 45-65.* The defeat of the Treaty of Versailles (1920) resulted from the Wilson administration's failure to make concessions to domestic political imperatives. Experience with the SALT and Panama treaties (1978) indicates that oversensitivity to Congress and domestic politics can complicate rather than resolve foreign policy problems. Preoccupation with domestic matters can cause an administration to raise unrealistic expectations, convey a sense of weakness to foreign governments, and lead to diplomatic failure. Diplomatic failure weakens an administration by giving an impression of incompetence, while diplomatic successes, such as the Camp David agreements (1978) can strengthen it. 4 notes.

T. L. Powers

2693. Dhanani, Gulshan. DULLES AND WEST ASIA. *Int. Studies [India] 1976 15(2): 217-228.* John Foster Dulles' first acquaintance with the Middle East came in 1948 when he cosponsored the UN resolution on Palestinian partition. In Dulles' world view, the threat of war came from Communism, to which he was irreconcilably opposed. His defense strategy, based on massive retaliation, assigned a great strategic importance to the Middle East. As Secretary of State, he visited the Middle East in 1953. He was encouraged by Arab support against Communism. He returned home determined to rid himself of pro-Israeli charges. His policy initiatives included: opposition to British domination, new efforts in the Arab-Israeli conflict, and strengthening the anti-Communist alliance. Secondary sources, interviews; 55 notes.

R. E. Stack

2694. Diebel, Terry L. A GUIDE TO INTERNATIONAL DIVORCE. *Foreign Policy 1978 (30): 17-35.* The United States should be pragmatic enough to view the termination of security commitments as a viable and not necessarily unscrupulous policy. New realities make old promises irrelevant and dangerously restrictive. Periodic analyses of the costs and benefits of ending an agreement, rather than of the agreement itself, should determine decisions. If termination is indicated, careful procedures in accomplishing it can minimize unfavorable repercussions. President Jimmy Carter is approaching this issue wrongly, for he is publicly reinforcing the expendable commitment to Taiwan, while abruptly and undiplomatically weakening the critically important one to South Korea. Note.

T. L. Powers

2695. Dingman, Roger V. THEORIES OF, AND APPROACHES TO, ALLIANCE POLITICS. Lauren, Paul Gordon, ed. *Diplomacy: New Approaches in History, Theory, and Policy* (New York: Free Pr., 1979): 245-266. Reflects on "the limitations of much of the existing literature on the theory of alliance; the historian's need for a working conceptual understanding of alliances; and the relative utility of various methods, new and old, for analyzing alliances." Examines particularly the unequal 1951 treaty of alliance negotiated by John Foster Dulles and Yoshida Shigeru between the United States and Japan which allowed US troops stationed in Japan to put down internal disturbances at Japan's request. Based on *Foreign Relations of the United States,* other primary and secondary sources; 52 notes.

S

2696. Divine, Robert A. EISENHOWER, DULLES, AND THE NUCLEAR TEST BAN ISSUE: MEMORANDUM OF A WHITE

HOUSE CONFERENCE, 24 MARCH 1958. *Diplomatic Hist. 1978 2(3): 321-330.* Discusses General Andrew Goodpaster's memorandum, recently declassified, of a White House conference on nuclear testing held on 24 March 1958. The Soviets at this time were staging an apparently accelerated series of tests, with the purpose, as the CIA correctly surmised, of following up their tests with the highly embarrassing announcement of a unilateral suspension of testing. Secretary of State John Foster Dulles convened the meeting to discuss the possibility of stealing a march on the Soviets by announcing a two-year test suspension before the USSR's expected announcement. Dulles dropped the idea in response to adverse comment from Atomic Energy Commission Chairman Lewis Strauss and various defense spokesmen. Discussion based on archival, contemporary press and periodical, other primary and secondary sources; 14 notes.
L. W. Van Wyk

2697. Dobriansky, Lev E. WHAT HAPPENED TO HUMAN RIGHTS? *Ukrainian Q. 1978 34(2): 125-134.* President Jimmy Carter's human rights foreign policy has lapsed, particularly in regard to the captive nations. Observance of Captive Nations Week dwindles. A lack of awareness or understanding of national rights afflicts the public, Congress, and the highest government officials. 9 notes.
K. N. T. Crowther

2698. Doenecke, Justus D. PRINCIPLE AND EXPEDIENCY: THE STATE DEPARTMENT AND PALESTINE, 1948. *J. of Libertarian Studies 1978 2(4): 343-356.* Far from consistently supporting Israel's claims to independence, as reports like those of Clark Clifford, his Special Counsel at the time indicated, President Harry S. Truman approved a UN trusteeship in March, and recognized Israel two months later only to secure the Jewish vote in his campaign for reelection.

2699. Donno, Antonio. GLI ANNI DI TRUMAN ED IL LIBERALISMO DELLA GUERRA FREDDA [The Truman years and Cold War liberalism]. *Nuova Riv. Storica [Italy] 1981 65(3-4): 380-398.* Truman perceived the postwar international and domestic situation in terms of a threat of Soviet imperialism, pro-Communist sympathies in certain American political circles, and a majority of Republicans and Democrats in Congress who were hostile to his Fair Deal policies and favored a return to pre-Depression laissez faire. This led to the Cold War and global projection of American power in defense of the liberal tradition and to a consequent loss of innocence. 69 notes.
J. V. Coutinho

2700. Dugard, John. SILENCE IS NOT GOLDEN. *Foreign Policy 1982 (46): 37-48.* Eschewing President Jimmy Carter's vocal opposition to South Africa's racial policies, the Reagan administration has opted for quiet diplomacy. Quiet diplomacy has not encouraged reform within South Africa and has permitted further racial injustices in South Africa. "Silence becomes collaboration" at a certain point, and the United States should stridently condemn violations of human rights in South Africa.
M. K. Jones

2701. Dunn, William N. THE SCHOLAR-DIPLOMAT SEMINAR ON LATIN AMERICAN AFFAIRS: THE PROMISE AND ILLUSIONS OF THE STATE DEPARTMENT REFORM MOVEMENT. *Latin Am. Res. Rev. 1971 6(2): 77-84.* Sponsored by the State Department, the International Studies Association, and the American Foreign Service Association, a week-long seminar in April 1970 attempted to open communication and improve relations between professionals in and out of government, to provide resource materials for scholars, and to improve US policymaking toward Latin America. All but the last objective were adequately achieved. Possibilities of change in policy formulation and execution through a brief seminar are limited due to resistance to innovation within the State Department. Based on the seminar, State Department documents, and secondary sources; 5 notes.
J. K. Pfabe

2702. Dutt, Gargi. CHINA AND THE SHIFT IN SUPER-POWER RELATIONS. *Int. Studies [India] 1974 13(4): 635-662.* Examines the implications of detente for China's foreign policy in the 1970's; assesses the impact of President Richard M. Nixon's visit to China in 1972.

2703. Eggleston, Noel C. AMERICA'S FIRST WITHDRAWAL FROM INDOCHINA. *Res. Studies 1976 44(4): 217-228.* US foreign policy changed from stout defense of self-determination for colonial peoples under Franklin D. Roosevelt to laissez-faire trusteeship in Indochina under Harry S. Truman and Dwight D. Eisenhower, 1945-52.

2704. El-Khawas, Mohamed A. and Hope, Constance Morris. A BIBLIOGRAPHICAL ESSAY ON U. S. DIPLOMATIC RELATIONS WITH SOUTH AFRICA. *J. of Southern African Affairs 1979 4(1): 81-115.* A brief treatment of US-South African relations, centering on attitudes toward South Africa within the executive branch, from the Eisenhower administration through the first years of the Carter administration. Publications on Washington-Pretoria relations are categorized and listed, with those from sources close to the US discussed in the body of the article.
L. W. Truschel

2705. Ellsworth, Robert F. and Adelman, Kenneth L. FOOLISH INTELLIGENCE. *Foreign Policy 1979 (36): 147-159.* The major shortcoming of America's intelligence community is not unrestrained excesses but inadequate performance. The community long has been dominated by a clique, centered in the Central Intelligence Agency's Operations Directorate, which is dedicated to the view that cooperation with the USSR is "the biggest game in town." As a result, information indicating potentially hostile Soviet attitudes has been discounted. The agencies repeatedly have failed to give adequate warning of Soviet military build-ups and technological break-throughs. Decentralization of the intelligence structure would prevent clique domination and permit the thorough collection and unvarnished presentation of realistic intelligence data. 2 charts.
T. L. Powers

2706. Erokhin, A. V. RUBEZHI KLANA KENNEDI [The borders of the Kennedy clan]. *Novaia i Noveishaia Istoriia [USSR] 1973 (6): 97-115.* Examines President John F. Kennedy's foreign policy and its political origins, especially his emphasis on arms expenditure, the strategy of the "flexible response," and US military involvement in the early 1960's in Cuba, Vietnam, and the Dominican Republic. Reviews other foreign policy tactics, such as support for pro-American regimes and the formation of the Peace Corps. Studies the political career of Edward M. Kennedy, including his private life and his views on American society. Primary and secondary sources; 73 notes.
C. R. Pike

2707. Etherington, Norman. THEORIES OF EMPIRE AND MODERN AMERICAN IMPERIALISM. *Australian J. of Pol. and Hist. [Australia] 1974 20(2): 210-222.* Challenges Harry Magdoff's New Left interpretation of modern American foreign policy in *The Age of Imperialism* (New York, 1969), by reexamining alternative explanations of imperialism: Schumpeter's "objectless" imperialism, Fieldhouse's emphasis on colonial counters to European power rivalries, and the role ascribed to nationalism by Hobson, Van Alstyne, and others. These explanations are tested against policy speeches of John F. Kennedy. Documented from interpretive essays and published speeches.
W. D. McIntyre

2708. Etzioni, Amitai. THE KENNEDY EXPERIMENT. *Peace Research Rev. [Canada] 1979 8(1): 53-89.* Discusses the events which took place between 10 June and 22 November 1963 in US/Soviet relations which proved to be a test for a theory of international relations which states that the gestures and responses between two countries will reduce tension which will then reduce the possibility of international conflict and warfare.

2709. Etzold, Thomas H. INDIVIDUALS, IDEAS AND INSTITUTIONS: RECENT WRITINGS ON AMERICAN FOREIGN POLICY. *Naval War Coll. Rev. 1977 30(2): 109-122.* Review article prompted by 10 books (1975-76) dealing with current American foreign policy; they seem to hold that Henry A. Kissinger years were transitional, the US political and economic role in world affairs is changing, and an immediate policy adjustment supporting domestic institutions is needed to meet public opinion demands.

2710. Fagen, Richard R. THE CARTER ADMINISTRATION AND LATIN AMERICA: BUSINESS AS USUAL? *Foreign Affairs 1979 57(3): 652-669.* Like its predecessors, the Carter administration has failed to appreciate the difficult choices necessary if US-Latin American relations are to succeed on a permanent basis. Latin America is enormously troubled; the gap between rich and poor continues to increase, unemployment is disturbingly high, and external debts have reached unparalleled levels. For relations to succeed, the United States " ... cannot, for example, honestly claim to be interested in supporting significant improvements in economic and social rights without at the same time being willing to accept and even support much more radical, nationalist,

and potentially 'anti-American' politics and economics than this or any other Administration has been willing to countenance." 10 notes.
M. R. Yerburgh

2711. Fagen, Richard R. DATELINE NICARAGUA: THE END OF THE AFFAIR. *Foreign Policy 1979 (36): 178-191.* The Carter administration's reactions to the collapse of the regime of Anastasio Somoza Debayle in Nicaragua revealed the persistence of Washington's inability to comprehend "the nature and implications of a popular insurrection against tyranny." Seeing only opportunities for communist gain in a victory for the anti-Somoza Sandinista National Liberation Front, the administration continued to support Somoza almost until the bitter end, and then attempted vainly to insure the succession of a non-Sandinista government. The result was the further degrading of America's already low reputation in Latin America. T. L. Powers

2712. Falk, Richard A. WHAT'S WRONG WITH HENRY KISSINGER'S FOREIGN POLICY? *Alternatives 1975 1(1): 79-100.* This article analyzes the reasons why Henry Kissinger has exercised such an extraordinary influence upon all sectors of world politics. It argues that Mr. Kissinger's role has not been beneficial because it has reflected his indifference to issues of morality and justice and his insensitivity to the obsolescence of the state system. To overcome Kissingerism is absolutely necessary for the achievement of political independence in the Third World and the sort of global reform which will be needed for the construction of a just and peaceful world order capable of meeting present challenges. J

2713. Farer, Tom J. SEARCHING FOR DEFEAT. *Foreign Policy 1980 (40): 155-174.* US foreign policy from 1945 to 1977 assumed that developing nations were only pawns in the great game between the United States and the USSR, and that every event involving them constituted a victory for one player and a defeat for the other. President Jimmy Carter (1977-81) attempted to depart from this pattern, assuming that other countries and peoples acted according to their own interests, without necessarily lining up on either side. His inability to establish a coherent policy based on these neorealist assumptions encouraged a resurgence of the old diplomacy, "a recipe for ultimate defeat or the collective destruction of the game." T. L. Powers

2714. Feldman, Elliot J. and Feldman, Lily Gardner. THE SPECIAL RELATIONSHIP BETWEEN CANADA AND THE UNITED STATES. *Jerusalem J. of Int. Relations [Israel] 1980 4(4): 56-85.* Although both countries now eschew the term "special," and although the relationship between the United States and Canada suffered in the early 1970's as a result of the Vietnam War and Richard Nixon's refusal to give Canada its accustomed preferential treatment, the special relationship between the two countries is stronger than ever now thanks to the rapport between the Carter and Trudeau administrations and, more important, a century-long tradition of military, economic, and cultural interdependence, based on a common border, a common language, a common history, and common or complementary needs.

2715. Ferrari, Silvio. IL VATICANO E LA QUESTIONE DI GERUSALEMME NEL CARTEGGIO SPELLMAN-TRUMAN [The Vatican and the question of Jerusalem in the Spellman-Truman correspondence]. *Storia Contemporanea [Italy] 1982 13(2): 285-320.* When the correspondence began in the spring of 1949, Jerusalem was divided between Jordanian and Israeli forces. Two UN resolutions passed by a large majority favored internationalization of the city, and a UN commission was trying to sort out the question of right from the de facto situation. The Vatican, the Arab states, with the exception of Jordan, and the countries with a Catholic majority were in favor of internationalization. The attitude of the great powers, in particular the United States, was unclear. The Vatican won the battle for internationalization, diplomatically, but the partition continued due to the incapacity of the General Assembly to enforce its resolutions. Reproduces the letters of Harry S. Truman and Francis Joseph Spellman on the issue. Based on primary material in the National Archives and the Public Record Office, London; 58 notes. J. V. Coutinho

2716. Ferrell, Robert H., ed. TRUMAN AT POTSDAM. *Am. Heritage 1980 31(4): 36-47.* Reprints the portion of Harry S. Truman's diary written en route to the Potsdam Conference in Berlin in 1945.

2717. Feuerwerger, Marvin C. THE FORD ADMINISTRATION AND ISRAEL: EARLY SIGNALS. *Midstream 1974 20(10): 13-19.*

2718. Feuerwerger, Marvin C. FORD AND ISRAEL. *Midstream 1975 21(8): 30-36.* Discusses the changes in President Ford's attitudes toward American foreign policy regarding Israel (1974-75). S

2719. Fischer, Dana D. THE INTERNATIONAL PROTECTION OF HUMAN RIGHTS. *Pro. of the Acad. of Pol. Sci. 1977 32(4): 44-55.* Since 1945 the United Nations has been a focal point for the development of a policy for the protection of individual human rights. The United States has remained outside these developments until recently when President Jimmy Carter made several proposals to strengthen UN human rights policies. The fate of these proposals is highly uncertain, however, as wholehearted support for them is lacking in many countries, including the United States. 7 notes. K. N. T. Crowther

2720. Fishlow, Albert. FLYING DOWN TO RIO: PERSPECTIVES ON U.S.-BRAZIL RELATIONS. *Foreign Affairs 1978-79 57(2): 387-405.* President Jimmy Carter's visit to Brazil in April 1978 assuaged many of the tensions that have separated the two nations during the past 20 years. But events of an episodic and purely ceremonial nature will not suffice. With a domestic economy of $165 billion, Brazil ranks first among the developing nations of the world. The United States must " . . . seek to seduce Brazil from its present preoccupation with national economic advantage to a more global role, and from its fears of political exclusion to active exercise of responsibility." M. R. Yerburgh

2721. Forsythe, David P. AMERICAN FOREIGN POLICY AND HUMAN RIGHTS: RHETORIC AND REALITY. *Universal Human Rights 1980 2(3): 35-54.* Identifies a tension between two traditions in American foreign policy—the ethical, represented by Jimmy Carter, and the machtpolitik, represented by Henry A. Kissinger—and then explores the disjunction which has often existed between ethical rhetoric and political reality.

2722. Frade, Fernando. LA DIFÍCIL POLÍTICA AMERICANA EN ORIENTE MEDIO [The difficult US policy in the Middle East]. *Rev. de Pol. Int. [Spain] 1979 (166): 57-62.* The resignation of Andrew Young, US ambassador at the UN, had a broad impact on US policy in the Middle East. President Carter had to fight against time to regain control of his Camp David policy, between the contrasting demands of the Jewish and black public opinions at home. The problems of meeting the Palestinian claims and of involving them in the peace talks were made more complicated. Time, however, works for the Palestinians. 9 notes. D. Ardia

2723. Francis, Samuel T. CONFLICT IN THE HORN OF AFRICA. *J. of Social and Pol. Studies 1978 2(3): 155-168.* Recent American expulsions (commercial and military) and slackening of American aid due to the moralistic policies of the Carter Administration portends increased Soviet influence in this strategically vital area.

2724. Freedman, Robert O. THE SOVIET IMAGE OF THE CARTER ADMINISTRATION'S POLICY TOWARD THE USSR FROM THE INAUGURATION TO THE INVASION OF AFGHANISTAN: A PRELIMINARY ANALYSIS. *Korea & World Affairs [South Korea] 1980 4(2): 229-267.* Analyzes the Soviet image of the Carter administration, 1977-79, and its impact on the USSR's international politics, the Strategic Arms Limitation Talks, and Soviet dissidents in 1977.

2725. Freymond, Jacques. L'EUROPE DANS LE POLITIQUE EXTÉRIEURE DE HENRY KISSINGER [Europe in the foreign policy of Henry Kissinger]. *Relations Int. [France] 1977 (11): 249-264.* Paying tribute to Henry A. Kissinger as "an artist of politics and diplomacy," the author contrasts his words and actions in regard to Europe's place in his strategy. While Kissinger spoke much of the importance of European unity and Euro-American cooperation, in fact he spent far more time on other regions, including China, the USSR, and the Middle East, to the alarm of many Europeans. Concludes that there was a gap between Kissinger's long-term and short-term objectives. R. Stromberg

2726. Friedman, Murray. AWACS AND THE JEWISH COMMUNITY. *Commentary 1982 73(4): 29-33.* Discusses the Reagan administration's successful attempt to pass legislation on 28 October 1981 for the sale of AWACS to Saudi Arabia, with special attention to the opposed lobbying positions of Jews and the business community.

2727. Fuller, Daniel J. and Ruddy, T. Michael. MYTH IN PROGRESS: HARRY TRUMAN AND *MEETING AT POTSDAM. Am. Studies (Lawrence, KS) 1977 18(2): 99-106.* A review essay about the popular rehabilitation of Harry S. Truman, one of the few remaining American presidents with dramatic potential. Image-makers have enthusiastically seized upon Truman, but the accuracy of their portrayals is questionable. The film skirts the major issues of the Potsdam Conference and focuses on personalities. This raises the broader issue of historical license on the part of authors and film-makers. Primary and secondary sources; 18 notes.
J. A. Andrew

2728. Gaddis, John Lewis. RECONSIDERATIONS: WAS THE TRUMAN DOCTRINE A REAL TURNING POINT? *Foreign Affairs 1974 52(2): 386-402.* Critics and defenders of the Truman Doctrine agree on two points: Truman's comments marked a turning point in U.S. foreign policy, and U.S. involvement grew out of that. The policy was in keeping with precedents. In spite of the administration's pronouncements, it had neither the intention nor the capability of policing the world. The policy of treating Communism as a monolith began with proof (Korea, 1950) that Communism was militarily aggressive. Until that point, one must distinguish between the *language* of the Truman Doctrine and the actual *policies* carried out by that administration. Based on U.S. Government publications, other primary works, and secondary works; 35 notes.
R. Riles

2729. Gaddis, John Lewis. STRATEGIES OF CONTAINMENT: THE 1980 STUART L. BERNATH MEMORIAL LECTURE. *Soc. for Hist. of Am. Foreign Relations. Newsletter 1980 11(2): 1-14.* Discusses the implementation of George F. Kennan's original containment strategy by the Truman administration during 1947-49, the 1950-53 containment due to the Korean War, the Eisenhower-Dulles strategy during 1953-61, the Kennedy-Johnson strategy during 1961-69, the idea of detente from the early 1970's to the end of 1979, and finally the new strategy of containment that has resulted from Soviet imperialism in Afghanistan.

2730. Gallagher, Nancy E. and Wilson, Dunning S. SUPPRESSION OF INFORMATION OR PUBLISHER'S ERROR?: KERMIT ROOSEVELT'S MEMOIR OF THE 1953 IRANIAN COUNTERCOUP. *Middle East Studies Assoc. Bull. 1981 15(1): 14-17.* Traces the publishing history of Central Intelligence Agency (CIA) agent Kermit Roosevelt's *Countercoup: The Struggle for Control of Iran* (1979-80), an account of the 1953 coup that restored the Shah to power. The book was first published in 1979, withdrawn, revised, and republished in 1980, all under pressure from British intelligence, the CIA, and British Petroleum. Compares selected passages from the two editions, in which discrepancies undermine the book's value as an accurate account of Iran in 1953.

2731. Ganin, Zvi. THE LIMITS OF AMERICAN JEWISH POLITICAL POWER: AMERICA'S RETREAT FROM PARTITION, NOVEMBER 1947-MARCH 1948. *Jewish Social Studies 1977 39(1-2): 1-36.* Forces within the Truman administration sought to undo the US commitment to the United Nations' Partition of Palestine resolution of 29 November 1947. These oppositionists included important members of the State Department, Secretary of Defense James Forrestal and members of the National Security Council and Central Intelligence Agency. Outside the government important sources of opposition were represented by James Reston of the *New York Times* and Kermit Roosevelt. President Truman was irritated by the interference of the American Jewish community into foreign policy matters by injecting the issue into domestic politics. Domestic Jewish groups and individuals failed to stem the retreat from supporting partition because they were unable to persuade the American foreign policy elite that the creation of a Jewish state was in the national interest. The foreign policy elite was able to effectively counter the presumed great strength of domestic Jewish political pressure.
N. Lederer

2732. Garfinkle, Adam M. NEGOTIATING BY PROXY: JORDANIAN FOREIGN POLICY AND U.S. OPTIONS IN THE MIDDLE EAST. *Orbis 1981 24(4): 847-880.* Examines the place of King Hussein of Jordan in US policy options in the Middle East, 1948-80. Discusses the Hashemite monarchy and Palestinian nationalism, the Rabat summit in 1974, President Carter's relationship with Jordan, and Hussein's failure to support the Camp David accords. The Carter administration failed to get Hussein to join the peace process because it misunderstood the Jordanian position in inter-Arab politics and overestimated King Hussein's trust. 57 notes.
J. W. Thacker, Jr.

2733. Garrett, Stephen A. NIXONIAN FOREIGN POLICY: A NEW BALANCE OF POWER—OR A REVIVED CONCERT? *Polity 1976 8(3): 389-421.* The claim of the early Nixon Administration to have moved the international political system in the direction of the classical balance of power has been in the center of discussion among students of international relations. Garrett questions that the new policy has been properly characterized. He works out an incisive distinction between the classical balance of power of the eighteenth century with its conceptual and operational chaos and the nineteenth-century concert of power system as a rational and controlled management of power relations. He argues that the Nixon-Kissinger foreign policy is more properly seen as a revival of the concert system and traces in detail the parallels between the two policies. He focuses on features in the international environment indicating that a concert is in fact in operation; on motivations of the member states that lead them to want a concert; and on technical requirements to be met for a concert to become a reality. In trying to obtain a clearer understanding the article deals with an important theoretical and practical problem.
J

2734. Garruccio, Ludovico. KISSINGER L'OSCURO [Kissinger the obscure]. *Affari Esteri [Italy] 1974 6(23): 13-33.* Although many books have been written about Henry A. Kissinger, his mind remains an enigma. His essence seems to be pessimism while he works in the hope of developing a peaceful world based on great power stability. While Kissinger's diplomacy tends toward a higher morality he remains the "first statesman of nuclear diplomacy."
A. R. Stoesen

2735. Garson, Robert. THE ROLE OF EASTERN EUROPE IN AMERICA'S CONTAINMENT POLICY, 1945-1948. *J. of Am. Studies [Great Britain] 1979 13(1): 73-92.* Before 1947, US foreign policymakers believed it possible to restrain Soviet expansion into Eastern Europe. But such optimism faded; and, with the Truman Doctrine formulated and the European Recovery Plan started in 1947, President Harry Truman and his advisers made clear their calculations that the West could not immediately reverse the USSR's hegemony over Eastern European nations. US policy then prescribed containing the Soviets to their existing sphere until East European nationalism would erode the USSR's hold on the region. Based on US and British manuscript sources and secondary works; 42 notes.
H. T. Lovin

2736. Garthoff, Raymond L. BANNING THE BOMB IN OUTER SPACE. *Int. Security 1980-81 5(3): 25-40.* In 1963 the UN General Assembly passed Resolution 1884 banning nuclear arms in outer space, a resolution which President John F. Kennedy believed would gain more widespread American support than a treaty or executive agreement; this resolution paved the way for the 1967 Treaty on Outer Space negotiated with the USSR by President Lyndon B. Johnson and the 1972 Anti-Ballistic Missile Treaty, but ratification of the SALT II Treaty and negotiations on an antisatellite systems ban are jeopardized by the present rift in American-Soviet relations.

2737. Gawronski, Jas. VIAGGIO PRESIDENZIALE [Presidential travel]. *Affari Esteri [Italy] 1974 6(23): 120-136.* In spite of the availability of instant worldwide communications systems, American presidents continue to rely heavily on travel and the personal touch in dealing with the rest of the world. During 1973 President Nixon's major efforts took him to the Middle East on "journeys of peace." While the mass media played these trips up and gave them the appearance of success, it is more likely that their effect on diplomacy was minimal.
A. R. Stoesen

2738. Gawronski, Jas. ZBIGNIEW BRZEZINSKI E I NUOVI RAPPORTI TRA STATI UNITI E ITALIA [Zbigniew Brzezinski and the new relations between the United States and Italy]. *Affari Esteri [Italy] 1977 9(34): 181-194.* Examines key aspects of the Carter administration's foreign policy toward Italy; based on several articles by Brzezinski, the president's foreign affairs adviser.

2739. Gazit, Mordechai. MEDIATION AND MEDIATORS. *Jerusalem J. of Int. Relations [Israel] 1981 5(4): 80-104.* Reviews the history of Middle East mediation from the interventions of Ralph Bunche (1949) and Count Bernadotte (1948) to Henry Kissinger's diplomatic successes 1973-75.

2740. Gelb, Leslie H. and Lake, Anthony. LESS FOOD, MORE POLITICS. *Foreign Policy 1974-75 (17): 176-189.* Reviews the reaction of Washington to the international food crisis, and finds that the bureaucracies were confused and in disagreement concerning the best policies to support. A president was needed to provide leadership to develop a coherent and effective program. To add to the confusion, the United States felt obligated to present a humanitarian face to the world. Henry A. Kissinger persuaded President Gerald R. Ford to increase food aid, but Secretary of Agriculture Earl Butz also won his point that other nations must share in this program. Washington agrees in general that food is power, and the United States cannot disregard food politics in international diplomacy. Some congressional leaders, however, particularly Senators Hubert Humphrey and George McGovern, want more emphasis on humanitarian considerations. Based mainly on secondary sources.
                                                    R. F. Kugler

2741. Gelb, Leslie H. WASHINGTON DATELINE: THE STORY OF A FLAP. *Foreign Policy 1974 (16): 165-181.* Based on a New York Times story in June 1974 which charged that Secretary of State Henry A. Kissinger had made secret agreements with the USSR regarding strategic weapons without informing Congress. Kissinger refuted this charge, although he admitted that inconsequential secret agreements had been made. In addition, it appears that during the 1972 Moscow Summit Conference, President Richard M. Nixon provided a written unilateral pledge to the Soviet Union that the United States would not build up to the allowable 710 submarine launchers—an amount provided for in the disarmament agreement. The American SALT (Strategic Arms Limitation Talks) delegation was not informed of this in detail. Kissinger apparently had also made a secret agreement with Soviet leaders permitting them to construct certain strategic weapons in excess of the disarmament agreement. This "loophole" has now been closed, perhaps as a result of media exposure.   R. F. Kugler

2742. Geyelin, Philip. IMPEACHMENT AND FOREIGN POLICY. *Foreign Policy 1974 (15): 183-190.* Assesses the effects which Nixon's impending impeachment had on his ability to conduct foreign affairs.   S

2743. Gimbel, John. DIE VEREINIGTEN STAATEN, FRANKREICH UND DER AMERIKANISCHE VERTRAGSENTWURF ZUR ENTMILITARISIERUNG DEUTSCHLANDS. EINE STUDIE ÜBER LEGENDENBILDUNG IM KALTEN KRIEG [The United States, France, and the American Draft Treaty for the demilitarization of Germany. A study in legend-making in the Cold War]. *Vierteljahrshefte für Zeitgeschichte [West Germany] 1974 22(3): 258-286.* A case study of the draft treaty on the disarmament and demilitarization of Germany (1946) the author demonstrates the overwhelming influence of later Cold War attitudes on the historical interpretation of immediate postwar events. Documentary evidence proves that the draft treaty was not conceived as a Cold War maneuver against the Soviet Union, but rather as a lever against France, on the insistence of the War Department and the Office of Military Government, United States, to nudge the French toward cooperation with Germany. Personally angered by V. M. Molotov's critical reaction to the draft, swayed by State Department Francophiles and influenced by the anti-Soviet Cold War lobby in his Department, Secretary of State James Byrnes subsequently falsely underplayed the skepticism of the British and the French toward the draft and accused Molotov of a sudden and deceitful turnabout in his rejection of the proposal. For years historians followed that interpretation. Based on printed State Department records and primary sources from the OMGUS Papers, War Department papers, National Archives, and Truman Library; 95 notes.   D. Prowe

2744. Girling, J. L. S. CARTER'S FOREIGN POLICY: REALISM OR IDEOLOGY? *World Today [Great Britain] 1977 33(11): 417-424.* Because the USSR is willing to accept ideological constraints, President Jimmy Carter can pursue a human rights foreign policy.

2745. Girling, J. L. S. "KISSINGERISM": THE ENDURING PROBLEM. *Internat. Affairs [Great Britain] 1975 51(3): 323-343.* Analyzes the nature of "Kissingerism," as defined with reference to Kissinger's stress upon power and equilibrium. Examines the recent realignment of American foreign policy, especially the Nixon Doctrine which is a central theme of "Kissingerism." Concludes by discussing the application of the Nixon Doctrine in Indochina and the problems of "Kissingerism," for example, the credibility gap. Secondary sources; 27 notes.
                                                    P. J. Beck

2746. Gleijeses, Piero. THE ELUSIVE CENTER IN CENTRAL AMERICA. *Working Papers Mag. 1981 8(6): 30-37.* Traces political events in Central America since the Alliance for Progress promoted political and social reforms to prevent a Communist takeover; focuses on criticisms of President Jimmy Carter's Central American policy by President Reagan's Republican supporters, some of whom believe that the Carter administration's naiveté resulted in increased Communist presence in Nicaragua, Guatemala, and El Salvador, while others believe that Carter's leftist supporters worked to get the left-wing in power.

2747. Gnevushev, N. "NOVAIA IADERNAIA STRATEGIIA" SSHA I RAZVIVAIUSHCHIESIA STRANY [The US "new nuclear strategy" and the developing nations]. *Aziia i Afrika Segodnia [USSR] 1981 (9): 11-13.* Discusses the impact of Directive 59, issued by President Jimmy Carter in 1979 and implemented by President Ronald Reagan, on political and military stability in the world, focusing on the directive's strategy involving US military bases and nuclear arms. Russian.

2748. Goldstein, Daniel. RÜCKBLICK AUF KISSINGER [Retrospective on Kissinger]. *Schweizer Monatshefte [Switzerland] 1977 56(10): 874-883.* A critical purview of Henry A. Kissinger's conduct of US foreign policy, especially his European policy.

2749. Goodsell, James Nelson. KISSINGER VISIT REQUIRED TO MITIGATE DISENCHANTMENT. *Int. Perspectives [Canada] 1975 (5): 30-33.* Discusses the promised but unfulfilled diplomacy by Secretary of State Henry A. Kissinger to reassure Latin America of the aims of US foreign policy; emphasizes issues in trade and the Organization of American States, 1974-75.

2750. Gordon, David F. UNITED STATES FOREIGN AID IN PERSPECTIVE. *Current Hist. 1979 77(448): 1-4, 33-34.* Discusses the philosophy and role of foreign aid in US diplomacy from the Marshall Plan in 1948 to President Jimmy Carter's human rights campaign in the late 1970's.

2751. Gordon, Murray. KISSINGER'S TRAVAILS. *Midstream 1975 21(5): 7-17.* An account of Henry A. Kissinger's efforts for peace in the Middle East.

2752. Gormly, James L. SECRETARY OF STATE JAMES F. BYRNES, AN INITIAL BRITISH EVALUATION. *South Carolina Hist. Mag. 1978 79(3): 198-205.* Reproduces the report of Lord Halifax, British ambassador to the United States, concerning James F. Byrnes and discusses British estimates of his competence in 1945-46.

2753. Gottlieb, Amy Zahl. REFUGEE IMMIGRATION: THE TRUMAN DIRECTIVE. *Prologue 1981 13(1): 5-17.* Discusses the directive of 22 December 1945 by which President Harry S. Truman sought to relieve the distress of Germany in the aftermath of World War II and help alleviate the plight of the many war refugees and displaced persons throughout Europe. The purpose of the directive was to allow displaced persons in Europe to obtain immigrant visas to the United States within the limits of the preestablished immigration quotas. Truman took many steps to facilitate the processing of visa applications for this special group of immigrants. The visas issued under the Truman directive (35,515) continued until 1 July 1948 and were then terminated by a provision of the Displaced Persons Act. Based on the archives of the American Joint Distribution Committee, presidential papers, and newspapers; 9 photos, 36 notes.   M. A. Kascus

2754. Graebner, Norman A. HENRY KISSINGER AND AMERICAN FOREIGN POLICY: A CONTEMPORARY APPRAISAL. *Australian J. of Pol. and Hist. [Australia] 1976 22(1): 7-22.* Henry A. Kissinger's diplomacy marked the first major change in American foreign policy since World War II. Instead of containing Communism he sought a stabilization of relations with Russia and China, based on the notion that they were essentially status quo powers. Until 1974 he achieved great popularity, but his sanctioning of wire-tapping indicated flaws, and his neglect of the professionals demoralized the State Department. Although his reputation survived the Watergate crisis and Nixon's removal, critics noted that his success with Moscow and Peking stemmed largely from Russian and Chinese desire for better relations. His uniqueness lies in the fact that he was the first Secretary of State in three generations to think and act in political rather than judicial/moral terms. Documented from newspapers and periodicals. W. D. McIntyre

2755. Graml, Herman. ZWISCHEN JALTA UND POTSDAM: ZUR AMERIKANISCHEN DEUTSCHLANDSPLANUNG IM FRÜHJAHR 1945 [Between Yalta and Potsdam: On American plans for Germany in Spring, 1945]. *Vierteljahrshefte für Zeitgeschichte [West Germany] 1976 24(3): 308-323.* At the Yalta Conference in January, 1945 Allied leaders, Winston Churchill excepted, had talked of dividing Germany, but at the Potsdam Conference in July 1945 they decided on preserving its unity. Franklin D. Roosevelt favored partition, but Edward Stettinius, Secretary of State, dissuaded him. The creation of a part state, *Teilstaat,* was not originally intended, and was merely a later development. As a means of decentralizing Germany's political structure, the American group commander suggested federalism and the division of Prussia to remove the threat of its militarism. Based on the Decentralization Reports of the American Group Commander of 1 and 23 March, 1945; 21 notes. A. Alcock

2756. Granjon, Marie-Christine. LA POLITIQUE DES DROITS DE L'HOMME ET SON APPLICATION [The human rights policy and its application]. *Problèmes d'Amérique Latine [France] 1981 (60): 57-71.* A critical analysis of President Jimmy Carter's application of human rights considerations in foreign policy in Latin America.

2757. Gray, Colin S. NUCLEAR STRATEGY: THE DEBATE MOVES ON. *J. of the Royal United Services Inst. for Defence Studies [Great Britain] 1976 121(1): 44-50.* Discusses developments in nuclear deterrence theory in the 1970's, specifically the "Schlesinger doctrine" of greater flexibility in US strategic nuclear options and creation of a hard target counterforce capability for the United States to match that of the USSR. Opponents of the notion of nuclear parity have long tended to ignore the unchanged Soviet belief in the possibilities for political exploitation of nuclear imbalance. The core of the Schlesinger doctrine is the creation of limited strategic options below the level of the Single Integrated Operations Plan; however, "not all credible threats deter" and the United States may find that the Schlesinger strategy will prove inadequate in terms of operational realities. 17 notes. D. H. Murdoch

2758. Grayson, George W. THE U.S.-MEXICAN NATURAL GAS DEAL AND WHAT WE CAN LEARN FROM IT. *Orbis 1980 24(3): 573-607.* A detailed discussion of the complex negotiations between the United States and Mexico for the purchase of natural gas between 1977 and 1980. The failure of the negotiations was a result of misunderstandings on both sides and a lack of concerted action on the part of the US State Department. Concludes that the Mexican price was too high and that Energy Secretary James R. Schlesinger was right to veto the deal. Based on newspapers, government documents, and other published sources; map, table, 100 notes. J. W. Thacker, Jr.

2759. Green, William C. HUMAN RIGHTS AND DETENTE. *Ukrainian Q. 1980 36(2): 138-149.* Examines the interplay between detente and human rights policy under the Carter administration. Basket Three of the Helsinki Final Act on humanitarian issues gave impetus and international prominence to Soviet dissident groups. The Carter administration's emphasis on human rights brought strong reaction from the Soviets and exposed the limitations placed on American policy by detente. Ultimately human rights policy was downplayed by the United States in the hope of gaining some success in dealing with the USSR on SALT and other more pressing international issues. 33 notes. K. N. T. Crowther

2760. Gregg, Richard B. and Hauser, Gerald A. RICHARD NIXON'S APRIL 30, 1970 ADDRESS ON CAMBODIA: THE "CEREMONY" OF CONFRONTATION. *Speech Monographs 1973 40(3): 167-181.* "This essay examines President Nixon's April 30, 1970 address announcing the American incursion into Cambodia. Examining the perceptual patterns of the speech, the authors found that Nixon's remarks led to a climax which justified the war on ritualistic rather than Cold War premises. The last third of the speech was content analyzed. The resulting term clusters were then interpreted for their symbolic significance. The authors found the President's remarks in conformity with the potlatch ceremony of the Kwakiutl Indians. The essay concludes by relating the perceptual patterns and analogical matrix of the potlatch to trends which may be developing on the international scene, and calls for the rhetorical critic to become aware of ritualistic elements in public communication." J

2761. Gregor, A. James. THE UNITED STATES, THE REPUBLIC OF CHINA, AND THE TAIWAN RELATIONS ACT. *Orbis 1980 24(3): 609-623.* Analyzes the policy of the Carter administration toward the Republic of China on Taiwan from 1978 to 1980. Despite promises made to Taiwan and the American people, the Carter administration was either unable or unwilling to carry out the Taiwan Relations Act (US, 1979). "Accommodation of the People's Republic seems to have had so high a place in the Carter administration's priority list that the Taiwan Relations Act was to be gutted ... The Republic of China or Taiwan, regardless of all administration assurances, has been, in fact, largely abandoned in the fevered courtship of the People's Republic." Published sources and government documents; 30 notes. J. W. Thacker, Jr.

2762. Grindle, Merilee. ARMED INTERVENTION AND U.S.-LATIN AMERICAN RELATIONS. *Latin Am. Res. Rev. 1981 16(1): 207-217.* Reviews seven works on US intervention in Latin America. Latin American elites have manipulated US involvement to serve their own purposes. In recent years, the decision to use troops has passed from State Department functionaries to higher level decisionmakers. Since World War II global issues have played a larger role than previously. US intervention has altered significantly the outcome of internal Latin American conflicts and the political and economic development of the area. 7 notes. J. K. Pfabe.

2763. Gromyko, Antoli A. KARIBSKII KRIZIS [The Caribbean crisis]. *Voprosy Istorii [USSR] 1971 (7): 135-144, (8): 121-129.* Part I. Discusses the Cuban crisis of 1962, suggesting that the conflict with the USSR over Cuba was deliberately engineered by President John F. Kennedy and his administration. The president's military advisers sought either invasion or naval blockade. The United States failed to reassure the Russians on the question of the sighting of missile bases in Europe, directed at the USSR. 58 notes. Part II. Describes the buildup of US military forces in the Caribbean in October 1962. The USSR protested to the UN over the US blockade of Cuba. The Security Council debated, and U. Thant intervened. But the United States pursued a policy of political blackmail. The Soviet offer to withdraw its missiles from Cuba met with contradictory US responses. The United States delayed over the text of the joint declaration in the UN when agreement had been reached; Kennedy was forced to respect the accord with the USSR and lift the threat of attack on Cuba. 55 notes. E. R. Sicher

2764. Gropman, Alan. WHY IS THERE STILL A COLD WAR? *Air U. Rev. 1978 29(2): 77-84.* Presents a combined review of three books that deal with the Cold War confrontations between the United States and the USSR. Richard J. Walton's *Henry Wallace, Harry Truman and the Cold War,* (New York: Viking, 1976) argues that Harry Truman provoked the Russians into the Cold War and that it could have been avoided if he had listened to Henry Wallace. James A. Nathan's and James K. Oliver's *United States Foreign Policy and World Order,* (Boston: Little Brown and Company, 1976) blame both sides but seem to side with the revisionist position. Alexander Solzhenitsyn's *Warning to the West* (New York: Farrar Straus and Giroux, 1976) presents the opposite view, stating that the United States has invited Soviet expansion by its weakness. Illus., 8 notes. J. W. Thacker, Jr.

2765. Guidi, Roberto. KISSINGER E IL NUOVO ORDINE INTERNAZIONALE [Kissinger and the new international order]. *Affari*

Esteri [Italy] 1973 5(20): 1-20. The new international order envisioned by Henry A. Kissinger is based on agreement among the great powers. While many difficulties appear to lessen the prospect for stability, a strong foundation has been constructed in the recent past which increases the prospect for a future of peace.   A. R. Stoesen

2766. Gyllenstierna, Ebbe. VIETNAMKRIGET, PRESIDENT JOHNSON OCH RÅDGIVERNA I VITA HUSET [The Vietnam War, President Johnson, and the advisers in the White House]. *Kungliga Krigsvetenskaps Akademiens Handlingar och Tidskrift [Sweden] 1973 177(7-8): 220-226.* Describes the role of Lyndon B. Johnson's presidential advisers in decisionmaking about the expansion of the Vietnam War. After having increased military activities Johnson was constantly pressed by the Pentagon and the generals in Vietnam to expand the war even further. On the other side, defense ministers urged him to stop the war because of the enormous costs. This was one of the reasons Johnson bitterly withdrew. Based on David Halberstam's *The Best and the Brightest* (London: Barneham and Jenkins, 1972).   U. Bartels/S

2767. Hafner, Donald L. BUREAUCRATIC POLITICS AND "THOSE FRIGGING MISSILES": JFK, CUBA, AND U.S. MISSILES IN TURKEY. *Orbis 1977 21(2): 307-334.* For many years two myths have grown up about the 1962 Cuban Missile Crisis. One holds that President John F. Kennedy did not know that US Jupiter missiles were still in Turkey when the Soviets suggested they be removed in a trade-off for their missiles in Cuba. The second myth is the one of "bureaucratic entrapment," in which a president of the United States is prisoner of the Washington bureaucracy. It is obvious from the historical record that Kennedy did know the Jupiter missiles were still in Turkey and that much of what has been written about this matter is less than factual. Kennedy was not a prisoner of bureaucratic politics, nor is any president such a prisoner. The president must depend on the bureaucracies for intelligence and other matters, but he can control them and have them do his bidding. If he attempts to "stretch his personal concern" too far, though, he may do more damage than good. In fact, he may erode his own power base. Thus, the major lesson of the 1962 crisis is a "lesson of limits," and one that future presidents should heed. 67 notes.   A. N. Garland

2768. Haight, David J. THE DWIGHT D. EISENHOWER LIBRARY AS A RESEARCH CENTER FOR THE STUDY OF INTERNATIONAL AFFAIRS: OPPORTUNITIES AND PROSPECTS. *Soc. for Hist. of Am. Foreign Relations. Newsletter 1979 10(2): 11-20.* General survey of the holdings of the Dwight D. Eisenhower Library in Abilene, Kansas, relating to foreign relations, 1953-61.

2769. Haight, David J. THE PAPERS OF C. D. JACKSON: A GLIMPSE AT PRESIDENT EISENHOWER'S PSYCHOLOGICAL WARFARE EXPERT. *Manuscripts 1976 28(1): 27-37.* Among the more interesting manuscript collections in the Dwight D. Eisenhower Library at Abilene are the papers of Charles Douglas Jackson (1902-1964). Before being brought into the Eisenhower administration as an advisor dealing in psychological warfare and the cold war in order to balance the intransigence of John Foster Dulles, Jackson was a vice president in the Luce publishing enterprises. Although Jackson was never soft on communism, he represented the liberal element among Eisenhower's close advisors. His papers spanning the period from 1931-67 offer a potentially rich source for historians of the Eisenhower Administration. 25 notes.   D. A. Yanchisin

2770. Halász, Zoltán. FOREIGN POLICY MADE BY HISTORIANS. *New Hungarian Q. [Hungary] 1981 22(83): 183-188.* Reviews Rezső Békés's *Kissinger és Brzezinski* [Kissinger and Brzezinski] (1980). Examines the ideological foundations of Henry A. Kissinger's policy as a basis for discussing the role of the historian in shaping foreign policy. The record of Zbigniew Brzezinski is analyzed by reference to his previous writings. Note.   P. J. Beck

2771. Hamburg, Roger. MASSIVE RETALIATION REVISITED. *Military Affairs 1974 38(1): 17-23.* Suggests that the Nixon administration's post-Vietnam policies involve a revival of massive retaliation. Based on public statements and special studies; 38 notes.   K. J. Bauer

2772. Hamilton, John A. TO LINK OR NOT TO LINK. *Foreign Policy 1981 (44): 127-144.* Linkage, or the political practice of tying a concession by one party to a concession by the other, has achieved recent prominence as an essential tool of American diplomacy during the Carter years. Although the Reagan administration has declared its intent to use linkage diplomacy, it should avoid linking other matters to the strategic arms negotiations, which are too delicate and important to benefit from this practice.   L. J. Klass

2773. Hamm, Michael J. THE *PUEBLO* AND *MAYAGUEZ* INCIDENTS: A STUDY OF FLEXIBLE RESPONSE AND DECISION-MAKING. *Asian Survey 1977 17(6): 545-555.* The US policy of flexible response was conceived to meet small, limited crises by reacting in graduated and ever-increasing persuasion. Discusses this policy within the framework of the seizure of the *Pueblo* by the North Koreans in 1969 and the capture of the *Mayaguez* by Cambodia in 1975, and points out the reason for its failure in 1969 but its success in 1975. Examines why the US government did not resort to force in the *Pueblo* incident but did employ force in the *Mayaguez* incident. The *Pueblo* incident was a political setback for the United States, but the *Mayaguez* incident was a political victory for President Gerald Ford. Based on newspaper reports and secondary sources; 22 notes.   M. Feingold/S

2774. Han, Yung-Chul. THE CARTER ADMINISTRATION'S POLICY TOWARD EAST ASIA: WITH FOCUS ON KOREA. *Am. Studies Int. 1979 18(1): 35-48.* Traces the background of US involvement in Korea, emphasizing initial fear of monolithic communism and the change in attitude caused by Vietnam, detente, and the new China policy. Carter's decision to pull American ground troops out of South Korea had two major motives: normalize relations with North Korea and avoid involvement in another Asian land war. Carter may reconsider: the troops virtually guarantee no North Korean invasion, Japan sees them as an essential part of its US protection, China sees them as a check on Soviet expansion, and even the Soviet view is probably ambivalent. 2 illus., 13 notes.   R. E. Noble

2775. Hansen, Erik Arne. PRESIDENT JOHN F. KENNEDY'S DECLARATION OF INTERDEPENDENCE: A STUDY IN HIS PRESIDENTIAL RHETORIC. *Am. Studies in Scandinavia [Norway] 1981 13(2): 117-127.* On 4 July 1962 at the National Governors' Conference in Philadelphia, Pennsylvania, President John F. Kennedy gave a speech which served as a rhetorical springboard for the Trade Expansion Act (US, 1962). Kennedy aimed to further Atlantic economic interdependence. 76 notes.   E. E. Krogstad

2776. Harbutt, Fraser. AMERICAN CHALLENGE, SOVIET RESPONSE: THE BEGINNING OF THE COLD WAR, FEBRUARY-MAY, 1946. *Pol. Sci. Q. 1981-82 96(4): 623-639.* Traces the beginnings of the Cold War to early 1946. At the end of 1945, Great Britain was perceived by the Soviets as their main adversary. On 10 February, due to American perceptions of an increased Soviet threat, Truman repudiated the policy that prevented the United States from collaborating with Britain against the Soviets. By 12 February, the United States began challenging the Soviet position in Eastern Europe. There were further disagreements over the Soviet position in Iran. By May, the USSR and the United States recognized in each other their prime adversary, pursued increasingly unilateral goals, and consolidated distinct spheres of influence and allies. Secondary sources; 49 notes.   J. Powell

2777. Haron, Miriam Joyce. NOTE: UNITED STATES-BRITISH COLLABORATION ON ILLEGAL IMMIGRATION TO PALESTINE, 1945-1947. *Jewish Social Studies 1980 42(2): 177-182.* The problem of illegal Jewish immigration into Palestine strained Anglo-American relations between 1945 and 1947. The American public's interest in the settlement of displaced persons in Palestine conflicted with Great Britain's determination to restrict Jewish immigration there. The State Department sympathized with British efforts, and endeavored to stop tax-deductible donations in aid of illegal immigration. The crisis over the displaced persons ship *Exodus* (1947) brought tensions to their height, because the vessel was originally American, and because the operation was largely financed by private contributions collected in the United States. After the *Exodus* affair the State Department prevented the departure of the ship *Colonel Frederick C. Johnson,* fearing that it too would be used for illegal immigration. The ship was permitted to sail two months after the creation of Israel. Based on British and American government documents; 38 notes.   J. D. Sarna

2778. Haron, Miriam Joyce. PALESTINE AND THE ANGLO-AMERICAN CONNECTION. *Modern Judaism 1982 2(2): 199-211.* Discusses Harry S. Truman's Palestine policy, as it was influenced by his concern for the survivors of the Holocaust, his desire to secure the Jewish vote, and, especially, relations with Great Britain.

2779. Harrington, Daniel F. KENNAN, BOHLEN, AND THE RIGA AXIOMS. *Diplomatic Hist. 1978 2(4): 423-437.* Review article prompted by Daniel H. Yergin, *Shattered Peace: The Origins of the Cold War and the National Security State* (Boston, 1977). Takes issue with Yergin's assertion that George F. Kennan and Charles E. Bohlen must bear much of the responsibiltiy for the triumph within the State Department of a set of ideas which Yergin calls (miscalls, says the author) the "Riga axioms." These state that Soviet policy is guided mainly by Marxist ideology, and aims single-mindedly at world domination. Neither Kennan nor Bohlen enjoyed much influence after 1950, and neither subscribed to these extreme positions. Based partly on archival and other primary sources; 52 notes.   L. W. Van Wyk

2780. Harrison, Michael M. REAGAN'S WORLD. *Foreign Policy 1981 (43): 3-16.* Beyond the general idea of restoring US leadership and authority through a major strengthening of the US military, President Ronald Reagan has no foreign policy. His perceptions are contradictory, simplistic, and "based on a misunderstanding of the current international order that is likely to prove debilitating and even disastrous in the coming decade." In place of his vision of a bipolar world, where America's allies are subservient to its control, he should adopt a multilateral model such as that of Charles de Gaulle.   T. L. Powers

2781. Heinrichs, Waldo. ROOSEVELT AND TRUMAN: THE PRESIDENTIAL PERSPECTIVE. Borg, Dorothy and Heinrichs, Waldo, ed. *Uncertain Years: Chinese-American Relations, 1947-1950* (New York: Columbia U. Pr., 1980): 3-12. Reports on the first session of the Conference on Chinese-American Relations, sponsored by the East Asian Institute of Columbia University, at Mount Kisco, New York, 1978, devoted to US policy toward China 1944-48, discussing Franklin D. Roosevelt's postwar plans, Harry S. Truman's early Cold War policies, assistance to Jiang Jieshi (Chiang Kai-shek), and the Marshall mission.

2782. Hensley, Carl Wayne. HARRY S. TRUMAN: FUNDAMENTAL AMERICANISM IN FOREIGN POLICY SPEECHMAKING, 1945-1946. *Southern Speech Communication J. 1975 40(2): 180-190.* "During his first year as President, Harry S. Truman had to deal with concluding World War II and the postwar problem of seeking world peace. Thus, foreign policy was his primary consideration. Truman built a foreign policy on the foundation of 'fundamental Americanism,' i.e., his commitment to the traditional American dream. This policy, as revealed in his early Presidential speeches, is fundamental to understanding American foreign policy rhetoric during the Cold War era."   J

2783. Herring, George C. THE TRUMAN ADMINISTRATION AND THE RESTORATION OF FRENCH SOVEREIGNTY IN INDOCHINA. *Diplomatic Hist. 1977 1(2): 97-117.* For years the view persisted "that the Truman administration, preoccupied with other matters and uninterested in the fate of Indochina, stood by virtually unnoticing" while France regained control of its former colony at the close of World War II. It is now clear, however, that the administration consciously chose "to accept the restoration of French sovereignty in Indochina as a means of enlisting French cooperation in the San Francisco Conference and in opposing Soviet expansion in Europe." 67 notes.   G. H. Curtis

2784. Hills, Thomas R. MORALITY IN FOREIGN POLICY: AN EXPRESSION OF AMERICAN IDEALISM. *Contemporary Rev. [Great Britain] 1978 232(1344): 23-30.* Traces the influence of American idealism on US foreign policy in the 20th century and during President Jimmy Carter's administration, relating its principles to the Declaration of Independence.

2785. Hilton, Stanley E. THE UNITED STATES, BRAZIL, AND THE COLD WAR, 1945-1960: END OF THE SPECIAL RELATIONSHIP. *J. of Am. Hist. 1981 68(3): 599-624.* Analyzes US policy decisions during the Truman and Eisenhower years that drove Brazil away from its traditional special relationship with the United States and toward

a position of solidarity with Spanish America. US neglect of Brazil plus Brazil's demands for preferential treatment combined to alienate Brazil and cost the United States influence in Latin America. Based on State Department records and private correspondence; 89 notes.
                                      T. P. Linkfield

2786. Hoffman, Daniel N. and Halperin, Morton H. TOP SECRET: NATIONAL SECURITY AND THE RIGHT TO KNOW. *Dissent 1977 24(3): 241-247.* Discusses secrecy in the Johnson and Nixon administration (and continued in the Ford administration) over the bombing of Cambodia, 1969-70; also mentions the 1975 intervention in Angola.

2787. Hoffmann, Stanley. A VIEW FROM AT HOME: THE PERILS OF INCOHERENCE. *Foreign Affairs 1979 57(3): 463-491.* "The year 1978 was one of solid accomplishments, multiple frustrations, and varied crises for American diplomacy." It also revealed the continuation of major obstacles to American success in the global arena, e.g., an inability to prepare an appropriate strategy for dealing with the Soveit Union. The Carter administration must develop a more coherent, flexible approach to the formulation of foreign policy—one which will appeal to the Congress and to the American people.   M. R. Yerburgh

2788. Hoffmann, Stanley. AFTER THE CREATION, OR THE WATCH AND THE ARROW. *Internat. J. [Canada] 1973 28(2): 175-184.* Reviews George Frost Kennan's *Memoirs, II: 1950-1963* (Boston: Little, Brown and Company, 1972) and Gaddis Smith's *Dean Acheson* (New York: Cooper Square Publishers, Inc., 1972). Contrasts the clash of views on U.S. foreign policy and the personalities of the two diplomats.
                                      R. V. Kubicek

2789. Hoffmann, Stanley. FOREIGN POLICY TRANSITION: REQUIEM. *Foreign Policy 1981 (42): 3-26.* The Jimmy Carter administration's greatest foreign policy successes were its reassertion of American idealism, its attempt to deal with the world as it is, its determination to address long-range as well as immediate problems, and its initiation of major improvements in national defense. The study of this administration indicates that it is essential to insure a unity of domestic and foreign policies, but that this will be hindered by the tendency of the US public and leadership to prefer simple myth to complex reality. Secondary sources; 3 notes.   T. L. Powers

2790. Hoffmann, Stanley. MUSCLE AND BRAINS. *Foreign Policy 1979-80 (37): 3-27.* Jimmy Carter's administration has lacked a clear policy toward the USSR and, consequently, foreign policy lacks direction. America's international decline has been the result of the growth of Soviet military power, the recovery of Western Europe, and by the more recent deficiency in political analysis and the lack of will.   S

2791. Hoffmann, Stanley. OLD WINE, OLD BOTTLES: AMERICAN FOREIGN POLICY AND THE POLITICS OF NOSTALGIA. *Millennium: J. of Int. Studies [Great Britain] 1980 9(2): 91-107.* Examines President Jimmy Carter's foreign policy since 1977, its internal dissension, its inadequate analysis of the international political situation, and public opinion concerning it; and discusses the Atlantic alliance and the possibilities for US-European relations under President Ronald Reagan.

2792. Holsti, Ole R. WILL THE REAL DULLES PLEASE STAND UP. *Int. J. [Canada] 1974-75 30(1): 34-44.* Discusses recent historiography dealing with the diplomacy and foreign policy of US Secretary of State John Foster Dulles 1953-59.

2793. Howard, Michael. CONDUCTING THE CONCERT OF POWERS. *Armed Forces and Soc. 1980 6(4): 654-665.* Review article of Henry A. Kissinger's *White House Years* (1979), which presents the view that the world consists of powers pursuing their own interests according to their best perception of them and that the interest of those powers in the stability of the international system could override their mutual suspicion. Kissinger's years as negotiator for President Richard M. Nixon during 1968-72 were marked by a breakthrough in communications with China, the reconciliation of Egypt with the West, a stable settlement in Germany, and initiation of the SALT talks, but they were marred by the clandestine bombing of Hanoi and Cambodia, even though those bombings may well have helped bring North Vietnam to prefer peace by negotiation to military victory.   E. L. Keyser

2794. Hoxie, R. Gordon. PRESIDENTIAL LEADERSHIP AND AMERICAN FOREIGN POLICY: SOME REFLECTIONS ON THE TAIWAN ISSUE, WITH PARTICULAR CONSIDERATIONS ON ALEXANDER HAMILTON, DWIGHT EISENHOWER, AND JIMMY CARTER. *Presidential Studies Q. 1979 9(2): 131-143.* Discusses American foreign policy toward Taiwan during the presidencies of Dwight D. Eisenhower and Jimmy Carter, based on Alexander Hamilton's doctrine of presidential power set forth in 1793.

2795. Hsu, King-yi. SINO-AMERICAN RELATIONS AND THE SECURITY OF TAIWAN. *Asian Affairs: An Am. Rev. 1978 6(1): 48-66.* Explores the Taiwan issue as an obstacle to full diplomatic relations between Washington and Peking. Analyzes the Nixon and Ford administrations' formula for normalization and its ability to convince public opinion and Congress of its viability. Examines the Washington-Moscow-Peking triangular relationship, consequences for American business, Taiwan's security, the Peking regime, and international law. Primary and secondary sources; media and government reports; 81 notes.
R. B. Mendel

2796. Hughes, Thomas L. CARTER AND THE MANAGEMENT OF CONTRADICTIONS. *Foreign Policy 1978 (31): 34-55.* Foreign policy making within the Carter administration tends to studiously avoid or conveniently overlook inherent contradictions. One example is a long-term commitment to Israel as a stake in moderate Arab regimes. These and other contradictions persist and Carter foreign policies must ultimately deal with them.
H. R. Mahood

2797. Hutson, Thomas R. POLICY AND REALITY: FOREIGN SERVICE RECOLLECTIONS. *Int. Studies Notes 1981 8(2): 1-7.* Stating that "the Carter Administration doesn't have a clue how to conduct foreign policy," the author resigned from the Foreign Service on 11 April 1980; here he recollects how his policy recommendation of 1980 regarding the Soviet occupation of Afghanistan was not compatible with the State Department.

2798. Ingraham, Edward C. PRESENT AT THE FABRICATION. *Washington Monthly 1982 14(2): 50-54.* Secretary of State Henry A. Kissinger changed the format of the written accounts of high-level diplomatic and foreign policy meetings, known as memoranda of conversations or "memcons"; instead of "having nothing to do with the official communiques issued to a waiting world after an important meeting" they became, ostensibly, verbatim transcripts of the meetings.

2799. Inoue, Shigenobu. REAGAN'S ASIA-PACIFIC POLICY. *Issues & Studies [Taiwan] 1981 17(9): 27-34.* The Reagan administration has shifted the United States from geopolitics to the ideological values of the John Foster Dulles (1885-1959) era. It is actively working to upgrade the defense of non-Communist nations in the Asia-Pacific area, while limiting relations with mainland China to the common interest of opposition to the Soviet Union. International think tanks on anti-communism, located in the United States and Taiwan, could provide important support to this policy. Based on U.S. documents and Chinese, Japanese, and U.S. media reports; 12 notes.
J. A. Krompart

2800. Ivie, Robert L. IMAGES OF SAVAGERY IN AMERICAN JUSTIFICATIONS FOR WAR. *Communication Monographs 1980 47(4): 279-294.* Looks at the rhetoric in US justifications for war, starting with the Lyndon B. Johnson administration, and finds that the enemy is portrayed as a nation of barbarians and the United States as a representative of civilization and rationality.

2801. Jacchia, Enrico. UNA STRATEGIA PLANETARIA [A planetary strategy]. *Riv. Marittima [Italy] 1981 114(5): 9-11.* Examines the changes appearing in the Reagan administration's strategy in early 1981. Italian.

2802. Jackson, Scott. PROLOGUE TO THE MARSHALL PLAN: THE ORIGINS OF THE AMERICAN COMMITMENT FOR A EUROPEAN RECOVERY PROGRAM. *J. of Am. Hist. 1979 65(4): 1043-1068.* Traces the origins of the Marshall Plan to Europe's deteriorating economic conditions and to American perceptions of how economic collapse might influence European political stability. Several crucial factors combined to influence the decisionmaking process that led

to the plan outlined in Secretary of State George C. Marshall's address at Harvard on 5 June 1947. Such factors as Europe's economic distress, Great Britain's possible economic and financial collapse, Europe's balance of trade and dollar problems, and the threat of Communist expansion combined in 1947 to motivate Marshall's plan for European economic recovery. 67 notes.
T. P. Linkfield

2803. Jacobs, Arthur Lester. SHOULD THE U.S. USE COVERT ACTION IN THE CONDUCT OF FOREIGN POLICY? *Freedom at Issue 1976 35: 13-19.* Questions the use of government secrecy and covert action in US foreign policy from 1947-70's, emphasizing reasons for the creation of the Central Intelligence Agency in 1947 as a response to USSR expansionism in Europe.

2804. Jaśkowski, Marian. NIEMCY ZACHODNIE A STANY ZJEDNOCZONE W OKRESIE PREZYDENTURY L. B. JOHNSONA [West Germany and the United States at the time of L. B. Johnson's presidency]. *Przegląd Zachodni [Poland] 1969 25(6): 295-321.* Lyndon B. Johnson's foreign policy, 1963-69, followed Kennedy's precedent and, within the framework of NATO, West Germany remained America's most reliable ally in Western Europe.

2805. Jay, Peter. REGIONALISM AS GEOPOLITICS. *Foreign Affairs 1980 58(3): 485-514.* Analyzes US foreign policy in 1979 considered in terms of the competition between the United States and the USSR for control of other territories. In the years between the Truman and Nixon administrations, the United States supported foreign governments without regard to regional circumstances. The Carter administration recognized and attempted to correct this situation, which led to closer relations with nations in southern Africa, and opened possbilities for resolving the difficulties in the Near East. The Soviet arms buildup and invasion of Afghanistan threatened a return to cold war policies. Based on writings by Henry A. Kissinger; 6 notes.
A. A. Englard

2806. Johnston, Whittle. THE NEW DIPLOMACY OF PRESIDENT CARTER. *Australian J. of Pol. and Hist. [Australia] 1978 24(2): 159-173.* Comments on the significance of elections when the Presidency changes party hands. Analyzes the main tenets of Jimmy Carter's approach: moral principles, emphasis on arms control and limitation of the nuclear arms race, the reinforcement of bonds with democracies, and improved relations with the Third World. Concludes with examples of the constraints placed on foreign policy execution and a comparison with Woodrow Wilson. Documented from newspapers, journals, and addresses; 40 notes.
W. D. McIntyre

2807. Jonas, Susanne. CENTRAL AMERICA AS A THEATER OF U.S. COLD WAR POLITICS. *Latin Am. Perspectives 1982 9(3): 123-128.* Efforts by Reagan's administration to reactivate the Cold War consensus in Central America cannot succeed because of public skepticism, absence of former US preeminence, and international contradictions.
J. F. Vivian

2808. Joyce, James Avery. WAS CARTER TRAPPED OVER THE ILO? *Contemporary Rev. [Great Britain] 1978 232(1346): 129-133.* Examines the significance of President Jimmy Carter's decision to withdraw from the International Labor Organization in 1977 for American foreign policy.

2809. Kaiser, David E. VIETNAM: WAS THE SYSTEM THE SOLUTION? A REVIEW ESSAY. *Int. Security 1980 4(4): 199-218.* Review article of the US involvement in Vietnam through Leslie H. Gelb with Richard K. Betts, *The Irony of Vietnam: The System Worked* (Washington, D.C.: Brookings Inst., 1979), Richard M. Nixon, *R. N.: The Memoirs of Richard Nixon* (New York: Grosset & Dunlap, 1978), and William Shawcross, *Sideshow* (New York: Simon & Schuster, 1979).

2810. Kamins'kyi, Anatol. "EKONOMICHNA KOEKZYSTENT-SIIA" I II IMPLIKATSII DLIA VNUTRISHN'NOI SYTUATSII V SRSR [Economic coexistence and its implications for the internal situation in the USSR]. *Sučasnist [West Germany] 1973 (1): 86-99.* Discusses the proposals of President Richard M. Nixon and Henry A. Kissinger in Moscow and Peking in 1972 as a historical continuation of diplomatic relations affecting the USSR.

2811. Kaplan, Stephen S. UNITED STATES AID TO POLAND, 1957-1964: CONCERNS, OBJECTIVES AND OBSTACLES. *Western Pol. Q. 1975 28(1): 147-166.* The ascension of Wladyslaw Gomulka to power in Poland over Russian opposition in October 1956 caused the Eisenhower administration to reassess US policy toward Poland. Secretary of State John Foster Dulles backed proposals to extend aid to Poland despite strong congressional opposition. The Americans hoped to allow the Poles to be somewhat more independent of Soviet influence, but expected no dramatic breakthroughs. The total amount of the assistance, chiefly wheat shipments and farm equipment, was worth $588 million. In addition Poland was granted most favored nation trading status. The policy was continued without major changes during the Kennedy and early Johnson administrations. While it is difficult to assess whether the program was successful, the Eisenhower administration was correct in recognizing the need for a new policy. Based on government publications including the *Department of State Bulletin*; 79 notes.

G. B. McKinney

2812. Kaspi, André. CONTROVERSE: FALLAIT-IL BOMBARDER HIROSHIMA? [Debate: should the bomb have been dropped on Hiroshima?]. *Histoire [France] 1981 (32): 87-91.* Examines the significance of the use of the atomic bomb in the closing days of World War II after President Harry S. Truman returned from the Potsdam Conference. Its use was as a weapon of diplomacy, marking the beginning of the Cold War.

2813. Kaspi, André. UNITÉ EUROPÉENNE, PARTNERSHIP ATLANTIQUE [European Unity, Atlantic Partnership]. *Relations Int. [France] 1977 (11): 231-248.* Makes use of the personal archives of Jean Monnet to relate President John F. Kennedy's conception of partnership between the United States and a united Europe, first presented in his speech of 4 July 1962. Charles de Gaulle's veto of British entry into the Common Market and Kennedy's assassination doomed the plan in 1963, but there were deeper causes of the failure, including nuclear arms. That failure marked the end of an epoch in world affairs, and was the last time the United States prodded Europe to unite. R. Stromberg

2814. Kaufman, Burton I. MIDEAST MULTINATIONAL OIL, U.S. FOREIGN POLICY, AND ANTITRUST: THE 1950'S. *J. of Am. Hist. 1976 63(4): 937-959.* The Truman and Eisenhower administrations sought, through American-controlled multinational oil companies, to assure America a reliable oil supply and to prevent the spread of Soviet influence in the Third World. This policy worked admirably well in the 1950's, but it has failed in the 1970's. To use these corporations as instruments of foreign policy, Truman and Eisenhower granted the oil companies certain immunities from antitrust laws. In the process, they undermined their own case against international cartels, and may have contributed to the formation of OPEC (the Organization of Petroleum Exporting Nations). Based on US Senate documents, hearings, and secondary sources; 49 notes. W. R. Hively

2815. Kaufman, Burton I. OIL AND ANTITRUST: THE OIL CARTEL CASE AND THE COLD WAR. *Business Hist. Rev. 1977 51(1): 35-56.* The Truman administration initiated antitrust prosecution of the five largest American oil companies in 1952, seeking to force divestment of their integrated operations. However, the governmental commitment to antitrust was eventually subordinated to foreign policy requirements—specifically, to countering a perceived Soviet threat in the Middle East and to assuring the nation a cheap and plentiful supply of energy during the Cold War. Based principally on Department of Justice files; 58 notes. C. J. Pusateri

2816. Kegley, Charles W., Jr. and Wittkopf, Eugene R. THE REAGAN ADMINISTRATION'S WORLD VIEW. *Orbis 1982 26(1): 223-244.* Analyzes the world view of the Reagan administration and its effect on foreign policy during 1981-82. So far, the policy seems to be based on a global posture, anticommunism, containment of Soviet expansion either by linkage or use of military force, intervention, and "strategic consensus." The sources of foreign policy and its prospects are also discussed in detail. The authors conclude that President Reagan has not yet defined clearly the elements of his foreign policy and the means for achieving it. Based on periodical literature; 23 notes. J. W. Thacker, Jr.

2817. Kelly, Peter A. RAIDS AND NATIONAL COMMAND: MUTUALLY EXCLUSIVE! *Military Rev. 1980 60(4): 19-26.* Discusses the role of the national military and political command structure in decisionmaking about the planning and execution of military raids. Two recent raids, the Sontay prison camp rescue attempt in 1970 and the effort to free the crew of the *Mayaguez* in 1975, are good examples of raids that should not have been made and that failed largely because of the direct control over them by the national command, including the president. In future raids, the planning and control of the operations should rest not with the national command in Washington, D.C., but with the "lowest level commander capable of performing the mission." Based on government reports; 2 photos, 16 notes. D. H. Cline

2818. Kennedy, Edward M. BEYOND DETENTE. *Foreign Policy 1974 (16): 3-29.* Criticizes President Nixon's methods of achieving better relations with the USSR. For example, the tactic of developing new weapons systems for the purpose of having bargaining chips does more to increase tensions than to reduce them. Advocates five steps for the era beyond détente: 1) involve more people (congressmen, etc.) in the development of US-Soviet relations, 2) conduct this relationship in full public view, 3) emphasize a step-by-step-improvement in relations, 4) work with Soviets who are for improving relations, and seek a more sophisticated understanding about each other's domestic politics, and 5) relate the needs of US-Soviet relations to broader world problems.

R. F. Kugler

2819. Kerby, Robert L. AMERICAN MILITARY AIRLIFT DURING THE LAOTIAN CIVIL WAR, 1958-1963. *Aerospace Hist. 1977 24(1): 1-10.* Robert L. Kerby discusses the airlift operation in which he participated. His observations lead to the following conclusions: 1) conventional military forces, used in conjunction with diplomatic initiatives and covert forms of intervention, were committed in sufficient strength to affect the course of the conflict; 2) Presidents Dwight D. Eisenhower and John F. Kennedy employed show-of-force with considerable finesse; and 3) despite Kennedy's romantic enthusiasm for novel counterinsurgency tactics, the Laotian operation suggests that his appreciation of the uses of conventional military forces was more subtle and sophisticated than some historians admit. Primary sources, Air Force records; 7 photos, 27 notes. C. W. Ohrvall

2820. Kernell, Samuel. THE TRUMAN DOCTRINE SPEECH: A CASE STUDY OF THE DYNAMICS OF PRESIDENTIAL OPINION LEADERSHIP. *Social Sci. Hist. 1976 1(1): 20-44.* Was the Truman Doctrine speech of 1947 influential in the creation of a new public opinion? Using the limited opinion data available, the speech appears to have been a normal factor, hardly the dynamic force some have said. A wave of militant anti-Communism did not follow; Americans did not immediately and profoundly swing around to the view that America must play a dominant role in the world. The President's support was strongest precisely among those persons and groups who valued his opinions on other issues. Dramatic events may cause a reorientation of public thinking to a radical degree, but Presidents are not so powerful. 9 tables, fig., 34 notes. V. L. Human

2821. Kerr, Malcolm H. NIXON'S SECOND TERM: POLICY PROSPECTS IN THE MIDDLE EAST. *J. of Palestine Studies [Lebanon] 1973 2(3): 14-29.*

2822. Kessler, Francis P. KISSINGER'S LEGACY: A LATIN AMERICAN POLICY. *Current Hist. 1977 72(424): 76-78, 86-88.* Examines the evolution in US Latin American policy during the Nixon and Ford administrations while Henry A. Kissinger was Secretary of State, 1968-74; President Carter's administration is likely to follow a similar policy.

2823. Kessler, Frank. KISSINGER'S "NEW DIALOGUE" WITH LATIN AMERICA: NEW BEGINNINGS VS. REALITIES. *Midwest Q. 1975 16(2): 119-134.* Henry A. Kissinger has little familiarity with the "nuances of inter-American programs and politics," but US foreign policy in Latin America may be enhanced by Nelson A. Rockefeller, because he brings expertise in hemisphere affairs to Kissinger's interest in the area. Kissinger's "Good Partner" policy has recently increased US involvement with Latin America. Based on secondary sources.

H. S. Marks

2824. Khazanov, A. BELYI DOM I "CHERNYI KONTINENT" [The White House and the "Dark Continent"]. *Aziia i Afrika Segodnia [USSR] 1981 (9): 14-16.* Examines US attitudes toward the nations of Africa from 1978 to 1981, focusing on the dealings of Secretary of State Alexander Haig and National Security Adviser Richard Allen with African countries, and discusses the relationship between the United States and South Africa. Russian.

2825. Kimche, Jon. FABRICATING THE OIL CRISIS. *Midstream 1980 26(6): 3-6.* The federal government, including Secretary of the Treasury Michael Blumenthal and Secretary of the Department of Energy James R. Schlesinger, as well as the oil companies and the Organization of Petroleum Exporting Countries, deliberately fostered the hoax of a shortfall of crude oil when Iran decreased production in 1979.

2826. Kimche, Jon. KISSINGER DIPLOMACY AND THE ART OF LIMITED WAR. *Midstream 1974 20(9): 3-12.* Considers the Middle East.

2827. Kimche, Jon. SUPER POWERS IN THE MIDDLE EAST—BACKSTAGE. *Midstream 1975 21(6): 7-13.* Analyzes the failure of Henry Kissinger's diplomatic mission to the Middle East on 22 March 1975 and urges Russia and the United States to ensure a balance of power between Israeli and Arab interests.

2828. King, Larry L. MACHISMO IN THE WHITE HOUSE: LBJ AND VIETNAM. *Am. Heritage 1976 27(5): 8-13, 98-101.* Lyndon B. Johnson was an old-fashioned man, shaped by America's strength and destiny, who believed firmly in the survival of the fittest. Stressing strength, LBJ was insecure and obsessed by the spectre of failure. An enthusiastic and consistent Cold Warrior, he believed in a worldwide, monolithic Communist conspiracy. His pride and ego could not accept the unpopularity of his policies in Vietnam. He never understood where or how he had gone wrong. 6 illus.   J. F. Paul

2829. Kintner, William R. THE UNITED STATES AND THE IRANIAN REVOLUTION. *J. of Social, Pol. and Econ. Studies 1981 6(4): 379-385.* Discusses US-Iranian relations from 1978 to 1981, with special emphasis on President Jimmy Carter's role in bringing about the Iranian revolution.

2830. Kirkpatrick, Jeane J. ESTABLISHING A VIABLE HUMAN RIGHTS POLICY. *World Affairs 1981 143(4): 323-334.* Describes the human rights policies of the Jimmy Carter administration which, though highly moralistic in aim, alienated nondemocratic but friendly nations, enabled anti-Western opposition groups to come to power in Iran and Nicaragua, and reduced worldwide American influence.

2831. Kirkpatrick, Jeane J. U.S. SECURITY & LATIN AMERICA. *Commentary 1981 71(1): 29-40.* The ideology embodied in Zbigniew Brzezinski's *Between Two Ages,* the two Linowitz reports, and *The Southern Connection,* a report issued by the Institute for Policy Studies Ad Hoc Working Group on Latin America, all of which abandoned the Monroe Doctrine for a global, rather than hemispheric, approach, determined the Carter administration's policy toward Latin America; the resulting commitment to "change" in Latin America has led to a Cuban-backed takeover in Nicaragua, the probability of another in El Salvador, and, but for a military coup, the accession of Hernan Siles Zuazo, strongly Communist- and Castro-connected, in Bolivia.

2832. Kissinger, Henry. U.S. SECRETARY OF STATE HENRY KISSINGER'S PRESS CONFERENCE OCTOBER 25, 1973. *IDOC Middle East Q. 1974 1(1): 42-49.* Discusses US and USSR diplomacy in the October War (1973).

2833. Klare, Michael T. LA "VIA" DEL GOLPE VENNE DA WASHINGTON [The "way" to the coup comes from Washington]. *Ponte [Italy] 1973 29(10): 1378-1398.* The Nixon administration and multinational corporations were responsible for the eventual fall of the Popular Unity government in Chile in September 1973 by blocking credit and suffocating the economy as a preparatory phase to military intervention.

2834. Knapp, Manfred. DIE DEUTSCHLANDPROBLEM UND DIE URSPRUNG DES EUROPISCHEN WIEDERAUFBAUPROGRAMMS: EINE AUSEINANDERSETZUNG MIT JOHN GIMBELS UNTERSUCHUNG "THE ORIGINS OF THE MARSHALL PLAN" [The problem of Germany and the causes of the European reconstruction program: an examination of John Gimbel's *The Origins of the Marshall Plan]. Politische Vierteljahresschrift [West Germany] 1978 19(1): 48-65.* US policies with regard to Germany after 1948 cannot be considered in isolation from Europolitics and the European reconstruction program inaugurated and financed by the Marshall Plan. Material recently made available has been studied in John Gimbel's *The Origins of the Marshall Plan.* Gimbel wrongly denies any intention by the United States to regard the Marshall Plan as a deterrent against possible Soviet aggression in the future. However, the Marshall Plan was adopted because it would assure the reestablishment of a strong, free capitalist society in Western Europe, in which Germany would have the key position, and because it would create a strong bloc favorable to the West. Diagram, 64 notes.   S. Bonnycastle/S

2835. Knapp, Manfred. EIN "BERLINER" NAMENS JOHN F. KENNEDY: ZUR DEUTSCHLAND UND EUROPA-POLITIK DER KENNEDY-ADMINISTRATION [A "Berliner" named John F. Kennedy: On the German and European policy of the Kennedy administration]. *Frankfurter Hefte [West Germany] 1974 29(5): 326-336.* Reviews the German and European policies of the United States under Kennedy, with special attention to the problem of West Berlin, coming to the conclusion that the US-Europe relationship was smoother then than under Nixon and Kissinger.

2836. Knight, Jonathan. AMERICAN INTERNATIONAL GUARANTEES FOR THE STRAITS: PRELUDE TO THE TRUMAN DOCTRINE. *Middle Eastern Studies [Great Britain] 1977 13(2): 241-250.* Harry S. Truman proposed internationalization of the Turkish Straits in 1945. Believing that such waterways should be open to free passage, thus tying industrial and commercial interests together, somewhat like the rivers of America, he hoped that such free trade would serve the interests of international peace. The president's proposal failed because 1) Turkey doubted US ability to prevent Russian control of the Straits, 2) the USSR opposed any arrangement which denied it strategic control of the Straits, 3) State Department experts doubted that either the administration or the country was prepared to accept such obligations, and 4) the president was so preoccupied in 1945 that he did nothing to secure support for his proposal. Based on *Foreign Relations of the United States* and secondary works; 21 notes.   K. M. Bailor

2837. Knight, Jonathan. AMERICAN STATECRAFT AND THE 1946 BLACK SEA STRAITS CONTROVERSY. *Pol. Sci. Q. 1975 90(3): 451-475.* Jonathan Knight explores American diplomacy during the 1946 Black Sea Straits controversy between Turkey and the Soviet Union. He argues that while the Truman administration took forceful measures, including the deployment of naval forces, to bolster Turkey's position, it also was careful to refrain from any direct military confrontation with the Soviets.   J

2838. Kohl, Wilfrid L. THE NIXON-KISSINGER FOREIGN POLICY SYSTEM AND U.S.-EUROPEAN RELATIONS: PATTERNS OF POLICY MAKING. *World Pol. 1975 28(1): 1-43.* No single model adequately explains the American foreign policymaking process. At least six models are required, singly or in some combination, to understand recent American foreign policy formation under the Nixon Administration. The six models are: democratic politics, organizational process/bureaucratic politics, the royal-court model, multiple advocacy, groupthink, and shared images or mind-sets. After a review of the rules of the foreign policy game in Washington and the main elements of the Nixon-Kissinger National Security Council system, the article seeks to apply the models to a number of cases in recent American policy making toward Europe. U.S.-Soviet relations, the "Year of Europe," and Nixon's New Economic Policy of August 1971 are examined as cases of royal-court decision making. A second category of cases exhibits mixed patterns of decision making: SALT, the Berlin negotiations, U.S. troops in Europe, MBFR, and US trade policy. Bureaucratic variables alone explained policy outcomes in international economic policy-making in the autumn of 1971, and an organizational process model was found to be dominant generally in the formation of recent international monetary policy, led by the Treasury Department. The conclusion considers the relationships between the models and certain kinds of policies. J

2839. Kolko, Gabriel. L'AMMINISTRAZIONE REAGAN A UN-'IMPASSE [The Reagan administration at an impasse]. *Ponte [Italy] 1982 38(1-2): 69-79.* President Ronald Reagan started with the intention of radically modifying both the US economic policy and the world balance of forces, but he has only succeeded in leading the country to an impasse which seriously limits his foreign policy options. Italian.

2840. Kolko, Gabriel. STRATEGIA DEL GOVERNO NIXON NEL VIETNAM [Strategy of the Nixon Administration in Vietnam]. *Ponte [Italy] 1973 29(2-3): 276-300.* Discusses US military and economic aid to the Republic of South Vietnam after the Paris agreement of 1973.

2841. Kolodziej, Edward A. CONGRESS AND FOREIGN POLICY: THE NIXON YEARS. *Pro. of the Acad. of Pol. Sci. 1975 32(1): 167-179.* Increased Congressional participation in foreign policy formulation during the Nixon Administration brought about the War Powers Act, led to amendment of the US role in world politics, and raised serious questions about the applicability of the Cold War thesis to modern international relations, 1968-72.

2842. Kolodziej, Edward A. FOREIGN POLICY AND THE POLITICS OF INTERDEPENDENCE: THE NIXON PRESIDENCY. *Polity 1976 9(2): 121-157.* The Nixon foreign policy has been subject to varying interpretations. In a recent issue of *Polity* (Spring 1976) [see abstract 14A:7275] it was analyzed in terms of overriding foreign-policy objectives, such as changes in the balance of power or creation of a concert of nations. Kolodziej argues here that conventional analysis in terms of foreign-policy objectives or decisional processes fails to provide adequate explanation. Constituting a fundamental departure from previous administrations, the Nixonian conception is seen as a unified process of domestic and international politics usable by the presidential player as he chooses. Kolodziej evaluates the effectiveness of the policy for controlling international crises and building a workable global security order. J

2843. Koniakhina, T. V. "POMOSHCH" TURTSII PO DOKTRINE TRUMENA ["Aid" to Turkey according to Truman's doctrine]. *Narody Azii i Afriki [USSR] 1975 (3): 135-143.* President Harry S. Truman's 12 March 1947 address to Congress on the course of the US foreign policy, the Truman Doctrine, had an anti-Communist, anti-Soviet, and expansionist character. Truman asked Congress to assign $400 million in foreign aid to Turkey and Greece, with the condition that the countries that receive US aid allow American oversight on how the aid was used. His request was approved, $100 million was assigned to Turkey, and the American-Turkish aid treaty was signed on 12 July 1947. Describes the strategic military importance of Turkey to Great Britain and the United States, the notes and discussions between Great Britain and the United States concerning Turkey, and the discussions in the United States about military and/or economic aid to Turkey. Also mentions the false American reasons for the proclamation of the Truman Doctrine—the fantastic allegations concerning the USSR's aggressive plans, and the real reasons—the Middle East's oil fields. Based on the latest publications of documents of the US State Department, *Foreign Relations of the United States, volume V.; The Near East and Africa* (Washington, 1971); 12 notes. L. Kalinowski

2844. Korb, Lawrence J. THE ARMS CONTROL IMPLICATIONS OF THE CARTER DEFENSE BUDGET. *Naval War College Rev. 1978 31(2): 3-16.* Historical evidence suggests that the basic policies of the full term of a President can be deduced from an examination and analysis of his initial budget. The arms control philosophy of the present administration is examined here. J

2845. Korb, Lawrence J. THE ISSUES AND COSTS OF THE NEW UNITED STATES NUCLEAR POLICY. *Naval War Coll. R. 1974 27(3): 28-41.* "The changes in strategic defense policy recently articulated by Secretary of Defense Schlesinger have given rise to considerable speculation on the relative strengths found in United States and Soviet nuclear arsenals. The intrinsic complexities of measuring throw weight, accuracy, and both warhead and launch vehicle number, further complicated by the difficulty of President Nixon and Premier Brezhnev in achieving any significant progress toward limiting the new technology, have made such speculation relatively subjective and open to a wide variety of opinion. Unfortunately, any disequilibrium in the nuclear equation is bound to be one that, although created in the name of national security, makes the actors on both sides feel progressively less secure." J

2846. Korb, Lawrence J. THE JOINT CHIEFS OF STAFF: ACCESS AND IMPACT IN FOREIGN POLICY. *Policy Studies J. 1974 3(2): 170-173.* The Joint Chiefs of Staff have modified US foreign policy "because of their access to both the executive and legislative branches." S

2847. Kousoulas, D. George. THE TRUMAN DOCTRINE AND THE STALIN-TITO RIFT: A REAPPRAISAL. *South Atlantic Q. 1973 72(3): 427-439.* The prevailing view in the West was, and still is, that the Communist guerrilla campaign unleashed in Greece in 1946 was merely part of a Soviet plan to extend Moscow's control to the shores of the eastern Mediterranean. However, the evidence now indicates that Joseph Stalin did not favor another round of armed conflict initiated by the Communist Party in Greece. Josip Tito supported Communist operations in Greece in accordance with traditional cooperation between Athens and Belgrade. "A friendly government in Greece appeared to be almost a matter of survival for Tito's regime. The Truman Doctrine with its prospect of American presence in Greece made Stalin concerned with Tito's adventure. Stalin's effort however to split the Central Committee failed, most of the members siding with Tito. The American Government offered economic assistance in ways that would not compromise Tito." E. P. Stickney

2848. Kraus, Jon. AMERICAN FOREIGN POLICY IN AFRICA. *Current Hist. 1981 80(464): 97-100, 129, 138.* Explores the Jimmy Carter administration's policies in Africa and the results of their implementation and examines the validity of the criticism offered by conservatives.

2849. Krause, Walter. LA ALIANZA PARA EL PROGRESO [The Alliance for Progress]. *J. of Inter-American Studies 1963 5(1): 67-82.* The Alliance for Progress set up at the Punta del Este Conference, under the leadership of American President John F. Kennedy in August 1961, was in many respects a reaction to the emergence of a Communist regime in Cuba. The Alliance provided for an enlightened program of economic development, but required an enormous degree of cooperation and commitment both by the United States, which would provide the money, and the states of Latin America, which would provide the effort.

2850. Kulik, Sergei. "GIGANTSKOE FIASKO" TSRU [The CIA's "gigantic fiasco"]. *Aziia i Afrika Segodnia [USSR] 1982 (5): 16-20.* Discusses the involvement of South Africa and the Central Intelligence Agency in anti-Angolan and anti-Namibian movements, 1974-81, and comments on the purpose and activities of National Union for the Complete Independence of Angola (UNITA). Russian.

2851. Kulinich, M. A. VOIENNO-POLITYCHNA STRATEGIA SSHA V ZONI INDIYS'KOHO OKEANU (1970-1979 RR.) [US military-political strategy in the Indian Ocean zone, 1970-79]. *Ukrains'kyi Istorychnyi Zhurnal [USSR] 1980 (2): 74-81.* The fact that some 48 countries adjoin the Indian Ocean makes it one of the most important geopolitical zones. US foreign policy and military strategy for the Indian Ocean zone are closely connected with economic and political interests: strategic interest in the oil-bearing countries in the Persian gulf region; large-volume trade; security of sea routes; and the physical presence to threaten new independent states and hinder national liberation movements. The Nixon doctrine, the Ford doctrine and the Carter administration's new approach to the security of the US interests in the Indian Ocean are cited. Despite some modernization and concretization in US military-political strategy in the Indian Ocean, the continuity of its determining principles and elements has been preserved. Documents; US and Soviet press articles; 26 notes. I. Krushelnyckyj

2852. Kunina, A. E. NOVYE ISSLEDOVANIIA SOVETSKIKH ISTORIKOV O VNESHNEI POLITIKE SSHA [Soviet historians' new research on US foreign policy]. *Novaia i Noveishaia Istoriia [USSR] 1972 (6): 150-157.* In the late 1940's and early 1950's Soviet historians considered only limited periods of US foreign policy but in the 1960's they adopted a more extensive chronological and theoretical approach. Regional, biographical, and historiographical studies have emerged as well as works considering the struggle of the American nation against the imperialism of the government's foreign policy. Recent important studies have examined US foreign policy, 1945-71, neocolonialism in the 1960's, John F. Kennedy's presidency, US attitudes to European problems, and relations between the USSR and the United States. Soviet secondary sources; 8 notes.   L. Smith/S

2853. Kwak, Tae-Hwan. U.S.-SOVIET RELATIONS: TRUMAN'S CONTAINMENT POLICY REVISITED. *Korea & World Affairs* *[South Korea] 1980 4(4): 607-622.* Examines the US policy of containment of the USSR from the proclamation of the Truman Doctrine in 1947 to 1980. Reviews George F. Kennan's writings on American foreign policy, which championed the cause of realism in foreign policy, as opposed to the idealistic, legal-moralistic strain, which has predominated in the United States.

2854. LaFeber, Walter. KISSINGER AND ACHESON: THE SECRETARY OF STATE AND THE COLD WAR. *Pol. Sci. Q. 1977* *92(2): 189-197.* Both Dean Acheson and Henry A. Kissinger attempted to translate their personal world views into a new global order. Despite their similar grounding in 19th-century European diplomacy, their most important legacy might well become their policies toward non-Western, revolutionary areas. Both men valued order more than justice. Acheson's policies rested on an analysis of capitalist needs, while Kissinger's fatal flaw was his neglect of economics. Thus Kissinger lost the domestic consensus that was created by Acheson's Truman Doctrine. A successful Secretary of State must be a partisan in domestic politics as well as a diplomatic troubleshooter. Secondary sources; 27 notes.
                                                          W. R. Hively

2855. Lange, Peter and Vannicelli, Maurizio. CARTER IN THE ITALIAN MAZE. *Foreign Policy 1978-79 (33): 161-173.* The Carter administration is continuing Henry A. Kissinger's policy of opposing participation of the Italian Communist Party (PCI) in the government of Italy. Italy's social and economic problems probably cannot be solved without Communist participation. America must adopt a policy more consistent with Italian realities, recognizing that the Italian people must decide the future of the PCI. A policy of "critical coexistence" (accepting the legitimacy of the PCI while continuing to disagree with it) would serve this purpose, and would encourage the party to continue its independent evolution.   T. L. Powers

2856. Laqueur, Walter and Luttwak, Edward N. KISSINGER & THE YOM KIPPUR WAR. *Commentary 1974 58(3): 33-40.* Discusses two versions of Henry Kissinger's actions in the Yom Kippur War, October 1973.   S

2857. Laqueur, Walter. KISSINGER AND HIS CRITICS. *Commentary 1980 69(2): 57-61.* Discusses Henry A. Kissinger's diplomacy and his book, *The White House Years,* and defends the book against its critics; 1969-70's.

2858. Laqueur, Walter. THE WORLD AND PRESIDENT CARTER. *Commentary 1978 65(2): 56-63.* Discusses the current attitudes toward President Carter's foreign policy, specifically his administration's stands on the human rights issue.

2859. Laroche, Jean. CONTROVERSES SUR L'ORIGINE ET LES CAUSES DE LA GUERRE FROIDE [Controversies on the origin and causes of the Cold War]. *Études Int. [Canada] 1975 6(1): 47-65.* Examines some of the standard interpretations of the Cold War, classifying them into traditionalist, revisionist, or realist schools. The traditionalist school attributes the Cold War to Soviet expansion. Though the revisionist school has several subdivisions, all revisionist studies point to the United States as the responsible party in bringing on the Cold War. For some, American culpability lies in an inappropriate response to Soviet expansion; for others, in President Harry S. Truman's failure to cooperate with Stalin; and for the extremists, American expansionism was the causative force. The realist school suggests that the Cold War resulted from incomprehensible circumstances which caused a conflict between two modes of thought: American universalism and Soviet zones of influence. 93 notes.   J. F. Harrington, Jr./S

2860. Lavergne, Bernard. L'INQUALIFIABLE AGGRESSION MILITAIRE DES ETATS-UNIS CONTRE LE CAMBODGE, ORDONNÉE PAR M. NIXON EN VIOLATION DE LA CONSTITUTION AMÉRICAINE [The abominable military aggression by the United States against Cambodia, ordered by Nixon in violation of the American constitution]. *Année Pol. et Écon. [France] 1973 46(234): 221-225.* Condemns the bombing of Cambodia ordered by President Nixon without the knowledge of his own Secretary of State, or indeed of anybody except a handful of people already committed to the venture. Expresses pity for the American people for having a presidential system which permits an unworthy incumbent to make war and peace at will, and to violate his formal campaign promise to end the war. Americans are rightly indignant over Watergate, but they should be even more exercised over his action in Cambodia, and the fact that no ruler since Hitler has been responsible for the loss of so many lives.   G. E. Orchard

2861. Leacock, Ruth. JFK, BUSINESS, AND BRAZIL. *Hispanic Am. Hist. Rev. 1979 59(4): 636-673.* President John F. Kennedy's Alliance for Progress was launched without business support on the assumption that the Communist threat would come from the poor in Latin America. When leftist João Goulart became president of Brazil, this policy began to change. The expropriation of an ITT subsidiary by the Brazilian state of Rio Grande do Sul, the suggested nationalization of AMFORP, which wished to sell to Brazil, and Brazil's attempts to control iron properties of Hanna Mining Corporation were regarded as Communistic, anti-United States moves. The Kennedy administration became more business-oriented in its dealings with Brazil. US businessmen and the CIA played a financial part in the 1962 elections in Brazil in an attempt to overthrow Goulart. The roles of US Ambassador Lincoln Gordon and ITT president Harold S. Geneen are discussed. 128 notes.
                                                        B. D. Johnson

2862. Leacock, Ruth. "PROMOTING DEMOCRACY": THE UNITED STATES AND BRAZIL, 1964-68. *Prologue 1981 13(2):* *77-99.* Discusses the American effort to promote democracy in Brazil during the Johnson administration. In 1964 conditions seemed ideal for the encouragement of democratic institutions in Brazil, but during 1964-68 Brazil moved steadily toward a more authoritarian state. The American failure to promote democracy in Brazil is attributed in part to a lack of a clear definition or plan of action, a lack of understanding of the Brazilian military, and a general unwillingness to use economic aid as a leverage in bringing about political change when it could have been effectively used. 13 photos, 81 notes.   M. A. Kascus

2863. Lees, Loraine M. THE AMERICAN DECISION TO ASSIST TITO, 1948-1949. *Diplomatic Hist. 1978 2(4): 407-422.* Josip Tito's dispute with Joseph Stalin came to the attention of the West with great suddenness in June 1948 when the Cominform expelled Tito and called for his overthrow. The State Department Policy Planning Staff under George F. Kennan at first advised a wait-and-see posture, but by February 1949 the same body was advocating a quiet relaxation of export restrictions and even the removal of prohibitions on the shipment of munitions. In September the United States and Yugoslavia announced a politically and economically important agreement involving the sale of a steel booming mill. American foreign policy toward Tito, while based in part on hopes which remained unrealized, might with profit have been taken as a model in our policy toward Mao and Ho Chi Minh. Primary sources; 57 notes.   L. W. Van Wyk

2864. Lei, Joanna C. and Cheng Yu-p'ing. LUN MEI KUO KUO HUI CHIH LI FA CHIEN TU CHUNG MEI KUAN HSI CHUNG CHÜN SHIH SHOU YÜ CHIH KO AN YEN CHIU. [American congressional oversight: the case of American arms sales to the Republic of China]. *Ssu yü Yen (Thought and Word) [Taiwan] 1982 19(5): 13-38.* The US Congress has the power of oversight to induce the State Department to fully effect the Taiwan Relations Act (US, 1979), which provides for arms sales to meet the Republic of China's defense needs. Based on the Taiwan Relations Act; biblio., 70 notes.   J. A. Krompart

2865. Leitenberg, Milton. PRESIDENTIAL DIRECTIVE (P.D.) 59: UNITED STATES NUCLEAR WEAPON TARGETING POLICY. *J. of Peace Res. [Norway] 1981 18(4): 309-317.* At least since 1960, US nuclear weapons targeting has been primarily countermilitary and not directed in the first instance against the cities of the USSR. Focuses on the research leading up to Presidential Directive No. 59 of the Carter administration.   J/S

2866. Lellouche, Pierre. BREAKING THE RULES WITHOUT QUITE STOPPING THE BOMB: EUROPEAN VIEWS. *Int. Organization 1981 35(1): 39-58.* Beginning with the Ford administration policy and continuing with the Carter nonproliferation policy, a major nuclear controversy opposed the American and European nuclear suppliers throughout the 1970's. The first area of controversy was the question of conditions for technological transfers to the Third World, and the area of the plutonium economy. Most of the problems raised in the 1970's are still open. Major points of disagreement remain: full scope safeguards, the question of breeder reactors, and plutonium economy. The major uncertainty for the future will be whether nuclear energy as a whole will remain in depression or grow again.   J/S

2867. Lentz, Jean-Jacques. REGARDS SUR LA REPUBLIQUE IMPERIALE [Views of the imperial republic]. *Esprit [France] 1974 (3): 411-432.* Reviews the foreign policies and theories of Henry Kissinger. The period since 1968 has seen a reversal of the assumptions held in world affairs by the Kennedy administration. Instead of the foreign policy of the "American mission," the Kissinger foreign policy is based on cooperation with other nations. Realism, not paranoia, marks the Kissinger policy, and American influence is at an all-time high.   G. F. Jewsbury

2868. Levering, Ralph B. THE OVERSELLING OF HENRY WALLACE. *Rev. in Am. Hist. 1977 5(4): 554-559.* Review article prompted by Richard J. Walton's *Henry Wallace, Harry Truman, and the Cold War* (New York: The Viking Pr., 1976).

2869. Lewis, Anthony Marc. THE BLIND SPOT OF U.S. FOREIGN INTELLIGENCE. *J. of Communication 1976 26(1): 44-55.* Discusses the problem of ethnocentrism in the semantics of foreign intelligence reports of the Central Intelligence Agency, emphasizing psychological and political miscalculations of events in Vietnam 1954-63.

2870. Lipset, Seymour Martin and Schneider, William. CARTER VS. ISRAEL: WHAT THE POLLS REVEAL. *Commentary 1977 64(5): 21-29.* Carter administration interest in American public opinion on the Middle East conflict increased as the administration began to pressure Israel and moved closer to confrontation with it, while leaning toward support of the concept of an independent Palestinian state. Surveys since 1948 have never shown more American public support for Arabs than Israelis. Recent polls show that most Americans support Israel and that support is strongest among the well-educated and socially influential. Confrontation with Israel would deeply divide American society and endanger the reelection prospects of those responsible.
                                                            S. R. Herstein

2871. Lissakers, Karin. MONEY AND MANIPULATION. *Foreign Policy 1981 (44): 107-126.* The move in 1980 by the Carter administration to freeze all Iranian financial assets in the United States and in American banks abroad was motivated not so much in order to force release of the Americans held hostage in Iran, as to forestall the major currency and banking crisis that might have resulted from the sudden withdrawal of those funds from American banks. The Iranian threat and the drastic US response shattered the illusion that petrodollars were nonpolitical.   L. J. Klass

2872. Lo, Clarence Y. H. CIVILIAN POLICY MAKERS AND MILITARY OBJECTIVES: A CASE STUDY OF THE U.S. OFFENSIVE TO WIN THE KOREAN WAR. *J. of Pol. and Military Sociol. 1979 7(2): 229-242.* The civilians who directed the Truman administration's foreign policy formulated the "pragmatic doctrine" (Janowitz, 1960), which emphasized alliances and limited war for political objectives. Nevertheless, civilian policy makers during the Korean War supported some of the "absolutist" positions of General MacArthur. These included rolling back Communism in Korea, seeking a decisive military victory, ignoring allies' calls for restraint, and valuing displays of military strength. This article utilizes recently declassified government documents to argue that civilian policy makers favored and directly approved MacArthur's offensive to the Chinese border, which brought on a Chinese counterattack, with disastrous results for the U.N. forces. The evidence does not support the standard interpretation that attributes the offensive

to MacArthur's insubordination and a breakdown of civilian control of the military.   J

2873. Loaeza, Soledad. HENRY KISSINGER: DE LA AMENAZA COMO INSTRUMENTO PARA LA PAZ [Henry Kissinger: Of threat as an instrument for peace]. *Foro Int. [Mexico] 1976 17(2): 180-214.* Examines the dynamics of US foreign policy under Henry A. Kissinger and discusses the cases of Angola, Vietnam, and the Middle East. Primary and secondary sources; 56 notes.   D. A. Franz

2874. Lobban, Richard. AMERICAN MERCENARIES IN RHODESIA. *J. of Southern African Affairs 1978 3(3): 319-325.* Discusses the recruitment of US mercenary soldiers and their processing into the Rhodesian armed forces. Contends that the Carter government has supported the Smith government by allowing illegal recruitment of Americans to fight in the Rhodesian forces. Based on newspaper accounts; 35 notes.   L. W. Truschel

2875. Lockhart, Charles. THE VARYING FORTUNES OF INCREMENTAL COMMITMENT: AN INQUIRY INTO THE CUBAN AND SOUTHEAST ASIAN CASES. *Int. Studies Q. 1975 19(1): 46-66.* Compares John F. Kennedy's handling of the Cuban Missile Crisis (1962) and Lyndon B. Johnson's handling of the Vietnam War (1964-68). Both situations are examples of incremental commitment. Tries to account for Kennedy's success and Johnson's failure. 5 notes.
                                                            G. J. Boughton

2876. Lockwood, Edgar. THE FUTURE OF THE CARTER POLICY TOWARD SOUTHERN AFRICA. *Issue: A Q. J. of Opinion 1977 7(4): 11-16.* Assesses the Carter administration's foreign policy toward Southern Africa as one of economic interests, based on promoting capitalism and defeating militancy; compares Kennedy policy and asserts that power politic tactics will no longer work with developing nations.

2877. Loeb, Larry M. JUPITER MISSILES IN EUROPE: A MEASURE OF PRESIDENTIAL POWER. *World Affairs 1976 139(1): 27-39.* Discusses presidential influence in military strategy and NATO in the placing of Jupiter missiles in Europe 1957-63, emphasizing the power of presidents Dwight D. Eisenhower and John F. Kennedy.

2878. Loescher, G. D. US HUMAN RIGHTS POLICY AND INTERNATIONAL FINANCIAL INSTITUTIONS. *World Today [Great Britain] 1977 33(12): 453-463.* The Carter administration, having shown that its foreign policy is dictated to a large extent by human rights, is developing a systematic policy on participation of human rights violators in international financial institutions.

2879. Logue, Cal M. and Patton, John H. FROM AMBIGUITY TO DOGMA: THE RHETORICAL SYMBOLS OF LYNDON B. JOHNSON ON VIETNAM. *Southern Speech Communication J. 1982 47(3): 310-329.* Analyzes Lyndon B. Johnson's rhetorical strategy in defense of his policies in Vietnam.

2880. López Segrera, Francisco. LA POLITICA DEL IMPERIALISMO YANQUI HACIA CUBA DE EISENHOWER A REAGAN [Yankee imperialist policy toward Cuba from Eisenhower to Reagan]. *Casa de las Américas [Cuba] 1982 22(131): 22-33.* Traces the US policy of nonrecognition and, therefore, containment of the Cuban Revolution by seven administrations. After the failure of its policy of military aggression and economic blockade, the United States persisted in dealing with Cuba, a sovereign and independent nation, on the basis of strength and not on that of equality. This attitude, however, does not deter Cuba from pursuing its internationalistic foreign policy or from responding to the conflict with the United States as an equal. Based on opinion polls from the United States and other primary sources.   J. V. Coutinho

2881. Lowenthal, Abraham F. LATIN AMERICA: A NOT-SO-SPECIAL RELATIONSHIP. *Foreign Policy 1978 (32): 107-126.* The Carter administration has made a commendable start in improving US-Latin American relations by respecting the sovereignty and interests of the nations of that region. In the economic realm, considered of prime importance by the Latin American states, there has been little improvement. To solidify hemispheric amity, the administration must effect a fundamental change in the international economic order, accommodating the claims and aspirations of Latin American and other emerging countries, despite the "painful adjustment" such an alteration demands of the industrialized world. 4 notes.   T. L. Powers

2882. Lozinov, D.   EVOLUTION OF THE "NEW DIALOGUE." *Int. Affairs [USSR] 1975 (4): 49-57.* Discusses recent trends in US foreign policy toward Latin America, 1972-74, emphasizing the role of Secretary of State Henry A. Kissinger and the Organization of American States.

2883. Lun, Ngoh Geok.   TRUMAN AND CONTAINMENT: THE RATIONALE AND APPLICATION OF THE TRUMAN DOCTRINE. *J. of the Hist. Soc. [Singapore] 1978: 63-68.* Discusses the transformation in US foreign policy after 1945 under President Truman, from its extremes of isolationism and total warfare to a strategy of "Cold War" and "Containment" to cope with the rising threat of the USSR's expansionism.

2884. MacDonald, William W.   HENRY KISSINGER: THE MAN, THE MYSTIQUE, AND THE FOREIGN POLICY. *Res. Studies 1975 43(4): 264-276.* Discusses recent writings about Secretary of State Henry A. Kissinger and his foreign policy.

2885. Madar, Daniel.   PATRONAGE, POSITION, AND POLICY PLANNING: S/P AND SECRETARY KISSINGER. *J. of Pol. 1980 42(4): 1065-1084.* While Henry A. Kissinger's term as Secretary of State was characterized by secretive centralization and a highly personal treatment of those issues interesting him, the State Department's Policy Planning staff thrived under his direction. The planning function had been ignored by Dean Rusk and William P. Rogers, but Kissinger brought both key personnel, including Winston Lord as Director of Policy Planning, and the organizational structure of the National Security Council with him to the State Department. During the Kissinger era, the Policy Planning staff had nearly complete access to both the Secretary and the Department's information network, displacing bureau officials, and played a major role in the writing and editing of significant policy documents and speeches. 36 notes.   A. W. Novitsky

2886. Mader, Julius.   DIE SUBVERSION ALS MITTEL DER AMERIKANISCHEN AUSSENPOLITIK [Subversion as a means of the foreign policy of the United States]. *Deutsche Aussenpolitik [East Germany] 1962 7(1): 92-99.* Since the end of World War II the State Department, the Pentagon, and the CIA have concentrated their efforts on anti-Communist propaganda in Latin America, Asia, Africa, and Europe. The Peace Corps founded by President John F. Kennedy in 1961 is a disguised effort to spread American interests.

2887. Magubane, Bernard.   WHAT IS KISSINGER UP TO IN SOUTH AFRICA? *Freedomways 1976 16(3): 162-171.* Reviews Henry A. Kissinger's 1976 tour through Africa and the USA's general shift in foreign policy 1974-76.

2888. Maher, Theodore James.   THE KENNEDY AND JOHNSON RESPONSES TO LATIN AMERICAN COUPS D'ÉTAT. *World Affairs 1968 131(3): 184-198.* The threat of coups d'état in Latin America has posed a vexing dilemma for the United States. Traces the development of US foreign policy in the John F. Kennedy and Lyndon B. Johnson administrations (1961-69) with regard to their willingness to interfere in governmental processes in Latin America.

2889. Mahler, Oldřich.   POMĚR SIL A STRATEGIE USA V 70. LETECH [The relationship of US strength to strategy in the 1970's]. *Hist. a Vojenství [Czechoslovakia] 1980 29(6): 69-88.* The US strategy, elaborated during Carter's administration, is nothing but a mixture of doctrinal theses lacking political balance and realistic evaluation of the international situation. Its goal of military dominance is out of reach. The military policy of the 1980's replicates the unrealized plans of the early 1970's. The "new" doctrine also represents a menace to world peace and security, and returns to the Cold War. Secondary sources; 2 charts, 28 notes.   G. E. Pergl

2890. Maitland, Ian.   ONLY THE BEST AND THE BRIGHTEST? *Asian Affairs 1976 3(4): 263-272.* "Seeks to evoke something of the elements of the Vietnam era by recalling the views as to the stakes involved in Vietnam that were held in late 1964 and early 1965 by Neil

Sheehan," David Halberstam and Malcolm Browne. Concludes that "the argument that the acquiescence of Congress and the public in the US Vietnam policy was engineered by Executive Branch deception does not withstand examination." 29 notes.   E. P. Stickney

2891. Mark, Eduard.   CHARLES E. BOHLEN AND THE ACCEPTABLE LIMITS OF SOVIET HEGEMONY IN EASTERN EUROPE: A MEMORANDUM OF 18 OCTOBER 1945. *Diplomatic Hist. 1979 3(2): 201-213.* Charles E. Bohlen's memorandum indicates that as late as October 1945 the US State Department recognized that the USSR had a legitimate right to a secure western frontier and expected Soviet domination of the foreign relations of Eastern European countries. US policy did not harden against the Soviets until 1946 when Soviet totalitarian designs in Eastern Europe became apparent. Based on archival and published primary sources; 31 notes.   S

2892. Mark, Eduard.   "TODAY HAS BEEN A HISTORICAL ONE": HARRY S. TRUMAN'S DIARY OF THE POTSDAM CONFERENCE. *Diplomatic Hist. 1980 4(3): 317-326.* Contains the text of a hitherto-unpublished diary kept by President Harry S. Truman (1884-1972) while at the Potsdam Conference in 1945. Included in it are the president's comments on communism, the atomic bomb, Soviet dictator Joseph Stalin, British Prime Minister Winston Churchill, and other topics and personalities. Text of a primary document; 23 notes.
                                                                T. L. Powers

2893. Markowitz, Arthur A.   HUMANITARIANISM VERSUS RESTRICTIONISM: THE UNITED STATES AND THE HUNGARIAN REFUGEES. *Int. Migration Rev. 1973 7(1): 46-59.* Discusses Congressional attempts to subvert the Eisenhower administration's humanitarian immigration policy toward refugees from Hungary in 1956-57; considers the role of US public opinion.

2894. Marsot, Alain-Gerard.   BACKGROUND TO THE AMERICAN INTERVENTION IN CAMBODIA: SIHANOUK'S OVERTHROW. *Asian Profile [Hong Kong] 1973 1(1): 75-90.* Examines the overthrow of Prince Norodom Sihanouk and the 1970 American intervention in Cambodia. Although President Richard M. Nixon announced that the limited American incursions into Cambodia were solely to interdict North Vietnamese military supply lines and sanctuaries, the real reason for this action was a futile effort to sustain the tottering government of Lon Nol. During the French and early American phases of the post-World War II conflicts in Southeast Asia, Prince Sihanouk had succeeded in steering a neutralist path and avoiding military involvement. Sihanouk successfully played the role of *deva raja* (god king), nationalistic leader, and master politician. Lon Nol, his chief lieutenant, Sirik Matak, and Son Ngoc Thanh, leader of the Khumers Serei (Free Khumers) with the encouragement and assistance of the United States Central Intelligence Agency, engineered the coup d'etat. American efforts to depose the Cambodian leader, who seemed either unwilling or unable to forestall the North Vietnamese and Khumers Rouge (Cambodian communist troops) and the military invasion, brought the Cambodian nation into the conflict they had previously avoided. Secondary sources; 73 notes.   S. H. Frank

2895. Martin, Ben L.   THE NEW "OLD CHINA HANDS."
SHAPING A SPECIALTY. *Asian Affairs: An Am. Rev. 1975 3(2): 107-137.* Part I. Discusses the views of China scholars. After 1944 liberal criticism of Nationalist corruption rose to flood proportions. In 1945 the State Department policy shifted to a more evenhanded treatment of the Nationalist government and Chinese Communists. A round table conference in Washington in 1949 led to eventual recognition of the new Chinese Communist government. The conservative campaign of the early 1950's was traumatic for the liberals who were temporarily terrorized in the McCarthy era. In the 1960's the study of China was funded by the Ford Foundation on a large scale, and "the expansion of the number and quality of area centers provided a basis for the beginning of a self-sustaining process of growth of the China specialty." 52 notes.
RESHAPING AMERICAN OPINION. *Asian Affairs: An Am. Rev. 1976 3(3): 185-208.* Part II. President Kennedy chose liberals for top posts relevant to China policy. By 1960 public opinion supported a change in American China policy. The Fulbright hearings showed that the Kennedy Administration was far below the coun-

try's willingness to adopt new approaches. "Over three fourths of all current specialists on contemporary China were produced in the 1960's," and they are overwhelmingly liberal. By 1971 there was little consensus for the isolation of Communist China. 35 notes.

E. P. Stickney

2896. Martin, Edwin M. HAITI: A CASE STUDY IN FUTILITY. *SAIS Rev. 1981 (2): 61-70.* In the 1960's, the Alliance for Progress and the cold war with Cuba piqued President John F. Kennedy's interest in Haiti; despite massive aid programs, minuscule progress has been made, showing that direct efforts by foreigners to promote peaceful change in a society they do not know well and with which they have little in common cannot be counted on for quick results.

2897. Martin, Laurence. CHANGES IN AMERICAN STRATEGIC DOCTRINE—AN INITIAL INTERPRETATION. *Survival [Great Britain] 1974 16(4): 158-164.* Discusses US military strategy and nuclear arms potential in 1974, emphasizing Secretary of Defense James Schlesinger's policies toward ICBM's and the Strategic Arms Limitation Talks with the USSR.

2898. Marvel, W. Macy. DRIFT AND INTRIGUE: UNITED STATES RELATIONS WITH THE VIET-MINH 1945. *Millennium: J. of Int. Studies [Great Britain] 1975 4(1): 10-27.* There is considerable confusion regarding US relations with the Viet Minh in the immediate postwar period. Analyzes the course of US policy in Vietnam, and especially the activities of the American Office of Strategic Services (OSS), while stressing that in 1945 Vietnam was low on the US list of priorities. Based on primary and secondary sources; 40 notes. P. J. Beck

2899. Masi, Fernando Luis. PARTICULARISMO VERSUS GLOBALISMO: LA POLITICA EXTERIOR NORTEAMERICANA EN AFRICA (1977-1981) [Particularism versus globalism: North American foreign policy in Africa, 1977-81]. *Foro Int. [Mexico] 1981 22(2): 180-202.* Examines US foreign policy in Africa, especially southern Africa and the Horn of Africa, noting the Carter administration's initial application of "particularism" and its 1979 return to "globalism" under the impact of domestic political changes. Secondary sources; 53 notes.

D. A. Franz

2900. Matray, James I. AMERICA'S RELUCTANT CRUSADE: TRUMAN'S COMMITMENT OF COMBAT TROOPS IN THE KOREAN WAR. *Historian 1980 42(3): 437-455.* US intervention in the Korean War in June 1950 was a pivotal event in postwar history, but President Harry S. Truman's decision was not a major reversal of US foreign policy. A more accurate appraisal of Truman's response finds it consistent with past policy. Before the attack the United States had devoted its efforts in South Korea to supporting self-defense and military protection. The North Korean attack destroyed the intellectual foundations of Truman's policy, which had rested on the conviction that the USSR would not engage in open military aggression. Truman committed US troops only after South Korea demonstrated its inability to defend itself. Truman's decision to use combat troops marked the beginning of US dependence on military intervention rather than nationalism and indigenous hostility to Soviet domination as the best method for combating international communism. Primary sources; 62 notes.

R. S. Sliwoski

2901. Matray, James I. CAPTIVE OF THE COLD WAR: THE DECISION TO DIVIDE KOREA AT THE 38TH PARALLEL. *Pacific Hist. Rev. 1981 50(2): 145-168.* The partition of Korea at the 38th parallel was the consequence of deteriorating Soviet-American relations in 1945, President Truman's desire to prevent the Soviet occupation of all Korea, and Stalin's efforts to protect Russian national security interests in northeastern Asia. Truman accepted the American military leaders' recommendation that Soviet forces enter Korea and Manchuria to accept the Japanese surrender, but America's Korea policy was transformed during the Potsdam Conference, as American military leaders shifted to an anti-Soviet position. The early Soviet entry into the Pacific War and Japan's surrender were followed by the American military and State Department agreement to divide Korea at the 38th parallel into US and Soviet occupation zones. Based on US Department of State Papers, US Army Staff records and other primary sources; 84 notes.

R. N. Lokken

2902. Matray, James I. TRUMAN'S PLAN FOR VICTORY: NATIONAL SELF-DETERMINATION AND THE THIRTY-EIGHTH PARALLEL DECISION IN KOREA. *J. of Am. Hist. 1979 66(2): 314-333.* President Harry S. Truman's decision in 1950 to send General Douglas MacArthur across the Korean 38th Parallel was the culmination of US policy since World War II. Such a move would guarantee for all Koreans the right of national self-determination and would allow them to choose the US model, not the Soviet, for their future development. Because Truman interpreted the Korean War as part of a global, Soviet-US competition, a decisive victory in Korea would also be a great defeat for the Soviet policy of expansion. 84 notes. T. P. Linkfield

2903. May, Gary. THE "NEW CHINA HANDS" AND THE RAPE OF THE CHINA SERVICE. *Rev. in Am. Hist. 1976 4(1): 120-127.* Review article prompted by E. J. Kahn, Jr.'s *The China Hands: America's Foreign Service Officers and What Befell Them* (New York: Viking Pr., 1975) which discusses the State Department Foreign Service officers stationed in China during the 1940's and the ambivalent attitudes they received, domestically.

2904. Mayer, Klaus. ROBERT MCNAMARAS AMTSFÜHRUNG ALS SECRETARY OF DEFENSE UND DIE AMERIKANISCHE MARINE: EIN INTERPRETATIONSVERSUCH DER VERHALTENSMOTIVE VON ZIVILER UND MILITÄRISCHER GEWALT IN DEN USA IM ZUSAMMENHANG MIT DER TONKING-AFFÄRE (AUGUST 1964) [Robert McNamara's achievement in his office as Secretary of Defense and the US Navy: an attempt at interpretation of motives of conduct by civil and military authority in connection with the Tonkin affair (August 1964)]. *Militärgeschichtliche Mitteilungen [West Germany] 1977 (2): 43-92.* Deals with Robert S. McNamara's service as Secretary of Defense (1961-68), the impact of his politics on the development of the US Navy, and the Tonkin Gulf crisis.

2905. Mazrui, Ali A. NATIONALISTS AND STATESMEN: FROM NKRUMAH AND DE GAULLE TO NYERERE AND KISSINGER. *J. of African Studies 1979-80 6(4): 199-205.* A comparative typological analysis of four modern leaders. Distinguishes nationalists from statesmen; identifies Charles de Gaulle and Kwame Nkrumah as nationalists and Henry A. Kissinger as a statesman, and places Julius Nyerere into both categories. Nkrumah and Nyerere were assertive Pan-Africanist leaders, but neither succeeded in achieving economic or political integration of their respective regions in West or East Africa or in uniting Africa. L. W. Truschel

2906. Mazur, Zbigniew. ZBIGNIEWA BRZEZIŃSKIEGO KONCEPCJA STOSUNKÓW WSCHÓD-ZACHÓD [Zbigniew Brzezinski's concept of East-West relations]. *Przegląd Zachodni [Poland] 1980 36(2): 60-91.* Zbigniew Brzezinski has exerted strong influence on world affairs. A renowned specialist on Eastern European relations, he translated his views into action as director of the Trilateral Commission, State Department consultant, and National Security Advisor to President Jimmy Carter. In the aviary of Washington he is a hawk with original ideas. He criticized Nixon-Kissinger policies as diplomatic virtuosity without long-run political thought. Recognizing the declining power of the United States, he wants to build cooperation among the United States, Western Europe, and Japan. This group in turn is to open a dialog with the socialist countries. Those that liberalize their domestic policies are to be rewarded. As more and more economic and political relations develop, a new, more cooperative world will emerge. Because German unification is not possible without prior European agreement, Brzezinski opposed the Hallstein doctrine and the subsequent opening of West Germany to the East. Based on primary publications, newspaper reports and Brzezinski's own publications. M. Krzyzaniak

2907. Mazuzan, George T. UNITED STATES POLICY TOWARD PALESTINE AT THE UNITED NATIONS, 1947-48: AN ESSAY. *Prologue 1975 7(3): 163-176.* Although US policy toward Palestine has appeared inconsistent, recent evidence shows that the deepening Cold War shaped American policy. The State Department's support of a United Nations trusteeship, its support for partitioning Palestine, its reversal of that decision, and the final recognition of Israel are linked to American perception of Russian strategy and to concurrent events in Palestine. President Truman and some of his advisers subordinated their desire to create a national home for Jews to their fear of Soviet intervention. Arab friendship, initially considered vital to maintain strategic oil supplies and military bases, was also subordinated to containment. Primary and secondary sources; map, 67 notes.   W. R. Hively

2908. McLain, Glenn A. SOUTH KOREA: CARTER'S DILEMMA. *Contemporary Rev. [Great Britain] 1978 232(1349): 300-305.* Discusses changes in the American attitude toward South Korea under President Jimmy Carter during 1977-78.

2909. McLellan, David S. and Hange, Robert. THE JOINT CHIEFS AND THE EXPANDED WAR. *Worldview 1974 17(4): 40-44.* In 1964-65, the Joint Chiefs of Staff succeeded in convincing civilian foreign policymakers of the need to enlarge the Vietnam War to include bombing of the north, and to increase ground troops.

2910. McLellan, David S. WHO FATHERED CONTAINMENT? A DISCUSSION. *Internat. Studies Q. 1973 17(2): 205-226.* America's Cold War policy of containing the USSR resulted from State Department experience with aggressive Soviet behavior in Turkey and Iran during 1945-46.   S

2911. Mehlman, Maxwell J.; Milch, Thomas H.; and Toumanoff, Michael V. UNITED STATES RESTRICTIONS ON EXPORTS TO SOUTH AFRICA. *Am. J. of Int. Law 1979 73(4): 581-603.* Traces US policy since 1960. Indicates public laws have gone deliberately unenforced. Only in 1977 did the State Department admit that guidelines had been liberalized in 1970. During 1960 and 1977, the State Department approved more Munitions List items to South Africa than to any other African country. The 1978 level of aircraft and computer-related exports to South Africa was among the very highest for all countries. Recommends policy changes designed to improve enforcement. 94 notes.
R. J. Jirran

2912. Melnikov, I. M. "AZIATSKAIA DOKTRINA" PRESIDENTA L. JOHNSONA [The Asiatic Doctrine of President L. Johnson]. *Novaia i Noveishaia Istoriia [USSR] 1974 (1): 107-122, (2): 116-129.* Part I. President Lyndon B. Johnson formulated the Asiatic Doctrine in 1961 during his first international mission to Saigon. Its object was to strengthen and stabilize reactionary forces in Indochina and to weaken national liberation forces. As president he deviated from Kennedy's path, and increased aggression in Vietnam. 31 notes. Part II. The need to gain votes in the election campaign of 1964 and later to counteract growing opposition to US participation in the war in March and April 1965 motivated Johnson's Vietnam peace initiatives. His hypocrisy was underlined by Washington's intensification of aggression and its insistence on continued supremacy in Indochina. Ceasefires from 1965 to 1967 were designed to deceive, and so-called peace talks were arranged to coincide with visits of American politicians to foreign countries. 40 notes.
L. Smith

2913. Messer, Robert L. PATHS NOT TAKEN: THE UNITED STATES DEPARTMENT OF STATE AND ALTERNATIVES TO CONTAINMENT, 1945-1946. *Diplomatic Hist. 1977 1(4): 297-319.* During the winter of 1945-46, the State Department was called upon to formulate a general policy toward the USSR. Numerous alternatives were discussed before the policy of containment, set forth in George F. Kennan's "long telegram" from Moscow, won the day. A memorandum authored by Cloyce K. Huston, and later a study written by Charles E. Bohlen and Gerold T. Robinson, which incorporated some of Huston's recommendations, both advocated a policy of cooperation and conciliation, a passage from the latter going so far as to suggest the sharing of atomic secrets. Discusses the reasons for Kennan's dramatic success in winning adherents to his views. The text of the Bohlen-Robinson report is given on pages 389-399. Based on State Department files and secondary sources; 51 notes.   L. W. Van Wyk

2914. Mikulín, Antonín. OZBROJENÉ SÍLY USA—HLAVNÍ NÁSTROJ GLOBÁLNÍ STRATEGIE IMPERIALISMU [US Armed Forces: the main instrument of imperialist global strategy]. *Hist. a Vojenství [Czechoslovakia] 1978 27(5): 137-162, (6): 119-149.* Part I. A study of the system of American military strategy since 1945 that periodizes the past decades: 1945-53; the time of "balanced armed forces": the years 1954-60 were influenced by the idea of massive retaliation; 1960-69 was the time of "elastic reaction"; and in 1970 the military circles

began the strategy of "realistic deterrent." Dissects US military planning and the strategic thinking of top ranking leaders at that time. 27 notes. Part II. Outlines further development of American strategic thinking and examines basic military conceptions as they appear backed by the armed potential of the United States. Compares actions taken by the Nixon, Ford, and Carter administrations and the volume of armament of all capitalist countries. Views US conceptions of warfare in all dimensions as too unrealistic and unbalanced. Based on published printed sources; 42 notes.   G. E. Pergl

2915. Miller, Lawrence W. and Sigelman, Lee. IS THE AUDIENCE THE MESSAGE? A NOTE ON LBJ'S VIETNAM STATEMENTS. *Public Opinion Q. 1978 42(1): 71-80.* Content analysis of 77 of Lyndon B. Johnson's public statements about Vietnam showed that, depending on the audience, he did vary the content—which suggests that to some extent the audience *is* the message.   J

2916. Miller, Linda B. CARTER AND THE PALESTINIANS. *Jerusalem Q. [Israel] 1979 (11): 21-35.* The Camp David agreements indicate that Egypt, Israel, and the United States have found sufficient common ground to transform the Arab-Israel conflict into a manageable interstate dispute susceptible to bargaining, but difficulties over the ambiguous arrangements for the West Bank and Gaza will continue to test the resolve of the United States and the local parties for peace.

2917. Millet, Stephen M. THE AIR FORCE, THE COURTS, AND THE CONTROVERSIAL BOMBING OF CAMBODIA. *Air U. Rev. 1976 27(5): 80-88.* Examines the history and implications of the 1973 federal court suit to stop the bombing of Cambodia filed by Congresswoman Elizabeth Holtzman and four USAF officers. A discussion of the initial suit, the political compromise worked out in Washington, the appeals, the Court of Appeals decision, and the War Powers Act of 1973 is included. The courts ultimately decided that the president was empowered to bomb Cambodia and that the suit was inappropriate because it involved a political, not a judicial matter. Based on judicial records and published sources; 4 illus., 22 notes.   J. W. Thacker, Jr.

2918. Minter, William. U.S. POLICY IN ANGOLA AND MOZAMBIQUE. *Africa Today 1976 23(3): 55-60.* American foreign policy will be directed at reversing the success of the revolutionary regimes in Mozambique and Angola by encouraging moderation among black African nations, gradual reform in South Africa, and antirevolutionary groups. Henry Kissinger-inspired conferences are a mask covering the face of American economic interests. Based on secondary sources; 8 notes.   G. O. Gagnon

2919. Miscamble, Wilson D. ANTHONY EDEN AND THE TRUMAN-MOLOTOV CONVERSATIONS OF APRIL, 1945. *Diplomatic Hist. 1978 2(2): 167-180.* The Truman-Molotov conversation of 23 April 1945 did not indicate a reversal of America's wartime policy of cooperation with the USSR. British Foreign Secretary Sir Anthony Eden considered the intransigence of Soviet Foreign Minister V. M. Molotov the roadblock to an acceptable settlement of the crucial disagreement over Poland. At Eden's instigation, President Harry S. Truman held the unscheduled meeting with Molotov in an effort to convince him of the importance of a quick resolution of this issue. Truman, who had discussed questions of general policy with Molotov in the scheduled meeting the previous day, intended the famous "dressing down" for this limited purpose only. 56 notes.   T. L. Powers

2920. Miscamble, Wilson D. GEORGE F. KENNAN, THE POLICY PLANNING STAFF AND THE ORIGINS OF THE MARSHALL PLAN. *Mid-America 1980 62(2): 75-89.* In April 1947 Secretary of State George Marshall instructed George F. Kennan and the new Policy Planning Staff to investigate postwar European economic problems and to develop proposals for US assistance. Analyzes the role of the Policy Planning Staff in developing a program of economic aid. 63 notes.   M. J. Wentworth

2921. Miscamble, Wilson D. HARRY S. TRUMAN, THE BERLIN BLOCKADE AND THE 1948 ELECTION. *Presidential Studies Q. 1980 10(3): 306-316.* Examines President Harry S. Truman's actions during the Berlin blockade of 1948 to better understand their relationship with his presidential campaign of that year. His successful handling of the crisis definitely enhanced his standing with American voters, but there is little evidence to suggest that his decisons were taken on the basis of political goals. Truman pursued a strongly moderate course, often over the opposition of many of his advisors, a course that was not managed to increase his domestic political standing. Based on primary presidential and governmental sources and on secondary sources; 60 notes.

D. H. Cline

2922. Moch, Jules. JAURÈS: MARSHALL [Jaurès: Marshall]. *Nouvelle Rev. des Deux Mondes [France] 1980 (7): 58-63.* The author, a French statesman, relates his personal contacts with French Socialist leader and author Jean Léon Jaurès (1859-1914) and American Secretary of State and Nobel Prize winner George C. Marshall (1880-1959).

2923. Mojdehi, J. M. M. AMERICA AND THE THIRD WORLD: RETURN TO THE PAST. *Survival [Great Britain] 1982 24(2): 78-86.* Examines US policies and attitudes to the Third World, which have varied between the view that the region is simply the arena for US-Soviet competition and the view that sees only local sources of political conflict; focuses on the dangers of adopting the first view as has been done under the Reagan administration.

2924. Molineu, Harold. CARTER AND HUMAN RIGHTS: ADMINISTRATIVE IMPACT OF SYMBOLIC POLICY. *Policy Studies J. 1980 8(6): 879-885.* Argues that the Carter administration's human rights policy is largely an exercise in symbolic politics and thus can be considered successful in that it has achieved symbolic response from the bureaucracy.

2925. Morgenthau, Hans J. HENRY KISSINGER, SECRETARY OF STATE: AN EVALUATION. *Encounter [Great Britain] 1974 43(5): 57-61.* Discusses Henry A. Kissinger's ability to adjust intellectual conviction to political exigencies, both as Secretary of State since 1969 and even earlier when he published *Nuclear Weapons and Foreign Policy* (1957).

2926. Morley, Morris H. and Smith, Steven. IMPERIAL "REACH": U.S. POLICY AND THE CIA IN CHILE. *J. of Pol. and Military Sociol. 1977 5(2): 203-216.* This study of the role of U.S. covert politics in Chile between 1970 and 1973 has two basic purposes. First, it seeks to locate the CIA and its activities within the overall U.S. executive branch response to the Allende government—differentiating between specific institutional tasks and overlapping responsibilities with other imperial state agencies. The CIA is not a policy formation agency. On the contrary, it executes and applies already thought out policies, and any autonomy or freedom of action which may accrue to the CIA does so only at this level. In the case of Allende, the larger 'destabilization' policy was devised by the White House and the National Security Council. The CIA's operational effectiveness, however, resides precisely in its capacity to coordinate its actions with those of other imperial state agencies (State, Treasury, Defense, etc.) to promote the long-term interests of U.S. private corporate capital. Second, our study shows how peripheral nations with a history of investment, commercial and financial dependence on core capitalist countries are particularly susceptible to covert politics and subversion. This is especially the case where nationalist and/or anti-capitalist movements hostile to basic U.S. political and economic interests gain political power but not total control of the peripheral state structure. A brief examination of the historical roots of Chilean economic dependence on U.S. public and private capital, and the conditioning impact of this phenomenon on the internal class structure, allows us to locate the sources of instability that plagued the Allende government throughout its tenure in office. We conclude that the Popular Unity government in Chile was vulnerable to political and economic-financial manipulation 'from the outside', in large part, because of the ease with which the CIA was able to locate economic pressure points and set up 'liasons' inside the Chilean class structure, and state and private institutions. The CIA played a critical role in exacerbating the internal social struggles that eventually culminated in the military coup of September 1973. J

2927. Morley, Morris H. TOWARD A THEORY OF IMPERIAL POLICYMAKING. *J. of Contemporary Asia [Sweden] 1981 11(3): 333-350.* Previous theorists have used a model of bureaucratic competition and conflict for analyzing US foreign policymaking since 1945. An examination of US policy toward Cuba from the mid-1950's to the mid-

1970's, however, reveals an overriding consensus among such imperial agencies as the State, Treasury, Defense, and Commerce departments, the National Security Council, and the Central Intelligence Agency as to the necessity of combating the anticapitalist regime of Fidel Castro. Although state and nonstate bureaucracies may heartedly debate specific lines of action at the middle levels of decisionmaking, they are united on crucial issues by their common purpose of protecting and extending the capitalist mode of production. Primary sources; 36 notes.

E. L. Keyser

2928. Morris, Roger. APRÈS HENRY LE DÉLUGE. *Washington Monthly 1976 7(5/6): 7-17.* Comments on the foreign policy of Henry A. Kissinger since 1969 and theorizes on the nature of the State Department and its secretary after Kissinger departs.

2929. Morris, Roger. KISSINGER AND THE BROTHERS KALB. *Washington Monthly 1974 6(5/6): 51-60.* Reviews Marvin Kalb and Bernard Kalb's *Kissinger* (Boston: Little, Brown, 1974). S

2930. Moss, Robert. THE CLOAK-AND-DAGGER CONTROVERSY. *Int. Rev. [Great Britain] 1974 (3): 19-24, 61.* Discusses controversy surrounding the involvement of Cubans and the US Central Intelligence Agency in covert operations in the coup d'etat against Salvador Allende in Chile, 1972-73.

2931. Mrozek, Donald J. A NEW LOOK AT "BALANCED FORCES": DEFENSE CONTINUITIES FROM TRUMAN TO EISENHOWER. *Military Affairs 1974 38(4): 145-151.* The military policies of Presidents Harry S. Truman and Dwight D. Eisenhower formed a continuum despite contemporary belief to the contrary. Both stressed strategic deterrent air power and neither accepted "a balanced forces" concept. Based on material in the Eisenhower Library; 46 notes.

K. J. Bauer

2932. Nathan, James A. HUMAN RIGHTS AND INTERNATIONAL ORDER. *Foreign Service J. 1978 55(2): 9-12, 33-36.* Examines the issue of human rights, 19th-20th centuries, focusing on the Jimmy Carter administration, 1977-78, and its effects on foreign policy.

2933. Nathan, James A. ZBIGSCAM: U.S. FOREIGN POLICY, 1976-80. *Virginia Q. Rev. 1981 57(2): 210-226.* "Whatever coherent view of the world that could be found in the Carter Administration came from Zbigniew Brzezinski." The "Ford/Kissinger approach" to detente was abandoned for treating the Soviets as morally and politically unequal. By 1980 the human rights emphasis was abandoned for "the renascent climate of Cold War." But the uncertainty concerning military responses resulted in the Carter administration's turn to economic coercion. Diplomacy was traded for force.

O. H. Zabel

2934. Nicoloff, Olivier. VALUE OF FOOD AS WEAPON MORE SYMBOLIC THAN REAL: POLITICS OF FOOD. *Int. Perspectives [Canada] 1980 (Sept-Oct): 19-21.* The hope that America's food surplus could be used to secure extraordinary economic and political influence over other nations has not been realized. President Jimmy Carter's embargo on grain to the USSR was a fiasco because other countries, notably Argentina, supplied most of the Soviet requirement and American ships, controlled by multinational corporations, carried the grain to Soviet bloc countries. It is clear today that the food weapon was primarily a propaganda instrument for internal use and is not likely to be used in the future.

E. S. Palais

2935. Nikitin, N. and Petrov, S. TAINAIA VOINA IMPERIALIZMA SSHA [The secret war of American imperialism]. *Voenno-Istoricheskii Zhurnal [USSR] 1980 (2): 59-64.* The decree published by President Jimmy Carter in 1978 on the centralization of the intelligence service amounts to a call for its strengthening. The CIA's broad network allows it to have considerable influence on events at home and abroad. One of the main targets of the American intelligence service is to undermine the stability of the socialist countries. As America's aggressive foreign policies meet stronger resistance, the government increases its reliance on intelligence agencies. Secondary sources; 8 notes.

L. Waters

2936. Nikolayev, Y. THE VLADIVOSTOK MEETING: IMPORTANT PROGRESS. *Internat. Affairs [USSR] 1975 (2): 3-9.* Views the

Vladivostok Accord between Leonid Brezhnev and Gerald R. Ford as an important step of detente, especially in the area of strategic arms limitation. The success of the 1974 meeting has made detente irreversible and as such a triumph of the Soviet policy of peaceful coexistence. Despite these gains, however, there are still major areas of concern: the continuing opposition within the United States toward detente and the still unresolved Middle East question.   D. K. McQuilkin

2937. Niksch, Larry A.   DEFENSE BURDEN-SHARING IN THE PACIFIC: U.S. EXPECTATIONS AND JAPANESE RESPONSES. *Asian Affairs: An Am. Rev. 1981 8(6): 331-345.* Compares and contrasts the approaches and content of US-Japanese dialogue on defense matters in the Carter and Reagan administrations. Discusses Japanese responsibilities (sea control, mining and port-blockading strategies, air defense screening) and US responsibilities (possible offensive operations toward eastern Siberia, defense of South Korea), Japanese political environment and pacificism, Pacific power equilibrium, and US and Japanese financial considerations. Based on press and government sources; 15 notes.
R. B. Mendel

2938. Nixon, Richard M.   UNITED STATES FOREIGN POLICY FOR THE 70'S: SHAPING A DURABLE PEACE (AFRICA). *Africa Today 1973 20(2): 3-10.* An excerpt from President Nixon's "State of the World" speech to Congress in May 1973. Promises that America will support African nations' economic development, avoid interference in domestic politics, and continue seeking evolutionary change in Rhodesia and South Africa.   G. O. Gagnon

2939. Nowak, Kazimierz.   KILKA UWAG O POLITYCE ZAGRANICZNEJ ADMINISTRACJI CARTERA [A few remarks about foreign policy of the Carter administration]. *Nowe Drogi [Poland] 1977 337(6): 149-158.* Reviews President Carter's foreign policy problems, examined in domestic and global contexts. The most significant domestic factors affecting the President's world outlook are said to include unemployment, inflation, Watergate, and the post-Vietnam popular weariness with US interventionist policies. A review of foreign relations, including the human rights campaign, the upgrading of relations with Western Europe and Japan, and the increasing emphasis on Africa, is followed by an implicit "central question": How long will President Carter's initial, "bargaining" and "prestige" foreign policy positions be permitted to impede the return of realism to the White House and the establishment of a working relationship with America's "natural partners in solving world problems." Note.   W. J. Lukaszewski

2940. Nuechterlein, James A.   HENRY KISSINGER AND AMERICAN FOREIGN POLICY. *Queen's Q. [Canada] 1980 87(3): 369-386.* Henry A. Kissinger's memoirs, *White House Years* (Boston: Little, Brown, 1979), have occasioned debate about how Americans should arrange their relations with the rest of the world. Kissinger's goal was to moderate America's traditional fluctuations between manic internationalism and peevish isolationism. This meant, above all, coming to terms with the realities of power. His attitudes toward such issues as detente, Vietnam, and nuclear weapons was that America needed to avoid excesses both of conciliation and truculence. He looked for a kind of balance (neither euphoria nor despair) in American foreign policy.
L. V. Eid

2941. Nurse, Ronald J.   CRITIC OF COLONIALISM: JFK AND ALGERIAN INDEPENDENCE. *Historian 1977 39(2): 307-326.* Studies John F. Kennedy's views regarding Algeria's struggle for independence with a comparison of the Vietnamese situation. An examination of Kennedy's congressional record indicates that there was a steadfast Kennedy position that "the United States must ally itself with the new nationalism of Asia, Africa and the Middle East even at the expense of America's traditional allies in Western Europe." His position on Algerian independence was in harmony with his earlier attack on French colonial policies. But he was also strongly anti-Communist and the Algerian nationalists were not Communist; the nationalists of Indochina were. He "refused to believe that nationalism and communism could be synonymous." 64 notes.   R. V. Ritter

2942. Nye, Joseph S., Jr.   PROLIFERATION WATCH: WE TRIED HARDER (AND DID MORE). *Foreign Policy 1979 (36): 101-104.* President Jimmy Carter's policies have succeeded in slowing the rate of

nuclear nonproliferation. His style of leadership, while often criticized for being messy and messianic, has been effective as well. "His habit of asking for a whole loaf may produce half a loaf of global reform, while asking cautiously for an incremental slice would have produced half a slice of reform."   T. L. Powers

2943. Nye, Joseph S., Jr.   U.S. POWER AND REAGAN POLICY. *Orbis 1982 26(2): 391-411.* Examines the decline of US power during 1971-81. In 1950 the United States accounted for more than one-third of the total world defense and of the gross world product; today it is less than one-fourth. Four short-term reasons for this change are: Vietnam, Soviet military growth, energy vulnerability, and declining economic productivity; two long-term reasons are an increased dispersal in world economic growth and reduced potential for political control in an increasingly complex world. Concludes that although President Reagan's policies have been fairly successful at handling the short-term, they have made no headway with the long-term problems. Based on published sources; 14 notes.   J. W. Thacker, Jr.

2944. Nyström, Sune.   AMERIKANSKA PROBLEM [The American problem]. *Kungliga Krigsvetenskaps Akademiens Handlingar och Tidskrift [Sweden] 1969 173(3): 131-150; 1970 174(9): 525-542; 1971 175(4): 65-81, (8): 203-218; 1972 176(4): 115-126; 1973 177(2): 13-25, (7-8): 198-218.* Part VII. Analyzes the US Vietnam policy between the cessation of bombing in November 1968 and the change of presidents in January 1969 relating it to the 1968-69 and 1969-70 defense bills. Gives examples of cooperations in these matters between Lyndon B. Johnson and Richard M. Nixon. Official sources, newspaper articles, and secondary sources; table. Part VIII. Comments on the Fitzhugh report of July 1970 and its consequences for the organization of the defense. Discusses the influence gained by Defense Secretary Melvin Laird, the pay raises for defense proposed by Nixon, and the impact and consequences in Korea, Vietnam, and especially Europe of the American policy of help to self-help. Opposition to American troop withdrawals was expressed by West German Defense Secretary Helmut Schmidt in *Foreign Affairs* (September 1970). Considers the four American bases in Spain essential for the balance of power. Comments on the development of Minuteman-3 in the Multiple Independent Re-entry Vehicle (MIRV) and the robot Spartan in the antirobot system Safeguard. Official sources and secondary literature. Part IX. Comments on Richard M. Nixon's foreign policy report of February 1971 to Congress and the intended reductions of American troops in Western Europe. Discusses difficulties in following the Nixon doctrine of help to self-help and a compromise between American reductions and contributions of manpower and money from England and West Germany. Differentiated wages for American troops have been suggested due to the demands and economic strains on the army and to reductions in Europe, Korea, and South Vietnam. Official reports, newspaper articles. Part X. Discusses security policy and military-strategic relationships, especially with China, Japan, and Vietnam. US policy of help to self-help is carried out by continued withdrawal of troops from South Vietnam and in seeking a better proportion between resources and enterprises. The announced American withdrawal from Okinawa in April 1972 gives rise to the question of finding another base for the nuclear weapons. Guam is considered the most likely place. Comments on the critisism of the US Army in South Vietnam based on Robert Debs Heinl's article in *Armed Forces Journal* (June 1971). Official sources, newspaper articles, and secondary literature. Part XI. Comments on President Nixon's third foreign policy report to Congress, 1972, including the problem of defense policy and possible mutual troop reductions in Europe. Considers the better transport possibilities between Russia and the Warsaw Pact countries and the possibility of quicker troop reinforcement. Difficulties in Congress of approval of Nixon's defense budget for 1972-73, with increases due to suggestions of more nuclear arms, are anticipated. US Defense and State Department papers and NATO reports. Part XII. Examines the John D. Lavelle affair in Vietnam, 1971-72; George S. McGovern's defense program as presented in the 1972 presidential campaign; President Richard M. Nixon's subsequent choice of Elliot Richardson for defense secretary after the resignation of Melvin Laird; the US foreign relations with the USSR and Western Europe, and the attitude of the former to NATO cooperation after the failure of some member countries to fulfill the agreements. Part XIII. Outlines the situation in the US armed forces after the abolition of national conscription in January 1973, following the ending of the Vietnam War. Gives details of the resultant structural changes in military organization in the United States itself and in Europe, comparing Secretary of State Henry A. Kissinger's and President Richard M. Nixon's views on NATO cooperation with those of the West German General J. Benneck. Asserts that the energy crisis, combined with the shortage of raw materials, is bound to influence the US economy, and consequently its military strategy and defense policy.

U. G. Jeyes/B. Jacobsen

2945. Oberndörfer, Dieter. DIE LATEINAMERIKAPOLITIK DER USA: BILANZ UND NEUERE ENTWICKLUNG [U.S. policy in Latin America: Summary and recent developments]. *Jahrbuch für Amerikastudien [West Germany] 1973 18: 24-45.* Since 1945 U.S. policy in Latin America has been characterized by the failure to realize its aims and a subsequent decline of the political and economic importance of Latin America to the United States. U.S. aims in Latin America were to: 1) protect American economic interests, 2) combat communism, 3) isolate Cuba, and 4) promote social reform and economic growth in order to stabilize political systems along Western lines. Under President Nixon Latin America became a region of secondary interest for U.S. foreign policy, which manifested itself in America's adoption of a "low profile" and withdrawal from previous responsibilities. Nixon abandons the traditional American missionary goal of transforming Latin American society and government according to the U.S. model. Based on secondary sources and published government documents; 40 notes.
G. Bassler

2946. O'Connor, Raymond G. TRUMAN: NEW POWERS IN FOREIGN AFFAIRS. *Australian J. of Pol. and Hist. [Australia] 1979 25(3): 319-326.* Harry S. Truman added to the authority of the president in international affairs. He increased presidential control over: nuclear weapons; dependence on military force in foreign policy; membership of the United Nations; unilateral protection of the free world; the first of the peacetime alliances (North Atlantic Treaty); promotion of world prosperity (Marshall Plan); new machinery for foreign policymaking (the National Security Council and the Central Intelligence Agency). Most moves were initially controversial, but Truman was an experienced politician and a tradition of bipartisanship had developed during World War II. Truman's reputation as a statesman was greater in Washington community than with the general public. Based on memoirs and monographs; 21 notes.
W. D. McIntyre

2947. Odell, John S. THE U.S. AND THE EMERGENCE OF FLEXIBLE EXCHANGE RATES: AN ANALYSIS OF FOREIGN POLICY CHANGE. *Int. Organization 1979 33(1): 57-81.* United States international monetary policy changed twice in the early 1970s— first with the 1971 New Economic Policy and again with a second devaluation in February 1973. These shifts helped bring about the collapse of the Bretton Woods regime of fixed exchange rates. Though these changes were most of all responses to the persistent U.S. deficit and other changes in the international financial situation, policy beliefs of senior officials were also critical in influencing the timing of change and the choice of new policy content. President Nixon's and Secretary Connally's domestic political expectations accounted for some parts of the 1971 package. International military-political considerations shaped the partial settlement of December 1971 but had only distant influence earlier or later. Organizational factors were of relatively little importance in determining monetary policies. The policy-making process tends to be tightly closed and centralized during major changes. "Stands" do not necessarily reflect organizational aims, and interest groups do not necessarily act in their own supposed interest. Transnational actors are an important element of the financial situation. The analysis of these changes can be integrated with approaches used to analyze other foreign policies.

2948. Odell, John S. US-BEAMTE UND DIE ENTSTEHUNG FLEXIBLER WECHSELKURSE: EINE ANALYSE DES AUSSENPOLISCHEN WANDELS [US officials and the emergence of flexible exchange rates: An analysis of foreign political change]. *Politische Vierteljahresschrift [West Germany] 1977 18(1): 25-47.* Analyzes US monetary policy after the dollar's breaking away from the Gold Standard in 1971, with reference to the international and domestic political situation. In the mid-1960's President Johnson had used many officials as advisers, but after 1971 it was realized that collective policymaking was the only way; consequently President Nixon used only a few, e.g. Henry A. Kissinger, John Connally, and George Schultz; the latter two advised floating the dollar, so that other countries might not be able to gain an unfair economic advantage over the USA. Based on primary (including personal interviews conducted by the author) and secondary works; 27 notes.
A. Alcock

2949. Ogburn, Robert W. IMPLEMENTING THE CARTER HUMAN RIGHTS POLICY IN SOUTH KOREA: HISTORIC MILIEU. *Towson State J. of Int. Affairs 1980 14(2): 75-91.* Examines US-Korean relations since 1945, describing the regime of Park Chung-hee and US human rights policy.

2950. Ohlin, Göran. NIXON, VALUTORNA OCH VÄRLDSHANDELN [Nixon, exchanges, and world trade]. *Svensk Tidskrift [Sweden] 1971 58(10): 466-474.* Explains US measures in 1971 to improve the US balance of payments after the trade crisis started by the increase in Japanese exports to the United States.

2951. O'Leary, James P. ON GRADING THE PRESIDENT'S HUMAN RIGHTS PERFORMANCE. *J. of Intergroup Relations 1979 7(2): 26-29.* President Jimmy Carter's human rights campaign has ignored the commitment most nations have to national autonomy and, in general, has failed to deliver meaningful results; 1977-79.

2952. Olson, William Clinton. THE WORLD FROM BOTH ENDS OF PENNSYLVANIA AVENUE: PRESIDENT CARTER'S FOREIGN POLICY PROBLEMS. *Round Table [Great Britain] 1978 (272): 333-339.* US foreign policy follows a program adopted by Congress before President Jimmy Carter took office and may conflict with measures he would like to take.

2953. Ondes, Bruce. THE SACKING OF THE SECRETARY. *Africa Report 1975 20(1): 17-19.* Controversy over Henry A. Kissinger's firing of his Assistant Secretary for African Affairs, Donald Easum, in 1974.
S

2954. Osgood, Robert E. CARTER POLICY IN PERSPECTIVE. *SAIS Rev. 1981 (1): 11-22.* Assesses President Carter's foreign policy, with its emphasis on North-South "architecture" rather than East-West "acrobatics," as well as his human rights stance, and policy of containment in an era of declining American power.

2955. Osgood, Robert E. THE REVITALIZATION OF CONTAINMENT. *Foreign Affairs 1982 60(3): 465-502.* Reviews foreign policy in 1981. The Reagan administration's primary foreign policy goal was to contain Soviet expansion. To achieve this aim, the United States sought to reinvigorate its economy and military and that of its allies, to strengthen its relations with friendly nations, to encourage peace and progress in less industrialized nations, and to make Soviet restraint and reciprocity the basis of US-Soviet relations. Attempts to carry out this policy were hindered by a weak economy, differences between the United States and Western Europe over security matters, and tensions in various parts of the world. Note.
A. A. Englard

2956. Ottaway, David. AFRICA: U.S. POLICY ECLIPSE. *Foreign Affairs 1980 58(3): 637-658.* The Carter administration's policy toward Africa changed from "Africanist" to "globalist" in 1979, as indicated by the decision to indefinitely delay diplomatic recognition of the Angolan government, the decision to provide Morocco with military aid, and the decision to seek access rights to military facilities in Kenya and Somalia. President Carter's human rights policy may have led to the downfall of oppressive dictators in Uganda, Equatorial Guinea, and the Central African Republic. The establishment of civilian rule in Nigeria and Ghana furthered the human rights cause. A return to "globalist" policy might be detrimental to America's relations with most of Africa. Based on United Nations' publications and secondary sources; 11 notes.
A. A. Englard

2957. Oudes, Bruce. THE CIA AND AFRICA. *Africa Report 1974 19(4): 49-52.* Describes Central Intelligence Agency operations in Africa, based on *The CIA and the Cult of Intelligence* (Knopf, 1974) by Victor Marchetti and John Marks.
S

2958. Oudes, Bruce. SOUTHERN AFRICA POLICY WATERSHED. *Africa Report 1974 19(6): 46-50.* US foreign policy toward South Africa is turning away from the prowhite stance embodied in Henry Kissinger's 1970 recommendations to President Nixon, here reprinted in part.
S

2959. Ovinnikov, R. S.   KTO I KAK STAZHIRUET BUDUSH-CHIKH PREZIDENTOV SSHA   [Who schools new American presidents and how it is done]. *Voprosy Istorii [USSR] 1979 (11): 102-110.* Most presidential candidates lack foreign policy expertise. Since the 1950's, the US financial oligarchy provided guidance through political advisors drawn from large research institutions funded by financial magnates. The Carnegie Corporation and the Rockefellers' Chase Manhattan Bank financed and trained Dwight D. Eisenhower in 1952, the Brookings Institution assured a smooth transition to the Democratic administration of John F. Kennedy in 1960 and the Republican administration of Richard M. Nixon in 1968. The Trilateral Commission, formed by big business in 1973, shaped Jimmy Carter's foreign policy in 1976. Based on American publications; 29 notes.   N. Frenkley

2960. Pannoni, Gregory A.   OVERTHROW OF ALLENDE: AN ANALYSIS OF U.S. INVOLVEMENT. *Towson State J. of Int. Affairs 1979 13(2): 97-116.* Through economic pressure and covert weapons action (notably by the CIA) the United States sought to prevent Salvador Allende from coming to power in Chile, destabilize his government once it had attained power, and secure US owned multinational corporations, 1970-73.

2961. Park, Chang Jin.   AMERICAN FOREIGN POLICY IN KOREA AND VIETNAM: COMPARATIVE CASE STUDIES. *R. of Pol. 1975 37(1): 20-47.* In both the Korean War and the Vietnam War, the United States pursued a gradualistic policy of intervention to repel communist expansion. "The desire to help protect the territorial and political integrity of South Korea and South Vietnam, the politics of prestige and the moralistic approach to foreign affairs all influenced American decisions to fight in Korea and Vietnam." The Nixon-Kissinger team succeeded in ending the Vietnam War because they saw it as a conflict of nation-states rather than of moral forces. Primary and secondary sources; 57 notes.   L. E. Ziewacz

2962. Parmet, Herbert S.   THE GENERAL AND THE GOOD SOLDIER. *Rev. in Am. Hist. 1981 9(4): 543-548.* Reviews Warren I. Cohen's *Dean Rusk* (1980), which presents a biography of Rusk, focusing on his diplomatic career as Secretary of State in the Kennedy and Johnson administrations; and Robert A. Divine's *Eisenhower and the Cold War* (1981), which examines Dwight D. Eisenhower's foreign policy during the 1950's.

2963. Parzen, Herbert.   PRESIDENT TRUMAN AND THE PALESTINE QUANDARY: HIS INITIAL EXPERIENCE, APRIL-DECEMBER, 1945. *Jewish Social Studies 1973 35(1): 42-72.* When Harry S. Truman (1884-1972) became president in the spring of 1945, he at first routinely followed the positions of the State Department. Truman's pro-Zionist attitudes became more manifest as he sought a humanitarian solution to the problem of Jewish refugees in Europe. 48 notes, appendix.   P. E. Schoenberg

2964. Paterson, Thomas G.   BEARING THE BURDEN: A CRITICAL LOOK AT JFK'S FOREIGN POLICY. *Virginia Q. Rev. 1978 54(2): 193-212.* The foreign policy of John F. Kennedy's administration was "propelled by Cold War history, by its own bumptious 'can-do' style, and by its grandiose theories for world revival . . . ." The Kennedy legacy included a massive arms race, fear, "neglect of traditional diplomacy, . . . conspicuous reliance upon military force" and global overcommitment.   O. H. Zabel

2965. Paterson, Thomas G.   FOREIGN AID UNDER WRAPS: THE POINT FOUR PROGRAM. *Wisconsin Mag. of Hist. 1972/73 56(2): 119-126.* The Truman administration could no longer assume that developing nations would side with the West in the Cold War, so it boldly proclaimed the Point Four program which combined private investment and technical assistance to recipient nations. It evolved from pre-1949 discussions between White House assistants Clark Clifford and George Elsey and State Department assistant Ben Hardy. The program never realized its goals of peace, prosperity, and stability because of bureaucratic bickering between the State Department and the White House, greater concern over the conflict in Korea, limited congressional appropriations, and the slight enthusiasm, if not open hostility, from the business community. 40 notes.   N. C. Burckel

2966. Paterson, Thomas G.   PRESIDENTIAL FOREIGN POLICY, PUBLIC OPINION, AND CONGRESS: THE TRUMAN YEARS. *Diplomatic Hist. 1979 3(1): 1-18.* "In the making of America's cold war foreign policy, public opinion and Congress proved malleable, compliant, and permissive." President Harry S. Truman successfully freed himself on several occasions from political and constitutional restraints in carrying out his foreign policy preferences. "Public opinion and Congress enjoyed supporting roles in foreign policy." 80 notes.   T. L. Powers

2967. Patkó, Imre.   AZ EGYESÜLT ÁLLAMOK KÉT TAK-TIKÁJA AZ "EMBERI JOGOKTÓL" A "NEMZETKÖZI TER-RORIZMUSIG"   [The two tactics of United States: from "human rights" to "international terrorism"]. *Társadalmi Szemle [Hungary] 1981 36(3): 61-72.* The abnormal stress on human rights, introduced as a political red herring by the Carter government did not pay the dividend expected. Consequently it was replaced in the Reagan administration by the more impressive sounding "fight against international terrorists."   T. Kuner

2968. Patrick, Richard.   PRESIDENTIAL LEADERSHIP IN FOREIGN AFFAIRS REEXAMINED: KENNEDY AND LAOS WITHOUT RADICAL REVISIONISM. *World Affairs 1978 140(3): 245-258.* Henry Fairlie (*The Kennedy Promise: The Politics of Expectation*, New York, 1972) and Richard J. Walton (*Cold War and Counter-Revolution: The Foreign Policy of John F. Kennedy*, New York, 1972) view John F. Kennedy as a Cold Warrior, but the President's response to the Laotian crisis (1960-62) was calm, restrained, and realistic, not militant and strident.

2969. Patrizio, Gabriele.   KISSINGER E IL TRAMONTO DELL-'EQUILIBRIO   [Kissinger and the decline of international equilibrium]. *Riv. di Studi Politici Int. [Italy] 1975 42(1): 85-88.* Since Watergate, international crises have become more complex and more difficult for Kissinger to solve. Before the fall of Nixon, the Secretary of State's diplomacy was aimed at maintaining the principle of international equilibrium, stability, and legitimacy. Since Watergate, however, the international system has been revolutionized by the conflict between the great powers (USSR, China), encouraging smaller nations to defy Kissinger's system, and succeeding in breaking the balance of power that American diplomacy worked out. Hence it seems that the Kissingerian theory for international equilibrium is no longer a viable tool for peace.   A. Sbacchi

2970. Patrizio, Gabriele.   KISSINGER E MOSCA: VARIAZIONI SUL TEMA DELLA DISTENSIONE   [Kissinger and Moscow: variations on a theme of détente]. *Civitas [Italy] 1974 25(10): 17-30.* Discusses Henry A. Kissinger's theories of foreign relations and how they might apply to the changing US relations with the USSR, NATO, the European Economic Community, and the Middle East.   S

2971. Patrizio, Gabriele.   KISSINGER, IL SISTEMA E L'EQUI-LIBRIO IMPOSSIBILE   [Kissinger, the system and the impossible equilibrium]. *Civitas [Italy] 1975 26(5): 51-62.* Analyzes the faults and merits of Henry Kissinger, and points out contradictory valuations among the frequent reproaches addressed to Kissinger's diplomacy. The prevailing tendency formerly was to lay special stress on pragmatism, with its innovations, compared with the idealistic tradition of American foreign policy. The most important points of Kissinger's style were not only diplomatic realism and a refined technique of negotiation, but also a nearly Machiavellian freedom from prejudice. More recently, however, particular stress has been placed on Kissinger's abstract scientific concept of diplomacy, deep-rooted doctrinairism, and a strict international affairs philosophy. It if is true that Kissinger has two different "souls," the soul of an historian and the soul of a statesman, we must understand how these two souls influence his actions as Secretary of State.   J

2972. Patrizio, Gabriele.   TEORIA DEL POLI: LOGICA E RISCHI DELLA DIPLOMAZIA KISSINGERIANA   [Polarity theory: logic and risk in Kissinger diplomacy]. *Civitas [Italy] 1974 25(7): 3-12.* "In this essay the author goes back to the origins of the multipolar theory, a correction of bipolarism. Multipolarism is bound to help American diplomacy carry out its disengagement from the difficult rôle of the world's gendarme. It becomes clear that multipolarism was founded on a hierarchy of responsibilities, which is the most serious obstacle to its working."   J and S

2973.   Pearson, Frederic S.; Reynolds, J. Martin; and Meyer, Keith E. THE CARTER FOREIGN POLICY AND THE USE OF INTERNATIONAL ORGANIZATION: THE LIMITS OF POLICY INNOVATION. *World Affairs 1979 142(2): 75-97.* Examines foreign policy innovation made by the Carter Administration, including a breaking-down of containment policy and a more positive attitude toward the UN, 1977-79.

2974.   Pellicanò, Gerolamo.   DA METTERNICH A KISSINGER: DALLA RESTAURAZIONE ALLA CONSERVAZIONE [From Metternich to Kissinger: From the restoration to conservation]. *Nuova Antologia [Italy] 1973 519(2076): 469-478.* Critiques Henry A. Kissinger's *The Diplomacy of the Restoration* and discusses his life and accomplishments as Secretary of State in comparison to the Austrian statesman Klemens von Metternich.   M. T. Wilson

2975.   Pelz, Stephen E.   JOHN F. KENNEDY'S 1961 VIETNAM WAR DECISIONS.   *J. of Strategic Studies [Great Britain] 1981 4(4): 356-385.* Discusses the expansion of the US commitment to South Vietnam by President John F. Kennedy during 1961. Kennedy decided from the outset that he was going to pay a high price to hold South Vietnam. He and his advisors expected their new counterinsurgency techniques to work. He considered only escalatory options. He misperceived the nature of Communist strategy in South Vietnam and proposed inappropriate military measures to turn the tide. Kennedy never seriously considered a graceful exit, and the deployment of advisers to the provinces led to American casualties, which in turn deepened Kennedy's commitment. Primary sources; 114 notes.   A. M. Osur

2976.   Pelz, Stephen E.   "WHEN DO I HAVE TIME TO THINK?" JOHN F. KENNEDY, ROGER HILSMAN, AND THE LAOTIAN CRISIS OF 1962.   *Diplomatic Hist. 1979 3(2): 215-229.* Publishes Roger Hilsman's memorandum chronicling the decisions of President John F. Kennedy and his advisers, 9-12 May 1962, on the Laotian crisis. As the result of these deliberations the United States sent the Seventh Fleet to the Gulf of Siam and troops to Thailand, and the warring Laotian parties reached a compromise position. 32 notes.   S

2977.   Pelz, Stephen E.   WHEN THE KITCHEN GETS HOT, PASS THE BUCK: TRUMAN AND KOREA IN 1950. *Rev. in Am. Hist. 1978 6(4): 548-555.* Review article prompted by US Department of State's *Foreign Relations of the United States, 1950, vol. 7, Korea* (Washington, D.C.: US Government Printing Office, 1976).

2978.   Percy, Charles H.   THE PARTISAN GAP.   *Foreign Policy 1981-82 (45): 3-15.* Bipartisanship is vitally important for the maintenance of American leadership in world affairs. Achievement of US foreign policy goals of worldwide peace, freedom, and economic progress depends upon Congressional and public support. In addition to the built-in institutional avenues for consultation between Congress and the Executive Branch, the Reagan administration must take the intiative to consult with Congress more often in order to form this bipartisan consensus on foreign policy.   M. K. Jones

2979.   PérezLlana, Carlos E.   EL LEGADO DE HENRY KISSINGER: ALGUNAS IMPLICANCIAS DE SU GESTIÓN [The legacy of Henry Kissinger: Some implications of his work]. *Estudios Int. [Chile] 1977 10(37): 68-91.* Henry A. Kissinger was US Secretary of State during 1973-77.

2980.   Perkins, Bradford.   RELUCTANT MIDWIFE: AMERICA AND THE BIRTH OF ISRAEL. *Rev. in Am. Hist. 1981 9(1): 138-143.* Review essay of Kenneth Ray Bain's *The March to Zion: United States Policy and the Founding of Israel* (1979), Zvi Ganin's *Truman, American Jewry, and Israel, 1945-1948* (1979), and Evan M. Wilson's *Decision on Palestine: How the U.S. Came to Recognize Israel* (1979).

2981.   Perlmutter, Amos.   CRISIS MANAGEMENT: KISSINGER'S MIDDLE EAST NEGOTIATIONS (OCTOBER, 1973-JUNE, 1974). *Int. Studies Q. 1975 19(3): 316-343.* Analyzes Henry A. Kissinger as a "super diplomat" and the prototype of a modern crisis manager. Contrasts institutionalized crisis management with Kissinger's personalized diplomatic management during the first phase of negotiations in the Middle East during October 1973-June 1974. 6 notes.   G. J. Boughton

2982.   Perlmutter, Amos.   REAGAN'S MIDDLE EAST POLICY: A YEAR-ONE ASSESSMENT.   *Orbis 1982 26(1): 26-29.* Evaulates President Reagan's Middle East policy during 1981, which has been characterized by a shift toward closer relations with Saudi Arabia and worsened relations with Israel. The linchpin of Middle East policy, "strategic consensus," is in reality no policy at all and has not even contained the USSR threat in South Yemen.   J. W. Thacker, Jr.

2983.   Petras, James.   U.S. FOREIGN POLICY: THE REVIVAL OF INTERVENTIONISM.   *Monthly Rev. 1980 31(9): 15-27.* President Jimmy Carter's human rights campaign is a device to overcome internal and external opposition while the United States recreates its capacity to intervene in foreign countries.

2984.   Pfau, Richard.   CONTAINMENT IN IRAN, 1946: THE SHIFT TO AN ACTIVE POLICY. *Diplomatic Hist. 1977 1(4): 359-372.* For some months following the first enunciation of the policy of containment by George F. Kennan in February 1946, the State Department attempted to achieve containment in Iran by verbal means. But following the admission of three members of the pro-Soviet Tūdeh Party to the Iranian cabinet in July, the United States determined to give Iran weapons and credit on a scale sufficient to assure its independence and to make American influence paramount. Even before this new policy became effective, able maneuvering by Ambassador George Allen had secured the ejection of the Tūdeh ministers from the cabinet. Later, concrete evidence of American commitment encouraged wavering Prime Minister Qavām-al-Saltana to send troops into the Soviet-controlled province of Azerbaidzhan, bringing an end to significant Soviet influence in Iran. Based on archival material and secondary sources; 32 notes.   L. W. Van Wyk

2985.   Piper, Don C.   THE CUBAN MISSILE CRISIS AND INTERNATIONAL LAW: PRECIPITOUS DECLINE OR UNILATERAL DEVELOPMENT.   *World Affairs 1975 138(1): 26-31.* Treats the incident with reference to the unilateral assertion of new rules by national decisionmakers.

2986.   Podet, Allen H.   ANTI-ZIONISM IN A KEY U.S. DIPLOMAT: LOY HENDERSON AT THE END OF WORLD WAR II. *Am. Jewish Arch. 1978 30(2): 155-187.* Describes Loy Henderson as the "single diplomat most centrally involved in questions of Zionism, of Palestine, and of the world Jewish movement that centered on these issues," at the end of World War II. The case of Loy Henderson must be seen as central to any understanding and evaluation of State Department policy during this important and controversial period leading to the creation of Israel.   J

2987.   Podhoretz, Norman.   KISSINGER   RECONSIDERED. *Commentary 1982 73(6): 19-28.* Reviews Henry Kissinger's *Years of Upheaval,* in which he establishes himself as an excellent writer, explains and defends his achievements as a diplomat, and reveals himself to be a practitioner of the art of diplomacy rather than the "conceptualizer" he was praised as being.

2988.   Poole, Peter A.   THE UNITED STATES AND SOUTHEAST ASIA: A NEW THEME.   *Current Hist. 1979 77(452): 193-196, 226.* A favorable evaluation of President Jimmy Carter's foreign policy in southeast Asia during the 1970's.

2989.   Poole, Walter S.   FROM CONCILIATION TO CONTAINMENT: THE JOINT CHIEFS OF STAFF AND THE COMING OF THE COLD WAR, 1945-1946. *Military Affairs 1978 42(1): 12-16.* Between 1944 and 1946, the Joint Chiefs of Staff's (JCS) view of Soviet-American relations changed completely. At first the JCS saw the United States as simply mediating Anglo-Soviet quarrels, but gradually the wheel turned full circle and they saw the US role as the prime mover in stopping Soviet aggression; by late 1945 they viewed the USSR as an expansionist power. Discusses Cold War historiography, saying that JCS's recommendations were defensive reactions and not offensive threats. Based on JCS papers; 25 notes.   A. M. Osur

2990.   Porter, Gareth.   THE DECLINE OF U.S. DIPLOMACY IN SOUTHEAST ASIA.   *SAIS Rev. 1981 (1): 149-159.* Discusses American influence in Southeast Asia since the end of the Vietnam War, particularly during the Carter administration, with special reference to relations with Vietnam and China.

2991. Postbrief, Sam. DEPARTURE FROM INCREMENTALISM IN U.S. STRATEGIC PLANNING: THE ORIGINS OF NSC-68. *Naval War Coll. Rev. 1980 33(2): 34-57.* Recently declassified documents and other materials make reexamination of the Truman administration national security planning apparatus a valuable example of policy formation in crises. The arguments formed and advanced in the present strategic debate are strikingly similar to those offered in the debate on NSC-68, the first major official American policy planning document of the Cold War. 76 notes.   J

2992. Poulose, T. T. SOME RECENT BOOKS ON DETENTE. *Int. Studies [India] 1974 13(4): 843-852.* Reviews four 1971-73 books dealing with the detente between the United States and Russia; includes the implications of detente for China and Richard M. Nixon's diplomacy.

2993. Power, Paul F. THE INDO-AMERICAN NUCLEAR CONTROVERSY. *Asian Survey 1979 19(6): 574-596.* Indo-US relations have improved since 1977, but not without controversy over the US nuclear nonproliferation policy and law and Indian reaction to them. President Carter and Prime Minister Desai have met to try to work out differences, but India will not agree to US demands for full-scope safeguards before delivering fuel supplies and continuing nuclear cooperation with India. Soviet offers of assistance to India with fewer strings attached complicate the issue, as does Pakistan's nuclear development project. 33 notes.   M. A. Eide

2994. Quandt, William B. KISSINGER AND THE ARAB-ISRAELI DISENGAGEMENT NEGOTIATIONS. *J. of Internat. Affairs 1975 29(1): 19-32.* Kissinger has been successful by segmenting issues, negotiating secretly, building personal rapport and public support, excluding the Soviets, and keeping each side aware of the other's domestic constraints. Ultimately, the United States will have to guarantee Israeli security, and the Israelis will have to deal with the Soviets, the Palestinians, and a relatively united Arab effort.   R. D. Frederick

2995. Raditsa, Leo. MOYNIHAN AT THE U.N. *Midstream 1980 26(8): 39-47.* Reviews *A Dangerous Place* by Daniel Patrick Moynihan with Suzanne Weaver (New York: Little, Brown, 1978) on the career of the US ambassador to the UN.

2996. Randall, Stephen J. THE AMERICANIZATION OF HENRY KISSINGER. *Can. Rev. of Am. Studies [Canada] 1977 8(2): 221-228.* In *Kisssinger, The European Mind in American Policy* (New York: Basic Books, 1976), Bruce Mazlish ascribes to Secretary of State Henry A. Kissinger (1973-76) a unique position in the formulation and execution of US foreign policy. Mazlish believes that German antecedents and a conservatism derived from continental intellectuals such as Oswald Spengler (1880-1936) shaped Kissinger's views on international relations and caused him to apply balance of power concepts to produce order and detente in the world. 5 notes.   H. T. Lovin

2997. Ranger, Robin. DESPITE FLAWS, KISSINGER SYSTEM COULD MEAN AN ERA OF STABILITY. *Internat. Perspectives [Canada] 1974 (1): 23-27.* Discusses the diplomacy of Secretary of State Henry Kissinger and the United States.   S

2998. Ravenal, Earl C. NIXON'S CHALLENGE TO CARTER: NO MORE MR. NICE GUY. *Foreign Policy 1977-78 (29): 27-42.* The Watergate scandal appeared to be the perfect illustration of the liberal tenet that bad policies derive from the bad character and/or bad motives of policymakers. In fact, that situation was the direct result of Richard M. Nixon's foreign policy, which most Americans supported. Grand goals sometimes require questionable means. President Jimmy Carter will have little diplomatic success until he realizes this and accepts that "secrecy, executive impunity, license for immoral external behavior, and forgiveness for internal actions that abridge the rights of citizens" are sometimes necessary for an effective foreign policy. 2 notes.
                                                             T. L. Powers

2999. Ravenal, Earl C. SECRECY, CONSENSUS, AND FOREIGN POLICY: THE LOGIC OF CHOICE. *Towson State J. of Internat.*

Affairs 1975 10(1): 1-12. Compares the use of secrecy in the foreign policy of the Nixon Admininstration and the Ford Administration in the 1970's, emphasizing the style of Henry Kissinger.

3000. Reich, Bernard. UNITED STATES POLICY IN THE MIDDLE EAST. *Current Hist. 1976 70(412): 1-4, 42.* Discusses US foreign policy in the Middle East, 1967-75, emphasizing the role of Secretary of State Henry A. Kissinger.

3001. Reichard, Gary W. DIVISIONS AND DISSENT: DEMOCRATS AND FOREIGN POLICY, 1952-1956. *Pol. Sci. Q. 1978 93(1): 51-72.* Traces the evolution of Democratic party thought and action on significant foreign policy issues during the first Eisenhower administration. Refuting the idea that bipartisanship prevailed in foreign policy during the 1950's, describes how Democratic leaders differed with Eisenhower's policies from 1952 to 1956 and why they developed a coherent alternative policy of their own after 1956.   J

3002. Reischauer, Edwin O. BACK TO NORMALCY. *Foreign Policy 1975 (20): 199-208.* Reviews recent US foreign relations and predicts new trends and policies. US interventionism, particularly in Vietnam, was based on false premises, as events in Southeast Asia have contradicted the domino theory. The failure of the Ford administration to understand the world situation led it into the ill-advised Mayaguez affair. We should avoid a repetition of the Vietnamese tragedy in Korea; after consulting with Japan, we should withdraw gradually. Our defeat in Vietnam should be looked upon as an opportunity to formulate a sound US foreign policy.   R. F. Kugler

3003. Roberts, Adam. KISSINGER AND THE STRUCTURING OF UNITED STATES FOREIGN POLICY. *Pol. Studies [Great Britain] 1981 29(4): 626-631.* Relates the basic theoretical problems found in American diplomacy during the last 20 years. Provides a brief analysis of the recent memoirs of Henry A. Kissinger, secretary of state in the Nixon and Ford administrations, and the major omissions that are quite evident in these memoirs. American foreign policy, as directed by Kissinger, definitely lacked a clear conception of intellectual statesmanship. Secondary sources.   W. D. Wrigley

3004. Roberts, Adam. KISSINGER AND THE STRUCTURING OF US FOREIGN POLICY. *Contemporary Rev. [Great Britain] 1982 240(1395): 169-176.* Discusses the process of US foreign policymaking and the influence of Henry A. Kissinger, as revealed in his recently published memoirs, with particular reference to Indochina, White House control, and the down-grading of the State Department.

3005. Roberts, Chalmers M. FOREIGN POLICY UNDER A PARALYZED PRESIDENCY. *Foreign Affairs 1974 52(4): 675-689.* The Watergate Scandal has robbed the nation of its ability to resolve problems in foreign relations and President Nixon has had to retreat from spectacular initiatives to maintain momentum. One must agree with Henry A. Kissinger that "one cannot have a crisis of authority without paying a price somewhere along the line."   R. Riles

3006. Rode, Reinhard. US-HANDELSPOLITIK IN DER ÄRA NIXON/FORD [US trade policies in the Nixon-Ford era]. *Neue Politische Literatur [West Germany] 1977 22(3): 346-360.* US trade policy between 1968 and 1976 was characterized by complex bargaining among the legislative and executive branches and diverse economic and social lobbies, free traders, and protectionists, and by the global political role of the United States.

3007. Rogers, Benjamin. "DEAR MR. PRESIDENT": THE HOOVER-TRUMAN CORRESPONDENCE. *Palimpsest 1974 55(5): 152-158.* Chronicles the correspondence between Herbert Hoover and Harry S. Truman concerning the World Famine Mission, 1945-48.   S

3008. Rondot, Philippe. LE PRÉSIDENT CARTER ET LE PROCHE-ORIENT: UN AN D'EFFORTS POUR LA PAIX [President Carter and the Near East: one year of efforts for peace]. *Pol. Étrangère [France] 1978 43(1): 59-86.* Describes and recounts the several stages of President Jimmy Carter's efforts to bring peace to the Middle East, concluding with the Egyptian initiative of 9 November 1977.

3009. Rosati, Jerel A. DEVELOPING A SYSTEMATIC DECISION-MAKING FRAMEWORK: BUREAUCRATIC POLITICS IN PERSPECTIVE. *World Pol. 1981 33(2): 234-252.* Too often the popular term "bureaucratic politics" is used by scholars and practitioners without clearly stating its policy application. The decisionmaking behavior that occurred during the Johnson and Nixon administrations for SALT I serves to illustrate many of the limits of the model. To provide a clearer understanding of policymaking behavior, a more systematic decisionmaking framework is offered, which should contribute to the development of better model- and theory-building.   J/S

3010. Rosenberg, David Alan. AMERICAN ATOMIC STRATEGY AND THE HYDROGEN BOMB DECISION. *J. of Am. Hist. 1979 66(1): 62-87.* Utilizes recently declassified material to analyze the development of American plans for a possible atomic war against the USSR between 1945 and 1950 and the military's role in President Harry S. Truman's decision in 1950 to develop the hydrogen bomb. Concerned over the strength of Soviet conventional forces, the United States by 1949 was firmly committed to a defensive strategy based on atomic weapons. The military's concern over how to counter Soviet conventional capability and possible technological advances prompted the Joint Chiefs of Staff to recommend development of the hydrogen bomb. President Truman accepted the position of the Joint Chiefs on thermonuclear development. 95 notes.   T. P. Linkfield

3011. Rosenberg, J. Philip. THE BELIEF SYSTEM OF HARRY S. TRUMAN AND ITS EFFECT ON FOREIGN POLICY DECISION-MAKING DURING HIS ADMINISTRATION. *Presidential Studies Q. 1982 12(2): 226-238.* Examines the recognition of the new state of Israel and the decision to defy the Russian blockade of Berlin through Truman's belief system. His deep commitment to God and his view of an ethical life shaped his commitment to both Israel, and to the German people in the face of the Russian threat. 2 tables, 92 notes.
                                                        D. H. Cline

3012. Rosenfeld, Stephen S. FROM WASHINGTON: THE PENTAGON TILT. *Present Tense 1977 4(3): 18-20.* Describes the Pentagon's Middle East policymaking apparatus, procedures, and options during the administrations of Richard Nixon, Gerald Ford, and Jimmy Carter. Primary sources; illus.   R. B. Mendel

3013. Rositzke, Harry. AMERICA'S SECRET OPERATIONS: A PERSPECTIVE. *Foreign Affairs 1975 53(2): 334-351.* Traces the history of American secret intelligence operations and raises questions concerning their objectives today. Founded by William J. Donovan in the Second World War as the OSS (Office of Strategic Services), this service was later put under the umbrella of the Central Intelligence Agency. Long-term national objectives should make for "clean-cut" missions for the AIS, not limited to war and politics. 2 notes.   C. W. Olson

3014. Rossi, Mario. LES RELATIONS AMÉRICANO-SOVIETIQUES [American-Soviet relations]. *Pol. Étrangère [France] 1976 41(5): 423-432.* The delicate balance in world peace has been dependent on US-USSR agreement since the Cuban crisis of October 1962; views the presidencies of Kennedy, Johnson, Nixon, and Ford, with speculation on future relations under Carter.

3015. Rostow, Eugene V. THE GIANT STILL SLEEPS. *Orbis 1980 24(2): 311-321.* Examines the impact of the Camp David agreements, the upheaval in Iran, and the Soviet invasion of Afghanistan on US foreign policy to ascertain why it has not changed. Concludes that the Carter administration is trying to maintain the post-1945 world when it is already changing, that it perceives the Soviets as being basically friendly and that the problems of Vietnam still haunt US policy.
                                                    J. W. Thacker, Jr.

3016. Rouquié, Alain. LA PRÉSIDENCE CARTER ET L'AMÉRIQUE LATINE: PARENTHÈSE OU MUTATION? [The Carter presidency and Latin America: parenthesis or change?]. *Problèmes d'Amérique Latine [France] 1981 (60): 49-56.* A critical analysis of President Jimmy Carter's policy toward Latin America.

3017. Rourke, Francis E. STYLES OF PRESIDENTIAL SECRECY. *Towson State J. of Internat. Affairs 1975 10(1): 19-26.* Discusses the use of foreign policy secrecy by US presidents since 1945, emphasizing the styles of John F. Kennedy and Lyndon B. Johnson.

3018. Rowe, David N. THE NIXON CHINA POLICY AND THE BALANCE OF POWER. *Issues & Studies [Taiwan] 1973 9(8): 12-28.* Discusses the Nixon Administration's foreign policy of improving relations with China, 1969-72, to maintain the balance of power between the USSR and China and to take advantage of the hostility between the two Communist countries.

3019. Rowe, David N. THE STATE DEPARTMENT WHITE PAPER: A SUGGESTED RESPONSE. *Issues & Studies [Taiwan] 1981 17(9): 35-59.* A discussion of the "White Paper on China": Department of State, *Relations with China, 1944-1949* (1949). This collection of documents was politically oriented toward promoting a military alliance between the United States and the Chinese Communists. Full disclosure of restricted materials, 1944-49, in government archives on Taiwan is necessary to refute the views contained in this volume, which still have an unfortunate influence on US politics.   J. A. Krompart

3020. Rozek, Edward J. WHITEWASHING THE WHITE HOUSE. *Survey [Great Britain] 1980 25(2): 32-40.* Reviews Henry A. Kissinger's *White House Years* (1979). The memoir depicts minuscule achievements as monumental triumphs and monumental blunders and defeats as nonexistent or the machinations of others, hence, in effect, the memoir should be viewed as an attempt at whitewashing the Nixon-Kissinger policies that led to the disastrous strategic retreat of the United States politically and militarily.   V. Samaraweera

3021. Rubin, Barry. AMERICA AND THE EGYPTIAN REVOLUTION, 1950-1957. *Pol. Sci. Q. 1982 97(1): 73-90.* American policy toward Egypt was transformed during this critical period from one oriented toward eventual Egyptian participation in an anti-Soviet collective security network to a belief that Gamal Abdel Nasser was the key force behind political upheaval and anti-Americanism in the Arab world. Chronicles the events leading up to Nassar's nationalization of the Suez Canal Company and the creation of the Eisenhower Doctrine. Based upon extensive interviews, newly released documents, and secondary sources; 67 notes.   L. J. Klass

3022. Rudnick, David. DEATH OF AN EMBARGO: WHY AMERICA RESUMED ARMS SALES TO TURKEY. *Round Table [Great Britain] 1978 (272): 355-361.* The US placed an embargo on arms sales to Turkey in February 1975, pending a settlement of the dispute with Cyprus, but lifted it in July 1978 because of increased goodwill and the influence of President Jimmy Carter's administration with both countries.

3023. Rudnick, David. THE WINDING ROAD OF GOOD INTENTIONS: A CONSIDERATION OF PRESIDENT CARTER'S FOREIGN POLICIES. *Round Table [Great Britain] 1977 (268): 345-350.* Examines changes in US foreign policy under President Jimmy Carter. Describes the replacement of Kissinger's realpolitik with Carter's moralpolitik, his attitude toward the Soviet Union, South America, South Africa, and the Communist regimes of Southeast Asia. Although President Carter's idealistic rhetoric has suggested a dramatic change in foreign policy, economic pressures and the need to maintain influential and powerful allies has kept the United States in the arms-exporting business.
                                                        C. Anstey

3024. Rushford, Gregory G. MAKING ENEMIES: THE PIKE COMMITTEE'S STRUGGLE TO GET THE FACTS. *Washington Monthly 1976 8(5-6): 42-53.* Reveals the noncooperative action by the executive branch, especially by the Central Intelligence Agency and Henry A. Kissinger, as the House Select Committee on Intelligence Activities (the Pike Committee) investigated and discovered mismanagement and distortion in the intelligence service in the 1970's.

3025. Rushkoff, Bennett C. EISENHOWER, DULLES AND THE QUEMOY-MATSU CRISIS, 1954-55. *Pol. Sci. Q. 1981 96(3): 465-480.* Examines high-level decisionmaking in the Eisenhower adminstration during the Quemoy-Matsu crisis of 1954-55. Dwight D. Eisenhower's personal handling of the crisis was responsible for a relaxation in early 1955 of the American commitment to the defense of the offshore islands.
                                                            J

3026. Rustin, Bayard and Gershman, Carl. AFRICA, SOVIET IM-PERIALISM AND THE RETREAT OF AMERICAN POWER. *Commentary 1977 64(4): 33-43.* Africa has suddenly become the focus of increased attention in Washington. American failure to halt Soviet intervention in Angola is the clearest demonstration since Munich of the impotence of the democratic world when faced by totalitarian aggression. American liberals opened the door to Soviet and Cuban intervention in Angola by applying their opposition to American policy in Vietnam to the African situation. Soviet foreign policy aims to control the supply of Southern Africa's minerals and to dominate the sea route around the Cape of Good Hope. The Carter administration has followed a noninterventionist policy toward Cuban intervention in Africa despite clearly expressed dismay by African leaders at Soviet and Cuban incursions in the area.　　　　　　　　　　　　　　S. R. Herstein

3027. Ryan, Henry Butterfield, Jr. THE AMERICAN INTELLEC-TUAL TRADITION REFLECTED IN THE TRUMAN DOCTRINE. *Am. Scholar 1973 42(2): 294-307.* The Truman Doctrine (1947) pledged the United States to support free nations against threatening totalitarian regimes. When the British embassy informed the Department of State that it would have to discontinue financial and military aid to Greece and Turkey, the US government made a strenuous effort to convert public opinion away from isolationism. The process of formulating the new policy and drafting Truman's speech is discussed at length.
　　　　　　　　　　　　　　　　　　E. P. Stickney

3028. Safford, Jeffrey J. THE NIXON-CASTRO MEETING OF 19 APRIL 1959. *Diplomatic Hist. 1980 4(4): 425-431.* Reprints the text of a memorandum written by US Vice-President Richard M. Nixon on his conversation with Cuban revolutionary Fidel Castro, who visited the United States in 1959. Nixon judged Castro as non-Communist, but "incredibly naive with regard to the Communist threat," praised his "indefinable qualities which make him a leader of man," and criticized his "almost slavish subservience to prevailing majority opinion," his shallow understanding of how to run a government or an economy, and his reluctance to welcome American investment in Cuba. In addition, the document reveals Nixon's concept of leadership. 5 notes.
　　　　　　　　　　　　　　　　　　T. L. Powers

3029. Said, Edward. THE UNITED STATES AND THE CON-FLICT OF POWERS IN THE MIDDLE EAST. *J. of Palestine Studies [Lebanon] 1973 2(3): 30-50.* Discusses the basis and formulation of US foreign policy in the Middle East, especially during the first Nixon administration, 1969-73.

3030. Sale, Richard T. AMERICA IN IRAN. *SAIS Rev. 1981-82 (3): 27-39.* Examines the geopolitical and economic goals of US involvement in Iran, 1941-82, commenting on differences between US and Iranian perceptions of the region's social and economic needs; discusses the foreign policy of presidential administrations from Roosevelt to Carter; and comments on the interference of Great Britain, the USSR, and the United States in the region.

3031. Salzberg, John P. THE HUMAN RIGHTS PROGRAM IN CONGRESS: SOME POLICY IMPLICATIONS FROM THE 1977 HEARINGS. *Int. Studies Notes 1977 4(4): 1-5.* The Carter administration has concentrated on human rights issues, but it is still important for Congress to maintain interest in these issues; 1977 hearings before the House Subcommittee on International Organizations monitored the executive branch and the actions of foreign governments and kept foreign and domestic public informed.

3032. Sanders, Sol W. DOCTOR KISSINGER'S ASIA: BALANCE OR VERTIGO? *Asian Affairs 1973 1(1): 1-16.* Evaluates Henry A. Kissinger's policy of a balance of forces in Asia (1968-73).　　　S

3033. Sanders, Sylvia. DATA PRIVACY: WHAT WASHINGTON DOESN'T WANT YOU TO KNOW. *Reason 1981 12(9): 24-37.* Created out of the Armed Forces Security Agency by President Harry Truman in 1952, the National Security Agency (NSA) has tried in vain to keep a monopoly on cryptography; now that the ability to construct secure codes outstrips the ability to break them, the NSA should give up its self-defeating suppressive measures and grant both individuals and businesses the security and privacy they need.

3034. Sapin, Burton M. ISN'T IT TIME FOR A *MODEST* PRESI-DENCY IN FOREIGN AFFAIRS? REFLECTIONS ON THE CARTER PERFORMANCE. *Presidential Studies Q. 1980 10(1): 19-27.* Reflects on President Jimmy Carter's performance in foreign policy and in foreign affairs. Both mistakes and notable accomplishments are summarized for lessons to be gleaned. Stronger staff work at the presidential level should help the president put his various problems into better perspective, thus contributing to a better sense of priority and overall strategy.　　　　　　　　　　　　　　　　G. E. Pergl

3035. Sato, Hideo. JAPANESE-AMERICAN RELATIONS. *Current Hist. 1978 75(441): 145-148, 180-181.* With the elections in 1976 of Jimmy Carter and Takeo Fukuda, a new era in Japanese-American relations began, strained initially because of disagreements over nuclear energy development and Carter's intention of withdrawing 32,000 American troops from South Korea.

3036. Saunders, Richard M. THE 1954 INDOCHINA CRISIS. *Military Rev. 1978 58(4): 68-78.* President Dwight D. Eisenhower's refusal to commit US forces to relieve the beleaguered garrison of Dien Bien Phu was not the result of US indecision. Eisenhower refused to intervene without the support of Congress, a pledge of joint intervention by the other Allied powers, and French renunciation of colonial claims to the area. 43 notes.　　　　　　　　　　　　　C. Hopkins

3037. Schlesinger, Arthur M., Jr. HUMAN RIGHTS AND THE AMERICAN TRADITION. *Foreign Affairs 1979 57(3): 503-526.* The Carter administration's efforts to make human rights a basic factor in the formulation of foreign policy has produced considerable confusion and misunderstanding here and abroad. Though human rights has always been a cherished component of the American tradition, its force must be applied primarily at the domestic level. Other countries will learn by our example. "The more the United States presses human rights as a unilateral initiative, the more it risks becoming a high court of indignation." 52 notes.　　　　　　　　　　　　　　M. R. Yerburgh

3038. Schoenbaum, David. THE UNITED STATES AND THE BIRTH OF ISRAEL. *Wiener Lib. Bull. [Great Britain] 1978 31(45-46): 87-100.* In 1946-47, three possibilities existed for US policy toward Palestine: support partition, oppose it, or adopt neutrality. The first one raised the possibility of military responsibility for the protection of the Jews; neutrality would open the area to the Russians. What remained was a cantonized federal Palestine under some kind of trusteeship. However, Jewish successes led US foreign policy to recognize a de facto partition. Shows variety of pressures on Harry S. Truman, from domestic political concerns to the exigencies of the Cold War, and concludes that his policy was "neither an opportunistic nor an incompetent one." It helped create Israel while maintaining the Anglo-American alliance, keeping up the ties with the Arab states, and avoiding being pulled into a major war. Summarizes contemporary opinions, for example, Secretary Forrestal's note in his diary in 1948 that unless the United States had access to Middle Eastern oil, American motorcar companies would have to design a four-cylinder motorcar. 77 notes.　　　　　　　　　R. V. Layton

3039. Schonberger, Howard B. U.S. POLICY IN POST-WAR JA-PAN: THE RETREAT FROM LIBERALISM. *Sci. & Soc. 1982 46(1): 39-59.* US policy in occupied Japan greatly contributed to, not simply reflected, the bipolarization that occurred in the late 1940's. George F. Kennan of the State Department and Undersecretary of the Army William H. Draper, Jr., combined to force General Douglas MacArthur to retreat from the reformist policy of deconcentrating Japanese industry into a policy that sought to make Japan the Asian workshop of a global capitalist order dominated by the United States. Mainly primary sources; 54 notes.　　　　　　　　　　　　　　　　L. V. Eid

3040. Schönfeld, Roland. DIE USA IN DEN WIRTSCHAFTS-BEZIEHUNGEN ZWISCHEN OST UND WEST [The United States and East-West economic relations]. *Osteuropa [West Germany] 1973 23(11): 837-847.* American "stagflation" and the emerging energy crisis induced the Nixon administration to back away from the accustomed embargo-oriented trade policy toward the USSR. Soviet and Chinese needs for American capital and technology meet the new American policy halfway, but on the Soviet side trade is limited by economic priorities and capabilities. Unlike Western Europe or Japan, the United States and the

USSR see foreign trade largely as a stopgap to help them overcome internal economic problems. 14 notes. R. E. Weltsch

3041. Schröder, Dieter. M. KISSINGER, L'EUROPE ET LA FRANCE [Mr. Kissinger, Europe, and France]. *Documents [France] 1974 29(2): 6-9.* A German editorial exposing an evolution in European public opinion, which no longer holds France responsible for European stagnation and lack of solidarity in the Atlantic Alliance, as Henry A. Kissinger and the Nixon administration did, 1969-73.

3042. Schulz, Donald E. KENNEDY AND THE CUBAN CONNECTION. *Foreign Policy 1977 (26): 57-64, 121-139.* Advocates the resumption of the investigation of the assassination of John F. Kennedy in order to clear up some of the leads uncovered by the Senate Select Committee. In light of the Central Intelligence Agency's attempts on Castro's life, the possible role of Cuban agents in the assassination needs to be examined thoroughly. The investigation will also reveal much about the conduct of US foreign policy. Primary and secondary sources; 22 notes. E. Hopkins

3043. Schulzinger, Robert D. THE NAIVE AND SENTIMENTAL DIPLOMAT: HENRY KISSINGER'S MEMOIRS. *Diplomatic Hist. 1980 4(3): 303-315.* "Naive" and "sentimental" are two of the favorite terms of abuse employed by Henry A. Kissinger in his memoirs, *White House Years* (Boston, 1979); yet those words best describe his diplomacy. "He is naively out of touch with the way modern democratic states conduct their diplomacy; and he is sentimentally attached to a vision of foreign policy, called geopolitics, which is almost pure fantasy." Based on *White House Years* and secondary sources; 16 notes.
T. L. Powers

3044. Schweigler, Gebhard. CARTER'S DETENTE POLICY: CHANGE OR CONTINUITY? *World Today [Great Britain] 1978 34(3): 81-88.* Originally President Jimmy Carter's foreign policy was one of tactical changes, but need of popular support has led to continue previous foreign relations while maintaining advocacy of human rights which originally gained him popular appeal.

3045. Schweigler, Gebhard. DIE AMERIKANISCHE ENTSPANNUNGSPOLITIK: WANDEL ODER KONTINUITÄT? [The American policy of detente: Change or continuity?]. *Europa Archiv [West Germany] 1977 32(22): 791-799.* President Jimmy Carter is continuing a policy of detente despite rising opposition in Congress and among the American people.

3046. Scoville, Herbert, Jr. FLEXIBLE MADNESS? *Foreign Policy 1974 (14): 164-177.* Criticizes the "flexible response" strategy of nuclear policies of the Nixon administration. S

3047. Seidman, Ann and Seidman, Neva. UNITED STATES MULTINATIONALS IN SOUTH AFRICA. *J. of Southern African Affairs 1976 1(special issue): 125-166.* A handful of the biggest firms in the United States have provided over three-fourths of US investments in South Africa. They are linked with each other, as well as with most of the nearly 400 other US companies which have invested in South Africa, through their boards of directors. Together, these firms comprised the growing economic interest which, even when it was smaller, apparently helped to convince the US National Security Council that in 1969 the US government should maintain cordial relations with the South African government. It was these interests which Secretary of State Henry Kissinger was seeking to protect by his shuttle-diplomacy, designed to prevent major upheavals in South Africa. Secondary sources; 5 tables, 53 notes.
A. W. Howell

3048. Sellen, Robert W. OLD ASSUMPTIONS VERSUS NEW REALITIES: LYNDON JOHNSON AND FOREIGN POLICY. *Internat. J. [Canada] 1973 28(2): 205-229.* Though Johnson's political skills were vast, his narrow outlook and personality flaws prevented him from pursuing an effective foreign policy. 83 notes.
R. V. Kubicek

3049. Semidei, Manuela. TRENTE ANS DE POLITIQUE EXTÉRIEURE DES ÉTATS-UNIS (1944-1974): QUELQUES LIVRES RÉCENTS [Thirty years of US foreign policy (1944-1974): Some recent

books]. *Rev. Française de Science Politique [France] 1974 24(5): 1056-1082.* A bibliographical essay covering a wide range of recent (primarily English-language) works on US foreign policy from Truman through Nixon. Scholars have returned to such basic issues as whether policy objectives or merely policy means have altered, the relations among containment, detente, and neoisolationism, and the degree to which specific presidents, secretaries of state, the bureaucracy, and public opinion have been responsible for decisions. 74 notes. W. J. Reedy

3050. Serfaty, Simon. BRZEZINSKI: PLAY IT AGAIN, ZBIG. *Foreign Policy 1978 (32): 3-21.* An 'enduring penchant for fashionable ideas and concepts that are adopted or discarded in the light of changing circumstances" and an "unbecoming reliance on the intellectual cliché of the moment" have prevented Zbigniew Brzezinski from forming a coherent structure for US foreign policy. Relying on first one analysis of international relations, then another, he has recommended different postures at different times. The result has been "a series of uncoordinated improvisations that could not add up to a policy, but created an impression of easily yielding under pressure." 11 notes. T. L. Powers

3051. Serfaty, Simon. THE KISSINGER LEGACY: OLD OBSESSIONS AND NEW LOOK. *World Today [Great Britain] 1977 33(3): 81-89.* Examines Henry A. Kissinger's foreign policy as a continuation of American policy of the 1960's under the auspices of the New Look, 1970's.

3052. Sergeev, F. ROL' TSRU V VOENNO-FASHISTSKOM PEREVOROTE V CHILI [The role of the CIA in the military-fascist coup in Chile]. *Novaia i Noveishaia Istoriia [USSR] 1977 (3): 91-102, (4): 101-116.* Examines the role of the Central Intelligence Agency in the right-wing military coup d'etat which displaced the Communist government of Salvador Allende in Chile in 1973. The CIA began plotting the coup as early as 1970, when Allende was elected. The investigative journalism and disclosures of the American press about their government's involvement in Chilean politiics were stage-managed by the CIA. The US interference in Chile must be seen as a part of a larger pattern of interference in Latin American politics. Based on US newspapers and on secondary sources; 55 notes. D. N. Collins/S

3053. Sewell, James P. MASTER BUILDER OR CAPTAIN OF THE DIKE? NOTES ON THE LEADERSHIP OF KISSINGER. *Int. J. [Canada] 1976 31(4): 648-665.* Examines the accomplishments of the former Secretary of State through terms of reference which Henry A. Kissinger developed in his own writings on historical figures. 43 notes.
R. V. Kubicek

3054. Shamberg, V. SSHA V SOVREMENNOM MIRE [The United States in the contemporary world]. *Mirovaia Ekonomika i Mezhdunarodnye Otnosheniia [USSR] 1980 (7): 43-57.* Examines the failure of the Carter administration to reverse the declining position of the United States, caused partly by declining economic power but also by cardinal changes in world political and economic forces. 2 tables, 22 notes. English summary.

3055. Shao-hsien, Ch'en. UNITED STATES FOREIGN POLICY AFTER THE DEBACLE IN SOUTHEAST ASIA. *Issues and Studies [Taiwan] 1975 11(7): 24-29.* Discusses US foreign policy toward Southeast Asia following the Vietnam War, 1972-75, emphasizing statements by President Gerald R. Ford and Secretary of State Henry A. Kissinger.

3056. Shapiro, Edward S. THE MILITARY OPTIONS TO HIROSHIMA: A CRITICAL EXAMINATION OF GAR ALPEROVITZ'S *ATOMIC DIPLOMACY. Amerikastudien/Am. Studies [West Germany] 1978 23(1): 60-72.* Gar Alperovitz's *Atomic Diplomacy* (1965) is a polemical revisionist tract. At no time was President Harry S. Truman advised by his military chiefs that Japan was on the verge of surrender or that Japanese capitulation would occur without use of the atomic bomb. Of little value in understanding the circumstances surrounding the dropping of the atomic bomb in 1945, *Atomic Diplomacy* reveals much about the outlook and methodology of one representative revisionist diplomatic historian. J/S

3057. Shattan, Joseph J. ISRAEL, THE UNITED STATES, AND THE UNITED NATIONS. *World Affairs 1981 143(4): 335-345.* Describes anti-Zionist UN resolutions from 1975 to 1980, the role of the Palestine Liberation Organization, and President Ronald Reagan's resolution to bring an end to UN scapegoating of Israel.

3058. Sheehan, Edward. STEP BY STEP IN THE MIDDLE EAST. *J. of Palestine Studies [Lebanon] 1976 5(3-4): 3-53.* Traces Henry A. Kissinger's step-by-step diplomacy in the Middle East from the 1973 October War to the 1975 Sinai agreement, drawing on highly secret US government documents; see also abstract 15A:1532.

3059. Shrivastava, B. K. AMERICAN PERSPECTIVES ON *DETENTE*. *Int. Studies [India] 1974 13(4): 577-607.* Discusses the role of strategic arms limitation negotiations and economic relations in the Nixon administration's policy of detente toward the USSR 1969-73.

3060. Sigelman, Lee. THE COMMANDER IN CHIEF AND THE PUBLIC: MASS RESPONSE TO JOHNSON'S MARCH 31, 1968 BOMBING HALT SPEECH. *J. of Pol. and Military Sociol. 1980 8(1): 1-14.* President [Lyndon B.] Johnson's 1968 bombing halt speech is employed as a case study of mass response to presidential actions. Many political scientists have written of a diffuse public support for presidential foreign policy initiatives. But analysis reveals that people's evaluations of the bombing halt were tied to their feelings about the president and even more closely to their general preferences concerning the American role in Vietnam. More speculatively, the primary opinion impact of the bombing halt announcement appears to have been the reimposition of balance on attitude structures that had fallen out of balance several weeks earlier. These findings suggest some revisions in the widely accepted interpretation of mass response to presidential actions in the international arena. 5 tables, 4 notes, 30 ref.   J

3061. Sigelman, Lee. RALLYING TO THE PRESIDENT'S SUPPORT: A REAPPRAISAL OF THE EVIDENCE. *Polity 1979 11(4): 542-561.* This article examines the extent of the president's influence on American public opinion in questions of major policy and challenges the validity of the widespread "followership concept." The author finds that the concept is not very helpful in explaining an important change in public opinion at a critical juncture in the Vietnam War. He points to the problem posed by the wording of poll questions and demonstrates the compelling force of such alternative explanations of public opinion changes as compassion for a discredited president. He also reverses the more commonly accepted causal link between Lyndon Johnson's resignation speech and the massive change in public opinion. His reappraisal gives us a better understanding of the complex relationship between president, public opinion, and foreign policy.   J

3062. Sigmund, Paul E. LATIN AMERICA: CHANGE OR CONTINUITY? *Foreign Affairs 1982 60(3): 629-657.* Discusses US policy toward Latin America in 1981. The Reagan administration based its policy on considerations of security and anti-Communism. Relations with Mexico were improved and the Caribbean Basin Initiative was developed. In these respects, the Reagan Administration's policy differed from that of the Carter administration, but questions regarding the appropriations of US policy regarding Latin America remain to be answered. Based on State Department publications and secondary sources; 13 notes.
                                                                A. A. Englard

3063. Sinitskii, A. AGRESSIYA SSHA V KAMBODZHE I LAOSE [American aggression in Cambodia and Laos]. *Voenno-Istoricheskii Zhurnal [USSR] 1971 (7): 46-52.* Talks about Nixon's policy of "Vietnamization" and outlines the diplomatic and military preparations behind the American invasions of Cambodia (May 1970) and Laos (February 1971). The United States overrated its strength and underrated that of its opponents.

3064. Siracusa, Joseph M. THE UNITED STATES, VIET-NAM, AND THE COLD WAR: A REAPPRAISAL. *J. of Southeast Asian Studies [Singapore] 1974 5(1): 82-101.* Reviews early US diplomatic involvement in Vietnam, 1944-50; considers President Franklin D. Roosevelt's determination to keep the United States out of Indochina and President Harry S. Truman's decision to aid France in Vietnam due to the pressures of Soviet imperialism.

3065. Škvařil, Jaroslav. ČÍNA NA JEDNÉ LODI S AMERICKÝM IMPERIALISMEM [China in the same boat as American imperialism]. *Hist. a Vojenství [Czechoslovakia] 1980 29(5): 110-127, (6): 149-167.* Part I: NĚKTERE ASPEKTY VÝVOJE ČÍNSKO-AMERICKÝCH VZTAHŮ [aspects of the development of Chinese-American relations]. The ideology of the current Chinese leadership can be traced to traditional nationalism, which increasingly influences the Chinese Communist Party, and to the victory of popular revolution in China, which created the desire for ideological and political hegemony in the worker's movement and the world. The story of American-Chinese approaches is thus a tale about the common desire to pragmatically use the other partner for one's own imperialistic plans. What the United States reactivated in 1971 had already begun in 1942. Part II: CESTA PLNÁ ROZPORŮ [On the way to conflict]. After President Richard M. Nixon's visit in 1972, the Chinese leaders accepted the theory that an alliance with the United States was possible and desirable in the struggle against the USSR. However, normalization during 1973-76 raised questions about bilateral relations. President Jimmy Carter's "new China policy" increased these tensions. Based on published diplomatic accounts, newspapers, and secondary sources; 105 notes.
                                                                G. E. Pergl

3066. Slany, William Z. HISTORY OF THE FOREIGN RELATIONS SERIES. *Soc. for Hist. of Am. Foreign Relations. Newsletter 1981 12(1): 10-19.* Discusses the history of the *Foreign Relations of the United States*, the official documentary record of American foreign policy, published by the State Department since 1861, focusing on the Acheson, Dulles, and Rusk periods, the 1970's, and the future.

3067. Slonim, Shlomo. THE 1948 AMERICAN EMBARGO ON ARMS TO PALESTINE. *Pol. Sci. Q. 1979 94(3): 495-514.* Loy Henderson, head of the Office of Near Eastern and African Affairs, first raised the suggestion of an arms embargo on Palestine. President Harry S. Truman's decision, based on the recommendations of Secretary of State George C. Marshall and others in the State Department, to support the embargo was an anomaly in the otherwise supportive US policy toward the formation of the modern state of Israel. Based on newly opened US State Department correspondence; 84 notes.   S

3068. Smith, Gaddis. RECONSIDERATIONS: THE SHADOW OF JOHN FOSTER DULLES. *Foreign Affairs 1974 52(2): 403-408.* Discusses Townsend Hoopes' *The Devil and John Foster Dulles* (Boston: Atlantic/Little Brown, 1973). The book depicts the former secretary of state as having been more flexible in his positions on foreign affairs before 1953 than afterward. Criticizes the book for not developing that point. Dulles' attitudes were not unique; rather they reflected the prevailing ideas of the nation's leaders, including Truman, Acheson, and (later) John Kennedy. 4 notes.   R. Riles.

3069. Smith, Gerard and Rathjens, George. REASSESSING NUCLEAR NONPROLIFERATION POLICY. *Foreign Affairs 1981 59(4): 875-894.* The Carter Administration's nuclear nonproliferation policy had limited success because it saw in the spread of nuclear power facilities an increased weapons production capability. This logic led to controls on exports of nuclear power technology which proved ineffective in preventing foreign nations from achieving nuclear capability. Future policy should emphasize international cooperation in setting guidelines for nuclear technology and materials exports, and in achieving greater international security and energy self-sufficiency. 10 notes.
                                                                A. A. Englard

3070. Smith, Joseph Burkholder. THE CIA IN VIETNAM: NATION-BUILDERS, OLD PROS, PARAMILITARY BOYS, AND MISPLACED PERSONS. *Washington Monthly 1978 9(12): 22-31.* Examines Central Intelligence Agency activities in Vietnam, 1963-75.

3071. Smith, Joseph Burkholder. WHAT CARTER DIDN'T KNOW ABOUT MEXICO AND WHY HE DIDN'T KNOW IT. *Washington Monthly 1979 11(4): 42-47.* Describes the US State Department's attitudes toward Mexico and Latin America, and the operation of the US embassy in Mexico.

3072. Smoke, Richard. THEORIES OF ESCALATION. Lauren, Paul Gordon, ed. *Diplomacy: New Approaches in History, Theory, and*

Policy (New York: Free Pr., 1979): 162-182. Nuclear weaponry sparked interest in escalation as a subject of study only recently separated from diplomacy and war. The Cuban missile crisis made "escalation" part of everyone's vocabulary, but the sources of escalation theory in the United States occurred after World War II. Sketches the roles of 1) Otto von Bismarck and the Franco-Prussian War of 1870 and 2) John F. Kennedy, Robert McNamara and the Cuban missile crisis of 1962 in order to illustrate the significance and implications of escalation decisionmaking. 31 notes.   S

3073. Soapes, Thomas F. A COLD WARRIOR SEEKS PEACE: EISENHOWER'S STRATEGY FOR NUCLEAR DISARMAMENT. *Diplomatic Hist. 1980 4(1): 57-71.* "[President Dwight D.] Eisenhower's efforts to reduce nuclear armaments, the potential for surprise attack, and East-West tensions illustrate his earnest desire for a cessation of the nuclear arms race, his ability to make decisions independently of his advisers, and his ability to formulate a plan for achieving his objectives. The historian's estimate of Eisenhower's effort to achieve these objectives must be tempered, however, by the fact that Eisenhower's conventional Cold War attitude toward the Soviet Union placed a major obstacle in his path. It was an obstacle he did not overcome." 41 notes.

T. L. Powers

3074. Solberg, Carl. THE TYRANNY OF OIL: HOW AND WHY THE UNITED STATES GOT INVOLVED IN THE MIDDLE EAST. *Am. Heritage 1976 28(1): 9-13, 78-83.* Traces the relationship of oil to US foreign policy from just before World War I to the present. Although the Wilson administration recognized the importance of Middle Eastern oil, it was not until the early 1940's that the United States became committed to oil diplomacy. After World War II, the Truman administration saw oil as an important tool in Cold War diplomacy. US support for Israel added a complicating factor because the United States backed Israel publicly but indirectly supported the Arabs through oil company diplomacy. The establishment of OPEC in 1960 signalled the beginning of the energy problems of the 1970's. 8 illus.   J. F. Paul

3075. Sonnenfeldt, Helmut. RUSSIA, AMERICA AND DÉTENTE. *Foreign Affairs 1978 56(2): 275-294.* The Carter administration hoped to deemphasize America's preoccupation with the USSR, yet Russia's steady accumulation of military strength dictates that such cannot be the case. Specific negotiations will have little effect on the Soviet compulsion to amass power. World peace hinges on the US and others' ability " . . . to draw the Soviet Union into the constraints and disciplines but also the advantages of the international system." 3 notes.

M. R. Yerburgh

3076. Soppelsa, Jacques. LE COMPLEXE MILITARO-INDUS-TRIEL AMÉRICAIN ET LA POLITIQUE EXTÉRIEURE DE JIMMY CARTER [The US military-industrial complex and Jimmy Carter's foreign policy]. *Défense Natl. [France] 1979 35(Jan): 99-108.* Examines the evolution of the military-industrial complex during the early years of Jimmy Carter's presidency, and concludes that presidential addresses on arms limitation notwithstanding, the military-industrial complex still plays an important role in US foreign policy.

3077. Sorensen, Theodore C. WATERGATE UND DIE AMERIKANISCHE AUSSENPOLITIK [Watergate and American foreign policy]. *Europa Archiv [West Germany] 1974 29(22): 749-756.* Compares the negative impact of the Watergate scandal, 1972-74, on American foreign policy with the Bay of Pigs operation in 1961 and the Tonkin Gulf escalation of the Vietnam War in 1964 under the Johnson administration.   R. Wagnleitner

3078. Spiegel, Steven L. CAMP DAVID DIPLOMACY. *Center Mag. 1979 12(3): 12-31.* Discusses the Camp David summit meeting held in January 1979 and provides the background of events surrounding the meeting, dating to 1977, involving the United States, Egypt, and Israel. Concludes with a discussion among the author and several scholars.

3079. Spiegel, Steven L. DOES THE UNITED STATES HAVE OPTIONS IN THE MIDDLE EAST? *Orbis 1980 24(2): 395-410.* Analyzes the foreign policy of the United States between 1977 and 1980 and the ideas of the man who shaped it, in order to ascertain why it failed. Although Zbigniew Brzezinski and Cyrus Vance had the usual experience

of National Security Affairs advisor and Secretary of State, they were not effective in their jobs. Details US global and regional policy, the problems of Iran and Afghanistan, and divisions within the Carter administration. Concludes that the major reason for the failure of US policy was President Jimmy Carter's view of the world.   J. W. Thacker, Jr.

3080. Spillmann, Kurt R. DIE STADT AUF DEM BERGE [The city on the hill]. *Schweizer Monatshefte [Switzerland] 1978 58(3): 179-182.* President Jimmy Carter's policies of human rights are part of the strategy of the American dream of religious and political dissenters who left Europe from the 17th through the 19th century.

R. Wagnleitner

3081. Stargardt, A. W. A FAR AWAY COUNTRY: THE FRUITS OF UNREALISTIC DIPLOMACY TOWARDS CAMBODIA. *Pacific Affairs [Canada] 1980 53(2): 298-305.* Reviews *Sideshow: Kissinger, Nixon and the Destruction of Cambodia* by William Shawcross, an indictment of the American escalation of hostilities in 1970 that brought the terror of the Vietnam War to Cambodia. Analyzes the US decision to secretly bomb Communist "sanctuaries" in neutral Cambodia. Examines the 1970 coup led by Sirik Matak and Lon Nol to depose Prince Norodom Sihanouk. Compares Richard M. Nixon and Henry A. Kissinger's lack of restraint in Cambodia in 1970 to Metternich's breach of Swiss neutrality in 1813. Secondary sources; 16 notes.

S. H. Frank

3082. Starr, Harvey. THE KISSINGER YEARS: STUDYING INDIVIDUALS AND FOREIGN POLICY. *Int. Studies Q. 1980 24(4): 465-496.* As Secretary of State, Henry A. Kissinger possessed and acted on a clear and consistent world view. His memoirs *(White House Years* [Little, Brown, 1979]) indicate that he both recalled and described his behavior in a manner consistent with his personality and belief system. There is also a remarkable congruence betwen the self-analysis of the memoirs and previous analyses of Kissinger, which have employed such varied techniques as operations code analysis, formal content analysis, events-data analysis, and psychohistory. Such high consistency provides confidence in the memoirs as a data source. 62 notes.

E. S. Palais

3083. Starr, Harvey. KISSINGER'S OPERATIONAL CODE. *Korea & World Affairs [South Korea] 1980 4(4): 582-606.* Analyzes Henry A. Kissinger's preoffice scholarly writings, including his doctoral thesis, in order to sketch his political theory and to find possible motivations for foreign policy decisions he made as secretary of state during the 1970's; compares these early writings with Kissinger's comments and memoirs after he left office.

3084. Steinbruner, John D. NUCLEAR DECAPITATION. *Foreign Policy 1981-82 (45): 16-28.* The command structure—the organizational and technical network of communication and command centers—of US strategic nuclear forces in the 1980's is extremely vulnerable to Soviet nuclear attack. Though President Ronald Reagan's defense policy has recognized this and called for strengthening the security of the command structure, technical solutions to command structure vulnerability probably are not possible at an affordable cost.

M. K. Jones

3085. Stern, Laurence. BITTER LESSONS: HOW WE FAILED IN CYPRUS. *Foreign Policy 1975 (19): 34-78.* Reviews events in Cyprus since 1974. Secretary of State Henry Kissinger's policies failed to save the Greek Cypriots from an aggressive Turkish regime. Turkey invaded following the Greek military junta's attempt to seize the island and assassinate Archbishop Makarios—apparently with Kissinger's approval. When the junta was overthrown, Kissinger seemed to become more pro-Turkish, opposing the congressional cutoff of military shipments to Turkey. Apparently Kissinger believes that Turkey can do more for US national interests than Greece, but that Turkey might look less favorably on US bases on Cyprus than the Makarios government. Anti-American sentiment in Greece has resulted in Greek withdrawal from NATO. Such developments might outweigh the benefits of having Turkey on our side, indicating that Kissinger has failed in this situation.

R. F. Kugler

3086. Stevens, Georgiana G.   1967-1977: AMERICA'S MOMENT IN THE MIDDLE EAST?   *Middle East J. 1977 31(1): 1-15.* Since the June War of 1967, the overriding aim of US policy in the Middle East has been to prevent Soviet dominance. President Johnson stressed that the Arabs must abandon the idea of destroying Israel but that Israel must persuade the world community that it had no expansionist designs. Details the positions of Nixon and Rogers. Under Ford and Kissinger it became clear that the United States was looking ahead to preserve a more equal bargaining status between the Arabs and Israel. "In 1977 new teams of negotiators start with strong assets. Future peace-making seems inevitably to involve safety for Israel, fewer weapons all around, and a base which Palestinians can call home, wherever that may be." 29 notes.
E. P. Stickney

3087. Stille, Ugo.   LA POLITICIA ESTERA DI UN'AMERICA IN CRISI [The foreign policy of an America in crisis]. *Affari Esteri [Italy] 1975 7(26): 218-224.* In the turbulent days of the Watergate scandal in early August 1974, Henry A. Kissinger stood as a symbol of stability amid the debris of the crumbling Nixon administration; today, despite his great skills, he finds himself forced to respond to growing attacks from within the United States.

3088. Stoler, Mark A.   AIKEN, MANSFIELD AND THE TONKIN GULF CRISIS: NOTES FROM THE CONGRESSIONAL LEADERSHIP MEETING AT THE WHITE HOUSE, AUGUST 4, 1964. *Vermont Hist. 1982 50(2): 80-94.* President Lyndon Johnson called the meeting to disarm opposition to an escalated war in Vietnam, claiming in his memoirs that the leaders had unanimously approved. "Johnson used [Walter] Jenkins'[s] notes very selectively, however," revealing "neither the range of issues discussed nor the dissent expressed." Mike Mansfield and George Aiken asked about Chinese retaliation in Korea, Taiwan, or Vietnam. They were not told of the South Vietnamese raids that provoked the torpedo attack, evoking the Tonkin resolution. By voting for the resolution with misgivings, Aiken and Mansfield preserved their "enormous influence" in the Senate, which would have been lost by their futile, negative votes. Publishes Jenkins's version of the conference notes, recently declassified, with list of attenders. 9 notes.
T. D. S. Bassett

3089. Stupak, Ronald J. and McLellan, David S.   THE BANKRUPTCY OF SUPER-ACTIVISM AND THE RESURGENCY OF DIPLOMACY AND THE DEPARTMENT OF STATE. *Foreign Service J. 1975 52(4): 23-28.* Examines US foreign relations with the developing nations in the 1960's-70's.
S

3090. Sudol, Ronald A.   THE RHETORIC OF STRATEGIC RETREAT: CARTER AND THE PANAMA CANAL DEBATE. *Q. J. of Speech 1979 65(4): 379-391.* In his televised address on the Canal Treaties, President Carter failed to employ the commonsense arguments that a policy of retreat requires. Five *topoi* for a rhetoric of retreat—timeliness, urgency, value, advantage, and shrewdness—help connect persuasion to policy, a rhetorical fact Carter more often accomplished in informal, impromptu speeches.
J

3091. Suhrke, Astri and Morrison, Charles E.   CARTER AND KOREA: THE DIFFICULTIES OF DISENGAGEMENT. *World Today [Great Britain] 1977 33(10): 366-375.* Discusses current Carter administration aims to withdraw all US ground troops in South Korea, 1977-81; southern strength may cause North Korea to go to desperate lengths, which may spur the arms race and cause closer connections between North Korea and either Communist China or the USSR.

3092. Suter, Keith D.   IN PRAISE OF DR. HENRY KISSINGER. *Army Q. and Defence J. [Great Britain] 1977 107(3): 345-353.* Henry A. Kissinger has shifted America's approach toward international diplomacy to less moralism and more sophistication, overcoming numerous obstacles to this approach.

3093. Swanson, Roger Frank.   THE FORD INTERLUDE AND THE U.S.-CANADIAN RELATIONSHIP. *Am. Rev. of Can. Studies 1978 8(1): 3-17.* During his presidency, Gerald R. Ford met with Canadian Prime Minister Pierre Elliott Trudeau five times. Their first meeting (Washington, 1974) did much to relieve strained US-Canadian relations as each leader agreed to notify the other of proposed policy changes affecting their respective countries. They also discussed energy, security, trade, and environmental matters. Subsequent meetings at Brussels and Helsinki (1975) and Washington and Puerto Rico (1976) featured discussions of NATO, NORAD, energy, world affairs, and US-Canadian issues. Overall, "the Ford interlude normalized a highly unstable period in the US-Canadian relationship." Based on confidential interviews; 16 notes.
G.-A. Patzwald

3094. Swearingen, Rodger.   REAGAN AND RUSSIA: THE NEW COURSE. *Korea & World Affairs [South Korea] 1982 6(2): 292-311.* Supporting President Ronald Reagan's condemnation of detente as an instrument of foreign policy, discusses the president's foreign policy during 1981-82 and looks at improving US military power, limiting Cuba's influence, and controlling terrorism.

3095. Szulc, Tad.   BEHIND THE VIETNAM CEASE-FIRE AGREEMENT. *Foreign Policy 1974 (15): 21-69.* Discusses the diplomacy, political dealings, and secret agreements formulated by Henry A. Kissinger to facilitate the cease-fire agreement.
S

3096. Szulc, Tad.   DATELINE WASHINGTON: THE VICAR VANQUISHED. *Foreign Policy 1981 (43): 173-186.* President Ronald Reagan's promised deemphasis on the role of the National Security Advisor in the conduct of US foreign policy has not left Secretary of State Alexander Haig in his expected position as the nation's chief diplomatic voice. Instead, Haig has been relegated to lesser status, competing for primacy in the field with Secretary of Defense Casper Weinberger and White House Counsellor Edwin Meese. President Reagan's style of administration and diplomatic inexperience have worked against effective coordination of this trio, resulting in a confused and incoherent foreign policy.
T. L. Powers

3097. Szulc, Tad.   KISSINGER'S (NEW) CONCERT OF NATIONS. *Present Tense 1974 1(3): 35-39.* Kissinger's foreign policy reveals his ideas on détente and power politics, and his lack of concern for humanitarian ideals.
S

3098. Szulc, Tad.   LISBON AND WASHINGTON: BEHIND PORTUGAL'S REVOLUTION. *Foreign Policy 1975 (21): 3-62.* Surveys US policy toward Portugal since 1974. In April 1974 leftist Portuguese military officers overthrew the Caetano dictatorship. Secretary of State Henry A. Kissinger during the Nixon and Ford administrations has vacillated, unable to follow a consistent policy toward Portugal. He has been most inclined to isolate Portugal, but has sometimes lapsed into "the ambassador's policy," which calls for supporting the moderate socialists. His tendency toward isolating Portugal flows from his pessimistic attitude, which views Portugal as moving inevitably toward Communist dominance; however, events have not entirely sustained Kissinger's pessimism. Based mainly on private and confidential accounts by American, Portuguese, and other officials.
R. F. Kugler

3099. Taylor, Maxwell D.   THE LEGITIMATE CLAIMS OF NATIONAL SECURITY. *Foreign Affairs 1974 52(3): 577-594.* The most serious threat to the United States is of nonmilitary nature. The National Security Council should be expanded to deal with all forms of security threats. Note.
R. Riles

3100. Theoharis, Athan G.   THE DECLINE OF AN ANTICOLONIAL TRADITION: OFFICIAL ATTITUDES TOWARDS REVOLUTIONS DURING THE COLD WAR YEARS. *J. of the Hellenic Diaspora 1977 4(3): 14-23.* Chronicles changing administrative attitudes towards anti-colonialist sentiment, 1789-1975, concentrating on the period 1945-75 when political fears brought on by the Cold War exacerbated CIA interference in foreign affairs and domestic politics reflected antiradical sentiment.

3101. Theoharis, Athan G.   THE ORIGINS OF THE COLD WAR: A REVISIONIST INTERPRETATION. *Peace and Change 1976 4(1): 3-11.* President Franklin D. Roosevelt's vagueness at the Yalta Conference was a source of the Cold War during the Truman administration, 1945-47.

3102. Thompson, Mark E.   THE TRUMAN-MAC ARTHUR CONTROVERSY: A BIBLIOGRAPHICAL ESSAY. *Studies in Hist. and*

Soc. 1974 5(2): 66-73. Reviews the reasons President Harry S. Truman removed General Douglas MacArthur from his post as United Nations Commander during the Korean War. Supporters of the president generally argue that he had to remove the general in order to carry on the war as he saw fit. MacArthur's supporters claim that the general was either a victim of poor communications or a scapegoat for failure to win the war. The controversy clearly shows the political problems inherent in limited warfare.   V. L. Human

3103. Thompson, W. Scott.   U.S. POLICY TOWARD AFRICA: AT AMERICA'S SERVICE?   *Orbis 1982 25(4): 1011-1024.* Analyzes the evolution of American strategic policy toward Africa during 1974-81, emphasizing the early lack of realism demonstrated by both the Ford and, especially, the Carter administrations. Under the Reagan administration, the United States for the first time has a strategy toward Africa and a comparative advantage in the region.   Based primarily on secondary works; 33 notes.   J. W. Thacker, Jr.

3104. Thorpe, James A.   TRUMAN'S ULTIMATUM TO STALIN ON THE 1946 AZERBAIJAN CRISIS: THE MAKING OF A MYTH. *J. of Pol. 1978 40(1): 188-195.* The claim, first presented in 1952, that Harry S. Truman gave Joseph Stalin an ultimatum which forced the Russian evacuation of Azerbaijan in May 1946, is a myth created by Truman and perpetuated by scholars. Publication of his memoirs in 1956 and 1960 provided greater details of the alleged ultimatum, but the American representatives in Moscow during that period, W. Averell Harriman and George F. Kennan, dispute the claim, and the US State Department could find no supporting documentation. Still, scholars including Nasrollah S. Fatemi, Michael K. Sheehan, George Lenczowski and Arthur M. Schlesinger, Jr. have maintained the myth. 25 notes.
                                                          A. W. Novitsky

3105. Tilhere, Jacques.   ETATS UNIS: RELANCE DU DÉBAT STRATÉGIQUE   [U.S.A.: the restarting of the strategic debate]. *Défense Natl. [France] 1977 33(3): 133-136.* Examines the character of the international strategic debate as affected by the advent of the Carter administration and by the appointment of Harold Brown as Defense Secretary. Note.

3106. Toinet, Marie-France.   LA "NOUVELLE" STRATÉGIE AMÉRICAINE ET SALT II   [The "new" American strategy and SALT II]. *Défense Natl. [France] 1974 30(6): 45-57.* Examines the real motivations behind the official announcement of a more ambitious US nuclear arms policy in 1973, tracing its link with Strategic Arms Limitation Talks (II) and with President Richard M. Nixon's growing weakness in the United States.

3107. Toinet, Marie-France.   L'ASIE ET SES CONFLITS VUS DE WASHINGTON   [Asia and her conflicts, as seen from Washington]. *Défense Natl. [France] 1979 35(11): 51-61.* Contrasts the achievements of the Nixon/Kissinger approach to Far Eastern diplomacy after 1969 with the hesitancy and awkwardness shown by the Carter administration.

3108. Toinet, Marie-France.   LE PRÉSIDENT CARTER ET SALT II   [President Carter and SALT II]. *Défense Natl. [France] 1977 33(12): 9-24.* Sees continuing interaction of US internal policy with the negotiations for a SALT II agreement, and considers the conflicting demands President Jimmy Carter has to deal with, especially the demand for the maintenance of a diplomatic status quo with the USSR.

3109. Toinet, Marie-France.   LES DIFFICULTÉS INTÉRIEURES DE LA POLITIQUE ÉTRANGÈRE AMÉRICAINE   [The internal difficulties of US foreign policy]. *Défense Natl. [France] 1979 35(Jan): 63-82.* Despite President Jimmy Carter's promises to reduce the sale of US arms abroad and his efforts to secure peace in the Middle East, the first two years of the Carter presidency demonstrated that the internal difficulties of Congressional politics, public opinion and fears of Soviet aggression were serious obstacles in the path of peace initiatives.

3110. Toinet, Marie-France.   LES ETATS-UNIS, LE PROCHE-ORI-ENT ET LA SITUATION INTÉRIEURE AMÉRICAINE   [The United States, the Near East and the domestic situation in America]. *R. Française de Sci. Pol. [France] 1974 24(4): 770-784.* The variations in United States policy in the Near East in recent years, particularly during

the October war, are partly due to the influence of a public opinion which is less unanimous than it used to be. There are two pressure groups: a powerful Jewish community backed up by pro-Israeli public opinion, and a pressure group which is ideologically pro-Arab, is weak, but has the support of a powerful economic lobby anxious for a more neutral government policy. These contradictory pressures would have left the Government with considerable room for manoeuvre if it had not been handicapped by the differences which exist between it and the legislature, the opposition between the Pentagon and the State Department and, lastly, by the Watergate affair.   J

3111. Tozer, Warren W.   LAST BRIDGE TO CHINA: THE SHANGHAI POWER COMPANY, THE TRUMAN ADMINISTRA-TION AND THE CHINESE COMMUNISTS. *Diplomatic Hist. 1977 1(1): 64-78.* A study of the American-owned Shanghai Power Company during 1949-50 indicates that the United States "was primarily responsible for closing the Open Door in China. The People's Republic of China (PRC) not only appeared willing to tolerate American firms for the short term but sought to establish some type of relationship with the United States. . . . The Truman administration, pursuing a policy of containment, refused to deal with the Chinese Communists, except on its own terms, and attempted to control trade with the PRC in order to force compliance with American demands." Based primarily on the Boise Cascade Corporation Archives; 55 notes.   G. H. Curtis

3112. Trask, Roger R.   GEORGE F. KENNAN'S REPORT ON LATIN AMERICA (1950).   *Diplomatic Hist. 1978 2(3): 307-311.* George F. Kennan wrote this report for Secretary of State Dean Acheson following his tour of Latin America. It was recently published in full for the first time in the State Department's *Foreign Relations* series. It epitomizes Kennan's generally deficient understanding of the area. Kennan had a subjective, and often questionable, appreciation of the region's character, but this was partially offset by his realistic assessment of its importance for the United States. He argued for an anti-Communist policy characterized by a thorough application of realpolitik (Kennan used the term "total diplomacy"), and a great power posture entirely frank and free of cant. We should at all times make it clear, said Kennan, "that we are more concerned to be respected than to be liked or understood." 18 notes.   L. W. Van Wyk

3113. Trofimenko, G.   AZIATSKAIA POLITIKA VASHING-TONA   [Washington's policy in Asia]. *Aziia i Afrika Segodnia [USSR] 1981 (11): 9-11.* Examines US foreign policy in Asia during the Reagan and Carter administrations, especially the strategic interests of the United States, China, and Japan against the USSR. Russian.

3114. Trofimenko, G.   POLITIKA BEZ PERSPEKTIVY (O TAK NAZIVAIEMOI DOKTRINE KARTERA)   [A policy without prospects, or, the so-called Carter doctrine]. *Mirovaia Ekonomika i Mezh-dunarodnye Otnosheniia [USSR] 1980 (3): 17-27.* The freezing of relations with Moscow has become an integral part of the foreign policy of the Carter administration; the policy involves closer relations with the countries of Western Europe and with Japan, on the basis of anti-Sovietism and militarism, efforts to attract the support of developing nations, and the undermining of detente.

3115. Tsai Wei-ping.   MORALITY AND DIPLOMACY: PRESI-DENT CARTER'S FOREIGN POLICY ORIENTATION.   *Issues and Studies [Taiwan] 1977 13(4): 1-11.* Examines the general importance of the US in international affairs and then concentrates on the Carter administration's attitude toward foreign policy (incorporating human rights and moral values); touches on the US attitude toward China.

3116. Tsou, Tang.   STATESMANSHIP AND SCHOLARSHIP. *World Pol. 1974 26(3): 428-451.* Several recent scholarly works on American and Chinese policies clarify the alternatives confronting the United States in 1971, and give us a glimpse of the Nixon Administration's objectives, strategies, tactics, considerations, and calculations in the opening to China. Together with these works, the processes and results of the negotiations with China constitute the fullest public record to date of Henry A. Kissinger's and Richard M. Nixon's general approach to international politics. But their policy toward China has a unique feature: the frank acknowledgment of the uncertainty of both the immediate and final outcome. This posture has bolstered their courage to take audacious initiatives, giving their policy the necessary flexibility and strengthening their bargaining position. The scholarly works have built a consensus behind the new policy. Their findings point to the theoretical proposition that an accommodation may be achieved if the revolutionary state is given a fair stake in the system and if it cannot improve its position by revolutionary methods.   J

3117. Tucker, Robert W.   AMERICAN POWER & THE PERSIAN GULF. *Commentary 1980 70(5): 25-41.* Analyzes the present political situation in the Persian Gulf and area and the Carter administration's response to recent events; a permanent, sizable American force in the Sinai could substantially improve matters and deal with most contingencies.

3118. Tucker, Robert W.   IS PEACE STILL POSSIBLE IN THE MIDDLE EAST? THE ROLE OF THE UNITED STATES. *Commentary 1978 66(1): 17-28.* US foreign policy is based on a position of weakness: the Arab states hold economic leverage through oil exports and can always play the USSR against the United States militarily. The former policy of unrestrained support of Israel has disappeared. Henry A. Kissinger saw this and acted accordingly; the Carter administration has carried it much further.   V. L. Human

3119. Twitchett, Kenneth J.   EUROPE AND THE UNITED STATES: THE CHANGING RELATIONSHIP. *J. of Common Market Studies [Great Britain] 1976 14(4): 372-376.* Reviews the Forschungsinstitut für Internationale Politik und Sicherheit's *Zur Europolitik der Regierung Nixon* (Eggenberg: Stiftung Wissenschaft und Politik, 1975) and Gerhard Mally's *The New Europe and the United States* (Lexington: Lexington/D.C. Heath for the Atlantic Council of the United States, 1975).

3120. Ulam, Adam.   U.S.-SOVIET RELATIONS: UNHAPPY CO-EXISTENCE. *Foreign Affairs 1979 57(3): 555-571.* Though almost every President since World War II has entered the White House with the hope of improving US-Soviet relations, success has always eluded them. 1978 was consistent with the overall pattern. Soviet policy remains circumspect; US policy remains volatile and diffuse. American flirtations with China and Soviet adventures in Africa will make a meaningful breakthrough increasingly difficult. 11 notes.   M. R. Yerburgh

3121. Urban, George.   A LONG CONVERSATION WITH DR. ZBIGNIEW BRZEZINSKI: "THE PERILS OF FOREIGN POLICY." *Encounter [Great Britain] 1981 56(5): 12-30.* Interview with Zbigniew Brzezinski on such issues concerning foreign policy during the Jimmy Carter administration as consistency of foreign policy, the ability of a large democracy dominated by the mass media to pursue a complex policy, the question of human rights, the policy of détente, and Brzezinski's relationship with Carter.

3122. Urban, Josef.   VOJENSKOPOLITICKÉ ZÁMĚRY AMERICKÉHO IMPERIALISMU NA POČÁTKU 80. LET [Military and political intentions of American imperialism at the beginning of the 1980's]. *Hist. a Vojenství [Czechoslovakia] 1981 30(5): 109-127.* The Carter administration retreated from the principles of peaceful coexistence in 1977. An intensive ideological and psychological offensive against socialist lands was triggered. Its theme was the defense of human rights. A continuous effort was made to isolate the socialist world both economically and culturally. When Reagan entered the White House, military escalation took place, especially in the area of ballistic missiles. Even when there are some explanations for the defensive doctrine of the "new nuclear strategy," it is obvious that constant American aggression cannot be camouflaged by slogans. Only the strength of the socialist camp impedes American plans for world dominance. 25 notes.
                                                            G. E. Pergl

3123. Urofsky, Melvin I.   AMERICA AND ISRAEL: TRYING TO FIND THE STRAIGHT PATH. *Reviews in Am. Hist. 1975 3(3): 383-388.* Discusses the evolution, 1945-48, of President Truman's policy on Israel, analyzes the importance of the Zionist cause in the 1948 presidential election, and summarizes the social and theological responses of American Protestantism since the Puritans in this review of Hertzel Fishman's *American Protestantism and a Jewish State* (Detroit, Mich.: Wayne State U. Pr., 1973) and John Snetsinger's *Truman, the Jewish*

Vote, and the Creation of Israel (Hoover Institution Studies 39. Stanford, Calif.: Hoover Institution Pr., 1974).

3124. VanCleave, William R. and Barnett, Roger W.   STRATEGIC ADAPTABILITY. *Orbis 1974 18(3): 655-676.* Approves Secretary of Defense James R. Schlesinger's strategic flexibility proposals concerning the deployment of nuclear arms during the 1970's.   S

3125. VanCleve, John V.   THE LATIN AMERICAN POLICY OF PRESIDENT KENNEDY: A REEXAMINATION: CASE: PERU. *Inter-Am. Econ. Affairs 1977 30(4): 29-44.* Argues that the Latin American policy of the Kennedy Administration was pragmatic rather than idealistic, hardly a break from previous foreign policy, and geared to obtain favorable publicity. United States-Peruvian relations in 1962 are used as a case study. 52 notes.   D. A. Franz

3126. vanderKroef, Justus M.   SOUTHEAST ASIA: NEW PATTERNS OF CONFLICT AND COOPERATION. *World Affairs 1975/76 138(3): 179-200.* Discusses President Gerald R. Ford's foreign policy in Southeast Asia, notably Indonesia and Thailand in 1975.

3127. VanHollen, Christopher.   THE TILT POLICY REVISITED: NIXON-KISSINGER GEOPOLITICS AND SOUTH ASIA. *Asian Survey 1980 20(4): 339-361.* In connection with the Nixon administration's controversial handling of the 1971 Bangladesh crisis, the author asserts that the White House policies, which Henry A. Kissinger spiritedly defends in his memoirs, were badly flawed and ill served US interests. For both personal and political reasons Nixon wanted to tilt policy in favor of Pakistan and against India. American interests would have fared better if Nixon and Kissinger had adopted the realistic goal of trying to resolve the Indo-Pakistan conflict in the South Asian regional context rather than viewing it in superpower geopolitical terms. Based on "The Anderson Papers," *Congressional Record,* and secondary sources; 40 notes.   M. A. Eide

3128. Vargas Hidalgo, Rafael.   ESTADOS UNIDOS Y AMERICA LATINA BAJO LA PRESIDENCIA DE CARTER [The United States and Latin America during the Carter presidency]. *Estudios Int. [Chile] 1978 11(41): 83-119.* Discusses the influence of the past on present-day inter-American relations. Spanish.

3129. Venkataramani, M. S.   THE UNITED STATES AND THAILAND: THE ANATOMY OF SUPER-POWER POLICY-MAKING, 1948-1963. *Internat. Studies [India] 1973 12(1): 57-110.* Studies the evolution of American policy toward Thailand. American concern over Communism in Indochina and China led the Truman administration to utilize Thailand as a part of its Asian containment policy. As the United States became more deeply involved in Indochina, U.S. economic, political, and military commitments to Thailand also increased. This was reflected in the technical assistance agreement of 1950, the Southeast Asia Treaty Organization established in 1954, the administration's effort to build a strong counter-insurgency force, and the frequent pronouncements of American leaders committing the United States to protect its allies. President Johnson accepted the premises of American policy set by preceding administrations, so that by the end of 1963 the United States was fully committed to the defense of Thailand and other non-Communist states in Southeast Asia. Based on published U.S. government documents; 110 notes. Article to be continued.   G. R. Hess

3130. Verax.   LA TEORIA E LA PRASSI DEL DISIMPEGNO [The theory and practice of disengagement]. *Affari Esteri [Italy] 1974 6(23): 3-12.* Disengagement was first used at the Congress of Vienna (1815). Henry A. Kissinger illustrated this in his study of Metternich, *A World Restored.* Such policies require the negotiators to have adequate support at home and to exhibit a high degree of leadership. As the position of the United States in the world has tended to become more insular, Kissinger has sought to move the United States and the USSR toward a more systematic approach in dealing with each other. Thus, each side has become more willing to accept the legitimate rights of the other in the interest of world harmony.   A. R. Stoesen

3131. Vernant, Jacques.   LES ENTRETIENS DE VLADIVOSTOK [The Vladivostok talks]. *Défense Natl. [France] 1975 31(1): 105-111.* Discusses the significance of the arms limitation talks between Gerald R.

Ford, Leonid Brezhnev, and Henry A. Kissinger on 23 and 24 November 1974 in Vladivostok.

3132. Vernant, Jacques. MOYEN-ORIENT: LE PLAN CARTER [The Middle East: the Carter plan]. *Défense Natl. [France] 1977 33(5): 103-108.* Discusses President Jimmy Carter's plan for a solution to the Arab-Israeli Conflict.

3133. Vernant, Jacques. PROLIFÉRATION ET DÉVELOPPE-MENT [Proliferation and development]. *Défense Natl. [France] 1977 33(7): 115-121.* Briefly surveys current international relations, focusing on East-West relations and Jimmy Carter's foreign policy, on the occasion of the so-called "north-south" conference held in Paris (30 May-2 June 1977). Secondary sources; 5 notes.

3134. Vernant, Jacques. UNE NOUVELLE STRATÉGIE AMÉRI-CAINE? [A new American strategy?]. *Défense Natl. [France] 1978 34(5): 107-114.* Analyzes President Jimmy Carter's 17 March 1978 Winston-Salem speech, in which confrontation with the USSR becomes possible, not on military, but on political terms, globally interpreted.

3135. Vogelgesang, Sandra. WHAT PRICE PRINCIPLE? U.S. POLICY ON HUMAN RIGHTS. *Foreign Affairs 1978 56(4): 819-841.* Analyzes the Carter administration's emphasis on human rights as an important feature of its foreign policy. Though the United States has certainly made the other countries of the world generally more sensitive to this problem, Carter's "moral crusade" has been somewhat selective, e. g., aid to Nicaragua was slashed; support to Iran was not. Human rights must frequently be weighed against other less noble considerations. "In sum, the future of US policy on human rights lies in the response to the larger question that launched the Republic: what price principle?" 8 notes.   M. R. Yerburgh

3136. Vukadinović, Radovan. SJEDINJENE AMERICKE DRZAVE I ATLANTSKA SURADNJA [The United States and Atlantic cooperation]. *Medjunarodni Problemi [Yugoslavia] 1971 23(3): 103-122.* Describes the development of cooperation between the United States and the nations of Western Europe since World War II, with particular emphasis on NATO and the policy of Richard M. Nixon's administration.

3137. Vysockij, V. N. DIE DEUTSCHE FRAGE AUF DER LONDONER AUSSENMINISTERKONFERENZ 1947 [The German question at the London conference of foreign ministers in 1947]. *Zeitschrift für Geschichtswissenschaft [East Germany] 1974 22(9): 956-968.* Analyzes the growing gap that developed between the American and Russian policies toward Germany. In London, V. M. Molotov demanded the establishment of a democratic German government, the restoration of the political and economic unity of Germany, and the preparation of a German peace treaty according to the Potsdam conference decisions. George C. Marshall's refusal to discuss a Soviet compromise indicated that the American government continued with its revision of the policy decisions of Tehran, Yalta, and Potsdam, which resulted in the building of an anti-Soviet Western group, the restoration of German imperialism, and the sacrifice of German unity. Based on Soviet documents in the Archiv Vneshnei Politiki in Moscow, printed documents and secondary sources; 62 notes.   R. Wagnleitner

3138. Walker, J. Samuel. CONFESSIONS OF A COLD WARRIOR: CLINTON P. ANDERSON AND AMERICAN FOREIGN POLICY, 1945-1972. *New Mexico Hist. Rev. 1977 52(2): 117-134.* When President Richard M. Nixon announced that he would use American troops to destroy North Vietnamese sanctuaries in Cambodia, Senator Clinton P. Anderson was one of those who spoke against the policy. Traces the evolution of Anderson's position from the 1940's. In 1970, he argued that Nixon's decision was not a policy of self-defense, that it would extend the war, and that it involved the constitutional question about the role of the President and Congress in making war. Illus., 26 notes.
                                    J. H. Krenkel

3139. Walker, Stephen G. THE INTERFACE BETWEEN BELIEFS AND BEHAVIOR: HENRY KISSINGER'S OPERATIONAL CODE AND THE VIETNAM WAR. *J. of Conflict Resolution 1977 21(1): 129-168.* Examines Kissinger's personal beliefs and diplomacy, including a "comparison of his academic writings and his conduct of the Vietnam negotiations and application of game theory."

3140. Walters, Ronald W. THE CLARK AMENDMENT: ANALYSIS OF U.S. POLICY CHOICES IN ANGOLA. *Black Scholar 1981 12(4): 2-12.* The Clark Amendment (US, 1975), which ended US military or paramilitary operations in Angola unless authorized by Congress, was a direct response to Central Intelligence Agency operations against the Popular Movement for Liberation of Angola; focuses on attempts to repeal that amendment by the Carter and Reagan administrations.

3141. Ward, Dana. KISSINGER: A PSYCHOHISTORY. *Hist. of Childhood Q. 1975 2(3): 287-348.* Basic tensions in Henry A. Kissinger's psyche, traceable to traumatic childhood and adolescent experiences, influence his world view and hence his actions as Secretary of State. Notable among those events were his Jewish childhood near Hitler's Nuremberg and subsequent need to flee to the United States, his father's loss of economic status and importance in the family, and the presence of favored siblings or quasi-siblings. Examines development of the "depressive personality" resulting from these factors. Explains Kissinger's relationships with business and political leaders, his first wife, and other women in terms of ego fulfillment, and relates his decisions of state to his personality development. Based on interviews, newspapers and magazines, and other primary and secondary sources; 187 notes.
                                    R. E. Butchart

3142. Warshawsky, Howard. THE DEPARTMENT OF STATE AND HUMAN RIGHTS POLICY: A CASE STUDY OF THE HUMAN RIGHTS BUREAU. *World Affairs 1980 142(3): 188-215.* Assesses how the State Department has reacted to and implemented President Jimmy Carter's human rights policy; 1977-80.

3143. Watt, D. C. A RETURN TO AMERICANISM? THE FOREIGN POLICY OF PRESIDENT CARTER. *Pol. Q. [Great Britain] 1977 48(4): 429-439.* Examines changes in US foreign policy from Henry A. Kissinger to President Jimmy Carter; discusses the British press's view of US policy, 1968-77.

3144. Watt, David. KISSINGER'S TRACK BACK. *Foreign Policy 1979-80 (37): 59-66.* Review article of Henry Kissinger's *White House Years* (Boston: Little, Brown 1979), an account of his time as Richard M. Nixon's national security advisor, 1969-73. It indicates that the objective of American foreign policy was to base world peace on a stable balance of power. Kissinger's pursuit of bipolarity violated the Constitution.   S

3145. Weber, William T. KISSINGER AS HISTORIAN: A HISTORIOGRAPHICAL APPROACH TO STATESMANSHIP. *World Affairs 1978 141(1): 40-56.* Discusses Henry A. Kissinger's philosophies of history and statecraft to understand American foreign policy during the past eight years.

3146. Weeks, Albert L. MORALITY IN THE AFFAIRS OF NATIONS. *Freedom at Issue 1977 (41): 12-15.* Examines the Carter administration's dedication to human rights on a worldwide basis; the United States must rededicate itself to democratic and humanitarian principles in domestic and foreign policy, 1970's.

3147. Weise, Eric. MR. "X," RUSSIA, AND VIETNAM. *Modern Age 1975 19(4): 397-406.* Ambassador George Kennan (b. 1904) was prescient in his analysis of Soviet behavior. He redirected US foreign policy along a path which, after 28 years, has proved to be right. The Vietnam War is the best evidence for his accuracy. Primary and secondary sources; 17 notes.   M. L. Lifka

3148. Weissman, Stephen R. CIA COVERT ACTION IN ZAIRE AND ANGOLA: PATTERNS AND CONSEQUENCES. *Pol. Sci. Q. 1979 94(2): 263-286.* Describes the Central Intelligence Agency's intervention in the Third World through case studies of "covert action" in Zaire and Angola. The varying degrees of success of covert action depended upon collateral use of overt diplomacy, the internal organization of targeted groups, and the nature of the Soviet and Chinese responses.
                                    J

3149. Wells, Samuel F., Jr. THE ORIGINS OF MASSIVE RETALI-ATION. *Pol. Sci. Q. 1981 96(1): 31-52.* Examines the popular understanding of the concept of massive retaliation and its refinement in the early months of the Eisenhower administration. The Truman administration had developed both the doctrine and the defense programs that formed the basis of its successor's new declaratory policy.   J

3150. Whiting, Allen S. SINO-AMERICAN DETENTE. *China Q. [Great Britain] 1980 (82): 334-341.* A review of H. R. Haldeman's *The Ends of Power,* Henry A. Kissinger's *White House Years,* and Richard M. Nixon's *The Memoirs of Richard M. Nixon.* Though critical of all three, the author does praise the Kissinger volume for its insights into high-level diplomacy.   J. R. Pavia, Jr.

3151. Wiltz, John Edward. TRUMAN AND MACARTHUR: THE WAKE ISLAND MEETING. *Military Affairs 1978 42(4): 169-176.* Summarizes historical evaluations of the October 1950 meeting between President Harry S. Truman and General of the Army Douglas MacArthur at Wake Island, giving the background to and a detailed account of the meeting. Many accounts contain inaccuracies and mistaken assumptions. Truman's purpose in calling the meeting was "public relations" for the upcoming election, and historians should be careful not to assume exalted motives for exalted personages. Based on the *Log of President Truman's Trip,* interviews, and secondary sources; 34 notes.
                    A. M. Osur

3152. Windrich, Elaine. RHODESIA: THE ROAD FROM LUANDA TO GENEVA. *World Today [Great Britain] 1977 33(3): 101-110.* Examines US moves in the Rhodesia dispute, especially Henry A. Kissinger's role at Geneva in 1976.

3153. Wittner, Lawrence S. WHEN CIA HEARTS WERE YOUNG AND GAY: PLANNING THE COLD WAR (SPRING 1945). *Peace and Change 1978 5(2-3): 70-76.* Reprints 2 April and 5 May 1945 memos to Presidents Roosevelt and Truman respectively from the Office of Strategic Services outlining the nature of Soviet-American relations after World War II.

3154. Wofford, Harris. YOU'RE RIGHT, CHET. YOU'RE RIGHT. AND YOU'RE FIRED. *Washington Monthly 1980 12(5-6): 46-54, 56.* Surveys the career of Chester Bowles—former governor, ambassador, congressman, and Office of Price Administration chief—as advisor in the John F. Kennedy administration (1961-63) and concludes that his consistent correctness was largely ignored because of his diffident personality, indicating that aggressive personalities dominate even presidential decisionmaking sessions, with implications for the country's political leadership.

3155. Wolk, Herman S. THE NEW LOOK IN RETROSPECT. *Air Force Mag. 1974 57(3): 48-51.* Examines the national security policy of Dwight D. Eisenhower's administration, the "New Look" of the 1950's, and suggests that it was remarkably successful in retrospect.

3156. Woodard, Kim. THE SECOND TRANSITION: AMERICA IN ASIA UNDER CARTER. *SAIS Rev. 1981 (1): 129-148.* Reviews the relationships of America with Asian nations during the Carter administration, especially formal and informal military alliances.

3157. Yankelovich, Daniel and Kaagan, Larry. ASSERTIVE AMERICA. *Foreign Affairs 1981 59(3): 696-713.* Americans' opinions shifted decisively between 1976 and 1980. A desire for greater assertiveness, evident in 1980, resulted from anxiety over the perception of the nation's loss of control over its affairs. The Ford and Carter administrations restored the sense of morality following Watergate. The Reagan administration will have to restore the sense of control. Public opinion gives the new administration greater latitude to achieve this goal by favoring increased expenditures for defense and intelligence, and approval of trade as a foreign policy weapon. The Reagan administration's ability to succeed will determine the future course of national politics. Based on public opinion surveys and on journal and newspaper articles; 24 notes.
                    A. A. England

3158. Yankelovich, Daniel. FAREWELL TO "PRESIDENT KNOWS BEST." *Foreign Affairs 1979 57(3): 670-693.* Since the Viet-nam debacle, an enlarged public role in the formulation of public policy has materialized. Though some observers fear that the United States may merely be giving up the abuses of an imperial presidency for the more volatile abuses of an "imperial public," public attitudes toward the Panama Canal, strategic arms limitation talks (SALT), the Middle East, and South Africa represent a healthy "public mind." Under our system, public involvement is the only real alternative to an imperial presidency. 40 notes.
                    M. R. Yerburgh

3159. Yim, Yong Soon. SOUTH KOREA IN AMERICAN MILITARY STRATEGY. *Asian Thought and Soc. 1979 4(10): 60-72.* Explores the position of South Korea in US military strategy from the Truman to the Carter administration.

3160. Yizhar, Michael. THE FORMULATION OF THE UNITED STATES MIDDLE EAST RESOLUTION (1957). *Wiener Lib. Bull. [Great Britain] 1972/73 26(3/4): 2-7.* The 1957 resolution, although formally referred to as the Eisenhower doctrine, was the brainchild of the Secretary of State, John Foster Dulles (1888-1959). Politically dependent upon Eisenhower's trust for continued appointment, Dulles had virtually a free hand in decisions relating to foreign affairs. When the British left the Middle East in the early 1950's, Dulles, without consultation of the administration or the countries involved, expanded the United States' "containment" policy to include that area. Such a special doctrine has greater implications when viewed as a dwindling power of Congress to control foreign policy. Based on House and Senate Hearings and on secondary sources.   T. H. Bauhs

3161. Yizhar, Michael. ISRAEL AND THE EISENHOWER DOCTRINE. *Wiener Lib. Bull. [Great Britain] 1975 28(33/34): 58-64.* Examines Israeli and American interpretations of the United States Middle East Resolution, 1957, known popularly as the Eisenhower Doctrine, which referred to US military force to assist any Middle East nation against armed aggression from any country controlled by international communism. Until the Lebanese crisis (1958) the Americans insisted that the doctrine was inapplicable to the Arab-Israeli conflict; the Israelis demanded that American policy statements should have contained positive ideas about the conflict. Following the Lebanese crisis the Eisenhower administration admitted that the doctrine could be extended to cases not involving threats from international communism, emphasizing that the independence of Middle East countries was vital to peace and the national interest of the United States. Based on published documentary and secondary sources; 25 notes.   J. P. Fox

3162. Yurechko, John J. THE DAY STALIN DIED: AMERICAN PLANS FOR EXPLOITING THE SOVIET SUCCESSION CRISIS OF 1953. *J. of Strategic Studies [Great Britain] 1980 3(1): 44-73.* George F. Kennan in 1946 noted that the Soviet system would inevitably face a serious political crisis when Joseph Stalin died. American foreign policy experts, Democrats and Republicans alike, accepted Kennan's argument about this Soviet vulnerability, and they developed the idea that the United States could exploit the Soviet succession crisis. However, no detailed plans were drawn up, and Dwight D. Eisenhower's administration was not prepared to take advantage of Stalin's death in 1953. John Foster Dulles's belligerent pessimism about the true nature of the USSR totally dominated American foreign policy. Primary sources; 75 notes.
                    A. M. Osur

3163. Zobrist, Benedict K. RESOURCES OF PRESIDENTIAL LIBRARIES FOR THE HISTORY OF POST-WORLD WAR II AMERICAN MILITARY GOVERNMENT IN GERMANY AND JAPAN. *Military Affairs 1978 42(1): 17-19.* Presidential libraries present to the scholar almost boundless research resources on the major aspects of the history of American military government in Germany and Japan. The Franklin D. Roosevelt Library contains much material, especially the papers of Henry M. Morgenthau. The Truman and Eisenhower libraries contain relatively little material, while the John F. Kennedy Library has significant holdings. The Hoover Library has material on his views. A systematic study of the post-World War II occupation of Germany and Japan is still to be written. 2 notes.   A. M. Osur

3164. Zorgbibe, Charles. HENRY KISSINGER ET LA DIPLO-MATIE DE CRISE [Henry Kissinger and crisis diplomacy]. *Défense Natl. [France] 1975 31(4): 51-64.* Evaluates the significance of Henry A.

Kissinger's crisis diplomacy and the mechanism of this "choreography" of negotiations.

3165. Zorgbibe, Charles. UN STRATÈGE CIVIL: HENRY KISSINGER [A civil strategist: Henry Kissinger]. *Défense Natl. [France] 1974 30(1): 47-61.* Examines Henry A. Kissinger's diplomacy and philosophy of history regarding international security based on the great powers' moderation.

3166. Zutz, Robert. THE RECAPTURE OF THE S.S. *MAYAGUEZ*: FAILURE OF THE CONSULTATION CLAUSE OF THE WAR POWERS RESOLUTION. *New York U. J. of Int. Law and Pol. 1976 8(3): 457-478.* Examines the legality of President Gerald R. Ford's successful attempt to secure release of the S.S. *Mayaguez*, a merchant vessel of the United States which the Cambodians had seized on 12 May 1975, in light of Section 3 of the War Powers Resolution. Concludes that "poor drafting has caused this clause to be subject to a variety of interpretations, many of which do not comport with the stated legislative intent." Primary and secondary sources; 119 notes.

M. L. Frey

3167. Żyblikiewicz, Lubomir. W POSZUKIWANIU DOKTRYNY POLITYKI ZAGRANICZNEJ STANÓW ZJEDNOCZONYCH (EWOLUCJA POGLĄDÓW ZBIGNIEWA BRZEZIŃSKIEGO) [Searching for a US foreign-policy doctrine (the evolution of Zbigniew Brzezinski's views)]. *Studia Nauk Politycznych [Poland] 1979 (2): 153-171.* A prolific author, Brzezinski has expressed and elaborated his views on major issues of American foreign policy, including the energy crisis, American involvement in Europe, and relations with the USSR and the Third World. His writings also include a critique of the policies of the Republican administration. In the ongoing search for new concepts and new solutions, he aims at maintaining the position of the United States in the changing world and at achieving better results in the ideological struggle against the growth of socialism. 47 notes.

M. K. Montgomery

3168. —. [ACHESON AND HIS ADVISERS]. Borg, Dorothy and Heinrichs, Waldo, ed. *Uncertain Years: Chinese-American Relations, 1947-1950* (New York: Columbia U. Pr., 1980): 13-59.
Cohen, Warren I. ACHESON, HIS ADVISERS, AND CHINA, 1949-1950, pp. 13-52. Dean Acheson as US Secretary of State, 1949-50, was willing to ignore the advice of Asia desk subordinates as well as the China Lobby when they violated his policy of salutary neglect of China, sought accommodation with the Chinese Communists, and consistently resisted growing anti-Communist US public opinion until the final and fatal decision to cross the 38th parallel in Korea.
Heinrichs, Waldo. SUMMARY OF DISCUSSION, pp. 53-59. Response to Cohen's paper at the Conference on Chinese-American Relations, sponsored by the East Asian Institute of Columbia University at Mount Kisco, New York.

3169. —. AMERICAN-EUROPEAN RELATIONS: THE TROUBLED PARTNERSHIP REVISITED. *Round Table [Great Britain] 1974 (255): 319-330.* Discusses the development and growing strains in American-European foreign relations since 1945, the impact of economic tensions, and the gradual divergence of interests between the two blocs, intensified by the Arab-Israeli War of 1973 and the ensuing oil crisis. Secretary of State Henry A. Kissinger's call for a new Atlantic Charter encouraged the Europeans to oppose American efforts to link economic and security issues. His demand that American views be considered before European Economic Community decisions were made was interpreted as a threat to the Community's decisionmaking process. Concludes that America must now decide whether to dissociate itself from Europe, continue its support for NATO and rely exclusively on bilateral relations, or maintain its support for the Atlantic Alliance while encouraging the European Community to develop into a political entity capable of bearing its share of responsibility in a European international security system.

C. Anstey

3170. —. [CHINA AND THE FOREIGN SERVICE]. *Foreign Service J. 1973 50(3): 17-24.*
Unsigned. INTRODUCTION, *p. 17.*

Tuchman, Barbara. WHY POLICY MAKERS DO NOT LISTEN, *pp. 18-21.*
Service, John S. FOREIGN SERVICE REPORTING, *pp. 22-24.* Discusses the gap between Foreign Service officers' reports and foreign policy, focusing on the dismissal of John S. Service in 1952 for disloyalty.

S

3171. —. [CONTAINMENT].
Gaddis, John Lewis. CONTAINMENT: A REASSESSMENT. *Foreign Affairs 1977 55(4): 873-887.* The foreign policy concept of containment as developed by George F. Kennan in his celebrated article for *Foreign Affairs* has been misunderstood ever since its introduction 30 years ago. Certain declassified documents coupled with partial access to Kennan's personal papers now enable us to more accurately determine what he was in fact suggesting. "Kennan is not often regarded as a strategist, but if 'strategy' is thought of as the rational relationship of national objectives to national capabilities, then he has as good a claim as anyone to having devised a coherent American strategy for dealing with the postwar world." 32 notes.
Mark, Eduard. A REPLY TO JOHN LEWIS GADDIS. *Foreign Affairs 1978 56(2): 430-440.* Questions the accuracy of the Gaddis article. ". . .the policy tended to promote a broader interventionism than Kennan admits or Gaddis realizes." 43 notes.
Gaddis, John Lewis. JOHN LEWIS GADDIS RESPONDS. *Foreign Affairs 1978 56(2): 440-441.* Argues that Mark completely misunderstood the earlier Gaddis article. 3 notes.

M. R. Yerburgh

3172. —. DOCUMENTATION: US POLICIES ON ARMS TRANSFERS AND NON-PROLIFERATION. *Survival [Great Britain] 1981 23(5): 231-232.*
—. PRESIDENTIAL DIRECTIVE ON ARMS TRANSFER POLICY 8 JULY 1981, *pp. 231-232* Reproduces the Reagan administration's announcement of new policies on arms transfers.
—. PRESIDENTIAL STATEMENT ON NON-PROLIFERATION 16 JULY 1981, *pp. 232-233.* Reprints the Reagan administration's policy statement on nuclear nonproliferation.

3173. —. [GEORGE F. KENNAN AND CONTAINMENT]. *Slavic Rev. 1976 35(1): 1-36.*
Wright, C. Ben. MR. "X" AND CONTAINMENT, *pp. 1-31.* An essay on several still unanswered questions regarding George F. Kennan's Mr. "X" article regarding Soviet expansionism and his containment policy. Examines Kennan's writings in the years immediately preceding 1947 in relation to the new Soviet stance of expansionism, and the US tendency toward conciliation. Kennan was not consistent, but developed a theory of contradiction by which he explained his own ambivalence, and ultimately he placed the contradiction within the country itself. 96 notes.
Kennan, George F. REPLIES, *pp. 32-36.* Wright has made his case by taking words and phrases out of context, and in so doing has created a false picture. Wright's article demonstrates his failure to understand how an individual functions in a large governmental organization.

R. V. Ritter

3174. —. INTERVIEW: *HODDING CARTER III WITH PHILIP GEYELIN. SAIS Rev. 1981 (1): 33-46.* Hodding Carter III, Assistant Secretary of State for Public Affairs for the Carter administration, discusses his position, his background, and especially the role of public opinion in the conduct of foreign policy.

3175. —. [KISSINGER, THE MIDDLE EAST, AND SHEEHAN].
Sheehan, Edward R. F. HOW KISSINGER DID IT: STEP BY STEP IN THE MIDDLE EAST. *Foreign Policy 1976 (22): 3-70.* Analyzes Henry A. Kissinger's personal diplomacy in the Middle East since 1973, his strategy and tactics, and the results of his efforts. After flying some 300,000 miles, shuttling back and forth between capitals, talking endlessly with all concerned, and negotiating more or less successfully, Kissinger appears to have prevented a major war, but a conflict could break out nevertheless. Kissinger's diplomacy has produced the following results, among others: 1) he created a coherent US policy toward the Arabs—the first secretary of state to do so, 2) he has increased US influence in the Arab

nations by use of US technology and other forms of assistance, 3) he has moved the US away from a completely pro-Israeli position, and 4) he assured Arab leaders that the United States favors substantial restorations of the 1967 borders. Based on extensive interviews with Arab, Israeli, and US experts.

—. AFTERMATH: THE SHEEHAN AFFAIR. *Foreign Policy 1976 (23): 231-234.* Chronicles the official reaction to Edward R. F. Sheehan's controversial article. Kissinger originally declared he did not authorize the article, but by the end of the week he did admit he had approved "in general" a request by Sheehan for special help in his research. 2 cartoons.

R. F. Kugler and C. Hopkins

3176. —. [NSC 68 AND THE SOVIET THREAT].
Wells, Samuel F., Jr. SOUNDING THE TOCSIN: NSC 68 AND THE SOVIET THREAT. *Int. Security 1979 4(2): 116-158.* Discusses the decisionmaking that contributed to and resulted from NSC 68, a National Security Council report issued in 1950 which warned of a significant technological threat to US security from the USSR.
Gaddis, John Lewis. NSC 68 AND THE PROBLEM OF ENDS AND MEANS. *Int. Security 1980 4(4): 164-170.* Response to Wells on the governmental study, NSC 68, authored by Paul H. Nitze in April 1950, and the continued US anxiety about the USSR over three decades.
Nitze, Paul. THE DEVELOPMENT OF NSC 68. *Int. Security 1980 4(4): 170-176.* Discusses attitudes at the State Department's Policy Planning Staff, 1946-50, that led to the writing of NSC 68.

3177. —. [THE OFFICE OF NATIONAL SECURITY ADVISOR].
Foreign Policy 1980 (38): 80-91.
Destler, I. M. A JOB THAT DOESN'T WORK, *pp. 80-88.* The post of National Security Advisor should be abolished. Holders of the office tend to become more policy formulators and advocates than policy managers. This leads to conflict with the State Department and to confused foreign and domestic perceptions of US foreign policy. Chart, 2 notes.
Szanton, Peter. TWO JOBS, NOT ONE, *pp. 89-91.* Both functions, management and advocacy, are necessary and legitimate. Instead of being abolished, the office should be divided, allowing different individuals to fill each need.

T. L. Powers

3178. —. QUESTIONS OF POWER, MATTERS OF RIGHT.
Round Table [Great Britain] 1977 (267): 207-214. Examines the implications of Jimmy Carter's election to the Presidency for detente, human rights, and nuclear disarmament. Analyzes the effects of Henry A. Kissinger's policies on American attitudes toward foreign policy, particularly his support for undemocratic regimes in Indochina, the Middle East, and Latin America, his lack of foresight over the South African issue, and his treatment of the 1973 oil crisis.

C. Anstey

3179. —. [RICHARD NIXON AND ANTHONY EDEN].
Pol. Sci. [New Zealand] 1976 28(2): 141-171.
Henderson, John T. LEADERSHIP PERSONALITY AND WAR: THE CASES OF RICHARD NIXON AND ANTHONY EDEN, *pp. 141-164.* Comparative analysis of decisionmaking in wartime situations—Great Britain's Anthony Eden (Suez, 1956) and Richard Nixon (Cambodia, 1970)—especially ill-advised military interventions; concludes that though these men were considered to have an amount of expertise in foreign relations matters, decisionmaking was motivated by inner needs to meet a challenge and to counter deep-rooted personal feelings of insecurity and inferiority rather than any inherent domestic or foreign pressure.
Till, Amnon. DOGMATISM AND FOREIGN POLICY: A COMMENT ON HENDERSON'S PAPER, *pp. 165-169.* Examines Henderson's approach to political decisionmaking, pointing out that political decisions are subject to more than personal desires and these should also be included in any such analyses.
Henderson, John T. REPLY TO AMNON TILL, *pp. 170-171.* Responds to four major points of criticism brought up by Till.

3180. —. THE UNITED STATES AND HER ALLIES. *Round Table [Great Britain] 1970 (239): 231-234.* President Richard M. Nixon's State of the Union message to Congress, 18 February 1970, indicated that he and Henry A. Kissinger intended to continue United States leadership of the Allies.

3181. —. WORLD AFFAIRS: AN INTERVIEW. *Encounter [Great Britain] 1978 51(5): 9-27.* Interview with Henry A. Kissinger deals with his opinions on the foreign policy of the Carter administration, 1977-78.

The Presidency: Limits of Power

3182. Abraham, Henry J. THE PRESIDENCY AT THE THRESHOLD OF THE LAST QUARTER OF THE CENTURY. *Southern Q. 1977 15(3): 231-244.* Reviews the growth of power and responsibilities associated with the American presidency. Primary focus is on the abuse of power during Richard M. Nixon's terms. Proposals to limit presidential authority or modify the role of the chief executive are evaluated. Concludes that the citizenry must become more involved in the affairs of government. 21 notes.

R. W. Dubay

3183. Adler, Emanuel. EXECUTIVE COMMAND AND CONTROL IN FOREIGN POLICY: THE CIA'S COVERT ACTIVITIES. *Orbis 1979 23(3): 671-696.* Evaluates the control and command of Central Intelligence Agency (CIA) covert activities by presidents between 1947 and 1979. Details the command and control process, the historical development of command and control, institutional and procedural deficiencies in the system, and a theoretical consideration of the CIA's covert actions using Chile as an example. Based on government documents and published sources; 111 notes.

J. W. Thacker, Jr.

3184. Agria, John J. CONSTITUTIONAL BASIS OF EXECUTIVE IMPOUNDMENT. *Michigan Academician 1974 7(2): 157-165.*

3185. Ahrari, Mohammed E. CONTEMPORARY CONSTRAINTS ON PRESIDENTIAL LEADERSHIP. *Presidential Studies Q. 1981 11(2): 233-243.* Recent presidents seem to be more or less crippled by a confluence of crises, characterized by an intermingling of domestic and international affairs. The president is currently beset by a stronger Congress, lowered public confidence in political institutions, and economic polycentrism. There is a need for new concepts of presidential leadership and for evaluating presidential performance. Based on a paper presented to the 1979 Summer Seminar for College Teachers; table, fig., 30 notes.

A. Drysdale

3186. Ahrari, Mohammed E. THE NATURE OF EXTERNAL CHALLENGES TO PRESIDENTIAL LEADERSHIP IN A CHANGING INTERNATIONAL POLITICAL ECONOMY. *Presidential Studies Q. 1980 10(3): 434-442.* Because this is an age of world-wide interdependence, a president can no longer view questions of foreign policy and those of domestic policy as separate. The United States is no longer the de facto leader in international economic or military affairs, and the president must act increasingly as a mediator when dealing with allies or foes in these areas. 29 notes.

D. H. Cline

3187. Alexander, Jon. PLEBISCITARY POLITICS: REQUIEM FOR THE AMERICAN DREAM? *Can. Rev. of Am. Studies [Canada] 1981 12(1): 89-99.* Review article prompted by William Dean Burnham, ed., and Martha Weinberg, ed., *American Politics and Public Policy* (1978), John W. Ceaser's *Presidential Selection: Theory and Development* (1979), Edwin Diamond's *Good News, Bad News* (1978), and Robert E. DiClerico's *The American President* (1979). The books focus on contemporary Americans' distrust of their political institutions because of the Vietnam War, the Watergate scandal, and the tottering US economy of the 1970's. 12 notes.

H. T. Lovin

3188. Allison, Graham T. AN EXECUTIVE CABINET. *Society 1980 17(5): 41-47.* Discusses the shortcomings of the cabinet as a collegial body, including its loose composition, fragmented power, and conflicting objectives; a solution would be an executive committee of the cabinet as the chief forum for high-level review and decision on all major policy issues.

3189. Andrew, Christopher. GOVERNMENTS AND SECRET SERVICES: A HISTORICAL PERSPECTIVE. *Int. J. [Canada] 1979 34(2): 167-186.* Neglect is the major vice of the British, French, and American governments toward their respective intelligence services.

Modern intelligence systems grew through haphazard bureaucracy rather than through a central government plan. The Truman and Eisenhower administrations let the Central Intelligence Agency develop so that the CIA was not accountable to political controls. Accountability and political controls are necessary for public confidence in intelligence tasks, but the western democracies have been reluctant to address this problem.

M. J. Wentworth

3190. Andrews, William G. PRESIDENCY STUDIES: AN AMERICAN DIALECTIC. *Polity 1977 10(1): 104-110.* Reviews Thomas E. Cronin's *The State of the Presidency* (Boston: Little, Brown and Co., 1975), Erwin C. Hargrove's *The Power of the Modern Presidency* (New York: Alfred A. Knopf, Inc., 1974), Emmet John Hughes's *The Living Presidency* (New York: Coward, McCann & Geoghegan, Inc., 1972), Louis W. Koenig's *The Chief Executive* (New York: Harcourt Brace Jovanovich, Inc., 1975), and Arthur M. Schlesinger, Jr.'s *The Imperial Presidency* (Boston: Houghton Mifflin Co., 1973). These authors, once champions of a strong presidency, do penance for themselves and their profession, but they fall short of providing political science with a theoretical base for understanding the American presidency.

W. R. Hively

3191. Anisuzzaman, Mohammad and Mohabbat Khan, Mohammad. PRESIDENTIAL POWER: A VIEW FROM THE PRESIDENT-ADVISORS INTERACTION PROCESS. *Indian Pol. Sci. Rev. [India] 1978 12(1): 88-106.* Emphasizes the personal element in the process of choosing advisors and taking advice. Describes three models of interaction between the President and his advisors: the alter-ego model, the free-wheeling model, and the appeals court model. These models are exemplified by Presidents John F. Kennedy, Lyndon B. Johnson, and Richard M. Nixon, respectively. Cites the harmful trend of each President's tendency to choose advisors whose ideas coincide with his own.

J. C. English

3192. Arcui, Alan F. THE IMPERIAL PRESIDENCY: THE TUG TOWARD ISOLATION. *Presidential Studies Q. 1977 7(2-3): 136-144.* Focuses on some of the causes and consequences of the Regal Presidency. Despite changes in personality, character, and political style, a pattern of presidential isolation has emerged. The Imperial Presidency is now institutionalized. Too much reverence is given to the President, and it only serves to isolate him. Presidents need to hear disagreement and dissent; they must not surround themselves with like-minded advisors who try to protect them. There is little indication, though, that modern Presidents are willing to become less isolated. Secondary sources; 57 notes.

R. D. Hurt

3193. Arnhart, Larry. THE GOD-LIKE PRINCE: JOHN LOCKE EXECUTIVE PREROGATIVE, AND THE AMERICAN PRESIDENCY. *Presidential Studies Q. 1979 9(2): 121-130.* Discusses John Locke's definition of presidential prerogative, and discusses Locke's doctrine as it applies to the American presidency, particularly to ex-President Richard M. Nixon's claims to discretionary powers as discussed in Arthur M. Schlesinger, Jr., *The Imperial Presidency* (Boston: Houghton Mifflin Co., 1973).

3194. Arnold, Peri E. THE FIRST HOOVER COMMISSION AND THE MANAGERIAL PRESIDENCY. *J. of Pol. 1976 38(1): 46-70.* Discusses the work of the Hoover Commission to reorganize the executive branch of government in 1947-48, emphasizing its influence in bringing about the political concept of managerial presidency.

3195. Arnold, Peri E. and Roos, L. John. TOWARD A THEORY OF CONGRESSIONAL-EXECUTIVE RELATIONS. *R. of Pol. 1974 36(3): 410-429.*

3196. Arterton, F. Christopher. THE IMPACT OF WATERGATE ON CHILDREN'S ATTITUDES TOWARD POLITICAL AUTHORITY. *Pol. Sci. Q. 1974 89(2): 269-288.* "Presents new attitude data showing how drastically Watergate has eroded the idealization of the presidency widely held in the past by children. Since many political scientists believe that it is precisely this early childhood idealization from which are derived adult feelings about the legitimacy of governmental authority in general, Arterton discusses the potentially serious implications of his findings for the future stability of our political system."

J

3197. Arterton, F. Christopher. WATERGATE AND CHILDREN'S ATTITUDES TOWARD POLITICAL AUTHORITY REVISITED. *Pol. Sci. Q. 1975 90(3): 477-496.* Contrasting data gathered in 1962, 1973, and 1975, F. Christopher Arterton finds that the attitudes of children toward the post-Watergate president have not recovered the idealism which characterized images reported during the early 1960s. If childhood idealization of the president is the basis of adult feelings about the legitimacy of government, the 1975 data suggest that our political system may be susceptible to a long-run legitimacy crisis as a product of Watergate.

J

3198. Bacchus, William I. OBSTACLES TO REFORM IN FOREIGN AFFAIRS: THE CASE OF NSAM 341. *Orbis 1974 18(1): 266-276.* Discusses why reorganization of the US government's foreign policy bureaucracy failed under the plan developed in 1966 in National Security Action Memorandum 341.

3199. Balutis, Alan P. CONGRESS, THE PRESIDENT, AND THE PRESS. *Journalism Q. 1976 53(3): 509-515.* Since 1958 newspaper coverage of the President has increased significantly in relation to that given to the Congress. Further studies are needed to determine the influence this may have on the growing power of the Presidency. Based on a survey of the *New York Times* and the Buffalo *Evening News;* 21 notes.

E. Gibson

3200. Barger, Harold M. THE PROMINENCE OF THE CHIEF OF STATE ROLE IN THE AMERICAN PRESIDENCY. *Presidential Studies Q. 1978 8(2): 127-139.* The public view of the president is based not on political achievements but on symbolic, emotional, and personal images generated by the chief of state role. The symbols, myths, and rituals surrounding the Presidency serve vital needs of the public and national government. The Presidency provides a sense of well-being and a simplification of complex political realities, assuring political consensus and stability. The ceremonial aspects of the Presidency are enhanced by the mass media with the obvious potential for demagoguery and abuse of power. The American people must learn to differentiate between the myth and the specific incumbent through educational curricula changes. Table, 31 notes, biblio.

S. C. Strom

3201. Barrett, Raymond J. THE WAR POWERS: CONSTITUTIONAL CRISIS. *US Naval Inst. Pro. 1973 99(11): 18-25.* Analyzes the current debate over adjustment in the constitutional war powers between the President and the Congress. The formal declaration of war is no longer a viable instrument of government. Therefore, an arrangement must be effected in which the Congress can exercise a controlling voice in the use of the armed forces, while simultaneously permitting the President to have flexibility in meeting emergency situations without a deadline that might frustrate his actions. Illus.

J. K. Ohl

3202. Beck, Nathaniel. PRESIDENTIAL INFLUENCE ON THE FEDERAL RESERVE IN THE 1970S. *Am. J. of Pol. Sci. 1982 26(3): 415-445.* Examines presidential influence on Federal Reserve monetary policy in the 1970's, studying the influences of elections and administration. The Federal Reserve did not appear to manipulate the money supply in 1972 to aid President Nixon's reelection. The reaction function shifted between the Nixon and Ford administrations; it did not shift with the ascension of Carter, and it did not shift with the replacement of Chairman Arthur Burns by Chairman William Miller.

J/S

3203. Beer, Sam H. GOVERNMENT AND POLITICS: AN IMBALANCE. *Center Mag. 1974 7(2): 10-22.* Also mentions the Watergate Scandal and executive powers.

S

3204. Benadom, Gregory A. and Goehlert, Robert U. THE CIA: ITS HISTORY, ORGANIZATION, FUNCTIONS, AND PUBLICATIONS. *Government Publ. Rev. 1979 6(3): 195-212.* This history of the Central Intelligence Agency, 1940-78, includes organizational structure, responsibilities and activities of major offices, and reorganization by the Carter administration, 1978; an extensive bibliography includes the CIA's relationship with the Foreign Broadcast Information Service and the Joint Publication Research Service.

3205. Benda, Charles G. STATE ORGANIZATION AND POLICY FORMATION: THE 1970 REORGANIZATION OF THE POST OF-

FICE DEPARTMENT. *Pol. and Soc. 1979 9(2): 123-151.* Case study that challenges pluralistic and Marxist instrumentalist and structuralist viewpoints on the role of the state in policy formation. Examination of the events leading to the reorganization of the Post Office Department in 1970, and its subsequent operation as a government corporation, reveals that the state itself is capable of structuring the demands placed upon it by various interest groups. Based on government documents; table, 28 notes.
    D. G. Nielson

3206. Bergren, Orville V. THE NEW LOOK IN DEFENSE ORGANIZATION. *Marine Corps Gazette 1958 42(12): 40-48.* Examines the changes wrought in the organization of the Defense Department and the high command of the US armed forces by the Defense Reorganization Act (US, 1958).

3207. Berman, Larry. THE OFFICE OF MANAGEMENT AND BUDGET THAT ALMOST WASN'T. *Pol. Sci. Q. 1977 92(2): 281-303.* Analyzes Bureau of the Budget (BOB) resistance to reorganization since the Eisenhower administration. Previously unstudied archival material shows that Presidents have intended to reorganize the BOB for more than three decades, but that it struggled to preserve its special status in the Executive Office of the President since 1939. Therefore, contrary to the commonly expressed view, the reorganization of the BOB into the Office of Management and Budget (OMB) in 1970 was not an isolated attempt by the Nixon administration to control a hostile bureaucracy. The OMB has apparently inherited its predecessor's management problems. Based on archival material from presidential libraries, government records, and secondary sources; 75 notes.
    W. R. Hively

3208. Berry, Jeffrey M. CONSUMERS AND THE HUNGER LOBBY. *Pro. of the Acad. of Pol. Sci. 1982 34(3): 68-78.* Examines the relationships between public interest advocacy groups and the Agriculture Department. The major points focus on the source of group influence and on why their power varied so greatly within one cabinet department. Public interest groups do represent legitimate views of the Americans who judge Agriculture Department policy without economic self-interest. Secondary sources; 3 notes.
    T. P. Richardson

3209. Best, James J. PRESIDENTIAL CABINET APPOINTMENTS: 1953-1976. *Presidential Studies Q. 1981 11(1): 62-66.* An examination of original and replacement cabinet appointments indicates a substantial difference in the experience and background of those appointed. Replacements are generally less well known to the public but more experienced in Washington and bureaucratic politics than were the initial appointments, loyalty not being as important as ability to manage the departments. 4 tables, 6 notes.
    D. H. Cline

3210. Bloomfield, Lincoln P. PLANNING FOREIGN POLICY: CAN IT BE DONE? *Pol. Sci. Q. 1978 93(3): 369-391.* Reviews the experience of policy planning staffs in the United States State Department and in foreign governments and sharply questions their effectiveness. Concludes with suggestions for how to improve the incorporation of long-range thinking into foreign policy planning.
    J/S

3211. Boiko, K. DISKUSSIIA O PREZIDENTSKOI VLASTI V SSHA (OBZOR RABOT AMERIKANSKIKH POLITOLOGOV) [The discussion about Presidential power in the USA (a survey of the works of American political commentators)]. *Mirovaia Ekonomika i Mezhdunarodnye Otnosheniia [USSR] 1976 (8): 124-128.* Surveys recent American writing on the presidency in light of the Watergate scandal and its aftermath.

3212. Bombardier, Gary. THE MANAGERIAL FUNCTION OF OMB: INTERGOVERNMENTAL RELATIONS AS A TEST CASE. *Public Policy 1975 23(3): 317-354.* Analyzes the changing functions of the Bureau of the Budget as it evolved into the Office of Management and Budget in the 1960's. The increasing importance of the managerial function of the OMB, especially its role in ad hoc interagency and intergovernmental problem-solving, is stressed. Studies the OMB's strivings to increase consultation with state and local government, mayors and governors, and some of its failings to do so. Examines the attempts of the OMB to rationalize the grant-in-aid system, and the opposition it encountered by those who felt OMB was becoming a too-powerful policymaker. With budget functions that generally are critical and negative, the difficulty of

the OMB's positive and creative management function is emphasized. Recommends a traditional, nonactivist role of the OMB in a time of economizing and checking the growth of the Presidency. Based on government documents and secondary sources; 51 notes.
    J. M. Herrick

3213. Borosage, Robert. SECRECY VS. THE CONSTITUTION. *Society 1975 12(3): 71-75.* By constitutional law the executive protects the secrets of intelligence services, like the Central Intelligence Agency.
    S

3214. Bowers, Douglas E. THE RESEARCH AND MARKETING ACT OF 1946 AND ITS EFFECTS ON AGRICULTURAL MARKETING RESEARCH. *Agric. Hist. 1982 56(1): 249-263.* The Research and Marketing Act (US, 1946) set up a greatly expanded program of marketing research by the US Agriculture Department (USDA) and the state experiment stations designed to lessen the effects of postwar surpluses. The act, however, was never funded at the levels originally provided by Congress, nor did marketing research succeed in narrowing the spread between wholesale and retail prices. By the time the USDA reorganized in 1953 to administer marketing research separately, marketing had become a well established research area, but policymakers were once again relying on production controls rather than research to control agricultural prices. Based on USDA and congressional documents; 44 notes.
    D. E. Bowers

3215. Boyer, Neil A. DECISIONS, OPTIONS, CLEARANCES, SECOND-GUESSING: WHATEVER HAPPENED TO PROFESSIONAL OBJECTIVITY? *Foreign Service J. 1977 54(8): 9-11.* The Foreign Service fails to provide decisionmaking offices within the State Department with adequate options and relevant information for the bureaucracy to make efficient and intelligent decisions, 1977.

3216. Braden, Tom. THE BIRTH OF THE CIA. *Am. Heritage 1977 28(2): 4-13.* Surveys the development of the Central Intelligence Agency. The efforts of General William J. Donovan, founder of the US intelligence service during World War II, led to the postwar Central Intelligence Group, created in 1946. The CIA emerged from the National Security Act of 1947. 10 illus.
    J. F. Paul

3217. Bradley, John P. SHAPING ADMINISTRATIVE POLICY WITH THE AID OF CONGRESSIONAL OVERSIGHT: THE SENATE FINANCE COMMITTEE AND MEDICARE. *Western Pol. Q. 1980 33(4): 492-501.* The oversight function of Congress may contribute to the accomplishment of policies sought by administrators. Secondly, committee-bureau cooperation was found in opposition to interest groups rather than there being a "cozy triangle" relationship. Evidence is presented concerning Medicare reimbursement issues where the committee and administrators in the Bureau of Health Insurance shared similar policies. Higher-level administrators did not accept the BHI policies until after the committee undertook oversight activities. Although relations changed somewhat after 1972, the committee continued its interest in Medicare reimbursement policies.
    J/S

3218. Brady, Linda P. PLANNING FOR FOREIGN POLICY: A FRAMEWORK FOR ANALYSIS. *Int. J. [Canada] 1977 32(4): 829-848.* Traces the successes and failures of the Policy Planning Staff of the US Department of State from its formation through subsequent transformation and rejuvenation. 44 notes.
    R. V. Kubicek

3219. Bravo Nuche, Ramón. SERVICIOS DE INTELIGENCIA [Intelligence services]. *Rev. General de Marina [Spain] 1977 193(8-9): 185-197.* The development of US intelligence services demonstrates the complexity of the interrelationships among the various armed services and agencies of government. During World War II, intelligence services were highly decentralized among the various services and only coordinated at the joint chiefs of staff level. This was clearly inadequate and led to the establishment of the Central Intelligence Agency in 1947. Intelligence functions then became too heavily centralized, leading to a partial decentralization after 1961 with the establishment of the Defense Intelligence Agency. The resulting balance between centralization and decentralization serves as a basis for the author's model intelligence organization, in which the armed services and governmental agencies individually provide intelligence requirements to a centralized evaluative department which compiles data from various sources and provides intelligence estimations to a central director of intelligence who oversees the entire process. 3 fig., biblio.   W. C. Frank

3220. Bray, Charles W. THE MEDIA AND FOREIGN POLICY. *Foreign Policy 1974 16: 109-125.* Discusses the pros and cons of the adversary relationship between the media and the US Department of State. While excessive secrecy and other undesirable State tendencies are admitted, much of the fault rests with the media. Reporters overemphasize the need to challenge everything the State does, rather than giving credit where credit is due. In addition, the press— particularly television —treats most stories superficially. The complexities of foreign policy require analysis in depth, and television tends to oversimplify the issues. Media often fail to report public opinion (polls aren't much help). If both the State Department and the media overcame such weaknesses, they could contribute to a more effective foreign policy. Primary sources; 6 notes.   R. F. Kugler

3221. Brisbin, Richard A., Jr. SEPARATION OF POWERS, THE RULE OF LAW, & THE STUDY OF POLITICAL INSTITUTIONS. *Polity 1982 15(1): 123-132.* Reviews Jesse H. Choper's *Judicial Review and the National Political Process: A Functional Reconsideration of the Role of the Supreme Court* (1980), Louis Fisher's *The Constitution between Friends: Congress, the President, and the Law* (1978), Michael A. Genovese's *The Supreme Court, the Constitution, and Presidential Power* (1980), Iredell Jenkins's *Social Order and the Limits of Law: A Theoretical Essay* (1980), and Henry J. Merry's *Five-Branch Government: The Full Measure of Constitutional Checks and Balances* (1980) that discuss American political institutions including the three branches of national government, the rule of law, and the bureaucracy. 5 notes.
                                    J. Powell

3222. Brown, Roger G. PARTY AND BUREAUCRACY: FROM KENNEDY TO REAGAN. *Pol. Sci. Q. 1982 97(2): 279-294.* Attempts to determine patterns of party affiliation among top-level presidential appointees, 1961-80. Distribution of prestigious positions is less a matter of patronage than of politics, of bargaining chips to further legislative goals and to insure support for executive policy. Staffs in the Executive Branch are less influenced by national parties than in former years. 3 tables, 51 notes.   J. Powell

3223. Bruce Lockhart, J. M. CIA AND THE POWERS OF DARKNESS? *J. of the Royal United Services Inst. for Defence Studies [Great Britain] 1975 120(1): 82-84.* A review article discussing Victor Marchetti and John D. Marks's *The CIA and the Cult of Intelligence* (London: Jonathan Cape, 1974). Ridicules the author's requirement that the US secret service should ensure that its operations are ethical and undertaken with a view to the moral consequences, and rejects their contention that the CIA is "a state within a state, accountable only to itself." CIA errors derived from the politics of the McCarthy era and an excess of funds and personnel. The real motive of the authors was not sinister but "a mixture of innocence, arrogance and personal gain." Their revelations raise the question of a definition of treason in a democracy.
                                    D. H. Murdoch

3224. Casey, Gregory. THE THEORY OF PRESIDENTIAL ASSOCIATION: A REPLICATION. *Am. J. of Pol. Sci. 1975 19(1): 19-26.* "This note tests, with 1968 Missouri survey data, Dolbeare and Hammond's proposition that evaluations of incumbent presidents govern public confidence in the Supreme Court more than do party loyalties. The data show that although independents generalize their evaluations of the president to the Supreme Court, partisans are less affected by the 'presidential association.' "   J

3225. Casey, William J. THE AMERICAN INTELLIGENCE COMMUNITY. *Presidential Studies Q. 1982 12(2): 150-153.* The intelligence community, institutionalized by President Truman in 1947, has been too limited and must be strengthened. Recent legislation, such as the Freedom of Information Act (US, 1966), must be modified to assure the same confidentiality for the intelligence service as other professions receive.   D. H. Cline

3226. Chambers, Raymond L. THE EXECUTIVE POWER: A PRELIMINARY STUDY OF THE CONCEPT AND OF THE EFFICACY

OF PRESIDENTIAL DIRECTIVES. *Presidential Studies Q. 1977 7(1): 21-37.* The public's reaction against presidential abuses of power could threaten the foundations of American democracy. Limiting of presidential power could prevent effective executive action. Discusses the concepts of power and the bureaucratic responses to Presidential directives. Suggests increasing vigilance over the President rather than changing the office itself. Based on secondary sources; table, 85 notes.
                                    R. D. Hurt

3227. Clifford, Clark M. COUNSELING THE PRESIDENT. *Center Mag. 1974 7(3): 22-26.* Clark Clifford, advisor to presidents Truman, Kennedy, and Johnson, discusses in an interview the presidency, the psychological effects of the office on its incumbent, and the difficulties involved in counseling him.   S

3228. Clubb, O. Edmund. SECURITY RISKS: NATIONAL SECURITY AND THE STATE DEPARTMENT. *Worldview 1973 16(8): 43-45.* Discusses the role of the State Department in the formation of US foreign policy 1945-70's, including so-called security risks among Foreign Service officers who accurately foresaw the taking of China by Communists in the 1940's.

3229. Clubb, O. Edmund. SECURITY RISKS: NATIONAL SECURITY AND THE STATE DEPARTMENT. *Foreign Service J. 1973 50(12): 13-15.* Discusses the Foreign Service's position within the State Department, its downgrading during the 1950's (through actions of persons such as McCarthy), its role in foreign policy formulation, and the present need to place more emphasis and trust in the Foreign Service.
                                    S

3230. Coletta, Paolo E. THE DEFENSE UNIFICATION BATTLE, 1947-50: THE NAVY. *Prologue 1975 7(1): 6-17.* From the passage of the National Security Act (1947) to the outbreak of the Korean War, the Office of the Secretary of Defense grew at the expense of the Navy, which had to scrap its plans for a supercarrier and drastically cut naval air power and the Marine Corps. Based on primary and secondary sources; 3 illus., 59 notes.   R. W. Tissing, Jr.

3231. Commager, Henry Steele. ON THE AMERICAN PRESIDENCY. *Massachusetts Rev. 1980 21(3): 561-567.* The Presidency is the most difficult office in the world; however, the caliber of those occupying it has declined since World War II.   E. R. Campbell

3232. Cook, J. Frank. "PRIVATE PAPERS" OF PUBLIC OFFICIALS. *Am. Archivist 1975 38(3): 299-324.* Reviews the legal precedents and traditions pertaining to the ownership of presidential papers and argues that ownership of papers of public officials should rest with the government. Urges archivists to support reforms insuring greater public access to officials' acts and decisions. Primary and secondary sources; 67 notes.   J. A. Benson

3233. Coontz, Stephanie. WATERGATE AND THE CONSTITUTION. *Internat. Socialist R. 1974 35(1): 12-17, 31-33.* Discussion of the Constitution, how it came into being, its interpretation by various presidents, and its relation to the Watergate Scandal.   S

3234. Cornwell, Elmer E., Jr. THE PRESIDENT AND THE PRESS: PHASES IN THE RELATIONSHIP. *Ann. of the Am. Acad. of Pol. and Social Sci. 1976 427: 53-64.* Approaches the relationship of the president to the press first by discussing the key importance of the president's ability to develop public support for his policies. This is his primary reliance since he has few constitutional powers for influencing policy and his role as party leader is not much help. Because the president's relationship with the public is so important, his dependence on the press to maintain that link is very great. The nation gains news about the president and what he is doing and forms opinions of him and his policies, through the news media. A president's relations with the press, though based on interdependence, rarely involve cordial cooperation. Rather, they tend to go through phases of "seasons" related closely to the more readily measured phases through which general presidential popularity passes during an administration. Using data gathered by the Gallup Poll on public approval of how the president is doing his job, the pattern can be studied. It usually involves high initial ratings and subsequent declines. The rate of decline depends partly on whether a president was elected or succeeded as vice-president. How wisely he uses this key asset in efforts to influence policy and how skillfully he deals with the media "middlemen" will determine much of his presidency's success.   J

3235.   Cotter, Richard D.   NOTES TOWARD A DEFINITION OF NATIONAL SECURITY.   *Washington Monthly 1975 7(10): 4-16*. Discusses recent findings in the hearings conducted by Senator Frank Church's Select Committee on Intelligence Activities and traces the history of the Federal Bureau of Investigation since the 1930's.   S

3236.   Cronin, Thomas E.   AN IMPERILED PRESIDENCY? *Society 1978 16(1): 57-64*. Examines the problems President Gerald R. Ford and President Jimmy Carter have encountered since Richard M. Nixon's imperial presidency, in effectively governing the United States during the 1970's.

3237.   Cronin, Thomas E.   PRESIDENTIAL POWER REVISED AND REAPPRAISED.   *Western Pol. Q. 1979 32(4): 381-395*. While concern over the imperial presidency has receded for the most part in the Ford-Carter era, this article argues that how social scientists portray presidential power and the presidency may promote misleading as well as helpful conceptions of presidential effectiveness. Using Richard E. Neustadt's 1960 and 1976 editions of *Presidential Power* as focal illustrations, the article summarizes contemporary mainstream thinking about the power of presidents and the study of presidential leadership. Basic criticisms of the Neustadt model are raised and discussed. Questions are raised about the validity and desirability of studying the means of presidential influence divorced from the content or ends of political influence. How does the Neustadt model hold up in the light of the Johnson and Nixon abuses of power? The limitations of the Neustadt approach are appraised. Finally, the article reviews the contemporary rebirth of yearning for a more assertive and effective presidency and notes the striking similarity between these views and the general premises of Richard Neustadt's work. Fig., 34 notes.   J

3238.   Cronin, Thomas E.   A RESURGENT CONGRESS AND THE IMPERIAL PRESIDENCY.   *Pol. Sci. Q. 1980 95(2): 209-237*. Assesses the argument that Congress has successfully reasserted itself in national policymaking and seriously curbed the imperial presidency. He finds that Congress has indeed become more involved in national policymaking and that constraints have been added to the way presidents exercise their powers. Cronin concludes that whatever reassertion has taken place may not last and that, in any event, the presidency has not been weakened as much as some commentators have claimed.   J

3239.   Cutler, Lloyd N.   TO FORM A GOVERNMENT.   *Foreign Affairs 1980 59(1): 126-143*. The separation of powers between the executive and legislative branches of the US government fails to meet contemporary needs for effective governing. A president is elected on the basis of his program, but its realization depends on congressional approval. If the president could form a government, as in a parliamentary system, with close cooperation between the executive and legislative branches, a coherent program could be carried out. Methods of improving the existing relationship between the two governmental branches ought to be discussed. 7 notes.   A. A. Englard

3240.   Daddario, Emilio Q.   SCIENCE POLICY: RELATIONSHIPS ARE THE KEY.   *Daedalus 1974 103(3): 135-142*. Although the federal government must assume primary responsibility for support and application of science programs, it is not clear that science and technology receive serious consideration at the highest levels of government. The new procedure of *ad hoc* committees called in response to emergencies should be supplemented by programs based on continuity and predictability of support. Past accomplishments argue for the value of a presidential science advisor, but the relationship between the advisor, the president, and the legislature depends on wise appointments by the president. Based on secondary sources; 5 notes.   E. McCarthy

3241.   Darling, W. Stuart and Mense, D. Craig.   RETHINKING THE WAR POWERS ACT.   *Presidential Studies Q. 1977 7(2-3): 126-136*. The nation needs a good war powers act, but the present War Powers Act (1973) is inadequate. The conference committee erred by not requiring prior congressional consent for limiting presidential warmaking in other than emergency situations. Return to the original Senate bill would clarify

the situations in which the President can act unilaterally, and would specify when he could act only with prior congressional authorization. That bill would help prevent the President from committing the nation to policies it will not accept. Primary and secondary sources and government documents; 30 notes, biblio.   R. D. Hurt

3242.   Dauer, Manning J.   A CRITIQUE OF SAMUEL HENDEL'S "SEPARATION OF POWERS REVISITED IN LIGHT OF WATERGATE."   *Western Political Q. 1974 27(4): 589-592*. Comments on Hendel's article; provides overviews on the historical meaning of separation of powers and the implications of Watergate upon this doctrine.

3243.   Dauses, Manfred A. and Wolf, Dieter O. A.   DIE VERFASSUNGSRECHTLICHE PROBLEMATIK DER "WAR POWERS" IN DEN VEREINIGTEN STAATEN   [The legal-constitutional problems of the war powers in the United States]. *Politische Vierteljahresschrift [West Germany] 1974 15(2): 213-244*. Analyzes three areas: the right to start a war, the right to carry it on, and restoring the constitutional balance through strengthened parliamentarism. Congress has the right to start a defensive war, but the President also has "sudden repulse power" and does not require the assent of Congress. As the commander-in-chief the President can carry on and end a war, but Congress controls the budget. Since Vietnam Congress has become more vocal about its right to influence foreign policy. An important recent development is the Javits Bill, 1971, which seeks to limit the presidential sudden repulse powers. This is a step toward parliamentarism as distinct from sole presidential control. Based on secondary works and newspapers; 141 notes.   A. Alcock

3244.   Davis, Paul B.   THE RESULTS AND IMPLICATIONS OF THE ENACTMENT OF THE TWENTY-SECOND AMENDMENT. *Presidential Studies Q. 1979 9(3): 289-303*. Discusses the results and future implications of the 22d Amendment which limits a president's terms to two and was passed during Harry Truman's administration in 1950, and presents the views of Presidents Truman through Carter on the amendment.

3245.   Dennis, Jack and Webster, Carol.   CHILDREN'S IMAGES OF THE PRESIDENT AND OF GOVERNMENT IN 1962 AND 1974. *Am. Pol. Q. 1975 3(4): 386-405*. Discusses political socialization by comparing children's attitudes and stereotypes of the presidency and of government in 1962 and 1974, emphasizing a decline in idealization.

3246.   Dennis, Jack.   WHO SUPPORTS THE PRESIDENCY? *Society 1976 13(5): 48-53*. Discusses public opinion of the presidency and governmental authority from 1972-74 in light of President Richard M. Nixon's involvement in the Watergate scandal and the Vietnam War.

3247.   Destler, I. M.   DATELINE WASHINGTON: CONGRESS AS BOSS.   *Foreign Policy 1981 (42): 167-180*. Despite expectations, the 1980 elections are unlikely to bring an end to the persistent foreign policy conflict between Congress and the executive branch. The Congressional revolt against executive authority in the 1970's brought institutional changes which enlarged the role of the legislature and encouraged its foreign policy activism. These changes cannot easily be reversed, but their divisive effects can be overcome by executive initiatives involving "reasonable policy convergence, professionalism in the administration, and the right personal connections between the branches." 2 notes.   T. L. Powers

3248.   Destler, I. M.   NATIONAL SECURITY MANAGEMENT: WHAT PRESIDENTS HAVE WROUGHT.   *Pol. Sci. Q. 1980-81 95(4): 573-588*. After analyzing the evolution of the National Security Council staff, argues that responding to immediate presidential demands has undercut the government's capacity for continuity and coherence in foreign policy.   J/S

3249.   Destler, I. M.   NATIONAL SECURITY ADVICE TO U.S. PRESIDENTS: SOME LESSONS FROM THIRTY YEARS.   *World Pol. 1977 29(2): 143-176*. Since 1947 the major formal institution for channeling national security advice to Presidents has been the National Security Council. The Council has operated (1) as a forum where senior officials meet with the President; (2) as a focal point for formal policy planning and decision processes; and (3) as an umbrella for establishment of a Presidential foreign policy staff. The first was the goal of its proponents; the last is what it has most importantly become. But the N.S.C. has reflected the relationships among each administration's top officials more than it has shaped them; hence the need to think of broader advisory "systems" combining the formal and the informal. Among the variables shaping such systems are: a President's particular organizational sense; his attitude toward formality and regularity; whether he has (and wants) strong Cabinet officials; how his key advisers work out their role relationships and jurisdictional boundaries; how widely he casts his net for advice; how broad a range of substantive issue involvement he seeks; how much he seeks operational involvement; and his attitude toward divided counsel and interpersonal conflict. Prescriptions about foreign policy advisory systems tend to stress the President's role as decision maker; they should focus also on the oft-competing role of effective Presidential leadership in getting policies and decisions executed. The importance of execution argues for giving the Secretary of State primary over other advisers; the need to protect the President's decision authority argues for a White House assistant independent of the Secretary, though perhaps with reduced rank. Presidents also need better advice on the domestic politics of U.S. foreign policy, and each could profit from a "mid-term system review" after his institutions and advisory relationships have taken shape.

J

3250. Donovan, J. A. IT IS DIFFICULT TO MAKE A PROPER BLENDING OF THE PRESIDENT'S CONTROL OF THE MILITARY WITH THE POWER OF THE CONGRESS TO DECLARE WAR. *Marine Corps Gazette 1977 61(9): 28-36.* Discusses the president's war powers versus those of the Congress during 1940-73 and details the provisions of the War Powers Act (1973) from a military standpoint.

3251. Donovan, Thomas A. THE CIA INVESTIGATION: ASKING THE UNTHINKABLE? *Foreign Service J. 1975 52(10): 19-20.* Discusses the Senate investigation of intelligence service and the Central Intelligence Agency in 1975, including a brief history of the CIA from its origins in 1945.

S

3252. Dunham, Roger G. and Mauss, Armand L. WAVES FROM WATERGATE: EVIDENCE CONCERNING THE IMPACT OF THE WATERGATE SCANDAL UPON POLITICAL LEGITIMACY AND SOCIAL CONTROL. *Pacific Sociol. Rev. 1976 19(4): 469-490.* Discusses the impact of the Watergate scandal on public opinion toward the Nixon administration, political leadership, and the US political system in general in 1973-74.

3253. Edwards, George C., III. PRESIDENTIAL INFLUENCE IN THE HOUSE: PRESIDENTIAL PRESTIGE AS A SOURCE OF PRESIDENTIAL POWER. *Am. Pol. Sci. Rev. 1976 70(1): 101-113.* Presidential prestige or popularity has often been cited as an important source of presidential influence in Congress. It has not been empirically and systematically demonstrated, however, that such a relationship exists. This study examines a variety of relationships between presidential prestige and presidential support in the U.S. House of Representatives. The relationships between overall national presidential popularity on the one hand and overall, domestic, and foreign policy presidential support in the House as a whole and among various groups of congressmen on the other are generally weak. Consistently strong relationships *are* found between presidential prestige among Democratic party identifiers and presidential support among Democratic congressmen. Similar relationships are found bewteen presidential prestige among the more partisan Republican party identifiers and the presidential support by Republican congressmen. Explanations for these findings are presented, and the findings are related to broader questions of American politics.

J

3254. Edwards, George C., III. PRESIDENTIAL INFLUENCE IN THE SENATE: PRESIDENTIAL PRESTIGE AS A SOURCE OF PRESIDENTIAL POWER. *Am. Pol. Q. 1977 5(4): 481-500.* Statistically investigates whether, and the extent to which, presidential prestige is a source of presidential power in the Senate, and how Senate insulation from its public (because of six-year terms) compares with House responsiveness. Correlates presidential prestige and presidential support in the Senate in several ways. 6 tables, 2 fig.

R. V. Ritter

3255. Edwards, George C., III. PRESIDENTIAL LEGISLATIVE SKILLS AS A SOURCE OF INFLUENCE IN CONGRESS. *Presi-*

dential Studies Q. 1980 10(2): 211-223. Presidential legislative skills are not the predominant factor in determining presidential support in Congress for most roll-call votes. By studying roll-call voting patterns during 1953-78, it is seen that presidents who vary in legislative skills do not necessarily vary in support in Congress attributable to those skills. Presidential influence can help, but it is not the deciding factor in congressional support. 7 tables, 30 notes.

D. H. Cline

3256. English, John W. DEAN RUSK VIEWS THE WASHINGTON PRESS CORPS. *Foreign Service J. 1974 51(6): 18-21, 39.* Comments by Dean Rusk on persistent problems between the press and the government.

S

3257. Entin, Kenneth. THE HOUSE ARMED SERVICES COMMITTEE: PATTERNS OF DECISION-MAKING DURING THE MC NAMARA YEARS. *J. of Pol. and Military Sociol. 1974 2(1): 73-87.* "This article focuses on the group life of the House Armed Services Committee from 1965 to 1968. Committee processes during this period were influenced by the existence of widely accepted norms which helped promote committee integration. However, contrasting interpretations of the general goal of insuring a strong national defense led to the formation of two bipartisan factions. The majority faction, containing the great bulk of committee members, and guided by the most senior legislators, equated this goal with the advancement of military interests in the policy-making process. Executive-legislative antagonisms were magnified when these congressmen perceived that centralization in the Department of Defense under Robert McNamara had an adverse effect on military access to the committee. The minority faction, centered in a small group called the 'fearless five,' challenged the majority's interpretation and defended the McNamara innovations and actions. The data point to the continued dominance of the pro-military faction."

J

3258. Epstein, Edward Jay. THE WAR WITHIN THE CIA. *Commentary 1978 66(2): 35-39.* It has become clear that Seymour Hersh's exposé, in the 22 December 1974 *New York Times,* of Central Intelligence Agency (CIA) violations of its own charter, which prompted House and Senate investigations in 1975 that hamstrung the CIA, was leaked to Hersh by CIA Director William E. Colby, who was engaged in a power struggle within the CIA. Colby disagreed with CIA Counterintelligence Director James J. Angleton, who for years had identified Soviet double agents among supposed defectors and other Soviet sources and discounted their "disclosures" as purposeful KGB disinformation. Plagued by inability to make any recruits not regarded by Angleton as unreliable, Colby wished to accept any Soviet volunteers as US agents. Colby pressured Angleton to resign, but Angleton refused to do that, until the *Times* story forced him to. The Soviets promptly planted a KGB double agent, utterly befuddling the CIA and enabling the Soviets to arrest and sentence Anatoly Scharansky.

V. L. Human/D. J. Engler

3259. Evans, Les. WATERGATE AND THE WHITE HOUSE: FROM KENNEDY TO NIXON AND BEYOND. *Internat. Socialist R. 1973 34(11): 4-11, 25-40.* Consistent accumulation of presidential power, especially in the Nixon administration, culminated in the Watergate Scandal.

S

3260. Fallows, James. CRAZIES BY THE TAIL: BAY OF PIGS, DIEM, AND LIDDY. *Washington Monthly 1974 6(7): 50-58.* Charts the "traditional" presidential aversion from disquieting truths and the resulting political misdeeds through the Kennedy, Johnson, and Nixon administrations.

S

3261. Fedler, Fred; Meeske, Mike; and Hall, Joe. *TIME* MAGAZINE REVISITED: PRESIDENTIAL STEREOTYPES PERSIST. *Journalism Q. 1979 56(2): 353-359. Time,* the weekly news magazine, has used selective explanation and word-choice, along with photographs, cartoons, and captions, to express editorial views on the four most recent US presidents. These same techniques in reporting on presidential administrations were noted in a 1965 study of the magazine's coverage. *Time's* editors appear to have been ambivalent toward Lyndon B. Johnson, strongly favorable toward Richard M. Nixon until the Watergate scandal, moderately favorable toward Gerald R. Ford, and critical of Jimmy Carter. Based on a study of 10 consecutive issues published during each of the four administrations; table, 8 notes.

R. P. Sindermann, Jr.

3262. Feigenbaum, Edward D. STAFFING, ORGANIZATION, AND DECISION-MAKING IN THE FORD AND CARTER WHITE HOUSES. *Presidential Studies Q. 1980 10(3): 364-377*. Analyzes the structure, functions, and roles of the Gerald R. Ford and Jimmy Carter White House presidential staffs. Ford, trying to make his congressional staff into a presidential staff, experienced serious organizational problems at first and only managed to get things working smoothly at the end of his term. Carter issued dual mandates to his Cabinet and staff, but found that this collegiality had too many problems. After a reorganization, by 1978 his staff ran without friction and in response to his needs.
D. H. Cline

3263. Fisher, Louis. A POLITICAL CONTEXT FOR LEGISLATIVE VETOES. *Pol. Sci. Q. 1978 93(2): 241-254*. Discusses the struggle between Congress and the president over the "legislative veto" by Congress.

3264. Fisher, Louis and Moe, Ronald C. PRESIDENTIAL REORGANIZATION AUTHORITY: IS IT WORTH THE COST? *Pol. Sci. Q. 1981 96(2): 301-318*. The authority of the president to propose executive reorganization plans to Congress, subject to veto in either house, expired on 6 April 1981. Both houses, at the request of President Ronald Reagan, must once again consider the value of this process. The decision in 1932 to give the president authority to submit reorganization proposals was the logical outgrowth of two powerful concepts that enjoyed favor at the time: the notion that a theory of administration could be developed that was at once apolitical and scientific, and the idea that the president should actively manage the executive branch. The drawbacks of the reorganization plan process are so serious and the premises behind it are so weak that both branches would benefit by not renewing the authority. Based on the *Congressional Record*, presidential papers, and other primary sources; 53 notes.
J. Powell

3265. Florestano, Patricia S. THE CHARACTERISTICS OF WHITE HOUSE STAFF APPOINTEES FROM TRUMAN TO NIXON. *Presidential Studies Q. 1977 7(4): 184-189*. Presents results of an examination of the characteristics of White House staff appointees from Harry S. Truman to Richard Nixon. Truman's staff was well-organized, but lacking in power; Dwight D. Eisenhower's, hierarchical; John F. Kennedy's, flexible and responsible; Nixon's, an isolationist minibureaucracy. Nevertheless, there was in common among staffs their age (median 42), race and sex (white male), and education (advanced, private, and eastern); and they were primarily from the private sector on the East Coast. Table, 15 notes, biblio.
J. Tull

3266. Foust, James D. U.S. BANKERS VS. THE DEPARTMENT OF JUSTICE: THE 1966 AMENDMENT TO THE BANK MERGER ACT, BANKING STRUCTURE, AND REGULATION. *Rev. Int. d'Hist. de la Banque [Italy] 1974 9: 80-106*. The Sherman and Clayton anti-trust laws were deficient with respect to bank mergers. Prior to 1960 most banking legislation neglected mergers and consolidation. This lack of legislation led to numerous clashes in the early 1960's between the Comptroller of the Currency and the Board of Governors of the Federal Reserve System, who tended to look favorably on mergers, and the Justice Department which viewed mergers in the light of antimonopoly legislation. Although the Bank Merger Act of 1966 provided additional guidelines regarding mergers, it left the banking authorities and the Justice Department in adversary positions. Based on federal court cases, government documents, and secondary sources; 4 tables, 105 notes.
D. McGinnis

3267. Frank, Thomas M. AFTER THE FALL: THE NEW PROCEDURAL FRAMEWORK FOR CONGRESSIONAL CONTROL OVER THE WAR POWER. *Am. J. of Int. Law 1977 71(4): 605-641*. Reviews the war power in historical perspective. Considers the fight (1969-73) for congressional control over warmaking. Examines the War Powers Resolution (1973) in practice with reference to the presidential duty to consult and to report. Treats the presidential perspective on the effect of the War Powers Resolution on "inherent" presidential powers. Ponders the legislative perspective of the War Powers Resolution's effect on inherent powers of the commander-in-chief. Challenges the constitutionality of the congressional veto in the War Powers context. Discusses treaty commitments. Suggests reforms for the War Powers Resolution. Concludes that the War Powers Resolution "weakens the congressional

power to prevent military action by conceding, without effectively limiting or defining it, a presidential power to start wars while only marginally strengthening the power of Congress to terminate them."
R. J. Jirran

3268. Freeman, J. Leiper. INVESTIGATING THE EXECUTIVE INTELLIGENCE: THE FATE OF THE PIKE COMMITTEE. *Capitol Studies 1977 5(2): 103-118*. Discusses the Pike Committee investigations into executive power and use of intelligence services during 1975-76; examines the effectiveness of investigations conducted by the House of Representatives.

3269. Frug, Gerald. REPORT ON COMMITTEE III. *Ann. of the Am. Acad. of Pol. and Social Sci. 1976 426: 152-158*. Political parties have been the traditional means by which the various groups in our society are able to articulate their views and goals; however, there has been a significant decline in the role of political parties in our society. One basic cause has been the primary system. Problems created by reliance on primaries are that this process encourages more extreme candidates and reliance on style rather than program. It is argued in favor of primaries that conflict between Congress and the president is not a bad thing and the primary system is more democratic than the party system. A possible resolution to this debate is the idea of the regional primary. Concerning the separation of powers, there is an increasing tendency of Congress to delegate unchecked authority to the Executive branch. Possible solutions to the problem are congressional oversight, unconstitutional delegation of powers, congressional veto, and the power of impeachment. Finally, there is the problem of Legislative effectiveness and the Executive function of planning. Congress must work as a whole on plans to deal with the country's problems, but this is a difficult change for Congress to make. [A report on Committee III of the AAPSS Bicentennial Constitutional Conference, 1976].
J

3270. Garnham, David. ATTITUDE AND PERSONALITY PATTERNS OF UNITED STATES FOREIGN SERVICE OFFICERS. *Am. J. of Pol. Sci. 1974 18(3): 525-548*. "The study examines relationships between the rank and functional specialization of United States Foreign Service officers and three psycho-attitudinal variables: 1) psychological flexibility, 2) international-mindedness, and 3) career satisfaction. Data analyses test generalizations concerning relationships between these variables which are prominent in the literature. Attitudes are found to relate more to rank than to function. Data consist of 274 responses to a mail questionnaire."
J

3271. Garnham, David. STATE DEPARTMENT RIGIDITY: TESTING A PSYCHOLOGICAL HYPOTHESIS. *Internat. Studies Q. 1974 18(1): 31-40*.

3272. Garnham, David. STATE DEPARTMENT RIGIDITY: TESTING A PSYCHOLOGICAL HYPOTHESIS. *Foreign Service J. 1974 51(10): 32-34*. Discusses the behavior of Foreign Service Officers.
S

3273. Gibson, Dirk Cameron. HALE BOGGS ON J. EDGAR HOOVER: RHETORICAL CHOICE AND POLITICAL DENUNCIATION. *Southern Speech Communication J. 1981 47(1): 54-66*. Thomas Hale Boggs's 1971 denunciation of J. Edgar Hoover was an unexpected and highly controversial rhetorical act; explains why only Boggs stood in Congress to complain about Federal Bureau of Investigation behavior by considering his public and private motives: Boggs's anger at discovering his home telephone tapped, his philosophy regarding responsible government, and his distrust of Hoover.

3274. Gilbert, Robert E. TELEVISION AND PRESIDENTIAL POWER. *J. of Social, Pol. and Econ. Studies 1981 6(1): 75-93*. Presidential use of television addresses has served to strengthen the power, popularity, and public image of the presidency at the expense of both the legislative branch and the opponents of presidential prerogatives; 1952-81.

3275. Gordon, George J. OFFICE OF MANAGEMENT AND BUDGET CIRCULAR A—95: PERSPECTIVES AND IMPLICATIONS. *Publius 1974 4(1): 45-68*. Discusses political factors in the competition among federal, state, and local government for budget planning and programming rights in the 1970's.

3276. Graber, Doris A. EXECUTIVE DECISION-MAKING. *Pro. of the Acad. of Pol. Sci. 1982 34(4): 75-87.* Discusses communications factors and their relationships to those known as decisionmakers, to the revealing of data pertinent to decisions, and to the winning of support for and the implementation of specific decisions. These are examined using examples taken mostly from the Executive Branch. Primary sources; 7 notes.   T. P. Richardson

3277. Graves, Thomas J. IGR AND THE EXECUTIVE BRANCH: THE NEW FEDERALISM. *Ann. of the Am. Acad. of Pol. and Social Sci. 1974 416: 40-51.* [Intergovernmental relations] "and the New Federalism are synonymous. Former President Nixon summarized the New Federalism as 'A cooperative venture among governments at all levels . . in which power, funds, and authority are channeled increasingly to those governments which are closest to the people.' IGR is essentially an art and primarily an exercise in the behavioral field. The thread which binds government officials intergovernmentally is the financing and administration of federal grants-in-aid and other forms of federal financial assistance. Concern in the executive branch for IGR developed in the last 20 years; thus its roots in American governance are not yet very deep. The views and support of public interest groups as well as the sympathetic attention of Congress are essential to the pursuit of IGR goals and objectives in the executive branch. In relations between levels of government, partnership rather than paternalism must prevail. The rise of stronger chief executives and decentralization of power from Washington are noted. Confidence of Americans in their own government is essential to achieving a federal system working in all parts, well-managed and equitably financed."   J

3278. Green, Barbara and Hurwitz, Leon. PRESS VIEWS OF EXECUTIVE VS. SENATORIAL POWERS. *Journalism Q. 1978 55(4): 775-778.* Compares the news and editorial coverage by the *New York Times* and the *Chicago Tribune* of the 1954 Army-McCarthy hearings and the 1973 Ervin Committee hearings in the US Senate. Although both series of hearings dealt with confrontations between the executive and legislative branches over jurisdictions and Senate access to executive sources, each newspaper's editorials supported the executive in one case, but Congress in the other. The *Times* sided with the President in 1954 but with the Senate in 1973; the *Tribune* took stands that were just the opposite. Table, 3 notes.   R. P. Sindermann, Jr.

3279. Greenberg, George D. REORGANIZATION RECONSIDERED: THE U.S. PUBLIC HEALTH SERVICE 1960-1973. *Public Policy 1975 23(4): 483-522.* Considers the effectiveness of bureaucratic reorganization, based on the experience of the Public Health Service. The PHS was reorganized in 1966 and again in 1968, but not much really changed. Shifting of high positions allowed the infusion of new personnel amenable to administration ideas, but on lower levels the organization functioned as before. Too many external constraints on the PHS's power negative effective change. Congress and the states modify its programs, its objectives are multiple and conflicting, and its resources are limited and insufficient—hard facts which reorganization is powerless to change. 6 figs., 35 notes.   V. L. Human

3280. Greenstein, Fred I. THE BENEVOLENT LEADER REVISITED: CHILDREN'S IMAGES OF POLITICAL LEADERS IN THREE DEMOCRACIES. *Am. Pol. Sci. Rev. 1975 69(4): 1371-1398.* This analysis of open-ended interviews conducted in 1969-70 with small samples of English, French, and white and black American children focuses on orientations toward the heads of state of the three nations and the Prime Ministers of Britain and France. The English children exhibit remarkably positive views of the Queen. Many of them believe her to be the nation's effective leader rather than a figurehead. Any political animus they express is directed toward the Prime Minister. The French children tend to describe the President of the Republic positively when they express feelings toward him at all but expect him to behave harshly and arrogantly in actual situations. Their descriptions of political leaders exude authoritarian imagery and perceptions; they perceive the President of the Republic in an impersonal, undifferentiated manner, and are only barely aware of the Premier. The general descriptions of the President of the United States by white American children interviewed in 1969-70 are remarkably similar to the benevolent-leader perceptions of children in the Eisenhower-Kennedy years, but the 1969-70 children exhibit much less idealized views of a president depicted as a law-breaker. A post-Watergate

white American comparison group interviewed in June 1973 is generally aware of, but puzzled by, the Watergate events. At this early stage in the Watergate revelations, white children were only slightly less likely than the 1969-70 respondents to idealize the President, but were substantially more likely to perceive the president depicted as a law-breaker in terms implying that the President is "above the law." The American black comparison group, which is too small and special in its geographical circumstances to offer more than suggestive findings, is the most negative of the four groups in general responses to the head of state, but is more like the white American group than like the English or French children in expectations about the actual behavior of the leader. Even though the black and white American children seem to be similar in their expectations about how certain political encounters would ensue, interpretations of encounters are strikingly different.   J

3281. Gromadzki, Grzegorz. ROLA PREZYDENTA W REALIZACJI POLITYKI ZAGRANICZNEJ STANÓW ZJEDNOCZONYCH AMERYKI [The role of the president in realizing US foreign policy]. *Studia Nauk Politycznych [Poland] 1980 (4): 45-61.* Each postwar president had ambitions to develop his own "style of governing." Each administration attempted also to adapt the existing administration machine to its needs. In spite of differences, each president, as chief executive, plays the essential role in administrating the US foreign policy. These tasks are directly realized by the appropriate offices of the State Department, but the president is responsible for their activity. The president as an institution has much greater power than established by the authors of the Constitution. Decisions are made in the White House that shape US foreign policy. An important role is played by the president's advisers, who share his powers.   J/S

3282. Grossman, Michael Baruch and Rourke, Francis E. THE MEDIA AND THE PRESIDENCY: AN EXCHANGE ANALYSIS. *Pol. Sci. Q. 1976 91(3): 455-470.* Contends that what has been traditionally characterized as an adversary relationship between the president and the press has been taking more of the form of a mutually beneficial exchange of news for publicity. They also believe that the press has recently been improving its position in the trading relationship that historically has been dominated by the White House.   J

3283. Grossman, Michael Baruch and Kumar, Martha Joynt. THE WHITE HOUSE AND THE NEWS MEDIA: THE PHASES OF THEIR RELATIONSHIP. *Pol. Sci. Q. 1979 94(1): 37-54.* Michael Baruch Grossman and Martha Joynt Kumar explore what they define as phases that have occurred in the relationship between the president and the news media in all administrations since 1960. They suggest that there are three such phases—alliance, competition, and detachment—that have recurred in spite of the major differences in policies and personalities of the incumbents.   J

3284. Gustafson, Merlin. OUR PART-TIME CHIEF OF STATE. *Presidential Studies Q. 1979 9(2): 163-171.* Discusses the role of the president of the United States as chief of state, whose function is as ceremonial leader, 1970's.

3285. Gustafson, Milton O. THE SUPREME COURT AND KISSINGER'S TELEPHONE RECORDS. *Soc. for Hist. of Am. Foreign Relations. Newsletter 1980 11(2): 18-22.* Discusses the background of Henry A. Kissinger's Supreme Court victory on 4 March 1980 that prevented public disclosure of transcripts of phone conversations recorded from 1969 to 1976 from his White House and State Department offices while he was Assistant to the President for National Security Affairs from 1969 to 1975 and Secretary of State from 1973 to 1977, and whether there will be more cases to try to disclose the contents of the telephone transcripts.

3286. Haftendorn, Helga. STUDIEN ZUM AUSSENPOLITISCHEN ENTSCHEIDUNGSPROZESS IN DEN USA [Studies on the decisionmaking process in foreign policy in the USA]. *Politische Vierteljahresschrift [West Germany] 1976 17(2): 245-254.* Analyzes post-Vietnam America's overhauling of its foreign policymaking. Examines the relationship between the White House and Congress under Presidents Kennedy and Nixon. In recent years Congress has seen the necessity of exercising a restraining influence on the President. In the last 30 years the USA has moved from a totally controlling power to one facing difficulties;

it is therefore necessary to understand how decisions are made. Investigates the intelligence machine which monitors American interests around the world. Based on secondary works; 31 notes.   A. Alcock

3287. Hall, F. Whitney. UNDERSTANDING THE JOINT CHIEFS OF STAFF. *Armed Forces and Soc. 1979 5(2): 321-328.* An essay reviewing Richard K. Betts's *Soldiers, Statesmen, and Cold War Crises* (Cambridge, Mass.: Harvard U. Pr., 1977), Paul R. Ignatius's *Department Headquarters Study: A Report to the Secretary of Defense* (Washington, D.C.: 1978), and Richard C. Steadman's *The National Military Command Structure: Report of a Study Requested by the President and Conducted in the Department of Defense* (Washington, D.C.: 1978). The Betts volume provides insights into the functioning of the Joint Chiefs of Staff since the environment for its activities has now changed in the National Security Council, the Department of Defense, and the increasing influence of Congress on defense policy. This provides a good background for understanding the implications of the other two volumes, which are essentially reorganization studies.   R. V. Ritter

3288. Halpert, Leon. LEGISLATIVE OVERSIGHT AND THE PARTISAN COMPOSITION OF GOVERNMENT. *Presidential Studies Q. 1981 11(4): 479-491.* Examines the oversight role of the Congress when dealing with the Executive Branch. Oversight was set up in pursuance of a myriad set of goals, all fitting into the constitutional checks and balance scheme. This rigorous review is a healthy part of the system. 2 tables, 12 notes, biblio.   D. H. Cline

3289. Hamilton, Charles V. AMERICA IN SEARCH OF ITSELF: A REVIEW ESSAY. *Pol. Sci. Q. 1982 97(3): 487-493.* Reviews Theodore H. White's *America in Search of Itself: The Making of the Presidents, 1956-1980* (1982), which places special emphasis on the 1980 election and sees the era as a time of national self-questioning regarding the nature of federal power.   J. Powell

3290. Hamilton, Lee H. CONGRESS AND FOREIGN POLICY. *Presidential Studies Q. 1982 12(2): 133-137.* The president and Congress are engaged in a continual struggle to control foreign policy. In the wake of Watergate and the Vietnam War, Congress has become a partner with the president in these decisions. While Congress has occasionally acted too aggressively in curbing presidential authority, the president must recognize the new reality of the situation and engage in genuine dialogue and consultation with Congress.   D. H. Cline

3291. Hamilton, Lee H. and Van Dusen, Michael H. MAKING THE SEPARATION OF POWERS WORK. *Foreign Affairs 1978 57(1): 17-39.* Over the past decade, Congress has assumed a greatly expanded role in the formulation of foreign policy. Though Congress contains diverse, highly politicized elements, its continued participation is inevitable (and essential). Members of both the executive and legislative branches " . . . must be willing to listen, as well as advocate, and show a sensitive understanding of their respective constitutional roles."
                                               M. R. Yerburgh

3292. Handberg, Robert and Bledsoe, Robert. SHIFTING PATTERNS IN THE AMERICAN MILITARY BUDGET PROCESS: AN OVERVIEW. *J. of Strategic Studies [Great Britain] 1979 2(3): 348-361.* In the 1950's and the 1960's, Congress basically ratified executive budgetary decisions. The Vietnam War changed Congress's attitude from support to critical or skeptical acceptance. The result has been more frequent attempts to reduce defense spending; military services, like other government agencies, are being forced to justify their funding levels to Congress, which determines US military capability. Table, 4 fig., 15 notes.
                                               A. M. Osur

3293. Harrison, Stanley L. PRESIDENT AND CONGRESS: THE WAR POWERS WRANGLE. *Military R. 1974 54(7): 40-49.* Discusses implications of the 1973 resolution in Congress to curb the war-making powers of the presidency.

3294. Hart, John. PRESIDENTIAL POWER REVISITED. *Pol. Studies [Great Britain] 1977 25(1): 48-61.* Richard Neustadt's *Presidential Power* (New York, 1960) represented a major advance in the study of the American presidency with its focus on the informal aspects of power. However, certain facets of the work require modification in the

light of recent history; "the methodology restricts the area of enquiry and . . . the criterion for comparing and judging Presidents, although a step towards objectivity, is still unsatisfactory." 59 notes.
                                               R. Howell

3295. Havard, William C. THE PRESIDENCY: THE OFFICE, THE MAN, AND THE CONSTITUENCIES. *Virginia Q. R. 1974 50(4): 497-514.* Analyzes the post-Watergate demands for changes in the Constitution by arguing that the real problem is political rather than structural. Discusses four major presidential constituencies: the body politic, party organization, Congress and the administrative bureaucracy. Describes the constituency relations of each president from Franklin D. Roosevelt through Nixon. Fears paralysis of the presidency and argues that the present structure is viable if constituency relations do "not break down completely."   O. H. Zabel

3296. Havens, Murray Clark and McNeil, Dixie Mercer. PRESIDENTS, IMPEACHMENT, AND POLITICAL ACCOUNTABILITY. *Presidential Studies Q. 1978 8(1): 5-18.* The Watergate experience has highlighted the inadequacy of present restraints on the chief executive. The quasi-legal impeachment procedure, the election process, and the party system have not prevented presidential incompetence or malfeasance. Impeachment is viewed as a time consuming, paralyzing process to determine the personal guilt or innocence of an office holder. The feasibility of alternative methods of removal is discussed. Impeachment based on the concept of the collective executive is the only realistic solution. Congress must abandon its parochial concerns and assume a watchdog function by refusing to pass legislation, appropriate funds, or confirm nominations, by casting censure votes, and finally by impeaching the president for poor performance by any member of the administration. 32 notes.   S. C. Strom

3297. Haynes, Richard F. THE DEFENSE UNIFICATION BATTLE, 1947-50: THE ARMY. *Prologue 1975 7(1): 27-31.* During the unification of defense (1947-50) the War Department lost its aviation component but tried to maintain budgetary parity with the other services. This resulted in the Army becoming larger in size and smaller in prestige as an administrative subdivision of the Defense Department. Based on primary and secondary sources; illus., 30 notes.
                                               R. W. Tissing, Jr.

3298. Hazlewood, Leo; Hayes, John J.; and Brownell, James R., Jr. PLANNING FOR PROBLEMS IN CRISIS MANAGEMENT: AN ANALYSIS OF POST-1945 BEHAVIOR IN THE U.S. DEPARTMENT OF DEFENSE. *Int. Studies Q. 1977 21(1): 75-106.* Examines problems encountered by the US Defense Department in managing domestic and international crises during 1946-75. A statistical study of all incidents involving the use of military force identifies patterns in the crisis environment and isolates the types of decisions required. Failures of intelligence have been caused by faulty analysis rather than lack of information, and training based on studies of crisis behavior can improve the quality and speed of decisionmaking and response execution. Primary and secondary sources; 9 tables, fig., 26 notes.   E. S. Palais

3299. Heclo, Hugh. OMB AND THE PRESIDENCY—THE PROBLEM OF "NEUTRAL COMPETENCE." *Public Interest 1975 (38): 80-98.* Discusses the nonpartisan advisory role of the Office of Management and Budget since 1970.   S

3300. Heclo, Hugh. POLITICAL EXECUTIVES AND THE WASHINGTON BUREAUCRACY. *Pol. Sci. Q. 1977 92(3): 395-424.* Examines strategies used by political executives who arrive with each new administration to "take control of the bureaucracy" in Washington. Suggests a statecraft of "conditional cooperation" rather than the "nice guy" or "tough guy" approach. Exchanging favors is far less effective than giving bureaucrats a stake in the future performance of the administration, for grasping rather than gratitude drives executive politics. Prudence for any President interested in controlling the bureaucracy consists in using the inevitable executive tensions constructively rather than in trying to eliminate them. Wholesale reorganization is impossible without a genuine crisis. Based on interviews with 200 political and career executives, adapted from the author's *A Government of Strangers: Executive Politics in Washington* (Washington, D.C.: The Brookings Institution, 1977); 10 notes.   W. R. Hively

3301. Helmer, John and Maisel, Louis. ANALYTICAL PROBLEMS IN THE STUDY OF PRESIDENTIAL ADVICE: THE DOMESTIC COUNCIL IN FLUX. *Presidential Studies Q. 1978 8(1): 45-67.* Discusses the relationship between organizational patterns and the outcome of policy processes, in the context of an expanding Executive Office of the President (EOP). Proposes several hypotheses on staff growth, delegation of authority, and policy formulation. Tests these theories by comparing policy processes of recent presidents and their use of EOP staff units. The changing role of the Domestic Council under Richard M. Nixon and Gerald R. Ford is examined through historical documents, interviews, quantitative analysis of contact networks, allocation of staff time, internal working relationships, and relative budget allocations. 6 tables, chart, 5 notes, biblio. S. C. Strom

3302. Hendel, Samuel. SEPARATION OF POWERS REVISITED IN LIGHT OF "WATERGATE." *Western Pol. Q. 1974 27(4): 575-588.* Presents an overview of the historical meaning (1688-1974) of separation of powers and the effect of the Watergate Scandal on this doctrine. S

3303. Hershey, Marjorie Randon and Hill, David B. THE PRESIDENT AND POLITICAL SOCIALIZATION: APPLYING SOCIAL LEARNING THEORY TO TWO LONG-STANDING HYPOTHESES. *Youth and Soc. 1977 9(2): 125-150.* Among young children, feelings of political power and an interest in government correlate with feelings of the power of the President and his responsiveness. Social learning theory appears to provide the best explanation for these findings. Based on a survey of Florida public schools in 1973-74 and on other primary and secondary sources; fig., 5 tables, 12 notes, biblio. J. H. Sweetland

3304. Herzik, Eric B. and Dodson, Mary L. THE PRESIDENT AND PUBLIC EXPECTATIONS: A RESEARCH NOTE. *Presidential Studies Q. 1982 12(2): 168-173.* In *The Presidential Character* (1977) James Barber presents a concept of "climate of expectations" to explain public opinion regarding the role and responsibilities of the presidency. The concept, however, is relatively undefined and its implications undocumented. 3 tables, 24 notes. D. H. Cline

3305. Heubel, E. J. EL ESTUDIO DE LA PRESIDENCIA NORTEAMERICANA: DEL MITO A LA REALIDAD [Study of the North American presidency: from myth to reality]. *Rev. de Estudios Pol. [Spain] 1980 (15): 161-174.* Analyzes recent literature on the nature of tensions and constrictions within the American presidency. Finds three major points of focus: the assessment that the president does not have the power or resources necessary to carry out the increasingly large responsibilities of his charge, emphasis on the extremely personal nature of the office which enhances the character and personality attributes of the man, and the need to augment presidential powers in order to solve the complex and difficult problems of contemporary society. 29 notes. N. A. Rosenblatt

3306. Hill, Kim Quaile and Plumlee, John Patrick. PRESIDENTIAL SUCCESS IN BUDGETARY POLICYMAKING: A LONGITUDINAL ANALYSIS. *Presidential Studies Q. 1982 12(2): 174-185.* President Ford noted that "the budget reflects the President's sense of priorities." Since Truman, a president's success at getting his budget enacted is largely dependent upon his poll popularity and the size and support of his partisan followers in Congress. Reagan has tried to drastically alter the existing budget patterns and has been successful only where these two factors have been strong. Table, 2 graphs, 12 notes, biblio. D. H. Cline

3307. Hirshon, Arnold. RECENT DEVELOPMENTS IN THE ACCESSIBILITY OF PRESIDENTIAL PAPERS AND OTHER PRESIDENTIAL HISTORICAL MATERIALS. *Government Publ. Rev. 1979 6(2): 343-357.* Access to presidential papers and related historical documents has been advanced by the Freedom of Information Act (and its amendments), Supreme Court rulings on Watergate materials, and the Presidential Records Act of 1978.

3308. Hoeksema, Renze L. THE PRESIDENT'S ROLE IN INSURING EFFICIENT, ECONOMICAL, AND RESPONSIBLE INTELLIGENCE SERVICES. *Presidential Studies Q. 1978 8(2): 187-199.* Efficiency, economy, and responsibility are the requirements of an effective intelligence service. The current disrepute of intelligence work is the result of presidential misuse of intelligence agencies. Reforms are needed to attain a professional, effective intelligence service. Despite its modest budget and relative effectiveness, the Central Intelligence Agency (CIA) has suffered more from recent cost-cutting than the less analytical Defense Department intelligence units. A tough, apolitical CIA director with intellectual honesty and access to the President must be appointed. In Congress, a joint committee for intelligence is needed, and release of nonsensitive documents should be encouraged. More emphasis on human analysis with restrained use of covert activity would improve the quality of the information provided to the President. 30 notes, biblio. S. C. Strom

3309. Hoekstra, Douglas J. THE "TEXTBOOK PRESIDENCY" REVISITED. *Presidential Studies Q. 1982 12(2): 159-167.* Thomas Cronin's "Textbook Presidency" in *Perspectives on the Presidency* (1970), edited by Stanley Bach and George T. Sulzner, argued that Americans viewed the presidency as all-powerful and imperial. Using the same techniques, it is seen that the emphasis has shifted to the limitations and constraints on the presidency. While accurate, the function of the presidency in the education of the citizenry concerning the political system must not be overlooked. 63 notes. D. H. Cline

3310. Hoffman, Kenneth E. STABILIZING THE PRESIDENCY. *Presidential Studies Q. 1979 9(2): 172-179.* Discusses the means which allow the president to gain the knowledge and experience required to serve the domestic and foreign policy needs of the country, including the Presidential Council, the vice-president, the president-elect, and the president, 1979.

3311. Hogan, Jerry H. TRANSLATING NATIONAL OBJECTIVES INTO SPECIFIC PROGRAMS—THE PPBS. *Military Rev. 1975 55(1): 35-39.* Examines the Planning, Programming and Budgeting System of the Department of Defense, showing how it provides the structure in which broad national policy objectives are translated into specific defense programs. Fig. J. K. Ohl

3312. Hopkins, Bruce R. CONGRESS CURTAILS PRESIDENTIAL IMPOUNDMENTS. *Am. Bar Assoc. J. 1974 60(9): 1053-1057.* "The Impoundment Control Act of 1974, signed into law by President Nixon on 12 July 1974 represents the response of Congress to the wave of executive department impoundments during recent years. Now the executive must follow specified steps if impoundment is desired, and the Congress is given opportunities of exercising final control over spending and impoundment." J

3313. Hopkins, Raymond F. FOOD POLICY MAKING. *Pro. of the Acad. of Pol. Sci. 1982 34(3): 12-24.* Where interagency decisionmaking proves to be effective and authoritative, representation of commericial interest by sympathetic bureaucrats or others should be opened to congressional and public scrutiny. The executive branch makes food policy. For this policy to be soundly based and farsighted, it needs continual democratization as well as the infusion of interagency collaboration on long-term planning. Based on primary and secondary sources; 7 notes. T. P. Richardson

3314. Hopkins, Raymond F. THE INTERNATIONAL ROLE OF "DOMESTIC" BUREAUCRACY. *Int. Organization 1976 30(3): 405-432.* Many agencies of the United States Government with nominally "domestic" mandates play important roles in international affairs, and collaborate extensively with other governments and international organizations in the performance of their tasks. In some areas, these agencies rather than intergovernmental organizations play key management roles. Data gathered from a variety of sources indicate the extensiveness of this involvement, and suggest that it continues to expand, although not in linear fashion. Certain trends in governmental reorganization, such as those in the Agriculture Department, suggest similar patterns to those observed in business firms as they become more heavily involved abroad. More attention needs to be paid to international networks involving "domestic" governmental bureaucracies and governmental agencies traditionally oriented toward international affairs. From a conceptual point of view, we should think of "international organization" as including not only formally intergovernmental organizations, but all officials who participate significantly in these networks. J

3315. Hoxie, R. Gordon. THE NATIONAL SECURITY COUN-
CIL. *Presidential Studies Q. 1982 12(1): 108-113.* A general overview
of the evolution of the National Security Council from its origins. 3 notes,
biblio.   D. H. Cline

3316. Hoxie, R. Gordon. THE NOT SO IMPERIAL PRESI-
DENCY: A MODEST PROPOSAL. *Presidential Studies Q. 1980
10(2): 194-210.* The "imperial" presidency is not a new notion, but the
congressional curbs on presidential power in the 1970's represent tremendous dangers in terms of national security policy. In the
past, there has been a swinging pendulum in congressional vis-à-vis presidential power relations, but this change seems more permanent today.
Much of the change has been good, but Congress cannot remain the
leader in terms of foreign policy. We must reach a consensus, where the
president has his hand on the tiller but is willing to reach out and consult
with Congress. 89 notes.   D. H. Cline

3317. Hoxie, R. Gordon. STAFFING THE FORD AND CARTER
PRESIDENCIES. *Presidential Studies Q. 1980 10(3): 378-401.* Examines the roles and functions of the White House presidential staffs of both
Gerald R. Ford and Jimmy Carter. Ford restored much respect and
openness to the presidency, and was well-prepared by his service in Congress. His staff was effective and worked well together. It took Carter
more than three years to realize how an effective staff works, and to reach
out beyond his loyal Georgians to include experienced people in his staff.
86 notes.   D. H. Cline

3318. Hunter, Robert W. BLUE SUITERS IN THE WHITE
HOUSE. *Air Force Mag. 1973 56(2): 36-39.* The White House Fellows
Programs brings outstanding young American professionals, including
Air Force men, to serve as temporary members of the White House staff,
1964-73.

3319. Hurst, James Willard. WATERGATE: SOME BASIC IS-
SUES. *Center Mag. 1974 7(1): 11-25.* Views the work of the Senate's
"Watergate Committee" against the background of Congressional investi-
gative functions and of separation-of-powers issues.   S

3320. Hutchins, Robert M. and Wheeler, Harvey. THE CONSTITU-
TION UNDER STRAIN. *Center Mag. 1974 7(2): 43-52.* Mentions
Congress and executive power since the 1960's.   S

3321. Hyman, Sidney. THE GOVERNANCE OF THE MILITARY.
Ann. of the Am. Acad. of Pol. and Social Sci. 1973 (406): 38-47. "First,
this paper traces the root sources of the crisis of legitimacy now gripping
both the civil and military components in the governance of the American
military establishment. Then it shows how our national reactions to revolutionary changes in post-World War II military technology and in world
politics shattered the long-standing 1789 constitutional formula for a controlled military impulse. Next it focuses on certain aspects of the legitimacy crisis. Constitutional assumptions underlying amateur-expert
relations in military governance have been unhinged by the tendency of
the civil order to subordinate its own judgment of an 'emergency need'
to the judgment of the professional military experts. Further, old constitutional fiscal controls over the military establishment have been shattered
by the Congress, and Congress has allowed its own constitutional power
to 'declare war' to be swallowed up by the grants to the president or his
assumption of a unilateral discretionary power to 'make war.' Finally, it
examines some remedies for the crisis of legitimacy, focusing not only on
congressional reform, but on the role of the electorate and the indispens-
able need for a president to place himself under a self-denying ordinance."
                                                                     J

3322. Jacobs, James B. THE ROLE OF MILITARY FORCES IN
PUBLIC SECTOR LABOR RELATIONS. *Industrial and Labor Relations Rev. 1982 35(2): 163-180.* Examines the use of military forces as
replacements in public sector strikes, a practice employed in over 40 cases
since President Nixon established the modern precedent by deploying
troops in the 1970 postal strike. Despite the dubious legality of Nixon's
action, legal constraints on the president and particularly on the governors in this context are very weak. Political and philosophical qualms
about breaking strikes with military replacements may have more vitality
as constraints, but they are subject to erosion if the appropriate role of
military forces in public sector labor relations does not become a subject

of public debate. The use of troops as strike replacements is primarily a
political rather than legal problem.   J/S

3323. Jacobs, Richard F. THE STATUS OF THE NIXON PRESI-
DENTIAL HISTORICAL MATERIALS. *Am. Archivist 1975 38(3):
337.* Records of the Nixon presidency are in custody of the government
under court order which forbids their processing, disposal, or disclosure
except for court actions and on matters of current government business.
The constitutionality of the Presidential Recordings and Materials Preservation Act (1974) is presently being tested in the Federal District Court.
Until court actions are completed, the materials will remain in closed
custody.   J. A. Benson

3324. Jeffreys-Jones, Rhodri. THE HISTORIOGRAPHY OF THE
CIA. *Hist. J. [Great Britain] 1980 23(2): 489-496.* Reviews six new
works, suggesting an embryonic historiography of the Central Intelligence Agency, moving away from recriminatory questions to more
thoughtful analyses.   A. R. Gross

3325. Johannes, John R. EXECUTIVE REPORTS TO CONGRESS.
J. of Communication 1976 26(3): 53-61. Discusses bureaucratic problems
for legislators in presidential and Executive Branch reports to the Congress in intergovernmental communications, 1945-73.

3326. Johannes, John R. THE PRESIDENT PROPOSES AND THE
CONGRESS DISPOSES—BUT NOT ALWAYS: LEGISLATIVE INI-
TIATIVE ON CAPITOL HILL. *R. of Pol. 1974 36(3): 356-370.*

3327. Johnson, Loch K. THE C.I.A.: CONTROLLING THE
QUIET OPTION. *Foreign Policy 1980 (39): 143-153.* Recent international events have encouraged the demand that the American intelligence
community be "unleashed." This sentiment threatens to destroy labori-
ously constructed safeguards whose disappearance would again permit
the infrequent but real abuses of intelligence functions that haunted the
United States before the post-Watergate reforms. If anything, such reins
as the Hughes-Ryan Act (US, 1974) need to be strengthened. The Intelligence Oversight Act (US, 1980) has much to commend itself, but still
leaves too many loopholes.   T. L. Powers

3328. Johnson, Loch K. and McCormick, James M. FOREIGN POL-
ICY BY EXECUTIVE FIAT. *Foreign Policy 1977 (28): 117-138.* Analyzes congressional legislation aimed at institutional sharing of power in
foreign affairs, especially with respect to treaties and executive agreements. Legislation has been drafted in three areas to enhance congressional involvement: reporting all executive agreements to congress,
permitting a veto of unwarranted executive agreements, and requirement
of a positive majority in military agreements or a special procedures for
significant international agreements. Covers 1946-77.
                                                              H. R. Mahood

3329. Johnson, Loch K. and McCormick, James M. THE MAKING
OF INTERNATIONAL AGREEMENTS: A REAPPRAISAL OF
CONGRESSIONAL INVOLVEMENT. *J. of Pol. 1978 40(2): 468-478.*
Analysis of US foreign policy during 1946-72 indicates the predominance
of statutory agreements. Executive agreements are used rarely and treaties are used least of all. From the Truman through the Nixon administration, the use of treaties has declined. Executive agreements were used
most often by Truman and least often by Kennedy. They have been used
most frequently for military and diplomatic policy. Treaties have been
used most frequently for diplomatic and transportation/communication
policy, less often for economic policy, and least often for military and
cultural/technical policy. Congress has played a greater *procedural,* if not
substantive, role than conventional wisdom would suggest. Primary and
secondary sources; 2 tables, 16 notes.   A. W. Novitsky

3330. Jones, David C. WHY THE JOINT CHIEFS OF STAFF
MUST CHANGE. *Presidential Studies Q. 1982 12(2): 138-149.* Discusses procedures, organizational structure, achievements, and failures of
the Joint Chiefs of Staff since establishment of the office in 1942.
                                                               D. H. Cline

3331. Jones, H. G. PRESIDENTIAL LIBRARIES: IS THERE A
CASE FOR A NATIONAL PRESIDENTIAL LIBRARY? *Am. Ar-
chivist 1975 38(3): 325-328.* Presidential papers are now considered pri-

vate property, but the theory that past presidents may decide whether to disclose information is not justified by any constitutional principle. The private ownership tradition should be terminated by a precedent-setting presidential executive order acknowledging public ownership. Edited version of commentary on papers given at the 1971 meeting of the American Historical Association.   J. A. Benson

3332. Joslyn, Richard A. and Galderisi, Peter F. THE IMPACT OF ADOLESCENT PERCEPTIONS OF THE PRESIDENT: A TEST OF THE "SPILLOVER" HYPOTHESIS. *Youth and Soc. 1977 9(2): 151-170.* During the last 15 years, teenagers' attitudes toward the President have declined on measures such as trust and his benevolence. Perceptions of presidential power are inconsistent with trust in government in general. Formation of political attitudes among youth thus appears more complex than merely a result of attitudes toward the President. Based on an eight-city survey of youths in the early 1960's, another of three upstate New York cities in 1973 and 1976, and other primary and secondary sources; 6 tables, 6 notes, biblio.   J. H. Sweetland

3333. Joyner, Conrad. A LIBERAL DILEMMA: PRESIDENTIAL POWER AND SEPARATION OF POWERS. *Western Pol. Q. 1974 27(4): 593-596.* Agrees with those who argue for a more stringent system of checks and balances, but argues that if the president is to be an effective leader he must have power.   S

3334. Kahn, Gilbert N. IN PERPETUAL TENSION: EXECUTIVE-LEGISLATIVE RELATIONS AND THE CASE OF THE LEGISLATIVE VETO. *Presidential Studies Q. 1981 11(2): 271-279.* The framers of the American Constitution envisioned Congress and the executive as existing in a competitive, contentious relationship. Recently, the legislative veto has been used increasingly and in wider areas, and is becoming a point of conflict. As this controversy is resolved, the presidency will again receive strong support in the balance between the institutions. Based on a paper presented to the 1979 Summer Seminar for College Teachers. Primary sources; 3 charts, 26 notes.

A. Drysdale

3335. Kassebaum, Nancy Landon. THE ESSENCE OF LEADERSHIP. *Presidential Studies Q. 1979 9(3): 239-242.* The President should exhibit moral leadership and present an example of broad values and unity of purpose since the demoralization of the American people in the 1960's and 1970's due to the Vietnam War, the economy, unemployment, and lack of natural resources.

3336. Kellerman, Barbara. THE POLITICAL FUNCTIONS OF THE PRESIDENTIAL FAMILY. *Presidential Studies Q. 1978 8(3): 303-318.* With the advent of television, the growing visibility of the presidency, the increasing number of primaries, and the rise of the women's movement, the President's family has assumed a political function during the last 18 years. Six roles are defined: Decorations, Extensions, Humanizers, Helpmates, Moral Supporters, and Alter Egos. Examines the political functions of six family members from the administrations of John F. Kennedy to Jimmy Carter and predicts the continuing political impact of presidential relatives. Fig., 63 notes.   S. C. Strom

3337. Kernell, Samuel. EXPLAINING PRESIDENTIAL POPULARITY. *Am. Pol. Sci. Rev. 1978 72(2): 506-522.* Within the last ten years a new conventional wisdom has surfaced in political science which tells us that presidents inexorably become less popular over time. Not much else matters. Neither the economy, nor the Vietnam War, not even Watergate seems to have had much independent effect on presidential popularity once time is taken into account. Before embracing these conclusions we need to reconsider the method that produced them. I argue that previous research too willingly accepted time as an explanatory variable, enshrouding it with theoretical meaning. To preserve its explanatory power alternative, substantive variables were shortchanged in their operational definitions and measurement. In this article I reverse the emphasis. Here, time is rejected as an explanatory variable and is employed only as a diagnostic indicator of the adequacy of the equations. A variety of alternative representations of real-world forces such as the economy and war are tested and some considerably improve the time-series correlation between the environment and presidential popularity. With these substantive variables I propose a simpler, if less glamorous, theory of presidential popularity consisting of two hypotheses: first, popu-

larity is related to real events and conditions, and second, that it responds slowly to environmental change. Popularity is then both experiential and incremental. The findings for Presidents Truman through Nixon support this common-sense view. The Korean War (measured by U.S. casualties), the Vietnam War (measured by the number of bombing missions over North Vietnam and the U.S. war dead), the economy (especially six-month changes in consumer prices), Watergate, international "rally" events, and early term surges of approval all contribute independently to short-term fluctuations in presidential popularity. Moreover, as predicted, popularity appears to be autoregressive even when represented by an instrumental variables surrogate measure to minimize serial correlation. When the equations are specified in this way, time proves to be unnecessary in order to explain trends in presidential popularity.   J

3338. Kessel, John H. THE PARAMETERS OF PRESIDENTIAL POLITICS. *Social Sci. Q. 1974 55(1): 8-24.* "Presents a computer content analysis of the 26 State of the Union messages delivered between 1946 and 1969. . . . Notes that the messages concern six distinctive policy areas: international involvement, social benefits, economic management, civil rights, natural resources, and agriculture (with the first three areas consuming most of the presidents' time and attention). Temporal variations in presidential involvement and some implications of the findings are also discussed."   J

3339. Kessler, Frank. PRESIDENTIAL-CONGRESSIONAL BATTLES: TOWARD A TRUCE ON THE FOREIGN POLICY FRONT. *Presidential Studies Q. 1978 8(2): 115-127.* Examines recent White House-Capitol Hill imbroglios over foreign policy use of executive agreements, executive privilege, and war powers. By blocking access to information, the executive branch has successfully discouraged Congressional participation and oversight of foreign policy. Reform proposals include: 1) internal legislative refinements, 2) adaptive approaches to interbranch relations, 3) constitutional innovation, and 4) improvement of nonexecutive information sources to Congress. Foreign affairs conflicts are symptomatic of a deeper imbalance of information which Congress has done little to correct. Congress cannot rely on executive goodwill alone in carrying out its oversight function, but must develop effective information-gathering and analytical capabilities. 98 notes.

S. C. Strom

3340. Kinder, Donald R. PRESIDENTS, PROSPERITY, AND PUBLIC OPINION. *Public Opinion Q. 1981 45(1): 1-21.* A president skillful enough, or fortunate enough, to preside over a healthy economy is rewarded with public support. A president's popularity might decline when economic times are bad because citizens in effect blame him for their personal hardships—the pocketbook citizen hypothesis—or because they see the president as failing to cope adequately with national economic problems, quite apart from the economic dislocations of private life—the sociotropic citizen hypothesis. Across a variety of tests, results from national surveys covering the Nixon, Ford, and Carter presidencies consistently supported the sociotropic hypothesis.   J/S

3341. Klieman, Aaron S. PREPARING FOR THE HOUR OF NEED: THE NATIONAL EMERGENCIES ACT. *Presidential Studies Q. 1979 9(1): 47-64.* Examines provisions of the War Powers Act (US, 1973), the findings of the Senate Special Committee on the Termination of the National Emergency, which led eventually to passage of the National Emergencies Act (US, 1976), and the effects of this latter act on presidential power and safeguarding democracy.

3342. Kochetkov, G. B. and Savelev, V. A. INFORMATSIONNYE PROBLEMY ZAKONODATEL'NYKH ORGANOV SSHA [Information problems of legislative bodies in the United States]. *Sovetskoe Gosudarstvo i Pravo [USSR] 1974 (11): 117-121.* Reviews the information crisis in American federal and state legislative bodies and discusses the means taken to overcome it, including increased use of computers and other data-processing equipment, appointment of special committees and of additional staff for the existing standing committees, and letting of private contracts for research and data gathering, etc. Finds an increasing tendency to circumvent the constitutional limitations on the powers of the executive by appointing persons responsible directly to the President who are not approved or controlled by the legislature. Based on Congressional documents and special publications on data processing; 9 notes.

S. P. Dunn

3343. Koenig, Louis W. THE PRESIDENCY TODAY. *Current Hist. 1974 66(394): 249-253, 272.* Since World War II American presidents have extended the power of their office, achieving virtual autonomy in foreign affairs. One of six articles in this issue on "The American Presidency."   S

3344. Kotler, Neil G. THE POLITICS OF THE BUDGETARY PROCESS. *Society 1977 14(3): 67-72.* Discusses the implications of the Budget and Impoundment Control Act (1974) and the Tax Reform Act (1976) for congressional budget reform, 1974-76.

3345. Krasner, Michael. WHY GREAT PRESIDENTS WILL BECOME MORE RARE. *Presidential Studies Q. 1979 9(4): 367-375.* The presidential nominating process introduced in 1960 has created problems. Since a presidential candidate requires the support of his party's rank and file rather than its leaders, practical experience in political give and take now means less in political campaigns than does charisma or media appeal. Skills required of a successful campaigner are not necessarily those of political leadership. The present system bodes ill for the consensus, compromise, and intergovernmental cooperation without which presidents such as Jimmy Carter can hardly translate legislative proposals into national policy. Based on newspapers and secondary sources; 28 notes.   S

3346. Kress, Paul F. OF ACTION AND VIRTUE: NOTES ON THE PRESIDENCY, WATERGATE AND LIBERAL SOCIETY. *Polity 1978 10(4): 510-523.* The Watergate syndrome and the underlying social pathology have been the subject of numerous scholarly analyses; however, the argument is far from being settled. In a recent issue of *Polity* (Summer 1977) it was argued that a value-neutral political science was responsible for the intellectual climate banishing moral concerns from the domain of political action. Paul Kress, too, sees the fundamental cause in the lack of moral purpose but attributes the political malpractice to theoretical and structural flaws inherent in modern liberalism in general and American constitutionalism in particular. He concludes with a speculation concerning the future prospects of liberal society and raises questions concerning the effect of its inadequacies on the problem of distributive justice in a no-growth economy.   J

3347. Lammers, William W. PRESIDENTIAL PRESS-CONFERENCE SCHEDULES: WHO HIDES, AND WHEN? *Pol. Sci. Q. 1981 96(2): 261-278.* Examines press conferences held by American presidents during 1929-79. Sharply increased international involvement, televised conferences, and presidential personality differences have all influenced the shift toward less frequent and less regular press conferences during 1950-79. The importance of international involvement as an underlying force has been underscored by both the declining frequency and regularity of conferences between the end of World War II and both the arrival of televised conferences in 1955 and the preponderence of foreign policy crises as situations contributing to conference avoidance. Personality differences are a third factor, but none of the presidents since Eisenhower has been able consistently to return to the pre-1950's level of frequency and regularity in conference scheduling. Personality differences have had their impact, but within an underlying set of forces tending to move presidents away from regular and frequent press conferences. Based on press conference records; 19 notes.   J. Powell

3348. Larson, Arthur. SOME MYTHS ABOUT THE EXECUTIVE BRANCH. *Center Mag. 1974 7(5): 53-60.* The role of the presidency in relation to the Congress.   S

3349. Larson, David L. EXECUTIVE AGREEMENTS. *Social Sci. 1981 56(2): 67-81.* Reviews the history of executive agreements in the United States and moves made by Congress to get more control over them. Executive agreements permit speed, avoid embarrassing disclosures, and enable the executive branch to dodge Senate ratification, which would be required of a treaty. The Korean War, which was never a declared war, provided the beginnings of opposition to the process, and the undeclared Vietnam War added to the momentum. Few restrictions, however, have been placed on executive agreement. 2 fig., 39 notes, biblio.   V. L. Human

3350. Lasch, Christopher. PARANOID PRESIDENCY. *Center Mag. 1974 7(2): 23-31.* Expansion of the executive branch since the 1930's has increasingly isolated the president from reality.   S

3351. Lee, Frederick Paul. "THE TWO PRESIDENCIES" REVISITED. *Presidential Studies Q. 1980 10(4): 620-628.* Tests Aaron Wildavsky's 1966 "Two Presidencies" thesis, which states that the president is perceived as being stronger and more powerful in foreign than domestic affairs. Testing the 1976 national party conventions, this thesis still seems valid. 3 tables, 35 notes.   D. H. Cline

3352. Leech, Noyes. REPORT ON COMMITTEE IV. *Ann. of the Am. Acad. of Pol. and Social Sci. 1976 426: 204-212.* Professor [Covey T.] Oliver [in this issue of *AAAPSS*] observed that the current expression of Congress' will to participate in foreign policy and the unrelieved separation of powers impose serious impediments on the ability of the Executive branch to enter into reliable, immediate foreign commitments. The committee appeared to recognize that the crisis in the exercise of our foreign relations power existed and was in some measure created by congressional will to participate and complicated by our separation of powers; but it did not agree that the U.S. was unduly hampered in its power to carry on foreign relations effectively. The committee dealt with the relationship between the Executive and Congress as one of continuing political balance that could be accommodated within our present Constitution. It considered how certain problems of congressional-Executive branch organization related to international agreements might be approached. In looking to the future, the committee projected that the U.S. would want to join international organizations of an increasingly sophisticated type. The view was expressed that constitutional problems arising from joining such organizations, if the matter were approached without amendments, could be quite complex. [A report on Committee IV of the AAPSS Bicentennial Constitutional Conference, 1976].   J

3353. Lees, John D. REORGANIZATION AND REFORM IN CONGRESS—LEGISLATIVE RESPONSES TO POLITICAL AND SOCIAL CHANGE. *Government and Opposition [Great Britain] 1973 8(2): 195-216.* Discusses Congress' attempts to reform executive branch and federal administration and bureaucracy in the 1960's and 70's.

3354. Leloup, Lance T. and Shull, Steven A. CONGRESS VERSUS THE EXECUTIVE: THE "TWO PRESIDENCIES" RECONSIDERED. *Social Sci. Q. 1979 59(4): 704-719.* Analyzes the contention that the United States has two presidencies: Congress for matters of domestic concern, and the President for foreign affairs. Suggestions that this system is no longer operable have led to this study. Analysis of presidential success with Congress in regard to foreign and domestic issues in recent years does indeed reveal that the President now enjoys less success than previously with issues of a foreign nature. Despite this, the correlation still exists; though less successful than formerly, presidents still fare better on foreign issues, and their popularity is also more dependent on success in foreign affairs. 2 fig., 3 tables, ref.   V. L. Human

3355. Lenchner, Paul. CONGRESSIONAL PARTY UNITY AND EXECUTIVE-LEGISLATIVE RELATIONS. *Social Sci. Q. 1976 57(3): 589-596.* Uses factor analysis to examine senate voting patterns in five years. Concludes that control of the presidency promotes legislative party unity and that majority status in Congress may make an additional contribution to party unity.   J

3356. Light, Paul C. PASSING NONINCREMENTAL POLICY: PRESIDENTIAL INFLUENCE IN CONGRESS, KENNEDY TO CARTER. *Congress & the Presidency 1981-82 9(1): 61-82.* Defines and discusses nonincremental policy, which involves new projects and large-scale spending by the federal government, and chronicles the difficulty experienced by Kennedy, Johnson, Nixon, Ford, and Carter in gaining congressional approval for these programs.

3357. Lugato, Giuseppe. LA PRESIDENZA AMERICANA DI FRONTE AL WATERGATE [The American presidency after Watergate]. *Civitas [Italy] 1974 25(10): 31-48.* "Here in Italy we have analyzed the relation between Watergate scandal and the American institutions mostly from a European point of view: that is the stability of the American democracy, its reactive apparatus, its possibilities of eliminating or at least containing the arbitrary acts. But we have much less considered a fact which is, on the contrary, the chief point in the analyses of American publicists: the Watergate scandal did not emerge from nothing; there is an evolution of the presidential doctrine, of the powers of the executive, all along the 200 years of US history. And this is the subject chosen by the author for this article."   J

3358. Macomber, William B. THE DIPLOMAT AND CONGRESS. *Foreign Service J. 1975 52(10): 14-18, 29.* Discusses the clash between Congress and the State Department over the determination of foreign policy.   S

3359. Maechling, Charles, Jr. FOREIGN POLICY-MAKERS: THE WEAKEST LINK? *Virginia Q. Rev. 1976 52(1): 1-23.* American foreign policymaking is a "collective process" involving hundreds of people. A "top managerial layer" above the bureaucracy is made up of outside appointees, military officers, senior Foreign Service officers and academics. Advocates recognition of the importance of the specialists, analysis of the "sociology of the foreign affairs establishment," changes in the organization and process of policymaking, and reduction of "the vagaries of a high-level spoils system."   O. H. Zabel

3360. Manheim, Jarol B. THE HONEYMOON'S OVER: THE NEWS CONFERENCE AND THE DEVELOPMENT OF PRESIDENTIAL STYLE. *J. of Pol. 1979 41(1): 55-74.* The administration of John F. Kennedy and the advent of live television coverage have transformed presidential press conferences. Study of transcripts of such conferences by Kennedy, Johnson, Nixon, and Ford indicates an in-role socialization process. Each president has used a developmental period to experiment with approaches to agenda control, become decreasingly assertive of both intent and accountability, and revise the manner of dealing with both journalists and the general public. 3 tables, 2 graphs, 25 notes.
                                                                A. W. Novitsky

3361. Marcy, Carl. THE IMPACT OF SECRECY ON CONGRESSIONAL ABILITY TO PARTICIPATE IN FOREIGN POLICY DECISION MAKING. *Towson State J. of Internat. Affairs 1975 10(1): 13-18.* Discusses Congress' lack of access to information regarding US foreign policy in the 1970's, emphasizing the executive branch's policy of secrecy.

3362. Mathias, Charles McC., Jr. NATIONAL EMERGENCIES AND THE CONSTITUTION. *Congressional Studies 1979 7(1): 5-9.* Discusses the perennial power struggle between the legislative and executive branches of government, 1933-78, and notes the importance of President Gerald Ford's decision to sign the National Emergencies Act on 14 September 1976 as a move to restore power to the Congress.

3363. McCarthy, Eugene J. THE EXPANSION OF THE WHITE HOUSE. *Center Mag. 1973 6(2): 53-55.* The trend toward personalization of presidential powers should be reversed to provide balance among the three branches of federal government.   S

3364. Mead, Lawrence M. FOREIGN SERVICE REFORM: A VIEW FROM HEW. *Foreign Service J. 1975 52(10): 21-24.* Compares the State Department and the Department of Health, Education, and Welfare, proposing reforms in the former.   S

3365. Meier, Kenneth John and Van Lohuizen, J. R. BUREAUS, CLIENTS, AND CONGRESS: THE IMPACT OF INTEREST GROUP SUPPORT ON BUDGETING. *Administration and Soc. 1978 9(4): 447-466.* Tests the hypothesis that budgets are influenced by interest groups, by studying 20 bureaus within the Agriculture Department; finds that for the fiscal years 1971-76 clientele support aided the bureaus' positions and helped avoid budget cuts.

3366. Menard, Orville D. THE ULTIMATE ILLUSION. *Midwest Q. 1974 15(2): 198-203.* Too many Americans believe that the president will solve all our social problems.   S

3367. Miller, Linda B. PRESIDENTS AND BUREAUCRATS: THE POLITICS OF FOREIGN POLICY. *Polity 1976 9(2): 228-236.* Review article prompted by eight books concerning the policymaking processes involved in determining foreign policy. Domestic constraints and politics influence the actions of presidents and bureaucrats on defense and security issues. There also is a gap between policy theory and diplomatic practice. Together, the eight volumes "illustrate the strengths and weaknesses of most broad surveys and case-studies of American foreign policy."   E. P. Stickney

3368. Miller, Nancy. PUBLIC ACCESS TO PUBLIC RECORDS: SOME THREATENING REFORMS. *Wilson Lib. Bull. 1981 56(2): 95-99.* Briefly traces the philosophies and traditions leading to the passage of the Freedom of Information Act (US, 1966), focusing on threats to the act under the administration of Ronald Reagan, 1917-81.

3369. Miroff, Bruce. BEYOND WASHINGTON. *Society 1980 17(5): 66-72.* Discusses shortcomings in contemporary presidential studies, and examines the nature of present understanding of the presidency, profoundly influenced by Richard E. Neustadt's *Presidential Power: The Politics of Leadership from FDR to Carter* (New York: John Wiley & Sons, 1979), suggesting new ventures in conceptualization and research.

3370. Mondale, Walter F. RESTORING THE BALANCE. *Center Mag. 1974 7(5): 30-39.* Restoring the balance of power between Congress and the presidency.   S

3371. Morris, Roger. CLIENTISM IN THE FOREIGN SERVICE. *Foreign Service J. 1974 51(2): 24-26, 30-31.* Some US diplomats resist any policy that client regimes might dislike; this "clientism" sometimes has tragic results.   S

3372. Mowery, David C.; Kamlet, Mark S.; and Crecine, John P. PRESIDENTIAL MANAGEMENT OF BUDGETARY AND FISCAL POLICYMAKING. *Pol. Sci. Q. 1980 95(3): 395-425.* The authors examine presidential management of three parallel executive branch budgetary policy processes—domestic budgeting, defense budgeting, and fiscal policy. After surveying the Eisenhower, Kennedy, and Johnson administrations, the authors offer recommendations on how a president can balance the competing demands of fiscal and budgetary policy planning.   J

3373. Moynihan, Daniel P. IMPERIAL GOVERNMENT. *Commentary 1978 65(6): 25-32.* Discusses one aspect of the national government's gigantism, the "Iron Law of Emulation." Gives examples in which an institution or procedure initiated by the Presidency has been emulated by Congress, or vice-versa. Even the Supreme Court seems to be moving toward emulation of the other branches of government, thus perpetuating the proliferation of new agencies or procedures. To break this "Iron Law," it must first be recognized that it is in operation, thus limiting the chances that it will continue to be exercised.   J. Tull

3374. Nathan, James A. and Oliver, James K. PUBLIC OPINION AND U.S. SECURITY POLICY. *Armed Forces and Soc. 1975 2(1): 46-62.* Discusses public opinion toward US foreign policy, defense policy, and the presidency in the 1970's, emphasizing the influence of the Vietnam War and the Watergate scandal.

3375. Natoli, Marie D. ABOLISH THE VICE PRESIDENCY? *Presidential Studies Q. 1979 9(2): 202-206.* Questions Arthur M. Schlesinger, Jr. in his belief that the vice-presidency should be abolished because it serves no vital function, as set forth in his "The Vice Presidency: A Modest Proposal," Appendix to *The Imperial Presidency* (Boston: Houghton Mifflin Co., 1973, 1974), and suggests that a restructuring of the vice-presidency is a more plausible remedy.

3376. Naveh, David. THE POLITICAL ROLE OF ACADEMIC ADVISERS: THE CASE OF THE U.S. PRESIDENT'S COUNCIL OF ECONOMIC ADVISERS, 1946-1976. *Presidential Studies Q. 1981 11(4): 492-510.* Examines the roles played by the Council of Economic Advisers for different presidents. Since its creation in 1946, the council has been made up mostly of academicians. This nonbureaucratic system has been highly informal, its membership based primarily on universal expertise, and it has been based on limited loyalty in time and scope. As a result, the council tends to add to presidential power and legitimacy. 3 tables, 66 notes, biblio.   D. H. Cline

3377. Nelson, Anna K. FOREIGN POLICY RECORDS AND PAPERS. *Soc. for Hist. of Am. Foreign Relations. Newsletter 1977 8(4): 2-16.* Part III. Discusses preservation and storage of presidential, State Department, and personal papers, concluding that the most serious issue facing archivists is guaranteeing the accessibility of all records and making certain that when public records are retired they are placed in the National Archives, 1950's-70's.

3378. Nelson, Anna K. FOREIGN POLICY RECORDS AND PAPERS: A CASE STUDY OF THE PRESERVATION AND ACCESSIBILITY OF ONE GROUP OF DOCUMENTS. *Soc. for Hist. of Am. Foreign Relations Newsletter 1977 8(2): 14-26, (3): 18-32.* Part I. Deals with State and Defense Department and National Security Council records preservation and the accessibility of these papers to the general public. Part II. Discusses the preservation and accessibility of official documents; discusses official histories and presidential papers and their accessibility to researchers and the general public. Article to be continued.

3379. Nelson, Michael. THE WHITE HOUSE, BUREAUCRACY, AND FOREIGN POLICY: LESSONS FROM CAMBODIA. *Virginia Q. Rev. 1980 56(2): 193-215.* To discover how US foreign policy should be made and implemented, investigates the extent of Henry A. Kissinger's revision of his Cambodia chapter in *The White House Years* after William Shawcross's critical *Sideshow* was published. Since the liberal attacks on the diplomatic bureaucracy in the 1960's, the State Department has lost influence in foreign policy. The Cambodia experience in the Nixon-Kissinger era suggests that the State Department needs to be rejuvenated so that it has real influence in both forming and implementing foreign policy.   O. H. Zabel

3380. Nicholas, H. G. THE INSULATION OF THE PRESIDENCY. *Government and Opposition [Great Britain] 1973 8(2): 156-176.* Discusses the possible isolation of the presidency from Congress, political parties, and cabinets 1950's-70's, emphasizing the Eisenhower and Nixon administrations.

3381. Nichols, W. Thomas. BEFORE REFORMING THE "INTELLIGENCY COMMUNITY," WHAT QUESTIONS MUST BE ASKED? *Freedom at Issue 1976 35: 20-23.* Discusses the respective places of various Intelligence Services in the US government from the 1940's-70's, emphasizing the roles of Congress and the Executive Branch in supervising intelligence activities.

3382. Nuechterlein, James A. LIBERALISM & THEODORE H. WHITE. *Commentary 1982 74(3): 32-38.* Traces the career of Theodore H. White, author and liberal thinker, and reviews his *America in Search of Itself: The Making of the President, 1956-1980.*

3383. Nufer, Harold F. FOUR MOMENTOUS EVENTS IN 1971-72: CATALYSTS FOR REFORM OF THE NATIONAL SECURITY CLASSIFICATION SYSTEM? *Air U. Rev. 1977 28(5): 56-63.* Examines the effect of the release of the Pentagon Papers and the publication of certain minutes of the National Security Council's deliberations during 1971-72 on the National Security Classification System. Discusses the use of national security as a shield of the Executive Branch of the federal government, the conduct of the Supreme Court on the issue of the Pentagon Papers, and the efforts of declassification of documents by Executive Branch departments since 1971. Based on government documents; 35 notes.   J. W. Thacker, Jr.

3384. O'Leary, Michael K.; Coplin, William D.; Shapiro, Howard B.; and Dean, Dale. THE QUEST FOR RELEVANCE: QUANTITATIVE INTERNATIONAL RELATIONS RESEARCH AND GOVERNMENT FOREIGN AFFAIRS ANALYSIS. *Internat. Studies Q. 1974 18(2): 211-238.* Focuses on the State Department (Bureau of Intelligence and Research); sees a "disjunction" between academic and policy research.

3385. Olson, William Clinton. PRESIDENT, CONGRESS AND AMERICAN FOREIGN POLICY: CONFRONTATION OR COLLABORATION? *Int. Affairs [Great Britain] 1976 52(4): 565-581.* Discusses Congressional participation in foreign policy, isolationist tendencies, and the nature of the relationship between Congress, the Secretary of State, and the President in respect to foreign policy. Speculates on the possible consequences of the 1976 presidential election. Secondary sources; 19 notes.   P. J. Beck

3386. Orman, John M. and Rudoni, Dorothy. EXERCISE OF THE PRESIDENT'S DISCRETIONARY POWER IN CRIMINAL JUSTICE POLICY. *Presidential Studies Q. 1979 9(4): 415-427.* The discretionary power of the president in the administration of criminal justice has symbolic as well as practical importance. Whether the dominant

theme is, as in 1968, law and order, or whether it is, as it has been since Watergate, trust in government, the social environment reflects the political, and expectations of justice for all have ramifications beyond the narrowly legal. Accordingly, the president's discretionary power should be depoliticized, so that the president will base his discretionary decisions on more theoretical and impact-oriented grounds. Democracy will benefit. 47 notes.   S

3387. Ortona, Egidio. L'ARDUA RELAZIONE FRA PRESIDENZA A CONGRESSO [The difficult relations between Presidency and Congress]. *Affari Esteri [Italy] 1977 9(33): 31-42.*

3388. Osborne, Trudi. THE WHITE HOUSE PRESS: LET AP COVER THE ASSASSINATIONS. *Washington Monthly 1977 8(12): 16-24.* Examines the press corps which follows the President despite high costs and stories of dubious value, 1970's.

3389. Packwood, Robert W. CONGRESS'S RESPONSIBILITY. *Center Mag. 1974 7(5): 40-52.* The responsibility of Congress in relation to the presidency.   S

3390. Paine, Christopher. SECRETS. *Bull. of the Atomic Sci. 1982 38(4): 11-16.* Discusses the conflict of national security and political freedom in the United States, focusing on Federal Bureau of Investigation and Central Intelligence Agency policies and on the history of the Freedom of Information Act (US, 1966), which has been challenged by several bills in Congress and by the Reagan administration.

3391. Pastor, Robert A. COPING WITH CONGRESS'S FOREIGN POLICY. *Foreign Service J. 1975 52(12): 15-18, 23.* Discusses the 1974-75 Constitutional struggle between Congress and the executive branch for control of US foreign policy.

3392. Payne, William C. IMPLEMENTING FEDERAL NONDISCRIMINATION POLICIES IN THE DEPARTMENT OF AGRICULTURE, 1964-1976. *Policy Studies J. 1978 6(4): 507-509.* Assesses attempts at integration and nondiscriminatory federal policy followed by the Agriculture Department's personnel policy, 1964-76. One of 16 articles in this issue on agricultural policy.

3393. Pellicanò, Gerolamo. GIUDIZIO SOSPESO SU NIXON [Judgment suspended on Nixon]. *Nuova Antologia [Italy] 1974 521(2082): 214-223.* Discusses the House impeachment proceedings as the conclusion of a long conflict between legislative and executive branches of government, 1969-74.

3394. Pellicanò, Gerolamo. L'AMERICA DOPO NIXON [America after Nixon]. *Nuova Antologia [Italy] 1974 521(2084): 490-500.* Reviews Richard Nixon's resignation from the presidency 9 August 1974, concluding that the outcome of the Watergate Scandal demonstrates the democratic nature of American political institutions.

M. T. Wilson

3395. Perlmutter, Amos. THE PRESIDENTIAL POLITICAL CENTER AND FOREIGN POLICY: A CRITIQUE OF THE REVISIONIST AND BUREAUCRATIC-POLITICAL ORIENTATIONS. *World Pol. 1974 27(1): 87-106.* Fundamental to modern politics is the fact that politics of security and diplomacy are central to society. Historically, foreign and security politics have been the main priorities of the political center, conducted primarily on that level. Since 1945, these political centers have gained predominance in the US. In the absence of well-integrated political elites, a highly centralized political party or parties, and powerful and permanent bureaucracies and civil service, the presidential political center has become the pivotal political center with almost exclusive control over foreign affairs and national security. The locus and degree of power within the American political and constitutional context, rather than elite orientations and practices, are identified to explain who dominates American foreign policy.   J

3396. Pious, Richard M. IS PRESIDENTIAL POWER "POISON"? *Pol. Sci. Q. 1974 89(3): 627-643.* " . . . Surveys recent books on the American presidency, describing dominant trends in the mode of analysis and the assessment of the office."   J

3397. Poole, Frederick. CONGRESS V. KISSINGER: THE NEW EQUALIZERS. *Washington Monthly 1975 7(3): 23-32.* Former Foreign Service officers are working on the Hill to restore the balance between the White House and Congress in foreign policymaking.

3398. Pynn, Ronald E. WATERGATE: RETROSPECTIVE POLICY IMPLICATIONS. *Policy Studies J. 1975 4(1): 63-68.* The Watergate scandal has stimulated a critical evaluation of such areas as presidential-congress relations, civil liberties, the presidential establishment, and campaign reform, as well as increased public cynicism towards government.

3399. Ransom, Harry Howe. CONGRESS AND REFORM OF THE C.I.A. *Policy Studies J. 1977 5(4): 476-480.* Covers 1974-76.

3400. Ransom, Harry Howe. CONGRESS AND THE INTELLIGENCE AGENCIES. *Pro. of the Acad. of Pol. Sci. 1975 32(1): 153-166.* The accountability of intelligence agencies in the federal government to Congress has been difficult to control during 1947-74, due to the nebulous definition of agency functions, their secrecy, and the complexity and dynamism of the separation of powers.

3401. Ransom, Harry Howe. SECRET INTELLIGENCE AGENCIES AND CONGRESS. *Society 1975 12(3): 33-38.* Dispute over the requirements of secrecy for national security and those of disclosure for government.   S

3402. Reed, Leonard. THE BUDGET GAME AND HOW TO WIN IT. *Washington Monthly 1979 10(10): 24-33.* Describes tractics of federal agencies in their continuing battles with the Office of Management and Budget over dispensation of the President's annual federal budget.

3403. Reedy, George E. NATIONAL SYMBOLS. *Society 1980 17(5): 61-65.* Discusses the presidency as a national symbol, the significance of the augmenting role of Congress in foreign policy, the insufficiency of presidential prestige to carry controversial proposals, and the effect of the Vietnam War and the Watergate Scandal on the office of the chief executive.

3404. Reedy, George E. THE OMNISCIENT PRESIDENT. *Worldview 1975 18(7-8): 10-14.* Discusses changing attitudes toward executive power from the 1940's-70's, emphasizing war-making powers, foreign policy and the implications of the Watergate scandal for the Nixon Administration.

3405. Reedy, George E. THE PRESIDENCY IN 1976: FOCAL POINT OF POLITICAL UNITY? *J. of Pol. 1976 38(3): 228-238.* Studies the nature of the Presidency and the realities of political life which make the office significant. Both Congress and the courts must look to the Presidency to translate their agreements into effective action. Regardless of Viet Nam, Watergate, and periodic calls for "smaller" government, every sign points to more governmental action. The world is too complicated and too interdependent for anything else. The Presidency cannot be exempted from the social ferment in America, but it will remain at the center of the political process, despite changing constituencies.
                    R. V. Ritter

3406. Reichard, Gary W. EISENHOWER AND THE BRICKER AMENDMENT. *Prologue 1974 6(2): 88-99.* Considers the nature and fate of the Bricker Amendment, designed to curb growing presidential power. Disturbed by federal policies in Asia which culminated in the communization of China and the disastrous Korean War, Senator Bricker's amendment quickly won many supporters in Congress. The election of President Dwight D. Eisenhower, who opposed it, weakened the proposal's chances, as did Bricker's own view of the need for quick action against marauding communism. The amendment failed, to the delight of liberals, many of whom now support similar measures. 3 photos, 48 notes.
                    V. L. Human

3407. Reilly, John E. THE AMERICAN MOOD: A FOREIGN POLICY OF SELF-INTEREST. *Foreign Policy 1979 (34): 74-86.* A 1978 poll of public opinion and national leadership reveals that Americans are more concerned with national self-interest in foreign policy than with past altruistic goals. The "missionary zeal" of the 1960's is gone, and

human rights is not perceived as important. There is increasing support for selective overseas involvement, but not for widespread commitments. Arms limitation and increased joint Soviet-American projects are favored. Overall interest in foreign policy is declining among the American people, most of whom rely on the President and the mass media for their information. 7 charts.
                    T. L. Powers

3408. Rhoads, James B. THE PAPERS OF THE PRESIDENTS. *Massachusetts Hist. Soc. Pro. 1976 88: 94-104.* A number of problems involved in preserving the papers of the Presidents have been raised by the question of the disposition of the Nixon administration papers. Traditionally, American Presidents took their papers with them when leaving office. Under the Presidential Libraries Act (1955), however, six presidential libraries have been established, and a 1974 Act of Congress created the Public Documents Commission to study the situation. The central dilemma they face is the balance between public access and the individual's liberty and privacy. Based on the author's experience as Archivist of the United States; 2 notes, index.
                    G. W. R. Ward

3409. Roberts, Adam. THE CIA: REFORM IS NOT ENOUGH. *Millennium: J. of Int. Studies [Great Britain] 1977 6(1): 64-72.* Comments on the recent increased interest in the Central Intelligence Agency which has been accused of criminal actions. Although reforms have been introduced, such as making the CIA responsible to the Senate Intelligence Oversight Committee, it is difficult to have confidence in reform, in view of precedents of contempt of Congress. Key questions are often ignored: Should the CIA be abolished? Should the CIA be deprived of some of its functions? Is the CIA the most appropriate body to exercise such functions? Examines the main functions of the CIA, and concludes that it should be abolished. Based on US government reports, and the Church Committee Report of 1975; 29 notes.
                    P. J. Peck

3410. Robinson, D. L. PRESIDENTIAL AUTOCRACY AND THE RULE OF LAW. *Worldview 1973 16(3): 5-12.* Argues the existence of autocracy in the formulation of foreign policy in the presidency and Executive Branch in the 1970's, including issues in Constitutional law.

3411. Rockman, Bert A. AMERICA'S *DEPARTMENTS* OF STATE: IRREGULAR AND REGULAR SYNDROMES OF POLICY MAKING. *Am. Pol. Sci. Rev. 1981 75(4): 911-927.* Sketches a general explanation for the growth of coordinative machinery and of irregular personnel in modern governments, identifies both general and specific reasons for this phenomenon in the United States with special reference to foreign policymaking, identifies within the American foreign policymaking context the modal characteristics of irregular and regular syndromes of policymaking, and the conjunction between personnel and institutional base, traces the implications arising from these different policy syndromes, and evaluates proposals for improving the coherence and knowledge base of American foreign policymaking.
                    J/S

3412. Rodgers, Harrell R., Jr.; Eisenberg, Norman; Miller, George; Reilly, Patrick; and Nadasty, Dean. CHILDREN'S IMAGES OF PRESIDENTS: PERSONALIZATION VERSUS ROLE. *J. of Pol. Sci. 1977 5(1): 27-37.* That children recognize the president as a specific individual and associate particular acts with him does not necessarily alter their perception of his role in the political system. Affect, not personalization, seems to determine the role of the presidency in the political socialization process. The distinction between man and office may be an important support mechanism for children as well as for adults. Based on 671 student questionnaires from nine schools in a large midwestern city; table, 13 notes.
                    T. P. Richardson

3413. Rose, Richard. THE PRESIDENT: A CHIEF BUT NOT AN EXECUTIVE. *Presidential Studies Q. 1977 7(1): 5-20.* A President can maximize his influence by presenting a positive image, maintaining popular and Congressional support, and acting forcefully within constitutional prerogatives. He should establish buffers between himself and major problems. The President's staff should influence policy decisions. The staff's size and responsibilities determine the President's strategies: absolute monarchy, saturation, rule-of-law feudalism, or free enterprise. Based on interviews with White House and Executive Office officials, public documents, and secondary sources; 51 notes.
                    R. D. Hurt

3414. Rothstein, Lawrence E. WHY NO RELEVANT RESPONSES TO THE PROBLEMS UNDERLYING WATERGATE? *J. of Intergroup Relations 1975 4(3): 33-47.* The lack of adequate response to the problems underlying the Watergate Scandal is due to the failure of Americans to recognize the basic defects in their systems of government and politics which caused the scandal.   S

3415. Rourke, John T. CONGRESS, THE EXECUTIVE, AND FOREIGN POLICY: A PROPOSITIONAL ANALYSIS. *Presidential Studies Q. 1980 10(2): 179-193.* Examines the relationship between Congress and the executive in foreign policy formulation and action since World War II. Using the influence theory, it can be seen through values, means, and scope how the executive, while sensitive to the wishes of Congress, is in a very powerful position to influence and change congressional desires, and to achieve many of the administration's programs. Congressional reassertiveness of the last five years is unlikely to last, due to a lack of institutional will and its constitutional position. With strong leadership, presidential power will again be dominant in the area of foreign affairs. 100 notes.   D. H. Cline

3416. Rourke, John T. THE FUTURE IS HISTORY: CONGRESS AND FOREIGN POLICY. *Presidential Studies Q. 1979 9(3): 275-283.* Discusses the legislative role of Congress in foreign policy, an area dominated by the President from World War II until the early 1970's; the turning point occurred in 1973 with the War Powers Resolution enacted by Congress over a Nixon veto.

3417. Rutkus, Denis S. PRESIDENTIAL TELEVISION. *J. of Communication 1976 26(2): 73-78.* Discusses problems in the easy accessibility of the presidency to television coverage, 1966-75, emphasizing the ability of presidents to influence public opinion through this medium.

3418. Sanders, Ralph. BUREAUCRATIC PLOYS AND STRATEGEMS: THE CASE OF THE U.S. DEPARTMENT OF DEFENSE. *Jerusalem J. of Int. Relations [Israel] 1979 4(2): 1-15.* Examines the Defense Department's bureaucracy, 1960's-70's.

3419. Scarrow, Howard A. PARLIAMENTARY AND PRESIDENTIAL GOVERNMENT COMPARED. *Current Hist. 1974 66(394): 264-267, 272.* One of six articles in this issue on "The American Presidency."   S

3420. Schechter, Stephen L. ON THE COMPATIBILITY OF FEDERALISM AND INTERGOVERNMENTAL MANAGEMENT. *Publius 1981 11(2): 127-141.* Defines and discusses the term intergovernmental management. Examines intergovernmental management as it relates to federalism, and as it developed during presidential administrations from Johnson to Carter. Primary sources; 26 notes, table.   G. Smith

3421. Schick, Allen. THE BATTLE OF THE BUDGET. *Pro. of the Acad. of Pol. Sci. 1975 32(1): 51-70.* Assesses the budgets process instituted with the Congressional Budget and Impoundment Control Act (US, 1974) and the conflict between the legislative and executive branches due to the budgetary role of the federal government.

3422. Schlesinger, Arthur M., Jr. ON THE PRESIDENTIAL SUCCESSION. *Pol. Sci. Q. 1974 89(3): 475-506.* . . . Examines the present manner of filling vacancies in the offices of president and vice president. Schlesinger, concluding that the vice presidency is a pointless and even mischievous office which should be abolished, recommends that vacancies in the presidency be filled, as he contends the founding fathers intended, by the formula of a temporary acting President and a special election."   J

3423. Schlesinger, Arthur M., Jr. WHO OWNS A PRESIDENT'S PAPERS? *Manuscripts 1975 27(3): 178-182.* Attacks the decision of US District Judge Charles R. Richey, 31 January 1975, against Richard M. Nixon's claim to ownership of his presidential papers and tapes. Because those materials included political as well as state papers, to make all materials generated by a President public property would impose unreasonable restrictions on the personal and political activities of the officeholder. Moreover, while the tapes belong to the government as long as they are required for evidence, a blanket ruling such as Richey's

interpretation would not give scholars automatic and expedious access to presidential papers and would not provide the public protection from dishonorable presidents. Suggests the Public Documents Commission, appointed by President Gerald Ford, avoid the Richey decision and set to work without delay in establishing guidelines for the ownership of public records. Reprinted from *The Wall Street Journal*.   D. A. Yanchisin

3424. Schultz, L. Peter. *GOLDWATER V. CARTER:* THE SEPERATION OF POWERS AND THE PROBLEM OF EXECUTIVE PREROGATIVE. *Presidential Studies Q. 1982 12(1): 34-41.* The Supreme Court decision in *Goldwater* v. *Carter* (US, 1979) did not answer the question of whether or not a president, under the Constitution, may unilaterally terminate a treaty of the United States. In viewing this issue in terms of the constitutional relationship between the Executive Branch and Congress, Carter's action is constitutionally unsound and potentially dangerous. 41 notes.   D. H. Cline

3425. Schwartzman, Robert Berman. FISCAL OVERSIGHT OF THE CENTRAL INTELLIGENCE AGENCY: CAN ACCOUNTABILITY AND CONFIDENTIALITY COEXIST? *New York U. J. of Internat. Law and Pol. 1974 7(3): 493-544.* Stresses that "both oversight and legislative power over the Central Intelligence Agency in House and Senate subcommittees is not fully effective." Seeks to outline "a middle course whereby the CIA's accountability to Congress might be increased without compromising the agency's legitimate need for confidentiality." Primary and secondary sources; 214 notes.   M. L. Frey

3426. Semidei, Manuela. FACTEURS INTERNES DE LA POLITIQUE ETRANGERE AMERICAINE [Internal factors of American foreign policy]. *Études Int. [Canada] 1974 5(4): 657-672.* Influenced by the thinking of Jean-Baptiste Duroselle, examines the effect of permanent institutions and pressure groups, such as the Presidency and its attendant bureaucracy, the power of Congress, and the role of political parties, minorities, labor groups, multinational corporations, and lobbyists in the formulation of foreign policy. Secondary sources; 42 notes.   J. F. Harrington, Jr.

3427. Semmel, Andrew K. SOME CORRELATES OF ATTITUDES TO MULTILATERAL DIPLOMACY IN THE U.S. DEPARTMENT OF STATE. *Int. Studies Q. 1976 20(2): 301-324.* The foreign policy attitudes of Foreign Service officers toward multilateral diplomacy are shaped by their immediate work milieu, not their individual social backgrounds or the orientation of the State Department.

3428. Seymour-Ure, Colin. PRESIDENTIAL POWER, PRESS SECRETARIES AND COMMUNICATION. *Pol. Studies [Great Britain] 1980 28(2): 253-270.* A president's control over how he is publicly understood is weak; this implies that presidential power itself is weak. The ability of the president and press secretary to communicate the President's message is jeopardized both by the secretary's personality and performance and by the nature of the presidency and the incumbent's style. The access of press corps and secretary to the president can also be crucial. This has been true since Franklin D. Roosevelt took office. 69 notes.   D. J. Nicholls

3429. Shannon, William V. IS GERALD FORD REALLY NECESSARY? *Worldview 1974 17(7): 13-18.* Discusses the office of the vice-presidency since 1945, recommending political reform in selection of the president's successor.

3430. Shapiro, Walter. WILDLY OUT OF CONTROL. *Washington Monthly 1976 8(1): 24-26.* A Brookings Institution study of 1975, "Uncontrollable Spending for Social Services Grants," reveals the irrational methods of the Health, Education and Welfare Department's bureaucracy.

3431. Shull, Steven A. ASSESSING MEASURES OF PRESIDENTIAL-CONGRESSIONAL POLICY FORMATION. *Presidential Studies Q. 1981 11(2): 151-157.* Since the *Congressional Quarterly* discontinued its "Boxscore" measure of proposals to Congress in 1976, many other measures of presidential-congressional relations in policy formation have been offered. An assessment of six measures related to the functions of agenda-setting, presenting alternatives, and adoption of preferred choices is given. None of the measures is perfect, and there are considerable problems. Data must be available to improve measurement. 3 graphs, 19 notes.   A. Drysdale

3432. Shull, Steven A. BUDGETARY POLICY-MAKING: CONGRESS AND THE PRESIDENT COMPARED. *Presidential Studies Q. 1979 9(2): 180-191*. Provides a determination of the budgets of eight federal executive branch agencies, and assesses presidential and congressional support of the agencies from fiscal years 1960 to 1971.

3433. Shull, Steven A. PRESIDENTIAL INTERACTIONS: AN ANNOTATED BIBLIOGRAPHY. *Presidential Studies Q. 1978 8(1): 79-95*. An annotated bibliography of recent secondary works on the presidency and its interaction with governmental and nongovernmental groups. Includes works on new concepts of presidential power, greatness, and personality.   S. C. Strom

3434. Sigelman, Lee and Carter, Robert. AMERICAN INDIANS IN THE POLITICAL KINGDOM: A NOTE ON THE BUREAU OF INDIAN AFFAIRS. *Administration and Soc. 1976 8(3): 343-354*. Discusses occupational stratification and wages in the employment of American Indians in the Bureau of Indian Affairs in the 1970's.

3435. Sigelman, Lee. A REASSESSMENT OF THE TWO PRESIDENCIES THESIS. *J. of Pol. 1979 41(4): 1195-1205*. Disputes Aaron Wildavsky's "The Two Presidencies," *Trans-Action*, 4 (Dec. 1966). In votes on key issues since 1957 most presidents have not enjoyed a freer hand in foreign and defense than domestic policies. Especially dramatic has been the erosion of support for the President's foreign policy among opposition members of Congress since 1972. While presidents won congressional victories on almost 75% of key votes during 1957-72, they have subsequently succeeded on fewer than 60% of such votes. While power tends to gravitate toward the president in crisis periods, Congress eventually reasserts its power in foreign as well as domestic affairs. Table, 18 notes.   A. W. Novitsky

3436. Silberman, Laurence H. TOWARD PRESIDENTIAL CONTROL OF THE STATE DEPARTMENT. *Foreign Affairs 1979 57(4): 872-893*. "Challenges the notion that it is appropriate for Foreign Service officers to routinely occupy senior policymaking positions in the State Department." The President needs individuals at this level who are compatible with him and his views. Moreover, Foreign Service officers are trained to implement policy, not to create it. State is the only executive department in which major appointments are not almost automatically awarded to presidential supporters. 21 notes.   M. R. Yerburgh

3437. Silver, Howard J. PRESIDENTIAL POWER AND THE POST-WATERGATE PRESIDENCY. *Presidential Studies Q. 1978 8(2): 199-214*. In *Presidential Power: The Politics of Leadership* (N.Y.: Wiley, 1975), Richard Neustadt contends that executive power is the "power to persuade." According to this thesis, successful bargaining depends on the personality of the President, political experience, public reputation, staff use, and relations with Congress. Neustadt's model is tested in the post-Watergate environment of Presidents Gerald R. Ford and Jimmy Carter. Despite Ford's nonpower-seeking nature and divergence from Neustadt's formula for success, he wielded power and controlled policy through veto politics. Conversely, Carter follows the course outlined by Neustadt and has achieved poor results, suggesting that alternate formulas for presidential leadership are needed. Fig., 82 notes.   S. C. Strom

3438. Simpson, Stephen J. CAN THE PRESIDENCY BE MADE SAFE FOR DEMOCRACY? *Antioch R. 1975 33(2): 60-72*. A profound disillusionment with the American presidency as an instrument of democracy has stimulated a plethora of reform proposals since the mid-1960's, focusing on the formal organizational structure and social psychology of the president's advisory system, and on the uses and abuses of executive power.   S

3439. Slonim, Solomon. CONGRESSIONAL-EXECUTIVE AGREEMENTS. *Columbia J. of Transnat. Law 1975 14(3): 434-450*. Discusses principles of constitutional law involved in agreements between Congress and the executive branch regarding control of US foreign policy and treatymaking powers, 1969-74.

3440. Smith, Margaret Chase. HOW MARGARET CHASE SMITH WOULD MONITOR THE CIA. *Freedom at Issue 1976 35: 11-13*. Presents the author's opinions regarding Congress' role in preventing presidential abuse of the Central Intelligence Agency from the 1950's-70's.

3441. Sniderman, Paul M.; Nauman, W. Russell; Citrin, Jack; McClosky, Herbert; and Shanks, J. Merrill. STABILITY OF SUPPORT FOR THE POLITICAL SYSTEM: THE INITIAL IMPACT OF WATERGATE. *Am. Pol. Q. 1975 3(4): 437-457*. Discusses the initial and subsequent impact of the Watergate scandal on attitudes toward the political system in the San Francisco Bay area of California in 1972-73.

3442. Spitzer, Robert J. THE PRESIDENT AND PUBLIC POLICY: A PRELIMINARY INQUIRY. *Presidential Studies Q. 1979 9(4): 441-457*. Policy analysis identifies variables useful in the analysis of presidential power. The political system produces policies; the kinds of policies engaging the president systematically affect his ability to influence political processes and events. The policy approach to the administrations of Presidents Eisenhower through Nixon suggests that policy analysis will develop into a valuable research tool for studying the institution of the Presidency. 6 tables, 2 fig., 39 notes.   S

3443. Spragens, William C. OUTSIDER'S VIEWS OF WHITE HOUSE REFORM. *Presidential Studies Q. 1977 7(2-3): 153-158*. A reaction has developed on Capitol Hill to the centralization of power in the White House which began in 1933 and has occurred in both Democratic and Republican administrations. The independent voting block has now caused Congress to be less complacent regarding the continued aggrandizement of White House power. Public opinion, however, ultimately will determine whether Executive power will be checked adequately. Interviews and secondary sources; 2 notes.   R. D. Hurt

3444. Stebbins, Phillip. POWERS, INHERENT AND PLENARY: THE MODERN PRESIDENCY AND FOREIGN POLICY—AN ESSAY REVIEW. *Pennsylvania Hist. 1974 41(1): 113-120*. Reviews five recent works discussing and criticizing the power of the presidency in foreign relations. To provide background, the author considers two decisions written by Justice George Sutherland and various works approving the growth of executuve power over foreign relations. Covers Hugh C. Gallaher, *Advise and Obstruct* (1969), Merlo J. Pusey, *The Way We Go to War* (Boston: Houghton Mifflin, 1969), George Reedy, *The Twilight of the Presidency* (New York: Norton, 1970), Dale Vinyard, *The Presidency* (New York: Scribners, 1971), and Anthony Austin, *The President's War* (Philadelphia: Lippincott, 1971).   D. C. Swift

3445. Stegmaier, John L. TOWARD A MORE EFFECTIVE PRESIDENCY. *Presidential Studies Q. 1977 7(2-3): 145-153*. Presidential failures in foreign affairs stem from deficiencies in the counsel available. The effective conduct of foreign affairs demands that the President have access to sound conceptual advice free from the pressures of interest groups. Proposes a Council of State, a bipartisan, continuing institution that would function independently to raise the level of presidential performance in the formulation and execution of broad foreign policy. Primary and secondary sources; 36 notes.   R. D. Hurt

3446. Stevenson, Adlai E., III. A CALL FOR NATIONAL LEADERSHIP. *Presidential Studies Q. 1979 9(1): 8-10*. Speculates on the apparent ineptitude and impotence of presidents in an ever more complicated economic and political melange.

3447. Stimson, James A. PUBLIC SUPPORT FOR AMERICAN PRESIDENTS: A CYCLICAL MODEL. *Public Opinion Q. 1976 40(1): 1-21*. The approval accorded to Presidents by the American public is found to follow a cyclical pattern over time. All Presidents begin their terms with great popularity, experience parabolic declines, steadily lose popular support for about three years, and then recover some at the ends of their terms. These distinctive cycles, it is argued, reflect regular expectation/disillusionment cycles among the less well-informed segments of the public and are tied to the four-year election calendar. The extraordinary fit of parabolic curves to actual presidential approval leads to the suspicion that presidential approval may be almost wholly independent of the President's behavior in office, a function largely of inevitable forces associated with time.   J

3448. Strong, Frank R. COURTS, CONGRESS, JUDICIARY: ONE IS MORE EQUAL THAN THE OTHERS. *Am. Bar Assoc. J. 1974 60(10): 1203-1206.* When the Supreme Court exercised 'constitutional review' in *United States* v. *Nixon*, it not only put a noose on an imperial presidency but also signaled that, had an impeachment 'conviction' come in the Senate, it would have been willing to exercise ultimate review over that also. This makes all the more important the manner, extent, and objectives by which the Court uses this power.   J

3449. Strong, Frank R. PRESIDENT, CONGRESS, JUDICIARY: ONE IS MORE EQUAL THAN THE OTHERS. *Am. Bar Assoc. J. 1974 60(9): 1050-1052.* United States v. Nixon was approached as a case of 'judicial review' under conventional separation of powers doctrine, but in truth it was an exercise of 'constitutional review,' which finds little analytical support in that doctrine. In the field of 'constitutional review,' the Supreme Court is more equal than its 'coequal' branches of government. *United States* v. *Nixon* was in this grand tradition.   J

3450. Sullivan, John L. and Minns, Daniel Richard. "THE BENEVOLENT LEADER REVISITED": SUBSTANTIVE FINDING OR METHODOLOGICAL ARTIFACT? *Am. J. of Pol. Sci. 1976 20(4): 763-772.* Greenstein (1975) presents data purporting to prove that the 'benevolent leader" phenomenon is alive and well after Vietnam and Watergate. He presents his respondents (children) with a hypothetical situation whereby a child from another country comes to the respondents' school and asks for information about the president, legislature, mayor, and so on. Greenstein finds that grade school children in three countries give almost unanimously positive responses to this series of questions, even during Watergate. Our analysis of an independent data set suggests that his findings are the result of the cue "child from *another country"* rather than the result of truly positive affect toward the president or the presidency.   J

3451. Tays, Dwight L. PRESIDENTIAL REACTION TO SECURITY: A LONGITUDINAL STUDY. *Presidential Studies Q. 1980 10(4): 600-609.* By examining presidential reaction to the intensive national security measures needed for protection, three types of presidents emerge. The least restrictive presidents (F. Roosevelt, Truman, Kennedy, Ford) enjoyed their freedom and public access. The passive-cooperative type (Eisenhower) was less resistant to security measures but still did not emphasize security. The final type, supportive-preference (Johnson, Nixon), did not enjoy contact with the public and preferred strong support or isolation. These categories seemingly support James Barber's Presidential Character Model. 68 notes, biblio.   D. H. Cline

3452. Thatcher, Terence L. THE BRICKER AMENDMENT: 1952-54. *Northwest Ohio Q. 1977 49(3): 107-120.* In 1952 Senator John W. Bricker (R.-Ohio) proposed a constitutional amendment to limit executive power, particularly in conducting foreign policy; traces the origin of the Bricker amendment to the American Bar Association arguments in 1948 opposing several treaties proposed at the UN.

3453. Theoharis, Athan G. THE FREEDOM OF INFORMATION ACT AND THE INTELLIGENCE AGENCIES. *Government Publ. Rev.: An Int. J. of Issues and Information Resources 1982 9(1): 37-44.* Discusses the activities of the Federal Bureau of Investigation and the Central Intelligence Agency to exempt their files from the search and disclosure provisions of the Freedom of Information Act (US, 1966), and challenges this exemption.

3454. Thomas, Norman C. THE PRESIDENCY AND POLICY STUDIES. *Policy Studies J. 1981 9(7): 1072-1082.* Assesses recent studies of presidential policymaking, including literature that deals with organization and staffing, and offers suggestions for streamlining bureaucratic structure.

3455. Thomas, Norman C. PRESIDENTIAL ACCOUNTABILITY SINCE WATERGATE. *Presidential Studies Q. 1978 8(4): 417-434.* Institutional accountability is viewed as a structural problem of executive-legislative relations and Constitutional interpretation which varies with the national political mood. Recent executive abuses have brought efforts to improve accountability through 1) reduction of presidential dominance of foreign and military policy, 2) curbing executive power in general, and 3) strengthening Congress. The War Powers Act of 1973 and the National

Emergencies Act of 1976 limit unilateral presidential action. The Nixon impeachment proceedings, the Impoundment Control Act, the use of congressional veto, oversight, and confirmation limit executive power. The congressional resurgence includes the establishment of the Congressional Budget Office, increasing subcommittee independence, and campaign financing reform. Discusses proposals not acted upon and assesses the outlook for continued congressional assertiveness. 54 notes.
S. C. Strom

3456. Thomson, Harry C. THE WAR POWERS RESOLUTION OF 1973: CAN CONGRESS MAKE IT STICK? *World Affairs 1976 139(1): 3-9.* Discusses the constitutional implications for the presidency and the executive branch of Congress' passing of the War Powers Resolution (1973).

3457. Tiwari, S. C. WATERGATE CRISIS: A VIEW FROM THE THIRD WORLD. *India Q. [India] 1973 29(4): 340-346.* Examines the feelings of Third World countries toward the Watergate Scandal in terms of political trust and efficacy and the potential effect of such feelings on foreign relations, 1972.

3458. Tower, John G. CONGRESS VERSUS THE PRESIDENT: THE FORMULATION AND IMPLEMENTATION OF AMERICAN FOREIGN POLICY. *Foreign Affairs 1981-82 60(2): 229-246.* The conflict between Congress and the president over the right to make and implement foreign policy turned in favor of Congress during the 1970's with passage of legislation limiting the president's foreign policy powers. This is an unfavorable situation because Congress lacks the flexibility and unified national outlook needed to deal with foreign affairs. 3 notes.   A. A. Englard

3459. Trager, Frank N. THE NATIONAL SECURITY ACT OF 1947: IT'S THIRTIETH ANNIVERSARY. *Air U. Rev. 1977 29(1): 2-15.* Discusses the US defense establishment and the effect of the National Security Act (1947), which created the Defense Department, on US policy. Includes the main features of the 1947 act, the 1958 amendment, and an evaluation of its work. Provides suggestions for reforming the system. Based on published works; an organizational chart and 12 notes.
J. W. Thacker, Jr.

3460. Triboulet, Raymond. NIXON ET LA PRESSE: L'AFFAIRE NIXON OU DU MAUVAIS USAGE DE LA PRESSE [Nixon and the press: the Nixon affair or bad usage of the press]. *Nouvelle Rev. des Deux Mondes [France] 1977 (6): 568-573.* Analyzes the Nixon affair as a case of political assassination by the United States and French press, recognizing the services and contributions of Nixon while in office, and arguing that public opinion in France does not correspond to journalistic claims.

3461. Vale, Vivian. THE OBLIGATION TO SPEND: PRESIDENTIAL IMPOUNDMENT OF CONGRESSIONAL APPROPRIATIONS. *Pol. Studies [Great Britain] 1977 25(4): 508-522.* Studies the executive impoundment of congressional appropriations by the President through the Office of Management and Budget. Examines and substantially rejects President Richard M. Nixon's claims to constitutional and statutory authority and historical precedent. Discusses limitation of the practice by statute to prevent the substitution of presidential legislative priorities for those of Congress. A new and more healthy equilibrium of responsibility has been achieved. 39 notes.   R. Howell

3462. VanDerSlik, Jack R. THE PRESIDENT IN A PARADIGM OF POLICY MAKING. *Presidential Studies Q. 1979 9(1): 65-70.* Explores to what extent the office of the president should participate in phases of policymaking: initiation, formulation, promotion, adoption, application, and termination.

3463. Vatz, Richard E. PUBLIC OPINION AND PRESIDENTIAL ETHOS. *Western Speech Communication 1976 40(3): 196-206.* Examines sources of estimating public opinion, assesses prevailing concepts and practices, and shows importance to the Presidency.

3464. Vaughn, Jacqueline. THE FUNCTIONS OF THE (CHIEF) EXECUTIVE: HOW CHESTER BARNARD MIGHT VIEW THE PRESIDENCY. *Presidential Studies Q. 1978 8(1): 18-27.* Examines the applicability to the American presidency of Chester Barnard's (1886-

1961) general model of the executive as expressed in his *Functions of the Executive* (Cambridge, Mass.: Harvard University Press, 1966). Barnard's primary executive functions, maintenance of organizational communication, securing essential services from individuals, and formulation of objectives, are defined and compared with presidential duties. Executive responsibility for leadership and moral creativeness is illustrated with examples from recent presidential behavior. Barnard's model provides an accurate portrait of presidential work and discredits the theory that the office is sui generis, a one-of-a-kind operation. 38 notes.

S. C. Strom

3465. Vendegrift, A. A. VICIOUS INFIGHTING. Karsten, Peter, ed. *The Military in America: From the Colonial Era to the Present* (New York: Free Pr., 1980): 363-369. Discusses the furor over the Collins Plan, introduced in 1946 by General J. Lawton Collins, which called for unification of the military under a Secretary of Defense and Armed Forces Chief of Staff, and for the reduction of the role and activities of the Marine Corps.

3466. Vialle, Pierre. LE CONGRÈS, LE PRÉSIDENT ET LA POLITIQUE ÉTRANGÈRE [Congress, the president, and foreign policy]. *Rev. Int. de Droit Comparé [France] 1979 31(3): 603-614.* Discusses the respective powers of Congress and the president, centers on changes in their relations since 1964, and mentions their influence on US foreign policy.

3467. Warwick, Donald P. BUREAUCRATIZATION IN THE U.S. DEPARTMENT OF STATE. *Sociol. Inquiry 1974 44(2): 75-91.*

3468. Wayne, Stephen J.; Cole, Richard L.; and Hyde, James F. C., Jr. ADVISING THE PRESIDENT ON ENROLLED LEGISLATION: PATTERNS OF EXECUTIVE INFLUENCE. *Pol. Sci. Q. 1979 94(2): 303-317.* Analyzes presidential decisions to approve or veto enrolled bills during the Nixon and Ford years. The authors show that presidential action was closely related to advice from the agency most directly affected by the proposed legislation and especially the Office of Management and Budget.

J

3469. Wayne, Stephen J. and Hyde, James F. C., Jr. PRESIDENTIAL DECISION-MAKING ON ENROLLED BILLS. *Presidential Studies Q. 1978 8(3): 284-296.* Describes the development of a formalized process to advise presidents on enrolled bills. Beginning with the administration of Franklin D. Roosevelt, the Bureau of the Budget dominated the process of coordinating and evaluating departmental recommendations. The growth of the White House Staff and the Domestic Council in the late 1960's affected the handling of enrolled bills but did not significantly diminish the influence of the Office of Management and Budget. Consensus was the rule; when controversy occurred, OMB was generally the veto proponent, less prone to politicalization and sycophancy. 2 tables, 28 notes.

S. C. Strom

3470. Weaver, Paul H. LIBERALS AND THE PRESIDENCY. *Commentary 1975 60(4): 48-53.* A spectacular reversal of ideological roles in recent American politics has resulted in the abandonment by American liberals of their commitment to a strong presidency. The presidency, in the traditional liberal view, could give authority and legitimacy to political and social programs, which would be hamstrung by the "inherently obstructionist procedures of the national legislature." Now, in a complete turnabout, liberals attack the strong presidency as the spearhead of imperialism. The true growth sector in American government today is in the Congress, but Congress is incapable of acting with coherence, responsibility and democratic accountability. A new class of liberals ("college-educated professionals and managers") espouses policy objectives that cannot be achieved without the political resources which a strong presidency can provide.

S. R. Herstein

3471. Weinstein, Edwin A. PRESIDENTIAL ASSASSINATION: AN AMERICAN PROBLEM. *Psychiatry 1976 39(3): 291-293.* Discusses psychological, sociopathological, and political aspects of assassination and assassination attempts on presidents, 1950's-70's, including public opinion toward the presidency and gun control.

3472. Werner, Simcha B. THE POLITICAL REVERSIBILITY OF ADMINISTRATIVE REFORM: A CASE STUDY OF THE UNITED STATES POSTAL SERVICE. *Public Administration [Great Britain] 1982 60(3): 320-338.* The 1971 reform of the US Post Office Department to a public corporation, the US Postal Service, allows examination of the idea that opposition to reform does not subside once reform is initiated, and shows that, in fact, interests scrutinize reform in hopes of showing a failure and thus a returning to the status quo.

3473. West, F. J. SECRETARIES OF DEFENSE: WHY MOST HAVE FAILED. *Naval War Coll. Rev. 1981 34(2): 86-92.* Reviews the careers of the 14 defense secretaries since their post was created in 1947, offering some reasons for their almost universal failure. The main cause of unsatisfactory performance rests in the numerous roles of the secretary, several of which tend to be, or to become, contradictory. To benignly administer an existing establishment, and yet to seek to change it; to seek to maintain favorable relations with a squabbling president and Congress —these are difficult tasks which perhaps no man can ideally perform. Table.

V. L. Human

3474. Wiatr, Jerzy J. UPADEK PREZYDENTA NIXONA [The downfall of President Nixon]. *Kultura i Społeczeństwo [Poland] 1974 18(4): 71-91.* The resignation of President Nixon on 9 August 1974 had many favorable repercussions in the political life of the United States. Caused by the Watergate scandal, personal political ambitions of Nixon, the Vietnam War, and the desire to strengthen the position of the president at the expense of Congress and the Court, the resignation resulted in a shifting of strength to the Democratic Party, blocking of executive power, and placing of the government before public judgment.

M. Swiecicka-Ziemianek

3475. Wildavsky, Aaron. THE PAST AND FUTURE PRESIDENCY. *Public Interest 1975(41): 56-76.* Considers the changing role of the president since the 1930's.

S

3476. Wilson, Graham K. ARE DEPARTMENTAL SECRETARIES REALLY A PRESIDENT'S NATURAL ENEMIES? *British J. of Pol. Sci. [Great Britain] 1977 7(3): 273-299.* Cabinet secretaries are more loyal to the president than to their department.

3477. Wilson, James Q. and Rachal, Patricia. CAN THE GOVERNMENT REGULATE ITSELF? *Public Interest 1977 (46): 3-14.* A government agency will have much difficulty in accomplishing its goals, if, to do so, it must change or modify the behavior of another government agency. Illustrations include the Office of Management and Budget and the VA hospitals, the Environmental Protection Agency and the Tennessee Valley Authority, the Federal Aviation Administration and the Defense Department, and, in Boston, the Housing Inspection Department and the Boston Housing Authority. The clearest example is affirmative action employment policies, which the Office of Federal Contracts Compliance has failed to get other federal agencies to follow. Interagency control is not always difficult. One agency can control the behavior of another if the second agency does not regard the constraint as a threat to its political autonomy.

S. Harrow

3478. Wilson, James Q. THE CHANGING FBI: THE ROAD TO ABSCAM. *Public Interest 1980 (59): 3-14.* The Federal Bureau of Investigation (FBI) has not launched a vendetta against Congress with Operation Abscam. Changing priorities of the FBI during the 1970's because of congressional pressure led to emphasis on white-collar and organized crime rather than on domestic security cases. Investigation of Congress itself is a logical outgrowth of the FBI's increasing undercover investigation of white-collar crime.

J. M. Herrick

3479. Witze, Claude. WHO'S IN CHARGE OF THE MONEY? *Air Force Mag. 1973 56(4): 30-33.* Examines the conflict between presidential and congressional authority over military finance, 1973.

3480. Wright, Esmond. FIRST IN WAR, FIRST IN PEACE: THE AMERICAN PRESIDENCY UNDER CHALLENGE. *Round Table [Great Britain] 1975 (260): 389-399.* Discusses the relationship between Congress and the Presidency, focusing on the growth of executive leadership in foreign affairs during the 20th century. Although Congress controls the purse strings and can veto presidential policy, it cannot formulate its own foreign policy or compete with the President's wartime role as Commander-in-Chief. Despite Watergate, Vietnam, and the increased willingness of Congress to veto overseas commitments, the Presidency has dominated both foreign and domestic policy.

C. Anstey

3481. Yarwood, Dean L. OVERSIGHT OF PRESIDENTIAL FUNDS BY THE APPROPRIATIONS COMMITTEES: LEARNING FROM THE WATERGATE CRISIS. *Administration and Soc. 1981 13(3): 299-346.* Examines congressional oversight of the use of the Special Projects Fund, the lack of distinction between it and the Emergency Fund for the President, and the absence of authorization for the White House Office, Salaries and Expenses Fund; though some lessons were learned about oversight of executive funds as a result of Watergate, other more basic lessons have been ignored.

3482. Zahniser, Marvin R., ed. JOHN W. BRICKER REFLECTS UPON THE FIGHT FOR THE BRICKER AMENDMENT. *Ohio Hist. 1978 87(3): 322-333.* Discusses the 1954 Senate Joint Resolution 102 (the Bricker Amendment) and includes Bricker's explanation and defense of that proposed constitutional amendment in the form of an after-dinner speech to a convention of foreign policy historians in 1976. Bricker argued that the amendment, which was intended to limit the president's abilities to negotiate treaties and executive agreements, to limit the widening powers of the Supreme Court, and to halt interference from the UN and One Worlders, was undermined by the opposition of John J. McCloy and John Foster Dulles of the Eisenhower administration. It lost in the Senate, by one vote. Based on the Bricker Amendment, the Congressional Record, and the Journal of the Senate; photo, 13 notes.

L. A. Russell

3483. Zeidenstein, Harvey G. PRESIDENTIAL POPULARITY AND PRESIDENTIAL SUPPORT IN CONGRESS: EISENHOWER TO CARTER. *Presidential Studies Q. 1980 10(2): 224-233.* During 1953-78, presidential popularity has led to more presidential support in Congress. The variation of presidential support during this period can be explained by the variation in his popularity in the Gallup polls: the more popular the president, the more likely he is to gain support for his programs in Congress. Eisenhower was the major exception, but his case can suggest links between popularity and support. 2 tables, fig., 13 notes.

D. H. Cline

3484. Zeidenstein, Harvey G. THE REASSERTION OF CONGRESSIONAL POWER: NEW CURBS ON THE PRESIDENT. *Pol. Sci. Q. 1978 93(3): 393-409.* Surveys the provisions legislated by Congress from 1972 to 1977 to restrict the freedom of action of presidents in foreign policy, military deployments, weapons procurement and sales, intelligence activities, and impoundment of funds. He shows how some of these provisions go beyond strengthening the influence of Congress in its traditional legislative role and extend to giving Congress vetoes over specific administrative acts.   J

3485. Zeidenstein, Harvey G. THE TWO PRESIDENCIES THESIS IS ALIVE AND WELL AND HAS BEEN LIVING IN THE U.S. SENATE SINCE 1973. *Presidential Studies Q. 1981 11(4): 511-525.* Reexamines Aaron Wildavsky's two presidencies thesis. In studying congressional votes between 1957 and 1980, the two presidencies can be seen as less a function of high foreign policy and defense support than of relatively low domestic program support. This is largely due to a decrease in Senate support for presidential domestic policy. Based primarily on congressional roll calls; 5 tables, 16 notes.   D. H. Cline

3486. Zimmerman, Deirdre A. CHIEF EXECUTIVES AND THE BUDGET: CONTROLLING THE CONTROLLERS. *Natl. Civic Rev. 1981 70(7): 356-360.* A major source of congressional irritation with

presidents has been executive impoundments of appropriations, which became more common by the early 1970's. The 1974 Congressional Budget and Impoundment Control Act dealt with policies and priorities and review of impoundments, in effect establishing a legislative veto the constitutionality of which has never been clearly established. In New York, the legislature has not challenged the governor's impoundment authority, but a county did so in 1980 and won.   J

3487. —. [PRESIDENTIAL POPULARITY POLLS]. *Am. Pol. Sci. Rev. 1979 73(2): 543-546.*
Darcy, R. and Schramm, Sarah Slavin. COMMENT ON KERNELL, *pp. 543-545.* Criticizes Samuel Kernell for relying so heavily on Gallup polls. Polls frequently inquire about presidential popularity after asking other questions about the president; they can thereby prejudice the results. Polls sample individuals at a given time and place, but there is no sampling of polls. Some opinion sampling on a "before" question has taken place during or after the event. Ref.
Kernell, Samuel. REPLY, *pp. 545-546.* Darcy and Schramm do not provide evidence of bias in Gallup polls. Available data suggests no such bias. Possible bias should be considered, but these authors have blown it out of proportion. Ref.   V. L. Human

3488. —. [PRESIDENTS AND STAFFS]. *Administration and Soc. 1977 9(3): 267-304.*
Dexter, Lewis. COURT POLITICS: PRESIDENTIAL STAFF RELATIONS AS A SPECIAL CASE OF A GENERAL PHENOMENON, *pp. 267-284.* Examines "courts," the habit which leaders display of surrounding themselves with agents, cabinets, surrogates, etc., and this tendency in the presidency, 1940's-70's.
Marvick, Elizabeth W.; Fenn, Dan H., Jr.; and Rourke, Francis E. COMMENTS ON LEWIS DEXTER'S "COURT POLITICS," *pp. 285-304.* Reactions to Dexter's theories on staff relations and internal policymaking, both in the broad historical sense and as a direct application to the presidency.

3489. —. RICHARD NEUSTADT'S *PRESIDENTIAL POWER* TWENTY YEARS LATER: THE TEST OF TIME. *Presidential Studies Q. 1981 11(3): 341-363.*
Wegee, David G. NEUSTADT'S *PRESIDENTIAL POWER:* THE TEST OF TIME AND EMPIRICAL RESEARCH ON THE PRESIDENCY, *pp. 342-347.* Neustadt's landmark study has contributed an adequate model on researching the presidency, but it needs much more work in the development of an empirical theory.
Thomas, Norman C. NEUSTADT'S *PRESIDENTIAL POWER* AFTER TWENTY YEARS, *pp. 348-350.* Neustadt's power-maximizing model of presidential leadership provided a much needed counterweight to Edward Corwin's earlier institutional model based on the formal powers of the president.
Bailey, Harry A., Jr. NEUSTADT'S THESIS REVISITED: TOWARD THE TWO FACES OF PRESIDENTIAL POWER, *pp. 351-357.* Neustadt's view of the presidency is at its best when used in coordination with Corwin's earlier thesis. Neither can stand alone, but both are still valuable.
Rockman, Bert A. NEUSTADT'S *PRESIDENTIAL POWER:* SOME RESIDUAL ISSUES, *pp. 358-360.* Trust is the main glue that can hold a democracy together and help it work smoothly. It legitimizes an administration and allows it to be effective.
Neustadt, Richard E. PRESIDENTIAL POWER: A REFLECTIVE VIEW, *pp. 361-363.* Neustadt's book was inspired by a sense of shock over how the presidency was analyzed in literature as opposed to his experience as an aide to Roosevelt and Truman. The literature, even 20 years later, however, is still incomplete.

D. H. Cline

SUBJECT INDEX

Subject Profile Index (ABC-SPIndex) carries both generic and specific index terms. Begin a search at the general term but also look under more specific or related terms. Cross-references are included.

Each string of index descriptors is intended to present a profile of a given article; however, no particular relationship between any two terms in the profile is implied. Terms within the profile are listed alphabetically after the leading term. The variety of punctuation and capitalization reflects production methods and has no intrinsic meaning; e.g., there is no difference in meaning between "History, study of" and "History (study of)."

Cities, towns, and counties are listed following their respective states or provinces; e.g., "Ohio (Columbus)." Terms beginning with an arabic numeral are listed after the letter Z. The chronology of the bibliographic entry follows the subject index descriptors. In the chronology, "c" stands for "century"; e.g., "19c" means "19th century."

Note that "United States" is not used as a leading index term; if no country is mentioned, the index entry refers to the United States alone. When an entry refers to both Canada and the United States, both "Canada" and "USA" appear in the string of index descriptors, but "USA" is not a leading term. When an entry refers to any other country and the United States, only the other country is indexed.

The last number in the index string, in italics, refers to the bibliographic entry number.

A

Ability. Attitudes. Economic opportunity. Lincoln, Abraham. Military Service. ca 1830-65. *408*

Abolition Movement *See also* Antislavery Sentiments; Emancipation.

—. Constitutional Union Party. Political Campaigns (presidential). Republican Party. 1860. *661*

Abortion. Catholic Church. Democratic Party. Elections (presidential). 1976. *1914*

Abraham Lincoln Library and Museum. Lincoln and Lincolniana. Lincoln Memorial University. Tennessee (Harrogate). 1977. *580*

Abrahamsen, David. Nixon, Richard M. (review article). Psychohistory. 1913-78. *1758*

Abramson, Paul R. Aldrich, John H. Elections (review article). Pomper, Gerald. Ranney, Austin. Rohde, David W. 1980. *1975*

Accountability. Central Intelligence Agency. Confidentiality. Congress. 1940's-74. *3425*

—. Congress. Executive Power. 1973-78. *3455*

Acheson, Dean. Balance of power. Foreign policy. Kissinger, Henry A. 1945-76. *2581*

—. Baruch, Bernard. Cold War. Diplomacy. Foreign policy. Nuclear Arms. Roosevelt, Franklin D. Stimson, Henry L. Truman, Harry S. USSR. 1942-46. *1489*

—. China. Diplomacy. Foreign Relations. 1944-50. *3168*

—. Cold War. Kissinger, Henry A. Politics. State Secretaries. ca 1945-76. *2854*

—. Foreign policy (review article). Kennan, George F. Smith, Gaddis. 1948-63. *2788*

—. Intervention. Korean War. Truman, Harry S. USSR. 1950. *2597*

—. Letters. Truman, Harry S. 1953-65. *1708*

ACTION (agency). Brown, Sam. Carter, Jimmy (administration). Federal Programs. VISTA. 1977-78. *2460*

—. Brown, Sam. Peace Corps. 1977-78. *2234*

Actors and Actresses. Films. Lincoln, Abraham. 1809-65. 1900-77. *466*

Adair, Douglass. *Federalist* No. 10. Hume, David. Madison, James. Political Theory. Republicanism. Wills, Garry. 1788. *238*

Adams, Abigail. Adams, John. Letters. 1762-84. *283*

—. Adams, John Quincy. Adolescence. 1767-1800. *483*

—. American Revolution. Warren, Mercy Otis. Washington, Martha. Women. 18c. *312*

—. Massachusetts. 1744-1818. *210*

Adams, Abigail Amelia. Tyler, Royall. 1782-85. *251*

Adams, Brooks. Adams, Henry Brooks. Adams, John Quincy. Historiography. 1767-1848. 1880-1920. *509*

Adams family. Archival Catalogs and Inventories. Belknap, Jeremy. Jefferson, Thomas. Massachusetts Historical Society. Washington, George. 1791-1960. *554*

—. Attitudes. Communications Behavior. Family. Generations. 1764-1919. *113*

Adams, Henry Brooks. Adams, Brooks. Adams, John Quincy. Historiography. 1767-1848. 1880-1920. *509*

—. Historiography. Jackson, Andrew. 1801-17. *753*

Adams, Henry Brooks *(Democracy)*. Presidential transitions. Reagan, Nancy. 1880-1981. *1773*

Adams, John. Adams, Abigail. Letters. 1762-84. *283*

—. American Revolution. Appointments to office. Congress. Military General Staff. Washington, George. 1775. *304*

—. American Revolution. Books. Emigration. Great Britain. Political Theory. 1776. *182*

—. American Revolution. Founding Fathers. Madison, James. Pufendorf, Samuel von *(On the Law of Nature and Nations)*. Sweden. Washington, George. 1632-1776. *315*

—. American Revolution (antecedents). Boston Massacre. Common law. Lawyers. Massachusetts. 1770. *328*

—. American Revolution (antecedents). Boston Massacre. Lawyers. Morality. Political Speeches. 1768-70. *190*

—. American Revolution (antecedents). Episcopal Church, Protestant. Letters. Weller, George. 1770's. 1824-25. *258*

—. American Revolution (antecedents). Government. Great Britain. Law. Massachusetts. 1760's-70's. *364*

—. American Revolution (antecedents). Hutchinson, Thomas. Massachusetts. Otis, James, Jr. Patriotism. 1761-76. *343*

—. Armies. Elections (presidential). Legislation. Military appointments. Politics and the Military. 1798-1800. *743*

—. Autobiography. Franklin, Benjamin. Jefferson, Thomas. Woolman, John. 18c. *183*

—. Beccaria, Cesare. Crime and Criminals. Declaration of Independence. Founding Fathers. Jefferson, Thomas. Madison, James. 1764-89. *246*

—. Books (editions). Editors and Editing (review article). 1775-76. 1977-79. *383*

—. Brown, Mather. Jefferson, Thomas. Portraits. 1785-88. *300*

—. Buchanan, James. Eisenhower, Dwight D. Harding, Warren G. Taft, William H. 1797-1961. *158*

—. Burke, Edmund. Government. Political Power. Senate. 1770-1800. *230*

—. Conservatism. DeLolme, Jean Louis. Political theory. Radicals and Radicalism. Turgot, Anne Robert. 1760-1800. *179*

—. Constitutions, State. Lee, Richard Henry. Virginia. 1775-76. *341*

—. Constitutions, State. Massachusetts. 1779. *267*

—. Constitutions, State. Massachusetts. 1780. *327*

—. Consular Service. Foreign Relations. Franklin, Benjamin. 1780. *360*

—. Courts. Executive Branch. Extradition. Foreign Relations. Great Britain. Jay Treaty. Robbins, Jonathan. Separation of powers. 1796-1804. *980*

—. Diplomats. Netherlands. 1780-82. *386*

—. Duane, William. Exiles. Great Britain. Journalists. Press. 1790-1800. *712*

—. Europe. Foreign policy. Free trade. Mercantilism. 1775-85. *209*

—. Federalist Party. Hamilton, Alexander. Jefferson, Thomas. Political Factions. Washington, George. 1775-90's. *720*

—. Founding Fathers. Jefferson, Thomas. Language. Washington, George. 1760's-70's. *218*

—. Friendship. Jefferson, Thomas. 1775-1826. *249*

—. Jefferson, Thomas. Madison, James. Monroe, James. Presidents. Role models. Washington, George. ca 1750's-1820's. *292*

—. Jefferson, Thomas. Presidents. Rush, Benjamin. 1796-1811. *323*

—. Lawyers. Massachusetts (Braintree, Worcester). Putnam, James. Teaching. 1755-58. *252*

—. Science. Technology. 1770-1825. *263*

—. Vice-presidency. 1789-97. *759*

Adams, John ("Plan of Treaties"). American Revolution. France. Franklin, Benjamin. Treaties. 1776. *287*

Adams, John (review article). Behavior. Brown, Ralph Adams. Political Power. Shaw, Peter. 1760's-1801. 1975-76. *197*

Adams, John Quincy. Adams, Abigail. Adolescence. 1767-1800. *483*

—. Adams, Brooks. Adams, Henry Brooks. Historiography. 1767-1848. 1880-1920. *509*

—. Americas (North and South). Letters. Monroe Doctrine. 1823. *979*

—. Antislavery Sentiments. Censorship. House of Representatives. South. 1831-48. *566*

—. Assimilation. Attitudes. Indians. Removals, forced. 1802-41. *526*

—. Book collecting (German). Libraries. Massachusetts (Quincy). 1781-ca 1801. *508*

—. Cuba. Expansionism. Monroe Doctrine. 1823. *967*

—. Democratic Party. Elections (presidential). Jackson, Andrew. Slavery. Whig Party. 1828-44. *923*

—. Diplomacy. Fishing. Great Britain. Monroe, James. Newfoundland. 1815-18. *991*

—. Diplomacy. Monroe Doctrine. Monroe, James. Pacific Northwest. Russia. 1812-23. *1000*

—. Elections (presidential). Jackson, Andrew. Missouri. 1828. *654*

—. Foreign policy. House of Representatives. Secession. 1842. *527*

—. Foreign Relations. Latin America. Monroe Doctrine. 1823. *974*

—. House of Representatives. 1831-48. *469*

—. House of Representatives. Political Leadership. Presidency. 1783-1848. *486*

—. Poetry. Rhey, Mary E. 1843. *412*

Adams, John Quincy *(Conquest of Ireland)*. Adultery. Ireland. Jackson, Andrew. MacMurrogh, Dermot. Politics. 1828-31. *489*

Adams, John Quincy (death). Nationalism. 1848. *528*

Adams, Louisa Catherine Johnson. First Ladies. 1775-1852. *415*

Addams, Jane. Foreign policy. Ideology. Open Door Policy. Wilson, Woodrow. 1900-20. *1623*

Adee, Alvey A. Diplomacy. Foreign relations. State Department. 1870-1924. *1700*

Aden. Florida (Escambia County). Mass media. Political Campaigns (presidential). Television. Voting and Voting Behavior. 1976. *2046*

Adolescence *See also* Youth.

—. Adams, Abigail. Adams, John Quincy. 1767-1800. *483*

—. Political attitudes. Presidents. 1960's-77. *3332*

Adultery. Adams, John Quincy *(Conquest of Ireland).* Ireland. Jackson, Andrew. MacMurrogh, Dermot. Politics. 1828-31. *489*

—. Harding, Warren G. Letters. Ohio (Marion). Phillips, Carrie. 1905-20. 1963-78. *1119*

Advertising *See also* Marketing; Propaganda; Public Relations; Publicity; Salesmen and Salesmanship.

—. Americas (North and South). Commercial Bureau of the American Republics. Foreign Relations. International Union. State Department. 1894-1902. *1053*

—. Campaign Finance. Elections (presidential). Television. Voting and Voting Behavior. 1972. *2021*

—. Children. Federal Regulation. Television. 1970-81. *2360*

—. Children. Political Campaigns (presidential). Reporters and reporting. Television. 1976. *1795*

—. Fugitive Slaves. Historiography. Jackson, Andrew. *Tennessee Gazette* (newspaper). 1804. 1977. *471*

—. Political Campaigns. Television. 1960-76. *1939*

—. Political Campaigns (presidential). Reporters and Reporting. Television. 1972. *1919*

Advisory committees. Industrial Relations. Presidents. 1955-80. *2447*

Aesthetics. Documentaries. Eisenhower, Dwight D. Heroism. *Ike* (program). Television. World War II. ca 1941-45. 1979. *1720*

Afghanistan. Carter, Jimmy (administration). Cold War. Decisionmaking. Defense spending. Inflation. Iran. USSR. 1979-80. *2284*

—. Carter, Jimmy (administration). Foreign policy. Hutson, Thomas R. Invasions. Personal narratives. USSR. 1980-81. *2797*

AFL-CIO. Carter, Jimmy. Democratic Party. Labor Unions and Organizations. Public welfare. 1976. *2063*

Africa. Carter, Jimmy (administration). Foreign policy. 1975-80. *2848*

—. Carter, Jimmy (administration). Foreign Policy. Human rights. 1979. *2956*

—. Central Intelligence Agency. Intelligence Service (review article). Marchetti, Victor. Marks, John D. 1974. *2957*

—. Cuba. Foreign policy. Intervention. USSR. ca 1970-77. *3026*

—. Easum, Donald. Kissinger, Henry A. State Department. 1969-75. *2953*

—. Foreign Policy. 1974-81. *3103*

—. Foreign policy. 1977-81. *2899*

—. Foreign policy. Kissinger, Henry A. 1974-76. *2887*

—. Foreign Policy. Kissinger, Henry A. 1976. *2656*

—. Foreign Policy. Nixon, Richard M. State of the World address. 1973. *2938*

—. Foreign Relations. 1978-81. *2824*

Africa, East. Carter, Jimmy (administration). Foreign Policy. 1970's. *2723*

Africa, Southern. Carter, Jimmy (administration). Economic interests. Foreign policy. 1976-77. *2876*

Afro-Americans. *See* Negroes.

Age. Elections, presidential. Voting and Voting Behavior. 1964-78. *1813*

Aged *See also* Death and Dying; Public Welfare.

—. Politics. White House Conferences on Aging. 1950-71. *2469*

Agendas. Carter, Jimmy. Debates. Ford, Gerald R. Political Campaigns (presidential). 1976. *1799*

—. Decisionmaking. Domestic Policy. Presidents. 1961-80. *2424*

Agent General. Appointments to Office. Coolidge, Calvin (administration). Diplomacy. Finance. Germany. Reparations. 1923-24. *1572*

Agnew, Spiro T. Ethics. Morality. Political Corruption. Watergate Scandal. 1960's-70's. *2490*

—. Greek Americans. Public Opinion. 1960's-70's. *2466*

—. McGovern, George S. Nixon, Richard M. Political speechwriting. Reagan, Ronald. Rhetoric. 1968-70's. *2261*

Agnew, Spiro T. (resignation). Political Speeches. Reporters and Reporting. Rhetoric. 1973. *2243*

Agrarianism. Classicism. Jefferson, Thomas. 1780-1825. *379*

Agricultural Adjustment Act (US, 1933). Commodities. Federal Programs. Iowa. New Deal. Wallace, Henry A. 1933-34. *1357*

Agricultural Adjustment Administration. Federal Government. National Recovery Administration. 1933-39. *1436*

—. New Deal. Soil Conservation Service. 1933-41. *1422*

Agricultural Adjustment Administration (Office of the General Counsel). Dale, Chester. Frank, Jerome. Wallace, Henry A. 1935. *1362*

Agricultural Commodities. Elections (presidential). Farmers. Iowa. Prices. Voting and Voting Behavior. 1948. *2055*

Agricultural Labor. California. Labor Unions and Organizations. National Industrial Recovery Act (US, 1933). 1933-34. *1282*

Agricultural Marketing Act (US, 1929). Coolidge, Calvin. Federal Farm Board. Hoover, Herbert C. McNary, Charles L. Prices. Surpluses. 1924-29. *1340*

Agricultural policy. Commerce Department. Economic policy. Hoover, Herbert C. 1921-29. *1351*

—. Congress. Democratic Party. Federal Programs. Presidents. South. 1933-61. *141*

—. Corporatism, concept of. Hoover, Herbert C. Politics. Roosevelt, Franklin D. 1929-33. *1295*

—. Economic development. Hoover, Herbert C. 1921-28. *1458*

—. Patent Office. 1836-62. *1039*

Agriculture *See also* Agricultural Labor; Conservation of Natural Resources; Dairying; Forests and Forestry; Land; Land Tenure; Livestock; Plantations.

—. Droughts. Kansas. New Deal. Political Campaigns (presidential). 1936. *1194*

—. Federal Programs. Indian-White Relations. Missions and Missionaries. Old Northwest. 1789-1820. *818*

—. Hamilton, Alexander. Jefferson, Thomas. Manufactures. Political Theory. ca 1775-1800. *823*

—. Missouri. Truman, Harry S. 1906-17. *1753*

Agriculture Department. Benson, Ezra Taft. Cattle raising. Eisenhower, Dwight D. (administration). Livestock. Prices. 1953-60. *2493*

—. Benson, Ezra Taft. Idaho. Mormons. Personal narratives. State Government. 1940's-61. *2299*

—. Budgets. Congress. Interest groups. 1971-76. *3365*

—. Butz, Earl. Food Supply. 1974. *2446*

—. Butz, Earl (resignation). Public Opinion. Racism. 1970's. *2403*

—. Citizen Lobbies. 1960-80. *3208*

—. Dyes. Federal regulation. Food. Public Health. 1913-19. *1334*

—. Employment. Equal opportunity. Federal policy. 1964-76. *3392*

—. Federal Government. Interest groups. 1974-76. *2436*

—. Marketing. Research and Marketing Act (US, 1946). 1940-55. *3214*

—. Mobilization. World War I. 1910's. *1281*

—. Scientists. Women. 1862-1975. *3*

Aid to Families with Dependent Children. Bureaucracies. Executive Power. Federal Policy. Nixon, Richard M. (administration). 1969-74. *2472*

Aides-de-camp. American Revolution. Washington, George. 1775-94. *208*

Aiken, George. Congress. Documents. Jenkins, Walter. Johnson, Lyndon B. Mansfield, Mike. Tonkin Gulf Crisis (conference). Vietnam War. 1964. *3088*

Air Forces *See also* Air Warfare.

—. Bombing. Cambodia. Executive power. Holtzman, Elizabeth. Trials. 1973. *2917*

—. Bombing. Japan (Kyoto). Stimson, Henry L. World War II. 1940-45. *1502*

—. Defense Policy. F-111 (aircraft). McNamara, Robert S. Navies. Vietnam War. 1960-70. *2675*

—. Hastie, William Henry. Race relations. World War II. 1940-43. *1377*

—. White House Fellows Programs. 1964-73. *3318*

Air Lines. Civil Aeronautics Board. Kuter, Laurence S. Personal Narratives. Truman, Harry S. 1948. *2408*

Air mail service. Black, Hugo. Contracts. Farley, James A. Hoover, Herbert C. (administration). Legislative Investigations. 1933-34. *1440*

Air power. Eisenhower, Dwight D. Military strategy. Truman, Harry S. 1947-55. *2931*

Air Warfare *See also* Airplanes, Military; Atomic Warfare.

—. Bombing. Churchill, Winston. Military General Staff. Normandy Invasion. Roosevelt, Franklin D. World War II. 1944. *1684*

Airlift, military. Eisenhower, Dwight D. Kennedy, John F. Kerby, Robert L. Laos. War. 1958-63. *2819*

Airplane Industry and Trade. Business. Defense policy. Military-industrial complex. Truman, Harry S. 1945-53. *2231*

—. Joint Aircraft Committee. National Defense Advisory Commission. Office of Production Management. Technological change. World War II. 1940-45. *1226*

Airplanes, Military. Greece. Military Aid. Roosevelt, Franklin D. (administration). World War II. 1940-41. *1618*

Alabama. Clergy. New Deal. Roosevelt, Franklin D. 1935-36. *1259*

—. Democratic Party. Federal Elections Bill. Political Campaigns. South. Stevenson, Adlai E. (1835-1914). 1889-93. *685*

—. Dinsmoor, Silas. Indian agents. Jackson, Andrew. Mississippi. Passports. 1811-12. *590*

—. Harding, Warren G. Washington (Seattle). 1923. *1299*

—. Indian-White Relations. Jackson, Andrew. Mississippi. 1789-1817. *448*

—. Politics. Wallace, George C. 1958-70. *1807*

Alabama (Dothan). Civil Service. Clayton, Henry D. Patronage. Postal Service. Taft, William H. Wilson, Woodrow (administration). 1900-13. *1415*

Alabama (Florence). Architecture. Wakefield (mansion). Washington, George. 1825-1979. *253*

Alabama (Mobile). Cuba. Economic conditions. McKinley, William. Petitions. Spanish-American War. 1897-98. *1005*

Alabama (Montgomery). 1885-87. *903*

Alaska *See also* Far Western States.

—. Emmons, George T. Roosevelt, Theodore. Tongass National Forest. 1902. *1274*

—. Harding, Warren G. Travel. 1923. *1456*

Alaska Reorganization Act (US, 1936). Aleuts. Eskimos. Federal Policy. Indians. 1936-45. *1400*

Alcohol. Bureau of Alcohol, Tobacco and Firearms. Federal Policy. Food additives. 1972-81. *2388*

Aldrich, John H. Abramson, Paul R. Elections (review article). Pomper, Gerald. Ranney, Austin. Rohde, David W. 1980. *1975*

Aleuts. Alaska Reorganization Act (US, 1936). Eskimos. Federal Policy. Indians. 1936-45. *1400*

Alexander, Charles C. Cold War. Eisenhower, Dwight D. (review article). Foreign policy. 1952-61. *2146*

—. Congress. Eisenhower, Dwight D. (review article). Reichard, Gary. 1953-61. *2247*

Algeria. Communism. Kennedy, John F. Nationalism. Vietnam War. 1950's-63. *2941*

Aliano, Richard A. Defense Policy (review article). Eisenhower, Dwight D. (administration). Killian, James R., Jr. Kinnard, Douglas. Kistiakowsky, George B. Military Strategy. 1953-61. *2627*

Alien Anarchist Act (US, 1918). Anti-Communist Movements. Congress. Law Enforcement. Leftism. Post, Louis F. 1919-20. *1268*

Alien Property Custodian. Banking. Crowley, Leo T. Federal Deposit Insurance Corporation. Politics. Roosevelt, Franklin D. (administration). 1934-45. *1454*

Aliens *See also* Immigration.

—. California. Japan. Johnson, Hiram W. Land Tenure. Webb-Heney Act (1913). Wilson, Woodrow. 1911-13. *1231*

Aliens, illegal. Amnesty. Carter, Jimmy. Legislation. 1976-77. *2348*

Allende, Salvador. Central Intelligence Agency. Chile. Coups d'etat. 1972-73. *2930*

—. Central Intelligence Agency. Chile. Foreign Policy. Multinational corporations. 1970-73. *2960*

—. Chile. Intervention. Kissinger, Henry A. *(White House Years).* 1973. *2612*

Alliance for Progress. Brazil. Kennedy, John F. (administration). Multinational Corporations. Nationalization. 1961-63. *2861*

—. Economic development. Latin America. 1961-62. *2849*

Alliances *See also* International Relations (discipline); Treaties.

—. Brzezinski, Zbigniew. National security. 1966-78. *2669*

Boer War. Anglo-Saxonism. Hay, John Milton. Public Opinion. Racism. Rhetoric. Roosevelt, Theodore. 1899-1900. *969*

Boggs, Thomas Hale. Federal Bureau of Investigation. Hoover, J. Edgar. Speeches, Addresses, etc. 1971. *3273*

Bohlen, Charles E. Cold War (origins). Kennan, George F. State Department. Yergin, Daniel H. (review article). 1945-50. *2779*

—. Containment. Kennan, George F. Robinson, Gerold T. State Department. USSR. 1945-46. *2913*

—. Documents. Europe, Eastern. Foreign Policy. State Department. USSR. 1945-46. *2891*

Bombing. Air Forces. Cambodia. Executive power. Holtzman, Elizabeth. Trials. 1973. *2917*

—. Air Forces. Japan (Kyoto). Stimson, Henry L. World War II. 1940-45. *1502*

—. Air Warfare. Churchill, Winston. Military General Staff. Normandy Invasion. Roosevelt, Franklin D. World War II. 1944. *1684*

—. Cambodia. Impeachment. Nixon, Richard M. Vietnam War. 1969-74. *2673*

—. Cambodia. Nixon, Richard M. Political Systems. Vietnam War. 1970. *2860*

Bombing halt. Foreign policy. Johnson, Lyndon B. Political Speeches. Public Opinion. Vietnam War. 1968-78. *3060*

Bonneville Power Administration. Electric utilities. New Deal. Pacific Northwest. Public Utilities. 1937-42. *1302*

Book Collecting See also Rare Books.

—. Jefferson, Thomas. 1770's-1820's. *282*

—. Presidents. 1789-1976. *87*

Book collecting (German). Adams, John Quincy. Libraries. Massachusetts (Quincy). 1781-ca 1801. *508*

Books See also Authors; Copyright; Libraries; Literature; Press; Publishers and Publishing; Rare Books.

—. Adams, John. American Revolution. Emigration. Great Britain. Political Theory. 1776. *182*

—. Biographers. Politics. Values. Washington, George. Weems, Mason. ca 1790-1820. 1980. *378*

—. Jefferson, Thomas. Madison, James. 1781-1832. *337*

Books (editions). Adams, John. Editors and Editing (review article). 1775-76. 1977-79. *383*

Books, subscription. Hayes, Rutherford B. Salesmen and Salesmanship. 1870's. *431*

Booth, John Wilkes. Assassination. Diaries. *Lincoln Conspiracy* (book, film). Stanton, Edwin M. 1865. 1977. *262*

—. Assassination. District of Columbia. Lincoln, Abraham. Personal narratives. Sawyer, Frederick A. 1865. *552*

—. Assassination. Lincoln, Abraham. 1865. *393*

—. Conspiracy. Defense Department. Eisenschiml, Otto. Kidnapping. Lincoln, Abraham. Research. 1865. ca 1930-80. *835*

Borglum, Gutzon. Mount Rushmore. Public opinion. Sculpture. South Dakota. 1923-73. *68*

Boritt, G. S. (review article). American Dream. Economic Theory. Lincoln, Abraham. Political Leadership. Social mobility. 1840's-64. 1978. *452*

Bossism. Barnes, William, Jr. Lawsuits. New York. Republican Party. Roosevelt, Theodore. 1915. *1062*

Boston Massacre. Adams, John. American Revolution (antecedents). Common law. Lawyers. Massachusetts. 1770. *328*

—. Adams, John. American Revolution (antecedents). Lawyers. Morality. Political Speeches. 1768-70. *190*

Boston *Pilot*. Catholic Church. Civil War. Irish Americans. Lincoln, Abraham. Massachusetts. Reporters and Reporting. 1840-72. *955*

Boundaries See also Annexation; Geopolitics.

—. Anglophobia. Aroostook War. Canada. Great Britain. VanBuren, Martin. 1837-39. *999*

—. Bowman, Isaiah. East Prussia. Germany. Oder-Neisse Line. Poland. State Department (Advisory Committee on Post-War Foreign Policy). Welles, Sumner. World War II. 1942-45. *1649*

—. Foreign Policy. Great Britain. Italy. World War II. Yugoslavia. 1941-45. *1493*

—. Foreign Policy. Oder-Neisse Line. Poland. Roosevelt, Franklin D. State Department. Truman, Harry S. World War II. 1941-45. *1609*

—. Foreign Relations. Italy. League of Nations. Paris Peace Conference. Wilson, Woodrow (administration). 1919-22. *1577*

Bounties. Civil War. Lincoln, Abraham. Military Recruitment. Staples, John Summerfield. 1864. *947*

Bourgeoisie. See Middle Classes.

Bourgois, Philippe. El Salvador. Foreign policy. Personal narratives. Reagan, Ronald (administration). Revolution. 1981. *2613*

Boutwell, George S. House of Representatives. Impeachment. Johnson, Andrew. 1865-68. *812*

Bowles, Chester. Decisionmaking. Kennedy, John F. (administration). Personality. Political leadership. 1953-78. *3154*

Bowman, Isaiah. Boundaries. East Prussia. Germany. Oder-Neisse Line. Poland. State Department (Advisory Committee on Post-War Foreign Policy). Welles, Sumner. World War II. 1942-45. *1649*

Boyd, Ben. Body snatching. Kinealy, James. Lincoln, Abraham. 1874-88. *557*

Boyd, Julian Parks (obituary). Editors and Editing. Historians. Jefferson, Thomas. 1943-80. *375*

Braeman, John (review article). Historiography. New Deal. Reform. State government. 1930's-40's. *1354*

—. New Deal. Politics. Roosevelt, Franklin D. 1930's. *1363*

Branch, Taylor (review article). Dean, John. Nixon, Richard M. (administration). Watergate scandal. 1972. *2462*

Brandeis, Louis D. Frankfurter, Felix. New Deal. Politics. Roosevelt, Franklin D. World War I. 1917-33. *1287*

Brauer, Carl M. (review article). Civil rights. Kennedy, John F. Legislation. 1961-63. *2527*

Brazil. Alliance for Progress. Kennedy, John F. (administration). Multinational Corporations. Nationalization. 1961-63. *2861*

—. Carter, Jimmy. Foreign Policy. 1978-79. *2720*

—. Cold war. Foreign Relations. 1945-60. *2785*

—. Democracy. Foreign Policy. 1964-68. *2862*

Breckinridge, John C. Buchanan, James. Democratic Party. Iowa (Pella). Michigan. Political Campaigns (presidential). Scholte, Henry (Hendrick) P. 1846-56. *706*

—. Secession crisis. South. Voting and Voting Behavior. 1856-61. *660*

Breeding. Lafayette, Marquis de. Mules. Spain. Washington, George. 1780-99. *324*

Brennan, Peter J. Labor Department. Nixon, Richard M. Personal narratives. 1972-74. *2448*

Brezhnev, Leonid. Arms control. Ford, Gerald R. Foreign Relations. Kissinger, Henry A. USSR. Vladivostok Accord. 1974. *3131*

—. Detente. Ford, Gerald R. Vladivostok Accord. 1974. *2936*

Bricker Amendment. American Bar Association. Executive power. Foreign Policy. 1948-54. *3452*

—. Anti-Communist Movements. Eisenhower, Dwight D. Executive power. 1951-58. *3406*

—. Bricker, John W. Dulles, John Foster. Executive agreements. McCloy, John J. Personal narratives. Presidency. Senate. Treaties. 1951-54. 1976. *3482*

Bricker, John W. Bricker Amendment. Dulles, John Foster. Executive agreements. McCloy, John J. Personal narratives. Presidency. Senate. Treaties. 1951-54. 1976. *3482*

Brinkerhoff, Roeliff. Assassination. Lincoln, Abraham. Personal narratives. 1865. *504*

Bristow, Benjamin Helm. Hayes, Rutherford B. Kentucky. Political Campaigns (presidential). Republican Party. 1876. *703*

British Columbia. Annexation. Foreign Policy. Seward, William H. 1865-69. *1020*

British Navy Office. Jones, William. Military Reform. Navy Department. 1813-14. *722*

British Security Coordination. Great Britain. Latin America. Military Intelligence. Office of Coordinator of Commercial and Cultural Relations. Rockefeller, Nelson A. World War II (antecedents). 1940-45. *1586*

Brodie, Fawn M. Children. Historiography. Jefferson, Thomas. Slaves. ca 1771-89. 1974-76. *279*

—. Hemings, Sally. Jefferson, Thomas (review article). Slavery. 1743-1826. *376*

—. Jefferson, Thomas. Mormons. Smith, Joseph. 18c-1844. 1946-79. *303*

—. Nixon, Richard M. Research. 1913-80. *1716*

—. Nixon, Richard M. (review article). 1920's-70's. *1737*

Brookings Institution. Bureaucracies. Health, Education, and Welfare Department. Social Services Grants. 1975. *3430*

Brooks, Noah. Civil War. District of Columbia. Lincoln, Abraham. Reporters and Reporting. 1862-1903. *741*

Brooks, Phillips. Assassination. Episcopal Church, Protestant. Lincoln, Abraham. Pennsylvania (Philadelphia). Sermons. Slavery. 1865. 1893. *421*

Brooks, Preston S. Civil War (antecedents). Congress. Republican Party. Sumner, Charles. Violence. 1856. *635*

Brough, Charles Hillman. Arkansas. Baptists. Elections (presidential). 1928-29. *1169*

Brown, Edmund G. Appointments to office. Brown, Jerry. California. Governors. Judges. Political attitudes. Reagan, Ronald. 1959-79. *1721*

Brown, Harold. Carter, Jimmy. Defense spending. USSR. 1964-80. *2617*

—. Carter, Jimmy (administration). Defense Department. Military Strategy. Strategic Arms Limitation Talks. 1977. *3105*

Brown, Harry J. Civil War. Garfield, James A. (review article). Leech, Margaret. Peskin, Allan. Political Leadership. 1850-81. 1978. *503*

Brown, Jerry. Appointments to office. Brown, Edmund G. California. Governors. Judges. Political attitudes. Reagan, Ronald. 1959-79. *1721*

—. Carter, Jimmy. Democratic Party. Political campaigns (presidential). Political campaigns (Presidential). 1976. *1816*

—. Carter, Jimmy. Federal Policy. Kennedy, Edward M. Politics. 1977-79. *2210*

Brown, John Henry. Lincoln, Abraham. Portraits. 1860-1976. *521*

Brown, Mather. Adams, John. Jefferson, Thomas. Portraits. 1785-88. *300*

Brown, Ralph Adams. Adams, John (review article). Behavior. Political Power. Shaw, Peter. 1760's-1801. 1975-76. *197*

Brown, Sam. ACTION (agency). Carter, Jimmy (administration). Federal Programs. VISTA. 1977-78. *2460*

—. ACTION (agency). Peace Corps. 1977-78. *2234*

Browne, William Garl. Chase, William Merritt. Hayes, Rutherford B. Personality. Portraits. 1870's. 1976. *463*

Brownlow, William G. Civil War. Elections. Johnson, Andrew. State Government. Tennessee. 1860-65. *899*

Bruce, Frederick. Foreign policy. Great Britain. Johnson, Andrew. Letters. Reconstruction. 1866. *821*

Brussels Conference. China. Diplomacy. Japan. Roosevelt, Franklin D. War. 1937. *1661*

Bryan, Charles Wayland. Democratic Party. Political Campaigns (presidential). South Dakota. Vice-Presidents. 1924. *1207*

Bryan, William Jennings. Chafin, Eugene W. Corn Palace. Political Campaigns (presidential). South Dakota (Mitchell). Taft, William H. 1908. *1206*

—. Chile (Santiago). Pan American Conference, 5th. Wilson, Woodrow. World War I. 1914. *1678*

—. Delaware. Foreign Policy. Political Campaigns (presidential). Stevenson, Adlai E. (1835-1914). 1900. *682*

—. Democratic Party. Imperialism. Philippines. Political Campaigns (presidential). Stevenson, Adlai E. (1835-1914). 1900. *690*

—. Democratic Party. Maine (Bath). Political Campaigns (vice-presidential). Sewall, Arthur. 1896. *686*

—. Democratic Party. Political Campaigns (presidential). Stevenson, Adlai E. (1835-1914). 1892-1900. *684*

—. Democratic Party. Political Conventions. Wilson, Woodrow. 1912. *1148*

—. Diplomacy. Lansing, Robert. Wilson, Woodrow. World War I (antecedents). 1913-17. *1511*

—. Elections, presidential. McKinley, William. Nebraska. 1900. *1142*

—. Elections (presidential). Political parties. Reagan, Ronald. Revivals. Social Change. 1730-1980. *175*

—. International Harvester Company. Intervention. Mexico (Yucatán). 1913-15. *1508*

—. McKinley, William. Political Campaigns (presidential). Rhetoric. Voting and Voting Behavior. 1896. *616*

—. Newspapers. Red River of the North (valley). Republican Party. 1890-96. *627*

—. Political Campaigns (presidential). Towne, Charles A. Vice-presidency. 1900. *687*

Brzezinski, Zbigniew. Alliances. National security. 1966-78. *2669*

—. Békés, Rezső. Foreign Policy (review article). Historians. Kissinger, Henry A. 1960's-70's. *2770*

—. Carter, Jimmy (administration). Foreign Policy. 1958-79. *2906*

—. Carter, Jimmy (administration). Foreign policy. 1976-80. *2933*

—. Carter, Jimmy (administration). Foreign policy. Italy. 1977. *2738*

—. Carter, Jimmy (administration). Foreign policy. Middle East. Vance, Cyrus. 1977-80. *3079*

—. Foreign policy. 1954-79. *3167*

—. Foreign policy. 1977-78. *3050*

Brzezinski, Zbigniew (interview). Carter, Jimmy (administration). Foreign policy. 1976-80. *3121*

Buchanan, James. Adams, John. Eisenhower, Dwight D. Harding, Warren G. Taft, William H. 1797-1961. *158*

—. Breckinridge, John C. Democratic Party. Iowa (Pella). Michigan. Political Campaigns (presidential). Scholte, Henry (Hendrick) P. 1846-56. *706*

—. Civil War (antecedents). Kansas. Lecompton Constitution. 1857-61. *873*

—. Democratic Party. Douglas, Stephen A. Elections. Kansas. Lecompton Constitution. Slavery. 1854-60. *624*

—. Democratic Party. Patronage. 1857-61. *892*

—. Douglas, Stephen A. Patronage. Political campaigns (Presidential). 1852-60. *893*

—. Federal Government. Holt, Joseph. Post Office Department. Reform. 1856-60. *776*

—. Federal Policy. Historiography. Mormons. Utah Expedition (1857-58). 1857-58. *881*

—. Historiography. Kansas. Lecompton Constitution. Political Leadership. Slavery. Suffrage. 1857. 20c. *894*

Buchwald, Art. Nixon, Richard M. Political Commentary. Satire. Watergate Scandal. 1972-74. *2471*

Budgets. Agriculture Department. Congress. Interest groups. 1971-76. *3365*

—. Bureau of the Budget. Executive Branch. Office of Management and Budget. ca 1939-70. *3207*

—. Carter, Jimmy. Congress. Decisionmaking. Water projects. 1977. *2494*

—. Carter, Jimmy (administration). Defense Policy. 1978. *2844*

—. Carter, Jimmy (administration). Etzioni, Amitai. Inflation. Personal narratives. 1980. *2341*

—. Congress. Congressional Budget and Impoundment Control Act (US, 1974). Reform. Tax Reform Act (US, 1976). 1974-76. *3344*

—. Congress. Defense spending. Military capability. 1945-78. *3292*

—. Congress. Executive Branch. Impoundment. Nixon, Richard M. (administration). Separation of powers. 1972-73. *2219*

—. Congress. Executive Power. Nixon, Richard M. 1972. *2346*

—. Congress. Fiscal Policy. Impoundment. Nixon, Richard M. Office of Management and Budget. Separation of Powers. 1969-77. *3461*

—. Congressional Budget and Impoundment Control Act (US, 1974). Executive branch. Impoundment. 1974. *3421*

—. Congressional Budget and Impoundment Control Act (US, 1974). Executive Power. Government. Impoundment. New York. 1974-80. *3486*

—. Executive branch. Fiscal policy. Presidents. Public administration. 1953-69. *3372*

—. Executive Branch. House of Representatives (Appropriations Committee). Intergovernmental Relations. Senate Appropriations Committee. Watergate Scandal. 1973-75. *3481*

—. Federal Government. 1960-71. *3432*

—. Federal Government. Office of Management and Budget. 1970's. *3402*

—. Intergovernmental Relations. Office of Management and Budget. Politics. 1970's. *3275*

—. New Deal. Reagan, Ronald. 1930-81. *2502*

—. New Deal. States. 1933-39. *1409*

—. Policymaking. Presidents. 1948-82. *3306*

—. Presidency. 1789-1974. *39*

Buell, Don Carlos. Civil War. Grant, Ulysses S. Lincoln, Abraham. Military General Staff. Political Leadership. 1862-98. *811*

Buffon, Georges Louis Leclerc de. France. Jefferson, Thomas. Moose. Sullivan, John. 1787. *239*

Buildings, public. Artists. Federal Programs. New Deal. 1930's. *1401*

Bulgaria. Alliances. Foreign Policy. Hungary. Romania. World War II. 1943-44. *1666*

Bullard, Arthur. Censorship. Committee on Public Information. Constitutional Amendments (1st). Creel, George. Press. Propaganda. World War I. 1917-20. *1451*

Bullitt, William C. *(For the President)*. Diplomats. Letters. Roosevelt, Franklin D. 1933-41. *1558*

Bundy, McGeorge. Foreign Relations. Historians. Journalism. Kennedy, John F. Personal narratives. 1960-64. *2153*

Burdick v. *United States* (US, 1915). Constitutional Amendments (5th). New York *Tribune*. Pardons. Supreme Court. Wilson, Woodrow. 1913-15. *1262*

Bureau of Alcohol, Tobacco and Firearms. Alcohol. Federal Policy. Food additives. 1972-81. *2388*

—. Civil Rights. Constitutional Amendments (2d). 1970-80. *2420*

Bureau of Health Insurance. Interest groups. Medicare. Oversight, congressional. Public Administration. Senate Finance Committee. 1965-78. *3217*

Bureau of Indian Affairs. Anthropology. Collier, John. Federal Programs. Indians. New Deal. 1930's. *1345*

—. Anthropology. Collier, John. New Deal. Public Administration. 1933-45. *1447*

—. Civil War. Coffin, William G. Federal policy. Indian Territory. Indians. 1861-65. *844*

—. Collier, John. Federal policy. Indians. New Deal. 1933-45. *1448*

—. Conscription, Military. Goshiute Indians. Indians (reservations). Nevada. Political protest. 1917-19. *1294*

—. Criminal law. Federal Programs. Indian Self-Determination and Educational Assistance Act (US, 1975). 1970-82. *2455*

—. Employment. Indians. Wages. 1970's. *3434*

Bureau of Indian Affairs (commissioners). Appointments to Office. Collier, John. Ickes, Harold L. Interior Department. Roosevelt, Franklin D. 1933. *1346*

Bureau of Labor Statistics. Lubin, Isador. New Deal. Perkins, Frances. Statistics. Unemployment. 1920-49. *1314*

Bureau of Labor Statistics (antecedents). Labor Department. Labor unions and organizations. Statistics. 1864-85. *1038*

Bureau of the Budget. Budgets. Executive Branch. Office of Management and Budget. ca 1939-70. *3207*

Bureaucracies. Aid to Families with Dependent Children. Executive Power. Federal Policy. Nixon, Richard M. (administration). 1969-74. *2472*

—. Appointments to Office. Executive Branch. Politics. 1961-80. *3222*

—. Brookings Institution. Health, Education, and Welfare Department. Social Services Grants. 1975. *3430*

—. Cabinet. Foreign policy. Kennedy, John F. (administration). Presidential staffs. State Department. 1961-63. *2647*

—. Cambodia. Foreign policy. Kissinger, Henry A. Nixon, Richard M. (administration). Shawcross, William. State Department. Vietnam War. 1960's-80. *3379*

—. Columbia Valley Authority. Congress. Corporations. Electric Power. Truman, Harry S. (administration). 1945-50. *2330*

—. Congress. Executive Branch. Political Change. Reform. Social change. 1960's-70's. *3353*

—. Congress. Presidency. Supreme Court. 20c. *3373*

—. Corporations. Labor. Poor. Social Classes. War on Poverty. 1964. *2350*

—. Cuban Missile Crisis. Foreign Policy. Kennedy, John F. Turkey. 1962. *2767*

—. Decisionmaking. Foreign Policy. Johnson, Lyndon B. (administration). Nixon, Richard M. (administration). Strategic Arms Limitation Talks. 1966-74. *3009*

—. Decisionmaking. State Department (Foreign Service). 1977. *3215*

—. Defense Department. 1960's-70's. *3418*

—. Economic Policy. Europe. International trade. Wilson, Woodrow. 1917-21. *1229*

—. Economic Policy. Mellon, Andrew W. Taxation. Treasury Department. 1918-32. *1390*

—. Executive Behavior. Federal Government. Politics. ca 1973-76. *3300*

—. Executive branch. Nixon, Richard M., administration. Reform. Watergate scandal. 1970-74. *2497*

—. Executive Power. Nixon, Richard M. (administration). Reform. Watergate scandal. 1968-74. *2275*

—. Federal Government. Foreign Relations. 1950-76. *3314*

—. Federal Government. Hoover, Herbert C. Public administration. 1917-32. *1215*

—. Foreign policy. 1976. *3359*

—. Lobbying. Medical care. Pemberton, William E. Poen, Monte M. Truman, Harry S. (administration; review article). 1945-50. *2445*

—. Nixon, Richard M. Presidency. Public administration. 1970's. *2451*

—. Office of Management and Budget. Presidency. 1970-75. *3299*

—. Policymaking. Presidency. 1970-80. *3454*

—. Public Health Service. Reform. 1960-73. *3279*

Bureaucratization. Business. State Department. 1886-1905. *1048*

—. State Department. 1965-74. *3467*

Bureaucrats. Decisionmaking. Foreign Policy (review article). Politics. Presidents. 1945-75. *3367*

Burials. Armies. Discrimination. Johnson, Lyndon B. Longoria, Felix. Mexican Americans. Texas (Three Rivers). 1945-49. *1724*

Burke, Edmund. Adams, John. Government. Political Power. Senate. 1770-1800. *230*

Burleson, Albert Sidney. Politics. Postmasters general. Progressivism. Wilson, Woodrow (administration). 1913-21. *1252*

Burnham, William Dean. Ceaser, John W. Diamond, Edwin. DiClerico, Robert E. Political Attitudes (review article). Presidency. Weinberg, Martha. 1970-79. *3187*

Burns, Arthur F. Council of Economic Advisers. Economic policy. Eisenhower, Dwight D. Jacoby, Neil H. Keynesianism. Recessions. 1953-54. *2337*

Burr, Aaron. Executive privilege. Jefferson, Thomas. Judicial review. Marshall, John. Supreme Court. 1804. *1033*

—. Executive privilege. Presidency. Supreme Court (subpoenas). Watergate Tapes. 1807. *1046*

Bush, George. Debates. Primaries (presidential). Reagan, Ronald. Republican Party. Texas (Houston). 1980. *1908*

Bushnell, Horace. Church and state. Congregationalism. Jefferson, Thomas. ca 1800-60. *185*

Business *See also* Advertising; Banking; Corporations; Credit; Manufactures; Marketing; Multinational Corporations; Salesmen and Salesmanship.

—. Airplane Industry and Trade. Defense policy. Military-industrial complex. Truman, Harry S. 1945-53. *2231*

—. Armies. Johnson, Hugh S. Military supplies. War Industries Board. World War I. 1918. *1395*

—. Attitudes. Interpersonal Relations. Lincoln, Abraham. Owen, Mary. Todd, Mary. 1831-42. *576*

—. Bureaucratization. State Department. 1886-1905. *1048*

—. Cabinet. Elites. Mills, C. Wright. 1897-1973. *56*

—. Carter, Jimmy. Negroes. Trilateral Commission. 1973-77. *1709*

—. Commerce Department. International Trade. State Department (Foreign Service). 1903-12. *1706*

—. Economic Conditions. Morality. Nixon, Richard M. Public opinion. Watergate scandal. 1969-74. *2322*

—. Federal regulation. Hoover, Herbert C. Political Theory. 1910-76. *1106*

—. McKinley, William. Reick, William C. Spanish-American War. Telegrams. Young, John Russell. 1898. *992*

—. New York. Political Reform. Roosevelt, Theodore. State Legislatures. 1882. *1098*

Business Advisory Council. Committee for Economic Development. Keynesianism. New Deal. Roosevelt, Franklin D. (administration). Scholars. 1933-42. *1272*

Businessmen *See also* Entrepreneurs.

—. Appointments to office. Eisenhower, Dwight D. Senate. Wealth. Wilson, Charles E. 1952. *2356*

—. Foreign policy. Human rights. Latin America.
1977-80. *2756*
—. Foreign policy. Human rights. Materialism.
Morality. 1977-79. *2571*
—. Foreign policy. Human rights. USSR.
1976-77. *2744*
—. Foreign policy. International Labor
Organization. 1977. *2808*
—. Foreign policy. Middle East. ca 1967-77.
2564
—. Foreign policy. Morality. 1913-77. *125*
—. Foreign policy. Morality. Pragmatism.
1776-1970's. *74*
—. Foreign Policy. Nuclear nonproliferation.
Political Leadership. 1977-79. *2942*
—. Foreign Policy. Nuclear nonproliferation.
Political Leadership. 1979. *2621*
—. Foreign Policy. Panama Canal. Political
Speeches. Rhetoric. Television. 1977-78.
3090
—. Foreign policy. Presidency. 1977-80. *3034*
—. Foreign Policy. Speeches, Addresses, etc.
USSR. 1978. *3134*
—. Foreign Relations. Iran. Revolution. 1972-79.
2652
—. Foreign relations. Latin America. 1977-78.
2565
—. Foreign Relations. Middle East. 1977. *3008*
—. Georgia. Higher education. 1960's-76. *1760*
—. Georgia (Plains). Interviews. 1928-76. *1726*
—. Group fantasy. National Characteristics.
War. 1946-76. *2165*
—. Hostages. Iran. Kentucky (Lexington).
Presidents. Public opinion. 1979. *2672*
—. Human rights. State Department (Human
Rights Bureau). 1977-80. *3142*
—. Human rights. UN. 1945-77. *2719*
—. Iran. Revolution. 1978-81. *2829*
—. Kennedy, Edward M. Political Campaigns.
Reagan, Ronald. 1980. *2081*
—. Kennedy, John F. Political Campaigns
(presidential). Religion. 1960-76. *2119*
—. Kraft, Tim. Pennsylvania. Primaries
(presidential). 1976. *2065*
—. Mass Media. Political Campaigns (presidential).
Rhetoric. Voting and Voting Behavior. 1976.
2038
—. Negroes. Political power. Voting and voting
behavior. 1976-77. *2084*
—. Nixon, Richard M. Political Commentary.
Presidency. Press. 1968-79. *2178*
—. Political Campaigns (presidential). Reagan,
Ronald. 1972-80. *2029*
—. Political Campaigns (presidential). Religion.
1976. *1761*
—. Political Campaigns (presidential). South.
Values. 1976. *1965*
—. Political Leadership. 1976-77. *2230*
—. Political leadership. Psychology. 1976. *2171*
—. Political power. Press. 1977-80. *2239*
—. Political Speeches. Rhetoric. 1975-76. *2022*
—. Political strategy. Public Opinion. 1979.
2152
—. Politics. Press. State of the Union message.
1978. *2186*
—. Presidency. 1975-80. *2250*
—. Press. Public Relations. 1977-78. *2214*
—. Strategic Arms Limitation Talks. USSR.
1972-77. *3108*
Carter, Jimmy (administration). 1945-78. *2159*
—. 1976-80. *2213*
—. 1977. *2208*
—. ACTION (agency). Brown, Sam. Federal
Programs. VISTA. 1977-78. *2460*
—. Afghanistan. Cold War. Decisionmaking.
Defense spending. Inflation. Iran. USSR.
1979-80. *2284*
—. Afghanistan. Foreign policy. Hutson, Thomas
R. Invasions. Personal narratives. USSR.
1980-81. *2797*
—. Africa. Foreign policy. 1975-80. *2848*
—. Africa. Foreign Policy. Human rights. 1979.
2956
—. Africa, East. Foreign Policy. 1970's. *2723*
—. Africa, Southern. Economic interests. Foreign
policy. 1976-77. *2876*
—. Appointments to office. National security.
Politics. Vietnam War. 1970's. *2229*
—. Armies. Foreign Policy. Korea. 1977. *3091*
—. Arms Trade. 1977-79. *2569*
—. Arms Trade. Conventional Arms Transfers
Talks. Developing nations. Foreign Policy.
Military aid. USSR. 1977-82. *2607*
—. Arms Trade. Cyprus. Embargoes. Turkey.
1975-78. *3022*
—. Arms Trade. Foreign Policy. 1977-79. *2570*
—. Asia. Diplomacy. Kissinger, Henry A. Nixon,
Richard M. 1969-79. *3107*

—. Asia. Foreign Relations. Military. 1976-80.
3156
—. Asia, South. Foreign Policy. 1977-80. *2579*
—. Attitudes. Foreign policy. Human rights.
1977-78. *2858*
—. Attitudes. Korea, South. 1977-78. *2908*
—. Balance of Power. Foreign policy.
Regionalism. USSR. 1979. *2805*
—. Banking. Foreign policy. Human rights.
1977. *2878*
—. Brown, Harold. Defense Department. Military
Strategy. Strategic Arms Limitation Talks.
1977. *3105*
—. Brzezinski, Zbigniew. Foreign Policy. 1958-79.
2906
—. Brzezinski, Zbigniew. Foreign policy. 1976-80.
2933
—. Brzezinski, Zbigniew. Foreign policy. Italy.
1977. *2738*
—. Brzezinski, Zbigniew. Foreign policy. Middle
East. Vance, Cyrus. 1977-80. *3079*
—. Brzezinski, Zbigniew (interview). Foreign
policy. 1976-80. *3121*
—. Budgets. Defense Policy. 1978. *2844*
—. Budgets. Etzioni, Amitai. Inflation. Personal
narratives. 1980. *2341*
—. Cabinet. Presidency. Reagan, Ronald
(administration). 1976-81. *2160*
—. Carter, Hodding, III. Foreign policy. Personal
narratives. Public opinion. 1976-80. *3174*
—. China. Foreign policy. Human rights.
Morality. 1976-77. *3115*
—. China. Foreign Relations. Taiwan Relations
Act (US, 1979). 1978-80. *2761*
—. Cities. Decisionmaking. Federal policy.
Planning. Presidential staffs. 1977-80. *2533*
—. Civil rights. Congress. Political Campaigns
(presidential). 1977-78. *2498*
—. Communism. Foreign Policy. Latin America.
National Security. 1977-80. *2831*
—. Communist Countries. Foreign Policy.
Military Strategy. Reagan, Ronald
(administration). 1980. *3122*
—. Communist Party. Foreign Policy. Italy.
Kissinger, Henry A. 1960's-70's. *2855*
—. Congress. Domestic policy. Foreign Policy.
Inflation. Interest groups. 1977-78. *2200*
—. Congress. Economic planning. Energy.
Federal Policy. Politics. 1976-78. *2364*
—. Congress. Energy. Federal Policy. Interest
Groups. 1977-78. *2421*
—. Congress. Executive Branch. Legislative
liaisons. 1977-78. *2161*
—. Congress. Foreign policy. Public Opinion.
1978. *2787*
—. Crime and Criminals. Law Enforcement
Assistance Administration. 1970's. *2321*
—. Declaration of Independence. Foreign policy.
Idealism. Morality. ca 1918-78. *2784*
—. Defense spending. Foreign policy. Military.
NATO. Politics. 1976. *2625*
—. Defense spending. Foreign Relations. 1977-80.
2270
—. Detente. Developing nations. Europe, Western.
Foreign policy. Japan. USSR. 1977-80. *3114*
—. Detente. USSR. 1970's. *3075*
—. Domestic policy. 1977-79. *2425*
—. Domestic policy. Foreign policy. 1976. *2191*
—. Domestic Policy. Foreign policy. Human
rights. 1977-79. *3037*
—. Domestic Policy. Foreign Policy. Morality.
1977. *2271*
—. Economic Conditions. Foreign Relations.
1977-80. *3054*
—. Economic Policy. Reagan, Ronald
(administration). 1979-81. *2399*
—. Energy. 1979-80. *2517*
—. Energy. Federal Policy. 1973-78. *2510*
—. Energy. Federal Programs. Oil industry and
trade. 1978-80. *2429*
—. Europe, Western. Foreign policy. USSR.
1970's. *2790*
—. Executive Branch. Reform. Roosevelt,
Franklin D. (administration). 1937-38. 1977-78.
1403
—. Federal Policy. McKelvey, Vincent. Natural
resources. Oil and Petroleum Products. US
Geological Survey. 1978. *2295*
—. Foreign policy. 1976-80. *2954*
—. Foreign policy. 1977-79. *2973*
—. Foreign policy. 1977-81. *2789*
—. Foreign policy. 1977. *2939*
—. Foreign policy. 1978. *2632*
—. Foreign Policy. Foreign Policy. 1976-78.
2796
—. Foreign policy. Human rights. 1970's. *3146*
—. Foreign policy. Human rights. 1977-78.
3135

—. Foreign policy. Human rights. 1977-79.
2690
—. Foreign Policy. Human rights. 1977-79.
2924
—. Foreign Policy. Human rights. 1977-81.
2830
—. Foreign policy. Human rights. Korea, South.
1945-79. *2949*
—. Foreign policy. Human rights. Race Relations.
South Africa. 1973-78. *2668*
—. Foreign policy. Institute for Palestine Studies.
Israel. Palestine. 1980. *2577*
—. Foreign Policy. International trade.
1950's-70's. *2588*
—. Foreign Policy. Israel. Political Surveys.
1948-77. *2870*
—. Foreign policy. Kissinger, Henry A. 1977-78.
3181
—. Foreign Policy. Korea. 1950-79. *2774*
—. Foreign Policy. Latin America. 1977-80.
3016
—. Foreign Policy. Military Strategy. Persian Gulf
and area. ca 1979-80. *3117*
—. Foreign policy. Military-industrial complex.
1976-78. *3076*
—. Foreign policy. Nixon, Richard M.
(administration). 1968-76. *2575*
—. Foreign Policy. Nuclear nonproliferation.
1977-81. *3069*
—. Foreign Policy. Race Relations. Reagan,
Ronald (administration). South Africa.
1981-82. *2700*
—. Foreign policy. USSR. 1980. *3015*
—. Foreign policy. Young, Andrew. 1977. *2606*
—. Foreign Relations. Latin America. 1977-79.
2710
—. Foreign relations. Latin America. 19c-20c.
3128
—. Foreign Relations. Nicaragua. Revolution.
Sandinistas. Somoza, Anastasio. 1978-79.
2711
—. Foreign Relations. Strategic Arms Limitation
Talks. USSR. 1977-79. *2724*
—. Foreign relations. USSR. 1977-78. *2623*
—. Inflation. 1977-79. *2310*
—. Interest Groups. 1976-79. *2437*
—. Jordan, Hamilton. Political Campaigns.
1974-78. *2415*
—. Military Strategy. Nuclear Arms. Presidential
Directive No. 59. USSR. 1960-80. *2865*
—. Political Leadership. 1976-81. *2145*
—. Powell, Jody. Press secretaries. 1975-76.
2463
—. Strategic Arms Limitation Talks. USSR.
1977. *2578*
Carter, Jimmy (and family). Family. Politics.
Psychohistory. 1928-76. *1713*
Carter, Jimmy (interview). *Playboy* (periodical).
Political Campaigns (presidential). Public
Opinion. Rhetoric. 1976. *2077*
Carter, Jimmy (review article). DeMause, Lloyd.
Ebel, Henry. Presidency. Psychohistory.
1977. *1728*
Carter, William H. Military general staff. Root,
Elihu. World War I (antecedents). 1903-16.
1703
Cartoons. Editorials. *Harper's Weekly* (periodical).
Political Campaigns (presidential). Scandals.
Wasp (periodical). 1876-77. *667*
—. Jackson, Andrew. Satire. 1828-36. *941*
—. Political Campaigns (presidential). Voting and
Voting Behavior. 1976. *1812*
—. Presidency. 1776-1976. *89*
Cass, Lewis. Foreign policy. Webster, Daniel.
1842-43. *1019*
Castel, Albert. Johnson, Andrew (review article).
Reconstruction. Riddleberger, Patrick W.
Sefton, James E. 1865-69. *773*
Castro, Fidel. Cuba. Documents. Foreign
Relations. Nixon, Richard M. Political
Leadership. 1959. *3028*
—. Cuba. Foreign policy. Imperialism.
Policymaking. 1945-80. *2927*
Catholic Church *See also* religious orders by name,
e.g. Franciscans, Jesuits, etc.; Vatican.
—. Abortion. Democratic Party. Elections
(presidential). 1976. *1914*
—. Boston *Pilot*. Civil War. Irish Americans.
Lincoln, Abraham. Massachusetts. Reporters
and Reporting. 1840-72. *955*
—. Church and state. Kennedy, John F. Political
Campaigns (presidential). Presbyterian Church.
1959-60. *2120*
—. Civil War. Copperheads. Editors and Editing.
Metropolitan Record (newspaper). Mullaly,
John. New York City. 1861-64. *824*

—. Acheson, Dean. Diplomacy. Foreign Relations. 1944-50. *3168*
—. Angola. Central Intelligence Agency. Covert operations. Diplomacy. USSR. Zaire. 1960-76. *3148*
—. Asia, East. Cold War (review article). Committee of One Million. Truman, Harry S. 1947-71. 1976-77. *2667*
—. Balance of power. Detente. Foreign policy. USSR. 1945-79. *2616*
—. Balance of power. Foreign policy. Nixon, Richard M. (administration). USSR. 1969-72. *3018*
—. Blockades. Chamberlain, Neville. Great Britain. Japan. Roosevelt, Franklin D. World War II (antecedents). 1937-38. *1549*
—. Brussels Conference. Diplomacy. Japan. Roosevelt, Franklin D. War. 1937. *1661*
—. Carter, Jimmy (administration). Foreign policy. Human rights. Morality. 1976-77. *3115*
—. Carter, Jimmy (administration). Foreign Relations. Taiwan Relations Act (US, 1979). 1978-80. *2761*
—. China. Cultural relations. Foreign Aid. State Department. 1942-45. *1622*
—. China. Cultural relations. Foreign Aid. State Department. 1942-45. *1622*
—. Churchill, Winston. Colonialism. deGaulle, Charles. Foreign Policy. France. Indochina. Roosevelt, Franklin D. 1942-45. *1588*
—. Cold War (origins). Communism. Foreign policy. 1945. *2648*
—. Communist Party. Foreign Policy. State Department. Stuart, John Leighton. 1949. *2631*
—. Communists. Foreign Policy. Liberals. Scholars. 1944-71. *2895*
—. Communists. Foreign Policy. Shanghai Power Company. Truman, Harry S. (administration). 1948-50. *3111*
—. Decisionmaking. Eisenhower, Dwight D. Taiwan Strait crisis. 1954-55. *3025*
—. Detente. Nixon, Richard M. 1970's. *2702*
—. Detente (review article). Nixon, Richard M. USSR. 1971-73. *2992*
—. Diplomacy. Foreign Policy (review article). Imperialism. Philippines. Reinsch, Paul S. 1899-1945. *1564*
—. Diplomacy. Hurley, Patrick J. Jiang Jieshi. Mao Zedong. State Department. Vincent, John Carter. 1944-45. *1591*
—. Diplomacy. Service, John Stewart (dismissal). State Department (Foreign Service). 1932-73. *3170*
—. Diplomacy. State Department. Vatican. World War I. 1918. *1476*
—. Diplomacy. Vietnam. 1975-80. *2990*
—. Diplomatic recognition. Missions and Missionaries. Revolution. Sun Zhongshan. 1911-13. *1610*
—. Diplomatic recognition. Sprouse, Philip D. Truman, Harry S. (administration). 1949-50. *2666*
—. Elections (presidential). Foreign Policy. Korean War. 1949-52. *1790*
—. Exports. Foreign policy. Geopolitics. USSR. 1969-80. *2686*
—. Foreign Policy. Kissinger, Henry A. Nixon, Richard M. 1960's-70's. *3116*
—. Foreign policy. Kissinger, Henry A. USSR. 1969-76. *2754*
—. Foreign policy. Korean War. Military strategy. 38th Parallel. 1950-52. *2594*
—. Foreign Policy. League of Nations. Paris Peace Conference. Treaties. Wilson, Woodrow. 1919. *1505*
—. Foreign Policy. Roosevelt, Franklin D. Truman, Harry S. 1944-48. 1978. *2781*
—. Foreign policy. Security risks. State Department (Foreign Service). 1945-70's. *3228*
—. Foreign Policy. State Department. Sun Zhongshan. 1920-24. *1540*
—. Foreign Policy. Taiwan. 1950's-70's. *2691*
—. Foreign policy. Taiwan. USSR. 1972-78. *2795*
—. Foreign policy (review article). Korean War. MacArthur, Douglas. Politics and the Military. Truman, Harry S. 1949-52. *2689*
—. Foreign Relations. 1942-80. *3065*
—. Foreign Relations. Great Britain. Hong Kong. Sovereignty. World War II. 1941-45. *1503*
—. Foreign Relations. Kahn, E. J., Jr. (review article). Politics. State Department (Foreign Service). 1940's-50's. *2903*
—. Foreign Relations. Loans (consortium). Wilson, Woodrow. 1910-13. *1606*

—. Foreign Relations. Nixon, Richard M. (administration). 1969-72. *2555*
—. Foreign Relations (review article). Haldeman, H. R. Kissinger, Henry A. Nixon, Richard M. 1968-76. *3150*
—. Hay, John Milton. Historiography. International Trade. International trade. 1899-1901. *975*
—. Historiography (Chinese). Jefferson, Thomas. Liu Zuochang. Virginia, University of. 1770-1826. 1976-81. *272*
—. Japan. Navies. Shanghai (battle). Stimson, Henry L. Taylor, Montgomery Meigs. Western nations. 1931-32. *1645*
—. *Keys of the Kingdom* (film). Office of War Information. Propaganda. Roosevelt, Franklin D. Stereotypes. World War II. 1940-45. *1495*
China (Gailan). Chinese Engineering and Mining Company. Fraud. Great Britain. Hoover, Herbert C. 1900-28. *1069*
China, Republic of (1949-). *See* Taiwan.
Chinese. Elections (presidential). Garfield, James A. Letters. Morey, H. L. Racism. 1875-85. *643*
Chinese Engineering and Mining Company. China (Gailan). Fraud. Great Britain. Hoover, Herbert C. 1900-28. *1069*
Chinese Exclusion Act (US, 1882). Argell, James B. Congress. Diplomacy. Immigration. 1876-82. *968*
—. Congress. Executive Branch. Immigration. Politics. 1876-82. *998*
Chiniquy, Charles P. T. Anti-Catholicism. Lincoln, Abraham. 1855-65. *462*
Choper, Jesse H. Federalism (review article). Fisher, Louis. Genovese, Michael A. Jenkins, Iredell. Law. Merry, Henry J. 1978-80. *3221*
Christenson, Reo M. Beitzinger, A. J. Equality. Hanley, Thomas O'Brien. Jaffa, Harry V. Lincoln, Abraham. Political Theory. Values (review article). 1770-1973. *446*
Christian Right. Conservatism. Elections (presidential). Indiana (Muncie). Reagan, Ronald. 1980. *1937*
Christianity *See also* Catholic Church; Missions and Missionaries; Protestantism.
—. Attitudes. Carter, Jimmy. Political Campaigns (presidential). Political Speeches. Rhetoric. 1976. *1861*
—. Gospel. Jefferson, Thomas. Morality. Russia. Tolstoy, Leo (*Christ's Christianity*). 1800-85. *285*
—. Jackson, Andrew (death). Jackson, Andrew, Jr. Personal narratives. 1845. *550*
—. Jefferson, Thomas. Religion. 1784-1800. *373*
—. Presidents. 1788-1979. *11*
Church and State *See also* Religious Liberty.
—. Bushnell, Horace. Congregationalism. Jefferson, Thomas. ca 1800-60. *185*
—. Catholic Church. Kennedy, John F. Political Campaigns (presidential). Presbyterian Church. 1959-60. *2120*
—. Civil religion. Lincoln, Abraham. 1812-65. *442*
—. Hoover, Herbert C. Protestantism. 1928-32. *1319*
Church, Frank. Federal Bureau of Investigation. National security. Senate (Intelligence Activities Committee). 1930's-75. *3235*
Churchill, Winston. Air Warfare. Bombing. Military General Staff. Normandy Invasion. Roosevelt, Franklin D. World War II. 1944. *1684*
—. Atomic Bomb. Diplomacy. Great Britain. Military Strategy. Normandy invasion. Roosevelt, Franklin D. World War II. 1942-44. *1675*
—. China. Colonialism. deGaulle, Charles. Foreign Policy. France. Indochina. Roosevelt, Franklin D. 1942-45. *1588*
—. Communism. Diaries. Nuclear Arms. Potsdam Conference. Stalin, Joseph. Truman, Harry S. 1945. *2892*
—. Disarmament. Einstein, Albert. Eisenhower, Dwight D. Europe. Khrushchev, Nikita. Memoirs. Moch, Jules. 1932-55. *2226*
—. Eisenhower, Dwight D. France. Great Britain. Resistance. World War II. 1943-44. *1733*
—. Espionage. Foreign Relations. Kent, Tyler. Roosevelt, Franklin D. World War II. 1940-45. *1581*
—. Foreign policy. Political Leadership. Roosevelt, Franklin D. Stalin, Joseph. World War II. 1939-45. *1698*

—. Foreign Relations. Great Britain. Roosevelt, Franklin D. World War II. 1939-45. *1641*
—. Germany. Partition. Potsdam Conference. Roosevelt, Franklin D. Stettinius, Edward Reilley. Truman, Harry S. Yalta Conference. 1945. *2755*
—. Great Britain. Joint Chiefs of Staff. Malta Conference. Military Strategy. Roosevelt, Franklin D. World War II. 1945. *1663*
—. Great Britain. Letters. Neutrality. Roosevelt, Franklin D. World War II. 1939-40. *1589*
—. Great Britain. Roosevelt, Franklin D. 1938-45. *1579*
—. Poland. Roosevelt, Franklin D. Stalin, Joseph. USSR. World War II. Yalta Conference. 1945. *1580*
Cities *See also* headings beginning with the word city and the word urban; names of cities and towns by state; Housing.
—. Carter, Jimmy. Domestic Policy. 1977-78. *2405*
—. Carter, Jimmy. Domestic Policy. New Federalism. State government. 1977. *2504*
—. Carter, Jimmy. Federal policy. 1978. *2505*
—. Carter, Jimmy. Federal policy. Urban and Regional Policy Group. 1978. *2383*
—. Carter, Jimmy. Negroes. 1977. *2395*
—. Carter, Jimmy (administration). Decisionmaking. Federal policy. Planning. Presidential staffs. 1977-80. *2533*
Cities, Port. Economic independence. Madison, James. State Government. Virginia. 1784-88. *298*
Citizen Lobbies *See also* Community Participation in Politics.
—. Agriculture Department. 1960-80. *3208*
Citizenship (definition of). Foreign policy. Morality. Self-determination. Wilson, Woodrow. 1917-24. *1617*
City Life. Elections (presidential). Vietnam War. 1968. 1972. *1889*
City Planning *See also* Housing; Urban Renewal.
—. Greenbelt new towns. Poor. Resettlement Administration. Rural areas. Tugwell, Rexford Guy. 1935-36. *1392*
City politics (review article). Democratic Party. Dorsett, Lyle W. Fine, Sidney. Roosevelt, Franklin D. Trout, Charles H. 1930-40. *1328*
—. Depressions. Massachusetts (Boston). New Deal. Roosevelt, Franklin D. (administration). Trout, Charles H. 1929-39. 1977. *1292*
Civil Aeronautics Board. Air Lines. Kuter, Laurence R. Personal Narratives. Truman, Harry S. 1948. *2408*
Civil Disobedience. Ideology. Watergate Scandal. 1939-74. *2307*
Civil Disturbances *See also* Revolution; Riots.
—. Executive Power. Military. 1789-1978. *132*
—. Governors. McKinley, William. National Guard. Ohio. 1894. *530*
Civil Liberty. *See* Civil Rights.
Civil religion. Church and State. Lincoln, Abraham. 1812-65. *442*
—. Croly, Herbert. Millenarianism. Politics. Wilson, Woodrow. 1909-19. *1261*
—. Eisenhower, Dwight D. Government. Values. 1954. *2380*
—. Elections (presidential). Nixon, Richard M. Voting and Voting Behavior. 1972. *2116*
—. Inaugural addresses. Political leadership. Presidency. 1789-1980. *50*
Civil Rights *See also* Freedom of Speech; Human Rights; Religious Liberty.
—. Attitudes. Johnson, Lyndon B. Negroes. 1930's-68. *1715*
—. Attitudes. South. Truman, Harry S. Whites. 1945-52. *2308*
—. Brauer, Carl M. (review article). Kennedy, John F. Legislation. 1961-63. *2527*
—. Bureau of Alcohol, Tobacco and Firearms. Constitutional Amendments (2d). 1970-80. *2420*
—. Butler, Thomas. Courts Martial and Courts of Inquiry. Haircuts. Jackson, Andrew. Military discipline. Tennessee. 1801. *472*
—. Carter, Jimmy. Georgia. State politics. 1950's-76. *1776*
—. Carter, Jimmy (administration). Congress. Political Campaigns (presidential). 1977-78. *2498*
—. Civil War. Constitution. Lincoln, Abraham. 1861-65. *920*
—. Civil War. Democracy. Lincoln, Abraham. Property. Slavery. 1861-65. *786*
—. Civil War. Emancipation Proclamation. Lincoln, Abraham. 1854-63. *908*

—. Cold War. Detention, preventive. Federal Bureau of Investigation. National security. Truman, Harry S. (administration). 1945-52. *2516*

—. Congress. Democratic Party. Kennedy, John F. 1960-63. *2376*

—. Congress. Discrimination, employment. Fair Employment Practices Committee. Roosevelt, Franklin D. (administration). World War II. 1941-46. *1394*

—. Congress. Negroes. Truman, Harry S. 1949-50. *2524*

—. Courts. Executive branch. Health, Education, and Welfare Department. Integration. Politics. 1960's-79. *2438*

—. Declaration of Independence. Negroes. Slavery. 1776-1976. *41*

—. Donovan, Robert J. (review article). Truman, Harry S. 1945-52. *2304*

—. Ervin, Sam J., Jr. Political Commentary. Senate. Vietnam War. Watergate Scandal. 1954-74. *2530*

—. Executive Power. Kennedy, John F. Legislation. 1961-64. *2428*

—. Federal Bureau of Investigation. Nixon, Richard M. (administration). Police. Violence. 1960-72. *2514*

—. Federal Bureau of Investigation. Roosevelt, Franklin D. 1936-80. *8*

—. Federal Policy. Interest Groups. Populism. Private enterprise. Racism. Wallace, George C. 1960's. *2107*

—. Ford, Gerald R. Negroes. 1949-74. *2441*

—. Johnson, Lyndon B. Louisiana (New Orleans). Political campaigns (presidential). Political Speeches. 1964. *1907*

—. Johnson, Lyndon B. Negroes. Political Reform. Suffrage. 1960's. *2413*

—. Johnson, Lyndon B. (administration). 1963-69. *2440*

—. Presidents. 1940-76. *172*

Civil Rights Act (US, 1957). Johnson, Lyndon B. 1957. *1768*

Civil Rights Act (US, 1964). Democratic Party. Indiana. Primaries (presidential). Wallace, George C. Welsh, Matthew E. 1964. *2111*

Civil Rights Bill (US, 1963). Johnson, Lyndon B. Kennedy, John F. 1963. *2479*

Civil rights movement. Credibility gap. Johnson, Lyndon B. Peace movements. Political Culture. 1960's. *2278*

—. Federal policy. Integration. Johnson, Lyndon B. Kennedy, John F. 1945-76. *2402*

—. Johnson, Lyndon B. Long, Huey P. Radicals and Radicalism. South. 1920-70. *1779*

Civil Service *See also* Federal Government; Public Administration; Public Employees.

—. Alabama (Dothan). Clayton, Henry D. Patronage. Postal Service. Taft, William H. Wilson, Woodrow (administration). 1900-13. *1415*

—. Carter, Jimmy. Equal Opportunity. Labor Department. 1977-78. *2410*

—. Carter, Jimmy. Reform. Supreme Court. 1950's-70's. *2398*

—. Executive Power. Nixon, Richard M. 1969-74. *2324*

—. Federal policy. Kennedy, John F. (administration). Peterson, Esther. President's Commission on the Status of Women. Sex Discrimination. Wages. Women. 1961-63. *2374*

—. Indians (reservations). Roosevelt, Theodore. Western States. 1892. *862*

—. Nixon, Richard M. (administration). 1969-74. *2417*

Civil Service Commissioners. Indian Rights Association. Indian-White Relations. Roosevelt, Theodore. Welsh, Herbert. 1889-95. *831*

Civil Service Reform Act (US, 1978). Carter, Jimmy. Reform. 1978. *2385*

Civil Service Reform Bill. Carter, Jimmy. 1978. *2392*

Civil War *See also* battles and campaigns by name; Confederate States of America; Reconstruction; Secession; Slavery.

—. American Freedmen's Inquiry Commission. Freedmen. Johnson, Andrew. 1863. *568*

—. Appointments to office. Indian Wars. Lincoln, Abraham. Military officers. Pope, John. 1861-64. *942*

—. Armies. Elections (presidential). Lincoln, Abraham. Propaganda. Sherman, William Tecumseh. 1864. *622*

—. Ashton, J. Hubley. Executive Power. Lincoln, Abraham. Personal narratives. 1864. *771*

—. Assassination. Attitudes. Australia (Melbourne). Lincoln, Abraham. Newspapers. 1865. *468*

—. Assassination. Films. *Lincoln Conspiracy* (film). Public Opinion. 1865. 1970's. *432*

—. Assassination. Kautz, August V. Lincoln, Abraham. Personal narratives. Trials. 1865. *424*

—. Attitudes. Illinois. Lincoln, Abraham. Military Service. 1832-65. *416*

—. Attitudes. Lincoln, Abraham. Political Speeches. Sectionalism. Slavery. 1850's-65. *456*

—. Belmont (battle). Grant, Ulysses S. Missouri. 1861. *506*

—. Belmont (battle). Grant, Ulysses S. Missouri. 1861. *569*

—. Blair, Francis Preston, Sr. (review article). Jackson, Andrew. Politics. Smith, Elbert B. 1830-79. 1980. *855*

—. Boston *Pilot*. Catholic Church. Irish Americans. Lincoln, Abraham. Massachusetts. Reporters and Reporting. 1840-72. *955*

—. Bounties. Lincoln, Abraham. Military Recruitment. Staples, John Summerfield. 1864. *947*

—. Brooks, Noah. District of Columbia. Lincoln, Abraham. Reporters and Reporting. 1862-1903. *741*

—. Brown, Harry J. Garfield, James A. (review article). Leech, Margaret. Peskin, Allan. Political Leadership. 1850-81. 1978. *503*

—. Brownlow, William G. Elections. Johnson, Andrew. State Government. Tennessee. 1860-65. *899*

—. Buell, Don Carlos. Grant, Ulysses S. Lincoln, Abraham. Military General Staff. Political Leadership. 1862-98. *811*

—. Bureau of Indian Affairs. Coffin, William G. Federal policy. Indian Territory. Indians. 1861-65. *844*

—. Calamity, use of. Lincoln, Abraham. Puritans. Rhetoric. 1650-1870. *782*

—. Canals. Grant, Ulysses S. Louisiana, northeastern. Mississippi River. Vicksburg campaign. 1863. *487*

—. Catholic Church. Copperheads. Editors and Editing. *Metropolitan Record* (newspaper). Mullaly, John. New York City. 1861-64. *824*

—. Censorship. Chicago *Times*. Lincoln, Abraham. Newspapers. 1863-64. *948*

—. Chambrun, Adolphe de. Letters. Lincoln, Abraham. 1865-68. *916*

—. Chaplains. Grant, Ulysses S. Jews. Lincoln, Abraham. 1861-62. *902*

—. Chase, Salmon P. Florida. Lincoln, Abraham. Olustee (battle). Political Campaigns (presidential). 1864. *891*

—. Chickamauga (battle). Garfield, James A. Rosecrans, William S. Tennessee. 1862-80. *583*

—. Civil Rights. Constitution. Lincoln, Abraham. 1861-65. *920*

—. Civil Rights. Democracy. Lincoln, Abraham. Property. Slavery. 1861-65. *786*

—. Civil Rights. Emancipation Proclamation. Lincoln, Abraham. 1854-63. *908*

—. Civil-Military Relations. Lincoln, Abraham. Military Strategy. 1861-65. *945*

—. Congress. Historiography. Lincoln, Abraham. 1861-65. *861*

—. Congress. Joint Congressional Committee on the Conduct of the Civil War. Lincoln, Abraham. 1861-65. *960*

—. Connecticut (New London). Letters. Lincoln, Abraham. Loomis, Francis B. Military finance. 1864. *796*

—. Constitution. Lincoln, Abraham. War Powers. 1860-66. *730*

—. Constitutional Amendments (13th). Emancipation. Lincoln, Abraham. Republicans, radical. 1861-65. *909*

—. Consular Service. Espionage. Great Britain. Lincoln, Abraham. Patronage. Shipping. 1861-63. *1012*

—. Consular Service. Espionage. Ireland. Lincoln, Abraham. Patronage. Scotland. 1861-63. *1013*

—. Copperheads. Democratic Party. Illinois. Lincoln, Abraham. 1861-65. *872*

—. Cotton. Davis, Jefferson. Lincoln, Abraham. Mississippi. Teasdale, Thomas Cox. War Relief. 1865. *795*

—. Crane, James L. Grant, Ulysses S. Illinois Volunteers, 21st. Personal narratives. 1861. *426*

—. Davis, Jefferson. Lincoln, Abraham. Political Leadership. 1861-65. *863*

—. Democratic Party. Lincoln, Abraham. Phelps, Richard Harvey. Political Protest. 1861-64. *777*

—. Democrats. Navy Secretaries. Niven, John (review article). Welles, Gideon. 1820's-70's. *740*

—. District of Columbia. Letters. Lincoln, Abraham. Mann, Horace, Jr. Peabody, Elizabeth. 1865. *952*

—. Dole, William P. Indians. Lincoln, Abraham. Treaties. 1861-64. *868*

—. Domestic Policy. Lincoln, Abraham. Negroes. 1850-65. *783*

—. Elections (presidential). Negroes. Political Participation. Republican Party. 1864. *666*

—. Emancipation. Kentucky. Lincoln, Abraham. 1861-65. *837*

—. Federalism. Grant, Ulysses S. Greeley, Horace. Nationalism. Political Campaigns (presidential). 1872. *658*

—. Five Civilized Tribes. Indian Territory. Lincoln, Abraham. Proclamations. Ross, John. 1860's. *790*

—. Florida (Amelia Island; Fernandina). Johnson, Andrew. Land Tenure. Military Occupation. Property Tax. Unionists. 1860's-90's. *934*

—. Foreign Relations. Lincoln, Abraham. Spain. Tassara, Gabriel Garcia. 1858-73. *978*

—. Fort Donelson (battle). Fort Henry (battle). Grant, Ulysses S. Military Strategy. Tennessee. 1862. *423*

—. Fort Sumter. Lincoln, Abraham. Seward, William H. 1861. *914*

—. Fox, Gustavus Vasa. Naval administration. Welles, Gideon. 1861-65. *744*

—. Grant, Ulysses S. Hampton Roads Peace Conference. Military General Staff. Telegraph. 1865. *601*

—. Habeas corpus. Lincoln, Abraham. Taney, Roger B. 1861. *886*

—. Halleck, Henry W. Lincoln, Abraham. Military strategy. 1862-63. *838*

—. Hampton Roads Peace Conference. Lincoln, Abraham. 1865. *961*

—. Historiography. Military Strategy. 1861-1979. *953*

—. Hitchcock, Ethan Allen. Lincoln, Abraham. Military Strategy. Peninsular Campaign. Shenandoah Valley (campaign). Virginia. 1862. *950*

—. Illinois (Charleston). Lincoln, Abraham (family). Riots. 1863-64. *769*

—. Inaugural Addresses. Lincoln, Abraham. Rhetoric. 1865. *832*

—. Letters. Lincoln, Abraham. Maryland (Baltimore). Military medicine. Wool, John E. 1862. *458*

—. Lincoln, Abraham. Lloyd, William Alvin. Military Intelligence. 1861-65. *772*

—. Lincoln, Abraham. *Merrimack* (vessel; capture). Military strategy. Norfolk (battle). Virginia. 1862. *866*

—. Lincoln, Abraham. Military General Staff. Political Leadership. 1862-64. *856*

—. Lincoln, Abraham. New York City. Theater. 1861-1900. *588*

—. Lincoln, Abraham. Political Leadership. Stillé, Charles Janeway ("How a Free People Conduct a Long War"). 1862. *825*

—. Lincoln, Abraham. Political Theory. 1861-65. *959*

—. Lincoln, Abraham. Political Theory. Revolution. Slavery. Social change. 1850-65. *912*

—. Lincoln, Abraham. Portraits. Washington, George. 19c. *72*

—. Lincoln, Abraham. Prisoners of War (exchanges). Underwood, John Cox. 1861-1913. *836*

—. Lincoln, Abraham. Puritans. Self-government. 1630-1865. *717*

—. Lincoln, Abraham. Working class. 1861-65. *865*

—. Lincoln, Abraham (Gettysburg Address). Pennsylvania. 1863. *895*

—. Melville, Herman. Poetry. 1861-66. *400*

—. Military General Staff. Military Strategy. 1861-65. *839*

—. Military General Staff. Politics. 1861-65. *436*

Civil War (antecedents). Brooks, Preston S. Congress. Republican Party. Sumner, Charles. Violence. 1856. *635*

—. Buchanan, James. Kansas. Lecompton Constitution. 1857-61. *873*

—. China. Churchill, Winston. deGaulle, Charles. Foreign Policy. France. Indochina. Roosevelt, Franklin D. 1942-45. *1588*
Colonization *See also* Settlement.
—. Arab-Israeli conflict. Carter, Jimmy. Military Occupation. New York. Political Campaigns (presidential). UN Security Council Resolution 465. 1978-80. *2600*
—. Attitudes. Douglas, Stephen A. Lincoln, Abraham. Negroes. Race. 1858-65. *819*
—. Attitudes. Lincoln, Abraham. Negroes. 1860's. *905*
—. Butler, Benjamin F. *(Butler's Book).* Lincoln, Abraham. Negroes. 1864-65. *904*
—. Emancipation. Lincoln, Abraham. Negroes. 1852-65. *567*
Colorado *See also* Western States.
—. Ammons, Elias. Coal. Federal regulation. Strikes. Wilson, Woodrow. 1914. *1338*
—. Antiquities Act (US, 1906). Holy Cross Mountain National Monument. Hoover, Herbert C. Roosevelt, Theodore. Wheeler National Monument. 1906-50. *1445*
—. Cleveland, Grover. Conservation of Natural Resources. Forest reserve controversy. McKinley, William. 1890-1900. *888*
—. Elections. 1980. *1798*
—. Johnson, Andrew. Newspapers. Reconstruction. Republican Party. 1865-67. *779*
Colson, Charles. International Telephone and Telegraph. Watergate Scandal. 1972-73. *2391*
Columbia (allegory). King, William. Myths and Symbols. Poetry. Washington, George. Wheatley, Phillis ("To his Excellency George Washington"). 1790. *356*
Columbia Broadcasting System. Associated Press. Political Campaigns (presidential). Reporters and Reporting. Television. 1972. *1980*
—. Nixon, Richard M. Political Commentary. Presidents. Television. 1970's. *2238*
Columbia Valley Authority. Bureaucracies. Congress. Corporations. Electric Power. Truman, Harry S. (administration). 1945-50. *2330*
Commerce *See also* Banking; Business; International Trade; Prices; Statistics; Tariff; Transportation.
—. Madison, James. Plantations. Politics. Social classes. 1770's-1816. *354*
Commerce Department. Agricultural policy. Economic policy. Hoover, Herbert C. 1921-29. *1351*
—. American Petroleum Institute. Ecology. Hoover, Herbert C. Oil Industry and Trade. Politics. Pollution. 1921-26. *1290*
—. Business. International Trade. State Department (Foreign Service). 1903-12. *1706*
—. Economic Regulations. Federal Government. Hoover, Herbert C. 1920's. *1380*
—. Federal regulation. Hoover, Herbert C. Industry. Labor. 1921-28. *1331*
—. Federal Regulation. Hoover, Herbert C. Licensing. Radio. 1918-22. *1416*
—. Federal Regulation. Hoover, Herbert C. Radio Act (US, 1927). 1921-28. *1305*
—. Mitchell, Ewing Young. Pendergast, Thomas J. Political machines. Roosevelt, Franklin D. 1933-36. *1426*
Commercial Bureau of the American Republics. Advertising. Americas (North and South). Foreign Relations. International Union. State Department. 1894-1902. *1053*
Commercials. *See* Advertising.
Committee for Economic Development. Business Advisory Council. Keynesianism. New Deal. Roosevelt, Franklin D. (administration). Scholars. 1933-42. *1272*
Committee of One. Clark, Bennett Champ. Democratic Party. Missouri. Political Campaigns (presidential). 1936. *1197*
Committee of One Million. Asia, East. China. Cold War (review article). Truman, Harry S. 1947-71. 1976-77. *2667*
Committee of State Security (KGB). Assassination. Epstein, Edward J. Kennedy, John F. McMillan, Priscilla Johnson. Oswald, Lee Harvey (review article). 1960-78. *1746*
—. Communism. Espionage (review article). Hiss, Alger. Oswald, Lee Harvey. USSR. 1938-78. *1759*
Committee on Public Information. Bullard, Arthur. Censorship. Constitutional Amendments (1st). Creel, George. Press. Propaganda. World War I. 1917-20. *1451*
Committee to Re-Elect the President. Mass Media. Nixon, Richard M. Political Campaigns (presidential). 1972. *2039*

Commodities. Agricultural Adjustment Act (US, 1933). Federal Programs. Iowa. New Deal. Wallace, Henry A. 1933-34. *1357*
Common law. Adams, John. American Revolution (antecedents). Boston Massacre. Lawyers. Massachusetts. 1770. *328*
Common Market. *See* European Economic Community.
Communications *See also* Language; Mass Media; Newspapers; Postal Service.
—. Decisionmaking. Executive Branch. 1930-82. *3276*
—. Political Campaigns (presidential). Voting and Voting Behavior. 1972. *2090*
Communications Behavior. Adams family. Attitudes. Family. Generations. 1764-1919. *113*
—. Carter, Jimmy. Debates. Ford, Gerald R. Illinois, University of. Political Campaigns (presidential). Students. Television. 1976. *2091*
—. Carter, Jimmy. Debates. Ford, Gerald R. Political Campaigns (presidential). Public opinion. Television. 1976. *1962*
—. Carter, Jimmy. Debates. Ford, Gerald R. Political Campaigns (presidential). Television. 1976. *2050*
—. Carter, Jimmy. Debates. Ford, Gerald R. Political Campaigns (presidential). Television. 1976. *2097*
—. Carter, Jimmy. House of Representatives. Legislation. Politics. 1977. *2223*
—. Dean, John (resignation). Executive Behavior. Watergate Scandal. 1973. *2496*
—. Nixon, Richard M. 1968-73. *2142*
—. Political Campaigns (presidential). 1960's-70's. *1895*
Communism *See also* Anti-Communist Movements; Leftism.
—. Algeria. Kennedy, John F. Nationalism. Vietnam War. 1950's-63. *2941*
—. Carter, Jimmy (administration). Foreign Policy. Latin America. National Security. 1977-80. *2831*
—. China. Cold War (origins). Foreign policy. 1945. *2648*
—. Churchill, Winston. Diaries. Nuclear Arms. Potsdam Conference. Stalin, Joseph. Truman, Harry S. 1945. *2892*
—. Committee of State Security (KGB). Espionage (review article). Hiss, Alger. Oswald, Lee Harvey. USSR. 1938-78. *1759*
—. Containment. Foreign Policy. Kennan, George F. USSR. 1944-47. *3173*
—. Documents. Foreign Relations. State Department *(Relations with China).* 1944-81. *3019*
—. Elections, presidential. Political Attitudes. 1976. *2015*
—. Foreign policy. Human Rights. Presidents. Religious liberty. USSR. 20c. *151*
—. Foreign policy. Korea. Truman Doctrine. 1945-50. *2728*
—. Foreign policy. Korean War. Truman, Harry S. USSR. 1950. *2900*
—. Foreign relations. Human rights. Liberty. USSR. 1940's-76. *2682*
—. Greece. Guerrilla Warfare. Stalin, Joseph. Tito, Josip. Truman Doctrine. 1946-53. *2847*
—. Hungary. Kun, Bela. Paris Peace Conference. Political Attitudes. Wilson, Woodrow. 1919. *1660*
—. Political Speeches. Public opinion. Rhetoric. Truman, Harry S. USSR. 1945-50. *2263*
Communist Countries *See also* Western Nations.
—. Carter, Jimmy (administration). Foreign Policy. Military Strategy. Reagan, Ronald (administration). 1980. *3122*
Communist Party. Allis-Chalmers Corporation. House of Representatives (Education and Labor Committee). Kennedy, John F. Legislative Investigations. Strikes. United Automobile Workers of America, Local 248. Wisconsin (Milwaukee). 1947. *1723*
—. Carter, Jimmy (administration). Foreign Policy. Italy. Kissinger, Henry A. 1960's-70's. *2855*
—. China. Foreign Policy. State Department. Stuart, John Leighton. 1949. *2631*
Communists. China. Foreign Policy. Liberals. Scholars. 1944-71. *2895*
—. China. Foreign Policy. Shanghai Power Company. Truman, Harry S. (administration). 1948-50. *3111*
Community Participation in Politics. Nebraska. Political Reform. Primaries (presidential). 1948-79. *2073*
Competency commissions. Federal Policy. Indians. Land allotment. 1913-20. *1374*

Compromise of 1850. Austria. Foreign policy. Politics. Spain. Webster, Daniel. 1850-52. *1017*
Compromise of 1877. Democratic Party. Elections (presidential). Historiography. Reconstruction. Republican Party. Woodward, C. Vann. 1876-77. *708*
Comptroller of the Currency. Banking. Federal Reserve System (Board of Governors). Justice Department. Mergers. 1950-66. *3266*
Confederate States of America *See also* names of individual states; Reconstruction.
—. Amnesty. California (San Francisco). *J. M. Chapman* (vessel). Lincoln, Abraham. 1863-65. *792*
—. Canada. Davis, Jefferson. Lincoln, Abraham. Peace missions. Virginia (Richmond). 1864. *789*
—. Letters. Lincoln, Abraham. Maynard, Lizzie Green. 1865. *842*
—. Lincoln, Abraham. Theater. 1861-65. *758*
Conference on Security and Cooperation in Europe. Europe. Ford, Gerald R. (administration). International Security. Public opinion. 1975. *2638*
Conferences. Eddy, William A. Foreign Relations. Ibn Saud, King. Roosevelt, Franklin D. Saudi Arabia. 1945. *1576*
Confidentiality. Accountability. Central Intelligence Agency. Congress. 1940's-74. *3425*
Conflict and Conflict Resolution. Foreign Relations. Kennedy, John F. USSR. 1963. *2708*
Conflict of interest. Antibiotics. Federal regulation. Food and Drug Administration. Periodicals. Pharmaceutical Industry. Welch, Henry. 1959-62. *2434*
Conger, Clement E. Decorative Arts. Onassis, Jacqueline Kennedy. White House. 19c-1980. *2353*
Congo Republic (Leopoldville). *See* Zaire.
Congregationalism *See also* Calvinism; Puritans.
—. Bushnell, Horace. Church and state. Jefferson, Thomas. ca 1800-60. *185*
Congress *See also* House of Representatives; Legislation; Senate.
—. 1974-76. *3399*
—. Accountability. Central Intelligence Agency. Confidentiality. 1940's-74. *3425*
—. Accountability. Executive Power. 1973-78. *3455*
—. Adams, John. American Revolution. Appointments to office. Military General Staff. Washington, George. 1775. *304*
—. Agricultural Policy. Democratic Party. Federal Programs. Presidents. South. 1933-61. *141*
—. Agriculture Department. Budgets. Interest groups. 1971-76. *3365*
—. Aiken, George. Documents. Jenkins, Walter. Johnson, Lyndon B. Mansfield, Mike. Tonkin Gulf Crisis (conference). Vietnam War. 1964. *3088*
—. Alexander, Charles C. Eisenhower, Dwight D. (review article). Reichard, Gary. 1953-61. *2247*
—. Alien Anarchist Act (US, 1918). Anti-Communist Movements. Law Enforcement. Leftism. Post, Louis F. 1919-20. *1268*
—. Anderson, Clinton P. Executive Power. Foreign policy. Nixon, Richard M. Vietnam War. 1945-72. *3138*
—. Antiwar sentiment. Lincoln, Abraham. Mexican War. Whig Party. 1846-49. *514*
—. Argell, James B. Chinese Exclusion Act (US, 1882). Diplomacy. Immigration. 1876-82. *968*
—. Arms Trade. Oversight, congressional. State Department. Taiwan Relations Act (US, 1979). 1979-81. *2864*
—. Autonomy. Politics. Puerto Rico. Roosevelt, Franklin D. (administration). World War II. 1940-45. *1258*
—. Brooks, Preston S. Civil War (antecedents). Republican Party. Sumner, Charles. Violence. 1856. *635*
—. Budgets. Carter, Jimmy. Decisionmaking. Water projects. 1977. *2494*
—. Budgets. Congressional Budget and Impoundment Control Act (US, 1974). Reform. Tax Reform Act (US, 1976). 1974-76. *3344*
—. Budgets. Defense spending. Military capability. 1945-78. *3292*
—. Budgets. Executive Branch. Impoundment. Nixon, Richard M. (administration). Separation of powers. 1972-73. *2219*
—. Budgets. Executive Power. Nixon, Richard M. 1972. *2346*

Crisis management. Cambodia. Decisionmaking. Ford, Gerald R. *Mayaguez* (incident). 1975. *2641*

—. Decisionmaking. Defense Department. Military Intelligence. 1946-75. *3298*

—. Decisionmaking. Diplomacy. Kissinger, Henry A. *Mayaguez* incident. 1975. *2573*

—. Diplomacy. Kissinger, Henry A. Middle East. 1973-74. *2981*

Critical election theory. Elections, presidential. Hoover, Herbert C. Smith, Al. 1916-40. 1928. *1168*

Crittenden, John. Constitutional Union Party. Lawrence, Amos A. 1850-60. *625*

Croly, Herbert. Civil religion. Millenarianism. Politics. Wilson, Woodrow. 1909-19. *1261*

Cromwell, Oliver. Carter, Jimmy. Great Britain. Political Leadership. Religion. Rickover, Hyman. Roosevelt, Theodore. 20c. *73*

Cronin, Thomas E. Hargrove, Erwin C. Hughes, Emmet John. Koenig, Louis W. Presidency (review article). Schlesinger, Arthur M., Jr. 1972-75. *3190*

Crowley, Leo T. Alien Property Custodian. Banking. Federal Deposit Insurance Corporation. Politics. Roosevelt, Franklin D. (administration). 1934-45. *1454*

Cruise missile. Attitudes. Defense Department. Politics and the Military. Weapons. 1964-76. *2212*

Cryptography. Information Storage and Retrieval Systems. National Security Agency. Privacy. 1952-80. *3033*

Cuba. Adams, John Quincy. Expansionism. Monroe Doctrine. 1823. *967*

—. Africa. Foreign policy. Intervention. USSR. ca 1970-77. *3026*

—. Alabama (Mobile). Economic conditions. McKinley, William. Petitions. Spanish-American War. 1897-98. *1005*

—. Appointments to office. Dallas, George M. Diplomats. Elections (presidential). Pierce, Franklin. 1852-56. *611*

—. Assassination. Foreign policy. Kennedy, John F. 1963-77. *3042*

—. Bay of Pigs Invasion. Foreign policy. Vietnam War. Watergate scandal. 1961-74. *3077*

—. Castro, Fidel. Documents. Foreign Relations. Nixon, Richard M. Political Leadership. 1959. *3028*

—. Castro, Fidel. Foreign policy. Imperialism. Policymaking. 1945-80. *2927*

—. Economic policy. Foreign policy. 1933-34. *1487*

—. Estrada Palma, Thomás. Imperialism. Intervention. Roosevelt, Theodore. 1901-06. *1568*

—. Foreign policy. 1961-81. *2880*

—. Foreign Policy. Mexico. Multinational Corporations. Roosevelt, Theodore. Taft, William H. 1880-1915. *1562*

Cuban missile crisis. Atomic Warfare. Diplomacy. Kennedy, John F. Khrushchev, Nikita. 1962. *2591*

—. Atomic warfare. Kennedy, John F. Khrushchev, Nikita. Military strategy. 1962. *2596*

—. Bismarck, Otto von. Diplomacy. Escalation theory. Franco-Prussian War. Kennedy, John F. McNamara, Robert S. 1870. 1962. *3072*

—. Bureaucracies. Foreign Policy. Kennedy, John F. Turkey. 1962. *2767*

—. Decisionmaking. International law. 1962-75. *2985*

—. Foreign Policy. Johnson, Lyndon B. Kennedy, John F. Vietnam War. 1962-68. *2875*

—. Foreign Policy. Kennedy, John F. (administration). UN. USSR. 1962-63. *2763*

—. Jupiter missiles. Kennedy, John F. (administration). Turkey. USSR. 1957-63. *2592*

Cubans. Central Intelligence Agency. Federal Bureau of Investigation. Louisiana (New Orleans). Oswald, Lee Harvey. 1963. *1757*

Cultural relations. China. China. Foreign Aid. State Department. 1942-45. *1622*

Cummings, Homer Stillé. Attorneys General. Federal Bureau of Investigation. Films. *G-Men* (film). Hoover, J. Edgar. 1933-35. *1405*

Cunningham, Noble E., Jr. Jefferson, Thomas (review article). Johnstone, Robert M., Jr. Political Leadership. 1801-09. 1978. *746*

Currie, Lauchlin. Fiscal policy. Income. Keynesianism. New Deal. 1920's-30's. *1469*

Custis, Daniel Parke. Virginia. Washington, George. Washington, Martha. 1732-1802. *211*

Custis, Eleanor Parke. Washington, George. 1785-1852. *273*

Cutting, Bronson M. Democratic Party. New Mexico. Political Campaigns. Roosevelt, Franklin D. Senate. 1934. *1462*

Cyprus. Arms Trade. Carter, Jimmy (administration). Embargoes. Turkey. 1975-78. *3022*

—. Foreign Policy. Greece. Kissinger, Henry A. Turkey. 1974-75. *3085*

—. Foreign policy. Kissinger, Henry A. 1969-74. *2676*

Czolgosz, Leon F. Assassination. McKinley, William. Stockton, Charles G. Surgery. 1901. *392*

D

Daily Life *See also* Popular Culture.

—. Coolidge, Calvin. Massachusetts (Northampton). 1929-33. *1108*

—. Hayes, Rutherford B. Political Leadership. 1877. *840*

Dairying. Federal Regulation. Food Administration. Hoover, Herbert C. 1917-18. *1320*

Dale, Chester. Agricultural Adjustment Administration (Office of the General Counsel). Frank, Jerome. Wallace, Henry A. 1935. *1362*

Dallas, Alexander James. Defense Department. Military Organization. 1815. *763*

Dallas, George M. Appointments to office. Cuba. Diplomats. Elections (presidential). Pierce, Franklin. 1852-56. *611*

—. Barton, William P. C. Courts Martial and Courts of Inquiry. Executive Power. Monroe, James. Witnesses. 1818-23. 1973-74. *938*

—. Democratic Party. Pennsylvania. Political Campaigns. 1844. *614*

Dallek, Robert (review article). Foreign Policy. Roosevelt, Franklin D. 1932-45. 1979. *1569*

Daniels, Jonathan W. Negroes. Race relations. Roosevelt, Franklin D. (administration). World War II. 1943-45. *1291*

Daugherty, Harry M. Antitrust. Attorneys General. Federal Government. Pennsylvania (Philadelphia). Political Corruption. United Gas Improvement Company. 1914-24. *1309*

Davies, Samuel. Eulogies. National Self-image. Washington, George. 1789-1815. *189*

Davis, James John. Labor Secretaries. Pennsylvania. Political Leadership. Republican Party. 1873-1947. *1466*

Davis, Jefferson. Canada. Confederate States of America. Lincoln, Abraham. Peace missions. Virginia (Richmond). 1864. *789*

—. Civil War. Cotton. Lincoln, Abraham. Mississippi. Teasdale, Thomas Cox. War Relief. 1865. *795*

—. Civil War. Lincoln, Abraham. Political Leadership. 1861-65. *863*

—. Defense Secretaries. Firearms. Mexican War. Military officers. Political feuds. Scott, Winfield. 1845-57. *757*

Davis, John W. American Liberty League. New Deal. Political Campaigns. 1932-36. *1161*

Davis, Nathaniel. Angola. Central Intelligence Agency. Intervention. Personal narratives. State Department. 1975. *2687*

Davison, Kenneth E. Hayes, Rutherford B. Research. 1860-1972. *718*

Dawes, Charles Gates. Democratic Party. LaFollette, Robert Marion. Political Campaigns (presidential). Republican Party. South Dakota (Sioux Falls). 1924. *1208*

Dawes, Henry L. Johnson, Andrew. Politics. Reconstruction. Republican Party. 1865-75. *770*

Dayton, Elias. American Revolution. Armies. Letters. New Jersey Regiment, 3d. Washington, George. 1780. *275*

Dayton, William L. Elections (presidential). Frémont, John C. Political conventions. Republican Party. 1854-56. *662*

Dean, John. Branch, Taylor (review article). Nixon, Richard M. (administration). Watergate scandal. 1972. *2462*

Dean, John (resignation). Communications Behavior. Executive Behavior. Watergate Scandal. 1973. *2496*

Death and Dying *See also* Aged.

—. Armies. Chancellorsville (battle). Hospitals (military). Letters. Lincoln, Abraham. 1863. *897*

Death Penalty. *See* Capital Punishment.

Debates. Agendas. Carter, Jimmy. Ford, Gerald R. Political Campaigns (presidential). 1976. *1799*

—. Bush, George. Primaries (presidential). Reagan, Ronald. Republican Party. Texas (Houston). 1980. *1908*

—. Carter, Jimmy. Communications Behavior. Ford, Gerald R. Illinois, University of. Political Campaigns (presidential). Students. Television. 1976. *2091*

—. Carter, Jimmy. Communications Behavior. Ford, Gerald R. Political Campaigns (presidential). Public opinion. Television. 1976. *1962*

—. Carter, Jimmy. Communications Behavior. Ford, Gerald R. Political Campaigns (presidential). Television. 1976. *2050*

—. Carter, Jimmy. Communications Behavior. Ford, Gerald R. Political Campaigns (presidential). Television. 1976. *2097*

—. Carter, Jimmy. Eye contact. Ford, Gerald R. Political Campaigns (presidential). Public Opinion. Television. 1976. *1842*

—. Carter, Jimmy. Ford, Gerald R. Mass Media. Voting and Voting Behavior. Wisconsin. 1976. *1828*

—. Carter, Jimmy. Ford, Gerald R. Political Campaigns (presidential). Public Opinion. Television. 1976. *2000*

—. Carter, Jimmy. Ford, Gerald R. Political Campaigns (presidential). Television. 1976. *1961*

—. Democratic Party. Political Attitudes. Political campaigns, presidential. Republican Party. 1960-76. *1992*

—. Douglas, Stephen A. Illinois. Lincoln, Abraham. Political Campaigns (senatorial). Slavery. 1774-1858. *401*

—. Elections (presidential). Journalism. Kennedy, John F. Nixon, Richard M. Television. White, Theodore H. 1960. *1789*

—. Mass Media. Political Campaigns (presidential). Rhetoric. 1980. *1804*

—. New Mexico (Albuquerque). Political campaigns. 1980. *1972*

—. Political Campaigns (presidential). Political issues. Television. 1960. 1976. *1995*

—. Political Campaigns (presidential). Public Opinion. Television. 1960-76. *1932*

—. Political Campaigns (presidential). Television. Voting and Voting Behavior. 1960-76. *1827*

Decentralization. Central Intelligence Agency (Operations Directorate). USSR. 1945-79. *2705*

Decisionmaking *See also* Elites; Foreign Policy.

—. Afghanistan. Carter, Jimmy (administration). Cold War. Defense spending. Inflation. Iran. USSR. 1979-80. *2284*

—. Agendas. Domestic Policy. Presidents. 1961-80. *2424*

—. Alperovitz, Gar (review article). Atomic Warfare. Historiography. Japan (Hiroshima). World War II. 1945-65. *3056*

—. Atomic Warfare. Japan (Hiroshima, Nagasaki). Military Strategy. World War II. 1944-45. *1536*

—. Berlin Blockade. Foreign policy. Ideology. Israel. Truman, Harry S. 1944-48. *3011*

—. Berlin Crisis. Foreign Relations. Germany. Intelligence Service. Kennedy, John F. 1961. *2644*

—. Bowles, Chester. Kennedy, John F. (administration). Personality. Political leadership. 1953-78. *3154*

—. Budgets. Carter, Jimmy. Congress. Water projects. 1977. *2494*

—. Bureaucracies. Foreign Policy. Johnson, Lyndon B. (administration). Nixon, Richard M. (administration). Strategic Arms Limitation Talks. 1966-74. *3009*

—. Bureaucracies. State Department (Foreign Service). 1977. *3215*

—. Bureaucrats. Foreign Policy (review article). Politics. Presidents. 1945-75. *3367*

—. Cambodia. Civil-Military Relations. *Mayaguez* incident. Military Strategy. Raids. Sontay raid. Vietnam War. 1970-79. *2817*

—. Cambodia. Crisis management. Ford, Gerald R. *Mayaguez* (incident). 1975. *2641*

—. Cambodia. Korea, North. *Mayaguez* incident. *Pueblo* incident. 1969-75. *2773*

—. Carter, Jimmy. Conscription, Military. Deserters. Draft dodgers. Pardons. Vietnam War. 1964-77. *2499*

—. Carter, Jimmy. Executive Behavior. Politics. 1977-78. *2211*

—. Carter, Jimmy. Ford, Gerald R. Nixon, Richard M. 1970's. *3236*

—. Carter, Jimmy. Foreign policy. 1977-78. 2582
—. Carter, Jimmy (administration). Cities. Federal policy. Planning. Presidential staffs. 1977-80. 2533
—. China. Eisenhower, Dwight D. Taiwan Strait crisis. 1954-55. 3025
—. Cold War. Disarmament. Eisenhower, Dwight D. Nuclear arms. USSR. 1953-61. 3073
—. Communications. Executive Branch. 1930-82. 3276
—. Congress. Executive branch. Foreign policy. Secrecy. 1970's. 3361
—. Congress. Foreign policy. Kennedy, John F. Nixon, Richard M. Presidents. 1970's. 3286
—. Connally, John. Economic Policy. Exchange rates. Foreign policy. Nixon, Richard M. (administration). 1944-73. 2947
—. Crisis management. Defense Department. Military Intelligence. 1946-75. 3298
—. Crisis management. Diplomacy. Kissinger, Henry A. Mayaguez incident. 1975. 2573
—. Cuban Missile Crisis. International law. 1962-75. 2985
—. Defense Department. House of Representatives (Armed Services Committee). McNamara, Robert S. Politics and the Military. 1965-68. 3257
—. Delbecq, André L. Presidential Staffs. Public administration. 1933-74. 58
—. Delegates. Goffman, Erving. Political Conventions. Professionalism. 1976. 2008
—. Economic conditions. Europe. Foreign Policy. Marshall Plan. 1946-47. 2802
—. Economists. Johnson, Lyndon B. (administration). 1963-69. 2323
—. Eden, Anthony. Great Britain. Nixon, Richard M. Political Leadership. War. 1956-70. 3179
—. Enrolled bills. Legislation. Office of Management and Budget. Presidents. 1932-77. 3469
—. Executive Branch. Food. Interest Groups. 1970-81. 3313
—. Executive Power. Steel industry seizure. Truman, Harry S. 1952-75. 2368
—. Federal Policy. Ideology. Presidents (review article). 1961-76. 2256
—. Foreign Policy. 1947-80. 3411
—. Foreign policy. Intelligence Service. Kissinger, Henry A. National Security Council. Nixon, Richard M. (administration). 1961-75. 2660
—. Foreign policy. Jackson, Henry. Kissinger, Henry A. Political Change. 1970-75. 2508
—. Foreign policy. Latin America. Methodology. 1965-80. 2645
—. Foreign Policy. Roosevelt, Franklin D. 1937-43. 1595
—. Foreign Relations. Forgeries. Peter I. Propaganda. Truman, Harry S. USSR. Wills. 1725-1948. 2659
—. Intergovernmental relations. Office of Management and Budget. 1921-74. 3212
—. Johnson, Lyndon B. Presidential advisers. Vietnam War. 1963-69. 2766
—. National Security Council (NSC 68). State Department (Policy Planning Staff). Technology. USSR. 1946-80. 3176
—. Presidency. 1960's-77. 3192
Declaration of Independence. Adams, John. Beccaria, Cesare. Crime and Criminals. Founding Fathers. Jefferson, Thomas. Madison, James. 1764-89. 246
—. Carter, Jimmy (administration). Foreign policy. Idealism. Morality. ca 1918-78. 2784
—. Civil rights. Negroes. Slavery. 1776-1976. 41
—. Conservatism. Jefferson, Thomas (review article). Property. Wills, Garry. 1776. 1978-80. 288
—. Enlightenment. Jefferson, Thomas (review article). Locke, John. Political Theory. Scotland. Wills, Garry. 1690's-1776. 1970's. 261
—. Equality. Jaffa, Harry V. Lincoln, Abraham. Political Theory. 1860's. 1950's-70's. 411
—. Jefferson, Thomas. Slavery. 1776. 250
—. Jefferson, Thomas. Virginia. 1743-1826. 207
—. Jefferson, Thomas (review article). Philosophy. Wills, Garry. 1776. 290
DeConde, Alexander (review article). France. Jefferson, Thomas. Louisiana Purchase. 1800-03. 985
Decorative Arts. Conger, Clement E. Onassis, Jacqueline Kennedy. White House. 19c-1980. 2353

—. Diplomatic reception rooms. State Department. 18c-1981. 167
Defense Department. Armaments. Laird, Melvin. McNamara, Robert S. Politics and the Military. 1960-76. 2215
—. Armies. Hastie, William Henry. Negroes. Racism. Stimson, Henry L. World War II. 1940-43. 1376
—. Armies. Military Organization. National Security Act (US, 1947). 1947-50. 3297
—. Attitudes. Cruise missile. Politics and the Military. Weapons. 1964-76. 2212
—. Booth, John Wilkes. Conspiracy. Eisenschiml, Otto. Kidnapping. Lincoln, Abraham. Research. 1865. ca 1930-80. 835
—. Brown, Harold. Carter, Jimmy (administration). Military Strategy. Strategic Arms Limitation Talks. 1977. 3105
—. Bureaucracies. 1960's-70's. 3418
—. Civil-Military Relations. Eisenhower, Dwight D. (administration). Wilson, Charles E. 1953-57. 2185
—. Civil-Military Relations. McNamara, Robert S. Vietnam War. 1961-68. 2206
—. Congress. Military finance. 1974. 2179
—. Crisis management. Decisionmaking. Military Intelligence. 1946-75. 3298
—. Dallas, Alexander James. Military Organization. 1815. 763
—. Decisionmaking. House of Representatives (Armed Services Committee). McNamara, Robert S. Politics and the Military. 1965-68. 3257
—. Defense Reorganization Act (US, 1958). Military General Staff. Military Organization. 1958. 3206
—. Democratic Party. Military bases. Negroes. Politics and the Military. 1962-73. 2379
—. Democratic Party. Nominations for office. Pennsylvania. Porter, James M. Tyler, John. 1824-43. 822
—. Economic Growth. Propaganda. State Department. World War II. 1939-45. 1468
—. Federal Programs. 1970's. 3311
—. Foreign Policy. Middle East. 1965-77. 3012
—. Hastie, William Henry. Military reform. Racism. World War II. 1940-43. 1378
—. Housing. Integration. Military. Social change. 1967-68. 2503
—. Marines. Military Organization. National Security Act (US, 1947). Navies. 1947-50. 3230
—. McNamara, Robert S. Navies. Tonkin Gulf crisis. Vietnam War. 1961-68. 2904
—. Military intelligence. VanDeman, Ralph H. 1897-1919. 1704
—. National Security Act (US, 1947). 1947-77. 3459
—. Schlesinger, James R. 1973-75. 2205
Defense Policy See also National Security.
—. Air Forces. F-111 (aircraft). McNamara, Robert S. Navies. Vietnam War. 1960-70. 2675
—. Airplane Industry and Trade. Business. Military-industrial complex. Truman, Harry S. 1945-53. 2231
—. Americas (North and South). Monroe Doctrine. Roosevelt, Franklin D. (administration). 1930's-40. 1550
—. Armaments. Reagan, Ronald (administration). USSR. 1981. 2624
—. Arms race. McNamara, Robert S. Technology. 1960's. 2282
—. Betts, Richard K. Ignatius, Paul R. Joint Chiefs of Staff (review article). Military Organization. Steadman, Richard C. 1958-78. 3287
—. Budgets. Carter, Jimmy (administration). 1978. 2844
—. Canada. Great Britain. Navies. Ogdensburg Agreement. Permanent Joint Board on Defense. Roosevelt, Franklin D. 1940. 1635
—. Carter, Jimmy. Executive Order No. 59. 1973-80. 2237
—. Congress. Europe. Nixon, Richard M. (administration). USSR. Vietnam War. 1968-73. 2944
—. Counterforce. Massive Retaliation. Military Strategy. 1952-75. 2553
—. Deterrence. Mobilization. Planning. 1978. 2642
—. Documents. Truman, Harry S. (administration). 1946-75. 2991
—. Dulles, John Foster. Eisenhower, Dwight D. Goodpaster, Andrew. Nuclear test ban issue. Strauss, Lewis. USSR. 1958. 2696
—. Economic Conditions. Reagan, Ronald (administration). 1981-82. 2344

—. Eisenhower, Dwight D. Massive retaliation. Truman, Harry S. 1950-61. 3149
—. Eisenhower, Dwight D. Wilson, Charles E. 1953-57. 2184
—. Federal Policy. Industry. Labor Unions and Organizations. World War II. 1939-41. 1435
—. Foreign policy. Presidency. Public opinion. Vietnam War. Watergate scandal. 1970's. 3374
—. Foreign Relations. Japan. 1979-81. 2937
—. Hamilton, Alexander. Madison, James. Tariff. Trans-Appalachian West. Washington, George. 1791-92. 715
—. ICBM's. Johnson, Lyndon B. Kennedy, John F. Kuter, Lawrence S. Personal Narratives. 1962. 2209
—. McNamara, Robert S. Planning-Programming-Budgeting System. Systems analysis. 1961-68. 2232
—. Navy Department. 1929-41. 1702
—. Nixon, Richard M. Nuclear arms. Strategic Arms Limitation Talks. 1973. 3106
—. Nuclear Arms. Reagan, Ronald (administration). USSR. 1980-81. 3084
Defense Policy (review article). Aliano, Richard A. Eisenhower, Dwight D. (administration). Killian, James R., Jr. Kinnard, Douglas. Kistiakowsky, George B. Military Strategy. 1953-61. 2627
Defense Reorganization Act (US, 1958). Defense Department. Military General Staff. Military Organization. 1958. 3206
Defense secretaries. 1947-80. 3473
—. Davis, Jefferson. Firearms. Mexican War. Military officers. Political feuds. Scott, Winfield. 1845-57. 757
Defense spending. Afghanistan. Carter, Jimmy (administration). Cold War. Decisionmaking. Inflation. Iran. USSR. 1979-80. 2284
—. Brown, Harold. Carter, Jimmy. USSR. 1964-80. 2617
—. Budgets. Congress. Military capability. 1945-78. 3292
—. Carter, Jimmy (administration). Foreign policy. Military. NATO. Politics. 1976. 2625
—. Carter, Jimmy (administration). Foreign Relations. 1977-80. 2270
—. Documents. Foreign policy. Truman, Harry S. (administration). 1947-79. 2608
—. Eisenhower, Dwight D. Military strategy. 1952-60. 2207
deGaulle, Charles. China. Churchill, Winston. Colonialism. Foreign Policy. France. Indochina. Roosevelt, Franklin D. 1942-45. 1588
—. Kissinger, Henry A. Nationalism. Nkrumah, Kwame. Nyerere, Julius. Political Leadership. 1940's-70's. 2905
Delaware See also Southeastern States.
—. Bryan, William Jennings. Foreign Policy. Political Campaigns (presidential). Stevenson, Adlai E. (1835-1914). 1900. 682
Delbecq, André L. Decisionmaking. Presidential Staffs. Public administration. 1933-74. 58
Delegates. Attitudes. Political Conventions. 1968. 1916
—. California. Democratic Party. Political Conventions. 1968-76. 2129
—. California (Los Angeles). Democratic Party. Kansas. Political campaigns (Presidential). Political Conventions. 1960. 1899
—. Carter, Jimmy. Democratic Party. Political Attitudes. Political Conventions. 1976. 1930
—. Caucuses. Political conventions. Republican Party. 1976. 2032
—. Decisionmaking. Goffman, Erving. Political Conventions. Professionalism. 1976. 2008
—. Democratic Party. Lengle, James. Political Theory. Primaries, presidential. Reform. Shafer, Byron. 1972. 1900
—. Democratic Party. Michigan. Political conventions. Political Conventions. 1972. 1985
—. Democratic Party. Minorities. Political Conventions. 1964-72. 1931
—. Democratic Party. Political Conventions. 1972. 1904
—. Democratic Party. Political Conventions. Political Reform. South. 1972. 1847
—. Democratic Party. Political Conventions. Politicians. 1968-74. 1915
—. Ford, Gerald R. Political conventions. Reagan, Ronald. Republican Party. 1976. 2009
—. Lincoln, Abraham. New Hampshire. Political conventions. Republican Party. 1860. 657
—. Political Conventions. 1972. 1814
—. Political Conventions. 1972. 1905

—. Political Conventions. Political Participation. Republican Party. 1972. *2043*
—. Political Conventions. Primaries, presidential. 1968-76. *1982*
—. Political conventions. Republican Party. Roosevelt, Theodore. Taft, William H. Texas. 1912. *1150*
DeLolme, Jean Louis. Adams, John. Conservatism. Political theory. Radicals and Radicalism. Turgot, Anne Robert. 1760-1800. *179*
DeMause, Lloyd. Carter, Jimmy (review article). Ebel, Henry. Presidency. Psychohistory. 1977. *1728*
—. Ebel, Henry. Kearns, Doris. Mazlish, Bruce. Presidency. Psychohistory (review article). 1960-80. *1742*
Dement'ev, I. P. American Historical Association (meeting). Historians. Methodology. Political parties. Roosevelt, Franklin D. Sivachev, N. V. 1981. *1433*
Demilitarization. Byrnes, James F. Cold War. Germany. Great Powers. Molotov, V. M. Treaties. 1946. *2743*
Democracies. Developing Nations. Dictatorships. Foreign policy. Nixon, Richard M. 1790-1975. *2634*
Democracy *See also* Aristocracy; Federal Government; Middle Classes; Referendum; Suffrage.
—. American Revolution. Law. Lincoln, Abraham. 1775-83. 1850's-65. *525*
—. Attitudes. Federal Reserve System. Income tax. Reform. Wilson, Woodrow. 1913-21. *1353*
—. Authoritarianism. Elections (presidential). Nixon, Richard M. Political Corruption. Watergate scandal. 1968-72. *1850*
—. Brazil. Foreign policy. 1964-68. *2862*
—. Civil Rights. Civil War. Lincoln, Abraham. Property. Slavery. 1861-65. *786*
—. Dominican Republic. Ideology. Intervention. Mexico. 1914-65. *67*
—. Emergency powers. Presidents. 17c-1979. *61*
—. Executive power. Political Reform. Social psychology. 1960's-75. *3438*
—. Foreign Policy (review article). 1865-1950. *20*
—. Inaugural addresses. Political Speeches. Roosevelt, Franklin D. Values. 1901-77. *52*
—. Nixon, Richard M. (resignation). Watergate Scandal. 1972-74. *3394*
—. Political parties. Presidency. Tocqueville, Alexis de. 1830's. *1035*
—. Presidency. Press. Public Opinion. 1789-1978. *101*
Democratic Party. Abortion. Catholic Church. Elections (presidential). 1976. *1914*
—. Adams, John Quincy. Elections (presidential). Jackson, Andrew. Slavery. Whig Party. 1828-44. *923*
—. AFL-CIO. Carter, Jimmy. Labor Unions and Organizations. Public welfare. 1976. *2063*
—. Agricultural Policy. Congress. Federal Programs. Presidents. South. 1933-61. *141*
—. Alabama. Federal Elections Bill. Political Campaigns. South. Stevenson, Adlai E. (1835-1914). 1889-93. *685*
—. Armies. Military training. Preparedness. South. Wilson, Woodrow. 1915-20. *1452*
—. Arvey, Jacob M. Illinois (Chicago). Political Conventions. Stevenson, Adlai E. 1932-52. *1806*
—. Barkley, Alben W. Political Conventions. Political Speeches. Vice-Presidents. 1948. *1832*
—. Barkley, Alben W. Political Conventions. Vice-presidency. 1948. *2105*
—. Barkley, Alben W. Roosevelt, Franklin D. Senate. Taxation. 1944. *1285*
—. Barkley, Alben W. Roosevelt, Franklin D. Senate (majority leader). Supreme Court. 1937. *1286*
—. Bland, Richard Parks. Free Silver movement. Missouri. Political Campaigns. 1878-96. *692*
—. Breckinridge, John C. Buchanan, James. Iowa (Pella). Michigan. Political Campaigns (presidential). Scholte, Henry (Hendrick) P. 1846-56. *706*
—. Brown, Jerry. Carter, Jimmy. Political campaigns (Presidential). Political campaigns (Presidential). 1976. *1816*
—. Bryan, Charles Wayland. Political Campaigns (presidential). South Dakota. Vice-Presidents. 1924. *1207*

—. Bryan, William Jennings. Imperialism. Philippines. Political Campaigns (presidential). Stevenson, Adlai E. (1835-1914). 1900. *690*
—. Bryan, William Jennings. Maine (Bath). Political Campaigns (vice-presidential). Sewall, Arthur. 1896. *686*
—. Bryan, William Jennings. Political Campaigns (presidential). Stevenson, Adlai E. (1835-1914). 1892-1900. *684*
—. Bryan, William Jennings. Political Conventions. Wilson, Woodrow. 1912. *1148*
—. Buchanan, James. Douglas, Stephen A. Elections. Kansas. Lecompton Constitution. Slavery. 1854-60. *624*
—. Buchanan, James. Patronage. 1857-61. *892*
—. Byrd, Harry F. Eisenhower, Dwight D. Elections (presidential). Virginia. 1952. *2094*
—. Byrd, Harry F. Elections (congressional). Glass, Carter. Patronage. Politics. Roosevelt, Franklin D. Senate. Virginia. 1938. *1324*
—. Byrd, Harry F. Elections (presidential). Roosevelt, Franklin D. State Politics. Virginia. 1932. *1205*
—. Byrd, Harry F. Elections, presidential. Truman, Harry S. Virginia. 1948. *2093*
—. Byrd, Harry F. Patronage. Senate. Virginia. 1935-39. *1350*
—. Byrd, Harry F. Political Campaigns (presidential). Political campaigns (presidential). Political Conventions. Roosevelt, Franklin D. 1932. *1158*
—. Byrnes, James F. Political conventions. Political Factions. Roosevelt, Franklin D. Truman, Harry S. Vice-Presidency. Wallace, Henry A. 1944. *1181*
—. Calhoun, John C. Economic policy. Slavery. South. VanBuren, Martin. 1837-41. *814*
—. California. Civil War (antecedents). Political Conventions. 1860. *704*
—. California. Delegates. Political Conventions. 1968-76. *2129*
—. California (Los Angeles). Delegates. Kansas. Political campaigns (Presidential). Political Conventions. 1960. *1899*
—. Campaign finance. Economic theory. Elections, presidential. Federal Regulation. 1976. *1783*
—. Campaign Finance Act (US, 1974; amended, 1976). Carter, Jimmy. Primaries (presidential). 1974-76. *1969*
—. Carter, Jimmy. Caucuses. Iowa. Political Campaigns (presidential). 1975-76. *1906*
—. Carter, Jimmy. Caucuses. Iowa. Political Campaigns (presidential). 1975. *2118*
—. Carter, Jimmy. Delegates. Political Attitudes. Political Conventions. 1976. *1930*
—. Carter, Jimmy. Group fantasy. Political Conventions. 1974-76. *1902*
—. Carter, Jimmy. Kennedy, Edward M. Political Campaigns (presidential). Press. 1979. *2037*
—. Carter, Jimmy. Kennedy, John F. Politics. 1961-63. 1977-80. *2257*
—. Carter, Jimmy. Primaries (presidential). 1976. *2131*
—. *Catholic Herald and Visitor*. Lincoln, Abraham. Newspapers. Pennsylvania (Philadelphia). Political Commentary. 1861-65. *826*
—. City politics (review article). Dorsett, Lyle W. Fine, Sidney. Roosevelt, Franklin D. Trout, Charles H. 1930-40. *1328*
—. Civil rights. Congress. Kennedy, John F. 1960-63. *2376*
—. Civil Rights Act (US, 1964). Indiana. Primaries (presidential). Wallace, George C. Welsh, Matthew E. 1964. *2111*
—. Civil War. Copperheads. Illinois. Lincoln, Abraham. 1861-65. *872*
—. Civil War. Lincoln, Abraham. Phelps, Richard Harvey. Political Protest. 1861-64. *777*
—. Clark, Bennett Champ. Committee of One. Missouri. Political Campaigns (presidential). 1936. *1197*
—. Clement, Frank Goad. Political Conventions. Political Speeches. Tennessee. 1956. *1834*
—. Cleveland, Grover. 1884-97. *723*
—. Cleveland, Grover. Political Campaigns (presidential). Stevenson, Adlai E. (1835-1914). 1888-92. *688*
—. Compromise of 1877. Elections (presidential). Historiography. Reconstruction. Republican Party. Woodward, C. Vann. 1876-77. *708*
—. Congress. Elections (congressional). George, Walter F. Roosevelt, Franklin D. 1938. *1270*
—. Congress. Panama Canal. South. Tolls controversy. Wilson, Woodrow. 1901-13. *1497*

—. Conservatism. Kennedy, John F. Political Campaigns (presidential). Political Conventions. South. 1956-60. *1959*
—. Constitutional Amendments (18th and 21st). Political Conventions. Prohibition repeal. Raskob, John J. Roosevelt, Franklin D. 1928-33. *1166*
—. Cutting, Bronson M. New Mexico. Political Campaigns. Roosevelt, Franklin D. Senate. 1934. *1462*
—. Dallas, George M. Pennsylvania. Political Campaigns. 1844. *614*
—. Dawes, Charles Gates. LaFollette, Robert Marion. Political Campaigns (presidential). Republican Party. South Dakota (Sioux Falls). 1924. *1208*
—. Debates. Political Attitudes. Political campaigns, presidential. Republican Party. 1960-76. *1992*
—. Defense Department. Military bases. Negroes. Politics and the Military. 1962-73. *2379*
—. Defense Department. Nominations for office. Pennsylvania. Porter, James M. Tyler, John. 1824-43. *822*
—. Delegates. Lengle, James. Political Theory. Primaries, presidential. Reform. Shafer, Byron. 1972. *1900*
—. Delegates. Michigan. Political conventions. Political Conventions. 1972. *1985*
—. Delegates. Minorities. Political Conventions. 1964-72. *1931*
—. Delegates. Political Conventions. 1972. *1904*
—. Delegates. Political Conventions. Political Reform. South. 1972. *1847*
—. Delegates. Political Conventions. Politicians. 1968-74. *1915*
—. Dewey, Thomas E. Elections, gubernatorial. Farley, James A. New York. Roosevelt, Franklin D. State Politics. 1942. *1444*
—. Domestic Policy. Internationalism. New Deal. Political Campaigns. Roosevelt, Franklin D. 1938-40. *1223*
—. Douglas, Stephen A. Letters. Political Conventions. South Carolina (Charleston). Stephens, Alexander H. Vallandigham, Clement L. 1860. *634*
—. Eaton Affair. Ely, Ezra Stiles. Jackson, Andrew. 1829-30. *805*
—. Eisenhower, Dwight D. (administration). Foreign policy. 1952-56. *3001*
—. Elections. Indiana. Kern, John W. Political Leadership. Senate. Wilson, Woodrow. 1916. *1414*
—. Elections. Political leadership. Roosevelt, Franklin D. 1942. *1298*
—. Elections. Political Systems. Republican Party. 1976. *2113*
—. Elections (presidential). Foreign policy. McGovern, George S. 1972. *1866*
—. Elections, presidential. Illinois (Cook County). Political Corruption. 1960. *1940*
—. Elections (presidential). Iowa. Roosevelt, Franklin D. 1932. *1154*
—. Elections (presidential). Jews. Political attitudes. Voting and Voting Behavior. 1972-80. *1912*
—. Elections (presidential). Lichtman, Allan J. (review article). Louisiana. Smith, Al. 1928. *1147*
—. Elections (presidential). Louisiana. Smith, Al. 1928. *1211*
—. Elections (presidential). Massachusetts. Roosevelt, Franklin D. Smith, Al. 1928-32. *1153*
—. Elections, presidential. McGovern, George S. 1972. *1974*
—. Elections (presidential). McGovern, George S. Voting and voting behavior. Wisconsin. 1972. *1860*
—. Elections (presidential). Political Conventions. 1968. 1972. *2078*
—. Elections (presidential). Rocky Mountain states. Voting and Voting Behavior. Wilson, Woodrow. 1916. *1190*
—. Elections (presidential). Stevenson, Adlai E. (1835-1914). 1896. *678*
—. Elections, presidential. Voting and Voting Behavior. 1972. *2134*
—. Elections (senatorial). Georgia. New Deal. Roosevelt, Franklin D. Talmadge, Eugene. 1926-38. *1271*
—. Elections (senatorial). Missouri. New Deal. Primaries. Truman, Harry S. 1934. *1736*
—. Executive power. Nixon, Richard M. (resignation). Watergate scandal. 1974. *3474*
—. Filibusters. House of Representatives. Race Relations. Reconstruction. Roll-call voting. 1876-77. *615*

—. Florida (Miami). McGovern, George S.
Political Campaigns (presidential). Radicals and
Radicalism. 1972. *1926*
—. Garner, John Nance. Political Conventions.
Rayburn, Sam. Roosevelt, Franklin D. 1932.
1182
—. Georgia. Political Campaigns (presidential).
Press. Russell, Richard B. 1952. *1890*
—. Gillette, Guy M. House of Representatives.
Iowa. Political Campaigns. Roosevelt, Franklin
D. 1932-48. *1326*
—. Good Neighbor League Colored Committee.
Negroes. Political Campaigns (presidential).
Roosevelt, Franklin D. 1936. *1198*
—. Hague, Frank. New Deal. New Jersey.
Roosevelt, Franklin D. 1932-40. *1289*
—. Higgins, Andrew J. Political Campaigns
(presidential). Roosevelt, Franklin D. 1944.
1175
—. Historiography. Illinois (Chicago). Mass
media. Political Conventions. Public opinion.
Violence. 1968. *1921*
—. Illinois (Chicago). Law Enforcement. Political
Conventions. Political Protest. Students.
1856-1978. *1973*
—. Jackson, Andrew. Politics. VanBuren, Martin.
1823-40. *804*
—. Kennedy, John F. Political conventions.
Roosevelt, Eleanor. 1958-61. *1877*
—. Kennedy, John F. Primaries (presidential).
West Virginia. 1960. *1815*
—. Kentucky. Political Campaigns
(vice-presidential). Stevenson, Adlai E.
(1835-1914). 1892. *679*
—. McAdoo, William G. Murray, Robert K.
(review article). New York City. Political
Conventions. Smith, Al. 1924. *1180*
—. McGovern, George S. Political Conventions.
Political Reform. 1972. *2031*
—. Meredith, Edwin T. Political Conventions.
Vice-presidency. 1924. *1183*
—. Michigan. Political Reform. Primaries
(presidential). 1970-76. *1984*
—. Missouri. Pendergast, Thomas J. Political
Conventions. Roosevelt, Franklin D. State
Politics. 1932. *1193*
—. New Deal. Ohio. Political Campaigns
(presidential). 1936. *1196*
—. New Deal. Pennsylvania (Pittsburgh). Political
Theory. Quantitative Methods. Voting and
Voting Behavior. Wisconsin. 1912-40. *1185*
—. Parker, Alton Brooks. Political Campaigns
(presidential). 1904. *1191*
—. Political Ambition. Presidency. Roll-call
voting. Senate. 1969-70. *2025*
—. Political ambition. Presidency. Schlesinger,
Joseph. Senate. 1952-76. *2102*
—. Political Campaigns (presidential). Primaries
(presidential). Smith, Al. South Dakota.
1928. *1184*
—. Political Campaigns (presidential). Republican
Party. 1976. *2126*
—. Political Campaigns (vice-presidential).
Populism. South. Stevenson, Adlai E.
(1835-1914). 1892. *681*
—. Political Campaigns (vice-presidential).
Stevenson, Adlai E. (1835-1914). Virginia.
1892. *683*
—. Political Conventions. Political Reform. 1972.
1826
—. Political Conventions. Political Reform. 1972.
1883
—. Political Conventions. Sex Discrimination.
Women. 1972. *1990*
—. Politics. Stevenson, Adlai E. (1835-1914).
1893-97. *931*
—. Politics. VanBuren, Martin. 1837-41. *813*
—. Primaries (presidential). Reynolds, John.
Wallace, George C. Wisconsin. 1964. *1901*
—. Stevenson, Adlai E. (1835-1914). 1876-1908.
562
Democratic-Republican Party. Antifederalists.
Jefferson, Thomas. 1780's-1800's. *229*
—. Armies. Jefferson, Thomas. Lewis,
Meriwether. 1800-03. *731*
—. Elections (presidential). Federalists. Pinckney,
Thomas. South Carolina. 1796. *677*
—. Embargoes. Great Britain. Madison, James.
Non-Intercourse Act (US, 1809). 1808-09.
1027
—. Madison, James. Political Factions. War of
1812. 1800-15. *1025*
Democrats. Calhoun, John C. Congress. Mexican
War. Polk, James K. Whig Party. 1846-48.
1016
—. Civil War. Navy Secretaries. Niven, John
(review article). Welles, Gideon. 1820's-70's.
740

Demonstrations *See also* Riots.
—. American Civil Liberties Union. Federal
Bureau of Investigation. Hoover, J. Edgar.
Political surveillance. Trade Union Education
League. 1924-36. *1457*
Deportation. Anti-Communist Movements.
Immigrants. Justice Department. Labor
Department. Palmer, A. Mitchell. Post, Louis
F. Wilson, William B. 1919-20. *1307*
Depressions *See also* Recessions.
—. Arkansas. Federal Aid to Education. Federal
Emergency Relief Administration. Hopkins,
Harry. Public schools. 1933-36. *1412*
—. Charities. Food. Hoover, Herbert C. Red
Cross. Wheat, surplus. 1932-33. *1356*
—. City Politics (review article). Massachusetts
(Boston). New Deal. Roosevelt, Franklin D.
(administration). Trout, Charles H. 1929-39.
1977. *1292*
—. Civil Works Administration. Louisiana.
1932-34. *1386*
—. Disarmament. Hoover, Herbert C. Washington
Conference. 1920-22. *1674*
—. Economic Policy. Germany. Nazism. New
Deal. ca 1933-36. *1304*
—. Economic Reform. Fisher, Irving. Roosevelt,
Franklin D. 1930's. *1251*
—. Elections (presidential). Hoover, Herbert C.
Missouri. Roosevelt, Franklin D. 1932. *1152*
—. Fausold, Martin L. Hoover, Herbert C. (review
article). Mazuzan, George T. Wilson, Joan
Hoff. 1929-33. 1974-75. *1224*
—. Federal Theatre Project. Flanagan, Hallie.
Hopkins, Harry. Politics. Theater. Works
Progress Administration. 1935-39. *1266*
—. Hoover, Herbert C. Hopkins, Harry. Lewis,
John L. Wallace, Henry A. 1930-69. *1425*
—. Hoover, Herbert C. New Deal. Political
Commentary. Republican Party. 1933-35.
1059
—. LaFollette, Philip F. New Deal. Progressivism.
Roosevelt, Franklin D. Wisconsin Works Bill.
1935. *1383*
—. Roosevelt, Franklin D. (administration). Social
Security Act (US, 1935). ca 1933-37. *1283*
DePriest, Oscar. Hoover, Herbert C.
(administration). House of Representatives.
Negroes. Politics. Republican Party. 1929.
1288
Deregulation. Filibusters. Mondale, Walter F.
Natural gas. Senate. Vice-presidency. 1977.
2454
DeSantis, Hugh (review article). Cold War.
Diplomacy. State Department (Foreign Service).
USSR. 1933-47. *1552*
Desegregation *See also* Segregation.
—. Federal regulation. Health, Education, and
Welfare Department. Public Schools. South.
1954-73. *2335*
Deserters. Carter, Jimmy. Conscription, Military.
Decisionmaking. Draft dodgers. Pardons.
Vietnam War. 1964-77. *2499*
Design. Naval administration. *Nevada* (vessel).
Warships. 1911. *1227*
Desks. Gifts. Hayes, Rutherford B. *Resolute*
(vessel). Victoria, Queen. White House (oval
office). 1880. *977*
Detente *See also* Balance of Power.
—. ca 1970-80. *2635*
—. Balance of power. China. Foreign policy.
USSR. 1945-79. *2616*
—. Balance of power. Europe. USSR. 1648-1973.
2636
—. Brezhnev, Leonid. Ford, Gerald R.
Vladivostok Accord. 1974. *2936*
—. Carter, Jimmy. Disarmament. Human rights.
Kissinger, Henry A. 1970-77. *3178*
—. Carter, Jimmy. Human rights. 1977-78.
3044
—. Carter, Jimmy. USSR. 1977. *3045*
—. Carter, Jimmy (administration). Developing
nations. Europe, Western. Foreign policy.
Japan. USSR. 1977-80. *3114*
—. Carter, Jimmy (administration). USSR. 1970's.
3075
—. China. Nixon, Richard M. 1970's. *2702*
—. Europe, Eastern. Ford, Gerald R. Political
Campaigns (presidential). USSR. 1976-77.
1849
—. Foreign Policy. Human rights. USSR.
1973-79. *2759*
—. Foreign Policy. Kissinger, Henry A. Political
power. 1970-74. *3097*
—. International trade. Nixon, Richard M.
(administration). Strategic arms limitation
Talks. USSR. 1969-73. *3059*
—. Kissinger, Henry A. 1969-70's. *2580*

Detente (review article). China. Nixon, Richard M.
USSR. 1971-73. *2992*
Detention, preventive. Civil Rights. Cold War.
Federal Bureau of Investigation. National
security. Truman, Harry S. (administration).
1945-52. *2516*
Deterrence. Defense Policy. Mobilization.
Planning. 1978. *2642*
—. Military Strategy. Nuclear Arms. 1966-76.
2757
—. Military strategy. Nuclear Arms. 1972-74.
3046
Developing nations. Arms Trade. Carter, Jimmy
(administration). Conventional Arms Transfers
Talks. Foreign Policy. Military aid. USSR.
1977-82. *2607*
—. Carter, Jimmy. Foreign policy. USSR.
1945-80. *2713*
—. Carter, Jimmy (administration). Detente.
Europe, Western. Foreign policy. Japan.
USSR. 1977-80. *3114*
—. Cold War. Foreign aid. Point Four program.
1949-68. *2965*
—. Democracies. Dictatorships. Foreign policy.
Nixon, Richard M. 1790-1975. *2634*
—. Diplomacy. State Department. 1960's-70's.
3089
—. Economic Policy. Political Attitudes. Reagan,
Ronald (administration). 1980. *2149*
—. Foreign Policy. Reagan, Ronald
(administration). 1980-82. *2923*
—. Foreign relations. Watergate Scandal. 1972.
3457
—. Nuclear arms. 1979-81. *2747*
Devine, Michael J. Diplomacy (review article).
Foster, John W. Spanish-American War.
State Department. Trask, David F. 1873-1917.
989
Devlin, Patrick (review article). Historiography.
Neutrality. Wilson, Woodrow. World War I.
1914-17. 1947-74. *1516*
Dewey, Thomas E. Democratic Party. Elections,
gubernatorial. Farley, James A. New York.
Roosevelt, Franklin D. State Politics. 1942.
1444
—. Elections (presidential). Pearl Harbor, attack
on. Roosevelt, Franklin D. (administration).
1944. *1177*
—. Elections (presidential). Thurmond, J. Strom.
Truman, Harry S. Virginia. 1948. *1891*
—. Elections, presidential. Truman, Harry S.
1948. *2106*
Diamond, Edwin. Burnham, William Dean. Ceaser,
John W. DiClerico, Robert E. Political
Attitudes (review article). Presidency.
Weinberg, Martha. 1970-79. *3187*
Diamond, Martin. Elections. Kirkpatrick, Jeane J.
Political parties. Political Reform (review
article). Ranney, Austin. 1950-80. *1843*
Diaries *See also* Personal Narratives.
—. Assassination. Booth, John Wilkes. *Lincoln
Conspiracy* (book, film). Stanton, Edwin M.
1865. 1977. *262*
—. Ayers, Eben A. Press. Truman, Harry S.
(administration). 1945-53. *2345*
—. Blaine, James G. Donaldson, Thomas Corwin.
Hayes, Rutherford B. Politics. 1872-93. *737*
—. Churchill, Winston. Communism. Nuclear
Arms. Potsdam Conference. Stalin, Joseph.
Truman, Harry S. 1945. *2892*
—. Diplomacy. Potsdam Conference. Truman,
Harry S. World War II. 1945. *2716*
—. Foreign Policy (review article). Roosevelt,
Franklin D. (administration). Stettinius, Edward
Reilley. World War II. 1943-46. 1975. *1582*
—. Gates, Guerdon. Monroe, James. Pennsylvania
(Washington). 1817. *830*
—. Letters. Mount Vernon. Virginia. Washington,
George. 1760-86. *331*
Dicey, Albert Venn. Blaine, James G. Cleveland,
Grover. Godkin, Edwin L. Great Britain.
Ireland. Political Campaigns (presidential).
1884. *633*
Dickens, Charles *(David Copperfield)*. Childhood.
Great Britain. Hoover, Herbert C. Poverty.
1812-1964. *1085*
DiClerico, Robert E. Burnham, William Dean.
Ceaser, John W. Diamond, Edwin. Political
Attitudes (review article). Presidency.
Weinberg, Martha. 1970-79. *3187*
Dictatorships. Democracies. Developing Nations.
Foreign policy. Nixon, Richard M. 1790-1975.
2634
Dien Bien Phu (battle). Eisenhower, Dwight D.
Foreign Policy. France. Vietnam War.
1953-54. *3036*

—. Israel. Politics. Truman, Harry S. ca 1945-49. *2658*

Diplomatic recognition (review article). Bain, Kenneth Ray. Ganin, Zvi. Independence. Israel. Wilson, Evan M. 1945-48. *2980*

—. Ganin, Zvi. Israel. Truman, Harry S. Wilson, Evan M. 1940-49. *2603*

Diplomats *See also* Consular Service.

—. Adams, John. Netherlands. 1780-82. *386*

—. Appointments to Office. Campaign Finance. Eisenhower, Dwight D. (administration). Gluck, Maxwell H. Nixon, Richard M. (administration). Symington, J. Fife. 1957-74. *2194*

—. Appointments to office. Cuba. Dallas, George M. Elections (presidential). Pierce, Franklin. 1852-56. *611*

—. Appointments to office. Grant, Ulysses S. Jews. Palestine. Sneersohn, Hayyim Zevi. 1869-70. *1026*

—. Bullitt, William C. *(For the President)*. Letters. Roosevelt, Franklin D. 1933-41. *1558*

—. Clientism. Foreign Policy. 1967-68. *3371*

Disability. Presidents. 1880-1980. *154*

Disarmament *See also* Arbitration, International; International Security; Strategic Arms Limitation Talks.

—. Carter, Jimmy. Detente. Human rights. Kissinger, Henry A. 1970-77. *3178*

—. Carter, Jimmy. Foreign policy. Inaugural Addresses. Morality. 1976. *2554*

—. Churchill, Winston. Einstein, Albert. Eisenhower, Dwight D. Europe. Khrushchev, Nikita. Memoirs. Moch, Jules. 1932-55. *2226*

—. Cold War. Decisionmaking. Eisenhower, Dwight D. Nuclear arms. USSR. 1953-61. *3073*

—. Depressions. Hoover, Herbert C. Washington Conference. 1920-22. *1674*

Disclosure. Kissinger, Henry A. Supreme Court. Telephone transcripts. 1969-80. *3285*

Discrimination *See also* Civil Rights; Minorities; Racism; Segregation; Sex Discrimination.

—. Armies. Burials. Johnson, Lyndon B. Longoria, Felix. Mexican Americans. Texas (Three Rivers). 1945-49. *1724*

—. Elites. Georgia (Savannah). Negroes. New Deal. Works Progress Administration. ca 1930-39. *1343*

—. Foreign Relations. International Trade. Jews. Public Opinion. Russia. Visas. 1906-13. *1465*

—. Freedmen's Bureau. Johnson, Andrew. Law. Reconstruction. 1865-66. *907*

Discrimination, employment. Civil rights. Congress. Fair Employment Practices Committee. Roosevelt, Franklin D. (administration). World War II. 1941-46. *1394*

Diseases *See also* names of diseases, e.g. diphtheria, etc.

—. Presidents. 1789-1975. *135*

Disengagement. Congress of Vienna. Foreign Relations. Kissinger, Henry A. USSR. 1815. 1969-74. *3130*

Dissent. American dream. Carter, Jimmy. Europe. Human rights. 17c-1978. *3080*

District of Columbia *See also* Southeastern States.

—. Appointments to office. Judges. Negroes. Racism. Terrell, Robert H. Wilson, Woodrow. 1914. *1384*

—. Architecture. Capitols. House of Representatives Chamber. Jefferson, Thomas. Latrobe, Benjamin Henry. 1803-12. *224*

—. Architecture. Restoration. White House. 1947-52. *2414*

—. Art. Houses. Mondale, Joan. Vice-presidency. 1974-77. *2336*

—. Assassination. Booth, John Wilkes. Lincoln, Abraham. Personal narratives. Sawyer, Frederick A. 1865. *552*

—. Assassination. Conspiracy. Lincoln, Abraham. Prisons. Washington Arsenal. 1803-1903. *488*

—. Assassination. Criminal investigations. Lincoln, Abraham. Police. Richards, A. C. Trials. 1865-69. *536*

—. Assassination. Ford's Theater. Grant, Ulysses S. Lincoln, Abraham. Lincoln, Mary Todd. 1865. *572*

—. Assassination. Heiss, William H., Sr. Lincoln, Abraham. Military. Telegraph. 1865. *499*

—. Blair, Francis Preston, Sr. Editors and Editing. *Globe* (newspaper). Jackson, Andrew. Politics. 1830. *935*

—. Brooks, Noah. Civil War. Lincoln, Abraham. Reporters and Reporting. 1862-1903. *741*

—. Calhoun, John C. Editors and Editing. Elections (presidential). Green, Duff. *United States Telegraph.* 1825-28. *631*

—. Calhoun, John C. Editors and Editing. Green, Duff. Jackson, Andrew. *United States Telegraph.* 1823-28. *630*

—. Capitols. Tombs. Washington, George. Washington, Martha. 1799-1832. *217*

—. Civil War. Letters. Lincoln, Abraham. Mann, Horace, Jr. Peabody, Elizabeth. 1865. *952*

—. Elections (presidential). Inaugurations. Jackson, Andrew. 1828-29. *896*

—. Entertainment. Madison, Dolly Payne. Upper Classes. 1836-49. *308*

—. Federal government. Lincoln, Abraham. Pennsylvania (Philadelphia). Speeches, Addresses, etc. 1861. *438*

—. Federal Policy. Johnson, Lyndon B. (administration). March on Washington for Jobs and Freedom. Poverty. 1968. *2357*

—. Gales, Joseph, Jr. Jackson, Andrew. *National Intelligencer.* Political Commentary. Political parties. Republicanism. Seaton, William Winston. 1827-35. *887*

—. Government. Politics and Media. Press. Rusk, Dean. 1974. *3256*

—. Hayes, Rutherford B. Keeler, Lucy Elliott. Ohio (Fremont). Personal narratives. Travel. White House. 1881. *867*

—. Inaugurations. Jackson, Andrew. 1829. *802*

—. Johnson, Andrew. Lincoln, Abraham. Schurz, Carl. Seance. 1865. *492*

Divine, Robert A. Cohen, Warren I. Eisenhower, Dwight D. Foreign Policy (review article). Rusk, Dean. 1953-69. *2962*

Divine, Robert A. (review article). Elections, presidential. Foreign policy. 1940-60. 1974. *2012*

Divorce *See also* Family; Marriage.

—. Blair, James. Documents. Jefferson, Thomas. Legislation. Virginia. 1770-73. *232*

Dix, I. F. Hoover, Herbert C. Local politics. Self-help. Unemployed Citizens' League. Washington (Seattle). 1931-32. *1389*

Dixon, James. Doolittle, James R. Impeachment. Johnson, Andrew. Norton, Daniel S. Republican Party. 1860-70. *768*

Documentaries. Aesthetics. Eisenhower, Dwight D. Heroism. *Ike* (program). Television. World War II. ca 1941-45. 1979. *1720*

Documents. Aiken, George. Congress. Jenkins, Walter. Johnson, Lyndon B. Mansfield, Mike. Tonkin Gulf Crisis (conference). Vietnam War. 1964. *3088*

—. Anderson, Maxwell. Cobb, Frank I. Wilson, Woodrow. World War I. 1917. *1481*

—. Anti-Communist Movements. Diplomacy. Germany. Office of Strategic Services. Papen, Franz von. USSR. World War II. 1942-45. *1599*

—. Armaments. Federal Policy. Nuclear nonproliferation. 1981. *3172*

—. Armenia. Foreign Relations. Harding, Warren G. Senate Foreign Relations Subcommittee. 1919. *1140*

—. Arthur, Chester A. 1880-1970. *549*

—. Benson, Ezra Taft. Cabinet. Construction. Eisenhower, Dwight D. Federal aid to education. Flemming, Arthur S. 1959. *2334*

—. Bentham, Edith. Lansing, Robert (resignation). State Department. Tumulty, Joseph. Wilson, Edith Bolling Galt. Wilson, Woodrow. 1919-20. *1682*

—. Blair, James. Divorce. Jefferson, Thomas. Legislation. Virginia. 1770-73. *232*

—. Bohlen, Charles E. Europe, Eastern. Foreign Policy. State Department. USSR. 1945-46. *2891*

—. Byrnes, James F. Great Britain. Halifax, 1st Earl of. State Department. 1945-46. *2752*

—. Castro, Fidel. Cuba. Foreign Relations. Nixon, Richard M. Political Leadership. 1959. *3028*

—. Clark, J. Reuben. Latin America. Monroe Doctrine. 1928-30. *1656*

—. Cold War. Dwight D. Eisenhower Library. Foreign Relations. India. 1953-60. *2602*

—. Cold War. Office of Strategic Services. USSR. World War II. 1945. *3153*

—. Collectors and Collecting. Garfield, James A. Presidency. 1881. *725*

—. Communism. Foreign Relations. State Department *(Relations with China).* 1944-81. *3019*

—. Copyright. House of Representatives (Printing Committee). Presidents. Richardson, James Daniel *(Messages and Papers of the Presidents).* Spofford, Ainsworth Rand. 1900. *1049*

—. Defense Policy. Truman, Harry S. (administration). 1946-75. *2991*

—. Defense spending. Foreign policy. Truman, Harry S. (administration). 1947-79. *2608*

—. Diplomacy. Foreign policy. Kissinger, Henry A. Memoranda. Publicity. 1970's. *2798*

—. Dulles, John Foster. Foreign Relations. India. Nehru, Jawaharlal. 1953-59. *2601*

—. Editors and Editing. Historians. Sparks, Jared. Washington, George. 1815-30. *199*

—. Eisenhower, Dwight D. (review article). Military. 1945-48. 1978. *1738*

—. Elections (congressional). Foreign Relations. Johnson, Andrew. Mexico. Romero, Matias. 1866. *1015*

—. Federal Policy. Harry S. Truman Library. Truman, Harry S. Western States. 1940-66. *2394*

—. Federal Policy. Libraries, Presidential. Ownership. 1971. *3331*

—. Foreign Policy. Hilsman, Roger. Kennedy, John F. Laos. 1962. *2976*

—. Foreign Policy. Kennan, George F. Latin America. 1950. *3112*

—. Foreign policy. Kissinger, Henry A. South Africa. 1967-74. *2958*

—. Foreign Policy. Palestine. State Department. Truman, Harry S. (administration). 1948. *2664*

—. Foreign policy. Preservation. Research. 1945-77. *3378*

—. Foreign relations. Hay, John Milton. Michael, William H. Publishers and Publishing. State Department. 1898-1906. *976*

—. Franklin D. Roosevelt Library. Information Access. Military finance. Security classification. 1970-75. *1130*

—. Franklin D. Roosevelt Library. New York (Hyde Park). 1935-51. *1096*

—. *Halperin et al. v. Kissinger et al* (US, 1976). Nixon, Richard M. Shattuck, John. 1976. *1777*

—. Historiography. Lincoln, Abraham. Lincoln, Mary Todd. Marriage. 1842-65. 1885. 1947-82. *457*

—. Illinois (Springfield). Land Tenure. Lincoln, Abraham. Walters, William. 1839-45. *473*

—. Information access. Law. Presidents. 1968-78. *3307*

—. Jefferson, Thomas. 18c-1976. *347*

—. Judicial Review. Nixon, Richard M. Ownership. Presidential Recordings and Materials Preservation Act (US, 1974). 1974-75. *3323*

—. Law Reform. Nixon, Richard M. Ownership. Public records. 1974-75. *3423*

—. Law Reform. Ownership. Presidents. Public officials. 1782-1975. *3232*

—. Nixon, Richard M. Watergate Scandal. 1973-74. *2228*

—. *Nixon v. Administrator of General Services.* Ownership. 1791-1981. *110*

—. Ownership. Presidents. 1789-1974. *108*

—. Presidents. 1934-76. *3408*

—. Virginia. Washington, George. 1797-99. *332*

Doenecke, Justus D. Arthur, Chester A. Garfield, James A. Gould, Lewis L. McKinley, William. Presidents (review article). 1880-1901. *736*

Dole, William P. Cherokee Indians. Federal policy. Indians. Lincoln, Abraham. Ross, John. 1860-65. *900*

—. Civil War. Indians. Lincoln, Abraham. Treaties. 1861-64. *868*

Domestic Policy *See also* Federal Policy.

—. Agendas. Decisionmaking. Presidents. 1961-80. *2424*

—. Anticolonialism. Cold War. Political Attitudes. Revolution. 1945-75. *3100*

—. Arms Trade. Carter, Jimmy. Foreign policy. Middle East. 1976-78. *3109*

—. Carter, Jimmy. Cities. 1977-78. *2405*

—. Carter, Jimmy. Cities. New Federalism. State government. 1977. *2504*

—. Carter, Jimmy (administration). 1977-79. *2425*

—. Carter, Jimmy (administration). Congress. Foreign Policy. Inflation. Interest groups. 1977-78. *2200*

—. Carter, Jimmy (administration). Foreign policy. 1976. *2191*

—. Carter, Jimmy (administration). Foreign policy. Human rights. 1977-79. *3037*

—. Carter, Jimmy (administration). Foreign Policy. Morality. 1977. *2271*

—. Civil War. Lincoln, Abraham. Negroes. 1850-65. *783*

—. Congress. Executive branch. 1970-75. *2467*

—. Politics. Public Opinion. 1976. *1917*
—. Populism. Racism. Texas. Wallace, George C. 1968. *2124*
—. Public opinion. 1940-76. *2068*
—. Radio. Reporters and Reporting. Television. 1952-76. *1809*
—. Regionalism. 1976. *2092*
—. Reporters and reporting. Voting and voting behavior. 1968. *1887*
—. Roosevelt, Theodore. Taft, William H. Wilson, Woodrow. 1910-12. *1187*
—. Smith, Al. West Virginia. 1928. *1146*
—. Socialist Party. Wisconsin (Milwaukee). Zeidler, Frank P. 1912-80. *1903*
—. States. 1952-76. *1943*
—. Voting and Voting Behavior. 1956-72. *1844*
—. Voting and Voting Behavior. 1960-76. *2061*
—. Voting and voting behavior. 1964-68. *1952*
Elections (review article). Abramson, Paul R. Aldrich, John H. Pomper, Gerald. Ranney, Austin. Rohde, David W. 1980. *1975*
—. Presidency. White, Theodore H. 1956-80. *3289*
Elections (senatorial). California. Douglas, Helen Gahagan. Nixon, Richard M. 1950. *1771*
—. Democratic Party. Georgia. New Deal. Roosevelt, Franklin D. Talmadge, Eugene. 1926-38. *1271*
—. Democratic Party. Missouri. New Deal. Primaries. Truman, Harry S. 1934. *1736*
Elections (special). Presidential succession. Vice-presidency. 1967-74. *3422*
Electoral College See also Presidents.
—. Bayh, Birch. Constitutional Amendments. Senate Judiciary Committee (Constitutional Subcommittee). 1977. *1848*
—. Constitutional Convention. Founding Fathers. 1787. *1051*
—. Constitutional Convention. Founding Fathers. Republicanism. 1787-1970's. *1040*
—. Elections (presidential). 1960's-70's. *1839*
—. Elections, presidential. Partisanship. Political Indicators. 1932-76. *2011*
—. Elections (presidential). Political Representation. 1860. 1980. *155*
—. Elections, Presidential. Voting and Voting Behavior. 1860-1972. *156*
—. Elections (presidential). 3/2's rule. 1960-72. *2128*
—. Political Campaigns (presidential). 1932-76. *159*
—. Political reform. 1787-1974. *102*
—. Political Theory. Voting and Voting Behavior. 1960. 1970. *2082*
Electric Power. Bureaucracies. Columbia Valley Authority. Congress. Corporations. Truman, Harry S. (administration). 1945-50. *2330*
Electric utilities. Bonneville Power Administration. New Deal. Pacific Northwest. Public Utilities. 1937-42. *1302*
Eliot, Charles William. Harvard University. Roosevelt, Theodore. Sports. 1908. *1129*
Elites See also Decisionmaking; Social Classes.
—. Appointments to Office. Cabinet. Presidents. 1932-72. *17*
—. Behavior. Campaign Finance. Elections (presidential). Political participation. 1972. *1819*
—. Business. Cabinet. Mills, C. Wright. 1897-1973. *56*
—. Campaign Finance. Political Attitudes. 1972. *1818*
—. Discrimination. Georgia (Savannah). Negroes. New Deal. Works Progress Administration. ca 1930-39. *1343*
—. Elections. Political Leadership. 1960's-70's. *1879*
Ely, Ezra Stiles. Democratic Party. Eaton Affair. Jackson, Andrew. 1829-30. *805*
Emancipation See also Freedmen.
—. Civil War. Constitutional Amendments (13th). Lincoln, Abraham. Republicans, radical. 1861-65. *909*
—. Civil War. Kentucky. Lincoln, Abraham. 1861-65. *837*
—. Colonization. Lincoln, Abraham. Negroes. 1852-65. *567*
—. Economics. South. 1860's. *884*
Emancipation Proclamation. Carpenter, Francis Bicknell. Herline, Edward. Lincoln, Abraham. Painting. Prints. Ritchie, Alexander Hay. 1864-66. *851*
—. Civil Rights. Civil War. Lincoln, Abraham. 1854-63. *908*
—. Engraving. Lincoln, Abraham. Ritchie, Alexander Hay *(First Reading of the Emancipation Proclamation before the Cabinet).* 1864. *853*

—. Lincoln, Abraham. Lithographers. Printers. 1862-65. *852*
—. Lincoln, Abraham. New Jersey. Peace. Public opinion. State legislatures. 1864. *829*
—. Lincoln, Abraham. Republican Party. 1863-64. *874*
Embargo Acts (US, 1807-08). Gallatin, Albert. Jefferson, Thomas. Madison, James. 1808-13. *1002*
Embargoes. Armaments. Isolationism. Neutrality Act (US, 1935). 1935. *1695*
—. Arms Trade. Carter, Jimmy (administration). Cyprus. Turkey. 1975-78. *3022*
—. Democratic-Republican Party. Great Britain. Madison, James. Non-Intercourse Act (US, 1809). 1808-09. *1027*
—. Foreign Policy. Japan. Oil and Petroleum Products. Roosevelt, Franklin D. 1941. *1479*
—. Foreign Policy. Palestine. Truman, Harry S. Weapons. 1947-48. *3067*
Emergency Energy Conservation Act (US, 1979). Congress. Energy Department. Governors. 1973-79. *2422*
Emergency powers. Democracy. Presidents. 17c-1979. *61*
—. Executive power. Habeas corpus. Martial law. War. 1861-1944. *134*
—. National Emergencies Act (US, 1976). Presidents. Senate Special Committee on the Termination of the National Emergency. War Powers Act (US, 1973). 1973-79. *3341*
Emigration See also Immigration; Population; Race Relations; Refugees.
—. Adams, John. American Revolution. Books. Great Britain. Political Theory. 1776. *182*
Emmons, George T. Alaska. Roosevelt, Theodore. Tongass National Forest. 1902. *1274*
Employment See also Discrimination, Employment; Unemployment.
—. Agriculture Department. Equal opportunity. Federal policy. 1964-76. *3392*
—. Bureau of Indian Affairs. Indians. Wages. 1970's. *3434*
—. Construction. Ickes, Harold L. Negroes. Public Works Administration. Quotas. 1933-40. *1355*
—. Equal opportunity. Labor Department (Division of Negro Economics). Negroes. World War I. 1917-21. *1322*
—. Minorities in Politics. Negroes. New Deal. Roosevelt, Franklin D. 1930-42. *1429*
Employment, part-time. National Youth Administration. New Deal. South Dakota. Struble, Anna C. Youth. 1935-43. *1333*
Energy See also Fuel.
—. Atomic Energy. Carter, Jimmy. Federal Policy. 1977-78. *2288*
—. Carter, Jimmy. Federal Policy. 1930's-78. *111*
—. Carter, Jimmy. Sermons. Speeches, Addresses, etc. 1979. *2369*
—. Carter, Jimmy (administration). 1979-80. *2517*
—. Carter, Jimmy (administration). Congress. Economic planning. Federal Policy. Politics. 1976-78. *2364*
—. Carter, Jimmy (administration). Congress. Federal Policy. Interest Groups. 1977-78. *2421*
—. Carter, Jimmy (administration). Federal Policy. 1973-78. *2510*
—. Carter, Jimmy (administration). Federal Programs. Oil industry and trade. 1978-80. *2429*
—. Congress. Economic growth. Ford, Gerald R. (administration). Planning. ca 1970's. *2293*
—. Conservation of Natural Resources. Federal Policy. Intergovernmental Relations. State Government. 1974-79. *2476*
—. Economic Policy. Eisenhower, Dwight D. (administration). Federal Policy. Truman, Harry S. (administration). 1945-60. *2543*
—. Economic Policy. Politics. Presidents. 1961-80. *2544*
—. Federal Policy. 1979. *2423*
Energy Department. Congress. Emergency Energy Conservation Act (US, 1979). Governors. 1973-79. *2422*
Engraving. Emancipation Proclamation. Lincoln, Abraham. Ritchie, Alexander Hay *(First Reading of the Emancipation Proclamation before the Cabinet).* 1864. *853*
—. Lincoln, Abraham. Lithographs. Political Campaigns (presidential). 1860. *645*
Enlightenment See also Rationalism.

—. Declaration of Independence. Jefferson, Thomas (review article). Locke, John. Political Theory. Scotland. Wills, Garry. 1690's-1776. 1970's. *261*
—. Ethics. Jefferson, Thomas. Race relations. 18c. *236*
—. *Federalist* No. 10. Madison, James. Political theory. 1760-87. *213*
—. Gallatin, Albert. Politics. Swiss Americans. Treasury Secretaries. 1780-1849. *929*
—. Government. Jefferson, Thomas. Science. 18c. *186*
—. Government. Madison, James. Scotland. Social Organization. ca 1760's-1829. *194*
—. Jefferson, Thomas *(Notes on the State of Virginia).* Law. Political Theory. 1780-87. *242*
Enrolled bills. Decisionmaking. Legislation. Office of Management and Budget. Presidents. 1932-77. *3469*
—. Federal Government. Legislation. Office of Management and Budget. Presidents. 1960's-78. *3468*
Entertainment. District of Columbia. Madison, Dolly Payne. Upper Classes. 1836-49. *308*
Entertainment industry. Federal Bureau of Investigation. Hoover, J. Edgar. Public relations. 1930's-60's. *131*
Entrepreneurs. Heroes. Lincoln, Abraham. Men. Pioneers. Social Change. 18c-19c. *558*
Environmental Protection Agency. Federal Policy. Reagan, Ronald (administration). 1981. *2361*
Episcopal Church, Protestant. Adams, John. American Revolution (antecedents). Letters. Weller, George. 1770's. 1824-25. *258*
—. Assassination. Brooks, Phillips. Lincoln, Abraham. Pennsylvania (Philadelphia). Sermons. Slavery. 1865. 1893. *421*
Epistemology. Jefferson, Thomas. Locke, John. Political theory. 17c-19c. *205*
Epstein, Edward J. Assassination. Committee of State Security (KGB). Kennedy, John F. McMillan, Priscilla Johnson. Oswald, Lee Harvey (review article). 1960-78. *1746*
Equal opportunity. Agriculture Department. Employment. Federal policy. 1964-76. *3392*
—. Bethune, Mary McLeod. Federal Policy. National Youth Administration. Negroes. Youth. 1935-44. *1438*
—. Carter, Jimmy. Civil Service. Labor Department. 1977-78. *2410*
—. Civilian Conservation Corps. Negroes. New Deal. 1933-42. *1317*
—. Education. Health, Education, and Welfare Department. Justice Department. South. 1968-74. *2509*
—. Employment. Labor Department (Division of Negro Economics). Negroes. World War I. 1917-21. *1322*
—. Federal aid to education. Nixon, Richard M. Political Speeches. Public schools. School integration. 1970's. *2456*
Equality. Beitzinger, A. J. Christenson, Reo M. Hanley, Thomas O'Brien. Jaffa, Harry V. Lincoln, Abraham. Political Theory. Values (review article). 1770-1973. *446*
—. Declaration of Independence. Jaffa, Harry V. Lincoln, Abraham. Political Theory. 1860's. 1950's-70's. *411*
—. Lincoln, Abraham. Mormons. Polygamy. Slavery. Smith, Joseph. 1840-64. *563*
Ervin, Sam J., Jr. Civil rights. Political Commentary. Senate. Vietnam War. Watergate Scandal. 1954-74. *2530*
Escalation theory. Bismarck, Otto von. Cuban missile crisis. Diplomacy. Franco-Prussian War. Kennedy, John F. McNamara, Robert S. 1870. 1962. *3072*
Eskimos. Alaska Reorganization Act (US, 1936). Aleuts. Federal Policy. Indians. 1936-45. *1400*
Espionage See also Counterintelligence; Military Intelligence.
—. Central Intelligence Agency. Covert operations. Foreign Policy. 1947-75. *2655*
—. Churchill, Winston. Foreign Relations. Kent, Tyler. Roosevelt, Franklin D. World War II. 1940-45. *1581*
—. Civil War. Consular Service. Great Britain. Lincoln, Abraham. Patronage. Shipping. 1861-63. *1012*
—. Civil War. Consular Service. Ireland. Lincoln, Abraham. Patronage. Scotland. 1861-63. *1013*
Espionage (review article). Committee of State Security (KGB). Communism. Hiss, Alger. Oswald, Lee Harvey. USSR. 1938-78. *1759*

Estrada Palma, Thomás. Cuba. Imperialism. Intervention. Roosevelt, Theodore. 1901-06. *1568*
Ethics *See also* Morality; Political Ethics; Values.
—. Agnew, Spiro T. Morality. Political Corruption. Watergate Scandal. 1960's-70's. *2490*
—. Carter, Jimmy. Foreign policy. Human rights. Kissinger, Henry A. Political Theory. 1973-80. *2721*
—. Enlightenment. Jefferson, Thomas. Race relations. 18c. *236*
—. Public administration. 1900-76. *60*
Ethnic Groups *See also* Minorities.
—. Elections (presidential). Nativism. Ohio (Cleveland). Republican Party. 1860. *653*
—. Elections (presidential). Religion. Roosevelt, Franklin D. Social Classes. 1940. *1162*
Ethnicity. Assimilation. Elections (presidential). Greek Americans. Republican Party. 1968. *1925*
—. Cherokee Indians. Indians. Jefferson, Thomas. Removals, forced. Tennessee. Willstown, Treaties of. 1794-1817. *890*
—. Elections (presidential). Kennedy, John F. Pennsylvania (Schuylkill County). Religion. Voting and Voting Behavior. 1960. *1896*
Ethnocentrism. Central Intelligence Agency. Intelligence Service. Language. Vietnam. 1954-63. *2869*
Ethnography. Diplomacy. Gallatin, Albert. Politics. Treasury Department. 1780-1849. *880*
Etiquette. Diplomacy. Jefferson, Thomas. Republicanism. 1800-04. *981*
Etzioni, Amitai. Budgets. Carter, Jimmy (administration). Inflation. Personal narratives. 1980. *2341*
Eulogies. Clay, Henry. Lincoln, Abraham. Nationalism. Seward, William H. 1852. *513*
—. Clergy. Presidency. Sermons. Washington, George. 1799. *351*
—. Davies, Samuel. National Self-image. Washington, George. 1789-1815. *189*
Europe *See also* Europe, Eastern; Europe, Western.
—. Adams, John. Foreign policy. Free trade. Mercantilism. 1775-85. *209*
—. American dream. Carter, Jimmy. Dissent. Human rights. 17c-1978. *3080*
—. Art. Classicism. Jefferson, Thomas. 1784-1807. *367*
—. Balance of power. Detente. USSR. 1648-1973. *2636*
—. Bismarck, Otto von. Foreign policy. Kissinger, Henry A. 19c. 1968-74. *2646*
—. Bureaucracies. Economic Policy. International trade. Wilson, Woodrow. 1917-21. *1229*
—. Central Intelligence Agency. Foreign policy. 1946-56. *2576*
—. Churchill, Winston. Disarmament. Einstein, Albert. Eisenhower, Dwight D. Khrushchev, Nikita. Memoirs. Moch, Jules. 1932-55. *2226*
—. Civil War (antecedents). Foreign Policy. Lincoln, Abraham. Seward, William H. War threats. 1861. *713*
—. Conference on Security and Cooperation in Europe. Ford, Gerald R. (administration). International Security. Public opinion. 1975. *2638*
—. Congress. Defense policy. Nixon, Richard M. (administration). USSR. Vietnam War. 1968-73. *2944*
—. Connecticut. International Trade. Jefferson, Thomas. Travel. Treaties. 1784. *191*
—. Decisionmaking. Economic conditions. Foreign Policy. Marshall Plan. 1946-47. *2802*
—. Diplomacy. Foreign Aid. Great Powers. Marshall Plan. 1947. *2679*
—. Diplomacy. Partition. Roosevelt, Franklin D. 1939-45. *1475*
—. Diplomacy. Roosevelt, Franklin D. (death). World War II. 1945. *2585*
—. Economic aid. Kennan, George F. Marshall Plan. State Department (Policy Planning Staff). 1947. *2920*
—. Eisenhower, Dwight D. Elections (presidential). Foreign Policy. Public Opinion. Reagan, Ronald. 1952-80. *1786*
—. Eisenhower, Dwight D. Military General Staff. World War II. 1942-69. *1744*
—. Executive Power. Jupiter missiles. Military strategy. NATO. 1957-63. *2877*
—. Federal Policy. Genocide. Jews. Roosevelt, Franklin D. (administration). World War II. 1942-44. *1608*
—. Foreign Aid. Immigration. Refugees. Truman, Harry S. Visas. 1945-48. *2753*

—. Foreign policy. 1782-1976. *34*
—. Foreign policy. 1917-78. *2*
—. Foreign Policy. Germany (Berlin). Kennedy, John F. (administration). 1961-63. *2835*
—. Foreign policy. Kissinger, Henry A. 1968-77. *2725*
—. Foreign policy. Kissinger, Henry A. 1969-77. *2748*
—. Foreign policy. Kissinger, Henry A. Nixon, Richard M., administration. Policymaking. 1971-75. *2838*
—. Foreign Relations. Mally, Gerhard. Nixon, Richard M. (administration). 1970's. *3119*
—. Foreign Relations. Nuclear proliferation. 1954-80. *2866*
—. Foreign Relations. USSR. 1970-73. *2599*
—. Kennedy, John F. Political Integration. 1962-65. *2813*
—. Newspapers. Nixon, Richard M. (resignation). Pardons. Political Commentary. 1974. *2197*
Europe, Eastern. Bohlen, Charles E. Documents. Foreign Policy. State Department. USSR. 1945-46. *2891*
—. Carter, Jimmy. Foreign policy. Human rights. Self-determination. USSR. 1977-78. *2697*
—. Containment. USSR. 1945-48. *2735*
—. Detente. Ford, Gerald R. Political Campaigns (presidential). USSR. 1976-77. *1849*
Europe, Southeastern. Roosevelt, Theodore. World War I. 1917-18. *1138*
Europe, Western. Carter, Jimmy (administration). Detente. Developing nations. Foreign policy. Japan. USSR. 1977-80. *3114*
—. Carter, Jimmy (administration). Foreign policy. USSR. 1970's. *2790*
—. Economic policy. Foreign policy. Nixon, Richard M. Political Factions. 1971. *2221*
—. Foreign Policy. Germany, West. Gimbel, John. Marshall Plan. 1946-56. *2834*
—. Foreign Policy. NATO. Nixon, Richard M. (administration). 1945-71. *3136*
European Economic Community. Foreign relations. Kissinger, Henry A. Middle East. NATO. USSR. 1970's. *2970*
—. Foreign relations. NATO. 1945-74. *3169*
Evans, Daniel S. Political conventions. Political speeches. Republican Party. Rhetoric. 1968. *2075*
Exchange rates. Connally, John. Decisionmaking. Economic Policy. Foreign policy. Nixon, Richard M. (administration). 1944-73. *2947*
Executive agreements. Bricker Amendment. Bricker, John W. Dulles, John Foster. McCloy, John J. Personal narratives. Presidency. Senate. Treaties. 1951-54. 1976. *3482*
—. Congress. 1918-80. *3349*
—. Congress. Foreign policy. Legislation. Treaties. 1946-72. *3329*
Executive Behavior. Attitudes. Foreign policy. Political Protest. Roosevelt, Franklin D. 1940-72. *1697*
—. Barber, James David. Carter, Jimmy. Presidents. Rhetoric. 1909-78. *22*
—. Bureaucracies. Federal Government. Politics. ca 1973-76. *3300*
—. Carter, Jimmy. Decisionmaking. Politics. 1977-78. *2211*
—. Communications Behavior. Dean, John (resignation). Watergate Scandal. 1973. *2496*
—. Congress. Public Opinion. Watergate Scandal. 1972. *2532*
—. Domestic Policy. Foreign policy. Nixon, Richard M. 1940's-74. *2276*
—. Eisenhower, Dwight D. Political Leadership. 1953-61. *2188*
—. Federal government. Political Ethics. Public administration. Richardson, Elliot. 1969-73. *2464*
—. Johnson, Lyndon B. Kennedy, John F. Nixon, Richard M. Presidency. Vietnam War. Watergate scandal. 1961-74. *3260*
Executive Branch *See also* Presidency.
—. 1970's. *3477*
—. Adams, John. Courts. Extradition. Foreign Relations. Great Britain. Jay Treaty. Robbins, Jonathan. Separation of powers. 1796-1804. *980*
—. Angola. Cambodia. Intervention. National security. Secrecy. Vietnam War. 1969-75. *2786*
—. Anti-Communist Movements. Historiography. 1945-54. *2268*
—. Appointments to Office. Bureaucracies. Politics. 1961-80. *3222*
—. Appointments to office. Eisenhower, Dwight D. Morrow, E. Frederick. Negroes. 1952-60. *2397*

—. Budgets. Bureau of the Budget. Office of Management and Budget. ca 1939-70. *3207*
—. Budgets. Congress. Impoundment. Nixon, Richard M. (administration). Separation of powers. 1972-73. *2219*
—. Budgets. Congressional Budget and Impoundment Control Act (US, 1974). Impoundment. 1974. *3421*
—. Budgets. Fiscal policy. Presidents. Public administration. 1953-69. *3372*
—. Budgets. House of Representatives (Appropriations Committee). Intergovernmental Relations. Senate Appropriations Committee. Watergate Scandal. 1973-75. *3481*
—. Bureaucracies. Congress. Political Change. Reform. Social change. 1960's-70's. *3353*
—. Bureaucracies. Nixon, Richard M., administration. Reform. Watergate scandal. 1970-74. *2497*
—. Cabinet. 1776-1976. *37*
—. Cabinet. 1970-80. *3188*
—. Cabinet. Congress. Executive power. Nixon, Richard M., administration. Reform. 1970-74. *2375*
—. Calvinism. National Security Council. Reform. Revivals. ca 1880-1930's. *1036*
—. Carter, Jimmy (administration). Congress. Legislative liaisons. 1977-78. *2161*
—. Carter, Jimmy (administration). Reform. Roosevelt, Franklin D. (administration). 1937-38. 1977-78. *1403*
—. Central Intelligence Agency. House of Representatives (Intelligence Activities Committee). Intelligence service. Kissinger, Henry A. 1970's. *3024*
—. *Chicago Tribune*. Editorials. Legislative Investigations. McCarthy, Joseph R. *New York Times*. Senate. Watergate scandal. 1954-73. *3278*
—. Chinese Exclusion Act (US, 1882). Congress. Immigration. Politics. 1876-82. *998*
—. Civil Rights. Courts. Health, Education, and Welfare Department. Integration. Politics. 1960's-79. *2438*
—. Communications. Decisionmaking. 1930-82. *3276*
—. Congress. Constitution. Federal Policy. National Emergencies Act (US, 1976). Political power. 1933-78. *3362*
—. Congress. Constitution. Foreign policy. 1969-74. *3439*
—. Congress. Constitution. Foreign policy. 1974-75. *3391*
—. Congress. Constitution. Presidency. War Powers Resolution. 1973. *3456*
—. Congress. Decisionmaking. Foreign policy. Secrecy. 1970's. *3361*
—. Congress. Domestic policy. 1970-75. *2467*
—. Congress. Fall, Albert B. Teapot Dome Scandal. Watergate Scandal. 1923-32. 1974. *7*
—. Congress. Foreign policy. 1969-80. *3247*
—. Congress. Foreign policy. Separation of powers. 1970's. *3352*
—. Congress. Government. Intelligence Service. 1940's-70's. *3381*
—. Congress. Intergovernmental communications. 1945-73. *3325*
—. Congress. Intergovernmental relations. Oversight, congressional. 1952-80. *3288*
—. Congress. Legislation. 1958-74. *3326*
—. Congress. Legislation. 1974-75. *2387*
—. Congress. Political Theory. 1947-74. *3195*
—. Congress. Reform. 1932-81. *3264*
—. Congress. Veto, legislative. 20c. *3263*
—. Constitutional Amendments (12th). Political Parties. 1800-04. *1052*
—. Decisionmaking. Food. Interest Groups. 1970-81. *3313*
—. Federal Regulation. Regulatory commissions. 1900-81. *12*
—. Foreign Policy. Political Commentary. Vietnam War. 1964-65. *2890*
—. Government. Nixon, Richard M. (administration). Political representation. Social services. 1968-74. *2287*
—. Hamilton, Alexander. Political theory. Public Administration. 1787-90's. *1043*
—. Hoover Commission. Public administration. 1947-48. *3194*
—. Intergovernmental relations. New Federalism. Nixon, Richard M. 1974. *3277*
—. National Security Classification System. Pentagon Papers. Supreme Court. 1971-72. *3383*
—. Nixon, Richard M. Office of Management and Budget. Reform. 1970's. *2522*

—. Oil Industry and Trade. Political Corruption. Teapot Dome scandal. Walsh, Thomas J. ca 1920-24. *1441*

Family *See also* Divorce; Marriage; Women.
—. Adams family. Attitudes. Communications Behavior. Generations. 1764-1919. *113*
—. Behavior. Kennedy family. Risk-taking. Violence. ca 1940-79. *1780*
—. Carter, Jimmy (and family). Politics. Psychohistory. 1928-76. *1713*
—. Hayes, Rutherford B. Social Conditions. 19c-20c. *461*
—. Political Campaigns (presidential). 1960-80. *1942*
—. Political Campaigns (presidential). Voting and Voting Behavior. 1976. *1792*
—. Politics. Presidents. 1961-77. *3336*

Family Assistance Program. Nixon, Richard M. Political leadership. Public opinion. 1971. *2485*

Family Planning Act (US, 1970). Health, Education, and Welfare Department. Hellman, Louis M. Personal narratives. Women. 1965-77. *2378*

Famine relief. Charities. Congress. Foreign Policy. Ireland. Philanthropy. Polk, James K. 1845-49. *1014*

Far Western States *See also* individual states (including Alaska and Hawaii).
—. Conservation of natural resources. Politics. Progressivism. Roosevelt, Theodore. 1909-12. *1115*
—. Elections (presidential). Mass Media. Voting and Voting Behavior. 1960-80. *1858*

Farley, James A. Air mail service. Black, Hugo. Contracts. Hoover, Herbert C. (administration). Legislative Investigations. 1933-34. *1440*
—. Democratic Party. Dewey, Thomas E. Elections, gubernatorial. New York. Roosevelt, Franklin D. State Politics. 1942. *1444*

Farmers. Agricultural Commodities. Elections (presidential). Iowa. Prices. Voting and Voting Behavior. 1948. *2055*
—. All-Party Agricultural Committee. Great Plains. North Central States. Political Campaigns (presidential). Roosevelt, Franklin D. 1936. *1201*
—. Labor. Ohio. Political Campaigns (presidential). 1892-96. *705*

Farming. Articles of Confederation. Jefferson, Thomas. Land Tenure. Property rights. Republicanism. 1776-87. *278*
—. Plantations. Virginia (Mount Vernon). Washington, George. 1797-99. *220*

Fascism. Italy. Monetary policy. Mussolini, Benito. New Deal. Roosevelt, Franklin D. 1922-36. *1398*
—. Italy. Mussolini, Benito. New Deal. Roosevelt, Franklin D. 1930's. *1296*

Fassett, Samuel M. Illinois (Chicago). Lincoln, Abraham. Mendel, Edward. Photography. Political Campaigns (presidential). Portraits. 1860. *646*

Faulkner, William. Eisenhower, Dwight D. (administration). Foreign Relations. National Commission for UNESCO. People-to-People Program (Writers' Group). Rabb, Maxwell M. State Department. 1954-61. *2148*

Fausold, Martin L. Depressions. Hoover, Herbert C. (review article). Mazuzan, George T. Wilson, Joan Hoff. 1929-33. 1974-75. *1224*

Favretti, Rudy J. Jefferson, Thomas. Landscaping. Monticello. Restorations. Virginia. 1775-1826. 1977-80. *305*

Federal Aid to Education. Arkansas. Depressions. Federal Emergency Relief Administration. Hopkins, Harry. Public schools. 1933-36. *1412*
—. Benson, Ezra Taft. Cabinet. Construction. Documents. Eisenhower, Dwight D. Flemming, Arthur S. 1959. *2334*
—. Equal opportunity. Nixon, Richard M. Political Speeches. Public schools. School integration. 1970's. *2456*

Federal Bureau of Investigation. American Civil Liberties Union. Demonstrations. Hoover, J. Edgar. Political surveillance. Trade Union Education League. 1924-36. *1457*
—. Attorneys General. Cummings, Homer Stillé. Films. *G-Men* (film). Hoover, J. Edgar. 1933-35. *1405*
—. Barnes, Harry Elmer. Crime and Criminals (organized). Hoover, J. Edgar. World War II. 1936-44. *1449*
—. Boggs, Thomas Hale. Hoover, J. Edgar. Speeches, Addresses, etc. 1971. *3273*

—. Central Intelligence Agency. Cubans. Louisiana (New Orleans). Oswald, Lee Harvey. 1963. *1757*
—. Central Intelligence Agency. Freedom of Information Act (US, 1966). 1966-82. *3453*
—. Central Intelligence Agency. Freedom of Information Act (US, 1966). National security. 1960's-81. *3390*
—. Church, Frank. National security. Senate (Intelligence Activities Committee). 1930's-75. *3235*
—. Civil Rights. Cold War. Detention, preventive. National security. Truman, Harry S. (administration). 1945-52. *2516*
—. Civil rights. Nixon, Richard M. (administration). Police. Violence. 1960-72. *2514*
—. Civil Rights. Roosevelt, Franklin D. 1936-80. *8*
—. Congress. Crime and Criminals (white-collar). Operation Abscam. 1970-80. *3478*
—. Courts. Crime and Criminals. Recidivism. 1967-73. *2540*
—. Crime and Criminals. Justice Department. Law enforcement. 1933-34. *1332*
—. Entertainment industry. Hoover, J. Edgar. Public relations. 1930's-60's. *131*
—. Hoover, J. Edgar. Nazism. 1934-76. *44*
—. Hoover, J. Edgar. Political Surveillance. Radicals and Radicalism. 1919-21. *1707*
—. Law Enforcement. 1790-1978. *157*
—. Leftism. Operation Cointelpro. Political surveillance. 1956-71. *2461*
—. Political protest. Presidential directives. 1936-53. *161*

Federal Deposit Insurance Corporation. Alien Property Custodian. Banking. Crowley, Leo T. Politics. Roosevelt, Franklin D. (administration). 1934-45. *1454*

Federal Drug Administration. Kelsey, Frances Oldham. Thalidomide. William S. Merrell Company. 1960's. *2435*

Federal Election Campaign Act (US, 1971). Campaign Finance. 1966-80. *1805*

Federal Election Campaign Act (US, 1971; amended, 1974). Campaign Finance. Political Campaigns (presidential). Political parties. 1974. *1948*

Federal Election Commission. Campaign Finance. Elections (presidential). Income tax. Legislation. 1966-76. *2004*
—. Campaign Finance. Primaries (presidential). 1976-80. *2098*

Federal Elections Bill. Alabama. Democratic Party. Political Campaigns. South. Stevenson, Adlai E. (1835-1914). 1889-93. *685*

Federal Emergency Relief Administration. Arkansas. Depressions. Federal Aid to Education. Hopkins, Harry. Public schools. 1933-36. *1412*

Federal Energy Administration. Federal Policy. Oil Industry and Trade. Petitions. 1974-80. *2475*

Federal Farm Board. Agricultural Marketing Act (US, 1929). Coolidge, Calvin. Hoover, Herbert C. McNary, Charles L. Prices. Surpluses. 1924-29. *1340*

Federal Government *See also* names of individual agencies, bureaus, and departments, e.g. Bureau of Indian Affairs, Office of Education, but State Department, Defense Department, etc.; Chiefs of State; Civil Service; Congress; Executive Branch; Government; Legislation; Supreme Court.
—. Agricultural Adjustment Administration. National Recovery Administration. 1933-39. *1436*
—. Agriculture Department. Interest groups. 1974-76. *2436*
—. Antitrust. Attorneys General. Daugherty, Harry M. Pennsylvania (Philadelphia). Political Corruption. United Gas Improvement Company. 1914-24. *1309*
—. Appointments to office. Carter, Jimmy. Harris, Patricia Roberts. Politics. 1976. *2240*
—. Appointments to office. Courts. Hall, Kermit L. (review article). Political Parties. Politics. 1829-61. *1037*
—. Arkansas (Little Rock). Eisenhower, Dwight D. India (Kerala). Segregation. State government. 1957. 1968. *2523*
—. Attorneys General. Black, Jeremiah Sullivan. Secession crisis. South Carolina. 1860-61. *859*
—. Banking. Hoover, Herbert C. Nevada. Reconstruction Finance Corporation. 1932-33. *1396*
—. Behavior. State Department (Foreign Service). 1974. *3272*

—. Bigelow, William Sturgis. Letters. Letters. Lodge, Henry Cabot. Politics. Roosevelt, Theodore. 1887-1919. *1101*
—. Blumenthal, Michael. Iran. Oil Industry and Trade. Organization of Petroleum Exporting Countries. Schlesinger, James R. 1979-80. *2825*
—. Buchanan, James. Holt, Joseph. Post Office Department. Reform. 1856-60. *776*
—. Budgets. 1960-71. *3432*
—. Budgets. Office of Management and Budget. 1970's. *3402*
—. Bureaucracies. Executive Behavior. Politics. ca 1973-76. *3300*
—. Bureaucracies. Foreign Relations. 1950-76. *3314*
—. Bureaucracies. Hoover, Herbert C. Public administration. 1917-32. *1215*
—. Carter, Jimmy. Economic Policy. Recessions. 1920's-70's. *2315*
—. Central Intelligence Agency. Senate. 1945-75. *3251*
—. Collier, John. Indians. Liberalism. Roosevelt, Franklin D. (administration). Truman, Harry S. (administration). 1933-53. *86*
—. Commerce Department. Economic Regulations. Hoover, Herbert C. 1920's. *1380*
—. Coolidge, Calvin. Harding, Warren G. Negroes. Segregation. 1916-29. *1344*
—. Crime and Criminals. Justice Department. Law enforcement. 1789-1976. *163*
—. District of Columbia. Lincoln, Abraham. Pennsylvania (Philadelphia). Speeches, Addresses, etc. 1861. *438*
—. Eisenhower, Dwight D. (administration). Fuel, liquid. Politics. Synthetic Products. Truman, Harry S. (administration). 1944-54. *2525*
—. Enrolled bills. Legislation. Office of Management and Budget. Presidents. 1960's-78. *3468*
—. Executive Behavior. Political Ethics. Public administration. Richardson, Elliot. 1969-73. *2464*
—. Executive power. Separation of powers. 1974. *3333*
—. Federalists. Foreign relations. Political Attitudes. Publicity. Secrecy. 1800-12. *719*
—. Food Administration. Hoover, Herbert C. Voluntarism. World War I. 1917-18. *1517*
—. Foreign policy. National Security Action Memorandum 341. Reform. 1965-69. *3198*
—. Great Britain. Jews. Morgenthau, Henry, Jr. Relief organizations. War Refugee Board. World War II. 1940-44. *1633*
—. Hoover, Herbert C. Public welfare. Roosevelt, Franklin D. 1920-37. *1257*
—. Intelligence service. 1941-77. *3219*
—. Medical care. Poor. Public Health. 1960-77. *2449*
—. Military Strategy. Nuclear Arms. Public Opinion. Strategic Arms Limitation Talks. 1945-78. *2643*
—. New Federalism. Nixon, Richard M., administration. Political power. 1960's-70's. *2501*
—. New Federalism. Nixon, Richard M. (administration). State Government. Texas (El Paso). 1966-79. *2386*
—. Political Corruption. Watergate Scandal. 1974. *2549*
—. Presidential science adviser (proposed). Science and Government. 1970's. *3240*
—. Segregation. Trotter, William Monroe. Wilson, Woodrow. 1913-14. *1367*

Federal Policy *See also* Domestic Policy.
—. Agriculture Department. Employment. Equal opportunity. 1964-76. *3392*
—. Aid to Families with Dependent Children. Bureaucracies. Executive Power. Nixon, Richard M. (administration). 1969-74. *2472*
—. Alaska Reorganization Act (US, 1936). Aleuts. Eskimos. Indians. 1936-45. *1400*
—. Alcohol. Bureau of Alcohol, Tobacco and Firearms. Food additives. 1972-81. *2388*
—. American Revolution. Military Strategy. Washington, George. 1770's-90's. *309*
—. Armaments. Documents. Nuclear nonproliferation. 1981. *3172*
—. Atomic Energy. Carter, Jimmy. Energy. 1977-78. *2288*
—. Attitudes. New Deal. Technology. 1927-40. *1406*
—. Bethune, Mary McLeod. Equal opportunity. National Youth Administration. Negroes. Youth. 1935-44. *1438*
—. Brown, Jerry. Carter, Jimmy. Kennedy, Edward M. Politics. 1977-79. *2210*

—. Buchanan, James. Historiography. Mormons. Utah Expedition (1857-58). 1857-58. *881*
—. Bureau of Indian Affairs. Civil War. Coffin, William G. Indian Territory. Indians. 1861-65. *844*
—. Bureau of Indian Affairs. Collier, John. Indians. New Deal. 1933-45. *1448*
—. Carter, Jimmy. Cities. 1978. *2505*
—. Carter, Jimmy. Cities. Urban and Regional Policy Group. 1978. *2383*
—. Carter, Jimmy. Energy. 1930's-78. *111*
—. Carter, Jimmy. Johnson, Lyndon B. Nixon, Richard M. Public welfare. Roosevelt, Franklin D. Truman, Harry S. 1933-78. *118*
—. Carter, Jimmy (administration). Cities. Decisionmaking. Planning. Presidential staffs. 1977-80. *2533*
—. Carter, Jimmy (administration). Congress. Economic planning. Energy. Politics. 1976-78. *2364*
—. Carter, Jimmy (administration). Congress. Energy. Interest Groups. 1977-78. *2421*
—. Carter, Jimmy (administration). Energy. 1973-78. *2510*
—. Carter, Jimmy (administration). McKelvey, Vincent. Natural resources. Oil and Petroleum Products. US Geological Survey. 1978. *2295*
—. Cherokee Indians. Dole, William P. Indians. Lincoln, Abraham. Ross, John. 1860-65. *900*
—. Cherokee Indians. Indian-White Relations. Treaties. 1835-1900. *815*
—. Civil rights. Interest Groups. Populism. Private enterprise. Racism. Wallace, George C. 1960's. *2107*
—. Civil rights movement. Integration. Johnson, Lyndon B. Kennedy, John F. 1945-76. *2402*
—. Civil Service. Kennedy, John F. (administration). Peterson, Esther. President's Commission on the Status of Women. Sex Discrimination. Wages. Women. 1961-63. *2374*
—. Clergy. Johnson, Andrew. Protestant Churches. Public Opinion. Reconstruction. 1865-68. *788*
—. Coleraine, Treaty of. Creek Indians. Georgia. Indian-White Relations. 1796. *820*
—. Competency commissions. Indians. Land allotment. 1913-20. *1374*
—. Congress. Constitution. Executive branch. National Emergencies Act (US, 1976). Political power. 1933-78. *3362*
—. Congress. Eisenhower, Dwight D. (administration). Hungarians. Immigration. Public opinion. Refugees. 1956-57. *2893*
—. Congress. Methodology. Presidents. 1976-81. *3431*
—. Conservation of Natural Resources. Energy. Intergovernmental Relations. State Government. 1974-79. *2476*
—. Decisionmaking. Ideology. Presidents (review article). 1961-76. *2256*
—. Defense Policy. Industry. Labor Unions and Organizations. World War II. 1939-41. *1435*
—. District of Columbia. Johnson, Lyndon B. (administration). March on Washington for Jobs and Freedom. Poverty. 1968. *2357*
—. Documents. Harry S. Truman Library. Truman, Harry S. Western States. 1940-66. *2394*
—. Documents. Libraries, Presidential. Ownership. 1971. *3331*
—. Economic planning. New Deal. 1932-41. *1361*
—. Economic Policy. Eisenhower, Dwight D. (administration). Energy. Truman, Harry S. (administration). 1945-60. *2543*
—. Eisenhower, Dwight D. (administration). Legislation. Public Welfare. Reform. 1950-60. *2302*
—. Energy. 1979. *2423*
—. Environmental Protection Agency. Reagan, Ronald (administration). 1981. *2361*
—. Europe. Genocide. Jews. Roosevelt, Franklin D. (administration). World War II. 1942-44. *1608*
—. Executive Power. Justice. Law Enforcement. Politics. Social Conditions. 1960-79. *3386*
—. Federal Energy Administration. Oil Industry and Trade. Petitions. 1974-80. *2475*
—. Federal Programs. Health, Education, and Welfare Department. Historians. Workmen's compensation. 1910's-70's. *2300*
—. Hamilton, Alexander. International Trade. Madison, James. Republicanism. 1789-94. *297*
—. Hayes, Rutherford B. Indians. 1877-81. *808*

—. Hoover, Herbert C. Inventions. Roosevelt, Franklin D. (administration). Technology. 1930's-77. *1337*
—. Hoover, Herbert C. (administration). Public lands. Western states. Wilbur, Ray Lyman. 1920's. *1293*
—. Hopkins, Harry. New Deal. Poverty. Roosevelt, Franklin D. Unemployment. 1910's-38. *1369*
—. Indians. Jackson, Andrew. Psychohistory. Rogin, Michael Paul (review article). 1800-50. *545*
—. Indians. Lincoln, Abraham. 1861-65. *906*
—. Indians (review article). New Deal. Parman, Donald L. Philp, Kenneth R. Taylor, Graham D. 1934-74. *1329*
—. Indochina. Military Intelligence. World War II. 1943-45. *1662*
—. Industry. Investments. Reagan, Ronald (administration). 1982. *2363*
—. Interest groups. Post Office Department. Reform. 1966-80. *3205*
—. Mississippi. Negroes. Nixon, Richard M. (administration). Poverty. 1967-73. *2294*
—. National Security Council. 1974. *3099*
—. Naval strategy. Pacific area. Roosevelt, Franklin D. 1933-39. *1239*
—. Political issues. Political parties. Voting and Voting Behavior. 1960-72. *1964*
—. Political Speeches. Presidents. State of the Union message. 1946-69. *3338*
—. Presidency. Research. 1954-74. *3442*
—. Presidents. 1979. *3462*
—. Puerto Rico. Self-government. Truman, Harry S. (administration). 1945-47. *2306*
—. Works Progress Administration. 1930's-70's. *1427*
Federal Programs. ACTION (agency). Brown, Sam. Carter, Jimmy (administration). VISTA. 1977-78. *2460*
—. Agricultural Adjustment Act (US, 1933). Commodities. Iowa. New Deal. Wallace, Henry A. 1933-34. *1357*
—. Agricultural Policy. Congress. Democratic Party. Presidents. South. 1933-61. *141*
—. Agriculture. Indian-White Relations. Missions and Missionaries. Old Northwest. 1789-1820. *818*
—. Anthropology. Bureau of Indian Affairs. Collier, John. Indians. New Deal. 1930's. *1345*
—. Artists. Buildings, public. New Deal. 1930's. *1401*
—. Bureau of Indian Affairs. Criminal law. Indian Self-Determination and Educational Assistance Act (US, 1975). 1970-82. *2455*
—. Carter, Jimmy (administration). Energy. Oil industry and trade. 1978-80. *2429*
—. Congress. Presidency. 1961-80. *3356*
—. Defense Department. 1970's. *3311*
—. Federal policy. Health, Education, and Welfare Department. Historians. Workmen's compensation. 1910's-70's. *2300*
—. Roosevelt, Franklin D. State Legislatures. 1933-70's. *1360*
Federal Regulation *See also* Economic Regulations, Regulatory Commissions.
—. Advertising. Children. Television. 1970-81. *2360*
—. Agriculture Department. Dyes. Food. Public Health. 1913-19. *1334*
—. Ammons, Elias. Coal. Colorado. Strikes. Wilson, Woodrow. 1914. *1338*
—. Antibiotics. Conflict of interest. Food and Drug Administration. Periodicals. Pharmaceutical Industry. Welch, Henry. 1959-62. *2434*
—. Automobile Industry and Trade. Pollution. 1970's. *2529*
—. Avery, Sewell. Illinois (Chicago). Labor Disputes. Montgomery Ward. War Labor Board. World War II. 1941. *1348*
—. Business. Hoover, Herbert C. Political Theory. 1910-76. *1106*
—. Campaign finance. Democratic Party. Economic theory. Elections, presidential. 1976. *1783*
—. Commerce Department. Hoover, Herbert C. Industry. Labor. 1921-28. *1331*
—. Commerce Department. Hoover, Herbert C. Licensing. Radio. 1918-22. *1416*
—. Commerce Department. Hoover, Herbert C. Radio Act (US, 1927). 1921-28. *1305*
—. Congress. Ickes, Harold L. Oil Industry and Trade. Roosevelt, Franklin D. 1933. *1358*
—. Conservatism. Eisenhower, Dwight D. (administration). Republican Party. 1953-61. *2515*

—. Dairying. Food Administration. Hoover, Herbert C. 1917-18. *1320*
—. Desegregation. Health, Education, and Welfare Department. Public Schools. South. 1954-73. *2335*
—. Economic Policy. 1957-78. *2320*
—. Executive branch. Regulatory commissions. 1900-81. *12*
—. Federal Trade Commission. National Labor Relations Board. Presidents. Securities and Exchange Commission. 1945-77. *2442*
—. Food and Drug Administration. Pharmaceutical Industry. Scientific Experiments and Research. 1962-71. *2500*
—. Forests and Forestry. Oregon. Pinchot, Gifford. Washington. 1902-10. *1297*
—. Inflation. Nixon, Richard M. (administration). 1969-77. *2352*
—. Nixon, Richard M. O'Brien, Mary-Win. Occupational Safety and Health Act (US, 1970). Page, Joseph A. 1970-74. *2291*
Federal Reserve System. Attitudes. Democracy. Income tax. Reform. Wilson, Woodrow. 1913-21. *1353*
—. Economic Policy. Political Parties. Presidents. 1958-73. *2362*
—. Elections (presidential). Presidents. 1970's. *3202*
Federal Reserve System (Board of Governors). Banking. Comptroller of the Currency. Justice Department. Mergers. 1950-66. *3266*
Federal systems. Canada. Editorials. Political Campaigns. 1972. *2076*
Federal Theatre Project. Depressions. Flanagan, Hallie. Hopkins, Harry. Politics. Theater. Works Progress Administration. 1935-39. *1266*
Federal Trade Commission. Federal Regulation. National Labor Relations Board. Presidents. Securities and Exchange Commission. 1945-77. *2442*
Federalism *See also* Federal Government; New Federalism; Revenue Sharing.
—. Calhoun, John C. Jefferson, Thomas. Natural Rights. Rationalism. Taylor, John (of Caroline). 1770's-1832. *264*
—. Civil War. Grant, Ulysses S. Greeley, Horace. Nationalism. Political Campaigns (presidential). 1872. *658*
—. Congress. Political power. Presidency. 1776-1976. *75*
—. Hamilton, Alexander. Madison, James. Politicians. 1770's-80's. 1970's. *387*
—. Nixon, Richard M. (administration). Social Problems. 1968-70. *2526*
—. Political Campaigns (presidential). Political Speeches. Reagan, Ronald. 1980-81. *2114*
—. Presidency. Public administration. 1787-1979. *3420*
—. Presidents. Supreme Court. 1796-1973. *1044*
—. Washington, George. 1789-96. *879*
Federalism (review article). Choper, Jesse H. Fisher, Louis. Genovese, Michael A. Jenkins, Iredell. Law. Merry, Henry J. 1978-80. *3221*
Federalist. Constitutional Convention. Government. Madison, James. Political Theory. 1783-90. *302*
—. Hamilton, Alexander. Jay, John. Liberty. Madison, James. Political Theory. 1787-88. *181*
Federalist No. 10. Adair, Douglass. Hume, David. Madison, James. Political Theory. Republicanism. Wills, Garry. 1788. *238*
—. Enlightenment. Madison, James. Political theory. 1760-87. *213*
—. General will (concept). Interest groups. Madison, James. Rousseau, Jean Jacques. 1787. *214*
—. Madison, James. Political Representation. Political Systems. 1740-88. *311*
—. Madison, James. Political Theory. 1787-20c. *192*
Federalist Party. Adams, John. Hamilton, Alexander. Jefferson, Thomas. Political Factions. Washington, George. 1775-90's. *720*
—. Navy Secretaries. Politics. Stoddert, Benjamin. ca 1783-1812. *928*
Federalists. Democratic-Republican Party. Elections (presidential). Pinckney, Thomas. South Carolina. 1796. *677*
—. Federal Government. Foreign relations. Political Attitudes. Publicity. Secrecy. 1800-12. *719*
—. France. Great Britain. Jefferson, Thomas. 1780-1805. *276*

—. Hamilton, Alexander. Madison, James. Political Representation. Republicanism. 1780's. *388*
—. Jefferson, Thomas. Nicholas, John, Jr. Politics. Virginia (Albemarle County). 1770's-1836. *254*
—. Politics. Presidency. Washington, George. 1789-97. *733*
Feminism. Elections (presidential). 1976-80. *1856*
Ferrell, Robert H. Gosnell, Harold F. Heller, Francis H. Presidency. Theoharis, Athan. Truman, Harry S. (review article). 1979-80. 1884-1953. *2189*
Filibusters. Democratic Party. House of Representatives. Race Relations. Reconstruction. Roll-call voting. 1876-77. *615*
—. Deregulation. Mondale, Walter F. Natural gas. Senate. Vice-presidency. 1977. *2454*
Fillmore, Millard. Anti-Catholicism. Know-Nothing Party. Nativism. Political Campaigns (presidential). Whig Party. 1850-56. *561*
—. Mormons. Territorial government. Utah. 1850-53. *843*
Films *See also* Actors and Actresses; Documentaries.
—. Actors and Actresses. Lincoln, Abraham. 1809-65. 1900-77. *466*
—. Assassination. Civil War. *Lincoln Conspiracy* (film). Public Opinion. 1865. 1970's. *432*
—. Attorneys General. Cummings, Homer Stillé. Federal Bureau of Investigation. *G-Men* (film). Hoover, J. Edgar. 1933-35. *1405*
—. Library of Congress. Roosevelt, Theodore. Women. 1891-1934. *1077*
—. *Meeting at Potsdam* (film). Potsdam Conference. Truman, Harry S. World War II. 1945. 1970's. *2727*
Finance *See also* subjects with the subdivision finance, e.g. Education (finance), World War I (finance), etc.; Business; Campaign Finance; Commerce; Economics.
—. Agent General. Appointments to Office. Coolidge, Calvin (administration). Diplomacy. Germany. Reparations. 1923-24. *1572*
—. Foreign relations. Great Britain. McAdoo, William G. Morgan, J. P. & Company. Wilson, Woodrow (administration). World War I. 1914-20. *1222*
—. Hayes, Rutherford B. Kenyon College. Ohio (Gambier). 1838-41. *500*
Fine, Sidney. Andersen, Kristi. Blumberg, Barbara. Jeffries, John W. New Deal (review article). Roosevelt, Franklin D. Swain, Martha H. 1933-39. *1263*
—. City politics (review article). Democratic Party. Dorsett, Lyle W. Roosevelt, Franklin D. Trout, Charles H. 1930-40. *1328*
Firearms *See also* Gun Control.
—. Davis, Jefferson. Defense Secretaries. Mexican War. Military officers. Political feuds. Scott, Winfield. 1845-57. *757*
Fireworks. Cosway, Maria. France. Jefferson, Thomas. 1786-89. *281*
First Ladies. Adams, Louisa Catherine Johnson. 1775-1852. *415*
—. Associated Press. Hickok, Lorena A. Reporters and Reporting. Roosevelt, Eleanor. 1932-68. *1056*
—. Attitudes. Hayes, Lucy Webb. 1831-89. *460*
—. Hayes, Lucy Webb. Women. 1877-1889. *459*
First Ladies, former. Bly, Nellie (Elizabeth C. Seaman). Hayes, Lucy Webb. Keeler, Lucy Elliott. Ohio (Fremont; Spiegel Grove). Reporters and Reporting. 1888. *422*
Fiscal Policy. Budgets. Congress. Impoundment. Nixon, Richard M. Office of Management and Budget. Separation of Powers. 1969-77. *3461*
—. Budgets. Executive branch. Presidents. Public administration. 1953-69. *3372*
—. Congress. Congressional Budget and Impoundment Control Act (US, 1974). Executive Power. Impoundment. 1974. *3312*
—. Conservatism. Economy Act (US, 1933). New Deal. Roosevelt, Franklin D. 1932-36. *1424*
—. Currie, Lauchlin. Income. Keynesianism. New Deal. 1920's-30's. *1469*
Fisher, Irving. Depressions. Economic Reform. Roosevelt, Franklin D. 1930's. *1251*
Fisher, Louis. Choper, Jesse H. Federalism (review article). Genovese, Michael A. Jenkins, Iredell. Law. Merry, Henry J. 1978-80. *3221*

Fisher, Walter Lowrie. Ballinger-Pinchot Controversy. Conservation of Natural Resources. Interior Department. 1911-13. *1315*
Fishing *See also* Whaling Industry and Trade.
—. Adams, John Quincy. Diplomacy. Great Britain. Monroe, James. Newfoundland. 1815-18. *991*
Fitzgerald, F. Scott. Franklin, Benjamin. Innocence (concept). National Characteristics. Nixon, Richard M. Thoreau, Henry David. Values. Watergate scandal. 18c-1978. *1762*
Five Civilized Tribes. Civil War. Indian Territory. Lincoln, Abraham. Proclamations. Ross, John. 1860's. *790*
Flanagan, Hallie. Depressions. Federal Theatre Project. Hopkins, Harry. Politics. Theater. Works Progress Administration. 1935-39. *1266*
Flemming, Arthur S. Benson, Ezra Taft. Cabinet. Construction. Documents. Eisenhower, Dwight D. Federal aid to education. 1959. *2334*
Florida *See also* Southeastern States.
—. Chase, Salmon P. Civil War. Lincoln, Abraham. Olustee (battle). Political Campaigns (presidential). 1864. *891*
—. Elections (presidential). Hayes, Rutherford B. Patronage. State politics. Wallace, Lew. 1876-78. *698*
—. Hoover, Herbert C. (administration). Patronage. Republican Party. State Politics. 1928-33. *1312*
—. Indian-White Relations. Jackson, Andrew. Remini, Robert V. (review article). Removals, forced. Tennessee. 1780's-1821. *560*
—. Jackson, Andrew. Seminole War, 1st. 1818. *599*
—. Mass Media. Primaries (presidential). Wallace, George C. 1972. *2005*
—. Public opinion. Roosevelt, Theodore. South. Washington, Booker T. White House dinners. 1901. *1431*
Florida (Amelia Island; Fernandina). Civil War. Johnson, Andrew. Land Tenure. Military Occupation. Property Tax. Unionists. 1860's-90's. *934*
Florida (Dry Tortugas Island, Fort Jefferson). Assassination. Johnson, Andrew. Lincoln, Abraham. Mudd, Samuel A. Pardons. 1865-96. *537*
Florida (Escambia County). Aden. Mass media. Political Campaigns (presidential). Television. Voting and Voting Behavior. 1976. *2046*
—. Political campaigns. Primaries (presidential). Public Relations. Voting and Voting Behavior. 1976. *2045*
Florida (Miami). Assassination. Cermak, Anton. Roosevelt, Franklin D. Zangara, Giuseppe. 1933. *1284*
—. Assassination. Roosevelt, Franklin D. Zangara, Giuseppe. 1933. *1118*
—. Democratic Party. McGovern, George S. Political Campaigns (presidential). Radicals and Radicalism. 1972. *1926*
Florida (Umatilla). Baptists. Lincoln, Abraham. Southern Baptist winter assembly grounds. 1865. 1925-29. *394*
Florville, William. Illinois (Springfield). Lincoln, Abraham. 1832-68. *519*
Floto, Inga. Foreign Policy. House, Edward Mandell. Paris Peace Settlements. Wilson, Woodrow (review article). 1919. *1592*
Folk culture. Carter, Jimmy. Niebuhr, Reinhold. Populism. Protestantism. South. 1976. *1875*
Folklore *See also* Myths and Symbols.
—. Historiography. Lincoln, Abraham. 1816-20c. *403*
Food. Agriculture Department. Dyes. Federal regulation. Public Health. 1913-19. *1334*
—. Butz, Earl. Diplomacy. Ford, Gerald R. Kissinger, Henry A. 1973-75. *2740*
—. Charities. Depressions. Hoover, Herbert C. Red Cross. Wheat, surplus. 1932-33. *1356*
—. Decisionmaking. Executive Branch. Interest Groups. 1970-81. *3313*
—. Wage-price controls. Wilson, Woodrow. World War I. 1917. *1325*
Food additives. Alcohol. Bureau of Alcohol, Tobacco and Firearms. Federal Policy. 1972-81. *2388*
Food Administration. Dairying. Federal Regulation. Hoover, Herbert C. 1917-18. *1320*
—. Federal government. Hoover, Herbert C. Voluntarism. World War I. 1917-18. *1517*
—. Hoover, Herbert C. Pork-packing. Prices. Voluntarism. World War I. 1917-19. *1277*

Food and Drug Administration. Antibiotics. Conflict of interest. Federal regulation. Periodicals. Pharmaceutical Industry. Welch, Henry. 1959-62. *2434*
—. Federal Regulation. Pharmaceutical Industry. Scientific Experiments and Research. 1962-71. *2500*
Food Supply. Agriculture Department. Butz, Earl. 1974. *2446*
—. Carter, Jimmy. Foreign Policy. Surpluses. USSR. 1974-80. *2934*
Foraker, Joseph B. Elections (presidential). Negroes. Republican Party. Taft, William H. 1908. *1157*
Force, concept of. Diplomacy. Wilson, Woodrow. World War I. 1917-18. *1668*
Ford, Gerald R. Agendas. Carter, Jimmy. Debates. Political Campaigns (presidential). 1976. *1799*
—. Amnesty. Justice. Nixon, Richard M. Pardons. Vietnam War. 1974. *2317*
—. Appointments to office. House of Representatives. Perjury. Watergate Scandal. 1973-75. *2311*
—. Arms control. Brezhnev, Leonid. Foreign Relations. Kissinger, Henry A. USSR. Vladivostok Accord. 1974. *3131*
—. Asia, Southeast. Foreign policy. Kissinger, Henry A. Vietnam War. 1972-75. *3055*
—. Asia, Southeast. Foreign relations. Intervention. 1900-75. *3002*
—. Brezhnev, Leonid. Detente. Vladivostok Accord. 1974. *2936*
—. Butz, Earl. Diplomacy. Food. Kissinger, Henry A. 1973-75. *2740*
—. Cambodia. Crisis management. Decisionmaking. *Mayaguez* (incident). 1975. *2641*
—. Cambodia. *Mayaguez* (incident). War Powers Resolution. 1975. *3166*
—. Campbell, Angus. Carter, Jimmy. Elections (presidential). Political Theory. 1976. *2066*
—. Canada. Foreign Relations. Trudeau, Pierre Elliott. 1974-76. *3093*
—. Carter, Jimmy. Communications Behavior. Debates. Illinois, University of. Political Campaigns (presidential). Students. Television. 1976. *2091*
—. Carter, Jimmy. Communications Behavior. Debates. Political Campaigns (presidential). Public opinion. Television. 1976. *1962*
—. Carter, Jimmy. Communications Behavior. Debates. Political Campaigns (presidential). Television. 1976. *2050*
—. Carter, Jimmy. Communications Behavior. Debates. Political Campaigns (presidential). Television. 1976. *2097*
—. Carter, Jimmy. Debates. Eye contact. Political Campaigns (presidential). Public Opinion. Television. 1976. *1842*
—. Carter, Jimmy. Debates. Mass Media. Voting and Voting Behavior. Wisconsin. 1976. *1828*
—. Carter, Jimmy. Debates. Political Campaigns (presidential). Public Opinion. Television. 1976. *2000*
—. Carter, Jimmy. Debates. Political Campaigns (presidential). Television. 1976. *1961*
—. Carter, Jimmy. Decisionmaking. Nixon, Richard M. 1970's. *3236*
—. Carter, Jimmy. Economic Policy. Elections (presidential). 1976. *2112*
—. Carter, Jimmy. Elections (presidential). Reagan, Ronald. Republican Party. 1976. *2085*
—. Carter, Jimmy. Executive power. Neustadt, Richard E. (review article). 1974-78. *3437*
—. Carter, Jimmy. Nixon, Richard M. Personality. Presidency. 1968-76. *2139*
—. Carter, Jimmy. Political Campaigns (presidential). Reporters and reporting. Television. 1976. *2089*
—. Carter, Jimmy. Political Conventions. Primaries (presidential). Reagan, Ronald. 1974-76. *1927*
—. Carter, Jimmy. Presidential staffs. 1974-80. *3262*
—. Carter, Jimmy. Presidential staffs. 1974-80. *3317*
—. Civil rights. Negroes. 1949-74. *2441*
—. Congress. Executive Power. Models. 1974-77. *2216*
—. Conservatism. Nixon, Richard M. Reagan, Ronald. 1969-80. *2477*
—. Delegates. Political conventions. Reagan, Ronald. Republican Party. 1976. *2009*
—. Detente. Europe, Eastern. Political Campaigns (presidential). USSR. 1976-77. *1849*
—. Domestic policy. Politics. 1974-76. *2273*

—. Elections (presidential). Republican Party. Vice-presidency. 1973-76. *2187*

—. Executive Office of the President (Domestic Council). Nixon, Richard M. 1967-76. *3301*

—. Foreign policy. Indonesia. Thailand. 1975. *3126*

—. Foreign policy. Israel. 1974-75. *2718*

—. Foreign policy. Kissinger, Henry A. Nixon, Richard M. Secrecy. 1970's. *2999*

—. Inflation. Political Speeches. Rhetoric. War metaphor. 1974. *2507*

—. Michigan (Mackinac Island). Travel. 1975. *2465*

—. Nixon, Richard M. Pardons. Political Speeches. 1974. *2404*

—. Nixon, Richard M. Political Participation. Reagan, Ronald. Republican Party. 1972-76. *2044*

—. Political conventions. Reagan, Ronald. Republican Party. 1976. *1794*

—. Political reform. Vice-presidency. 1945-74. *3429*

—. Political speechwriting. 1976. *2074*

—. Politics. 1974-77. *2141*

Ford, Gerald R. (administration). Conference on Security and Cooperation in Europe. Europe. International Security. Public opinion. 1975. *2638*

—. Congress. Economic growth. Energy. Planning. ca 1970's. *2293*

—. Foreign Policy. Israel. Middle East. Nixon, Richard M. (administration). 1969-77. *2589*

Ford's Theater. Assassination. District of Columbia. Grant, Ulysses S. Lincoln, Abraham. Lincoln, Mary Todd. 1865. *572*

Foreign Aid *See also* Economic Aid; Military Aid.

—. 1948-79. *2750*

—. China. China. Cultural relations. State Department. 1942-45. *1622*

—. Cold War. Developing nations. Point Four program. 1949-68. *2965*

—. Diplomacy. Europe. Great Powers. Marshall Plan. 1947. *2679*

—. Dulles, John Foster. Gomulka, Wladyslaw. Poland. 1957-64. *2811*

—. Europe. Immigration. Refugees. Truman, Harry S. Visas. 1945-48. *2753*

—. Haiti. Kennedy, John F. Social Change. 1960's-80. *2896*

—. Italy. Politics. Roosevelt, Franklin D. 1943-44. *1611*

—. Truman Doctrine. Turkey. 1947. *2843*

Foreign Assistance Act (US, 1974). Human rights. Military aid. 1973-82. *2665*

Foreign Exchange *See also* Exchange Rates.

—. Nixon, Richard M. (administration). Politics. Presidential advisers. 1960's-70's. *2948*

Foreign Investments. Diplomacy. Gómez, Juan. Great Britain. Oil Industry and Trade. Venezuela. 1908-29. *1638*

—. Diplomacy. Kissinger, Henry A. Multinational Corporations. South Africa. 1969-76. *3047*

Foreign Ministers conference (London). Germany. Marshall, George C. Molotov, V. M. USSR. 1947. *3137*

Foreign Office. Great Britain. State Department. War. 20c. *170*

Foreign Policy *See also* Defense Policy; Detente; International Relations (discipline).

—. Acheson, Dean. Balance of power. Kissinger, Henry A. 1945-76. *2581*

—. Acheson, Dean. Baruch, Bernard. Cold War. Diplomacy. Nuclear Arms. Roosevelt, Franklin D. Stimson, Henry L. Truman, Harry S. USSR. 1942-46. *1489*

—. Adams, John. Europe. Free trade. Mercantilism. 1775-85. *209*

—. Adams, John Quincy. House of Representatives. Secession. 1842. *527*

—. Addams, Jane. Ideology. Open Door Policy. Wilson, Woodrow. 1900-20. *1623*

—. Afghanistan. Carter, Jimmy (administration). Hutson, Thomas R. Invasions. Personal narratives. USSR. 1980-81. *2797*

—. Africa. 1974-81. *3103*

—. Africa. 1977-81. *2899*

—. Africa. Carter, Jimmy (administration). 1975-80. *2848*

—. Africa. Carter, Jimmy (administration). Human rights. 1979. *2956*

—. Africa. Cuba. Intervention. USSR. ca 1970-77. *3026*

—. Africa. Kissinger, Henry A. 1974-76. *2887*

—. Africa. Kissinger, Henry A. 1976. *2656*

—. Africa. Nixon, Richard M. State of the World address. 1973. *2938*

—. Africa, East. Carter, Jimmy (administration). 1970's. *2723*

—. Africa, Southern. Carter, Jimmy (administration). Economic interests. 1976-77. *2876*

—. Alexander, Charles C. Cold War. Eisenhower, Dwight D. (review article). 1952-61. *2146*

—. Allende, Salvador. Central Intelligence Agency. Chile. Multinational corporations. 1970-73. *2960*

—. Alliances. Bulgaria. Hungary. Romania. World War II. 1943-44. *1666*

—. Allies. Kissinger, Henry A. Nixon, Richard M. State of the Union message. 1970. *3180*

—. American Bar Association. Bricker Amendment. Executive power. 1948-54. *3452*

—. American Dream. Rhetoric. Truman, Harry S. 1945-46. *2782*

—. Anderson, Chandler. Mexico. Multinational Corporations. Wilson, Woodrow. 1913-20. *1555*

—. Anderson, Clinton P. Congress. Executive Power. Nixon, Richard M. Vietnam War. 1945-72. *3138*

—. Angola. 1960-81. *2583*

—. Angola. Clark Amendment (US, 1975). 1975-81. *3140*

—. Angola. Mozambique. South Africa. 1970-76. *2918*

—. Annexation. British Columbia. Seward, William H. 1865-69. *1020*

—. Anti-Communist Movements. Asia. Reagan, Ronald (administration). Taiwan. 1981. *2799*

—. Antitrust. Cold War. Middle East. Oil industry and trade. 1950-65. *2815*

—. Antitrust. Middle East. Multinational Corporations. Oil Industry and Trade. 1945-61. *2814*

—. Appeasement. Chamberlain, Neville. Great Britain. Roosevelt, Franklin Delano. 1937-39. *1679*

—. Appeasement. Germany. Great Britain. International Trade. 1933-40. *1626*

—. Appeasement. Germany. Roosevelt, Franklin D. 1933-36. *1652*

—. Arab States. Israel. Pressure groups. 1973-75. *3110*

—. Arab States. Israel. USSR. 1973-78. *3118*

—. Arab-Israeli Conflict. Carter, Jimmy. 1977. *3132*

—. Arab-Israeli conflict. Kissinger, Henry A. Middle East. 1969-79. *2584*

—. Archives, National. Information access. Presidents. Public records. State Department. 1950's-70's. *3377*

—. Argentina. Hull, Cordell. Ramírez, Pedro. 1943. *1685*

—. Armies. Carter, Jimmy (administration). Korea. 1977. *3091*

—. Arms Control and Disarmament Agency. Reagan, Ronald (administration). 1960-81. *2657*

—. Arms Trade. Carter, Jimmy. Domestic Policy. Middle East. 1976-78. *3109*

—. Arms Trade. Carter, Jimmy (administration). 1977-79. *2570*

—. Arms Trade. Carter, Jimmy (administration). Conventional Arms Transfers Talks. Developing nations. Military aid. USSR. 1977-82. *2607*

—. Asia. 1975-80. *3113*

—. Asia. Balance of power. Kissinger, Henry A. 1968-73. *3032*

—. Asia, East. Lansing, Robert. State Department. World War I (antecedents). 1914-17. *1557*

—. Asia, South. Carter, Jimmy (administration). 1977-80. *2579*

—. Asia, Southeast. Carter, Jimmy. 1970's. *2988*

—. Asia, Southeast. Colonialism. Great Britain. Roosevelt, Franklin D. (administration). 1942-44. *1681*

—. Asia, Southeast. Ford, Gerald R. Kissinger, Henry A. Vietnam War. 1972-75. *3055*

—. Asia, Southeast. Japan. Military strategy. Pearl Harbor, attack on. Roosevelt, Franklin D. World War II. 1941. *1506*

—. Assassination. Central Intelligence Agency. Covert operations. 1947-70's. *2654*

—. Assassination. Cuba. Kennedy, John F. 1963-77. *3042*

—. Atomic Warfare. Diplomacy. Roosevelt, Franklin D. Truman, Harry S. 1945-51. *1490*

—. Atomic Warfare. Massive Retaliation. 1954-73. *2771*

—. Attitudes. Carter, Jimmy (administration). Human rights. 1977-78. *2858*

—. Attitudes. Executive Behavior. Political Protest. Roosevelt, Franklin D. 1940-72. *1697*

—. Attitudes. Executive power. Nixon, Richard M. (administration). War. Watergate scandal. 1940's-70's. *3404*

—. Austria. Compromise of 1850. Politics. Spain. Webster, Daniel. 1850-52. *1017*

—. Axis Powers. Latin America. Office of the Coordinator of Inter-American Affairs. Rockefeller, Nelson A. Roosevelt, Franklin D. (administration). 1933-42. *1551*

—. Balance of Power. Carter, Jimmy (administration). Regionalism. USSR. 1979. *2805*

—. Balance of power. China. Detente. USSR. 1945-79. *2616*

—. Balance of power. China. Nixon, Richard M. (administration). USSR. 1969-72. *3018*

—. Balance of power. Kissinger, Henry A. (review article). Mazlish, Bruce. 1973-76. *2996*

—. Balance of power. Kissinger, Henry A. (review article). Nixon, Richard M. 1969-73. *3144*

—. Bangladesh. India. Kissinger, Henry A. Nixon, Richard M. (administration). Pakistan. 1971-76. *3127*

—. Banking. Carter, Jimmy (administration). Human rights. 1977. *2878*

—. Bay of Pigs Invasion. Cuba. Vietnam War. Watergate scandal. 1961-74. *3077*

—. Berlin Blockade. Decisionmaking. Ideology. Israel. Truman, Harry S. 1944-48. *3011*

—. Bibliographies. 1944-74. *3049*

—. Biddle, A. J. Drexel. Poland. 1918-45. *1494*

—. Bipartisanship. Intergovernmental Relations. 1981. *2978*

—. Bipartisanship. Taft, Robert A. Truman, Harry S. (administration). 1943-52. *2586*

—. Bismarck, Otto von. Europe. Kissinger, Henry A. 19c. 1968-74. *2646*

—. Blaine, James G. International Trade. Latin America. Reciprocity. 1884-94. *1009*

—. Bohlen, Charles E. Documents. Europe, Eastern. State Department. USSR. 1945-46. *2891*

—. Bombing halt. Johnson, Lyndon B. Political Speeches. Public Opinion. Vietnam War. 1968-78. *3060*

—. Boundaries. Great Britain. Italy. World War II. Yugoslavia. 1941-45. *1493*

—. Boundaries. Oder-Neisse Line. Poland. Roosevelt, Franklin D. State Department. Truman, Harry S. World War II. 1941-45. *1609*

—. Bourgois, Philippe. El Salvador. Personal narratives. Reagan, Ronald (administration). Revolution. 1981. *2613*

—. Brazil. Carter, Jimmy. 1978-79. *2720*

—. Brazil. Democracy. 1964-68. *2862*

—. Bruce, Frederick. Great Britain. Johnson, Andrew. Letters. Reconstruction. 1866. *821*

—. Bryan, William Jennings. Delaware. Political Campaigns (presidential). Stevenson, Adlai E. (1835-1914). 1900. *682*

—. Brzezinski, Zbigniew. 1954-79. *3167*

—. Brzezinski, Zbigniew. 1977-78. *3050*

—. Brzezinski, Zbigniew. Carter, Jimmy (administration). 1958-79. *2906*

—. Brzezinski, Zbigniew. Carter, Jimmy (administration). 1976-80. *2933*

—. Brzezinski, Zbigniew. Carter, Jimmy (administration). Italy. 1977. *2738*

—. Brzezinski, Zbigniew. Carter, Jimmy (administration). Middle East. Vance, Cyrus. 1977-80. *3079*

—. Brzezinski, Zbigniew (interview). Carter, Jimmy (administration). 1976-80. *3121*

—. Bureaucracies. 1976. *3359*

—. Bureaucracies. Cabinet. Kennedy, John F. (administration). Presidential staffs. State Department. 1961-63. *2647*

—. Bureaucracies. Cambodia. Kissinger, Henry A. Nixon, Richard M. (administration). Shawcross, William. State Department. Vietnam War. 1960's-80. *3379*

—. Bureaucracies. Cuban Missile Crisis. Kennedy, John F. Turkey. 1962. *2767*

—. Bureaucracies. Decisionmaking. Johnson, Lyndon B. (administration). Nixon, Richard M. (administration). Strategic Arms Limitation Talks. 1966-74. *3009*

—. Cambodia. Kissinger, Henry A. Nixon, Richard M. Shawcross, William. Vietnam War (review article). 1953-70. *3081*

—. Camp David Agreement. Middle East. 1977-81. *2567*

—. Canada. Economics. Great Britain. Madison, James. Sheffield, 1st Earl of. War of 1812. West Indies. 1783-1812. *355*

—. Cannon, Mary. Labor Department (Women's Bureau). Latin America. Women. 1930-39. *1654*

—. Carter, Hodding, III. Carter, Jimmy (administration). Personal narratives. Public opinion. 1976-80. *3174*

—. Carter, Jimmy. 1820's-1970's. *2806*

—. Carter, Jimmy. 1977-80. *2791*

—. Carter, Jimmy. 1977. *2671*

—. Carter, Jimmy. 1977. *3023*

—. Carter, Jimmy. 1977. *3133*

—. Carter, Jimmy. Congress. ca 1975-78. *2952*

—. Carter, Jimmy. Decisionmaking. 1977-78. *2582*

—. Carter, Jimmy. Developing nations. USSR. 1945-80. *2713*

—. Carter, Jimmy. Disarmament. Inaugural Addresses. Morality. 1976. *2554*

—. Carter, Jimmy. Eisenhower, Dwight D. Executive Power. Hamilton, Alexander. Taiwan. 1793-1979. *2794*

—. Carter, Jimmy. Ethics. Human rights. Kissinger, Henry A. Political Theory. 1973-80. *2721*

—. Carter, Jimmy. Europe, Eastern. Human rights. Self-determination. USSR. 1977-78. *2697*

—. Carter, Jimmy. Executive Power. Nixon, Richard M. Watergate scandal. 1973-78. *2998*

—. Carter, Jimmy. Food Supply. Surpluses. USSR. 1974-80. *2934*

—. Carter, Jimmy. Great Britain. Kissinger, Henry A. Press. 1968-77. *3143*

—. Carter, Jimmy. Hostages. Iran. Terrorism. 1979-81. *2605*

—. Carter, Jimmy. Human rights. 1977-78. *2932*

—. Carter, Jimmy. Human rights. 1977-79. *2951*

—. Carter, Jimmy. Human rights. Intervention. 1977-80. *2983*

—. Carter, Jimmy. Human rights. Latin America. 1977-80. *2756*

—. Carter, Jimmy. Human rights. Materialism. Morality. 1977-79. *2571*

—. Carter, Jimmy. Human rights. USSR. 1976-77. *2744*

—. Carter, Jimmy. International Labor Organization. 1977. *2808*

—. Carter, Jimmy. Middle East. ca 1967-77. *2564*

—. Carter, Jimmy. Morality. 1913-77. *125*

—. Carter, Jimmy. Morality. Pragmatism. 1776-1970's. *74*

—. Carter, Jimmy. Nuclear nonproliferation. Political Leadership. 1977-79. *2942*

—. Carter, Jimmy. Nuclear nonproliferation. Political Leadership. 1979. *2621*

—. Carter, Jimmy. Panama Canal. Political Speeches. Rhetoric. Television. 1977-78. *3090*

—. Carter, Jimmy. Presidency. 1977-80. *3034*

—. Carter, Jimmy. Speeches, Addresses, etc. USSR. 1978. *3134*

—. Carter, Jimmy (administration). 1976-80. *2954*

—. Carter, Jimmy (administration). 1977-79. *2973*

—. Carter, Jimmy (administration). 1977-81. *2789*

—. Carter, Jimmy (administration). 1977. *2939*

—. Carter, Jimmy (administration). 1978. *2632*

—. Carter, Jimmy (administration). China. Human rights. Morality. 1976-77. *3115*

—. Carter, Jimmy (administration). Communism. Latin America. National Security. 1977-80. *2831*

—. Carter, Jimmy (administration). Communist Countries. Military Strategy. Reagan, Ronald (administration). 1980. *3122*

—. Carter, Jimmy (administration). Communist Party. Italy. Kissinger, Henry A. 1960's-70's. *2855*

—. Carter, Jimmy (administration). Congress. Domestic policy. Inflation. Interest groups. 1977-78. *2200*

—. Carter, Jimmy (administration). Congress. Public Opinion. 1978. *2787*

—. Carter, Jimmy (administration). Declaration of Independence. Idealism. Morality. ca 1918-78. *2784*

—. Carter, Jimmy (administration). Defense spending. Military. NATO. Politics. 1976. *2625*

—. Carter, Jimmy (administration). Detente. Developing nations. Europe, Western. Japan. USSR. 1977-80. *3114*

—. Carter, Jimmy (administration). Domestic policy. 1976. *2191*

—. Carter, Jimmy (administration). Domestic Policy. Human rights. 1977-79. *3037*

—. Carter, Jimmy (administration). Domestic Policy. Morality. 1977. *2271*

—. Carter, Jimmy (administration). Europe, Western. USSR. 1970's. *2790*

—. Carter, Jimmy (administration). Foreign Policy. 1976-78. *2796*

—. Carter, Jimmy (administration). Foreign Policy. 1976-78. *2796*

—. Carter, Jimmy (administration). Human rights. 1970's. *3146*

—. Carter, Jimmy (administration). Human rights. 1977-78. *3135*

—. Carter, Jimmy (administration). Human rights. 1977-79. *2690*

—. Carter, Jimmy (administration). Human rights. 1977-79. *2924*

—. Carter, Jimmy (administration). Human rights. 1977-81. *2830*

—. Carter, Jimmy (administration). Human rights. Korea, South. 1945-79. *2949*

—. Carter, Jimmy (administration). Human rights. Race Relations. South Africa. 1973-78. *2668*

—. Carter, Jimmy (administration). Institute for Palestine Studies. Israel. Palestine. 1980. *2577*

—. Carter, Jimmy (administration). International trade. 1950's-70's. *2588*

—. Carter, Jimmy (administration). Israel. Political Surveys. 1948-77. *2870*

—. Carter, Jimmy (administration). Kissinger, Henry A. 1977-78. *3181*

—. Carter, Jimmy (administration). Korea. 1950-79. *2774*

—. Carter, Jimmy (administration). Latin America. 1977-80. *3016*

—. Carter, Jimmy (administration). Military Strategy. Persian Gulf and area. ca 1979-80. *3117*

—. Carter, Jimmy (administration). Military-industrial complex. 1976-78. *3076*

—. Carter, Jimmy (administration). Nixon, Richard M. (administration). 1968-76. *2575*

—. Carter, Jimmy (administration). Nuclear nonproliferation. 1977-81. *3069*

—. Carter, Jimmy (administration). Race Relations. Reagan, Ronald (administration). South Africa. 1981-82. *2700*

—. Carter, Jimmy (administration). USSR. 1980. *3015*

—. Carter, Jimmy (administration). Young, Andrew. 1977. *2606*

—. Cass, Lewis. Webster, Daniel. 1842-43. *1019*

—. Castro, Fidel. Cuba. Imperialism. Policymaking. 1945-80. *2927*

—. Cease-fire agreements. Kissinger, Henry A. USSR. Vietnam War. 1971-73. *3095*

—. Central America. Cold War. Reagan, Ronald (administration). 1954-81. *2807*

—. Central America. Reagan, Ronald (administration). 1981. *2609*

—. Central Intelligence Agency. Chile. Coups d'Etat. Covert operations. Politics. 1970-73. *2926*

—. Central Intelligence Agency. Coups d'Etat. Iran. Publishers and Publishing. Roosevelt, Kermit *(Countercoup: The Struggle for Control of Iran)*. 1953-80. *2730*

—. Central Intelligence Agency. Covert operations. 1947-75. *2670*

—. Central Intelligence Agency. Covert operations. Espionage. 1947-75. *2655*

—. Central Intelligence Agency. Covert operations. Presidents. 1947-79. *3183*

—. Central Intelligence Agency. Europe. 1946-56. *2576*

—. Central Intelligence Agency. Expansionism. Secrecy. USSR. 1947-70's. *2803*

—. Charities. Congress. Famine relief. Ireland. Philanthropy. Polk, James K. 1845-49. *1014*

—. China. Churchill, Winston. Colonialism. deGaulle, Charles. France. Indochina. Roosevelt, Franklin D. 1942-45. *1588*

—. China. Cold War (origins). Communism. 1945. *2648*

—. China. Communist Party. State Department. Stuart, John Leighton. 1949. *2631*

—. China. Communists. Liberals. Scholars. 1944-71. *2895*

—. China. Communists. Shanghai Power Company. Truman, Harry S. (administration). 1948-50. *3111*

—. China. Elections (presidential). Korean War. 1949-52. *1790*

—. China. Exports. Geopolitics. USSR. 1969-80. *2686*

—. China. Kissinger, Henry A. Nixon, Richard M. 1960's-70's. *3116*

—. China. Kissinger, Henry A. USSR. 1969-76. *2754*

—. China. Korean War. Military strategy. 38th Parallel. 1950-52. *2594*

—. China. League of Nations. Paris Peace Conference. Treaties. Wilson, Woodrow. 1919. *1505*

—. China. Roosevelt, Franklin D. Truman, Harry S. 1944-48. 1978. *2781*

—. China. Security risks. State Department (Foreign Service). 1945-70's. *3228*

—. China. State Department. Sun Zhongshan. 1920-24. *1540*

—. China. Taiwan. 1950's-70's. *2691*

—. China. Taiwan. USSR. 1972-78. *2795*

—. Churchill, Winston. Political Leadership. Roosevelt, Franklin D. Stalin, Joseph. World War II. 1939-45. *1698*

—. Citizenship (definition of). Morality. Self-determination. Wilson, Woodrow. 1917-24. *1617*

—. Civil War (antecedents). Europe. Lincoln, Abraham. Seward, William H. War threats. 1861. *713*

—. Civil-Military Relations. Joint Chiefs of Staff. 1968-74. *2846*

—. Clientism. Diplomats. 1967-68. *3371*

—. Cold War. Dulles, John Foster. 1952-59. *2680*

—. Cold War. Palestine. USSR. 1947-48. *2907*

—. Cold War (origins). Historiography. New Left. Wilson, Woodrow. 20c. *1477*

—. Colombia. Panama. Senate. Thomson-Urrutia Treaty. Wilson, Woodrow. 1913-22. *1587*

—. Colonial Government. France. Indochina. Truman, Harry S. (administration). 1943-45. *2783*

—. Colonial Government. Philippines. Taft, William H. 1900-05. *1103*

—. Communism. Containment. Kennan, George F. USSR. 1944-47. *3173*

—. Communism. Human Rights. Presidents. Religious liberty. USSR. 20c. *151*

—. Communism. Korea. Truman Doctrine. 1945-50. *2728*

—. Communism. Korean War. Truman, Harry S. USSR. 1950. *2900*

—. Congress. Constitution. Executive branch. 1969-74. *3439*

—. Congress. Constitution. Executive branch. 1974-75. *3391*

—. Congress. Constitution. Presidents. War powers. 19c-1974. *3243*

—. Congress. Decisionmaking. Executive branch. Secrecy. 1970's. *3361*

—. Congress. Decisionmaking. Kennedy, John F. Nixon, Richard M. Presidents. 1970's. *3286*

—. Congress. Domestic policy. Johnson, Lyndon B. Kennedy, John F. Nixon, Richard M. 1961-74. *2258*

—. Congress. Executive agreements. Legislation. Treaties. 1946-72. *3329*

—. Congress. Executive branch. 1969-80. *3247*

—. Congress. Executive branch. Separation of powers. 1970's. *3352*

—. Congress. Executive Power. 1970-81. *3458*

—. Congress. Executive Power. National security. 1973-80. *3316*

—. Congress. Executive Power. Reform. 1968-78. *3339*

—. Congress. Executive Power. Two presidencies thesis. Wildavsky, Aaron. 1957-79. *3435*

—. Congress. Lobbying. Presidency. 1970's. *3397*

—. Congress. Madison, James. Political Leadership. Roll-call voting. War of 1812. 1789-1812. *970*

—. Congress. Myths and Symbols. Presidency. Vietnam War. Watergate Scandal. 1961-80. *3403*

—. Congress. Nixon, Richard M. (administration). 1968-72. *2841*

—. Congress. Panama. Politics. Strategic Arms Limitation Talks. Treaties. 1977-78. *2692*

—. Congress. Political Leadership. Presidents. 1945-80. *3415*

—. Congress. Political parties. Presidency. Pressure groups. 1950-75. *3426*

—. Congress. Presidency. 1970-82. *3290*

—. Congress. Presidency. 20c. *3480*

—. Congress. Presidency. War powers. 1787-1972. *133*

—. Isolationism. Political Leadership. Roosevelt, Franklin D. Senate. World Court. 1935. *1573*

—. Israel. Middle East. 1974. *2717*

—. Israel. Palestine Liberation Organization. Reagan, Ronald. UN. 1975-81. *3057*

—. Israel. Protestantism. Zionism (review article). 1945-48. *3123*

—. Israel. Reagan, Ronald (administration). Saudi Arabia. USSR. 1981. *2982*

—. Jackson, Andrew. 1829-37. *972*

—. Japan. Korea. Roosevelt, Theodore. Russia. 1901-05. *1578*

—. Japan. World War II (antecedents). 1940-41. *1488*

—. Jews. Palestine. Partition. Political power. Truman, Harry S. (administration). 1947-48. *2731*

—. Johnson, Lyndon B. 1963-68. *3048*

—. Johnson, Lyndon B. Kennedy, John F. Secrecy. 1945-75. *3017*

—. Johnson, Lyndon B. Kennedy, John F. Vietnam War. 1960-68. *2561*

—. Johnson, Lyndon B. Political Speeches. Public opinion. Vietnam War. 1967-69. *3061*

—. Johnson, Lyndon B. Political Speeches. Tonkin Gulf crisis. Vietnam War. 1964. *2649*

—. Johnson, Lyndon B. Vietnam War. 1960's-73. *2912*

—. Joint Chiefs of Staff. Politics and the Military. Vietnam War. 1964-65. *2909*

—. Jordan. 1948-80. *2732*

—. Kennan, George F. State Department Policy Planning Staff. Tito, Josip. Yugoslavia. 1948-49. *2863*

—. Kennan, George F. USSR. Vietnam War. ca 1946-70's. *3147*

—. Kennedy, Edward M. Kennedy, John F. Politics. 1961-73. *2706*

—. Kennedy, John F. (administration). 1961-63. *2964*

—. Kennedy, John F. (administration). Kissinger, Henry A. 1974. *2867*

—. Kennedy, John F. (administration). Latin America. Peru. 1960-62. *3125*

—. Kissinger, Henry A. 1950-76. *2873*

—. Kissinger, Henry A. 1960's-70's. *3051*

—. Kissinger, Henry A. 1968-77. *3004*

—. Kissinger, Henry A. 1969-77. *3082*

—. Kissinger, Henry A. 1969-80. *3003*

—. Kissinger, Henry A. 1970's. *2884*

—. Kissinger, Henry A. 1975. *2712*

—. Kissinger, Henry A. Latin America. 1968-77. *2822*

—. Kissinger, Henry A. Latin America. Organization of American States. 1972-74. *2882*

—. Kissinger, Henry A. Latin America. Rockefeller, Nelson A. 1968-74. *2823*

—. Kissinger, Henry A. Middle East. 1967-75. *3000*

—. Kissinger, Henry A. Newhouse, John (review article). Nuclear arms. Strategic Arms Limitation Talks. 1973. *2556*

—. Kissinger, Henry A. Nixon, Richard M. 1970-75. *2552*

—. Kissinger, Henry A. Nixon, Richard M. (administration). 1968-73. *2733*

—. Kissinger, Henry A. Nixon, Richard M. (administration). USSR. 1919-70's. *116*

—. Kissinger, Henry A. Nixon, Richard M., administration. Watergate scandal. 1974-75. *3087*

—. Kissinger, Henry A. Philosophy of History. Political Leadership. 1970-78. *3145*

—. Kissinger, Henry A. Political Leadership. 1969-70's. *3053*

—. Kissinger, Henry A. Political theory. 1973-77. *3083*

—. Kissinger, Henry A. Portugal. 1974-75. *3098*

—. Kissinger, Henry A. Pragmatism. 1960-74. *2630*

—. Kissinger, Henry A. State Department. 1969-76. *2928*

—. Kissinger, Henry A. (White House Years). 1968-79. *2590*

—. Kissinger, Henry A. (White House Years). 1979. *2940*

—. Korea. Partition. World War II. 1945. *2901*

—. Korea. World War II. 1941-45. *1605*

—. Korean War. MacArthur, Douglas. Self-determination. Truman, Harry S. USSR. 38th Parallel. 1943-50. *2902*

—. Korean War. Vietnam War. 1950-53. 1961-73. *2961*

—. Latin America. 1981. *3062*

—. Latin America. Monroe Doctrine. Roosevelt, Franklin D. 1933-41. *1690*

—. Legislation. Presidents. 1946-77. *3328*

—. Link, Arthur S. Wilson, Woodrow (review article). 1913-20. 1979. *1471*

—. Lobbying. Presidents. Zionism. 1912-73. *84*

—. Mexico. Oil Industry and Trade. State Department. 1921-28. *1575*

—. Mexico. Revolution. Wilson, Woodrow. 1913-15. *1509*

—. Mexico (Ciudad Juárez). Taft, William H. 1908-12. *1657*

—. Middle East. 1967-77. *3086*

—. Middle East. Nixon, Richard M. (administration). 1969-73. *3029*

—. Middle East. Nixon, Richard M. (administration). 1972-73. *2821*

—. Middle East. Palestine. Roosevelt, Franklin D. 1943-45. *1631*

—. Middle East. State Department. 1919-45. *1484*

—. Military. Reagan, Ronald (administration). 1970's-81. *2626*

—. Military. State Department (Foreign Service). 1776-1976. *117*

—. Models. Presidency. 1947-65. *2677*

—. Munro, Dana G. (review article). State Department. West Indies. 1921-30. 1974. *1672*

—. Myths and Symbols. Osgood, Robert E. *(Ideals and Self-Interest in America's Foreign Relations).* Roosevelt, Theodore. Wilson, Woodrow. 1900-20. *1515*

—. National Security Advisor. State Department. 1980. *3177*

—. National Security Council. Presidency. 1953-81. *3248*

—. National Security Council. Presidents. 1947-70's. *3249*

—. National Security Council. South Africa. 1969-76. *2685*

—. Nixon, Richard M. 1970-72. *2629*

—. Nixon, Richard M. (administration). 1968-72. *2842*

—. Nixon, Richard M. (administration). Peace. 1971-74. *2628*

—. Nixon, Richard M. (administration). Vietnam War. 1968-73. *2620*

—. Nixon, Richard M. (administration). Watergate scandal. 1973. *2157*

—. Palestine. Partition. Truman, Harry S. Zionism. 1945-49. *3038*

—. Palestine. Truman, Harry S. Truman, Margaret. 1945-47. *2551*

—. Planning. 1947-78. *3210*

—. Planning. State Department (Policy Planning Staff). 1947-77. *3218*

—. Poland. Roosevelt, Franklin D. 1932-33. *1687*

—. Polish Americans. Political Campaigns (presidential). Roosevelt, Franklin D. Rozmarek, Charles. USSR. 1944. *1178*

—. Political Campaigns (presidential). 1952-80. *1910*

—. Political Campaigns (presidential). Rhetoric. 1976. *1838*

—. Political Leadership. Roosevelt, Franklin D. (administration). World Court. 1930's. *1472*

—. Politics. Roosevelt, Theodore. 1880's-1919. *1057*

—. Politics and Media. State Department. 1945-74. *3220*

—. Politics and the Military. Roosevelt, Franklin D. USSR. Warships. 1930's. *1596*

—. Presidency. 1970's. *3410*

—. Presidents. 1945-80. *3281*

—. Presidents. Public opinion. 1939-75. *94*

—. Presidents. State Department (Foreign Service). 1979. *3436*

—. Public opinion. 1978. *3407*

—. Public opinion. Reagan, Ronald (administration). 1980. *3157*

—. Public opinion. Roosevelt, Franklin D. 1932-45. *1533*

—. Public opinion. Roosevelt, Franklin D. USSR. World War II. 1941-45. *1624*

—. Reagan, Ronald. 1980-81. *2604*

—. Reagan, Ronald. 1981. *2780*

—. Reagan, Ronald. USSR. 1981-82. *3094*

—. Reagan, Ronald (administration). 1980-81. *2839*

—. Reagan, Ronald (administration). 1981-82. *2816*

—. Reagan, Ronald (administration). South Africa. USSR. 1980-82. *2633*

—. Reagan, Ronald (administration). Taiwan. 1981-82. *2566*

—. Revolutionary movements. 1900's-79. *143*

—. Romania. Self-determination. Transylvania. Unification. Wilson, Woodrow. 1917-18. *1560*

—. Roosevelt, Franklin D. 1940-45. *1620*

—. Roosevelt, Franklin D. USSR. 1933-45. *1567*

—. Russia (Transcaucasia). Smith, Felix Willoughby. World War I. 1917-18. *1561*

—. Separation of powers. 1970's. *3291*

—. State Department (Foreign Service). 1950's-73. *3229*

—. Viet Minh. Vietnam. 1940-50. *2898*

—. Wilson, Woodrow. 1913-21. *1538*

—. Wilson, Woodrow. 1913-21. *1655*

—. Wilson, Woodrow. Wister, Owen. World War I. 1912-17. *1604*

—. Wilson, Woodrow. World War I. 1914-19. *1688*

Foreign policy (review article). Acheson, Dean. Kennan, George F. Smith, Gaddis. 1948-63. *2788*

—. Békés, Rezső. Brzezinski, Zbigniew. Historians. Kissinger, Henry A. 1960's-70's. *2770*

—. Bureaucrats. Decisionmaking. Politics. Presidents. 1945-75. *3367*

—. China. Diplomacy. Imperialism. Philippines. Reinsch, Paul S. 1899-1945. *1564*

—. China. Korean War. MacArthur, Douglas. Politics and the Military. Truman, Harry S. 1949-52. *2689*

—. Cohen, Warren I. Divine, Robert A. Eisenhower, Dwight D. Rusk, Dean. 1953-69. *2962*

—. Democracy. 1865-1950. *20*

—. Diaries. Roosevelt, Franklin D. (administration). Stettinius, Edward Reilley. World War II. 1943-46. 1975. *1582*

—. Kissinger, Henry A. Public opinion. 1975-76. *2709*

—. Military strategy. Nixon, Richard M. 1980. *1712*

Foreign Relations *See also* Boundaries; Detente; Diplomacy; Disarmament; Geopolitics; International Relations (discipline); Tariff; Treaties.

—. Acheson, Dean. China. Diplomacy. 1944-50. *3168*

—. Adams, John. Consular Service. Franklin, Benjamin. 1780. *360*

—. Adams, John. Courts. Executive Branch. Extradition. Great Britain. Jay Treaty. Robbins, Jonathan. Separation of powers. 1796-1804. *980*

—. Adams, John Quincy. Latin America. Monroe Doctrine. 1823. *974*

—. Adee, Alvey A. Diplomacy. State Department. 1870-1924. *1700*

—. Advertising. Americas (North and South). Commercial Bureau of the American Republics. International Union. State Department. 1894-1902. *1053*

—. Africa. 1978-81. *2824*

—. Anglo-American Committee. Bevin, Ernest. Great Britain. Palestine. Truman, Harry S. (administration). 1945-47. *2662*

—. Arab-Israeli conflict. Carter, Jimmy. 1977-78. *2568*

—. Armenia. Documents. Harding, Warren G. Senate Foreign Relations Subcommittee. 1919. *1140*

—. Arms control. Brezhnev, Leonid. Ford, Gerald R. Kissinger, Henry A. USSR. Vladivostok Accord. 1974. *3131*

—. Asia. Carter, Jimmy (administration). Military. 1976-80. *3156*

—. Asia, Southeast. Ford, Gerald R. Intervention. 1900-75. *3002*

—. Assets, frozen. Economic Conditions. Iran. 1979-80. *2871*

—. Attitudes. Mexico. State Department (Foreign Service). 1950-79. *3071*

—. Axis powers. Hull, Cordell. Latin America. Rio Conference. Welles, Sumner. World War II. 1941-42. *1535*

—. Azerbaidzhan. Iran. Stalin, Joseph. Truman, Harry S. USSR. 1946-75. *3104*

—. Bennett, Richard Bedford, Viscount. Canada. Hoover, Herbert C. 1930-31. *1585*

—. Berlin blockade. Political Campaigns (presidential). Truman, Harry S. 1948-49. *2921*

—. Berlin Crisis. Decisionmaking. Germany. Intelligence Service. Kennedy, John F. 1961. *2644*

—. Bibliographies. South Africa. 1953-78. *2704*

—. Boundaries. Italy. League of Nations. Paris Peace Conference. Wilson, Woodrow (administration). 1919-22. *1577*
—. Brazil. Cold war. 1945-60. *2785*
—. Bundy, McGeorge. Historians. Journalism. Kennedy, John F. Personal narratives. 1960-64. *2153*
—. Bureaucracies. Federal Government. 1950-76. *3314*
—. Canada. 1970-80. *2714*
—. Canada. Ford, Gerald R. Trudeau, Pierre Elliott. 1974-76. *3093*
—. Canada. Hoover, Herbert C. St. Lawrence Seaway Treaty of 1932. 1932. *1583*
—. Canada. Hoover, Herbert C. Smoot-Hawley Tariff. 1929-33. *1584*
—. Carter, Jimmy. Iran. Revolution. 1972-79. *2652*
—. Carter, Jimmy. Latin America. 1977-78. *2565*
—. Carter, Jimmy. Middle East. 1977. *3008*
—. Carter, Jimmy (administration). China. Taiwan Relations Act (US, 1979). 1978-80. *2761*
—. Carter, Jimmy (administration). Defense spending. 1977-80. *2270*
—. Carter, Jimmy (administration). Economic Conditions. 1977-80. *3054*
—. Carter, Jimmy (administration). Latin America. 1977-79. *2710*
—. Carter, Jimmy (administration). Latin America. 19c-20c. *3128*
—. Carter, Jimmy (administration). Nicaragua. Revolution. Sandinistas. Somoza, Anastasio. 1978-79. *2711*
—. Carter, Jimmy (administration). Strategic Arms Limitation Talks. USSR. 1977-79. *2724*
—. Carter, Jimmy (administration). USSR. 1977-78. *2623*
—. Castro, Fidel. Cuba. Documents. Nixon, Richard M. Political Leadership. 1959. *3028*
—. Central America. 1960's-81. *2746*
—. Central America. 1979-81. *2598*
—. Central Intelligence Agency. Hughes-Ryan Act (US, 1974). Intelligence Oversight Act (US, 1980). 1974-80. *3327*
—. China. 1942-80. *3065*
—. China. Great Britain. Hong Kong. Sovereignty. World War II. 1941-45. *1503*
—. China. Kahn, E. J., Jr. (review article). Politics. State Department (Foreign Service). 1940's-50's. *2903*
—. China. Loans (consortium). Wilson, Woodrow. 1910-13. *1606*
—. China. Nixon, Richard M. (administration). 1969-72. *2555*
—. Churchill, Winston. Espionage. Kent, Tyler. Roosevelt, Franklin D. World War II. 1940-45. *1581*
—. Churchill, Winston. Great Britain. Roosevelt, Franklin D. World War II. 1939-45. *1641*
—. Civil War. Lincoln, Abraham. Spain. Tassara, Gabriel Garcia. 1858-73. *978*
—. Cold War. Documents. Dwight D. Eisenhower Library. India. 1953-60. *2602*
—. Cold war. Economic policy. Historiography. Political Systems. 1945-52. *2684*
—. Cold War (review article). USSR. 1945-76. *2764*
—. Communism. Documents. State Department (*Relations with China*). 1944-81. *3019*
—. Communism. Human rights. Liberty. USSR. 1940's-76. *2682*
—. Conferences. Eddy, William A. Ibn Saud, King. Roosevelt, Franklin D. Saudi Arabia. 1945. *1576*
—. Conflict and Conflict Resolution. Kennedy, John F. USSR. 1963. *2708*
—. Congress. Domestic Policy. Presidents. 1950-79. *3354*
—. Congress of Vienna. Disengagement. Kissinger, Henry A. USSR. 1815. 1969-74. *3130*
—. Decisionmaking. Forgeries. Peter I. Propaganda. Truman, Harry S. USSR. Wills. 1725-1948. *2659*
—. Defense Policy. Japan. 1979-81. *2937*
—. Developing Nations. Watergate Scandal. 1972. *3457*
—. Discrimination. International Trade. Jews. Public Opinion. Russia. Visas. 1906-13. *1465*
—. Documents. Dulles, John Foster. India. Nehru, Jawaharlal. 1953-59. *2601*
—. Documents. Elections (congressional). Johnson, Andrew. Mexico. Romero, Matias. 1866. *1015*
—. Documents. Hay, John Milton. Michael, William H. Publishers and Publishing. State Department. 1898-1906. *976*

—. Drug Abuse. Mexico. Operation Intercept. 1969. *2678*
—. Dwight D. Eisenhower Library. Eisenhower, Dwight D. Kansas (Abilene). 1953-61. *2768*
—. Economic Aid. Great Britain. Saudi Arabia. State Department (Near East Affairs Division). World War II. 1941-45. *1647*
—. Economic Conditions. Reagan, Ronald (administration). 1971-81. *2943*
—. Economic policy. Germany. Neutrality. Roosevelt, Franklin D. (administration). World War II (antecedents). 1933-41. *1602*
—. Economic policy. Gold standard. Roosevelt, Franklin D. (administration). 1933-34. *1230*
—. Economic Policy. International Trade. Nixon, Richard M. (administration). USSR. 1970's. *3040*
—. Egypt. Nasser, Gamal Abdel. 1950-57. *3021*
—. Eisenhower, Dwight D. (administration). Faulkner, William. National Commission for UNESCO. People-to-People Program (Writers' Group). Rabb, Maxwell M. State Department. 1954-61. *2148*
—. Elections, presidential. Political Parties. USSR. 1976. *1963*
—. Europe. Mally, Gerhard. Nixon, Richard M. (administration). 1970's. *3119*
—. Europe. Nuclear proliferation. 1954-80. *2866*
—. Europe. USSR. 1970-73. *2599*
—. European Economic Community. Kissinger, Henry A. Middle East. NATO. USSR. 1970's. *2970*
—. European Economic Community. NATO. 1945-74. *3169*
—. Executive Power. Presidency. 1945-74. *3343*
—. Extradition. Illinois (Chicago). Refugees. Root, Elihu. Rudowitz, Christian Ansoff. Russia. 1908-09. *1542*
—. Federal Government. Federalists. Political Attitudes. Publicity. Secrecy. 1800-12. *719*
—. Finance. Great Britain. McAdoo, William G. Morgan, J. P. & Company. Wilson, Woodrow (administration). World War I. 1914-20. *1222*
—. France. Jaurès, Jean Léon. Marshall, George C. Memoirs. Moch, Jules. 1911-51. *2922*
—. Germany. Roosevelt, Theodore. William II. 1901-09. *1658*
—. Great Britain. Hitler, Adolf. Letters. Lothian, 11th Marquis of. Roosevelt, Franklin D. 1938-39. *1642*
—. Great Britain. Immigration, illegal. Jews. Palestine. 1945-47. *2777*
—. Great Britain. Nuclear Arms. Roosevelt, Franklin D. World War II. 1940-45. *1491*
—. Hamilton, Alexander. Lycan, Gilbert L. Republicanism. Stourzh, Gerald. 1780-1800. 1970. *1031*
—. Hay, John Milton. Kidnapping. Morocco. Perdicaris, Ion. Raisuli, Ahmed ibn-Muhammed. Roosevelt, Theodore. 1904. *1528*
—. Historiography. Paris Peace Settlements. Wilson, Woodrow (administration). 1918-81. *1482*
—. India. Nuclear nonproliferation. 1977-79. *2993*
—. India. Pakistan. 1947-73. *2681*
—. Indians. Jefferson, Thomas. Privy Council. Public Records. South Carolina. 1787-89. *358*
—. Intelligence service. 1947-80. *2935*
—. International Trade. Kissinger, Henry A. Nixon, Richard M. USSR. 1972. *2810*
—. Intervention. Mexico. Pershing, John J. Wilson, Woodrow. 1916. *1664*
—. Intervention (review article). Latin America. ca 1900-79. *2762*
—. Japan. 1976-78. *3035*
—. Japan. Military Intelligence. Roosevelt, Franklin D. World War II (antecedents). 1940-41. *1554*
—. Kennedy, John F. Political Speeches. Rhetoric. Trade Expansion Act (US, 1962). 1962. *2775*
—. Kissinger, Henry A. 1970-75. *2969*
—. Kissinger, Henry A. 1970-80. *2653*
—. Kissinger, Henry A. Middle East. October War. 1973. *2856*
—. Kissinger, Henry A. Middle East. Peace. 1975. *2751*
—. Kissinger, Henry A. Nixon, Richard M. Political Authority. Watergate Scandal. 1974. *3005*
—. Kissinger, Henry A. Nixon, Richard M. Secrecy. Strategic Arms Limitation Talks. USSR. 1972-74. *2741*
—. Kissinger, Henry A. Peace. 1973. *2765*

—. Kissinger, Henry A. *(White House Years).* Middle East. Vietnam War. 1969-73. *2650*
—. Knox, Philander C. Latin America. Travel. West Indies. 1912. *1541*
—. Latin America. 1823-1961. *177*
—. Latin America. 1945-72. *2945*
—. Mexico. 1973-80. *2639*
—. Middle East. 1820's-1970's. *14*
—. Nixon, Richard M. (resignation). Politics. Watergate scandal. 1974. *2279*
—. Palestine. Truman, Harry S. 1945. *2963*
—. Pipes, Richard. USSR. 1976-81. *2558*
—. Presidency (review article). Sutherland, George. 1974. *3444*
—. Roosevelt, Franklin D. USSR. 1933-45. *1545*
—. Thailand. Truman, Harry S. (administration). 1948-63. *3129*
—. USSR. 1962-76. *3014*
—. USSR. 1969-74. *2818*
—. USSR. 1978. *3120*
—. Watergate Scandal. 1974. *2262*
Foreign relations analysis. International relations (discipline). Quantitative Methods. State Department (Intelligence and Research Bureau). 1974. *3384*
Foreign Relations of the United States. Publishers and Publishing. State Department. 1861-1981. *3066*
Foreign Relations (review article). China. Haldeman, H. R. Kissinger, Henry A. Nixon, Richard M. 1968-76. *3150*
—. Kissinger, Henry A. *(White House Years).* 1968-72. *2793*
—. Korean War. Truman, Harry S. 1950. 1976. *2977*
Foreign Relations (seminar). American Foreign Service Association. International Studies Association. Latin America. State Department. 1970. *2701*
Foreign Trade. *See* International Trade.
Forest reserve controversy. Cleveland, Grover. Colorado. Conservation of Natural Resources. McKinley, William. 1890-1900. *888*
Forest Service. Conservation of Natural Resources. Legislation. 1872-1976. *109*
Forests and Forestry. Federal regulation. Oregon. Pinchot, Gifford. Washington. 1902-10. *1297*
Forgeries. *Atlantic Monthly.* Courtship. Letters. Lincoln, Abraham. Minor, Wilma Frances. Periodicals. Rutledge, Ann. Sedgwick, Ellery. 1928. *450*
—. Decisionmaking. Foreign Relations. Peter I. Propaganda. Truman, Harry S. USSR. Wills. 1725-1948. *2659*
Forgie, George (review article). Lincoln, Abraham. Politics. 1820's-61. 1979. *564*
Formosa. *See* Taiwan.
Fort Donelson (battle). Civil War. Fort Henry (battle). Grant, Ulysses S. Military Strategy. Tennessee. 1862. *423*
Fort Henry (battle). Civil War. Fort Donelson (battle). Grant, Ulysses S. Military Strategy. Tennessee. 1862. *423*
Fort Sumter. Civil War. Lincoln, Abraham. Seward, William H. 1861. *914*
—. Civil War (antecedents). Lincoln, Abraham. Secession crisis. South. Union Party. 1860-61. *801*
Fortas, Abe. Interior Department. Lawyers. Letters. Peres, Hardwig. Roosevelt, Franklin D. 1930-44. *1342*
Forts. *See* names of specific forts, e.g. Fort Bragg.
Foster, John W. Devine, Michael J. Diplomacy (review article). Spanish-American War. State Department. Trask, David F. 1873-1917. *989*
Founding Fathers. Adams, John. American Revolution. Madison, James. Pufendorf, Samuel von (*On the Law of Nature and Nations*). Sweden. Washington, George. 1632-1776. *315*
—. Adams, John. Beccaria, Cesare. Crime and Criminals. Declaration of Independence. Jefferson, Thomas. Madison, James. 1764-89. *246*
—. Adams, John. Jefferson, Thomas. Language. Washington, George. 1760's-70's. *218*
—. Constitutional Convention. Electoral college. 1787. *1051*
—. Constitutional Convention. Electoral College. Republicanism. 1787-1970's. *1040*
—. Historiography. Jefferson, Thomas. Washington, George. 1760-1800. 1970-79. *353*
—. Kansas-Nebraska Act (US, 1854). Lincoln, Abraham. Reconstruction. Republicanism. 1854-65. *910*

Fox, Gustavus Vasa. Civil War. Naval administration. Welles, Gideon. 1861-65. *744*

France. Adams, John ("Plan of Treaties"). American Revolution. Franklin, Benjamin. Treaties. 1776. *287*

—. American Revolution. Jefferson, Thomas. Lafayette, Marquis de. Monticello. Virginia. 1777-1824. *206*

—. Arbitration, International. Great Britain. Lodge, Henry Cabot. Senate. Taft, William H. Treaties. 1911-12. *1531*

—. Arbitration, International. Great Britain. Roosevelt, Theodore. Taft, William H. Treaties. ca 1910-12. *1559*

—. Belgium. Great Britain. Roosevelt, Eleanor. Travel. 1929. *1068*

—. Buffon, Georges Louis Leclerc de. Jefferson, Thomas. Moose. Sullivan, John. 1787. *239*

—. Chambrun, Adolphe de. Civil War. Letters. Lincoln, Abraham. 1865-68. *916*

—. Children. Great Britain. Political Leadership. Public opinion. 1969-70. *3280*

—. China. Churchill, Winston. Colonialism. deGaulle, Charles. Foreign Policy. Indochina. Roosevelt, Franklin D. 1942-45. *1588*

—. Churchill, Winston. Eisenhower, Dwight D. Great Britain. Resistance. World War II. 1943-44. *1733*

—. Cold War. USSR. Vietnam. 1944-50. *3064*

—. Colonial Government. Foreign Policy. Indochina. Truman, Harry S. (administration). 1943-45. *2783*

—. Cosway, Maria. Fireworks. Jefferson, Thomas. 1786-89. *281*

—. DeConde, Alexander (review article). Jefferson, Thomas. Louisiana Purchase. 1800-03. *985*

—. Dien Bien Phu (battle). Eisenhower, Dwight D. Foreign Policy. Vietnam War. 1953-54. *3036*

—. Diplomacy. Germany. Morocco. Roosevelt, Theodore. 1904-06. *1590*

—. Diplomacy. Jefferson, Thomas. National Characteristics. Social Conditions. 1776-1826. *245*

—. Federalists. Great Britain. Jefferson, Thomas. 1780-1805. *276*

—. Foreign Policy. Jackson, Andrew. Shipping. 1834-36. *1029*

—. Foreign policy. Neutrality. Public Opinion. Washington, George. 1792-93. *996*

—. Foreign Relations. Jaurès, Jean Léon. Marshall, George C. Memoirs. Moch, Jules. 1911-51. *2922*

—. Government. Great Britain. Intelligence service. 1941-70's. *3189*

—. Houdon, Jean Antoine *(Washington).* Sculpture. Virginia (Richmond). Washington, George. ca 1784-96. *260*

—. Kissinger, Henry A. NATO. Nixon, Richard M., administration. 1969-73. *3041*

—. Nixon, Richard M. Press. Watergate Scandal. 1972-74. *3460*

—. Roosevelt, Franklin D. World War II. 1938-45. *1529*

France (Languedoc, Provence). Aristocracy. Jefferson, Thomas. Social conditions. Travel. 1787. *382*

—. Jefferson, Thomas. Short, William. Travel. 1787. *381*

France (southern). Jefferson, Thomas. Letters. Occitan language. 1787. *326*

Franchise. *See* Citizenship; Suffrage.

Franco-Prussian War. Bismarck, Otto von. Cuban missile crisis. Diplomacy. Escalation theory. Kennedy, John F. McNamara, Robert S. 1870. 1962. *3072*

Frank, Jerome. Agricultural Adjustment Administration (Office of the General Counsel). Dale, Chester. Wallace, Henry A. 1935. *1362*

Frankfurter, Felix. Brandeis, Louis D. New Deal. Politics. Roosevelt, Franklin D. World War I. 1917-33. *1287*

—. Lippmann, Walter. New Deal. Roosevelt, Franklin D. World War II. 1932-45. *1107*

Franklin, Benjamin. Adams, John. Autobiography. Jefferson, Thomas. Woolman, John. 18c. *183*

—. Adams, John. Consular Service. Foreign Relations. 1780. *360*

—. Adams, John ("Plan of Treaties"). American Revolution. France. Treaties. 1776. *287*

—. American Revolution. Historiography. Hungary. Washington, George. Zinner, János. 1775-78. *248*

—. Fitzgerald, F. Scott. Innocence (concept). National Characteristics. Nixon, Richard M. Thoreau, Henry David. Values. Watergate scandal. 18c-1978. *1762*

Franklin D. Roosevelt Library. Documents. Information Access. Military finance. Security classification. 1970-75. *1130*

—. Documents. New York (Hyde Park). 1935-51. *1096*

—. Dwight D. Eisenhower Library. Harry S. Truman Library. Herbert Hoover Presidential Library and Museum. John Fitzgerald Kennedy Library. Libraries, presidential. Lyndon Baines Johnson Library. 1940-79. *70*

—. Manuscripts Society. 1939-73. *1084*

Fraud. China (Gailan). Chinese Engineering and Mining Company. Great Britain. Hoover, Herbert C. 1900-28. *1069*

Free ports. Diplomacy. Norway. Roosevelt, Franklin D. USSR. World War II. 1941-43. *1644*

Free Silver movement. Bland, Richard Parks. Democratic Party. Missouri. Political Campaigns. 1878-96. *692*

Free Trade *See also* Tariff.

—. Adams, John. Europe. Foreign policy. Mercantilism. 1775-85. *209*

—. Great Britain. Hamilton, Alexander. Washington, George (Farewell Address). 1796. *987*

Free World. *See* Western Nations.

Freedmen. American Freedmen's Inquiry Commission. Civil War. Johnson, Andrew. 1863. *568*

Freedmen's Bureau. Discrimination. Johnson, Andrew. Law. Reconstruction. 1865-66. *907*

Freedom of Information Act (US, 1966). Central Intelligence Agency. Federal Bureau of Investigation. 1966-82. *3453*

—. Central Intelligence Agency. Federal Bureau of Investigation. National security. 1960's-81. *3390*

—. Intelligence service. National Security. 1970-82. *3225*

—. Public Records. Reagan, Ronald (administration). 1917-81. *3368*

Freedom of speech. Censorship. Constitutional Amendments (1st). Libraries. Nixon, Richard M. 1974. *2381*

—. Mass media. Nixon, Richard M. (administration). 1969-73. *2396*

Freidel, Frank (review article). Economic policy. New Deal. Political leadership. Roosevelt, Franklin D. 1930's. *1273*

Frémont, John C. Cluseret, Gustave Paul. Editors and Editing. *New Nation* (periodical). Political Campaigns (presidential). 1864. *691*

—. Dayton, William L. Elections (presidential). Political conventions. Republican Party. 1854-56. *662*

—. Lincoln, Abraham. Material culture. Political Campaigns (presidential). Republican Party. 1856. 1860. *632*

French, Daniel Chester. Lincoln Memorial. Sculpture. 1911-26. *551*

French language. Jefferson, Thomas *(Notes on the State of Virginia).* Morellet, André. Translating and Interpreting. 1780-88. *299*

Frieden, Bernard J. Haar, Charles M. Kaplan, Marshall. Model Cities program (review article). Urban Renewal. 1960's-70's. *2331*

Friedman, Saul S. (review article). Foreign Policy. Genocide. Jews. Refugees. Roosevelt, Franklin D. (administration). World War II. 1938-45. 1973. *1646*

Friendship. Adams, John. Jefferson, Thomas. 1775-1826. *249*

—. American Revolution. Georgia (Mulberry Grove). Greene, Caty. Washington, George. 1775-91. *357*

—. Historiography. National Characteristics. Roosevelt, Theodore. Western States. Wister, Owen. 1890's-1900's. *1116*

—. Land Tenure. Pennsylvania, western. Settlement. Simpson, Gilbert. Washington, George. 1740-94. *255*

Frontier thesis. Historiography. Roosevelt, Theodore *(Winning of the West).* Turner, Frederick Jackson. 1890-1905. *1088*

Fuel, liquid. Eisenhower, Dwight D. (administration). Federal government. Politics. Synthetic Products. Truman, Harry S. (administration). 1944-54. *2525*

Fugitive Slaves. Advertising. Historiography. Jackson, Andrew. *Tennessee Gazette* (newspaper). 1804. 1977. *471*

Fullam, William F. Marines. Navies. Reform. Roosevelt, Theodore. Sims, William S. 1890's-1909. *1243*

Fund raising. Howard, Oliver Otis. Lincoln Memorial University. Twain, Mark. 1901-09. *444*

Funston, Richard. "Greatness" (measures). Judges. Lame-duck hypothesis. Nominations for office. Presidents. Supreme Court. 1789-1976. *106*

F-111 (aircraft). Air Forces. Defense Policy. McNamara, Robert S. Navies. Vietnam War. 1960-70. *2675*

G

Gaddis, John Lewis. Containment. Kennan, George F. 1947-49. *2674*

Gage, Lyman. Counterintelligence. McKinley, William. Quebec (Montreal). Spanish-American War. Wilkie, John. 1898. *732*

Gales, Joseph, Jr. District of Columbia. Jackson, Andrew. *National Intelligencer.* Political Commentary. Political parties. Republicanism. Seaton, William Winston. 1827-35. *887*

Gallatin, Albert. Crawford, William H. Political Campaigns. 1780's-1824. *642*

—. Diplomacy. Ethnography. Politics. Treasury Department. 1780-1849. *880*

—. Embargo Acts (US, 1807-08). Jefferson, Thomas. Madison, James. 1808-13. *1002*

—. Enlightenment. Politics. Swiss Americans. Treasury Secretaries. 1780-1849. *929*

Gallup poll. Bias. Political Surveys. Presidents. 1970's. *3487*

—. Congress. Political Surveys. Presidents. 1953-78. *3483*

—. Political surveys. Presidency. Voting and voting behavior. Women. 1958-72. *1872*

Ganin, Zvi. Bain, Kenneth Ray. Diplomatic recognition (review article). Independence. Israel. Wilson, Evan M. 1945-48. *2980*

—. Diplomatic Recognition (review article). Israel. Truman, Harry S. Wilson, Evan M. 1940-49. *2603*

Garfield, Harry A. Coal. Wilson, Woodrow (administration). World War I. 1917-18. *1339*

Garfield, James A. Arthur, Chester A. Doenecke, Justus D. Gould, Lewis L. McKinley, William. Presidents (review article). 1880-1901. *736*

—. Assassination. Capital Punishment. Guiteau, Charles. Trials. 1881-82. *582*

—. Blaine, James G. Latin America. Pan-Americanism. 1881. *1008*

—. Chickamauga (battle). Civil War. Rosecrans, William S. Tennessee. 1862-80. *583*

—. Chinese. Elections (presidential). Letters. Morey, H. L. Racism. 1875-85. *643*

—. Collectors and Collecting. Documents. Presidency. 1881. *725*

—. Congress. House of Representatives (Appropriations Committee). Political leadership. 1872-81. *745*

—. Grant, Ulysses S. Politics. Presidents. Reconstruction. 1868-81. *533*

—. Historians. 1850-80. *532*

—. National characteristics. Reform. Republican Party. 1881. *919*

—. Negroes. Republican Party. South. Suffrage. 1881. *918*

—. Pineton, Charles Adolphe de, Marquis de Chambrun. 1873-75. *575*

—. Politics. 1831-81. *531*

Garfield, James A. (review article). Brown, Harry J. Civil War. Leech, Margaret. Peskin, Allan. Political Leadership. 1850-81. 1978. *503*

—. Peskin, Allan. 1848-81. 1978. *516*

Garland, Augustus Hill. Attorneys General. Cleveland, Grover. Letters. Politics. 1885-88. *930*

Garner, John Nance. Democratic Party. Political Conventions. Rayburn, Sam. Roosevelt, Franklin D. 1932. *1182*

—. New Deal. Roosevelt, Franklin D. 1933-38. *1397*

Gasoline. *See* Oil and Petroleum Products.

Gates, Guerdon. Diaries. Monroe, James. Pennsylvania (Washington). 1817. *830*

Gates, Horatio. American Revolution. Military strategy. Washington, George. 1777-80. *306*

Gelb, Leslie H. Betts, Richard K. Nixon, Richard M. Political Systems. Shawcross, William. Vietnam War (review article). 1954-79. *2809*

General Motors Corp. Antitrust. DuPont, E. I. and Company. Supreme Court. *United States v. E. I. Du Pont de Nemours and Company et al.* (US, 1957). 1948-65. *2407*

—. Japan. Naval Strategy. Pacific Area. World
War II. 1941-45. *1486*
—. Jefferson, Thomas. Travel. 1786. *368*
—. Presidency. Scholars. 1888-1980. *55*
Great Plains *See also* Midwest; North Central
States.
—. All-Party Agricultural Committee. Farmers.
North Central States. Political Campaigns
(presidential). Roosevelt, Franklin D. 1936.
1201
—. Cattle raising. North Dakota (Medora).
Remington, Frederic. Roosevelt, Theodore.
1880's. *1073*
Great Powers. Byrnes, James F. Cold War.
Demilitarization. Germany. Molotov, V. M.
Treaties. 1946. *2743*
—. Diplomacy. Europe. Foreign Aid. Marshall
Plan. 1947. *2679*
—. Diplomacy. International security. Kissinger,
Henry A. Philosophy of history. 1804-1973.
3165
Great Society. Johnson, Lyndon B. Political
Attitudes. 1933-69. *1731*
—. Johnson, Lyndon B. Public Welfare. Rhetoric.
1963-65. *2538*
—. Johnson, Lyndon B. Social reform. Vietnam
War. 1964-65. *2547*
—. Johnson, Lyndon B. War on Poverty. 1964-69.
2535
—. Johnson, Lyndon B. (administration). Public
Welfare. Social Conditions. 1964-76. *2418*
"Greatness" (measures). Funston, Richard. Judges.
Lame-duck hypothesis. Nominations for office.
Presidents. Supreme Court. 1789-1976. *106*
—. Presidents. Supreme Court. 18c-20c. *59*
Greece *See also* Ottoman Empire.
—. Airplanes, Military. Military Aid. Roosevelt,
Franklin D. (administration). World War II.
1940-41. *1618*
—. Communism. Guerrilla Warfare. Stalin,
Joseph. Tito, Josip. Truman Doctrine.
1946-53. *2847*
—. Cyprus. Foreign Policy. Kissinger, Henry A.
Turkey. 1974-75. *3085*
—. Foreign Policy. Paris Peace Settlements.
1919. *1613*
Greek Americans. Agnew, Spiro T. Public
Opinion. 1960's-70's. *2466*
—. Assimilation. Elections (presidential).
Ethnicity. Republican Party. 1968. *1925*
Greeley, Horace. Civil War. Federalism. Grant,
Ulysses S. Nationalism. Political Campaigns
(presidential). 1872. *658*
—. Elections, presidential. Politics. 1860-72.
629
—. Political campaigns (Presidential). 1872.
675
Green, Duff. Calhoun, John C. District of
Columbia. Editors and Editing. Elections
(presidential). *United States Telegraph.*
1825-28. *631*
—. Calhoun, John C. District of Columbia.
Editors and Editing. Jackson, Andrew. *United
States Telegraph.* 1823-28. *630*
Greenbelt new towns. City planning. Poor.
Resettlement Administration. Rural areas.
Tugwell, Rexford Guy. 1935-36. *1392*
Greene, Caty. American Revolution. Friendship.
Georgia (Mulberry Grove). Washington,
George. 1775-91. *357*
Grigsby, Melvin. Politics. Roosevelt, Theodore.
Rough Riders. Spanish-American War. Torrey,
Jay L. Wood, Leonard. 1898. *1095*
Gromyko, Anatoli (review article). Kennedy, John
F. USSR. 1960-63. *2286*
Group fantasy. Carter, Jimmy. Democratic Party.
Political Conventions. 1974-76. *1902*
—. Carter, Jimmy. National Characteristics.
War. 1946-76. *2165*
—. Presidency. 1953-79. *2164*
Guano. Diplomacy. Peru (Lobos Islands).
Webster, Daniel. 1841-52. *1018*
Guerrilla Warfare *See also* Resistance; Terrorism.
—. Communism. Greece. Stalin, Joseph. Tito,
Josip. Truman Doctrine. 1946-53. *2847*
Guiteau, Charles. Assassination. Capital
Punishment. Garfield, James A. Trials.
1881-82. *582*
Gun Control. Assassination. Presidency. Public
opinion. Sociopaths. 1950's-70's. *3471*
Gurewitsch, Edna P. Personal narratives.
Roosevelt, Eleanor. ca 1950-62. *1078*

H

Haar, Charles M. Frieden, Bernard J. Kaplan,
Marshall. Model Cities program (review article).
Urban Renewal. 1960's-70's. *2331*
Habeas corpus. Civil War. Lincoln, Abraham.
Taney, Roger B. 1861. *886*
—. Emergency powers. Executive power. Martial
law. War. 1861-1944. *134*
Hague, Frank. Democratic Party. New Deal.
New Jersey. Roosevelt, Franklin D. 1932-40.
1289
Haig, Alexander. Foreign policy. Meese, Edwin.
Reagan, Ronald. Weinberger, Casper. 1981.
3096
Haircuts. Butler, Thomas. Civil rights. Courts
Martial and Courts of Inquiry. Jackson,
Andrew. Military discipline. Tennessee. 1801.
472
Haiti. Foreign Aid. Kennedy, John F. Social
Change. 1960's-80. *2896*
—. Military Aid. Slave revolts. Washington,
George. 1791-1804. *1003*
Haldeman, H. R. China. Foreign Relations (review
article). Kissinger, Henry A. Nixon, Richard
M. 1968-76. *3150*
Halifax, 1st Earl of. Byrnes, James F. Documents.
Great Britain. State Department. 1945-46.
2752
Hall, Kermit L. (review article). Appointments to
office. Courts. Federal Government. Political
Parties. Politics. 1829-61. *1037*
Halleck, Henry W. Civil War. Lincoln, Abraham.
Military strategy. 1862-63. *838*
Halperin et al. v. *Kissinger et al* (US, 1976).
Documents. Nixon, Richard M. Shattuck,
John. 1976. *1777*
Hamilton, Alexander. Adams, John. Federalist
Party. Jefferson, Thomas. Political Factions.
Washington, George. 1775-90's. *720*
—. Agriculture. Jefferson, Thomas. Manufactures.
Political Theory. ca 1775-1800. *823*
—. Caesar, Julius. Jefferson, Thomas. 1789-1811.
256
—. Carter, Jimmy. Eisenhower, Dwight D.
Executive Power. Foreign policy. Taiwan.
1793-1979. *2794*
—. Coxe, Tench. Manufactures. Society for
Establishing Useful Manufactures. 1790-92.
797
—. Defense policy. Madison, James. Tariff.
Trans-Appalachian West. Washington, George.
1791-92. *715*
—. Economic policy. Industry. 1789-95. *946*
—. Executive Branch. Political theory. Public
Administration. 1787-90's. *1043*
—. Executive Power. Political Systems. Wilson,
Woodrow. 1780-1980. *1094*
—. Federal policy. International Trade. Madison,
James. Republicanism. 1789-94. *297*
—. Federalism. Madison, James. Politicians.
1770's-80's. 1970's. *387*
—. *Federalist.* Jay, John. Liberty. Madison,
James. Political Theory. 1787-88. *181*
—. Federalists. Madison, James. Political
Representation. Republicanism. 1780's. *388*
—. Foreign Relations. Lycan, Gilbert L.
Republicanism. Stourzh, Gerald. 1780-1800.
1970. *1031*
—. Free trade. Great Britain. Washington, George
(Farewell Address). 1796. *987*
—. International law. 1790's. *1011*
—. Jefferson, Thomas. Pennsylvania. Taxation.
Whiskey Rebellion. 1791-1801. *915*
—. Political Theory. Presidency. 1785-1950.
103
Hamlin, Hannibal. Lincoln, Abraham. Republican
Party. Vermont. Wide-Awake clubs. 1860.
651
Hammer, Armand. Historic Sites. New Brunswick.
Roosevelt Campobello International Park.
1959-74. *1136*
Hammond, Jabez D. Elections (presidential).
Monroe, James. Tompkins, Daniel D.
VanBuren, Martin. 1816. *674*
Hampton Roads Peace Conference. Civil War.
Grant, Ulysses S. Military General Staff.
Telegraph. 1865. *601*
—. Civil War. Lincoln, Abraham. 1865. *961*
Handwriting. Lincoln, Abraham. 1826-65. *397*
Hanley, Thomas O'Brien. Beitzinger, A. J.
Christenson, Reo M. Equality. Jaffa, Harry V.
Lincoln, Abraham. Political Theory. Values
(review article). 1770-1973. *446*

Hanna, Marcus. Fairbanks, Charles W. Gould,
Lewis L. Personal narratives. Political
Conventions. Republican Party. Roosevelt,
Theodore. 1900. *636*
Hanoi, bombing of. Foreign policy. Kissinger,
Henry A. Vietnam War. 1972. *2572*
Harding, Warren G. Adams, John. Buchanan,
James. Eisenhower, Dwight D. Taft, William
H. 1797-1961. *158*
—. Adultery. Letters. Ohio (Marion). Phillips,
Carrie. 1905-20. 1963-78. *1119*
—. Alabama. Washington (Seattle). 1923. *1299*
—. Alaska. Travel. 1923. *1456*
—. Armenia. Documents. Foreign Relations.
Senate Foreign Relations Subcommittee. 1919.
1140
—. Congress. Germany. Military Occupation.
Wilson, Woodrow. 1919-23. *1544*
—. Coolidge, Calvin. Federal Government.
Negroes. Segregation. 1916-29. *1344*
—. Cox, James M. Newspapers. Political
Campaigns (presidential). 1920. *1141*
—. Foreign policy. Johnson, Hiram W. Politics.
Republican Party. 1920-22. *1519*
—. Georgia. Johnson, Henry Lincoln. Philips,
John Louis. Republican Party. 1920-24. *1330*
—. Historiography. Presidents. ca 1920-44.
1110
—. Lenroot, Irvine L. Political conventions.
Republican Party. Vice-Presidency. Wisconsin.
1920. *1171*
—. Radio. 1920-23. *1455*
—. Senate. World Court. 1920-23. *1473*
—. Teapot Dome Scandal. 1923-24. *1391*
Harding, Warren G. (death). Reporters and
Reporting. 1923. *1135*
Hargrove, Erwin C. Cronin, Thomas E. Hughes,
Emmet John. Koenig, Louis W. Presidency
(review article). Schlesinger, Arthur M., Jr.
1972-75. *3190*
Harlem Heights (battle). American Revolution.
Virginia Regiment (3rd). Washington, George.
1776. *277*
Harper's Ferry Armory. Economic Development.
Washington, George. West Virginia. 1790-99.
937
Harper's Weekly (periodical). Cartoons. Editorials.
Political Campaigns (presidential). Scandals.
Wasp (periodical). 1876-77. *667*
Harris, Gibson W. Elections. Illinois. Letters.
Lincoln, Abraham. Mormons. 1846. *414*
Harris, J. Will. Colleges and Universities. Coolidge,
Calvin. Education, Finance. Hoover, Herbert
C. Inter-American University. Personal
narratives. Puerto Rico. ca 1920-30. *1327*
Harris, Patricia Roberts. Appointments to office.
Carter, Jimmy. Federal Government. Politics.
1976. *2240*
Harrison, Benjamin (administration). Blaine, James
G. Canada. Tariff. 1891-92. *1022*
Harrison, Byron Patton (Pat). Political friendship.
Roosevelt, Franklin D. Senate. 1920-41.
1443
Harrison, William Henry. Diplomacy. Gran
Colombia (Bogotá). 1829-30. *602*
—. Indian Wars. Indiana. Personal narratives.
Peters, George P. Tippecanoe (battle). 1811.
417
—. Indiana. 1798-1840. *597*
—. Music. Political Campaigns (presidential).
Song sheets. 1840. *709*
Harry S. Truman Library. Documents. Federal
Policy. Truman, Harry S. Western States.
1940-66. *2394*
—. Dwight D. Eisenhower Library. Franklin D.
Roosevelt Library. Herbert Hoover Presidential
Library and Museum. John Fitzgerald Kennedy
Library. Libraries, presidential. Lyndon Baines
Johnson Library. 1940-79. *70*
Harvard University. Archival catalogs and
inventories. Roosevelt, Theodore. 1919-76.
1066
—. Eliot, Charles William. Roosevelt, Theodore.
Sports. 1908. *1129*
—. Roosevelt, Franklin D. Students. 1901-04.
1074
Harvey Mudd College (Sprague Memorial Library;
Herbert Hoover Collection of Mining and
Metallurgy). California (Claremont). Hoover,
Herbert C. Metallurgy. Mines. Rare Books.
1470-1980. *1111*
Hastie, William Henry. Air Forces. Race relations.
World War II. 1940-43. *1377*
—. Armies. Defense Department. Negroes.
Racism. Stimson, Henry L. World War II.
1940-43. *1376*
—. Defense Department. Military reform. Racism.
World War II. 1940-43. *1378*

—. Hopkins, Harry. Iowa. Lewis, John L. Wallace, Henry A. 1870's-1960's. *1121*

—. Hopkins, Harry. Iowa. Lewis, John L. Wallace, Henry A. 1870's-90's. 1930's. *1122*

—. Hopkins, Harry. Iowa. Lewis, John L. Wallace, Henry A. 1874-1930. *1123*

—. Ideology. Individualism. 1885-1925. *1102*

—. Indians. Public Administration. Rhoads, Charles J. Scattergood, J. Henry. Wilbur, Ray Lyman. 1929-33. *1413*

—. Intervention. Isolationism. Peace. Totalitarianism. USSR. World War II. 1939-41. *1061*

—. Johnson, Lyndon B. Kennedy, John F. Nixon, Richard M. (administration). Presidency. Public administration. Secrecy. 1929-74. *139*

—. Johnson, Lyndon B. Nixon, Richard M. Protestant ethic. Public welfare. Rhetoric. Roosevelt, Franklin D. Weber, Max. 1905-79. *51*

—. Landon, Alfred M. Political Leadership. Republican Party (conference; proposed). 1937-38. *1058*

—. Letters. Truman, Harry S. World Famine Mission. 1945-48. *3007*

—. Negroes. Racism. Social change. ca 1910-33. *1075*

—. Political Campaigns (presidential). Smith, Al. Tennessee, west. 1928. *1173*

—. Political leadership. Republican Party. 1920-32. *1393*

—. Politics. 1900-33. 1970-80. *1236*

—. Presidents. Sullivan, Mark. 1920-52. *1090*

—. Press. Reporters and Reporting. 1929-32. *1411*

Hoover, Herbert C. (administration). Air mail service. Black, Hugo. Contracts. Farley, James A. Legislative Investigations. 1933-34. *1440*

—. DePriest, Oscar. House of Representatives. Negroes. Politics. Republican Party. 1929. *1288*

—. Federal policy. Public lands. Western states. Wilbur, Ray Lyman. 1920's. *1293*

—. Florida. Patronage. Republican Party. State Politics. 1928-33. *1312*

—. Georgia. Patronage. Political factions. Race Relations. Republican Party. 1928-32. *1311*

—. Howard, Perry W. Mississippi. Patronage. Political Campaigns (presidential). Political Factions. Race. Republican Party. State Politics. 1928-33. *1310*

—. Negroes. Republican Party. 1928-32. *1303*

—. Senate. World Court. 1929-33. *1470*

Hoover, Herbert C. (review article). Depressions. Fausold, Martin L. Mazuzan, George T. Wilson, Joan Hoff. 1929-33. 1974-75. *1224*

Hoover, J. Edgar. American Civil Liberties Union. Demonstrations. Federal Bureau of Investigation. Political surveillance. Trade Union Education League. 1924-36. *1457*

—. Attorneys General. Cummings, Homer Stillé. Federal Bureau of Investigation. Films. *G-Men* (film). 1933-35. *1405*

—. Barnes, Harry Elmer. Crime and Criminals (organized). Federal Bureau of Investigation. World War II. 1936-44. *1449*

—. Boggs, Thomas Hale. Federal Bureau of Investigation. Speeches, Addresses, etc. 1971. *3273*

—. Entertainment industry. Federal Bureau of Investigation. Public relations. 1930's-60's. *131*

—. Federal Bureau of Investigation. Nazism. 1934-76. *44*

—. Federal Bureau of Investigation. Political Surveillance. Radicals and Radicalism. 1919-21. *1707*

Hoover, Joseph. Lincoln, Abraham (family). Lithographs. Spokny, George. 1861-65. *854*

Hopkins, Harry. Arkansas. Depressions. Federal Aid to Education. Federal Emergency Relief Administration. Public schools. 1933-36. *1412*

—. Coan, George W., Jr. North Carolina. Patronage. Works Progress Administration. 1935. *1370*

—. Depressions. Federal Theatre Project. Flanagan, Hallie. Politics. Theater. Works Progress Administration. 1935-39. *1266*

—. Depressions. Hoover, Herbert C. Lewis, John L. Wallace, Henry A. 1930-69. *1425*

—. Federal Policy. New Deal. Poverty. Roosevelt, Franklin D. Unemployment. 1910's-38. *1369*

—. Foreign policy. Roosevelt, Franklin D. USSR. World War II. 1938-46. *1598*

—. Hoover, Herbert C. Iowa. Lewis, John L. Wallace, Henry A. 1870's-1960's. *1121*

—. Hoover, Herbert C. Iowa. Lewis, John L. Wallace, Henry A. 1870's-90's. 1930's. *1122*

—. Hoover, Herbert C. Iowa. Lewis, John L. Wallace, Henry A. 1874-1930. *1123*

—. Marshall, George C. Military reorganization. Roosevelt, Franklin D. World War II. 1942-45. *1634*

—. New Deal. Politics. 1912-40. *1407*

Hospitality. Washington, George. Washington, Martha. 1732-99. *318*

Hospitals (community). Mississippi. Mound Bayou Community Hospital and Health Center. New federalism. 1968-73. *2390*

Hospitals (military). Armies. Chancellorsville (battle). Death and Dying. Letters. Lincoln, Abraham. 1863. *897*

Hostages. Carter, Jimmy. Foreign Policy. Iran. Terrorism. 1979-81. *2605*

—. Carter, Jimmy. Iran. Kentucky (Lexington). Presidents. Public opinion. 1979. *2672*

—. Inaugurations. Iran. Reagan, Ronald. Reporters and Reporting. Television. 1980-81. *2147*

Houdon, Jean Antoine *(Washington)*. France. Sculpture. Virginia (Richmond). Washington, George. ca 1784-96. *260*

Hough, Charles. Appointments to office. Courts. New York. Roosevelt, Theodore. 1906. *1387*

House, Edward Mandell. Floto, Inga. Foreign Policy. Paris Peace Settlements. Wilson, Woodrow (review article). 1919. *1592*

—. Foreign Policy. Historiography. Paris Peace Conference. Wilson, Woodrow. 1919. *1532*

House of Representatives *See also* Legislation; Senate.

—. Adams, John Quincy. 1831-48. *469*

—. Adams, John Quincy. Antislavery Sentiments. Censorship. South. 1831-48. *566*

—. Adams, John Quincy. Foreign policy. Secession. 1842. *527*

—. Adams, John Quincy. Political Leadership. Presidency. 1783-1848. *486*

—. Appointments to office. Ford, Gerald R. Perjury. Watergate Scandal. 1973-75. *2311*

—. Bell, Rudolph M. McDonald, Forrest. Political Parties. Presidency. Washington, George (review article). 1789-1801. 1973-74. *727*

—. Boutwell, George S. Impeachment. Johnson, Andrew. 1865-68. *812*

—. Carter, Jimmy. Communications behavior. Legislation. Politics. 1977. *2223*

—. Democratic Party. Filibusters. Race Relations. Reconstruction. Roll-call voting. 1876-77. *615*

—. Democratic Party. Gillette, Guy M. Iowa. Political Campaigns. Roosevelt, Franklin D. 1932-48. *1326*

—. DePriest, Oscar. Hoover, Herbert C. (administration). Negroes. Politics. Republican Party. 1929. *1288*

—. Elections. Presidency. 1962-75. *1971*

—. Elections, presidential. Presidents. Public opinion. 1953-72. *1853*

—. Executive Power. Logan-Walter Bill. Rayburn, Sam. Sumners, Hatton. Texas. Veto. 1939. *1404*

—. Executive Power. Political Attitudes. 1953-72. *3253*

—. Executive Power. Political Leadership. Wilson, Woodrow. 1913-17. *1216*

—. Executive privilege. Intelligence transmittals. Sonnenfeldt, Helmut. State Department. 1958-73. *2136*

—. Impeachment. State Secretaries. Webster, Daniel. 1846. *864*

House of Representatives (Appropriations Committee). Budgets. Executive Branch. Intergovernmental Relations. Senate Appropriations Committee. Watergate Scandal. 1973-75. *3481*

—. Congress. Garfield, James A. Political leadership. 1872-81. *745*

House of Representatives (Armed Services Committee). Decisionmaking. Defense Department. McNamara, Robert S. Politics and the Military. 1965-68. *3257*

House of Representatives Chamber. Architecture. Capitols. District of Columbia. Jefferson, Thomas. Latrobe, Benjamin Henry. 1803-12. *224*

House of Representatives (Committee of Thirty-three). Civil War (antecedents). Diplomacy. Lincoln, Abraham. Peace. 1860. *841*

House of Representatives (Education and Labor Committee). Allis-Chalmers Corporation. Communist Party. Kennedy, John F. Legislative Investigations. Strikes. United Automobile Workers of America, Local 248. Wisconsin (Milwaukee). 1947. *1723*

House of Representatives (Intelligence Activities Committee). Central Intelligence Agency. Executive branch. Intelligence service. Kissinger, Henry A. 1970's. *3024*

—. Executive power. Intelligence service. 1975-76. *3268*

House of Representatives (International Organizations Subcommittee). Foreign Policy. Human rights. 1977. *3031*

House of Representatives (Judiciary Committee). Historians. Impeachment (review article). Presidents. Woodward, C. Vann. 1789-1974. *5*

—. Ideology. Impeachment. Nixon, Richard M. Partisanship. 1974. *2351*

House of Representatives (Printing Committee). Copyright. Documents. Presidents. Richardson, James Daniel *(Messages and Papers of the Presidents)*. Spofford, Ainsworth Rand. 1900. *1049*

House of Representatives (Rules Committee). Johnson, Lyndon B. (administration). Kennedy, John F. (administration). Legislation. 1961-69. *2419*

Houses. Art. District of Columbia. Mondale, Joan. Vice-presidency. 1974-77. *2336*

—. Historic sites. Illinois (Springfield). Letters. Lincoln, Abraham (residence). Lincoln, Robert Todd. 1865-1909. *475*

Housing *See also* City Planning; Public Housing; Urban Renewal.

—. Defense Department. Integration. Military. Social change. 1967-68. *2503*

Housing and Urban Development Department. Planning. Public Housing. Urban government councils. 1970-75. *2431*

Howard, Oliver Otis. Fund raising. Lincoln Memorial University. Twain, Mark. 1901-09. *444*

Howard, Perry W. Hoover, Herbert C. (administration). Mississippi. Patronage. Political Campaigns (presidential). Political Factions. Race. Republican Party. State Politics. 1928-33. *1310*

Howells, William Cooper. *Ashtabula Sentinel*. Hayes, Rutherford B. Newspapers. Political Campaigns (presidential). Republican Party. 1875-76. *669*

Howells, William Dean. Authors. Biography. Hayes, Rutherford B. 1876-1930. *529*

—. Hayes, Rutherford B. Political Speeches. Republican Party. Twain, Mark. 1876. *612*

Hoxie, Vinnie Ream. Congress. Impeachment. Johnson, Andrew. Lincoln, Abraham. Sculpture. 1865-71. *573*

—. Lincoln, Abraham. Sculpture. 1866-81. *433*

Hughes, Charles Evans. Banking. Diplomacy. International Committee of Bankers on Mexico. Lamont-de la Huerta Agreement. Mexico. 1921-24. *1574*

—. California (San Francisco). Labor. Political Campaigns (presidential). Republican Party. 1916. *1161*

Hughes, Emmet John. Cronin, Thomas E. Hargrove, Erwin C. Koenig, Louis W. Presidency (review article). Schlesinger, Arthur M., Jr. 1972-75. *3190*

Hughes-Ryan Act (US, 1974). Central Intelligence Agency. Foreign Relations. Intelligence Oversight Act (US, 1980). 1974-80. *3327*

Hulbert, Mary. Wilson, Woodrow. 1907-35. *1120*

Hull, Cordell. Argentina. Foreign Policy. Ramírez, Pedro. 1943. *1685*

—. Axis powers. Foreign Relations. Latin America. Rio Conference. Welles, Sumner. World War II. 1941-42. *1535*

—. Diplomacy. Indochina. Japan. Philippines. World War II (antecedents). 1941. *1499*

—. Exports. Foreign policy. Japan. Oil and Petroleum Products. Roosevelt, Franklin D. State Department. 1940-41. *1673*

—. Foreign policy. Japan. Roosevelt, Franklin D. Stimson, Henry L. 1933-36. *1570*

Human rights. Africa. Carter, Jimmy (administration). Foreign Policy. 1979. *2956*

—. American dream. Carter, Jimmy. Dissent. Europe. 17c-1978. *3080*

—. Attitudes. Carter, Jimmy (administration). Foreign policy. 1977-78. *2858*

—. Banking. Carter, Jimmy (administration). Foreign policy. 1977. *2878*

—. Carter, Jimmy. Detente. 1977-78. *3044*
—. Carter, Jimmy. Detente. Disarmament. Kissinger, Henry A. 1970-77. *3178*
—. Carter, Jimmy. Ethics. Foreign policy. Kissinger, Henry A. Political Theory. 1973-80. *2721*
—. Carter, Jimmy. Europe, Eastern. Foreign policy. Self-determination. USSR. 1977-78. *2697*
—. Carter, Jimmy. Foreign policy. 1977-78. *2932*
—. Carter, Jimmy. Foreign Policy. 1977-79. *2951*
—. Carter, Jimmy. Foreign policy. Intervention. 1977-80. *2983*
—. Carter, Jimmy. Foreign policy. Latin America. 1977-80. *2756*
—. Carter, Jimmy. Foreign policy. Materialism. Morality. 1977-79. *2571*
—. Carter, Jimmy. Foreign policy. USSR. 1976-77. *2744*
—. Carter, Jimmy. State Department (Human Rights Bureau). 1977-80. *3142*
—. Carter, Jimmy. UN. 1945-77. *2719*
—. Carter, Jimmy (administration). China. Foreign policy. Morality. 1976-77. *3115*
—. Carter, Jimmy (administration). Domestic Policy. Foreign policy. 1977-79. *3037*
—. Carter, Jimmy (administration). Foreign policy. 1970's. *3146*
—. Carter, Jimmy (administration). Foreign policy. 1977-78. *3135*
—. Carter, Jimmy (administration). Foreign policy. 1977-79. *2690*
—. Carter, Jimmy (administration). Foreign Policy. 1977-79. *2924*
—. Carter, Jimmy (administration). Foreign Policy. 1977-81. *2830*
—. Carter, Jimmy (administration). Foreign Policy. Korea, South. 1945-79. *2949*
—. Carter, Jimmy (administration). Foreign policy. Race Relations. South Africa. 1973-78. *2668*
—. Communism. Foreign policy. Presidents. Religious liberty. USSR. 20c. *151*
—. Communism. Foreign relations. Liberty. USSR. 1940's-76. *2682*
—. Detente. Foreign Policy. USSR. 1973-79. *2759*
—. Foreign Assistance Act (US, 1974). Military aid. 1973-82. *2665*
—. Foreign policy. 1789-1978. *78*
—. Foreign Policy. House of Representatives (International Organizations Subcommittee). 1977. *3031*
—. Foreign Policy. Kissinger, Henry A. National security. 1971-76. *2562*
—. Foreign Policy. Terrorism. 1975-81. *2967*
Hume, David. Adair, Douglass. *Federalist* No. 10. Madison, James. Political Theory. Republicanism. Wills, Garry. 1788. *238*
—. Banking. Economic theory. Jefferson, Thomas. 1775-1816. *289*
Humor *See also* Satire.
—. Lincoln, Abraham. 1860-65. *755*
—. Lincoln, Abraham. Politics. Prose. 1847-65. *404*
—. Politics. 1933-76. *2183*
Hungarians. Congress. Eisenhower, Dwight D. (administration). Federal policy. Immigration. Public opinion. Refugees. 1956-57. *2893*
Hungary. Alliances. Bulgaria. Foreign Policy. Romania. World War II. 1943-44. *1666*
—. American Revolution. Franklin, Benjamin. Historiography. Washington, George. Zinner, János. 1775-78. *248*
—. Communism. Kun, Bela. Paris Peace Conference. Political Attitudes. Wilson, Woodrow. 1919. *1660*
Hunting. Naturalists. Roosevelt, Theodore. Sportsmanship. Upper Classes. 1880's-1900. *1055*
Hurley, Edward Nash. Economic Policy. Foreign policy. Shipping Board. Wilson, Woodrow. 1918-19. *1650*
Hurley, Patrick J. China. Diplomacy. Jiang Jieshi. Mao Zedong. State Department. Vincent, John Carter. 1944-45. *1591*
Hutchins, Thomas. Geography. Jefferson, Thomas. Letters. Old Northwest. Old Southwest. Rivers. 1784. *266*
Hutchinson, Thomas. Adams, John. American Revolution (antecedents). Massachusetts. Otis, James, Jr. Patriotism. 1761-76. *343*
Hutson, Thomas R. Afghanistan. Carter, Jimmy (administration). Foreign policy. Invasions. Personal narratives. USSR. 1980-81. *2797*

Hydrogen bomb. Joint Chiefs of Staff. Military Strategy. Nuclear Arms. Truman, Harry S. USSR. 1945-50. *3010*

I

Ibn Saud, King. Conferences. Eddy, William A. Foreign Relations. Roosevelt, Franklin D. Saudi Arabia. 1945. *1576*
ICBM's. Defense Policy. Johnson, Lyndon B. Kennedy, John F. Kuter, Lawrence S. Personal Narratives. 1962. *2209*
—. Military strategy. Nuclear arms. Schlesinger, James R. Strategic Arms Limitation Talks. 1974. *2897*
Ickes, Harold L. Appointments to Office. Bureau of Indian Affairs (commissioners). Collier, John. Interior Department. Roosevelt, Franklin D. 1933. *1346*
—. Congress. Federal Regulation. Oil Industry and Trade. Roosevelt, Franklin D. 1933. *1358*
—. Construction. Employment. Negroes. Public Works Administration. Quotas. 1933-40. *1355*
—. Douglas, Lewis W. Public Administration. Public Works Administration. 1933. *1410*
—. Interior Department. Political Leadership. Psychohistory. 1874-1941. *1371*
Idaho *See also* Far Western States.
—. Agriculture Department. Benson, Ezra Taft. Mormons. Personal narratives. State Government. 1940's-61. *2299*
—. Elections. Republican Party. 1980. *1989*
Idealism. Carter, Jimmy (administration). Declaration of Independence. Foreign policy. Morality. ca 1918-78. *2784*
—. League of Nations. Morality. Paris Peace Conference. Wilson, Woodrow. 1918-19. *1612*
Identity. Lincoln, Abraham. Personality. Rhetoric. 1831-61. *480*
Ideology. Addams, Jane. Foreign policy. Open Door Policy. Wilson, Woodrow. 1900-20. *1623*
—. Berlin Blockade. Decisionmaking. Foreign policy. Israel. Truman, Harry S. 1944-48. *3011*
—. Civil Disobedience. Watergate Scandal. 1939-74. *2307*
—. Conservatism. Pressure Groups. Reagan, Ronald (administration). 1964-80. *2389*
—. Decisionmaking. Federal Policy. Presidents (review article). 1961-76. *2256*
—. Democracy. Dominican Republic. Intervention. Mexico. 1914-65. *67*
—. Elections. Politics. 1972. *2083*
—. Elections. Politics. Sisson, Daniel (review article). 1776-1800. 1974. *650*
—. Hoover, Herbert C. Individualism. 1885-1925. *1102*
—. House of Representatives (Judiciary Committee). Impeachment. Nixon, Richard M. Partisanship. 1974. *2351*
—. Military Strategy. 1981. *2563*
—. Political Conventions. Political Factions. Political Parties. Voting and Voting Behavior. 1940-76. *1836*
—. Political conventions. Pressure groups. Public opinion. Roll-call voting. 1944-76. *2013*
—. Political Surveys. Self-evaluation. Voting and Voting Behavior. 1960's-70's. *1920*
—. Politics. Rhetoric. ca 1800-1975. *147*
Ignatius, Paul R. Betts, Richard K. Defense policy. Joint Chiefs of Staff (review article). Military Organization. Steadman, Richard C. 1958-78. *3287*
Ike (program). Aesthetics. Documentaries. Eisenhower, Dwight D. Heroism. Television. World War II. ca 1941-45. 1979. *1720*
Illegitimacy. Hemings, Sally. Jefferson, Thomas. 1770's-1979. *223*
Illinois *See also* North Central States.
—. Attitudes. Civil War. Lincoln, Abraham. Military Service. 1832-65. *416*
—. Black Hawk War. Indian Wars. Lincoln, Abraham. Military intelligence. Spy Battalion. Wisconsin. 1832. *581*
—. Chicago Historical Society. Dioramas. Lincoln, Abraham. 1809-65. *447*
—. Civil War. Copperheads. Democratic Party. Lincoln, Abraham. 1861-65. *872*
—. Debates. Douglas, Stephen A. Lincoln, Abraham. Political Campaigns (senatorial). Slavery. 1774-1858. *401*

—. Douglas, Stephen A. Lincoln, Abraham. Political Campaigns (senatorial). Slavery. 1858. *485*
—. Education. Jefferson, Thomas. Lincoln, Abraham. 1820-62. *439*
—. Elections. Harris, Gibson W. Letters. Lincoln, Abraham. Mormons. 1846. *414*
—. Elections (congressional). Johnson, Andrew. Reconstruction. 1866. *911*
—. Grant, Ulysses S. Military Service. 1861. *587*
—. Hatch, Ozias M. Knapp, Nathan. Letters. Lincoln, Abraham. Republican Party. 1859. *710*
—. Herndon, William H. Letters. Lincoln, Abraham. Oglesby, Richard J. 1865. 1873. *605*
—. Indiana. Kentucky. Lincoln, Abraham. 1814-31. *518*
—. Internal improvements. Lincoln, Abraham. National development. 1830-61. *465*
—. Johnson, Lyndon B. Politics. 1952-68. *1857*
—. Lawyers. Lincoln, Abraham. 1837-60. *517*
—. Letters. Lincoln, Abraham. Shields, James. 1842. *498*
—. Lincoln, Abraham. Politics. Todd, Robert Smith. 1841-44. *476*
—. Lincoln, Abraham. State Legislatures. Unionism. 1860-61. *584*
Illinois Central Railroad. Dubois, Jesse K. Lawyers. Lincoln, Abraham. State Government. 1858. *406*
—. Elections (presidential). Lawyers. Lincoln, Abraham. 1855-60. *619*
Illinois (Charleston). Civil War. Lincoln, Abraham (family). Riots. 1863-64. *769*
Illinois (Chicago). Arvey, Jacob M. Democratic Party. Political Conventions. Stevenson, Adlai E. 1932-52. *1806*
—. Avery, Sewell. Federal regulation. Labor Disputes. Montgomery Ward. War Labor Board. World War II. 1941. *1348*
—. Democratic Party. Historiography. Mass media. Political Conventions. Public opinion. Violence. 1968. *1921*
—. Democratic Party. Law Enforcement. Political Conventions. Political Protest. Students. 1856-1978. *1973*
—. Extradition. Foreign Relations. Refugees. Root, Elihu. Rudowitz, Christian Ansoff. Russia. 1908-09. *1542*
—. Fassett, Samuel M. Lincoln, Abraham. Mendel, Edward. Photography. Political Campaigns (presidential). Portraits. 1860. *646*
—. Foreign policy. Poland. Polish-American Congress. Roosevelt, Franklin D. World War II. 1944. *1420*
—. Kelly, Edward J. New Deal. Political machines. Roosevelt, Franklin D. 1932-40. *1341*
—. Letters. Lincoln, Abraham. Lithography. Mendel, Edward. Portraits. 1827-84. *707*
—. Lincoln, Abraham. Politics. Rivers and Harbors Convention. 1847-82. *437*
Illinois (Cook County). Democratic Party. Elections, presidential. Political Corruption. 1960. *1940*
Illinois (Logan County). Hoblit family. Lincoln, Abraham. ca 1840-66. *522*
Illinois (New Salem, Springfield). Indiana. Lincoln, Abraham. Political Campaigns. 1817-37. *578*
Illinois (Sangamon County). Legislation. Lincoln, Abraham. Musick, Sam. Politics. Smoot, Coleman. 1827-46. *399*
Illinois (Springfield). Atwood, Elbridge. Letters. Lincoln, Abraham. 1860-65. *606*
—. Bailey, Gilbert S. Baptists. Chicago, University of. Lincoln, Abraham. 1822-91. *535*
—. Body snatching. Lincoln, Abraham. Mullen, Terrance. 1876. *494*
—. Converts. Jacquess, James F. Lincoln, Abraham. Methodist Church. 1847. *593*
—. Documents. Land Tenure. Lincoln, Abraham. Walters, William. 1839-45. *473*
—. Elder, Samuel S. Lincoln, Abraham. Tinsmiths. Tools. 1865. 1978. *585*
—. Florville, William. Lincoln, Abraham. 1832-68. *519*
—. Herndon, Archer G. Lincoln, Abraham. 1835-36. *586*
—. Historic sites. Houses. Letters. Lincoln, Abraham (residence). Lincoln, Robert Todd. 1865-1909. *475*
—. Illinois State Historical Library. Land Tenure. Lincoln, Abraham. 1837-53. *608*

—. Competency commissions. Federal Policy. Land allotment. 1913-20. *1374*
—. Education. Morgan, Thomas Jefferson. 1890's-1910's. *858*
—. Federal policy. Hayes, Rutherford B. 1877-81. *808*
—. Federal policy. Jackson, Andrew. Psychohistory. Rogin, Michael Paul (review article). 1800-50. *545*
—. Federal policy. Lincoln, Abraham. 1861-65. *906*
—. Foreign Relations. Jefferson, Thomas. Privy Council. Public Records. South Carolina. 1787-89. *358*
—. Hoover, Herbert C. Public Administration. Rhoads, Charles J. Scattergood, J. Henry. Wilbur, Ray Lyman. 1929-33. *1413*
—. Jackson, Andrew. Liberalism. Removals, forced. Rogin, Michael Paul (review article). 19c. 1975. *453*
—. Lincoln, Abraham. Peace. Plains Indians. Southwest. 1863. *871*
—. Madison, James. Political Theory. Religion. 1751-1836. *385*
—. Washington Monument. 1848-84. *198*
Indians (reservations). Bureau of Indian Affairs. Conscription, Military. Goshiute Indians. Nevada. Political protest. 1917-19. *1294*
—. Chickasaw. Jackson, Andrew. Land Tenure. Shelby, Isaac. South. 1818. *794*
—. Civil Service. Roosevelt, Theodore. Western States. 1892. *862*
Indians (review article). Federal Policy. New Deal. Parman, Donald L. Philp, Kenneth R. Taylor, Graham D. 1934-74. *1329*
Indian-White Relations. Agriculture. Federal Programs. Missions and Missionaries. Old Northwest. 1789-1820. *818*
—. Alabama. Jackson, Andrew. Mississippi. 1789-1817. *448*
—. Cherokee Indians. Federal Policy. Treaties. 1835-1900. *815*
—. Cherokee Indians. Jackson, Andrew. Removals, forced. 1835. *965*
—. Cherokee Indians. Jefferson, Thomas. Removals, forced. Southeastern States. Speeches, Addresses, etc. 1809. *966*
—. Civil Service Commissioners. Indian Rights Association. Roosevelt, Theodore. Welsh, Herbert. 1889-95. *831*
—. Coleraine, Treaty of. Creek Indians. Federal Policy. Georgia. 1796. *820*
—. Florida. Jackson, Andrew. Remini, Robert V. (review article). Removals, forced. Tennessee. 1780's-1821. *560*
—. Marquette, Pierre. Peace pipes. Presidents. 17c-19c. *817*
Individualism. Hoover, Herbert C. Ideology. 1885-1925. *1102*
Indochina See also Asia, Southeast.
—. China. Churchill, Winston. Colonialism. deGaulle, Charles. Foreign Policy. France. Roosevelt, Franklin D. 1942-45. *1588*
—. Colonial Government. Foreign Policy. France. Truman, Harry S. (administration). 1943-45. *2783*
—. Credibility gap. Foreign policy. Kissinger, Henry A. Nixon Doctrine. 1968-75. *2745*
—. Diplomacy. Hull, Cordell. Japan. Philippines. World War II (antecedents). 1941. *1499*
—. Federal Policy. Military Intelligence. World War II. 1943-45. *1662*
—. Foreign policy. 1945-52. *2703*
Indonesia See also Netherlands East Indies.
—. Ford, Gerald R. Foreign policy. Thailand. 1975. *3126*
Industrial democracy. Corporations. Hoover, Herbert C. Labor Unions and Organizations. 1919-29. *1467*
Industrial Relations See also Labor Unions and Organizations; Strikes.
—. Advisory committees. Presidents. 1955-80. *2447*
Industry See also individual industries, e.g. Iron Industry, etc.; Manufactures.
—. Commerce Department. Federal regulation. Hoover, Herbert C. Labor. 1921-28. *1331*
—. Defense Policy. Federal Policy. Labor Unions and Organizations. World War II. 1939-41. *1435*
—. Economic policy. Hamilton, Alexander. 1789-95. *946*
—. Federal Policy. Investments. Reagan, Ronald (administration). 1982. *2363*
—. Labor Unions and Organizations. Roosevelt, Franklin D. (administration). War Manpower Commission. War Production Board. 1939-45. *1352*

Inflation. Afghanistan. Carter, Jimmy (administration). Cold War. Decisionmaking. Defense spending. Iran. USSR. 1979-80. *2284*
—. Budgets. Carter, Jimmy (administration). Etzioni, Amitai. Personal narratives. 1980. *2341*
—. Carter, Jimmy (administration). 1977-79. *2310*
—. Carter, Jimmy (administration). Congress. Domestic policy. Foreign Policy. Interest groups. 1977-78. *2200*
—. Federal Regulation. Nixon, Richard M. (administration). 1969-77. *2352*
—. Ford, Gerald R. Political Speeches. Rhetoric. War metaphor. 1974. *2507*
—. Kernell, Samuel. Presidents. Public Opinion. 1950-78. *2444*
—. Office of Price Administration. O'Mahoney, Joseph C. Politics. Truman, Harry S. Wage-price controls. Wyoming. 1945-47. *2534*
—. Presidents. Public Opinion. 1953-72. *2400*
—. Public opinion. Public opinion. Unemployment. 1952-72. *2203*
Information. Congress. Executive Power. 1970's. *3342*
Information access. Archives, National. Foreign policy. Presidents. Public records. State Department. 1950's-70's. *3377*
—. Documents. Franklin D. Roosevelt Library. Military finance. Security classification. 1970-75. *1130*
—. Documents. Law. Presidents. 1968-78. *3307*
Information Storage and Retrieval Systems. Cryptography. National Security Agency. Privacy. 1952-80. *3033*
Ingham, Samuel Delucenna. Berrien, John M. Cabinet. Eaton Affair. Jackson, Andrew. Letters. 1829-31. *889*
Inheritance and Transfer Tax. Coolidge, Calvin. Income tax. Mellon, Andrew W. Republican Party. 1925-28. *1347*
Innocence (concept). Fitzgerald, F. Scott. Franklin, Benjamin. National Characteristics. Nixon, Richard M. Thoreau, Henry David. Values. Watergate scandal. 18c-1978. *1762*
Insanity. See Mental Illness.
Institute for Palestine Studies. Carter, Jimmy (administration). Foreign policy. Israel. Palestine. 1980. *2577*
Integration See also Assimilation.
—. Civil Rights. Courts. Executive branch. Health, Education, and Welfare Department. Politics. 1960's-79. *2438*
—. Civil rights movement. Federal policy. Johnson, Lyndon B. Kennedy, John F. 1945-76. *2402*
—. Defense Department. Housing. Military. Social change. 1967-68. *2503*
Intellectuals. Beard, Charles A. Historians. Isolationism. Liberalism. New Deal. Roosevelt, Franklin D. 1932-48. *1219*
—. Foreign policy. Kissinger, Henry A. Political Attitudes. 1957-74. *2925*
—. Jefferson, Thomas. Virginia. 17c-19c. *349*
Intelligence Oversight Act (US, 1980). Central Intelligence Agency. Foreign Relations. Hughes-Ryan Act (US, 1974). 1974-80. *3327*
Intelligence Service See also Espionage; Military Intelligence; Secret Service.
—. American Revolution. Jefferson, Thomas. Political Attitudes. 1775-83. *178*
—. Berlin Crisis. Decisionmaking. Foreign Relations. Germany. Kennedy, John F. 1961. *2644*
—. Central Intelligence Agency. Constitution. Executive Power. 1933-74. *3213*
—. Central Intelligence Agency. Covert operations. Donovan, William J. National Security. 1940's-74. *3013*
—. Central Intelligence Agency. Donovan, William J. 1942-54. *3216*
—. Central Intelligence Agency. Ethnocentrism. Language. Vietnam. 1954-63. *2869*
—. Central Intelligence Agency. Executive branch. House of Representatives (Intelligence Activities Committee). Kissinger, Henry A. 1970's. *3024*
—. Congress. 1947-74. *3400*
—. Congress. Executive Branch. Government. 1940's-70's. *3381*
—. Congress. National security. 1946-74. *3401*
—. Decisionmaking. Foreign policy. Kissinger, Henry A. National Security Council. Nixon, Richard M. (administration). 1961-75. *2660*

—. Executive power. House of Representatives (Intelligence Activities Committee). 1975-76. *3268*
—. Federal Government. 1941-77. *3219*
—. Foreign Relations. 1947-80. *2935*
—. France. Government. Great Britain. 1941-70's. *3189*
—. Freedom of Information Act (US, 1966). National Security. 1970-82. *3225*
—. Presidents. 1973-78. *3308*
Intelligence Service (review article). Africa. Central Intelligence Agency. Marchetti, Victor. Marks, John D. 1947-80. *2957*
—. Central Intelligence Agency. Powers, Thomas. Roosevelt, Kermit. 1947-80. *2550*
Intelligence transmittals. Executive privilege. House of Representatives. Sonnenfeldt, Helmut. State Department. 1958-73. *2136*
Inter-American University. Colleges and Universities. Coolidge, Calvin. Education, Finance. Harris, J. Will. Hoover, Herbert C. Personal narratives. Puerto Rico. ca 1920-30. *1327*
Interest Groups See also Political Factions; Pressure Groups.
—. Agriculture Department. Budgets. Congress. 1971-76. *3365*
—. Agriculture Department. Federal Government. 1974-76. *2436*
—. Bureau of Health Insurance. Medicare. Oversight, congressional. Public Administration. Senate Finance Committee. 1965-78. *3217*
—. Carter, Jimmy (administration). 1976-79. *2437*
—. Carter, Jimmy (administration). Congress. Domestic policy. Foreign Policy. Inflation. 1977-78. *2200*
—. Carter, Jimmy (administration). Congress. Energy. Federal Policy. 1977-78. *2421*
—. Civil rights. Federal Policy. Populism. Private enterprise. Racism. Wallace, George C. 1960's. *2107*
—. Decisionmaking. Executive Branch. Food. 1970-81. *3313*
—. Federal Policy. Post Office Department. Reform. 1966-80. *3205*
—. *Federalist* No. 10. General will (concept). Madison, James. Rousseau, Jean Jacques. 1787. *214*
—. Government. Madison, James. Political theory. 19c-20c. *200*
—. Political conditions. Presidents. 1961-79. *2195*
Intergovernmental communications. Congress. Executive Branch. 1945-73. *3325*
Intergovernmental Relations. Bipartisanship. Foreign policy. 1981. *2978*
—. Budgets. Executive Branch. House of Representatives (Appropriations Committee). Senate Appropriations Committee. Watergate Scandal. 1973-75. *3481*
—. Budgets. Office of Management and Budget. Politics. 1970's. *3275*
—. Congress. Executive Branch. Oversight, congressional. 1952-80. *3288*
—. Conservation of Natural Resources. Energy. Federal Policy. State Government. 1974-79. *2476*
—. Decisionmaking. Office of Management and Budget. 1921-74. *3212*
—. Executive branch. New Federalism. Nixon, Richard M. 1974. *3277*
—. Labor Department. Public Administration. World War I. 1917-18. *1278*
—. Local government. Nixon, Richard M. (administration). Roosevelt, Franklin D. (administration). Social problems. State Government. 1933-45. 1969-74. *95*
Interior decoration. Hayes, Rutherford B. White House. 1877-81. *806*
Interior Department. Anti-Communist movements. Chapman, Oscar L. Loyalty. Schoeppel, Andrew F. Senate Interior and Insular Affairs Committee. 1950. *2406*
—. Appointments to Office. Bureau of Indian Affairs (commissioners). Collier, John. Ickes, Harold L. Roosevelt, Franklin D. 1933. *1346*
—. Ballinger-Pinchot Controversy. Conservation of Natural Resources. Fisher, Walter Lowrie. 1911-13. *1315*
—. California (Mineral King Valley). Land development. *Sierra Club v. Morton* (US, 1972). Wilderness. 1969-72. *2333*
—. Fall, Albert B. New Mexico. Political Corruption. Teapot Dome Scandal. 1910-30. *1463*

—. Assassination. Conspiracy. District of Columbia. Prisons. Washington Arsenal. 1803-1903. *488*

—. Assassination. Conspiracy. Due process. 1865-68. *491*

—. Assassination. Conspiracy. Mental Illness. Trials. Weichmann, Louis J. 1865. 1895. *484*

—. Assassination. Conspiracy. Personal narratives. Risvold, Floyd (review article). Trials. Weichmann, Louis J. 1864-66. *594*

—. Assassination. Courts Martial and Courts of Inquiry. 1861-66. *574*

—. Assassination. Criminal investigations. District of Columbia. Police. Richards, A. C. Trials. 1865-69. *536*

—. Assassination. District of Columbia. Ford's Theater. Grant, Ulysses S. Lincoln, Mary Todd. 1865. *572*

—. Assassination. District of Columbia. Heiss, William H., Sr. Military. Telegraph. 1865. *499*

—. Assassination. Eisenschiml, Otto *(Why Was Lincoln Murdered?)*. Historiography. Stanton, Edwin M. 1865-1930's. *467*

—. Assassination. Florida (Dry Tortugas Island, Fort Jefferson). Johnson, Andrew. Mudd, Samuel A. Pardons. 1865-96. *537*

—. Assassination. Historiography. Stanton, Edwin McMasters. Trials. 1865-1980. *781*

—. Assassination. Leale, Charles Augustus. Physicians. 1865. *548*

—. Assassination. Lincoln, Robert Todd. 1864-1947. *418*

—. *Atlantic Monthly.* Courtship. Forgeries. Letters. Minor, Wilma Frances. Periodicals. Rutledge, Ann. Sedgwick, Ellery. 1928. *450*

—. Attitudes. Business. Interpersonal Relations. Owen, Mary. Todd, Mary. 1831-42. *576*

—. Attitudes. Civil War. Illinois. Military Service. 1832-65. *416*

—. Attitudes. Civil War. Political Speeches. Sectionalism. Slavery. 1850's-65. *456*

—. Attitudes. Colonization. Douglas, Stephen A. Negroes. Race. 1858-65. *819*

—. Attitudes. Colonization. Negroes. 1860's. *905*

—. Attitudes. Constitution. 1861-65. *724*

—. Attitudes. Negroes. Women. ca 1840-65. *398*

—. Attitudes. Nixon, Richard M. Presidency. Sacrifice. Wilson, Woodrow. ca 1850-1976. *137*

—. Attitudes. Race relations. 1830's-65. *454*

—. Attitudes. Slavery. 1837-63. *451*

—. Atwood, Elbridge. Illinois (Springfield). Letters. 1860-65. *606*

—. Bagehot, Walter. Constitution. Great Britain. Political Theory. 19c. *762*

—. Bailey, Gilbert S. Baptists. Chicago, University of. Illinois (Springfield). 1822-91. *535*

—. Baptists. Florida (Umatilla). Southern Baptist winter assembly grounds. 1865. 1925-29. *394*

—. Baptists. Indiana. Pigeon Creek Baptist Church. 1822-30. *604*

—. Barnard, George Grey. Letters. Lincoln, Robert Todd. Sculpture. 1910-22. *474*

—. Beards. Portraits. 1860-61. *845*

—. Beds. 1850's-1981. *520*

—. Beitzinger, A. J. Christenson, Reo M. Equality. Hanley, Thomas O'Brien. Jaffa, Harry V. Political Theory. Values (review article). 1770-1973. *446*

—. Belz, Herman. Louisiana. McCrary, Peyton. Politics. Reconstruction. Social Organization. 1861-77. *962*

—. Bennett, James Gordon. Elections (national). Negroes. *New York Herald.* 1819-64. *699*

—. Bibliographies. Scholarship. Warren, Louis A. 1920-76. *571*

—. Black Hawk War. Illinois. Indian Wars. Military intelligence. Spy Battalion. Wisconsin. 1832. *581*

—. Body snatching. Boyd, Ben. Kinealy, James. 1874-88. *557*

—. Body snatching. Illinois (Springfield). Mullen, Terrance. 1876. *494*

—. Booth, John Wilkes. Conspiracy. Defense Department. Eisenschiml, Otto. Kidnapping. Research. 1865. ca 1930-80. *835*

—. Boston *Pilot.* Catholic Church. Civil War. Irish Americans. Massachusetts. Reporters and Reporting. 1840-72. *955*

—. Bounties. Civil War. Military Recruitment. Staples, John Summerfield. 1864. *947*

—. Brooks, Noah. Civil War. District of Columbia. Reporters and Reporting. 1862-1903. *741*

—. Brown, John Henry. Portraits. 1860-1976. *521*

—. Buell, Don Carlos. Civil War. Grant, Ulysses S. Military General Staff. Political Leadership. 1862-98. *811*

—. Butler, Benjamin F. Elections (presidential). New York City. 1864. *648*

—. Butler, Benjamin F. Vice-Presidency. 1864. *647*

—. Butler, Benjamin F. *(Butler's Book).* Colonization. Negroes. 1864-65. *904*

—. Cabinet. Chase, Salmon P. Civil War (antecedents). Gilmer, John Adams. Nominations for office. North Carolina. Seward, William H. 1860-61. *800*

—. Calamity, use of. Civil War. Puritans. Rhetoric. 1650-1870. *782*

—. Canada. Confederate States of America. Davis, Jefferson. Peace missions. Virginia (Richmond). 1864. *789*

—. Cannibals. Kekela, James Hunnewell. Marquesas Islands (Hiva Oa). Whaling Industry and Trade. Whalon, Jonathan. 1864. *1030*

—. Carpenter, Francis Bicknell. Emancipation Proclamation. Herline, Edward. Painting. Prints. Ritchie, Alexander Hay. 1864-66. *851*

—. *Catholic Herald and Visitor.* Democratic Party. Newspapers. Pennsylvania (Philadelphia). Political Commentary. 1861-65. *826*

—. Censorship. Chicago *Times.* Civil War. Newspapers. 1863-64. *948*

—. Chambrun, Adolphe de. Civil War. France. Letters. 1865-68. *916*

—. Chaplains. Civil War. Grant, Ulysses S. Jews. 1861-62. *902*

—. Chase, Salmon P. Civil War. Florida. Olustee (battle). Political Campaigns (presidential). 1864. *891*

—. Chase, Salmon P. Nominations for office. Supreme Court. Treasury Department. 1848-64. *799*

—. Cherokee Indians. Dole, William P. Federal policy. Indians. Ross, John. 1860-65. *900*

—. Chicago Historical Society. Dioramas. Illinois. 1809-65. *447*

—. Church and State. Civil religion. 1812-65. *442*

—. Civil Rights. Civil War. Constitution. 1861-65. *920*

—. Civil Rights. Civil War. Democracy. Property. Slavery. 1861-65. *786*

—. Civil Rights. Civil War. Emancipation Proclamation. 1854-63. *908*

—. Civil War. Civil-Military Relations. Military Strategy. 1861-65. *945*

—. Civil War. Congress. Historiography. 1861-65. *861*

—. Civil War. Congress. Joint Congressional Committee on the Conduct of the Civil War. 1861-65. *960*

—. Civil War. Connecticut (New London). Letters. Loomis, Francis B. Military finance. 1864. *796*

—. Civil War. Constitution. War Powers. 1860-66. *730*

—. Civil War. Constitutional Amendments (13th). Emancipation. Republicans, radical. 1861-65. *909*

—. Civil War. Consular Service. Espionage. Great Britain. Patronage. Shipping. 1861-63. *1012*

—. Civil War. Consular Service. Espionage. Ireland. Patronage. Scotland. 1861-63. *1013*

—. Civil War. Copperheads. Democratic Party. Illinois. 1861-65. *872*

—. Civil War. Cotton. Davis, Jefferson. Mississippi. Teasdale, Thomas Cox. War Relief. 1865. *795*

—. Civil War. Davis, Jefferson. Political Leadership. 1861-65. *863*

—. Civil War. Democratic Party. Phelps, Richard Harvey. Political Protest. 1861-64. *777*

—. Civil War. District of Columbia. Letters. Mann, Horace, Jr. Peabody, Elizabeth. 1865. *952*

—. Civil War. Dole, William P. Indians. Treaties. 1861-64. *868*

—. Civil War. Domestic Policy. Negroes. 1850-65. *783*

—. Civil War. Emancipation. Kentucky. 1861-65. *837*

—. Civil War. Five Civilized Tribes. Indian Territory. Proclamations. Ross, John. 1860's. *790*

—. Civil War. Foreign Relations. Spain. Tassara, Gabriel Garcia. 1858-73. *978*

—. Civil War. Fort Sumter. Seward, William H. 1861. *914*

—. Civil War. Habeas corpus. Taney, Roger B. 1861. *886*

—. Civil War. Halleck, Henry W. Military strategy. 1862-63. *838*

—. Civil War. Hampton Roads Peace Conference. 1865. *961*

—. Civil War. Hitchcock, Ethan Allen. Military Strategy. Peninsular Campaign. Shenandoah Valley (campaign). Virginia. 1862. *950*

—. Civil War. Inaugural Addresses. Rhetoric. 1865. *832*

—. Civil War. Letters. Maryland (Baltimore). Military medicine. Wool, John E. 1862. *458*

—. Civil War. Lloyd, William Alvin. Military Intelligence. 1861-65. *772*

—. Civil War. *Merrimack* (vessel; capture). Military strategy. Norfolk (battle). Virginia. 1862. *866*

—. Civil War. Military General Staff. Political Leadership. 1862-64. *856*

—. Civil War. New York City. Theater. 1861-1900. *588*

—. Civil War. Political Leadership. Stillé, Charles Janeway ("How a Free People Conduct a Long War"). 1862. *825*

—. Civil War. Political Theory. 1861-65. *959*

—. Civil War. Political Theory. Revolution. Slavery. Social change. 1850-65. *912*

—. Civil War. Portraits. Washington, George. 19c. *72*

—. Civil War. Prisoners of War (exchanges). Underwood, John Cox. 1861-1913. *836*

—. Civil War. Puritans. Self-government. 1630-1865. *717*

—. Civil War. Working class. 1861-65. *865*

—. Civil War (antecedents). Diplomacy. House of Representatives (Committee of Thirty-three). Peace. 1860. *841*

—. Civil War (antecedents). Europe. Foreign Policy. Seward, William H. War threats. 1861. *713*

—. Civil War (antecedents). Fort Sumter. Secession crisis. South. Union Party. 1860-61. *801*

—. Clay, Henry. Eulogies. Nationalism. Seward, William H. 1852. *513*

—. Clay, Henry. Historiography. Nationalism. Webster, Daniel. 19c-1974. *512*

—. Clay, Henry. Jefferson, Thomas. Political Leadership. Taylor, Zachary. 19c. *429*

—. Clergy. Lewis, Lloyd. Myths and symbols. Unionists. 1861-65. *543*

—. Colonization. Emancipation. Negroes. 1852-65. *567*

—. Confederate States of America. Letters. Maynard, Lizzie Green. 1865. *842*

—. Confederate States of America. Theater. 1861-65. *758*

—. Congress. Hoxie, Vinnie Ream. Impeachment. Johnson, Andrew. Sculpture. 1865-71. *573*

—. Conservatism. Law. Order (concept). ca 1840-65. *455*

—. Converts. Illinois (Springfield). Jacquess, James F. Methodist Church. 1847. *593*

—. Crady, John W. Gollaher, Austin. Kentucky (Larue County; Knob Creek). Rescues. ca 1815. *425*

—. Debates. Douglas, Stephen A. Illinois. Political Campaigns (senatorial). Slavery. 1774-1858. *401*

—. Declaration of Independence. Equality. Jaffa, Harry V. Political Theory. 1860's. 1950's-70's. *411*

—. Delegates. New Hampshire. Political conventions. Republican Party. 1860. *657*

—. District of Columbia. Federal government. Pennsylvania (Philadelphia). Speeches, Addresses, etc. 1861. *438*

—. District of Columbia. Johnson, Andrew. Schurz, Carl. Seance. 1865. *492*

—. Documents. Historiography. Lincoln, Mary Todd. Marriage. 1842-65. 1885. 1947-82. *457*

—. Documents. Illinois (Springfield). Land Tenure. Walters, William. 1839-45. *473*

—. Douglas, Stephen A. Illinois. Political Campaigns (senatorial). Slavery. 1858. *485*

—. Douglas, Stephen A. *Illinois State Journal* (newspaper). *Illinois State Register* (newspaper). Political Campaigns (senatorial). Slavery. 1858. *413*

—. Douglas, Stephen A. Morality. Political Attitudes. Slavery. 1850's. *553*

—. Douglass, Frederick. Slavery. 1860's. *784*
—. Dubois, Jesse K. Illinois Central Railroad. Lawyers. State Government. 1858. *406*
—. Economic Policy. Executive Power. Mexican War. Political Theory. Polk, James K. 1840's. *515*
—. Education. Illinois. Jefferson, Thomas. 1820-62. *439*
—. Elder, Samuel S. Illinois (Springfield). Tinsmiths. Tools. 1865. 1978. *585*
—. Elections. Harris, Gibson W. Illinois. Letters. Mormons. 1846. *414*
—. Elections. Letters. Political Commentary. Trumbull, Lyman. 1856. *464*
—. Elections (presidential). Illinois Central Railroad. Lawyers. 1855-60. *619*
—. Emancipation Proclamation. Engraving. Ritchie, Alexander Hay (*First Reading of the Emancipation Proclamation before the Cabinet*). 1864. *853*
—. Emancipation Proclamation. Lithographers. Printers. 1862-65. *852*
—. Emancipation Proclamation. New Jersey. Peace. Public opinion. State legislatures. 1864. *829*
—. Emancipation Proclamation. Republican Party. 1863-64. *874*
—. Engraving. Lithographs. Political Campaigns (presidential). 1860. *645*
—. Entrepreneurs. Heroes. Men. Pioneers. Social Change. 18c-19c. *558*
—. Equality. Mormons. Polygamy. Slavery. Smith, Joseph. 1840-64. *563*
—. Fassett, Samuel M. Illinois (Chicago). Mendel, Edward. Photography. Political Campaigns (presidential). Portraits. 1860. *646*
—. Federal policy. Indians. 1861-65. *906*
—. Florville, William. Illinois (Springfield). 1832-68. *519*
—. Folklore. Historiography. 1816-20c. *403*
—. Forgie, George (review article). Politics. 1820's-61. 1979. *564*
—. Founding Fathers. Kansas-Nebraska Act (US, 1854). Reconstruction. Republicanism. 1854-65. *910*
—. Frémont, John C. Material culture. Political Campaigns (presidential). Republican Party. 1856. 1860. *632*
—. Hamlin, Hannibal. Republican Party. Vermont. Wide-Awake clubs. 1860. *651*
—. Handwriting. 1826-65. *397*
—. Hatch, Ozias M. Illinois. Knapp, Nathan. Letters. Republican Party. 1859. *710*
—. Herndon, Archer G. Illinois (Springfield). 1835-36. *586*
—. Herndon, William H. 1865-91. *445*
—. Herndon, William H. Illinois. Letters. Oglesby, Richard J. 1865. 1873. *605*
—. Herndon, William H. Letters. Oglesby, Richard J. 1866. *538*
—. Herndon, William H. Mexican War. Political attitudes. 1837-1962. *407*
—. Heroes. Myers, Alonzo (*Tragedy: A View of Life*). 1861-65. 1956. *534*
—. Historiography. Holland, Josiah G. 1866. *510*
—. Historiography. Literature. 1840's-65. 20c. *395*
—. History. National characteristics. 1858-65. *409*
—. Hoblit family. Illinois (Logan County). ca 1840-66. *522*
—. Hohenstein, Anton. Lithographers. Pennsylvania (Philadelphia). 1860's. *846*
—. Hoxie, Vinnie Ream. Sculpture. 1866-81. *433*
—. Humor. 1860-65. *755*
—. Humor. Politics. Prose. 1847-65. *404*
—. Identity. Personality. Rhetoric. 1831-61. *480*
—. Illinois. Indiana. Kentucky. 1814-31. *518*
—. Illinois. Internal improvements. National development. 1830-76. *465*
—. Illinois. Lawyers. 1837-60. *517*
—. Illinois. Letters. Shields, James. 1842. *498*
—. Illinois. Politics. Todd, Robert Smith. 1841-44. *476*
—. Illinois. State Legislatures. Unionism. 1860-61. *584*
—. Illinois (Chicago). Letters. Lithography. Mendel, Edward. Portraits. 1827-84. *707*
—. Illinois (Chicago). Politics. Rivers and Harbors Convention. 1847-82. *437*
—. Illinois (New Salem, Springfield). Indiana. Political Campaigns. 1817-37. *578*
—. Illinois (Sangamon County). Legislation. Musick, Sam. Politics. Smoot, Coleman. 1827-46. *399*

—. Illinois (Springfield). Illinois State Historical Library. Land Tenure. 1837-53. *608*
—. Inaugural addresses. 1865. *898*
—. Indians. Peace. Plains Indians. Southwest. 1863. *871*
—. Judges. Taney, Roger B. (death). 1864. *810*
—. Kennedy, John A. Letters. Lewis, Enoch. Pennsylvania (Philadelphia). Pinkerton, Allen. Travel. 1861-67. *497*
—. Kentucky. 1809-19. *577*
—. Letters. Lincoln, Robert Todd. 1865-1980. *477*
—. Lincoln, Mary Todd. 1846-65. *495*
—. Lincoln, Mary Todd. Spiritualism. 1848-64. *556*
—. Lloyd, H. H. and Company. New York City (Manhattan). Political Campaigns (presidential). Posters. 1860. *644*
—. Lowell, James Russell ("Commemoration Ode"). 1865. *507*
—. Lutheran Church (Evangelical). 1862-63. *816*
—. Marfan Syndrome. 1809-1977. *435*
—. Massachusetts. Political Speeches. Slavery. Taylor, Zachary. Whig Party. 1848. *640*
—. Ohio. Portraits. Prints. 1860-65. *848*
—. Personal narratives. Stanton, Robert Livingston. 1861-64. *751*
—. Personality. Political leadership. 1860-65. *756*
—. Political Conventions. Political Speeches. Republican Party. 1860. *655*
—. Political Factions. Republican Party. Rhode Island. Travel. 1860. *639*
—. Political Leadership. Presidency. 1861. *427*
—. Political Leadership. Shakespearean tragedy. 1861-65. *449*
—. Political Speeches. 1830's-65. *410*
—. Politics. 1832-65. *603*
—. Portraits. 1858-66. *478*
—. Portraits. 1860-1977. *850*
—. Printmakers. 1861-65. *849*
—. Psychohistory. 1840's-65. *547*
—. Reconstruction. Republicans, Radical. 1861-69. *982*
—. Sandburg, Carl. 1809-65. 1926-39. *434*
—. Scholarship. 19c-1978. *546*
—. Science. Social Change. Technology. 1840's-59. *470*
—. Stereoscopes. 1863. *913*
—. Trials. Truett, Henry B. 1838. *493*
—. Vidal, Gore. 1806-63. *419*
Lincoln, Abraham (ancestors). Ireland. Lincoln, Samuel. Lyford, Martha. 1624-49. *490*
Lincoln, Abraham (Cooper Union Address). Political Speeches. Rhetorical Criticism (theory of). 1860. ca 1900-74. *664*
Lincoln, Abraham (death). Poetry. 1865. *443*
Lincoln, Abraham (estate). 1865-82. *591*
Lincoln, Abraham (family). Civil War. Illinois (Charleston). Riots. 1863-64. *769*
—. Hoover, Joseph. Lithographs. Spokny, George. 1861-65. *854*
Lincoln, Abraham (Gettysburg Address). 1863. *925*
—. 1863. *957*
—. Bible. Covenants. Legitimation. 1863. *926*
—. Civil War. Pennsylvania. 1863. *895*
—. Pennsylvania. 1863. 1973. *949*
—. Rhetoric. 1863. *780*
Lincoln, Abraham (life mask). Mills, Clark. 1865. *523*
Lincoln, Abraham (residence). Historic sites. Houses. Illinois (Springfield). Letters. Lincoln, Robert Todd. 1865-1909. *475*
—. Illinois (Springfield). Photographs. Prints. 1860-66. *479*
Lincoln, Abraham (review article). Herndon, William H. Weik, Jesse W. 1850-1920. *592*
—. Nichols, David. Oates, Stephen B. Potter, David. 1831-65. 1970-79. *539*
—. Oates, Stephen B. 1809-65. 1977. *482*
Lincoln and Lincolniana. Abraham Lincoln Library and Museum. Lincoln Memorial University. Tennessee (Harrogate). 1977. *580*
—. Beckwith, Robert Todd Lincoln. Illinois State Historical Library. 1809-65. 1978. *609*
—. Collectors and Collecting. Library of Congress. Stern, Alfred Whital. 1923-61. *565*
—. New England. 19c-1979. *496*
Lincoln Conspiracy (book, film). Assassination. Booth, John Wilkes. Diaries. Stanton, Edwin M. 1865. 1977. *262*
—. Balsinger, David. Sellier, Charles, Jr. Sunn Classics Pictures. 1865. 1970's. *481*
Lincoln Conspiracy (film). Assassination. Civil War. Films. Public Opinion. 1865. 1970's. *432*

Lincoln, Mary Todd. Assassination. District of Columbia. Ford's Theater. Grant, Ulysses S. Lincoln, Abraham. 1865. *572*
—. Attitudes. Domesticity. Stanton, Elizabeth Cady. Stowe, Harriet Beecher. 1830-80. *570*
—. Documents. Historiography. Lincoln, Abraham. Marriage. 1842-65. 1885. 1947-82. *457*
—. Lincoln, Abraham. 1846-65. *495*
—. Lincoln, Abraham. Spiritualism. 1848-64. *556*
—. Neurosis. Reporters and reporting. 1819-82. *505*
Lincoln Memorial. French, Daniel Chester. Sculpture. 1911-26. *551*
Lincoln Memorial University. Abraham Lincoln Library and Museum. Lincoln and Lincolniana. Tennessee (Harrogate). 1977. *580*
—. Fund raising. Howard, Oliver Otis. Twain, Mark. 1901-09. *444*
Lincoln Memorial University (Colonel Harland Sanders Center for Lincoln Studies). 1973. *607*
Lincoln, Robert Todd. Assassination. Lincoln, Abraham. 1864-1947. *418*
—. Barnard, George Grey. Letters. Lincoln, Abraham. Sculpture. 1910-22. *474*
—. Historic sites. Houses. Illinois (Springfield). Letters. Lincoln, Abraham (residence). 1865-1909. *475*
—. Letters. Lincoln, Abraham. 1865-1980. *477*
Lincoln, Samuel. Ireland. Lincoln, Abraham (ancestors). Lyford, Martha. 1624-49. *490*
Link, Arthur S. Anderson, James William. Historiography. Weinstein, Edwin A. Wilson, Woodrow. 1896-1921. *1076*
—. Diplomacy. Wilson, Woodrow (review article). 1913-14. *1514*
—. Foreign Policy. Wilson, Woodrow (review article). 1913-20. 1979. *1471*
—. New Jersey. Princeton University. Wilson, Woodrow (review article). 1896-1902. *1126*
Lippmann, Walter. Frankfurter, Felix. New Deal. Roosevelt, Franklin D. World War II. 1932-45. *1107*
Literature *See also* Authors; Autobiography; Biography; Books; Humor; Journalism; Language; Memoirs; Novels; Poetry; Satire; Travel Accounts.
—. Autobiography. Jefferson, Thomas. 1743-1826. 1830. *219*
—. Historiography. Lincoln, Abraham. 1840's-65. 20c. *395*
—. Jefferson, Thomas (*Notes on the State of Virginia*). Virginia. 1781-89. *286*
Lithographers. Emancipation Proclamation. Lincoln, Abraham. Printers. 1862-65. *852*
—. Hohenstein, Anton. Lincoln, Abraham. Pennsylvania (Philadelphia). 1860's. *846*
Lithographs. Engraving. Lincoln, Abraham. Political Campaigns (presidential). 1860. *645*
—. Hoover, Joseph. Lincoln, Abraham (family). Spokny, George. 1861-65. *854*
Lithography. Illinois (Chicago). Letters. Lincoln, Abraham. Mendel, Edward. Portraits. 1827-84. *707*
Liu Zuochang. China. Historiography (Chinese). Jefferson, Thomas. Virginia, University of. 1770-1826. 1976-81. *272*
—. Jefferson, Thomas. Political Theory. 1776-1820. *391*
Livestock *See also* Cattle Raising; Dairying.
—. Agriculture Department. Benson, Ezra Taft. Cattle raising. Eisenhower, Dwight D. (administration). Prices. 1953-60. *2493*
Living generation (concept). Jefferson, Thomas. Political Theory. 1790's. 1976. *321*
Lloyd, H. H. and Company. Lincoln, Abraham. New York City (Manhattan). Political Campaigns (presidential). Posters. 1860. *644*
Lloyd, William Alvin. Civil War. Lincoln, Abraham. Military Intelligence. 1861-65. *772*
Loans (consortium). China. Foreign Relations. Wilson, Woodrow. 1910-13. *1606*
Lobbying *See also* Citizen Lobbies; Interest Groups; Political Factions.
—. Bureaucracies. Medical care. Pemberton, William E. Poen, Monte M. Truman, Harry S. (administration; review article). 1945-50. *2445*
—. Congress. Foreign Policy. Presidency. 1970's. *3397*
—. Congress. White House Office of Congressional Relations. 1961-63. *2192*
—. Foreign policy. Presidents. Zionism. 1912-73. *84*

M

McCrary, Peyton. Belz, Herman. Lincoln, Abraham. Louisiana. Politics. Reconstruction. Social Organization. 1861-77. *962*

McCumber, Porter J. League of Nations. Letters. North Dakota. Republican Party. Senate. Taft, William H. 1919. *1124*

McDonald, Forrest. Bell, Rudolph M. House of Representatives. Political Parties. Presidency. Washington, George (review article). 1789-1801. 1973-74. *727*

—. Jefferson, Thomas (review article). 1801-09. 1976. *711*

McDonald, James. Jews. Refugees. Roosevelt, Franklin D. (administration). State Department. 1933-40's. *1539*

McDonough, Gordon L. Letters. Marines. Truman, Harry S. 1947-52. *2225*

McFeely, William S. (review article). Grant, Ulysses S. 1830-79. *428*

McGovern, George S. Agnew, Spiro T. Nixon, Richard M. Political speechwriting. Reagan, Ronald. Rhetoric. 1968-70's. *2261*

—. Conservatism. Elections (presidential). Nixon, Richard M. 1972. *2125*

—. Democratic Party. Elections, presidential. 1972. *1974*

—. Democratic Party. Elections (presidential). Foreign policy. 1972. *1866*

—. Democratic Party. Elections (presidential). Voting and voting behavior. Wisconsin. 1972. *1860*

—. Democratic Party. Florida (Miami). Political Campaigns (presidential). Radicals and Radicalism. 1972. *1926*

—. Democratic Party. Political Conventions. Political Reform. 1972. *2031*

—. Eagleton, Thomas F. Interpersonal Relations. Political campaigns (Presidential). Political Surveys. 1972. *2017*

—. Eagleton, Thomas F. Political Campaigns (presidential). Public Opinion. 1972. *1811*

—. Elections (presidential). Language. Nixon, Richard M. Watergate scandal. 1972-73. *2024*

—. Elections (presidential). Nixon, Richard M. 1972. *2014*

—. Elections (presidential). Nixon, Richard M. Political Change. 1972. *1888*

—. LaFollette, Robert Marion. Newspapers. Political Campaigns (presidential). 1924. 1972. *1172*

—. Nixon, Richard M. Political Campaigns (presidential). Religion. Rhetoric. Voting and Voting Behavior. 1972. *1851*

—. Organizational structure. Political campaigns (presidential). 1972. *1941*

—. Political Campaigns (presidential). 1972. *2064*

—. Political Campaigns (presidential). Protest movements. 1972. *2069*

McKelvey, Vincent. Carter, Jimmy (administration). Federal Policy. Natural resources. Oil and Petroleum Products. US Geological Survey. 1978. *2295*

McKinley, William. Alabama (Mobile). Cuba. Economic conditions. Petitions. Spanish-American War. 1897-98. *1005*

—. Arthur, Chester A. Doenecke, Justus D. Garfield, James A. Gould, Lewis L. Presidents (review article). 1880-1901. *736*

—. Assassination. Czolgosz, Leon F. Stockton, Charles G. Surgery. 1901. *392*

—. Bryan, William Jennings. Elections, presidential. Nebraska. 1900. *1142*

—. Bryan, William Jennings. Political Campaigns (presidential). Rhetoric. Voting and Voting Behavior. 1896. *616*

—. Business. Reick, William C. Spanish-American War. Telegrams. Young, John Russell. 1898. *992*

—. Civil Disturbances. Governors. National Guard. Ohio. 1894. *530*

—. Cleveland, Grover. Colorado. Conservation of Natural Resources. Forest reserve controversy. 1890-1900. *888*

—. Counterintelligence. Gage, Lyman. Quebec (Montreal). Spanish-American War. Wilkie, John. 1898. *732*

—. Editorials. Nevada. Newspapers. Spanish-American War. 1896-98. *986*

—. Elections. Ohio. Republican Party. Working class. 1891-93. *598*

—. Executive Power. 1897-1901. *728*

—. Historiography. Political Leadership. Spanish-American War. 1898. 1905-77. *988*

—. Labor disputes. Letters. Murphy, S. W. Railroads and State. West Virginia. 1893. *954*

McMillan, Priscilla Johnson. Assassination. Committee of State Security (KGB). Epstein, Edward J. Kennedy, John F. Oswald, Lee Harvey (review article). 1960-78. *1746*

McNamara, Robert S. Air Forces. Defense Policy. F-111 (aircraft). Navies. Vietnam War. 1960-70. *2675*

—. Armaments. Defense Department. Laird, Melvin. Politics and the Military. 1960-76. *2215*

—. Arms race. Defense Policy. Technology. 1960's. *2282*

—. Bismarck, Otto von. Cuban missile crisis. Diplomacy. Escalation theory. Franco-Prussian War. Kennedy, John F. 1870. 1962. *3072*

—. Civil-Military Relations. Civil-military relations. 1953-64. *2427*

—. Civil-Military Relations. Defense Department. Vietnam War. 1961-68. *2206*

—. Decisionmaking. Defense Department. House of Representatives (Armed Services Committee). Politics and the Military. 1965-68. *3257*

—. Defense Department. Navies. Tonkin Gulf crisis. Vietnam War. 1961-68. *2904*

—. Defense policy. Planning-Programming-Budgeting System. Systems analysis. 1961-68. *2232*

McNary, Charles L. Agricultural Marketing Act (US, 1929). Coolidge, Calvin. Federal Farm Board. Hoover, Herbert C. Prices. Surpluses. 1924-29. *1340*

—. Chamberlain, George E. League of Nations. Oregon (Portland). Wilson, Woodrow. 1919. *1670*

Medals. American Revolution. Purple Heart Medal. Washington, George. 1780-1961. *371*

Medical care. Bureaucracies. Lobbying. Pemberton, William E. Poen, Monte M. Truman, Harry S. (administration; review article). 1945-50. *2445*

—. Federal Government. Poor. Public Health. 1960-77. *2449*

—. Roosevelt, Franklin D. (administration). Works Progress Administration. 1935. 1975. *112*

Medicare. Bureau of Health Insurance. Interest groups. Oversight, congressional. Public Administration. Senate Finance Committee. 1965-78. *3217*

Meese, Edwin. Foreign policy. Haig, Alexander. Reagan, Ronald. Weinberger, Casper. 1981. *3096*

Meeting at Potsdam (film). Films. Potsdam Conference. Truman, Harry S. World War II. 1945. 1970's. *2727*

Mellon, Andrew W. Bureaucracies. Economic Policy. Taxation. Treasury Department. 1918-32. *1390*

—. Coolidge, Calvin. Income tax. Inheritance and Transfer Tax. Republican Party. 1925-28. *1347*

Melville, Herman. Civil War. Poetry. 1861-66. *400*

Memoirs *See also* Autobiography; Diaries; Personal Narratives.

—. Churchill, Winston. Disarmament. Einstein, Albert. Eisenhower, Dwight D. Europe. Khrushchev, Nikita. Moch, Jules. 1932-55. *2226*

—. Diplomacy. Geopolitics. Kissinger, Henry A. (*White House Years*). 1969-77. *3043*

—. Diplomacy. Kissinger, Henry A. (review article). 1969-72. *3020*

—. Diplomacy. Moynihan, Daniel Patrick. UN (review article). Weaver, Suzanne. 1975-78. *2995*

—. Foreign Relations. France. Jaurès, Jean Léon. Marshall, George C. Moch, Jules. 1911-51. *2922*

—. Navies. Zumwalt, Elmo R., Jr. 1970's. *2267*

Memoranda. Diplomacy. Documents. Foreign policy. Kissinger, Henry A. Publicity. 1970's. *2798*

Men. Entrepreneurs. Heroes. Lincoln, Abraham. Pioneers. Social Change. 18c-19c. *558*

Mendel, Edward. Fassett, Samuel M. Illinois (Chicago). Lincoln, Abraham. Photography. Political Campaigns (presidential). Portraits. 1860. *646*

—. Illinois (Chicago). Letters. Lincoln, Abraham. Lithography. Portraits. 1827-84. *707*

Mental Illness. Assassination. Conspiracy. Lincoln, Abraham. Trials. Weichmann, Louis J. 1865. 1895. *484*

—. Health, Education, and Welfare Department. National Institute of Mental Health. President's Commission on Mental Health. 1976-77. *2314*

—. Mitchell, Martha. Nixon, Richard M. (administration). Press. Watergate scandal. 1972-76. *2483*

Mental Retardation Facilities and Community Mental Health Centers Construction Act (US, 1963). Domestic Policy. Kennedy, John F. Politics. Social Security Act (US, 1935; amended, 1963). 1961-63. *2301*

Mercantilism. Adams, John. Europe. Foreign policy. Free trade. 1775-85. *209*

Mercenaries. Military Recruitment. Rhodesia. 1975-78. *2874*

Meredith, Edwin T. Democratic Party. Political Conventions. Vice-presidency. 1924. *1183*

Mergers. Banking. Comptroller of the Currency. Federal Reserve System (Board of Governors). Justice Department. 1950-66. *3266*

Merriam, Frank. Bank of America. California. Elections, gubernatorial. Giannini, Amadeo P. Roosevelt, Franklin D. Sinclair, Upton. ca 1923-34. *1254*

Merrimack (vessel; capture). Civil War. Lincoln, Abraham. Military strategy. Norfolk (battle). Virginia. 1862. *866*

Merry, Henry J. Choper, Jesse H. Federalism (review article). Fisher, Louis. Genovese, Michael A. Jenkins, Iredell. Law. 1978-80. *3221*

Messersmith, George S. Austria (Vienna). Diplomacy. Patronage. Roosevelt, Franklin D. 1932-36. *1474*

Metallism, theory of. Bank of the United States, 2d. Jackson, Andrew. Monetary systems. 1820-37. *885*

Metallurgy *See also* Steel Industry.

—. California (Claremont). Harvey Mudd College (Sprague Memorial Library; Herbert Hoover Collection of Mining and Metallurgy). Hoover, Herbert C. Mines. Rare Books. 1470-1980. *1111*

Methadone programs. Krogh, Egil, Jr. Law enforcement. Nixon, Richard M. Politics. 1968-72. *2339*

Methodist Church. Converts. Illinois (Springfield). Jacquess, James F. Lincoln, Abraham. 1847. *593*

Methodist Episcopal Church, South. Candler, Warren A. Political Campaigns (presidential). Prohibition. Religion. Smith, Al. 1928. *1143*

Methodology *See also* Models; Quantitative Methods; Research.

—. American Historical Association (meeting). Dement'ev, I. P. Historians. Political parties. Roosevelt, Franklin D. Sivachev, N. V. 1981. *1433*

—. Congress. Federal Policy. Presidents. 1976-81. *3431*

—. Creativity. Jefferson, Thomas. Paraphrasing. Political Theory. Psychoanalysis. 1743-1826. 1979. *363*

—. Decisionmaking. Foreign policy. Latin America. 1965-80. *2645*

—. Elections (presidential). 1964. *1876*

—. Elections (presidential). Minnesota. 1928. 1979. *1156*

—. Elections (presidential). Sociological theory. Voting and Voting Behavior. 1975. *1950*

—. Elections (presidential). Voting and Voting Behavior. 1956-72. *2060*

—. Executive Power. Neustadt, Richard E. Political Theory. 1960-77. *3294*

—. Political science. Voting and Voting Behavior. 1952-60. *1841*

Metropolitan Record (newspaper). Catholic Church. Civil War. Copperheads. Editors and Editing. Mullaly, John. New York City. 1861-64. *824*

Metternich. Diplomacy. Kissinger, Henry A. (*Diplomacy of the Restoration*). 18c-20c. *2974*

Mexican Americans. Armies. Burials. Discrimination. Johnson, Lyndon B. Longoria, Felix. Texas (Three Rivers). 1945-49. *1724*

—. Newspapers. Panama Canal. Political Campaigns (presidential). Reagan, Ronald. Treaties. 1976-80. *2053*

Mexican War. Annexation. Editorials. Louisiana. Newspapers. Polk, James K. 1846-48. *990*

—. Antiwar sentiment. Congress. Lincoln, Abraham. Whig Party. 1846-49. *514*

—. Beach, Moses Y. Diplomacy. National Security. Polk, James K. Secret agents. 1846-47. *1006*

—. Biography. Hawthorne, Nathaniel. Pierce, Franklin. Political Campaigns (presidential). 1847. 1852. *702*

—. Black, John. Diplomacy. Peña, Manuel de la. Polk, James K. Slidell, John. Taylor, Zachary. 1845-46. *1004*

—. Calhoun, John C. Congress. Democrats. Polk, James K. Whig Party. 1846-48. *1016*

—. Connor, David. Marcy, William L. Military strategy. Navies. Polk, James K. Scott, Winfield. Vera Cruz (siege). 1847. *1010*

—. Davis, Jefferson. Defense Secretaries. Firearms. Military officers. Political feuds. Scott, Winfield. 1845-57. *757*

—. Diplomacy. Politics. Polk, James K. 1847-48. *993*

—. Economic Policy. Executive Power. Lincoln, Abraham. Political Theory. Polk, James K. 1840's. *515*

—. Herndon, William H. Lincoln, Abraham. Political attitudes. 1837-1962. *407*

—. Historiography. 1846-48. 1960's-79. *973*

Mexican War (causes). California. Diplomacy. Great Britain. Military. Polk, James K. Texas. 1846. *994*

Mexican War (review article). Antiwar sentiment. Expansionism. Pletcher, David M. Polk, James K. Schroeder, John H. 1830's-40's. *983*

Mexico. Anderson, Chandler. Foreign policy. Multinational Corporations. Wilson, Woodrow. 1913-20. *1555*

—. Annexation. Clay, Henry. Elections (presidential). Polk, James K. Texas. 1844. *689*

—. Attitudes. Foreign Relations. State Department (Foreign Service). 1950-79. *3071*

—. Banking. Diplomacy. Hughes, Charles Evans. International Committee of Bankers on Mexico. Lamont-de la Huerta Agreement. 1921-24. *1574*

—. Cabrera, Luis. Carranza, Venustiano. Diplomacy. Revolution. Wilson, Woodrow. 1914-17. *1507*

—. Carranza, Venustiano. Diplomacy. Pershing, John J. Villa, Pancho. Wilson, Woodrow. 1915-17. *1651*

—. Cuba. Foreign Policy. Multinational Corporations. Roosevelt, Theodore. Taft, William H. 1880-1915. *1562*

—. Democracy. Dominican Republic. Ideology. Intervention. 1914-65. *67*

—. Diplomacy. Intervention. Revolution. Scott, Hugh Lenox. Wilson, Woodrow. 1914-17. *1553*

—. Diplomacy. Natural gas. State Department. 1977-80. *2758*

—. Diplomacy. Revolution. 1906-11. *1637*

—. Diplomatic recognition. Fall, Albert B. Wilson, Woodrow (administration). 1920-21. *1671*

—. Documents. Elections (congressional). Foreign Relations. Johnson, Andrew. Romero, Matias. 1866. *1015*

—. Drug Abuse. Foreign Relations. Operation Intercept. 1969. *2678*

—. Foreign policy. Oil Industry and Trade. State Department. 1921-28. *1575*

—. Foreign Policy. Revolution. Wilson, Woodrow. 1913-15. *1509*

—. Foreign Relations. 1973-80. *2639*

—. Foreign relations. Intervention. Pershing, John J. Wilson, Woodrow. 1916. *1664*

Mexico (Ciudad Juárez). Foreign Policy. Taft, William H. 1908-12. *1657*

Mexico (Yucatán). Bryan, William Jennings. International Harvester Company. Intervention. 1913-15. *1508*

Meyer, George von Lengerke. Diplomacy. Germany. Roosevelt, Theodore. Russo-Japanese War. William II. 1902-14. *1680*

Michael, William H. Documents. Foreign relations. Hay, John Milton. Publishers and Publishing. State Department. 1898-1906. *976*

Michigan *See also* North Central States.

—. Appointments to office. Courts. Jackson, Andrew. Territorial government. 1828-32. *834*

—. Breckinridge, John C. Buchanan, James. Democratic Party. Iowa (Pella). Political Campaigns (presidential). Scholte, Henry (Hendrick) P. 1846-56. *706*

—. Delegates. Democratic Party. Political conventions. Political Conventions. 1972. *1985*

—. Democratic Party. Political Reform. Primaries (presidential). 1970-76. *1984*

—. Impeachment. Johnson, Andrew. 1865-68. *870*

Michigan (Mackinac Island). Ford, Gerald R. Travel. 1975. *2465*

Michigan, southern. Johnson, Andrew. Political Speeches. Reconstruction. 1866. *869*

Middle classes. American Revolution. Washington, George. 1732-99. *339*

Middle East. Antitrust. Cold War. Foreign policy. Oil industry and trade. 1950-65. *2815*

—. Antitrust. Foreign policy. Multinational Corporations. Oil Industry and Trade. 1945-61. *2814*

—. Arab-Israeli conflict. Foreign Policy. Kissinger, Henry A. 1969-79. *2584*

—. Arms Trade. Carter, Jimmy. Domestic Policy. Foreign policy. 1976-78. *3109*

—. Begin, Menahem. Camp David Agreement. Carter, Jimmy. Diplomacy. Sadat, Anwar. 1978. *2615*

—. Brzezinski, Zbigniew. Carter, Jimmy (administration). Foreign policy. Vance, Cyrus. 1977-80. *3079*

—. Camp David Agreement. Diplomacy. Young, Andrew. 1975-79. *2722*

—. Camp David Agreement. Foreign Policy. 1977-81. *2567*

—. Carter, Jimmy. Foreign policy. ca 1967-77. *2564*

—. Carter, Jimmy. Foreign Relations. 1977. *3008*

—. Congress. Containment. Dulles, John Foster. Eisenhower Doctrine. 1947-57. *3160*

—. Crisis management. Diplomacy. Kissinger, Henry A. 1973-74. *2981*

—. Defense Department. Foreign Policy. 1965-77. *3012*

—. Diplomacy. Israel. Peace. Rogers, William. 1969-70. *2619*

—. Diplomacy. Kissinger, Henry A. 1973-75. *3058*

—. Diplomacy. Kissinger, Henry A. 1973-76. *3175*

—. Diplomacy. Kissinger, Henry A. USSR. 1975. *2827*

—. Diplomacy. Kissinger, Henry A. War, limited. 1973-74. *2826*

—. Diplomacy. Oil Industry and Trade. ca 1915-77. *3074*

—. Dulles, John Foster. Foreign Policy. 1948-53. *2693*

—. Eisenhower Doctrine. Foreign Policy. Israel. 1957-58. *3161*

—. European Economic Community. Foreign relations. Kissinger, Henry A. NATO. USSR. 1970's. *2970*

—. Ford, Gerald R. (administration). Foreign Policy. Israel. Nixon, Richard M. (administration). 1969-77. *2589*

—. Foreign Policy. 1967-77. *3086*

—. Foreign Policy. Israel. 1974. *2717*

—. Foreign policy. Kissinger, Henry A. 1967-75. *3000*

—. Foreign policy. Nixon, Richard M. (administration). 1969-73. *3029*

—. Foreign Policy. Nixon, Richard M. (administration). 1972-73. *2821*

—. Foreign policy. Palestine. Roosevelt, Franklin D. 1943-45. *1631*

—. Foreign policy. State Department. 1919-45. *1484*

—. Foreign Relations. 1820's-1970's. *14*

—. Foreign Relations. Kissinger, Henry A. October War. 1973. *2856*

—. Foreign Relations. Kissinger, Henry A. Peace. 1975. *2751*

—. Foreign Relations. Kissinger, Henry A. *(White House Years)*. Vietnam War. 1969-73. *2650*

Midwest *See also* Great Plains; North; North Central States.

—. Canada. Politics. Public opinion. Reciprocity. Taft, William H. 1909-11. *1669*

Military *See also* headings beginning with the words military and paramilitary; Air Warfare; Armaments; Armies; Artillery; Civil-Military Relations; Conscription, Military; Defense Policy; Disarmament; Guerrilla Warfare; Navies; Politics and the Military; Psychological Warfare; Veterans; War.

—. Asia. Carter, Jimmy (administration). Foreign Relations. 1976-80. *3156*

—. Assassination. District of Columbia. Heiss, William H., Sr. Lincoln, Abraham. Telegraph. 1865. *499*

—. California. Diplomacy. Great Britain. Mexican War (causes). Polk, James K. Texas. 1846. *994*

—. Carter, Jimmy (administration). Defense spending. Foreign policy. NATO. Politics. 1976. *2625*

—. Civil Disturbances. Executive Power. 1789-1978. *132*

—. Civil-Military Relations. 1945-73. *3321*

—. Congress. Presidency. War Powers Act (US, 1973). 1940-73. *3250*

—. Defense Department. Housing. Integration. Social change. 1967-68. *2503*

—. Diplomacy. Wilson, Woodrow. World War I. 1914-18. *1667*

—. Documents. Eisenhower, Dwight D. (review article). 1945-48. 1978. *1738*

—. Foreign policy. Reagan, Ronald (administration). 1970's-81. *2626*

—. Foreign policy. State Department (Foreign Service). 1776-1976. *117*

—. National Science Foundation. Nixon, Richard M. Scientific Experiments and Research. Technology. 1973. *2426*

—. Public Employees. Strikes. 1970-81. *3322*

—. Washington, George. 1751-77. *244*

Military Aid. Airplanes, Military. Greece. Roosevelt, Franklin D. (administration). World War II. 1940-41. *1618*

—. Alliances. Carter, Jimmy. Korea, South. Taiwan. 1970's. *2694*

—. Arms Trade. Carter, Jimmy (administration). Conventional Arms Transfers Talks. Developing nations. Foreign Policy. USSR. 1977-82. *2607*

—. Economic aid. Nixon, Richard M. (administration). Vietnam War. 1973. *2840*

—. Foreign Assistance Act (US, 1974). Human rights. 1973-82. *2665*

—. Haiti. Slave revolts. Washington, George. 1791-1804. *1003*

Military appointments. Adams, John. Armies. Elections (presidential). Legislation. Politics and the Military. 1798-1800. *743*

Military Bases *See also* names of military bases, e.g. Travis Air Force Base.

—. Defense Department. Democratic Party. Negroes. Politics and the Military. 1962-73. *2379*

Military capability. Budgets. Congress. Defense spending. 1945-78. *3292*

Military discipline. Butler, Thomas. Civil rights. Courts Martial and Courts of Inquiry. Haircuts. Jackson, Andrew. Tennessee. 1801. *472*

Military finance. Carter, Jimmy. Economic development. 1976. *2245*

—. Civil War. Connecticut (New London). Letters. Lincoln, Abraham. Loomis, Francis B. 1864. *796*

—. Civil-Military Relations. Newburgh Conspiracy. Washington, George. 1782-83. *372*

—. Congress. Defense Department. 1974. *2179*

—. Congress. Executive Power. 1973. *3479*

—. Documents. Franklin D. Roosevelt Library. Information Access. Security classification. 1970-75. *1130*

Military General Staff *See also* Joint Chiefs of Staff.

—. Adams, John. American Revolution. Appointments to office. Congress. Washington, George. 1775. *304*

—. Air Warfare. Bombing. Churchill, Winston. Normandy Invasion. Roosevelt, Franklin D. World War II. 1944. *1684*

—. Appointments to office. Eisenhower, Dwight D. Marshall, George C. Normandy Invasion. Roosevelt, Franklin D. World War II. 1942-44. *1534*

—. Buell, Don Carlos. Civil War. Grant, Ulysses S. Lincoln, Abraham. Political Leadership. 1862-98. *811*

—. Carter, William H. Root, Elihu. World War I (antecedents). 1903-16. *1703*

—. Civil War. Grant, Ulysses S. Hampton Roads Peace Conference. Telegraph. 1865. *601*

—. Civil War. Lincoln, Abraham. Political Leadership. 1862-64. *856*

—. Civil War. Military Strategy. 1861-65. *839*

—. Civil War. Politics. 1861-65. *436*

—. Defense Department. Defense Reorganization Act (US, 1958). Military Organization. 1958. *3206*

—. Eisenhower, Dwight D. Europe. World War II. 1942-69. *1744*

Military Government *See also* Military Occupation.

—. Germany. Japan. Libraries, Presidential. Research. 1945-78. *3163*

Military Intelligence. Astor, Vincent. Great Britain. New York. ROOM (group). Roosevelt, Franklin D. Upper Classes. 1933-42. *1525*

—. Black Hawk War. Illinois. Indian Wars. Lincoln, Abraham. Spy Battalion. Wisconsin. 1832. *581*

—. British Security Coordination. Great Britain. Latin America. Office of Coordinator of Commercial and Cultural Relations. Rockefeller, Nelson A. World War II (antecedents). 1940-45. *1586*

—. Civil War. Lincoln, Abraham. Lloyd, William Alvin. 1861-65. *772*

—. Crisis management. Decisionmaking. Defense Department. 1946-75. *3298*

—. Defense Department. VanDeman, Ralph H. 1897-1919. *1704*

—. Eisenhower, Dwight D. World War II. 1941-45. *1710*

—. Federal Policy. Indochina. World War II. 1943-45. *1662*

—. Foreign Relations. Japan. Roosevelt, Franklin D. World War II (antecedents). 1940-41. *1554*

Military medicine. Civil War. Letters. Lincoln, Abraham. Maryland (Baltimore). Wool, John E. 1862. *458*

Military mind (concept). Civil-Military Relations. Eisenhower, Dwight D. Marshall, George C. 1945-61. *2253*

Military Occupation *See also* Military Government; Resistance.

—. Arab-Israeli conflict. Carter, Jimmy. Colonization. New York. Political Campaigns (presidential). UN Security Council Resolution 465. 1978-80. *2600*

—. Civil War. Florida (Amelia Island; Fernandina). Johnson, Andrew. Land Tenure. Property Tax. Unionists. 1860's-90's. *934*

—. Congress. Germany. Harding, Warren G. Wilson, Woodrow. 1919-23. *1544*

—. Economic Policy. Foreign Policy. Japan. 1945-49. *3039*

—. Gilbert, Prentiss B. Japan. Kellogg-Briand Pact. League of Nations. Manchuria. Stimson, Henry L. 1931. *1524*

Military officers. Appointments to office. Civil War. Indian Wars. Lincoln, Abraham. Pope, John. 1861-64. *942*

—. Davis, Jefferson. Defense Secretaries. Firearms. Mexican War. Political feuds. Scott, Winfield. 1845-57. *757*

Military officers, retired. Constitutional Convention. Pennsylvania (Philadelphia). Society of the Cincinnati. Washington, George. 1783-87. *377*

Military Organization *See also* Military General Staff.

—. Armies. Calhoun, John C. 1817-25. *752*

—. Armies. Defense Department. National Security Act (US, 1947). 1947-50. *3297*

—. Betts, Richard K. Defense policy. Ignatius, Paul R. Joint Chiefs of Staff (review article). Steadman, Richard C. 1958-78. *3287*

—. Collins, J. Lawton. 1946. *3465*

—. Dallas, Alexander James. Defense Department. 1815. *763*

—. Defense Department. Defense Reorganization Act (US, 1958). Military General Staff. 1958. *3206*

—. Defense Department. Marines. National Security Act (US, 1947). Navies. 1947-50. *3230*

—. Joint Chiefs of Staff. 1942-82. *3330*

Military Peace Establishment Act (US, 1802). Armies. Jefferson, Thomas. Politics. 1793-1802. *716*

Military records. Dwight D. Eisenhower Library. Kansas (Abilene). Research. World War II. 1916-52. 1977. *1740*

Military Recruitment *See also* Conscription, Military.

—. Bounties. Civil War. Lincoln, Abraham. Staples, John Summerfield. 1864. *947*

—. Mercenaries. Rhodesia. 1975-78. *2874*

Military Reform. British Navy Office. Jones, William. Navy Department. 1813-14. *722*

—. Defense Department. Hastie, William Henry. Racism. World War II. 1940-43. *1378*

Military reorganization. Hopkins, Harry. Marshall, George C. Roosevelt, Franklin D. World War II. 1942-45. *1634*

Military Service. Ability. Attitudes. Economic opportunity. Lincoln, Abraham. ca 1830-65. *408*

—. Attitudes. Civil War. Illinois. Lincoln, Abraham. 1832-65. *416*

—. Grant, Ulysses S. Illinois. 1861. *587*

—. Roosevelt, Theodore. World War I. 1917-19. *1091*

—. Truman, Harry S. 1905-42. *1754*

Military Strategy *See also* Naval Strategy.

—. 1970-80. *2889*

—. Air power. Eisenhower, Dwight D. Truman, Harry S. 1947-55. *2931*

—. Aliano, Richard A. Defense Policy (review article). Eisenhower, Dwight D. (administration). Killian, James R., Jr. Kinnard, Douglas. Kistiakowsky, George B. 1953-61. *2627*

—. American Revolution. Federal Policy. Washington, George. 1770's-90's. *309*

—. American Revolution. Gates, Horatio. Washington, George. 1777-80. *306*

—. American Revolution. Washington, George. 1776-81. *350*

—. Armaments. 1945-78. *2914*

—. Asia. Foreign policy. 1960's-70's. *2651*

—. Asia, Southeast. Foreign Policy. Japan. Pearl Harbor, attack on. Roosevelt, Franklin D. World War II. 1941. *1506*

—. Atomic Bomb. Churchill, Winston. Diplomacy. Great Britain. Normandy invasion. Roosevelt, Franklin D. World War II. 1942-44. *1675*

—. Atomic warfare. Cuban Missile Crisis. Kennedy, John F. Khrushchev, Nikita. 1962. *2596*

—. Atomic Warfare. Decisionmaking. Japan (Hiroshima, Nagasaki). World War II. 1944-45. *1536*

—. Berlin blockade. Elections (presidential). Germany. Truman, Harry S. 1945-48. *2611*

—. Brown, Harold. Carter, Jimmy (administration). Defense Department. Strategic Arms Limitation Talks. 1977. *3105*

—. Cambodia. Civil-Military Relations. Decisionmaking. *Mayaguez* incident. Raids. Sontay raid. Vietnam War. 1970-79. *2817*

—. Carter, Jimmy (administration). Communist Countries. Foreign Policy. Reagan, Ronald (administration). 1980. *3122*

—. Carter, Jimmy (administration). Foreign Policy. Persian Gulf and area. ca 1979-80. *3117*

—. Carter, Jimmy (administration). Nuclear Arms. Presidential Directive No. 59. USSR. 1960-80. *2865*

—. China. Foreign policy. Korean War. 38th Parallel. 1950-52. *2594*

—. Churchill, Winston. Great Britain. Joint Chiefs of Staff. Malta Conference. Roosevelt, Franklin D. World War II. 1945. *1663*

—. Civil War. Civil-Military Relations. Lincoln, Abraham. 1861-65. *945*

—. Civil War. Fort Donelson (battle). Fort Henry (battle). Grant, Ulysses S. Tennessee. 1862. *423*

—. Civil War. Halleck, Henry W. Lincoln, Abraham. 1862-63. *838*

—. Civil War. Historiography. 1861-1979. *953*

—. Civil War. Hitchcock, Ethan Allen. Lincoln, Abraham. Peninsular Campaign. Shenandoah Valley (campaign). Virginia. 1862. *950*

—. Civil War. Lincoln, Abraham. *Merrimack* (vessel; capture). Norfolk (battle). Virginia. 1862. *866*

—. Civil War. Military General Staff. 1861-65. *839*

—. Connor, David. Marcy, William L. Mexican War. Navies. Polk, James K. Scott, Winfield. Vera Cruz (siege). 1847. *1010*

—. Counterforce. Defense Policy. Massive Retaliation. 1952-75. *2553*

—. Defense spending. Eisenhower, Dwight D. 1952-60. *2207*

—. Deterrence. Nuclear Arms. 1966-76. *2757*

—. Deterrence. Nuclear Arms. 1972-74. *3046*

—. Eisenhower, Dwight D. Germany (Berlin). Great Britain. USSR. World War II. 1945. *1756*

—. Eisenhower, Dwight D. Normandy invasion. World War II. 1944. *1711*

—. Europe. Executive Power. Jupiter missiles. NATO. 1957-63. *2877*

—. Federal Government. Nuclear Arms. Public Opinion. Strategic Arms Limitation Talks. 1945-78. *2643*

—. Foreign policy. Geopolitics. Indian Ocean and Area. 1970-79. *2851*

—. Foreign policy. Hoover, Herbert C. Truman, Harry S. (administration). 1950. *1099*

—. Foreign Policy (review article). Nixon, Richard M. 1980. *1712*

—. Hydrogen bomb. Joint Chiefs of Staff. Nuclear Arms. Truman, Harry S. USSR. 1945-50. *3010*

—. ICBM's. Nuclear arms. Schlesinger, James R. Strategic Arms Limitation Talks. 1974. *2897*

—. Ideology. 1981. *2563*

—. Korea, South. 1947-78. *3159*

—. National security. Nuclear Arms. USSR. 1954-74. *2845*

—. Nuclear arms. Schlesinger, James R. 1970's. *3124*

—. Reagan, Ronald (administration). 1981. *2801*

Military supplies. Armies. Business. Johnson, Hugh S. War Industries Board. World War I. 1918. *1395*

Military training. Armies. Democratic Party. Preparedness. South. Wilson, Woodrow. 1915-20. *1452*

Military-industrial complex. Airplane Industry and Trade. Business. Defense policy. Truman, Harry S. 1945-53. *2231*

—. Carter, Jimmy (administration). Foreign policy. 1976-78. *3076*

Millenarianism. Civil religion. Croly, Herbert. Politics. Wilson, Woodrow. 1909-19. *1261*

Miller, John Chester (review article). Jefferson, Thomas. Slavery. 1760's-1826. 1977. *226*

Mills, C. Wright. Business. Cabinet. Elites. 1897-1973. *56*

Mills, Clark. Lincoln, Abraham (life mask). 1865. *523*

Mills, Wilbur. Legislation. Local government. Nixon, Richard M. Revenue sharing. 1958-75. *2450*

Milton, John. Education. Great Britain. Jefferson, Thomas. 17c-19c. *203*

Mines. California (Claremont). Harvey Mudd College (Sprague Memorial Library; Herbert Hoover Collection of Mining and Metallurgy). Hoover, Herbert C. Metallurgy. Rare Books. 1470-1980. *1111*

Ministers. See Clergy.

Minnesota *See also* North Central States.

—. Eisenhower, Dwight D. Political Campaigns (write-in). Primaries (presidential). Republican Party. 1952. *1892*

—. Elections (presidential). Methodology. 1928. 1979. *1156*

—. Mondale, Walter F. Natural resources. Social Change. 1928-77. *1734*

Minor, Wilma Frances. *Atlantic Monthly.* Courtship. Forgeries. Letters. Lincoln, Abraham. Periodicals. Rutledge, Ann. Sedgwick, Ellery. 1928. *450*

Minorities *See also* Discrimination; Ethnic Groups; Nationalism; Population; Racism; Segregation.

—. Delegates. Democratic Party. Political Conventions. 1964-72. *1931*

—. Economic conditions. Labor Department. Office of Contract Compliance. 1960's-72. *2347*

Minorities in Politics. Employment. Negroes. New Deal. Roosevelt, Franklin D. 1930-42. *1429*

Miroff, Bruce. Johnson, Lyndon B. Kearns, Doris. Kennedy, John F. Politics. 1961-69. 1976. *2163*

Miscegenation. Hemings, Sally. Jefferson, Thomas (and descendants). Virginia. ca 1780-1976. *195*

Missions and Missionaries. Agriculture. Federal Programs. Indian-White Relations. Old Northwest. 1789-1820. *818*

—. American Board Commissioners for Foreign Missions. Internal Macedonian Revolutionary Organization. Kidnapping. Macedonia. Roosevelt, Theodore. Stone, Ellen M. Terrorism. 1901-02. *1686*

—. China. Diplomatic recognition. Revolution. Sun Zhongshan. 1911-13. *1610*

—. Diplomacy. Navies. Ottoman Empire. Roosevelt, Theodore. 1903-04. *1566*

Mississippi. Alabama. Dinsmoor, Silas. Indian agents. Jackson, Andrew. Passports. 1811-12. *590*

—. Alabama. Indian-White Relations. Jackson, Andrew. 1789-1817. *448*

—. Civil War. Cotton. Davis, Jefferson. Lincoln, Abraham. Teasdale, Thomas Cox. War Relief. 1865. *795*

—. Elections, presidential. Voting and Voting Behavior. 1948-72. *1803*

—. Federal policy. Negroes. Nixon, Richard M. (administration). Poverty. 1967-73. *2294*

—. Hoover, Herbert C. (administration). Howard, Perry W. Patronage. Political Campaigns (presidential). Political Factions. Race. Republican Party. State Politics. 1928-33. *1310*

—. Hospitals (community). Mound Bayou Community Hospital and Health Center. New federalism. 1968-73. *2390*

—. Political Campaigns (presidential). Republican Party. 1960. *1960*

—. Foreign policy. Kissinger, Henry A. 1968-76. *2733*

—. Foreign policy. Kissinger, Henry A. USSR. 1919-70's. *116*

—. Foreign policy. Kissinger, Henry A. Watergate scandal. 1974-75. *3087*

—. Foreign policy. Middle East. 1969-73. *3029*

—. Foreign Policy. Middle East. 1972-73. *2821*

—. Foreign policy. Peace. 1971-74. *2628*

—. Foreign Policy. Vietnam War. 1968-73. *2620*

—. Foreign policy. Watergate scandal. 1973. *2157*

—. France. Kissinger, Henry A. NATO. 1969-73. *3041*

—. Freedom of speech. Mass media. 1969-73. *2396*

—. Grants. Hispanic Americans. Political Campaigns (presidential). Revenue sharing. 1960-72. *1845*

—. Hoover, Herbert C. Johnson, Lyndon B. Kennedy, John F. Presidency. Public administration. Secrecy. 1929-74. *139*

—. Impeachment. Public opinion. 1974. *2409*

—. Intergovernmental relations. Local government. Roosevelt, Franklin D. (administration). Social problems. State Government. 1933-45. 1969-74. *95*

—. Legislation. Public welfare. 1969-73. *2489*

—. Mass Media. Porter, William E. (review article). Reporters and Reporting. 1969-74. 1976. *2513*

—. Mental Illness. Mitchell, Martha. Press. Watergate scandal. 1972-76. *2483*

—. New Federalism. Professionalism. State Politics. 1969-80. *2495*

—. New Federalism. Social policy. 1969-79. *2482*

—. Newspapers. Political Commentary. USSR. Watergate scandal. 1972-73. *2198*

—. Political Corruption. Public opinion. Watergate scandal. 1972-74. *2342*

—. Political Corruption. Watergate Scandal. 1968-73. *2249*

—. Political Ethics. Watergate scandal. 1972-74. *2319*

—. Political leadership. Public opinion. Social control. Watergate scandal. 1973-74. *3252*

—. Political surveillance. Watergate Scandal. 1969-73. *2309*

—. Politics. Poverty. Public welfare. Social reform. 1969-72. *2382*

—. Politics. South. Watergate Scandal. 1970's. *2492*

—. Presidency. Science Advisory Committee (dismissal). Science and Government. 1970-74. *2297*

—. Wage-price controls. 1970-73. *2292*

—. Wage-price controls. 1971-72. *2412*

Nixon, Richard M. (resignation). Democracy. Watergate Scandal. 1972-74. *3394*

—. Democratic Party. Executive power. Watergate scandal. 1974. *3474*

—. Elections, congressional. Watergate scandal. 1974-75. *2269*

—. Europe. Newspapers. Pardons. Political Commentary. 1974. *2197*

—. Foreign relations. Politics. Watergate scandal. 1974. *2279*

—. Legislative Investigations. Television. Watergate scandal. 1973-74. *2182*

—. Political Systems. 1974. *2252*

Nixon, Richard M. (review article). Abrahamsen, David. Psychohistory. 1913-78. *1758*

—. Brodie, Fawn M. 1920's-70's. *1737*

—. Morality. Political Attitudes. 1979. *1766*

—. Political corruption. White, Theodore H. 1950-72. *2201*

—. Psychohistory. 1913-78. *1747*

Nixon, Richard M. (*Six Crises*). Kennedy, John F. (*Profiles in Courage*). Values. 1955-75. *1751*

Nixon v. Administrator of General Services. Documents. Ownership. 1791-1981. *110*

Nkrumah, Kwame. deGaulle, Charles. Kissinger, Henry A. Nationalism. Nyerere, Julius. Political Leadership. 1940's-70's. *2905*

Nobel Peace Prize. Kissinger, Henry A. 1902-74. *2614*

Nominations for Office *See also* Appointments to Office.

—. Arthur, Chester A. Labor commissioners. Wright, Carroll. 1884-1905. *882*

—. Cabinet. Chase, Salmon P. Civil War (antecedents). Gilmer, John Adams. Lincoln, Abraham. North Carolina. Seward, William H. 1860-61. *800*

—. Chase, Salmon P. Lincoln, Abraham. Supreme Court. Treasury Department. 1848-64. *799*

—. Congress. Senate. Supreme Court. Tyler, John (administration). 1844-45. *944*

—. Defense Department. Democratic Party. Pennsylvania. Porter, James M. Tyler, John. 1824-43. *822*

—. Funston, Richard. "Greatness" (measures). Judges. Lame-duck hypothesis. Presidents. Supreme Court. 1789-1976. *106*

—. New Deal. Political Factions. Roosevelt, Franklin D. Rural Electrification Administration. Williams, Aubrey W. 1945. *1421*

—. Presidents. Supreme Court. 1789-1967. *168*

Non-Intercourse Act (US, 1809). Democratic-Republican Party. Embargoes. Great Britain. Madison, James. 1808-09. *1027*

Nonvoters. Political campaigns (presidential). Voting and Voting Behavior. 1976. *1977*

Norfolk (battle). Civil War. Lincoln, Abraham. *Merrimack* (vessel; capture). Military strategy. Virginia. 1862. *866*

Normandy Invasion. Air Warfare. Bombing. Churchill, Winston. Military General Staff. Roosevelt, Franklin D. World War II. 1944. *1684*

—. Appointments to office. Eisenhower, Dwight D. Marshall, George C. Military General Staff. Roosevelt, Franklin D. World War II. 1942-44. *1534*

—. Atomic Bomb. Churchill, Winston. Diplomacy. Great Britain. Military Strategy. Roosevelt, Franklin D. World War II. 1942-44. *1675*

—. Eisenhower, Dwight D. Military Strategy. World War II. 1944. *1711*

Norodom Sihanouk. Cambodia. Coups d'Etat. Invasions. Nixon, Richard M. (administration). 1970. *2894*

Norris, George W. Congress. Roosevelt, Franklin D. Supreme Court. 1937. *1364*

—. New Deal. Roosevelt, Franklin D. Tennessee Valley Authority. 1933. *1365*

North. Jefferson, Thomas. Political Theory. Republicanism. South. 1785-1826. *342*

North Carolina *See also* Southeastern States.

—. Cabinet. Chase, Salmon P. Civil War (antecedents). Gilmer, John Adams. Lincoln, Abraham. Nominations for office. Seward, William H. 1860-61. *800*

—. Coan, George W., Jr. Hopkins, Harry. Patronage. Works Progress Administration. 1935. *1370*

—. Domestic policy. Political Attitudes. Truman, Harry S. 1944-48. *2366*

—. Political Attitudes. Rural areas. Wallace, George C. 1920's-73. *1894*

North Carolina (Charlotte). Mass media. Political attitudes. Voting and Voting behavior. Watergate scandal. 1972-73. *2274*

North Central States *See also* individual states; Great Plains; Midwest; North; Old Northwest.

—. All-Party Agricultural Committee. Farmers. Great Plains. Political Campaigns (presidential). Roosevelt, Franklin D. 1936. *1201*

North Dakota *See also* Western States.

—. League of Nations. Letters. McCumber, Porter J. Republican Party. Senate. Taft, William H. 1919. *1124*

—. Roosevelt, Theodore. 1884-86. *1117*

North Dakota (Medora). Cattle raising. Great Plains. Remington, Frederic. Roosevelt, Theodore. 1880's. *1073*

Norton, Daniel S. Dixon, James. Doolittle, James R. Impeachment. Johnson, Andrew. Republican Party. 1860-70. *768*

Norway. Diplomacy. Free ports. Roosevelt, Franklin D. USSR. World War II. 1941-43. *1644*

Novels. Cooke, John Esten. Virginia. Washington, George. 1750-1870. *316*

Nuclear accidents. Licensing. Reform. Three Mile Island power plant. 1977-79. *2512*

Nuclear Arms *See also* terms beginning with the word atomic.

—. Acheson, Dean. Baruch, Bernard. Cold War. Diplomacy. Foreign policy. Roosevelt, Franklin D. Stimson, Henry L. Truman, Harry S. USSR. 1942-46. *1489*

—. Carter, Jimmy (administration). Military Strategy. Presidential Directive No. 59. USSR. 1960-80. *2865*

—. Churchill, Winston. Communism. Diaries. Potsdam Conference. Stalin, Joseph. Truman, Harry S. 1945. *2892*

—. Cold War. Decisionmaking. Disarmament. Eisenhower, Dwight D. USSR. 1953-61. *3073*

—. Cold War. Diplomacy. Roosevelt, Franklin D. 1941-45. *1659*

—. Defense Policy. Nixon, Richard M. Strategic Arms Limitation Talks. 1973. *3106*

—. Defense policy. Reagan, Ronald (administration). USSR. 1980-81. *3084*

—. Deterrence. Military Strategy. 1966-76. *2757*

—. Deterrence. Military strategy. 1972-74. *3046*

—. Developing nations. 1979-81. *2747*

—. Federal Government. Military Strategy. Public Opinion. Strategic Arms Limitation Talks. 1945-78. *2643*

—. Foreign Policy. Kissinger, Henry A. Newhouse, John (review article). Strategic Arms Limitation Talks. 1973. *2556*

—. Foreign Relations. Great Britain. Roosevelt, Franklin D. World War II. 1940-45. *1491*

—. Hydrogen bomb. Joint Chiefs of Staff. Military Strategy. Truman, Harry S. USSR. 1945-50. *3010*

—. ICBM's. Military strategy. Schlesinger, James R. Strategic Arms Limitation Talks. 1974. *2897*

—. Military Strategy. National security. USSR. 1954-74. *2845*

—. Military strategy. Schlesinger, James R. 1970's. *3124*

—. Space. Treaties. USSR. 1962-80. *2736*

Nuclear nonproliferation. Armaments. Documents. Federal Policy. 1981. *3172*

—. Carter, Jimmy. Foreign Policy. Political Leadership. 1977-79. *2942*

—. Carter, Jimmy. Foreign Policy. Political Leadership. 1979. *2621*

—. Carter, Jimmy (administration). Foreign Policy. 1977-81. *3069*

—. Foreign Relations. India. 1977-79. *2993*

Nuclear proliferation. Europe. Foreign Relations. 1954-80. *2866*

Nuclear test ban issue. Defense Policy. Dulles, John Foster. Eisenhower, Dwight D. Goodpaster, Andrew. Strauss, Lewis. USSR. 1958. *2696*

Nuclear war. Jet command posts. Nixon, Richard M. Presidency. 1960's-74. *2222*

Nullification *See also* Secession; States' Rights.

—. Augusta Arsenal. Georgia. Jackson, Andrew. Scott, Winfield. South Carolina. 1832. *787*

—. Jackson, Andrew. Republicanism. 1828-33. *878*

Nye Committee. Foreign policy. Isolationism. Johnson, Hiram W. Roosevelt, Franklin D. (administration). ca 1933-34. *1518*

Nyerere, Julius. deGaulle, Charles. Kissinger, Henry A. Nationalism. Nkrumah, Kwame. Political Leadership. 1940's-70's. *2905*

O

Oates, Stephen B. Lincoln, Abraham (review article). 1809-65. 1977. *482*

—. Lincoln, Abraham (review article). Nichols, David. Potter, David. 1831-65. 1970-79. *539*

O'Brien, Mary-Win. Federal regulation. Nixon, Richard M. Occupational Safety and Health Act (US, 1970). Page, Joseph A. 1970-74. *2291*

Observatories (proposed). Architecture. Jefferson, Thomas. 18c. *237*

Occitan language. France (southern). Jefferson, Thomas. Letters. 1787. *326*

Occupational Safety and Health Act (US, 1970). Federal regulation. Nixon, Richard M. O'Brien, Mary-Win. Page, Joseph A. 1970-74. *2291*

October War. Diplomacy. Israel. Kissinger, Henry A. Kosygin, Aleksei. USSR. 1973. *2618*

—. Diplomacy. USSR. 1967-73. *2832*

—. Foreign Relations. Kissinger, Henry A. Middle East. 1973. *2856*

Oder-Neisse Line. Boundaries. Bowman, Isaiah. East Prussia. Germany. Poland. State Department (Advisory Committee on Post-War Foreign Policy). Welles, Sumner. World War II. 1942-45. *1649*

—. Boundaries. Foreign Policy. Poland. Roosevelt, Franklin D. State Department. Truman, Harry S. World War II. 1941-45. *1609*

Office of Contract Compliance. Economic conditions. Labor Department. Minorities. 1960's-72. *2347*

Office of Coordinator of Commercial and Cultural Relations. British Security Coordination. Great Britain. Latin America. Military Intelligence. Rockefeller, Nelson A. World War II (antecedents). 1940-45. *1586*

Office of Economic Opportunity. Public Welfare. War on Poverty. 1974. *2289*

Office of Management and Budget. Archives, National. Diplomacy. Public Records. 1910-82. *136*

—. Budgets. Bureau of the Budget. Executive Branch. ca 1939-70. *3207*

—. Budgets. Congress. Fiscal Policy. Impoundment. Nixon, Richard M. Separation of Powers. 1969-77. *3461*

—. Budgets. Federal Government. 1970's. *3402*

—. Budgets. Intergovernmental Relations. Politics. 1970's. *3275*

—. Bureaucracies. Presidency. 1970-75. *3299*

—. Decisionmaking. Enrolled bills. Legislation. Presidents. 1932-77. *3469*

—. Decisionmaking. Intergovernmental relations. 1921-74. *3212*

—. Enrolled bills. Federal Government. Legislation. Presidents. 1960's-78. *3468*

—. Executive branch. Nixon, Richard M. Reform. 1970's. *2522*

Office of Price Administration. Inflation. O'Mahoney, Joseph C. Politics. Truman, Harry S. Wage-price controls. Wyoming. 1945-47. *2534*

Office of Production Management. Airplane Industry and Trade. Joint Aircraft Committee. National Defense Advisory Commission. Technological change. World War II. 1940-45. *1226*

Office of Strategic Services. Anti-Communist Movements. Diplomacy. Documents. Germany. Papen, Franz von. USSR. World War II. 1942-45. *1599*

—. Cold War. Documents. USSR. World War II. 1945. *3153*

Office of the Coordinator of Inter-American Affairs. Axis Powers. Foreign Policy. Latin America. Rockefeller, Nelson A. Roosevelt, Franklin D. (administration). 1933-42. *1551*

Office of War Information. China. *Keys of the Kingdom* (film). Propaganda. Roosevelt, Franklin D. Stereotypes. World War II. 1940-45. *1495*

—. Italian Americans. Liberalism. Loyalty. Propaganda. 1939-40. *1382*

Ogden, John C. Elections (presidential). Illuminati controversy. Philadelphia *Aurora*. Religious liberty. 1798-1800. *621*

Ogdensburg Agreement. Canada. Defense Policy. Great Britain. Navies. Permanent Joint Board on Defense. Roosevelt, Franklin D. 1940. *1635*

Oglesby, Richard J. Herndon, William H. Illinois. Letters. Lincoln, Abraham. 1865. 1873. *605*

—. Herndon, William H. Letters. Lincoln, Abraham. 1866. *538*

Ohio *See also* North Central States.

—. Art. Hayes, Rutherford B. Rutherford B. Hayes Library. Turner, William E. 1822-93. 1971-76. *596*

—. Chase, Salmon P. Politics. Republican Party. State Government. 1850-73. *617*

—. Civil Disturbances. Governors. McKinley, William. National Guard. 1894. *530*

—. Democratic Party. New Deal. Political Campaigns (presidential). 1936. *1196*

—. Elections. McKinley, William. Republican Party. Working class. 1891-93. *598*

—. Elections (presidential). Political Parties. Voting and Voting Behavior. 1824. *673*

—. Farmers. Labor. Political Campaigns (presidential). 1892-96. *705*

—. Lincoln, Abraham. Portraits. Prints. 1860-65. *848*

Ohio (Cincinnati). Blaine, James G. Hayes, Rutherford B. Political conventions. Republican Party. 1876. *623*

—. Elections (presidential). Women. 1920. *1210*

Ohio (Cleveland). Elections (presidential). Ethnic Groups. Nativism. Republican Party. 1860. *653*

Ohio (Fremont). Barnard, Harry. Hayes, Rutherford B. Hayes, Webb Cook. Psychohistory. Research. 1822-93. 1950's. *396*

—. District of Columbia. Hayes, Rutherford B. Keeler, Lucy Elliott. Personal narratives. Travel. White House. 1881. *867*

—. Hayes, Rutherford B. 1845-49. *501*

Ohio (Fremont; Spiegel Grove). Bly, Nellie (Elizabeth C. Seaman). First Ladies, former. Hayes, Lucy Webb. Keeler, Lucy Elliott. Reporters and Reporting. 1888. *422*

Ohio (Gambier). Finance. Hayes, Rutherford B. Kenyon College. 1838-41. *500*

—. Hayes, Rutherford B. Higher education. Kenyon College. 1838-42. *600*

Ohio (Marion). Adultery. Harding, Warren G. Letters. Phillips, Carrie. 1905-20. 1963-78. *1119*

Ohio Valley. Washington, George. Westward Movement. 1750's-90's. *212*

Oil and Petroleum Products *See also* Oil Industry and Trade.

—. Carter, Jimmy (administration). Federal Policy. McKelvey, Vincent. Natural resources. US Geological Survey. 1978. *2295*

—. Embargoes. Foreign Policy. Japan. Roosevelt, Franklin D. 1941. *1479*

—. Exports. Foreign policy. Hull, Cordell. Japan. Roosevelt, Franklin D. State Department. 1940-41. *1673*

Oil Industry and Trade. American Petroleum Institute. Commerce Department. Ecology. Hoover, Herbert C. Politics. Pollution. 1921-26. *1290*

—. Antitrust. Cold War. Foreign policy. Middle East. 1950-65. *2815*

—. Antitrust. Foreign policy. Middle East. Multinational Corporations. 1945-61. *2814*

—. Blumenthal, Michael. Federal government. Iran. Organization of Petroleum Exporting Countries. Schlesinger, James R. 1979-80. *2825*

—. Carter, Jimmy (administration). Energy. Federal Programs. 1978-80. *2429*

—. Congress. Continental Trading Company. Fall, Albert B. Teapot Dome Scandal. 1921-29. *1308*

—. Congress. Federal Regulation. Ickes, Harold L. Roosevelt, Franklin D. 1933. *1358*

—. Diplomacy. Foreign Investments. Gómez, Juan. Great Britain. Venezuela. 1908-29. *1638*

—. Diplomacy. Middle East. ca 1915-77. *3074*

—. Exports. Great Britain. Japan. Roosevelt, Franklin D. World War II. 1940-41. *1526*

—. Fall, Albert B. Political Corruption. Teapot Dome scandal. Walsh, Thomas J. ca 1920-24. *1441*

—. Federal Energy Administration. Federal Policy. Petitions. 1974-80. *2475*

—. Foreign policy. Great Britain. Private enterprise. State Department. 1918-24. *1563*

—. Foreign policy. Mexico. State Department. 1921-28. *1575*

Oklahoma *See also* Indian Territory.

—. Progressive Party. Roosevelt, Theodore. Statehood. 1900-12. *1437*

Old Northwest *See also* North Central States.

—. Agriculture. Federal Programs. Indian-White Relations. Missions and Missionaries. 1789-1820. *818*

—. Geography. Hutchins, Thomas. Jefferson, Thomas. Letters. Old Southwest. Rivers. 1784. *266*

Old Southwest. Geography. Hutchins, Thomas. Jefferson, Thomas. Letters. Old Northwest. Rivers. 1784. *266*

Olustee (battle). Chase, Salmon P. Civil War. Florida. Lincoln, Abraham. Political Campaigns (presidential). 1864. *891*

O'Mahoney, Joseph C. Inflation. Office of Price Administration. Politics. Truman, Harry S. Wage-price controls. Wyoming. 1945-47. *2534*

Onassis, Jacqueline Kennedy. Conger, Clement E. Decorative Arts. White House. 19c-1980. *2353*

Open Door Policy. Addams, Jane. Foreign policy. Ideology. Wilson, Woodrow. 1900-20. *1623*

Operation Abscam. Congress. Crime and Criminals (white-collar). Federal Bureau of Investigation. 1970-80. *3478*

Operation Cointelpro. Federal Bureau of Investigation. Leftism. Political surveillance. 1956-71. *2461*

Operation Intercept. Drug Abuse. Foreign Relations. Mexico. 1969. *2678*

Order (concept). Conservatism. Law. Lincoln, Abraham. ca 1840-65. *455*

Oregon *See also* Far Western States.

—. Elections. Republican Party. 1980. *1951*

—. Federal regulation. Forests and Forestry. Pinchot, Gifford. Washington. 1902-10. *1297*

Oregon (Portland). Chamberlain, George E. League of Nations. McNary, Charles L. Wilson, Woodrow. 1919. *1670*

Organization of American States. Diplomacy. International Trade. Kissinger, Henry A. Latin America. 1974-75. *2749*

—. Foreign policy. Kissinger, Henry A. Latin America. 1972-74. *2882*

Organization of Petroleum Exporting Countries. Blumenthal, Michael. Federal government. Iran. Oil Industry and Trade. Schlesinger, James R. 1979-80. *2825*

Organizational structure. McGovern, George S. Political campaigns (presidential). 1972. *1941*

Organizational Theory *See also* Public Administration.

—. Congress. Presidency. 1905-37. *1699*

Osgood, Robert E. *(Ideals and Self-Interest in America's Foreign Relations)*. Foreign policy. Myths and Symbols. Roosevelt, Theodore. Wilson, Woodrow. 1900-20. *1515*

Oswald, Lee Harvey. Central Intelligence Agency. Cubans. Federal Bureau of Investigation. Louisiana (New Orleans). 1963. *1757*

—. Committee of State Security (KGB). Communism. Espionage (review article). Hiss, Alger. USSR. 1938-78. *1759*

Oswald, Lee Harvey (review article). Assassination. Committee of State Security (KGB). Epstein, Edward J. Kennedy, John F. McMillan, Priscilla Johnson. 1960-78. *1746*

Oswego Emergency Refugee Shelter. Bergson, Peter. Jews. Morgenthau, Henry, Jr. New York. Refugees. Roosevelt, Franklin D. (administration). War Refugee Board. World War II. 1943-45. *1594*

Otis, James, Jr. Adams, John. American Revolution (antecedents). Hutchinson, Thomas. Massachusetts. Patriotism. 1761-76. *343*

Ottoman Empire *See also* constituent parts, e.g. Palestine, Armenia, etc.; Bulgaria; Cyprus; Turkey.

—. Arabs. Self-determination. Wilson, Woodrow. 1915-20. *1648*

—. Diplomacy. Missions and Missionaries. Navies. Roosevelt, Theodore. 1903-04. *1566*

Oversight, congressional. Arms Trade. Congress. State Department. Taiwan Relations Act (US, 1979). 1979-81. *2864*

—. Bureau of Health Insurance. Interest groups. Medicare. Public Administration. Senate Finance Committee. 1965-78. *3217*

—. Congress. Executive Branch. Intergovernmental relations. 1952-80. *3288*

Owen, Mary. Attitudes. Business. Interpersonal Relations. Lincoln, Abraham. Todd, Mary. 1831-42. *576*

Ownership. Documents. Federal Policy. Libraries, Presidential. 1971. *3331*

—. Documents. Judicial Review. Nixon, Richard M. Presidential Recordings and Materials Preservation Act (US, 1974). 1974-75. *3323*

—. Documents. Law Reform. Nixon, Richard M. Public records. 1974-75. *3423*

—. Documents. Law Reform. Presidents. Public officials. 1782-1975. *3232*

—. Documents. *Nixon* v. *Administrator of General Services*. 1791-1981. *110*

—. Documents. Presidents. 1789-1974. *108*

P

Pacific area. Federal Policy. Naval strategy. Roosevelt, Franklin D. 1933-39. *1239*

—. Great Britain. Japan. Naval Strategy. World War II. 1941-45. *1486*

—. Joint Chiefs of Staff. MacArthur, Douglas. Nimitz, Chester W. Roosevelt, Franklin D. World War II. 1941-42. *1513*

Pacific Dependencies (US). Atlantic Dependencies (US). Imperialism. Roosevelt, Franklin D. 1910-45. *1689*

Pacific Northwest. Adams, John Quincy. Diplomacy. Monroe Doctrine. Monroe, James. Russia. 1812-23. *1000*

—. Bonneville Power Administration. Electric utilities. New Deal. Public Utilities. 1937-42. *1302*

Pacifism *See also* Peace Movements.

—. Jefferson, Thomas. Social Conditions. War. 1783-1812. *362*

Page, Joseph A. Federal regulation. Nixon, Richard M. O'Brien, Mary-Win. Occupational Safety and Health Act (US, 1970). 1970-74. *2291*

Page, Thomas Nelson. Appointments to office. Diplomacy. Progressivism. Wilson, Woodrow (administration). 1913. *1537*

Paint. Mount Vernon. Preservation. Virginia. Washington, George. 1790's-1982. *370*

Painting. Carpenter, Francis Bicknell. Emancipation Proclamation. Herline, Edward. Lincoln, Abraham. Prints. Ritchie, Alexander Hay. 1864-66. *851*

—. Kempton, Greta. Truman, Harry S. (family). 1946-68. *1752*

Pakistan See also Bangladesh; India.

—. Bangladesh. Foreign Policy. India. Kissinger, Henry A. Nixon, Richard M. (administration). 1971-76. *3127*

—. Foreign Relations. India. 1947-73. *2681*

Palestine See also Israel; Jordan.

—. Anglo-American Committee. Bevin, Ernest. Foreign Relations. Great Britain. Truman, Harry S. (administration). 1945-47. *2662*

—. Appointments to office. Diplomats. Grant, Ulysses S. Jews. Romania. Sneersohn, Hayyim Zevi. 1869-70. *1026*

—. Arab states. Kennedy, John F. Kennedy, Robert F. Letters. 1939. 1948. *1767*

—. Carter, Jimmy (administration). Foreign policy. Institute for Palestine Studies. Israel. 1980. *2577*

—. Cold War. Foreign Policy. USSR. 1947-48. *2907*

—. Diplomacy. Foreign Policy. Henderson, Loy. Jews. Zionism. 1945-48. *2986*

—. Diplomacy. Historiography. Politics. Truman, Harry S. (administration). 1945-48. *2663*

—. Documents. Foreign Policy. State Department. Truman, Harry S. (administration). 1948. *2664*

—. Embargoes. Foreign Policy. Truman, Harry S. Weapons. 1947-48. *3067*

—. Foreign Policy. Great Britain. Truman, Harry S. 1945-48. *2778*

—. Foreign policy. Jews. Partition. Political power. Truman, Harry S. (administration). 1947-48. *2731*

—. Foreign Policy. Middle East. Roosevelt, Franklin D. 1943-45. *1631*

—. Foreign policy. Partition. Truman, Harry S. Zionism. 1945-49. *3038*

—. Foreign policy. Truman, Harry S. Truman, Margaret. 1945-47. *2551*

—. Foreign Relations. Great Britain. Immigration, illegal. Jews. 1945-47. *2777*

—. Foreign Relations. Truman, Harry S. 1945. *2963*

Palestine Liberation Organization. Foreign policy. Israel. Reagan, Ronald. UN. 1975-81. *3057*

Palestinians. Camp David Agreement. Carter, Jimmy. Diplomacy. Egypt. Israel (occupied territories). 1967-79. *2916*

Palm Beach *Times*. Graves, John Temple, II. Liberalism. New Deal. South. 1933-40. *1255*

Palmer, A. Mitchell. Anti-Communist Movements. Deportation. Immigrants. Justice Department. Labor Department. Post, Louis F. Wilson, William B. 1919-20. *1307*

Pan American Conference, 5th. Bryan, William Jennings. Chile (Santiago). Wilson, Woodrow. World War I. 1914. *1678*

Panama See also Central America; Latin America.

—. Colombia. Foreign Policy. Senate. Thomson-Urrutia Treaty. Wilson, Woodrow. 1913-22. *1587*

—. Congress. Foreign policy. Politics. Strategic Arms Limitation Talks. Treaties. 1977-78. *2692*

—. Intervention. Navies. Revolution. Roosevelt, Theodore. 1903. *1621*

Panama Canal. Carter, Jimmy. Foreign Policy. Political Speeches. Rhetoric. Television. 1977-78. *3090*

—. Congress. Democratic Party. South. Tolls controversy. Wilson, Woodrow. 1901-13. *1497*

—. Mexican Americans. Newspapers. Political Campaigns (presidential). Reagan, Ronald. Treaties. 1976-80. *2053*

Pan-Americanism. Anti-Imperialism. Blaine, James G. Latin America. Martí, José. ca 1870-1902. *1021*

—. Blaine, James G. Garfield, James A. Latin America. 1881. *1008*

—. Diplomacy. Latin America. Regionalism. Wilson, Woodrow. 1914-17. *1543*

Papen, Franz von. Anti-Communist Movements. Diplomacy. Documents. Germany. Office of Strategic Services. USSR. World War II. 1942-45. *1599*

Paraphrasing. Creativity. Jefferson, Thomas. Methodology. Political Theory. Psychoanalysis. 1743-1826. 1979. *363*

Pardons. Amnesty. Ford, Gerald R. Justice. Nixon, Richard M. Vietnam War. 1974. *2317*

—. Assassination. Florida (Dry Tortugas Island, Fort Jefferson). Johnson, Andrew. Lincoln, Abraham. Mudd, Samuel A. 1865-96. *537*

—. *Burdick* v. *United States* (US, 1915). Constitutional Amendments (5th). New York *Tribune*. Supreme Court. Wilson, Woodrow. 1913-15. *1262*

—. Carter, Jimmy. Conscription, Military. Decisionmaking. Deserters. Draft dodgers. Vietnam War. 1964-77. *2499*

—. Europe. Newspapers. Nixon, Richard M. (resignation). Political Commentary. 1974. *2197*

—. Ford, Gerald R. Nixon, Richard M. Political Speeches. 1974. *2404*

Paris Peace Conference. Boundaries. Foreign Relations. Italy. League of Nations. Wilson, Woodrow (administration). 1919-22. *1577*

—. China. Foreign Policy. League of Nations. Treaties. Wilson, Woodrow. 1919. *1505*

—. Clemenceau, Georges. Germany. Wilson, Woodrow. 1919. *1478*

—. Communism. Hungary. Kun, Bela. Political Attitudes. Wilson, Woodrow. 1919. *1660*

—. Diplomacy. Great Britain. League of Nations Commission. Wilson, Woodrow. 1918-20. *1639*

—. Diplomacy (review article). Wilson, Woodrow. World War I. 1918-19. *1615*

—. Foreign Policy. Historiography. House, Edward Mandell. Wilson, Woodrow. 1919. *1532*

—. Idealism. League of Nations. Morality. Wilson, Woodrow. 1918-19. *1612*

—. Italy. Peace. Socialist Party. Wilson, Woodrow. World War I. 1916-19. *1665*

—. Wilson, Woodrow. World Court. 1900-20. *1632*

Paris Peace Settlements See also individual treaties by name; World War I.

—. Austria. Germans, Austrian. Self-determination. Wilson, Woodrow. 1918-19. *1619*

—. Diplomacy. Economic Conditions. Great Britain. Wilson, Woodrow (administration). 1919-20. *1480*

—. Floto, Inga. Foreign Policy. House, Edward Mandell. Wilson, Woodrow (review article). 1919. *1592*

—. Foreign Policy. Greece. 1919. *1613*

—. Foreign Relations. Historiography. Wilson, Woodrow (administration). 1918-81. *1482*

Parker, Alton Brooks. Democratic Party. Political Campaigns (presidential). 1904. *1191*

Parliaments. Presidency. 1974. *3419*

Parman, Donald L. Federal Policy. Indians (review article). New Deal. Philp, Kenneth R. Taylor, Graham D. 1934-74. *1329*

Parties, Political. See Political Parties.

Partisanship. Elections, presidential. 1972. 1976. *2001*

—. Elections, presidential. Electoral college. Political Indicators. 1932-76. *2011*

—. Elections, presidential. Political parties. Voting and voting behavior. 1952-72. *2100*

—. House of Representatives (Judiciary Committee). Ideology. Impeachment. Nixon, Richard M. 1974. *2351*

Partition. Churchill, Winston. Germany. Potsdam Conference. Roosevelt, Franklin D. Stettinius, Edward Reilley. Truman, Harry S. Yalta Conference. 1945. *2755*

—. Diplomacy. Europe. Roosevelt, Franklin D. 1939-45. *1475*

—. Foreign policy. Jews. Palestine. Political power. Truman, Harry S. (administration). 1947-48. *2731*

—. Foreign Policy. Korea. World War II. 1945. *2901*

—. Foreign policy. Palestine. Truman, Harry S. Zionism. 1945-49. *3038*

Passports. Alabama. Dinsmoor, Silas. Indian agents. Jackson, Andrew. Mississippi. 1811-12. *590*

Patent Office. Agricultural policy. 1836-62. *1039*

Patriotism See also Loyalty.

—. Adams, John. American Revolution (antecedents). Hutchinson, Thomas. Massachusetts. Otis, James, Jr. 1761-76. *343*

—. American Revolution. Elections (presidential). Lafayette, Marquis de. 1824. *641*

Patronage. Alabama (Dothan). Civil Service. Clayton, Henry D. Postal Service. Taft, William H. Wilson, Woodrow (administration). 1900-13. *1415*

—. Austria (Vienna). Diplomacy. Messersmith, George S. Roosevelt, Franklin D. 1932-36. *1474*

—. Buchanan, James. Democratic Party. 1857-61. *892*

—. Buchanan, James. Douglas, Stephen A. Political campaigns (Presidential). 1852-60. *893*

—. Byrd, Harry F. Democratic Party. Elections (congressional). Glass, Carter. Politics. Roosevelt, Franklin D. Senate. Virginia. 1938. *1324*

—. Byrd, Harry F. Democratic Party. Senate. Virginia. 1935-39. *1350*

—. Civil War. Consular Service. Espionage. Great Britain. Lincoln, Abraham. Shipping. 1861-63. *1012*

—. Civil War. Consular Service. Espionage. Ireland. Lincoln, Abraham. Scotland. 1861-63. *1013*

—. Coan, George W., Jr. Hopkins, Harry. North Carolina. Works Progress Administration. 1935. *1370*

—. Elections (presidential). Florida. Hayes, Rutherford B. State politics. Wallace, Lew. 1876-78. *698*

—. Florida. Hoover, Herbert C. (administration). Republican Party. State Politics. 1928-33. *1312*

—. Georgia. Hoover, Herbert C. (administration). Political factions. Race Relations. Republican Party. 1928-32. *1311*

—. Historiography. Jackson, Andrew. 1828-36. 20c. *901*

—. Hoover, Herbert C. (administration). Howard, Perry W. Mississippi. Political Campaigns (presidential). Political Factions. Race. Republican Party. State Politics. 1928-33. *1310*

—. Kissinger, Henry A. Planning. Policymaking. State Department. 1969-74. *2885*

Payne-Aldrich Tariff. Political leadership. Republican Party. Sectionalism. Taft, William H. Tariff. Western States. 1909. *1316*

Peabody, Elizabeth. Civil War. District of Columbia. Letters. Lincoln, Abraham. Mann, Horace, Jr. 1865. *952*

Peace See also Arbitration, International; Disarmament; International Security; Pacifism.

—. Allies. Roosevelt, Franklin D. Surrender, Unconditional. World War II. ca 1942-45. *1483*

—. Benedict XV, Pope. Diplomacy. Wilson, Woodrow. World War I. 1914-17. *1693*

—. Cease-fire agreements. Diplomacy. Eisenhower, Dwight D. Korean War. UN. 1952-53. *1774*

—. Civil War (antecedents). Diplomacy. House of Representatives (Committee of Thirty-three). Lincoln, Abraham. 1860. *841*

—. Diplomacy. Israel. Middle East. Rogers, William. 1969-70. *2619*

—. Eisenhower, Dwight D., administration. Prosperity. Revisionism. 1953-61. *2166*

—. Emancipation Proclamation. Lincoln, Abraham. New Jersey. Public opinion. State legislatures. 1864. *829*

—. Foreign policy. Nixon, Richard M. (administration). 1971-74. *2628*

—. Foreign Relations. Kissinger, Henry A. 1973. *2765*

—. Foreign Relations. Kissinger, Henry A. Middle East. 1975. *2751*

—. Hoover, Herbert C. Intervention. Isolationism. Totalitarianism. USSR. World War II. 1939-41. *1061*

—. Indians. Lincoln, Abraham. Plains Indians. Southwest. 1863. *871*

—. Italy. Paris Peace Conference. Socialist Party. Wilson, Woodrow. World War I. 1916-19. *1665*

—. Japan. Potsdam Conference. Roosevelt, Franklin D. Surrender, unconditional. World War II. 1945. *1676*

Peace Corps. ACTION (agency). Brown, Sam. 1977-78. *2234*

Peace missions. Canada. Confederate States of America. Davis, Jefferson. Lincoln, Abraham. Virginia (Richmond). 1864. *789*

Peace Movements See also Antiwar Sentiment.

—. Civil rights movement. Credibility gap. Johnson, Lyndon B. Political Culture. 1960's. *2278*

—. Delegates. Democratic Party. Minorities. 1964-72. *1931*

—. Delegates. Democratic Party. Political Reform. South. 1972. *1847*

—. Delegates. Democratic Party. Politicians. 1968-74. *1915*

—. Delegates. Ford, Gerald R. Reagan, Ronald. Republican Party. 1976. *2009*

—. Delegates. Lincoln, Abraham. New Hampshire. Republican Party. 1860. *657*

—. Delegates. Political Participation. Republican Party. 1972. *2043*

—. Delegates. Primaries, presidential. 1968-76. *1982*

—. Delegates. Republican Party. Roosevelt, Theodore. Taft, William H. Texas. 1912. *1150*

—. Democratic Party. Douglas, Stephen A. Letters. South Carolina (Charleston). Stephens, Alexander H. Vallandigham, Clement L. 1860. *634*

—. Democratic Party. Elections (presidential). 1968. 1972. *2078*

—. Democratic Party. Garner, John Nance. Rayburn, Sam. Roosevelt, Franklin D. 1932. *1182*

—. Democratic Party. Historiography. Illinois (Chicago). Mass media. Public opinion. Violence. 1968. *1921*

—. Democratic Party. Illinois (Chicago). Law Enforcement. Political Protest. Students. 1856-1978. *1973*

—. Democratic Party. Kennedy, John F. Roosevelt, Eleanor. 1958-61. *1877*

—. Democratic Party. McAdoo, William G. Murray, Robert K. (review article). New York City. Smith, Al. 1924. *1180*

—. Democratic Party. McGovern, George S. Political Reform. 1972. *2031*

—. Democratic Party. Meredith, Edwin T. Vice-presidency. 1924. *1183*

—. Democratic Party. Missouri. Pendergast, Thomas J. Roosevelt, Franklin D. State Politics. 1932. *1193*

—. Democratic Party. Political Reform. 1972. *1826*

—. Democratic Party. Political Reform. 1972. *1883*

—. Democratic Party. Sex Discrimination. Women. 1972. *1990*

—. Evans, Daniel S. Political speeches. Republican Party. Rhetoric. 1968. *2075*

—. Fairbanks, Charles W. Gould, Lewis L. Hanna, Marcus. Personal narratives. Republican Party. Roosevelt, Theodore. 1900. *636*

—. Ford, Gerald R. Reagan, Ronald. Republican Party. 1976. *1794*

—. Harding, Warren G. Lenroot, Irvine L. Republican Party. Vice-Presidency. Wisconsin. 1920. *1171*

—. Historiography. McClure, Alexander K. Pennsylvania. Republican Party. Seward, William H. 1860. 1892. *626*

—. Ideology. Political Factions. Political Parties. Voting and Voting Behavior. 1940-76. *1836*

—. Ideology. Pressure groups. Public opinion. Roll-call voting. 1944-76. *2013*

—. Legitimation. Rites and Ceremonies. 1976. *1868*

—. Lincoln, Abraham. Political Speeches. Republican Party. 1860. *655*

—. Missouri (St. Louis). 1876-1917. *149*

—. Negroes. 1868-1972. *169*

—. Political campaigns (presidential). Reform. 1972-74. *2019*

—. Political campaigns (Presidential). Television. 1972. *2018*

—. Political commentary. Reporters and reporting. Rogers, Will. 1924-32. *1209*

—. Presidents. 1848-1980. *32*

—. Republican Party. Senate. Smoot, Reed. Utah. 1920. *1204*

—. Republican Party (platform). 1976. *2109*

—. Roll-call voting. 1940-76. *1835*

—. Television. 1948. *1840*

—. Television. 1952-80. *1867*

Political Corruption *See also* Elections; Lobbying; Political Reform.

—. Agnew, Spiro T. Ethics. Morality. Watergate Scandal. 1960's-70's. *2490*

—. Antitrust. Attorneys General. Daugherty, Harry M. Federal Government. Pennsylvania (Philadelphia). United Gas Improvement Company. 1914-24. *1309*

—. Authoritarianism. Democracy. Elections (presidential). Nixon, Richard M. Watergate scandal. 1968-72. *1850*

—. Belknap, William W. Impeachment. War Secretaries. 1869-76. *921*

—. Campaign Finance. Watergate scandal. 1972-73. *2035*

—. Capitalism. Corporations. Nixon, Richard M. 1968-73. *2303*

—. Constitution. Presidents. Watergate Scandal. 1787-1973. *3233*

—. Democratic Party. Elections, presidential. Illinois (Cook County). 1960. *1940*

—. Elections. Political parties. 19c-1970's. *19*

—. Elections (presidential). Louisiana. Potter, Clarkson N. 1876-78. *700*

—. Executive power. Kennedy, John F. (administration). Nixon, Richard M. (administration). Watergate Scandal. 1940's-73. *3259*

—. Executive Power. Watergate scandal. 1974. *3357*

—. Fall, Albert B. Interior Department. New Mexico. Teapot Dome Scandal. 1910-30. *1463*

—. Fall, Albert B. Oil Industry and Trade. Teapot Dome scandal. Walsh, Thomas J. ca 1920-24. *1441*

—. Federal Government. Watergate Scandal. 1974. *2549*

—. Nixon, Richard M. Watergate scandal. 1972. *2433*

—. Nixon, Richard M., administration. Public opinion. Watergate scandal. 1972-74. *2342*

—. Nixon, Richard M. (administration). Watergate Scandal. 1968-73. *2249*

—. Nixon, Richard M. (review article). White, Theodore H. 1950-72. *2201*

—. Presidency. Public administration. 1927-79. *57*

—. Public Opinion. Watergate scandal. 1970-73. *2432*

Political Crimes *See also* Impeachment; Political Corruption; Terrorism.

—. Government. Watergate Scandal. 1900-74. *3414*

—. Nixon, Richard M. Values. Watergate Scandal. 1972-74. *2506*

—. Public opinion. Watergate Scandal. 1972-73. *2470*

Political Culture. Civil rights movement. Credibility gap. Johnson, Lyndon B. Peace movements. 1960's. *2278*

—. Congress. Truman, Harry S. 1947-48. *2305*

—. Watergate Scandal. 1945-74. *2536*

Political Economy *See also* Economics.

—. Historians. Libraries, presidential. Presidents. 1938-76. *30*

Political Ethics *See also* Citizenship; Morality; Political Corruption; Political Crimes.

—. Executive Behavior. Federal government. Public administration. Richardson, Elliot. 1969-73. *2464*

—. Executive power. Watergate Scandal. 1972. *2370*

—. Kress, Paul. Liberalism. Presidency. Watergate scandal. 18c. 20c. *3346*

—. Language. Watergate Scandal. 1972-73. *2354*

—. Mass Media. Political campaigns (presidential). Public Opinion. 1976. *1880*

—. Nixon, Richard M. (administration). Watergate scandal. 1972-74. *2319*

—. Watergate Scandal. 1973. *2349*

Political Factions *See also* Interest Groups; Lobbying.

—. Adams, John. Federalist Party. Hamilton, Alexander. Jefferson, Thomas. Washington, George. 1775-90's. *720*

—. Byrnes, James F. Democratic Party. Political conventions. Roosevelt, Franklin D. Truman, Harry S. Vice-Presidency. Wallace, Henry A. 1944. *1181*

—. Cabinet. Calhoun, John C. Eaton Affair. Jackson, Andrew. VanBuren, Martin. 1828-31. *876*

—. Congress. Jefferson, Thomas. 1775. *366*

—. Democratic-Republican Party. Madison, James. War of 1812. 1800-15. *1025*

—. Economic policy. Europe, Western. Foreign policy. Nixon, Richard M. 1971. *2221*

—. Georgia. Hoover, Herbert C. (administration). Patronage. Race Relations. Republican Party. 1928-32. *1311*

—. Grant, Ulysses S. Republican Party. 1880. *656*

—. Hoover, Herbert C. (administration). Howard, Perry W. Mississippi. Patronage. Political Campaigns (presidential). Race. Republican Party. State Politics. 1928-33. *1310*

—. Ideology. Political Conventions. Political Parties. Voting and Voting Behavior. 1940-76. *1836*

—. Lincoln, Abraham. Republican Party. Rhode Island. Travel. 1860. *639*

—. New Deal. Nominations for Office. Roosevelt, Franklin D. Rural Electrification Administration. Williams, Aubrey W. 1945. *1421*

—. Political Campaigns (presidential). 1964-76. *2041*

Political feuds. Davis, Jefferson. Defense Secretaries. Firearms. Mexican War. Military officers. Scott, Winfield. 1845-57. *757*

Political friendship. Harrison, Byron Patton (Pat). Roosevelt, Franklin D. Senate. 1920-41. *1443*

Political Indicators. Elections, presidential. Electoral college. Partisanship. 1932-76. *2011*

Political Integration. Europe. Kennedy, John F. 1962-65. *2813*

Political issues. Debates. Political Campaigns (presidential). Television. 1960. 1976. *1995*

—. Elections, presidential. 1952-76. *2027*

—. Elections, presidential. 1956-76. *1823*

—. Elections (presidential). Mass media. Political Participation. 1976. *2095*

—. Elections (presidential). Political parties. 1964-75. *1929*

—. Federal Policy. Political parties. Voting and Voting Behavior. 1960-72. *1964*

—. Political campaigns, presidential. Voting and Voting Behavior. 1972. *1947*

—. Voting and Voting Behavior. 1972. *1979*

—. Voting and Voting Behavior. 1972. *1998*

Political Leadership. Adams, John Quincy. House of Representatives. Presidency. 1783-1848. *486*

—. American Dream. Boritt, G. S. (review article). Economic Theory. Lincoln, Abraham. Social mobility. 1840's-64. 1978. *452*

—. Appointments to office. Cabinet. Carter, Jimmy. Nixon, Richard M. 1970's. *2241*

—. Barnard, Chester *(Functions of the Executive)*. Models. Presidency. 1968-78. *3464*

—. Bell, Terrel Howard. Education Department. Hatch, Orrin Grant. Mormons. Reagan, Ronald (administration). Utah. 1980-82. *2325*

—. Bibliographies. Hoover, Herbert C. Isolationism. Political Attitudes. 1929-41. *1070*

—. Bowles, Chester. Decisionmaking. Kennedy, John F. (administration). Personality. 1953-78. *3154*

—. Brown, Harry J. Civil War. Garfield, James A. (review article). Leech, Margaret. Peskin, Allan. 1850-81. 1978. *503*

—. Buchanan, James. Historiography. Kansas. Lecompton Constitution. Slavery. Suffrage. 1857. 20c. *894*

—. Buell, Don Carlos. Civil War. Grant, Ulysses S. Lincoln, Abraham. Military General Staff. 1862-98. *811*

—. Carter, Jimmy. 1976-77. *2230*

—. Carter, Jimmy. Cromwell, Oliver. Great Britain. Religion. Rickover, Hyman. Roosevelt, Theodore. 20c. *73*

—. Carter, Jimmy. Eisenhower, Dwight D. Presidency. Roosevelt, Franklin D. Truman, Harry S. 1933-80. *115*

—. Carter, Jimmy. Elections, presidential. Faith. 1976. *1938*

—. Carter, Jimmy. Foreign Policy. Nuclear nonproliferation. 1977-79. *2942*

—. Carter, Jimmy. Foreign Policy. Nuclear nonproliferation. 1979. *2621*

—. Carter, Jimmy. Psychology. 1976. *2171*

—. Carter, Jimmy (administration). 1976-81. *2145*

—. Castro, Fidel. Cuba. Documents. Foreign Relations. Nixon, Richard M. 1959. *3028*

—. Charisma. Public Opinion. Roosevelt, Theodore. ca 1898-1919. *1221*

—. Children. France. Great Britain. Public opinion. 1969-70. *3280*

—. Children. Presidency. Public opinion. 1960's-70's. *3450*

—. Churchill, Winston. Foreign policy. Roosevelt, Franklin D. Stalin, Joseph. World War II. 1939-45. *1698*

—. Civil religion. Inaugural addresses. Presidency. 1789-1980. *50*

—. Civil War. Davis, Jefferson. Lincoln, Abraham. 1861-65. *863*

—. Civil War. Lincoln, Abraham. Military General Staff. 1862-64. *856*

—. *Foreign Relations of the United States.* State Department. 1861-1981. *3066*
Pueblo incident. Cambodia. Decisionmaking. Korea, North. *Mayaguez* incident. 1969-75. *2773*
Puerto Rico. Autonomy. Congress. Politics. Roosevelt, Franklin D. (administration). World War II. 1940-45. *1258*
—. Colleges and Universities. Coolidge, Calvin. Education, Finance. Harris, J. Will. Hoover, Herbert C. Inter-American University. Personal narratives. ca 1920-30. *1327*
—. Federal Policy. Self-government. Truman, Harry S. (administration). 1945-47. *2306*
Pufendorf, Samuel von *(On the Law of Nature and Nations).* Adams, John. American Revolution. Founding Fathers. Madison, James. Sweden. Washington, George. 1632-1776. *315*
Puritans *See also* Calvinism; Congregationalism.
—. Calamity, use of. Civil War. Lincoln, Abraham. Rhetoric. 1650-1870. *782*
—. Civil War. Lincoln, Abraham. Self-government. 1630-1865. *717*
Purple Heart Medal. American Revolution. Medals. Washington, George. 1780-1961. *371*
Putnam, James. Adams, John. Lawyers. Massachusetts (Braintree, Worcester). Teaching. 1755-58. *252*

Q

Qavām-al-Saltana. Containment. Foreign Policy. Iran. Tūdeh Party. USSR. 1943-53. *2984*
Quantitative Methods *See also* Methodology.
—. Democratic Party. New Deal. Pennsylvania (Pittsburgh). Political Theory. Voting and Voting Behavior. Wisconsin. 1912-40. *1185*
—. Foreign relations analysis. International relations (discipline). State Department (Intelligence and Research Bureau). 1974. *3384*
—. Political Science. Presidency. 1789-1980. *48*
—. Roosevelt, Franklin D. Supreme Court. 1937. 1970's. *1301*
—. Roosevelt, Franklin D. Supreme Court. 1937. 1970's. *1388*
Quebec (Montreal). Counterintelligence. Gage, Lyman. McKinley, William. Spanish-American War. Wilkie, John. 1898. *732*
Quotas. Construction. Employment. Ickes, Harold L. Negroes. Public Works Administration. 1933-40. *1355*

R

Rabb, Maxwell M. Eisenhower, Dwight D. (administration). Faulkner, William. Foreign Relations. National Commission for UNESCO. People-to-People Program (Writers' Group). State Department. 1954-61. *2148*
Race. Attitudes. Colonization. Douglas, Stephen A. Lincoln, Abraham. Negroes. 1858-65. *819*
—. Hoover, Herbert C. (administration). Howard, Perry W. Mississippi. Patronage. Political Campaigns (presidential). Political Factions. Republican Party. State Politics. 1928-33. *1310*
Race Relations *See also* Discrimination; Emigration; Immigration; Indian-White Relations; Negroes.
—. Air Forces. Hastie, William Henry. World War II. 1940-43. *1377*
—. Arkansas. Republican Party. Roosevelt, Theodore. 1901-12. *1306*
—. Attitudes. Lincoln, Abraham. 1830's-65. *454*
—. Carter, Jimmy (administration). Foreign policy. Human rights. South Africa. 1973-78. *2668*
—. Carter, Jimmy (administration). Foreign Policy. Reagan, Ronald (administration). South Africa. 1981-82. *2700*
—. Daniels, Jonathan W. Negroes. Roosevelt, Franklin D. (administration). World War II. 1943-45. *1291*
—. Democratic Party. Filibusters. House of Representatives. Reconstruction. Roll-call voting. 1876-77. *615*
—. Du Bois, W. E. B. (essay). Wilson, Woodrow. 1911-18. *1313*
—. Enlightenment. Ethics. Jefferson, Thomas. 18c. *236*
—. Georgia. Hoover, Herbert C. (administration). Patronage. Political factions. Republican Party. 1928-32. *1311*

—. Political Systems. Wallace, George C. 1960's-70's. *2052*
—. South. Voting and Voting Behavior. Wallace, George C. 1968. *2123*
Racism. Agriculture Department. Butz, Earl (resignation). Public Opinion. 1970's. *2403*
—. American Revolution. Economic conditions. Historiography. Jefferson, Thomas. Negroes. Washington, George. 1776-1976. *202*
—. Anglo-Saxonism. Boer War. Hay, John Milton. Public Opinion. Rhetoric. Roosevelt, Theodore. 1899-1900. *969*
—. Appointments to office. District of Columbia. Judges. Negroes. Terrell, Robert H. Wilson, Woodrow. 1914. *1384*
—. Armies. Defense Department. Hastie, William Henry. Negroes. Stimson, Henry L. World War II. 1940-43. *1376*
—. California. Elections (presidential). Republican Party. Slavery. 1860. *695*
—. Chinese. Elections (presidential). Garfield, James A. Letters. Morey, H. L. 1875-85. *643*
—. Civil rights. Federal Policy. Interest Groups. Populism. Private enterprise. Wallace, George C. 1960's. *2107*
—. Defense Department. Hastie, William Henry. Military reform. World War II. 1940-43. *1378*
—. Elections (presidential). Hoover, Herbert C. Smith, Al. Tennessee, west. 1928. *1174*
—. Elections (presidential). Populism. Texas. Wallace, George C. 1968. *2124*
—. Hoover, Herbert C. Negroes. Social change. ca 1910-33. *1075*
Radicals and Radicalism *See also* Leftism; Political Reform; Revolution; Social Reform.
—. Adams, John. Conservatism. DeLolme, Jean Louis. Political theory. Turgot, Anne Robert. 1760-1800. *179*
—. Civil Rights movement. Johnson, Lyndon B. Long, Huey P. South. 1920-70. *1779*
—. Democratic Party. Florida (Miami). McGovern, George S. Political Campaigns (presidential). 1972. *1926*
—. Federal Bureau of Investigation. Hoover, J. Edgar. Political Surveillance. 1919-21. *1707*
Radio. Carter, Boake. New Deal. Political commentary. Roosevelt, Franklin D. 1935-38. *1280*
—. Commerce Department. Federal Regulation. Hoover, Herbert C. Licensing. 1918-22. *1416*
—. Coolidge, Calvin. Politics. 1924-28. *1144*
—. Elections (presidential). Reporters and Reporting. Television. 1952-76. *1809*
—. Harding, Warren G. 1920-23. *1455*
—. Newspapers. Political Campaigns (presidential). Political participation. Public Opinion. Television. 1972. *1918*
Radio Act (US, 1927). Commerce Department. Federal Regulation. Hoover, Herbert C. 1921-28. *1305*
Raids. Cambodia. Civil-Military Relations. Decisionmaking. *Mayaguez* incident. Military Strategy. Sontay raid. Vietnam War. 1970-79. *2817*
Railroads. Hayes, Rutherford B. (and family). Travel. Western states. 1880. *807*
Railroads and State *See also* Railroads.
—. Labor disputes. Letters. McKinley, William. Murphy, S. W. West Virginia. 1893. *954*
Raisuli, Ahmed ibn-Muhammed. Foreign Relations. Hay, John Milton. Kidnapping. Morocco. Perdicaris, Ion. Roosevelt, Theodore. 1904. *1528*
Ramirez, Pedro. Argentina. Foreign Policy. Hull, Cordell. 1943. *1685*
Ranney, Austin. Abramson, Paul R. Aldrich, John H. Elections (review article). Pomper, Gerald. Rohde, David W. 1980. *1975*
—. Diamond, Martin. Elections. Kirkpatrick, Jeane J. Political parties. Political Reform (review article). 1950-80. *1843*
Rapid response capability. Foreign policy. Intervention. 1954-73. *2557*
Rare Books. California (Claremont). Harvey Mudd College (Sprague Memorial Library; Herbert Hoover Collection of Mining and Metallurgy). Hoover, Herbert C. Metallurgy. Mines. 1470-1980. *1111*
Raskob, John J. Constitutional Amendments (18th and 21st). Democratic Party. Political Conventions. Prohibition repeal. Roosevelt, Franklin D. 1928-33. *1166*
Rationalism *See also* Enlightenment.
—. Calhoun, John C. Federalism. Jefferson, Thomas. Natural Rights. Taylor, John (of Caroline). 1770's-1832. *264*

Rationality. Downs, Anthony *(An Economic Theory of Democracy).* Political Theory. Voting and Voting Behavior. 1972. *1996*
—. Voting and Voting Behavior. Wyoming. 1970's. *1797*
Rayburn, Sam. Democratic Party. Garner, John Nance. Political Conventions. Roosevelt, Franklin D. 1932. *1182*
—. Executive Power. House of Representatives. Logan-Walter Bill. Sumners, Hatton. Texas. Veto. 1939. *1404*
Reading interests. Wilson, Woodrow. 1870's-1924. 1975. *1081*
Reagan, Nancy. Adams, Henry Brooks *(Democracy).* Presidential transitions. 1880-1981. *1773*
Reagan, Ronald. Agnew, Spiro T. McGovern, George S. Nixon, Richard M. Political speechwriting. Rhetoric. 1968-70's. *2261*
—. Appalachia. Conservatism. Elections (presidential). Voting and Voting Behavior. 1980. *2088*
—. Appointments to office. Brown, Edmund G. Brown, Jerry. California. Governors. Judges. Political attitudes. 1959-79. *1721*
—. Bryan, William Jennings. Elections (presidential). Political parties. Revivals. Social Change. 1730-1980. *175*
—. Budgets. New Deal. 1930-81. *2502*
—. Bush, George. Debates. Primaries (presidential). Republican Party. Texas (Houston). 1980. *1908*
—. California. Public welfare. State Government. Statistics. 1971-73. *1745*
—. Capitalism. Economic Policy. Elections, presidential. 1970-80. *1822*
—. Carter, Jimmy. Elections (presidential). 1980. *1833*
—. Carter, Jimmy. Elections (presidential). Ford, Gerald R. Republican Party. 1976. *2085*
—. Carter, Jimmy. Ford, Gerald R. Political Conventions. Primaries (presidential). 1974-76. *1927*
—. Carter, Jimmy. Kennedy, Edward M. Political Campaigns. 1980. *2081*
—. Carter, Jimmy. Political Campaigns (presidential). 1972-80. *2029*
—. Christian Right. Conservatism. Elections (presidential). Indiana (Muncie). 1980. *1937*
—. Conservatism. Elections. New Right. Religion. 1978-81. *1865*
—. Conservatism. Ford, Gerald R. Nixon, Richard M. 1969-80. *2477*
—. Delegates. Ford, Gerald R. Political conventions. Republican Party. 1976. *2009*
—. Economic policy. 1981. *2340*
—. Eisenhower, Dwight D. Elections (presidential). Europe. Foreign Policy. Public Opinion. 1952-80. *1786*
—. Elections. 1980. *1911*
—. Federalism. Political Campaigns (presidential). Political Speeches. 1980-81. *2114*
—. Ford, Gerald R. Nixon, Richard M. Political Participation. Republican Party. 1972-76. *2044*
—. Ford, Gerald R. Political conventions. Republican Party. 1976. *1794*
—. Foreign policy. 1980-81. *2604*
—. Foreign policy. 1981. *2780*
—. Foreign policy. Haig, Alexander. Meese, Edwin. Weinberger, Casper. 1981. *3096*
—. Foreign policy. Israel. Palestine Liberation Organization. UN. 1975-81. *3057*
—. Foreign policy. USSR. 1981-82. *3094*
—. Heroes. Presidents. Romanticism. 1960's-81. *2180*
—. Hostages. Inaugurations. Iran. Reporters and Reporting. Television. 1980-81. *2147*
—. Inaugural Addresses. Political Speeches. 1967-81. *2158*
—. Mass media. Political Campaigns (presidential). Primaries, presidential. 1824-1980. *1953*
—. Mexican Americans. Newspapers. Panama Canal. Political Campaigns (presidential). Treaties. 1976-80. *2053*
—. Political attitudes. 1981. *2196*
—. Political campaigns, presidential. Reporters and Reporting. 1976-80. *1787*
—. Politics. States' rights. 1981. *2326*
—. Republican Party. 1930-81. *1725*
Reagan, Ronald (administration). Anti-Communist Movements. Asia. Foreign Policy. Taiwan. 1981. *2799*
—. Armaments. Defense Policy. USSR. 1981. *2624*
—. Arms Control and Disarmament Agency. Foreign policy. 1960-81. *2657*

—. Carter, Jimmy. Kennedy, John F. Political Campaigns (presidential). 1960-76. *2119*

—. Carter, Jimmy. Political Campaigns (presidential). 1976. *1761*

—. Christianity. Jefferson, Thomas. 1784-1800. *373*

—. Conservatism. Elections. New Right. Reagan, Ronald. 1978-81. *1865*

—. Eisenhower, Dwight D. Presidency. 1952-61. *2177*

—. Elections (presidential). Ethnic groups. Roosevelt, Franklin D. Social Classes. 1940. *1162*

—. Elections (presidential). Ethnicity. Kennedy, John F. Pennsylvania (Schuylkill County). Voting and Voting Behavior. 1960. *1896*

—. Inaugural addresses. Presidents. 1789-1941. *90*

—. Indians. Madison, James. Political Theory. 1751-1836. *385*

—. Jefferson, Thomas. 1800-25. *270*

—. McGovern, George S. Nixon, Richard M. Political Campaigns (presidential). Rhetoric. Voting and Voting Behavior. 1972. *1851*

Religious Liberty *See also* Church and State; Persecution.

—. Communism. Foreign policy. Human Rights. Presidents. USSR. 20c. *151*

—. Elections (presidential). Illuminati controversy. Ogden, John C. Philadelphia *Aurora*. 1798-1800. *621*

—. Madison, James. Political Theory. 1780-1830. *369*

Religious Persecution. *See* Persecution.

Religious Revivals. *See* Revivals.

Remington, Frederic. Cattle raising. Great Plains. North Dakota (Medora). Roosevelt, Theodore. 1880's. *1073*

Remini, Robert V. (review article). Expansionism. Jackson, Andrew. 1767-1821. 1977. *540*

—. Florida. Indian-White Relations. Jackson, Andrew. Removals, forced. Tennessee. 1780's-1821. *560*

Removals, forced. Adams, John Quincy. Assimilation. Attitudes. Indians. 1802-41. *526*

—. Cherokee Indians. Ethnicity. Indians. Jefferson, Thomas. Tennessee. Willstown, Treaties of. 1794-1817. *890*

—. Cherokee Indians. Indian-White Relations. Jackson, Andrew. 1835. *965*

—. Cherokee Indians. Indian-White Relations. Jefferson, Thomas. Southeastern States. Speeches, Addresses, etc. 1809. *966*

—. Florida. Indian-White Relations. Jackson, Andrew. Remini, Robert V. (review article). Tennessee. 1780's-1821. *560*

—. Indians. Jackson, Andrew. Liberalism. Rogin, Michael Paul (review article). 19c. 1975. *453*

Reparations. Agent General. Appointments to Office. Coolidge, Calvin (administration). Diplomacy. Finance. Germany. 1923-24. *1572*

—. Morgan Guaranty Trust Company. State Department. World War I. 1930's. *1527*

Reparations (review article). Diplomacy. Germany. Wilson, Woodrow. World War I. 1918-30. 1975. *1523*

Reporters and Reporting *See also* Editors and Editing; Journalism; Press.

—. Advertising. Children. Political Campaigns (presidential). Television. 1976. *1795*

—. Advertising. Political Campaigns (presidential). Television. 1972. *1919*

—. Agnew, Spiro T. (resignation). Political Speeches. Rhetoric. 1973. *2243*

—. Associated Press. Columbia Broadcasting System. Political Campaigns (presidential). Television. 1972. *1980*

—. Associated Press. First ladies. Hickok, Lorena A. Roosevelt, Eleanor. 1932-68. *1056*

—. Bias. Great Britain. Nixon, Richard M. *Times* (London). Watergate scandal. 1973-74. *2511*

—. Bly, Nellie (Elizabeth C. Seaman). First Ladies, former. Hayes, Lucy Webb. Keeler, Lucy Elliott. Ohio (Fremont; Spiegel Grove). 1888. *422*

—. Boston *Pilot*. Catholic Church. Civil War. Irish Americans. Lincoln, Abraham. Massachusetts. 1840-72. *955*

—. Brooks, Noah. Civil War. District of Columbia. Lincoln, Abraham. 1862-1903. *741*

—. Canal Zone. Roosevelt, Theodore. Speeches, Addresses, etc. 1911. *1677*

—. Carter, Jimmy. Elections (Presidential). Income tax. Political campaigns (presidential). Reform. 1976. *2026*

—. Carter, Jimmy. Ford, Gerald R. Political Campaigns (presidential). Television. 1976. *2089*

—. Eagleton, Thomas F. Politics and Media. Television. 1972. *1855*

—. Elections (presidential). Political Surveys. 1976. *1817*

—. Elections (presidential). Radio. Television. 1952-76. *1809*

—. Elections, presidential. Voting and voting behavior. 1968. *1887*

—. Harding, Warren G. (death). 1923. *1135*

—. Hoover, Herbert C. Press. 1929-32. *1411*

—. Hostages. Inaugurations. Iran. Reagan, Ronald. Television. 1980-81. *2147*

—. Johnson, Lyndon B. (administration). 1963-68. *2265*

—. Lincoln, Mary Todd. Neurosis. 1819-82. *505*

—. Mass Media. Nixon, Richard M. (administration). Porter, William E. (review article). 1969-74. 1976. *2513*

—. McCarthy, Eugene J. Periodicals. Political Campaigns (presidential). Third Parties. 1976. *1854*

—. Political campaigns (presidential). 1960-76. *1968*

—. Political Campaigns (presidential). 1976. *1796*

—. Political Campaigns (presidential). 1976. *2067*

—. Political Campaigns (presidential). Presidents. *Time* (periodical). 1966-77. *3261*

—. Political campaigns, presidential. Reagan, Ronald. 1976-80. *1787*

—. Political Campaigns (presidential). Television. Voting and Voting Behavior. 1976. *1999*

—. Political commentary. Political conventions. Rogers, Will. 1924-32. *1209*

Republican Party. Abolition Movement. Constitutional Union Party. Political Campaigns (presidential). 1860. *661*

—. Appointments to office. Clarkson, James S. New York City. Political Campaigns (presidential). Progressivism. Roosevelt, Theodore. 1901-04. *1276*

—. Arizona. Elections. 1980. *1997*

—. Arkansas. Race Relations. Roosevelt, Theodore. 1901-12. *1306*

—. *Ashtabula Sentinel*. Hayes, Rutherford B. Howells, William Cooper. Newspapers. Political Campaigns (presidential). 1875-76. *669*

—. Assimilation. Elections (presidential). Ethnicity. Greek Americans. 1968. *1925*

—. Attitudes. Impeachment. Johnson, Andrew. Letters. Ross, Edmund. 1867-68. *778*

—. Barnes, William, Jr. Bossism. Lawsuits. New York. Roosevelt, Theodore. 1915. *1062*

—. Behavior. 1976. *2087*

—. Benson, Lee. Historiography. Massachusetts. Mugwumps. Voting and Voting Behavior. 1880's. *613*

—. Blaine, James G. Hayes, Rutherford B. Ohio (Cincinnati). Political conventions. 1876. *623*

—. Bristow, Benjamin Helm. Hayes, Rutherford B. Kentucky. Political Campaigns (presidential). 1876. *703*

—. Brooks, Preston S. Civil War (antecedents). Congress. Sumner, Charles. Violence. 1856. *635*

—. Bryan, William Jennings. Newspapers. Red River of the North (valley). 1890-96. *627*

—. Bush, George. Debates. Primaries (presidential). Reagan, Ronald. Texas (Houston). 1980. *1908*

—. California. Elections (presidential). Racism. Slavery. 1860. *695*

—. California. Elections, presidential. Slavery. 1856. *694*

—. California (San Francisco). Hughes, Charles Evans. Labor. Political Campaigns (presidential). 1916. *1167*

—. Carter, Jimmy. Elections (presidential). Ford, Gerald R. Reagan, Ronald. 1976. *2085*

—. Caucuses. Delegates. Political conventions. 1976. *2032*

—. Chase, Salmon P. Ohio. Politics. State Government. 1850-73. *617*

—. Civil War. Elections (presidential). Negroes. Political Participation. 1864. *666*

—. Colorado. Johnson, Andrew. Newspapers. Reconstruction. 1865-67. *779*

—. Compromise of 1877. Democratic Party. Elections (presidential). Historiography. Reconstruction. Woodward, C. Vann. 1876-77. *708*

—. Conkling, Roscoe. Elections (presidential). New York (Oneida County). 1884. *668*

—. Conservatism. Eisenhower, Dwight D. (administration). Federal Regulation. 1953-61. *2515*

—. Conservatism. Goldwater, Barry M. Political Campaigns (presidential). 1952-64. *1793*

—. Coolidge, Calvin. Income tax. Inheritance and Transfer Tax. Mellon, Andrew W. 1925-28. *1347*

—. Crawford, Coe Isaac. Progressivism. Roosevelt, Theodore. South Dakota. State Politics. 1912-14. *1192*

—. Davis, James John. Labor Secretaries. Pennsylvania. Political Leadership. 1873-1947. *1466*

—. Dawes, Charles Gates. Democratic Party. LaFollette, Robert Marion. Political Campaigns (presidential). South Dakota (Sioux Falls). 1924. *1208*

—. Dawes, Henry L. Johnson, Andrew. Politics. Reconstruction. 1865-75. *770*

—. Dayton, William L. Elections (presidential). Frémont, John C. Political conventions. 1854-56. *662*

—. Debates. Democratic Party. Political Attitudes. Political campaigns, presidential. 1960-76. *1992*

—. Delegates. Ford, Gerald R. Political conventions. Reagan, Ronald. 1976. *2009*

—. Delegates. Lincoln, Abraham. New Hampshire. Political conventions. 1860. *657*

—. Delegates. Political Conventions. Political Participation. 1972. *2043*

—. Delegates. Political conventions. Roosevelt, Theodore. Taft, William H. Texas. 1912. *1150*

—. Democratic Party. Elections. Political Systems. 1976. *2113*

—. Democratic Party. Political Campaigns (presidential). 1976. *2126*

—. Depressions. Hoover, Herbert C. New Deal. Political Commentary. 1933-35. *1059*

—. DePriest, Oscar. Hoover, Herbert C. (administration). House of Representatives. Negroes. Politics. 1929. *1288*

—. Dixon, James. Doolittle, James R. Impeachment. Johnson, Andrew. Norton, Daniel S. 1860-70. *768*

—. Eisenhower, Dwight D. Minnesota. Political Campaigns (write-in). Primaries (presidential). 1952. *1892*

—. Elections. Idaho. 1980. *1989*

—. Elections. McKinley, William. Ohio. Working class. 1891-93. *598*

—. Elections. Montana. 1980. *1898*

—. Elections. New Mexico. 1980. *1831*

—. Elections. Oregon. 1980. *1951*

—. Elections. South. 1972-76. *2033*

—. Elections. Utah. 1980. *1923*

—. Elections. Washington. 1980. *1897*

—. Elections, congressional. New Deal. Roosevelt, Franklin D. 1937-38. *1402*

—. Elections, congressional. Nixon, Richard M. 1972. *1933*

—. Elections (presidential). Ethnic Groups. Nativism. Ohio (Cleveland). 1860. *653*

—. Elections (presidential). Foraker, Joseph B. Negroes. Taft, William H. 1908. *1157*

—. Elections (presidential). Ford, Gerald R. Vice-presidency. 1973-76. *2187*

—. Elections (presidential). Hoover, Herbert C. Progressivism. Senate. 1930-32. *1149*

—. Elections (presidential). New York. Prohibition Party. 1884. *671*

—. Emancipation Proclamation. Lincoln, Abraham. 1863-64. *874*

—. Evans, Daniel S. Political conventions. Political speeches. Rhetoric. 1968. *2075*

—. Fairbanks, Charles W. Gould, Lewis L. Hanna, Marcus. Personal narratives. Political Conventions. Roosevelt, Theodore. 1900. *636*

—. Florida. Hoover, Herbert C. (administration). Patronage. State Politics. 1928-33. *1312*

—. Ford, Gerald R. Nixon, Richard M. Political Participation. Reagan, Ronald. 1972-76. *2044*

—. Ford, Gerald R. Political conventions. Reagan, Ronald. 1976. *1794*

—. Foreign policy. Harding, Warren G. Johnson, Hiram W. Politics. 1920-22. *1519*

—. Frémont, John C. Lincoln, Abraham. Material culture. Political Campaigns (presidential). 1856. 1860. *632*

—. Garfield, James A. National characteristics. Reform. 1881. *919*

—. Garfield, James A. Negroes. South. Suffrage. 1881. *918*

—. Georgia. Harding, Warren G. Johnson, Henry Lincoln. Philips, John Louis. 1920-24. *1330*

—. Georgia. Hoover, Herbert C. (administration). Patronage. Political factions. Race Relations. 1928-32. *1311*

—. Grant, Ulysses S. Political factions. 1880. *656*

—. Hamlin, Hannibal. Lincoln, Abraham. Vermont. Wide-Awake clubs. 1860. *651*

—. Harding, Warren G. Lenroot, Irvine L. Political conventions. Vice-Presidency. Wisconsin. 1920. *1171*

—. Hatch, Ozias M. Illinois. Knapp, Nathan. Letters. Lincoln, Abraham. 1859. *710*

—. Hayes, Rutherford B. Howells, William Dean. Political Speeches. Twain, Mark. 1876. *612*

—. Historiography. McClure, Alexander K. Pennsylvania. Political Conventions. Seward, William H. 1860. 1892. *626*

—. Hoover, Herbert C. Political leadership. 1920-32. *1393*

—. Hoover, Herbert C. (administration). Howard, Perry W. Mississippi. Patronage. Political Campaigns (presidential). Political Factions. Race. State Politics. 1928-33. *1310*

—. Hoover, Herbert C. (administration). Negroes. 1928-32. *1303*

—. LaFollette, Philip F. MacArthur, Douglas. Political Campaigns. Primaries (presidential). Wisconsin. 1948. *2058*

—. LaFollette, Robert Marion. Political campaigns (presidential). Roosevelt, Theodore. 1910-12. *1170*

—. League of Nations. Letters. McCumber, Porter J. North Dakota. Senate. Taft, William H. 1919. *1124*

—. Lincoln, Abraham. Political Conventions. Political Speeches. 1860. *655*

—. Lincoln, Abraham. Political Factions. Rhode Island. Travel. 1860. *639*

—. Mail, constituency. New Hampshire. Personal narratives. Political Commentary. Public Opinion. Squires, J. Duane. 1952-56. *2080*

—. Mississippi. Political Campaigns (presidential). 1960. *1960*

—. Nixon, Richard M. Watergate scandal. 1973-74. *2443*

—. Payne-Aldrich Tariff. Political leadership. Sectionalism. Taft, William H. Tariff. Western States. 1909. *1316*

—. Political conventions. Senate. Smoot, Reed. Utah. 1920. *1204*

—. Primaries (presidential). South Dakota. Taft, Robert A. 1952. *1893*

—. Reagan, Ronald. 1930-81. *1725*

Republican Party (conference; proposed). Hoover, Herbert C. Landon, Alfred M. Political Leadership. 1937-38. *1058*

Republican Party (platform). Political Conventions. 1976. *2109*

Republicanism. Adair, Douglass. *Federalist* No. 10. Hume, David. Madison, James. Political Theory. Wills, Garry. 1788. *238*

—. Articles of Confederation. Farming. Jefferson, Thomas. Land Tenure. Property rights. 1776-87. *278*

—. Congress. Legaré, Hugh Swinton. Presidency. Tyler, John (administration). 1841-43. *791*

—. Constitutional Convention. Electoral College. Founding Fathers. 1787-1970's. *1040*

—. Diplomacy. Etiquette. Jefferson, Thomas. 1800-04. *981*

—. District of Columbia. Gales, Joseph, Jr. Jackson, Andrew. *National Intelligencer.* Political Commentary. Political parties. Seaton, William Winston. 1827-35. *887*

—. Elections (presidential). Jefferson, Thomas. Virginia. 1796. *676*

—. Federal policy. Hamilton, Alexander. International Trade. Madison, James. 1789-94. *297*

—. Federalists. Hamilton, Alexander. Madison, James. Political Representation. 1780's. *388*

—. Foreign Relations. Hamilton, Alexander. Lycan, Gilbert L. Stourzh, Gerald. 1780-1800. 1970. *1031*

—. Founding Fathers. Kansas-Nebraska Act (US, 1854). Lincoln, Abraham. Reconstruction. 1854-65. *910*

—. Jackson, Andrew. Nullification. 1828-33. *878*

—. Jefferson, Thomas. North. Political Theory. South. 1785-1826. *342*

—. Labor. Madison, James. Manufactures. Population. ca 1780-1836. *296*

—. Madison, James. Political Leadership. Political parties. Presidency. 1780-1820. *1041*

Republicans, radical. Civil War. Constitutional Amendments (13th). Emancipation. Lincoln, Abraham. 1861-65. *909*

—. Grand Army of the Republic. Impeachment. Johnson, Andrew. Veterans. 1867-68. *809*

—. Lincoln, Abraham. Reconstruction. 1861-69. *982*

Rescues. Crady, John W. Gollaher, Austin. Kentucky (Larue County; Knob Creek). Lincoln, Abraham. ca 1815. *425*

Research *See also* Methodology.

—. Barnard, Harry. Hayes, Rutherford B. Hayes, Webb Cook. Ohio (Fremont). Psychohistory. 1822-93. 1950's. *396*

—. Booth, John Wilkes. Conspiracy. Defense Department. Eisenschiml, Otto. Kidnapping. Lincoln, Abraham. 1865. ca 1930-80. *835*

—. Brodie, Fawn M. Nixon, Richard M. 1913-80. *1716*

—. Children's Literature. Hayes, Rutherford B. Myers, Elisabeth P. Regnery, Henry. 1822-93. 1967-69. *511*

—. Davison, Kenneth E. Hayes, Rutherford B. 1860-1972. *718*

—. Diplomatic history. Johnson, Lyndon B. Lyndon Baines Johnson Library. Texas (Austin). 1937-69. *1727*

—. Documents. Foreign policy. Preservation. 1945-77. *3378*

—. Dwight D. Eisenhower Library. Educational Policy. Eisenhower, Dwight D. Libraries, presidential. 1900's-61. *2254*

—. Dwight D. Eisenhower Library. Kansas (Abilene). Military records. World War II. 1916-52. 1977. *1740*

—. Federal policy. Presidency. 1954-74. *3442*

—. Germany. Japan. Libraries, Presidential. Military government. 1945-78. *3163*

—. Political campaigns, presidential. 1978. *1791*

—. Presidency. 1960's-81. *126*

—. Public opinion. 1943-78. *2259*

Research and Marketing Act (US, 1946). Agriculture Department. Marketing. 1940-55. *3214*

Resettlement Administration. Appalachia. Leftism. Mountaineers. Music. Seeger, Charles. Social Organization. 1935-37. *1453*

—. City planning. Greenbelt new towns. Poor. Rural areas. Tugwell, Rexford Guy. 1935-36. *1392*

Resistance *See also* Military Occupation.

—. Churchill, Winston. Eisenhower, Dwight D. France. Great Britain. World War II. 1943-44. *1733*

Resolute (vessel). Desks. Gifts. Hayes, Rutherford B. Victoria, Queen. White House (oval office). 1880. *977*

Restorations *See also* Preservation.

—. Architecture. District of Columbia. White House. 1947-52. *2414*

—. Favretti, Rudy J. Jefferson, Thomas. Landscaping. Monticello. Virginia. 1775-1826. 1977-80. *305*

—. Jefferson, Thomas. Kuper, Theodore Fred. Monticello. Virginia. 1826-1935. *243*

—. Monticello. Virginia (Charlottesville). 1826-1954. *196*

Reunions. Roosevelt, Theodore. Rough Riders. Texas (San Antonio). 1905. *1399*

Revenue sharing. Congress. Nixon, Richard M. (administration). 1968-72. *2312*

—. Grants. Hispanic Americans. Nixon, Richard M. (administration). Political Campaigns (presidential). 1960-72. *1845*

—. Legislation. Local government. Mills, Wilbur. Nixon, Richard M. 1958-75. *2450*

Revisionism. Eisenhower, Dwight D., administration. Peace. Prosperity. 1953-61. *2166*

Revivals. Bryan, William Jennings. Elections (presidential). Political parties. Reagan, Ronald. Social Change. 1730-1980. *175*

—. Calvinism. Executive branch. National Security Council. Reform. ca 1880-1930's. *1036*

Revolution *See also* specific revolutions by name, e.g. Glorious Revolution, French Revolution, etc.; American Revolution; Civil Disturbances; Coups d'Etat; Radicals and Radicalism; Riots.

—. Anticolonialism. Cold War. Domestic Policy. Political Attitudes. 1945-75. *3100*

—. Bourgois, Philippe. El Salvador. Foreign policy. Personal narratives. Reagan, Ronald (administration). 1981. *2613*

—. Cabrera, Luis. Carranza, Venustiano. Diplomacy. Mexico. Wilson, Woodrow. 1914-17. *1507*

—. Carter, Jimmy. Foreign Relations. Iran. 1972-79. *2652*

—. Carter, Jimmy. Iran. 1978-81. *2829*

—. Carter, Jimmy (administration). Foreign Relations. Nicaragua. Sandinistas. Somoza, Anastasio. 1978-79. *2711*

—. China. Diplomatic recognition. Missions and Missionaries. Sun Zhongshan. 1911-13. *1610*

—. Civil War. Lincoln, Abraham. Political Theory. Slavery. Social change. 1850-65. *912*

—. Diplomacy. Intervention. Mexico. Scott, Hugh Lenox. Wilson, Woodrow. 1914-17. *1553*

—. Diplomacy. Mexico. 1906-11. *1637*

—. Foreign Policy. Mexico. Wilson, Woodrow. 1913-15. *1509*

—. Intervention. Navies. Panama. Roosevelt, Theodore. 1903. *1621*

Revolutionary movements. Foreign policy. 1900's-79. *143*

Reynolds, John. Democratic Party. Primaries (presidential). Wallace, George C. Wisconsin. 1964. *1901*

Rhetoric *See also* Political Speeches.

—. Agnew, Spiro T. McGovern, George S. Nixon, Richard M. Political speechwriting. Reagan, Ronald. 1968-70's. *2261*

—. Agnew, Spiro T. (resignation). Political Speeches. Reporters and Reporting. 1973. *2243*

—. American Dream. Foreign policy. Truman, Harry S. 1945-46. *2782*

—. Anglo-Saxonism. Boer War. Hay, John Milton. Public Opinion. Racism. Roosevelt, Theodore. 1899-1900. *969*

—. Attitudes. Carter, Jimmy. Christianity. Political Campaigns (presidential). Political Speeches. 1976. *1861*

—. Barber, James David. Carter, Jimmy. Executive Behavior. Presidents. 1909-78. *22*

—. Bryan, William Jennings. McKinley, William. Political Campaigns (presidential). Voting and Voting Behavior. 1896. *616*

—. Calamity, use of. Civil War. Lincoln, Abraham. Puritans. 1650-1870. *782*

—. Carter, Jimmy. Foreign Policy. Panama Canal. Political Speeches. Television. 1977-78. *3090*

—. Carter, Jimmy. Mass Media. Political Campaigns (presidential). Voting and Voting Behavior. 1976. *2038*

—. Carter, Jimmy. Political Speeches. 1975-76. *2022*

—. Carter, Jimmy (interview). *Playboy* (periodical). Political Campaigns (presidential). Public Opinion. 1976. *2077*

—. Civil War. Inaugural Addresses. Lincoln, Abraham. 1865. *832*

—. Communism. Political Speeches. Public opinion. Truman, Harry S. USSR. 1945-50. *2263*

—. Debates. Mass Media. Political Campaigns (presidential). 1980. *1804*

—. Elections, presidential. Jackson, Andrew. Madison, James. Monroe, James. 1828. *697*

—. Evans, Daniel S. Political conventions. Political speeches. Republican Party. 1968. *2075*

—. Executive Power. Historians. Presidents. 1789-1970's. *130*

—. Ford, Gerald R. Inflation. Political Speeches. War metaphor. 1974. *2507*

—. Foreign policy. Political Campaigns (presidential). 1976. *1838*

—. Foreign Relations. Kennedy, John F. Political Speeches. Trade Expansion Act (US, 1962). 1962. *2775*

—. Great Society. Johnson, Lyndon B. Public Welfare. 1963-65. *2538*

—. Hoover, Herbert C. Johnson, Lyndon B. Nixon, Richard M. Protestant ethic. Public welfare. Roosevelt, Franklin D. Weber, Max. 1905-79. *51*

—. Identity. Lincoln, Abraham. Personality. 1831-61. *480*

—. Ideology. Politics. ca 1800-1975. *147*

—. Inaugural Addresses. Moley, Raymond. Roosevelt, Franklin D. 1933. *1418*

—. Inaugural addresses. Presidents. 1789-1976. *27*

—. Byrd, Harry F. Democratic Party. Elections (presidential). State Politics. Virginia. 1932. *1205*

—. Byrd, Harry F. Democratic Party. Political Campaigns (presidential). Political campaigns (presidential). Political Conventions. 1932. *1158*

—. Byrnes, James F. Democratic Party. Political conventions. Political Factions. Truman, Harry S. Vice-Presidency. Wallace, Henry A. 1944. *1181*

—. Canada. Defense Policy. Great Britain. Navies. Ogdensburg Agreement. Permanent Joint Board on Defense. 1940. *1635*

—. Carter, Boake. New Deal. Political commentary. Radio. 1935-38. *1280*

—. Carter, Jimmy. Eisenhower, Dwight D. Political Leadership. Presidency. Truman, Harry S. 1933-80. *115*

—. Carter, Jimmy. Federal Policy. Johnson, Lyndon B. Nixon, Richard M. Public welfare. Truman, Harry S. 1933-78. *118*

—. China. Churchill, Winston. Colonialism. deGaulle, Charles. Foreign Policy. France. Indochina. 1942-45. *1588*

—. China. Foreign Policy. Truman, Harry S. 1944-48. 1978. *2781*

—. China. *Keys of the Kingdom* (film). Office of War Information. Propaganda. Stereotypes. World War II. 1940-45. *1495*

—. Churchill, Winston. Espionage. Foreign Relations. Kent, Tyler. World War II. 1940-45. *1581*

—. Churchill, Winston. Foreign policy. Political Leadership. Stalin, Joseph. World War II. 1939-45. *1698*

—. Churchill, Winston. Foreign Relations. Great Britain. World War II. 1939-45. *1641*

—. Churchill, Winston. Germany. Partition. Potsdam Conference. Stettinius, Edward Reilley. Truman, Harry S. Yalta Conference. 1945. *2755*

—. Churchill, Winston. Great Britain. 1938-45. *1579*

—. Churchill, Winston. Great Britain. Joint Chiefs of Staff. Malta Conference. Military Strategy. World War II. 1945. *1663*

—. Churchill, Winston. Great Britain. Letters. Neutrality. World War II. 1939-40. *1589*

—. Churchill, Winston. Poland. Stalin, Joseph. USSR. World War II. Yalta Conference. 1945. *1580*

—. City politics (review article). Democratic Party. Dorsett, Lyle W. Fine, Sidney. Trout, Charles H. 1930-40. *1328*

—. Civil Rights. Federal Bureau of Investigation. 1936-80. *8*

—. Clergy. Massachusetts. New Deal. Social problems. 1933-36. *1260*

—. Cold War. Diplomacy. Nuclear Arms. 1941-45. *1659*

—. Cold War. International trade. Truman, Harry S. USSR. 1941-50. *1683*

—. Cold War (origins). Truman, Harry S. (administration). Yalta Conference. 1945-47. *3101*

—. Commerce Department. Mitchell, Ewing Young. Pendergast, Thomas J. Political machines. 1933-36. *1426*

—. Conferences. Eddy, William A. Foreign Relations. Ibn Saud, King. Saudi Arabia. 1945. *1576*

—. Congress. Democratic Party. Elections (congressional). George, Walter F. 1938. *1270*

—. Congress. Federal Regulation. Ickes, Harold L. Oil Industry and Trade. 1933. *1358*

—. Congress. New Deal. Social Security Act (US, 1935). Unemployment insurance. 1934-35. *1256*

—. Congress. Norris, George W. Supreme Court. 1937. *1364*

—. Congress of Industrial Organizations. Elections (presidential). Labor Non-Partisan League. Pennsylvania. 1936. *1199*

—. Conservatism. Economy Act (US, 1933). Fiscal Policy. New Deal. 1932-36. *1424*

—. Constitutional Amendments (18th and 21st). Democratic Party. Political Conventions. Prohibition repeal. Raskob, John J. 1928-33. *1166*

—. Cutting, Bronson M. Democratic Party. New Mexico. Political Campaigns. Senate. 1934. *1462*

—. Dallek, Robert (review article). Foreign Policy. 1932-45. 1979. *1569*

—. Decisionmaking. Foreign Policy. 1937-43. *1595*

—. Democracy. Inaugural addresses. Political Speeches. Values. 1901-77. *52*

—. Democratic Party. Dewey, Thomas E. Elections, gubernatorial. Farley, James A. New York. State Politics. 1942. *1444*

—. Democratic Party. Domestic Policy. Internationalism. New Deal. Political Campaigns. 1938-40. *1223*

—. Democratic Party. Elections. Political leadership. 1942. *1298*

—. Democratic Party. Elections (presidential). Iowa. 1932. *1154*

—. Democratic Party. Elections (presidential). Massachusetts. Smith, Al. 1928-32. *1153*

—. Democratic Party. Elections (senatorial). Georgia. New Deal. Talmadge, Eugene. 1926-38. *1271*

—. Democratic Party. Garner, John Nance. Political Conventions. Rayburn, Sam. 1932. *1182*

—. Democratic Party. Gillette, Guy M. House of Representatives. Iowa. Political Campaigns. 1932-48. *1326*

—. Democratic Party. Good Neighbor League Colored Committee. Negroes. Political Campaigns (presidential). 1936. *1198*

—. Democratic Party. Hague, Frank. New Deal. New Jersey. 1932-40. *1289*

—. Democratic Party. Higgins, Andrew J. Political Campaigns (presidential). 1944. *1175*

—. Democratic Party. Missouri. Pendergast, Thomas J. Political Conventions. State Politics. 1932. *1193*

—. Depressions. Economic Reform. Fisher, Irving. 1930's. *1251*

—. Depressions. Elections (presidential). Hoover, Herbert C. Missouri. 1932. *1152*

—. Depressions. LaFollette, Philip F. New Deal. Progressivism. Wisconsin Works Bill. 1935. *1383*

—. Diplomacy. Europe. Partition. 1939-45. *1475*

—. Diplomacy. Free ports. Norway. USSR. World War II. 1941-43. *1644*

—. Diplomacy. Germany. USSR. 1934-39. *1597*

—. Diplomacy. Great Britain. 1936-37. *1556*

—. Diplomacy. Japan. Konoe Fumimaro. 1934-41. *1565*

—. Diplomacy. Politics. USSR. 1920's-40's. *1238*

—. Domestic Policy. Elections (presidential). Foreign policy. Lewis, John L. 1936-40. *1188*

—. Domestic Policy. Foreign Policy. 1920-79. *1246*

—. Domestic Policy. Foreign policy. 1933-36. *1241*

—. Douglas, Lewis W. Economic Policy. New Deal. 1933-34. *1423*

—. Economic conditions. Elections (presidential). Hoover, Herbert C. Political Parties. South Dakota. 1932. *1151*

—. Economic policy. Foreign Policy. New Deal. 1933. *1234*

—. Economic policy. Freidel, Frank (review article). New Deal. Political leadership. 1930's. *1273*

—. Economic Policy. Hoover, Herbert C. New Deal. 1930's. *1464*

—. Education. Jackson, Robert H. Presidency. 1933-45. *1139*

—. Eisenhower, Dwight D. Historiography. Hoover, Herbert C. Presidents. Truman, Harry S. 1928-74. *107*

—. Elections, congressional. New Deal. Republican Party. 1937-38. *1402*

—. Elections (presidential). Ethnic groups. Religion. Social Classes. 1940. *1162*

—. Elections (presidential). German Americans. Iowa. 1936-40. *1189*

—. Elections (presidential). Long, Huey P. Share Our Wealth movement. 1932-36. *1195*

—. Elections (presidential). Poland. Polish Americans. 1942-44. *1155*

—. Embargoes. Foreign Policy. Japan. Oil and Petroleum Products. 1941. *1479*

—. Employment. Minorities in Politics. Negroes. New Deal. 1930-42. *1429*

—. Executive Power. 1933-45. *1245*

—. Exports. Foreign policy. Hull, Cordell. Japan. Oil and Petroleum Products. State Department. 1940-41. *1673*

—. Exports. Great Britain. Japan. Oil Industry and Trade. World War II. 1940-41. *1526*

—. Fascism. Italy. Monetary policy. Mussolini, Benito. New Deal. 1922-36. *1398*

—. Fascism. Italy. Mussolini, Benito. New Deal. 1930's. *1296*

—. Federal Government. Hoover, Herbert C. Public welfare. 1920-37. *1257*

—. Federal Policy. Hopkins, Harry. New Deal. Poverty. Unemployment. 1910's-38. *1369*

—. Federal Policy. Naval strategy. Pacific area. 1933-39. *1239*

—. Federal programs. State Legislatures. 1933-70's. *1360*

—. Foreign Aid. Italy. Politics. 1943-44. *1611*

—. Foreign policy. 1940-45. *1620*

—. Foreign Policy. Genocide. Jews. World War II. 1939-45. *1530*

—. Foreign Policy. Hawaii. Preparedness. Works Progress Administration. 1935-40. *1240*

—. Foreign policy. Hopkins, Harry. USSR. World War II. 1938-46. *1598*

—. Foreign policy. Hull, Cordell. Japan. Stimson, Henry L. 1933-36. *1570*

—. Foreign policy. Illinois (Chicago). Poland. Polish-American Congress. World War II. 1944. *1420*

—. Foreign Policy. International Labor Organization. Isolationism. New Deal. Perkins, Frances. 1921-34. *1628*

—. Foreign policy. Isolationism. Political Leadership. Senate. World Court. 1935. *1573*

—. Foreign Policy. Latin America. Monroe Doctrine. 1933-41. *1690*

—. Foreign Policy. Middle East. Palestine. 1943-45. *1631*

—. Foreign Policy. Poland. 1932-33. *1687*

—. Foreign Policy. Polish Americans. Political Campaigns (presidential). Rozmarek, Charles. USSR. 1944. *1178*

—. Foreign Policy. Politics and the Military. USSR. Warships. 1930's. *1596*

—. Foreign policy. Public opinion. 1932-45. *1533*

—. Foreign Policy. Public opinion. USSR. World War II. 1941-45. *1624*

—. Foreign Policy. USSR. 1933-45. *1567*

—. Foreign Relations. Great Britain. Hitler, Adolf. Letters. Lothian, 11th Marquis of. 1938-39. *1642*

—. Foreign Relations. Great Britain. Nuclear Arms. World War II. 1940-45. *1491*

—. Foreign Relations. Japan. Military Intelligence. World War II (antecedents). 1940-41. *1554*

—. Foreign Relations. USSR. 1933-45. *1545*

—. Fortas, Abe. Interior Department. Lawyers. Letters. Peres, Hardwig. 1930-44. *1342*

—. France. World War II. 1938-45. *1529*

—. Frankfurter, Felix. Lippmann, Walter. New Deal. World War II. 1932-45. *1107*

—. Garner, John Nance. New Deal. 1933-38. *1397*

—. Georgia (Warm Springs). Henderson, F. P. Marines. Personal narratives. 1937. *1225*

—. Germany. National Reich Church. Propaganda. World War II (antecedents). 1941. *1512*

—. Harrison, Byron Patton (Pat). Political friendship. Senate. 1920-41. *1443*

—. Harvard University. Students. 1901-04. *1074*

—. Historiography. Liberalism. Reform. Truman, Harry S. 1932-53. 1960-75. *129*

—. Historiography. World War II. 1930's-79. *1521*

—. Hoover, Herbert C. Johnson, Lyndon B. Nixon, Richard M. Protestant ethic. Public welfare. Rhetoric. Weber, Max. 1905-79. *51*

—. Hopkins, Harry. Marshall, George C. Military reorganization. World War II. 1942-45. *1634*

—. Illinois (Chicago). Kelly, Edward J. New Deal. Political machines. 1932-40. *1341*

—. Inaugural Addresses. Moley, Raymond. Rhetoric. 1933. *1418*

—. Inaugural addresses. Political Speechwriters. 1944-45. *1419*

—. Japan. Peace. Potsdam Conference. Surrender, unconditional. World War II. 1945. *1676*

—. Joint Chiefs of Staff. MacArthur, Douglas. Nimitz, Chester W. Pacific Area. World War II. 1941-42. *1513*

—. Leftism. New Deal. 1933-79. *1217*

—. Navies. Preparedness. Vinson, Carl. 1932-40. *1249*

—. New Deal. New Hampshire. Political Campaigns (presidential). 1936. *1200*

—. New Deal. Nominations for Office. Political Factions. Rural Electrification Administration. Williams, Aubrey W. 1945. *1421*

—. New Deal. Norris, George W. Tennessee Valley Authority. 1933. *1365*

Shafer, Byron. Delegates. Democratic Party. Lengle, James. Political Theory. Primaries, presidential. Reform. 1972. *1900*

Shakespearean tragedy. Lincoln, Abraham. Political Leadership. 1861-65. *449*

Shanghai (battle). China. Japan. Navies. Stimson, Henry L. Taylor, Montgomery Meigs. Western nations. 1931-32. *1645*

Shanghai Power Company. China. Communists. Foreign Policy. Truman, Harry S. (administration). 1948-50. *3111*

Share Our Wealth movement. Elections (presidential). Long, Huey P. Roosevelt, Franklin D. 1932-36. *1195*

Shattuck, John. Documents. *Halperin et al. v. Kissinger et al* (US, 1976). Nixon, Richard M. 1976. *1777*

Shaw, Peter. Adams, John (review article). Behavior. Brown, Ralph Adams. Political Power. 1760's-1801. 1975-76. *197*

Shawcross, William. Betts, Richard K. Gelb, Leslie H. Nixon, Richard M. Political Systems. Vietnam War (review article). 1954-79. *2809*

—. Bureaucracies. Cambodia. Foreign policy. Kissinger, Henry A. Nixon, Richard M. (administration). State Department. Vietnam War. 1960's-80. *3379*

—. Cambodia. Foreign Policy. Kissinger, Henry A. Nixon, Richard M. Vietnam War (review article). 1953-70. *3081*

Sheffield, 1st Earl of. Canada. Economics. Foreign Policy. Great Britain. Madison, James. War of 1812. West Indies. 1783-1812. *355*

Shelby, Isaac. Chickasaw. Indians (reservations). Jackson, Andrew. Land Tenure. South. 1818. *794*

Shenandoah Valley (campaign). Civil War. Hitchcock, Ethan Allen. Lincoln, Abraham. Military Strategy. Peninsular Campaign. Virginia. 1862. *950*

Sherman, John. Impeachment. Johnson, Andrew. Reconstruction. 1867-68. *785*

Sherman, William Tecumseh. Armies. Civil War. Elections (presidential). Lincoln, Abraham. Propaganda. 1864. *622*

Shields, James. Illinois. Letters. Lincoln, Abraham. 1842. *498*

Shipping. Civil War. Consular Service. Espionage. Great Britain. Lincoln, Abraham. Patronage. 1861-63. *1012*

—. Foreign Policy. France. Jackson, Andrew. 1834-36. *1029*

Shipping Board. Economic Policy. Foreign policy. Hurley, Edward Nash. Wilson, Woodrow. 1918-19. *1650*

Short, William. France (Languedoc, Provence). Jefferson, Thomas. Travel. 1787. *381*

Shriver, Sargent. Political attitudes. Political campaigns (Presidential). 1976. *1986*

Sierra Club v. *Morton* (US, 1972). California (Mineral King Valley). Interior Department. Land development. Wilderness. 1969-72. *2333*

Sihanouk, Norodom. *See* Norodom Sihanouk.

Simpson, Gilbert. Friendship. Land Tenure. Pennsylvania, western. Settlement. Washington, George. 1740-94. *255*

Sims, William S. Fullam, William F. Marines. Navies. Reform. Roosevelt, Theodore. 1890's-1909. *1243*

Sinclair, John. Land. Letters. Natural Resources. Washington, George. 1796. *939*

Sinclair, Upton. Bank of America. California. Elections, gubernatorial. Giannini, Amadeo P. Merriam, Frank. Roosevelt, Franklin D. ca 1923-34. *1254*

Sirica, John J. Stans, Maurice H. Watergate Scandal (review article). 1962-79. *2457*

Sisson, Daniel (review article). Elections. Ideology. Politics. 1776-1800. 1974. *650*

Sivachev, N. V. American Historical Association (meeting). Dement'ev, I. P. Historians. Methodology. Political parties. Roosevelt, Franklin D. 1981. *1433*

Slave revolts. Haiti. Military Aid. Washington, George. 1791-1804. *1003*

Slavery *See also* Abolition Movement; Antislavery Sentiments; Emancipation; Freedmen; Fugitive Slaves; Negroes.

—. Adams, John Quincy. Democratic Party. Elections (presidential). Jackson, Andrew. Whig Party. 1828-44. *923*

—. Assassination. Brooks, Phillips. Episcopal Church, Protestant. Lincoln, Abraham. Pennsylvania (Philadelphia). Sermons. 1865. 1893. *421*

—. Attitudes. Civil War. Lincoln, Abraham. Political Speeches. Sectionalism. 1850's-65. *456*

—. Attitudes. Lincoln, Abraham. 1837-63. *451*

—. Brodie, Fawn M. Hemings, Sally. Jefferson, Thomas (review article). 1743-1826. *376*

—. Buchanan, James. Democratic Party. Douglas, Stephen A. Elections. Kansas. Lecompton Constitution. 1854-60. *624*

—. Buchanan, James. Historiography. Kansas. Lecompton Constitution. Political Leadership. Suffrage. 1857. 20c. *894*

—. Calhoun, John C. Democratic Party. Economic policy. South. VanBuren, Martin. 1837-41. *814*

—. California. Elections (presidential). Racism. Republican Party. 1860. *695*

—. California. Elections, presidential. Republican Party. 1856. *694*

—. Civil Rights. Civil War. Democracy. Lincoln, Abraham. Property. 1861-65. *786*

—. Civil rights. Declaration of Independence. Negroes. 1776-1976. *41*

—. Civil War. Lincoln, Abraham. Political Theory. Revolution. Social change. 1850-65. *912*

—. Debates. Douglas, Stephen A. Illinois. Lincoln, Abraham. Political Campaigns (senatorial). 1774-1858. *401*

—. Declaration of Independence. Jefferson, Thomas. 1776. *250*

—. Douglas, Stephen A. Illinois. Lincoln, Abraham. Political Campaigns (senatorial). 1858. *485*

—. Douglas, Stephen A. *Illinois State Journal* (newspaper). *Illinois State Register* (newspaper). Lincoln, Abraham. Political Campaigns (senatorial). 1858. *413*

—. Douglas, Stephen A. Lincoln, Abraham. Morality. Political Attitudes. 1850's. *553*

—. Douglass, Frederick. Lincoln, Abraham. 1860's. *784*

—. Equality. Lincoln, Abraham. Mormons. Polygamy. Smith, Joseph. 1840-64. *563*

—. Jefferson, Thomas. Miller, John Chester (review article). 1760's-1826. 1977. *226*

—. Lincoln, Abraham. Massachusetts. Political Speeches. Taylor, Zachary. Whig Party. 1848. *640*

—. Louisiana. Newspapers. Political Campaigns (presidential). Political parties. 1834-36. *637*

Slaves. Brodie, Fawn M. Children. Historiography. Jefferson, Thomas. ca 1771-89. 1974-76. *279*

Slidell, John. Black, John. Diplomacy. Mexican War. Peña, Manuel de la. Polk, James K. Taylor, Zachary. 1845-46. *1004*

Slums. *See* Cities.

Slush funds. Central Intelligence Agency. International Telephone and Telegraph. Nixon, Richard M. (administration). Political surveillance. Watergate scandal. 1968-72. *2541*

Smith, Adam. American Revolution. Economic Theory. Jefferson, Thomas. Nationalism. Utilitarianism. 1770's-90's. *257*

Smith, Al. Attitudes. Louisiana. Political Campaigns (presidential). Religion. Voting and Voting Behavior. 1920-28. *1212*

—. Candler, Warren A. Methodist Episcopal Church, South. Political Campaigns (presidential). Prohibition. Religion. 1928. *1143*

—. Critical election theory. Elections, presidential. Hoover, Herbert C. 1916-40. 1928. *1168*

—. Democratic Party. Elections (presidential). Lichtman, Allan J. (review article). Louisiana. 1928. *1147*

—. Democratic Party. Elections (presidential). Louisiana. 1928. *1211*

—. Democratic Party. Elections (presidential). Massachusetts. Roosevelt, Franklin D. 1928-32. *1153*

—. Democratic Party. McAdoo, William G. Murray, Robert K. (review article). New York City. Political Conventions. 1924. *1180*

—. Democratic Party. Political Campaigns (presidential). Primaries (presidential). South Dakota. 1928. *1184*

—. Elections (presidential). Hoover, Herbert C. Racism. Tennessee, west. 1928. *1174*

—. Elections (presidential). West Virginia. 1928. *1146*

—. Hoover, Herbert C. Political Campaigns (presidential). Tennessee, west. 1928. *1173*

Smith, Elbert B. Blair, Francis Preston, Sr. (review article). Civil War. Jackson, Andrew. Politics. 1830-79. 1980. *855*

Smith, Felix Willoughby. Foreign policy. Russia (Transcaucasia). World War I. 1917-18. *1561*

Smith, Gaddis. Acheson, Dean. Foreign policy (review article). Kennan, George F. 1948-63. *2788*

Smith, Joseph. Brodie, Fawn M. Jefferson, Thomas. Mormons. 18c-1844. 1946-79. *303*

—. Equality. Lincoln, Abraham. Mormons. Polygamy. Slavery. 1840-64. *563*

Smithsonian Institution. Ball gowns. Bible. Inaugurations. 1789-1972. *162*

Smoot, Coleman. Illinois (Sangamon County). Legislation. Lincoln, Abraham. Musick, Sam. Politics. 1827-46. *399*

Smoot, Reed. Political conventions. Republican Party. Senate. Utah. 1920. *1204*

Smoot-Hawley Tariff. Canada. Foreign Relations. Hoover, Herbert C. Tariff. 1929-33. *1584*

Sneersohn, Hayyim Zevi. Appointments to office. Diplomats. Grant, Ulysses S. Jews. Palestine. Romania. 1869-70. *1026*

Social Change *See also* Economic Growth.

—. Bryan, William Jennings. Elections (presidential). Political parties. Reagan, Ronald. Revivals. 1730-1980. *175*

—. Bureaucracies. Congress. Executive Branch. Political Change. Reform. 1960's-70's. *3353*

—. Civil War. Lincoln, Abraham. Political Theory. Revolution. Slavery. 1850-65. *912*

—. Defense Department. Housing. Integration. Military. 1967-68. *2503*

—. Entrepreneurs. Heroes. Lincoln, Abraham. Men. Pioneers. 18c-19c. *558*

—. Foreign Aid. Haiti. Kennedy, John F. 1960's-80. *2896*

—. Hoover, Herbert C. Negroes. Racism. ca 1910-33. *1075*

—. Johnson, Lyndon B. Kennedy, John F. New Left. Nixon, Richard M. Popular culture. 1960-69. *2260*

—. Lincoln, Abraham. Science. Technology. 1840's-59. *470*

—. Minnesota. Mondale, Walter F. Natural resources. 1928-77. *1734*

Social Classes *See also* Aristocracy; Elites; Middle Classes; Social Mobility; Upper Classes; Working Class.

—. Bureaucracies. Corporations. Labor. Poor. War on Poverty. 1960's. *2350*

—. Commerce. Madison, James. Plantations. Politics. 1770's-1816. *354*

—. Elections (presidential). Ethnic groups. Religion. Roosevelt, Franklin D. 1940. *1162*

—. Elections (presidential). Political Parties. Whites. 1948-76. *1784*

Social Conditions *See also* Cities; Daily Life; Economic Conditions; Family; Labor; Marriage; Popular Culture; Social Classes; Social Mobility; Social Problems; Social Reform.

—. Aristocracy. France (Languedoc, Provence). Jefferson, Thomas. Travel. 1787. *382*

—. Atlanta University. Labor Department. Negroes. 1897-1907. *1318*

—. Diplomacy. France. Jefferson, Thomas. National Characteristics. 1776-1826. *245*

—. Executive Power. Federal Policy. Justice. Law Enforcement. Politics. 1960-79. *3386*

—. Family. Hayes, Rutherford B. 19c-20c. *461*

—. Great Society. Johnson, Lyndon B. (administration). Public Welfare. 1964-76. *2418*

—. Jefferson, Thomas. Pacifism. War. 1783-1812. *362*

—. Myths and symbols. Public Opinion. Washington, George. 1865-1900. *325*

Social control. Nixon, Richard M. (administration). Political leadership. Public opinion. Watergate scandal. 1973-74. *3252*

Social mobility. American Dream. Boritt, G. S. (review article). Economic Theory. Lincoln, Abraham. Political Leadership. 1840's-64. 1978. *452*

Social movements. Johnson, Lyndon B. Rhetoric. Social reform. War on Poverty. 1965-66. *2539*

Social Organization. Appalachia. Leftism. Mountaineers. Music. Resettlement Administration. Seeger, Charles. 1935-37. *1453*

—. Belz, Herman. Lincoln, Abraham. Louisiana. McCrary, Peyton. Politics. Reconstruction. 1861-77. *962*

—. Enlightenment. Government. Madison, James. Scotland. ca 1760's-1829. *194*

Social policy. New Federalism. Nixon, Richard M. (administration). 1969-79. *2482*

T

Weik, Jesse W. Herndon, William H. Lincoln, Abraham (review article). 1850-1920. *592*

Weinberg, Martha. Burnham, William Dean. Ceaser, John W. Diamond, Edwin. DiClerico, Robert E. Political Attitudes (review article). Presidency. 1970-79. *3187*

Weinberger, Casper. Foreign policy. Haig, Alexander. Meese, Edwin. Reagan, Ronald. 1981. *3096*

Weinstein, Edwin A. Anderson, James William. Historiography. Link, Arthur S. Wilson, Woodrow. 1896-1921. *1076*

—. Presidents. Wilson, Woodrow (review article). 1856-1924. *1105*

Welch, Henry. Antibiotics. Conflict of interest. Federal regulation. Food and Drug Administration. Periodicals. Pharmaceutical Industry. 1959-62. *2434*

Welfare. *See* Public Welfare.

Weller, George. Adams, John. American Revolution (antecedents). Episcopal Church, Protestant. Letters. 1770's. 1824-25. *258*

Welles, Gideon. Civil War. Democrats. Navy Secretaries. Niven, John (review article). 1820's-70's. *740*

—. Civil War. Fox, Gustavus Vasa. Naval administration. 1861-65. *744*

Welles, Sumner. Axis powers. Foreign Relations. Hull, Cordell. Latin America. Rio Conference. World War II. 1941-42. *1535*

—. Boundaries. Bowman, Isaiah. East Prussia. Germany. Oder-Neisse Line. Poland. State Department (Advisory Committee on Post-War Foreign Policy). World War II. 1942-45. *1649*

Welsh, Herbert. Civil Service Commissioners. Indian Rights Association. Indian-White Relations. Roosevelt, Theodore. 1889-95. *831*

Welsh, Matthew E. Civil Rights Act (US, 1964). Democratic Party. Indiana. Primaries (presidential). Wallace, George C. 1964. *2111*

West Indies *See also* individual islands by name.

—. Canada. Economics. Foreign Policy. Great Britain. Madison, James. Sheffield, 1st Earl of. War of 1812. 1783-1812. *355*

—. Foreign policy. Munro, Dana G. (review article). State Department. 1921-30. 1974. *1672*

—. Foreign Relations. Knox, Philander C. Latin America. Travel. 1912. *1541*

—. Germany. Imperialism. Intervention. 1898-1917. *1522*

West Virginia *See also* Southeastern States.

—. Congress. Impeachment. Johnson, Andrew. Reconstruction. VanWinkle, Peter G. 1868. *857*

—. Democratic Party. Kennedy, John F. Primaries (presidential). 1960. *1815*

—. Economic Development. Harper's Ferry Armory. Washington, George. 1790-99. *937*

—. Elections (presidential). Smith, Al. 1928. *1146*

—. Labor disputes. Letters. McKinley, William. Murphy, S. W. Railroads and State. 1893. *954*

—. Political Campaigns (presidential). Stevenson, Adlai E. (1835-1914). 1892. 1900. *680*

Western Nations *See also* Communist Countries.

—. China. Japan. Navies. Shanghai (battle). Stimson, Henry L. Taylor, Montgomery Meigs. 1931-32. *1645*

—. Elections (presidential). Political participation. 1960-78. *2051*

Western States *See also* individual states; Far Western States; Southwest.

—. Civil Service. Indians (reservations). Roosevelt, Theodore. 1892. *862*

—. Documents. Federal Policy. Harry S. Truman Library. Truman, Harry S. 1940-66. *2394*

—. Federal policy. Hoover, Herbert C. (administration). Public lands. Wilbur, Ray Lyman. 1920's. *1293*

—. Friendship. Historiography. National Characteristics. Roosevelt, Theodore. Wister, Owen. 1890's-1900's. *1116*

—. Hayes, Rutherford B. (and family). Railroads. Travel. 1880. *807*

—. Johnson, Lyndon B. Politics. 1930's-73. *1732*

—. Payne-Aldrich Tariff. Political leadership. Republican Party. Sectionalism. Taft, William H. Tariff. 1909. *1316*

Westward Movement *See also* Pioneers.

—. Jackson, Donald. Jefferson, Thomas (review article). 1780's-1820's. *344*

—. Ohio Valley. Washington, George. 1750's-90's. *212*

Whaling Industry and Trade. Cannibals. Kekela, James Hunnewell. Lincoln, Abraham. Marquesas Islands (Hiva Oa). Whalon, Jonathan. 1864. *1030*

Whalon, Jonathan. Cannibals. Kekela, James Hunnewell. Lincoln, Abraham. Marquesas Islands (Hiva Oa). Whaling Industry and Trade. 1864. *1030*

Wheat, surplus. Charities. Depressions. Food. Hoover, Herbert C. Red Cross. 1932-33. *1356*

Wheatley, Phillis ("To his Excellency George Washington"). Columbia (allegory). King, William. Myths and Symbols. Poetry. Washington, George. 1790. *356*

Wheeler National Monument. Antiquities Act (US, 1906). Colorado. Holy Cross Mountain National Monument. Hoover, Herbert C. Roosevelt, Theodore. 1906-50. *1445*

Whig Party. Adams, John Quincy. Democratic Party. Elections (presidential). Jackson, Andrew. Slavery. 1828-44. *923*

—. Anti-Catholicism. Fillmore, Millard. Know-Nothing Party. Nativism. Political Campaigns (presidential). 1850-56. *561*

—. Antiwar sentiment. Congress. Lincoln, Abraham. Mexican War. 1846-49. *514*

—. Calhoun, John C. Congress. Democrats. Mexican War. Polk, James K. 1846-48. *1016*

—. Lincoln, Abraham. Massachusetts. Political Speeches. Slavery. Taylor, Zachary. 1848. *640*

—. Politics. Presidents. Tyler, John. 1820-62. *729*

—. Presidential succession. Tyler, John. 1841. *754*

Whiskey Rebellion. Hamilton, Alexander. Jefferson, Thomas. Pennsylvania. Taxation. 1791-1801. *915*

White House. Architecture. District of Columbia. Restoration. 1947-52. *2414*

—. Conger, Clement E. Decorative Arts. Onassis, Jacqueline Kennedy. 19c-1980. *2353*

—. District of Columbia. Hayes, Rutherford B. Keeler, Lucy Elliott. Ohio (Fremont). Personal narratives. Travel. 1881. *867*

—. Hayes, Rutherford B. Interior decoration. 1877-81. *806*

White House Conferences on Aging. Aged. Politics. 1950-71. *2469*

White House dinners. Florida. Public opinion. Roosevelt, Theodore. South. Washington, Booker T. 1901. *1431*

White House Fellows Programs. Air Forces. 1964-73. *3318*

White House Office of Congressional Relations. Congress. Lobbying. 1961-63. *2192*

White House (oval office). Desks. Gifts. Hayes, Rutherford B. *Resolute* (vessel). Victoria, Queen. 1880. *977*

White House transcripts. Bibliographies. Nixon, Richard M. Watergate scandal. 1974. *2519*

White, Theodore H. Debates. Elections (presidential). Journalism. Kennedy, John F. Nixon, Richard M. Television. 1960. *1789*

—. Elections, presidential. Historiography. Political Commentary. 1960-75. *1871*

—. Elections (review article). Presidency. 1956-80. *3289*

—. Liberalism. Presidency (review article). 1956-80. *3382*

—. Nixon, Richard M. (review article). Political corruption. 1950-72. *2201*

Whites. Attitudes. Behavior. Negroes. Public opinion. Voting and Voting Behavior. Wallace, George C. 1968. *1928*

—. Attitudes. Civil rights. South. Truman, Harry S. 1945-52. *2308*

—. Elections (presidential). Negroes. South. Voting and voting behavior. 1952-76. *1824*

—. Elections (presidential). Political Parties. Social Classes. 1948-76. *1784*

—. Political Attitudes. Voting and voting behavior. 1960's-70's. *2042*

Wickliffe, Charles A. Elections (presidential). Kentucky (Louisville). Letters. Pope, Warden. 1828. *620*

Wide-Awake clubs. Hamlin, Hannibal. Lincoln, Abraham. Republican Party. Vermont. 1860. *651*

Wilbur, Ray Lyman. Federal policy. Hoover, Herbert C. (administration). Public lands. Western states. 1920's. *1293*

—. Hoover, Herbert C. Indians. Public Administration. Rhoads, Charles J. Scattergood, J. Henry. 1929-33. *1413*

Wildavsky, Aaron. Congress. Executive Power. Foreign policy. Two presidencies thesis. 1957-79. *3435*

—. Domestic Policy. Foreign Policy. Presidency. 1976. *3351*

—. Domestic Policy. Foreign Policy. Presidency. Senate. Voting and Voting Behavior. 1973-80. *3485*

Wilde, Richard Henry. Assassination. Jackson, Andrew. Lawrence, Richard. Letters. 1834-35. *951*

Wilderness *See also* Conservation of Natural Resources; Forests and Forestry; Nature.

—. California (Mineral King Valley). Interior Department. Land development. *Sierra Club* v. *Morton* (US, 1972). 1969-72. *2333*

Wildlife Conservation *See also* Forests and Forestry; Great Plains; Natural Resources.

—. Montana. National Park Service. Roosevelt, Theodore. Yellowstone National Park. 1883-1918. *1125*

Wilkie, John. Counterintelligence. Gage, Lyman. McKinley, William. Quebec (Montreal). Spanish-American War. 1898. *732*

William II. Diplomacy. Germany. Meyer, George von Lengerke. Roosevelt, Theodore. Russo-Japanese War. 1902-14. *1680*

—. Foreign Relations. Germany. Roosevelt, Theodore. 1901-09. *1658*

William S. Merrell Company. Federal Drug Administration. Kelsey, Frances Oldham. Thalidomide. 1960's. *2435*

Williams, Aubrey W. New Deal. Nominations for Office. Political Factions. Roosevelt, Franklin D. Rural Electrification Administration. 1945. *1421*

Williams, Herbert Lee. Personal narratives. Truman, Harry S. 1954. *1778*

Willkie, Wendell. Edison, Charles. Elections (Gubernatorial, Presidential). Hendrickson, Robert. Hoffman, Harold G. New Jersey. 1940. *1203*

Wills. Decisionmaking. Foreign Relations. Forgeries. Peter I. Propaganda. Truman, Harry S. USSR. 1725-1948. *2659*

Wills, Garry. Adair, Douglass. *Federalist* No. 10. Hume, David. Madison, James. Political Theory. Republicanism. 1788. *238*

—. Conservatism. Declaration of Independence. Jefferson, Thomas (review article). Property. 1776. 1978-80. *288*

—. Declaration of Independence. Enlightenment. Jefferson, Thomas (review article). Locke, John. Political Theory. Scotland. 1690's-1776. 1970's. *261*

—. Declaration of Independence. Jefferson, Thomas (review article). Philosophy. 1776. *290*

—. Jefferson, Thomas (review article). Liberalism. Nixon, Richard M. 18c. 20c. *173*

Willstown, Treaties of. Cherokee Indians. Ethnicity. Indians. Jefferson, Thomas. Removals, forced. Tennessee. 1794-1817. *890*

Wilson, Charles E. Appointments to office. Businessmen. Eisenhower, Dwight D. Senate. Wealth. 1952. *2356*

—. Civil-Military Relations. Defense Department. Eisenhower, Dwight D. (administration). 1953-57. *2185*

—. Defense policy. Eisenhower, Dwight D. 1953-57. *2184*

Wilson, Edith Bolling Galt. Bentham, Edith. Documents. Lansing, Robert (resignation). State Department. Tumulty, Joseph. Wilson, Woodrow. 1919-20. *1682*

—. Letters. Politics. Wilson, Woodrow. Wives. 1893-1961. *1083*

Wilson, Evan M. Bain, Kenneth Ray. Diplomatic recognition (review article). Ganin, Zvi. Independence. Israel. 1945-48. *2980*

—. Diplomatic Recognition (review article). Ganin, Zvi. Israel. Truman, Harry S. 1940-49. *2603*

Wilson (film). International Organizations. Public Opinion. Zanuck, Darryl F. 1944. *1089*

Wilson, Joan Hoff. Depressions. Fausold, Martin L. Hoover, Herbert C. (review article). Mazuzan, George T. 1929-33. 1974-75. *1224*

Wilson, William B. Anti-Communist Movements. Deportation. Immigrants. Justice Department. Labor Department. Palmer, A. Mitchell. Post, Louis F. 1919-20. *1307*

Wilson, Woodrow. 1856-1924. *1097*

—. Addams, Jane. Foreign policy. Ideology. Open Door Policy. 1900-20. *1623*

—. Aliens. California. Japan. Johnson, Hiram W. Land Tenure. Webb-Heney Act (1913). 1911-13. *1231*

Y

Z

AUTHOR INDEX

A

Aberbach, Joel D. 1782 2287
Abraham, Henry J. 3182
Abrams, Burton A. 1783
Abrams, Rochonne 767
Abramson, Paul R. 1784
Accinelli, Robert D. 1470
  1471 1472 1473
Acheson, Dean 1708
Adams, D. K. 1474
Adams, John Clarke 1785
Adelman, Kenneth L. 2550
  2705
Adkison, Danny 1
Adler, Emanuel 3183
Adler, Frank J. 2551
Adler, Selig 392
A.G 2288
Aga Rossi, Elena 1475
Agnoletti, Enzo Enriques
  1786
Agria, John J. 3184
Ahmad, Eqbal 2552
Ahrari, Mohammed E. 3185
  3186
Aiken, Ann 1951
Alberts, D. J. 2553
Albin, Mel 113
Albright, Claude 768
Alexander, Jon 3187
Allen, H. C. 2554
Allen, Mark 1709
Allen, T. Harrell 2555
Allen, William R. 1251
Allison, Graham T. 2556
  2557 3188
Allison, Hildreth M. 1213
Alsop, Joseph 1054
Alter, Jonathan 1787 2558
Altherr, Marco 2559
Altherr, Thomas L. 1055
Altschuler, Bruce E. 1788
Altschull, J. Herbert 1789
Alvarez, David J. 1476
Alvarez Pedroso, Antonio 967
Ambacher, Bruce 611
Ambri, Mariano 2560
Ambrose, Stephen E. 1710
  1711
Ambrosius, Lloyd E. 1477
  1478
Ammon, Harry 1032
Anderson, Adrian 1252
Anderson, David L. 968 1790
Anderson, Donald F. 1214
  1791
Anderson, Fenwick 1141
Anderson, Irvine H., Jr. 1479
Anderson, James A. 1792
Anderson, James E. 2289
Anderson, James William
  1133
Anderson, Ken 769
Anderson, Stuart 969
Andrew, Christopher 3189
Andrews, Robert Hardy 178
Andrews, William G. 3190
Anikin, A. 2290
Anisuzzaman, Mohammad
  3191
Annunziata, Frank 1253 1793
Antognini, Richard 1254
Appleby, Joyce 179 180
Aragonnès, Claude 393
Arbatov, A. G. 2561
Arconti, Steven J. 770
Arcui, Alan F. 3192
Armbrester, Margaret E. 1255
Armour, Rollin S. 394
Arnhart, Larry 3193
Arnold, Hugh M. 2562
Arnold, Peri E. 1215 1699
  3194 3195
Aron, Raymond 2563
Aronson, Shlomo 2564
Artaud, Denise 2 1480
Arterton, F. Christopher 1794
  3196 3197
Artzi, Pinhas 1539
Ashbrook, John M. 2136
Ashenfelter, Orley 2132
Asher, Robert 2291

Ashton, J. Hubley 771
Astiz, Carlos A. 2565
Atkin, Charles K. 1795
Auw, David C. L. 2566
Avery, Laurence G. 1481
Avery, Robert K. 1792
Avineri, Shlomo 2567 2568
Azevedo, Ross E. 2292

B

Baas, Larry A. 2517
Babcock, William A. 2236
Babu, B. Ramesh 181 1256
Bacchus, William I. 3198
Baer, Emily Angel 395
Baetzhold, Howard G. 612
Bailey, George 1796
Bailey, Gil 2293
Bailey, Harry A., Jr. 3489
Bailey, John W., Jr. 1142
Bailey, Thomas A. 1482
Bailyn, Bernard 182
Bakeless, John 772
Baker, Gladys L. 3
Baker, James T. 2137
Baker, Kendall L. 1797
Baker, Stephen C. 1163
Baker, Tod A. 2033
Balch, Stephen H. 1216
Balfour, Michael 1483
Balfour, Nancy 2138
Ball, Nicole 2569 2570
Balthazar, Louis 2571
Balutis, Alan P. 4 3199
Banes, Ruth A. 183
Banfi, Arialdo 2572
Banner, James M., Jr. 5
Banning, Lance 184
Baral, Jaya Krishna 2573
  2574
Baram, Phillip 1484 1485
Baranovski, V. 1712
Barber, James David 2139
  2140
Barber, Rims 2294
Barenboim, P. D. 6
Barger, Harold M. 3200
Barnard, Harry 396
Barnds, William J. 2575
Barnes, Howard A. 185
Barnes, Trevor 2576
Barnet, Richard 2577
Barnett, Roger W. 3124
Barney, William L. 773
Baron, Sherry 186
Baroody, William J., Jr. 2141
Barrett, Raymond J. 3201
Barrett, Wayne 187
Bartlett, Bruce 1581 2295
Bartlett, Merrill 1486
Basler, Roy P. 397 398
Bates, J. Leonard 7
Baudhuin, E. Scott 2142
Bauer, Charles J. 399
Baum, Dale 613 660
Bauman, Mark K. 1143
Beard, Robin 2578
Beasley, Maurine 1056
Beatty, Kathleen Murphy
  1798
Bechtolt, Warren E., Jr. 1799
Beck, Kent M. 2143
Beck, Nathaniel 3202
Becker, Lee B. 2296
Beckler, David Z. 2297
Beer, Sam H. 3203
Beeton, Beverly 774
Beglova, N. 2579
Beil, Cheryl 2108
Beisel, David R. 1713
Beliavskaia, I. A. 1057
Bell, B. Tartt 1800
Bell, Charles G. 1801
Bell, Coral 2580 2581 2582
Bell, Rudolph M. 970
Bellush, Jewel 1217
Beloff, Max 188
Belohlavek, John M. 614 971
  972
Benadom, Gregory A. 3204
Benda, Charles G. 3205
Bender, Gerald J. 2583

Benedict, Michael Les 615
  775
Beniger, James R. 1802
Benjamin, Jules R. 1487
Benjamin, Thomas 973
Bennett, James D. 776
Bennett, Janet 1812
Bennett, Stephen E. 2016
Bennett, W. Lance 616
Bennett, William E. 1803
Benoit, William L. 2144
Bensman, Joseph 2298
Benson, Ezra Taft 2299
Ben-Zvi, Abraham 1488 2584
Bérard, Armand 2585
Berens, John F. 8 189
Berger, Harriet F. 9
Berger, Henry W. 2586
Berger, Raoul 10 1033
Bergquist, Harold E., Jr. 974
Bergren, Orville V. 3206
Bergsten, C. Fred 2587 2588
Berkowitz, Edward D. 1257
  2300 2301 2302
Berman, Bruce J. 2303
Berman, Larry 3207
Berman, Sylvan M. 2589
Berman, William C. 2146
  2590
Bernard, Kenneth A. 400
Bernard, Kenneth H. 777
Bernstein, Barton J. 1489
  1490 1491 2304 2305
  2591 2592 2593 2594
  2595 2596 2597
Berquist, Goodwin F. 1804
Berry, Jeffrey M. 3208
Berryman, Phillip 2598
Bertram, Christoph 2599
Berwanger, Eugene H. 778
  779
Bessette, Joseph M. 24
Best, Gary Dean 1058 1059
  1060 1061 1492
Best, James J. 3209
Bethell, Thomas N. 1714 2600
Beveridge, John W. 401
Bezayiff, David 190
Bhagat, G. 2601
Bhagat, Sheela 2602
Bhana, Surendra 1258 2306
Bibbee, M. Jane 1854
Bibby, John F. 1805
Biber, Dušan 1493
Bickel, Alexander M. 2307
Bickerton, Ian J. 975 2603
Biles, Roger 1806
Billington, Monroe 1259 1260
  1715 2308
Birnbaum, Norman 2604
Bishirjian, Richard J. 1261
Bishop, Joseph W., Jr. 2605
Biskupski, M. B. 1494
Bissell, Richard E. 2606
Black, Earl 1807
Black, Edwin 1808
Black, Gregory D. 1495
Black, Merle 1807
Blair, John L. 1144 1218
Blake, May Belle 402
Blakey, George T. 1062
Blanchard, Margaret A. 1262
Blank, Robert H. 1989
Blayney, Michael Stewart
  1145 1496
Blechman, Barry M. 2607
Bledsoe, Robert 3292
Blinder, Alan S. 2362
Block, Fred 2608
Block, Robert Hoyt 1497
Bloom, Robert L. 780
Bloomfield, Lincoln P. 3210
Blue, Frederick J. 617
Blue, Merle D. 403
Bohmer, David A. 618
Bohn, Thomas W. 1809
Bohne, Regina 2309
Boiko, K. 3211
Boller, Paul F., Jr. 11 404
Bolt, Robert 405
Bombardier, Gary 3212
Bonazzi, Tiziano 1810
Bone, Beverly 781

Bonior, David E. 2609
Borden, Morton 711
Borg, Dorothy 2781 3168
Borisov, K. 2610
Borisov, V. 2344
Boritt, G. S. 406 407 408 619
Bormann, Ernest G. 782 1811
  1812 2147
Borosage, Robert 3213
Borowski, Harry R. 2611
Borst, William A. 409
Bosch, Juan 2612
Bosha, Francis J. 2148
Bosworth, Barry P. 2310
Bosworth, Richard 1693
Bottorff, William K. 191
Bourgois, Philippe 2613
Bourke, Paul F. 192
Bourne, Tom 1716
Bouzas, Roberto 2149
Bovey, John A., Jr. 2614
Bovin, A. 2615
Bowers, Douglas E. 3214
Boyd, Julian P. 193
Boyd, Marjorie 2311
Boyd, Richard W. 1813
Boyer, Neil A. 3215
Boyett, Gene W. 1034
Boyett, Joseph H. 1814
Brach, Hans Günter 2616
Brademas, John 2312
Braden, Tom 3216
Bradford, M. E. 410 411 783
Bradford, Richard H. 1146
  1815
Bradley, John P. 3217
Brady, Linda P. 3218
Braeman, John 1219 1263
  1498
Braestrup, Peter 2617
Brams, Steven J. 2128
Branson, Roy 194
Branton, Harriet K. 412
Brauer, Carl M. 2313
Brauer, Kinley J. 713
Bravo Nuche, Ramón 3219
Bray, Charles W. 3220
Brecher, Michael 2618 2619
Breiseth, Christopher N. 413
  784
Bremer, William W. 1264
Bremner, John Evan 1816
Brenner, Michael J. 2620
  2621
Brescia, Anthony M. 620
Briceland, Alan V. 621
Bridges, Robert D. 785
Bridges, Roger D. 414 786
Brigman, William E. 12
Brinkley, Alan 1265
Brisbin, Richard A., Jr. 3221
Brodie, Bernard 2622
Brodie, Fawn M. 13 195 1717
Brogan, Hugh 1035
Brogdan, Frederick W. 1452
Broh, C. Anthony 1817
Brody, Richard 1930
Brown, Barbara L. 1930
Brown, Bertram S. 2314
Brown, Clifford W., Jr. 1818
  1819
Brown, Jesse C. 1930
Brown, Lorraine 1266
Brown, Richard C. 1267
Brown, Roger G. 3222
Brown, Russel K. 787
Brown, Seyom 2623
Brown, Steven R. 2150
Brown, Thad A. 2134
Brownell, James R., Jr. 3298
Brownlow, Paul C. 788
Brozen, Yale 2315
Bruce Lockhart, J. M. 3223
Brumgardt, John R. 622 789
Brummett, Barry 2151 2152
Brundtland, Arne Olav 2626
Brune, Lester H. 1499 2627
Bruns, Roger 714
Bryson, Thomas A. 14 1500
Brzezinski, Zbigniew 2628
  2629
Buchan, Alastair 2630
Buhite, Russell D. 2631

Buice, David 790
Bull, Hedley 2632 2633
Bullitt, William C. 1558
Bullock, Charles S., III 2316
  2509
Bullock, Paul 1718
Bulman, Raymond F. 2317
Bundy, McGeorge 2153 2154
Bundy, William P. 2634
Burk, Robert F. 15
Burnham, James 16
Burstein, Jerome S. 1878
Burstein, Paul 17
Burton, Agnes Rose 18
Burton, D. H. 1501
Burton, William L. 19
Bushnell, Eleanore 1820
Buss, Terry F. 1918 1980
Butler, Broadus N. 2318
Butow, R. J. C. 1220
Butterfield, L. H. 415
Bybee, Carl R. 1799
Byers, R. B. 2635

C

Cable, Mary 196
Cain, Marvin R. 416 791
Caldwell, Dan 2636
Caldwell, Lawrence T. 2637
Calhoon, Robert M. 197
Calkin, Homer L. 976
Campbell, A. E. 20
Campbell, Bruce A. 1821
Campbell, Janet 198
Campbell, John 2638
Campen, Jim 1822
Campos, Icardo Salvador
  2639
Candee, Dan 2319
Candeloro, Dominic 1268
Cane, Guy 1063
Canon, David 2640
Cantor, Milton 21
Cappon, Lester J. 199
Caputo, David A. 2324
Caraley, Demetrios 2155
Carey, George W. 200 201
Carlile, Donald E. 2641
Carlson, Richard G. 417
Carmines, Edward G. 1823
Carpenter, Joseph 202
Carpenter, Ronald H. 22
Carreras Matas, Narciso 2642
Carroll, James D. 2502
Carson, S. L. 418
Carter, Barry E. 2643
Carter, Paul A. 1147
Carter, Robert 3434
Cary, Otis 1502
Casey, Gregory 3224
Casey, William J. 3225
Cash, Kenneth P. 419
Cassel, Carol A. 1824 1825
Catudal, Honoré M., Jr. 2644
Cauthen, Irby B., Jr. 203
Cavala, William 2129
Cavalla, Antonio 2645
Ceaser, James W. 23 24
Centeno, José 1692
Center, Judith A. 1826
Chace, James 2646
Chaffee, Steven H. 1827 1828
Chai, Jai Hyung 2647
Chambers, John Whiteclay, II
  1719
Chambers, Raymond L. 1829
  3226
Chambrun, René de 420
Chan, Kit-cheng 1503
Chan, Loren B. 1504
Chandler, Robert T. 792
Chapel, Gage William 2156
Chastenet, Jacques 25
Chaudhuri, Joyotpaul 204 205
Cheatham, Edgar 206
Cheatham, Patricia 206
Cheng Yu-p'ing 2864
Chern, Kenneth S. 2648
Cherne, Leo 2157
Cherwitz, Richard A. 2649
Chesebro, James W. 2069
Chesteen, Richard D. 883

Chester, Edward W. 26 2158
Chi, Madeleine 1505
Chianese, Mary Lou 207
Childs, Catherine Murtaugh 208
Childs, Richard S. 1830
Chizhov, Iu 2320
Choe, Sun Yuel 1828
Chomsky, Noam 2159 2545 2650
Christensen, Bonniejean 27
Christenson, Reo M. 28
Christie, Jean 1269
Chu, Shao-hsien 2651
Chubin, Shahram 2652
Chuinard, E. G. 793
Chung, Chong-Wook 2653
Church, Frank 2654 2655
Churchill, Mae 2321
Cigliana, Carlo 1506
Citrin, Jack 3441
Clar, Bayard S. 421
Clarfield, Gerald H. 209
Clarfield, Gerard H. 715
Clark, Cal 1260 1831
Clark, Dick 2656
Clark, Janet M. 1831 2322
Clark, Thomas D. 794
Clarke, Duncan L. 2657
Claussen, E. Neal 1832
Clements, Kendrick A. 1507 1508 1509
Clifford, Clark M. 2658 3227
Clifford, J. Garry 2659
Cline, Ray S. 2660
Cloud, Preston 29
Clubb, O. Edmund 3228 3229
Coaldrake, Peter 2160
Cobb, James C. 1270 1271
Cobbey, Robin E. 2296
Cochran, William C. 623
Cochrane, Elizabeth 422
Cochrane, James L. 30 2323
Coffey, John W. 2661
Cohen, Jeffrey 31
Cohen, Michael 1036
Cohen, Michael J. 2662 2663 2664
Cohen, Stephan J. 1878
Cohen, Stephen B. 2665
Cohen, Warren I. 2666 2667 3168
Coker, Christopher 2668
Colantoni, Claude S. 2128
Colard, Daniel 2669
Colby, William 2670
Cole, Adelaide M. 210 211
Cole, Richard L. 2324 3468
Cole, Terrence 977
Coletta, Paolo E. 1148 1510 1511 1512
Colgate, Gilbert, Jr. 795
Colket, Meredith B., Jr. 212
Collat, Donald S. 32
Collier, Bonnie B. 796
Colling, B. F. 423
Collins, Bruce W. 624
Collins, Larry 2671
Collins, Robert M. 1272
Combs, James 1720
Commager, Henry Steele 3231
Conforto, Bruce M. 2542
Conkin, Paul K. 1273
Connell, Christopher 2325
Conniff, James 213 214
Conover, Pamela Johnston 2672
Conrad, David E. 1274
Conway, John S. 1512
Conyers, John, Jr. 2673
Coogan, John W. 2674
Cook, Charles O., Jr. 1513
Cook, J. Frank 3232
Cooke, J. W. 215
Cooke, Jacob E. 216 797
Cooney, Charles F. 217 424 798
Coontz, Stephanie 3233
Cooper, John Milton, Jr. 1064 1514 1515 1516
Coplin, William D. 3384
Corbetta, Piergiorgio 1833
Corgan, Michael T. 1065
Corlew, Robert E., III 1834
Cormier, Raymond J. 218
Cornwell, Elmer E., Jr. 3234
Cortada, James W. 978
Cosmas, Graham A. 1243

Costain, Anne N. 1835 1836
Cotter, Cornelius P. 1805
Cotter, Richard D. 3235
Couch, Stephen R. 1896
Coughlan, Margaret N. 33
Coulam, Robert F. 2675
Couloumbis, Theodore A. 2676
Court, Susan J. 799
Coveyou, Michael R. 1837
Cowhey, Peter F. 2677
Cox, James M. 219
Crackel, Theodore J. 716
Crady, Wilson 425
Cragan, John F. 1838
Craig, Gordon A. 34
Craig, Richard B. 2678
Crane, James L. 426
Crane, Sylvia E. 2326
Crapol, Edward P. 979
Crecine, John P. 3372
Cresciani, Gianfranco 1693
Cress, Larry D. 980
Crevelli, John P. 2327
Crews, Clyde F. 35
Croce, Lewis H. 427
Crofts, Daniel W. 800 801
Cromwell, William C. 2679
Cronin, Thomas E. 1839 2328 2329 3236 3237 3238
Crosby, Earl W. 1275
Crosson, David 1276
Crotts, Gail 1840
Crouch, Barry A. 625
Crowl, Philip A. 2680
Cuff, Robert D. 1277 1278 1279 1517
Culbert, David H. 1280
Cullen, Joseph P. 220 802
Culver, John H. 1721
Cunliffe, Marcus 221 222
Cunningham, Noble E. 428 429 717
Currie, Lauchlin 1469
Curry, Earl R. 626
Curtis, David 430
Curtis, George H. 1740
Curtis, James C. 803 804
Curtis, Kenneth M. 36
Cutler, Lloyd N. 3239
Cyr, A. Bruce 1841

D

Dabney, Virginius 223
Daddario, Emilio Q. 3240
Dahiya, M. S. 2681
Dahl, Curtis 805
Daiker, Virginia 224
Dailey, Wallace Finley 1066
Dainelli, Luca 2682
Dallek, Robert 1698
Dallin, Alexander 1698
Dalton, Kathleen 1221
Daly, James J. 627
Damiloff, Nicholas 2683
Damon, Allan L. 37 38 39 40
Danbom, David B. 1281
Daniel, Cletus E. 1282
Daniels, James D. 628
Daniels, O. C. Bobby 41
Darcy, R. 3487
Darling, W. Stuart 3241
D'Attorre, Pier Paolo 2684
Dauer, Manning J. 3242
Dauses, Manfred A. 3243
David, Beverly R. 431
David, Charles 2685
Davidson, Frederic 2686
Davis, Cullom 398 408 413 455 465 570 576 717 724
Davis, Edwin S. 225
Davis, Eric L. 2161 2162
Davis, Glenn 1067
Davis, Kenneth S. 1068 1283 1284
Davis, Leslie K. 1842
Davis, Morton D. 2128
Davis, Nathaniel 2687
Davis, Paul B. 3244
Davis, Polly Ann 1285 1286 1722
Davis, Robert R., Jr. 981
Davis, Vincent 2688
Davis, William C. 432
Davison, Kenneth E. 42 718 806 807 808

Dawidoff, Robert 226
Dawson, Nelson L. 1287
Day, David S. 1288
Dayer, Roberta Allbert 1222
Dean, Dale 3384
Deane, Hugh 1069
Dearing, Mary R. 809
Dearmont, Nelson S. 719
DeBats, Donald A. 1843
DeBirny, Cecile Ream 433
deChambrun, René 227
Declercq, Eugene 1844
Degler, Carl N. 2163
DelaIsla, José 1845
Delaplaine, Edward S. 810
D'Elia, Donald J. 228
Dell, Christopher 982
Dellinger, David 2577
Delmas, Claude 2689
DeLuna, P. R. 2330
DeMaio, Gerald 1846
DeMause, Lloyd 2164 2165
Demuth, Christopher C. 2331
Denhardt, Robert B. 1847
Dennis, Jack 3245 3246
DeNovo, John A. 1700
Deren, Štefica 229 720
Derian, Patricia M. 2690
DeSantis, Vincent P. 721 2166
DeSimone, Silvio 2691
Destler, I. M. 2167 2692 3177 3247 3248 3249
Deutrich, Mabel E. 1083 1092 1438
Devine, Francis E. 230
Devol, Edward 43
Dewey, Frank L. 231 232 233 234
DeWitt, Howard A. 1518 1519
Dexter, Lewis 3488
Dhanani, Gulshan 2693
Diamond, Martin 1848
Diamond, Sigmund 1723
Dickson, Charles Ellis 235
Diebel, Terry L. 2694
Diggins, John P. 236
Dilks, David 1698
Dillon, Merton L. 983
Dillon, Rodney E., Jr. 811
Dingman, Roger V. 2695
D'Innocenzo, Michael 699
Divine, Robert A. 2168 2169 2696
Dobriansky, Lev E. 1849 2697
Dobson, Douglas 2057
Dodd, Thomas J. 1520
Dodson, Mary L. 3304
Doeker, Günther 1850
Doenecke, Justus D. 1070 1521 2698
Doerries, Reinhard R. 1522 1523
Domer, Thomas 812
Donahue, Bernard F. 1851
Donnelly, J. B. 1524
Donnelly, Marian C. 237
Donner, Frank 44 2332
Donno, Antonio 2699
Donovan, J. A. 3250
Donovan, Thomas A. 3251
Dorsett, Lyle W. 1289
Dorwart, Jeffery M. 1525
Douglas, William O. 2333
Dowding, Nancy E. 434
Drake, Douglas C. 1290
Draper, Theodore 238
Dreyer, Edward C. 1943
Driggs, Don W. 1820
Drischler, Alvin Paul 2170
Drummond, Roscoe 2157
Dubovitski, G. A. 813 814
Dugard, John 2700
Dumbauld, Edward 984
Dumbrell, John W. 45
Duncan, Mary B. 2038
Dunham, Roger G. 3252
Dunn, William N. 2701
Duram, James C. 2334
Durbin, Louise 46
Durham, Harriet F. 435
Dutt, Gargi 2702
Dyer, Stanford P. 1724
Dyer, Thomas G. 1071

E

Eagles, Charles W. 1291
Easterbrook, Gregg 1725
Ebel, Henry 2171
Ebner, Michael H. 1292
Eckert, Edward K. 436 722
Eckstein, George Günther 2172
Edelman, Marian Wright 2335
Edward, C. 239
Edwards, George C., III 47 48 1852 1853 3253 3254 3255
Edwards, John Carver 1293
Edwards, Tom 629
Eggert, Gerald G. 723
Eggleston, Noel C. 2703
Einhorn, Lois J. 240
Einsiedel, Edna F. 1854 1855
Eisenberg, Norman 3412
Eisendrath, Joseph L. 437
Eisenhower, Dwight D. 2173
Eisenstein, Zillah 1856
Eismeier, Dana L. 1526
Ekirch, Arthur A., Jr. 2174
Elazar, Daniel J. 438
Elfin, Margery 2336
El-Khawas, Mohamed A. 2704
Ellis, Richard N. 1294
Ellsworth, Edward W. 439
Ellsworth, Robert F. 2705
Elovitz, Paul H. 1726
Elson, Martha 2018
Ely, James W., Jr. 440 441
Elzy, Martin I. 1727 1857
Endy, Melvin B. 442
Engel, Bernard F. 443
Engelbourg, Saul 2337
Engeman, Thomas S. 49
Englund, Donald R. 815
English, John W. 3256
Ensor, Allison R. 444
Entin, Kenneth 3257
Entman, Robert M. 2239
Epstein, Edward Jay 2338 2339 3258
Epstein, Laurily K. 1858
Epstein, Leon D. 1859 1860
Erickson, Gary Lee 445 816
Erickson, Keith V. 1861 1862
Erikson, Robert S. 1863
Erler, Edward J. 446
Erokhin, A. V. 2175 2176 2706
Errico, Charles J. 1223
Eskilsson, Sture 2340
Etheredge, Lloyd S. 1728
Etherington, Norman 2707
Etzioni, Amitai 2341 2708
Etzold, Thomas H. 1527 1528 2709
Eubank, Robert B. 1954
Eulenberg, Ed 447
Evans, Les 3259
Evarts, Dru 1864
Ewers, John C. 817
Ewing, Gretchen Garst 630 631
Eyal, Chaim 2186

F

Fagen, Richard R. 2710 2711
Fairbanks, James David 50 1865 2177
Fairlie, Henry 1866 2342
Falk, Gerhard 51
Falk, Jay 2108
Falk, Richard A. 2577 2712
Fallert, J. Cecilia 2236
Fallows, James 2178 2343 3260
Fant, Charles H. 1867
Faramazian, R. 2344
Farer, Tom J. 2713
Farrar, Ronald 2345
Farrell, Richard 818
Farrell, Thomas B. 1868
Fausold, Martin L. 1295
Faust, Richard H. 448
Fay, Bernard 1529
Feder, Donald 1296
Fedler, Fred 3261

Fehrenbacher, Don E. 449 450 724 819
Feigenbaum, Edward D. 3262
Feingold, Henry L. 1530
Feinman, Ronald L. 1149
Feldman, Elliot J. 2714
Feldman, Lily Gardner 2714
Felkins, Patricia K. 2358
Fellman, Michael 923
Felson, Marcus 1869
Feltner, Paula 1870
Fenn, Dan H., Jr. 1729 3488
Ferguson, Clyde R. 820
Ferguson, Henry N. 241
Ferguson, Robert A. 242
Ferling, John E. 1871
Ferrari, Silvio 2715
Ferree, Myra Marx 1872
Ferrell, Robert H. 2716
Feuerwerger, Marvin C. 2717 2718
Ficken, Robert E. 1297 1298 1299
Finch, Gerald B. 2548
Finegold, Kenneth 1436
Fink, Gary M. 1730
Finkelstein, Leo, Jr. 52
Finn, Dallas 610
Fiorina, Morris P. 1873
Fisch, Dov 1300
Fischer, Dana D. 2719
Fischer, Robert 1072 1531
Fischer, Roger A. 53 632
Fischhoff, Baruch 1301
Fisher, Everett 725
Fisher, Louis 54 726 2179 2346 3263 3264
Fisher, Walter R. 2180
Fishlow, Albert 2720
Fitzgerald, Michael R. 1949
Flanagan, Robert J. 2347
Flatto, Elie 2181 2182
Fleischman, Richard K. 451
Fleming, Thomas 243
Flexner, James Thomas 244
Florestano, Patricia S. 3265
Floto, Inga 1532
Fohlen, Claude 245 985 1533
Foner, Eric 452 821
Ford, Trowbridge H. 633
Forsythe, David P. 2721
Foust, James D. 3266
Fowler, John G., Jr. 1534
Fox-Genovese, Elizabeth 453
Frade, Fernando 2722
Fragomen, Austin T., Jr. 2348
Francis, Michael J. 1535
Francis, Samuel T. 2723
Frank, Thomas M. 3267
Franks, Kenny A. 1073
Frantz, Joe B. 1731 1732
Frazer, Catherine S. 2349
Fredman, L. E. 55
Fredrickson, George M. 454 455
Freedman, Lawrence 1536
Freeland, Roger 2350
Freedman, Jean E. 822
Friedman, Murray 2726
Friedman, Norman 1227
Friedmann, F. G. 1875
Fries, Sylvia D. 456
Frisch, Morton J. 823
Frohlich, Norman 1876
Frug, Gerald 3269
Fry, Brian R. 2351
Fry, Joseph A. 986 987 988
Fry, William F. 2183
Frye, Jon 2352
Fuchs, Lawrence H. 1877
Fuller, Daniel J. 2727
Fullington, Michael Gregory 57 58
Funigiello, Philip J. 1302
Funk, Arthur L. 1733
Funston, Janet 246
Funston, Richard 59 246
Furlong, William Barry 1734

McAnaw, Richard L. 1984 1985
McAndrew, William J. 1372
McCarthy, Colman 1986
McCarthy, Eugene J. 3363
McCarthy, G. Michael 888 1173 1174
McClelland, Stewart W. 607
McClosky, Herbert 3441
McClure, Robert D. 1987 2021
McCombs, Maxwell E. 2186 2274
McCormick, James M. 3328 3329
McCoy, Donald R. 107 1096 1373 2218
McCoy, Drew R. 295 296 297 298
McCrary, Peyton 660
McCrary, Royce C., Jr. 889
McDonald, Forrest 739
McDonnell, Janet 1374
McDonnell, Richard A. 1988
McDonough, John 108
McFadyen, Richard E. 2434 2435
McFarland, Charles K. 1375
McFeeley, Neil D. 1989
McFeely, William S. 740
McGee, Gale 2219
McGeever, Patrick J. 2548
McGhee, James E. 506
McGinty, Brian 741
McGrath, Wilma E. 1990 2078
McGregor, Eugene B., Jr. 1991
McGuire, Jack B. 1175
McGuire, John R. 109
McGuire, Phillip 1376 1377 1378
McInerney, Thomas J. 2220
McIntosh, Richard A. 2121
McKay, Pamela R. 110
McLain, Glenn A. 2908
McLellan, David S. 2909 2910 3089
McLoughlin, William G. 890
McMurry, Richard 891
McMurtry, R. Gerald 507 607
McNeil, Dixie Mercer 3296
McQuaid, Kim 1257 2302
McWilliams, Tennant S. 1005
Mead, Lawrence M. 3364
Mead, Walter J. 111
Meadow, Robert G. 1932 1992 1993 1994 1995
Medick, Monika 2221
Medlin, Dorothy 299
Meehan, Mary 2222
Meeker, Joseph W., ed 2333
Meerse, David E. 892 893 894
Meeske, Mike 3261
Mehlman, Maxwell J. 2911
Meier, Kenneth John 1996 2436 3365
Melcher, Daniel P. 1176
Melnikov, I. M. 2912
Melosi, Martin V. 1177 1379
Meltzer, Allan H. 2130
Menard, Orville D. 3366
Mendel, Roberta 1097
Mense, D. Craig 3241
Merget, Astrid E. 2533
Mering, John V. 661
Merrill, Bruce D. 1997
Merrill, F. T., Jr. 2223
Merrill, Jeffrey 112
Merrin, Mary Beth 1964 1998
Mervin, David 1233
Meschutt, David 300 301
Messer, Robert L. 2913
Metallo, Michael V. 1610
Metcalf, Evan B. 1380
Metzger, H. Peter 2437
Meyer, Keith E. 2973
Meyer, Lysle E. 662
Meyers, Marvin 302
Meyers, Renee A. 1999
Michel, Dorothy 895
Michelman, Irving S. 1381
Middleton, Lorenzo 2438
Midgley, Louis 303
Miglian, Robert Murken 663
Mikulín, Antonín 2914
Milch, Thomas H. 2911
Miles, Edwin A. 896

Miller, Arthur H. 2000 2001 2134
Miller, Ben R. 2439
Miller, Bud 897
Miller, Clark 660
Miller, George 3412
Miller, James Edward 1382 1611
Miller, John E. 1383
Miller, Lawrence W. 2915
Miller, Linda B. 2916 3367
Miller, M. Sammy 1384
Miller, Nancy 3368
Miller, Randall M. 304
Miller, Richard G. 742
Miller, Sue Freeman 305
Miller, Warren E. 2134
Miller, William Lee 898
Millet, Stephen M. 2917
Minns, Daniel Richard 3450
Minow, Newton N. 2002
Minter, William 2918
Mintz, Max M. 306
Miroff, Bruce 2003 2224 2440 3369
Miscamble, William G. 899
Miscamble, Wilson D. 1385 1765 2919 2920 2921
Misse, Fred B. 1178
Mitchell, Clarence 2441
Mitchell, David 1612
Mitchell, Franklin D. 2225
Mitchell, Kell 1613
Mitchell, Lee M. 2002
Mitchell, Virgil L. 1386
Moch, Jules 2226 2922
Moe, Ronald C. 153 2227 3264
Moe, Terry M. 2442
Mohabbat Khan, Mohammad 3191
Mohrmann, G. P. 655 664
Mojdehi, J. M. M. 2923
Molineu, Harold 2924
Molnar, Thomas 2443
Mondale, Walter F. 3370
Monroe, Kristen R. 2444
Montero Gibert, José Ramón 2004
Mooney, Christopher F. 1614
Moore, James R. 1234 1615
Moore, Jamie W. 1616
Moore, John Hammond 307
Moore, Virginia 308
Morehead, Joe 2228
Moreland, Laurence W. 2033
Morgan, Anne Hodges 2445
Morgan, Edmund S. 309
Morgan, Robert J. 310 311
Morgenthau, Hans J. 2925
Morison, Elting E. 1387
Morison, Samuel Eliot 312
Morlando, Anne 832
Morley, Morris H. 2926 2927
Morris, Edmund 1098 1235
Morris, Roger 2229 2446 2928 2929 3371
Morris, Walter J. 508
Morrison, Charles E. 3091
Morrison, Katherine L. 509
Morrison, Rodney J. 1388
Morrissey, Charles T. 510
Morrow, Lance 2230
Moss, Robert 2930
Moulton, Gary E. 900
Mowery, David C. 3372
Moye, William T. 2447
Moynihan, Daniel P. 1617 3373
Mrozek, Donald J. 1099 2231 2931
Mugleston, William F. 901 1179
Mulder, John M. 1100
Mullaney, Thomas R. 2448
Mullen, William F. 1897
Mullins, William H. 1389
Murakata, Akiko 1101
Murdock, Clark A. 2232
Murphy, William J., Jr. 743
Murray, Crosby 607
Murray, G. E. Patrick 1618
Murray, Lawrence L. 1390
Murray, Michael D. 2005
Murray, Richard K. 1391
Murray, Robert K. 1180
Musto, David F. 113
Muzzio, Douglas 1846

Myers, Beverlee A. 2449
Myers, David S. 2006 2007
Myers, Duane 1619
Myers, Elisabeth P. 511
Myers, James E. 902
Myers, Will S. 2450
Myhra, David 1392

N

Nadasty, Dean 3412
Nadler, Solomon 665
Nakamura, Robert T. 2008 2009
Nash, George H. 1102
Nathan, James A. 2932 2933 3374
Nathan, Richard P. 2451 2452
Natoli, Marie D. 2010 2453 2454 3375
Nauman, W. Russell 3441
Naveh, David 3376
Neal, Nevin B. 1375
Neeley, Mary Ann 903
Neely, Mark E., Jr. 512 513 514 515 904
Nelsen, Clair E. 1393
Nelson, Anna K. 1006 3377 3378
Nelson, Larry E. 666
Nelson, Michael 114 3379
Nelson, Michael C. 2011
Nelson, Paul David 905
Nelson, Robert A. 2455
Ness, Gary C. 1103 1104
Neu, Charles E. 1105
Neumann, Gerd 2233
Neumann, Robert G. 115
Neumann, William L. 1620
Neustadt, Richard E. 2285 3489
Newhouse, Thomas L. 1999
Newman, Ralph G. 607
Newman, William J. 2012
Ney, Virgil 313
Nice, David 2013
Nicholas, David 2186
Nicholas, H. G. 2014 3380
Nichols, David A. 906
Nichols, W. Thomas 3381
Nicoloff, Olivier 2934
Nieman, Donald G. 907
Nikitin, N. 2935
Nikol, John 1621
Nikolayev, Y. 116 117 2015 2936
Niksch, Larry A. 2937
Ninkovich, Frank 1622 1623
Nitze, Paul 3176
Niven, John 744
Nixon, Richard M. 2456 2938
Nocera, Joseph 2234
Noelte, Earl 1624
Nolan, Janne E. 2607
Nordham, George Washington 314
Norton, Douglas M. 1625
Nowak, Kazimierz 2939
Nuechterlein, James A. 1394 1766 2457 2940 3382
Nufer, Harold F. 3383
Nugent, Walter 516
Nurse, Ronald J. 1767 2941
Nye, Joseph S., Jr. 2942 2943
Nyquist, Ewald B. 315
Nyström, Sune 2944

O

Oates, Stephen B. 517 518 908 909 910
Oberndörfer, Dieter 2945
O'Brien, Matthew C. 316
O'Brien, Patrick G. 1236 1237
O'Connor, Raymond G. 2946
Odell, John S. 2947 2948
Oder, Broeck N. 911
Offner, Arnold A. 1626
Ogburn, Floyd, Jr. 317
Ogburn, Robert W. 2949
Oh, John C. H. 118
Ohl, John Kennedy 1395
Ohlin, Goran 2950
Okuneva, M. A. 1627
Oldendick, Robert W. 2016

O'Leary, James P. 2951
O'Leary, Michael K. 3384
Oleinikova, L. V. 2458
Oliver, James K. 3374
Olmsted, Roger 667
Olsen, Otto H. 912
Olson, Dolores 119
Olson, James S. 1106 1396
Olson, William Clinton 2952 3385
Ondes, Bruce 2953
O'Neill, James E. 120
Oppenheimer, Joe A. 1876
Ordeshook, Peter C. 2128
Orman, John 121
Orman, John M. 3386
Ornstein, Norman J. 123
O'Rourke, Timothy G. 2133
Orr, C. Jack 2069
Ortona, Egidio 3387
Osborne, Leonard L. 2235
Osborne, Thomas J. 668
Osborne, Trudi 3388
Osgood, Robert E. 2954 2955
Ostendorf, Lloyd 519 520 521 522 523 850 913
Ostlund, Lyman E. 2017
Ostman, Ronald E. 2236
Ostrower, Gary B. 1628 1629
Ottaway, David 2956
Oudes, Bruce 2957 2958
Outrey, Georges 2237
Overland, Doris 2459
Ovinnikov, R. S. 2959
Owsley, Harriet Chappell 524

P

Packwood, Robert W. 3389
Padvaiskas, Edmund R. 1630
Paige, Connie 2460
Paine, Christopher 3390
Paletz, David L. 2018 2238 2239
Palmer, Lilla Rachel 318
Paludan, Phillip S. 525
Pannoni, Gregory A. 2960
Parish, P. J. 914
Park, Chang Jin 2961
Parker, Harold T. 1658
Parker, Iola B. 915
Parkhomenko, V. K. 2461
Parmet, Herbert S. 2962
Parris, Judith H. 122 2019
Parsons, Lynn H. 526
Parsons, Lynn Hudson 527 528
Partin, John W. 1181
Parzen, Herbert 1631 2963
Pastor, Robert A. 3391
Patenaude, Lionel V. 1182 1397
Paterson, Thomas G. 2964 2965 2966
Patkó, Imre 2967
Patrick, Rembert 2968
Patrizio, Gabriele 2969 2970 2971 2972
Patterson, David S. 1632
Patterson, Kirby W. 1045
Patterson, Thomas E. 1987 2020 2021
Patton, John H. 2022 2879
Payne, Alma J. 529 669
Payne, James L. 915
Peabody, Robert L. 123 1948
Pearson, Frederic S. 2973
Pechatnov, Vladimir O. 1107
Peckham, Charles A. 530
Peden, William 319
Pederson, Johannes T. 2023
Pederson, William D. 124
Pei, Mario 2024
Pellanda, Anna 1398
Pellicanò, Gerolamo 2974 3393 3394
Peltier, Michel 916 1007 1238
Pelz, Stephen E. 2975 2976 2977
Penkower, Monty Noam 1633
Percy, Charles H. 2978
PérezLlana, Carlos E. 2979
Perkins, Bradford 2980
Perlmutter, Amos 2981 2982 3395
Perman, Michael 917
Pernacciaro, Samuel J. 2025

Perry, Lewis 923
Perry, Phillip M. 1108
Peskin, Allan 531 532 533 708 745 918 919 1008
Peters, Charles 2026 2240 2462 2463 2464
Petersen, Eugene T. 2465
Petersen, Peter L. 1183 1184
Peterson, Barbara Bennett 1239
Peterson, Merrill D. 320 321 746
Petras, James 125 2983
Petrocik, John R. 2027
Petropoulos, Nikos 2466
Petrov, S. 2935
Pettigrew, Thomas F. 2052
Petz, Weldon 607
Pfau, Richard 2984
Pfeiffer, David G. 1837
Phillips, Charles 2134
Phillips, Edward Hake 1399
Phillips, Kim T. 670
Phillips, Steven L. 1908
Phillips, William 2545
Philp, Kenneth R. 1400
Pickens, Buford 322
Piereson, James E. 1979
Pika, Joseph A. 126
Pilcher, George William 127
Pilling, Ron 323
Pingree, Suzanne 2193
Pious, Richard M. 128 2467 3396
Piper, Don C. 2985
Planck, Gary R. 534 535 536 537
Platschek, Hans 1401
Plekhanov, S. M. 2028
Plesur, Milton 51 392 1402
Pletcher, David M. 1009
Ploughman, Piers (pseud.) 2286
Plumlee, John Patrick 3306
Plummer, Mark A. 538
Pocock, Emil 671
Podet, Allen H. 2986
Podhoretz, Norman 2029 2987
Pogue, Forrest C. 1634
Poland, Charles P., Jr. 920
Polenberg, Richard 129 1403
Polinard, Jerry L. 2124
Polk, John Fleming 1010
Pollin, Burton R. 1109
Pollock, Fred E. 1635
Polsby, Nelson W. 130 2241 2286
Pomerance, Michla 1636
Pomper, Gerald M. 2030 2060 2468
Poole, Frederick 3397
Poole, Peter A. 2988
Poole, Walter S. 2989
Popkin, Samuel 2134
Porter, David 1404
Porter, Gareth 2990
Porter, Laurinda W. 2038
Postbrief, Sam 2991
Potts, Louis W. 1110
Poulose, T. T. 2992
Powe, Marc B. 1703 1704
Powell, J. H. 324
Powell, Lynda Watts 1818 1819
Power, Paul F. 2993
Powers, Richard Gid 131 1405
Prager, Annabelle 196
Pratt, Alan 2607
Pratt, Henry J. 2469
Pressly, Thomas J. 539
Pressman, Jeffrey L. 2031 2032
Prindle, David F. 1185
Prucha, Francis Paul 540
Prysby, Charles L. 2033
Pukl, Joseph M., Jr. 541 542
Purcell, L. Edward 921
Purdy, Virginia C. 1083 1092 1438
Purnell, Sandra E. 2034
Pursell, Carroll W., Jr. 1406
Pynn, Ronald E. 3398

LIST OF PERIODICALS

A

Administration & Society
Administrative Science Quarterly
Aerospace Historian
Affari Esteri [Italy]
Africa Report
Africa Today
Agricultural History
Air Force Magazine
Air University Review
Alabama Historical Quarterly
Alabama Review
Alaska Journal (ceased pub 1980)
Amerasia Journal
American Archivist
American Art Journal
American Bar Association Journal
American Behavioral Scientist
American Economic Review
American Heritage
American Historical Review
American History Illustrated
American Indian Art Magazine
American Jewish Archives
American Jewish Historical Quarterly (see American
     Jewish History)
American Jewish History
American Journal of Economics and Sociology
American Journal of International Law
American Journal of Legal History
American Journal of Political Science
American Literature
American Neptune
American Political Science Review
American Politics Quarterly
American Quarterly
American Review of Canadian Studies
American Scholar
American Society of International Law. Proceedings
     (issues for 1970-73 appeared under the title
     American Journal of International Law)
American Studies in Scandinavia [Norway]
American Studies International
American Studies (Lawrence, KS)
American Studies (Washington, DC) (see American
     Studies International)
American West
Americas: A Quarterly Review of Inter-American
     Cultural History (Academy of American
     Franciscan History)
Américas (Organization of American States)
Amerikastudien/American Studies [German Federal
     Republic]
Annales du Midi [France]
Annales Historiques de la Révolution Française
     [France]
Annals of Iowa
Annals of the American Academy of Political and
     Social Science
Année Politique et Économique (ceased pub 1975)
     [France]
Antioch Review
ANU Historical Journal [Australia]
Appalachian Journal
Arizona and the West
Arkansas Historical Quarterly
Armed Forces and Society
Armenian Review
Army Quarterly and Defence Journal [Great
     Britain]
Art & Antiques
Art in America
Asian Affairs: An American Review
Asian Profile [Hong Kong]
Asian Survey
Asian Thought and Society
Atlantic Community Quarterly
Atlantis: A Women's Studies Journal [Canada]
Australian Foreign Affairs Record [Australia]
Australian Journal of Politics and History
     [Australia]
Australian Quarterly [Australia]
Aziia i Afrika Segodnia [Union of Soviet Socialist
     Republic]
Aztlán

B

Baptist History and Heritage
Belfagor: Rassegna di Varia Umanità [Italy]
Biography
Black Scholar

Brigham Young University Studies
British Journal of International Studies (see Review
     of International Studies) [Great Britain]
British Journal of Political Science [Great Britain]
Bulgarian Historical Review = Revue Bulgare
     d'Histoire [Bulgaria]
Bulletin of the Atomic Scientists (briefly known as
     Science and Public Affairs)
Bulletin of the History of Medicine
Bulletin of the Institute of Modern History.
     Academia Sinica [Taiwan]
Business History [Great Britain]
Business History Review

C

California Historical Quarterly (see California
     History)
California History
Canadian Dimension [Canada]
Canadian Historical Association Historical Papers
     (see Historical Papers) [Canada]
Canadian Journal of History = Annales Canadiennes
     d'Histoire [Canada]
Canadian Review of American Studies [Canada]
Canadian Review of Studies in Nationalism = Revue
     Canadienne des Études sur le Nationalisme
     [Canada]
Canadian Slavonic Papers = Revue Canadienne des
     Slavistes [Canada]
Capitol Studies (see Congressional Studies)
Casa de las Américas [Cuba]
Catholic Historical Review
Centennial Review
Center Magazine
Central European History
Change
Chicago History
China Quarterly [Great Britain]
Chinese Studies in History
Chronicle: Magazine of the Historical Society of
     Michigan
Chronicles of Oklahoma
Church History
Cincinnati Historical Society Bulletin
Cithara
Civil Liberties Review (ceased pub 1979)
Civil War History
Civil War Times Illustrated
Civitas [Italy]
Clio Medica [Netherlands]
Colorado Heritage
Colorado Magazine (superseded by Colorado
     Heritage)
Colorado Quarterly
Columbia Journal of Transnational Law
Commentary
Communication Monographs
Comparative Politics
Comunità [Italy]
Conflict
Congress and the Presidency: A Journal of Capital
     Studies
Congressional Studies (see Congress and the
     Presidency)
Contemporary Review [Great Britain]
Continuity
Crisis
Cry California
Current History
Current Notes on International Affairs (see
     Australian Foreign Affairs Record) [Australia]

D

Daedalus
Dalhousie Review [Canada]
Daughters of the American Revolution Magazine
Défense Nationale [France]
Delaware History
Deutsche Aussenpolitik * [German Democratic
     Republic]
Diplomatic History
Dissent

E

Early American Life
Early American Literature
East Europe
East European Quarterly

East Tennessee Historical Society's Publications
Eastern Horizon [Hong Kong]
Economia e Storia [Italy]
Écrits de Paris [France]
Eighteenth-Century Life
Éire-Ireland
Encounter [Great Britain]
Esprit [France]
Essex Institute Historical Collections
Estudios Internacionales [Chile]
Estudios Sociales Centroamericanos [Costa Rica]
Ethnic Groups
Ethnicity
Études [France]
Études Internationales [Canada]
Europa Archiv [German Federal Republic]
European Review (superseded by International
     Review) [Great Britain]
Explorations in Economic History

F

Feminist Studies
Fides et Historia
Filson Club History Quarterly
Florida Historical Quarterly
Foreign Affairs
Foreign Policy
Foreign Service Journal
Forest History (see Journal of Forest History)
Foro Internacional [Mexico]
Frankfurter Hefte [German Federal Republic]
Freedom at Issue
Freedomways

G

Gateway Heritage
Gazette: International Journal for Mass
     Communication Studies [Netherlands]
Gegenwartskunde [German Federal Republic]
Geographical Review
Georgia Historical Quarterly
Georgia Life (ceased pub 1980)
Geschichte in Wissenschaft und Unterricht
     [German Federal Republic]
Gilcrease: Magazine of American History and Art
Government and Opposition [Great Britain]
Government Publications Review: An International
     Journal of Issues and Information Resources
Great Plains Journal

H

Halcyon: A Journal of the Humanities
Harvard Library Bulletin
Hayes Historical Journal
Hispanic American Historical Review
Histoire [France]
Historia Mexicana [Mexico]
Historian
Historic Preservation
Historical Journal [Great Britain]
Historical Journal of Massachusetts
Historical Journal of Western Massachusetts (see
     Historical Journal of Massachusetts)
Historical Magazine of the Protestant Episcopal
     Church
Historical New Hampshire
Historical Papers = Communications Historiques
     [Canada]
Historie a Vojenství [Czechoslovakia]
Historische Zeitschrift [German Federal Republic]
Historisk Tidsskrift [Denmark]
History and Theory
History of Childhood Quarterly: The Journal of
     Psychohistory (see Journal of Psychohistory)
History of Political Economy
History Teacher
History Today [Great Britain]
Horizon
Human Rights Quarterly

I

Idaho Heritage (ceased pub 1978)
IDOC Middle East Quarterly (suspended pub)
India Quarterly: Journal of International Affairs
     [India]
Indian Archives [India]
Indian Journal of American Studies [India]

Indian Journal of Politics [India]
Indian Political Science Review [India]
Indiana History Bulletin
Indiana Magazine of History
Indiana Social Studies Quarterly
Industrial and Labor Relations Review
Inter-American Economic Affairs
Internasjonal Politikk [Norway]
International Affairs [Great Britain]
International Affairs [Union of Soviet Socialist Republic]
International Journal [Canada]
International Migration Review
International Organization
International Perspectives [Canada]
International Problems [Israel]
International Review (ceased pub 1975) [Great Britain]
International Security
International Social Science Journal [France]
International Social Science Review
International Socialist Review
International Studies [India]
International Studies Notes
International Studies Quarterly
Investigación Económica [Mexico]
Issue: A Quarterly Journal of Opinion
Issues & Studies [Taiwan]
Italia Contemporanea [Italy]

J

Jahrbuch für Amerikastudien (see Amerikastudien/American Studies) [German Federal Republic]
Jahrbuch für Wirtschaftsgeschichte [German Democratic Republic]
Japan Quarterly [Japan]
Jerusalem Journal of International Relations [Israel]
Jerusalem Quarterly [Israel]
Jewish Social Studies
Journal for the Scientific Study of Religion
Journal of African Studies
Journal of American History
Journal of American Studies [Great Britain]
Journal of Cherokee Studies
Journal of Church and State
Journal of Common Market Studies [Great Britain]
Journal of Communication
Journal of Conflict Resolution
Journal of Contemporary Asia [Sweden]
Journal of Contemporary History [Great Britain]
Journal of Economic History
Journal of Ethnic Studies
Journal of Forest History
Journal of Human Relations (suspended pub 1973)
Journal of Indian History [India]
Journal of Inter-American Studies (see Journal of Interamerican Studies and World Affairs)
Journal of Interamerican Studies and World Affairs
Journal of Interdisciplinary History
Journal of Intergroup Relations
Journal of International Affairs
Journal of Latin American Studies [Great Britain]
Journal of Law & Economics
Journal of Libertarian Studies
Journal of Library History, Philosophy, and Comparative Librarianship
Journal of Mississippi History
Journal of Modern African Studies [Great Britain]
Journal of Modern History
Journal of NAL Associates
Journal of Negro Education
Journal of Negro History
Journal of Palestine Studies [Lebanon]
Journal of Peace Research [Norway]
Journal of Political and Military Sociology
Journal of Political Economy
Journal of Political Science
Journal of Politics
Journal of Popular Culture
Journal of Popular Film and Television
Journal of Presbyterian History
Journal of Psychohistory
Journal of Social and Political Studies (see Journal of Social, Political and Economic Studies)
Journal of Social Issues
Journal of Social, Political and Economic Studies
Journal of Social Sciences and Humanities [South Korea]
Journal of Southeast Asian History (see Journal of Southeast Asian Studies) [Singapore]
Journal of Southeast Asian Studies [Singapore]
Journal of Southern African Affairs
Journal of Southern History
Journal of Sport History
Journal of Strategic Studies [Great Britain]

Journal of the American Academy of Religion
Journal of the American Institute of Planners (see Journal of the American Planning Association)
Journal of the American Planning Association
Journal of the Early Republic
Journal of the Hellenic Diaspora: Critical Thoughts on Greek and World Issues
Journal of the History of Ideas
Journal of the History of the Behavioral Sciences
Journal of the History Society. University of Singapore [Singapore]
Journal of the Hong Kong Branch of the Royal Asiatic Society [Hong Kong]
Journal of the Illinois State Historical Society
Journal of the Lancaster County Historical Society
Journal of the Royal United Services Institute for Defence Studies [Great Britain]
Journal of the Rutgers University Library
Journal of the Society of Architectural Historians
Journal of the United Service Institution of India [India]
Journal of the University of Bombay [India]
Journal of the West
Journal of Urban History
Journalism History
Journalism Quarterly

K

Kansas Historical Quarterly (superseded by Kansas History)
Kansas History
Kansas Quarterly
Kleio [Netherlands]
Korea and World Affairs [South Korea]
Kultura i Społeczeństwo [Poland]
Kungliga Krigsvetenskaps Akademiens Handlingar och Tidskrift [Sweden]

L

Labor History
Latin American Perspectives
Latin American Research Review
Library Quarterly
Lincoln Herald
Literature of Liberty
Lituanus
Lock Haven Review (suspended pub 1974)
Louisiana History
Louisiana Studies (see Southern Studies: An Interdisciplinary Journal of the South)

M

Magazin Istoric [Romania]
Maine Historical Society Quarterly
Mankind
Manuscripta
Marine Corps Gazette
Maryland Historian
Maryland Historical Magazine
Massachusetts Historical Society Proceedings
Massachusetts Review
Medjunarodni Problemi [Yugoslavia]
Mezhdunarodnaia Zhizn' (see International Affairs edition) [Union of Soviet Socialist Republic]
Michigan Academician
Michigan History
Michigan Journal of Political Science
Mid-America
Middle East Journal
Middle East Studies Association Bulletin
Middle Eastern Studies [Great Britain]
Midstream
Midwest Quarterly
Militärgeschichte [German Democratic Republic]
Militärgeschichtliche Mitteilungen [German Federal Republic]
Military Affairs
Military Review
Millennium: Journal of International Studies [Great Britain]
Milwaukee History
Minnesota History
Miroir de l'Histoire [France]
Mirovaia Ekonomika i Mezhdunarodnye Otnosheniia [Union of Soviet Socialist Republic]
Mississippi Quarterly
Missouri Historical Review
Missouri Historical Society. Bulletin (superseded by Gateway Heritage)
Modern Age
Modern Judaism
Mondo Cinese [Italy]

Montana: Magazine of Western History
Monthly Labor Review
Monthly Review

N

Narody Azii i Afriki [Union of Soviet Socialist Republic]
National Civic Review
Nautical Research Journal
Naval War College Review
Nebraska History
Negro History Bulletin
Neue Politische Literatur [German Federal Republic]
Nevada Historical Society Quarterly
New England Quarterly
New England Social Studies Bulletin
New Hungarian Quarterly [Hungary]
New Jersey History
New Mexico Historical Review
New Review: A Journal of East-European History (see New Review of East-European History) [Canada]
New Review of East-European History [Canada]
New South (superseded by Southern Voices)
New York Affairs
New York History
New York University Journal of International Law and Politics
New-England Galaxy
New-York Historical Society Quarterly (suspended pub 1979)
Niagara Frontier
Nineteenth Century
North American Review
North Carolina Historical Review
North Dakota History
North Dakota Quarterly
North Louisiana Historical Association Journal
Northwest Ohio Quarterly: a Journal of History and Civilization
Nouvelle Revue des Deux Mondes [France]
Novaia i Noveishaia Istoriia [Union of Soviet Socialist Republic]
Nowe Drogi [Poland]
Nuova Antologia [Italy]
Nuova Rivista Storica [Italy]

O

Ohio History
Old Northwest
Orbis
Oregon Historical Quarterly
Osteuropa [German Federal Republic]

P

Pacific Affairs [Canada]
Pacific Historian
Pacific Historical Review
Pacific Northwest Quarterly
Pacific Sociological Review
Palimpsest
Pan-African Journal [Kenya]
Papers of the Bibliographical Society of America
Parameters
Parliamentary Affairs [Great Britain]
Partisan Review
Peace and Change
Peace Research Reviews [Canada]
Pennsylvania History
Pennsylvania Magazine of History and Biography
Perspectives in American History
Phylon
Policy Studies Journal
Policy Studies Review
Polish American Studies
Polish Review
Political Quarterly [Great Britain]
Political Science [New Zealand]
Political Science Quarterly
Political Science Review [India]
Political Studies [Great Britain]
Political Theory: an International Journal of Political
Politička Misao [Yugoslavia]
Politico [Italy]
Politics [Australia]
Politics & Society
Politique Étrangère [France]
Politische Vierteljahresschrift [German Federal Republic]
Polity

Ponte [Italy]
Potomac Review
Present Tense
Presidential Studies Quarterly
Problèmes d'Amérique Latine [France]
Problemi di Ulisse [Italy]
Proceedings of the Academy of Political Science
Proceedings of the American Antiquarian Society
Proceedings of the American Philosophical Society
Proceedings of the Annual Meeting of the Western
 Society for French History
Proceedings of the British Academy [Great Britain]
Proceedings of the South Carolina Historical
 Association
Prologue: the Journal of the National Archives
Przegląd Zachodni [Poland]
PS
Psychiatry: Journal for the Study of Interpersonal
 Processes
Psychohistory Review
Public Administration [Great Britain]
Public Historian
Public Interest
Public Opinion Quarterly
Public Policy
Publius

Q

Quarterly Journal of Speech
Quarterly Journal of the Library of Congress
Quarterly Review of Economics and Business
Quarterly Review of Historical Studies [India]
Queen's Quarterly [Canada]

R

Radical America
Reason
Red River Valley Historical Review
Register of the Kentucky Historical Society
Relations Internationales [France]
Religion in Life (ceased pub 1980)
Rendezvous
Research Studies
Review of International Studies [Great Britain]
Review of Politics
Reviews in American History
Revista de Estudios Internacionales (supersedes
 Revista de Política Internacional) [Spain]
Revista de Estudios Políticos [Spain]
Revista de la Biblioteca Nacional "José Martí"
 [Cuba]
Revista de Política Internacional (superseded by
 Revista de Estudios Internacionales) [Spain]
Revista de Política Social [Spain]
Revista del Pensamiento Centroamericano
 [Nicaragua]
Revista Española de la Opinión Pública [Spain]
Revista General de Marina [Spain]
Revista Interamericana (see Revista/Review
 Interamericana) [Puerto Rico]
Revista Mexicana de Ciencias Políticas y Sociales
 [Mexico]
Revista/Review Interamericana [Puerto Rico]
Revue des Travaux de l'Académie des Sciences
 Morales et Politiques & Comptes Rendus de ses
 Séances [France]
Revue d'Histoire de la Deuxième Guerre Mondiale
 [France]
Revue Française de Science Politique [France]
Revue Française d'Études Américaines [France]
Revue Internationale de Droit Comparé [France]
Revue Internationale d'Histoire de la Banque
 [Italy]
Revue Militaire Générale (suspended pub 1973)
 [France]
Revue Roumaine d'Histoire [Romania]
Rhode Island History
Richmond County History
Rivista di Studi Politici Internazionali [Italy]
Rivista Italiana di Scienza Politica [Italy]
Rivista Marittima [Italy]
Rivista Militare [Italy]
Rocky Mountain Social Science Journal (see Social
 Science Journal)
Round Table (ceased pub 1981) [Great Britain]
Rural Sociology

S

SAIS Review
San José Studies
Scandinavian Review
Schweizer Monatshefte [Switzerland]
Schweizerische Zeitschrift für Geschichte = Revue
 Suisse d'Histoire = Rivista Storica Svizzera
 [Switzerland]
Science and Public Affairs (see Bulletin of the
 Atomic Scientists)
Science and Society
Secolas Annals
Seiyō Shigaku [Japan]
Serials Librarian
Shakaikeizaishigaku (Socio-Economic History)
 [Japan]
Shih-ta Hsüeh-pao = Bulletin of National Taiwan
 Normal University [Taiwan]
Shvut [Israel]
Slavic Review: American Quarterly of Soviet and
 East European Studies
Smithsonian
Social Forces
Social Policy
Social Problems
Social Science (see International Social Science
 Review)
Social Science History
Social Science Journal
Social Science Quarterly
Social Science Research Council Items
Social Service Review
Social Studies
Society
Society for Historians of American Foreign
 Relations. Newsletter
Sociological Inquiry
South Atlantic Quarterly
South Carolina Historical Magazine
South Dakota History
Southern California Quarterly
Southern Exposure
Southern Humanities Review
Southern Quarterly
Southern Review
Southern Speech Communication Journal
Southern Studies: An Interdisciplinary Journal of the
 South
Southern Voices (ceased pub 1974)
Southwest Review
Southwestern Historical Quarterly
Sovetskie Arkhivy [Union of Soviet Socialist
 Republic]
Sovetskoe Gosudarstvo i Pravo [Union of Soviet
 Socialist Republic]
Soviet Studies in History
Speech Monographs (see Communication
 Monographs)
Spiegel Historiael [Netherlands]
Ssu yü Yen = Thought and Word [Taiwan]
State Government
Stimmen der Zeit [German Federal Republic]
Storia Contemporanea [Italy]
Storia e Politica [Italy]
Studia Nauk Politycznych [Poland]
Studies in Comparative Communism
Studies in Eighteenth-Century Culture
Studies in History and Society (suspended pub 1977)
Sučasnist [German Federal Republic]
Supreme Court Historical Society Yearbook
Survey [Great Britain]
Survival [Great Britain]
Svensk Tidskrift [Sweden]
Swedish American Historical Quarterly
Swedish Pioneer Historical Quarterly (see Swedish
 American Historical Quarterly)
Swiss American Historical Society Newsletter
Synthesis
Századok [Hungary]

T

Társadalmi Szemle [Hungary]
Technology and Culture
Tennessee Historical Quarterly
Texana (ceased pub 1974)
Thought
Towson State Journal of International Affairs

U

UCLA Historical Journal
Ukrainian Quarterly
Ukrains'kyi Istorychnyi Zhurnal [Union of Soviet
 Socialist Republic]
United States Naval Institute Proceedings
Universal Human Rights (see Human Rights
 Quarterly)
Urban and Social Change Review
Utah Historical Quarterly

V

Vermont History
Vestnik Leningradskogo Universiteta: Seriia Istorii,
 Iazyka i Literatury [Union of Soviet Socialist
 Republic]
Vestnik Moskovskogo Universiteta:
 Istoriko-Filologicheskaia Seriia (superseded by
 Vestnik Moskovskogo Universiteta, Seriia 9:
 Istoriia) [Union of Soviet Socialist Republic]
Vestnik Moskovskogo Universiteta, Seriia 8: Istoriia
 [Union of Soviet Socialist Republic]
Vestnik Moskovskogo Universiteta, Seriia 9: Istoriia
 (superseded by Vestnik Moskovskogo
 Universiteta, Seriia 8: Istoriia) [Union of Soviet
 Socialist Republic]
Vierteljahrshefte für Zeitgeschichte [German
 Federal Republic]
Virginia Cavalcade
Virginia Magazine of History and Biography
Virginia Quarterly Review
Voenno-Istoricheskii Zhurnal [Union of Soviet
 Socialist Republic]
Vojnoistorijski Glasnik [Yugoslavia]
Voprosy Istorii [Union of Soviet Socialist Republic]

W

Washington Monthly
West Georgia College Studies in the Social Sciences
West Tennessee Historical Society Papers
West Texas Historical Association Year Book
West Virginia History
Western American Literature
Western Folklore
Western Historical Quarterly
Western Humanities Review
Western Journal of Speech Communication
Western Pennsylvania Historical Magazine
Western Political Quarterly
Western Speech (see Western Journal of Speech
 Communication)
Western Speech Communication (see Western
 Journal of Speech Communication)
Western States Jewish Historical Quarterly
Wiener Library Bulletin [Great Britain]
William and Mary Quarterly
Wilson Library Bulletin
Wilson Quarterly
Winterthur Portfolio
Wisconsin Magazine of History
Wissenschaftliche Zeitschrift der Friedrich-Schiller
 Universität Jena. Gesellschafts- und
 Sprachwissenschaftliche Reihe [German
 Democratic Republic]
Wissenschaftliche Zeitschrift der Humboldt
 Universität zu Berlin. Gesellschafts- und
 Sprachwissenschaftliche Reihe [German
 Democratic Republic]
Working Papers for a New Society (see Working
 Papers Magazine)
Working Papers Magazine
World Affairs
World Politics
World Today [Great Britain]
Worldview

Y

Yale University Library Gazette
Youth and Society

Z

Zeitschrift für Geschichtswissenschaft [German
 Democratic Republic]
Zgodovinski Časopis [Yugoslavia]

LIST OF ABSTRACTERS

A

Aimone, A. C.
Alcock, A.
Aldrich, R.
Alexander, G. M.
Alltmont, R. C.
Alvis, R.
Andrew, J. A.
Andrews, H. D.
Anstey, C.
Aoki, Y.
Ardia, D.
Athey, L. L.

B

Bailey, E. C.
Bailor, K. M.
Balmuth, D.
Bamber, J.
Bartels, U.
Bassett, T. D. S.
Bassler, G.
Bauer, K. J.
Bauhs, T. H.
Bazillion, R. J.
Beaber, P. A.
Beck, P. J.
Belles, A. G.
Benson, J. A.
Bett, M. A.
Billigmeier, J. C.
Bishop, D. M.
Blaser, L. K.
Bobango, G. J.
Boehnke, St.
Bonnycastle, S.
Boughton, G. J.
Bowers, D. E.
Bradford, J. C.
Brewster, D. E.
Broussard, J. H.
Brown, C. C.
Brown, J.
Burckel, N. C.
Burkholder, M. A.
Busachi, F.
Buschen, J. J.
Bushnell, D.
Butchart, R. E.

C

Cameron, D. D.
Campbell, E. R.
Canavero, A.
Carp, E. W.
Carr, S. P.
Casada, J. A.
Chard, D. F.
Charles, J. S. S.
Cimbala, D. J.
Cline, D. H.
Cohen, P. M.
Coleman, J. S.
Coleman, P. J.
Collins, D. N.
Costello, E. P.
Coutinho, J. V.
Crapster, B. L.
Crowther, K. N. T.
Curtis, G. H.
Cushnie, J.

D

D'Aniello, C. A.
Davis, D. G.
Davis, G. H.
Davison, S. R.
Dempsey, A. C.
Dewees, A. C.
Dibert, M. D.
Dodd, D.
Drysdale, A.
Dubay, R. W.
Dunn, S. P.
Durell, P. J.

E

Egerton, F. N.
Eid, L. V.
Eide, M. A.
Elzy, M. I.
Eminhizer, E. E.
Englard, A. A.
Engler, D. J.
English, J. C.
Erlebacher, A.
Estes, K. W.
Evans, J. L.

F

Fahl, R. J.
Feingold, M.
Fenlon, I.
Fenske, B. L.
Findling, J. E.
Fitzgerald, C. B.
Fox, J. P.
Frame, R. M., III
Frank, S. H.
Frank, W. C.
Franz, D. A.
Frederick, R. D.
Frenkley, N.
Frey, M. L.
Friedel, J. N.
Fulton, R. T.
Furdell, E. L.

G

Gagnon, G. O.
Garfinkle, R. A.
Garland, A. N.
Gassner, J. S.
Geist, C. D.
Genung, M.
Gibson, E.
Gillam, M. R.
Glasrud, B. A.
Glovins, G. A.
Grant, C. L.
Grant, J. R.
Gross, A. R.

H

Harling, F. F.
Harrington, J. F.
Harrow, S.
Harvey, K. A.
Hazelton, J. L.
Held, C.
Herrick, J. M.
Herstein, S. R.
Hess, G. R.
Heston, T. J.
Hetzron, R.
Hewlett, G. A.
Hilliker, J. F.
Hillje, J. W.
Hively, W. R.
Hobson, W. K.
Hoffman, A.
Holland, B.
Holsinger, J. C.
Hopkins, C.
Hopkins, E.
Horn, D. E.
Hough, C. M.
Houston, R. C.
Howell, A. W.
Howell, R.
Human, V. L.
Hurt, R. D.

J

Jacobsen, B.
Jewsbury, G. F.
Jeyes, U. G.
Jirran, R. J.
Johnson, B. D.
Johnson, D. W.
Johnson, E. S.

Johnson, L. F.
Jones, M. K.
Jordan, D. P.

K

Kalinowski, L.
Kascus, M. A.
Kaufman, M.
Keller, R. A.
Kennedy, P. W.
Keyser, E. L.
Kicklighter, J. A.
Klass, L. J.
Knafla, L. A.
Koppel, T.
Krenkel, J. H.
Krogstad, E. E.
Krompart, J. A.
Krukones, J. H.
Krushelnyckyj, I.
Krzyzaniak, M.
Kubicek, R. V.
Kugler, R. F.
Kuner, T.
Kuntz, N. A.
Kurland, G.

L

LaBue, B. J.
Lambert, D. K.
Larson, A. J.
Layton, R. V.
Ledbetter, B. D.
Lederer, N.
Lee, J. M.
Leedom, J. W.
Legan, M. S.
Lester, E. R.
Lewis, J. A.
Lifka, M. L.
Linkfield, T. P.
Lokken, R. N.
Lovin, C. R.
Lovin, H. T.
Lowitt, R.
Lucas, M. B.
Lukaszewski, W. J.

M

Mahood, H. R.
Marks, H. S.
Marshall, P. C.
Marti, D. B.
Mattar, P. J.
Maxted, L. R.
McCarthy, E.
McGinnis, D.
McGinty, G. W.
McIntyre, W. D.
McKinney, G. B.
McKinney, G. M.
McKinstry, E. R.
McLaughlin, P. L.
McQuilkin, D. K.
Meier, H. K.
Mendel, R. B.
Migliazzo, A. C.
Miller, H. J.
Miller, R. M.
Moen, N. W.
Montgomery, M. K.
Moore, J.
Mulligan, W. H.
Munro, G. E.
Murdoch, D. H.
Murdock, E. C.
Myers, J. P. H.
Myers, R. C.
Myres, S. L.

N

Neville, R. G.
Newton, P. T.
Nicholls, D. J.
Nielson, D. G.
Noble, R. E.
Novitsky, A. W.

O

Oaks, R. F.
Ohl, J. K.
Ohrvall, C. W.
Olbrich, W. L.
Olson, C. W.
Olson, G. L.
Orchard, G. E.
Osur, A. M.
Owen, G. L.
Oxley, A. P.

P

Palais, E. S.
Panting, G. E.
Papalas, A. J.
Parker, H. M.
Patzwald, G.-A.
Paul, B. J.
Paul, J. F.
Pavia, J. R.
Peck, P. J.
Pergl, G. E.
Petersen, P. L.
Pfabe, J. K.
Pickens, D. K.
Piersen, W. D.
Pike, C. R.
Pliska, S. R.
Porter, B. S.
Powell, J.
Powell, L. N.
Powers, T. L.
Prowe, D.
Puffer, K. J.
Pusateri, C. J.

Q

Quéripel, S. R.
Quinlan, S. J.
Quinlivan, M. E.

R

Rahmes, R. D.
Raife, L. R.
Read, C. J.
Reedy, W. J.
Reith, L. J.
Richardson, T. P.
Rilee, V. P.
Riles, R.
Ring, D. F.
Ritter, R. V.
Rollins, R. M.
Rosenblatt, N. A.
Rosenthal, F.
Russell, L. A.
Ryan, E. E.

S

Samaraweera, V.
Sapper, N. G.
Sarna, J. D.
Sassoon, T.
Sather, L. B.
Savitt, T. L.
Sbacchi, A.
Schoenberg, P. E.
Schoonover, T.
Schroeder, G. R.
Schultz, C. B.
Schulz, C. B.
Seymour, L. J.
Shaw, F. J.
Sicher, E. R.
Simmerman, T.
Sindermann, R. P.
Sliwoski, R. S.
Smith, C. O.
Smith, D. L.
Smith, G.

Smith, L.
Smith, L. C.
Smith, T. W.
Sobeslavsky, V.
Soff, H. G.
Souby, A. R.
Sprague, S. S.
Stack, R. E.
Stickney, E. P.
Stoesen, A. R.
Strausbaugh, M. R.
Street, J. B.
Street, N. J.
Strom, S. C.
Stromberg, R.
Summers, N.
Sweetland, J. H.
Swiecicka-Ziemianek, M.
Swift, D. C.

T

Talalay, S. J.
Tate, M. L.
Taylorson, P. J.
Thacker, J. W.
Thomas, J.
Thomson, H. F.
Tissing, R. W.
Tomlinson, R. H.
Touchstone, D. B.
Trauth, M. P.
Travis, P.
Truschel, L. W.
Tull, J.
Tutorow, N. E.

V

Valliant, R. B.
VanBenthuysen, R. F.
Vance, M. M.
VanWyk, L. W.
Velicer, L. F.
Verardo, D. R.
Vignery, J. R.
Vivian, J. F.

W

Waalwijk, H. P.
Wagnleitner, R.
Walker, W. T.
Ward, G. W. R.
Ward, H. M.
Ware, R. J.
Wasson, G. V.
Waters, L.
Watson, D. H.
Weltsch, R. E.
Wendel, T. H.
Wentworth, M. J.
West, K. B.
Wharton, D. P.
Wiederrecht, A. E.
Wiegand, W. A.
Wilcox, L. D.
Wilson, M. T.
Woehrmann, P. J.
Wood, C. W.
Woodward, R. L.
Woolfe, L.
Wrigley, W. D.

Y

Yanchisin, D. A.
Yerburgh, M. R.

Z

Zabel, O. H.
Ziewacz, L. E.
Zolota, M.
Zornow, W. F.

LIST OF ABBREVIATIONS

A.	Author-prepared Abstract
Acad.	Academy, Academie, Academia
Agric.	Agriculture, Agricultural
AIA	Abstracts in Anthropology
Akad.	Akademie
Am.	America, American
Ann.	Annals, Annales, Annual, Annali
Anthrop.	Anthropology, Anthropological
Arch.	Archives
Archaeol.	Archaeology, Archaeological
Art.	Article
Assoc.	Association, Associate
Biblio.	Bibliography, Bibliographical
Biog.	Biography, Biographical
Bol.	Boletim, Boletin
Bull.	Bulletin
c.	century (in index)
ca.	circa
Can.	Canada, Canadian, Canadien
Cent.	Century
Coll.	College
Com.	Committee
Comm.	Commission
Comp.	Compiler
DAI	Dissertation Abstracts International
Dept.	Department
Dir.	Director, Direktor
Econ.	Economy, Econom-.
Ed.	Editor, Edition
Educ.	Education, Educational
Geneal.	Genealogy, Genealogical, Genealogique
Grad.	Graduate
Hist.	History, Hist-.
IHE	Indice Historico Espanol

Illus.	Illustrated, Illustration
Inst.	Institute, Institut-.
Int.	International, Internacional, Internationaal, Internationaux, Internazionale
J.	Journal, Journal-prepared Abstract
Lib.	Library, Libraries
Mag.	Magazine
Mus.	Museum, Musee, Museo
Nac.	Nacional
Natl.	National, Nationale
Naz.	Nazionale
Phil.	Philosophy, Philosophical
Photo.	Photograph
Pol.	Politics, Political, Politique, Politico
Pr.	Press
Pres.	President
Pro.	Proceedings
Publ.	Publishing, Publication
Q.	Quarterly
Rev.	Review, Revue, Revista, Revised
Riv.	Rivista
Res.	Research
RSA	Romanian Scientific Abstracts
S.	Staff-prepared Abstract
Sci.	Science, Scientific
Secy.	Secretary
Soc.	Society, Societe, Sociedad, Societa
Sociol.	Sociology, Sociological
Tr.	Transactions
Transl.	Translator, Translation
U.	University, Universi-.
US	United States
Vol.	Volume
Y.	Yearbook

Abbreviations also apply to feminine and plural forms.
Abbreviations not noted above are based on *Webster's Third New International Dictionary*
and the *United States Government Printing Office Style Manual*.